Lecture Notes in Computer Science   13044

More information about this subseries at http://www.springer.com/series/7410

Kobbi Nissim · Brent Waters (Eds.)

Theory
of Cryptography

19th International Conference, TCC 2021
Raleigh, NC, USA, November 8–11, 2021
Proceedings, Part III

 Springer

Editors
Kobbi Nissim
Georgetown University
Washington, WA, USA

Brent Waters
The University of Texas at Austin
Austin, TX, USA

NTT Research
Sunnyvale, CA, USA

ISSN 0302-9743   ISSN 1611-3349   (electronic)
Lecture Notes in Computer Science
ISBN 978-3-030-90455-5   ISBN 978-3-030-90456-2   (eBook)
https://doi.org/10.1007/978-3-030-90456-2

LNCS Sublibrary: SL4 – Security and Cryptology

This Springer imprint is published by the registered company Springer Nature Switzerland AG
The registered company address is: Gewerbestrasse 11, 6330 Cham, Switzerland

Preface

The 19th Theory of Cryptography Conference (TCC 2021) was held during November 8–11, 2021 at North Carolina State University in Raleigh, USA. It was sponsored by the International Association for Cryptologic Research (IACR). The general chair of the conference was Alessandra Scafuro.

The conference received 161 submissions, of which the Program Committee (PC) selected 66 for presentation giving an acceptance rate of 41%. Each submission was reviewed by at least four PC members. The 43 PC members (including PC chairs), all top researchers in our field, were helped by 197 external reviewers, who were consulted when appropriate. These proceedings consist of the revised version of the 66 accepted papers. The revisions were not reviewed, and the authors bear full responsibility for the content of their papers.

As in previous years, we used Shai Halevi's excellent Web Submission and Review software, and are extremely grateful to him for writing it, and for providing fast and reliable technical support whenever we had any questions.

This was the seventh year that TCC presented the Test of Time Award to an outstanding paper that was published at TCC at least eight years ago, making a significant contribution to the theory of cryptography, preferably with influence also in other areas of cryptography, theory, and beyond. This year the Test of Time Award Committee selected the following paper, published at TCC 2005: "Keyword Search and Oblivious Pseudorandom Functions" by Michael Freedman, Yuval Ishai, Benny Pinkas, and Omer Reingold. The award committee recognized this paper for "introducing and formalizing the notion of Oblivious Pseudorandom Functions, and identifying connections to other primitives such as keyword search, inspiring a vast amount of theoretical and practical work".

We are greatly indebted to many people who were involved in making TCC 2021 a success. A big thanks to the authors who submitted their papers and to the PC members and external reviewers for their hard work, dedication, and diligence in reviewing the papers, verifying the correctness, and in-depth discussions. A special thanks goes to the general chair Alessandra Scafuro, Kevin McCurley, Kay McKelly, and the TCC Steering Committee.

October 2021

Kobbi Nissim
Brent Waters

Organization

General Chair

Alessandra Scafuro   North Carolina State University, USA

Program Chairs

Kobbi Nissim   Georgetown University, USA
Brent Waters   NTT Research and University of Texas at Austin, USA

Program Committee

Masayuki Abe   NTT, Japan
Ittai Abraham   VMware, Israel
Benny Applebaum   Tel Aviv University, Israel
Gilad Asharov   Bar-Ilan University, Israel
Amos Beimel   Ben-Gurion University, Israel
Andrej Bogdanov   Chinese University of Hong Kong, Hong Kong
Elette Boyle   IDC Herzliya, Israel
Chris Brzuska   Aalto University, Finland
Mark Bun   Boston University, USA
Yilei Chen   Tsinghua University, China
Itai Dinur   Ben-Gurion University, Israel
Pooya Farshim   University of York, UK
Sanjam Garg   NTT Research and UC Berkeley, USA
Rishab Goyal   MIT, USA
Siyao Guo   NYU Shanghai, China
Iftach Haitner   Tel Aviv University, Israel
Mohammad Hajiabadi   University of Waterloo, Canada
Carmit Hazay   Bar-Ilan University, Israel
Yuval Ishai   Technion, Israel
Abhishek Jain   Johns Hopkins University, USA
Stacey Jeffery   CWI, The Netherlands
Lisa Kohl   CWI, The Netherlands
Ilan Komargodski   NTT Research and Hebrew University, Israel
Benoit Libert   CNRS and ENS de Lyon, France
Huijia Lin   University of Washington, USA
Alex Lombardi   MIT, USA
Vadim Lyubashevsky   IBM Research - Zurich, Switzerland
Jesper Buus Nielsen   Aarhus University, Denmark
Ryo Nishimaki   NTT, USA
Omkant Pandey   Stony Brook University, USA

Omer Paneth	Tel Aviv University, Israel	
Manoj Prabhakaran	ITT Bombay, India	
Leo Reyzin	Boston University, USA	
Alon Rosen	Bocconi University, Italy, and IDC Herzliya, Israel	
Guy Rothblum	Weizmann Institute of Science, Israel	
Christian Schaffner	QuSoft and University of Amsterdam, The Netherlands	
Peter Scholl	Aarhus University, Denmark	
Gil Segev	Hebrew University, Israel	
Justin Thaler	Georgetown University, USA	
Muthu Venkitasubramaniam	Georgetown University, USA	
Mark Zhandry	NTT Research and Princeton University, USA	

External Reviewers

Christian Badertscher	Leo De Castro	Jiaxin Guan
Mingyuan Wang	Suvradip Chakraborty	Divya Gupta
Damiano Abram	Sun Chao	Shai Halevi
Anasuya Acharya	Nai-Hui Chia	Mathias Hall-Andersen
Shweta Agrawal	Arka Rai Choudhuri	Hamidreza Khoshakhlagh
Adi Akavia	Ashish Choudhury	Patrick Harasser
Gorjan Alagic	Hao Chung	Dominik Hartmann
Bar Alon	Kai-Min Chung	Brett Hemenway
Pedro Alves	Michele Ciampi	Justin Holmgren
Miguel Ambrona	Geoffroy Couteau	Thibaut Horel
Prabhanjan Ananth	Jan Czajkowski	Pavel Hubacek
Ananya Appan	Amit Deo	Aayush Jain
Anirudh C.	Jelle Don	Dingding Jia
Gal Arnon	Xiaoqi Duan	Zhengzhong Jin
Thomas Attema	Leo Ducas	Eliran Kachlon
Benedikt Bünz	Yfke Dulek	Gabriel Kaptchuk
Laasya Bangalore	Christoph Egger	Pihla Karanko
James Bartusek	Jaiden Keith Fairoze	Akinori Kawachi
Balthazar Bauer	Islam Faisal	Jiseung Kim
Sina Shiehian	Luca de Feo	Fuyuki Kitagawa
Ward Beullens	Cody Freitag	Susumu Kiyoshima
Rishabh Bhadauria	Georg Fuchsbauer	Anders Konrig
Kaartik Bhushan	Chaya Ganesh	Venkata Koppula
Nir Bitansky	Juan Garay	Ben Kuykendall
Olivier Blazy	Rachit Garg	Changmin Lee
Alex Block	Romain Gay	Baiyu Li
Estuardo Alpirez Bock	Nicholas Genise	Xiao Liang
Jonathan Bootle	Ashrujit Ghoshal	Wei-Kai Lin
Lennart Braun	Niv Gilboa	Jiahui Liu
Konstantinos Brazitikos	Aarushi Goel	Qipeng Liu
Ignacio Cascudo	Junqing Gong	Tianren Liu

Contents – Part III

Covert Learning: How to Learn with an Untrusted Intermediary

Ran Canetti and Ari Karchmer[✉]

Boston University, Boston, MA 02215, USA
{canetti,arika}@bu.edu

Abstract. We consider the task of learning a function via oracle queries, where the queries and responses are monitored (and perhaps also modified) by an untrusted intermediary. Our goal is twofold: First, we would like to prevent the intermediary from gaining any information about either the function or the learner's intentions (e.g. the particular hypothesis class the learner is considering). Second, we would like to curb the intermediary's ability to meaningfully interfere with the learning process, even when it can modify the oracles' responses.

Inspired by the works of Ishai et al. (Crypto 2019) and Goldwasser et al. (ITCS 2021), we formalize two new learning models, called *Covert Learning* and *Covert Verifiable Learning*, that capture these goals. Then, assuming hardness of the Learning Parity with Noise (LPN) problem, we show:

- Covert Learning algorithms in the agnostic setting for parity functions and decision trees, where a polynomial time eavesdropping adversary that observes all queries and responses learns nothing about either the function, or the learned hypothesis.
- Covert Verifiable Learning algorithms that provide similar learning and privacy guarantees, even in the presence of a polynomial-time adversarial intermediary that can modify all oracle responses. Here the learner is granted additional random examples and is allowed to abort whenever the oracles responses are modified.

Aside theoretical interest, our study is motivated by applications to the secure outsourcing of automated scientific discovery in drug design and molecular biology. It also uncovers limitations of current techniques for defending against model extraction attacks.

1 Introduction

A Motivating Scenario. Imagine a biologist, Alice, who wishes to learn a model—within some class of hypothesized models—for the relationship between the structure of a molecule and its "activity" (e.g. whether or not the molecule binds to a certain protein). Alice plans to conduct a variety of lab experiments in order to learn her model.

Supported by the DARPA SIEVE program, Agreement Nos. HR00112020020 and HR00112020021. A full version of this work appears in [CK21].

K. Nissim and B. Waters (Eds.): TCC 2021, LNCS 13044, pp. 1–31, 2021.
https://doi.org/10.1007/978-3-030-90456-2_1

However, in Alice's lab all experiments are public: they are observable by anyone. Can Alice design experiments so that only she will learn her model? Furthermore, can Alice design the experiments so that they will not leak her initial hypotheses on the possible models, which encode Alice's innovative, secret list of molecule features that are likely to influence activity? In fact, can Alice design the experiments so that no one else but her learns *anything at all* from her experiments?

To complicate things further, suppose that after starting the experiments, Alice is notified that she has been exposed to COVID-19 and has to quarantine at home; she has no choice but to delegate the recording of the results from her experiments to an untrusted colleague, Bob. Thus, in addition to concealing her learned model, hypothesized class of models, and any information about the molecular relationship, Alice needs a way to verify the results reported by Bob. In summary, Alice needs a learning algorithm that will carry the following (informal) guarantees:

- *Learning*: If Bob reports the results correctly, then Alice is guaranteed to acquire some satisfactory model for the studied molecular relationship.
- *Verifiability*: Even if Bob behaves maliciously, Alice is guaranteed to acquire a satisfactory model, *as long as she does not decide to reject Bob's report.*
- *Hypothesis-hiding*: Bob does not learn anything about the model Alice has learned or about Alice's hypothesized class of models.
- *Concept-hiding*: Bob learns nothing about the molecular relationship.

The learning requirement mimics classic learning-theoretic formalisms. In particular, it naturally corresponds to agnostic learning with membership queries: the molecular relationship corresponds to a concept, Alice's experiments correspond to queries to the concept at arbitrary points, and Alice's task of finding a model within a class of models corresponds to learning a hypothesis out of a given hypothesis class (e.g. polynomial size decision trees).

Put in these terms, our work is focused on the following questions: Can we devise agnostic learning algorithms in the membership query model that satisfy the above verifiability and hiding guarantees? If so, then for which hypothesis classes, and under what computational assumptions? In fact, how should we even define these (so far informal) goals?

Before proceeding to present our contributions, we note that this work has been inspired by the works of Ishai et al. [IKOS19] and Goldwasser et al. [GRSY20] that consider related models. We elaborate on these works in Sect. 1.3 and in the full version [CK21] of this paper.

1.1   Our Contributions

We define and construct learning algorithms that satisfy the above requirements. We first present our definitions, then state our results, and finally overview our techniques.

New Learning Models: Covert and Verifiable Learning. We propose two new learning models: the basic *Covert Learning* model, which considers a passive adversary only, and the *Covert Verifiable Learning* model, which considers an intermediary who may observe queries and even modify responses.

The Covert Learning Model. Our model is grounded in the learning with membership queries setting, where a learner is allowed to directly query the concept, with an added twist: every query and response obtained by the learner is also obtained by a computationally bounded adversary. The high level goal is for the learner to construct queries that are useful to herself, but are completely unintelligible to any adversary.

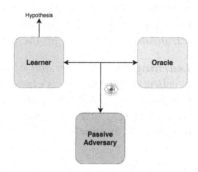

Fig. 1. A Covert Learning scenario. The learner interacts with the concept by making queries to an oracle that implements access to the concept at arbitrary points. Meanwhile, an adversary attempts to deduce information about the learner's hypothesis or about the concept itself, given a view: the set of queries and responses obtained by the learner.

One may be tempted to formulate this property by requiring that the adversary gains nothing from the interaction between the learner and the concept. However, this would be too much to demand, since the adversary does (at the very least) learn the responses to the learner's queries. We thus somewhat relax the hiding property to say that the adversary learns nothing *except for some number of random examples from the concept.* In other words, the view of the adversary can be *simulated* in probabilistic polynomial time (p.p.t.), given only random examples from the concept. This in particular means that the notion of Covert Learning is meaningful only when the learning task at hand is computationally hard in the traditional PAC learning model, where a concept must be learned from random examples only.

A bit more formally, Let $\mathcal{X}$ be a set, and consider a distribution D over $\mathcal{X} \times \{0, 1\}$. We will call a sample $(x, y) \sim D$ an example, where x is an *input* and y is a *label*, and call D a *concept*[1]. Let $\mathcal{H}$ denote a *hypothesis class*, which is a subset of functions $h : \mathcal{X} \to \{0, 1\}$. A learning algorithm under the Covert Learning model is tasked with finding an hypothesis $h \in \mathcal{H}$ that best approximates the concept D on unobserved examples $(x, y) \sim D$. This notion is captured by a *loss*

---

[1] Alternatively, one may think of a concept as a tuple consisting of a distribution $D_{\mathcal{X}}$ over the input domain $\mathcal{X}$ and a target function $f : \mathcal{X} \to \{0, 1\}$ which labels inputs. However, the notion described above (and used in the rest of this paper) is more general, as a joint distribution allows concepts which are *probabilistic*.

function (with respect to a concept). For example: $\mathcal{L}_D(h) = \Pr_{(x,y)\sim D}[h(x) \neq y]$. The learning goal of the Covert Learning model is then the requirement that the learner outputs $h \in \mathcal{H}$ such that $\mathcal{L}_D(h) \leq \mathcal{L}_D(\mathcal{H}) + \epsilon = \inf_{h\in\mathcal{H}} \mathcal{L}_D(h) + \epsilon$ with high probability, and we will call such an h ϵ-good. In order to achieve this goal, the learner is given access to a (possibly probabilistic) oracle that labels a queried input $x_j \in \mathcal{X}$ with a corresponding y_j. The novelty of the Covert Learning model is the guarantee that—in addition to the learning goal—no information about the hypothesis class or the concept is leaked to a passive adversary, except some random examples from the concept. *This guarantee holds even when the adversary has access to extraneous information on the concept.*

Definition 1. *Covert Learning* *(informal version of Definition 9). A covert learning algorithm—for a collection of hypothesis classes and with respect to a class of concepts and a loss function—is an algorithm that, for any concept in the class and accuracy parameters ϵ, δ, takes as input a target hypothesis class in the collection, and interacts with an oracle that labels queries to the concept such that the following are true:*

- ***Completeness.*** *The learning algorithm outputs an ϵ-good hypothesis for the concept with probability $1 - \delta$.*
- ***Privacy.*** *There exists a p.p.t. simulation algorithm that, given access to additional random examples from the concept, generates a distribution of queries and responses which is computationally indistinguishable from that of the real interaction. The simulation algorithm should function without further access to the oracle, or knowledge of the target hypothesis class within the collection.*

On Hypothesis-Hiding. In addition to hiding the learned concept, the above definition also requires that a covert learning algorithm hides the initial hypothesis class. Let us motivate this requirement. Indeed, when operating in a setting where the concept is included in a fixed class and can be learned fully, there is little motivation for hypothesis-hiding. However, in the more realistic setting of agnostic learning—where no assumptions are made about the concept—one resorts to learning the best approximation to the concept that is contained in some chosen hypothesis class. Clearly, the choice of hypothesis class is crucial in determining the value of the resulting approximation. Therefore, the chosen hypothesis class reflects the learner's prior beliefs about the concept, and is *itself* valuable information in need of protection. Indeed, the main motivation of *tolerance testing*[2] is to decide if a class of hypotheses contains a good approximator to an unknown concept. Concretely, the learner could be motivated to hide the results of a tolerant testing procedure that were received as advice. Alternatively, relating back to the motivating scenario, the specific domain knowledge that Alice has might influence her choices of experiments, which could in turn

---

[2] In tolerance testing [PRR06], a generalization of property testing, the goal is to distinguish the case where a function is "close" to a class of functions, or "far." A further generalization is the problem of estimating the distance of a function to a certain class of functions.

reveal information about her sensitive domain knowledge. Alice may be motivated to conceal her sensitive domain knowledge.

As a matter of fact, digging deeper into real world applications of learning with membership queries reveals further motivation for hypothesis-hiding, even when the concept is known to be from a fixed class (and therefore may be learned fully). In some specific practical applications (see Sect. 1.2 for more details), arbitrarily synthesized membership queries are difficult or expensive (in some measure) to obtain. For example, conducting a biological assay using an unstable compound. As is the case, and despite the fact that a concept may be known to be contained in a fixed class, the learner might voluntarily submit itself to an agnostic learning setting (i.e., settle for a hypothesis from a less expressive, easier to learn class, that does *not* contain the full set of potential concepts). Doing so is motivated by either the desire to reduce the *total* number of membership queries needed, or avoid making contrived or artificial queries (e.g. the inclusion of a highly unstable chemical in the biological assay).

The Covert Verifiable Learning (CVL) Model. The Covert Verifiable Learning model considers the case where, in addition to observing all queries and responses, the adversary (henceforth, the adversarial *intermediary*) also actively modifies the oracle's responses. Still, we require the learner to either detect the modifications and abort, or else come up with a good approximation of the actual concept represented by the oracle (which may in and of itself be an arbitrary function).

To make this requirement meaningful—namely, to allow the learner to meaningfully distinguish between responses that were modified by the adversarial intermediary and those that were not—we give the learner access to some number of ground truth random examples from the concept (see Fig. 2). We consider three variants of the CVL model, depending when the adversarial intermediary learns these additional random examples: In the weakest variant, the ground truth examples remain completely hidden throughout. In the intermediate model, we consider the case where the examples become known *once the learning process completes.* Finally, we consider our strongest variant, where these examples are publicly known *in advance.*

In more detail, the Covert Verifiable Learning model requires that, like Covert Learning, the output of the learner is a hypothesis $h \in \mathcal{H}$ that such that (with respect to the concept D) $\mathcal{L}_D(h) \leq \mathcal{L}_D(\mathcal{H}) + \epsilon$ with high probability, *but only when the adversarial intermediary simply observes and does not tamper with oracle responses.* The Covert Verifiable Learning model then augments the Covert Learning model by requiring that, for any adversarial intermediary that tampers with the oracle, the output of the learner is an $h \in \mathcal{H}$ that such that $\mathcal{L}_D(h) > \mathcal{L}_D(\mathcal{H}) + \epsilon$ with low probability, *assuming that the learner did not reject the interaction all together.*

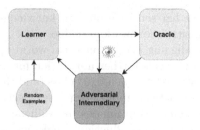

Fig. 2. The "intermediate model" Covert Verifiable Learning scenario. A learner, given a set of random examples of a concept, accesses supplementary data using an oracle in the presence of an adversarial intermediary. While attempting to deduce information about the concept or the learner's hypothesis, the adversarial intermediary may tamper with the oracle responses (both to help steal information and to simply deceive the learner). The learner aims to output a hypothesis that models the concept.

The concept-hiding and hypothesis-hiding guarantees should still hold—albeit with an adversarial intermediary. To capture this stronger requirement, we adapt the simulation-based privacy of Covert Learning to embrace the active nature of the adversarial intermediary. Basically, we require that for any adversarial intermediary, there is a simulator that can interact with the adversarial intermediary such that no computationally bounded adversary be able to tell whether the adversarial intermediary is interacting with the actual learner or with the simulator. As in Covert Learning, the simulator will access random examples from the concept, but operate with no further knowledge about the concept and no knowledge of the learner's hypothesis class. Depending on the variant we consider, the adversary may have access to the learner's random examples (recall that in the intermediate setting, they leak subsequent the interaction).

Definition 2. *Covert Verifiable Learning* *(informal version of Definition 25) A covert verifiable learning algorithm—for a collection of hypothesis classes and with respect to a class of concepts and a loss function—is a learning algorithm that, for any concept in the class and accuracy parameters ϵ, δ, takes as input a target hypothesis class in the collection, a set of random examples from the concept, and interacts with an oracle that labels queries on the concept such that the following are true:*

- ***Completeness.*** *If the adversarial intermediary acts honestly (i.e. no oracle responses are corrupted), then the learning algorithm outputs an ϵ-good hypothesis for the concept with probability $1 - \delta$.*
- ***Soundness.*** *For any computationally bounded adversarial intermediary who tampers with oracle responses, if the learning algorithm does not reject then it outputs a hypothesis which is not ϵ-good with probability at most δ.*
- ***Privacy (intermediate model).*** *For any adversarial intermediary, there exists a simulator such the following two random variables are indistinguishable to an external adversarial entity which chooses the concept, the target hypothesis class, and accuracy parameters:*

Real execution: *The output of the intermediary from a real interaction with the learning algorithm and the oracle, along with the set of random examples that the learner received in this interaction (the intermediary does not see the random examples).*

Ideal execution: *The output of the simulator, along with the set of random examples that the learning algorithm received in the interaction. The simulator is given access to the set of random examples that were known to the learning algorithm, plus an additional set of random examples. However, the simulator can neither have further access to the concept nor have knowledge of the target hypothesis class.*

If the output of the real execution does not include the random examples given to the learning algorithm, then we say that the algorithm is a covert verifiable learning algorithm with fully private examples.

If the random examples given to the learning algorithm are also given to the intermediary, then we say that the protocol is a public covert verifiable learning algorithm.

For simplicity, we don't give the intermediary the ability to modify the queries. Indeed, an intermediary that is able to modify the learner's queries is arguably able to learn the function to begin with.

Overview of Results. As discussed, meaningful covert learning algorithms can exist only for learning problems where learning from random examples is hard, whereas learning with membership queries is feasible. However, it is not a priori clear that meaningful covert learning algorithms exist at all. In fact, to the best of our knowledge, for all known learning algorithms in the membership query model, an external observer can learn the function by just observing the queries and responses. This holds even when no efficient learning algorithms are known in the traditional PAC model (for instance, consider the algorithm of Kushilevitz and Mansour for decision trees [KM93], which is thought to be hard in the traditional PAC model [Blu03, OS07]).

This works constructs polynomial time, covert learning algorithms for salient learning tasks within the two new learning models.

First, we consider the problem of Covert Learning for noisy parity functions. In this problem, a secret n-bit parity function is generated by drawing an n-bit vector k, where each bit is sampled i.i.d. from a Bernoulli random variable with mean $1/\sqrt{n}$, and defining the parity function to be $f(x) = \langle x, k \rangle$. An example (x, y) is generated from a concept D_{LPN}^k which draws a uniformly random input x, and returns $y = f(x) \oplus 1$ with probability $1/\sqrt{n}$, and $y = f(x)$ otherwise. By the low-noise LPN assumption [Ale03], learning the hidden vector parity function from examples $(x, y) \sim D_{\mathsf{LPN}}^k$ is not possible in polynomial time. On the other hand, oracle queries to D_{LPN}^k make the problem tractable. Let $D_{\mathsf{LPN}} = \{D_{\mathsf{LPN}}^k \mid k \in \{0,1\}^n\}$. To this end, we define a hypothesis class $\mathcal{H}_T$ as the set of all parity functions on a subset of $T \subseteq [n]$. We show:

Theorem 1. *(Informal version of Theorem 7) Assuming hardness of the low-noise LPN assumption, there is a covert learning algorithm for the collection* $\mathcal{C} = \{\mathcal{H}_T \mid T \subseteq [n]\}$, *w.r.t. the concept class* D_{LPN} *and loss function* $\mathcal{L}_D$.

Next, we consider the following concept class. Let $\mathcal{F}$ be a class of functions $f : \{0,1\}^n \to \{-1,1\}$. $D_{\mathcal{F}}$ is a concept class indexed by $f \in \mathcal{F}$, where for any $D_f \in D_{\mathcal{F}}$, an example $(x, y) \sim D_f$ is generated by first sampling an input x uniformly at random, and then a returning $(x, f(x))$.

The first problem we consider is that of learning the "heavy" Fourier coefficients of a function. In this problem, the goal of a learner (given a function $f : \{0,1\}^n \to \{-1,1\}$) is to find the set of all k such that $\mathbb{E}_x[f(x)\chi_k(x)] \geq \tau$, where $\tau \geq 1/\mathrm{poly}(n)$ is a given parameter and $\chi_k(x) = (-1)^{\langle k, x \rangle}$. We denote by $\hat{f}_b^{\geq \tau}$ the aforementioned set of k with the added stipulation that $|k| \leq b$. Achieving this goal using only examples $(x, y) \sim D_f$ is known to be as hard many longstanding open problems in computational learning theory, such as PAC learning DNF formulas, even when it is only required to find k such that $|k| = O(\log n)$ [Blu03, Jac97, OS07]. On the other hand, membership queries make the problem tractable [GL89]. With this in mind, we define a hypothesis class $\mathcal{H}_T^b = \{\chi_k \mid k_i = 0 \implies i \notin T, |k| \leq b\}$, where $T \subseteq [n]$, and a loss function $\mathcal{L}^{\tau,b} : \mathcal{P}([n]) \to [0,1]$ given by

$$\mathcal{L}^{\tau,b}(T) = \Pr_{k \sim \hat{f}_b^{\geq \tau}} \left[\chi_k \in T \right]$$

where $k \sim \hat{f}_b^{\geq \tau}$ is a uniformly random sample $k \in \hat{f}_b^{\geq \tau}$ and $\mathcal{P}(S)$ denotes the powerset of a set S (we also require that $|T| \leq \mathrm{poly}(n)$). We show:

Theorem 2. *(Informal version of Theorem 9) Let* $\mathcal{F}$ *be the class of all n-bit boolean functions. Assuming sub-exponential hardness of the standard LPN problem, there is a covert learning algorithm for the collection* $\mathcal{C} = \{\mathcal{H}_T^b \mid T \subseteq [n]\}$, *with respect to the concept* $D_{\mathcal{F}}$ *and the loss function* $\mathcal{L}^{\tau,b}$ *and for* $b \leq O(\log n)$, $\tau \geq 1/\mathrm{poly}(n)$.

In the problem of agnostically learning decision trees, a learner is given access to $D_f \in D_{\mathcal{F}}$ and tasked with finding (close to) the best decision tree that minimizes some loss function with respect to D_f. This learning problem, too, is thought to be difficult in the traditional PAC model, but is known to be efficiently learnable with membership queries [KM93, Blu03]. Building on top of the covert learning algorithm for $O(\log n)$-degree Fourier coefficients, we show:

Theorem 3. *(Informal version of Theorem 10) Assuming sub-exponential hardness of the standard LPN problem, there is a covert learning algorithm for the collection of all subsets of functions computable by* $\mathrm{poly}(n)$ *size decision trees with respect to the concept class* $D_{\mathcal{F}}$ *and the loss function* $\mathcal{L}_D$.

Unsatisfied with only the covert learning algorithms, we demonstrate how to transform our covert learning algorithms into covert verifiable learning algorithms. We do so both according to the intermediate setting and the stronger public variant. Specifically, in the intermediate setting we show:

Theorem 4. *(Informal version of Theorem 11) Assuming sub-exponential hardness of the standard LPN problem, there is a covert verifiable learning algorithm for the collection $\mathcal{C} = \{\mathcal{H}_T^b \mid T \subseteq [n]\}$, with respect to the concept $D_{\mathcal{F}}$ and the loss function $\mathcal{L}^{\tau,b}$, and for $b \leq O(\log n)$, $\tau \geq 1/\mathrm{poly}(n)$.*

Theorem 5. *(Informal version of Theorem 12) Assuming sub-exponential hardness of the standard LPN problem, there is a covert verifiable learning algorithm for the collection of all subsets of functions computable by $\mathrm{poly}(n)$ size decision trees with respect to the concept class $D_{\mathcal{F}}$ and the loss function $\mathcal{L}_D$.*

In the public variant, we prove:

Theorem 6. *(Informal version of Theorem 13) Let $s\text{-}\mathcal{DNF}_n$ be the class of all $f : \{0,1\}^n \to \{-1,1\}$ computable by a size s DNF formula. Assuming sub-exponential hardness of the standard LPN problem, there is a public covert verifiable learning algorithm for the collection $\mathcal{C} = \{\mathcal{H}_T^b \mid T \subseteq [n]\}$, with respect to the concept class $D_{s\text{-}\mathcal{DNF}_n}$ and loss function and the loss function $\mathcal{L}^{\tau,b}$, for $s \leq \mathrm{poly}(n)$, $b \leq O(\log n)$, and $\tau \geq 1/\mathrm{poly}(n)$.*

In particular, the result of Theorem 13 gives the first verifiable PAC learning protocol without any private examples, even in the model of [GRSY20] which does not consider privacy.

Due to space constraints, we have omitted all proofs and refer the reader to [CK21]. Furthermore, we have removed two results, namely, a key exchange algorithm that arises from Theorem 7 and a statistically sound and perfectly private covert learning algorithm for the "junta problem" in the fully private examples model. These results may also be found in the [CK21].

Algorithmic Ideas. We give high level descriptions of the algorithmic techniques. Formal overviews precede the constructions in the following sections.

Covert Learning of Noisy Parities. Our Covert Learning algorithm for learning noisy parities employs a "masked query" technique which works as follows. To mask a query $q \in \{0,1\}^n$, the learner starts by requesting n uniformly random examples from the oracle. Then, by taking the inputs of those random examples and drawing a random LPN secret, a "mask" is produced by multiplying the random inputs with the secret, and corrupting the resulting vector with independent random noise for each entry. Each query desired by the learner is then "masked" by adding the resulting sequence of LPN samples. In other words, each query is one-time-padded with an LPN instance. By the LPN assumption, a single masked query is pseudorandom. Moreover, the joint distribution for a set of masked queries is pseudorandom. The learner proceeds by sending the set of masked queries to the oracle, and upon receiving the results, decodes each one using the LPN secrets, the random examples, and by leveraging natural homomorphic properties provided by the LPN problem (with low noise). The simulation algorithm works by simply sampling queries from the uniform distribution, and pairing them with uniformly random results. We reduce the hardness of distinguishing the simulated transcript from the real transcript to solving the low-noise LPN problem.

Covert Learning of Low-Degree Fourier Coefficients and Decision Trees. The covert learning algorithms for low-degree Fourier coefficients and decision trees use the same "masked query" technique as the covert learning algorithm for noisy parities.

In particular, we use our "masked query" technique to run Goldreich-Levin queries on the (arbitrary) function in question. In contrast to the noisy parity setting, each individual query is not correctly decoded. Instead, the entire set of results is aggregated in a way resembling the original technique of Goldreich and Levin [GL89]. This allows us to then recover heavy Fourier coefficients belonging to $O(\log n)$-degree parity functions. Due to the noise of the masking, the technique fails to extract higher degree coefficients. Once the set of $O(\log n)$-degree parities that have noticeable Fourier coefficients is known, we employ standard techniques to produce a hypothesis which is the sign of a low-degree polynomial. We give a Fourier-based analysis that obtains agnostic learning guarantees on the hypothesis for the class of polynomial size decision trees. To demonstrate privacy, we adopt a variant of the LPN assumption that works over sparse secrets. The variant is due to [YZ16], whose hardness is implied by a sub-exponential hardness assumption on the standard LPN problem. We then construct a simulator that returns uniformly random examples of the function. We reduce solving the variant of the LPN problem to a constructing putative distinguisher between a real execution and a simulated execution.

Augmenting the Covert Learning Algorithms with Verifiability. In order to engineer the verifiability guarantee into our covert learning algorithms, we use one main technique which works as follows. We take the covert learning algorithms and wrap them with an outer loop, which at each iteration randomly decides to do a "learning" phase, where the covert learning algorithm is executed, or do a "test" phase. In a test phase, the algorithm sends a subset of the privately held queries to the oracle. Naturally, if the intermediary modifies any responses in this case, then the algorithm will detect that. Crucially, the distribution of queries in the learning phase (pseudorandom) is computionally indistinguishable from the distribution of queries in the test phase (uniformly random), due to the masking technique (and the LPN assumption). Therefore, this allows us to formalize the notion that no computationally bounded adversarial intermediary can reliably lie on the learning phase but not the testing phase—it would entail breaking the indistinguishability of the distributions of queries of the two phases and therefore the LPN hardness assumption.

When considering verifiability in the Public Covert Verifiable Learning setting (recall, here the learner does not have any private examples to leverage), the above technique does not immediately work. However, we can modify it in a simple way as follows. As before, the learning phase consists of executing a covert learning algorithm. The testing phase is instead conducted by taking the public random examples and applying the same masking technique as used on the learning queries. Now, the test phase and the learning phase are still computationally indistinguishable to the adversarial intermediary, but the queries of the testing phase cannot be linked back to the public random examples. The learner can then decide if the intermediary is lying on the masked public examples by using the secret keys of the masks to unlock and measure a correlation between the oracle's responses on the masked public examples and the public labels. Like above, the adversarial intermediary generating an "acceptable" correlation, while reliably lying on the learning phase, would entail breaking the indistinguishability of the distributions of queries of the two phases and therefore the LPN hardness assumption.

Unconditional Covert Verifiable Learning with Fully Private Examples. We design a Covert Verifiable Learning with fully private examples algorithm for $O(\log n)$-juntas. The algorithm works by requesting random hamming neighbors of the privately held uniformly random example set, and using them to find all the $O(\log n)$ relevant variables. Clearly, this means that the distribution of the membership queries is also uniform, despite the joint distribution being far from the concatenation of independent and uniformly random distributions. Since the adversary cannot see one component of the joint distribution, this suffices to give perfect privacy. By planting other private random examples (those which did not have random hamming neighbors requested), we may also prove that the protocol achieves statistical soundness against computationally unbounded adversarial intermediaries.

1.2   Real World Applications

Outsourcing of Drug Design and Discovery. The drug design and discovery process begins by searching a massive space of chemical compounds for an "active" compound [LPP04, DAG06, DGRDR08]. A compound is called active (with respect to some biological structure) if it produces a reaction under some biological test (e.g. whether or not a molecule or compound binds with a protein). Quickly finding (and optimizing) active compounds among a massive search space is a primary goal of the drug discovery process.

The recent trend of drug companies delegating elements of the R&D process to well-equipped and specialized third parties who can carry out the necessary biological experiments on behalf of the drug companies has greatly enhanced the efficiency of the drug discovery process (for more information, see [Cla11] and the references therein). However, currently the outsourcing of experiments carries within it the risk of exposure of both the experimental design and experimental results. Indeed, much of the proprietary knowledge and intellectual property underpinning pharmaceutical science is generated in this way, but only until relatively recently was it not conducted in-house [Cla11].

One of the famous methods for carrying out drug discovery is *Quantitive Structure-Activity Relationship* modelling, or QSAR (for more information, see [DAG06] and the references therein). The QSAR methodology attempts to identify a relationship between compound activity and compound structure. As noted in [BHZ19], a compound or molecule may be described using a predefined set of features, which may then be linked to positive classification if it is active, and a negative classification if inactive. A membership query can be simulated by assembling a compound according to the specific attributes defined by the algorithm's query and submitting it to face some biological test. Thus, the process of privately and verifiably delegating QSAR modelling can be distilled to the following covert verifiable learning setting: Drug company A contracts a private lab to gather relevant data labelled by a function f, with the end goal of learning a model that provides a good approximation to f. In this case, A may want to prevent the private lab from:

1. Reselling or releasing the data (queries to f) to a competing drug company B, after collecting the data for A.
2. Leaking to B that A is interested in a certain type of model, or certain trade secrets like cutting edge domain knowledge that is revealed by the design of the queries.
3. Charging more money for arbitrary, complex or "high value" data (that is, data needed to learn expressive models like polynomial size DNF formulas).
4. Cutting costs by providing faulty data.

Using a covert verifiable learning algorithm in this setting achieves each of the above points, while maintaining the usual learning guarantees of the plain learning with membership queries setting. In particular, the concept-hiding guarantee prevents (1), as the queries requested by A are essentially useless to any other (computationally bounded) party. Meanwhile, hypothesis-hiding (for a relevant collection of hypothesis classes) counters (2) and (3), as ability to efficiently do either would clearly violate the guarantee. Ultimately, the verifiability requirement also prohibits a private lab from (4).

We note that decision trees are one of the standard ways used in QSAR modelling to obtain a relationship between molecule features and activity. Thus, the decision tree learning algorithms in this work are highly relevant.

1.3   Related Work

Two recent works explore models related to ours and have influenced this work.

Cryptographic Sensing. Ishai et al. study a related scenario, called Cryptographic Sensing [IKOS19]. Like the present work, Cryptographic Sensing focuses on the goal of sensing (or, learning) properties of a physical object, while keeping these same properties secret to any passive adversary who does not have access to the internal randomness of the sensing algorithm. However, Cryptographic Sensing does not consider our notion of hypothesis-hiding, nor does it consider active intermediaries and verifiability. Furthermore, [IKOS19] chiefly focuses on *exact* learning of the object, where the aim is to decode the object exactly with non-noisy queries, and hiding is achieved for any high-entropy object. In contrast, our focus is on agnostic learning, where membership queries may return noisy responses. As a result, our model allows learning parities, whereas [IKOS19] only obtain learning algorithms for linear functions over larger moduli or over the integers. Another effect of noisy membership queries is that they allow concept-hiding even when there is a large and public labeled data set (the latter would rule out hiding a linear function in the noiseless setting of [IKOS19]). Indeed, our simulation-based definition will allow us to consider hiding in relation to auxiliary information about the concept, in a strong, zero-knowledge-like way.

PAC-Verification. Goldwasser et al. initiated the study of PAC-verification [GRSY20], which aims to answer questions about the complexity of verifying machine learning models via interactive proofs. Among other scenarios, they consider the task where a prover, having learned a concept (perhaps via membership queries), wishes to convey the learned model to a distrusting third party (a verifier) that has only random examples from the concept. In this setting, they obtain a protocol for PAC-verification for the heavy Fourier coefficients (of any degree) of arbitrary functions. Their protocol is statistically sound in a model that corresponds to our CVL with fully private random examples model. That is, the prover has no access to the random examples available to the verifier. We note, however, that Goldwasser et al. do not consider (or obtain) any hiding requirements—neither concept hiding nor hypothesis hiding. Furthermore, while our covert verifiable learning algorithms offer only computational soundness, some of them provide soundness even in the setting where the random examples are known to the prover in advance.

Other Related Models

Delegation of Computation. Though bearing some resemblance to the traditional cryptographic task of delegation of computation, our setting focuses on the specific task of learning. In this respect, we are focused on good *outcomes*, that is, guarantees on the efficacy of the learned hypothesis. In contrast, delegation of computation provides guarantees on the correctness of the computation steps themselves, and provides no guarantees on the learned hypothesis. For example, the delegation of computation model does not address the use of incorrect or poisoned data.

The PAC+MQ Model. The power of membership queries in the agnostic setting was studied by Feldman in [Fel09]. Feldman defines an agnostic PAC+MQ learning model and, assuming existence of one-way functions, shows a particular learning problem that is computationally hard to learn in the agnostic PAC model with uniformly random examples, while efficiently learnable in the agnostic PAC+MQ model. Essentially, the agnostic PAC+MQ model augments the agnostic PAC learning model with query access to a membership oracle for the concept. It is possible to view our Covert Learning algorithms as working in a model that is between PAC and PAC+MQ, where the membership queries cannot be synthesized arbitrarily (as in PAC+MQ), but must be generated in a way that can be emulated by a simulation algorithm.

r-Local Membership Queries. Another learning model lying between PAC and PAC+MQ was introduced in [AFK13]. There, *r-local* membership queries are permitted, in that any membership query must have hamming distance r from an example received from the concept D. This requirement forces the membership queries to "look" like they are distributed according to D, but it falls short of our model. In contrast, we require that the membership queries, *in conjunction* with the examples from D, can be emulated by a simulation algorithm.

Differentially Private Learning. The study of differentially private learning was initiated in [KLN+11]. Roughly, the work of [KLN+11] asks what can hypothesis classes can learned by an algorithm whose output does not depend too heavily on any one specific training example. In essence, differentially private learning is concerned with maintaining the privacy of sensitive *training data* used by the learner. In contrast, our notion of privacy is orthogonal, as it pertains to the secrecy (with respect to third parties) of the underlying concept, and the hypothesis of the learner itself.

2   Covert Learning

In this section, we concentrate on the basic Covert Learning setting, which considers only eavesdropping attacks. We give a formal definition of Covert Learning. Next, we demonstrate how to construct a Covert Learning algorithm for a noisy parity learning problem as a warm-up. Then we extend the techniques used in the warm-up and show a Covert Learning algorithm for learning the $O(\log n)$-degree Fourier coefficients of any function $f : \{0,1\}^n \to \{-1,1\}$. Using this algorithm as a subroutine, we obtain a Covert Learning algorithm for functions computable by polynomial size decision trees.

2.1   Preliminaries

We briefly recall here the standard terminology and notation which we use throughout the paper.

Definition 3. *A concept D_n is a joint distribution over an input domain $\mathcal{X}_n$ and label domain $\mathcal{Y}_n$.*

Definition 4. *A hypothesis class $\mathcal{H}_n$ is a set of functions $\mathcal{H}_n = \{h : \mathcal{X}_n \to \mathcal{Y}_n\}$.*

We call a sampled $(x, y) \sim D_n$ an *example*, where x is the *input* and y is the *label*. We use $\mathcal{X}_n = \{0,1\}^n$, and either $\mathcal{Y}_n = \{0,1\}$ or $\mathcal{Y}_n = \{-1,1\}$. We will use the term *concept class* denoted by $\mathcal{D}_n$ to signify a set of concepts (which are joint distributions over the input domain $\{0,1\}^n$ and label domain $\{0,1\}$).

Definition 5. *A concept oracle $\mathcal{O}_{D_n}$ for a concept D_n is a (probabilistic) oracle with the property that on query $z \in \{0,1\}^n$, $\mathcal{O}_{D_n}(z) = y$ with probability $\Pr_{D_n}[(x,y)|x = z]$, and $y \oplus 1$ otherwise.*

Finally, we very often use the notation to denote random variables of n-bit vectors.

Definition 6. β_μ^n *denotes the distribution over an n-bit vector where each of the bits is drawn i.i.d. from a Bernoulli random variable with mean μ.*

2.2 Definition of Covert Learning

In defining Covert Learning, we wish to require that the transcript of the interaction between a learner and a membership oracle reveals no information to a passive adversary about either:

– the concept, or
– the learner's chosen hypothesis class, or any auxiliary information that the learner has on the concept prior to the interaction.

Furthermore, these requirements should hold even when there is auxiliary information (in the form of random examples from the concept) available to the adversary.

As a starting point, we consider the learning with membership queries model, where the learner is given query access to a probabilistic oracle that responses queries about a concept (a concept oracle $\mathcal{O}_{D_n}$ for the concept D_n). The learner's goal is to find a hypothesis, out of some given class of hypotheses $\mathcal{H}_n$, that best approximates the concept D_n with respect to a loss function. For example, a loss function $\mathcal{L}_{D_n}(h) = \Pr_{(x,y)\sim D_n}[h(x) \neq y]$. This gives us a baseline model for accuracy guarantees in the learning with access to membership queries setting. However, we diverge from this model in an important way. Rather than define learning with respect to a single, fixed hypothesis class (as is common in learning theory), we use a *collection* of hypothesis classes. This will provide a natural way to model the desire to hide auxiliary information on the concept, as well as the chosen hypothesis class.

In more detail, we fix a collection of hypothesis classes $\mathcal{C}_n$, and require accuracy guarantees *for every* hypothesis class $\mathcal{H}_n \in \mathcal{C}_n$: the learning algorithm will receive as input a description of a specific target hypothesis class within the collection, along with accuracy parameters $\epsilon, \delta > 0$. Then, the learning algorithm will *agnostically* learn the target hypothesis class with respect to a given loss function. For example, using the above example loss function, the learner will try to find an $h \in \mathcal{H}_n$ such that $\Pr_{(x,y)\sim D_n}[h(x) \neq y] \leq \inf_{h \in \mathcal{H}_n} \Pr_{(x,y)\sim D_n}[h(x) \neq y] + \epsilon$, with probability at least $1 - \delta$. That is, the algorithm should output a hypothesis—within the given target class—that best approximates the concept (up to the given accuracy parameters and a distribution over inputs). The input to the learner naturally models the *intent* of the learner, by capturing the particular choice of hypothesis class within the collection, and any auxiliary information used to select the class (e.g. the results of a tolerant testing algorithm or specific domain knowledge).

Finally, we will require that the transcript of the communication between the learner and the concept oracle does not leak any knowledge to an eavesdropper, in the following sense: we require that there exists a p.p.t. algorithm (a simulator) that generates an (ideal) simulated transcript of the (real) interaction between the learner and the concept oracle, with access to random examples from the concept, but not further access to the concept oracle. Furthermore, the simulator should operate without knowledge of the learner's target hypothesis class. The simulated transcript should be indistinguishable from a real transcript, even to a (polynomial time) adversary that has access to auxiliary information on the concept. We define two distributions, $\{\text{real}_{\mathcal{A}}^{\mathcal{O}_{\mathcal{D}_n}}\}$ and $\{\text{ideal}_{Sim}\}$ as follows.

Definition 7. *Let $\mathcal{D}_n$ be a concept class, and $\mathcal{C}_n$ a collection of hypothesis classes. We define $\{\text{real}_{\mathcal{A}}^{\mathcal{O}_{\mathcal{D}_n}}\}$ to be the distribution generated by the following process.*

1. *An adversary (a distinguisher) selects $\epsilon, \delta > 0$, a hypothesis class $\mathcal{H}_n \in \mathcal{C}_n$, and a concept $D_n \in \mathcal{D}_n$.*
2. *A set of examples $\mathcal{S}$ is drawn from D_n.*
3. *A learner $\mathcal{A}$ receives ϵ, δ and $\mathcal{H}_n$, and begins interacting with the concept by querying the oracle $\mathcal{O}_{D_n}$ on examples of his choosing, receiving back responses for each queried example. $\mathcal{A}$ tries to agnostically learn $\mathcal{H}_n$ using this oracle. Denote the queries and responses as $\text{transcript}_{\mathcal{A}^{\mathcal{O}_{D_n}}(\mathcal{H}_n, \epsilon, \delta)}$.*
4. *Output $\left(\mathcal{H}_n, \epsilon, \delta, \text{transcript}_{\mathcal{A}^{\mathcal{O}_{D_n}}(\mathcal{H}_n, \epsilon, \delta)}\right)$*

Definition 8. *Let Sim be a p.p.t. algorithm, which takes as input a set of random examples to a concept, and a length parameter which denotes the number of queries requested by the learner in the real interaction. We define $\{\text{ideal}_{Sim}\}$ to be the distribution generated by the following process.*

1. *An adversary (a distinguisher) selects $\epsilon, \delta > 0$, a hypothesis class $\mathcal{H}_n \in \mathcal{C}_n$, and a concept $D_n \in \mathcal{D}_n$.*
2. *A set of examples $\mathcal{S}$ is drawn from D_n.*
3. *A p.p.t. simulator Sim receives $\mathcal{S}, \ell$, and "interacts" with the $\mathcal{O}_{D_n}$ and outputs the set queries and responses denoted as $\text{transcript}_{Sim(\mathcal{S}, \ell)}$. Here ℓ is the number of queries that the learner requests in the real interaction.*
4. *Output $\left(\mathcal{H}_n, \epsilon, \delta, \text{transcript}_{Sim(\mathcal{S}, \ell)}\right)$*

We note that the size of the random example set obtained by the simulator is given as a parameter of the definition of Covert Learning. Formally,

Definition 9. *Covert Learning.* *Let $\mathcal{C}_n$ be a collection of hypothesis classes, let $\mathcal{D}_n$ be a concept class, let $\mathcal{O}_{\mathcal{D}_n}$ be a class of oracles indexed by $D_n \in \mathcal{D}_n$, and let $\mathcal{L}$ be a loss function. $\mathcal{A}$ is a $(m(n), \alpha)$-covert learning algorithm for $\mathcal{C}$ with respect to $\mathcal{D}_n$, $\mathcal{O}_{\mathcal{D}_n}$ and $\mathcal{L}$ if for every $\epsilon, \delta > 0$, $\mathcal{A}$ satisfies the following:*

- *Completeness. For every distribution $D_n \in \mathcal{D}_n$, and every $\mathcal{H}_n \in \mathcal{C}_n$, the random variable $h = \mathcal{A}^{\mathcal{O}_{D_n}}(\mathcal{H}_n, \epsilon, \delta)$ satisfies*

$$\Pr_h \left[\mathcal{L}(h) \leq \alpha \cdot \mathcal{L}(\mathcal{H}_n) + \epsilon \right] \geq 1 - \delta$$

*The loss function may depend on the distribution D_n. For **proper** Covert Learning, the output of $\mathcal{A}$ must be an element of $\mathcal{H}$, i.e. $h \in \mathcal{H}_n$.*

– *Privacy. There exists a p.p.t. simulator Sim such that:*

$$\left\{ \mathsf{real}_{\mathcal{A}}^{\mathcal{O}_{D_n}} \right\} \overset{c}{\approx} \left\{ \mathsf{ideal}_{Sim} \right\}$$

where $\overset{c}{\approx}$ denotes computational indistinguishability. We stipulate that the number of random examples given to the simulator is $O(m(n))$.

See Fig. 3 for an illustration of the model. Often, we will use the terminology from the computational learning theory literature, and say that a collection of hypothesis classes $\mathcal{C}$ is α-*covertly learnable* if there exists an α-covert learning algorithm for $\mathcal{C}$.

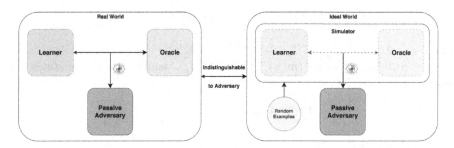

Fig. 3. Privacy of Covert Learning. The "real world," where the adversary views the learner access the oracle, should be indistinguishable from the "ideal world," where the adversary interacts with a simulator that simulates the learner accessing the oracle. The adversary gets to choose the concept which is implemented by oracle (within the given class). Observe that, the simulator is also allowed random examples from the concept, and these are "leaked."

About the Simulation. We note that the simulation paradigm lends itself well to our setting: It allows formalizing the requirement that sensitive information is not revealed by the interaction, while maintaining the overall usefulness of the interaction. In this case, we formalize the notion that whatever could have been learned by a passive adversary about the concept or learner's hypothesis after the interaction, could have been learned *before* the interaction (given access to random examples). Furthermore, we can model the presence of other, unavoidable information leakage (e.g. random examples on the concept).

Our Focus Is on Collections of Hypothesis Classes That Are Not Efficiently PAC Learnable. When every hypothesis class in a collection is efficiently learnable without membership queries (i.e. with random examples only), Covert Learning is considered trivial. This is because in this case the privacy requirement is easily satisfied by a transcript full of random examples (and it does not even rule out leakage, because the adversary can learn the function from them). We thus concentrate on the case where the hypothesis classes within the collection need (or are assumed to need) membership queries to be learned.

2.3   A Warm-Up: Covert Learning of Noisy Parity Functions

In this section, we concentrate on Covert Learning of parity functions with noise. Indeed, this class of learning problems is broadly assumed to not be efficiently agnostically PAC-learnable in a very strong sense, as per the Learning Parity with Noise (LPN) assumption:

Definition 10. *Search/Decision LPN assumption: For $\mu \in (0, 0.5), n \in \mathbb{N}$, the $(m(n), T(n))$-DLPN$_{\mu,n}$ assumption states that for every distinguisher $\mathbb{D}$ running in time $T(n)$,*

$$\left| \Pr_{s, A, e}[\mathbb{D}(A, As \oplus e)] = 1 - \Pr_{r, A}[\mathbb{D}(A, r)] = 1 \right| \leq \frac{1}{T(n)}$$

where $s \xleftarrow{\$} \mathbb{Z}_2^n, A \xleftarrow{\$} \mathbb{Z}_2^{m(n) \times n}, e \xleftarrow{\$} \beta_\mu^{m(n)}, r \xleftarrow{\$} \mathbb{Z}_2^{m(n)}$.
For $\mu \in (0, 0.5), n \in \mathbb{N}$, the $(m(n), T(n))$−SLPN$_{\mu,n}$ search assumption states that for every inverter $\mathbb{I}$ running in time $T(n)$,

$$\Pr_{s, A, e}[\mathbb{I}(A, As \oplus e) = s] \leq \frac{1}{T(n)}$$

where $s \xleftarrow{\$} \mathbb{Z}_2^n, A \xleftarrow{\$} \mathbb{Z}_2^{m(n) \times n}, e \xleftarrow{\$} \beta_\mu^{m(n)}$.

Remark 1. The search and decisional LPN$_{\mu,n}$ assumptions are polynomially equivalent, in that an algorithm that breaks one of them can be turned into an algorithm that breaks the other in polynomial time. For more information, consult [Pie12] and the references therein.

One typical setting of parameters gives the DLPN$_{1/\sqrt{n},n}$ problem, which is conjectured to be $(O(n), \text{poly}(n))$-hard [Ale03]. However, for even super polynomial queries, the best known attacks are not asymptotically better than the $O(n)$ case [YS16]. Furthermore, an important variant was introduced in [ACPS09]. Specifically, it was shown that solving the decisional LPN problem when drawing the secret from the same distribution as the noise vector is as hard as drawing the secret from the uniform distribution. Henceforth, when referring to the DLPN$_{\mu,n}$ problem, we refer to this setting.

In the remainder of this section, we construct a Covert Learning algorithm for the learning parity with noise problem using only the assumption that DLPN$_{1/\sqrt{n},n}$ is hard itself—the minimal assumption that keeps the problem nontrivial: for any rate of noise bounded away from one half by an inverse polynomial, it easy (using majority voting) to solve DLPN$_{\mu,n}$ when membership queries are available, and even in the "adversarial" noise case [GL89]. However, this is not enough for Covert Learning. It is clear that running membership query algorithms "in the open" (like Fig. 1) may violate all our previously mentioned privacy goals.

The Learning Problem. As a warm-up, we will consider a distributional variant of Covert Learning. Here, the learning and privacy guarantees are required when the concept is drawn from a distribution over the concept class, rather than for every concept in the class. For privacy, this means that the distinguisher will not have the privilege of choosing the concept from the class, but instead it is sampled from the distribution. Our concept class is the following:

Definition 11. *Let $\mathcal{X}_n = \{0,1\}^n$. We define the concept class $\mathcal{D}_{\mathsf{LPN}}^{\mu,n}$ to be the family of distributions over $\mathcal{X}_n \times \{0,1\}$ indexed by a $k \in \{0,1\}^n$, that have the following properties,*

- *The input (marginal) distribution over $\mathcal{X}$ of any $D_k \in \mathcal{D}_{\mathsf{LPN}}^{\mu,n}$ is uniform.*
- *For any $D_k \in \mathcal{D}_{\mathsf{LPN}}^{\mu,n}$, the label $y \in \{0,1\}$ of the input x is generated by taking $\langle k, x \rangle$ and flipping the result with probability μ.*

For our learning problem, the concept will be drawn using a distribution over $\mathcal{D}_{\mathsf{LPN}}^{\mu,n}$:

Definition 12. *We define a distribution $\mathcal{M}_{\mathsf{LPN}}^n$ over the concept class $\mathcal{D}_{\mathsf{LPN}}^{\mu,n}$ as follows. $D_k \in \mathcal{D}_{\mathsf{LPN}}^{\mu,n}$ is selected by drawing $k \xleftarrow{\$} \beta_{1/\sqrt{n}}^n$.*

The learner will get membership access to the concept by using the following class of oracles:

Definition 13. *Let $\mathcal{O}_D$ be a concept oracle for a concept D. Recall the concept oracle that implements "membership query access" to a distribution D over $\mathcal{X} \times \mathcal{Y}$ in the following sense: on a query q to the oracle, a sample from the conditional distribution over $\mathcal{Y}$ is returned, given that $\mathcal{X} = q$.*

Hence, when the concept D_k is drawn from $\mathcal{M}_{\mathsf{LPN}}^n$, the learner will obtain access to $\mathcal{O}_{D_k}$. We will do Covert Learning for the following collection of hypothesis classes:

Definition 14. *For $a \in \{0,1\}^n$, let $\ell_a : \{0,1\}^n \to \{0,1\}$, defined by $\ell_a(x) = \langle a, x \rangle$. Let $\mathsf{PARITY}_{A,n} = \{\ell_a \mid i \notin A \implies a_i = 0\}$. Let $\mathcal{C}_{\mathsf{PARITY},n} = \{\mathsf{PARITY}_{A,n} \mid A \subseteq [n]\}$.*

Our Covert Learning task is then as follows. We would like to design a learning algorithm that takes as input any hypothesis class $\mathsf{PARITY}_{A,n} \in \mathcal{C}_{\mathsf{PARITY},n}$ (we will call A the *relevant set*). Then, given access to $\mathcal{O}_{D_k}$, the learning algorithm outputs $\ell_a \in \mathsf{PARITY}_{A,n}$ which minimizes the following loss (with respect to D_k):

Definition 15. *Let the loss function $\mathcal{L}_D$ be defined as*

$$\mathcal{L}_D(h) = \Pr_{(x,y)\sim D}[h(x) \neq y]$$

for a concept D.

Meanwhile, the privacy guarantee of Covert Learning should be satisfied. In particular, any information about A or k should be hidden.

The Construction

Overview. We will refer to $\mathcal{D}_{\mathsf{LPN}}^{\frac{1}{\sqrt{n}},n}$ as $\mathcal{D}_{\mathsf{LPN}}^{\mathsf{Low}}$. We construct Covert Learning for $\mathcal{C}_{\mathsf{PARITY},n}$ with respect to $\mathcal{D}_{\mathsf{LPN}}^{\mathsf{Low}}$, $\mathcal{O}_{\mathcal{D}_{\mathsf{LPN}}^{\mathsf{Low}}}$, and $\mathcal{L}_D$, and where learning is considered when the concept is drawn from $\mathcal{M}_{\mathsf{LPN}}^n$. The Covert Learning algorithm begins by requesting "masked queries" from $\mathcal{O}_{D_k}$. For $x_1, \cdots, x_n \xleftarrow{\$} \beta_{1/2}^n$, let

$$\mathbf{X} = \begin{bmatrix} x_1 \ x_2 \ x_3 \ \cdots \ x_n \end{bmatrix}$$

Note that, each x_i is a column of $\mathbf{X}$. Furthermore, let $e, s \xleftarrow{\$} \beta_{1/\sqrt{n}}^n$. A masked query $\hat{q} \in \{0,1\}^n$ for query $q \in \{0,1\}^n$ is generated by taking

$$\hat{q} = \mathbf{X}s \oplus e \oplus q$$

In our algorithm, each query q requested by the learner is a unit vector under the above masking, plus requests for the columns of $\mathbf{X}$. Indeed, the ith unit vector is only masked and requested if the ith index is in the relevant set A. Upon receiving the results to the masked unit vectors, denoted by $\mathcal{O}_{D_k}(\hat{q})$, the algorithm decodes each one by taking $\mathcal{O}_{D_k}(\hat{q}) \oplus \langle y, s \rangle$, where $y = (\mathcal{O}_{D_k}(x_1), \cdots, \mathcal{O}_{D_k}(x_n))$. It turns out that,

$$\Pr\left[\mathcal{O}_{D_k}(\hat{q}) \oplus \langle y, s \rangle = \langle k, q \rangle\right] > 0.501$$

Hence, our algorithm requests each masked unit vector some constant number of times—the final decoding for each is done by taking the majority bit over the set of results from the duplicate queries. Note that, for a pair duplicate queries (say, two copies of the ith unit vector), the masks are independently generated. Once the decoded results to the masked unit vectors are obtained, the algorithm produces a hypothesis in the natural way: if r_i is the decoded result of the masking query of the ith unit vector, then the output hypothesis is $r(x) = \langle (r_1, \cdots, r_n), x \rangle$.

Theorem 7. *Assuming* $\mathsf{DLPN}_{\mu,n}$ *is* $(O(n), \mathrm{poly}(n))$-*hard,* $\mathcal{C}_{\mathsf{PARITY},n}$ *is* $(\mathrm{poly}(n), 1)$-*covertly learnable with respect to* $\mathcal{D}_{\mathsf{LPN}}^{\mathsf{Low}}$, $\mathcal{O}_{\mathcal{D}_{\mathsf{LPN}}^{\mathsf{Low}}}$, *and* $\mathcal{L}_D$, *and where the concept is drawn according to* $\mathcal{M}_{\mathsf{LPN}}^n$.

The algorithm (called CLP and presented in [CK21]) is efficient. The queries are constructed in time polynomial in n, and the same is true for the decoding process. From there, it's easy to see that since we run $O(\log(n/\delta))$ iterations, the entire algorithm runs in time polynomial in n and $\log(1/\delta)$.

2.4   Covert Learning of Low-Degree Fourier Coefficients

In this section, we will extend our techniques from the warm-up to present a Covert Learning algorithm for "heavy" $O(\log n)$-degree Fourier coefficients.

This learning problem will no longer live in the distributional learning case, as in the warm-up.

The learning problem is nontrivial for Covert Learning: the problem of efficiently identifying heavy, even $O(\log n)$-degree, Fourier coefficients from random examples is a fundamental problem that has so far evaded intense research effort from the learning theory community. In particular, such an algorithm would imply the PAC learnability of DNFs via a "weak learning" parity function and boosting results [Jac97]. Moreover, such an algorithm would be considered a massive breakthrough in computational learning theory [Blu03, OS07].

Our Task. We consider the following natural class of concepts.

Definition 16. *Let $\mathcal{X}_n = \{0,1\}^n$, and $\mathcal{F}_n$ be a class of functions $f : \mathcal{X}_n \to \{-1,1\}$. We define $\mathcal{D}_{\mathcal{F}_n}$ to be the concept class containing all distributions over $\mathcal{X}_n \times \{-1,1\}$ that have the following properties,*

- *The input (marginal) distribution over $\mathcal{X}_n$ of any $D_f \in \mathcal{D}_{\mathcal{F}_n}$ is uniform.*
- *For any $D_f \in \mathcal{D}_{\mathcal{F}_n}$, there exists a polynomial time computable target function $f : \mathcal{X}_n \to \{-1,1\}$ such that $f \in \mathcal{F}_n$ and*

$$\Pr_{(x,y) \sim D_f} [f(x)y = 1] = 1$$

The learner will be allowed to interact with a membership query oracle to any concept in $\mathcal{D}_{\mathcal{F}_n}$.

Definition 17. *Let $\mathcal{O}_{\mathcal{F}_n}$ be a class of membership oracles indexed by $D_f \in \mathcal{D}_{\mathcal{F}_n}$, such that $\mathcal{O}_f$ implements membership query access to f. To simplify notation, we may write $\mathcal{O}_f$ instead of $\mathcal{O}_{D_f}$.*

Hence, the learner will have access to $\mathcal{O}_f$ when tasked with learning the "heavy" Fourier coefficients of the target function of D_f.

In plain English, the task is as follows. The learner chooses a hypothesis class characterized by a subset T of $[n]$ and a bound $b < n$, where the hypothesis class consists of a subset of all n-bit parity functions. A parity function is in the hypothesis class if it is of degree less than b and if all it's relevant variables are included in T. The learner must then find all parity functions in the hypothesis class which have Fourier coefficients larger than some given threshold τ.

More formally, the goal is to learn the following hypothesis class with respect to the following loss function:

Definition 18. *Let $k \in \{0,1\}^n$. Define the parity function $\chi_k : \{0,1\}^n \to \{-1,1\}$ as*

$$\chi_k(x) = (-1)^{\langle k,x \rangle}$$

We will call $|k|$ the degree of χ_k.

Definition 19. *Let $T \subseteq [n]$. Define the hypothesis class* $\mathsf{FOURIER}_{T,b,n} = \mathcal{P}\{\chi_k \mid k_i \notin T \implies k_i = 0, \wedge |k| \leq b\}$. *In other words,* $\mathsf{FOURIER}_{T,b,n}$ *is the powerset of the set all parity functions on subsets of $[n]$ contained in T, with degree at most b. Let the collection of hypothesis classes* $\mathcal{C}_{\mathsf{FOURIER},b,n} = \{\mathsf{FOURIER}_{T,b,n} \mid T \subseteq [n]\}$. *For any hypothesis class* $\mathsf{FOURIER}_{T,b,n} \in \mathcal{C}_{\mathsf{FOURIER},b,n}$, *we will call T the relevant set.*

Definition 20. *Let $f : \{0,1\}^n \to \{0,1\}$ be a function. Let $P = \mathcal{P}\{\chi_k \mid k \in \{0,1\}^n\}$. Also, let $\hat{f}_b^{\geq \tau} = \{\chi_k \mid \hat{f}(k) \geq \tau, |k| \leq b\}$. $\mathcal{L}^{\tau,b} : P \to [0,1]$ is a loss function given by*

$$\mathcal{L}^{\tau,b}(T) = \begin{cases} \Pr_{\chi_k \sim \hat{f}_b^{\geq \tau}} [\chi_k \in T] & when \ |T| \leq \mathrm{poly}(n) \\ 1 & otherwise \end{cases}$$

where $\chi_k \sim \hat{f}_b^{\geq \tau}$ is a uniformly random sample $\chi_k \in \hat{f}_b^{\geq \tau}$.

The learning algorithm, given a hypothesis class $\mathsf{FOURIER}_{T,b,n} \in \mathcal{C}_{\mathsf{FOURIER},b,n}$, should hide any information about the relevant set T, as well as any information about f, as formalized by the privacy guarantee of Covert Verifiable Learning. Finally, the protocol should achieve computational soundness and be efficient (i.e. run in time $poly(n, 1/\tau, log(1/\delta)$ for a soundness parameter δ).

The Construction

Overview. We construct Covert Verifiable Learning for $\mathcal{C}_{\mathsf{FOURIER},b,n}$ with respect to $\mathcal{D}_{\mathcal{F}_n}$, $\mathcal{O}_{\mathcal{F}_n}$, and $\mathcal{L}^{\tau,b}$. The overall flow of the algorithm will be similar to that of our Covert Learning algorithm for noisy parities. Instead of using the masking technique to encode unit vectors, we instead use masking to run Goldreich-Levin queries.

Theorem 8. *Goldreich-Levin learning algorithm. Given query access to a function $f : \{0,1\}^n \to \{-1,1\}$ and given parameters τ, δ, there exists a $poly(n, \frac{1}{\tau}, \frac{1}{\delta})$ time algorithm that outputs a list $L = \{S_1, ..., S_\ell\}$ such that the following hold,*

1. *if $|\hat{f}(S)| \geq \tau$, then $S \in L$.*
2. *if $S \in L$, $|\hat{f}(S)| \geq \frac{\tau}{2}$.*

with probability $1 - \delta$.

The Goldreich-Levin queries are those that are selected by the above algorithm. Using the Goldreich-Levin algorithm, all the Fourier coefficients satisfying $|\hat{f}(S)| \geq 1/\mathrm{poly}(n)$ can be found in polynomial time (with high probability).

For any subset $T \subseteq [n]$, the Goldreich-Levin algorithm can be executed in a way that it only outputs subsets S such that $S \subseteq T$. In this case, the algorithm skips doing majority voting on the indices not in T, and uses less queries. In the event that the algorthim is executed in the described restricted manner, we will refer to the queries as the Goldreich-Levin queries on T.

For our construction, we will need the following "chopped tail" binomial distribution.

Definition 21. *Define the distribution, $\tilde{\beta}_\mu^n$, as the output of the following process. Draw $y \sim \beta_\mu^n$, and if $\mu n/2 \le |y| \le 3\mu n/2$ output y, else output $\perp$.*

For $\mu = \log(n)/n$, $\tilde{\beta}_\mu^n$ can be seen to have min-entropy $\Theta(log^2 n)$ [YZ16].

Fixing a $D_f \in \mathcal{D}_{\mathcal{F}_n}$, the Covert Learning algorithm begins by requesting "masked queries" from $\mathcal{O}_f$. Let $\ell = \Theta(log^2 n)$. For $x_1, \cdots, x_n \overset{\$}{\leftarrow} \beta_{1/2}^\ell$ and $y_1, \cdots, y_\ell \overset{\$}{\leftarrow} \beta_{1/2}^n$, let

$$\mathbf{U}_1 = \begin{bmatrix} x_1\, x_2\, x_3 \cdots x_n \end{bmatrix}, \mathbf{U}_2 = \begin{bmatrix} y_1\, y_2\, y_3 \cdots x_\ell \end{bmatrix}$$

Note that, each x_i or y_i is a column of $\mathbf{U}_1, \mathbf{U}_2$. Now, let $\mathbf{X} = \mathbf{U}_2\mathbf{U}_1$ Furthermore, let $s \overset{\$}{\leftarrow} \tilde{\beta}_\mu^n$ for $\mu = \log(n)/n$. A masked query $\hat{q} \in \{0,1\}^n$ for query $q \in \{0,1\}^n$ is generated by taking

$$\hat{q} = \mathbf{X}s \oplus e \oplus q$$

In the algorithm, each query q requested by the learner is a Goldreich-Levin query under the above masking. Indeed, the Goldreich-Levin queries are only masked and requested if they are one of the Goldreich-Levin queries on the relevant set T given by the target hypothesis class (as discussed above).

Upon receiving the responses to the masked Goldreich-Levin queries, denoted by $\mathcal{O}_f(\hat{q})$, the secret s for the masked query $\hat{q}$ is utilized to post-process $\mathcal{O}_f(\hat{q})$. The post-processed responses correlate with $f'(q)$, where f' is a function whose $O(\log n)$-degree Fourier coefficients are greater than $\Omega(\tau n^{-c})$ (for some small constant $c > 0$) wherever f has a Fourier coefficient greater than τ. By following the technique of Goldreich and Levin, we recover all the $O(\log n)$-degree Fourier coefficients of f' greater than $\Omega(\tau n^{-c})$—and therefore all the $O(\log n)$-degree Fourier coefficients of f greater than τ.

To prove privacy of the algorithm, the idea is to produce a simulator that first emulates the learner's queries, and then interacts with an AI by also passing as the oracle to the concept. It turns out that, assuming subexponential hardness of LPN, the masking procedure described above maps each query to a pseudorandom distribution. Thus, we will construct a simulator that requests truly random queries. Intuitively, it can then be shown that if there exists and AI such that an adversary distinguishes between the simulated interaction and the real interaction (where the requested queries are pseudorandom), then an adversary distinguishes the pseudorandom masked queries from random queries.

Theorem 9. *Under the $(2^{\omega(n^{\frac{1}{2}})}, 2^{\omega(n^{\frac{1}{2}})})$–$\mathsf{SLPN}_{\mu,n}$ assumption and for sufficiently large n, there exists a proper $(\mathrm{poly}(n), 1)$-covert learning algorithm for $\mathcal{C}_{\mathrm{FOURIER},b,n}$ with respect to $\mathcal{D}_{\mathcal{F}_n}, \mathcal{O}_{\mathcal{F}_n}$, and $\mathcal{L}^{\tau,b}$, and where $b \le O(\log n), \tau \ge 1/\mathrm{poly}(n), \delta \ge \exp(-n)$.*

The algorithm, called CLF, is presented in [CK21]. An important ingredient in the proof is the following hardness lemma due to [YZ16].

Lemma 1. *LPN on squared-log entropy (Simplified from [YZ16]).* Let n be a security parameter and let $\mu \leq 1/2$ be a constant. Assume that the $\mathsf{SLPN}_{\mu,n}$ problem is $(2^{\omega(n^{\frac{1}{2}})}, 2^{\omega(n^{\frac{1}{2}})})$-hard, then for every $\lambda = \Theta(log^2 \, n)$, $q = \mathrm{poly}(n)$, and every polynomial time sampleable $x \in \{0,1\}^n$ with $\boldsymbol{H}_\infty(x) \geq 2\lambda$,

$$(\boldsymbol{A}, \boldsymbol{A}x + e) \overset{c}{\approx} (\boldsymbol{A}, u)$$

where $\boldsymbol{A} = U_{q \times \lambda} U_{\lambda \times n}$ and $U_{m \times n}$ is a uniformly random $m \times n$ binary matrix, and $e \sim \beta_\mu^q$, $u \sim \{0,1\}^q$. We will call the task of distinguishing the above distributions the decisional squared-log entropy LPN problem.

Proof Idea. We first analyze the "unmasking" procedure ϕ defined in line 24. Essentially, the unmasking ϕ_i, which is applied to the response for the ith masked query, reintroduces a dependency on the secret used to construct the masking for the ith query. In this way, we may cancel some noisy terms in an expanded analysis of the oracle responses. We then leverage the pseudorandomness of the masked queries to show that, roughly, the responses to the unmasked queries can be written as noisy inner products with any $O(\log n)$-degree parity function which the target function of the concept has a "heavy" Fourier coefficient attached. Using this fact, we prove that running a "local decoding" of each bit of any $O(\log n)$-degree parity function where this is true suffices to recover the parity functions we are interested in. We prove that this is the case by using techniques inspired by the original analysis of the Goldreich-Levin algorithm [GL89].

2.5   Covert Learning of Polynomial Size Decision Trees

In this section, we supply a natural application of Covert Learning for low-degree Fourier coefficients. Specifically, we will show that the collection of hypothesis classes given by taking all subsets of polynomial size decision trees is covertly learnable. Recall that we are focused on collections that contain hypothesis classes which are not (or not known to be) efficiently agnostically PAC learnable from uniformly random examples. The problem of learning decision trees under the uniform distribution has long been considered, and yet no polynomial time (in the size of the smallest decision tree) algorithms exist for arbitrary functions, and some distributions over functions [BFKL93,IKOS19] (even in the realizable case). In fact, any such algorithm would be considered a massive breakthrough in computational learning theory [Blu03, OS07][3].

Definition 22. *Let* $\mathsf{DT}_{n,s}$ *be the hypothesis class of all* $f : \{0,1\}^n \to \{-1,1\}$ *computable by a size* s *decision tree. Let* $\mathcal{C}_{\mathsf{DT}_{n,s}} = \{\mathcal{H}_n | \mathcal{H}_n \subseteq \mathsf{DT}_{n,s}\}$.

This collection of hypothesis classes is motivated for the following simple reason. If an adversary has no information about which subset of decision trees has been learned, then the adversary has no information about the learned decision tree. This claim is easily seen to be true from the contrapositive. The algorithm is presented as CLDT in [CK21].

Theorem 10. *Under the* $(2^{\omega(n^{\frac{1}{2}})}, 2^{\omega(n^{\frac{1}{2}})})$–$\mathsf{SLPN}_{\mu,n}$ *assumption, the collection* $\mathcal{C}_{\mathsf{DT}_{n,s}}$ *for* $s = \mathrm{poly}(n)$ *is* $(\mathrm{poly}(n), 4)$*- covertly learnable, with respect to* $\mathcal{D}_{\mathcal{F}_n}$, $\mathcal{O}_{\mathcal{F}_n}$, *and* $\mathcal{L}_D$, *and where* $\epsilon \geq 1/\mathrm{poly}(n)$, *and* $\delta \geq \exp(-n)$.

3   Covert Verifiable Learning

In this section we define and construct the notion of Covert *Verifiable* Learning. The Covert Verifiable Learning setting can be viewed as an interactive protocol between a learner and an *adversarial intermediary* (AI). Here, the adversarial intermediary monitors access to the membership oracle. Figure 2 depicts this perspective. In this context, the learner must request queries from the oracle, but the responses are intercepted by the AI who then either truthfully reports the oracle's responses, or lies.

3.1   Definition of Covert Verifiable Learning

For Covert Verifiable Learning, we augment the desired properties of Covert Learning by allowing the learner to abort, and requiring: If the AI corrupts any queries or results, the learner will not output an incorrect hypothesis except with small probability. In addition, we will extend the privacy requirements of Covert Learning to capture the active nature of the adversarial intermediary. Let us informally describe the Covert Verifiable Learning setting in more detail.

---

[3] Not much formal work has been done on identifying "hard distributions" over DNF formulas (or other function classes) [BFKL93, IKOS19], as it is not relevant in the usual learning models. However, even some relatively simple distributions appear to defy all known techniques. For example, consider the distribution over polynomial size DNFs (also, decision trees), constructed as follows. Select at random two disjoint subsets of $[n]$ of size $\log n$ each. Let the first subset be denoted S and the second T. The distribution over DNFs induced by defining $f(x) = \chi_S(x) \oplus \mathsf{majority}_T(x)$ seems hard to even weakly predict over the uniform distribution [BFKL93]. Indeed, such a distribution over DNF formulas could be used to instantiate our Covert Learning algorithms of this section.

The Learner's Inputs: Similarly to the Covert Learning setting, the learner will receive as input a specific target hypothesis class $\mathcal{H}_n$ (within a fixed collection $\mathcal{C}_n$), in addition to accuracy parameters ϵ, δ. The learner will *also* receive a set of auxiliary random examples from a concept D_n within a concept class $\mathcal{D}_n$ which are private—the AI has no information on the identity of these random examples.

The Interaction: The learner will interact with an oracle $\mathcal{O}_{D_n}$ that implements query access to the concept. However, the responses have the potential to be corrupted by an AI who lives between the learner and the oracle. The learner tries to learn $\mathcal{H}_n$ with respect to the concept D_n.

The Security Experiment: We define a real and ideal experiment.

Definition 23. *Let $\mathcal{D}_n$ be a concept class, and let $\mathcal{C}_n$ be a collection of hypothesis classes. Let $\mathcal{I}$ be a p.p.t adversarial intermediary algorithm, which takes as input ϵ, δ, and a set of queries and the oracle's responses on those queries. We define $\{\mathsf{Vreal}_{A,\mathcal{I}}^{\mathcal{O}_{D_n}}\}$ to be the distribution generated by the following process.*

1. *An adversary (a distinguisher) chooses a target hypothesis class $\mathcal{H}_n \in \mathcal{C}_n$, a concept $D_n \in \mathcal{D}_n$, and accuracy parameters $\epsilon, \delta > 0$.*
2. *A set of random examples $\mathcal{S}$ is drawn from D_n. $\mathcal{S}$ is given to the learner, along with $\mathcal{H}_n, \epsilon, \delta$, while the adversarial intermediary $\mathcal{I}$ is given ϵ, δ.*
3. *The learner begins to interact with the concept oracle $\mathcal{O}_{D_n}$ by requesting membership queries in order to agnostically learn $\mathcal{H}_n$. $\mathcal{I}$ sees the learner's queries and responses and is given the chance to modify the responses. At the end of the interaction, $\mathcal{I}$ outputs a string denoted by $\mathsf{real}_{A,\mathcal{I}}^{\mathcal{O}_{D_n}}$.*
4. *Output $\left(\mathcal{H}_n, \epsilon, \delta, \mathcal{S}, \mathsf{real}_{A,\mathcal{I}}^{\mathcal{O}_{D_n}} \right)$*

Definition 24. *Let Sim be a p.p.t. algorithm, which takes as input two sets of random examples from the concept and a length parameter ℓ which signifies the number of queries requested by the learner in the real interaction. Let $\mathcal{I}$ be a p.p.t adversarial intermediary algorithm, which takes as input ϵ, δ, and a set of queries and oracle's responses. We define $\{\mathsf{Videal}_{Sim,\mathcal{I}}\}$ to be the distribution generated by the following process.*

1. *An adversary (a distinguisher) chooses a target hypothesis class $\mathcal{H}_n \in \mathcal{C}_n$, a concept $D_n \in \mathcal{D}_n$, and accuracy parameters $\epsilon, \delta > 0$.*
2. *A set of random examples $\mathcal{S}'$ is drawn from D_n.*
3. *The simulator is given $\epsilon, \delta, \mathcal{S}, \mathcal{S}'$ (where $\mathcal{S}$ is the set of examples given to the learner in the real interaction), while an adversarial intermediary $\mathcal{I}$ is given ϵ, δ.*
4. *Sim begins to "interact" with the $\mathcal{O}_{D_n}$ by "requesting" membership queries. $\mathcal{I}$ "views" the queries and responses, and is given the chance to change the responses. The simulator outputs a string, which is denoted by $\mathsf{ideal}_{\mathcal{I}}^{Sim}$.*
5. *Output $\left(\mathcal{H}_n, \epsilon, \delta, \mathcal{S}, \mathsf{ideal}_{\mathcal{I}}^{Sim} \right)$*

Definition 25. *Covert Verifiable Learning. Let C_n be a collection of hypothesis classes, let $\mathcal{D}_n$ be a class of concepts, let $\mathcal{O}_{\mathcal{D}_n}$ be a class of oracles indexed by $D_n \in \mathcal{D}_n$, and let $\mathcal{L}$ be a loss function. An algorithm $\mathcal{A}$ is an $(m(n), \alpha)$-covert verifiable learning algorithm for C_n, with respect to $\mathcal{D}_n$, $\mathcal{O}_{\mathcal{D}_n}$ and $\mathcal{L}$, if for every $\epsilon, \delta > 0$, the following are true.*

– *Completeness. If for any distribution $D_n \in \mathcal{D}_n$, any hypothesis class $\mathcal{H}_n \in C_n$, and where $\mathcal{S}$ is a set of size $m(n)$ of examples drawn i.i.d. from D_n, the randomized output of $h = \mathcal{A}^{\mathcal{O}_{D_n}}(\mathcal{H}_n, \epsilon, \delta, \mathcal{S})$ satisfies*

$$\Pr_h \left[\mathcal{L}(h) \leq \alpha \cdot \mathcal{L}(\mathcal{H}_n) + \epsilon \right] \geq 1 - \delta$$

– *Soundness. If for any distribution $D_n \in \mathcal{D}_n$, any hypothesis class $\mathcal{H}_n \in C_n$, and where $\mathcal{S}$ is a set of size $m(n)$ of examples drawn i.i.d. from D_n, then for any adversarial intermediary $\mathcal{I}$ that corrupts queries or responses from $\mathcal{A}$ to $\mathcal{O}_{D_n}$, the random variable $h = \mathcal{A}^{\mathcal{O}_{D_n}}(\mathcal{H}_n, \epsilon, \delta, \mathcal{S})$ satisfies*

$$\Pr_h \left[\mathcal{L}(h) > \alpha \cdot \mathcal{L}(\mathcal{H}_n) + \epsilon \;\middle|\; h \neq \text{reject} \right] < \delta$$

We say that soundness is computational if $\mathcal{I}$ is p.p.t..
– *Privacy. For any adversarial intermediary $\mathcal{I}$, there exists a p.p.t. simulation algorithm Sim that satisfies:*

$$\left\{ \mathsf{Vreal}_{\mathcal{A},\mathcal{I}}^{\mathcal{O}_{\mathcal{D}_n}} \right\} \overset{c}{\approx} \left\{ \mathsf{Videal}_{Sim,\mathcal{I}} \right\}$$

We stipulate that each of the sets of random examples given to the simulator are of size $m(n)$.

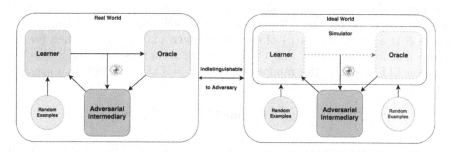

Fig. 4. Privacy of Covert Verifiable Learning. The "real world," where the AI interacts with the learner and oracle, should be indistinguishable from the "ideal world," where the AI interacts with a simulator that plays both roles of learner and oracle. Importantly, the simulator works without knowledge of the underlying hypothesis classes or the actual oracle, though it does have access to random examples from the concept.

In keeping with the terminology from the computational learning theory literature, we will often say that a collection of hypothesis classes $\mathcal{C}$ is verifiably $(m(n), \alpha)$-*verifiably covertly learnable* if there exists a $(m(n), \alpha)$-covert verifiable learning algorithm for $\mathcal{C}$ (Fig. 4).

Discussion

Variants. We would like to highlight some salient variants of the model that we have presented above. The variants are on the nature of the random examples that are present in the interaction. For example, we could also consider the case that the learner's random examples are publicly known. We call this setting the *public* Covert Verifiable learning variant. In this public variant, achieving soundness and privacy is much more difficult, as the learner has no private examples to leverage against the AI. However, this variant significantly increases the practicality of the model because it may be infeasible for the learner to acquire private examples. In Sect. 3.4, we focus on this case. Another variant of the formally stated model involves weakening the privacy requirement to require indistinguishability of only the membership queries, and not for the joint distribution of the private random examples and membership queries. This model (called the *fully private examples* variant), may be justified, as we already consider private examples in order to achieve soundness. In the full version [CK21] of this paper, we show that this model is quite powerful, even if we require *perfect* privacy and *statistical* soundness. We opt to focus (in Sect. 2.4 and Sect. 2.5) on the case where privacy is with respect to the joint distribution since it seems to be the "right" level of difficulty. Additionally, this model provides strong "zero-knowledge-style" guarantees in a forward focused manner. That is, even if private examples used for verification (a one time event) become known in the future, then the privacy guarantees remain intact.

3.2   Making CLF **Verifiable**

In this section, we show how to add the soundness guarantee of Covert Verifiable Learning to CLF. More specifically, we want to provide the guarantee that if for any concept $D_f \in \mathcal{D}_{\mathcal{F}_n}$, any hypothesis class $\text{FOURIER}_{T,b,n} \in \mathcal{C}_{\text{FOURIER},b,n}$, and where $\mathcal{S}$ is a set of size $m(n)$ of examples drawn i.i.d. from D_f, then for any adversarial intermediary $\mathcal{I}$ that corrupts oracle responses from the interaction between CLF and $\mathcal{O}_f$, the random variable $h = \text{CLF}^{\mathcal{O}_f}(\text{FOURIER}_{T,b,n}, \epsilon, \delta, \mathcal{S})$ satisfies

$$\Pr_h \left[\mathcal{L}^{\tau,b}(h) > \alpha \cdot \mathcal{L}^{\tau,b}(\text{FOURIER}_{T,b,n}) + \epsilon \; \middle| \; h \neq \text{reject} \right] < \delta$$

Our basic idea to achieve verifiability is to wrap the CLF algorithm with an outer loop, which attempts to catch the adversarial intermediary cheating by randomly deciding to either execute CLF (the "learning" case) or send queries which are part of the learner's private example set $\mathcal{S}$ (the "test" case). The crucial point is: the queries of the learning case can be shown to be computationally indistinguishable from the test queries (which are simply uniformly random). This system gives an easy proof idea for soundness: The (p.p.t.) adversarial intermediary must lie a similar amount on the learning case and the test case, else it would contradict the pseudorandomness of the queries made by CLF. Therefore, since the AI can always be detected if it lies in the test case, it cannot reliably lie on the learning case, without being detected.

Theorem 11. *Under the $(2^{\omega(n^{\frac{1}{2}})}, 2^{\omega(n^{\frac{1}{2}})})$–$\mathsf{SLPN}_{\mu,n}$ assumption, there exists a $(\mathrm{poly}(n), 1)$-covert verifiable learning algorithm for $\mathcal{C}_{\mathsf{FOURIER},b,n}$ with respect to $\mathcal{D}_{\mathcal{F}_n}$, $\mathcal{O}_{\mathcal{F}_n}$, and $\mathcal{L}^{\tau,b}$, and where the degree bound $b \leq O(\log n)$ and $\tau \geq 1/\mathrm{poly}(n)$.*

3.3 Making CLDT Verifiable

To make CLDT verifiable, almost all of the work has already been done by constructing CVLF. We may modify CLDT by replacing the subroutine of CLF in CVLF, and this alone suffices. The resulting algorithm, called CVLDT, is presented [CK21].

All three guarantees of Covert Verifiable Learning intuitively hold for CLDT, as all the communication of CVLDT is contained in CVLDT.

Theorem 12. *Under the $(2^{\omega(n^{\frac{1}{2}})}, 2^{\omega(n^{\frac{1}{2}})})$–$\mathsf{SLPN}_{\mu,n}$ assumption, the collection $\mathcal{C}_{\mathsf{DT}_{n,s}}$ for $s \leq \mathrm{poly}(n)$ is $(\mathrm{poly}(n), 4)$- covertly verifiably learnable, with respect to $\mathcal{D}_{\mathcal{F}_n}$, $\mathcal{O}_{\mathcal{F}_n}$, and $\mathcal{L}_D$, and where $\epsilon \geq 1/\mathrm{poly}(n)$, and $\delta \geq \exp(-n)$.*

3.4 Verifiability Without Secret Examples

In this section, we pose the question: *can we achieve Covert Verifiable Learning in a setting where the learner has no private examples to leverage against the adversarial intermediary?* Indeed, we are considering the *public* Covert Verifiable Learning model briefly discussed in Sect. 3.1.

We will demonstrate that our CVL protocol for low-degree Fourier coefficients of Sect. 2.4 can be adapted to fit the Public Covert Verifiable Learning (PCVL) model (formally defined in [CK21]). From there, we can conclude that an application to decision trees is suitable, similar to that of Sect. 2.5.

Our algorithm CVLF (and soundness proof) falls short of the PCVL model—it makes crucial use of secret examples. Specifically, the AI will always know when the learner is executing a "test" case, because it has access to the test examples before hand, and as a result can distinguish them from the learning case. Our idea to adapt is as follows. Instead of threatening to send private random examples at each iteration (with probability $1/2$), we threaten to send the public examples under the same masking that we use on the Goldreich-Levin queries. In this way, we can show that the computationally bounded AI will be caught lying with high probability; the AI will not be able to link the masked public examples with the real public examples. We will require that the concept is computed by a polynomial size DNF formula[4], and this will be essential to letting the learner detect an AI. Why this is the case will become clear shortly, but intuitively, we must assume some structure on the concept; otherwise the learner has no hope in obtaining any correlation on the public examples save querying for them. Clearly, if the learner cannot get any correlation on the public examples without querying them, then the AI will always be able to deceive the learner.

---

[4] Note that, this is still an agnostic setting, despite not being *fully* agnostic, as before.

Definition 26. *Let $s\text{-}\mathcal{DNF}_n$ be the class of all $f : \{0,1\}^n \to \{-1,1\}$ such that f is computable by a size s DNF formula. A DNF formula is said to have size s if it has s clauses.*

Theorem 13. *Under the $(2^{\omega(n^{\frac{1}{2}})}, 2^{\omega(n^{\frac{1}{2}})})\text{-}\mathsf{SLPN}_{\mu,n}$ assumption, there exists a proper $(\text{poly}(n), 1)$-Public covert verifiable learning algorithm for $\mathcal{C}_{\mathsf{FOURIER},b,n}$ with respect to $\mathcal{D}_{s\text{-}\mathcal{DNF}_n}$, $\mathcal{O}_{s\text{-}\mathcal{DNF}_n}$, and $\mathcal{L}^{\tau,b}$, and where $\delta \geq \exp(-n), b \leq O(\log n), 1/\text{poly}(n) \leq \tau \leq 1/2(2s+1)^2$, and the DNF size $s \leq \text{poly}(n)$.*

The algorithm is presented as PCVLF in [CK21].

Proof Idea. We begin with a lemma that establishes a correlation between the "test case" queries of the learner and the publicly available examples. Using this lemma, we can prove soundness by showing that if the AI lies on a "significant" amount of queries then the learner will be able to detect this using the correlation with the public examples. On the other hand, we observe that if the AI lies on a "less than significant" amount of queries, completeness still holds from the properties of CVLF—thus we conclude PCVLF is sound. For completeness, we need to prove that, essentially, the learner will not accidentally abort the interaction too often. This is done by bounding the probability that an honest AI is unlucky using standard probabilistic techniques. Finally, the proof of privacy is done by adapting the simulator and reduction of the proof of Theorem 11 to appropriately reflect the changes we made in the test case of the algorithm.

Acknowledgements. We would like to thank Shafi Goldwasser and Ronitt Rubinfeld for very helpful discussions on the model and its motivation.

References

[ACPS09] Applebaum, B., Cash, D., Peikert, C., Sahai, A.: Fast cryptographic primitives and circular-secure encryption based on hard learning problems. In: Halevi, S. (ed.) CRYPTO 2009. LNCS, vol. 5677, pp. 595–618. Springer, Heidelberg (2009). https://doi.org/10.1007/978-3-642-03356-8_35

[AFK13] Awasthi, P., Feldman, V., Kanade, V.: Learning using local membership queries. In: Conference on Learning Theory, pp. 398–431 (2013)

[Ale03] Alekhnovich, M.: More on average case vs approximation complexity. In: 44th Annual IEEE Symposium on Foundations of Computer Science 2003, Proceedings, pp. 298–307. IEEE (2003)

[BFKL93] Blum, A., Furst, M., Kearns, M., Lipton, R.J.: Cryptographic primitives based on hard learning problems. In: Stinson, D.R. (ed.) CRYPTO 1993. LNCS, vol. 773, pp. 278–291. Springer, Heidelberg (1994). https://doi.org/10.1007/3-540-48329-2_24

[BHZ19] Bshouty, N.H., Haddad-Zaknoon, C.A.: Adaptive exact learning of decision trees from membership queries. In: Algorithmic Learning Theory, pp. 207–234. PMLR (2019)

[Blu03] Blum, A.: Open problems-learning a function of r relevant variables. Lect. Notes Comput. Sci. **2777**, 731–733 (2003)

[CK21]   Canetti, R., Karchmer, A.: Covert learning: how to learn with an untrusted intermediary (2021). https://ia.cr/2021/764

[Cla11]   Clark, D.E.: Outsourcing lead optimization: the eye of the storm. Drug Discov. Today **16**(3–4), 147–157 (2011)

[DAG06]   Dudek, A.Z., Arodz, T., Gálvez, J.: Computational methods in developing quantitative structure-activity relationships (QSAR): a review. Comb. Chem. High Throughput Screening **9**(3), 213–228 (2006)

[DGRDR08]   De Grave, K., Ramon, J., De Raedt, L.: Active learning for high throughput screening. In: Jean-Fran, J.-F., Berthold, M.R., Horváth, T. (eds.) DS 2008. LNCS (LNAI), vol. 5255, pp. 185–196. Springer, Heidelberg (2008). https://doi.org/10.1007/978-3-540-88411-8_19

[Fel09]   Feldman, V.: On the power of membership queries in agnostic learning. J. Mach. Learn. Res. **10**, 163–182 (2009)

[GL89]   Goldreich, O., Levin, L.A.: A hard-core predicate for all one-way functions. In: Proceedings of the Twenty-First Annual ACM Symposium on Theory of Computing, pp. 25–32 (1989)

[GRSY20]   Goldwasser, S., Rothblum, G.N., Shafer, J., Yehudayoff, A.: Interactive proofs for verifying machine learning. Electronic Colloquium on Computational Complexity (ECCC), 27:58 (2020)

[IKOS19]   Ishai, Y., Kushilevitz, E., Ostrovsky, R., Sahai, A.: Cryptographic sensing. In: Boldyreva, A., Micciancio, D. (eds.) CRYPTO 2019. LNCS, vol. 11694, pp. 583–604. Springer, Cham (2019). https://doi.org/10.1007/978-3-030-26954-8_19

[Jac97]   Jackson, J.C.: An efficient membership-query algorithm for learning DNF with respect to the uniform distribution. J. Comput. Syst. Sci. **55**(3), 414–440 (1997)

[KLN+11]   Kasiviswanathan, S.P., Lee, H.K., Nissim, K., Raskhodnikova, S., Smith, A.: What can we learn privately? SIAM J. Comput. **40**(3), 793–826 (2011)

[KM93]   Kushilevitz, E., Mansour, Y.: Learning decision trees using the Fourier spectrum. SIAM J. Comput. **22**(6), 1331–1348 (1993)

[LPP04]   Landrum, G.A., Penzotti, J.E., Putta, S.: Machine-learning models for combinatorial catalyst discovery. Meas. Sci. Technol. **16**(1), 270 (2004)

[OS07]   O'Donnell, R., Servedio, R.A.: Learning monotone decision trees in polynomial time. SIAM J. Comput. **37**(3), 827–844 (2007)

[Pie12]   Pietrzak, K.: Cryptography from learning parity with noise. In: Bieliková, M., Friedrich, G., Gottlob, G., Katzenbeisser, S., Turán, G. (eds.) SOFSEM 2012. LNCS, vol. 7147, pp. 99–114. Springer, Heidelberg (2012). https://doi.org/10.1007/978-3-642-27660-6_9

[PRR06]   Parnas, M., Ron, D., Rubinfeld, R.: Tolerant property testing and distance approximation. J. Comput. Syst. Sci. **72**(6), 1012–1042 (2006)

[YS16]   Yu, Yu., Steinberger, J.: Pseudorandom functions in almost constant depth from low-noise LPN. In: Fischlin, M., Coron, J.-S. (eds.) EUROCRYPT 2016. LNCS, vol. 9666, pp. 154–183. Springer, Heidelberg (2016). https://doi.org/10.1007/978-3-662-49896-5_6

[YZ16]   Yu, Yu., Zhang, J.: Cryptography with auxiliary input and trapdoor from constant-noise LPN. In: Robshaw, M., Katz, J. (eds.) CRYPTO 2016. LNCS, vol. 9814, pp. 214–243. Springer, Heidelberg (2016). https://doi.org/10.1007/978-3-662-53018-4_9

Random-Index PIR and Applications

Craig Gentry[1($\boxtimes$)], Shai Halevi[1], Bernardo Magri[2,3], Jesper Buus Nielsen[2,3], and Sophia Yakoubov[3]

[1] Algorand Foundation, New York, USA
shaih@alum.mit.edu
[2] Concordium Blockchain Research Center, Aarhus University, Aarhus, Denmark
{magri,jbn}@cs.au.dk
[3] Aarhus University, Aarhus, Denmark

Abstract. Private information retrieval (PIR) lets a client retrieve an entry from a database without the server learning which entry was retrieved. Here we study a weaker variant that we call *random-index PIR* (RPIR), where the retrieved index is an *output* rather than an input of the protocol, and is chosen at random. RPIR is clearly weaker than PIR, but it suffices for some interesting applications and may be realized more efficiently than full-blown PIR.

We report here on two lines of work, both tied to RPIR but otherwise largely unrelated. The first line of work studies RPIR as a primitive on its own. Perhaps surprisingly, we show that RPIR is in fact equivalent to PIR when there are no restrictions on the number of communication rounds. On the other hand, RPIR can be implemented in a "noninteractive" setting (with pre-processing), which is clearly impossible for PIR. For two-server RPIR we even show a truly noninteractive solution, offering information-theoretic security without any pre-processing.

The other line of work, which was the original motivation for our work, uses RPIR to improve on the recent work of Benhamouda *et al.* (TCC'20) for maintaining secret values on public blockchains. Their solution depends on a method for selecting many random public keys from a PKI while hiding most of the selected keys from an adversary. However, the method they proposed is vulnerable to a double-dipping attack, limiting its resilience. Here we observe that a RPIR protocol, where the client is implemented via secure MPC, can eliminate that vulnerability. We thus get a secrets-on-blockchain protocol (and more generally large-scale MPC) which is resilient to any fraction $f < 1/2$ of corrupted parties, resolving the main open problem left from the work of Benhamouda *et al.*

As the client in this solution is implemented via secure MPC, it really brings home the need to make it as efficient as possible. We thus strive to

J. B. Nielsen—Partially funded by The Concordium Foundation; The Danish Independent Research Council under Grant-ID DFF-8021-00366B (BETHE); The Carlsberg Foundation under the Semper Ardens Research Project CF18-112 (BCM).

S. Yakoubov—Funded by the European Research Council (ERC) under the European Unions's Horizon 2020 research and innovation programme under grant agreement No 669255 (MPCPRO).

K. Nissim and B. Waters (Eds.): TCC 2021, LNCS 13044, pp. 32–61, 2021.
https://doi.org/10.1007/978-3-030-90456-2_2

explore whatever efficiency gains we can get by using RPIR rather than PIR. We achieve more gains by using *batch RPIR* where multiple indexes are retrieved at once. Lastly, we observe that this application can make do with a weaker security guarantee than full RPIR, and show that this weaker variant can be realized even more efficiently. We discuss one protocol in particular that may be attractive for practical implementations.

Keywords: Private information retrieval · Batch PIR · Random PIR · Large-scale MPC · Secrets on blockchain · Random ORAM

1   Introduction

A Private Information Retrieval (PIR) scheme lets a client fetch an entry from a database held by a server, without the server learning which entry was retrieved. The database is typically modelled as an n-bit string $DB \in \{0,1\}^n$, known in full to the server. The client has an input index $i \in [n]$, and its goal is to retrieve the bit $DB[i]$. A PIR scheme is secure if the server cannot distinguish between any two possible input indexes i, i' for the client, and it is *nontrivial* if the server sends to the client less than n bits. PIR was introduced by Chor et al. [6] who described a solution with multiple non-colluding servers; a single-server solution was first described by Kushilevitz and Ostrovsky [14].

1.1   Random-Index PIR (RPIR)

In this work we consider a similar setting, but with a twist. Rather than a specific index, in our setting the client wishes to retrieve *a random index* from the database, without the server learning which index was retrieved. Namely, instead of the index i being an input to the protocol, we consider it an output, and require that it be random. We call such a scheme random-index PIR (RPIR). While clearly a weaker variant of PIR, we show below that RPIR suffices for some interesting applications. Of course, RPIR can be easily implemented by having the client choose i at random and then run a PIR protocol. But being a weaker variant, we could hope that RPIR is easier and more efficient to implement than full blown PIR. Such improved efficiency could be critical for some applications, including our motivating application of large-scale secure MPC (which is described below).

One measure of efficiency is the number of communication rounds. We show that, unlike PIR, RPIR can be implemented in a "noninteractive" fashion. Namely, after a pre-processing stage in which the client sends to the server some string whose length depends only on the security parameter κ, we only allow server-to-client communication and we want to perform arbitrarily many RPIR executions. It is clear that no such nontrivial PIR protocols exist, since there is no way for such protocols to incorporate the client's input. However, we show that some existing interactive PIR protocols can be adapted to yield noninteractive

RPIR protocols. (These can be based on fully homomorphic encryption or one-way trapdoor permutations.) Moreover, for the two-server setting we show that a nontrivial noninteractive protocol is possible even without any pre-processing. Other examples of settings where RPIR is more efficient than PIR are discussed in Sect. 1.3 below.

On the other hand, we show that such efficiency gains are necessarily limited, since every RPIR protocol can be converted into a PIR protocol with only slightly more communication and rounds. Specifically, given a r-round RPIR protocol with server communication $m < n$, we show how to construct:

- A $((r+1)\log n)$-round PIR with server communication $1 + m\log n$; or
- A $(r+2)$-round PIR with server communication $O(\sqrt{mn})$.

We note that the latter transformation relies on a long client-to-server message. We also describe a simple variant with a short client-to-server message, where the server communication is $m + \frac{n}{2}$.

1.2   Applications

Computing on Public Blockchains. Our initial motivation for studying RPIR came from a recent work of Benhamouda *et al.* [2] (BGG+) about maintaining secret values on public blockchains. In that work they construct a scalable evolving-committee proactive secret-sharing (ECPSS) scheme, that allows dynamically-changing small committees to maintain a secret over a public blockchain. The main challenge in that work was to choose a small committee from within a large population in such a way that (a) everyone can send messages to committee members, and yet (b) a mobile adversary does not learn who they are and therefore cannot target them for corruption. Once chosen, such committees can execute the proactive secret sharing protocol (or more generally any secure-MPC protocol).

A drawback of the BGG+ scheme is that, in order to guarantee an honest majority within the committees, it can only tolerate up to about $1/4$ corruptions overall. The reason is that committee-selection is done by individual parties, who "nominate" members to the new committee by drawing their public keys from a list and then re-randomizing them. This nomination style enables a double-dipping adversarial strategy: corrupted parties can always nominate other corrupted parties, while honest parties nominate randomly selected parties (so they too sometimes nominate corrupted parties by chance).

To do better, we can try to delegate the nomination task to previous committees, who would emulate an honest nominator via secure MPC. Roughly, the function computed by the committee-selection procedure of [2] is

$$\text{Nominate}(n \text{ public keys, randomness}) = k \text{ re-randomized keys.}$$

We can let previous committees compute that randomized function, without the adversary learning anything about who the honest nominees are, hence depriving it of the double-dipping strategy above. The problem with this solution, however, is that it scales poorly with the total number of parties: The circuit of the Nominate function above has input of size linear in n, hence a naive secure-MPC protocol for it would have complexity more than n.

This is where RPIR comes in. The only role that the input plays in the Nominate function is of a database from which we choose $k \ll n$ random entries. We therefore employ a variant of MPC-in-the-head, letting previous committees play the role of the RPIR client while each committee member individually mentally plays the role of the RPIR server. (The database is the list of n public keys, which is known to everyone; so, the state of the RPIR server is public.)

The result of the RPIR protocol is the previous committee holding a set of k random keys, but since we have honest-majority in the committee then the adversary does not know whose keys were chosen. The committee then runs a secure-MPC protocol to re-randomize the chosen keys and output the result. This time, the circuit size depends on the complexity of the RPIR client. For some RPIR constructions, this depends only on k, not on the total number n of keys. Putting all these ideas together we get:

Theorem (informal): In the model of [2], there exists a scalable ECPSS scheme tolerating any fraction $f < 1/2$ of corrupted parties.

Of course, once we have the committees we can again let them compute on secrets rather than just pass them along, hence we have:

Theorem (informal): In the model of [2], there exists a scalable secure MPC scheme tolerating any fraction $f < 1/2$ of corrupted parties.

PIR with Preprocessing. In many applications it is interesting to consider offline preprocessing before the inputs are known, which can help improve the efficiency of the on-line computation once all the inputs are available. This approach is very popular in contemporary secure-MPC work, and was also used for PIR (e.g., [1,8]).

As it turns out, our PIR-to-RPIR reductions from Sect. 2.4 can be used for that purpose. These reductions have the following format: They first run the underlying RPIR protocol on the original database DB, letting the client learn a few random bits from it. The client then sends a single message to the server, from which the server computes a new database DB' of size $n' < n$. The parties then run a PIR protocol on the new (smaller) database, and the client uses what it learns to compute the bit that it needs from the original DB.

This format makes it possible to run the RPIR protocol in a pre-processing phase, before the client knowns what index it wants, and only execute the last part during the online phase. Using a standard PIR to implement the RPIR in the pre-processing step, we obtain a black-box method of shifting work from the online to the offline phase of a PIR protocol. If $CC(n, \kappa)$ is the server communication complexity of an underlying PIR protocol (as a function of the database size n and the security parameter κ), the online server communication complexity of the resulting protocol with preprocessing will be only $CC(n', \kappa)$. Specifically:

– Using the SimplePIR protocol from Sect. 2.4, we obtain a PIR-with-Preprocessing protocol with offline communication $CC(n, \kappa)$, online communication $CC(n/2, \kappa)$, and the client sending one more message of $\log n$ bits.
– Using the PartitionPIR protocol from Sect. 2.4, we get for any $t < n$ a PIR-with-Preprocessing protocol with offline communication $t \cdot CC(n, \kappa)$, online communication $CC(O(n/t), \kappa)$, and the client sending one more long message (of more than n bits).

1.3   Batch RPIR

In our first motivating application in Sect. 1.2, the client needs to fetch not one but k random entries from the database, so we would like to amortize the work and implement it in complexity less than that of k independent RPIR executions. Building such batch PIR protocols from PIR was studied by Ishai, Kushilevitz, Ostrovsky, and Sahai (IKOS) [13]. However, their solutions require the underlying protocol to be a full-blown PIR protocol (rather than RPIR). It is not clear how to build batch-RPIR protocols from an underlying RPIR protocol any better than either running k independent instances of RPIR, or converting to full-blown PIR and using the IKOS solutions.

But it turns out that our motivating application can make do with a weaker security notion than what RPIR provides. What we care about in this application is not quite that the indexes look random to the server, but rather that a server with limited "corruption budget" in the entire population cannot corrupt too many of the selected indexes (whp). Roughly, we can replace the pseudorandomness of the indexes from the server's perspective by unpredictability. Defining this property takes some care. In Sect. 5.1 we provide a definition in the real/ideal style.

Having lowered the security bar, we take another look at the constructions from [13] and note that we can use better parameters than are possible for batch-PIR (or batch-RPIR with strong security). Moreover, we describe in Sect. 5.2 an even simpler construction that cannot possibly work for batch PIR or strong-RPIR, but we prove that it meets our weaker security notion of batch RPIR. The simplicity and efficiency of this construction may be attractive for practical implementations.

1.4   Multi-server RPIR

It is known that nontrivial single-server PIR cannot offer information-theoretic privacy; nontrivial single-server RPIR has the same limitation. It is interesting to ask whether by involving multiple non-colluding servers (each with the same database as input) we can build RPIR that is (a) nontrivial, (b) information-theoretic and (c) noninteractive (meaning that only a single round of communication—from each server to the client—is required). We answer this question in the affirmative; we show a two-server nontrivial, information-theoretic noninteractive RPIR with communication complexity equal to half the size of the database.

While it seems that multi-server RPIR cannot be used directly in the application of secure computation on public blockchains, it can be used for PIR pre-processing (either for a multi-server PIR execution with the same servers that participated in the pre-processing, or perhaps even for a single-server PIR execution with only one of those servers).

1.5   Organization

In Sect. 2 we formally define (single-server and multi-server) RPIR, and study the relationship between RPIR and PIR. In Sect. 3 we describe some constructions of RPIR in the noninteractive setting. In Sect. 4 we describe the application of batch RPIR with weak security to the architecture of Benhamouda *et al.* [2] for large-scale MPC. Motivated by this application, we study in Sect. 5 more efficient constructions of batch-RPIR.

In Appendix A we describe the notion of a *random-index oblivious-RAM* (RORAM), which relates to ORAM in the same way that RPIR relates to PIR. In particular we show that RORAM can replace RPIR in the same context of large-scale MPC, offering a somewhat different performance profile. For completeness, in Appendix B we discuss a third approach for the large-scale MPC context that uses mix-nets.

2   Random-Index Private Information Retrieval

2.1   Background: Private Information Retrieval

A single-server Private Information Retrieval (PIR) scheme is a two-party protocol Π between a server holding a n-bit string $DB \in \{0, 1\}^n$ and a client holding an index $i \in [n]$. In addition, both parties know the security parameter κ.

We assume for simplicity that the server communication complexity, i.e. the number of bits sent by the server, depends only on n and κ, but not on the specific values of DB and i (or the protocol randomness), and denote it by $CC_\Pi(n, \kappa)$. The two properties of interest for a PIR protocol Π are its client-privacy (i.e. the index i is hidden from the server) and its communication complexity.

Definition 1 (Single-server PIR [14]**).** *A two-party protocol Π is a (semi-honest) single-server PIR if it satisfies:*

Correctness. *The client's output is $DB[i]$, except with probability negligible in κ.*
Client privacy. *For every n, database $DB \in \{0, 1\}^n$, and indexes $i, i' \in [n]$, the ensembles $\mathsf{serverView}(\Pi(\kappa, n;\ i, DB))_\kappa$ and $\mathsf{serverView}(\Pi(\kappa, n;\ i', DB))_\kappa$ are indistinguishable.*
Nontriviality. *For any κ and large enough n, it holds that $CC_\Pi(n, \kappa) < n$.*

Batch PIR. In this work we are also interested in amortized protocols in which the client queries more than a single entry of the database at a time, but rather k indexes at a time. The definition of batch PIR is identical to the above, except that the single index $i \in [n]$ is replaced with a vector $\vec{i} \in [n]^k$. Everything else remains the same.

Multi-server PIR. We additionally explore protocols involving multiple non-colluding servers. The definition of multi-server PIR is similar to the above, except that client privacy is defined with respect to each of the servers (individually).

Ideal Functionality. A different approach for defining PIR is via an ideal functionality that gives no output to the server and outputs $DB[i]$ to an honest client.[1] We will use that style of definition for random-PIR below, as it seems easier to work with than the one above, especially for the weaker-security variant from Sect. 5.1.

Nevertheless, defining security of PIR using an ideal functionality can sometimes be problematic. If the server is maliciously corrupted, then the simulator needs an extra input, the database, from the malicious server. However, the server communication is too small to even *define* the database, so this extraction cannot be performed. In this work we only consider semi-honest corruptions of the server, thus we do not run into this problem.

2.2   Defining RPIR

A random-index PIR (RPIR) protocol is different from PIR in that the index i is an output of the client, rather than an input. Namely, RPIR is a two-party protocol between a server holding a n-entry database $DB \in \{0,1\}^n$ and a client with no input. At the conclusion of the protocol, the client is supposed to get a pair $(i, DB[i])$, with i random in $[n]$.

Just like standard PIR, an RPIR protocol is parametrized by the security parameter κ and the database size n, both known to the two parties. As above, we assume that the server communication complexity depends only on n and κ but not on the specific value of DB or the randomness, and we denote it by $CC_\Pi(n, \kappa)$.

It will later (when we define batch RPIR) be convenient to define client-privacy by means of an "ideal RPIR functionality", i.e., via simulation-based security. We give both simulation-based and game-based definitions of RPIR below, and show that the two definitions are equivalent. Later we only use the simulation-based style.

---

[1] Note that standard PIR does not provide any privacy to the server, hence the functionality lets a corrupted client get the entire database.

The RPIR Functionality. The functionality $\mathcal{F}_{\mathsf{RPIR}}$ accepts from the server an input $DB \in \{0,1\}^*$. It leaks DB to the adversary, and waits for the client to ask for an output. When the client does, $\mathcal{F}_{\mathsf{RPIR}}$ sets $n = |DB|$, chooses $i \leftarrow [n]$ uniformly at random, and returns $(i, DB[i])$ to the client (when the adversary says it's time to give output).

Definition 2 (Single-server RPIR (simulation-based)). *A two-party protocol Π is a single-server RPIR if it realizes the functionality $\mathcal{F}_{\mathsf{RPIR}}$ above with semi-honest server and honest client in the UC framework [4]. It is nontrivial if for any κ and large enough n if it holds that $CC_\Pi(n,\kappa) < n$.*

Remarks on the Formalization. When defining RPIR we leak the entire database to the adversary. This models that the database is not required to be kept secret from the client or anyone in the network. (We only *require* that the client learns $DB[i]$; we do not give the database as output to the client as this would turn it into an implementation requirement.) Since we give the database to the adversary, the protocol is allowed to leak information on DB to the adversary even if the server and client are both honest. So, the protocol can run over an authenticated but unencrypted channel. One could have chosen a more complicated formulation where nothing is leaked to the adversary when both server and client are honest; this complicates the formulation and is not needed in our setting, so we opted for the simpler formulation.

It is important to consider a corrupt (semi-honest) server in order to ensure that such a server cannot learn i. However, we choose not to consider a corrupt (semi-honest) client, since our main application (where the client is run within an MPC, and thus honest) does not require this. Considering definitions for corrupt clients, as well as considering malicious corruptions, is left for future work.

Next, for clarity, we look at the relationship of the simulation-based definition given above to a game-based definition. We can adopt the definition of [14] to the case of a random index as follows.

Definition 3 (Single-server RPIR (game-based)). *A two-party protocol Π is a (semi-honest) single-server RPIR if it satisfies:*

Correctness. *The client's output is $(i, DB[i])$, where i is statistically close to uniform on $[n]$.*

Client privacy. *For every n, database $DB \in \{0,1\}^n$ and a run of the protocol, let i_{REAL} be the index output to the client and let i_{RAN} be a fresh uniform value from $[n]$. We require that the ensembles $(\mathsf{serverView}(\Pi(\kappa, n; DB))_\kappa, i_{\mathrm{REAL}})$ and $(\mathsf{serverView}(\Pi(\kappa, n; DB))_\kappa, i_{\mathrm{RAN}})$ are indistinguishable.*

Nontriviality. *For any κ and large enough n, it holds that $CC_\Pi(n,\kappa) < n$.*

In the statement of correctness, we ask that i is statistically close to uniform. We could have asked for only computational indistinguishability, but these are equivalent when i is on a domain of polynomial size.

Lemma 1. *Let Π be a two-party protocol. If it is an RPIR according to Definition 3 then it is an RPIR according to Definition 2.*

Proof (sketch). Assume the protocol Π fulfills the game-based definition. We construct a simulator for the simulation-based definition. Assume without loss of generality an environment $\mathcal{E}$ and a dummy adversary. This means the simulator is *de facto* interacting with $\mathcal{E}$.

Our simulator engages with $\mathcal{E}$ in an honest execution $\Pi(\kappa, n; DB)$, where the simulator plays the role of client. As a result of the interaction, $\mathcal{E}$ gets serverView$(\Pi(\kappa, n; DB))$; the simulator gets i_{REAL}. When that happens, the simulator will instruct $\mathcal{F}_{\text{RPIR}}$ to deliver output to the client. The effect of this is that $\mathcal{E}$ learns a uniformly random i_{RAN} from $\mathcal{F}_{\text{RPIR}}$ as client output. (It also learns $DB[i_{\text{RAN}}]$, but it can compute this value from i_{RAN} anyways, since it knows DB.) So, the view of $\mathcal{E}$ is (serverView$(\Pi(\kappa, n; DB)), i_{\text{RAN}}$).

Consider now a hybrid world with a hacked $\mathcal{F}_{\text{RPIR}}$, where we allow the simulator to give i_{REAL} to $\mathcal{F}_{\text{RPIR}}$ when it instructs delivery, and then $\mathcal{F}_{\text{RPIR}}$ gives i_{REAL} as output to the client instead of a fresh random value. This means that the view of $\mathcal{E}$ becomes (serverView$(\Pi(\kappa, n; DB)), i_{\text{REAL}}$). We can use a reduction to client privacy to prove that the simulation and the hybrid are indistinguishable. Notice that the view of $\mathcal{E}$ in the hybrid has the same distribution as the the view of $\mathcal{E}$ in a real protocol execution.

Lemma 2. *Let Π be a two-party protocol. If it is an RPIR according to Definition 2 then it is an RPIR according to Definition 3.*

This is clear, since any distinguisher that can break client privacy can be used to build an environment that can distinguish between the client output in a real execution and the ideal client output that it sees when interacting with the simulator.

2.3   Defining Multi-server RPIR

We also consider a multi-server version of RPIR. An ℓ-server RPIR protocol involves ℓ servers $\mathsf{Server}_1, \ldots, \mathsf{Server}_\ell$ each holding the same database $DB \in \{0,1\}^n$, and a client who wants to retrieve a random index i of the database. Multi-server RPIR is interesting since, while nontrivial single-server RPIR cannot provide information-theoretic privacy, nontrivial multi-server RPIR can. We therefore require *perfect* correctness and client-privacy for multi-server RPIR. Since we do not extend multi-server RPIR to the batch setting, we use the simple definitions of multi-server RPIR that are analogous to those for PIR (Sect. 2.1).

Definition 4 (Multi-server RPIR). *An $(\ell+1)$-party protocol Π is a (semi-honest) ℓ-server RPIR if it satisfies:*

Correctness. *For every n, every database $DB \in \{0,1\}^n$, and every index $i \in [n]$, the client's output in $\Pi(n; \perp, DB, \ldots, DB)$ is $(i, DB[i])$ with probability $\frac{1}{n}$.*

Client privacy. *For every n, every database $DB \in \{0,1\}^n$, and every server index $j \in [\ell]$, the view $\mathsf{serverView}_j(\Pi(n; \perp, DB, \ldots, DB))_\kappa$ is independent of the index i that the client outputs.*

Nontriviality. *For any κ and large enough n, it holds that $CC_\Pi(n, \kappa) < n$ (where the $CC_\Pi(n, \kappa)$ is communication complexity of all the servers).*

2.4   RPIR is equivalent to PIR

In terms of existence, it is obvious that PIR implies RPIR: the client chooses a random index $i \in [n]$ and the parties then run a PIR protocol in which the client learns $DB[i]$. The opposite direction is less clear: how can the client get a specific index in the database using the RPIR tool that only provides random indexes? Below we show, however, that RPIR *does imply* PIR with very small overhead. We begin with a simple PIR protocol that works when n is a power of two, makes a single RPIR call, and has the server send $n/2$ additional bits. This protocol is described in Fig. 1.

SimplePIR$\big[$Client$(i \in [n])$, Server$(DB \in \{0,1\}^n)\big]$ (n is a power of two)

1. Server and client run RPIR$[$Client, Server$(DB)]$, client gets $(j, DB[j])$;
2. Client sends to server $\delta = i \oplus j$ (i, j are viewed as $\log(n)$-bit strings)
3. Server partitions the index-set $[n]$ into $n/2$ pairs $p = \{k, k \oplus \delta\}$, computes for each pair $\sigma_p = DB[k] \oplus DB[k \oplus \delta]$, and sends these $n/2$ bits to the client;
4. Client computes $DB[i] = DB[j] \oplus \sigma_{\{i,j\}}$.

Fig. 1. A simple PIR protocol with one RPIR call and $n/2$ bits of communication

Lemma 3. *For n a power of two, the SimplePIR protocol from Fig. 1 is a non-trivial PIR protocol in the hybrid-RPIR model in which the client sends $\log n$ bits and the server sends $n/2$ bits.*

Proof. Correctness and complexity are obvious. For client privacy, note that in the hybrid-RPIR model the client gets a uniformly random index $j \in [n]$, and since n is a power of two then j is also a uniformly random $\log(n)$-bit string. Hence from the server's perspective, the message $\delta = i \oplus j$ from the client is also a uniformly random $\log(n)$-bit string, and in particular it carries no information about the client's input i.

Next, we note that Steps 3–4 in the SimplePIR protocol actually implement the trivial PIR protocol for a database of size $n/2$: The server sends all the $n/2$ bits and the client looks up the one that it needs. We can do better by replacing these steps with a recursive call for the same PIR protocol on this smaller database, as described in Fig. 2.

Theorem 1. *An r-round RPIR with server-communication $m = m(n, \kappa)$ and client-communication $k = k(n, \kappa)$ can be transformed into a PIR protocol with $(r+1)\lceil \log n \rceil$ rounds, server communication $1 + \sum_{i=1}^{\lceil \log n \rceil} m(2^i, \kappa) \leq 1 + m(n, \kappa) \cdot \lceil \log n \rceil$, and client communication $\sum_{i=1}^{\lceil \log n \rceil} i + k(2^i, \kappa) \leq \binom{\lceil \log(n) \rceil}{2} + k(n, \kappa) \cdot \lceil \log n \rceil$.*

Proof (sketch). On a size-n database, the server pads it to size the nearest power of two and then the parties run the RecursivePIR protocol from Fig. 2. The complexity is obvious, and correctness and privacy are argued by induction, following the same proof as for Lemma 3.

RecursivePIR$\big[$Client$(i \in [n])$, Server$(DB \in \{0,1\}^n)\big]$ (n is a power of two)

0. If $n = 1$ the server sends DB to the client. Else continue to Step 1.
1. The server and client run RPIR$\big[$Client, Server$(DB)\big]$, client gets $(j, DB[j])$
2. Client sends to server $\delta = i \oplus j$ (i, j are viewed as $\log(n)$-bit strings)
3. Server partitions the index-set $[n]$ into $n/2$ pairs $p = \{k, k \oplus \delta\}$ and computes for each pair the bit $\sigma_p = DB[k] \oplus DB[k \oplus \delta]$.
4. Let $DB' = (\sigma_p)_p$ be the resulting database of size $n/2$, and let $i' \in [n/2]$ be the index corresponding to the pair $\{i, j\}$ in this database.
   The parties run RecursivePIR$\big[$Client(i'), Server$(DB')\big]$, client gets $\sigma_{i'}$.
5. Client outputs $DB[i] = DB[j] \oplus \sigma_{i'}$.

Fig. 2. A recursive PIR protocol with $\log n$ calls to RPIR and one bit of communication

PIR from RPIR with Fewer Rounds. While the protocol in Fig. 2 has a low communication complexity, it has a large number of rounds. Below we describe instead a protocol that has the same number of rounds as the SimplePIR protocol from Fig. 1, but lower server communication complexity. The basic idea is for the client to learn more random indexes $DB[j]$, then partition the bits in DB into larger sets instead of the pairs $\{i, i \oplus \delta\}$ from SimplePIR. Specifically, we have a parameter t that tells us how large should these groups be (Fig. 3).

PartitionPIR$\big[$Client$(i \in [n])$, Server$(DB \in \{0,1\}^n)\big]$ (n is divisible by t)

1. Server and client run in parallel t' executions RPIR$\big[$Client, Server$(DB)\big]$, where t' is large enough to ensure that the client gets whp at least $t - 1$ distinct entries $(j_1, DB[j_1]), \ldots, (j_{t-1}, DB[j_{t-1}])$, all different from i.
2. Client chooses a random partition $\mathcal{P}$ of $[n]$ into sets of size t, with one of them being $I = \{i, j_1, j_2, \ldots, j_{t-1}\}$, and sends $\mathcal{P}$ to server.
3. For each t-subset $J \in \mathcal{P}$, the server computes the bit $\sigma_J = \oplus_{j \in J} DB[j]$, and sends these n/t bits to the client.
4. Client computes $DB[i] = DB[j_1] \oplus \cdots \oplus DB[j_{t-1}] \oplus \sigma_I$.

Fig. 3. A partition-based PIR protocol

Exactly the same proof as Lemma 3 shows that this is a secure PIR protocol in the RPIR-hybrid model, with t' executions of the RPIR protocol all on the same database DB, and additional server communication of n/t bits. If we have a r-round RPIR protocol with server communication $m = m(n, \kappa) < n/2$, we can set $t \approx \sqrt{n/m}$ and $t' = t(1 + o(1))$, and then we would get a $(r + 2)$-round PIR protocol with server communication $t'm + n/t = (1 + o(1))\sqrt{nm} + \sqrt{mn} \approx 2\sqrt{nm}$.

Theorem 2. *Given a r-round RPIR protocol with server-communication m, there is a PIR protocol with $r + 2$ rounds and server communication $O(\sqrt{mn})$.* $\square$

We note that the client communication in the protocol is large, since describing a random partition of $[n]$ into t-subsets takes more than n bits. Finding a protocol with few rounds and small client communication is an open problem.

3   RPIR Protocols

3.1   Noninteractive RPIR

While equivalent in terms of existence, RPIR can still be cheaper to implement than PIR by some measures. In particular, the fact that the client has no input in RPIR means that it can be (almost) *noninteractive*, something that is obviously impossible for PIR. Many interactive PIR protocols can be converted to noninteractive RPIR protocols; below we sketch two such protocols. One is based on FHE, and the other on trapdoor permutations (similar to Kushilevitz-Ostrovsky [15]). We suspect that many other PIR protocols can be similarly modified to obtain noninteractive RPIR; we leave it to future work to explore whether those other protocols can give better parameters.

In both of the protocols described in this section, the client sends a short "pre-processing message" to the server, and then the server can succinctly send to the client arbitrarily many random entries from the database, without learning what they are and without any more messages from the client. (These protocols can be upgraded to handle a malicious server by adding succinct proofs of correct behavior; however, we only need semi-honest security for our primary application, described in Sect. 4.)

Noninteractive RPIR from FHE. It is fairly easy to implement noninteractive RPIR from FHE. For example, the client sends to the server "once and for all" an encryption of a seed s for a PRF $f_s(\cdot)$ with range $[n]$. Then the server can run many instances of a protocol, where it chooses a random x, and homomorphically computes $i = f_s(x)$ and $y = DB[i]$. The server sends the ciphertexts encrypting (i, y) to the client, who can decrypt them.

Noninteractive RPIR from One-Way Trapdoor Permutations. This construction is based on the Kushilevitz-Ostrovsky PIR protocol from [15]. In this protocol the client sends the description of a permutation to the server, and then the server can send as many random indexes to the client as we want. As in the original Kushilevitz-Ostrovsky protocol, each random index costs just a little less than n bits of communication for an n-bit database.

Background: UOWHFs from One-Way Permutations. Recall that Naor and Yung described in [16] a construction for 2-to-1 universal one-way hash functions (UOWHF) based on one-way permutations. Namely, given a one-way permutation π over $\{0,1\}^k$ (and some other public randomness that we ignore here) they define a 2-to-1 function $h_\pi : \{0,1\}^k \to \{0,1\}^{k-1}$, such that given π and a random $x \in \{0,1\}^k$, it is hard to find the second pre-image $x' \neq x$ such that

$h_\pi(x') = h_\pi(x)$. However given a trapdoor π^{-1}, it is easy to compute the two pre-images of any $y \in \{0,1\}^{k-1}$. Finally, applying the Goldreich-Levin hard-core predicate [12], we also know that given the permutation π and random $x, r \in \{0,1\}^k$, the inner product $\langle r, x' \rangle$ mod 2 is pseudorandom, where x' is the second pre-image of $h_\pi(x)$.

A Noninteractive Variant of the Kushilevitz-Ostrovsky Construction. In a preprocessing phase, the client chooses a one-way permutation π over $\{0,1\}^k$ together with its trapdoor π^{-1}, and sends π to the server. Let $h_\pi(x)$ be a Naor-Yung UOWHF based on π, that has input length k and output length $k-1$.

The server partitions the database into pairs of k-bit blocks (x_i^0, x_i^1), $i = 1, 2, \ldots$. For simplicity, we assume below that $x_i^0 \neq x_i^1$ for all i (we mention at the end how to change the protocol when this is not the case). The server also chooses a random $r \in \{0,1\}^k$ that defines a Goldreich-Levin hard-core predicate [12] $\rho_r(x) = \langle x, r \rangle$ mod 2. The server sends to the client the k-bit string r, and also for each pair (x_i^0, x_i^1) it sends a tuple

$$\left(h_\pi(x_i^0), h_\pi(x_i^1), \rho_r(x_i^0) \oplus \rho_r(x_i^1)\right).$$

Note that each tuple is only $(2k-1)$-bits long, whereas the pair itself has $2k$ bits, so this is a nontrivial protocol (as long as there are more than k pairs).

For each received tuple (y_i^0, y_i^1, σ_i), the client uses its trapdoor to invert the hash function, computing the two possible pre-images $u_i^0, v_i^0 \in h_\pi^{-1}(y_i^0)$ and $u_i^1, v_i^1 \in h_\pi^{-1}(y_i^1)$. By construction, $x_i^0 = u_i^0$ or $x_i^0 = v_i^0$ and similarly $x_i^1 = u_i^1$ or $x_i^1 = v_i^1$. Next, the client finds an index i such that,

(a) either $\rho_r(u_i^0) = \rho_r(v_i^0)$ and $\rho_r(u_i^1) \neq \rho_r(v_i^1)$, or
(b) $\rho_r(u_i^0) \neq \rho_r(v_i^0)$ and $\rho_r(u_i^1) = \rho_r(v_i^1)$.

As r was chosen at random and $x_i^0 \neq x_i^1$ for all i, there is at least one such index whp. If there are more than one then the client chooses one of them at random. Moreover it can be shown that the index used by the client is uniform in $[n]$.

In case (a) the client knows that $\rho_r(x_i^0) = \rho_r(u_i^0) = \rho_r(v_i^0)$, and so it can use $\sigma = \rho_r(x_i^0) \oplus \rho_r(x_i^1)$ to determine the value of $\rho_r(x_i^1)$, and therefore decide whether $x_i^1 = u_i^1$ or $x_i^1 = v_i^1$. Similarly in case (b) the client knows that $\rho_r(x_i^1) = \rho_r(u_i^1) = \rho_r(v_i^1)$, so it can use σ to decide if $x_i^0 = u_i^0$ or $x_i^0 = v_i^0$. In either case, the client learns a single k-bit block of the database.

The security of this protocol follows from the OWUHF property and the Goldreich-Levin hard-core predicate, in exactly the same way as in [15].

Theorem 3. *If trapdoor one-way permutations exist, then there exists a nontrivial noninteractive random-PIR protocol.* □

Remark: To deal with generic databases where we could have $x_i^0 = x_i^1$ for some i, the server can choose another k-bit string $w \in \{0,1\}^n$ which is also sent to the client, and use $x_i'^1 = x_i^1 \oplus w$ instead of x_i^1 for all i. This ensures that $x_i^0 \neq x_i'^1$ except with exponentially small probability, and the client can mask-out w at the end of the protocol if needed.

3.2 Multi-server RPIR Protocols

It is well known that nontrivial single-server PIR cannot offer information-theoretic security, and RPIR is no different. To get nontrivial information-theoretic security we need to look at multi-server solutions, where two or more non-colluding servers are used. In this section, we describe two non-interactive multi-server solutions. The first one (Sect. 3.2) is an information-theoretic two-server RPIR; the second one (Sect. 3.2) uses some symmetric cryptography, and is based on Reed-Muller PIR.

Note that converting existing multi-server PIR schemes to noninteractive multi-server RPIR schemes is only possible under very specific conditions. Multi-server PIR schemes always have a message from the client to the servers, to encode the query; to convert multi-server PIR to noninteractive multi-server RPIR, we need the servers to generate these messages locally on their own. However, in many PIR schemes (such as the Reed-Muller and matching-vector PIR schemes), these messages need to be highly correlated, making local generation by the servers (instead of coordinated generation by the client) difficult. In Sect. 3.2, we describe a construction where the servers don't need any correlated messages; in Sect. 3.2, we adapt the Reed-Muller construction—which does require correlated messages—by giving the servers some correlated information as setup, which they are able to expand to support an arbitrary number of RPIR executions. (Note that not all forms of correlated messages are amenable to this kind of expansion from efficient cryptographic primitives. The randomness required for the matching vectors PIR construction does not appear to be, given the state of the art in non-interactive randomness expansion.)

Non-interactive Information-Theoretic Two-Server RPIR. In Fig. 4 below we describe a nontrivial two-server solution that offers information-theoretic security and in addition is completely noninteractive. Differently than the protocols from Sect. 3.1, this protocol does not even have a pre-processing phase. All it has are two messages, one from each server, from which the client can deduce $DB[i]$ for a random index i, with i independent of the view of each server (separately). In this protocol, one server sends a single database record, while the other sends $n/2$ values each of which correspond to the XOR of two database records. The client is able to use the record sent by the first server to recover another record from one of the values sent by the second server. (Reducing the communication complexity in this noninteractive multi-server setting below $n/2$ for a size-n database remains an interesting open problem.)

Lemma 4. *For even n, the SimpleMSPIR protocol from Fig. 4 is a noninteractive, nontrivial two-server RPIR protocol with information theoretic security in which the servers send $n/2 + \log(n) + 1$ bits.*

Proof. Correctness and complexity are obvious. For client privacy, we separately consider privacy against Server$_1$ and Server$_2$. Server$_1$, who chooses j, learns nothing about i since the random and uniform δ is unknown to Server$_1$, and

---

SimpleMSPIR$\big[$Client, Server$_1(DB)$, Server$_2(DB)$ where $DB \in \{0,1\}^n)\big]$

1. Server$_1$ chooses a random index $j \in [n]$ and sends $DB[j]$ to Client.
2. Server$_2$ chooses a random mask $\delta \in [n]$ (viewed as a $\log(n)$-bit string).
   (a) If $\delta = 0$, Server$_2$ sets $DB' = \bot$.
   (b) Otherwise, let $p_1, \ldots, p_{n/2}$ be the list of pairs of indices $p_k = (j_{k,1}, j_{k,2})$ such that $j_{k,1} \oplus j_{k,2} = \delta$ (ordered e.g. by increasing smallest value in the pair). These pairs are publicly computable given δ. Server$_2$ obtains the database DB' as $DB'[k] = DB[j_{k,1}] \oplus DB[j_{k,2}]$. ($DB'$ contains $n/2$ records.)
3. Server$_2$ sends (δ, DB') to Client.
4. If $\delta = 0$, Client returns $DB[j]$.
5. Otherwise, Client finds the pair p_k such that $j \in p_k$. Let i be the other index in p_k. Client returns $(i, DB'[k] \oplus DB[j])$.

Fig. 4. A simple multi-server RPIR protocol with $n/2$ bits of communication

each choice of δ leads to a different choice of i. Similarly, Server$_2$, who chooses δ, also learns nothing about i since the random and uniform index j is unknown to Server$_2$, and each choice of j leads to a different choice of i.

Non-interactive Computational Multi-server RPIR with a Better Rate. We can use Reed-Muller codes and ideas from pseudo-random secret sharing to get a non-interactive multi-server scheme based on the existence of pseudo-random generators. (Note that, since this scheme relies on computational assumptions, it meets only a weaker—computational—version of Definition 4.) The construction follows the usual roadmap to get PIR from Reed-Muller codes, and then uses pseudo-random secret sharing (PRSS) to generate the line of points usually sent to the servers by the client.

We will encode DB as a multivariate polynomial. Let v be the number of formal variables. Let d be the maximal degree of the polynomial. Let $q > d$ be a prime. We consider multivariate polynomials $f(\mathbf{x}) \in \mathbb{Z}_q[\mathbf{x}_1, \ldots, \mathbf{x}_v]$ of degree at most d. It is easy to see that there are $K = \binom{v+d}{v}$ unique monomials of degree at most d,[2] so we can use $f(\mathbf{x})$ to encode an element from $\mathbb{Z}_q^K$. This will allow us to encode at least $K(\log_2(q) - 1)$ bits of the database by encoding bits into positions in the binary representation of the field elements in $\mathbb{Z}_q$. Note that this is a locally-decodable encoding: To decode a bit we only need the field element it sits in. The codewode will be $f(\mathbb{Z}_q^v)$, i.e., we evaluate f on all points in $\mathbb{Z}_q^v$. There are $N = q^v$ such points. We can encode by placing the K elements DB$[i$

---

[2] Consider an array of length $v + d$. Consider placing a 0 in v positions and a 1 in the remaining d positions. Let the degree of $\mathbf{x}_i$ be the number of 1's between the i'th occurrence of a 0 and the $(i+1)$'th occurrence of a 0 (or the end of the array when $i = v$). Clearly this gives total degree at most d and there is a one-to-one correspondence between such assignments and monomials of degree at most d. There are $k = \binom{v+d}{v}$ ways to place the v entries which are 0.

in K evaluation points $f(a)$ and then use interpolation to compute $f(\mathbb{Z}_q^v)$. This gives a linear code

$$\mathsf{Enc} : \mathbb{Z}_q^K \to \mathbb{Z}_q^N .$$

Let $f_{\mathsf{DB}}(\mathbf{x})$ be the polynomial used to encode DB. Below we call a point a encoding entries $\mathsf{DB}[j]$ a *database point*. We assume that each database point encodes the same number of bits.

We let $d = q - 2$. This means that the rate is

$$\frac{K}{N} = \frac{\binom{v+q-2}{v}}{q^v}.$$

For a constant v we have that

$$\binom{v+q-2}{v} = \Theta_q(q^v) ,$$

which gives us a constant rate.

Interactive Information-Theoretic Multi-server RPIR. We can use the local decodability of Reed-Muller to get a multi-server RPIR for $c = q - 1$ servers $\mathsf{S}_1, \ldots, \mathsf{S}_c$ as follows.

1. Each server S_i forms the polynomial $f_{\mathsf{DB}}(\mathbf{x})$.
2. The client picks a uniformly random $a \in \mathbb{Z}_q^v$ and $b \in \mathbb{Z}_q^v$ and for $\lambda = 1, \ldots, q-1$ it lets $c_\lambda = a + \lambda b$. It queries S_i for $f_{\mathsf{DB}}(c_i)$.[3]
3. Let $\mathbf{y}$ be a formal variable over $\mathbb{Z}_q$ and consider the univariate polynomial $g(\mathbf{y}) = f_{\mathsf{DB}}(a + \mathbf{y}b)$. Since $f(\mathbf{x})$ has degree at most d, so does $g(\mathbf{y})$. The client knows $q - 1$ points on $g(\mathbf{y})$ as $g(i) = f_{\mathsf{DB}}(c_i)$. Since $d + 1 = q - 1$ the client can use interpolation to learn $g(0) = f_{\mathsf{DB}}(a)$.
4. If a happens to be a database point, then let j be uniform among the encoded entries j and output $(j, \mathsf{DB}[j])$. Otherwise, output $\perp$.

Privacy follows from $a + ib$ perfectly hiding a when $i \neq 0$. So a single server gets no information on a. Therefore, if a hits a database point j, then it hits a uniformly random database point in the view of the all servers. And each database point contains the same number of bits, so the position i will be uniform. The schemes has constant correctness. Namely, since the rate is constant it happens with constant probability that a hits a database point. This correctness can be amplified to any constant by a constant number of parallel repetitions and taking $(j, \mathsf{DB}[j])$ from the first correct instance. It can be amplified to negligible probability of error by repeating a linear number of times in the security parameter. For a batch scheme one can run $O(m)$ instances in parallel to get m correct instances except with negligible probability.

---

[3] For the reader familiar with Reed-Muller based PIR it looks odd to pick a at random. However, this leads up to the non-interactive versions, as detailed below.

Achieving Noninteractivity. In the above scheme the client can of course choose a to be a database point, yielding the well known Reed-Muller based multi-server PIR. Before showing how to derive a non-interactive version using pseudo-random secret sharing, we review the notion of pseudo-random secret sharing [9].

Consider servers $S_1, \ldots, S_c$ for $c = q - 1$. For each i we can pick a seed s_i for a pseudo-random generator and give s_i to all servers except S_i. By stretching the seed this will allow the servers to create any number of instances of pseudo-random $\alpha_1, \ldots, \alpha_c \in \mathbb{Z}_q$ where α_i is known to all servers $S_j \neq S_i$ and where α_i is indistinguishable from uniform in the view of S_i. Below we assume for simplicity that the elements are truly uniform.

Let $g_i(\mathsf{y}) \in \mathbb{Z}_q[\mathsf{y}]$ be a polynomial of degree 1 such that $g_i(0) = 1$ and $g_i(i) = 0$. Let $g_\alpha(\mathsf{y}) = \sum_{i=1}^c \alpha_i g_i(\mathsf{y})$. Note that $g_\alpha(0) = \sum_{i=1}^c \alpha_i$. This is an element uniformly random in the view of all servers. We can therefore take this to be one coordinate in our evaluation point $a \in \mathbb{Z}_q^v$. We can repeat v times in parallel to get all of a. Note also that S_i can compute $g_\alpha(i) = \sum_{j=1}^c \alpha_j g_j(i)$ as it knows α_j for $j \neq i$ and $g_j(i) = 0$ for $j = i$. This gives us the following non-interactive version.

1. The setup consists of seeds $s_1, \ldots, s_c$ for a PRG where s_i is given to all servers but S_i.
2. Each server S_i forms the polynomial $f_{\mathsf{DB}}(\mathsf{x})$.
3. The servers use v parallel instances of PRSS of lines (with $t = 1$) to implicitly generate uniformly random $a \in \mathbb{Z}^v$ and $b \in \mathbb{Z}^v$ such that for $\lambda = 1, \ldots, q - 1$ server S_λ knows $c_\lambda = a + \lambda b$. Then S_i sends $(c_i, f_{\mathsf{DB}}(c_i))$ to C.
4. Let $\mathsf{y} \in \mathbb{Z}_q$ and consider the univariate polynomial $g(\mathsf{y}) = f_{\mathsf{DB}}(a + \mathsf{y}b)$. The client uses interpolation to learn $g(0) = f_{\mathsf{DB}}(a)$.
5. If a happens to be a point where f_{DB} encodes a database entries, then let j be uniform among the encoded entries and output $(j, \mathsf{DB}[j])$. Otherwise, output $\bot$.

Again we can use parallel repetition to amplify correctness.

We now consider the communication complexity of the protocol. We can make the optimization that only S_1 and S_2 send c_1 and c_2, as $c_3, \ldots, c_{q-1}$ can be computed by interpolation: the evaluation points are on a line. This is $2v$ elements from $\mathbb{Z}_q$. All $q - 1$ servers have to send $f_{\mathsf{DB}}(c_i)$, which is an element from $\mathbb{Z}_q$. This is, all in all, less than $q + 2v$ elements from $\mathbb{Z}_q$. For constant v the communication is therefore $\Theta_q(q)$ elements from $\mathbb{Z}_q$. We have that $K = \Theta_q(q^v)$ so for constant v and growing K we have that the communication is $\Theta_K(K^{1/v} \log(K))$ bits. The database has size $K \log_2(K)$. The constant rate of the Reed-Muller code will deteriorate with growing constant v. Therefore the number of times to iterate the RPIR in parallel to get a given correctness level will grow with v. The communication for each iteration drops with growing v. This means that in practice for a fixed K there is a tradeoff to be found for v.

4 Applications to Large-Scale DoS-Resistant Computation

As described in the introduction, a strong motivation for RPIR is setting up communication channels to random parties who should remain anonymous. Below we call these *target-anonymous communication channels*. Imagine a very large number of parties (perhaps millions), that want to securely perform some computation in the presence of a powerful denial of service (DoS) adversary. While distributed computation requires sending and receiving messages, in this setting the parties run the risk of being knocked offline by a targeted DoS attack as soon as the adversary learns that they play an important role in the computation.

If the adversary is limited to attacking at most some fraction f of the parties, then one solution is to run a secure MPC protocol among all the parties. If the MPC protocol is resilient to f fraction of misbehaving participants, the DoS adversary will not be able to disable sufficiently many participants to thwart the computation. But this resilience comes at a steep price, as MPC protocols typically requires communication between all pairs of parties, which is completely infeasible at the scales that we consider.

Another approach entails assigning special roles to a small number of parties, and relying on them to carry out the computation. This could be much more efficient, but security is a challenge: as soon as the adversary discovers what parties are playing the special roles, it can target those parties and knock them offline. Hence, realizing these potential efficiency gains requires that the parties playing special roles *remain anonymous up until they speak*, and moreover they *can only speak once* before their special role is concluded, else the adversary can identify and target them. The parties playing special roles can be thought of in terms of a sequence of *committees*, where parties in committee i speak simultaneously in the i'th round.

Secure-MPC protocols where parties only need to speak once were described in several recent works [2,3,7,11]. But using these protocols in the presence of that powerful DoS adversary requires solving a delicate problem: How can you send messages to these parties, in order to provide them with the state that they need to carry out their task? This is where we want to use target-anonymous channels. We need to continuously establish communication channels to random parties, while preventing the adversary from learning who are the recipients, so that it cannot target them for attacks.

Benhamouda *et al.* (BGG+) proposed in [2] one approach using a "nomination" process. First, a nominating committee is established using standard tools (such as VRFs, or by solving moderately hard puzzles). Then, every (honest) nominator p chooses another random party q, looks up its public key, and broadcasts a re-randomized version of that key. This lets everyone send messages to q, without the adversary knowing who the recipient is. As pointed out in the introduction, a side-effect of this nomination technique is that the adversary knows the identity of the nominee if *either* the nominator *or* the nominee is corrupt. So, if overall only some fraction f of the parties are corrupt, the adversary will know the identities of around $f + (1 - f)f$ of the committee members. This doubling is unfortunate; it implies that honest majority among the nominees (which is crucial for secure computation with guaranteed output delivery), requires that the overall fraction is bounded by some $f < 0.29$. In the following, we outline an approach that does not have this adversarial doubling effect.

4.1   Target Anonymous Communication Channels from RPIR

Rather than let individual parties establish target anonymous channels to future committee members, our solution leverage past committees to do this job.

That is, past committees will run a secure-MPC protocol to choose a random small subset of the public keys, re-randomize them, and then broadcast the result. Since past committees are ensured (by induction) to have honest majority, we no longer allow corrupt nominators to choose corrupt nominees. We are ensured that all future committee members are chosen at random, and the adversary does not know who they are (unless it happened to corrupt them independently).

The only issue with this solution, is that the circuit describing the nominator's function is large: The input consists of everyone's keys (which could number in the millions), hence a naive MPC protocol will be too expensive. This is where we use RPIR, we let past committees simulate the RPIR client, while the state of the RPIR server remains completely public (and so can be simulated locally by each committee member). Specifically, the server state in our protocol consists of the list of public keys belonging to all the parties, as well as some public randomness (e.g., derived from a beacon). Since the client's work and communication is much smaller than the database size, we obtain a secure-MPC protocol that scales well with the total number of parties.

To simplify the presentation we describe this solution in terms of a noninteractive RPIR protocol, but of course it can be adapted to handle arbitrary RPIR protocols. Let $\Pi = (\mathsf{Setup}, \mathsf{Client}, \mathsf{Server})$ be a noninteractive RPIR protocol, where:

- $\mathsf{Setup}(1^\kappa) \to (\mathsf{sk}, \mathsf{pk})$ is the client's setup function;
- $\mathsf{Server}(\mathsf{pk}, DB, \rho) \to m$ is the server's processing function (where ρ is randomness); and
- $\mathsf{Client}(\mathsf{sk}, m) \to (i, DB[i])$ is the client's output function.

For simplicity, assume that we have a one-time trusted setup, which is used to run the Setup procedure, makes pk publicly known by anyone, and shares sk among the members of an initial committee. Let d be the number of rounds required to run Client *together* with a re-randomization of the obtained key. Assume we are given a public source of randomness, and target anonymous communication channels to d committees, each guaranteed to have an honest majority, and the first of which has secret shares of the RPIR secret key sk. Then, we can generate communication channels to an arbitrary additional number of committees by using our existing committees to run the RPIR protocol (followed by key randomization).

Server: All committee members *locally* obtain the randomness ρ (from a public source of randomness), and evaluate Server(pk, DB, ρ) $\to m$. Note that, because the client secret state is secret shared, this message is not enough to reveal the output to any individual committee member. Note also that, since this computation was entirely local, no committee member needs to speak during this computation.

Output: The members of the d committees run Client(sk, m) $\to$ $(i, DB[i])$, followed by a re-randomization of the retrieved public key, using techniques from [2,3,7,11] so that each committee only needs to speak once. Then they publicly reveal the output, thus establishing as many target-anonymous channels as needed to keep the process going.

This process consumes d committees, but can be used to make any desired number of key-selections and rerandomizations. In particular we can use it to establish d more committees that would handle the next selection, in addition to however many are needed to an external application. We can even let the same committee handle different steps of different RPIR instances: The last step in the protocol for the next committee, the second-to-last step in the protocol for the committee after that, *et cetera*. To conclude, we state the following informal theorem.

Theorem 4. *(informal) In the model of Benhamouda et al. [2] with a broadcast channel and mobile adversary, given anonymous PKE (for the target-anonymous channels) and a nontrivial weak RPIR protocol satisfying Definition 6, there exists a scalable evolving-committee proactive secret sharing scheme (ECPSS) as per [2, Def 2.3], tolerating any fraction $f < 1/2$ of corrupt parties.*

We note that the construction from [2] required other components (such as NIZK), but in our honest-majority setting those can be replaced by information-theoretic counterparts. We also comment that while the description above used public randomness, this can be replaced by the client generating the required randomness via a secure-MPC protocol. Also, we can use the same committees and the same techniques to get scalable secure-MPC for realizing arbitrary functions.

Theorem 5. *(informal) In the model of Benhamouda et al. [2] with a broadcast channel and mobile adversary, given anonymous PKE (for the target-anonymous channels) and a nontrivial weak RPIR protocol satisfying Definition 6, there exists scalable secure-MPC protocols for realizing any poly-time function, tolerating any fraction $f < 1/2$ of corrupt parties.*

5   Batch RPIR

We consider the application to large-scale secure-MPC as a "stress test" for RPIR efficiency. Not only do we need to run the RPIR client inside a secure-MPC protocol, but this protocol must use the only-speak-once pattern [11] which makes things hard, and we need to run very many copies of it to generate enough target-anonymous channels for it to sustain itself. It is therefore crucial to get the basic RPIR construction as efficient as can be for this application, which is what we do in this section. In particular, we consider a batch protocol that can choose multiple random indexes cheaper than choosing them one at a time, and also observe that the application can use a weaker security property than Definition 2, making it possible to do even better.

5.1   Definitions

Definition 2 can be easily adapted to amortized protocols in which the client gets more than a single entry of the database—say k entries at a time. The functionality for this case, denoted $\mathcal{F}_{\mathsf{RPIR}}^k$, is almost identical to the one from Sect. 2.2, except that the random single index $i \in [n]$ is replaced with a vector $\vec{i} \in [n]^k$. Everything else remains the same.

As we mentioned, it turns out that Definition 2 can sometimes be an overkill for applications of batch RPIR. In particular our motivating application uses RPIR to choose a random subset of indexes, where some subsets are "bad" (since they include too many corrupted parties), but they are very rare. In such an application, we may not really care about the chosen subset being random. Rather all we care about is that the odds of hitting a "bad subset" remains small. We thus weaken the security condition to only say that every collection of subsets that has negligible probability-mass by the uniform distribution, remains with a negligible probability-mass also in the RPIR output.

Formalizing this requirement using a game-based approach seems rather awkward, since the distribution of indexes that we care about is the a-posteriori distribution as seen by a computationally-bounded server. Fortunately it is easy to formulate it using the real/ideal approach of Definition 2. All we need to do is change the $\mathcal{F}_{\mathsf{RPIR}}^k$ functionality, so that instead of the uniform distribution, it chooses the indexes from some other distribution $\mathcal{D}$ which is "not too different" than uniform. Let us first define the statistical property of being not too different.

Definition 5 ((f, α)-domination). *Let D_1, D_2 be two distributions with X being the union of their support sets, and let $f, \alpha \in \mathbb{R}^+$ be positive numbers. We say that D_1 is (f, α)-dominated by D_2 if for any subset $S \subseteq X$ it holds that $D_1(S) \leq f \cdot D_2(S) + \alpha$.*

An ensemble $\mathcal{D}_1 = \{D_{1,k}\}_k$ is polynomially dominated by another ensemble $\mathcal{D}_2 = \{D_{2,k}\}_k$ if each $D_{1,i}$ is (f_i, α_i)-dominated by $D_{2,i}$, where $\{f_k\}_k$ is polynomially bounded and $\{\alpha_k\}_k$ is negligible.

It is clear that if $\mathcal{D}_1$ is polynomially dominated by $\mathcal{D}_2$, and some collection S has negligible probability in $\mathcal{D}_2$, then it also has negligible probability in $\mathcal{D}_1$.

The Parametrized RPIR Functionality $\mathcal{F}_{\mathsf{RPIR}}^{\mathcal{D}}$. The functionality is similar to the standard batch functionality $\mathcal{F}_{\mathsf{RPIR}}^k$, except that it is also parametrized by a distribution ensemble $\mathcal{D} = \{D_n\}_n$ (with D_n being a distribution over $[n]^k$).

When the client is honest and the server input is some $DB \in \{0,1\}^n$, the functionality draws an index set $\vec{i} \leftarrow D_n$ (rather than uniform in $[n]^k$) and returns to the client $(\vec{i}, DB[\vec{i}])$.

Definition 6 (Single-server batch weak RPIR). *A two-party protocol Π is a (semi-honest) single-server batch weak RPIR if it UC realizes the functionality $\mathcal{F}_{\mathsf{RPIR}}^{D}$ with semi-honest server and honest client for some D which is polynomially dominated by the uniform distribution over $[n]^\kappa$ (with κ the security parameter). It is nontrivial if the server sends less than n bits.*

5.2 Constructions

Ishai, Kushilevitz, Ostrovsky, and Sahai (IKOS) described in [13] several constructions for batch PIR from standard PIR protocols. Unfortunately, even if we wanted to use those constructions to fetch *random* indexes (rather than specific ones), the underlying protocol must still be full-blown PIR (rather than RPIR). Luckily, it turns out that we can use similar approaches with an underlying RPIR protocol if we are willing to settle for the weaker security from Definition 6, and we can even get must better parameters than what the IKOS constructions give.

Specifically, below we describe how to modify the IKOS "expander-based" construction from [13]. The original construction, used to fetch k entries out of an n-entry database, is parameterized by two more integers $m > d \geq 2$. Using public randomness which is shared by the server and client, the construction uses m bins and puts every database entry into d random bins. This created a degree-d bipartite expander, with the n database entries on one side and the m bins on the other. Then for every k-subset of entries that the client wants to fetch, it finds a perfect matching in that expander graph, with the k requested entries on one side and a k-subset of the bins on the other. The client then uses standard PIR to fetch these items from their bins (and dummy items from the other bins).

As we mentioned above, even if we wanted to use that construction to fetch k random items, we would still need to fetch specific items from selected bins, so the underlying protocol must be a PIR protocol, rather than RPIR. In terms of parameters, that construction has "rate" of $\rho = 1/d \leq 1/2$ (meaning the total space taken by all the bins is d times larger than the database size), and it requires $m = \Omega(k(nk)^{1/(d-1)})$, which is optimal for replication-based constructions. We can apply this construction with much better parameters, however, if we are willing to settle for the weak security notion (but the underlying protocol must still be PIR rather than RPIR).

Lemma 5. *There exists a weak-RPIR scheme as per Definition 6 based on the IKOS expander-based construction [13], with parameters (k, d, m) such that $m = (1 + O(e^{-d}))k$.*

Proof (sketch). When running the expander-based scheme above with a much smaller m, there will necessarily be some k-subsets of indexes that cannot be retrieved. The RPIR protocol will therefore have the client resample its indexes until it arrives at a subset that can be retrieved one per bin.

It is easy to see that the fraction of k-subsets that cannot be retrieved with some parameters d, m, corresponds exactly to the failure probability of inserting k random elements into a Cuckoo hash table [17] with d hash functions and table-size m. It is known that for $d = 2$ it is enough to use $m = (2 + \epsilon)k$ to get failure probability $o(1)$, and for larger d we get the same guarantee with $m = (1 + O(e^{-d}))k$ (see e.g., Fountoulakis-Panagiotou-Steger [10]). The probability mass of each of the achievable subsets is therefore increased only by a $1 + o(1)$ factor, which means that any negligible-probability collection of subsets remain negligible.   □

A Practically Appealing Weak Batch-RPIR. While the construction above has good parameters, the work that the client has to perform is far from simple, as it needs to resample indexes until some perfect matching can be found in the construction graph. In our motivating application this would have to be done via secure MPC, requiring a complex and costly protocol. One could attempt to simplify this construction by having the client simply choose k random bins and retrieve a random item from each bin, but analyzing this variant is very challenging. Instead, we describe and analyze below an even simpler and more efficient construction.

The Construction. In addition to n (the number of entries) and k (the number of indexes to fetch), the construction is also parametrized by m (the number of bins). We assume that both n and k are divisible by m, and note that k/m is playing a somewhat similar role to d in the expander-based construction. We deterministically partition the indexes in $[n]$ into m bins of size n/m each, for example $\{0, \ldots, \frac{n}{m} - 1\}, \{\frac{n}{m}, \ldots, \frac{2n}{m} - 1\}, \ldots$. Then we just fetch k/m random indexes from each bin using an underlying RPIR protocol. See Fig. 5.

Simple Batch-RPIR (parameters $m < k < n$, m divides k, n)
1. Partition DB into m "bins", $B_i = \{DB[\frac{i \cdot n}{m}], \ldots, DB[\frac{(i+1)n}{m} - 1]\}$
2. Client, Server run k copies of RPIR to retrieve k/m entries from each B_i.

Fig. 5. A simple batch-RPIR protocol.

Note that by replicating each bin k/m times and fetching one item from each replica, we can view this construction as a very specific instance of the IKOS construction from [13] with exactly k bins, where instead of putting each item in $d = k/m$ random bins we put the first n/m items in bins $0, \ldots \frac{k}{m} - 1$, then the next n/m items in bins $\frac{k}{m}, \ldots \frac{2k}{m} - 1$, and so on. Note that we may end up fetching the same item more than once in this protocol, but this is quite acceptable for our application for large-scale MPC.

Analysis of the Simple Batch-RPIR Protocol. Clearly, if the underlying RPIR protocol has work $w(\kappa, n)$ and communication $c(\kappa, n)$ on databases of size n, then this protocol has work $k \cdot w(\kappa, n/m)$ and communication $k \cdot c(\kappa, n/m)$. In particular if the work is $w(\kappa, n) = p(\kappa) \cdot n$ then the work in this protocol is $p(\kappa) \cdot kn/m$, which is m times better than the naive solution of just running k RPIR instances against the entire database.

Theorem 6. *The simple batch-RPIR protocol from Fig. 5 is a weak-RPIR protocol as per Definition 6, provided that the underlying RPIR protocol satisfies Definition 2 and that $m = O(\log \kappa / \log \log \kappa)$ (and $k = \text{poly}(\kappa)$).*

We show that when drawing k elements at random from a universe of size n which is split evenly between m bins, the probability drawing exactly k/m elements from each bin is only exponentially small in m, regardless of n. Since $m = O(\log \kappa / \log \log \kappa)$, it means a noticeable probability in κ. We state the following lemma.

Lemma 6. $\binom{n}{k} / \binom{n/m}{k/m}^m = \Theta(\frac{1}{\sqrt{k}}(C \cdot k/m)^{m/2})$ *for some constant C.*

Proof. We use Stirling's approximation (cf. [19]) – namely, there are constants $C_1 = \sqrt{2\pi}$, and $C_2 = e$, such that for all positive t

$$C_1 \sqrt{t} \cdot (t/e)^t < t! < C_2 \sqrt{t} \cdot (t/e)^t.$$

Using these bounds we have:

$$
\begin{aligned}
\binom{n}{k} / \binom{n/m}{k/m}^m &= \frac{n!(k/m)!^m(n/m - k/m)!^m}{k!(n-k)!(n/m)!^m} \\
&< \frac{C_2^{(1+2m)} \cdot n^{n+\frac{1}{2}} \cdot (k/m)^{k+\frac{m}{2}} \cdot ((n-k)/m)^{n-k+\frac{m}{2}}}{C_1^{(2+m)} \cdot k^{k+\frac{1}{2}} \cdot (n-k)^{n-k+\frac{1}{2}} \cdot (n/m)^{n+\frac{m}{2}}} \\
&= \frac{C_2^{(1+2m)} \cdot k^{(m-1)/2} \cdot (n-k)^{(m-1)/2}}{C_1^{(2+m)} \cdot n^{(m-1)/2} \cdot m^{m/2}} \\
&< \frac{C_2}{C_1^2 \cdot \sqrt{k}} \cdot \left(\frac{C_2^4}{C_1^2} \cdot \frac{k}{m}\right)^{m/2} < \frac{1}{2\sqrt{k}} \cdot (9k/m)^{m/2}. \quad (1)
\end{aligned}
$$

Lemma 6 implies that drawing k/m elements from each of the m bins (rather than drawing k elements uniformly from the entire universe) increases the probability of each k-subset by at most a factor of $\Theta(\frac{1}{\sqrt{k}}(C \cdot k/m)^{m/2})$ for some $C < 9$. For $k = \text{poly}(\kappa)$ and $m = O(\log \kappa / \log \log \kappa)$, this factor is polynomial in the security parameter. Finally, the underlying RPIR protocol satisfying Definition 2 implies that the server cannot distinguish the output of the protocol from drawing exactly k/m random elements from each bin. This concludes the proof of Theorem 6. □

Table 1. Some parameters for batch-RPIR with $n = 10000$ and security level=128.

f	m	k	f	m	k
0.2	10	440	0.3	10	1080
0.2	40	640	0.3	40	1560
0.25	10	680	0.35	10	1850
0.25	40	1000	0.40	10	3500

Setting the Parameters. While the general Theorem 6 only holds for very small $m = O(\log \kappa / \log \log \kappa)$, in the context of our motivating application we can choose much large values, linear in κ. The reason is that the probability mass of the "bad subsets" in this case is exponentially small, not just negligible. As we show below we can choose the committee-size k as a small multiple of the security parameter. Hence, we not only get much better resilience than Benhamouda *et al.* [2], but also much smaller committees, and the secure-MPC cost can be kept small by increasing the number of bins m.

In the application from Sect. 4 we have an adversary $\mathcal{A}$ that watches an execution of the batch-RPIR protocols (for choosing k parties from a universe of size n in m bins). Then $\mathcal{A}$ adaptively corrupts up to $f \cdot n$ parties (for some $f < 1/2$). For each corrupted party, $\mathcal{A}$ learns if that party was chosen or not, and its goal is to corrupt $k/2$ (or more) of the parties that were chosen by the protocol.

To get concrete parameters, we can start by analyzing the naive RPIR protocol with one bin, and then view Lemma 6 as quantifying the security loss by going to the more efficient protocol with m bins. By that lemma, the min-entropy of $\mathcal{D}$ (and hence the security level) decreases by roughly $\frac{m}{2} \log(9k/m)$ bits when switching from one to m bins. Analyzing the naive protocol is rather straightforward. For example, we can use the Chernoff bound, which says that for any $f \lesssim 1/2$ we can set $k = c \cdot \kappa$ for some $c = \Theta(f(\frac{1}{2} - f)^2)$ to get security level of (say) 2κ. We can then set $m = \kappa/\Theta(\log c) = k/\theta(c \log c)$ and lose only κ bits, obtaining security κ while selecting only a constant $\Theta(c \log c)$ parties from each bin.

It turns out that for our parameter regime the Chernoff bound is rather loose, and we get much better concrete parameters using an exact calculation. Specifically, for the one-bin protocol we need to compute the probability that a random f-subset of $[n]$ contains more than $1/2$ of the elements in $[k]$. The exact expression for this probability is

$$\sum_{i=k/2}^{k} \binom{fn}{i} \binom{(1-f)n}{k-i} / \binom{n}{k},$$

which is easy to compute for specific n, f, k values. Accounting for the "penalty" from Lemma 6 we therefore get:

Lemma 7. *For a specific setting of the parameters f, n, k, m, κ, if the underlying RPIR protocol satisfies Definition 2 then for any poly-time adversary $\mathcal{A}$ it holds that,*

$$\Pr[\mathcal{A} \text{ corrupts } k/2 \text{ or more selected parties}]$$

$$\leq \frac{\sum_{i=k/2}^{k} \binom{fn}{i}\binom{(1-f)n}{k-i}}{\binom{n}{k}} \cdot \frac{1}{2\sqrt{k}} \cdot \left(\frac{9k}{m}\right)^{m/2} + \mathsf{negligible}(\kappa).$$

$\square$

In Table 1 we list a few example parameters for $n = 10000$ parties, corrupt fractions $f \in [0.2, 0.4]$, and various k, m values that achieve security level $\kappa = 128$.

A   Random-Index Oblivious-RAM

In this section we note that a random-index ORAM (RORAM) can be used in our motivating application instead of RPIR, resulting is a somewhat different performance profile. We begin by defining RORAM.

A Random-Index ORAM (RORAM) is a two party protocol between a client and a server similar to Oblivious RAM (ORAM), except that the client does not choose the indexes to read from memory. Instead, these indexes are chosen at random (by the protocol), with the client getting (i, Mem_i) while hiding them from the server. Similarly to ORAM, we have procedures for Init, Read, and Write, except that the index to be read is not an input to Read but an output of it.

Definition 7 (RORAM Syntax). *A Random-Index ORAM protocol (RORAM) consists of the following components:*

- *Init$(1^{\kappa}, \mathsf{Mem}) \rightarrow (\mathsf{cst}; \mathsf{SST})$: The initialization algorithm takes as input the security parameter and initial memory $\mathsf{Mem} \in \{0,1\}^*$ (that could be empty), and generates an initial secret client state cst and a public server state SST.*
- *Read$(\mathsf{cst}, \mathsf{SST}) \rightarrow (i, x, \mathsf{SST}')$: The client fetches (i, Mem_i) (presumably for a random index $i \in |\mathsf{Mem}|$), and the server state is updated to SST'.[4]*
- *Write$(\mathsf{cst}, i, x, \mathsf{SST}) \rightarrow \mathsf{SST}'$: The content of the memory is modified by setting $\mathsf{Mem}[i] := x$ and the server state is updated to SST'.*

A RORAM protocol is nontrivial if the communication in each of Read *and* Write *operations is $o(|\mathsf{Mem}|)$.*

Desired Properties: The security notion for (computational) ORAM from [18] intuitively says that the server should not learn anything about which data and in what order it is being accessed. (We may also require that the server cannot learn if the operation is read or write.) As for RPIR, here too it is convenient to define security by means of an ideal functionality.

---

[4] We can assume wlog that the client state does not change throughout the protocol.

RORAM Functionality. The functionality $\mathcal{F}_{\mathsf{RORAM}}$ takes as input a (possibly empty) initial Mem $\in \{0,1\}^*$ from the client. It stores Mem internally and gives the size of the memory |Mem| to the server.

Thereafter, on input Read from the client it sets $n := |\mathsf{Mem}|$, chooses at random an index $i \leftarrow [n]$, returns $(i, \mathsf{Mem}[i])$ to the client, and outputs n to the server. On input Write(i, x) from the client (i in unary) it modifies $\mathsf{Mem}[i] := x$ (extending the memory if needed), and outputs the new |Mem| to the server.

Definition 8 (RORAM). *A two-party protocol Π is a Random ORAM if it realizes the functionality $\mathcal{F}_{\mathsf{RORAM}}$ above.*

A.1   Target Anonymous Channels from RORAM

One can use (batch) RORAM as an almost "drop-in" replacement for (batch) RPIR to establish target-anonymous channels. Here too we have previous committees playing the part of the RORAM client, where the server state is publicly known so every committee member can simulate the server in its head. However, there are a few differences.

In the RPIR-based solution, the server state only changes when the database contents change; that is, when public keys are added or removed due to a party joining or leaving the pool of participants (or parties changing their keys). When this happens, no additional communication is needed to run the RPIR server, since all parties can update the server state locally. In contrast, the RORAM server state is evolving dynamically with each read/write operation, and the state depends on the client secret. This has several consequences. First, setting up the server state takes $O(n)$ communication (where n is the number of parties in the pool of participants), since communication with the client (played by the committees) is necessary for every write. Second, every party in the pool of participants must continuously update the server state and keep a local copy of it, so that it can simulate the server for itself if it gets selected to one of these committees. Namely, whenever a client-simulating committee broadcasts an RORAM-client message, every party in the universe must update its local copy of the RORAM-server state accordingly.

The rest of the construction works just like the RPIR-based solution, with the committees implementing the RORAM client and any secrets that the client requires passed from committee to committee using the proactive secret sharing technique of Benhamouda *et al.* [2]. The result is summarized by the following informal theorem:

Theorem 7. *In the model of Benhamouda et al. [2] with a broadcast channel and mobile adversary, given anonymous PKE (for the target-anonymous channels) and a nontrivial RORAM protocol satisfying Definition 8, there exists a scalable ECPSS scheme as per [2, Def 2.3], tolerating any fraction $f < 1/2$ of corrupt parties.*

We remark that there is an interesting trade-off between the RPIR-based and the RORAM-based solutions: While both tools can provide a scalable solution (in that the amount of communication in each step is independent of the universe size n), they differ in how many parties need to perform local computation, and how much local computation each of them must do.

- When using RPIR, the only parties that need to perform local computations in each step are the current committee members (so only $O(\kappa)$ of them). However, each one of them must play the RPIR server, so it must do at least $\Omega(n)$ operations.
- When using RORAM, every party in the universe must keep up to date with the evolving server state, so every party must perform some computation in every step.[5] On the other hand, the computational complexity of one server-step is typically just polylog(n) (depending on the underlying RORAM protocol).

Hence we have a choice between $O(\kappa)$ parties performing $\Omega(n)$ operations each for RPIR, or all n parties performing only polylog(n) operations each for RORAM. It is an interesting open problem to find a solution where both the number of computing parties and the complexity of operations is sublinear in n (possibly using some combination of RPIR and RORAM).

B   Target Anonymous Channels from Mix-Nets

A different approach to setting up target anonymous communication channels is using Mix-Nets [5], i.e., by repeatedly shuffling and re-randomizing all the keys. This solution can be implemented simply by having individual parties self-select to shuffle and re-randomize all parties' public keys, then proves in zero knowledge that they did so correctly. Since the shuffling parties do not need any secret state, they can self-select using VRFs or by solving moderately-hard puzzles. There is no need to establish target-anonymous channels with these parties as recipients.

Notice that this setting is slightly different than traditional use of Mix-Nets, in that the shuffled and re-randomized entities are themselves public keys, with the corresponding secret keys held by individual parties. This means in particular that the adversary can always recognize its own keys in the shuffled list; only the honest parties' keys are hidden. Therefore, even after all the shuffling is done, we still require fresh public randomness—unpredictable by the adversary—to select the rerandomized keys from the shuffled database. (Otherwise a malicious last shuffler can plant keys belonging to corrupt parties in the positions from which keys are to be selected.)

This solution uses κ (security parameter) shuffles, so that at least one of the shufflers will be honest with overwhelming probability. As usual with Mix-Nets, all we need is one honest shuffler, as biased shuffles do no harm as long as at least one shuffle along the way is uniform. Also, we assume a synchronous model,

---

[5] Parties can perform these computations lazily, only when they are selected to a committee, but this does not change the total number of operations that they must perform.

so if one or more shufflers do not show up to play their roles, we simply skip their turns.

The major drawback here is communication; each of the κ shufflers needs to broadcast n public keys, or $O(n\kappa)$ bits. This gives us a total communication complexity of $O(n\kappa^2)$. On the other hand, this solution is very simple and requires no evolving secret state to be passed among the parties, making it appealing in some practical settings where the number of parties is not so large.

The solution can be optimized further, along somewhat similar lines to the batch-RPIR construction from Sect. 5.2: We divide the database of public keys into m bins each containing $\frac{n}{m}$ public keys. We then run the Mix-Net solution above on each bin separately, using independently-chosen set of shufflers for each bin. Finally we use fresh public randomness to select k/m committee members from each bin. Note that we can now use only $s \ll \kappa$ shuffling steps, maybe as little as $s = \Theta(1)$. Each bin has 2^{-s} probability of having all corrupt shufflers, hence starting from an f-fraction of corrupt parties the expected fraction of corrupt committee members per bin is $f' = 2^{-s} + f(1 - 2^{-s})$, and setting m large enough we can ensure that the actual fraction is very close to f' whp.

The total communication complexity of this modified scheme becomes $O(n\kappa s)$. For comparison, the FHE-based batch RPIR approach (Sect. 3) in combination with YOSO MPC gives total communication complexity of $\tilde{O}(\kappa^3)$, where both the size of a YOSO MPC committee and the number of keys being selected (for communication channels to the next committee) is $O(\kappa)$, and the length of an FHE decryption share is $\tilde{O}(\kappa)$. While the dependence of the communication complexity on n in the Mix-Nets solution may appear crippling, in practice the term $\tilde{O}(\kappa^3)$ may dwarf the number of participants n.

References

1. Beimel, A., Ishai, Y., Malkin, T.: Reducing the servers computation in private information retrieval: PIR with preprocessing. In: Bellare, M. (ed.) CRYPTO 2000. LNCS, vol. 1880, pp. 55–73. Springer, Heidelberg (2000). https://doi.org/10.1007/3-540-44598-6_4
2. Benhamouda, F., et al.: Can a public blockchain keep a secret? In: Pass, R., Pietrzak, K. (eds.) TCC 2020. LNCS, vol. 12550, pp. 260–290. Springer, Cham (2020). https://doi.org/10.1007/978-3-030-64375-1_10
3. Blum, E., Katz, J., Liu-Zhang, C.-D., Loss, J.: Asynchronous byzantine agreement with subquadratic communication. In: Pass, R., Pietrzak, K. (eds.) TCC 2020. LNCS, vol. 12550, pp. 353–380. Springer, Cham (2020). https://doi.org/10.1007/978-3-030-64375-1_13
4. Canetti, R.: Universally composable security: a new paradigm for cryptographic protocols. In: 42nd Annual Symposium on Foundations of Computer Science, FOCS 2001, Las Vegas, Nevada, USA, 14–17 October 2001, pp. 136–145. IEEE Computer Society (2001)
5. Chaum, D.: Untraceable electronic mail, return addresses, and digital pseudonyms. Commun. ACM 24(2), 84–88 (1981)
6. Chor, B., Goldreich, O., Kushilevitz, E., Sudan, M.: Private information retrieval. In: 36th FOCS, pp. 41–50. IEEE Computer Society Press, October 1995

7. Choudhuri, A.R., Goel, A., Green, M., Jain, A., Kaptchuk, G.: Fluid MPC: secure multiparty computation with dynamic participants. In: Malkin, T., Peikert, C. (eds.) CRYPTO 2021. LNCS, vol. 12826, pp. 94–123. Springer, Cham (2021). https://doi.org/10.1007/978-3-030-84245-1_4

8. Corrigan-Gibbs, H., Kogan, D.: Private information retrieval with sublinear online time. In: Canteaut, A., Ishai, Y. (eds.) EUROCRYPT 2020. LNCS, vol. 12105, pp. 44–75. Springer, Cham (2020). https://doi.org/10.1007/978-3-030-45721-1_3

9. Cramer, R., Damgård, I., Ishai, Y.: Share conversion, pseudorandom secret-sharing and applications to secure computation. In: Kilian, J. (ed.) TCC 2005. LNCS, vol. 3378, pp. 342–362. Springer, Heidelberg (2005). https://doi.org/10.1007/978-3-540-30576-7_19

10. Fountoulakis, N., Panagiotou, K., Steger, A.: On the insertion time of cuckoo hashing. SIAM J. Comput. **42**(6), 2156–2181 (2013). https://arxiv.org/abs/1006.1231

11. Gentry, C., et al.: YOSO: you only speak once. In: Malkin, T., Peikert, C. (eds.) CRYPTO 2021. LNCS, vol. 12826, pp. 64–93. Springer, Cham (2021). https://doi.org/10.1007/978-3-030-84245-1_3

12. Goldreich, O., Levin, L.A.: A hard-core predicate for all one-way functions. In: 21st ACM STOC, pp. 25–32. ACM Press, May 1989

13. Ishai, Y., Kushilevitz, E., Ostrovsky, R., Sahai, A.: Batch codes and their applications. In: Babai, L. (ed.) 36th ACM STOC, pp. 262–271. ACM Press, June 2004

14. Kushilevitz, E., Ostrovsky, R.: Replication is NOT needed: SINGLE database, computationally-private information retrieval. In: 38th FOCS, pp. 364–373. IEEE Computer Society Press, October 1997

15. Kushilevitz, E., Ostrovsky, R.: One-way trapdoor permutations are sufficient for non-trivial single-server private information retrieval. In: Preneel, B. (ed.) EUROCRYPT 2000. LNCS, vol. 1807, pp. 104–121. Springer, Heidelberg (2000). https://doi.org/10.1007/3-540-45539-6_9

16. Naor, M., Yung, M.: Universal one-way hash functions and their cryptographic applications. In: 21st ACM STOC, pp. 33–43. ACM Press, May 1989

17. Pagh, R., Rodler, F.F.: Cuckoo hashing. In: auf der Heide, F.M. (ed.) ESA 2001. LNCS, vol. 2161, pp. 121–133. Springer, Heidelberg (2001). https://doi.org/10.1007/3-540-44676-1_10

18. Stefanov, E., et al.: Path ORAM: an extremely simple oblivious RAM protocol. In: Sadeghi, A.-R., Gligor, V.D., Yung, M. (eds.) ACM CCS 2013, pp. 299–310. ACM Press, November 2013

19. Stirling's approximation. https://en.wikipedia.org/wiki/Stirling%27s_approximation. Accessed Oct 2020

Forward Secret Encrypted RAM: Lower Bounds and Applications

Alexander Bienstock[1]([✉]), Yevgeniy Dodis[1], and Kevin Yeo[2,3]

[1] New York University, New York City, USA
{abienstock,dodis}@cs.nyu.edu
[2] Google, Menlo Park, USA
kwlyeo@google.com
[3] Columbia University, New York City, USA

Abstract. In this paper, we study *forward secret encrypted RAMs* (FS eRAMs) which enable clients to outsource the storage of an n-entry array to a server. In the case of a catastrophic attack where both client and server storage are compromised, FS eRAMs guarantee that the adversary may not recover any array entries that were deleted or overwritten prior to the attack. A simple folklore FS eRAM construction with $O(\log n)$ overhead has been known for at least two decades. Unfortunately, no progress has been made since then. We show the lack of progress is fundamental by presenting an $\Omega(\log n)$ lower bound for FS eRAMs proving that the folklore solution is optimal. To do this, we introduce the *symbolic model* for proving cryptographic data structures lower bounds that may be of independent interest.

Given this limitation, we investigate applications where forward secrecy may be obtained without the additional $O(\log n)$ overhead. We show this is possible for oblivious RAMs, memory checkers, and multicast encryption by incorporating the ideas of the folklore FS eRAM solution into carefully chosen constructions of the corresponding primitives.

1 Introduction

In recent years, there is an increasing desire to outsource the storage of data to remote servers (such as cloud service providers). By outsourcing, organizations can avoid dealing with problems arising from storing data such as global availability, replication, handling outages, etc. On the other hand, outsourcing incurs new problems with respect to privacy. In many settings, the outsourced data is stored by third-party entities that may not be completely trustworthy. As a result, there is a need for cryptographic protocols that guarantee the outsourced data remains private even when stored by the potentially untrusted storage servers.

A straightforward attempt to obtain privacy is to encrypt all data before being sent to the servers. In more detail, the data owner (also referred to as the

---

The full version [5] is available as entry 2021/244 in the IACR eprint archive.

K. Nissim and B. Waters (Eds.): TCC 2021, LNCS 13044, pp. 62–93, 2021.
https://doi.org/10.1007/978-3-030-90456-2_3

client) will store a private key locally and encrypt all data that will be outsourced to the servers. The storage servers will never see the outsourced data in plaintext. Unfortunately, this protocol critically assumes that the client's storage always remains secure. In the case of a catastrophic attack where the client storage is compromised, the adversary may be able to decrypt all prior ciphertexts observed by the server to obtain the outsourced data in plaintext. Catastrophic attacks will inevitably leak the current state of outsourced data as the client should be able to retrieve the current outsourced data for use. However, we can still aim to provide strong privacy guarantees for prior iterations of outsourced data that may have been overwritten and/or deleted in the past. This is the core problem that we will study in our work.

In more precise terminology, we denote this primitive as *forward secret encrypted RAMs* or *FS eRAMs*. The notion of forward secret encrypted RAMs is not new and has been studied several times in the past two decades under different names such as "secure deletion" [3,35,37–39], "how to forget a secret" [14], "self-destruction" [16] and "revocability" [7] to list some examples. FS eRAMs consider the setting with a client and server where the client outsources the storage of an array with n entries to the potentially untrusted server that enables the client to perform read and write operations to any of the n array entries. Note that deletion is supported by simply writing $\perp$ to any array entry. For security, FS eRAMs guarantee that even after a catastrophic corruption of both the client and server storage (and with knowledge of the access pattern to server storage cells from reads and writes), the adversary may only decrypt the array's contents at the time of the compromise. Any array entries that have been overwritten prior to the attack may not be recovered.

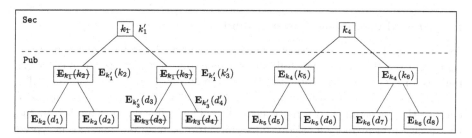

Fig. 1. Folklore Forward Secret Encrypted RAM construction from [14]. In this case, we have $s = 2, n = 8$, and so we have two trees rooted at the secret cells, each with four leaves corresponding to data cells. The two roots store encryption keys, while every other interior node stores an encryption of a key which was used to encrypt the contents of the node's children. All cells, except for the two roots, reside in public storage. We depict with red font the execution of the operation write(Sec, Pub, d'_4, 4) by showing that the keys at the interior nodes on the path of the leaf holding $\mathbf{E}_{k_3}(d_4)$ are replaced by new keys which in turn are used to re-encrypt their children (including new data d'_4). This operation reads and overwrites $O(\log(n/s))$ cells asymptotically and deletes from Sec any keys that could be used to recover the old data d_4.

All prior FS eRAM constructions may be unified with a single folklore solution with logarithmic overhead that was, to our knowledge, first presented in [14]. The folklore construction utilizes a binary tree with n leaf nodes that will be used to store array entries. Each internal node stores a symmetric encryption key that is used to encrypt the contents of its two children. The leaf nodes store array entries encrypted by their parent node's key. Finally, the root's encryption key is stored in client memory. To read an array entry, the corresponding root-to-leaf path is downloaded and decrypted sequentially starting from the root node. For writing to an array entry, the root-to-leaf path is downloaded along with the children of all nodes in the path and the leaf node's contents are replaced with the new entry. All encryption keys of internal nodes in the root-to-leaf path are re-generated randomly and all ciphertexts are re-encrypted using the new keys before being uploaded back to the server. Figure 1 presents a diagram of the folklore construction. For both operations, the communication and computation costs are $O(\log n)$. If the client has the capability to store $O(s)$ keys, the efficiency may be reduced to $O(\log(n/s))$ by storing the top $O(\log s)$ levels of the tree in client storage. This folklore construction has been extended in many interesting ways such as handling dynamic array sizes [38] and more complex tree structures like B-trees [39].

Even though this folklore solution has been known for more than two decades, there have been no improvements on the asymptotic efficiency. This leads to the very important question of "Is the folklore forward secret encrypted RAM construction optimal?". Another important question is "If the folklore solution is optimal, are there important applications or settings where one can incorporate forward secret encrypted RAMs without incurring the additional logarithmic overhead?". In this work, we study both questions and answer affirmatively.

1.1   Our Main Result: Lower Bound

As the main result of our work, we present a lower bound for forward secret encrypted RAMs showing the folklore construction is optimal. In the past, lower bounds for cryptographic data structures were mainly proved in either the balls-and-bins [8,17] or cell probe model [23,24,26,27,33,34,47] that lie on opposite ends of the spectrum in terms of flexibility. The balls-and-bins models insists that each server memory location (bins) may store at most one opaque encrypted array entry (balls). Nothing else may be stored in server memory. Therefore, the balls-and-bins model does not encompass the folklore FS eRAM construction that utilizes server memory to store encrypted keys. On the other hand, the cell probe model allows arbitrary encodings of array entries to be stored in server memory. Due to this flexibility, proving cell probe lower bounds is viewed as the holy grail. However, cell probe lower bounds are very difficult to prove and there are long-standing gaps between lower bounds in the cell probe model and more restrictive models.

At a high level, the cell probe model only charges data structures for probing (either reading/writing) a cell. Probing a single cell accounts for one unit cost of computation. All other resources of the data structure may be used without cost, including computation *besides* cell probes, randomness generation, etc. However, this does not apply to adversaries who are typically expected to be PPT. We refer readers to [47] for a formal definition with respect to data structures and [26] with respect to cryptographic data structures.

It turns out that when computation is free, we can construct a simple FS eRAM with only $O(1)$ cell probes. Each of the n entries are encrypted using authenticated encryption. To retrieve an entry, the data structure retrieves the ciphertext and tries to decrypt with all keys until succeeding. This is technically a valid, but practically infeasible, construction in the cell probe model.

To circumvent this problem, one could also require that the data structure is a PPT algorithm. However, this only rules out natural usages of encryption and other cryptographic primitives. Data structures may use cryptographic primitives in unnatural manners (like with weaker security parameters) trying to find an encryption scheme that is breakable by the data structure yet is intractable for the adversary. Unfortunately, this phenomenon occurs due to the assumptions of the adversary's and data structure's computational powers (along with the data structure's private state) as opposed to studying the hardness of the FS eRAM problem.

To address this gap, we introduce the *symbolic model* for proving lower bounds for cryptographic data structures inspired by prior works [4, 29] for other primitives. The symbolic model enables server cells to only store strings that are derived from a structured grammar that incorporates *natural usage* of important cryptographic primitives (encryption, (dual)PRFs, etc.). The symbolic model strikes a balance between the balls-and-bins and cell probe model by enabling more flexible server storage beyond just encrypted array entries (like the balls-and-bins model) but not arbitrary encodings (like the cell probe model). Importantly, our symbolic model encompasses the folklore solution. In the symbolic model, we prove our main result showing that the folklore solution is optimal.

Theorem 1 (Informal).   *For any client storage s, any forward secret encrypted RAM in the symbolic model must use $\Omega(\log(n/s))$ overhead.*

Our Lower Bound Techniques. We provide a simple, non-adaptive adversary that at each time t selects a random virtual cell to overwrite with new data. We show that after each of these operations, in expectation, the contents of logarithmically (in n/s) many public and secret cells that were used by the protocol become unusable by the protocol. I.e., because the protocol must force itself to delete some of the secrets which it used to recover the old data, for any encoding of some other secret in a public or secret cell, if decoding requires a deleted secret, the encoding is useless. Since we show that we can identify $\Omega(\log(n/s))$ different such cells at each instant, we reach our lower bound.

To show that the contents of logarithmically-many cells become useless at each t, we abstract the relationship between the contents of the secret cells, the keys that the protocol uses, and the virtual cells at each instant into a directed graph $\mathcal{G}$ in Definition 9, which we call the *key-data* graph. More specifically, the contents in each secret cell, the keys that the protocol uses (and can thus recover using the contents of the secret and public cells), and the virtual cells at some time t are the vertices of $\mathcal{G}$. Each key vertex has an edge to another vertex if it was used in a (d)PRF computation to generate the target vertex, or it was used in the generation of a string (e.g., as an encryption key) in one of the public or secret cells that encodes the target vertex. Additionally, each vertex corresponding to the contents of a secret cell that is not a key has an edge to another vertex if it encodes the target vertex.

By correctness, we show that at each instant of the protocol, for every data item stored in the virtual cells, there exists a collection of paths starting from vertices corresponding to secret cells and ending at the vertex corresponding to the data. These paths abstract the notion that together with the contents of the public cells at that instant, those secret cells (and not any subset of them) can recover the data. Moreover, these paths satisfy the special property that if the corresponding data cell is overwritten, all of the vertices along at least one of these paths must be made indefinitely inaccessible by the protocol for it to no longer be able to recover the old data. This choice of paths is completely determined by the protocol and indeed the protocol may make this choice in an effort to minimize the amount of computation it has to do. By proving a graph-theoretic lemma about the out-degrees of the nodes on any such chosen path in the key-data graph (i.e. that they sum to $\log n/s$), we show that in expectation over the virtual cell which the adversary chooses to overwrite, the number of cells which can no longer be used to access the secrets they encode as a consequence of all of the vertices on the path becoming inaccessible is $\Omega(\log(n/s))$ in expectation.

1.2 "Bypassing" the Lower Bound

Equipped with the knowledge that the folklore solution is optimal, we investigate applications where FS eRAMs may be incorporated without the additional logarithmic overhead. At a high level, we will show that the folklore FS eRAM construction may be overlaid into constructions that already utilize tree-like structures. We prove this is true for three such primitives.

Oblivious RAMs. Oblivious RAMs (ORAMs) [1,17,18,32,36,42] are cryptographic primitives in the client-server setting that obfuscate the client's access pattern to the underlying array entry even when the server observes physical accesses to server storage. Note ORAMs do not protect against client corruption. The best ORAM constructions require $O(\log n)$ overhead. A naive composition with FS eRAMs incurs $O(\log^2 n)$ overhead. In Sect. 5, we provide a construction that essentially avoids additional overhead over ORAM:

Theorem 2 (Informal). *There exists a construction that is both a forward secret encrypted RAM and an oblivious RAM with $O(\log n \cdot f(n))$ overhead and $O(1)$ client storage for any function $f(n) = \omega(1)$.*

As an additional contribution, we also show that stronger notions of forward secret obliviousness are expensive in the cell probe model. One natural notion might be to provide forward secrecy for access patterns. After client compromise, the server may not learn information about the prior accesses to data. We denote this as strong oblivious forward secret encrypted RAMs. We note a similar lower bound was presented in [39], but only in the balls-and-bins model. Our result is slightly stronger since it is proved in the cell probe model.

Theorem 3 (Informal). *For any client storage s, any strong oblivious forward secret encrypted RAM in the cell probe model must use $\Omega(n - s)$ overhead.*

Memory Checkers. Memory checkers (MCs) [6,11,31], are cryptographic primitives in the client-server setting which provide authenticity of an outsourced data array for the client. MCs require $\Omega(\log n / \log \log n)$ overhead [15], and the best known constructions require $O(\log n)$ overhead.[1] Again, a naive composition with FS eRAM also provides forward secrecy of the data, but requires $O(\log^2 n)$ overhead. In Sect. 6, we provide a construction that avoids the extra overhead:

Theorem 4 (Informal). *There exists a forward secret memory checker with $O(\log n)$ overhead and $O(1)$ client storage.*

Multicast Encryption. Multicast encryption (ME) is a primitive that allows a group manager to securely and efficiently distribute secrets to an evolving group of users. After each group membership change, a new epoch is initiated, and the group manager sends ciphertexts over a broadcast channel which allow only the *current* group members to derive the next group secret.[2] ME has been widely studied in the literature [9,21,22,30,41,45,46]. Indeed, these works can be unified into a folklore construction based on binary trees which tightly achieves optimal $O(\log n)$ communication and computational complexity per epoch with respect to the lower bound of [29]. However, this folklore construction has large group manager secret state and does not protect against corruption of this state. In the full version [5], we provide a construction that achieves group manager FS, while reducing its secret state to $O(1)$ size and retaining the optimal efficiency of the folklore solution, without an extra $O(\log n)$ factor of computational overhead:

Theorem 5 (Informal). *There exists an ME construction that is forward secret with respect to group manager corruptions, has $O(1)$ group manager secret storage, and $O(\log n)$ communication and computation per epoch.*

---

[1] In both cases, for *online* MCs that access the remote storage in a deterministic and non-adaptive manner. Online MCs report any inauthentic retrieval from the server immediately, as opposed to after a long sequence of retrievals. Recall that the folklore FS eRAM construction also makes deterministic, non-adaptive accesses.

[2] In the full version [5], we briefly compare ME with a harder setting called Continuous Group Key Agreement.

2   Lower Bound Model

In this section, we present a general framework for proving computational lower bounds on cryptographic or privacy-preserving data structures using a symbolic model, then formalize it for the case of FS eRAM. The symbolic model we present is inspired by the one used for communication complexity lower bounds originally by Micciancio and Panjwani in [29] for multicast encryption and also recently in [4] for concurrent group ratcheting.[3]

2.1   Framework for Symbolic Private Data Structure Lower Bounds

The first step in proving a lower bound on some private data structure in our symbolic framework is to decide which primitives are allowed in the constructions. Based on these primitives, one has to define a *grammar* within the model which specifies exactly the types of strings that can be created and stored in the structure to keep the data private. For example, if one of the allowed primitives is encryption, then the grammar must specify strings that correspond to encryption keys and encryptions of certain other strings derived from the grammar. If no other primitives are allowed, for example PRFs, then the constructions can only use such a key to generate more ciphertexts according to the grammar, and not other keys through PRF computations, for example. This grammar only defines the exact form of strings that can be generated by the allowed primitives, but does not on its own define how these strings can be used to recover the data.

The manner in which constructions can use sets of strings derived from the grammar to recover other strings, including data, is specified by an *entailment relation*. We emphasize that this relation takes as input strings derived from the grammar, generated by the functionality of the allowed primitives, and outputs other strings within the grammar, also based on the functionality of the allowed primitives. For example, if a construction stores a set of strings which include a ciphertext within the grammar that is generated by an encryption algorithm, along with the encryption key, the entailment relation specifies that the plaintext that also falls within the grammar can be recovered via the decryption algorithm. We note that unlike in traditional models, we only define the syntax and security of the allowed primitives implicitly within the grammar and entailment relation. Further utilizing the encryption example, if the key for a ciphertext is not available, then the entailment relation prohibits derivation of the underlying plaintext (and thus it is secure).

Grammars and corresponding entailment relations can generally be used for lower bounds on any private data structures. Indeed, we will provide our own in Sect. 2.2. However, we again stress that for some arbitrary private data structure, one might use a completely different grammar and entailment relation to show a lower bound in the symbolic framework. To apply the grammar and entailment relation to a lower bound for a specific private data structure, one has to provide syntax, correctness, and security definitions in the symbolic model. For

---

[3] The model is also related to that of automated protocol verification (see e.g., [25]).

correctness, in general, constructions must derive strings from the grammar to store in the data structure and later use these strings, along with the entailment relation, to derive the plaintext data that they store. For security, we use the implicit security definitions for the allowed primitives within the grammar and entailment relation to show that an adversary cannot derive certain data using certain other strings (e.g., encrypted storage). In general, such security definitions may not be as strong as the standard (e.g., indistinguishability based) definitions for private data structures. However, proving a lower bound based on a weaker adversarial model only strengthens the result.

2.2 Symbolic Definitions for Allowed Primitives

Our symbolic model allows the FS eRAM cells (secret and public) to store only certain types of strings generated by the functionality of our allowed primitives and specified by our grammar, which can only be interpreted and utilized via our entailment relation. We introduce the allowed primitives, the grammar and entailment relation in this section. Note again: our grammar and entailment relation for these primitives can be used for other private data structure lower bounds in the symbolic framework, but some such lower bounds may also allow for other primitives (e.g., public key techniques), and use some other grammar, and/or entailment relation.

Cryptographic Primitives. The primitives which we choose to consider in our lower bound encompass all of the reasonable primitives which one would use for FS eRAM, while excluding those that are too powerful and inefficient in practice. Indeed, a trivial construction exists from Puncturable Encryption (PE) [10,12, 13,19,20,43,44], by simply revoking all overwritten ciphertexts. However, PE is a strong primitive and is seen as too computationally inefficient for most practical applications (see e.g., [2]). Therefore, we do not consider PE in our model and indeed view a corollary of our lower bound as a lower bound on the overhead of PE schemes from practical primitives.

Thus, we choose to include only those primitives that are natural and useful for FS eRAM, as well as not too powerful as to make the problem trivial. Since FS eRAM protocols are carried out by a single entity, we only consider symmetric techniques. Namely, we include symmetric encryption, (dual) pseudorandom functions, and secret sharing. These are all of the primitives (and more) which the folklore construction and all other constructions in the literature use [7,14,38]. In fact, only symmetric encryption is used in these prior constructions. We include (dual) pseudorandom functions, as they have been shown to achieve speedups for many other primitives. We note that FS eRAMs are easy to achieve with two non-colluding servers as the array may be secret shared between the two servers. Therefore, we add secret sharing in the case that it may be useful even in the single-server setting. We introduce the primitives here, before defining them formally in our grammar and entailment relation.

An encryption algorithm $\mathbf{E}$ takes as input a key K and string C, and outputs a ciphertext $C' = \mathbf{E}_K(C)$. Informally, $\mathbf{E}_K(C)$ hides the string C. Symbolically, the string C can be recovered from the ciphertext, only by using the key K and corresponding decryption algorithm: $\mathbf{D}_K(\mathbf{E}_K(C)) = C$.

A PRF is an efficiently computable function $\mathbf{F}$ that takes as input a single key K_1 and some string C and outputs a pseudorandom and independent key K_2: $\mathbf{F}(K_1, C) = K_2$. Symbolically, K_2 can only be computed with $\mathbf{F}$ on input K_1 and not some other input key $K_1' \neq K_1$.

We also consider dPRFs which are efficiently computable functions $\mathbf{dF}$ that take as input two keys K_1 and K_2 and output a pseudorandom and independent key K_3: $\mathbf{dF}(K_1, K_2) = K_3$. Symbolically, K_3 can only be computed with $\mathbf{dF}$ on input K_1 and K_2 and not some other pair of keys (K_1', K_2') such that *either* $K_1' \neq K_1$ *or* $K_2' \neq K_2$. The output key of both PRFs and dPRFs can be used as encryption keys.

A secret sharing scheme allows one to *split* a string C into shares $\mathbf{S}_1(C), \ldots,$ $\mathbf{S}_n(C)$, for some fixed integer n, such that C can only be recovered from certain subsets of the shares. These subsets are defined using an *access structure* $\Gamma \subseteq 2^{\{1,\ldots,n\}}$. For each subset $I \in \Gamma$, if we are given the set of shares $\mathbf{S}_I(C) = \{\mathbf{S}_i(c)\}_{i \in I}$ of some string C, then we can efficiently recover C using the reconstruction function $\mathbf{R}$: $\mathbf{R}(I, S_I(C)) = C$. Symbolically, if we only have a set of shares $S_{I'}(C)$ for some $I' \notin \Gamma$, then we cannot recover C.

Grammar and Entailment Relation Definitions. We will allow cells of the FS eRAM to contain strings which are arbitrary nested combinations of encryption, PRFs, dPRFs, and secret sharing. We formally allow cell contents to be described by strings derived from the grammar in the left of Fig. 2.

$\begin{aligned} C &\to K \mid \mathbf{E}_K(C) \mid \mathbf{S}_1(C) \mid \ldots \mid \mathbf{S}_n(C) \mid D \\ K &\to R \mid \mathbf{F}(K, C) \mid \mathbf{dF}(K, K) \end{aligned}$	$\begin{aligned} c \in \mathsf{C} &\implies \mathsf{C} \vdash c \\ \mathsf{C} \vdash k &\implies \mathsf{C} \vdash \mathbf{F}(k, c), \forall c \\ \mathsf{C} \vdash k_1, k_2 &\implies \mathsf{C} \vdash \mathbf{dF}(k_1, k_2) \\ \mathsf{C} \vdash \mathbf{E}_k(c), k &\implies \mathsf{C} \vdash c \\ \exists I \in \Gamma : \forall i \in I, \mathsf{C} \vdash \mathbf{S}_i(c) &\implies \mathsf{C} \vdash c \end{aligned}$

Fig. 2. Definitions of: 1. (left) the grammar used in our symbolic model to describe the strings which any FS eRAM protocol can create and store in secret and public cells, and 2. (right) the entailment relation $\vdash$, where in the second through fourth rules, k, k_1, k_2 are of type K in our grammar.

The variables C and K in the grammar represent strings and keys, D is a variable that ranges over the arbitrarily large set of plaintext strings which we allow the user to write into the virtual cells of the FS eRAM, and R ranges over an arbitrarily large set of truly random keys. We will call strings created from variable K as keys and those from variable D as data throughout the next two sections. Observe that the input to PRFs that is not the key can be any string C derived from the grammar. Some remarks:

- We emphasize that the data cells can only hold strings of type D. We mainly make this restriction for simplicity so that data cannot be used as keys, secret shares, or ciphertexts in any protocol. Note: the adversary in the security definition, as will be later seen, chooses the contents of the data cells.
- For convenience, we do not allow ciphertexts or secret shares to be encryption keys or (d)PRF keys. Our proof may be modified to enable ciphertexts or secret shares to be keys if desired.
- We assume that all cells are of approximately the same length, and that each of them can hold any one string derived from the grammar. This means that the functions $\mathbf{E}, \mathbf{F}, \mathbf{dF}, \mathbf{S}$ have outputs of about the same length.

Again, it is important to observe that the strings specified by the above grammar are *purely syntactic* and without any meaning. Their only intended meaning is described by the entailment relation $\mathsf{C} \vdash c$, specifying which strings c can be recovered given a set of strings C. This entailment relation follows naturally from the standard cryptographic definitions for the primitives we consider (and inductively from the base case): 1. For PRFs, one can only compute the function if the key is revealed; 2. For dPRFs, one can only derive an output for a given input if they have *both* keys (security holds if only one key is revealed); 3. For encryption, one can only derive the underlying plaintext of a ciphertext if they have the key; and 4. For secret sharing, one can reconstruct a secret that has been shared only if they have all shares for a given subset of the access structure. We formally define the relation in the right part of Fig. 2 and add the following useful definition.

Definition 1. *For any C, we denote the set of strings that can be recovered from C using $\vdash$ as $Rec(\mathsf{C})$.*

2.3   FS eRAM Symbolic Definition

Now we provide the formal definition of FS eRAM in our symbolic model. Throughout the execution of an FS eRAM protocol Π, it forward secretly stores a user-chosen ordered n-element array D of virtual cells, which hold strings of type D in our grammar. We refer to these cells as the *data cells* and their initial contents as array D_0. We again emphasize that data cells can only hold strings of type D in our grammar, and thus cannot hold strings arbitrarily derived from C in our grammar.

At each instant t, Π is given one data cell $i \in [n]$ to overwrite with new data d so that the contents of the data cells at time t, D_t, satisfy: $\mathsf{D}_t[i] = d$ and $\mathsf{D}_t[j] = \mathsf{D}_{t-1}[j], \forall j \in [n] \setminus \{i\}$. Π proceeds using an array of s ($\ll n$) secret cells, Sec, and a (possibly arbitrarily large) array of public cells Pub, which can hold strings derived from our above grammar.[4] We emphasize that in normal protocol execution, the cells in Pub can always be viewed by an adversary $\mathcal{A}$, while the cells in Sec cannot be viewed by $\mathcal{A}$ until corruption. Π has the following syntax:

---

[4] Every cell of Sec and Pub initially contains the special *empty* symbol $\bot$.

Definition 2 (Syntax). *A Forward Secret Encrypted RAM protocol* Π = (init, write) *consists of the following algorithms:*

- init($D_0 = (d_1, \ldots, d_n)$)), *which takes in the* n *initial data cell contents* D_0 *and computes the initial state of the cells* Sec *and* Pub *using strings derived from* C *in our grammar.*
- write(i, d), *which takes in a cell index* i *and new data* d *and overwrites the contents of some cells of* Sec *and* Pub *using strings derived from* C *in our grammar.*
- read(i), *which takes in a cell index* i *and using the contents of the cells of* Sec *and* Pub *(and the entailment relation) returns the data* d_i *stored there.*

We note that Π need not be deterministic either in choosing contents of cells or in choosing which cells to write to, i.e., Π could have access to an arbitrarily long, finite random string $\mathcal{R}$ at each instant. However, as we will later describe, the adversary that we consider to reach our lower bound is agnostic to any randomness that Π uses.

An adversary $\mathcal{A}$ specifies the data D_0 input to the init algorithm, as well as for each $t > 0$, the cell i and data d input to the write algorithm. At each instant t, we refer to the contents of Sec and Pub as arrays Sec_t and Pub_t, respectively. For any sequence of data cells chosen by $\mathcal{A}$, $\widetilde{D}_t = (D_0, D_1, \ldots, D_t)$, let $\text{Pub}(\widetilde{D}_t)$ denote the union of all strings written to public cells by Π when $D_0, D_1, \ldots, D_t$ are specified by calls to init and write, i.e. $\text{Pub}(\widetilde{D}_t) = \cup_{i=0}^{t} \text{Pub}_i$. Similarly, let $\text{Sec}(\widetilde{D}_t)$ denote the union of all strings written to secret cells by Π as a result of $\widetilde{D}_t$, i.e., $\text{Sec}(\widetilde{D}_t) = \cup_{i=0}^{t} \text{Sec}_i$. Additionally, at any time t, we refer to all of the previous strings of each cell of D_t as $Prev(D_t) = (\bigcup_{j=0}^{t-1} D_j) \setminus D_t$.[5]

For correctness, we intuitively require that with Sec_t and Pub_t, Π should be able to recover and successfully return $D_t[i] \leftarrow \text{read}(i)$ for all $i \in [n]$. For forward secrecy, at each instant t, we also want to protect all data that used to be in D, but was since overwritten, in case of a corruption of Sec_t by $\mathcal{A}$. We abstract the above conditions (without explicitly providing read or corruption oracles to $\mathcal{A}$) using the following definition:

Definition 3 (Correctness and Security). Π *is correct and secure if for all* t, *and all sequences* $\widetilde{D}_t$ *determined by an adversary* $\mathcal{A}$:

- (Correctness): *All of the data cells* D_t *can be recovered by the contents of the secret and public cells and successfully returned at time* t: *For every* $i \in [n], d_i \leftarrow \text{read}(i)$, *where* $d_i = D_t[i]$ *and* $D_t[i] \in Rec(\text{Sec}_t \cup \text{Pub}_t)$.[6]

---

[5] All set operations specified in the definitions of $\text{Pub}(\widetilde{D}_t)$, $\text{Sec}(\widetilde{D}_t)$, $Prev(D_t)$, and the remainder of the proof are taken with respect to the sets containing the unique elements of the corresponding operands, ignoring cells with $\bot$. We may in fact directly refer to these defined arrays as sets in the remainder. While such definitions will not consider duplicate cells, our lower bound proof will not have to take into account the number of duplicates.

[6] Condition $D_t[i] \in Rec(\text{Sec}_t \cup \text{Pub}_t)$ forces Π to be a proper symbolic construction.

– (Security): *The previous contents of all cells in* D *with respect to time t cannot be recovered by the contents of the secret cells at time t and all public cells written to up to time t:* $\forall d \in Prev(\mathsf{D}_t), d \notin Rec(\mathsf{Sec}_t \cup \mathsf{Pub}(\widetilde{\mathsf{D}}_t))$.

Again, we note that the security of this definition is not as strong as an indistinguishability-based definition, as we require explicit recovery of previous data to break security. However, this only strengthens our lower bound.

We will measure the computational complexity of the protocol Π by amortizing over the number of unique strings derived from our grammar that are written to the public and secret cells throughout the execution of the protocol. This measure of course does not track *all* of the computation of some protocol Π, which only strengthens our lower bound. For example, we do not count the computational cost of any of our primitives. Formally, the computational cost $c(\widetilde{\mathsf{D}}_t)$, incurred by an execution of the protocol when run on input $\widetilde{\mathsf{D}}_t$, is defined as

$$c(\widetilde{\mathsf{D}}_t) := \frac{|\mathsf{Pub}(\widetilde{D}_t) \cup \mathsf{Sec}(\widetilde{D}_t)|}{t+1}.$$

3   Forward Secret Encrypted RAM Lower Bound

In this section, we prove the following Theorem in several steps.

Theorem 6. *There exists a non-adaptive, randomized adversarial sequence of* init *and* write *operations such that for any FS eRAM protocol Π that is correct and secure with respect to Definition 3, the amortized computational complexity cost incurred by the protocol when executed against that strategy is in expectation $\Omega(\log(n/s))$.*

Before we formalize our lower bound, we start with a simple example which demonstrates an important observation needed in our proof, and which we will refer to throughout the proof. Suppose that at time t, we have $s = 1$, $n = 4$ and keys k_1, k_2, k_3 such that $k_1 \in \mathsf{Sec}_t$. Further, we have $\{\mathbf{E}_{k_1}(k_2), \mathbf{E}_{k_1}(k_3), \mathbf{E}_{k_2}(d_1),$ $\mathbf{E}_{k_2}(d_2), \mathbf{E}_{k_2}(\mathbf{E}_{k_3}(d_3)), \mathbf{E}_{k_3}(d_4)\} \subseteq \mathsf{Pub}(\widetilde{\mathsf{D}}_t)$, for $\mathsf{D}_t = \{d_1, d_2, d_3, d_4\}$. We can informally abstract this into a graph depicting the relations between keys and data shown in Fig. 3.

The graph demonstrates that k_1 encodes information about k_2 and k_3, while k_2 and k_3 both encode some information about d_3. Additionally, k_2 encodes information about d_1 and d_2, while k_3 encodes information about d_4. Now suppose that virtual cell 3 (corresponding to d_3) is overwritten by some adversary. The goal of the protocol is effectively to create a new graph that retains as much reachability, in the graph theoretic sense, from the secret cells as possible (since we want to minimize the amount of computation needed to achieve correctness), while still disabling any ability to recover d_3 if any of the keys in the new graph are obtained by the adversary.

In our example, it is sufficient to remove k_1, as then k_2 and k_3, and thus d_3 cannot be recovered. However, this may be a rather inefficient method, as

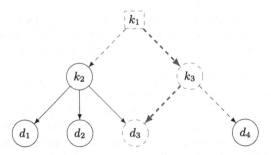

Fig. 3. Key-data graph $\mathcal{G}_\Pi(\widetilde{\mathsf{D}}_{t-1})$ at time $t-1$ as defined by Definition 9 for an execution of an FS eRAM protocol Π in which $s = 1$, $n = 4$, $k_1 \in \mathsf{Sec}_{t-1}$ (denoted by its square border), $\{\mathbf{E}_{k_1}(k_2), \mathbf{E}_{k_1}(k_3), \mathbf{E}_{k_2}(d_1), \mathbf{E}_{k_2}(d_2), \mathbf{E}_{k_2}(\mathbf{E}_{k_3}(d_3)), \mathbf{E}_{k_3}(d_4)\} \subseteq \mathsf{Pub}(\widetilde{\mathsf{D}}_{t-1})$, and $\mathsf{D}_{t-1} = \{d_1, d_2, d_3, d_4\}$. Since k_1 *minimally recovers* d_3 according to Definition 4, the collection of paths $\mathcal{P}_3^{t-1}$ that exist according to Lemma 1 are $P_{3,1} := k_1 \to k_2 \to d_3$, represented by blue edges, and $P_{3,2} := k_1 \to k_3 \to d_3$, represented by thick red edges. By Lemma 2, if at time t, d_3 is overwritten, all of the vertices on one of these paths must become indefinitely useless (see Definitions 5, 6). Since k_2 can be used to recover more data (besides d_3) than k_3 can, the protocol may choose to make the vertices of $P_{3,2}$ useless at time t (represented by dashed borders). In this case, all of the strings in $\mathsf{Pub}(\widetilde{\mathsf{D}}_t)$ corresponding to the dashed edges $k_1 \to k_2$, $k_1 \to k_3$, $k_3 \to d_3$, and $k_3 \to d_4$ become indefinitely useless at time t (see Definition 8), as the protocol can no longer recover the keys and data that they encapsulate. However, we stress that the choice of the path $P_{3,1}$ or $P_{3,2}$ on which all nodes must become useless at time t is determined by the protocol.

k_2 and k_3 also encode information about data d_1, d_2, d_4, and thus the protocol would have to generate fresh encodings of them for correctness. Unfortunately, we cannot retain reachability to both k_2 and k_3: it is necessary to remove *either* one of the edges $k_2 \to d_3$ or $k_3 \to d_3$ in the graph (which is done by removing k_2 or k_3, respectively), since together, they can be used to recover d_3 from $\mathbf{E}_{k_2}(\mathbf{E}_{k_3}(d_3))$, but the absence of one of them enables secrecy of d_3. Furthermore, it is still necessary to remove k_1, as it alone can recover d_3 by recovering k_2 and k_3. In this case, the protocol may want to remove just k_1 and k_3, as retaining reachability to k_2 retains reachability to two data cells, without any extra computation (as opposed to just one if reachability to k_3 is retained). However, we emphasize that the choice of which key to retain reachability to is indeed completely decided by the protocol, and the adversary does not have any control over this. The key to our proof is to lower bound the minimal amount of reachability, corresponding to edges in the graph and ciphertexts stored in public and secret cells in the protocol, that must be lost after each operation. Note that this is not the exact formalization, as the proof needs to handle several subtleties and complex cases, as later detailed in this section.

To do this, we will first abstract a meaningful graph-theoretic notion to determine the (amortized) minimum number of unique strings that any FS eRAM protocol, captured by our symbolic model, must write to its public and secret cells during each operation to preserve forward secrecy and correctness.

3.1   Minimality and Usefulness

We first introduce the notion of sets of strings defined by our grammar *minimally recovering* other sets of strings. Intuitively, a set C of strings minimally recovers another set C' of strings if the strings of C can together recover the strings of C' (using the contents of the public cells up to time t, too), but the removal of any string $c \in$ C prevents the recovery of at least one string $c' \in$ C'.

Definition 4. *A set* C *of strings minimally recovers set* C' *of strings if* $C' \subseteq Rec(C \cup Pub(\widetilde{D}_t))$ *and for any* $c \in C$, $C' \nsubseteq Rec((C \setminus \{c\}) \cup Pub(\widetilde{D}_t))$.

If C' contains a single element c', we may only write "C recovers c'" at certain points throughout our exposition (instead of C' or $\{c'\}$).

Now, for any execution of an FS eRAM protocol Π, at certain instants some of the keys that have been used by it may be accessible by the secret cells, while others may not. We call such keys *useful* and *useless*, respectively.

Definition 5. *A key* k *is* useful *at time* t *if* $\exists S \subseteq Sec_t$ *such that* S *minimally recovers* k. *It is* useless *otherwise.*

The set of useful keys at time t is denoted $UsefulKeys_{\Pi}(\widetilde{D}_t)$. The intuition behind this definition is that as data cells are overwritten, at least some of the keys that the protocol used to recover the previous data (if there are any) for correctness cannot be used anymore, for otherwise, previous data would be accessible, which would violate security. For example, in Fig. 3, keys k_1 and k_3 become useless at time t, because they can be used to recover d_3. Similarly, we can define data in terms of *usefulness*.

Definition 6. *Data* d *is* useful *at time* t *if* $d \in D_t$. *It is* useless *otherwise.*

We also define *usefulness* for strings derived by our grammar (that are not keys), based on the keys that are used to create them, and if they are accessible by the adversary at a given time. We first recall that there are four types of cryptographic operations we allow to derive strings from our grammar: encryptions, secret sharing, and (d)PRF computations. Based on this, we define how a string from our grammar can *encapsulate* a key or data:

Definition 7. *We say that a string* c *encapsulates* key or data c', *if* c *is the result of arbitrarily nested encryption and secret sharing operations on* c'; *i.e.,* $c = e_1(e_2(\ldots(e_l(c'))\ldots))$ *for some* $l \geq 1$, *where each* e_i *is either* $\mathbf{E}_{k_i}$ *for some key* k_i *or* $\mathbf{S}_j$ *for some* $j \in [n]$.

Definition 8. *A string* c *that encapsulates* c', *as in Definition 7 above, is* useless *at time* t *if*

- *at least one* e_i *corresponds to* $\mathbf{E}_{k_i}$ *for* $k_i \notin UsefulKeys_{\Pi}(\widetilde{D}_t)$, *or*
- $c \notin Sec_t \cup Pub(\widetilde{D}_t)$.[7]

Otherwise, it is useful.

---

[7] Note that we do not say $c \notin Rec(Sec_t \cup Pub(\widetilde{D}_t))$, since for our lower bound we want to only count those strings that were actually stored in some secret cell and are erased at some time. Also, as will be seen later, it must be that for any such string that we count in our lower bound, it must further be that $c \notin Rec(Sec_t \cup Pub(\widetilde{D}_t))$.

It is important to note that usefulness is dynamic: keys and strings that are useful at one instant may be useless at another instant. As noted above, every time a data cell is overwritten, some of the keys that can be used to recover its old contents must become useless for security and thus all strings that were in part generated by such keys (via the encryption algorithm, $\mathbf{E}$), as well as some strings which encapsulated these keys or the data, must become useless too. For example, in Fig. 3, since keys k_1 and k_3 become useless at time t, strings $\{\mathbf{E}_{k_1}(k_2), \mathbf{E}_{k_1}(k_3), \mathbf{E}_{k_2}(\mathbf{E}_{k_3}(d_3)), \mathbf{E}_{k_3}(d_4)\} \subseteq \mathrm{Pub}(\widetilde{\mathsf{D}}_t)$ must too.

Our goal is to show that after every write operation, logarithmically many (in n/s) strings stored in public and secret cells must become useless. Such strings may have been generated and stored in their respective cells at any time in the past, but the protocol incurs a computational cost of at least one per string.

3.2   Key-Data Graph

We will interpret secret cells, keys, and data using graph-theoretic terminology. For any execution of the protocol Π on a sequence of data cells $\widetilde{\mathsf{D}}_t$, we associate a directed graph $\mathcal{G}_\Pi(\widetilde{\mathsf{D}}_t)$ called the *key-data graph* at that time. Each vertex in the graph is either a string in a secret cell at time t, a useful key at time t, or a data cell at time t, and edges between the vertices abstract the process of key or data recovery (by use of the entailment relation $\vdash$).

Definition 9. *Let Π be a Forward Secret Encrypted RAM protocol executed with a sequence of data cells $\widetilde{\mathsf{D}}_t$. The Key-Data Graph for the protocol at time t is a directed graph $\mathcal{G}_\Pi(\widetilde{\mathsf{D}}_t) = (\mathcal{V}, \mathcal{E})$, where $\mathcal{V} = \mathrm{UsefulKeys}_\Pi(\widetilde{\mathsf{D}}_t) \cup \mathrm{Sec}_t \cup \mathsf{D}_t$ and $\mathcal{E}$ is the set of all ordered pairs $(v_1, v_2) \in \mathcal{V} \times \mathcal{V}$ such that at least one of the following is true:*

1. $\exists c \text{ s.t. } v_2 = \mathbf{F}(v_1, c)$.
2. $\exists k \in \mathrm{UsefulKeys}_\Pi(\widetilde{\mathsf{D}}_t) \text{ s.t. } v_2 = \mathbf{dF}(v_1, k) \text{ or } v_2 = \mathbf{dF}(k, v_1)$.
3. $\exists c \in \mathrm{Pub}(\widetilde{\mathsf{D}}_t) \cup \mathrm{Sec}_t \text{ s.t. } c = e_1(\mathbf{E}_{v_1}(e_2(v_2)))$ *(for arbitrary sequences of encryption and sharing operations e_1, e_2)*.
4. $v_1 \in \mathrm{Sec}_t, v_2 \in \mathrm{UsefulKeys}_\Pi(\widetilde{\mathsf{D}}_t) \cup \mathsf{D}_t$ *and* v_1 *encapsulates* v_2.

We note that in Fig. 3, we depict exactly $\mathcal{G}_\Pi(\widetilde{\mathsf{D}}_{t-1})$ for the simple example, which demonstrates that this definition can flexibly handle general schemes

In the following lemma, we show that if a set of vertices C in $\mathcal{G}_\Pi(\widetilde{\mathsf{D}}_t)$ minimally recovers some other vertex v_j, then there is a collection of paths from the vertices of C to v_j in $\mathcal{G}_\Pi(\widetilde{\mathsf{D}}_t)$ such that every vertex on the path (except for the vertices of C) is minimally recovered by its predecessors on these paths.

Lemma 1. *For any FS eRAM protocol Π, for every $t \geq 0$, for every sequence of data cell updates $\widetilde{\mathsf{D}}_t$ performed by $\mathcal{A}$ and for every useful key or data $v_j \in \mathcal{V}$ and (non-empty) set $\mathsf{C} \subseteq \mathcal{V}$, if C minimally recovers v_j, then there exists a collection of paths $\mathcal{P}$ from all $v_i \in \mathsf{C}$ to v_j (at least one per individual vertex v_i) in $\mathcal{G}_\Pi(\widetilde{\mathsf{D}}_t)$ such that for every v along these paths, except for the $v_i \in \mathsf{C}$, the set of strings $\{v_1, \ldots, v_\ell\} \subseteq \mathrm{UsefulKeys}_\Pi(\widetilde{\mathsf{D}}_t) \cup \mathrm{Sec}_t$ that have an edge to v on one of the paths minimally recover v.*

Proof. Consider some C and v_j satisfying the conditions in the lemma statement. Let $q \geq 1$ be the smallest number of applications of the entailment relation $\vdash$ required to recover v_j from C and $\mathsf{Pub}(\widetilde{D}_t)$. We prove the lemma using induction over q. I.e., for all $q \geq 1$ and every C that can minimally recover v_j in q steps, there is a collection of paths $\mathcal{P}$ originating from the v_i in C and ending at v_j in $\mathcal{G}_\Pi(\widetilde{D}_t)$ satisfying the lemma statement.

The statement is true for $q = 1$ since in this case $C = \{v_j\}$ and so there is a trivial path from v_j to itself. Now, suppose that the statement is true for all values of q smaller than an integer $Q > 1$. So, for all $q < Q$, every set $C \subseteq V$ that can minimally recover v_j in q steps has a collection of paths in $\mathcal{G}_\Pi(\widetilde{D}_t)$ leading from every $v_i \in C$ to v_j and for every vertex v along the paths, the vertices from which it has incoming edges along the paths form a set which minimally recovers v.

Consider any set $C \subseteq V$ that can minimally recover v_j in Q steps. It must be that there exists some set C' such that 1. C' can minimally recover v_j in less than Q steps, and 2. for each $c' \in C'$, either

(i) there exists some $k \in C$ and some string c such that $\mathbf{F}(k, c) = c'$ and k minimally recovers c', or

(ii) there exists keys $k_1, k_2 \in \mathtt{UsefulKeys}_\Pi(\widetilde{D}_t)$ such that 1. $k_1 \in C$, 2. $k_2 \in C$, or 3. both $k_1, k_2 \in C$ and $\mathbf{dF}(k_1, k_2) = c'$, where in cases (a), (b), (c), just k_1, just k_2, or $\{k_1, k_2\}$ minimally recovers c', respectively, or

(iii) c' is a key or data and there exists sets $C'' \subseteq \mathsf{Pub}(\widetilde{D}_t)$ and $C''' \subseteq \mathsf{Sec}_t \cap C$ (each possibly empty) whose strings encapsulate c' and $C_e \subseteq C$, a set of useful encryption keys used in the generation of these strings, such that $C''' \cup C_e$ minimally recovers c',[8] or

(iv) $c' \in C$.

Moreover, for any string $c' \in C'$ satisfying case (i), it must be $c' \in \mathtt{UsefulKeys}_\Pi(\widetilde{D}_t)$ because $c' \in Rec(\{k\}) \subseteq Rec(\mathsf{Sec}_t \cup \mathsf{Pub}(\widetilde{D}_t))$, since $k \in \mathtt{UsefulKeys}_\Pi(\widetilde{D}_t)$. For any string satisfying case (ii), it must be that $c' \in \mathtt{UsefulKeys}_\Pi(\widetilde{D}_t)$ because $c' \in Rec(\{k_1, k_2\}) \subseteq Rec(\mathsf{Sec}_t \cup \mathsf{Pub}(\widetilde{D}_t))$, since $k_1, k_2 \in \mathtt{UsefulKeys}_\Pi(\widetilde{D}_t)$. For any key or data $c' \in C'$ satisfying case (iii), it must be that $c' \in \mathtt{UsefulKeys}_\Pi(\widetilde{D}_t) \cup D_t$ because: If c' is a key, we have that $c' \in Rec(C_e \cup C'' \cup \mathsf{Pub}(\widetilde{D}_t)) \subseteq Rec(\mathsf{Sec}_t \cup \mathsf{Pub}(\widetilde{D}_t))$, since $C_e \subseteq \mathtt{UsefulKeys}_\Pi(\widetilde{D}_t)$ and $C''' \subseteq \mathsf{Sec}_t$. If c' is data, we must have that $v_j \in V$ so $c' = v_j \in D_t$, for otherwise, since data cells have no outgoing edges, C' does not minimally recover v_j. Thus, we have shown that $C' \subseteq V$.

We also note that we can choose to consider only C' that contain c' corresponding to case (iii) that are the keys or data which are encapsulated by C'' and C''' (and not some intermediary strings c_{bad} encapsulating c' in C', which could be in Sec_t, for example) because v_j in the lemma statement is a useful key or data. Therefore the encapsulated c' must either be v_j itself or some key that

---

[8] This is the case in which c' is recovered through secret share reconstruction (using $C'' \cup C'''$), decryption (using keys of C_e and possibly some that can be recovered using only $\mathsf{Pub}(\widetilde{D}_t)$, along with $C'' \cup C'''$), or possibly a combination of both.

must be used to minimally recover v_j. Thus, if C contains enough keys which were used in the generation of the strings of $C'' \cup C'''$ that (in addition to the cells of C''') can minimally recover c' anyway, then we can just directly include c' in C'. If C does not contain enough of those keys, then we can just choose C' that lessens the number of applications of the entailment relation needed to recover a sufficient set of those keys, and defer inclusion of c' until some later set.

Continuing, by the inductive hypothesis, there are a collection of paths from the $c' \in C'$ satisfying the lemma statement, and prepending the paths with:

- in case (i), the edge $k \to c'$,
- in case (ii,a), the edge $k_1 \to c'$, in case (ii,b) the edge $k_2 \to c'$, in case (ii,c) the edges $k_1 \to c'$ and $k_2 \to c'$,
- in case (iii), the edges $k \to c'$, for each $k \in C_e$, and the edges $c_{\mathsf{Sec}} \to c'$, for each $c_{\mathsf{Sec}} \in C'''$, and
- in case (iv), nothing,

extends these paths appropriately. Indeed, by the case analysis above, for each $c' \in C'$ the nodes in C corresponding to its incoming edges on the paths minimally recover c'. Furthermore, if any nodes $c \in C$ do not have any edges to nodes in C', then since C' minimally recovers v_j and all of the nodes in C' can be recovered by the other nodes of C, C does not minimally recover v_j, a contradiction. Thus we have shown the inductive step holds for all $Q > 1$. □

Now we show a quick proposition which establishes that at each time t, any data $d_i \in D_t$ cannot be solely recovered by the contents of the public cells up to time t and thus there must exist some non-empty set of strings in the secret cells that minimally recovers d_i:

Proposition 1. *For any $d_i \in D_t$, it must be that $d_i \notin Rec(\mathsf{Pub}(\widetilde{D}_t))$ and thus $\exists S_i \subseteq \mathsf{Sec}_t$ such that $S_i \neq \emptyset$ and S_i minimally recovers d_i.*

Proof. The proof for this is quite basic: if $d_i \in Rec(\mathsf{Pub}(\widetilde{D}_t))$, then if the adversary's next operation is write(i, d) for some data d, then at time $t + 1$, for example, it is clear that $d_i \in Prev(D_{t+1})$ and also that $d_i \in Rec(\mathsf{Pub}(\widetilde{D}_{t+1})) \subseteq Rec(\mathsf{Sec}_{t+1} \cup \mathsf{Pub}(\widetilde{D}_{t+1}))$, which violates security. Thus, a contradiction is reached.

Now, by correctness, it must be that $d_i \in Rec(\mathsf{Sec}_t \cup \mathsf{Pub}_t)$, so with the above, it must be that there exists some non-empty $S_i \subseteq \mathsf{Sec}_t$ such that S_i minimally recovers d_i. □

As a result of this proposition, we have that for each $d_i \in D_t$ at time t, there exists *at least one* collection of paths $\mathcal{P}_i^t$ from the $s_j \in S_i$ to d_i satisfying the conditions of Lemma 1. In the example of Fig. 3, the collection of paths $\mathcal{P}_3^{t-1} = \{P_{3,1}, P_{2,1}\}$, where $P_{3,1} := k_1 \to k_2 \to d_3$ and $P_{3,2} := k_1 \to k_3 \to d_3$, represents one such collection of paths that must exist as a result of Lemma 1, since $\{k_1\}$ minimally recovers d_3. Observe, however, that in general, there could be multiple such path collections (even from the same $S_i \subseteq \mathsf{Sec}_t$) for each d_i (for example, if in Fig. 3 we also have $\mathbf{E}_{k_1}(d_3) \in \mathsf{Pub}(\widetilde{D}_{t+1})$, then we also have the collection consisting of just $k_1 \to d_3$); we cannot restrict protocols to just one collection, even though having more does not seem fruitful. So, for each $i \in [n]$, there may exist r_i non-empty secret cell subsets $S_{i,j} \subseteq \mathsf{Sec}_t, j \in [r_i]$ that minimally recover d_i, and $r_i' \geq r_i$ corresponding path collections $\mathcal{P}_{i,l}^t, l \in [r_i']$, which therefore must exist by Lemma 1.

We also note that by the proof of Lemma 1, every string stored in a secret cell $c_{\mathsf{Sec}} \in \mathsf{Sec}_t$ that exists on these paths and is not a key or data has no incoming edges on the paths from other path nodes.

We now show how any FS eRAM protocol Π must handle such collections of paths at every time t in order to preserve security.

Lemma 2. *If at time t, an adversary $\mathcal{A}$ executes* write(i, d_i') *for $d_i' \neq \mathsf{D}_{t-1}[i]$, then, for every collection of paths $\mathcal{P}_{i,l}^{t-1}, l \in [r_i']$, from some non-empty $S_{i,j} \subseteq \mathsf{Sec}_{t-1}$ that minimally recovers $\mathsf{D}_{t-1}[i]$, all of the vertices (data, keys, and strings in secret cells) on at least one of the paths $P_i^* \in \mathcal{P}_{i,l}^{t-1}$, must become useless for all times $t' \geq t$.*

Proof. Since $\mathcal{A}$ queries write(i, d_i'), Π must alter the contents of the secret cells and the partition of useful and useless keys so that $d_i \notin Rec(\mathsf{Sec}_{t'} \cup \mathsf{Pub}(\widetilde{\mathsf{D}}_{t'}))$ for all $t' \geq t$, where d_i was the string stored in data cell i at time $t - 1$ (i.e., what d_i' replaces at time t).

Now, consider one such collection of paths $\mathcal{P}_{i,l}^{t-1}$. If $d_i \in \mathsf{Sec}_{t-1}$, i.e., $\mathcal{P}_{i,l}^{t-1}$ only consists of the trivial path from d_i to itself, then, looking ahead to Sect. 3.3, the adversary will never again write d_i to D, and thus d_i becomes useless for all $t' \geq t$. Otherwise, we will proceed inductively starting from the sink of all of these paths, d_i (and ending at a node right after the source of one of them). Let V_i and E_i be the set of vertices and edges in all of the paths of $\mathcal{P}_{i,l}^{t-1}$, respectively. We know from Lemma 1 that the set $R := \{v : v \in V_i, (v, d_i) \in E_i\}$, indeed minimally recovers d_i. Thus, for security, since we must have that $d_i \notin Rec(\mathsf{Sec}_{t'} \cup \mathsf{Pub}(\widetilde{\mathsf{D}}_{t'}))$, it must be that $\exists v^* \in R$ such that $v^* \notin Rec(\mathsf{Sec}_{t'} \cup \mathsf{Pub}(\widetilde{\mathsf{D}}_{t'}))$ for all $t' \geq t$, i.e., $v^* \notin \mathsf{UsefulKeys}_\Pi(\widetilde{\mathsf{D}}_{t'}) \cup \mathsf{Sec}_{t'}$. So, if v^* was in $\mathsf{UsefulKeys}_\Pi(\widetilde{\mathsf{D}}_{t-1})$ or Sec_{t-1}, it can no longer be useful at each time t' (it is deleted at time t and can never be generated again, by definition of the symbolic model). We must then recurse on v^*, continuing until we reach some source in $\mathcal{P}_{i,l}^{t-1}$, i.e., some key or string $c^* \in \mathsf{Sec}_{t-1}$, that must become useless.

Therefore, we conclude that all of the vertices on at least one of the paths $P_i^* \in \mathcal{P}_{i,l}^{t-1}$ must become indefinitely useless at time t. $\square$

It is important to note that the protocol Π has control over which path P_i^* in each $\mathcal{P}_{i,l}^{t-1}$ must have all of its nodes become useless at time t (and there could in fact be overlap between collections, even for the same i). For example, in Fig. 3, it may be that either of $P_{3,1}$ or $P_{3,2}$ have all of their nodes become useless at time t. We depict in that figure that the path which Π chooses is $P_{3,2}$.

The rest of the lower bound proof will proceed by considering for each t and $i \in [n]$, an arbitrary collection of paths $\mathcal{P}_i^t$ and for each such collection, the path P_i^* that minimizes the sum of the number of outgoing edges of type 3 or 4 in Definition 9 from its vertices. We do so to focus on the minimum number of strings that are actually stored in public and secret cells, corresponding to tangible actions that Π took in the past to put them there, that Π must make useless at each time t. In particular, we remove all edges (such as those for (d)PRFs) that may not require such storage. We do this by, in Definition 11, first choosing an arbitrary collection $\mathcal{P}_i^t$ for each $i \in [n]$ and considering only the edges on those paths, then restricting these paths to only edges of type 3 or 4, and finally further restricting to only those edges on path P_i^* for each $i \in [n]$. First, a helpful definition:

Definition 10. *Let $G = (\mathcal{V}, \mathcal{E})$ be a directed graph and let P be some path in G. The out-degree of P in G, denoted $out_G(P)$, is the number of edges in $\mathcal{E}$ that start from a node in P. That is,*

$$out_G(P) = \sum_{v \in P} out_G(v).$$

Definition 11. *For any FS eRAM protocol Π, executed with a sequence of data cell updates $\widetilde{D}_t$, the succinct key-data graph at time t, denoted $\hat{\mathcal{G}}_\Pi(\widetilde{D}_t)$, is a modification of $\mathcal{G}_\Pi(\widetilde{D}_t)$ formed by*

- *first, choosing for each $i \in [n]$ an arbitrary collection of paths $\mathcal{P}_i^t$ in $\mathcal{G}_\Pi(\widetilde{D}_t)$ specified by Lemma 1 and which must exist by Proposition 1, starting from the vertices of some arbitrary non-empty $S_i \in \mathsf{Sec}_t$ that minimally recovers d_i and ending at d_i,*
- *second, including an edge from $\mathcal{G}_\Pi(\widetilde{D}_t)$ if and only if it is contained in the collection of paths $\mathcal{P}_i^t$ for some $i \in [n]$,*
- *third, for each $i \in [n], l \in [\ell_i]$, where ℓ_i the number of paths in $\mathcal{P}_i^t$, for any non-empty sequence of edges $(e_1, \ldots, e_m)$ on path $P_{i,l} \in \mathcal{P}_i^t$ such that each $e_j = (v_{j-1}, v_j)$ for $j \in [m-1]$ is a (d)PRF edge of type 1 or 2, $e_m = (v_{m-1}, v_m)$ is not a (d)PRF edge, and v_0 does not have any incoming (d)PRF edges on $P_{i,l}$, removing all of the edges in the sequence and replacing them with the single edge $e = (v_0, v_m)$ for only $P_{i,l}$,*
- *fourth, taking the union of these edges for all $i \in [n]$, and finally*
- *including an edge if and only if it is contained in the path P_i^* for some $i \in [n]$ such that $out(P_i^*) = \min_{P_{i,l} \in \mathcal{P}_i^t} out(P_{i,l})$, where the outdegree of the nodes is over only the edges from the last step.*

One can observe that vertices representing data cells are of course sinks, i.e., they have no outgoing edges, in $\mathcal{G}_\Pi(\widetilde{D}_t)$ and $\hat{\mathcal{G}}_\Pi(\widetilde{D}_t)$. In addition, at most s secret cells can be represented in $\mathcal{G}_\Pi(\widetilde{D}_t)$ and $\hat{\mathcal{G}}_\Pi(\widetilde{D}_t)$, by definition. Furthermore, if a data cell d_i is not itself in Sec_t at time t, by Proposition 1, it must be that some non-empty subset $S_i \subseteq \mathsf{Sec}_t$ minimally recovers d_i, and so there must be some collection of paths $\mathcal{P}_i^t$ in $\mathcal{G}_\Pi(\widetilde{D}_t)$ starting at the secret cells of S_i and ending in edges of type 3 or 4 at d_i. Thus, there must still be one path in $\hat{\mathcal{G}}_\Pi(\widetilde{D}_t)$ starting at some secret cell $c_{\mathsf{Sec}} \in \mathsf{Sec}_t$ and ending at d_i. We will call such paths $\hat{P}_i^*$.

3.3 Adversarial Strategy

We now describe the strategy used by the adversary to prove the lower bound. The adversary will use a simple non-adaptive randomized strategy. Initially, the adversary inputs n distinct strings of type D to be stored in the data cells: $\mathsf{D}_0 = (d_1, \ldots, d_n)$ to the init algorithm. At each instant t, the adversary will pick a cell i uniformly at random to write data d that has never before been in $\mathsf{D}_{t'}$ for $0 \leq t' \leq t$, i.e. $\mathrm{write}(i, d)$. We will show that in expectation, the number of strings stored in secret and public cells combined that become *useless* after time t is logarithmically-many (in terms of n/s). Before proving Theorem 6, we provide an instrumental graph-theoretic lemma in proving our lower bound. We prove this lemma in the full version [5].

Lemma 3. *Let $G = (\mathcal{V}, \mathcal{E})$ be an arbitrary graph and let $S = \{u_1, \ldots, u_s\}$, $D = \{v_1, \ldots, v_n\}$ be any sets of nodes in the graph such that for each $v_i \in D$, $\exists u_j \in S$ such that there is a path P_i from u_j to v_i and there is no $k \neq i$ such that v_k occurs in P_i. Then if $i \in [n]$ is chosen uniformly at random:*

$$\mathbb{E}[out_G(P_i)] \geq \log_2(n/s).$$

Proof (Theorem 6). In the setting of succinct key-data graphs, sets S and D in Lemma 3 correspond to the secret cells and data cells, respectively, at time t, i.e., Sec_t and Pub_t. Each path $P_i = \widehat{P}_i^*$ corresponds to the path starting from some secret cell u_j to the data cell v_i that has the minimum number of outgoing edges over all $P_{i,l} \in \mathcal{P}_i^t$, for some arbitrary $\mathcal{P}_i^t$, which correspond to strings that must be stored in the public or secret cells of Π. Since no data cells have outgoing edges, for every $i \in [n]$, no data cell v_k, $k \neq i$ lies on the path $\widehat{P}_i^*$. Thus, Lemma 3 implies that for every $t \geq 1$, the data cell v_i replaced by $\mathcal{A}$ at time t is such that in expectation, $\widehat{P}_i^*$ will always have out-degree at least $\log_2(n/s)$ in $\hat{\mathcal{G}}_\Pi(\widetilde{\mathsf{D}}_t)$. Since $\widehat{P}_i^*$ corresponds to the path from a secret cell to d_i which minimizes the number of outgoing edges corresponding to strings that must be stored in the public or secret cells of Π, any other path that Π chooses whose nodes must become useless after time t (by Lemma 2) must have at least $\log_2(n/s)$ such edges in expectation.

Once all of the vertices on some such path become useless, all strings in public or secret cells that were in part generated by them become useless by definition. For example, in Fig. 3, since the vertices on $P_{3,2}$ become useless, each string $\mathbf{E}_{k_1}(k_2), \mathbf{E}_{k_1}(k_3), \mathbf{E}_{k_2}(\mathbf{E}_{k_3}(d_3)), \mathbf{E}_{k_3}(d_4)$ becomes useless. So, under the above adversarial strategy, at least $\log_2(n/s)$ strings stored in public or secret cells become useless after time t, in expectation. We only mark each string as useless once because:

- if a key in the set, which minimally recovers the key or data that the string encapsulates, using that string, is indefinitely inaccessible by the protocol, the protocol is indefinitely unable to recover the key or data using the string (and also the string can never be reproduced, by definition of the symbolic model),

- otherwise, if the string was stored in a secret cell on the path P_i^*, then from Lemma 2, we know that it must become useless indefinitely and therefore never be stored in a secret cell again.

Therefore, in both cases, there will never be any edge in any future succinct key-data graph that corresponds to the string. Moreover, since v_i is never added back to a data cell by the adversary, the strings remain useless for all $t' \geq t$.

Therefore, we have shown that throughout the execution of any protocol Π, at least $\frac{t}{t+1} \cdot \log_2(n/s) \geq (1 - \frac{1}{t}) \cdot \log_2(n/s) = (1 - o(1)) \cdot \log_2(n/s)$ strings which were stored in public or secret cells become useless in expectation through time t, proving Theorem 6. ∎

4 Stronger Forward Secret Encrypted RAM Definitions

We note that our FS eRAM computational lower bound in Sect. 3 uses a different, weaker definition in our symbolic model based on recoverability (which only makes our lower bound stronger). For our upper bounds, we will use the typical indistinguishability-based security that we define here in the standard model of computation.

Definition 12 (Forward Secret Encrypted RAM). *A Forward Secret Encrypted RAM (FS eRAM) protocol $\Pi = (\text{init}, \text{read}, \text{write})$ consists of the following algorithms:*

- *(Sec, Pub) $\leftarrow$ init($1^\lambda, s, n$), which initializes public cells Pub and s secret cells Sec, where n is the number of virtual cells and λ is the security parameter.*
- *(Sec', Pub', d) $\leftarrow$ read(Sec, Pub, i), which returns data d of virtual cell $i \in [n]$.*
- *(Sec', Pub') $\leftarrow$ write(Sec, Pub, d, i), which replaces the contents of virtual cell $i \in [n]$ with data d.*

Correctness. An FS eRAM scheme is *correct* if for any sequence of operations: $\Pr[(\cdot, \cdot, d^*) \leftarrow \text{read(Sec, Pub, } i) : d^* = d] = 1$, for any execution of read(Sec, Pub, i) in the sequence after an execution of write(Sec, Pub, d, i) and before a subsequent execution of write(Sec, Pub, d', i), for some data d', in the sequence where the probability is over the random coin tosses of the protocol.

Security. We define security with respect to the following game between a challenger and an adversary. We emphasize that the adversary has read-access to *all* of Pub (which is usually encrypted) on which the FS eRAM operates, as well as the access pattern to cells of Pub during operations.

The challenger initially chooses $b \in \{0, 1\}$ uniformly at random and runs (Sec, Pub) $\leftarrow$ init($1^\lambda, s, n$) (where $s \ll n = \text{poly}(\lambda)$). Then, the adversary has access to (polynomial-many queries of) the following oracles:

- **write**(d, i), which computes write(Sec, Pub, d, i).
- **corrupt**(), which simply returns Sec.
- **chall**(d_0, d_1, i), which computes write(Sec, Pub, d_b, i).

An adversary is not allowed to call **corrupt**() after a call to **chall**(d_0, d_1, i), without first using **write**(d, i) to overwrite the i-th virtual cell with some other data d, since otherwise they would trivially win. Observe that w.l.o.g. there is no oracle for read() since the adversary already knows the data in cells which they filled using **write**(), and should not know the data in cells filled via **chall**(). Further observe that the following definition provides forward secrecy, since upon some legal **corrupt**() call after some **chall**(d_0, d_1, i) call, the adversary $\mathcal{A}$ should not be able to guess the bit b, i.e. whether d_0 or d_1 was stored in virtual cell i.

Definition 13 (Forward Secret Encrypted RAM Security). *A Forward Secret Encrypted RAM protocol Π is secure if for every adversary $\mathcal{A}$ that runs in time* $\texttt{poly}(\lambda)$: $|\Pr[\mathcal{A} \to 1 | b = 1] - \Pr[\mathcal{A} \to 1 | b = 0]| \leq \texttt{negl}(\lambda)$.

Recall the folklore construction of Fig. 1. It is clear that this construction is secure with respect to Definition 13 due to standard IND-CPA security of symmetric encryption. Once the adversary queries **write**(d, i) after a **chall**(d_0, d_1, i) query, all of the keys on the path of cell i, including those in Sec, are refreshed, and encryptions of the children of the path nodes are recomputed. Thus no information about the challenge bit b can be garnered from a **corrupt**() query.

5   Oblivious Forward Secret Encrypted RAM

In this section, we consider combining the notion of forward secret encrypted RAMs with *oblivious RAMs* (or ORAMs). ORAMs are a well-studied cryptographic primitive (see [1,17,18,32,36,42] and references therein) that provides security for the patterns of data access. At a high level, ORAMs guarantee that adversaries may not distinguish between two equal-length operational sequences even when viewing accesses to encrypted data. We note that ORAMs do not consider the setting where adversaries corrupt client storage.

Looking forward, we first formally define oblivious forward secret encrypted RAMs. We present both a strong and a weak notion combining obliviousness and forward secrecy. First, we present a linear cell probe lower bound for the strong variant. To obtain sub-linear overhead, we consider the weaker notion and present an optimal construction with logarithmic overhead. As a result, we show that one can add a weaker notion of obliviousness to forward secret encrypted RAMs without asymptotic overhead.

5.1   Definitions

The syntax of ORAMs are identical to the syntax of FS eRAMs presented in Definition 12 where secret cells Sec are client storage and public cells Pub are server storage. Therefore, we omit a formal notion of ORAM syntax and refer readers back to FS eRAM syntax if needed.

We start by defining the most natural notion of oblivious forward secret encrypted RAMs. When the adversary corrupts client storage and views the current memory contents, the adversary should not be able to distinguish between any two equal-length operational sequences that result in the current memory contents. At a high level, this notion provides forward secrecy for both the memory contents as well as the access patterns performed by the client prior to corruption. We denote this notion as *strong* oblivious forward secret encrypted RAMs.

Definition 14 (Strong Oblivious Forward Secret Encrypted RAM). *Consider any two equal-length sequences of read and write operations O_1 and O_2 such that the contents of the array after both sequences are executed are identical. Let $\mathcal{V}(O)$ be the adversary's view when executing sequence O that includes contents of server (public) cells, all accesses to server cells and corrupted secret cells after O is executed. For any pair of such sequences O_1 and O_2 and any PPT adversary $\mathcal{A}$, a protocol Π is a strong oblivious forward secret encrypted RAM if $|\Pr[\mathcal{A}(\mathcal{V}(O_1)) = 1] - \Pr[\mathcal{A}(\mathcal{V}(O_2)) = 1]| \leq \mathsf{negl}(\lambda)$.*

We show in the full version [5] that this strong notion requires linear overhead in the cell probe model. As a result, we need to consider a weaker security notion to obtain reasonable (or even sub-linear) overhead. Another natural composition of forward secret encrypted RAMs and oblivious RAMs is to trivially combine the two security notions together. If we consider an adversary that never corrupts client storage, then the access pattern to data remains secure (identical to ORAM guarantees). When the adversary corrupts client storage, all deleted memory contents are not recoverable by the adversary (identical to forward secret guarantees). In the case of client corruption, no security guarantees are offered about the client's access patterns prior to corruption. We denote this security as *weak* oblivious forward secret encrypted RAMs. As this is the notion that enables interesting sub-linear constructions, we will also refer to this notion as simply oblivious forward secret encrypted RAMs. We start by defining oblivious RAM:

Definition 15 (Oblivious RAM). *Consider any two equal-length sequences of read and write operations O_1 and O_2. Let $\mathcal{V}(O)$ be the adversary's view when executing sequence O that includes contents of server (public) cells and all accesses to server cells. For any pair of such sequences O_1 and O_2 and any PPT adversary $\mathcal{A}$, a protocol Π is an oblivious RAM if $|\Pr[\mathcal{A}(\mathcal{V}(O_1)) = 1] - \Pr[\mathcal{A}(\mathcal{V}(O_2)) = 1]| \leq \mathsf{negl}(\lambda)$.*

Definition 16 ((Weak) Oblivious Forward Secret Encrypted RAM). *A protocol Π is a (weak) oblivious forward secret encrypted RAM if Π is both a forward secret encrypted RAM and an oblivious RAM.*

5.2 Oblivious Forward Secret Encrypted RAM Construction

We start by presenting a naive composition of oblivious RAM and forward secret encrypted RAM constructions. Throughout this section, we will measure overhead with respect to encrypted array entries. For example, $O(\log n)$ communication means $O(\log n)$ encrypted array entries. We make the natural assumption that cell size is $\Omega(\log n)$ bits, and also array entries are $O(\log n)$ bits. The idea is to take any forward secret encrypted RAM and replace each memory access using an oblivious RAM. While this guarantees both obliviousness and forward secrecy, the efficiency is not optimal. Note that forward secret encrypted RAMs use $O(\log n)$ memory accesses. Each memory access in an ORAM costs $O(\log n)$ overhead incurring a total $O(\log^2 n)$ overhead. We note that prior works have studied this primitive such as [39]. To our knowledge, the best current construction requires $O(\log^2 n)$ overhead.[9]

Our construction utilizes two observations. First, tree-based ORAMs are quite conducive to incorporate the folklore FS eRAM solution. However, all tree-based ORAMs [42] require $O(\log^2 n)$ overhead. On the other hand, hierarchical ORAMs [1,17,32,36] obtain $O(\log n)$ overhead but there is no straightforward way to incorporate the folklore FS eRAM solution. To obtain our result, we compose tree-based and hierarchical ORAMs to obtain a faster solution. At a high level, we use tree-based ORAMs and replace the recursive position map with a hierarchical ORAMs. We describe our new constructions below.

Overview. Our construction will avoid this additional logarithmic overhead incurred by ORAM over forward secret encrypted RAMs. Without loss of generality, suppose we are storing n array entries $D[0], \ldots, D[n-1]$ where n is a power of two. Our construction uses three components: a complete binary tree, a stash and an oblivious RAM. The binary tree is inspired by prior works for tree-based ORAMs [42]. The tree will have n leaf nodes and $\log n$ levels used to store the n array entries. Every node in the binary tree has capacity to store up to a constant number of array entries. Each of the n array entries, $D[i]$, will be uniquely assigned a uniformly random leaf node of the tree denoted by $\mathsf{Leaf}(i)$. The tree maintains the invariant that if any array entry $D[i]$ is stored in the binary tree, then $D[i]$ will be stored in a node that appears on the unique root-to-leaf path for leaf $\mathsf{Leaf}(i)$. If $D[i]$ is not stored in the tree, then it will be stored (along with $\mathsf{Leaf}(i)$) in the *stash* denoted by Stash. Additionally, we need to maintain a *position map*, PMAP, that stores the assigned leaf nodes for each array entry, that is, $\mathsf{PMAP}[i] = \mathsf{Leaf}(i)$.

Binary Tree. Whenever an array entry $D[i]$ is either read or overwritten, the root-to-leaf path to $\mathsf{Leaf}(i)$ will be accessed along with the stash Stash to obtain $D[i]$. Afterwards, $\mathsf{Leaf}(i)$ is re-initialized by picking amongst the n leaf nodes uniformly at random with PMAP being updated accordingly. Finally, $D[i]$ is stored in Stash with its updated $\mathsf{Leaf}(i)$. To ensure Stash remains small, entries in Stash are evicted in a greedy manner whenever a root-to-leaf path is accessed. If there is space in the root node, any item in Stash may be evicted into the root node (as the root appears on every root-to-leaf node path). Generally, for any node accessed in a root-to-leaf path, any data entry $D[i]$ whose leaf node $\mathsf{Leaf}(i)$ appears in the sub-tree rooted at the node may be evicted until reaching the node's capacity. Prior works proved that the Stash remains small except with

---

[9] To be fair, we note that these works appeared before recent developments leading to $O(\log n)$ overhead ORAMs [1,32].

negligible probability. Formally, Stash contains at most $\omega(\log n)$ items except with probability negligible in n. Additionally, it has been showing that accessing the tree is oblivious.

To obtain forward secrecy, we embed the folklore FS eRAM ideas into the binary tree. Each internal node in the binary tree will additionally store a random encryption key that will be used to encrypt the contents of both children. Each time a root-to-leaf path is accessed, all children of nodes in the root-to-leaf path will also be accessed. All encryption keys of nodes in the path will be re-generated. Furthermore, all nodes will be re-encrypted using their parent's new encryption key. The newly re-encrypted nodes will be uploaded back to the server for storage. This modification guarantees forward secrecy for the data.

Position Map and Stash. Next, we consider the position map PMAP. Note that PMAP only stores relationships between entries and leaf nodes. In particular, PMAP does not store any information about the array entry contents. As a result, we only need to focus on obliviousness for PMAP. We choose to store PMAP in any oblivious RAM. If we choose the construction in [1], reading or overwriting any entry PMAP[i] requires only $O(\log n)$ overhead as PMAP contains only n entries. Finally, the Stash is handled by encrypting the array entries D[i] that it contains, along with their corresponding leaves Leaf(i), and storing the ciphertexts on the server. Making the natural assumption that the cell size is $\Omega(\log n)$ bits and can fit memory addresses, we can encode Leaf(i) using $O(\log n)$ bits, and thus additionally storing Leaf(i) does not incur any extra overhead.

Read and Write Algorithms. Altogether, a read or write to the oblivious forward secure encrypted RAM works as follows. To read/overwrite D[i], the leaf node Leaf(i) is queried from PMAP using ORAM operations. Next, the root-to-leaf path to Leaf(i), children of nodes in the root-to-leaf path and Stash are downloaded and decrypted. D[i] is then retrieved and updated if needed. A new uniformly random Leaf(i) is generated and written back to PMAP, and D[i] is placed into Stash with its new Leaf(i). Items are greedily evicted from Stash into the downloaded root-to-leaf path using their Leaf(i) as guidance. Each node is padded to the maximum capacity with dummies if needed. All encryption keys of internal nodes are freshly sampled and all nodes are encrypted using the parent node's encryption keys before being uploaded back to the server. The root is encrypted with a freshly generated client-stored encryption key. Finally, Stash is padded to the maximum capacity with dummies and re-encrypted using the new client key before being uploaded to the server.

Theorem 7. *For any function $f(n) = \omega(1)$, there exists a (weak) oblivious forward secret encrypted RAM with $O(\log n \cdot f(n))$ overhead, $O(n)$ server storage and $O(1)$ client storage.*

We provide a proof of this Theorem in the full version [5]. Our construction is essentially optimal except for the multiplicative $\omega(1)$ factor as we already proved that forward secure encrypted RAMs require $\Omega(\log n)$ overhead. Similarly, it is known that ORAMs also require $\Omega(\log n)$ overhead [17,26].

6   Forward Secret Memory Checkers

In this section, we combine forward secret encrypted RAMs with memory checkers (MCs) to get forward secret memory checkers (FS MCs). Memory checking is a well-studied cryptographic notion [6,11,15,31] that provides authenticity for outsourced data storage. Intuitively, MCs use some small local storage to guarantee that an adversarial server cannot alter outsourced data entries without the MC noticing (and outputting that a bug has occurred).

We will first define our combined notion of FS MCs then provide a scheme which overlays the folklore FS eRAM scheme with a tree-based MC from [6] that uses ideas from Merkle Trees [28]. As a result, we will achieve $O(1)$ secret storage, $O(n)$ remote storage, and $O(\log n)$ overhead, i.e., a scheme which provides memory checking with no additional asymptotic overhead to the folklore FS eRAM scheme.[10] Our construction is optimal with respect to both our $\Omega(\log n)$ lower bound on the overhead of FS eRAM and the best known $O(\log n)$ overhead construction for MCs (and almost optimal with respect to the $\Omega(\log n/\log\log n)$ MC lower bound of [15]).[11]

6.1   Forward Secret Memory Checker Definition

For FS MCs, we alter the syntax of FS eRAMs presented in Definition 12 to highlight the interaction between the FS MC and the potentially malicious remote server. Before reading the data from a virtual cell i, the FS MC must first receive the relevant (but possibly maliciously fabricated) public cells from the server. Additionally, to write to a cell i, the FS MC must first receive the relevant public cells from the server as above, then send new public cells to the server, which the FS MC expects to be written in place of the old public cells.

Definition 17 (Forward Secret Memory Checker).   *A Forward Secret Memory Checker (FS MC)* $\Pi = (\mathrm{init}, \mathrm{retrieve}, \mathrm{read}, \mathrm{write}, \mathrm{commit})$ *consists of the following algorithms:*[12]

- $(\mathsf{Sec}, \mathsf{Pub}) \leftarrow \mathrm{init}(1^\lambda, n)$, *which initializes public cells* Pub *and secret cells* Sec, *where n is the number of virtual cells and λ is the security parameter.*
- $S \leftarrow \mathrm{index}(i)$, *which the server uses to identify* $S \subseteq \{1, \ldots, |\mathsf{Pub}|\}$, *a sparse subset of indices of the cells of* Pub *associated with virtual cell i. We refer to these cells of* Pub *as* $\mathsf{Pub}_{\mathrm{index}(i)}$.
- $(\mathsf{Sec}', d) \leftarrow \mathrm{read}(\mathsf{Sec}, \mathsf{C}, i)$, *which the FS MC uses to obtain the data d of virtual cell i, where in the case of an honest server, C is expected to be* $\mathsf{Pub}_{\mathrm{index}(i)}$. *In the case that the FS MC wants to report a loss of integrity, it may output* $d \leftarrow \mathsf{bug}$.

---

[10] Although the solution of [38] informally provides the same guarantees with a similar construction, we provide a complete formal model and construction.

[11] For online MCs that access server memory deterministically and non-adaptively.

[12] While our definition is not fully general, i.e., does not allow for arbitrary interaction between the FS MC and server, it suffices for our optimal construction.

- $(\mathsf{Sec}', \mathsf{C}') \leftarrow \mathrm{write}(\mathsf{Sec}, \mathsf{C}, d, i)$, *which the FS MC uses to replace the contents of virtual cell i with data d, where in the case of an honest server, C is expected to be $\mathsf{Pub}_{\mathrm{index}(i)}$. The FS MC will provide the server with new public cells C' relevant to virtual cell i with which an honest server will replace cells $\mathsf{Pub}_{\mathrm{index}(i)}$. In the case that the FS MC wants to report a loss of integrity, it may output $\mathsf{C}' \leftarrow \mathsf{bug}$.*

Correctness. An FS MC scheme is *correct* if for any sequence of operations executed by the FS MC and an honest server: $\Pr[(\cdot, d^*) \leftarrow \mathrm{read}(\mathsf{Sec}, \mathsf{Pub}_{\mathrm{index}(i)}, i) : d^* = d] = 1$, for any execution of $(\cdot, d^*) \leftarrow \mathrm{read}(\mathsf{Sec}, \mathsf{Pub}_{\mathrm{index}(i)}, i)$ in the sequence after an execution of $(\mathsf{Sec}', \mathsf{C}') \leftarrow \mathrm{write}(\mathsf{Sec}, \mathsf{Pub}_{\mathrm{index}(i)}, d, i)$, and before a subsequent execution of $(\mathsf{Sec}', \mathsf{C}') \leftarrow \mathrm{write}(\mathsf{Sec}, \mathsf{Pub}_{\mathrm{index}(i)}, d', i)$, where the probability is over the random coin tosses of the protocol.

Security. We now provide the security definition of FS MCs. The adversary in the game will adaptively specify the sequence of operations that the FS MC performs and have the ability to choose which cells C to provide to the FS MC challenger for read() and write() operations.

Throughout, the security game will store a dictionary $\mathsf{D}[\cdot]$ containing the correct data items at each index $i \in [n]$, corresponding to the most recent adversarial write or challenge to that index i. For every $i \in [n], \mathsf{D}[i] \leftarrow \bot$ initially. The challenger initially chooses $b \in \{0,1\}$ uniformly at random, runs $(\mathsf{Sec}, \mathsf{Pub}) \leftarrow \mathrm{init}(1^\lambda, n)$, sends Pub to the adversary $\mathcal{A}$, and deletes it. Then the adversary has access to (polynomial-many queries of) the following oracles:

- **read**(C, i): $\mathcal{A}$ sends public cells C for data cell i to the challenger who then computes $(\mathsf{Sec}', d) \leftarrow \mathrm{read}(\mathsf{Sec}, \mathsf{C}, i)$. If $d \notin \{\mathsf{D}[i], \mathsf{bug}\}$, the game outputs win and ends. Note: d is not sent to $\mathcal{A}$.
- **write**(C, d, i): $\mathcal{A}$ sends public cells C and data d to overwrite virtual cell i with to the challenger who then computes $(\mathsf{Sec}', \mathsf{C}') \leftarrow \mathrm{write}(\mathsf{Sec}, \mathsf{C}, d, i)$. The challenger then sends C' back to $\mathcal{A}$, and deletes it. Additionally, if $\mathsf{C}' \neq \mathsf{bug}$, the game sets $\mathsf{D}[i] \leftarrow d$.
- **chall**$(\mathsf{C}, d_0, d_1, i)$: $\mathcal{A}$ sends public cells C and data d_0, d_1 to overwrite data cell i with to the challenger who then computes $(\mathsf{Sec}', \mathsf{C}') \leftarrow \mathrm{write}(\mathsf{Sec}, \mathsf{C}, d_b, i)$. The challenger then sends C' back to $\mathcal{A}$, and deletes it. Additionally, if $\mathsf{C}' \neq \mathsf{bug}$, the game sets $\mathsf{D}[i] \leftarrow d_b$.
- **corrupt**(): The challenger simply sends the contents of Sec to $\mathcal{A}$.

Finally, $\mathcal{A}$ outputs a bit b' and the game outputs win if and only if $b' = b$.

As in the FS eRAM security definition, $\mathcal{A}$ is not allowed to call **corrupt**() after a call to **chall**$(\mathsf{C}, d_0, d_1, i)$, without first a call to **write**(C, d, i) to overwrite the i-th virtual cell with some other data d, in which the challenger returns $\mathsf{C}' \neq \mathsf{bug}$, since otherwise they would trivially win.

Definition 18 (Forward Secret Memory Checker Security). *A Forward Secret Memory checker is* secure *if for every PPT adversary $\mathcal{A}$, $\left| \Pr[\mathcal{A} \ wins] - \frac{1}{2} \right| \leq \mathrm{negl}(\lambda)$.*

6.2   Forward Secret Memory Checker Construction

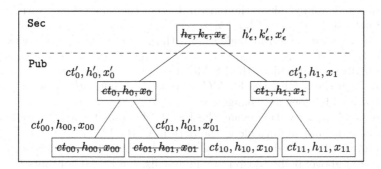

Fig. 4. Depiction of how our Forward Secret Memory Checker overwrites Sec and $\text{Pub}_{\text{index}(01)}$ after an execution of $\text{write}(\text{Sec}, \text{Pub}_{\text{index}(01)}, d'_{01}, 01)$. For every internal node v along the root-to-leaf path of leaf 01, as well as their siblings, the ciphertext $ct'_v = \mathbf{E}_{k'_p}(k'_v)$ is regenerated with the new keys k'_v, k'_p at v and its parent p, respectively (for siblings of path nodes, $k'_v = k_v$, the current key). For leaves 00 and 01, $ct'_{00} = \mathbf{E}_{k'_0}(d_{00})$, $ct'_{01} = \mathbf{E}_{k'_0}(d'_{01})$. For every node u on *only* the root-to-leaf path of leaf 01 (*not* their siblings), the hash function h'_u and corresponding hash value $x'_u = h'_u(ct'_{u.c_1}||h'_{u.c_1}||x'_{u.c_1}||ct'_{u.c_2}||h'_{u.c_2}||x'_{u.c_2})$ is regenerated, where one child $u.c_1$ or $u.c_2$, w.l.o.g., $u.c_1$, is not on the root-to-leaf path, and thus $h'_{u.c_1} = h_{u.c_1}, x'_{u.c_1} = x_{u.c_1}$ (their current values). Also, h_w and x_w are the all-zero string if w is a leaf.

Our FS MC construction is depicted in Fig. 4. We overlay the folklore FS eRAM solution, which uses IND-CPA secure symmetric encryption for forward secrecy, with the MC solution of [6], which uses universal one-way hash functions (UOWHF) for integrity. Both utilize a binary tree with n leaf nodes to store the data elements in Pub, and store the root in Sec. Note: It is possible to construct a family of UOWHF given any one-way function [40], but the use of UOWHFs requires the assumption that the word size of the RAM is $\ell = n^\epsilon$, for any $\epsilon > 0$.

More specifically, each leaf node i holds $ct_i = \mathbf{E}_{k_p}(d_i)$, where k_p is the encryption key of the parent p of i. Each internal node v holds $(h_v, ct_v = \mathbf{E}_{k_p}(k_v), x_v = h_v(ct_{v.c_1}||h_{v.c_1}||x_{v.c_1}||ct_{v.c_2}||h_{v.c_2}||x_{v.c_2}))$, where here and in the following, $||$ represents concatenation, k_v, k_p are the encryption keys of v and its parent p, respectively, $h_v, h_{v.c_1}, h_{v.c_2}$ are the description of the hash functions used at v and the children $v.c_1, v.c_2$ of v, respectively (which can be described in $O(\ell)$ bits), $ct_{v.c_1}, ct_{v.c_2}$ are the ciphertexts stored at the children $v.c_1, v.c_2$, respectively, and $x_{v.c_1}, x_{v.c_2}$ are the hashes at the children $v.c_1, v.c_2$, respectively. If $v.c_1, v.c_2$ are leaves, $h_{v.c_1}, x_{v.c_1}, h_{v.c_2}, x_{v.c_2}$ are the all-zero string. The root node, stored in Sec contains $(h_r, k_r, x_r = h_r(ct_{r.c_1}||h_{r.c_1}||x_{rc_1}||ct_{r.c_2}||h_{r.c_2}||x_{r.c_2}))$, where k_r is the root encryption key. The FS MC algorithms are as follows:

- $\text{init}(1^\lambda, n)$: Initializes a complete binary tree with n leaves in Pub, with data $\bot$ at each node, Sec $\leftarrow \bot$.

- index(i): Returns the indices of the cells of the root-to-leaf path nodes of leaf i, along with all path nodes' siblings.
- read(Sec, C, i): Given (what the FS MC believes to be) the root-to-leaf path of leaf i and siblings along the path in C from the server, the FS MC:
  - First checks $x_r = h_r(ct_{r.c_1}||h_{r.c_1}||x_{r.c_1}||ct_{r.c_2}||h_{r.c_2}||x_{r.c_2})$.
  - Then, for every internal node v along the path to i, the FS MC checks $x_v = h_v(ct_{v.c_1}||h_{v.c_1}||x_{v.c_1}||ct_{v.c_2}||h_{v.c_2}||x_{v.c_2})$ and decrypts $k_v \leftarrow \mathbf{D}_{k_p}(ct_v)$.
  - Finally, at leaf node i, the FS MC decrypts $d_i \leftarrow \mathbf{D}_{k_p}(ct_i)$.

  If any hash check fails, the FS MC outputs $d_i \leftarrow$ bug, otherwise, it outputs d_i. The FS MC does not change Sec.
- write(Sec, C, d'_i, i): Given (what the FS MC believes to be) the root-to-leaf path of leaf i and siblings along the path in C, the FS MC
  - First verifies and decrypts all of the nodes (including siblings) in C as in read() above; if the test on any node fails, the FS MC outputs C' $\leftarrow$ bug and does not change Sec. Otherwise,
  - For each internal node v on the root-to-leaf path of i, except for the parent of i, the FS MC regenerates k'_v and $ct'_{v.c_1} = \mathbf{E}_{k'_v}(k'_{v.c_1})$, $ct'_{v.c_2} = \mathbf{E}_{k'_v}(k'_{v.c_2})$, where if $v.c_1$ is not on the root-to-leaf path, $k'_{v.c_1} = k_{v.c_1}$ (its current key), and symmetrically if $v.c_2$ is not.
  - Then for the parent p of i, the FS MC regenerates k'_p and $ct'_i = \mathbf{E}_{k'_p}(d'_i)$ and for the sibling j of i, $ct'_j = \mathbf{E}_{k'_p}(d_j)$.
  - Next, for each internal node v on the root-to-leaf path of i, the FS MC regenerates h'_v and $x'_v = h'_v(ct'_{v.c_1}||h'_{v.c_1}||x'_{v.c_1}||ct'_{v.c_2}||h'_{v.c_2}||x'_{v.c_2})$ where if $v.c_1$ is not on the root-to-leaf path, $h'_{v.c_1} = h_{v.c_1}$, $x'_{v.c_1} = x_{v.c_1}$ (its current values), and symmetrically if $v.c_2$ is not.

  C' is set to store the updated ciphertexts, hash functions, and hash values at their corresponding nodes, and Sec' is set to store the regenerated hash function h'_r, root key k'_r, and hash value x'_r.

Intuitively, the root key and hash stored in Sec ensure that the ciphertexts at the root's children will decrypt to the correct keys, while still ensuring privacy. Then, inductively, the decrypted keys and corresponding hashes at level i ensure the ciphertexts at level $i + 1$ decrypt to the correct keys, while still ensuring privacy. We formalize this in the following theorem, which we prove in the full version [5].

Theorem 8. *There exists a secure Forward Secret Memory Checker with $O(\log n)$ overhead, $O(n)$ public storage and $O(1)$ secret storage.*

Remark 1. In practice, a single CRHF can be used in place of a UOWHF family so that there is no need to regenerate the hash functions at the nodes of the root-to-leaf path for every write(), nor include them in the hashes at each node. We use a UOWHF family since it is possible to construct one given any OWF.

Remark 2. For the same level of privacy, but weaker integrity (i.e., integrity only before any corruption of Sec), one can use *only* AEAD in place of *both* symmetric encryption *and* a UOWHF/CHRF. In this case also, the word size need not be polynomial. This is a generalization of a weaker MC construction from [6].

References

1. Asharov, G., Komargodski, I., Lin, W.-K., Nayak, K., Peserico, E., Shi, E.: OptORAMa: optimal oblivious RAM. In: Canteaut, A., Ishai, Y. (eds.) EURO-CRYPT 2020. LNCS, vol. 12106, pp. 403–432. Springer, Cham (2020). https://doi.org/10.1007/978-3-030-45724-2_14
2. Aviram, N., Gellert, K., Jager, T.: Session resumption protocols and efficient forward security for TLS 1.3 0-RTT. In: Ishai, Y., Rijmen, V. (eds.) EUROCRYPT 2019, Part II. LNCS, vol. 11477, pp. 117–150. Springer, Heidelberg (2019). https://doi.org/10.1007/978-3-030-17656-3_5
3. Bajaj, S., Sion, R.: Ficklebase: looking into the future to erase the past. In: 2013 IEEE 29th International Conference on Data Engineering (ICDE), pp. 86–97. IEEE (2013)
4. Bienstock, A., Dodis, Y., Rösler, P.: On the price of concurrency in group ratcheting protocols. In: Pass, R., Pietrzak, K. (eds.) TCC 2020. LNCS, vol. 12551, pp. 198–228. Springer, Cham (2020). https://doi.org/10.1007/978-3-030-64378-2_8
5. Bienstock, A., Dodis, Y., Yeo, K.: Forward secret encrypted ram: lower bounds and applications. Cryptology ePrint Archive, Report 2021/244 (2021). https://eprint.iacr.org/2021/244
6. Blum, M., Evans, W.S., Gemmell, P., Kannan, S., Naor, M.: Checking the correctness of memories. In: 32nd FOCS, pp. 90–99. IEEE Computer Society Press, San Juan (1991)
7. Boneh, D., Lipton, R.J.: A revocable backup system. In: USENIX Security Symposium, pp. 91–96 (1996)
8. Boyle, E., Naor, M.: Is there an oblivious ram lower bound? In: Proceedings of the 2016 ACM Conference on Innovations in Theoretical Computer Science, pp. 357–368 (2016)
9. Canetti, R., Garay, J., Itkis, G., Micciancio, D., Naor, M., Pinkas, B.: Multicast security: a taxonomy and some efficient constructions. In: IEEE INFOCOM '99. Conference on Computer Communications. Proceedings. Eighteenth Annual Joint Conference of the IEEE Computer and Communications Societies. The Future is Now (Cat. No.99CH36320), vol. 2, pp. 708–716 (1999)
10. Canetti, R., Raghuraman, S., Richelson, S., Vaikuntanathan, V.: Chosen-ciphertext secure fully homomorphic encryption. In: Fehr, S. (ed.) PKC 2017. LNCS, vol. 10175, pp. 213–240. Springer, Heidelberg (2017). https://doi.org/10.1007/978-3-662-54388-7_8
11. Clarke, D.E., Suh, G.E., Gassend, B., Sudan, A., van Dijk, M., Devadas, S.: Towards constant bandwidth overhead integrity checking of untrusted data. In: 2005 IEEE Symposium on Security and Privacy, pp. 139–153. IEEE Computer Society Press, Oakland (2005)
12. Cohen, A., Holmgren, J., Nishimaki, R., Vaikuntanathan, V., Wichs, D.: Watermarking cryptographic capabilities. In: Wichs, D., Mansour, Y. (eds.) 48th ACM STOC, pp. 1115–1127. ACM Press, Cambridge (2016)
13. Derler, D., Jager, T., Slamanig, D., Striecks, C.: Bloom filter encryption and applications to efficient forward-secret 0-RTT key exchange. In: Nielsen, J.B., Rijmen, V. (eds.) EUROCRYPT 2018, Part III. LNCS, vol. 10822, pp. 425–455. Springer, Heidelberg (2018). https://doi.org/10.1007/978-3-319-78372-7_14
14. Di Crescenzo, G., Ferguson, N., Impagliazzo, R., Jakobsson, M.: How to forget a secret. In: Meinel, C., Tison, S. (eds.) STACS 1999. LNCS, vol. 1563, pp. 500–509. Springer, Heidelberg (1999). https://doi.org/10.1007/3-540-49116-3_47

15. Dwork, C., Naor, M., Rothblum, G.N., Vaikuntanathan, V.: How efficient can memory checking be? In: Reingold, O. (ed.) TCC 2009. LNCS, vol. 5444, pp. 503–520. Springer, Heidelberg (2009). https://doi.org/10.1007/978-3-642-00457-5_30
16. Geambasu, R., Kohno, T., Levy, A.A., Levy, H.M.: Vanish: Increasing data privacy with self-destructing data. In: USENIX Security Symposium, vol. 316 (2009)
17. Goldreich, O., Ostrovsky, R.: Software protection and simulation on oblivious rams. J. ACM (JACM) **43**(3), 431–473 (1996)
18. Goodrich, M.T., Mitzenmacher, M.: Privacy-preserving access of outsourced data via oblivious RAM simulation. In: Aceto, L., Henzinger, M., Sgall, J. (eds.) ICALP 2011. LNCS, vol. 6756, pp. 576–587. Springer, Heidelberg (2011). https://doi.org/10.1007/978-3-642-22012-8_46
19. Green, M.D., Miers, I.: Forward secure asynchronous messaging from puncturable encryption. In: 2015 IEEE Symposium on Security and Privacy, pp. 305–320. IEEE Computer Society Press, San Jose (2015)
20. Günther, F., Hale, B., Jager, T., Lauer, S.: 0-RTT key exchange with full forward secrecy. In: Coron, J.-S., Nielsen, J.B. (eds.) EUROCRYPT 2017. LNCS, vol. 10212, pp. 519–548. Springer, Cham (2017). https://doi.org/10.1007/978-3-319-56617-7_18
21. Harney, H., Muckenhirn, C.: Rfc2093: group key management protocol (gkmp) specification (1997)
22. Harney, H., Muckenhirn, C.: Rfc2094: Group key management protocol (gkmp) architecture (1997)
23. Hubáček, P., Koucký, M., Král, K., Slívová, V.: Stronger lower bounds for online ORAM. In: Hofheinz, D., Rosen, A. (eds.) TCC 2019. LNCS, vol. 11892, pp. 264–284. Springer, Cham (2019). https://doi.org/10.1007/978-3-030-36033-7_10
24. Jacob, R., Larsen, K.G., Nielsen, J.B.: Lower bounds for oblivious data structures. In: Proceedings of the Thirtieth Annual ACM-SIAM Symposium on Discrete Algorithms, pp. 2439–2447. SIAM (2019)
25. Kobeissi, N., Nicolas, G., Bhargavan, K.: Noise explorer: fully automated modeling and verification for arbitrary noise protocols. In: 2019 IEEE European Symposium on Security and Privacy (EuroS P), pp. 356–370 (2019)
26. Larsen, K.G., Nielsen, J.B.: Yes, there is an oblivious RAM lower bound! In: Shacham, H., Boldyreva, A. (eds.) CRYPTO 2018. LNCS, vol. 10992, pp. 523–542. Springer, Cham (2018). https://doi.org/10.1007/978-3-319-96881-0_18
27. Larsen, K.G., Simkin, M., Yeo, K.: Lower bounds for multi-server oblivious rams. Theory of Cryptography Conference (to appear) (2020)
28. Merkle, R.C.: A certified digital signature. In: Brassard, G. (ed.) CRYPTO 1989. LNCS, vol. 435, pp. 218–238. Springer, New York (1990). https://doi.org/10.1007/0-387-34805-0_21
29. Micciancio, D., Panjwani, S.: Optimal communication complexity of generic multicast key distribution. In: Cachin, C., Camenisch, J.L. (eds.) EUROCRYPT 2004. LNCS, vol. 3027, pp. 153–170. Springer, Heidelberg (2004). https://doi.org/10.1007/978-3-540-24676-3_10
30. Mittra, S.: Iolus: a framework for scalable secure multicasting. In: Proceedings of the ACM SIGCOMM '97 Conference on Applications, Technologies, Architectures, and Protocols for Computer Communication, SIGCOMM '97, pp. 277–288. Association for Computing Machinery, New York (1997). https://doi.org/10.1145/263105.263179
31. Oprea, A., Reiter, M.K.: Integrity checking in cryptographic file systems with constant trusted storage. In: Provos, N. (ed.) USENIX Security 2007, pp. 6–10. USENIX Association, Boston (2007)

32. Patel, S., Persiano, G., Raykova, M., Yeo, K.: Panorama: oblivious ram with logarithmic overhead. In: 2018 IEEE 59th Annual Symposium on Foundations of Computer Science (FOCS), pp. 871–882. IEEE (2018)

33. Patel, S., Persiano, G., Yeo, K.: Lower bounds for encrypted multi-maps and searchable encryption in the leakage cell probe model. In: Micciancio, D., Ristenpart, T. (eds.) CRYPTO 2020. LNCS, vol. 12170, pp. 433–463. Springer, Cham (2020). https://doi.org/10.1007/978-3-030-56784-2_15

34. Persiano, G., Yeo, K.: Lower bounds for differentially private RAMs. In: Ishai, Y., Rijmen, V. (eds.) EUROCRYPT 2019. LNCS, vol. 11476, pp. 404–434. Springer, Cham (2019). https://doi.org/10.1007/978-3-030-17653-2_14

35. Peterson, Z.N., Burns, R.C., Herring, J., Stubblefield, A., Rubin, A.D.: Secure deletion for a versioning file system. In: FAST, vol. 5 (2005)

36. Pinkas, B., Reinman, T.: Oblivious RAM revisited. In: Rabin, T. (ed.) CRYPTO 2010. LNCS, vol. 6223, pp. 502–519. Springer, Heidelberg (2010). https://doi.org/10.1007/978-3-642-14623-7_27

37. Reardon, J., Basin, D., Capkun, S.: Sok: secure data deletion. In: 2013 IEEE Symposium on Security and Privacy, pp. 301–315. IEEE (2013)

38. Reardon, J., Ritzdorf, H., Basin, D., Capkun, S.: Secure data deletion from persistent media. In: Proceedings of the 2013 ACM SIGSAC Conference on Computer & Communications Security, pp. 271–284 (2013)

39. Roche, D.S., Aviv, A., Choi, S.G.: A practical oblivious map data structure with secure deletion and history independence. In: 2016 IEEE Symposium on Security and Privacy (SP), pp. 178–197. IEEE (2016)

40. Rompel, J.: One-way functions are necessary and sufficient for secure signatures. In: 22nd ACM STOC, pp. 387–394. ACM Press, Baltimore (1990)

41. Sherman, A.T., McGrew, D.A.: Key establishment in large dynamic groups using one-way function trees. IEEE Trans. Softw. Eng. 29(5), 444–458 (2003)

42. Stefanov, E., Van Dijk, M., Shi, E., Fletcher, C., Ren, L., Yu, X., Devadas, S.: Path oram: an extremely simple oblivious ram protocol. In: Proceedings of the 2013 ACM SIGSAC Conference on Computer & Communications Security, pp. 299–310 (2013)

43. Sun, S.-F., Sakzad, A., Steinfeld, R., Liu, J.K., Gu, D.: Public-key puncturable encryption: modular and compact constructions. In: Kiayias, A., Kohlweiss, M., Wallden, P., Zikas, V. (eds.) PKC 2020. LNCS, vol. 12110, pp. 309–338. Springer, Cham (2020). https://doi.org/10.1007/978-3-030-45374-9_11

44. Susilo, W., Duong, D.H., Le, H.Q., Pieprzyk, J.: Puncturable encryption: a generic construction from delegatable fully key-homomorphic encryption. In: Chen, L., Li, N., Liang, K., Schneider, S. (eds.) ESORICS 2020. LNCS, vol. 12309, pp. 107–127. Springer, Cham (2020). https://doi.org/10.1007/978-3-030-59013-0_6

45. Wallner, D., Harder, E., Agee, R.: Rfc2627: Key management for multicast: issues and architectures (1999)

46. Wong, C.K., Gouda, M., Lam, S.S.: Secure group communications using key graphs. In: Proceedings of the ACM SIGCOMM '98 Conference on Applications, Technologies, Architectures, and Protocols for Computer Communication, SIGCOMM '98, pp. 68–79. Association for Computing Machinery, New York (1998). https://doi.org/10.1145/285237.285260

47. Yao, A.C.C.: Should tables be sorted? J. ACM (JACM) 28(3), 615–628 (1981)

Laconic Private Set Intersection
and Applications

Navid Alamati[1(✉)], Pedro Branco[2(✉)] , Nico Döttling[3(✉)] , Sanjam Garg[1,4(✉)],
Mohammad Hajiabadi[5(✉)], and Sihang Pu[3(✉)]

[1] UC Berkeley, Berkeley, USA
sanjamg@berkeley.edu
[2] IT, IST - University of Lisbon, Lisbon, Portugal
[3] Helmholtz Center for Information Security (CISPA), Saarbrücken, Germany
[4] NTT Research, Palo Alto, USA
[5] University of Waterloo, Waterloo, Canada

Abstract. Consider a server with a *large* set S of strings $\{x_1, x_2 \ldots, x_N\}$ that would like to publish a *small* hash h of its set S such that any client with a string y can send the server a *short* message allowing it to learn y if $y \in S$ and nothing otherwise. In this work, we study this problem of two-round private set intersection (PSI) with low (asymptotically optimal) communication cost, or what we call *laconic* private set intersection (ℓPSI) and its extensions. This problem is inspired by the recent general frameworks for laconic cryptography [Cho et al. CRYPTO 2017, Quach et al. FOCS'18].

We start by showing the first feasibility result for realizing ℓPSI based on the CDH assumption, or LWE with polynomial noise-to-modulus ratio. However, these feasibility results use expensive non-black-box cryptographic techniques leading to significant inefficiency. Next, with the goal of avoiding these inefficient techniques, we give a construction of ℓPSI schemes making only black-box use of cryptographic functions. Our construction is secure against semi-honest receivers, malicious senders and reusable in the sense that the receiver's message can be reused across any number of executions of the protocol. The scheme is secure under the ϕ-hiding, decisional composite residuosity and subgroup decision assumptions.

Finally, we show natural applications of ℓPSI to realizing a semantically-secure encryption scheme that supports detection of encrypted messages belonging to a set of "illegal" messages (e.g., an illegal video) circulating online. Over the past few years, significant effort has gone into realizing laconic cryptographic protocols. Nonetheless, our work provides the first black-box constructions of such protocols for a natural application setting.

1 Introduction

Laconic cryptography [13,18,20,40] is an emerging paradigm which enables realizing cryptographic tasks with asymptotically-optimal communication in just

© International Association for Cryptologic Research 2021
K. Nissim and B. Waters (Eds.): TCC 2021, LNCS 13044, pp. 94–125, 2021.
https://doi.org/10.1007/978-3-030-90456-2_4

two messages. In this setting, the receiver has a potentially large input, and the size of her protocol message only depends on the security parameter, and not her input size. The second message, sent by the sender, may grow with the size of the sender's input, but should be independent of the receiver's input size.

The pioneering work of [13] introduced the notion of laconic oblivious transfer (laconic OT), which allows a receiver with a large input $D \in \{0,1\}^n$ to send a short hash digest h of her input D. Next, a sender with an input $(i \in [n], m_0, m_1)$, sends a short message ots to the receiver, enabling the receiver to learn $m_{D[i]}$, and nothing more. We require (a) the sizes of h and ots be $\mathsf{poly}(\log(n), \lambda)$, where λ is the security parameter; (b) the sender's computation time be $\mathsf{poly}(\log(n), \lambda)$ and (c) and receiver's second-phase computation time be $\mathsf{poly}(\log(n), \lambda)$.

The notion of laconic OT, and the techniques built around it, have led to breakthrough results in the last few years, which, among others, include the first construction of identity-based encryption from CDH [8,16,17,19], and two-round MPC protocols from minimal assumptions [4,24,25].

Laconism Beyond OT? Motivated by the developments enabled by laconic OT, it is natural to ask whether we can push the boundary further, realizing laconism for richer functionalities. Laconic OT by itself does not seem to be sufficient for this task (at least generically). Specifically, the general laconic OT+garbled circuit based approach for a function $f(\cdot, \cdot)$ results in protocols in which the size of the sender's protocol message grows with the receiver's input size.

The work of Quach, Wee and Wichs [40] shows how to realize laconic cryptography for general functionalities using LWE. However, two significant issues remain. Firstly, it is not clear whether we can achieve laconism from other assumptions, for functionalities beyond OT. As mentioned above, research in laconic OT has led to several breakthrough feasibility results, motivating the need for developing techniques that can be realized using wider assumptions and for richer functionalities. Secondly, existing constructions of laconic primitives are non-black-box, leading to inefficient constructions. Addressing the above shortcomings, our goals are twofold: (1) Feasibility: Can we realize laconic primitives beyond OT from assumptions other than LWE? and (2) Black-boxness: Can we make the constructions black-box?

Black-Box Techniques. We use the notion "black-box" techniques in the sense that the construction should not use an explicit circuit-level description of cryptographic primitives. In this sense, we think of constructions which e.g., compute cryptographic primitives inside garbled circuits (as previous laconic OT constructions) or use general purpose NIZK proofs (which express statements in terms of NP-complete languages) as "non-black-box" techniques.

Laconic PSI. We make the first progress toward the above two goals with respect to a non-trivial functionality: Laconic Private Set Intersection (ℓPSI) and its family. Private set intersection (PSI) is a cryptographic primitive that allows two parties to learn the intersection of their input sets and nothing else. Because of its usefulness and versatility, this cryptographic primitive has been extensively studied in numerous settings throughout the years (see e.g., [31,35,36,38,39,42] and references therein).

Laconic PSI allows a receiver to send a short digest of its large data set, which in turn can be used by a sender to compute a PSI second round message. We require that the total communication complexity as well as the sender's running time to be independent of the receiver's input size.

1.1 Our Results

As our first result, we give a generic construction of laconic PSI from a primitive called anonymous hash encryption, which in turn can be realized from CDH/LWE [8,16,17]. Our construction builds on the Merkle-tree garbled circuit based approach of [8,16,17,22,23,26], showing how to use garbled circuits to perform binary search on a set of sorted values. Prior to our work there did not exist any construction of a laconic primitive from CDH beyond OT. We also obtain an LWE instantiation with polynomial modulus to noise ration, improving the subexponential ratio of [40].

The above construction is non-black-box caused by the use of garbled circuits. As our second contribution, we achieve a black-box construction of laconic PSI from the ϕ-hiding assumption.

Both constructions above are only semi-honest secure, and can be made malicious (UC) secure by using Non-Interactive Zero Knowledge (NIZK).[1] However, the eventual protocol will be non-black-box. To enhance applicability, we show how to make our second construction secure against malicious senders, and semi-honest receivers in the CRS model, by additionally assuming decisional composite residuosity (DCR) and subgroup decision assumptions. We term this notion *reusable malicious* laconic PSI, meaning the receiver's message may be re-used.[2]

Applications. We show an application of laconic PSI in realizing a primitive that we dub self-detecting encryption. A self-detecting encryption acts like a normal public-key encryption with a key difference that it is possible to detect whether the underlying message of a given ciphertext belongs to a database of special (e.g., "illegal") messages. This can be determined just by knowing the database values, as opposed to the system's secret key. Such encryption systems provide a feature for detecting the presence of illegal contents, without compromising the privacy of legal messages. There has only been a limited number of proposals for this task so far, and all of them use heavy tools (e.g., FHE) for this purpose (see [28] for more details). We formally define this notion, and show how to realize it using laconic PSI.

In a self-detecting encryption, an authority (e.g., a government entity or a delegated NGO) publishes a small hash value of a (possibly large) database of

---

[1] Note that in the laconic setting we cannot prove malicious security against a receiver since it is information-theoretically impossible to extract its input. Thus, since the NIZK will only be computed by the sender, the protocol will remain laconic.

[2] We use the word reusability only in conjunction with malicious security, since in the semi-honest setting, reusability is satisfied by default.

special messages such that a user can encrypt a message using the system's public key and the hash value. If the message belongs to the database, then the authority can detect it; else, the message remains hidden to the authority. We require that the size of the hash and the encryption running time to be independent of the database size.

We note that attribute-based encryption does not provide a solution to the above problem, because either the authority should reveal its database to a master-key generator, or it should be the master-key generator itself – both of which defeat our security purposes.

Additional New Results: Labeled Laconic PSI and Malicious Laconic OT (LOT). We extend our laconic PSI techniques to build a reusable *labeled* laconic PSI. Labeled PSI [11,34] is a flavor of PSI, where the sender holds a *label* ℓ_i associated with each set element x_i, and the receiver will learn the labels corresponding to the intersection elements. Labeled PSI has several practical applications (e.g., private web service queries [11]).

Moreover, we show how to use our techniques to realize the first construction of a reusable LOT secure against malicious senders and semi-honest receivers.

DV-NIZK Range Proofs for DJ Ciphertexts. As a building block for our laconic PSI protocol, we propose a Designated-Verifier Non-Interactive Zero-Knowledge (DV-NIZK[3]) scheme for range proof with Damgård Jurik (DJ) ciphertexts, which may be of independent interest. Our DV-NIZK has statistical simulation soundness and computational zero-knowledge given that the subgroup decision (SD) assumption holds [5,29].

Such range proofs can also be constructed in the random oracle model (ROM) via the Fiat-Shamir transform (e.g., [3,9,15,43]), which might yield the best efficiency. As our LPSI construction is modular, this can be done independently of the remaining results in the paper. The goal of our DV-NIZK is to provide an efficient standard model construction which we see as a reasonable middle ground between feasibility from the weakest assumption (at the cost of unrealistic efficiency) and practical efficiency (at the cost of relying on strong heuristic assumptions such as the ROM).

1.2   Previous Work

Laconic PSI can be seen as a particular case of unbalanced PSI. Protocols for unbalanced PSI were presented in [2,11,12,41]. The protocol of [41] achieves linear communication complexity on the receiver's set size in the *pre-processing* model. The protocols of [11,12] rely on somewhat homomorphic encryption (SWHE) and proceed in two rounds. However, the communication complexity scales with the size of the receiver's set (and logarithmic with the size of the

---

[3] DV-NIZK *only* allows the designated prover to prove that it holds a witness for a certain NP statement to a verifier in just one message.

sender's set), in contrast with our protocol whose communication complexity
scales with the sender's set size.

Comparison with [2]. Ateniese et al. in [2] proposed a semi-honest size-hiding
PSI protocol[4] inspired by RSA accumulators that achieves communication complexity independent of the receiver's set size. However, we emphasize that their
scheme does not fit the framework of laconic cryptography since it requires the
sender to know the factorization of a CRS modulus N. Thus, either it requires
pre-processing (giving a designated secret key to the sender), or it requires three
rounds in the CRS model. In contrast, laconic cryptography requires (a) two
rounds and (b) no pre-processing (i.e., neither party receives a secret key correlated with the CRS). Both (a) and (b) are crucially used in applications of
laconic cryptography. Specifically, these restrictions prevent use of [2] in settings
with multiple senders, an aspect that has been critical for laconic cryptography
applications. Finally, we remark that the security of [2] relies on random oracles,
whereas we prove security in the standard model and achieve a substantially
stronger security notion without resorting to heavy generic tools.

All of above constructions are just secure against semi-honest adversaries,
except for [11] which achieves security against a malicious receiver.

1.3 Open Problems

The main open question is to realize laconic cryptography for functionalities
richer than PSI. A second question is to build laconic PSI in a black-box way
from assumptions not involving ϕ-hiding (e.g., pairings alone).

In this work, we build DV-NIZK for proving equality of plaintexts across
different encryption schemes, namely between the DJ [15] and the BGN [5,29]
encryption schemes. This scheme opens the door to new applications since it
allows us to extend the capabilities of GS/GOS proof systems [29,30] to non-
pairing-based primitives with additional properties (in our case to the DJ cryptosystem). We believe that these ideas will have applications beyond range
proofs, e.g., one can think of further uses of structure preserving cryptography,
so we leave this as an open problem for future works.

2 Technical Overview

2.1 Semi-Honest PSI from CDH/LWE

Our protocol uses hash encryption and garbled circuits, building on [8,17,22],
while introducing new techniques. A hash-encryption scheme allows one to
encrypt a message m to the output h of a hash function by specifying an
index/bit (i, b) (denoted $\mathsf{HEnc}(h, m, (i, b))$), so that knowledge of a consistent
pre-image value z allows for decryption ($\mathsf{Hash}(z) = h$ and $z_i = b$) while having semantic security against inconsistent pre-image values (i.e., against z where
$\mathsf{Hash}(z) = h$ but $z_i = \bar{b}$).[5]

---

[4] Such schemes were also studied in [32,33,37].

[5] Enc also takes as input a public parameter pp, which we ignore here.

In all discussion below we assume the sender's and receiver's elements are in $\{0,1\}^\lambda$ and that the output of Hash also has λ bits.

Receiver's Set Size is 2. We first assume the receiver has only two elements $S_R = \{\text{id}_1, \text{id}_2\}$ and the sender has a single element id. The receiver sends $\text{hr}_{\text{root}} :=$ Hash(id_1, id_2). Consider a circuit $F[\text{id}]$, with id hardwired, which on input (id', id'') outputs id if id $\in \{\text{id}', \text{id}''\}$; else, $\perp$. The sender garbles $F[\text{id}]$ to get $(\widetilde{C}_0, \{\text{lb}_{i,b}\})^6$ and sends $\text{psi}_2 := (\widetilde{C}_0, \{\text{ct}_{i,b}\})$, where $\text{ct}_{i,b} := \text{HEnc}(\text{hr}_{\text{root}}, \text{lb}_{i,b}, (i, b)))$. The receiver who has the pre-image $z := (\text{id}_1, \text{id}_2)$ can retrieve only the labels lb_{i,z_i}, and the rest will be hidden. Thus, by garbled circuit security the receiver will only learn the output of $F[\text{id}](\text{id}_1, \text{id}_2)$, as desired.

Moving Beyond $|S_R| = 2$. Suppose the receiver has four elements $S_R = \{\text{id}_1, \text{id}_2, \text{id}_3, \text{id}_4\}$ in ascending order. The receiver Merkle-hashes all these values and sends hr_{root}, the root hash. Let h_1 and h_2 be the two hash values at level one (i.e., $h_1 = \text{Hash}(\text{id}_1, \text{id}_2)$). If the sender knows the value of, say, h_1, he may hash-encrypt $\{\text{lb}_{i,b}\}$ (defined in the previous paragraph) under h_1, so that the receiver can only open the labels that correspond to the bits of $z = (\text{id}_1, \text{id}_2)$, revealing the value of $F[\text{id}](\text{id}_1, \text{id}_2)$. However, h_1 is statistically hidden given hr_{root}. Thus, we use the idea of deferred evaluation [8,13,16,17], delegating the task of hash-encrypting $\{\text{lb}_{i,b}\}$ to the receiver herself, via garbled circuits.

In essence, we want the receiver to be able to compute the hash encryption of $\{\text{lb}_{i,b}\}$ wrt either h_1 or h_2 (depending on whether id $\leq \text{id}_2$ or not), but not both; because obtaining both hash encryptions will allow the receiver to open both labels $\text{lb}_{i,0}$ and $\text{lb}_{i,1}$ for some indices i (because $(\text{id}_1, \text{id}_2) \neq (\text{id}_3, \text{id}_4)$), destroying garbled circuit security. Thus, the sender has to make sure that the receiver will be able to obtain only either of the above hash encryptions, the one whose sub-tree contains id. To enable this, we perform binary search.

Performing Binary Search. We handle the above difficulty by performing *binary search* using ideas developed in the context of registration-based encryption [22]. The hash of each node is now computed as the hash of the concatenation of its left child's hash, right child's hash, and the largest identity under its left child. For example, the hash root is $\text{hr}_{\text{root}} = \text{Hash}(h_1, h_2, \text{id}_2)$, where h_1 and h_2 are the hash values of the two nodes in the first level, and in turn $h_1 = \text{Hash}(\text{id}_1, \text{id}_2, \text{id}_1)$. Now let id be the sender's element, and change $F[\text{id}]$ to be a circuit that on input ($\text{id}', \text{id}'', *$) outputs id if id $\in \{\text{id}', \text{id}''\}$, else $\perp$. Letting $(\widetilde{C}_0, \{\text{lb}_{i,b}\})$ be the garbling of $F[\text{id}]$, consider a circuit $G[\text{id}, \{\text{lb}_{i,b}\}]$ which on input (h, h', id') outputs a hash-encryption of $\text{lb}_{i,b}$ either under h or under h', depending on whether id $\leq \text{id}'$ or id $> \text{id}'$. Let $(\widetilde{C}', \{\text{lb}'\}_{i,b})$ be the garbling of $G[\text{id}, \{\text{lb}_{i,b}\}]$, let $\{\text{ct}_{i,b}\}$ be the hash encryption of $\{\text{lb}'_{i,b}\}$ wrt hr_{root}, and return $\text{psi}_2 := (\widetilde{C}_0, \widetilde{C}', \{\text{ct}_{i,b}\})$. Using the pre-image $z := (h_1, h_2, \text{id}_2)$ of hr_{root}, the receiver can retrieve the labels $\{\text{lb}'_{i,z[i]}\}$, allowing to compute $G[\text{id}, \{\text{lb}_{i,b}\}](h_1, h_2, \text{id}_2)$, which will produce a hash encryption $\{\text{ct}'_{i,b}\}$ of $\{\text{lb}_{i,b}\}$ under either h_1 or h_2, depending on whether id $\leq \text{id}_2$,

---

[6] $\widetilde{C}_0$ stands for the garbled circuit and $\{\text{lb}_{i,b}\}_i$ are the corresponding labels of inputs.

or not. For concreteness, suppose $\text{id} \leq \text{id}_2$, meaning that $\{\text{ct}'_{i,b}\}$ are formed under h_1, and so the pre-image $z' = (\text{id}_1, \text{id}_2, \text{id}_1)$ of h_1 will lead to $\{\text{lb}_{i,z'_i}\}$, which along with $\widetilde{C}_0$ will reveal the value of $\text{F}[\text{id}](\text{id}_1, \text{id}_2, \text{id}_1)$. Of course, the receiver *a priori* does not know whether $\{\text{ct}'_{i,b}\}$ are encryptions under h_1 or h_2, so the receiver should try decrypting wrt both, and see which one succeeds.

Are We Done? Unfortunately, when arguing security, a subtle issue emerges. Suppose a hash-encryption ciphertext reveals its hash value (e.g., the hash is appended to the ciphertext). Then, the ciphertexts $\{\text{ct}'_{i,b}\}$ will reveal whether they were encrypted under h_1 or h_2; equivalently, whether $\text{id} \leq \text{id}_2$ or $\text{id} > \text{id}_2$. We cannot allow this information to be leaked if $\text{id} \notin S_R$. To fix this issue we assume the hash-encryption scheme is *anonymous*, meaning that, roughly, a random ciphertext leaks no information about the underlying hash value. This property was defined in [8] for achieving anonymous IBE. The use of anonymous hash encryption does not resolve the issue completely yet. For concreteness, suppose $\text{id} < \text{id}_1$. This means that $\{\text{ct}'_{i,b}\}$ is encrypted under h_1, and so by decrypting $\{\text{ct}'_{i,b}\}$ using $z' = (\text{id}_1, \text{id}_2, \text{id}_1)$, the receiver will obtain meaningful labels, evaluating the garbled circuit $\widetilde{C}_0$ to $\perp$ (rightly so, because $\text{id} \notin S_R$). On the other hand, if the receiver tries decrypting $\{\text{ct}'_{i,b}\}$ using $z'' = (\text{id}_3, \text{id}_4, \text{id}_3)$ which is not a pre-image of h_1, then the resulting labels will be meaningless, evaluating $\widetilde{C}_0$ to junk. This leaks which path is the right binary search path, giving information about id. To fix this issue, we change the circuit F so that if $\text{id} \notin S_R$, then decryption along any path will result in a random value. Specifically, sample two random values r and r', let $\text{F}[\text{id}, r, r'](\text{id}', \text{id}'', *)$ return r if $\text{id} \notin \{\text{id}', \text{id}''\}$ and r' otherwise. We will also include r in the clear in psi_2. Now the receiver can check decryption along which path (if any) yields r; in which case, the receiver can determine the intersection identity. To argue security, if we use anonymous garbled circuits [8], then we can argue if $\text{id} \notin S_R$, then psi_2 is pseudorandom to the receiver. Arguing this formally (especially for the general case) is non-trivial, requiring a delicate formulation of hybrids.

Receiver's Security? The receiver's hash hr_{root} is computed deterministically from S_R, so it cannot be secure. But this is easy to fix: On the leaf level we append the identities with random values, and only then will perform the Merkle hash.

2.2   Reusable Laconic PSI

We now outline our techniques for obtaining laconic PSI in a black-box way, for both semi-honest and malicious cases.

A Semi-Honestly Secure Protocol. Our starting point is a recent construction of a *one-way function with encryption* from the ϕ-hiding assumption due to Goyal, Vusirikala and Waters [27], and we remark that similar *accumulator-style* ideas were used before to construct PSI [2]. Since the protocol of [27] is "almost" a

PSI protocol, we will directly describe the underlying semi-honestly secure PSI based. Assume for a moment that both the receiver's input S_R and the sender's input S_S are subsets of a polynomially-sized universe $\mathcal{U} = \{1,\ldots,\ell\}$. We will later remove this size-restriction on $\mathcal{U}$. We have a common reference string crs which is composed of an RSA modulus $N = PQ$, a uniformly random generator $g \in \mathbb{Z}_N^*$ and pairwise distinct primes $p_1,\ldots,p_\ell$.

For the sake of simplicity, we will assume in this outline that the sender's input set S_S is a singleton set $\{w\} \subseteq \mathcal{U}$. The actual protocol will be obtained by running the protocol we will now sketch for every element in the sender's input set. The protocol commences as follows: The receiver first *hashes* its input set into

$$h = g^{r\,\prod_{i \in S_R} p_i} \mod N,$$

where r is chosen a uniformly chosen random from $[N]$ (and thus $r \bmod \phi(N)$ is statistically close to uniform). The receiver then sends h to the sender.

The sender, whose input is $S_S = \{w\}$, chooses a uniformly random value $\rho \leftarrow_\$ [N]$ and a uniformly random seed s for a suitable randomness extractor Ext, and computes the values $f \leftarrow g^{\rho p_w}$ and $R \leftarrow \mathsf{Ext}(s, h^\rho)$. It sends s, f and R to the receiver.

The receiver, upon receiving f and R, will check for all elements $i \in S_R$ whether it holds that $R_i \overset{?}{=} R$, for $R_i \leftarrow \mathsf{Ext}(s, f^{r\,\prod_{j \in S_R \setminus \{i\}} p_j})$. If it finds such an i, it outputs $\{i\}$ as the intersection of S_R and S_S. Correctness of this protocol follows routinely[7]. by noting that if $w \in S_R$ then

$$f^{r\,\prod_{j \in S_R \setminus \{w\}} p_j} = g^{\rho \cdot r \cdot \prod_{j \in S_R} p_j} = h^\rho.$$

Also, note that this scheme is laconic, as the size of the messages exchanged by the parties is independent of the size of the set S_R.

Arguing security against a semi-honest sender is also routine, as h is in fact statistically close to a uniformly random group element in $\mathbb{Z}_N^*$. Proving security against a semi-honest receiver is a bit more involved and proceeds via the following hybrid modifications. Let $S_S = \{w\}$ be the sender's input such that $w \notin S_R$. In the first hybrid, we will choose the modulus N such that p_w divides $\phi(N)$; under the ϕ-hiding assumption this change will go unnoticed. Now, via a standard lossiness-argument, we have that $f = g^{\rho p_w}$ loses information about g^ρ, i.e., g^ρ has high min-entropy given f. This means that $h^\rho = g^{\rho r \cdot \prod_{i \in S_R} p_i}$ has also high min-entropy as $w \notin S_R$ and thus p_w does not divide $r \cdot \prod_{i \in S_R} p_i$ (w.o.p). Consequently, as h^ρ has high min-entropy conditioned on f, in the next hybrid change we can replace $R = \mathsf{Ext}(s, h^\rho)$ with a uniformly random value, incurring only a negligible statistical distance via the extraction property of Ext. In the next hybrid change, we can switch the modulus N back to normal mode, i.e., such that p_w does not divide $\phi(N)$. But now $f = g^{\rho p_w}$ is statistically close to uniform in $\mathbb{Z}_N^*$. Thus, in the last hybrid change we can replace f with a uniformly random value in $\mathbb{Z}_N^*$ and get that the view of the receiver is independent of w, as required.

---

[7] We will not further discuss the small correctness-error of this protocol as our final protocol will not suffer from this defect.

For the case that the sender's input S_S contains more than a single element, we mount a hybrid argument repeating the above modifications for each element of S_S not in the receiver's set S_R.

Large Universes. The above protocol has the drawback that the size of the common reference string crs depends linearly on the size of the universe $\mathcal{U}$, which is highly undesirable. There is a standard way of overcoming this issue: Instead of explicitly listing all the primes p_i in crs, we will describe them implicitly via a pseudorandom function (PRF).[8] For this purpose, we need a PRF which maps into the set of primes of a certain size. This can e.g. be achieved by using rejection sampling: we first sample $y \leftarrow F_k(x|i)$ (starting with $i = 1$) and check if y is a prime number. If it is, we output y; else, we increment i until a prime is hit. Under standard number-theoretic assumptions, this process finds a prime after a logarithmic number of steps. One small issue is that, in the above security proof, we need to replace one of the primes with a prime provided by the ϕ-hiding experiment. We resolve this issue by making the PRF programmable in one point, e.g., by setting $F_{k,k'}(x|i) = F'_k(x|i) \oplus k_i$ for a PRF F', $k' = (k_1, \ldots, k_\xi)$ and a suitable choice of ξ.

A First Attempt at Malicious Sender Security. Our protocol thus far, however, offers no security against a malicious sender. The main issue is that a corrupted sender may choose the values f and R arbitrarily, and further, there is no mechanism for a simulator against a malicious sender to extract the senders input w. Of course, this protocol can be made secure against malicious senders by letting the sender prove via a general purpose NIZK proof that it follows the semi-honest protocol correctly. This however would necessitate to make non-black-box use of our semi-honest laconic PSI protocol, contrary to our goal of achieving a fully black-box protocol.

Re-inspecting the above protocol, we have not made full use of the fact that the extracted string R is uniformly random. Our first idea to make the sender extractable is to make better use of R. Instead of sending R in the plain, we will use R as random coins for a public key encryption (PKE) scheme to encrypt the sender's input w. More concretely, we will modify the above protocol as follows. We include a public key pk of a PKE scheme in the common reference string crs and, instead of having the sender include R in the plain in its message to the receiver, it will include a ciphertext $ct \leftarrow Enc(pk, i; R)$. We also need to modify the procedure of the receiver. The receiver will recover R_i as before, but will now use R_i to *re-encrypt* the index i, that is, for each $i \in S_R$ it will compute $ct_i \leftarrow Enc(pk, i; R_i)$.

First notice that, as a side bonus, this modification makes our laconic PSI scheme perfectly correct, given that the PKE scheme is perfectly correct, as now ct_i uniquely specifies the element i.

In terms of security, we first observe that this modification does not harm security against a semi-honest receiver given that the PKE scheme is IND-CPA

---

[8] We remark that we use a PRF, not because we want uniform outputs, but to implicitly define the set of primes. A similar trick was used in [6].

secure. In the above sketch of a security proof, we have argued that, if w is not in the set S_R, then R is uniformly random from the view of the receiver. This means now that ct is a freshly encrypted ciphertext, using fresh random coins (independent of ρ). Moreover, we can use IND-CPA security of the PKE to replace ct with an encryption of 0, and then continue as above to argue security against a semi-honest receiver.

To establish security against a malicious sender, we would like to argue as follows. The simulator can now generate the public key pk in crs together with a secret key sk. Given a message (s, f, ct) by a malicious sender, the simulator can recover the set element w by decrypting the ciphertext ct using sk. At a first glance this seems to provide us with security against malicious senders. And indeed, the simulator will recover all elements for which the receiver would have declared to be in the intersection. There is a grave issue however: The simulator has no means of detecting whether the honest receiver would actually have succeeded in re-encrypting the index i. In other words, the malicious sender can make the simulator *false positives*, such that the simulator declares an element i to be in the intersection, whereas an honest receiver would not have.

Switch Groups, Extract Everything! We briefly recall some facts about the Damgård-Jurik cryptosystem [15]. The group $\mathbb{Z}^*_{N^{\xi+1}}$ contains a cyclic subgroup $\mathbb{NR}_N$ of order $\phi(N)$[9]. Now let $g_0 \in \mathbb{NR}_N$ be a generator of $\mathbb{NR}_N$. Then we can generate the entire group $\mathbb{Z}^*_{N^{\xi+1}}$ by g_0 and $1 + N$, i.e. we can write every $h \in \mathbb{Z}^*_{N^{\xi+1}}$ as $h = g_0^t \cdot (1 + N)^m$ for some $t \in \mathbb{Z}_{\phi(N)}$ and $m \in \mathbb{Z}_{N^\xi}$. Furthermore, we can efficiently compute discrete logarithms relative to $1 + N$, i.e. if $h = (1 + N)^m$ for an $m \in \mathbb{Z}_{N^\xi}$, then we can efficiently compute m from h. Finally, the decisional composite residue (DCR) assumption in $\mathbb{Z}^*_{N^{\xi+1}}$ states that a random element in $\mathbb{NR}_N$ is indistinguishable from a random element in $\mathbb{Z}^*_{N^{\xi+1}}$. It follows that $g_1 = g_0^{t_1}$ and $g_2 = g_0^{t_2} \cdot (1 + N)$ (for uniformly random $t_1, t_2 \leftarrow_\$ \mathbb{Z}_{\phi(N)}$) are computationally indistinguishable. Moreover, if $h = g_2^t$ for a $t < N^{\xi-1}$, we can efficiently compute t from h using $\phi(N)$ as a trapdoor by first computing

$$h^{\phi(N)} = g_2^{t \cdot \phi(N)} = \underbrace{g_0^{t\phi(N)}}_{=1} \cdot (1+N)^{t \cdot \phi(N)} = (1+N)^{t \cdot \phi(N)} \mod N^{\xi+1},$$

from which we can efficiently compute $t \cdot \phi(N)$ (as $t \cdot \phi(N) < N^\xi$) and thus t.

Given this, we will now make the following additional modification to our PSI protocol. Instead of choosing the element g in the common reference string crs to be a random generator of $\mathbb{Z}^*_N$, we choose g to be a random generator of $\mathbb{NR}_N$, where $\mathbb{NR}_N$ is the subgroup of order $\phi(N)$ in $\mathbb{Z}^*_{N^{\xi+1}}$ (for a sufficiently large but

[9] Note that $\mathbb{NR}_N$ is not a cyclic group and we only assume this here for simplicity. Actually, if we choose N as a product of two safe primes, then we could find a cyclic subgroup $\mathbb{J}_N$ which is the group of elements with Jacobi symbol 1, and its subgroup $\mathbb{T}_N$ composing of N^ξ-th powers of $\mathbb{J}_N$ has order $\phi(N)/2$. Namely, just replace the group pair $(\mathbb{Z}^*_{N^{\xi+1}}, \mathbb{NR}_N)$ with $(\mathbb{J}_N, \mathbb{T}_N)$ to fix this issue. Please refer to Sect. 3.1 and Sect. 6 for details.

constant ξ). Our first observation is that this does not affect the security proof in the case of a semi-honest receiver, since $\mathbb{NR}_N$ is still a cyclic group of order $\phi(N)$ and the above argument using the ϕ-hiding assumption works analogously in this group.

Assume for a moment we had a mechanism which ensures that the group element f in the sender's message is of the form $f = g^a$ for an $a < N^{\xi-1}$. We can then argue security against a malicious sender as follows: First we make a hybrid change and choose the element g in the common reference string like g_2 above, i.e. we choose $g = g_0^t(1 + N)$; under the DCR assumption this change goes unnoticed. Now, given that $f = g^a$ for an $a < N^{\xi-1}$ and using $\phi(N)$ as a trapdoor, the simulator can efficiently compute a from f as described above. Since it can also recover the index w from the ciphertext ct as described above, it can now check if a is of the form $a = \rho \cdot p_w$. If so, it recovers ρ and performs the same re-encryption test for ct which the real receiver would perform. This makes the simulation indistinguishable from the real experiment.

2.3 DV-NIZK Range Proofs for DJ Ciphertexts

The final component which is missing to make the above argument succeed is a mechanism which ensures that the group element f is indeed of the form $f = g^a$ for a *small* a. For the sake of generality, we will make the following discussion for general DJ-ciphertexts, that is, ciphertexts of the form $c = h^t \cdot (1 + N)^a$ (where $h = g_1^z$ is the public key). If we can show that such a ciphertext encrypts a small value a, proving that $f = g^a$ and $c = h^t \cdot (1 + N)^a$ for the same a can be efficiently proven via a standard hash-proof system (HPS) [14].

First, we observe that, to show that $c = h^t \cdot (1 + N)^a$ encrypts a value $a < 2^k$ for some parameter k, it suffices to prove that some ciphertexts $c_0, \dots, c_{k-1}$ encrypt *bits* $b_1, \dots, b_{k-1}$. Assume for now we had a DV-NIZK protocol Π to prove that the ciphertexts $c_0, \dots, c_{k-1}$ all just encrypt bits. The prover can convince the verifier as follows that c encrypts a value $a < 2^k$. First the prover encrypts bit b_i in a ciphertext c_i and sets $c' = \prod_{i=0}^{k-1} c_i^{2^i}$ (it is not hard to see that c' encrypts a). Now, the prover uses Π to to convince the verifier that $c_0, \dots, c_{k-1}$ indeed encrypt bits. Furthermore, it can use a standard HPS to prove that c and c' indeed encrypt the same value. Zero-knowledge follows routinely. To see that this protocol is sound, observe that if the c_i indeed encrypt bits, then c' must encrypt a value bounded by 2^k.

A DV-NIZK Proof System for Ciphertext Equality Across Different Encryption Schemes. Alas, we do not know of a black-box DV-NIZK which proves that DJ ciphertexts encrypt bits. However, for the pairing-based Boneh-Goh-Nissim (BGN) cryptosystem [5], such a proof system was constructed by Groth, Ostrovsky and Sahai [29]. Consequently, if we could prove in a black box way that a BGN ciphertext encrypts the same value as DJ ciphertext we would be done.

Recall that, in the BGN cryptosystem, public keys are of the form (G, H), where G and H a generators of subgroups of a composite-order pairing group $\mathbb{G}$.

BGN ciphertexts are of the form $C = G^m H^r$, where m is the encrypted message and r are random coins.

Our final contribution is a DV-NIZK proof system which allows us to prove that a DJ ciphertext and a BGN ciphertext encrypt the same value.

To simplify the description of our prove system, assume we have BGN public keys $(G, H_1), \ldots, (G, H_\ell)$, i.e. each key sharing the same G but having fresh and random H_i, and an element H_0. Furthermore, assume that we have DJ public keys $h_1, \ldots, h_\ell$, and an element h_0. We will assume that both sequences of keys are in a public setup, together with the elements H_0, h_0.

Suppose further that we have BGN ciphertexts $C_1, \ldots, C_\ell$, where $C_i = G^{m_i} H_i^r$, i.e., all ciphertexts use the same random coins r but encrypt possibly different bits m_i.[10] As mentioned above, using the NIZK scheme from [29], we can prove that the ciphertexts $C_i = G^{m_i} H_i^r$ are indeed well-formed and that $m_i \in \{0, 1\}$. Moreover, we have $C_0 = H_0^r$, which can be proven well-formed using a standard hash proof system (HPS) [14].

Assume further that we are given DJ ciphertexts $c_1, \ldots, c_\ell$, where $c_i = h_i^t \cdot (1+N)^{m_i'}$, i.e., again the ciphertexts share the same random coins t.[11] Moreover, assume that we have a value h_0^r exactly as above. We want to prove that it holds for all $i \in [\ell]$ that $m_i = m_i'$. Our DV-NIZK proof system for equality of BGN and DJ ciphertexts now proceeds roughly as follows:

- The verifier starts by sampling a uniformly random binary string $\sigma \leftarrow_\$ \{0, 1\}^\ell$ and computes $F = H_0^A \prod H_i^{\sigma_i} \in \mathbb{G}$ and $f = h_0^\alpha \prod h_i^{\sigma_i} \in Z_{N^{\varepsilon+1}}^*$, for uniformly random values A, α. It sends $\mathsf{crs} = (F, f)$ to the prover and keeps σ as the designated-verifier key.
- The prover is given ciphertexts $C_1, \ldots, C_\ell$ and $c_1, \ldots, c_\ell$ with $C_i = G^{m^i} H_i^r$ and $c_i = h_i^t (1 + N)^{m_i}$, and the values $C_0 = H_0^r$ and $c_0 = h_0^t$. It computes $K = F^r G^\tau$ and $k = f^t (1+N)^\tau$ where τ is sampled according to a distribution which is wide enough to drown the m_i, but short enough such that it is bounded by N. The proof π is consists of (K, k).
- The verifier, given the proof $\pi = (K, k)$, computes the discrete log y (in base $(1 + N)$) of $k^{-1} c_0^\alpha \prod_{i=1}^\ell c_i^{\sigma_i}$ and checks if $G^y = K^{-1} C_0^A \prod_{i=1}^\ell C_i^{\sigma_i}$.

For completeness, note that

$$k^{-1} c_0^\alpha \prod c_i^{\sigma_i} = \left(h_0^\alpha \prod h_i^{\sigma_i} \right)^{-t} (1 + N)^{-\tau} \left(h_0^t \right)^\alpha \prod \left(h_i^t (1+N)^{m_i} \right)^{\sigma_i}$$
$$= (1 + N)^{\sum \sigma_i m_i - \tau},$$

from which the verifier can recover $y = \sum \sigma_i m_i - \tau$. Moreover

$$L = K^{-1} C_0^A \prod C_i^{\sigma_i} = \left(H_0^A \prod H_i^{\sigma_i} \right)^{-r} G^{-\tau} \left(H_0^r \right)^A \prod (H_i^r G^{m_i})^{\sigma_i} = G^{\sum \sigma_i m_i - \tau}$$

and thus $G^y = L$.

---

[10] Via a standard rerandomization argument we can show that reusing the same random coins across different keys does not harm CPA security.

[11] Same as above.

The zero-knowledge property can be established by noting that the term τ statistically drowns $\sum_i \sigma_i m_i$.

To prove *reusable statistical soundness* (or simulation soundness), we argue as follows. First note that σ is statistically hidden, given $F = H_0^A \prod H_i^{\sigma_i}$ and $f = h_0^\alpha \prod h_i^{\sigma_i}$, by the uniform values A, α. We need to show that if there is an index i for which $m_i \neq m_i'$, then the verifier will reject with high probability, irrespective of the (adversarial) choices of τ, τ' (which are not necessarily short)[12]. It follows from the above description that the verifier accepts a proof if the condition

$$\sum \sigma_{i,j} m_i - \tau_j \mod n = \left(\sum \sigma_{i,j} m_i' - \tau_j' \mod N^\xi\right) \mod n$$

is satisfied, where n is the order of the subgroup of $\mathbb{G}$ generated by G. In the main body we will show that, given that $n > N^\xi$, this condition will be violated with probability $\approx 1/2$ if the there exists an index i for which $m_i \neq m_i'$. By repeating the protocol λ times, we achieve negligible soundness error.

2.4 Labeled Laconic PSI and Laconic OT

Our laconic PSI construction can be easily extended into a labeled laconic PSI, in which the receiver also learns labels associated with set elements in the intersection. To achieve this, we simply use an extractor with an output size twice as large: the first half is used as above to perform the re-encryption step; the other half is used as an one-time pad to encrypt the corresponding label. It is easy to see that the receiver can only recover the labels for the elements within the intersection, since the security proof follows the same blueprint as before.

We also build an LOT using the same ideas as above. The receiver commits to a database $D \in \{0,1\}^\Gamma$ by computing $h = g_0^{r \prod_{i=1}^{\Gamma} e_{i,D_i}} \mod N^{\xi+1}$, where each prime $e_{i,b}$ is the output of a PRF (just as before). The sender computes $f_j = g_0^{\rho_j e_{L,j}}, F_j = g_1^{\rho_j e_{L,j}}(1+N)^{\rho_j e_{L,j}}$ for each $j \in \{0,1\}$, together with a range proof. Moreover, he encrypts each message as $\mathsf{ct}_j = k_j \oplus m_j$ where $k_j \leftarrow \mathsf{Ext}(s_j, h^{\rho_j})$. Again, security follows the same reasoning as above. Our LOT protocol is the first one to provide security against a malicious sender while incurring in communication complexity independent of the size of D.

3 Preliminaries

We use λ to denote the security parameter. By $\mathsf{negl}(\lambda)$, we denote a negligible function in λ. For an integer n, $[n]$ denotes $\{1,\dots,n\}$. If $\mathcal{A}$ is an algorithm, we denote by $y \leftarrow \mathcal{A}(x)$ the output y after running $\mathcal{A}$ on input x. For a S, $x \leftarrow_\$ S$ denotes sampling x uniformly at random from S. If D is a distribution, then $x \leftarrow_\$ D$ denotes sampling x according to D, and $y \in D$ indicates y is in the support of D. We say that D is B-bounded if for every $x \leftarrow_\$ D$, we have

---

[12] We assume that the verifier rejects if it fails to compute the discrete logarithm of $k^{-1} \prod d_i^{\sigma_i}$.

$|x| < B$, except with negligible probability. If D_0, D_1 are two distributions, we use $D_0 \approx_\varepsilon D_1$ to indicate that D_0 and D_1 are statistically indistinguishable. Throughout this work, ϕ will denote the Euler's totient function.

In terms of cryptographic primitives we need public-key encryption (PKE), designated-verifier zero-knowledge (DV-NIZK) proof systems, programmable pseudorandom functions (PPRF) [36] and strong randomness extractors. The hardness assumptions used in this work are the ϕ-hiding, decisional composite residuosity (DCR), subgroup decision (SD), computational Diffie-Hellman (CDH) and learning with errors (LWE). Apart from ϕ-hiding and DCR assumptions we described below, other primitives/assumptions are reviewed in the full version of this paper [1].

3.1 Hardness Assumptions

We start by introducing some notation. Let $\mathsf{Primes}(\kappa)$ denote the set of prime numbers of bit-length κ. Let

$$\mathsf{RSA}(\lambda) = \{N : N = PQ \text{ and } P, Q \in \mathsf{Primes}(\lambda/2) \text{ and } \gcd(P-1, Q-1) = 2\}$$

and

$$\mathsf{RSA}_e(\lambda) = \{N : e | \phi(N)\}$$

for any $e \leq 2^\lambda$.

Definition 1 (Phi-Hiding). *The* phi-hiding *assumption, denoted as ϕ-hiding, states that for all $\varepsilon > 0$ and $3 < e < 2^{\lambda/4-\varepsilon}$ and all PPT adversaries $\mathcal{A}$, we have that*

$$|\Pr[1 \leftarrow \mathcal{A}(N, e) : N \leftarrow_\$ \mathsf{RSA}(\lambda)] - \Pr[1 \leftarrow \mathcal{A}(N, e) : N \leftarrow_\$ \mathsf{RSA}_e(\lambda)]| \leq \mathsf{negl}(\lambda).$$

Let $N = PQ$ where P, Q are safe primes (that is, $P = 2p'+1$ and $Q = 2q'+1$ for primes p', q') and consider the multiplicative group $\mathbb{Z}^*_{N^{\xi+1}}$ where ξ is a fixed nonnegative integer. Recall that $\mathbb{Z}^*_{N^{\xi+1}}$ can be written as the product of two subgroups $\mathbb{H}_N \times \mathbb{NR}_N$ where $\mathbb{H}_N = \{(1+N)^i : i \in [N^\xi]\}$ and $\mathbb{NR}_N = \{x^{N^\xi} : x \in \mathbb{Z}^*_{N^{\xi+1}}\}$ (the subgroup of N^ξ-residues) which has order $\phi(N)$. Given $(1+N)^m \bmod N^{\xi+1}$, there is a polynomial-time algorithm that allows to recover m [15].

Furthermore, let $\mathbb{J}_N$ be the group of elements with Jacobi symbol 1, i.e., $\mathbb{J}_N = \{x : (x|N) = 1, x \in \mathbb{Z}^*_{N^{\xi+1}}\}$. Note that $\mathbb{J}_N$ can be written as the direct product of two cyclic groups $\mathbb{H}_N \times \mathbb{T}_N$ with order N^ξ and $\phi(N)/2$, respectively. Also, the subset membership problem for $(\mathbb{J}_N, \mathbb{T}_N)$ is still hard if DCR assumption holds as shown in Sect. 8.2 of [14].

The following lemma is straightforwardly adapted from [27].

Lemma 1 ([27]). *Assume that the ϕ-hiding assumption holds. Let Ext be a $(\kappa - 1, \mathsf{negl}(\lambda))$-strong extractor. For every admissible stateful PPT adversary $\mathcal{A}$ and for all λ, κ such that $\lambda \geq 5\kappa$, we have that*

$$\left| \Pr \left[b \leftarrow \mathcal{A}(y_b) : \begin{array}{c} N \leftarrow_\$ \mathsf{RSA}(\lambda); \ s \leftarrow_\$ \{0,1\}^\lambda \\ e \leftarrow_\$ \mathsf{Primes}(\kappa); \ g \leftarrow \mathbb{T}_N \\ G \leftarrow \mathcal{A}(N, s, e, g); \ b \leftarrow_\$ \{0,1\} \\ y_0 \leftarrow \mathsf{Ext}(s, g^{Ge^{-1}} \bmod N^{\xi+1}); \ y_1 \leftarrow_\$ \mathcal{Y} \end{array} \right] - \frac{1}{2} \right| \leq \mathsf{negl}(\lambda)$$

where an admissible adversary is one that outputs G *such that* e *does not divide* G.

In this work, we also make use of the DCR assumption which we define in the following. We present the DCR assumption as a subgroup indistinguishability assumption [7].

Definition 2 (Decisional Composite Residuosity). *Let* $N = \mathsf{RSA}(\lambda)$ *and let* $\xi \geq 0$ *be a fixed integer. The* decisional composite residuosity *(DCR) assumption states that for all PPT adversaries* $\mathcal{A}$,

$$\left| \Pr\left[1 \leftarrow \mathcal{A}(N, x) : x \leftarrow_\$ \mathbb{Z}_{N^{\xi+1}}^* \right] - \Pr\left[1 \leftarrow \mathcal{A}(N, x) : x \leftarrow_\$ \mathbb{NR}_N \right] \right| \leq \mathsf{negl}(\lambda).$$

Lemma 2 ([14]). $N = \mathsf{RSA}(\lambda)$ *and let* $\xi \geq 0$ *be a fixed integer. Assume that the DCR assumption holds. Then for all PPT adversaries* $\mathcal{A}$,

$$\left| \Pr\left[1 \leftarrow \mathcal{A}(N, x) : x \leftarrow_\$ \mathbb{J}_N \right] - \Pr\left[1 \leftarrow \mathcal{A}(N, x) : x \leftarrow_\$ \mathbb{T}_N \right] \right| \leq \mathsf{negl}(\lambda).$$

Proof (Proof (sketch)).

The proof follows from the following observation: The map $x \to x^2(-1)^b$ where $b \leftarrow_\$ \{0, 1\}$ sends the uniform distribution on $\mathbb{NR}_N$ to the uniform distribution on $\mathbb{T}_N$, and the uniform distribution on $\mathbb{H}_N \times \mathbb{NR}_N$ to the uniform distribution on $\mathbb{H}_N \times \mathbb{T}_N$.

3.2 Laconic Private Set Intersection

Laconic Private Set Intersection. An ℓPSI is a two-round protocol that implements a PSI functionality and has special compactness properties.

Definition 3. *A* ℓPSI *scheme* $\mathsf{LPSI} = (\mathsf{GenCRS}, \mathsf{R}_1, \mathsf{S}, \mathsf{R}_2)$ *is defined as follows:*

- $\mathsf{GenCRS}(1^\lambda)$: *Takes as input a security parameter* 1^λ, *and outputs a common reference string* crs.
- $\mathsf{R}_1(\mathsf{crs}, S_R)$: *Takes as input a* crs *and a set* S_R. *It outputs a first PSI message* psi_1 *and a state* st.
- $\mathsf{S}(\mathsf{crs}, S_S, \mathsf{psi}_1)$: *Takes as input a* crs, *a set* S_S *and a first PSI message* psi_1. *It outputs a second PSI message* psi_2.
- $\mathsf{R}_2(\mathsf{crs}, \mathsf{st}, \mathsf{psi}_2)$: *Takes as input a* crs, *a state* st *and a second message* psi_2. *It outputs a set* $\mathcal{I}$.

We require the following properties.

- **Correctness:** *The protocol satisfies PSI correctness in the standard sense.*
- **Efficiency Requirements.** *There exists a fixed polynomial* poly *such that the length of* psi_1 *and the running time of* S *are at most* $\mathsf{poly}(\lambda, \log |S_R|)$.

For malicious security, we work in the standard UC-framework [10] that allows us to prove security of protocols under arbitrary composition with other protocols. Let $\mathcal{F}$ be a functionality, π a protocol that implements $\mathcal{F}$ and $\mathcal{E}$ be a environment, an entity that oversees the execution of the protocol in both the real and the ideal worlds. Let $\mathsf{IDEAL}_{\mathcal{F},\mathsf{Sim},\mathcal{E}}$ be a random variable that represents the output of $\mathcal{E}$ after the execution of $\mathcal{F}$ with adversary Sim. Similarly, let $\mathsf{REAL}^{\mathcal{G}}_{\pi,\mathcal{A},\mathcal{E}}$ be a random variable that represents the output of $\mathcal{E}$ after the execution of π with adversary $\mathcal{A}$ and with access to the functionality $\mathcal{G}$.

Definition 4. *A protocol π UC-realizes $\mathcal{F}$ in the $\mathcal{G}$-hybrid model if for every PPT adversary $\mathcal{A}$ there is a PPT simulator Sim such that for all PPT environments $\mathcal{E}$, the distributions $\mathsf{IDEAL}_{\mathcal{F},\mathsf{Sim},\mathcal{E}}$ and $\mathsf{REAL}^{\mathcal{G}}_{\pi,\mathcal{A},\mathcal{E}}$ are computationally indistinguishable.*

We present the (reusable) PSI ideal functionality.

Reusable PSI Functionality. The functionality $\mathcal{F}_{\mathsf{rPSI}}$ is parametrized by a universe $\mathcal{U}$ and works as follows:

- **Setup phase.** R sends $(\mathsf{sid}, S_{\mathsf{R}})$ to $\mathcal{F}_{\mathsf{rPSI}}$ where $S_{\mathsf{R}} \subseteq \mathcal{U}$. It ignores future messages from R with the same sid.
- **Send phase.** S sends $(\mathsf{sid}, i, S_{\mathsf{S}} \subseteq \mathcal{U})$ to $\mathcal{F}_{\mathsf{rPSI}}$. $\mathcal{F}_{\mathsf{rPSI}}$ sends $(\mathsf{sid}, i, S_{\mathsf{R}} \cap S_{\mathsf{S}})$ to R. It ignores future messages from S with the same sid and $i \in \mathbb{N}$.

4 Semi-Honest Laconic PSI from CDH/LWE

We show how to realize semi-honest ℓPSI from CDH/LWE. Our construction is non-black-box, making use of garbled circuits. This leads to the first feasibility result based on CDH, and an alternative LWE construction to that of [40].

Our construction makes use of hash encryption schemes in conjunction with garbled circuits, which we review below.

Definition 5 (Hash Encryption [8,17]). *A hash encryption scheme* $\mathsf{HE} = (\mathsf{HGen}, \mathsf{Hash}, \mathsf{HEnc}, \mathsf{HDec})$ *is defined as follows.*

- $\mathsf{HGen}(1^\lambda, n)$: *Takes as input a security parameter 1^λ and an input size n and outputs a hash key* pp.
- $\mathsf{Hash}(\mathsf{pp}, z)$: *Takes as input a hash key* pp *and $z \in \{0,1\}^n$, and deterministically outputs $h \in \{0,1\}^\lambda$.*
- $\mathsf{HEnc}(\mathsf{pp}, h, \{m_{i,b}\}_{i \in [n], b \in \{0,1\}}; \{r_{i,b}\})$: *Takes as input a hash key* pp, *a hash output h, messages $\{m_{i,b}\}$ and randomness $\{r_{i,b}\}$, and outputs $\{\mathsf{cth}_{i,b}\}_{i \in [n], b \in \{0,1\}}$. We write it shortly as $\{\mathsf{cth}_{i,b}\}$. Overloading notation, each ciphertext $\mathsf{cth}_{i,b}$ is computed as $\mathsf{cth}_{i,b} = \mathsf{HEnc}(\mathsf{pp}, h, m_{i,b}, (i, b); r_{i,b})$.*
- $\mathsf{HDec}(z, \{\mathsf{cth}_{i,b}\})$: *Takes as input a hash input z and $\{\mathsf{cth}_{i,b}\}$ and outputs n messages $(m_1, \ldots, m_n)$.*

We require correctness meaning that for the variables above, $(m_1, \ldots, m_n) = (m_{1,z[1]}, \ldots, m_{n,z[n]})$. We define two notions of security.

- **Semantic Security:** *Given $z \in \{0,1\}^n$, no adversary can distinguish between encryptions of messages made to indices $(i, \bar{z}_i)$. For any PPT $\mathcal{A}$, sampling $\mathsf{pp} \leftarrow_\$ \mathsf{HGen}(1^\lambda, n)$, if $(z, \{m_{i,b}\}, \{m'_{i,b}\}) \leftarrow_\$ \mathcal{A}(\mathsf{pp})$ and if $m_{i,z[i]} = m'_{i,z[i]}$ for all $i \in [n]$, then $\mathcal{A}$ cannot distinguish between $\mathsf{HEnc}(\mathsf{pp}, h, \{m_{i,b}\})$ and $\mathsf{HEnc}(\mathsf{pp}, y, \{m'_{i,b}\})$, where $h := \mathsf{Hash}(\mathsf{pp}, z)$.*
- **Anonymous Semantic Security:** *For a random $\{m_{i,b}\}$ with equal rows (i.e., $m_{i,0} = m_{i,1}$), the output of $\mathsf{HEnc}(\mathsf{pp}, h, \{m_{i,b}\})$ is pseudorandom even in the presence of the hash input. Formally, for any $z \in \{0,1\}^n$, sampling $\mathsf{pp} \leftarrow_\$ \mathsf{HGen}(1^\lambda, n)$, $h := \mathsf{Hash}(\mathsf{pp}, z)$, and sampling $\{m_{i,b}\}$ uniformly at random with the same rows, then $\boldsymbol{v} := (\mathsf{pp}, z, \mathsf{HEnc}(\mathsf{pp}, h, \{m_{i,b}\}))$ is indistinguishable from another tuple in which we replace the hash-encryption component of $\boldsymbol{v}$ with a random string.*

We have the following results from [8, 21].

Lemma 3. *Assuming CDH/LWE there exists anonymous hash encryption schemes, where $n = 3\lambda$ (i.e., $\mathsf{Hash}(\mathsf{pp}, \cdot) \colon \{0,1\}^{3\lambda} \mapsto \{0,1\}^\lambda$).[13] Moreover, the hash function Hash satisfies robustness in the following sense: for any input distribution on z which samples at least 2λ bits of z uniformly at random, $(\mathsf{pp}, \mathsf{Hash}(\mathsf{pp}, z))$ and (pp, u) are statistically close, where $\mathsf{pp} \leftarrow_\$ \mathsf{HGen}(1^\lambda, 3\lambda)$ and $u \leftarrow_\$ \{0,1\}^\lambda$.*

We also review the notion of garbled circuits and the anonymous property, as defined in [8].

Definition 6 (Garbled Circuits). *A garbling scheme for a class of circuits $\{\mathsf{C} \colon \{0,1\}^n \mapsto \{0,1\}^m\}$ consists of $(\mathsf{Garb}, \mathsf{Eval}, \mathsf{Sim})$ satisfying the following.*

- **Correctness:** *for all $\mathsf{C} \in \mathcal{C}$, $\mathsf{m} \in \{0,1\}^n$, $\Pr[\mathsf{Eval}(\tilde{\mathsf{C}}, \{\mathsf{lb}_{i,\mathsf{m}[i]}\}) = \mathsf{C}(\mathsf{m})] = 1$, where $(\tilde{\mathsf{C}}, \{\mathsf{lb}_{i,b}\}) \leftarrow_\$ \mathsf{Garb}(1^\lambda, \mathsf{C})$.*
- **Simulation Security:** *For any $\mathsf{C} \in \mathcal{C}$ and $\mathsf{m} \in \{0,1\}^n$: $(\tilde{\mathsf{C}}, \{\mathsf{lb}_{i,\mathsf{m}[i]}\}) \overset{c}{\equiv} \mathsf{Sim}(1^\lambda, \mathsf{C}(\mathsf{m}))$, where $(\tilde{\mathsf{C}}, \{\mathsf{lb}_{i,b}\}) \leftarrow_\$ \mathsf{Garb}(1^\lambda, \mathsf{C})$.*
- **Anonymous Security [8]:** *For any $\mathsf{C} \in \mathcal{C}$, choosing $y \leftarrow_\$ \{0,1\}^m$, the output of $\mathsf{Sim}(1^\lambda, y)$ is pseudorandom.*

Lemma 4 ([8]). *Anonymous garbled circuits can be built from one-way functions (OWFs).*

Notation on Hash Encryption. Throughout this section we assume $\mathsf{Hash}(\mathsf{pp}, \cdot) \colon \{0,1\}^n \mapsto \{0,1\}^\lambda$, where $n = 3\lambda$. We use $\{\mathsf{lb}_{i,b}\}$ to define a sequence of pairs of labels, where (throughout this section) $i \in [n]$ and $b \in \{0,1\}$. For $\boldsymbol{r} := \{r_{i,b}\}$ we let $\mathsf{HEnc}(\mathsf{pp}, h, \{\mathsf{lb}_{i,b}\}; \boldsymbol{r})$ denote the ciphertexts $\{\mathsf{cth}_{i,b}\}$, where

---

[13] We note that the CDH construction of [8] satisfies a weaker notion of anonymity, in which only some part of the ciphertext is pseudorandom. But for ease of presentation we keep the notion as is, and remark that our ℓPSI construction works also with respect to that weaker notion.

Table 1. Circuits F, V and procedure DecPath

Circuit $F[\mathsf{id}, r, r'](\mathsf{id}', x, x')$:	**Circuit** $V[\mathsf{pp}, \mathsf{id}, \{\mathsf{lb}_{i,b}\}, r](h_1, h_2, \mathsf{id}')$:
– **Hardwired:** target identity id and randomness values r and r'. – **Operation:** Return $$y := \begin{cases} r & \mathsf{id} = \mathsf{id}' \\ r' & \text{else} \end{cases}$$	– **Hardwired:** Hash public parameter pp, target identity id, labels $\{\mathsf{lb}_{i,b}\}$, randomness r. – **Operation:** Return $$\mathsf{ct} := \begin{cases} \mathsf{HEnc}(\mathsf{pp}, h_1, \{\mathsf{lb}_{i,b}\}; r) & \mathsf{id} \leq \mathsf{id}' \\ \mathsf{HEnc}(\mathsf{pp}, h_2, \{\mathsf{lb}_{i,b}\}; r) & \text{else} \end{cases}$$

Procedure $\mathsf{DecPath}(\mathsf{pth}, \mathsf{psi}_2)$:

– **Input:** A leaf-root Path pth and ciphertext $\psi_2 := (\widetilde{C}_0, \dots, \widetilde{C}_d, \{\mathsf{cth}_{i,b}^{(d)}\})$.

– **Operation:** Parse $\mathsf{pth} := (\underbrace{(\mathsf{id}, x, x')}_{z_0}, \underbrace{(h_0, h_0', \mathsf{id}_0)}_{z_1}, \dots, \underbrace{(h_{d-1}, h_{d-1}', \mathsf{id}_{d-1})}_{z_d}, \mathsf{hr}_{\mathsf{root}})$.

For $w \in \{d, \dots, 1\}$:

1. Let $\{\mathsf{lb}_i^{(w)}\} := \mathsf{HDec}(z_w, \{\mathsf{cth}_{i,b}^{(w)}\})$.
2. Set $\{\mathsf{cth}_{i,b}^{(w-1)}\} := \mathsf{Eval}(\widetilde{C}_w, \{\mathsf{lb}_i^{(w)}\})$.

Let $\{\mathsf{lb}_i^{(0)}\} := \mathsf{HDec}(z_0, \{\mathsf{cth}_{i,b}^{(0)}\})$. Return $\mathsf{Eval}(\widetilde{C}_0, \{\mathsf{lb}_i^{(0)}\})$.

$\mathsf{cth}_{i,b} = \mathsf{HEnc}(\mathsf{pp}, h, \mathsf{lb}_{i,b}, (i, b); r_{i,b})$. We further overload the notation as follows. We use $\{\mathsf{lb}_i\}$ to denote a sequence of 3λ elements. For $r := \{r_{i,b}\}$ we let $\mathsf{HEnc}(\mathsf{pp}, h, \{\mathsf{lb}_i\}; r)$ denote a hash encryption where both plaintext rows are $\{\mathsf{lb}_i\}$; namely, the ciphertexts $\{\mathsf{cth}_{i,b}\}$, where $\mathsf{cth}_{i,b} = \mathsf{HEnc}(\mathsf{pp}, h, \{m_{i,b}\}; r_{i,b})$, where $m_{i,0} = m_{i,1} = \mathsf{lb}_i$, for all i.

Tree Terminology. Throughout this section we work with full binary trees. The depth of a tree is the length of a root-leaf path. We call the leaf level level 0, the level above it level one, and so on. We order the root-leaf paths from left to right; namely, the path from the root to the leftmost leaf node is the first root-leaf path, and the path from the root to the rightmost leaf node is the 2^dth root-leaf path, where d is the depth. Each node has an associated hash value, computed based on values associated to its children. Thus, when representing a root-leaf path, we include both children of each branching intermediate node.

Sender's Set Size is One. We assume without loss of generality that the sender holds a single element. For the general case where the sender may have multiple elements, we reuse the first message of the receiver for each element in the sender's set. The overall running time of the sender will only scale with its own set size, and not with the receiver's set size.

Construction 1 (ℓPSI Construction). *We require the following ingredients in our ℓPSI Construction.*

1. *A hash encryption scheme* $\mathsf{HE} = (\mathsf{HGen}, \mathsf{Hash}, \mathsf{HEnc}, \mathsf{HDec})$, *where*
   * $\mathsf{Hash}(\mathsf{pp}, \cdot) \colon \{0,1\}^{3\lambda} \mapsto \{0,1\}^{\lambda}$.
2. *A garbling scheme* $\mathsf{GS} = (\mathsf{Garb}, \mathsf{Eval}, \mathsf{Sim})$.
3. *Circuits* F *and* V, *as well as procedure* $\mathsf{DecPath}$, *defined in Table 1.*

We assume the elements of the receiver and the sender are strings in $\{0,1\}^{\lambda}$. *We refer to each element as an identity. Build* $(\mathsf{GenCRS}, \mathsf{R_1}, \mathsf{S}, \mathsf{R_2})$ *as follows.*

$\mathsf{GenCRS}(1^{\lambda})$: *Return* $\mathsf{crs} \leftarrow_{\$} \mathsf{HGen}(1^{\lambda}, 3\lambda)$.

$\mathsf{R_1}(\mathsf{crs}, S_\mathsf{R})$: *Assume* $|S_\mathsf{R}| = 2^d$. *(With small tweaks the same construction works if* S_R *is not a power of two.)*

- *Parse* $\mathsf{crs} := \mathsf{pp}$. *Let* $n := 2^d$, *and sort* $S_\mathsf{R} := \{\mathsf{id}_1, \ldots, \mathsf{id}_n\}$, *where* $\mathsf{id}_i < \mathsf{id}_{i+1}$ *for all* i. *Populate the leaf node values as follows. For each* $\mathsf{id}_i \in S_\mathsf{R}$, *sample* $x_i, x_i' \leftarrow_{\$} \{0,1\}^{\lambda}$, *and let* $h_i^{(0)} := \mathsf{Hash}(\mathsf{pp}, \mathsf{id}_i, x_i, x_i')$. *Set* $\mathsf{H}[v_i^{(0)}] := h_i^{(0)}$ *and* $\mathsf{ID}[v_i^{(0)}] := \mathsf{id}_i$.
  1. *For* $w \in [d]$, *populate the values for the nodes at level w as follows. Informally, the hash value for each node is the hash of the concatenation of its left child, right child, and the largest identity value under its left child. Formally, noting we have 2^{d-w} nodes on level w, for $j \in [2^{d-w}]$, set* $h_j^{(w)} := \mathsf{Hash}(\mathsf{pp}, (h_{2j-1}^{(w-1)}, h_{2j}^{(w-1)}, \mathsf{id}_{[j,w]}))$, *where* $\mathsf{id}_{[j,w]}$ *denotes the larges leaf identity under the left child of the current node (i.e., $\mathsf{id}_{[j,w]} = \mathsf{id}_f$, where $f := (2j-1)2^{w-1}$.) Set* $\mathsf{H}[v_j^{(w)}] = h_j^{(w)}$ *and* $\mathsf{ID}[v_j^{(w)}] = \mathsf{id}_{[j,w]}$.
  2. *Set* $\mathsf{psi}_1 := (d, \mathsf{hr}_{\mathsf{root}})$, *where* $\mathsf{hr}_{\mathsf{root}} := h_1^{(d)}$ *(i.e., the root hash value). Set* $\mathsf{st} := (S_\mathsf{R}, \{x_i\}, \{x_i'\}, \{v_j^{(w)}\})$ *for all values of* $i \in [n]$, $w \in \{0, \ldots, d\}$ *and* $j \in [2^{d-w}]$.

$\mathsf{S}(\mathsf{crs}, \mathsf{id}, \mathsf{psi}_1)$:

- *Parse* $\mathsf{psi}_1 := (d, \mathsf{hr}_{\mathsf{root}})$ *and* $\mathsf{crs} := \mathsf{pp}$. *Sample* $r, r' \leftarrow_{\$} \{0,1\}^{\lambda}$ *and let* $\mathsf{C}_0 := \mathsf{F}[\mathsf{id}, r, r']$ *(Table 1). Garble* $(\widetilde{\mathsf{C}}_0, \{\mathsf{lb}_{i,b}^{(0)}\}) \leftarrow_{\$} \mathsf{Garb}(\mathsf{C}_0)$. *For* $1 \leq w \leq d$
  1. *Sample* $\boldsymbol{r}_w$ *at random, and let* $\mathsf{C}_w := \mathsf{V}[\mathsf{pp}, \mathsf{id}, \{\mathsf{lb}_{i,b}^{(w-1)}\}, \boldsymbol{r}_w]$.
  2. *Garble* $(\widetilde{\mathsf{C}}_w, \{\mathsf{lb}_{i,b}^{(w)}\}) \leftarrow_{\$} \mathsf{Garb}(\mathsf{C}_w)$.
- *Let* $\{\mathsf{cth}_{i,b}\} \leftarrow_{\$} \mathsf{HEnc}(\mathsf{pp}, \mathsf{hr}_{\mathsf{root}}, \{\mathsf{lb}_{i,b}^{(d)}\})$. *Return* $\mathsf{psi}_2 := (\widetilde{\mathsf{C}}_0, \ldots, \widetilde{\mathsf{C}}_d, \{\mathsf{cth}_{i,b}\}, r)$.

$\mathsf{R_2}(\mathsf{crs}, \mathsf{st}, \mathsf{psi}_2)$:

- *Parse* $\mathsf{st} := (S_\mathsf{R}, \{x_i\}, \{x_i'\}, \{v_j^{(w)}\})$, $\mathsf{psi}_2 := (\widetilde{\mathsf{C}}_0, \ldots, \widetilde{\mathsf{C}}_d, \{\mathsf{cth}_{i,b}\}, r)$ *and* $S_\mathsf{R} := \{\mathsf{id}_1, \ldots, \mathsf{id}_n\}$. *For* $i \in [n]$ *let* $\mathsf{pth}_i := ((\mathsf{id}_i, x_i, x_i'), \ldots, \mathsf{hr}_{\mathsf{root}})$ *be the i'th leaf-root path in the tree, and let*

$$r_i := \mathsf{DecPath}(\mathsf{pth}_i, \widetilde{\mathsf{C}}_0, \ldots, \widetilde{\mathsf{C}}_d, \{\mathsf{cth}_{i,b}\}).$$

If for a unique index $i \in [n]$, $r_i = r$, *then output* id_i. *Otherwise, output* $\perp$.

Theorem 1. *Assuming the hash encryption* HE *is anonymous and robust (robustness defined in Lemma 3), and that the garbling scheme* GS *is anonymous, the ℓPSI protocol of Construction 1 is correct and provides statistical security for the receiver and semi-honest security for the sender. As a result, such ℓPSI protocols can be realized from CDH/LWE.*

Roadmap for the Proof of Theorem 1. The fact that the protocol provides statistical security for the receiver follows from the robustness of HE. In particular, robustness implies that $h_i^{(0)}$ values statistically hide S_R. We can continue this to argue that all the first-level hash values (i.e., $h_i^{(1)}$) also hide S_R, and hence, continuing like this, the root hash value $\mathsf{hr}_{\mathsf{root}}$ statistically hides S_R.

We now prove that the protocol provides sender security against semi-honest receivers. Let id be the sender's input message, and $S_R := \{\mathsf{id}_1, \ldots, \mathsf{id}_n\}$ be the receiver's set, where $\mathsf{id}_i < \mathsf{id}_{i+1}$. Assuming $\mathsf{id} \notin S_R$ we will show that the sender's protocol message is pseudorandom in the receiver's point of view. For simplicity suppose $\mathsf{id} < \mathsf{id}_1$; the general case follows via simple changes, which we will explain later. Let

$$\mathsf{pth} := (\underbrace{(\mathsf{id}_1, x_1, x_1')}_{z_0}, \underbrace{(h_0, h_0', \mathsf{id}_0)}_{z_1}, \ldots, \underbrace{(h_{d-1}, h_{d-1}', \mathsf{id}_{d-1})}_{z_d}, \mathsf{hr}_{\mathsf{root}}) \qquad (1)$$

be the leaf-root path from leaf id_1 to the root. Note $\mathsf{hr}_{\mathsf{root}} = \mathsf{Hash}(\mathsf{pp}, z_d)$, and $h_i = \mathsf{Hash}(\mathsf{pp}, z_i)$ for $i \in \{0, \ldots, d-1\}$. Noting that $\mathsf{hr}_{\mathsf{root}}$ is the receiver's protocol message produced based on her random coins st, we define the following hybrids for the sender's response message.

Hyb$_0$: The sender's response message psi_2 is formed as in the protocol.

Hyb$_1$: Sample $r, r' \leftarrow_{\$} \{0,1\}^\lambda$. Let $(\widetilde{\mathsf{C}}_0, \{\mathsf{lb}_i^{(0)}\}) \leftarrow_{\$} \mathsf{Sim}(\mathsf{F}, r')$. For $1 \leq w \leq d$

1. Sample $\{\mathsf{cth}_{i,b}^{(w-1)}\} \leftarrow_{\$} \mathsf{HEnc}(\mathsf{pp}, h_{w-1}, \{\mathsf{lb}_i^{(w-1)}\})$.
2. Let $(\widetilde{\mathsf{C}}_w, \{\mathsf{lb}_i^{(w)}\}) \leftarrow_{\$} \mathsf{Sim}(\mathsf{V}, \{\mathsf{cth}_{i,b}^{(w-1)}\})$.

Let $\{\mathsf{cth}_{i,b}\} \leftarrow_{\$} \mathsf{HEnc}(\mathsf{pp}, \mathsf{hr}_{\mathsf{root}}, \{\mathsf{lb}_i^{(d)}\})$. Return $\mathsf{psi}_2 := (\widetilde{\mathsf{C}}_0, \ldots, \widetilde{\mathsf{C}}_d, \{\mathsf{cth}_{i,b}\}, r)$.

Lemma 5. *Given* R*'s random coins,* **Hyb$_0$** *and* **Hyb$_1$** *are indistinguishable.*

Hyb$_2$: Sample psi_2 at random.

Lemma 6. *Given* R*'s random coins,* **Hyb$_1$** *and* **Hyb$_2$** *are indistinguishable.*

The above two lemmas establish sender's security; namely—if $\mathsf{id} \notin S_R$, then the sender's message psi_2 is pseudorandom for the receiver. We prove Lemma 5, Lemma 6 and correctness in the full paper [1].

5   Reusable DV-NIZK Range Proofs for DJ Ciphertexts

In this section, we construct a DV-NIZK scheme for ranges of DJ ciphertexts. The main idea of our construction is the following: the prover proves that a BGN ciphertext [5] is within a certain range (this can be done via the protocol of [29]). Then it proves that the DJ and BGN ciphertexts encrypt the same value.

We first recall the required cryptosystems used in this section.

BGN Cryptosystem. Recall that the BGN cryptosystem [5] is defined over a group $\mathbb{G}$ of order $n = pq$ for primes p, q. The public key is composed by $(\mathbb{G}, n, G, H)$ where G is a generator of $\mathbb{G}$ and H is an element of order p (let $p\mathbb{G}$ be the subgroup of order p). The public key is composed by $(\mathbb{G}, n, G, H)$ and a ciphertext for a message $m \in \{0, 1\}$ is of the form $C = G^m H^t$ for $t \leftarrow_\$ \mathbb{Z}_n$.

Damgård-Jurik Cryptosystem. The Damgård-Jurik (DJ) cryptosystem[14] [15] is defined over $\mathbb{Z}^*_{N^{\xi+1}}$ where $N \leftarrow_\$ \mathsf{RSA}(\lambda)$. The public key is formed by (N, ξ, g, h) where $g \leftarrow_\$ \mathbb{T}_N$ and $h = g^x$ for $x \leftarrow_\$ [N]$. A ciphertext has the form (c_1, c_2) where $c_1 = g^t \bmod N^{\xi+1}$ and $c_2 = h^t(1 + N)^m \bmod N^{\xi+1}$ for $t \leftarrow_\$ [N]$ and $m \in [N^\xi]$.

5.1   Equality of Plaintexts in DJ and BGN Ciphertexts

We now show how to prove that a BGN and a DJ ciphertexts encrypt the same value. Consider the following language

$$\mathcal{EQ}_\Delta = \left\{ D_0, h_0, \{D_i, c_{1,i}, c_{2,i}\}_{i \in [\ell]} : \exists (r, t, \{m_i\}) \text{ s.t.} \begin{array}{l} m_i \in \{0, 1\} \\ D_0 = H_0^r \in \mathbb{G} \\ D_i = G^m H_i^r \in \mathbb{G} \\ c_0 = h_0^t \in \mathbb{Z}_{N^{\xi+1}} \\ c_1 = g^t \in \mathbb{Z}_{N^{\xi+1}} \\ c_{2,i} = h_i^t(1 + N)^{m_i} \in \mathbb{Z}_{N^{\xi+1}} \end{array} \right\}$$

where $\Delta = (\mathbb{G}, n, G, H_0, \{H_i\}_{i \in [\ell]}, N, \xi, g, h_0, \{h_i\}_{i \in [\ell]})$, $G, H_0, \{H_i\}_{i \in [\ell]} \in \mathbb{G}$ and $g, h_0, \{h_i\}_{i \in [\ell]} \in \mathbb{Z}_{N^{\xi+1}}$.

The DV-NIZK construction for the language above is outlined in Sect. 2. We defer the full construction and its analysis to [1].

5.2   DV-NIZK for Range Proofs of DJ Ciphertexts with Equal Discrete Log

Let $N \leftarrow \mathsf{RSA}(\lambda)$ and $\xi \geq 0$ be a fixed integer. Consider the following language of ranges:

$$\mathcal{REDJ}_\Delta = \left\{ c_1 \in \{\mathbb{Z}^*_{N^{\xi+1}}\}^2 : \exists t \in \{\lceil -N^\xi/2 \rceil, \ldots, N^\xi/2 \rceil\} \text{ s.t.} \begin{array}{l} t \in [-B, B] \\ c_1 = g^t \bmod N^{\xi+1} \end{array} \right\}$$

---

[14] Here, we present a slightly different variant of the scheme in [15].

which is parametrized by $\Delta = (g, B, N, \xi)$ where $g \in \mathbb{T}_N$, $B \in \mathbb{Z}$, N and ξ.

In the following, we present a DV-NIZK scheme for the language above. The main idea is quite simple: The prover outputs BGN ciphertexts D_i encrypting bits m_i and DJ ciphertexts $(c_{1,i}, c_{2,i}$ that encrypt the same values as D_i (we can prove this using the scheme from the previous section). Then, the prover proves that (c_1, c_2) encrypts the same value as $\left(\prod_{i=0}^{\ell} c_{1,i}^{2^i}, \prod_{i=0}^{\ell} c_{2,i}^{2^i} \right)$. Since DJ is linearly-homomorphic, we conclude that (c_1, c_2) encrypts $m = \sum_{i=0}^{\ell} 2^i m_i \leq 2^{\ell-1}$.

Due to space restrictions, the full construction is presented in [1].

6   Reusable Laconic Private Set Intersection

In this section, we present a protocol that implements ℓPSI in a black-box fashion. We then prove that the protocol guarantees security against a semi-honest receiver and against a malicious sender. The input sets are subsets of a universe $\mathcal{U}$ of exponential size.

Protocol. We now present the construction for reusable PSI.

Construction 2 . *Let $\mathcal{U}$ be a universe which contains the input sets of the parties. Let $\kappa \in \mathbb{Z}$ such that $5\kappa \leq \lambda$ and $\xi \in \mathbb{N}$.*

We require the following ingredients in this construction:

1. A PPRF PPRF $: \mathcal{K} \times \mathcal{U} \to \text{Primes}(\kappa)$ which outputs a prime number.[15]
2. A DV-NIZK

   $$\text{NIZK}_{\mathcal{R}\mathcal{E}\mathcal{D}\mathcal{J}_\Delta} = (\text{NIZK.GenCRS}_{\mathcal{R}\mathcal{E}\mathcal{D}\mathcal{J}_\Delta}, \text{NIZK.Prove}_{\mathcal{R}\mathcal{E}\mathcal{D}\mathcal{J}_\Delta}, \text{NIZKVerify}_{\mathcal{R}\mathcal{E}\mathcal{D}\mathcal{J}_\Delta})$$

   for the language $\mathcal{R}\mathcal{E}\mathcal{D}\mathcal{J}_\Delta$ which is defined in Sect. 5, for some $\Delta = (g_0, B, N, \xi)$.
3. An IND-CPA PKE scheme PKE $= (\text{PKE.KeyGen}, \text{PKE.Enc}, \text{PKE.Dec})$
4. A $(\kappa - 1, \text{negl}(\lambda))$-strong extractor $\text{Ext} : \mathcal{S} \times \mathbb{Z}_{N^{\xi+1}} \to \{0, 1\}^\lambda$.

We assume that the receiver's set is of size M and the sender's set is of size m, where $M > m$. The protocol is composed by the following algorithms:

$\text{GenCRS}(1^\lambda)$:

- Sample $N \leftarrow_\$ \text{RSA}(\lambda)$, that is, $N = PQ$ where P, Q are safe prime numbers. Choose B such that $N^{\xi-1}/2 \geq B > N2^\kappa$.
- Sample a pair of public and secret keys $(\text{pk}, \text{sk}) \leftarrow \text{PKE.KeyGen}(1^\lambda)$. Additionally, sample a PPRF key $k \leftarrow_\$ \mathcal{K}$. Set $\Delta = (g_0, B, N, \xi)$ where $g_0 \leftarrow_\$ \mathbb{T}_N$.
- Output $\text{crs} = (N, \text{pk}, g_0, B, k, \Delta)$.

---

[15] We remark that we use a PPRF, not because we want uniform outputs, but to implicitly define the set of primes. A similar trick was used in [6].

$R_1(crs, S_R)$:

- Parse $crs := (N, pk, g_0, B, k, \Delta)$, and $S_R := \{id_i\}_{i \in [M]} \subseteq \mathcal{U}$
- Compute the prime numbers $p_i \leftarrow \mathsf{PPRF}(k, id_i)$, for all $i \in [M]$.
- Sample $r \leftarrow_\$ [N/4]$ and compute $h = g_0^{r \prod_{i \in [M]} p_i} \bmod N^{\xi+1}$.
- Run $(crs_1, td_1) \leftarrow \mathsf{NIZK.GenCRS}_{\mathcal{REDJ}_\Delta}(1^\lambda)$.
- Output $st = (r, td_1)$ and $psi_1 = (h, crs_1)$.

$S(crs, S_S, psi_1)$:

- Parse $crs := (N, pk, g_0, B, k, \Delta)$, $psi_1 := (h, crs_1)$ and $S_S := \{id'_i\}_{i \in [m]} \subseteq \mathcal{U}$.
- For $i \in [m]$ do the following:
  - Sample $\rho_i \leftarrow_\$ [N/4]$. Compute the prime numbers $p_i \leftarrow \mathsf{PPRF}(k, id'_i)$.
  - Sample an extractor seed $s_i \leftarrow_\$ S$ and compute $R_i \leftarrow \mathsf{Ext}(s_i, h^{\rho_i} \bmod N^{\xi+1})$
  - Compute $f_i = g_0^{\rho_i p_i} \bmod N^{\xi+1}$ and $ct_i \leftarrow \mathsf{PKE.Enc}(pk, id'_i; R_i)$.
  - Compute $\pi_i \leftarrow \mathsf{NIZK.Prove}_{\mathcal{REDJ}_\Delta}(crs_1, x_i, w_i)$ where $x_i = f_i$ and $w_i = \rho_i p_i$.
- Output $psi_2 = \{f_i, ct_i, s_i, \pi_i\}_{i \in [m]}$.

$R_2(crs, st, psi_2)$:

- Parse $st := (r, td_1)$ and $psi_2 := \{f_i, ct_i, s_i, \pi_i\}_{i \in [m]}$. Set $\mathcal{I} = \emptyset$
- For all $j \in [m]$ do the following:
  - If $0 \leftarrow \mathsf{NIZK.Verify}_{\mathcal{REDJ}_\Delta}(td_1, x_j, \pi_j)$ where $x_j = f_j$, abort the protocol.
  - If there is a $i \in [M]$ such that

$$ct_j = \mathsf{PKE.Enc}(pk, id_i; R'_i)$$

where $R'_i \leftarrow \mathsf{Ext}(s_j, f_j^{r_i} \bmod N^{\xi+1})$ and $r_i = r \prod_{\ell=1, \ell \neq i}^{M} p_\ell$, then add the element id_i to $\mathcal{I}$.
- Output $\mathcal{I}$.

Communication Cost. Here, we analyze the communication cost of the protocol as a function of the input set sizes $|S_S| = m$ and $|S_R| = M$ and we omit polynomial factors in the security parameter λ. The first message outputted by R_1 has size $\mathcal{O}(1)$. The second message outputted by S has size $\mathcal{O}(m)$. The overall communication cost is $\mathcal{O}(m)$, that is, it is independent of M.

Analysis. We now analyze the correctness and security of the protocol.

Theorem 2. *The protocol presented in Construction 2 is correct given that* $\mathsf{NIZK}_{\mathcal{REDJ}_\Delta}$ *is complete and* PKE *is correct.*

The proof is presented in the full paper [1].

Theorem 3. *The protocol presented in Construction 2 securely UC-realizes functionality $\mathcal{F}_{\mathsf{rPSI}}$ in the $\mathcal{G}_{\mathsf{CRS}}$-hybrid model against:*

- *a semi-honest receiver given that the ϕ-hiding assumption hold and $\mathsf{NIZK}_{\mathcal{R}\mathcal{E}\mathcal{D}\mathcal{J}_\Delta}$ is zero-knowledge;*
- *a malicious sender, given that the DCR assumption holds and $\mathsf{NIZK}_{\mathcal{R}\mathcal{E}\mathcal{D}\mathcal{J}_\Delta}$ is reusable sound.*

Proof. We start by proving that the protocol is secure against semi-honest adversaries corrupting the receiver.

Lemma 7. *The protocol is secure against a semi-honest receiver.*

We first show how the simulator $\mathsf{Sim}_{\mathsf{R}}$ works. In the following, let $\mathsf{Sim}_{\mathsf{NIZK}}$ be the zero-knowledge simulator from Lemma 7 for the $\mathsf{NIZK}_{\mathcal{R}\mathcal{E}\mathcal{D}\mathcal{J}_\Delta}$ scheme.

1. $\mathsf{Sim}_{\mathsf{R}}$ takes the input S_{R} of R and sends it to the ideal functionality $\mathcal{F}_{\mathsf{rPSI}}$.
2. **CRS generation.** To generate the CRS, Sim behaves as the honest algorithm would do.
3. The simulator creates the semi-honest receiver's view exactly as in the real protocol and keeps $\mathsf{st} = (r, \mathsf{td}_1)$ to itself.
4. Upon receiving a message $\mathsf{psi}_1 = (h, \mathsf{crs}_1)$ from R and a message $\mathcal{I}$ (of size m', that is, $|\mathcal{I}| = m'$) from the ideal functionality $\mathcal{F}_{\mathsf{rPSI}}$, the simulator does the following:
   - Sample a subset $\mathcal{X}$ of size $m - m'$ from the universe $\mathcal{U}$ and sets $S_{\mathcal{S}} = \mathcal{I} \cup \mathcal{X}$.
   - For all $i \in \mathcal{I}$, $\mathsf{Sim}_{\mathsf{R}}$ computes $(f_i, \mathsf{ct}_i, s_i, \pi_i)$ as in the real protocol.
   - For all $i \in S_{\mathsf{S}} \setminus \mathcal{I}$, $\mathsf{Sim}_{\mathsf{R}}$ simulates proofs $\pi_i \leftarrow \mathsf{Sim}_{\mathsf{NIZK}}(\mathsf{td}_1, x)$ for $x = f_i$ where $f_i \leftarrow_{\$} \mathbb{T}_N$. Then, it encrypts $\mathsf{ct}_i \leftarrow \mathsf{PKE}.\mathsf{Enc}(\mathsf{pk}, 0; R_i)$ where $R_i \leftarrow \{0, 1\}^\lambda$.

To prove indistinguishability between the real protocol and the simulated one, we consider the following sequence of hybrids:

Hyb$_0$: The is the real protocol.

Hyb$_1$: This hybrid is identical to the previous one, except that, for $i \in S_{\mathsf{S}} \setminus \mathcal{I}$, $\mathsf{Sim}_{\mathsf{R}}$ simulates the proofs $\pi_i \leftarrow \mathsf{Sim}_{\mathsf{NIZK}}(\mathsf{td}_1, x)$ for $x_i = f_i$.

Claim 1. *Hybrids* **Hyb$_0$** *and* **Hyb$_1$** *are statistically indistinguishable.*

The claim above follows directly from the statistical zero-knowledge of the scheme $\mathsf{NIZK}_{\mathcal{R}\mathcal{E}\mathcal{D}\mathcal{J}_\Delta}$.

Hyb$_{2,\ell}$: This hybrid is identical to the previous one, except that the simulator samples $f_{u_\ell} \leftarrow_{\$} \mathbb{T}_N$ and computes

$$R_{u_\ell} \leftarrow \mathsf{Ext}\left(s, f_{u_\ell}^{r q_{u_\ell}^{-1} \prod_j^M p_j} \bmod N^{\xi+1}\right)$$

where $q_{u_\ell} \leftarrow \mathsf{PPRF}(k, x_{u_\ell})$ for all $u_\ell \in \{i : x_i \in S_{\mathsf{S}} \setminus \mathcal{I}\}$ and $p_j \leftarrow \mathsf{PPRF}(k, y_j)$ for all $y_j \in S_{\mathsf{R}}$. The hybrid is defined for $\ell = 1, \ldots, m - m'$.

Claim 2. *Hybrids* $\mathbf{Hyb}_1$ *and* $\mathbf{Hyb}_{2,m-m'}$ *are indistinguishable.*

The proof of the claim is deferred to the full paper [1].

$\mathbf{Hyb}_{3,\ell}$: This hybrid is identical to the previous one except that Sim_R computes $R_{u_\ell} \leftarrow_{\$} \{0,1\}^\lambda$ for all $u_\ell \in \{i : x_i \in S_S \setminus \mathcal{I}\}$. The hybrid is defined for $\ell = 1, \ldots, m - m'$.

Claim 3. *Assume that* Ext *is a* $(\kappa - 1, \mathsf{negl}(\lambda))$*-strong extractor and that the* ϕ*-hiding assumption holds. Then hybrids* $\mathbf{Hyb}_{2,m-m'}$ *and* $\mathbf{Hyb}_{3,m-m'}$ *are indistinguishable.*

The proof of the claim is in [1].

$\mathbf{Hyb}_{4,\ell}$: This hybrid is identical to the previous one except that Sim_R encrypts $\mathsf{ct}_{u_\ell} \leftarrow \mathsf{PKE.Enc}(\mathsf{pk}, 0; R_{u_\ell})$ for all for all $u_\ell \in \{i : x_i \in S_S \setminus \mathcal{I}\}$. The hybrid is defined for $\ell = 1, \ldots, m - m'$. Hybrid $\mathbf{Hyb}_{4,m-m'}$ is identical to the simulation.

Claim 4. *Assume that* PKE *is an IND-CPA PKE. Then hybrids* $\mathbf{Hyb}_{3,m-m'}$ *and* $\mathbf{Hyb}_{4,m-m'}$ *are indistinguishable.*

The claim follows directly from the IND-CPA property of the underlying PKE. That is, given an adversary $\mathcal{A}$ that distinguishes both hybrids, we can easily build an adversary $\mathcal{B}$ against the IND-CPA property of PKE. This adversary $\mathcal{B}$ simply chooses as messages $m_0 = x_{u_\ell}$ (where $x_{u_\ell} \in S_S \setminus \mathcal{I}$) and $m_1 = 0$. It outputs whatever $\mathcal{A}$ outputs.

We first show how the simulator Sim_S extracts the sender's input:

1. **CRS generation.** Sim_S generates the crs following the algorithm GenCRS, except that it sets $g_0 = g_0'(1 + N)$ for $g_0' \leftarrow_{\$} \mathbb{T}_N$. It keeps $\phi(N)$ to itself (which can be computed using the prime numbers P, Q) and the secret key sk corresponding to pk. It outputs $\mathsf{crs} = (\mathsf{pk}, g_0, B, k, \Delta)$
2. Sim_S samples $h \leftarrow_{\$} \mathbb{T}_N$ and computes $(\mathsf{crs}_1, \mathsf{td}_1) \leftarrow \mathsf{NIZK.GenCRS}_{\mathcal{REDJ}_\Delta}(1^\lambda)$. It sends $\mathsf{psi}_1 = (h, \mathsf{crs}_1)$ to the malicious sender.
3. Whenever Sim_S receives a message $\mathsf{psi}_2 = \{f_i, \mathsf{ct}, s_i, \pi_i\}_{i \in [m]}$ from the sender, the simulator initially sets S_S and does the following for all $i \in [m]$:
   - It checks if $1 \leftarrow \mathsf{NIZK.Verify}_{\mathcal{REDJ}_\Delta}(\mathsf{td}_1, x_j, \pi_j)$ where $x_j = f_j$, and aborts otherwise.
   - It computes $\mathsf{id}_i' \leftarrow \mathsf{PKE.Dec}(\mathsf{sk}, \mathsf{ct}_i)$ and $p_i \leftarrow \mathsf{PPRF}(k, \mathsf{id}_i')$. Additionally, it extracts ζ_i by recovering ζ_i' from $(1 + N)^{\zeta_i'} = f_i^{\phi(N)}$ and computing $\zeta = \zeta'/\phi(N)$ over the integers. It computes $\rho_i' = \zeta_i/p_i$ over the integers. If $\mathsf{ct}_i = \mathsf{PKE.Enc}(\mathsf{pk}, \mathsf{id}_i'; R_i)$ where $R_i = \mathsf{Ext}(s_i, h^{\rho_i'} \bmod N^{\xi+1})$, then it adds id_i' to S_S.
4. It sends S_S to $\mathcal{F}_{\mathsf{PSI}}$ and halts.

We now show that the simulation is indistinguishable from the real protocol via the following sequence of hybrids.

$\mathbf{Hyb}_0$: This hybrid is the real protocol.

$\mathbf{Hyb}_1$: This hybrid is identical to the previous one except that the simulator computes the first message (sent by the receiver) as $h \leftarrow_{\$} \mathbb{T}_N$.

Claim 5. *Hybrids* $\mathbf{Hyb}_0$ *and* $\mathbf{Hyb}_1$ *are statistically indistinguishable.*

Since g_0 is a generator of $\mathbb{T}_N$, the distributions of g^x and $h \leftarrow_{\$} \mathbb{T}_N$ are identical. It follows that the hybrids are indistinguishable.

$\mathbf{Hyb}_2$: This hybrid is identical to the previous one, except that $g_0 = g_0'(1+N)$ for $g_0' \leftarrow_{\$} \mathbb{T}_N$ (instead of choosing $g_0 \leftarrow_{\$} \mathbb{T}_N$). Additionally, Sim_S keeps $(\phi(N), \mathsf{sk})$ while creating crs.

Claim 6. *Assume that the DCR assumption holds. Then hybrids* $\mathbf{Hyb}_1$ *and* $\mathbf{Hyb}_2$ *are indistinguishable.*

$\mathbf{Hyb}_3$: This hybrid is identical to the previous one except that the simulator, instead of checking if there is an index i for which

$$\mathsf{ct}_j = \mathsf{PKE.Enc}(\mathsf{pk}, \mathsf{id}_i; R_i')$$

where $R_i' = \mathsf{Ext}(s_j, f_j^{r_i})$ and $r_i = r \prod_{\ell=1, \ell \neq i}^{M} p_\ell$ (as in the real protocol), it does the checks as in the simulation. That is, it computes $\mathsf{id}_i' \leftarrow \mathsf{PKE.Dec}(\mathsf{sk}, \mathsf{ct}_i)$ and $p_i \leftarrow \mathsf{PPRF}(k, \mathsf{id}_i')$. Additionally, it extracts ζ_i by recovering ζ_i' from $(1+N)^{\zeta_i'} = f_i^{\phi(N)}$ and computing $\zeta = \zeta'/\phi(N)$. It computes $\rho_i' = \zeta_i/p_i$ over the integers. Then, it checks if $\mathsf{ct}_i = \mathsf{PKE.Enc}(\mathsf{pk}, \mathsf{id}_i'; R_i)$ where $R_i = \mathsf{Ext}(s_i, h^{\rho_i'})$.

Claim 7. *Hybrids* $\mathbf{Hyb}_2$ *and* $\mathbf{Hyb}_3$ *are indistinguishable given that* PKE *is correct and* $\mathsf{NIZK}_{\mathcal{REDJ}_\Delta}$ *is simulation sound.*

By the simulation soundness of $\mathsf{NIZK}_{\mathcal{REDJ}_\Delta}$, $\zeta_i < N^{\xi-1}/2$. Hence, $\zeta_i' < N^\xi/2$ and thus $\zeta_i' \bmod N^\xi$ is equal to ζ_i' as an integer. Computing $\zeta = \zeta_i'/\phi(N)$ yields $\rho_i p_i$ over $\mathbb{Z}$. Thus $\rho_i = \zeta_i/p_i$ over $\mathbb{Z}$.

Thus, performing the checks in this hybrid has the same outcome as in the real protocol. □

Setting the Parameters. The value B is such that $N^{\xi-1}/2 \geq B > N2^\kappa$ for $5\kappa \leq \lambda$. Then, it is enough to set $\xi = 3$, so that we can find a B that fulfills the condition.

Achieving Statistical Security Against the Sender. The protocol presented in Construction 2 achieves computational security against a malicious sender given that the DCR assumption holds (recall that $\mathsf{NIZK}_{\mathcal{REDJ}_\Delta}$ achieves statistical reusable soundness).

The only place where we use the DCR assumption in the proof of security against a malicious sender is when we replace $g_0 \leftarrow_{\$} \mathbb{T}_N$ by $g_0 = g_0'(1+N)$. Hence, consider the following modification of the protocol presented in Construction 2: In GenCRS, the element g_0 is chosen as $g_0'(1+N)$ for g_0'. This simple modification of the protocol yields a new one which is *statistically secure against a malicious sender*. On the other hand, security against a semi-honest receiver now relies on the hardness of ϕ-hiding (as before) *and* the DCR assumption.

7 Self-Detecting Encryption

In this section we define self-detecting encryption, and show how to build it from laconic PSI. We first give a semi-honest definition, and will present the malicious definition in the full paper [1].

Definition 7. *A Self-Detecting Encryption (SDE) scheme is tuple of (randomized) algorithms* SDE = (Prm, Gen, Hash, Enc, Dec, Detect) *such that:*

- Prm(1^λ): *Takes as input a security parameter* 1^λ, *and outputs a public parameter* pp.
- Gen(pp): *Takes as input a public parameter* pp, *and outputs a pair of keys* (pk, sk).
- Hash(pp, DB): *Takes as input a public parameter* pp *and a database* DB, *and outputs a hash value* h *and a private state* st. *We require* $|h| \leq$ poly(λ), *for a fixed polynomial* poly.
- Enc(pk, h, m): *Takes as input a public key* pk, *a hash value* h, *and a message* m, *and outputs a ciphertext* ct.
- Dec(sk, ct): *Takes as input a secret key* sk *and a ciphertext* ct, *and outputs a message* m *or* $\perp$.
- Detect(st, ct): *Takes as input a private state* st *and a ciphertext* ct, *and outputs a message* m *or* $\perp$.

  We require the following properties:

- **Correctness.** *For any message* m, *letting* pp $\leftarrow_\$$ Prm(1^λ) *and* (pk, sk) $\leftarrow_\$$ Gen(pp): Pr[Dec(sk, Enc(pk, m)) $\neq$ m] $\leq$ negl(λ).
- **Detection.** *For any* pp $\in$ Prm, *any* (pk, sk) $\in$ Gen(1^λ), *any database of strings* DB, *and any message* m, *letting* (h, st) $\leftarrow_\$$ Hash(pp, DB) *and* ct $\leftarrow_\$$ Enc(pk, h, m), *if* m $\in$ DB *then* Detect(st, ct) = m.
- **Efficiency.** *The size of* h *and running time of* Enc *are independent of the database size. There exists a polynomial* poly *s.t. for all* $n := n(\lambda)$, *any* DB $\in$ $\{0, 1\}^n$, *letting* h $\leftarrow_\$$ Hash(pp, DB) *and* pp, pk *be as above, then* $|h| \leq$ poly(λ) *and also the running time of* Enc(pk, h, m) *is upper bounded by* poly($|m|, \lambda$).
- **Database Hiding.** *For any two databases* (DB$_0$, DB$_1$) *of equal size, if* (h$_0$, $*$) $\leftarrow_\$$ Hash(pp, DB$_0$) *and* (h$_1$, $*$) $\leftarrow_\$$ Hash(pp, DB$_1$) *then* h$_0$ *and* h$_1$ *are indistinguishable where* pp $\leftarrow_\$$ Gen(1^λ).
- **Semantic Security.** *For any database of strings* DB *and any two messages* (m$_0$, m$_1$): (pk, h, Enc(pk, h, m_0)) $\overset{c}{\equiv}$ (pk, h, Enc(pk, h, m_1)), *where all the variables are sampled as above.*
- **Security Against the Authority.** *For any two messages* (m$_0$, m$_1$), *if* m$_0$ $\notin$ DB *and* m$_1$ $\notin$ DB *then*

$$\big(\mathsf{pk}, (\mathsf{h}, \mathsf{st}), \mathsf{Enc}(\mathsf{pk}, \mathsf{h}, m_0)\big) \overset{c}{\equiv} \big(\mathsf{pk}, (\mathsf{h}, \mathsf{st}), \mathsf{Enc}(\mathsf{pk}, \mathsf{h}, m_1)\big),$$

where pp $\leftarrow_\$$ Prm(1^λ), (pk, sk) $\leftarrow_\$$ Gen(pp), *and* (h, st) $\leftarrow_\$$ Hash(pp, DB).

We now show how to realize self-detecting encryption from semi-honest laconic PSI. Informally, the SDE hash is the receiver's first-round laconic PSI message, and the encryption of a message m consists of a PKE encryption of m as well as a second-round PSI message based on m.

Construction 3 . *Let* $\mathsf{PKE} = (\mathsf{KeyGen}', \mathsf{Enc}', \mathsf{Dec}')$ *be a CPA-secure PKE scheme*[16] *and* $\mathsf{LPSI} = (\mathsf{GenCRS}, \mathsf{R}_1, \mathsf{S}, \mathsf{R}_2)$ *a laconic PSI.*

- $\mathsf{Prm}(1^\lambda)$: *Sample* $\mathsf{crs} \leftarrow_\$ \mathsf{LPSI.GenCRS}(1^\lambda)$, *and let* $\mathsf{pp} := \mathsf{crs}$.
- $\mathsf{Gen}(\mathsf{pp})$: *Run* $\mathsf{PKE.Gen}'(1^\lambda)$ *to generate a pair of keys* $(\mathsf{pk}, \mathsf{sk})$.
- $\mathsf{Hash}(\mathsf{pp}, \mathsf{DB})$: *Let* h *be the output of the receiver on* DB *and* pp, *i.e.,* $\mathsf{h} \leftarrow_\$$ $\mathsf{LPSI.R}_1(\mathsf{pp}, \mathsf{DB})$. *In addition, let* st *be the private state of the receiver.*
- $\mathsf{Enc}(\mathsf{pk}, \mathsf{h}, \mathsf{m})$: *Output* $(\mathsf{ct}_1, \mathsf{ct}_2)$, *where* $\mathsf{ct}_1 \leftarrow_\$ \mathsf{PKE.Enc}'(\mathsf{pk}, \mathsf{m})$ *and* $\mathsf{ct}_2 \leftarrow_\$$ $\mathsf{LPSI.S}(\mathsf{pp}, \{\mathsf{m}\}, \mathsf{h})$.
- $\mathsf{Dec}(\mathsf{sk}, \mathsf{ct} = (\mathsf{ct}_1, \mathsf{ct}_2))$: *Output* $\mathsf{PKE.Dec}'(\mathsf{sk}, \mathsf{ct}_1)$.
- $\mathsf{Detect}(\mathsf{st}, \mathsf{ct} = (\mathsf{ct}_1, \mathsf{ct}_2))$: *Output* $\mathsf{R}_2(\mathsf{st}, \mathsf{ct}_2)$.

Correctness and efficiency follow immediately.

- **Statistical** database hiding follows from PSI-receiver statistical security.
- Semantic security and security against the authority property of the scheme follows from the CPA security of PKE scheme Π and the sender's security. Observe that if $\mathsf{m} \notin \mathsf{DB}$ then both ct_1 and ct_2 computationally hide the message even in the presence of the private state st of PSI. Specifically, one can argue that ct_1 computationally hides m because of the CPA security of PKE scheme Π, and ct_2 computationally hides m because of the sender's security of laconic PSI. The arguments above can be made formal via a routine hybrid argument, and we omit the details.

Acknowledgment. Pedro Branco thanks the support from DP-PMI and FCT (Portugal) through the grant PD/BD/135181/2017. This work is supported by Security and Quantum Information Group of Instituto de Telecomunicações, by the Fundação para a Ciência e a Tecnologia (FCT) through national funds, by FEDER, COMPETE 2020, and by Regional Operational Program of Lisbon, under UIDB/50008/2020.

Nico Döttling: This work is partially funded by the Helmholtz Association within the project "Trustworthy Federated Data Analytics" (TFDA) (funding number ZT-I-OO1 4).

Sanjam Garg is supported in part by DARPA under Agreement No. HR00 112020026, AFOSR Award FA9550-19-1-0200, NSF CNS Award 1936826, and research grants by the Sloan Foundation, Visa Inc., and Center for Long-Term Cybersecurity (CLTC, UC Berkeley). Any opinions, findings and conclusions or recommendations expressed in this material are those of the author(s) and do not necessarily reflect the views of the United States Government or DARPA.

Mohammad Hajiabadi is supported in part by NSF CNS Award 2055564.

---

[16] We proceed with an independent PKE scheme for the sake of simplicity.

References

1. Alamati, N., Branco, P., Döttling, N., Garg, S., Hajiabadi, M., Pu, S.: Laconic private set intersection and applications. Cryptology ePrint Archive, Report 2021/728 (2021). https://ia.cr/2021/728
2. Ateniese, G., De Cristofaro, E., Tsudik, G.: (If) size matters: size-hiding private set intersection. In: Catalano, D., Fazio, N., Gennaro, R., Nicolosi, A. (eds.) PKC 2011. LNCS, vol. 6571, pp. 156–173. Springer, Heidelberg (2011). https://doi.org/10.1007/978-3-642-19379-8_10
3. Baum, C., Bootle, J., Cerulli, A., del Pino, R., Groth, J., Lyubashevsky, V.: Sublinear lattice-based zero-knowledge arguments for arithmetic circuits. In: Shacham, H., Boldyreva, A. (eds.) CRYPTO 2018. LNCS, vol. 10992, pp. 669–699. Springer, Cham (2018). https://doi.org/10.1007/978-3-319-96881-0_23
4. Benhamouda, F., Lin, H.: k-round multiparty computation from k-round oblivious transfer via garbled interactive circuits. In: Nielsen, J.B., Rijmen, V. (eds.) EUROCRYPT 2018. LNCS, vol. 10821, pp. 500–532. Springer, Cham (2018). https://doi.org/10.1007/978-3-319-78375-8_17
5. Boneh, D., Goh, E.-J., Nissim, K.: Evaluating 2-DNF formulas on ciphertexts. In: Kilian, J. (ed.) TCC 2005. LNCS, vol. 3378, pp. 325–341. Springer, Heidelberg (2005). https://doi.org/10.1007/978-3-540-30576-7_18
6. Boyle, E., Gilboa, N., Ishai, Y.: Breaking the circuit size barrier for secure computation under DDH. In: Robshaw, M., Katz, J. (eds.) CRYPTO 2016. LNCS, vol. 9814, pp. 509–539. Springer, Heidelberg (2016). https://doi.org/10.1007/978-3-662-53018-4_19
7. Brakerski, Z., Goldwasser, S.: Circular and leakage resilient public-key encryption under subgroup indistinguishability. In: Rabin, T. (ed.) CRYPTO 2010. LNCS, vol. 6223, pp. 1–20. Springer, Heidelberg (2010). https://doi.org/10.1007/978-3-642-14623-7_1
8. Brakerski, Z., Lombardi, A., Segev, G., Vaikuntanathan, V.: Anonymous IBE, leakage resilience and circular security from new assumptions. In: Nielsen, J.B., Rijmen, V. (eds.) EUROCRYPT 2018. LNCS, vol. 10820, pp. 535–564. Springer, Cham (2018). https://doi.org/10.1007/978-3-319-78381-9_20
9. Bünz, B., Bootle, J., Boneh, D., Poelstra, A., Wuille, P., Maxwell, G.: Bulletproofs: short proofs for confidential transactions and more. In: 2018 IEEE Symposium on Security and Privacy, pp. 315–334. IEEE Computer Society Press, San Francisco (2018)
10. Canetti, R.: Universally composable security: a new paradigm for cryptographic protocols. In: 42nd Annual Symposium on Foundations of Computer Science, pp. 136–145. IEEE Computer Society Press, Las Vegas (2001)
11. Chen, H., Huang, Z., Laine, K., Rindal, P.: Labeled PSI from fully homomorphic encryption with malicious security. In: Lie, D., Mannan, M., Backes, M., Wang, X. (eds.) ACM CCS 2018: 25th Conference on Computer and Communications Security, pp. 1223–1237. ACM Press, Toronto (2018)
12. Chen, H., Laine, K., Rindal, P.: Fast private set intersection from homomorphic encryption. In: Thuraisingham, B.M., Evans, D., Malkin, T., Xu, D. (eds.) ACM CCS 2017: 24th Conference on Computer and Communications Security, pp. 1243–1255. ACM Press, Dallas (2017)
13. Cho, C., Döttling, N., Garg, S., Gupta, D., Miao, P., Polychroniadou, A.: Laconic oblivious transfer and its applications. In: Katz, J., Shacham, H. (eds.) CRYPTO 2017. LNCS, vol. 10402, pp. 33–65. Springer, Cham (2017). https://doi.org/10.1007/978-3-319-63715-0_2

14. Cramer, R., Shoup, V.: Universal hash proofs and a paradigm for adaptive chosen ciphertext secure public-key encryption. In: Knudsen, L.R. (ed.) EUROCRYPT 2002. LNCS, vol. 2332, pp. 45–64. Springer, Heidelberg (2002). https://doi.org/10.1007/3-540-46035-7_4

15. Damgård, I., Jurik, M.: A generalisation, a simplification and some applications of paillier's probabilistic public-key system. In: Kim, K. (ed.) PKC 2001. LNCS, vol. 1992, pp. 119–136. Springer, Heidelberg (2001). https://doi.org/10.1007/3-540-44586-2_9

16. Döttling, N., Garg, S.: From selective IBE to full IBE and selective HIBE. In: Kalai, Y., Reyzin, L. (eds.) TCC 2017. LNCS, vol. 10677, pp. 372–408. Springer, Cham (2017). https://doi.org/10.1007/978-3-319-70500-2_13

17. Döttling, N., Garg, S.: Identity-based encryption from the diffie-hellman assumption. In: Katz, J., Shacham, H. (eds.) CRYPTO 2017. LNCS, vol. 10401, pp. 537–569. Springer, Cham (2017). https://doi.org/10.1007/978-3-319-63688-7_18

18. Döttling, N., Garg, S., Goyal, V., Malavolta, G.: Laconic conditional disclosure of secrets and applications. In: Zuckerman, D. (ed.) 60th Annual Symposium on Foundations of Computer Science, pp. 661–685. IEEE Computer Society Press, Baltimore (2019)

19. Döttling, N., Garg, S., Hajiabadi, M., Masny, D.: New constructions of identity-based and key-dependent message secure encryption schemes. In: Abdalla, M., Dahab, R. (eds.) PKC 2018. LNCS, vol. 10769, pp. 3–31. Springer, Cham (2018). https://doi.org/10.1007/978-3-319-76578-5_1

20. Döttling, N., Garg, S., Ishai, Y., Malavolta, G., Mour, T., Ostrovsky, R.: Trapdoor hash functions and their applications. In: Boldyreva, A., Micciancio, D. (eds.) CRYPTO 2019. LNCS, vol. 11694, pp. 3–32. Springer, Cham (2019). https://doi.org/10.1007/978-3-030-26954-8_1

21. Garg, S., Gay, R., Hajiabadi, M.: New techniques for efficient trapdoor functions and applications. In: Ishai, Y., Rijmen, V. (eds.) EUROCRYPT 2019. LNCS, vol. 11478, pp. 33–63. Springer, Cham (2019). https://doi.org/10.1007/978-3-030-17659-4_2

22. Garg, S., Hajiabadi, M., Mahmoody, M., Rahimi, A.: Registration-based encryption: removing private-key generator from IBE. In: Beimel, A., Dziembowski, S. (eds.) TCC 2018. LNCS, vol. 11239, pp. 689–718. Springer, Cham (2018). https://doi.org/10.1007/978-3-030-03807-6_25

23. Garg, S., Hajiabadi, M., Mahmoody, M., Rahimi, A., Sekar, S.: Registration-based encryption from standard assumptions. In: Lin, D., Sako, K. (eds.) PKC 2019. LNCS, vol. 11443, pp. 63–93. Springer, Cham (2019). https://doi.org/10.1007/978-3-030-17259-6_3

24. Garg, S., Srinivasan, A.: Garbled protocols and two-round MPC from bilinear maps. In: Umans, C. (ed.) 58th Annual Symposium on Foundations of Computer Science, pp. 588–599. IEEE Computer Society Press, Berkeley (2017)

25. Garg, S., Srinivasan, A.: Two-round multiparty secure computation from minimal assumptions. In: Nielsen, J.B., Rijmen, V. (eds.) EUROCRYPT 2018. LNCS, vol. 10821, pp. 468–499. Springer, Cham (2018). https://doi.org/10.1007/978-3-319-78375-8_16

26. Goyal, R., Vusirikala, S.: Verifiable registration-based encryption. In: Micciancio, D., Ristenpart, T. (eds.) CRYPTO 2020. LNCS, vol. 12170, pp. 621–651. Springer, Cham (2020). https://doi.org/10.1007/978-3-030-56784-2_21

27. Goyal, R., Vusirikala, S., Waters, B.: New constructions of hinting PRGs, OWFs with encryption, and more. In: Micciancio, D., Ristenpart, T. (eds.) CRYPTO 2020. LNCS, vol. 12170, pp. 527–558. Springer, Cham (2020). https://doi.org/10.1007/978-3-030-56784-2_18

28. Green, M.: (2019). https://blog.cryptographyengineering.com/2019/12/08/on-client-side-media-scanning/

29. Groth, J., Ostrovsky, R., Sahai, A.: Perfect non-interactive zero knowledge for NP. In: Vaudenay, S. (ed.) EUROCRYPT 2006. LNCS, vol. 4004, pp. 339–358. Springer, Heidelberg (2006). https://doi.org/10.1007/11761679_21

30. Groth, J., Sahai, A.: Efficient non-interactive proof systems for bilinear groups. In: Smart, N. (ed.) EUROCRYPT 2008. LNCS, vol. 4965, pp. 415–432. Springer, Heidelberg (2008). https://doi.org/10.1007/978-3-540-78967-3_24

31. Hazay, C., Venkitasubramaniam, M.: Scalable multi-party private set-intersection. In: Fehr, S. (ed.) PKC 2017. LNCS, vol. 10174, pp. 175–203. Springer, Heidelberg (2017). https://doi.org/10.1007/978-3-662-54365-8_8

32. Hubacek, P., Wichs, D.: On the communication complexity of secure function evaluation with long output. In: Roughgarden, T. (ed.) ITCS 2015: 6th Conference on Innovations in Theoretical Computer Science, pp. 163–172. Association for Computing Machinery, Rehovot (2015)

33. Ishai, Y., Paskin, A.: Evaluating branching programs on encrypted data. In: Vadhan, S.P. (ed.) TCC 2007. LNCS, vol. 4392, pp. 575–594. Springer, Heidelberg (2007). https://doi.org/10.1007/978-3-540-70936-7_31

34. Jarecki, S., Liu, X.: Fast secure computation of set intersection. In: Garay, J.A., De Prisco, R. (eds.) SCN 2010. LNCS, vol. 6280, pp. 418–435. Springer, Heidelberg (2010). https://doi.org/10.1007/978-3-642-15317-4_26

35. Kissner, L., Song, D.: Privacy-preserving set operations. In: Shoup, V. (ed.) CRYPTO 2005. LNCS, vol. 3621, pp. 241–257. Springer, Heidelberg (2005). https://doi.org/10.1007/11535218_15

36. Kolesnikov, V., Matania, N., Pinkas, B., Rosulek, M., Trieu, N.: Practical multi-party private set intersection from symmetric-key techniques. In: Thuraisingham, B.M., Evans, D., Malkin, T., Xu, D. (eds.) ACM CCS 2017: 24th Conference on Computer and Communications Security, pp. 1257–1272. ACM Press, Dallas (2017)

37. Lindell, Y., Nissim, K., Orlandi, C.: Hiding the input-size in secure two-party computation. In: Sako, K., Sarkar, P. (eds.) ASIACRYPT 2013. LNCS, vol. 8270, pp. 421–440. Springer, Heidelberg (2013). https://doi.org/10.1007/978-3-642-42045-0_22

38. Pinkas, B., Schneider, T., Weinert, C., Wieder, U.: Efficient circuit-based PSI via cuckoo hashing. In: Nielsen, J.B., Rijmen, V. (eds.) EUROCRYPT 2018. LNCS, vol. 10822, pp. 125–157. Springer, Cham (2018). https://doi.org/10.1007/978-3-319-78372-7_5

39. Pinkas, B., Schneider, T., Zohner, M.: Faster private set intersection based on OT extension. In: Fu, K., Jung, J. (eds.) USENIX Security 2014: 23rd USENIX Security Symposium, pp. 797–812. USENIX Association, San Diego (2014)

40. Quach, W., Wee, H., Wichs, D.: Laconic function evaluation and applications. In: Thorup, M. (ed.) 59th Annual Symposium on Foundations of Computer Science, pp. 859–870. IEEE Computer Society Press, Paris (2018)

41. Resende, A.C.D., Aranha, D.F.: Faster unbalanced private set intersection. In: Meiklejohn, S., Sako, K. (eds.) FC 2018. LNCS, vol. 10957, pp. 203–221. Springer, Heidelberg (2018). https://doi.org/10.1007/978-3-662-58387-6_11

42. Rindal, P., Rosulek, M.: Malicious-secure private set intersection via dual execution. In: Thuraisingham, B.M., Evans, D., Malkin, T., Xu, D. (eds.) ACM CCS 2017: 24th Conference on Computer and Communications Security, pp. 1229–1242. ACM Press, Dallas (2017)
43. Thyagarajan, S.A.K., Bhat, A., Malavolta, G., Döttling, N., Kate, A., Schröder, D.: Verifiable timed signatures made practical. In: ACM CCS 20: 27th Conference on Computer and Communications Security, pp. 1733–1750. ACM Press (2020)

Amortizing Rate-1 OT and Applications to PIR and PSI

Melissa Chase[1], Sanjam Garg[2,3], Mohammad Hajiabadi[4], Jialin Li[2], and Peihan Miao[5(✉)]

[1] Microsoft Research, Redmond, USA
melissac@microsoft.com
[2] University of California, Berkeley, USA
{sanjamg,j.li98}@berkeley.edu
[3] NTT Research, Sunnyvale, USA
[4] University of Waterloo, Waterloo, Canada
mdhajiabadi@uwaterloo.ca
[5] University of Illinois at Chicago, Chicago, USA
peihan@uic.edu

Abstract. Recent new constructions of rate-1 OT [Döttling, Garg, Ishai, Malavolta, Mour, and Ostrovsky, CRYPTO 2019] have brought this primitive under the spotlight and the techniques have led to new feasibility results for private-information retrieval, and homomorphic encryption for branching programs. The receiver communication of this construction consists of a quadratic (in the sender's input size) number of group elements for a single instance of rate-1 OT. Recently [Garg, Hajiabadi, Ostrovsky, TCC 2020] improved the receiver communication to a linear number of group elements for a single string-OT. However, most applications of rate-1 OT require executing it multiple times, resulting in large communication costs for the receiver.

In this work, we introduce a new technique for amortizing the cost of multiple rate-1 OTs. Specifically, based on standard pairing assumptions, we obtain a two-message rate-1 OT protocol for which the amortized cost per string-OT is asymptotically reduced to only four group elements. Our results lead to significant communication improvements in PSI and PIR, special cases of SFE for branching programs.

1. *PIR*: We obtain a rate-1 PIR scheme with client communication cost of $O(\lambda \cdot \log N)$ group elements for security parameter λ and database size N. Notably, after a one-time setup (or one PIR instance), any following PIR instance only requires communication cost $O(\log N)$ number of group elements.

2. *PSI with unbalanced inputs*: We apply our techniques to private set

---

S. Garg—supported in part by DARPA under Agreement No. HR00112020026, AFOSR Award FA9550-19-1-0200, NSF CNS Award 1936826, and research grants by the Sloan Foundation and Visa Inc.

M. Hajiabadi—supported in part by NSF CNS Award 2055358 and a 2020 DPI Science Team Seed Grant.

P. Miao—supported in part by NSF CNS Award 2055564.

K. Nissim and B. Waters (Eds.): TCC 2021, LNCS 13044, pp. 126–156, 2021.
https://doi.org/10.1007/978-3-030-90456-2_5

intersection with unbalanced set sizes (where the receiver has a smaller set) and achieve receiver communication of $O((m + \lambda) \log N)$ group elements where m, N are the sizes of the receiver and sender sets, respectively. Similarly, after a one-time setup (or one PSI instance), any following PSI instance only requires communication cost $O(m \cdot \log N)$ number of group elements. All previous sublinear-communication non-FHE based PSI protocols for the above unbalanced setting were also based on rate-1 OT, but incurred at least $O(\lambda^2 m \log N)$ group elements.

1   Introduction

Oblivious transfer (OT) [Rab05] is a foundational primitive in cryptography. In this work, we are interested in *two-message* OT protocols between: (i) a receiver with an input bit b who sends the first message otr of the protocol, and (ii) a sender with input two (equal length) strings m_0, m_1 who sends the second message ots. Correctness requires that at the end of execution, the receiver should learn m_b, while security requires that the receiver does not learn m_{1-b} and that the sender does not learn the bit b. Over the years, significant progress has been made in constructing two-message OT protocols, either from general assumptions [EGL82, GMW87], or from specific assumptions but with enhanced security/functionality/efficiency, such as OT based on DDH [NP01, AIR01, PVW08], CDH [DGH+20], factoring related [HK12] and LWE [PVW08].

Rate-1 OT. In this work, we are interested in constructing rate-1 two-message OT protocols. We say that an OT protocol is rate-1 if the ratio $\frac{|m_0|}{|ots|}$ approaches 1, as n grows. As shown by Ishai and Paskin [IP07], rate-1 OT enables powerful applications such as (i) semi-compact homomorphic encryption for branching programs (where the ciphertext grows only with the depth but not the size of the program) as well as (ii) communication-efficient private-information retrieval (PIR) protocols.

The rate-1 property is crucial in realizing these applications, allowing a sender to compress a large database for a receiver who is interested only in a small portion of it. To give some intuition, suppose we want to use a rate-1 OT to implement a 1-out-of-4 OT for a sender with four elements $\mathbf{m} := (m_{00}, m_{01}, m_{10}, m_{11})$. Thinking about the corresponding binary tree, the receiver on an input $uw \in \{0, 1\}^2$ will send two messages otr and otr', the first one for choice bit u and the second one for w. The sender will use otr' once against (m_{00}, m_{01}) and once against (m_{10}, m_{11}) to get two outgoing messages ots_0 and ots_1. The receiver is only interested in ots_u, but the sender does not know which one it is. So, the sender compresses (ots_0, ots_1) using otr, allowing the receiver to learn ots_u, and consequently m_{uw}.

The above construction employs a *self-eating* process, where a pair of ots messages is used as the sender input for the next OT, and so on. Employing a low rate 1-out-of-2 OT to build 1-out-of-n OT will blow up the communication, falling short for PIR. To see this, suppose $|ots| \geq 2|m_0|$, as is the case with most 1-out-of-2 OT protocols. Then, if $n = 2^k$, as the sender packs up the tree from bottom-up, in each OT invocation the size of the resulting ots message (which either packs two previous ots messages, or two leaf messages) doubles, resulting in a final message of size at least $O(2^k u)$, where u is the size of each initial individual message of the sender. While the protocol is a 1-out-of-n OT, it is not a sublinear PIR, because the size of the sender's protocol message is not sublinear in its total input size, nu. Moreover, as we will see later, in some applications involving branching programs, such as Private Set Intersection (PSI) with unbalanced set sizes, the sender will need to pack a tree of depth polynomial in the security parameter (as opposed to logarithmic size as in PIR), so using low rate 1-out-of-2 OT will result in an exponential size blow-up.

Building Rate-1 OT. Recent work of Döttling, Garg, Ishai, Malavolta, Mour, and Ostrovsky [DGI+19] provides a framework for constructing rate-1 OT based on a variety of assumptions such as DDH, QR, and LWE. This in turn led to PIR protocols with sender messages of only a logarithmic size dependence on the server size, and, more generally, branching-program protocols with sender messages whose size only grows with the depth of the program. In addition to these applications, the underlying techniques have been used in building collision-intractable hash functions and non-interactive zero-knowledge (NIZK) proofs [BKM20]. This has made the notion of rate-1 OT fundamental both from a theory and applications point of view.

How About the Receiver Communication? An overlooked aspect of rate-1 OT is the receiver communication cost. This is an important metric because, as stated above, the self eating process involve producing many otr messages (proportional to the depth of the tree/program), and hence sending a fresh otr for each depth results in large first-round messages. Concretely, in the DDH-based rate-1 OT construction of [DGI+19], for a sender with $(m_0 \in \{0,1\}^n, m_1 \in \{0,1\}^n)$, the receiver should send a linear $(O(n))$ number of group elements for each bit of the sender, resulting in overall $O(n^2)$ group elements. This incurs high receiver communication in the respective applications. Addressing this issue, Garg, Hajiabadi and Ostrovsky [GHO20] obtained rate-1 OT for which otr consists of only a linear $O(n)$ number of group elements in total, as opposed to $O(n^2)$.

One limitation of [GHO20] is that it only improves the communication efficiency of the base rate-1 OT, but still requires the receiver to send a fresh otr message for each new OT execution. This constitutes a prohibitive overhead for the receiver in applications in which the depth of the branching program is large, and the receiver needs to engage with a sender holding a branching program BP on many different inputs $x_1, \ldots, x_n$ (e.g., PSI). Addressing this communication bottleneck is the goal of our paper. We achieve this by introducing and realizing a new primitive that we call receiver-amortized (or amortized, for short) rate-1 OT.

1.1   Our Results

We put forth a cryptographic primitive that we call *amortized* rate-1 OT, and show how to realize it using standard assumptions on bilinear groups. As applications we obtain significant efficiency improvements, shaving a factor of $\mathsf{poly}(\lambda)$

off the receiver communication in various protocols involving secure branching program computation (e.g., unbalanced PSI).

An amortized rate-1 OT breaks up the computation of a receiver into an *offline* and *online* phase. The offline phase is performed by the receiver once and for all, prior to receiving any choice bits. Specifically, we have an algorithm $\mathsf{PreP}(1^\lambda)$, run by the receiver, which outputs a private state str for the receiver, and a reusable parameter prm. Next, we have an algorithm OT_1 run by the receiver on a choice bit b to obtain $\mathsf{otr} \overset{\$}{\leftarrow} \mathsf{OT}_1(\mathsf{str}, b)$. A sender with messages $\mathbf{m} := (m_0 \in \{0,1\}^n, m_1 \in \{0,1\}^n)$ runs $\mathsf{OT}_2((\mathsf{prm}, \mathsf{otr}), \mathbf{m})$ to obtain ots. Finally, the receiver can recover m_b by running $\mathsf{OT}_3(\mathsf{str}, \mathsf{ots})$. One notable aspect is that the state str used by OT_1 and OT_3 is the same as the initial state outputted by PreP—the state is not updated as a result of OT_1 executions. This property is in fact exploited in some of our applications, such as PSI cardinality. Also, the message prm is reused across all communications, so the receiver may send it only once. We require the following properties:

1. Sender rate-1 communication: $|\mathsf{ots}| = n + \mathsf{poly}(\lambda)$, where poly is a fixed polynomial (e.g., the size of a group element) independent of how large n is.
2. Receiver non-reusable compactness: $|\mathsf{otr}| = \mathsf{poly}'(\lambda)$, where $\mathsf{poly}'(\lambda)$ is independent of n.
3. Receiver privacy: We require indistinguishability security for the receiver against adaptive adversaries. If $(\mathsf{str}, \mathsf{prm}) \overset{\$}{\leftarrow} \mathsf{PreP}(1^\lambda)$, an adaptive adversary who is given prm and who sends many pairs of choice bits in an adaptive fashion cannot determine whether his received otr messages (all made relative to str) were built using the first choice bits or the second choice bits of his submitted pairs. Notice that since otr messages are all produced based on the same private state str, we should give the adversary the ability to submit many pairs.
4. Sender privacy: Standard indistinguishability security against honest receivers.[1]

Assuming an SXDH-hard bilinear map $\mathrm{e}\colon \mathbb{G}_1 \times \mathbb{G}_2 \mapsto \mathbb{G}_T$ on prime-order groups, we give a construction of amortized rate-1 OT in which prm consists of $O(n^2)$ group elements in $\mathbb{G}_1$ and otr consists of 4 group elements in $\mathbb{G}_2$. Recall that the SXDH assumption [BGdMM05] (Symmetric External Diffie-Hellman) states that both $\mathbb{G}_1$ and $\mathbb{G}_2$ are DDH hard. Our construction is based on a new re-randomization trick that allows us to obtain a structured matrix, as required for rate-1 OT, from a reusable initial matrix and a re-randomizing term involving four group elements.

The above reusable parameter prm is still quite large, even though it can be amortized among many OT executions. We show by relying on a stronger assumption on $\mathbb{G}_1$, called $2n$-power-DDH, we can make prm consist only of $O(n)$

---

[1] For applications involving non-oblivious branching programs we need to strengthen sender privacy, along the lines of [IP07]. For oblivious branching programs, from which all our applications are obtained, the stated requirement suffices.

group elements in $\mathbb{G}_1$. We achieve this by relying on a sliding window technique, introduced in [GHO20], that implicitly builds a Toeplitz matrix in the exponent using a linear number of group elements. The t-power DDH assumption says the distribution $(g, g^a, \ldots, g^{a^t})$ is pseudorandom.

Efficiency Gained. For performing t rate-1 OTs where the size of each message of the sender is n, our receiver communication consists of $O(n^2)$ reusable group elements in $\mathbb{G}_1$ and $4t$ group elements in $\mathbb{G}_2$, relying on SXDH. Assuming power DDH on $\mathbb{G}_1$ the receiver communication becomes $O(n)$ group elements in $\mathbb{G}_1$ and $4t$ group elements in $\mathbb{G}_2$. In comparison, the most receiver compact bilinear SXDH-based rate-1 OT, due to [DGI+19], involves sending $O(tn\sqrt{n})$ both in $\mathbb{G}_1$ and $\mathbb{G}_2$. As we will see in Sect. 1.2 in many applications of rate-1 OT, we have $t \gg \sqrt{n}$, allowing us to cut off large multiplicative polynomial factors from the receiver communication. We compare our receiver communication with prior rate-1 OT protocols in Table 1. We only include receiver communication, since the sender communication in all these protocols is the same (rate-1 for each instance of the OT).

Table 1. Receiver communication complexity for t executions of a rate-1 OT. Here n denotes the bit size of each message of the sender in the OT executions.

Work	Receiver reusable comm	Receiver non-reusable comm	Receiver total comm	Assumption
[DGI+19]	N/A	$O(tn^2)$ $\mathbb{G}$	$O(tn^2)$ $\mathbb{G}$	DDH
[DGI+19]	N/A	$O(tn\sqrt{n})$ $\mathbb{G}_1 + O(tn\sqrt{n})$ $\mathbb{G}_2$	$O(tn\sqrt{n})$ $\mathbb{G}_1 + O(tn\sqrt{n})$ $\mathbb{G}_2$	Bilinear SXDH
[GHO20]	N/A	$O(tn)$ $\mathbb{G}$	$O(tn)$ $\mathbb{G}$	Power-DDH
Ours	$O(n^2)$ $\mathbb{G}_1$	$O(t)$ $\mathbb{G}_2$	$O(n^2)$ $\mathbb{G}_1 + O(t)$ $\mathbb{G}_2$	Bilinear SXDH
Ours	$O(n)$ $\mathbb{G}_1$	$O(t)$ $\mathbb{G}_2$	$O(n)$ $\mathbb{G}_1 + O(t)$ $\mathbb{G}_2$	Bilinear Power DDH

1.2   Applications

Our results allow us to realize SFE for branching programs with significantly lower receiver communication. To illustrate our improvements, we first review the concept of branching programs. A deterministic κ-bit input branching program BP is a directed acyclic graph, where every leaf node has a label 0 or 1 (reject or accept), and every non-leaf node v has a label $\mathsf{lb}(v) \in \{1, \ldots, \kappa\}$. The root node is labeled with 1. Every non-leaf node has two outgoing edges labeled 0 and 1. An input $x \in \{0,1\}^\kappa$ induces a unique computation path from the root to a leaf node, where the computation from a node v will branch out to one of its two children depending on the value of x_i, where $i = \mathsf{lb}(v)$. We say $\mathsf{BP}(x) = b$ if the underlying computation path ends in a b-labeled leaf node. The size of a branching program is the number of nodes, and the depth, ℓ, is the length of the longest path. A branching program is *oblivious* if $\kappa = \ell$ and if all nodes at level i (where the root is considered level 1) are labeled i.[2]

---

[2] The standard definition of oblivious branching programs is more general than what we give here, but we stick to our own definition since it captures our application needs.

As an example, consider a client who wants to know whether her input $x \in \{0,1\}^\lambda$ is in the set $\mathsf{D} \subset \{0,1\}^\lambda$ of a server. This reduces to evaluating an oblivious branching program PSI on x where PSI is constructed as follows: for every string $a \in \{\epsilon\} \cup \{0,1\} \cup \cdots \{0,1\}^\lambda$ such that a is a prefix of a string in D, we put a node v_a in the graph. We designate v_ϵ as the root node, and all v_a such that $a \in \{0,1\}^\lambda$ as accept leaf nodes. The label of a node v_a for $|a| < \lambda$ is $\mathsf{lb}(v_a) = |a| + 1$. For a node v_a, for $|a| < \lambda$, and for $b \in \{0,1\}$, if a node v_{ab} exists, we put a b-labeled edge from v_a to v_{ab}; otherwise, we create a new reject leaf node and put a b-labeled edge from v_a to this node. The depth of PSI is λ and its size is $O(\lambda|\mathsf{D}|)$.

Now if a client wants to learn the intersection of her set $\mathsf{S} = \{x_1, \ldots, x_m\}$ with D, she needs to learn the values of all $\mathsf{PSI}(x_i)$ for $i \in [m]$, leading to m evaluations of PSI.

Shorter Client Communication for PSI. Ishai and Paskin [IP07] give a construction of SFE for branching programs from rate-1 OT, where, for an oblivious branching program BP of depth d, the receiver sends d otr messages, each prepared for a sender whose input messages are of size $O(d\lambda)$. Returning to the PSI problem for a client with set $\mathsf{S} = \{x_1, \ldots, x_m\}$ and a server with set D, we need to evaluate the oblivious branching program PSI m times. Recall that the depth of PSI is λ. Hence, setting $t = m\lambda$ and $n = \lambda^2$ in Table 1, our PSI-client communication consists of $O(m\lambda)$ non-reusable group elements in $\mathbb{G}_2$ (in either SXDH or power-DDH cases) and $O(\lambda^4)$ reusable group elements in $\mathbb{G}_1$ (in the case of SXDH), and $O(\lambda^2)$ reusable group elements in $\mathbb{G}_1$ (in the case of bilinear power DDH). In contrast, [DGI+19] results in $O(m\lambda^4)$ group elements in both $\mathbb{G}_1$ and $\mathbb{G}_2$. Thus, we drop a multiplicative factor of m by relying on the same SXDH assumption, and a factor of $m\lambda^2$ by relying on bilinear power DDH. The results of [GHO20] give $O(m\lambda^3)$ group elements for the receiver using (pairing-free) power DDH. This is again significantly larger than what we achieve.

In Sect. 7.3 we describe some PSI optimization techniques that further reduce the client communication, replacing a multiplicative factor of λ with $\log N$, where $N = |\mathsf{D}|$. These techniques may be of independent interest. We also give more applications, involving PSI/PIR, in Sect. 7.

SFE for Non-oblivious Branching Programs. Ishai and Paskin [IP07] show how to realize SFE for non-oblivious branching programs (in which at any given level the program might branch over several variables, not known to the receiver) by relying on a stronger sender privacy notion for the underlying rate-1 OT. Informally, the stronger property requires that a sender's response message should hide the previous protocol message of the receiver, even for the receiver herself. In Sect. 8 we show that simple variants of our amortized rate-1 OT satisfy the stronger sender security requirement, without affecting the efficiency parameters. All our applications are obtained based on oblivious branching programs, however.

We summarize our efficiency parameters for branching programs in Table 2. See Table 3 for a more detailed comparison.

Table 2. Bit-complexity for receiver communication, omitting $O(\cdot)$ notation. We assume $O(\lambda)$ is the bit size of a group element (in the case of pairings, for both source and target group elements). m denotes the number of branching programs executions. For (oblivious) branching programs (BP), h is the bit size of the output, κ is the bit size of receiver message and ℓ is the depth of the BP program.

Work	Assumption	Primitive	Recv Reuse Comm	Recv Non-Reuse Comm
Ours	Bilinear SXDH	Oblivious BP	$\lambda(h+\lambda\ell)^2$	$m\lambda\ell$
Ours	Bilinear Power DDH	Oblivious BP	$\lambda(h+\lambda\ell)$	$m\lambda\ell$
[GHO20]	Power DDH	Oblivious BP	N/A	$m\lambda\ell(h+\lambda\ell)$
[DGI+19]	Bilinear SXDH	Oblivious BP	N/A	$O(m\lambda\ell(h+\lambda\ell)^{3/2})$
[DGI+19]	DDH	Oblivious BP	N/A	$O(m\lambda\ell(h+\lambda\ell)^2)$
Ours	Bilinear SXDH	BP	$\lambda(h+\lambda\ell)^2$	$m\kappa\lambda\ell$
Ours	Bilinear Power DDH	BP	$\lambda(h+\lambda\ell)$	$m\kappa\lambda\ell$
[GHO20]	Power DDH	BP	N/A	$m\kappa\lambda\ell(h+\lambda\ell)$
[DGI+19]	Bilinear SXDH	BP	N/A	$O(m\lambda\ell\kappa(h+\lambda\ell)^{3/2})$
[DGI+19]	DDH	BP	N/A	$O(m\lambda\ell\kappa(h+\lambda\ell)^2)$

1.3   Comparison with Prior Work

The rate-1 OT constructions of [DGI+19] built upon ideas developed in the context of trapdoor functions (TDFs) [GH18, GGH19], identity-based encryption [CDG+17, DG17, BLSV18] and homomorphic secret sharing [BGI16]. The TDF techniques in turn led to notions such as hinting PRGs [KW19], which found extensive applications, e.g., [LQR+19, KMT19, HKW20, GVW20].

OT Extension. One might wonder about the difference between amortized rate-1 OT and OT extension [Bea96, IKNP03]. The primary goal of OT extension is to minimize the number of public-key operations: Performing $n := n(\lambda)$ OTs at the cost of doing a fewer, λ, number of OTs and some private key operations. On the other hand, we are concerned with amortizing receiver communication for rate-1 OT; doing t rate-1 OTs, but in a way that the receiver total communication is less than the sum of t individual rate-1 OT executions. OT extension techniques do not provide this feature. Moreover, OT extension techniques destroy the rate-1 property of the sender. For example, Beaver's protocol, which is round preserving, results in sender's OT protocol messages which are larger than $|m_0| + |m_1|$, where (m_0, m_1) is the sender's initial input pair. We leave it as open problem whether one can achieve some form of OT extension and amortized rate-1 OT at the same time.

PSI. Private set intersection (PSI) enables two parties, each holding a private set of elements, to compute the intersection of the two sets while revealing nothing. PSI and its variants have found many real-world applications including online advertising [IKN+20], password breach alert [TPY+19, APP, MIC], mobile private contact discovery [KRS+19], privacy-preserving contact tracing [TSS+20, CCF+20]. In the recent years, there has been tremendous progress made towards realizing PSI efficiently in various settings, including Diffie-Hellman-based [HFH99, IKN+20], RSA-based [ADT11], OT-extension-based [KKRT16,

PRTY19, PRTY20, CM20], FHE-based [CLR17], circuit-based [HEK12, PSSZ15, PSWW18, PSTY19], Vector-OLE-based [RS21] approaches.

Most of the existing approaches require the communication complexity to grow with the size of the *larger* set, the only exception being the FHE-based protocol [CLR17] (where communication grows linearly in the receiver set and logistically in the sender set) and RSA-based protocol [ADT11] (where the receiver has the bigger set and the communication grows linearly in the smaller, sender set). We consider the dual setting of [ADT11], meaning that in our case the receiver has the smaller set. In many real-world applications such as password breach alert [TPY+19, APP, MIC] and mobile private contact discovery [KRS+19], we need to perform *unbalanced* PSI between a constrained device (e.g. cellphone) holding a small set and a service provider holding a large set, thus having communication grow the larger set (especially the sender set) is a big concern. Our work presents unbalanced PSI with communication complexity linear in the size of the receiver set and logarithmic in the sender set. Furthermore, our approach is easily adapted to PSI with advanced functionalities such as PSI-Cardinality, PSI-Sum, PSI-Test, etc., which could only be achieved from Diffie-Hellman-based or circuit-based approaches. See Sect. 7 for more details.

2   Technical Overview

One tool used in our constructions (and in all recent rate-1 OT constructions) is a compressed version of n-bit packed ElGamal encryption. We review these compression features, formalized in [BBD+20], building on [BGI16]. A secret key is an n-bit tuple of exponents $\mathsf{sk} := (\rho_1, \ldots, \rho_n)$ and the public key is $\mathsf{pk} := (g, g^{\rho_1}, \ldots, g^{\rho_n})$. Given $\mathsf{pk} := (g, g_1, \ldots, g_n)$ we can encrypt an n-bit message $\mathsf{Enc}(m_1, \ldots, m_n)$ as $\mathsf{ct} : (g^r, g_1^{r+m_1}, \ldots, g_n^{r+m_n})$. We have two additional algorithms Shrink and ShrinkDec, where $\mathsf{Shrink}(\mathsf{ct})$ shrinks $\mathsf{ct} \in \mathbb{G}^{n+1}$ to obtain $\mathsf{Shrink}(\mathsf{ct}) \to (g', K, b_1, \ldots, b_n) \in \mathbb{G} \times \{0,1\}^{\lambda+n}$. We have shrinking correctness: $\Pr[\mathsf{ShrinkDec}(\mathsf{sk}, \mathsf{Shrink}(\mathsf{ct})) = (m_1, \ldots, m_n)] = 1$.

Approach of [DGI+19]. Let $\mathbb{G}$ be a group of prime order p with a generator g. We let $\boldsymbol{e}_i \in \mathbb{G}^{2n}$ denote a vector which has g in its ith position, and the identity element 1 everywhere else.

The receiver on a choice bit b samples $\mathsf{hk} \xleftarrow{\$} \mathbb{G}^{2n}$ and for every $i \in [n]$ samples $\rho_i \xleftarrow{\$} \mathbb{Z}_p$ and sets $\mathsf{ek}_i := \mathsf{hk}^{\rho_i} \cdot \boldsymbol{e}_{i+nb}$, where hk^{ρ_i} denotes entry-wise exponentiation, and $(\cdot)$ denotes entry-wise group multiplication. She sends $\mathsf{otr} := (\mathsf{hk}, \{\mathsf{ek}_i\})$ to the sender.

Let $\boldsymbol{m} = (m_0, m_1) \in \{0,1\}^{2n}$ be a vector concatenating the two strings of the sender. Let $g' := \boldsymbol{m} \cdot \mathsf{hk}$, and for $i \in [n]$ let $g_i' := \boldsymbol{m} \cdot \mathsf{ek}_i$, where we overload the $(\cdot)$ notation to define $(b_1, \ldots, b_{2n}) \cdot (g_1, \ldots, g_{2n}) = \prod g_i^{b_i}$. Letting $\mathsf{pk} := (g, g^{\rho_1}, \ldots, g^{\rho_n})$, we have $(g', g_1', \ldots, g_n') \in \mathsf{Enc}(\mathsf{pk}, m_b)$, where Enc denotes n-bit packed ElGamal. With this in mind, the sender sends $\mathsf{ots} = \mathsf{Shrink}(\mathsf{ct})$ to the receiver, and the receiver, who has $\mathsf{sk} := (\rho_1, \ldots, \rho_n)$ can recover m_b as $\mathsf{ShrinkDec}(\mathsf{sk}, \mathsf{ots})$. We have $\mathsf{ots} \in \mathbb{G} \times \{0,1\}^{\lambda+n}$, so the OT is sender rate-1.

In the above, each vector $\mathbf{ek}_i$ is a ρ_i exponentiation of $\mathbf{hk}$ but with a *bump* on its $(n+ib)$'s location: namely, we multiply its $(n+b)$'s location by g.

Our Techniques: SXDH. We now give a new technique based on pairings that allows us to produce many bumpy vectors $\mathbf{ek}_i$'s in the target group, using only 4 group elements and a reusable initial parameter in the source groups. The receiver samples $2n$ vectors $r_i \xleftarrow{\$} \mathbb{Z}_p^2$, and let $\mathbf{M}$ contain all these vectors in the exponent in $\mathbb{G}_1$, namely

$$\mathbf{M} := ([r_1]_1, \ldots, [r_n]_1 \mid [r_{n+1}]_1, \ldots, [r_{2n}]_1),$$

where $[r]_1 := g^r$. We similarly define $[r]_2 := h^r$ and $[r]_T := e(g,h)^r$.

Also, let

$$\nu_1 := ([p_1 r_1 + u]_1, [p_1 r_2]_1, \cdots, [p_1 r_n]_1 \mid [p_1 r_{n+1} + u]_1, [p_1 r_{n+2}]_1, \cdots, [p_1 r_{2n}]_1)$$

$$\vdots$$

$$\nu_n := ([p_n r_1]_1, [p_n r_2]_1, \cdots, [p_n r_n + u]_1 \mid [p_n r_{n+1}]_1, [p_n r_{n+2}]_1, \cdots, [p_n r_{2n} + u]_1),$$

The receiver sets $\mathsf{prm} := (\mathbf{M}, \nu_1, \ldots, \nu_n)$ and her private state as $\mathsf{str} := (u, p_1, \ldots, p_n)$.

Receiver's Non-reusable Messages. To send a short otr message for a choice bit b, the receiver samples two random vectors (v, w) s.t. $\langle v, u \rangle = 0$ and $\langle w, u \rangle = 1$. The receiver sends $\mathsf{otr} := ([f]_2, [h]_2)$, where $(f, h) = (w, v)$ if $b = 0$, and $(f, h) = (v, w)$ if $b = 1$.

Sender's Protocol Messages. Given $\mathsf{prm} := (\mathbf{M}, \nu_1, \ldots, \nu_n)$ and $\mathsf{otr} := ([f]_2, [h]_2)$, the sender uses the pairing to computes the inner product of f with all the vectors in the left-hand side of $\mathbf{M}, \nu_1, \ldots, \nu_n$, and the inner product of h with all the vectors in the right-hand side of the $\mathbf{M}, \nu_1, \ldots, \nu_n$. That is, using the notation above, letting $\alpha_j := \langle r_j, f \rangle$ if $j \in [n]$, and $\alpha_j := \langle r_j, h \rangle$ if $j \in \{n+1, \ldots, 2n\}$ the sender will compute

$$\mathbf{hk} := ([\alpha_1]_T \cdots, [\alpha_n]_T \mid [\alpha_{n+1}]_T \cdots, [\alpha_{2n}]_T)$$

$$\mathbf{EK} := \begin{bmatrix} [p_1\alpha_1 + 1]_T & \cdots & [p_1\alpha_n]_T & \mid & [p_1\alpha_{n+1}]_T & \cdots & [p_1\alpha_{2n}]_T \\ \vdots & \ddots & \vdots & \mid & \vdots & \ddots & \vdots \\ ([p_n\alpha_1]_T & \cdots & [p_n\alpha_n + 1]_T & \mid & [p_n\alpha_{n+1}]_T & \cdots & [p_n\alpha_{2n}]_T \end{bmatrix} \quad \text{if } b = 0$$

$$\mathbf{EK} := \begin{bmatrix} [p_1\alpha_1]_T & \cdots & [p_1\alpha_n]_T & \mid & [p_1\alpha_{n+1} + 1]_T & \cdots & [p_1\alpha_{2n}]_T \\ \vdots & \ddots & \vdots & \mid & \vdots & \ddots & \vdots \\ ([p_n\alpha_1]_T & \cdots & [p_n\alpha_n]_T & \mid & [p_n\alpha_{n+1}]_T & \cdots & [p_n\alpha_{2n} + 1]_T \end{bmatrix} \quad \text{if } b = 1$$

The sender has now built $(\mathbf{hk}, \mathbf{IK})$ that satisfies the bump structure explained in the first paragraph. Namely, think of the ith row of $\mathbf{EK}$ as $\mathbf{ek}_i$ in that paragraph. Moreover, the receiver knows all the underlying exponent values $\mathsf{sk} := (p_1, \ldots, p_n)$. Now the sender can perform the step explained in the first paragraph to send a rate-1 message ots, and the receiver will be able to use sk to decrypt it to obtain m_b.

Notice that the protocol has rate-1 sender communication, and that otr consist of only 4 group elements in $\mathbb{G}_2$.

To argue about receiver privacy, let us, for simplicity, argue that an adversary $\mathcal{A}$ cannot distinguish between a world in which otr always encrypts the bit 0 from a world in which otr encrypts 1; the proof for the case where the adversary can submits adaptively-chosen pairs of choice bits will be similar. We should show that $\mathcal{A}$ for a random pair $([\boldsymbol{f}]_2, [\boldsymbol{h}]_2)$ of vectors cannot tell which one is orthogonal to $\boldsymbol{u}$ and which one has inner product one. This should be argued in the presence of prm, known to $\mathcal{A}$. We will first remove the presence of $\boldsymbol{u}$ from prm, relying on DDH for $\mathbb{G}_1$. Let prm' be the same as prm but with $\boldsymbol{u}$ removed. By DDH, $(\boldsymbol{u}, \mathsf{prm}) \overset{c}{\equiv} (\boldsymbol{u}, \mathsf{prm}')$. If we want to replace prm with prm' for $\mathcal{A}$, we should be able to reply to $\mathcal{A}$'s subsequent OT_1 queries. The reason this can be done is because OT_1 responses are produced based on only $\boldsymbol{u}$ and the underlying choice bit, and $\boldsymbol{u}$ is included in both distributions. Thus, we can remove $\boldsymbol{u}$ from the prm view of $\mathcal{A}$. Once this is done, we will then show that the entire otr view of $\mathcal{A}$ can be simulated by knowing a pair of vectors $(\boldsymbol{v}, \boldsymbol{w})$ where $\boldsymbol{v}$ is orthogonal to $\boldsymbol{u}$ and $\boldsymbol{w}$ has inner product one with $\boldsymbol{u}$. In particular, to sample from $\mathsf{OT}_1(\mathsf{str}, b)$, we return $(k_1\boldsymbol{v} + (1-b)\boldsymbol{w}, k_2\boldsymbol{v} + b\boldsymbol{w})$, where k_1 and k_2 are random exponents. Next we show that the distribution of $(\boldsymbol{v}, \boldsymbol{w})$ is identical to uniformly random vectors. This can be argued because information about $\boldsymbol{u}$ has been already removed from prm. Finally, we rely on DDH for $\mathbb{G}_2$ to show that by using a random $(\boldsymbol{v}, \boldsymbol{w})$ in the above simulation, the entire otr view of $\mathcal{A}$ will be pseudorandom, masking the value of the choice bit b.

Our Techniques: Bilinear Power DDH. We sketch how to adapt our cancellation technique to a sliding window setting, developed in [GHO20], to reduce the size of prm into a linear number of group elements. The receiver samples a random exponent a and a vector $\boldsymbol{r} \overset{\$}{\leftarrow} \mathbb{Z}_p^2$ and sets

$$\mathbf{M} := \left([a\boldsymbol{r}]_1, [a^2\boldsymbol{r}]_1, \cdots, [a^{2n}\boldsymbol{r}]_1\right)$$

$$\boldsymbol{w} := ([ka\boldsymbol{r}]_1, \cdots, [ka^{n-1}\boldsymbol{r}]_1, [ka^n\boldsymbol{r} + u]_1, [ka^{n+1}\boldsymbol{r}]_1, \cdots, [ka^{2n-1}\boldsymbol{r}]_1,$$
$$[ka^{2n}\boldsymbol{r} + u]_1, [ka^{2n+1}\boldsymbol{r}]_1, \cdots, [ka^{3n-1}\boldsymbol{r}]_1),$$

where k is a random exponent. The receiver sets $\mathsf{prm} := (\mathbf{M}, \boldsymbol{w})$.

The receiver samples a non-reusable message $\mathsf{otr} = ([\boldsymbol{f}]_2, [\boldsymbol{h}]_2)$ for a choice bit b exactly as in the SXDH case—by sampling it based on $\boldsymbol{u}$ and b.

A sender given $(\mathsf{prm}, \mathsf{otr})$ builds n vectors $\boldsymbol{\nu}_1, \ldots, \boldsymbol{\nu}_n$ as follows. For $i \in [n]$ let $\boldsymbol{\nu}_i = \boldsymbol{w}[n+1-i, 3n-i]$, where $\boldsymbol{w}[i, j]$ denotes the elements in positions i all the way up to j. Once the vectors $\boldsymbol{\nu}_1, \ldots, \boldsymbol{\nu}_n$ are formed, the sender will proceed exactly like the SXDH case. Correctness will then follow. The proof of receiver privacy follow similarly to the SXDH case, but we should replace DDH with power DDH in the appropriate places. We omit the details.

3   Preliminaries and Definitions

We use λ for the security parameter. We use $\overset{c}{\equiv}$ and $\overset{s}{\equiv}$ for computational and statistical indistinguishability, respectively. We let $\equiv$ denote that two distributions are identical. For a distribution $\mathbf{S}$ we use $x \overset{\$}{\leftarrow} \mathbf{S}$ to mean x is sampled according to $\mathbf{S}$ and use $y \in \mathbf{S}$ to mean $y \in \sup(\mathbf{S})$, where sup denotes the support of a distribution. For a set S we overload the notation to use $x \overset{\$}{\leftarrow} \mathsf{S}$ to indicate that x is chosen uniformly at random from S. If $\mathsf{A}(x_1, \ldots, x_n)$ is a randomized algorithm, then $\mathsf{A}(a_1, \ldots, a_n)$, for deterministic inputs $a_1, \ldots, a_n$, denotes the random variable obtained by sampling random coins r uniformly at random and returning $\mathsf{A}(a_1, \ldots, a_n; r)$. We use $[n] := \{1, \ldots, n\}$ and $[i, i+s] := \{i, i+1, \ldots, i+s\}$. For a vector $\boldsymbol{v} = (v_1, \ldots, v_n)$ we define $\boldsymbol{v}[i, i+s] := (v_i, v_{i+1}, \ldots, v_{i+s})$.

Definition 1 (Pairings and SXDH hardness). *A bilinear map is given by* $(\mathsf{e}, \mathbb{G}_1, \mathbb{G}_2, \mathbb{G}_T, p, g, h) \overset{\$}{\leftarrow} \mathsf{G}(1^\lambda)$, *where p is a prime number and is the order of* $\mathbb{G}_1$, $\mathbb{G}_2$ *and* $\mathbb{G}_T$, *and g and h are random generators of* $\mathbb{G}_1$ *and* $\mathbb{G}_2$, *respectively. The function e is a non-degenerate map, satisfying* $\mathsf{e}(g^a, h^b) = \mathsf{e}(g, h)^{ab}$ *for all exponents a and b. The Symmetric External Diffie-Hellman (SXDH) assumption [BGdMM05] says* $\mathbb{G}_1$ *and* $\mathbb{G}_2$, *sampled as above, are DDH-hard.*

Computing Inner Product in the Exponent. Given $\boldsymbol{g} := (g_1, \ldots, g_k) \in \mathbb{G}_1^k$ and $\boldsymbol{h} := (h_1, \ldots, h_k) \in \mathbb{G}_2^k$ we define $\mathsf{e}(\boldsymbol{g}, \boldsymbol{h}) := \prod_{i \in [k]} \mathsf{e}(g_i, h_i)$.

Inner Product with Integer Vectors. Given $\boldsymbol{b} := (b_1, \ldots, b_k) \in \mathbb{Z}_p^k$ and $\boldsymbol{g} := (g_1, \ldots, g_k) \in \mathbb{G}_1^k$, we define $\boldsymbol{b} \cdot \boldsymbol{g} := \prod_{i \in [k]} g_i^{b_i}$.

3.1   Amortized Rate-1 OT: Definition

We define our new notion of amortized rate-1 OT, which allows a receiver to reuse part of her protocol message across many independent OT executions. In the definition below, think of n as the maximum size of each input message of a sender. The receiver will generate a reusable parameter prm, based on n, which will allow her later to send a short protocol message otr whenever she wants to perform a new OT. The sender will use (prm, otr) to complete an OT transfer for any pair of messages ($m_0 \in \{0, 1\}^{n_1}, m_1 \in \{0, 1\}^{n_1}$), as long as $n_1 \leq n$.

Definition 2 (Amortized Rate-1 OT). *Let $n := n(\lambda)$ be a polynomial. An amortized rate-1 OT* $\mathsf{OT} := (\mathsf{PreP}, \mathsf{OT}_1, \mathsf{OT}_2, \mathsf{OT}_3)$ *is defined as follows.*

- $\mathsf{PreP}(1^\lambda, n) \to (\mathsf{str}, \mathsf{prm})$: *Takes as input a security parameter 1^λ and n, denoting the maximum length of each of the sender's messages, and outputs a private state str and a reusable message prm.*

- $OT_1(str, b) \rightarrow otr$: *Takes as input a security parameter 1^λ and a choice bit $b \in \{0,1\}$, and outputs a a protocol message otr. We refer to otr as a fresh receiver's message, to distinguish it from the reusable message prm.*
- $OT_2((prm, otr), (m_0, m_1)) \rightarrow ots$: *Takes as input a reusable message prm, a fresh message otr and a pair of messages $(m_0, m_1) \in \{0,1\}^{n_1} \times \{0,1\}^{n_1}$, for some $n_1 \leq n$, and outputs ots.*
- $OT_3(str, ots) \rightarrow m$: *Takes as input a private state str and ots and outputs $m \in \{0,1\}^n$.*

We require

- **Correctness:** *For any polynomial $n := n(\lambda)$, $b \in \{0,1\}$, $n_1 \leq n$ and $(m_0, m_1) \in \{0,1\}^{n_1} \times \{0,1\}^{n_1}$, $\Pr[OT_3(str, ots) = m_b] = 1$, where $(str, prm) \xleftarrow{\$} PreP(1^\lambda, n)$, $otr \xleftarrow{\$} OT_1(str, b)$ and $ots \xleftarrow{\$} OT_2((prm, otr), (m_0, m_1))$.*
- **Rate-1 sender communication:** *There exists a fixed polynomial poly such that for all n and $n_1 \leq n$, $|ots| = n_1 + poly(\lambda)$, where ots is formed as above.*
- **Receiver amortized compactness:** *The length of otr is independent of n. There exists a fixed polynomial poly' such that for all polynomials $n := n(\lambda)$, $|otr| = poly'(\lambda)$, where otr is formed as above.*
- **Receiver privacy:** *An adaptive sender cannot determine the choice bits of a receiver. Any PPT adversary $\mathcal{A}$ has at most $1/2 + negl(\lambda)$ advantage in the following game. The challenger samples $b \xleftarrow{\$} \{0,1\}$ and $(str, prm) \xleftarrow{\$} PreP(1^n, \lambda)$ and gives prm to $\mathcal{A}$. Then, $\mathcal{A}$ adaptively submits queries $(s_0, s_1) \in \{0,1\}^2$, and receives $OT_1(str, s_b)$. $\mathcal{A}$ has to guess the value of b.*

Sender Privacy? Notice that Definition 2 does not impose any sender security requirements. The reason for this is that sender security can be generically realized for rate-1 OT using known techniques [BGI+17], as sketched below. Let poly be the polynomial defined in the rate-1 sender property of Definition 2. The new sender on a pair of messages $(m_0, m_1) \in \{0,1\}^n \times \{0,1\}^n$ samples two seeds (r_0, r_1) whose length is sufficiently larger than $poly(\lambda)$ but independent of n. The sender sends (ots_1', ots_2') to the receiver, where $ots_1' \xleftarrow{\$} OT_2((r_0, r_1), (prm, otr))$ and $ots_2' \xleftarrow{\$} OT_2((ct_0, ct_1), (prm, otr))$, where $ct_0 := PRG(Ext(r_0)) \oplus m_0$ and $ct_1 := PRG(Ext(r_1)) \oplus m_1$, and Ext is a randomness extractor. The protocol is still sender rate-1. It now provides computational sender privacy against honest receivers: This is because given ots_1' the value of $Ext(r_{1-b})$ is statistically close to uniform, where b is the receiver's choice bit.

Finally, we mention that we may modify our constructions so that they achieve sender privacy for free, without using the above generic randomness extraction method.

4   Amortized Rate-1 OT from SXDH

Our amortized rate-1 OT protocol makes use of a shrinking algorithm, that allows one to shrink ciphertexts of ElGamal encryption, as long as the underlying plaintexts are coming from a small space, say, $\{0,1\}$. An n-bit packed

ElGamal encryption has a secret key $\mathsf{sk} := (x_1, \ldots, x_n)$ and a public key $\mathsf{pk} := (g, g^{x_1}, \ldots, g^{x_n})$. Given $\mathsf{pk} := (g, g_1, \ldots, g_n)$ we can encrypt an n-bit message $\mathsf{Enc}(m_1, \ldots, m_n)$ as $\mathsf{ct} : (g^r, g_1^{r+m_1}, \ldots, g_n^{r+m_n})$. We have a shrinking procedure for n-bit ElGamal encryption that will shrink a ciphertext into one group element plus n bits, while allowing for efficient decryption. The procedure below, presented in [BBD+20], enables perfect decryption correctness, improving upon the previous procedures [BGI16, DGI+19] that had a decryption error.

Lemma 1 ([BBD+20]). *There exists a pair of (expected) PPT algorithms* (Shrink, ShrinkDec) *such that if* $(\mathsf{pk}, \mathsf{sk})$ *is as above and* $\mathsf{ct} \xleftarrow{\$} \mathsf{Enc}(\mathsf{pk}, \mathbf{m})$ *is a packed ElGamal ciphertext encrypting a message* $\mathbf{m} \in \{0, 1\}^n$,

(1) $\mathsf{Shrink}(\mathsf{ct}) \to (g', K, b_1, \ldots, b_n) \in \mathbb{G} \times \{0, 1\}^{\lambda + n}$.
(2) $\Pr[\mathsf{ShrinkDec}(\mathsf{sk}, \mathsf{Shrink}(\mathsf{ct})) = \mathbf{m}] = 1$.

Our amortized rate-1 OT makes us of the following procedure OrthSam that given a vector $\boldsymbol{u} \in \mathbb{Z}_p^2$ and a bit $b \in \{0, 1\}$, samples two random vectors $\boldsymbol{v}$ and $\boldsymbol{w}$ such that $\langle \boldsymbol{u}, \boldsymbol{v} \rangle = 0$ and $\langle \boldsymbol{u}, \boldsymbol{w} \rangle = 1$, and it outputs these two vectors in a shuffled order based on the value of b.

Definition 3. *The algorithm* $\mathsf{OrthSam}(\boldsymbol{u} \in \mathbb{Z}_p^2, b \in \{0, 1\})$ *works as follows. It Samples random vectors* $\boldsymbol{w}, \boldsymbol{v}$ *such that* $\langle \boldsymbol{w}, \boldsymbol{u} \rangle = 1$ *and* $\langle \boldsymbol{v}, \boldsymbol{u} \rangle = 0$, *and returns* $(\boldsymbol{f}, \boldsymbol{h}) \in \mathbb{Z}_p^4$, *where*

$$(\boldsymbol{f}, \boldsymbol{h}) = \begin{cases} (\boldsymbol{w}, \boldsymbol{v}) & b = 0 \\ (\boldsymbol{v}, \boldsymbol{w}) & b = 1 \end{cases}$$

4.1 Our Construction

We now present our construction. For notational clarity, we assume the size of each message of the sender is exactly n, as opposed to an arbitrary value $n_1 \leq n$. Adapting the construction to work with respect to varying lengths for the sender messages will be immediate.

Construction 1 (Amortized rate-1 OT: SXDH). *Build* $\mathsf{OT} := (\mathsf{PreP}, \mathsf{OT}_1, \mathsf{OT}_2, \mathsf{OT}_3)$ *as follows.*

– $\mathsf{PreP}(1^\lambda, n)$: *Sample* $\mathsf{pp} := (e, \mathbb{G}_1, \mathbb{G}_2, \mathbb{G}_T, p, g, h) \xleftarrow{\$} \mathsf{G}(1^\lambda)$. *Then*
   1. *For* $i \in [2n]$, *sample* $\boldsymbol{r}_i \xleftarrow{\$} \mathbb{Z}_p^2$. *Let*

$$\mathbf{M} := [g^{\boldsymbol{r}_1}, g^{\boldsymbol{r}_2}, \cdots, g^{\boldsymbol{r}_n} \mid g^{\boldsymbol{r}_{n+1}}, g^{\boldsymbol{r}_{n+2}}, \cdots, g^{\boldsymbol{r}_{2n}}].$$

   2. *Sample* $\boldsymbol{u} \xleftarrow{\$} \mathbb{Z}_p^2$ *and for* $i \in [n]$ *sample a random exponent* $p_i \xleftarrow{\$} [p]$. *Let* $\mathbf{D} := (\boldsymbol{\nu}_1, \ldots, \boldsymbol{\nu}_n)$, *where*

$$\boldsymbol{\nu}_1 := [g^{p_1 \boldsymbol{r}_1 + u}, g^{p_1 \boldsymbol{r}_2}, \cdots, g^{p_1 \boldsymbol{r}_n} \mid g^{p_1 \boldsymbol{r}_{n+1} + u}, g^{p_1 \boldsymbol{r}_{n+2}}, \cdots, g^{p_1 \boldsymbol{r}_{2n}}]$$

$$\vdots \tag{1}$$

$$\boldsymbol{\nu}_n := [g^{p_n \boldsymbol{r}_1}, g^{p_n \boldsymbol{r}_2}, \cdots, g^{p_n \boldsymbol{r}_n + u} \mid g^{p_n \boldsymbol{r}_{n+1}}, g^{p_n \boldsymbol{r}_{n+2}}, \cdots, g^{p_n \boldsymbol{r}_{2n} + u}],$$

3. Return private state str $:= (\boldsymbol{u}, p_1, \ldots, p_n)$ *and reusable message* prm $:=$ (pp, $\mathbf{M}, \boldsymbol{\nu}_1, \ldots, \boldsymbol{\nu}_n$).

- OT$_1$(str, $b \in \{0,1\}$): *Parse* str *and all its inside variables as above. Sample* $(\boldsymbol{f}, \boldsymbol{h}) \xleftarrow{\$} \mathsf{OrthSam}(\boldsymbol{u}, b)$ *(Definition 3). Return return* otr $:= (h^f, h^h) \in \mathbb{G}_2^4$.
- OT$_2$((prm, otr), $(m_0, m_1)) \in \{0,1\}^n \times \{0,1\}^n)$: *Parse* prm $:= $ (pp, $\mathbf{M}, \boldsymbol{\nu}_1, \ldots, \boldsymbol{\nu}_n$), otr $:= (\boldsymbol{\chi}_1, \boldsymbol{\chi}_2) \in \mathbb{G}_2^4$, $\mathbf{M} := (\boldsymbol{m}_1, \ldots, \boldsymbol{m}_{2n})$ *and* $\boldsymbol{\nu}_i := (\nu_{i,1}, \ldots, \nu_{i,2n})$ *for* $i \in [n]$. *Let*

$$\boldsymbol{hk} := (\mathsf{e}(\boldsymbol{\chi}_1, \boldsymbol{m}_1), \ldots \mathsf{e}(\boldsymbol{\chi}_1, \boldsymbol{m}_n) \mid \mathsf{e}(\boldsymbol{\chi}_2, \boldsymbol{m}_{n+1}), \ldots \mathsf{e}(\boldsymbol{\chi}_2, \boldsymbol{m}_{2n}))$$

$$\mathbf{IK} := \begin{bmatrix} \mathsf{e}(\boldsymbol{\chi}_1, \nu_{1,1}) \cdots \mathsf{e}(\boldsymbol{\chi}_1, \nu_{1,n}) & \mathsf{e}(\boldsymbol{\chi}_2, \nu_{1,n+1}) \cdots \mathsf{e}(\boldsymbol{\chi}_2, \nu_{1,2n}) \\ \vdots \quad \ddots \quad \vdots & \vdots \quad \ddots \quad \vdots \\ \mathsf{e}(\boldsymbol{\chi}_1, \nu_{n,1}) \cdots \mathsf{e}(\boldsymbol{\chi}_1, \nu_{n,n}) & \mathsf{e}(\boldsymbol{\chi}_2, \nu_{n,n+1}) \cdots \mathsf{e}(\boldsymbol{\chi}_2, \nu_{n,2n}) \end{bmatrix}.$$

Let $\boldsymbol{m} := (m_0, m_1) \in \{0,1\}^{2n}$. *Let* $\boldsymbol{y}_j \in \mathbb{G}_T^{2n}$ *be the jth row of* $\mathbf{IK}$. *The sender then sends*

$$\mathsf{ots} := \mathsf{Shrink}(\boldsymbol{m} \cdot \boldsymbol{hk}, \boldsymbol{m} \cdot \boldsymbol{y}_1, \ldots, \boldsymbol{m} \cdot \boldsymbol{y}_n) \in \mathbb{G}_T \times \{0,1\}^{n+\lambda}.$$

- OT$_3$(str, ots): *Parse* str $:= (\boldsymbol{u}, p_1, \ldots, p_n)$ *and set* sk $:= (p_1, \ldots, p_n)$. *Return* $m' := \mathsf{ShrinkDec}(\mathsf{sk}, \mathsf{ots})$.

Correctness. We prove $m' = m_b$, where, following the notation of Construction 1, m' is the string output by OT$_3$, and (m_0, m_1) are the input strings to OT$_2$ and b is the choice bit for OT$_1$.

Let $\boldsymbol{f}, \boldsymbol{h}$ and $\boldsymbol{r}_1, \ldots, \boldsymbol{r}_{2n}$ be as in Construction 1. Let $\alpha_j := \langle \boldsymbol{r}_j, \boldsymbol{f} \rangle$ if $j \in [n]$, and $\alpha_j := \langle \boldsymbol{r}_j, \boldsymbol{h} \rangle$ if $j \in \{n+1, \ldots, 2n\}$. Letting $\boldsymbol{hk}$ and $\mathbf{IK}$ be as in Construction 1, we have

$$\boldsymbol{hk} := [\mathsf{e}(g, h)^{\alpha_1} \cdots, \mathsf{e}(g, h)^{\alpha_n} \mid \mathsf{e}(g, h)^{\alpha_{n+1}} \cdots, \mathsf{e}(g, h)^{\alpha_{2n}}] \in \mathbb{G}_T^{2n}$$

$$\mathbf{IK} := \begin{bmatrix} \mathsf{e}(g, h)^{p_1\alpha_1} \cdot \mathsf{e}(g, h) \cdots & \mathsf{e}(g, h)^{p_1\alpha_n} & \mathsf{e}(g, h)^{p_1\alpha_{n+1}} \cdots \mathsf{e}(g, h)^{p_1\alpha_{2n}} \\ \vdots \quad \ddots \quad \vdots & & \vdots \quad \ddots \quad \vdots \\ \mathsf{e}(g, h)^{p_n\alpha_1} & \cdots \mathsf{e}(g, h)^{p_n\alpha_n} \cdot \mathsf{e}(g, h) & \mathsf{e}(g, h)^{p_n\alpha_{n+1}} \cdots \mathsf{e}(g, h)^{p_n\alpha_{2n}} \end{bmatrix} \in \mathbb{G}_T^{n \times 2n} \text{ if } b = 0$$

$$\mathbf{IK} := \begin{bmatrix} \mathsf{e}(g, h)^{p_1\alpha_1} \cdots \mathsf{e}(g, h)^{p_1\alpha_n} & \mathsf{e}(g, h)^{p_1\alpha_{n+1}} \cdot \mathsf{e}(g, h) \cdots & \mathsf{e}(g, h)^{p_1\alpha_{2n}} \\ \vdots \quad \ddots \quad \vdots & \vdots \quad \ddots \quad \vdots \\ \mathsf{e}(g, h)^{p_n\alpha_1} \cdots \mathsf{e}(g, h)^{p_n\alpha_n} & \mathsf{e}(g, h)^{p_n\alpha_{n+1}} \quad \cdots \mathsf{e}(g, h)^{p_n\alpha_{2n}} \cdot \mathsf{e}(g, h) \end{bmatrix} \in \mathbb{G}_T^{n \times 2n} \text{ if } b = 1.$$

Thus, $(\boldsymbol{m} \cdot \boldsymbol{hk}, \boldsymbol{m} \cdot \boldsymbol{y}_1, \ldots, \boldsymbol{m} \cdot \boldsymbol{y}_n) \in \mathsf{Enc}(\mathsf{pk}, (m_b[1], \ldots, m_b[n]))$, where $\boldsymbol{m} = (m_0, m_1)$, $\boldsymbol{y}_j$ is the jth row of $\mathbf{IK}$, pk $:= (\mathsf{e}(g, h), \mathsf{e}(g, h)^{p_1}, \ldots, \mathsf{e}(g, h)^{p_n})$ and Enc is the packed ElGamal encryption algorithm as in Lemma 1. By Lemma 1, $m' = m_b$, as desired.

Rate-1 Sender Communication and Receiver Amortized Compactness. We have $|\mathsf{ots}| = n + \lambda + |g| = n + \mathsf{poly}(\lambda)$ and $|\mathsf{otr}| = 4|h|$.

4.2 Receiver Privacy

In the following we say a vector f is non-orthogonal to u if $\langle f, u \rangle = 1$. This is an abuse of terminology (because non-orthogonality refers to any non-zero inner product), but we stick to it below.

To prove receiver OT security, we should argue that a fresh receiver protocol message otr does not reveal the receiver's underlying choice bit. The main difficulty is that all otr values depend on the vector u.

The core of our argument is in showing that the vector u remains hidden in the following sense. Given a sequence of (g^{f_i}, g^{h_i}), an adversary cannot determine the order of orthogonality/non-orthogonality in any given pair, with respect to g^u. To this end, we will first remove u from all vectors $D := (\nu_1, \ldots, \nu_n)$, given in Eq. 1. Once u is removed from the reusable message prm, we will then show any receiver's future fresh message otr may be simulated by the underlying choice bit b and a pair of vectors (v, w) which are orthogonal/non-orthogonal to u, in a way that if the joint distribution of (v, w) is pseudorandom, then the entire simulated view will be pseudorandom as well, masking the choice bits. We will then show that the distribution of a random (v, w) subject to them being orthogonal/non-orthogonal to a random u is uniformly random. Taken all together, receiver security will follow.

Definition 4 (Distribution Dual). *For $u \in \mathbb{Z}_p^2$ the distribution* **Dual**(u) *returns (v, w), where v and w are sampled uniformly subject to $\langle v, u \rangle = 0$ and $\langle w, u \rangle = 1$.*

We now describe a way of simulating messages otr, for a given choice bit b, without knowing u, but by knowing a pair (v, w) sampled according to **Dual**(u).

Definition 5 (Simulator Sim). *The algorithm* Sim(v, w, b) *samples $k, k' \overset{\$}{\leftarrow} \mathbb{Z}_p$, and returns $(h^{kv+(1-b)w}, h^{k'v+bw})$.*

Hybrid Hyb$_1$: Real game. Sample $(\mathsf{str}, \mathsf{prm}) \overset{\$}{\leftarrow} \mathsf{PreP}(1^\lambda, 1^n)$, a challenge bit $b \overset{\$}{\leftarrow} \{0, 1\}$, and give prm to the adversary. Parse $\mathsf{str} := (u, p_1, \ldots, p_n)$. Reply to an adversary's query $(s_0, s_1) \in \{0, 1\}^2$ with $\mathsf{OT}_1(\mathsf{str}, s_b)$. The view of the adversary for otr messages can be produced just by knowing u, as opposed to $\mathsf{str} := (u, p_1, \ldots, p_n)$. In particular, the values $p_1, \ldots, p_n$ do not participate in producing the output of $\mathsf{OT}_1(\mathsf{str}, s_b)$, and are only used in OT_3, which is immaterial to the adversary's view.

Hybrid Hyb$_2$: Replace $D = (\nu_1, \ldots, \nu_n)$, Eq. 1, with uniformly random vectors of group elements. Thus, information about u will be removed from D, and hence from prm.

Hybrid Hyb$_3$: Same as Hybrid Hyb$_2$, except we sample $(v, w) \overset{\$}{\leftarrow}$ **Dual**(u), and reply to any adversary's query (s_0, s_1) as Sim(v, w, s_b). The whole view is produced by knowing only (v, w).

Hybrid Hyb$_4$: Same as Hyb$_3$, except we sample $(v, w) \overset{\$}{\leftarrow} \mathbb{Z}_p^4$.

Hybrid Hyb$_5$: Same as Hyb$_4$, except we reply to any adversary's query (s_0, s_1) with a uniformly random vector sampled from $\mathbb{G}_2^4$. This hybrid perfectly hides the value of the challenge bit b.

We will now show that any two adjacent hybrids produce computationally indistinguishable views.

Lemma 2 (Hyb$_1$ $\overset{c}{\equiv}$ Hyb$_2$). *Assuming DDH hardness of $\mathbb{G}_1$, $(\boldsymbol{u}, \mathbf{D}) \overset{c}{\equiv} (\boldsymbol{u}, \mathbf{D}')$, where $\boldsymbol{u}$ and $\mathbf{D}$ are as in Eq. 1, and $\mathbf{D}'$ is a uniformly random matrix of group elements.*

Proof. By DDH hardness of $\mathbb{G}_1$, $(\boldsymbol{u}, \mathbf{D}) \overset{c}{\equiv} (\boldsymbol{u}, \mathbf{D}')$. The views in Hybrid Hyb$_1$ and Hyb$_2$ can be produced just by knowing $(\boldsymbol{u}, \mathbf{D})$ and $(\boldsymbol{u}, \mathbf{D}')$, respectively. (See the explanation given in Hybrid Hyb$_1$ on why the view can be simulated just by knowing $(\boldsymbol{u}, \mathbf{D})$.) Thus, Hyb$_1$ $\overset{c}{\equiv}$ Hyb$_2$.

Lemma 3. Hyb$_2$ $\overset{s}{\equiv}$ Hyb$_3$.

Proof. Let $\boldsymbol{v}$ and $\boldsymbol{w}$ be as in Hyb$_3$, namely $(\boldsymbol{v}, \boldsymbol{w}) \overset{\$}{\leftarrow} \mathbf{Dual}(\boldsymbol{u})$. We show that for any choice bit $z \in \{0, 1\}$, the output of $\mathsf{Sim}(\boldsymbol{v}, \boldsymbol{w}, z)$ is statistically close to $(h^{\boldsymbol{f}}, h^{\boldsymbol{h}})$, where $(\boldsymbol{f}, \boldsymbol{h}) \overset{\$}{\leftarrow} \mathsf{OrthSam}(\boldsymbol{u}, z)$.

Let S_0 be the set of all vectors whose inner product with $\boldsymbol{u}$ is one, and S_1 be the set of all vectors orthogonal to $\boldsymbol{u}$. The vectors $\boldsymbol{f}$ and $\boldsymbol{h}$ are uniformly distributed over S_z and S_{1-z}, respectively. Also, recall that the output of $\mathsf{Sim}(\boldsymbol{v}, \boldsymbol{w}, z)$ is as $(h^{k\boldsymbol{v}+(1-z)\boldsymbol{w}}, h^{k'\boldsymbol{v}+z\boldsymbol{w}})$, where $k, k' \overset{\$}{\leftarrow} \mathbb{Z}_p$. In what follows, we show $(r\boldsymbol{v}, r'\boldsymbol{v} + \boldsymbol{w})$ for random r and r' is statistically close the uniform distribution over (S_0, S_1), and this will complete the proof.

Notice that S_1 is a subspace and has dimension one; i.e., any basis of it has only one vector. Letting $\boldsymbol{v} := (v_1, v_2)$ assume $v_1 \neq 0$ and $v_2 \neq 0$. (The probability that either is zero is negligible, so we may ignore it.) Since $v_1 \neq 0$ and $v_2 \neq 0$, if $r \overset{\$}{\leftarrow} \mathbb{Z}_p$, then $r\boldsymbol{v}$ is uniformly random in S_1.

Next, note that $S_0 = \boldsymbol{w} + S_1$; i.e., for any $\boldsymbol{m}' \in S_0$, there exists $\boldsymbol{m} \in S_1$ s.t. $\boldsymbol{m}' = \boldsymbol{w} + \boldsymbol{m}$. Since $\boldsymbol{v}$ spans S_1, the vector $r'\boldsymbol{v} + \boldsymbol{w}$ for a random $r' \overset{\$}{\leftarrow} \mathbb{Z}_p$ is uniformly distributed over S_0. The above was conditioned on $v_1 \neq 0$ and $v_2 \neq 0$, which is true with all but negligible probability. Thus, we have statistical indistinguishability.

Lemma 4 (Hyb$_3$ $\overset{s}{\equiv}$ Hyb$_4$). *Assuming $\boldsymbol{u} \overset{\$}{\leftarrow} \mathbb{Z}_p^2$, the output of $\mathbf{Dual}(\boldsymbol{u})$ is statistically close to the uniform distribution over $\mathbb{Z}_p^4$. Thus, the two hybrids are statistically indistinguishable.*

Proof. The only difference between these two hybrids lies in $(\boldsymbol{v}, \boldsymbol{w})$, sampled as $(\boldsymbol{v}, \boldsymbol{w}) \overset{\$}{\leftarrow} \mathbf{Dual}(\boldsymbol{u})$ in Hyb$_3$ and as completely random in Hyb$_4$. We show that the marginal distribution of $(\boldsymbol{v}, \boldsymbol{w})$ sampled as $(\boldsymbol{v}, \boldsymbol{w}) \overset{\$}{\leftarrow} \mathbf{Dual}(\boldsymbol{u})$ is statistically close to the uniform distribution over $\mathbb{Z}_p^4$, assuming $\boldsymbol{u}$ is uniformly random. This will complete the proof, because the view in either hybrid can be sampled by knowing (v, w), and by knowing prm, from which we have already removed u, so prm is information-theoretically independent of u.

Parse $u := (a, b) \in \mathbb{Z}_p^2$. First, we know that $u = 0$ with negligible probability. In case $u \neq 0$, without loss of generality assume $b \neq 0$, then we have $v = (x, -\frac{a}{b}x)$ and $w = (z, -\frac{a}{b}z + \frac{1}{b})$, where $x, z \xleftarrow{\$} \mathbb{Z}_p$. Let $(t, t') := (-\frac{a}{b}, \frac{1}{b})$, and note that (t, t') is uniform over $\mathbb{Z}_p^2$ with $t' \neq 0$, since u is uniformly random except that $b \neq 0$. We may then rewrite $v = (x, tx)$ and $w = (z, tz + t')$, where x, z, t, t' are all independent and uniformly random over $\mathbb{Z}_p$ with the constraint that $t' \neq 0$. Thus, (v, w) is statistically close to the uniform distribution over $\mathbb{Z}_p^4$.

Lemma 5 (Hyb$_4$ $\overset{c}{\equiv}$ Hyb$_5$). *Assuming DDH hardness of $\mathbb{G}_2$, Hyb$_4$ $\overset{c}{\equiv}$ Hyb$_5$.*

Proof. In Hyb$_4$ the receiver forms an otr message for an adversary's query $(s_0, s_1) \in \{0, 1\}^2$ as $(h^{kv+(1-s_b)w}, h^{k'v+s_b w})$. Since v and w are independent and uniformly random, and since $k, k' \xleftarrow{\$} \mathbb{Z}_p$, by DDH $(g^{kv}, g^{k'v})$ is pseudorandom, and hence $(h^{kv+(1-b_i)w}, h^{k'v+b_i w})$ is pseudorandom. The proof is now complete. ∎

Thus, we have the following theorem.

Theorem 1. *Assuming DDH hardness for $\mathbb{G}_1$ and $\mathbb{G}_2$, the amortized rate-1 OT protocol of Construction 1 provides receiver privacy.*

5   Amortized Rate-1 OT from Bilinear Power DDH

We show how to shorten the reusable parameter using the circulant structure imposed by power-DDH assumptions, following ideas from [GHO20]. We assume $\mathbb{G}_2$ is DDH-hard, and $\mathbb{G}_1$ is m-power-DDH hard, meaning that $(g, g^\alpha, g^{\alpha^2}, \ldots, g^{\alpha^m})$ is pseudorandom. We will need to set $m = O(n)$, where n is the bit length of each of the sender's messages. Concretely, $m = 3n - 1$ suffices.

Construction 2 (Amortized rate-1 OT: Bilinear Power DDH). *Build* OT $:= (\mathsf{PreP}, \mathsf{OT}_1, \mathsf{OT}_2, \mathsf{OT}_3)$ *as follows.*

- $\mathsf{PreP}(1^\lambda, n)$: *Sample* $\mathsf{pp} := (e, \mathbb{G}_1, \mathbb{G}_2, \mathbb{G}_T, p, g, h) \xleftarrow{\$} \mathsf{G}(1^\lambda)$. *Then*
  1. *Sample* $\mathbf{M} := [g^{ar}, g^{a^2 r}, \cdots, g^{a^{2n} r}]$, *where* $a \xleftarrow{\$} \mathbb{Z}_p$ *and* $r \xleftarrow{\$} \mathbb{Z}_p^2$.
  2. *Sample* $k \xleftarrow{\$} \mathbb{Z}_p$ *and let*

$$w := [g^{kar}, g^{ka^2 r}, \cdots, g^{ka^{n-1} r}, g^{ka^n r + u}, g^{ka^{n+1} r}, \cdots, g^{ka^{2n-1} r},$$
$$g^{ka^{2n} r + u}, g^{ka^{2n+1} r}, \cdots, g^{ka^{3n-1} r}] \tag{2}$$

  3. *Return private state* $\mathsf{str} := (u, k, a)$ *and reusable message* $\mathsf{prm} := (\mathsf{pp}, \mathbf{M}, w)$.

- $\mathsf{OT}_1(\mathsf{str}, b \in \{0,1\})$: *Parse* str *as above. Sample* $(\boldsymbol{f}, \boldsymbol{h}) \xleftarrow{\$} \mathsf{OrthSam}(\boldsymbol{u}, b)$ *(Definition 3). Return* return $\mathsf{otr} := (h^{\boldsymbol{f}}, h^{\boldsymbol{h}}) \in \mathbb{G}_2^4$.
- $\mathsf{OT}_2((\mathsf{prm}, \mathsf{otr}), (m_0, m_1) \in \{0,1\}^n \times \{0,1\}^n)$: *Parse* $\mathsf{otr} := (\boldsymbol{\chi}_1, \boldsymbol{\chi}_2) \in \mathbb{G}_2^4$, $\mathsf{prm} := (\mathsf{pp}, \mathbf{M}, \boldsymbol{w})$, $\mathbf{M} := (\boldsymbol{m}_1, \ldots, \boldsymbol{m}_{2n})$ *and* $\boldsymbol{w} := (\boldsymbol{w}_1, \ldots, \boldsymbol{w}_{3n-1})$. *For* $j \in [n]$ *let* $\boldsymbol{w}_j := \boldsymbol{w}[j, j + 2n - 1]$; *namely, the elements of* $\boldsymbol{w}$ *in the range* $[j, j + 2n - 1]$. *Parse* $\boldsymbol{w}_j := (\boldsymbol{w}_{j,1}, \ldots, \boldsymbol{w}_{j,2n})$. *Let*

$$\boldsymbol{hk} := (\mathsf{e}(\boldsymbol{\chi}_1, \boldsymbol{m}_1), \ldots \mathsf{e}(\boldsymbol{\chi}_1, \boldsymbol{m}_n) \mid \mathsf{e}(\boldsymbol{\chi}_2, \boldsymbol{m}_{n+1}), \ldots \mathsf{e}(\boldsymbol{\chi}_2, \boldsymbol{m}_{2n}))$$

$$\mathbf{IK} := \begin{bmatrix} \mathsf{e}(\boldsymbol{\chi}_1, \boldsymbol{w}_{n,1}) & \cdots & \mathsf{e}(\boldsymbol{\chi}_1, \boldsymbol{w}_{n,n}) & \mathsf{e}(\boldsymbol{\chi}_2, \boldsymbol{w}_{n,n+1}) & \cdots & \mathsf{e}(\boldsymbol{\chi}_2, \boldsymbol{w}_{n,2n}) \\ \vdots & \ddots & \vdots & \vdots & \ddots & \vdots \\ \mathsf{e}(\boldsymbol{\chi}_1, \boldsymbol{w}_{1,1}) & \cdots & \mathsf{e}(\boldsymbol{\chi}_1, \boldsymbol{w}_{1,n}) & \mathsf{e}(\boldsymbol{\chi}_2, \boldsymbol{w}_{1,n+1}) & \cdots & \mathsf{e}(\boldsymbol{\chi}_2, \boldsymbol{w}_{1,2n}) \end{bmatrix}.$$

Let $\boldsymbol{m} := (m_0, m_1) \in \{0,1\}^{2n}$. *Let* $\boldsymbol{y}_j \in \mathbb{G}_T^{2n}$ *be the jth row of* $\mathbf{IK}$. *The sender then sends*

$$\mathsf{ots} := \mathsf{Shrink}(\boldsymbol{m} \cdot \boldsymbol{hk}, \boldsymbol{m} \cdot \boldsymbol{y}_1, \ldots, \boldsymbol{m} \cdot \boldsymbol{y}_n) \in \mathbb{G}_T \times \{0,1\}^{n+\lambda}.$$

- $\mathsf{OT}_3(\mathsf{str}, \mathsf{ots})$: *Parse* $\mathsf{str} := (\boldsymbol{u}, k, a)$ *and set* $\mathsf{sk} := (ka^{n-1}, \ldots, ka, k)$. *Return* $m' := \mathsf{ShrinkDec}(\mathsf{sk}, \mathsf{ots})$.

Correctness. We prove $m' = m_b$, where, following the notation of Construction 2, m' is the string output by OT_3, and (m_0, m_1) are the input strings to OT_2 and b is the choice bit for OT_1.

Let $\boldsymbol{f}, \boldsymbol{h}, \boldsymbol{r}$ and $\boldsymbol{w}_j$ for $j \in [n]$ be as in Construction 2. Let $\beta = \langle \boldsymbol{r}, \boldsymbol{f} \rangle$ and $\mu = \langle \boldsymbol{r}, \boldsymbol{h} \rangle$. Letting $\boldsymbol{hk}$ and $\mathbf{IK}$ be as in Construction 2, we have

$$\boldsymbol{hk} := [\mathsf{e}(g,h)^{\beta a} \cdots, \mathsf{e}(g,h)^{\beta a^n} \mid \mathsf{e}(g,h)^{\mu a^{n+1}} \cdots, \mathsf{e}(g,h)^{\mu a^{2n}}]$$

$$\mathbf{IK} := \begin{bmatrix} \mathsf{e}(g,h)^{k\beta a^n} \cdot \mathsf{e}(g,h) \cdots & \mathsf{e}(g,h)^{k\beta a^{2n-1}} & \mathsf{e}(g,h)^{k\mu a^{2n}} & \cdots & \mathsf{e}(g,h)^{k\mu a^{3n-1}} \\ \vdots & \ddots & \vdots & \vdots & \ddots & \vdots \\ \mathsf{e}(g,h)^{k\beta a} & \cdots & \mathsf{e}(g,h)^{k\beta a^n} \cdot \mathsf{e}(g,h) & \mathsf{e}(g,h)^{k\mu a^{n+1}} & \cdots & \mathsf{e}(g,h)^{k\mu a^{2n}} \end{bmatrix} \quad \text{if } b_i = 0$$

$$\mathbf{IK} := \begin{bmatrix} \mathsf{e}(g,h)^{k\beta a^n} & \cdots & \mathsf{e}(g,h)^{k\beta a^{2n-1}} & \mathsf{e}(g,h)^{k\mu a^{2n}} \cdot \mathsf{e}(g,h) \cdots & \mathsf{e}(g,h)^{k\mu a^{3n-1}} \\ \vdots & \ddots & \vdots & \vdots & \ddots & \vdots \\ \mathsf{e}(g,h)^{k\beta a} & \cdots & \mathsf{e}(g,h)^{k\beta a^n} & \mathsf{e}(g,h)^{k\mu a^{n+1}} & \cdots & \mathsf{e}(g,h)^{k\mu a^{2n}} \cdot \mathsf{e}(g,h) \end{bmatrix} \quad \text{if } b_i = 1$$

Thus, $(\boldsymbol{m} \cdot \boldsymbol{hk}, \boldsymbol{m} \cdot \boldsymbol{y}_1, \ldots, \boldsymbol{m} \cdot \boldsymbol{y}_n) \in \mathsf{Enc}(\mathsf{pk}, (m_b[1], \ldots, m_b[n]))$, where $\boldsymbol{m} = (m_0, m_1)$, $\boldsymbol{y}_j$ is the jth row of $\mathbf{IK}$, $\mathsf{pk} := (\mathsf{e}(g,h), \mathsf{e}(g,h)^{ka^{n-1}}, \ldots, \mathsf{e}(g,h)^k)$ and Enc is the packed ElGamal encryption algorithm as in Lemma 1. By Lemma 1, $m' = m_b$, as desired.

5.1   Receiver Privacy

The proof of security follows the same sequence of hybrids as in Sect. 4.2, so we only sketch the hybrids and the proofs.

Hybrid $\mathsf{Hyb_1}$: Real game. Sample $(\mathsf{str}, \mathsf{prm}) \xleftarrow{\$} \mathsf{PreP}(1^\lambda, 1^n)$, a challenge bit $b \xleftarrow{\$} \{0,1\}$, and give prm to the adversary. Parse $\mathsf{str} := (\boldsymbol{u}, *)$. Reply to an adversary's query $(s_0, s_1) \in \{0,1\}^2$ with $\mathsf{OT_1}(\mathsf{str}, s_b)$. The view of the adversary for $\mathsf{OT_1}$ outputs can be produced just by knowing $\boldsymbol{u}$.

Hybrid $\mathsf{Hyb_2}$: Replace $\boldsymbol{w}$, Eq. 2, with uniformly random vectors of group elements. Thus, information about $\boldsymbol{u}$ will be removed from $\boldsymbol{D}$, and hence from prm.

Hybrid $\mathsf{Hyb_3}$: Same as Hybrid $\mathsf{Hyb_2}$, except we sample $(\boldsymbol{v}, \boldsymbol{w}) \xleftarrow{\$} \mathbf{Dual}(\boldsymbol{u})$ (Definition 4), and reply to any adversary's query $(s_0, s_1) \in \{0,1\}^2$ as $\mathsf{Sim}(\boldsymbol{v}, \boldsymbol{w}, s_b)$ (Definition 5). The whole view is produced by knowing only $(\boldsymbol{v}, \boldsymbol{w})$.

Hybrid $\mathsf{Hyb_4}$: Same as $\mathsf{Hyb_3}$, except we sample $(\boldsymbol{v}, \boldsymbol{w}) \xleftarrow{\$} \mathbb{Z}_p^4$.

Hybrid $\mathsf{Hyb_5}$: Same as $\mathsf{Hyb_4}$, except we reply to any adversary's query (s_0, s_1) with a uniformly random vector sampled from $\mathbb{G}_2^4$. This hybrid perfectly hides the value of the challenge bit b.

$\mathsf{Hyb_1} \overset{c}{\equiv} \mathsf{Hyb_2}$ is established exactly like Lemma 2, except we use the power-DDH assumption instead of DDH. We have $\mathsf{Hyb_2} \overset{s}{\equiv} \mathsf{Hyb_3}$, $\mathsf{Hyb_3} \equiv \mathsf{Hyb_4}$ and $\mathsf{Hyb_4} \equiv \mathsf{Hyb_5}$, and the proofs are exactly the same as those of Lemmas 3, 4 and 5, respectively. Thus, we have the following theorem.

Theorem 2. *Assuming $(3n-1)$-power DDH hardness for $\mathbb{G}_1$, and DDH hardness for $\mathbb{G}_2$, the amortized rate-1 OT protocol of Construction 2 provides receiver privacy.*

6 Optimization

In this section, we discuss some techniques to improve the concrete computational efficiency and lower the communication cost in amortized rate-1 OT. These optimizations work for both the basic amortized rate-1 OT from bilinear SXDH and the sliding-window construction from bilinear power DDH. In Sect. 7 when we describe the applications of amortized rate-1 OT, we will discuss further optimizations specific to these applications.

6.1 Delayed Pairing

Recall that when the sender computes her response message, she needs to compute the hash-key vector $\boldsymbol{hk}$, which requires $4n$ pairing operations. In addition, she needs to compute the matrix $\mathbf{IK}$, which requires $4n^2$ pairing operations in the basic construction and $6n$ pairing operations in the sliding-window construction. Since paring operations are orders of magnitude more expensive than the other group operations, we introduce a technique to minimize it.

On Basic Construction. The high-level idea is that we can leverage the bilinear property to delay the pairing operations. Instead of first performing the pairing operations and then computing inner products in the target group, we can first compute the inner products in $\mathbb{G}_1$ and then perform the pairings.

In more detail, in the basic construction, let

$$\mathbf{M}_0 := [g^{r_1}, g^{r_2}, \cdots, g^{r_n}],$$
$$\mathbf{M}_1 := [g^{r_{n+1}}, g^{r_{n+2}}, \cdots, g^{r_{2n}}].$$

Let $\boldsymbol{m} = (\boldsymbol{m}_0, \boldsymbol{m}_1) \in \{0,1\}^{2n}$ be the sender messages. With receiver message $\mathsf{otr} = (\boldsymbol{\chi}_1, \boldsymbol{\chi}_2) \in \mathbb{G}_2^4$, the inner product of $\boldsymbol{m} \cdot \boldsymbol{hk}$ can be computed as

$$\mathsf{e}(\boldsymbol{m}_0 \cdot \mathbf{M}_0, \boldsymbol{\chi}_1) \cdot \mathsf{e}(\boldsymbol{m}_1 \cdot \mathbf{M}_1, \boldsymbol{\chi}_2).$$

Here $\boldsymbol{m}_0 \cdot \mathbf{M}_0$ computes inner products for each vector component of $\mathbf{M}_0$ and results in a vector of two group elements in $\mathbb{G}_1$, and $\mathsf{e}(\mathbf{M}_0 \cdot \boldsymbol{m}_0, \boldsymbol{\chi}_1)$ takes the inner product on the exponent of the two vectors. $\mathsf{e}(\boldsymbol{m}_1 \cdot \mathbf{M}_1, \boldsymbol{\chi}_2)$ is computed in the same way. The same approach can be applied to compute $\boldsymbol{m} \cdot \boldsymbol{y}_1, \ldots, \boldsymbol{m} \cdot \boldsymbol{y}_n$.

The computational cost of $\boldsymbol{m} \cdot \boldsymbol{hk}$ in the basic construction includes $4n$ pairing operations and $4n$ multiplications in $\mathbb{G}_T$. By using the above technique, this cost can be reduced to 4 pairing operations, $4n$ multiplications in $\mathbb{G}_1$, and 3 multiplications in $\mathbb{G}_T$. The same improvement applies to each inner product $\boldsymbol{m} \cdot \boldsymbol{y}_1, \ldots, \boldsymbol{m} \cdot \boldsymbol{y}_n$. Therefore, the total computational cost of the sender is reduced to $4n$ pairing operations, $4n^2$ multiplications in $\mathbb{G}_1$, and $3n$ multiplications in $\mathbb{G}_T$.

On Sliding-Window Construction. The same technique can be applied on the sliding-window construction and the improvements on $\boldsymbol{m} \cdot \boldsymbol{hk}$ is the same as above. The total cost of computing $\boldsymbol{m} \cdot \boldsymbol{y}_1, \ldots, \boldsymbol{m} \cdot \boldsymbol{y}_n$ in the sliding-window construction includes $6n$ pairing operations and $(2n^2 + 3n)$ multiplications in $\mathbb{G}_T$. This can be improved to $4n$ pairing operations, $4n^2$ multiplications in $\mathbb{G}_1$, and $3n$ multiplications in $\mathbb{G}_T$.

6.2   Increasing Vector Dimension

Reducing Hash Value Size. The hash value $\boldsymbol{m} \cdot \boldsymbol{hk}$ currently contains a single group element in $\mathbb{G}_T$. Since the bit representation of group elements in $\mathbb{G}_T$ is much longer than group elements in $\mathbb{G}_1$, we can reduce that by sending 4 group elements in $\mathbb{G}_1$, namely $\boldsymbol{m}_0 \cdot \mathbf{M}_0$ and $\boldsymbol{m}_1 \cdot \mathbf{M}_1$, and then let the receiver perform the remaining pairing operations. In applications such as PIR and PSI, the sender message grows with the tree depth and this saving in communication gets accumulated throughout all the levels of the tree. Another benefit of this optimization is that it pushes the pairing operations in computing hashes to the receiver side, which significantly reduces the computational cost in computing hashes because the sender had to compute hashes in every node of the tree while the receiver only needs to compute hashes along a single path of the tree.

Next we discuss another technique to further reduce the cost to 3 group elements in $\mathbb{G}_1$.

On Basic Construction. At a high-level, we will unify f and h to a single vector by increasing the vector dimension from 2 to 3. In more detail, the base hash key $\mathbf{M}$ is the same as before except that each $r_i \overset{\$}{\leftarrow} \mathbb{Z}_p^3$ is of dimension 3. The receiver's reusable message is redefined by

$$\nu_1 := [g^{p_1 r_1 + u}, g^{p_1 r_2}, \cdots, g^{p_1 r_n} \mid g^{p_1 r_{n+1} + v}, g^{p_1 r_{n+2}}, \cdots, g^{p_1 r_{2n}}]$$

$$\vdots$$

$$\nu_n := [g^{p_n r_1}, g^{p_n r_2}, \cdots, g^{p_n r_n + u} \mid g^{p_n r_{n+1}}, g^{p_n r_{n+2}}, \cdots, g^{p_n r_{2n} + v}],$$

where all p_i's are random exponents and $u, v \overset{\$}{\leftarrow} \mathbb{Z}_p^3$. For a choice bit b, the receiver samples a single random vector f s.t. $\langle u, f \rangle = 1 - b$ and $\langle v, f \rangle = b$, and sends a single vector $\chi = h^f \in \mathbb{G}_2^3$.

Next the sender computes hk by taking the inner product in the exponent of $\mathbf{M}$ and χ. The matrix $\mathbf{IK}$ can be computed by taking the inner product in the exponent of ν_j's and χ. We can use delayed pairing to compute $m \cdot hk$ by

$$\mathsf{e}(m \cdot \mathbf{M}, \chi).$$

Again, we can reduce the hash value size by sending 3 group elements in the vector $m \cdot \mathbf{M}$ and postpone the pairing operations to the receiver side. It also reduces the receiver's non-reusable message from 4 group elements in $\mathbb{G}_2$ to 3.

To summarize, the receiver's reusable message is increased from $(4n^2 + 4n)$ to $(6n^2 + 6n)$ group elements in $\mathbb{G}_1$, but the non-reusable message is reduced from 4 to 3 group elements in $\mathbb{G}_2$. The hash value in the sender's message is reduced from 1 group element in $\mathbb{G}_T$ to 3 group elements in $\mathbb{G}_1$.

On Sliding-Window Construction. The same technique can be applied on the sliding-window construction and the improvements on the communication is the same as above. In particular, the receiver's reusable message is increased from $10n$ to $15n$ group elements in $\mathbb{G}_1$, but the non-reusable message is reduced from 4 to 3 group elements in $\mathbb{G}_2$. The hash value in the sender's message is reduced from 1 group element in $\mathbb{G}_T$ to 3 group elements in $\mathbb{G}_1$.

7 Applications

In this section, we discuss several applications of our amortized rate-1 OT and focus on the communication improvements over prior work. For certain applications, we will discuss optimizations that further improve the communication and/or computational complexity. The communication improvements are summarized in Table 3 at the end of the section.

7.1 Secure Function Evaluation on Branching Programs

The work of Ishai and Paskin [IP07] presents an approach to two-round secure function evaluation (SFE) on (oblivious) branching program (BP) from rate-1 OT where the communication complexity only grows with the depth of the branching program instead of its size. In particular, consider a sender holding a private branching program P and a receiver holding a private input x. They can jointly compute $P(x)$ in two rounds of communication, that is, the receiver first sends an encryption c of the input x to the sender, and the sender can compute a succinct ciphertext c' which allows the receiver to decrypt $P(x)$ without revealing any further information about P except its depth. The size of c' depends polynomially on the size of x and the depth of P, but does not further depend on the size of P.

In terms of concrete communication complexity, let ℓ be the depth of the oblivious BP and h be the bit length of the output. The recent work of Garg et al. [GHO20] achieves receiver's communication complexity of $O(\ell \cdot (h + \lambda \cdot \ell))$ group elements and sender's communication complexity of $O(h + \lambda \cdot \ell)$ bits, where the group elements are from a pairing-free group where the power DDH assumption holds. This improves upon prior work of Döttling et al. [DGI+19] based on DDH with receiver's communication complexity of $O(\ell \cdot (h + \lambda \cdot \ell)^2)$ group elements and sender's communication complexity of $O(h + \lambda \cdot \ell)$ bits.

In this work, we consider the problem in the *reusable* setting where the receiver first sends a one-time reusable message to the sender consisting of $O(h + \lambda \cdot \ell)$ group elements in $\mathbb{G}_1$. Afterwards, for any oblivious BP with depth ℓ and output length h and any input x, the receiver's communication complexity is $O(\ell)$ group elements in $\mathbb{G}_2$ and the sender's communication complexity is $O(h + \lambda \cdot \ell)$ bits. Note that the one-time messages can be reused for arbitrary polynomially many times.

Example: Secure Inference of Decision Trees. As an example, we consider a server holding a machine learning model of a decision tree, which takes as input a data point with multiple features. Starting from the root, each node of the tree is a function on some feature (e.g. testing if $x < 10$, $t = \mathtt{true}$) that determines whether to go to the left or right child. The client has a single data point and would like to perform a secure inference with the server on the decision tree. The decision tree can be formalized as a branching program and two-round secure inference can be achieved by two-round SFE described above, where the communication only grows with the depth of the tree.

7.2   PSI and PIR

In this section, we illustrate several useful applications that can be viewed as special cases of SFE on oblivious BP, hence they achieve the same improvements over prior work.

Unbalanced Private Set Intersection (PSI). Consider the PSI problem between a server holding a private set $X = \{x_1, \ldots, x_N\}$ and a client holding a private set $Y = \{y_1, \ldots, y_m\}$. They want to jointly compute the set intersection $X \cap Y$ without revealing any other information. Without loss of generality we assume all the set elements $x_i, y_j \in \{0,1\}^\lambda$.[3] We focus on the case with *unbalanced* set sizes, namely $N \gg m$, and present a solution for two-round PSI.

To learn the intersection $X \cap \{y\}$ for any $y \in Y$, we can construct an oblivious BP with depth λ and size $\lambda \cdot N$. To construct the oblivious BP, we can first think of it as a full binary tree of depth λ where each leaf node indicates whether the root-to-leaf path is an element in X. However, this branching program has exponential size. We can prune the full binary tree by replacing each subtree consisting of only 0's with a "dummy node" of the same depth. A dummy node of depth d is connected to two dummy nodes with depth $d - 1$.

Following this approach, the client only needs to performs m instances of SFE on the oblivious BP to learn the intersection $X \cap \{y\}$ for every $y \in Y$. The oblivious BP has depth $\ell = \lambda$, size $\lambda \cdot N$, and single-bit output.

Private Set Intersection (PIR). Consider a server (sender) holding a large database $D \in \{0,1\}^N$ and a client (receiver) who wants to retrieve $D[i]$ for $i \in [N]$ without revealing i to the server. As pointed out in [IP07], single-server two-round PIR can be viewed as two-round SFE on an oblivious BP with depth $\ell = \log N$ and single-bit output.

PIR-with-Default. Consider a PIR variant where the server holds N binary strings $s_1, \ldots, s_N \in \{0,1\}^t$ along with N values $v_1, \ldots, v_N \in \{0,1\}^k$. The server additionally holds a default value $v_{\mathsf{dflt}} \in \{0,1\}^k$. The client holds a binary string $w \in \{0,1\}^t$ and wants to learn a value v such that if $w = s_j$ for some $j \in [N]$, then $v = v_j$; otherwise $v = v_{\mathsf{dflt}}$, without revealing any information about w to the server. This problem is formalized by Lepoint et al. [LPR+20]. Two-round PIR-with-Default can be viewed as two-round SFE on a k-bit output oblivious BP with depth t and polynomial size. Hence the receiver and sender communication follow generically from oblivious BP with many-bit outputs. We mention this PIR variant because it will be used to construct PSI-Cardinality.

PSI-Cardinality. Consider a PSI variant where a server holding a private set $X = \{x_1, \ldots, x_N\}$ and a client holding a private set $Y = \{y_1, \ldots, y_m\}$ want to learn the cardinality of the intersection $|X \cap Y|$ instead of the intersection itself.

We can achieve PSI-Cardinality by the client querying PIR-with-Default on every element in the her set, where in each PIR-with-Default instance, the default value v_{dflt}^i is sampled at random such that all the default values sum up to 0, namely $\sum_{i=1}^m v_{\mathsf{dflt}}^i = 0$. All the non-default values in a single instance are set to $v_{\mathsf{dflt}}^i + 1$. At the end, the client sums up all the values retrieved from the PIR-with-Default instances. Similar to PSI, we should prune the full binary tree to obtain an oblivious BP with depth λ and polynomial size.

7.3   Optimization for PSI and PSI-Cardinality

We design optimizations for unbalanced PSI and PSI-Cardinality so as to achieve better communication than the above generic approaches.

---

[3] The set elements can be of arbitrary length, but the parties can first apply a collision-resistant hash function on the elements to make them all have length λ.

Optimized PSI. Note that the aforementioned oblivious BP for PSI has depth $\ell = \lambda$. To further improve the communication complexity, we replace small subtrees by small instances of two-round PSI (e.g. DDH-based PSI [HFH99]), which we denote by Π_{PSI}.

In particular, to compute $X \cap \{y\}$, the server first hashes his N elements into N random bins. We know that each bin has at most $O(\log N)$ elements. The client computes the same hash on y to identify the bin b that could possibly contain an element y. Now the client queries the server with PIR-with-Default on a string b. The client additionally sends the round-1 message of the two-round PSI protocol Π_{PSI} on a single element y. The server then computes a round-2 message of Π_{PSI} for each bin with elements in that bin. The server views his database for PIR-with-Default as all the N indices of the bins along with the associated values being the round-2 messages of Π_{PSI}, and generates the response for PIR-with-Default. Finally, the client first recovers the round-2 message of Π_{PSI} from PIR-with-Default, and then recovers the output of Π_{PSI}, namely $X \cap \{y\}$.

The receiver's reusable communication is reduced from $O(\lambda^2)$ to $O(\lambda \cdot \log N)$ group elements in $\mathbb{G}_1$. Then for each $X \cap \{y\}$ query, her online communication is reduced from $O(\lambda)$ to $O(\log N)$ group elements in $\mathbb{G}_2$. The sender's communication is reduced from $O(\lambda^2)$ to $O(\lambda \cdot \log N)$.

- Server has a set X of size N, client has a single element y. All the elements are λ-bit strings.
- Let $h : \{0,1\}^\lambda \to [N]$ be a hash function.
- Let Π_{PSI} and $\Pi_{\mathsf{PIR\text{-}Default}}$ be two-round PSI and PIR-with-Default protocols, respectively.

Round 1: Client does the following:

1. Compute $b := H(y)$.
2. Compute round-1 message of Π_{PSI} with a single element y, and round-1 message of $\Pi_{\mathsf{PIR\text{-}Default}}$ with query b, and send them to the server.

Round 2: Server does the following:

1. Let $B[i] := \emptyset$ for each bin $i \in [N]$.
2. For each $j \in [N]$, compute $b_j := H(x_j)$ and let $B[b_j] := B[b_j] \cup \{x_j\}$.
3. For each bin $i \in [N]$:
   (a) Pad $B[i]$ with dummy elements to be a total of $\log N$ elements.
   (b) Based on the round-1 message of Π_{PSI}, compute round-2 message of Π_{PSI} with set $B[i]$. Let the round-2 message be M_i.
4. Based on the round-1 message of $\Pi_{\mathsf{PIR\text{-}Default}}$, compute round-2 message of $\Pi_{\mathsf{PIR\text{-}Default}}$ with N values $M_1, \ldots, M_N$, and send it to the client.

Output: Client does the following:

1. Compute the output of the $\Pi_{\mathsf{PIR\text{-}Default}}$, which gives a round-2 message of Π_{PSI}, namely M_b.
2. Use the round-2 message M_b of Π_{PSI} to compute the PSI output.

Fig. 1. Optimized two-round PSI protocol with a single element on the client side.

PSI-Cardinality. We can optimize the PSI-Cardinality protocol by replacing small subtrees by small instances of two-round PSI-Cardinality (e.g. DDH-based PSI-Cardinality [IKN+20]), similarly as in the above PSI protocol. However, this would reveal which elements are in the intersection and which are not.

Nonetheless, we notice that in our reusable rate-1 OT protocol, any OT response from the sender can be decrypted by the receiver using the same secret state str, and the receiver cannot distinguish between different responses. Therefore, the server can randomly shuffle the responses for all the PIR-with-Default instances so that the client can only learn the cardinality of the intersection. This achieves the same improvement as in the above PSI protocol.

7.4   Other Variants of PSI and PIR

In this section, we discuss a few more useful variants of PSI and PIR problems.

PIR-by-Keywords. Consider a PIR variant where the server holds N binary strings $s_1, \ldots, s_N \in \{0,1\}^t$. The client holds a binary string $w \in \{0,1\}^t$, who wants to learn whether $w = s_j$ for some $j \in [N]$ without revealing any information about w to the server. This problem was introduced by Chor et al. [CGN98]. As pointed out in [IP07], two-round PIR-by-Keywords can be viewed as two-round SFE on a branching program with depth $\ell = t$ and single-bit-output.

PSI-Sum. Consider a server holding a set with weights $(X, W) = \{(x_1, w_1), \ldots, (x_N, w_N)\}$ and a client holding a set $Y = \{y_1, \ldots, y_m\}$. They want to jointly compute the PSI-Cardinality along with the sum of the weights associated with the elements in the intersection, namely $\sum_{i:x_i \in Y} w_i$. This functionality, introduced by Ion et al. [IKN+20], is a generalization of PSI-Cardinality.

We can achieve PSI-Sum from PIR-with-Default similarly as in the PSI-Cardinality protocol except that all the non-default values v_j in a single instance are set to $v_{\text{dflt}}^i + w_j$ where w_j is the corresponding weight. Note that this approach additionally hides the PSI-Cardinality and only reveals the PSI-Sum.

PSI-Test. Consider a PSI variant where a server holding a private set $X = \{x_1, \ldots, x_N\}$ and a client holding a private set $Y = \{y_1, \ldots, y_m\}$ want to learn whether the two sets intersect or not, namely whether $|X \cap Y| = \emptyset$.

We can achieve this from PIR-with-Default similarly as in PSI-Cardinality but all the non-default values in a single instance are all set to $v_{\text{dflt}}^i + r^i$ for some random r^i. At the end, the client checks if all the values obtained from the PIR-with-Default instances sum up to 0. The sum equals 0 if and only if $|X \cap Y| = \emptyset$ except with negligible probability.

Extended-PIR-with-Default. An extension to PIR-with-Default, also formalized in [LPR+20], enables two parties to learn random shares of the PIR-with-Default answer multiplied with a weight w supplied from the client. By using the techniques from [LPR+20], we can achieve the same complexity as PIR-with-Default with additively homomorphic encryption. In particular, we make the following changes to the PIR-with-Default protocol. The client additionally sends $\mathsf{Enc}(w)$ to the server (in the online phase) where Enc is an additively homomorphic encryption scheme. The server picks a random value α as his output of Extended-PIR-with-Default and replaces each value v in a leaf node of the PIR-with-Default tree by $\mathsf{Enc}(v \cdot w - \alpha)$. Finally the client needs to decrypt her output from PIR-with-Default to recover her output for Extended-PIR-with-Default. We mention this PIR variant because it will be useful in the following application.

Private Join and Compute (PJC) for Inner Product. Consider a server holding a set with weights $(X, W) = \{(x_1, w_1), \ldots, (x_N, w_N)\}$ and a client also holding a set with weights $Y = \{(y_1, v_1), \ldots, (y_m, v_m)\}$. They want to jointly compute the $\sum_{i,j:x_i=y_j} w_i \cdot v_j$. This functionality, introduced by Lepoint et al. [LPR+20], is a generalization of PSI-Sum.

We can achieve this by the client querying Extended-PIR-with-Default on every element in her set, where in each Extended-PIR-with-Default instance, the default values are set to 0 and the two parties learn a secret share of $w_i \cdot v_j$ if $X \cap \{y_j\} \neq \emptyset$. From this the two parties can sum up their own shares to obtain a secret sharing of the inner product result. The server only needs to additionally send the sum of his shares to the client, from which the client can recover the output. Note that this approach additionally hides the PSI-Cardinality and only reveals the result of the inner product.

Table 3. Summary of communication complexity in various applications of rate-1 OT. We compare our work based on bilinear power DDH with the state-of-the-art rate-1 OT based on power DDH [GHO20], and show improvements in terms of the receiver's communication while the sender's communication remain the same. Recall that ℓ is the depth of the oblivious BP and h is the output length in bits, m is the client's set size in PSI, N is the server's set size in PSI and the size of database in PIR, t is the length of the keywords in PIR-by-Keywords, k is the output length in PIR-with-Default. In all the applications, the one-time reusable message sent by the receiver can be reused for arbitrary polynomially many times.

Application	Receiver Comm [GHO20]	Receiver Comm Ours (reusable)	Receiver Comm Ours (online)	Sender Comm (same)
SFE on oblivious BP	$O(\ell \cdot (h + \lambda \cdot \ell))$ $\mathbb{G}$	$O(h + \lambda \cdot \ell)$ $\mathbb{G}_1$	$O(\ell)$ $\mathbb{G}_2$	$O(h + \lambda \cdot \ell)$
PSI/PSI-Cardinality/ PSI-Sum/PJC/PSI-Test	$O(\lambda^3 \cdot m)$ $\mathbb{G}$	$O(\lambda^2)$ $\mathbb{G}_1$	$O(\lambda \cdot m)$ $\mathbb{G}_2$	$O(\lambda^2 \cdot m)$
Optimized PSI/ Optimized PSI-Cardinality	$O(\lambda^2 \cdot \log N \cdot m)$ $\mathbb{G}$	$O(\lambda \cdot \log N)$ $\mathbb{G}_1$	$O(\log N \cdot m)$ $\mathbb{G}_2$	$O(\lambda \cdot \log N \cdot m)$
PIR	$O(\lambda \cdot \log^2 N)$ $\mathbb{G}$	$O(\lambda \cdot \log N)$ $\mathbb{G}_1$	$O(\log N)$ $\mathbb{G}_2$	$O(\lambda \cdot \log N)$
PIR-by-Keywords	$O(\lambda \cdot t^2)$ $\mathbb{G}$	$O(\lambda \cdot t)$ $\mathbb{G}_1$	$O(t)$ $\mathbb{G}_2$	$O(\lambda \cdot t)$
(Extended-)PIR-with-Default	$O(t \cdot (k + \lambda \cdot t))$ $\mathbb{G}$	$O(k + \lambda \cdot t)$ $\mathbb{G}_1$	$O(t)$ $\mathbb{G}_2$	$O(k + \lambda \cdot t)$

8   Amortized Rate-1 OT with Strong Sender Privacy

We will now show that variants of our amortized rate-1 OT constructions satisfy a stronger sender privacy requirement, essential for secure computation on non-oblivious branching programs, as required in [IP07].

Definition 6 (Strong sender privacy [IP07]**).** *Let* $\mathsf{OT} := (\mathsf{PreP}, \mathsf{OT}_1, \mathsf{OT}_2, \mathsf{OT}_3)$ *be as in Definition 2. We say* OT *provides strong sender privacy if there exists a PPT algorithm* OTSim *such that for any bit b and any pair of messages* (m_0, m_1), *sampling* $(\mathsf{str}, \mathsf{prm}) \xleftarrow{\$} \mathsf{PreP}(1^\lambda)$ *and* $\mathsf{otr} \xleftarrow{\$} \mathsf{OT}_1(\mathsf{str}, b)$, *the two distributions* $\mathsf{OT}_2((\mathsf{prm}, \mathsf{otr}), (m_0, m_1))$ *and* $\mathsf{OTSim}(\mathsf{prm}, m_b)$ *are statistically close.*

Our amortized rate-1 OT constructions, as presented in Sects. 4 and 5, do not provide strong sender privacy, because OT_2 is deterministic. Thus, we will consider a randomized OT_2 version of these constructions, obtained by using random extractors and PRGs, as explained in Sect. 3.1. Under these new OT_2 algorithms of our constructions, the following holds: for any choice b and any two pairs (m_0, m_1) and (m_0', m_1') such that $m_b = m_b'$, any $\mathsf{otr} \in \mathsf{OT}_1(\mathsf{str}, b)$, $\mathsf{otr}' \in \mathsf{OT}_1(\mathsf{str}, b')$, the two distributions $\mathsf{OT}_2((\mathsf{prm}, \mathsf{otr}), (m_0, m_1))$ and $\mathsf{OT}_2((\mathsf{prm}, \mathsf{otr}'), (m_0', m_1'))$ are statistically close. The simulation algorithm OTSim, which is only given m_b, should somehow sample from $\mathsf{OT}_2((\mathsf{prm}, \mathsf{otr}), (m_0, m_1))$. By what just mentioned, OTSim may, instead, sample from $\mathsf{OT}_2((\mathsf{prm}, \mathsf{otr}), (m_b, m_b))$. The main challenge in doing so is that OTSim is only given (prm, m_b), and not otr, which in turn is sampled based on str, not known to OTSim. Luckily, in our proofs we showed an oblivious way of sampling from OT_1 without knowing $\mathsf{str} := (\boldsymbol{u}, \dots)$. In particular, assuming OTSim is given $(\boldsymbol{v}, \boldsymbol{w})$ sampled as $(\boldsymbol{v}, \boldsymbol{w}) \xleftarrow{\$} \mathbf{Dual}(\boldsymbol{u})$ (Definition 4), then $\mathsf{Sim}(\boldsymbol{v}, \boldsymbol{w}, b)$ (Definition 5) samples an output statistically close to the output of $\mathsf{OT}_1(\mathsf{str}, b)$ (Lemma 3). We may include $(\boldsymbol{v}, \boldsymbol{w})$ in prm without harming security, as argued in the security of the constructions.

Once $(\boldsymbol{v}, \boldsymbol{w})$ is included as part of prm, the output of $\mathsf{OTSim}(\mathsf{prm}, m_b)$ is formed as follows: sample $\mathsf{otr} \xleftarrow{\$} \mathsf{Sim}(\boldsymbol{v}, \boldsymbol{w}, 0)$ and return $\mathsf{OT}_2((\mathsf{prm}, \mathsf{otr}), (m_b, m_b))$. In terms of efficiency, the size of otr remains the same, and the size of prm is increased by four group elements in $\mathbb{G}_1$.

References

[ADT11] Ateniese, G., De Cristofaro, E., Tsudik, G.: (If) size matters: size-hiding private set intersection. In: Catalano, D., Fazio, N., Gennaro, R., Nicolosi, A. (eds.) PKC 2011. LNCS, vol. 6571, pp. 156–173. Springer, Heidelberg (2011). https://doi.org/10.1007/978-3-642-19379-8_10

[AIR01] Aiello, B., Ishai, Y., Reingold, O.: Priced oblivious transfer: how to sell digital goods. In: Pfitzmann, B. (ed.) EUROCRYPT 2001. LNCS, vol. 2045, pp. 119–135. Springer, Heidelberg (2001). https://doi.org/10.1007/3-540-44987-6_8

[APP]   Password Monitoring - Apple Platform Security. https://support.apple.com/en-al/guide/security/sec78e79fc3b/web

[BBD+20]   Brakerski, Z., Branco, P., Döttling, N., Garg, S., Malavolta, G.: Constant ciphertext-rate non-committing encryption from standard assumptions. In: Pass, R., Pietrzak, K. (eds.) TCC 2020. LNCS, vol. 12550, pp. 58–87. Springer, Cham (2020). https://doi.org/10.1007/978-3-030-64375-1_3

[Bea96]   Beaver, D.: Correlated pseudorandomness and the complexity of private computations. In: 28th ACM STOC, Philadelphia, PA, USA, 22–24 May 1996, pp. 479–488. ACM Press (1996)

[BGdMM05]   Ballard, L., Green, M., de Medeiros, B., Monrose, F.: Correlation-resistant storage via keyword-searchable encryption. Cryptology ePrint Archive, Report 2005/417 (2005). https://eprint.iacr.org/2005/417

[BGI16]   Boyle, E., Gilboa, N., Ishai, Y.: Breaking the circuit size barrier for secure computation under DDH. In: Robshaw, M., Katz, J. (eds.) CRYPTO 2016. LNCS, vol. 9814, pp. 509–539. Springer, Heidelberg (2016). https://doi.org/10.1007/978-3-662-53018-4_19

[BGI+17]   Badrinarayanan, S., Garg, S., Ishai, Y., Sahai, A., Wadia, A.: Two-message witness indistinguishability and secure computation in the plain model from new assumptions. In: Takagi, T., Peyrin, T. (eds.) ASIACRYPT 2017. LNCS, vol. 10626, pp. 275–303. Springer, Cham (2017). https://doi.org/10.1007/978-3-319-70700-6_10

[BKM20]   Brakerski, Z., Koppula, V., Mour, T.: NIZK from LPN and trapdoor hash via correlation intractability for approximable relations. In: Micciancio, D., Ristenpart, T. (eds.) CRYPTO 2020. LNCS, vol. 12172, pp. 738–767. Springer, Cham (2020). https://doi.org/10.1007/978-3-030-56877-1_26

[BLSV18]   Brakerski, Z., Lombardi, A., Segev, G., Vaikuntanathan, V.: Anonymous IBE, leakage resilience and circular security from new assumptions. In: Nielsen, J.B., Rijmen, V. (eds.) EUROCRYPT 2018. LNCS, vol. 10820, pp. 535–564. Springer, Cham (2018). https://doi.org/10.1007/978-3-319-78381-9_20

[CCF+20]   Chan, J., et al.: PACT: privacy-sensitive protocols and mechanisms for mobile contact tracing. IEEE Data Eng. Bull. 43(2), 15–35 (2020)

[CDG+17]   Cho, C., Döttling, N., Garg, S., Gupta, D., Miao, P., Polychroniadou, A.: Laconic oblivious transfer and its applications. In: Katz, J., Shacham, H. (eds.) CRYPTO 2017. LNCS, vol. 10402, pp. 33–65. Springer, Cham (2017). https://doi.org/10.1007/978-3-319-63715-0_2

[CGN98]   Chor, B., Gilboa, N., Naor, M.: Private information retrieval by keywords. Cryptology ePrint Archive, Report 1998/003 (1998). https://eprint.iacr.org/1998/003

[CLR17]   Chen, H., Laine, K., Rindal, P.: Fast private set intersection from homomorphic encryption. In: ACM CCS 2017, Dallas, TX, USA, 31 October–2 November 2017, pp. 1243–1255. ACM Press (2017)

[CM20]   Chase, M., Miao, P.: Private set intersection in the internet setting from lightweight oblivious PRF. In: Micciancio, D., Ristenpart, T. (eds.) CRYPTO 2020. LNCS, vol. 12172, pp. 34–63. Springer, Cham (2020). https://doi.org/10.1007/978-3-030-56877-1_2

[DG17]   Döttling, N., Garg, S.: Identity-based encryption from the Diffie-Hellman assumption. In: Katz, J., Shacham, H. (eds.) CRYPTO 2017. LNCS, vol. 10401, pp. 537–569. Springer, Cham (2017). https://doi.org/10.1007/978-3-319-63688-7_18

[DGH+20] Döttling, N., Garg, S., Hajiabadi, M., Masny, D., Wichs, D.: Two-round oblivious transfer from CDH or LPN. In: Canteaut, A., Ishai, Y. (eds.) EUROCRYPT 2020. LNCS, vol. 12106, pp. 768–797. Springer, Cham (2020). https://doi.org/10.1007/978-3-030-45724-2_26

[DGI+19] Döttling, N., Garg, S., Ishai, Y., Malavolta, G., Mour, T., Ostrovsky, R.: Trapdoor hash functions and their applications. In: Boldyreva, A., Micciancio, D. (eds.) CRYPTO 2019. LNCS, vol. 11694, pp. 3–32. Springer, Cham (2019). https://doi.org/10.1007/978-3-030-26954-8_1

[EGL82] Even, S., Goldreich, O., Lempel, A.: A randomized protocol for signing contracts. In: CRYPTO 1982, Santa Barbara, CA, USA, pp. 205–210. Plenum Press, New York, USA (1982)

[GGH19] Garg, S., Gay, R., Hajiabadi, M.: New techniques for efficient trapdoor functions and applications. In: Ishai, Y., Rijmen, V. (eds.) EUROCRYPT 2019. LNCS, vol. 11478, pp. 33–63. Springer, Cham (2019). https://doi.org/10.1007/978-3-030-17659-4_2

[GH18] Garg, S., Hajiabadi, M.: Trapdoor functions from the computational Diffie-Hellman assumption. In: Shacham, H., Boldyreva, A. (eds.) CRYPTO 2018. LNCS, vol. 10992, pp. 362–391. Springer, Cham (2018). https://doi.org/10.1007/978-3-319-96881-0_13

[GHO20] Garg, S., Hajiabadi, M., Ostrovsky, R.: Efficient range-Trapdoor functions and applications: rate-1 OT and more. In: Pass, R., Pietrzak, K. (eds.) TCC 2020. LNCS, vol. 12550, pp. 88–116. Springer, Cham (2020). https://doi.org/10.1007/978-3-030-64375-1_4

[GMW87] Goldreich, O., Micali, S., Wigderson, A.: How to play any mental game or A completeness theorem for protocols with honest majority. In: 19th ACM STOC, New York City, NY, USA, 25–27 May, pp. 218–229. ACM Press (1987)

[GVW20] Goyal, R., Vusirikala, S., Waters, B.: New constructions of hinting prgs, owfs with encryption, and more. In: Micciancio, D., Ristenpart, T. (eds.) CRYPTO 2020. LNCS, vol. 12170, pp. 527–558. Springer, Cham (2020). https://doi.org/10.1007/978-3-030-56784-2_18

[HEK12] Huang, Y., Evans, D., Katz, J.: Private set intersection: are garbled circuits better than custom protocols? In: NDSS 2012, San Diego, CA, USA, 5–8 February 2012. The Internet Society (2012)

[HFH99] Huberman, B.A., Franklin, M.K., Hogg, T.: Enhancing privacy and trust in electronic communities. In: Proceedings of the 1st ACM Conference on Electronic Commerce, EC 1999, Denver, CO, USA, 3–5 November 1999, pp. 78–86. ACM (1999)

[HK12] Halevi, S., Kalai, Y.T.: Smooth projective hashing and two-message oblivious transfer. J. Cryptol. 25(1), 158–193 (2012)

[HKW20] Hohenberger, S., Koppula, V., Waters, B.: Chosen ciphertext security from injective trapdoor functions. In: Micciancio, D., Ristenpart, T. (eds.) CRYPTO 2020. LNCS, vol. 12170, pp. 836–866. Springer, Cham (2020). https://doi.org/10.1007/978-3-030-56784-2_28

[IKN+20] Ion, M., et al.: On deploying secure computing: Private intersection-sum-with-cardinality. In: IEEE European Symposium on Security and Privacy, EuroS&P 2020, Genoa, Italy, 7–11 September 2020, pp. 370–389. IEEE (2020)

[IKNP03] Ishai, Y., Kilian, J., Nissim, K., Petrank, E.: Extending oblivious trans-fers efficiently. In: Boneh, D. (ed.) CRYPTO 2003. LNCS, vol. 2729, pp. 145–161. Springer, Heidelberg (2003). https://doi.org/10.1007/978-3-540-45146-4_9

[IP07] Ishai, Y., Paskin, A.: Evaluating branching programs on encrypted data. In: Vadhan, S.P. (ed.) TCC 2007. LNCS, vol. 4392, pp. 575–594. Springer, Heidelberg (2007). https://doi.org/10.1007/978-3-540-70936-7_31

[KKRT16] Kolesnikov, V., Kumaresan, R., Rosulek, M., Trieu, N.: Efficient batched oblivious PRF with applications to private set intersection. In: ACM CCS 2016, Vienna, Austria, 24–28 October 2016, pp. 818–829. ACM Press (2016)

[KMT19] Kitagawa, F., Matsuda, T., Tanaka, K.: CCA security and trapdoor func-tions via key-dependent-message security. In: Boldyreva, A., Micciancio, D. (eds.) CRYPTO 2019. LNCS, vol. 11694, pp. 33–64. Springer, Cham (2019). https://doi.org/10.1007/978-3-030-26954-8_2

[KRS+19] Kales, D., Rechberger, C., Schneider, T., Senker, M., Weinert, C.: Mobile private contact discovery at scale. In: USENIX Security (2019)

[KW19] Koppula, V., Waters, B.: Realizing chosen ciphertext security generically in attribute-based encryption and predicate encryption. In: Boldyreva, A., Micciancio, D. (eds.) CRYPTO 2019. LNCS, vol. 11693, pp. 671–700. Springer, Cham (2019). https://doi.org/10.1007/978-3-030-26951-7_23

[LPR+20] Lepoint, T., Patel, S., Raykova, M., Seth, K., Trieu, N.: Private join and compute from PIR with default. Cryptology ePrint Archive, Report 2020/1011 (2020). https://eprint.iacr.org/2020/1011

[LQR+19] Lombardi, A., Quach, W., Rothblum, R.D., Wichs, D., Wu, D.J.: New constructions of reusable designated-verifier NIZKs. In: Boldyreva, A., Micciancio, D. (eds.) CRYPTO 2019. LNCS, vol. 11694, pp. 670–700. Springer, Cham (2019). https://doi.org/10.1007/978-3-030-26954-8_22

[MIC] Password Monitor: Safeguarding passwords in Microsoft Edge. https://www.microsoft.com/en-us/research/blog/password-monitor-safeguarding-passwords-in-microsoft-edge/

[NP01] Naor, M., Pinkas, B.: Efficient oblivious transfer protocols. In: 12th SODA, Washington, DC, USA, 7–9 January 2001, pp. 448–457. ACM-SIAM (2001)

[PRTY19] Pinkas, B., Rosulek, M., Trieu, N., Yanai, A.: SpOT-light: lightweight private set intersection from sparse OT extension. In: Boldyreva, A., Micciancio, D. (eds.) CRYPTO 2019. LNCS, vol. 11694, pp. 401–431. Springer, Cham (2019). https://doi.org/10.1007/978-3-030-26954-8_13

[PRTY20] Pinkas, B., Rosulek, M., Trieu, N., Yanai, A.: PSI from PaXoS: fast, mali-cious private set intersection. In: Canteaut, A., Ishai, Y. (eds.) EURO-CRYPT 2020. LNCS, vol. 12106, pp. 739–767. Springer, Cham (2020). https://doi.org/10.1007/978-3-030-45724-2_25

[PSSZ15] Pinkas, B., Schneider, T., Segev, G., Zohner, M.: Phasing: private set intersection using permutation-based hashing. In: USENIX Security 2015, Washington, DC, USA, 12–14 August 2015, pp. 515–530. USENIX Asso-ciation (2015)

[PSTY19] Pinkas, B., Schneider, T., Tkachenko, O., Yanai, A.: Efficient circuit-based psi with linear communication. In: Ishai, Y., Rijmen, V. (eds.) EUROCRYPT 2019. LNCS, vol. 11478, pp. 122–153. Springer, Cham (2019). https://doi.org/10.1007/978-3-030-17659-4_5

[PSWW18] Pinkas, B., Schneider, T., Weinert, C., Wieder, U.: Efficient circuit-based psi via Cuckoo hashing. In: Nielsen, J.B., Rijmen, V. (eds.) EUROCRYPT 2018. LNCS, vol. 10822, pp. 125–157. Springer, Cham (2018). https://doi.org/10.1007/978-3-319-78372-7_5

[PVW08] Peikert, C., Vaikuntanathan, V., Waters, B.: A framework for efficient and composable oblivious transfer. In: Wagner, D. (ed.) CRYPTO 2008. LNCS, vol. 5157, pp. 554–571. Springer, Heidelberg (2008). https://doi.org/10.1007/978-3-540-85174-5_31

[Rab05] Rabin, M.O.: How to exchange secrets with oblivious transfer. Cryptology ePrint Archive, Report 2005/187 (2005). https://eprint.iacr.org/2005/187

[RS21] Rindal, P., Schoppmann, P.: VOLE-PSI: fast OPRF and circuit-PSI from vector-OLE. In: International Conference on the Theory and Applications of Cryptographic Techniques, EUROCRYPT 2021. Advances in Cryptology (2021)

[TPY+19] Thomas, K., et al.: Protecting accounts from credential stuffing with password breach alerting. In: USENIX Security (2019)

[TSS+20] Trieu, N., Shehata, K., Saxena, P., Shokri, R., Song, D.: Epione: lightweight contact tracing with strong privacy. IEEE Data Eng. Bull. **43**(2), 95–107 (2020)

Ring-Based Identity Based Encryption – Asymptotically Shorter MPK and Tighter Security

Parhat Abla[1,2], Feng-Hao Liu[3], Han Wang[1,2(✉)], and Zhedong Wang[4]

[1] State Key Laboratory of Information Security, Institute of Information Engineering, Chinese Academy of Science, Beijing, China
{parhat,wanghan}@iie.ac.cn
[2] School of Cyber Security, University of Chinese Academy of Science, Beijing, China
[3] Florida Atlantic University, Boca Raton, FL, USA
liuf@fau.edu
[4] School of Cyber Science and Engineering, Shanghai Jiao Tong University, Shanghai, China

Abstract. This work constructs an identity based encryption from the ring learning with errors assumption (RLWE), with shorter master public keys and tighter security analysis. To achieve this, we develop three new methods: (1) a new homomorphic equality test method using nice algebraic structures of the rings, (2) a new family of hash functions with natural homomorphic evaluation algorithms, and (3) a new insight for tighter reduction analyses. These methods can be used to improve other important cryptographic tasks, and thus are of general interests.

Particularly, our homomorphic equality test method can derive a new method for packing/unpacking GSW-style encodings, showing a new non-trivial advantage of RLWE over the plain LWE. Moreover, our new insight for tighter analyses can improve the analyses of all the currently known partition-based IBE designs, achieving the best of the both from prior analytical frameworks of Waters (Eurocrypt '05) and Bellare and Ristenpart (Eurocrypt '09).

1 Introduction

Identity-based Encryption (IBE) was introduced by [33] as a generalization of the traditional public-key encryption (PKE) in which a publicly known string (id) of a party can serve as its public key pk_{id}. This primitive is particularly useful in scenarios that require to manage a large amount of public keys, without the need to access a public-key infrastructure (PKI). Since its first realization [11], there has been significant research in the past two decades [1,4,9,10,19,20,25,36–40], constructing various IBE schemes from different assumptions.

There have been two major security notions – selective security and adaptive security studied in the literature, where the former requires the adversary to choose the challenge id before seeing the master public key, yet the latter does

© International Association for Cryptologic Research 2021
K. Nissim and B. Waters (Eds.): TCC 2021, LNCS 13044, pp. 157–187, 2021.
https://doi.org/10.1007/978-3-030-90456-2_6

not have this restriction. Obviously the adaptive security is more desirable by providing stronger security for more realistic settings, yet realizing such a notion is quite challenging, especially when one aims at comparable efficiency in the plain model with the selectively secure designs.

Prior constructions from bilinear groups have achieved this task via the powerful framework of dual-system [36]. However, it is elusive whether the dual-system framework can be instantiated from other assumptions, especially from a post-quantum candidate such as lattices. For the post-quantum settings, even though there are adaptively secure lattice-based IBE, the current instantiations come at a rather higher cost in the size of mpk, ciphertext, and/or larger security loss in the reduction. How to improve these aspects is an important step towards realizing a practical post-quantum IBE.

In this work, we focus on adaptively secure lattice-based IBE with smaller mpk, comparable ciphertexts, and smaller security loss for the reduction. Below we discuss challenges for current approaches and then our new ideas.

Challenges in Current Techniques. Among the existing lattice-based IBE schemes, the most efficient one is the selectively secure scheme by [1], which only requires 2 public matrices in mpk (or ring vectors using Ring-LWE [27]) and has rather small ciphertexts. To achieve the adaptive security, there have been several proposals, but they all have various drawbacks as stated below.

There are two ways to achieve the shortest mpk that exactly matches the selectively secure one as [1], but both suffer from serious issues. The first one simply applies the generic complexity leveraging argument, yet the security reduction would lose 2^ℓ in advantage (ℓ is the bit length of ID), resulting in a much larger security parameter required in the underlying assumption. The second method is a new bootstrapping via a recent technique by [14,18], which transforms any selectively secure IBE into an adaptively secure one without blowing up the mpk at all. The resulting scheme is however, not considered even close to practical as each ciphertext consists of ℓ garbled circuits.

More efficient IBE can be achieved via a lattice vanishing technique by [1], yet the scheme has a larger mpk (i.e., $O(\lambda)$ basic matrices or ring vectors) and reduction running time (an additive $O(1/\epsilon^2)$ increase), compared with the selectively secure scheme.[1] Later, subsequent work [4,25,38,39] improved this technique by using homomorphic computation in novel ways [3,21,29] with more delicate security analyses. Yet these schemes still have several critical shortcomings.

- The best scheme (asymptotically) is the one by [39], which only has $\omega(\log \lambda)$ basic matrices (or ring vectors) in mpk and rather small ciphertexts. However, the IBE construction requires to use Barrington's Theorem [5] to compute an NC1 boolean circuit, which can be done in polynomial time in theory yet would not be expected to be efficient in practice. In fact, the work [39] did not (was not able to) present an explicit construction, making it hard to determine concrete bounds for the parameters for comparison.
- The follow up works [4,25,38,39] removed the $O(1/\epsilon^2)$ blowup of [1] in the reduction running time, but would incur an additional reduction loss of $O(\epsilon)$,

---

[1] λ is the security parameter and ϵ is the adversary's advantage in attacking the IBE scheme.

multiplicatively. Seemingly this tradeoff is inherent, i.e., the reduction either blows up its running time by $O(1/\epsilon^2)$ additively or loses its advantage by an extra $O(\epsilon)$ multiplicatively, under the current techniques.

1.1 Our Contributions

In this work, we significantly improve existing lattice-based IBE in the parameters and security analysis. The crux relies on new techniques related to homomorphic computation in the cyclotomic rings and new analytical insights to achieve tighter analysis for general partition-based IBE. We believe that these tools can be applied broadly and thus are of general interests. Below we summarize our two major contributions, and present our new techniques in Sect. 1.2.

- We construct an adaptively secure IBE based on Ring-LWE, with $\omega(1)$ ring vectors in the master public key. This improves the prior state-of-the-art [39] by a factor of $\log \lambda$. Additionally, every component in our construction is explicit, i.e., without relying the Barrington's Theorem as required by [39], and thus we are able to determine concrete bounds for all parameters.
- We identify an analytical insight that improves all (to our knowledge) prior security reductions of the partition-based designs (e.g., [1,4,25,38,39]). Particularly, our reduction only blows up the running time by a small fixed polynomial (independent of ϵ), and does not lose an additional $O(\epsilon)$ in advantage, breaking the seemingly unavoidable tradeoff as above.

Table 1. Comparison with Prior Lattice IBE Schemes in the Ring Setting.

Scheme	# of ring vectors in the mpk	Bit length of id	RLWE Param $\frac{1}{\alpha} = \frac{q}{\sigma_{RLWE}}$	# of ring vectors in ct/sk$_{id}$	Reduction cost
[1]	$O(\lambda)$	$\Theta(\lambda)$	$\tilde{O}(n^{3.5})$	$O(1)$	$T' = T + \tilde{O}(\lambda^5 \cdot Q/\epsilon^2)$, $\epsilon' = O(\epsilon/(\lambda^5 Q))$
[25]	$O(\lambda^{\frac{1}{\mu}})^\dagger$	$\Theta(\lambda)$	$O(n^{0.5+2\mu})$	$O(1)$	$T' = O(T)$, $\epsilon' = O(((\frac{\lambda\epsilon}{Q})^\mu/\lambda)^{\mu+1})$
[39] I +[24]	$\omega(\log^2(\lambda))$	$\Theta(\lambda)$	$\tilde{O}(n^{5.5})$	$O(1)$	$T' = O(T)$, $\epsilon' = O(\epsilon^{v+1}/Q^v)$
[39] II	$\omega(\log(\lambda))$	$\Theta(\lambda)$	$poly(n)^*$	$O(1)$	$T' = O(T)$, $\epsilon' = O(\epsilon^2/\lambda^2 Q)$
Ours A	$\omega(\log(\lambda))$	$\Theta(\lambda)$	$\tilde{O}(n^{4.5+\frac{4}{\kappa}})$	$O(1)$	$T' = T + \min\{\tilde{O}(\lambda^{1/\kappa} \cdot Q/\epsilon), O(\lambda^{(1+3/\kappa)} \cdot Q^{\kappa+3})\}$, $\epsilon' = O(\epsilon/\lambda^{1/\kappa}Q)^{\dagger\dagger}$
Ours B	$\omega(1)$	$\Theta(\lambda)$	$\tilde{O}(n^{7.5+\frac{4}{\kappa}})$	$O(1)$	$T' = T + \min\{\tilde{O}(\lambda^{1/\kappa} \cdot Q/\epsilon), O(\lambda^{(1+3/\kappa)} \cdot Q^{\kappa+3})\}$, $\epsilon' = O(\epsilon/\lambda^{1/\kappa}Q)^{\dagger\dagger}$

Notation: mpk, ct, and sk$_{id}$ denote the master public key, ciphertext, and secret key of the IBE. λ, n, q, σ_{RLWE} denote the security parameter, ring dimension, modulus, and gaussian parameter of RLWE. T, Q, and ϵ denote the adversary's running time, number of key queries and advantage in attacking the IBE scheme, and T', ϵ' denote the reduction's time and advantage in breaking RLWE. All the schemes have basic vector size of bit length $O(n \log^2 q)$. The size can be optimized to $O(n \log q)$ at the cost of increasing the size of q, which requires smaller RLWE parameter $1/\alpha$. All the schemes set the ring dimension $n = \Theta(\lambda)$. Here we use $\omega(f(\lambda))$ to denote any function that asymptotically dominates $f(\lambda)$, e.g., $\omega(1)$ can be $\log \log \lambda$ or $\log \log \log \lambda$, etc.
* poly(n) denotes some fixed but large polynomial. It is hard to determine an explicit bound for comparison due to the implicit construction of the work.
† $\mu \in \mathbb{N}$ is a constant that can be chosen arbitrary. Since the reduction cost is exponential in μ, this value typically set very small (e.g., $\mu = 2$ or 3).
‡ $v > 1$ is the constant that can be set small, depending on the underlying error correcting code.
†† $\kappa \geq 1$ can be any constant that satisfies $n^{\frac{1}{\kappa}} > 3 + \kappa$, e.g., 2 or 4, depending on how we set parameters of the underlying error correcting code.

In Table 1, we summarize our results and a comparison with prior published works[2] in the asymptotic setting. To compare fairly with some prior schemes described in the plain-LWE[3], we calculate the parameters of their ring variants and set the basic all vectors with the same bit length. We notice that parameters about some prior works in our table are different than the table of [39], which might over calculated some parameters. We also notice that there is a line of work, studying (almost) tightly secure IBE from lattices, e.g., [13,26]. These constructions are not partition-based designs, and in general they require to homomorphically compute a PRF, resulting in at least $O(\lambda)$ basic ring vectors in mpk. In the context of "compact" IBE (for mpk), we believe that partitioned-based IBE are more suitable, so we only include these schemes for comparison.

Our scheme can be instantiated with multiple sets of parameters. We present two of them – scheme A requires smaller RLWE parameter $1/\alpha$, but require longer mpk, yet scheme B requires a slightly larger $1/\alpha$ but smaller mpk. Assuming that the security level of RLWE is roughly the same for any $1/\alpha = \mathsf{poly}(n)$, then scheme B would have smaller overall size, asymptotically.

Remark. We point out that it is possible to further shrink the mpk size of [39] I +[24] to $\omega(\log \lambda)$ basic ring vectors without applying the Barrington Theorem, by using an ECC with larger alphabets, e.g., [8], even though this idea was not explicitly written. This approach is similar to our scheme A, yet our scheme enjoys a tighter analysis. It is highly non-trivial to further shrink the mpk size to $\omega(1)$ ring vectors (as our scheme B), and this is the main novelty of this work.

A prior draft of this work would require to set $n = O(\lambda^{1+\tau})$ for a small constant τ, thus resulting in a larger length per basic ring vector. This work removes the requirement, showing that the typical setting $n = O(\lambda)$ is sufficient. As we mentioned in the note of Table 1, all the basic ring vectors (of all the listed schemes) have bit length $O(n \log^2 q) = O(\lambda \log^2 \lambda)$, which can be further optimized to $O(n \log q) = O(\lambda \log \lambda)$ by using a larger base of the gadget matrix. Thus, counting the number of ring vectors would be an easier way to compare efficiency/size of the listed schemes.

1.2   Technical Overview

We present an overview of our new techniques in two parts: (1) new IBE designs, and (2) tighter reduction analysis.

Part I: IBE Design
We start with a quick recap of some common features of the existing partitioned based IBE since [1], and then describe our new insights.

---

[2] There is an unpublished work [4] that achieves essentially the same parameters as scheme II of [39], except [4] has an explicit bound on $q = O(n^{15.5})$.

[3] The plain-LWE schemes usually count how many basic matrices in mpk, where each matrix is larger than the basic ring vectors of Ring-LWE designs by at least a multiplicative factor of $O(\lambda)$.

Recap of Existing IBE Designs. At a high level, the public parameter of IBE [1] contains matrices $\mathbf{A}, \mathbf{B}_1, \ldots, \mathbf{B}_\ell$, where ℓ is the length of the identity, i.e., $\mathsf{id} \in \{0,1\}^\ell$. To derive a public key for an identity id, one just computes the matrix $\mathbf{F}_{\mathsf{id}} = [\mathbf{A} \mid \sum_{i \in [\ell]} (-1)^{\mathsf{id}[i]} \mathbf{B}_i]$. The encryption algorithm uses the dual-Regev scheme with respect to the matrix $\mathbf{F}_{\mathsf{id}}$. In the security proof, each public $\mathbf{B}_i$ is switched to $\mathbf{A} \cdot \mathbf{R}_i + h_i \mathbf{G}$ for some small-norm $\mathbf{R}_i$ and some random h_i. In this way, we can rewrite $\mathbf{F}_{\mathsf{id}} = [\mathbf{A} \mid \mathbf{A} \cdot \mathbf{R}_{\mathsf{id}} + H(\mathsf{id})\mathbf{G}]$, where $\mathbf{R}_{\mathsf{id}} = \sum_{i \in [\ell]} (-1)^{\mathsf{id}[i]} \mathbf{R}_i$, and $H(\mathsf{id}) = \sum_{i \in [\ell]} (-1)^{\mathsf{id}[i]} h_i$. The work [1] showed that suppose the hash function H isolates – with non-negligible probability, H separates the challenge id^* with the other query id's, then the scheme is adaptively secure. Later in subsequent works [4,38,39], it was observed that in fact we can view $\mathbf{B}_i$'s as GSW FHE ciphertexts [3,21], and thus the key derivation process can be viewed as homomorphic computation of $H(\mathsf{id})$, (id in the clear and the description of H encrypted). Thus, by allowing the hash function to compute beyond the linear combination, it is possible to apply a more succinct hash function that can be encoded by much fewer public matrices.

Moreover, the work [25] showed that the plain LWE-based approach can be ported to the Ring-LWE setting (in 2-th powers cyclotomic rings), with a generic parameter saving. Particularly, the matrices can be replaced by ring vectors $\boldsymbol{a}, \boldsymbol{b}_1, \ldots, \boldsymbol{b}_\ell$, and the intuition of homomorphic computation of the hash function works smoothly in the ring setting. Therefore, working in the ring has a generic advantage for smaller parameters than the plain LWE.

Challenges. Currently IBE with the shortest mpk (asymptotically) comes from the work [39], which proposed to use integer multiplication-then-modulo to design the hash function. Particularly, the hash function can be described by $a, b, \rho \in \mathbb{Z}$ such that $H_{a,b,\rho}(\mathsf{id}) = a \times \mathsf{id} + b \mod \rho$, where id is treated as an integer and the computation is in $\mathbb{Z}$. The work [39] showed that it suffices to encode $t = \omega(\log \lambda)$ bits of each a, b, ρ for the security analysis, and thus it suffices to use just ring vectors $\mathbf{b}_1, \ldots, \mathbf{b}_{3t}$ to encode the hash function, resulting in total $\omega(\log \lambda)$ matrices or ring vectors in the public parameter. Since integer multiplication-then-modulo is in NC1 [6], this homomorphic computation can be done within a polynomial modulus q by the Barrington's Theorem [23]. However, this approach does not give an explicit homomorphic computation method of the hash function, and it is hard to determine an explicit bound of q. This is one serious limitation of the current technique.

Our New Insights. Our goal is to tackle the challenge as described above, and additionally, determine new methods to further shrink the size of mpk. To achieve this, we develop two new techniques: (1) a new homomorphic equality testing method under the Ring-LWE, and (2) a new family of hash functions in the ring setting that can be naturally computed homomorphically. By using these two techniques, we only need $\ell' = \omega(1)$ ring vectors in the mpk and our IBE design can be computed explicitly without the Barrington's Theorem.

New Technique (1): As we discussed above, the design of IBE is highly related to homomorphic computation of a hash function. To shrink the size of mpk, it suffices to construct a more efficient GSW style encoding that can pack/unpack multiple bit encodings into one encoding. We then observe that this task is deeply connected to the homomorphic equality test as we elaborate how next.

The most general form of the homomorphic equality test is given an encoding Encode(α) and some β in the clear, homomorphically compute an encoded bit Encode(τ) such that $\tau = 1$ if and only if $\alpha = \beta$. Denote this family of functions as {Equal$_\beta(\alpha)$} where each function is parameterized by β in the clear. If we can achieve this task beyond bit compute, i.e., α can be some ring element, then we can homomorphically extract every single bit of α from Encode(α) by the equality test, by computing $\sum_{\beta \in Z}$ Equal$_\beta(\alpha)$ where Z is the set of all possible values that have consistent bit with α for the targeted bit we want to extract. (We present the detailed procedure in Sect. 3). However, the general task seems to incur a large blowup in the noise, and thus unclear whether it is feasible.

This work identifies a critical property of cyclotomic rings so that we can achieve an important subclass of the task. Particularly, let us take R as the m-th cyclotomic ring where m is a power of two. In this case, we know that $R = \mathbb{Z}[x]/(x^n + 1)$ where $n = \varphi(m) = m/2$. Then, we consider the case where α appears in the exponent of the monomial x (corresponding to a root of unity in cyclotomic rings); i.e., given Encode(x^α) and $\beta \in \mathbb{Z}$, compute the desired Encode(τ). To design a homomorphic equality test function in this ring setting, we first observe a critical fact in the rings. For any monomial $v = x^i$ where $i \neq 0$ mod m, we have $f(v) := \sum_{i=0}^{m-1} v^i = \frac{1-v^m}{1-v} = 0$, as the denominator $1 - v$ is not equal to 0, and $1 - v^m = 1 - x^{mi} = 0$ for $i \neq 0 \mod m$. On the other hand, if $v = 1$, i.e., $i = 0 \mod m$, then $f(v) = m$. Therefore, the function f naturally separates the two cases as: $f(x^i) = \begin{cases} 0 & \text{if } i \neq 0 \mod m \\ m & \text{otherwise.} \end{cases}$

Using this fact, we can design a simple algorithm for our goal: given $\boldsymbol{b} =$ Encode(x^α) and β, we compute the following three steps: (1) first we set $\boldsymbol{b}' =$ Encode($x^{\alpha-\beta}$) by a homomorphic scale multiplication of $x^{-\beta}$.

(2) Then we homomorphically compute $\boldsymbol{b}'' = f(\boldsymbol{b}') =$ Encode($f(x^{\alpha-\beta})$). (3) Finally, we output $\boldsymbol{b}^*$ by homomorphically multiply $\boldsymbol{b}''$ and Encode(m^{-1}).[4] Clearly, this procedure outputs Encode(τ) where $\tau = 1$ if $\alpha = \beta \mod m$ and otherwise 0. Our analysis crucially relies on that multiplying monomials does not blow up the norm of a matrix, and thus the noise behaves the same as the bit multiplication case.

By using the above techniques, we can pack/unpack $\log(m)$ bit encodings into one single encoding. This would imply that we can further shrink the size of mpk required in the work [39] by a factor of $O(\log m)$, resulting $t = \omega(1)$ ring vectors for mpk under the Ring-LWE setting. This algebraic structure of Ring-LWE demonstrates another non-trivial efficiency gain over the plain LWE, which may be of independent interests.

---

[4] We note that m^{-1} with respect to $\mathbb{Z}_q$ exists if we choose m and q to be co-prime.

New Technique (2): By building upon the equality test technique, we further design a new hash function that can be explicitly computed, homomorphically, without the Barrington's Theorem. We start with a nice observation by [4] that identifies that in fact (almost) pairwise independent hash functions suffice to isolate [35]. To design a suitable hash function, we propose to use an error-correcting code (ECC : $\{0,1\}^{\ell} \rightarrow \mathbb{Z}_p^{\mathsf{L}}$) with good relative distance. We first consider the hash function $H_{\alpha,\beta}(\mathsf{id}) = \mathsf{ECC}(\mathsf{id})[\alpha] + \beta$. It is not hard to show that this hash function behaves as an almost pairwise independent hash. The drawback is that the range might be too small in the application of IBE designs. To amplify the range, we can use a parallel repetition: $H_{\alpha,\beta}^{\|}(z) = \left(H_{\alpha_1,\beta_1}(z), \ldots, H_{\alpha_t,\beta_t}(z) \right)$. In fact, using error correcting codes to design a partition function has been explored in the context of IBE and VRF, e.g., [8,24,39], yet these generic designs are still not naturally compatible with the ring setting. Our new insight is to design an embedding method that maps the output $H_{\alpha,\beta}^{\|} \in \mathbb{Z}_p^t$ to the ring R of the underlying Ring-LWE. In this way, the homomorphic computation method can be designed based on the above equality test method, and therefore our IBE design can be explicit, avoiding the route of the Barrington's Theorem. The actual design requires to deal with further technical subtleties. We refer the readers to Sect. 4 for details.

Part II: Tighter Reduction Analysis
Next we present our new insights to achieve a tighter analysis for general partitioned-based IBE designs. We start with a recap of the existing proof framework.

Recap of the Proof Framework. As we discussed above, the security proof framework switches the public matrices (or ring vectors) $\mathbf{B}_i$ to $\mathbf{A} \cdot \mathbf{R}_i + h_i \mathbf{G}$, and then homomorphically computes $\mathbf{F}_{\mathsf{id}} = [\mathbf{A}|\mathbf{A} \cdot \mathbf{R}_{\mathsf{id}} + H(\mathsf{id})\mathbf{G}]$, for some suitable hash function H. Intuitively, the security reduction can respond to a key query id if $H(\mathsf{id}) \neq 0$, and then embeds the (Ring) LWE challenge if $H(\mathsf{id}^*) = 0$ for the challenge id^*. Therefore, if the hash function separates all the query id's from the challenge id^* as we just stated, then the reduction can be used to attack the underlying (Ring) LWE. On the other hand, if the adversary queries *some* id that $H(\mathsf{id}) = 0$, then the reduction simply aborts and outputs a random guess. By designing an appropriate parameters for H, we can show that with some noticeable probability, we will have $H(\mathsf{id}) \neq 0$ for all id's queried by the adversary and $H(\mathsf{id}^*) = 0$. This implies that the security reduction will still have sufficient advantage in attacking the underlying (Ring) LWE.

Challenges. To analyze the limitation of the current reduction approach, we delve into some further details. First we denote as the event abort if the adversary has queried some id such that $H(\mathsf{id}) = 0$ or $H(\mathsf{id}^*) \neq 0$, and ¬abort as the other case. Let $\gamma(I)$ denote the probability of ¬abort for the query pattern $I = \{\mathsf{id}_1, \ldots, \mathsf{id}_t\}$ for some $t \leq Q$, and $\gamma(I) \in [\gamma_{\min}, \gamma_{\max}]$ for every query pattern I.

The work [1,7,37] showed the following statement (simplified): suppose the adversary has advantage ϵ in breaking the IBE scheme, then by this partitioning strategy, the reduction would have advantage roughly $\epsilon\gamma_{\min} - (\gamma_{\max} - \gamma_{\min})/2$

in breaking the (Ring) LWE hard problem. Now (also pointed out by [1]), we would face a challenge in choosing the range $[\gamma_{\min}, \gamma_{\max}]$ (by setting appropriate the hash function parameters):

- If we aim to optimize the reduction's advantage, we can set $\gamma_{\max} \approx 1/Q$ and $\gamma_{\min} \approx 1/2Q$. However, as $\epsilon\gamma_{\min}$ might be smaller than the extra term $(\gamma_{\max} - \gamma_{\min})/2$, we need to apply the technique of Waters [37] that reduces the gap between $\gamma_{\min}$ and $\gamma_{\max}$ by adding an extra "artificial abort". However, this would require to blow up the running time by roughly $O(1/\epsilon^2)$.
- The other way to handle this is by Bellare and Ristenpart [7], which is then used by the follow up works [4,25,38,39]. Particularly, they choose $\gamma_{\max} \approx \epsilon/Q$ and $\gamma_{\min} \approx \epsilon(1-\epsilon)/Q$, so that the gap would be ϵ^2/Q, implying $\epsilon\gamma_{\min} - (\gamma_{\max}-\gamma_{\min})/2 \geq \epsilon^2/2Q$. This does not need to blow up the running time, yet the advantage would suffer from an extra multiplicative loss of ϵ compared with the above.

Our New Insights. To break the tradeoff, we first give a new method that can generally improve both of the above two cases: for the former, the running time blowup is improved to $O(1/\epsilon)$, and for the latter, the advantage only loses an extra multiplicative $\sqrt{\epsilon}$. Then we show how to further reduce the running time blowup for the first case, so that it can be upper bounded by a fixed polynomial (in n, Q) without relying on the advantage ϵ. The crux for the first idea relies on using the framework [30], on which we devise a better advantage bound than that of $\epsilon\gamma_{\min} - (\gamma_{\max} - \gamma_{\min})/2$. The second idea uses a critical property of the design of the hash function. We elaborate the insights below.

First we recall the work [30], which considers two quantities α, β, where the former is the probability that an adversary does not output $\perp$, and the latter is the conditional probability that the adversary outputs the correct bit, conditioned on the non-$\perp$ event. Then the work [30] defined the advantage in a decisional game $\epsilon := \alpha(1 - 2\beta)^2 = \alpha\delta^2$ where $\delta = |1 - 2\beta|$.

Now we analyze the reduction above under this framework. Consider an (α, β) adversary with advantage $\epsilon = \alpha\delta^2$. If we take the reduction as above, then the reduction has $\gamma_{\min}$ probability of $\neg$abort, resulting in non-$\perp$ probability $\alpha' = \alpha\gamma_{\min}$ as the hash is chosen independent of the adversary. By a careful analysis, the reduction's conditional success probability would be roughly $\beta' \approx (\gamma_{\min}/\gamma_{\max}) \cdot \beta$. In order to ensure a significant success (conditional) probability of the reduction, i.e., sufficiently large $\delta' = |1 - 2\beta'|$, we aim to set $\gamma_{\min}/\gamma_{\max} \approx 1 - \delta/4$, meaning that $\delta' = |1 - 2\beta'| \approx |1 - 2(1 - \delta/4)\beta| = |\pm\delta + \delta\beta/2| \geq \delta/2 \geq \sqrt{\epsilon}/2$. Now the reduction has advantage $\alpha'\delta'^2 \approx \alpha \cdot \gamma_{\min} \cdot \delta^2/4 \approx \epsilon \cdot \gamma_{\min}/4$.

Now we can improve the parameters with or without the artificial abort:

- We can improve the running time of the first case compared with the previous analysis. Particularly, we set $\gamma_{\max} \approx 1/Q$ and $\gamma_{\min} \approx 1/2Q$. The ratio of $\gamma_{\min}/\gamma_{\max}$ is 0.5, which needs to be increased to $(1-\delta/4)$ by the artificial abort technique of Waters [37]. Yet now, we only need precision $O(\delta) = O(\sqrt{\epsilon})$, which yield $O(1/\epsilon)$ samples, whereas the prior analysis needs precision $O(\epsilon)$, and thus $O(1/\epsilon^2)$ samples.

– We can also improve the reduction's advantage for the second case. Particularly, we can set $\gamma_{\max} \approx \delta/4Q$ and $\gamma_{\min} \approx \delta(1 - \delta/4)/4Q$. In this way, the ratio is $(1 - \delta/4)$ as needed, and the reduction's advantage would lose a multiplicative factor of $O(\delta) = O(\sqrt{\epsilon})$ compared with the above, whereas the prior analysis would lose $O(\epsilon)$.

Finally, we show how to further improve the reduction's running time for the first case, to get rid of the dependency on $O(1/\epsilon)$, which would be large when ϵ is small. As a result, our reduction has a smaller overhead in running time, i.e., $T + \text{poly}(\lambda)$ for some small polynomial that is independent of ε (recall that T is adversary's running time), and maintains the advantage, achieving the best of the both of the two cases.

To achieve this, we observe that the blowup in running time comes from the estimation of $\gamma(I)$ for the technique of Waters' artificial abort, which roughly needs $O(1/\epsilon)$ samples for the procedure. To get rid of this dependency, we observe that the sample space of the our design of hash function H (all possible choices of the hash function) is roughly bounded by a small fixed polynomial $\text{poly}(\lambda)$. Therefore, if the adversary has a larger advantage ϵ, then the reduction would use $O(1/\epsilon)$ samples to estimate $\gamma(I)$, whereas if the ϵ is small, then the reduction would enumerate all possible choices of the hash function to compute the *exact value* of $\gamma(I)$. Therefore, the running time in the worst case would be upper bounded by $T + \text{poly}(\lambda)$ as desired.

2 Preliminaries

This section includes the basic preliminaries. Readers who are already familiar with the concepts can skip the entire section and start to read from Sect. 3.

Notations. We denote $\mathbb{Z}$ as the set of the integers and $\mathbb{R}$ as the real numbers. For a positive integer k, let $[k]$ be set of integers $\{0, 1, ..., k - 1\}$. We denote $[a, b]$ as the set $[a, b] \cap \mathbb{Z}$ for any integers $a, b \in \mathbb{N}$ satisfying $a \leq b$. We use bold uppercase letters to denote matrices (e.g., $\mathbf{A}$), and bold lowercase letters for column vectors (e.g., $\boldsymbol{a}$), and denote the horizontal concatenation of two vectors $\boldsymbol{a}, \boldsymbol{b}$ by $[\boldsymbol{a}|\boldsymbol{b}]$. For any $1 \leq p \leq \infty$, the p-norm of a vector $\boldsymbol{a}$ is defined as $\|\boldsymbol{a}\|_p = (\sum_i \|\boldsymbol{a}_i\|^p)^{1/p}$, and p-norm of a matrix $\mathbf{A}$ is defined by $\|\mathbf{A}\|_p = \max_{\|\boldsymbol{x}\|_p = 1} \|\mathbf{A}\boldsymbol{x}\|_p$, assuming the dimensions match. We omit the subscript p if $p = 2$. We denote $s_1(\mathbf{A})$ as the largest singular value of $\mathbf{A}$, then we have $s_1(\mathbf{A}) = \|\mathbf{A}\|$. We say $\varepsilon : \mathbb{N} \to [0, 1)$ be a negligible function, if for any $c > 0$, we have $\varepsilon(n) < \frac{1}{n^c}$ starting from some integer $n_0(c) \in \mathbb{N}$. We say an event happens with overwhelmingly, if the probability of that event not happens is negligible. For any two random variables X and Y with support Ω, define the statistical distance, denoted $\Delta(X, Y)$, as $\Delta(X, Y) = \frac{1}{2} \sum_{s \in \Omega} |\Pr[X = s] - \Pr[Y = s]|$. We say X is statistically close(or ϵ-close) to Y, if the statistical distance $\Delta(X, Y)$ is negligible(or $\Delta(X, Y) \leq \epsilon$).

Definition 2.1 (Relative Distance). *Let $\mathbb{F}$ be some finite field and $\mathsf{L} \in \mathbb{N}$, $\mathcal{D}$ be some input domain, and $\mathsf{ECC} : \mathcal{D} \to \mathbb{F}^{\mathsf{L}}$ be some encoding, where the output* *vector is indexed by* $[1, \ldots, \mathsf{L}]$. *Define the relative distance of* ECC, *denoted* Υ, *as*

$$\Upsilon := \min \left\{ \Pr_{i \xleftarrow{\$} [1, \ldots, \mathsf{L}]} \left[\mathsf{ECC}(a)[i] \neq \mathsf{ECC}(b)[i] \right] \middle| a \neq b, a, b \in \mathcal{D} \right\}$$

2.1   Identity-Based Encryption (IBE)

Definition 2.2 (IBE [11,33]). *An identity-based encryption scheme* Π *consists of four algorithms* {Setup, KeyGen, Enc, Dec} *as follows.*

- Setup (1^λ): *On input the security parameter* λ, *the algorithm outputs the master public key* mpk *and the master secret key* msk.
- KeyGen (mpk, msk, id): *On input* (mpk, msk) *and an identity* id, *the key generation algorithm outputs a secret key* $\mathsf{sk}_{\mathsf{id}}$ *corresponding to the identity* id.
- Enc (mpk, id, μ): *On input the master public key* mpk, *identity* id *and the message* μ, *the encryption algorithm outputs a ciphertext* ct.
- Dec (mpk, $\mathsf{sk}_{\mathsf{id}}$, ct): *On input the master public key* mpk, *the secret key* $\mathsf{sk}_{\mathsf{id}}$ *and the ciphertext* ct, *the decryption algorithm outputs the message* μ' *or* $\bot$.

Correctness. We say an IBE scheme Π is correct, if for any message μ and any identity id, the following holds

$$\Pr \left[\mathsf{Dec}(\mathsf{sk}_{\mathsf{id}}, \mathsf{ct}) \neq \mu \, \middle| \, \begin{array}{l} (\mathsf{mpk}, \mathsf{msk}) \leftarrow \mathsf{Setup}(1^\lambda) \\ \mathsf{sk}_{\mathsf{id}} \leftarrow \mathsf{KeyGen}(\mathsf{mpk}, \mathsf{msk}, \mathsf{id}) \\ \mathsf{ct} \leftarrow \mathsf{Enc}(\mathsf{mpk}, \mathsf{id}, \mu) \end{array} \right] < \mathsf{negl}(\lambda).$$

Security. We use the following experiment to describe the security of IBE against adaptive adversaries. Formally, for any PPT adversary $\mathcal{A}$, we consider the experiment $\mathbf{Expt}_{\mathcal{A}}^{\mathsf{IBE}}(1^\lambda)$ between $\mathcal{A}$ and the challenger defined below:

Setup: At the beginning of the experiment, the adversary $\mathcal{A}$ sends a public parameter requirement to the challenger. After receiving the public parameter requirement, the challenger runs (mpk, msk) $\leftarrow$ Setup(1^λ), and sends mpk to the adversary $\mathcal{A}$.

Phase 1: Proceeding adaptively, the adversary $\mathcal{A}$ queries a sequence of identities $(\mathsf{id}_1, \cdots, \mathsf{id}_m)$. On the i-th query, the challenger runs KeyGen(msk, id_i), and sends the result $\mathsf{sk}_{\mathsf{id}_i}$ to the $\mathcal{A}$.

Challenge: In this phase, $\mathcal{A}$ chooses an identity $\mathsf{id}^* \notin \{\mathsf{id}_1, \cdots, \mathsf{id}_m\}$ and two length-equal messages μ_0, μ_1, and forwards them to the challenger. Upon receiving the $\mathsf{id}^*, \mu_0, \mu_1$, the challenger chooses a random bit $b \in \{0, 1\}$ and runs $\mathsf{ct}^* \leftarrow \mathsf{Enc}(\mathsf{mpk}, \mathsf{id}^*, \mu_b)$. Then, the challenger sends ct^* to $\mathcal{A}$.

Phase 2: $\mathcal{A}$ continues to make key queries $(\mathsf{id}_{m+1}, \cdots, \mathsf{id}_Q)$ such that $\mathsf{id}_j \neq \mathsf{id}^*$ for any $j \in [m+1, Q]$. The challenger responds as in Phase 1.

Guess: The adversary $\mathcal{A}$ outputs a bit b' as the guess of b.

We define the notion of asymptotic security: the IBE scheme is secure if for any PPT adversary $\mathcal{A}$, the probability that $\mathcal{A}$ outputs the right bit, i.e., $b' = b$ in $\mathbf{Expt}_{\mathcal{A}}^{\mathsf{IBE}}(1^\lambda)$ is bounded by $\frac{1}{2} + \mathsf{negl}(\lambda)$ for some negligible function $\mathsf{negl}(\lambda)$.

In addition to the asymptotic notion, our work also focuses on the concrete bit-security notion, which is more relevant in practice. In the following section, we present the framework established by the recent work [30].

2.2   Concrete Bit-Security

The work [30] considers concrete bit-security for security games that capture two types of general primitives – (1) search primitives where the adversary's goal is to output a string that satisfies a certain relation, and (2) decision primitives where the adversary only needs to output one bit, trying to distinguish two challenging distributions. Clearly, IBE is a decision primitive as the adversary in $\mathbf{Expt}_{\mathcal{A}}^{\mathsf{IBE}}(1^\lambda)$ above tries to guess the challenge bit. To capture its bit-security, we present the framework of [30] for decision primitives.

Given an adversary $\mathcal{A}$, we say $\mathcal{A}$ is a $(T_{\mathcal{A}}, \alpha_{\mathcal{A}}, \beta_{\mathcal{A}})$-adversary if its running time is at most $T_{\mathcal{A}}$, output probability $\alpha_{\mathcal{A}} = \Pr[\mathcal{A} \neq \bot]$, and conditional success probability $\beta_{\mathcal{A}} = \Pr[\mathcal{A} \text{ wins} \mid \mathcal{A} \neq \bot]$, where the probabilities are over the randomness of the entire game. For a decision primitive including IBE, define the advantage of the $(T_{\mathcal{A}}, \alpha_{\mathcal{A}}, \beta_{\mathcal{A}})$-adversary $\mathcal{A}$ as $\mathsf{Adv}_{\mathcal{A}} := \alpha_{\mathcal{A}}(2\beta_{\mathcal{A}} - 1)^2$.

Importantly, this formulation allows the adversary to output $\bot$, intuitively meaning "I don't know" even for decision primitives. As the work [30] showed, in some cases it is more advantageous if the adversary admits being defeated rather than guessing at random. In this work, we demonstrate that this is extremely crucial for partition-based IBE [1,7,37,39], allowing a much better security analysis over all these prior work. For the rationale of this definitional framework, we refer the reader to the original paper [30]. Next we present the notion of bit-security for IBE in the framework of [30] as a general decision primitive.

Definition 2.3 ([30]). *We say an* IBE *scheme is adaptively secure with λ-bit security, if for all (T, α, β)-adversary $\mathcal{A}$ in $\mathbf{Expt}_{\mathcal{A}}^{\mathsf{IBE}}(1^\lambda)$, we have $\frac{T}{\mathsf{Adv}_{\mathcal{A}}} \geq 2^\lambda$.*

Remark 2.4. *The term $T_{\mathcal{A}}$ can also be generalized to any measure of resources that is linear under repetition as stated in [30]. In this work, we use the running time for simplicity. Moreover, we assume that $T_{\mathcal{A}}$ is greater than the running time of the challenger. This is without loss of generality as the security game ends at the last guessing step of the adversary, whose total running time must be at least as long as that of experiment (including the challenger's time).*

Next we present a useful lemma for the relation between the statistical distance between two games and the difference of the corresponding (α, β)'s. Due to space limit, we put the proof of the lemma below in full version of our paper.

Lemma 2.5. *Let $\mathcal{S}^{\mathcal{P}}, \mathcal{S}^{\mathcal{Q}}$ be two indistinguishability games with black-box access to two probability distribution $\mathcal{P}$ and $\mathcal{Q}$, respectively, with $\Delta(\mathcal{P}, \mathcal{Q}) \leq \varepsilon$. For any $(T_{\mathcal{A}}, \alpha_{\mathcal{A}}^{\mathcal{P}}, \beta_{\mathcal{A}}^{\mathcal{P}})$-adversary $\mathcal{A}$ with $\alpha_{\mathcal{A}}^{\mathcal{P}} > \varepsilon$ in the game $\mathcal{S}^{\mathcal{P}}$, the same $\mathcal{A}$ in the game $\mathcal{S}^{\mathcal{Q}}$ is a $(T_{\mathcal{A}}, \alpha_{\mathcal{A}}^{\mathcal{Q}}, \beta_{\mathcal{A}}^{\mathcal{Q}})$-adversary, where $\alpha_{\mathcal{A}}^{\mathcal{Q}} \geq \alpha_{\mathcal{A}}^{\mathcal{P}} - \varepsilon$ and $\beta_{\mathcal{A}}^{\mathcal{Q}} \geq \beta_{\mathcal{A}}^{\mathcal{P}} - \varepsilon/(\alpha_{\mathcal{A}}^{\mathcal{P}} - \varepsilon)$.*

2.3   Lattices and Gaussian Distributions

Lattices. A lattice is a discrete additive subgroup of $\mathbb{R}^n$. Let $\mathbf{B} = (\boldsymbol{b}_1, \ldots, \boldsymbol{b}_m) \subset \mathbb{R}^{n \times m}$ consist of m linearly independent vectors, the n-dimensional lattice Λ generated by the basis $\mathbf{B}$ is $\Lambda = \mathcal{L}(\mathbf{B}) = \{\mathbf{B} \cdot \boldsymbol{c} = \sum_{i \in [m]} c_i \cdot \boldsymbol{b}_i : \boldsymbol{c} = (c_0, \ldots, c_{m-1}) \in$

$\mathbb{Z}^m\}$. We denote $\widetilde{\mathbf{B}}$ as the Gram-Schmidt orthogonalization of $\mathbf{B}$, and $\|\mathbf{B}\|_{\mathsf{GS}}$ as the length of the longest vector of $\widetilde{\mathbf{B}}$.

In this paper, we focus on a particular family of integer lattices. Let $\mathbf{A} \in \mathbb{Z}_q^{m \times n}$ for integers m, n, q, where m and q are functions of n. We consider the following two kinds of full-rank m-dimensional integer lattices defined by $\Lambda_q^{\perp}(\mathbf{A}) = \{e \in \mathbb{Z}^m : \mathbf{A}^\top \cdot e = 0 \bmod q\}$ and its shift $\Lambda_q^u(\mathbf{A}) = \{e \in \mathbb{Z}^m : \mathbf{A}^\top \cdot e = u \bmod q\}$.

Gaussian Distributions. For any real number $s > 0$ and an n-dimensional vector c, let $\rho_{s,c}(x) := \exp(-\pi\|x - c\|^2/s^2)$ be the gaussian function with parameter s and centered at c. The discrete gaussian distribution over a lattice coset $\Lambda + u$ is defined as $D_{\Lambda+u,s}(x) = \frac{\rho_s(x)}{\rho_s(\Lambda+u)}$. Let $\eta_{\epsilon_s}(\Lambda)$ be the smoothing parameter. For a gaussian over lattices, we have the following tail bound.

Lemma 2.6 ([20,29]). *Let $\Lambda \subset \mathbb{R}^n$ be a lattice and $s > \eta_{\epsilon_s}(\Lambda)$ for some $\epsilon_s \in (0, 1/2)$. For any $c \in \mathrm{span}(\Lambda)$, we have $\Pr[\|D_{\Lambda+c,s}\| \geq s\sqrt{n}] \leq 2^{-n} \cdot \frac{1+\epsilon_s}{1-\epsilon_s}$. Furthermore, if $c = 0$, the bound holds for any $r > 0$ with $\epsilon_s = 0$.*

We say a polynomial $a = \sum_{i \in [n]} a_i x^i$ is sampled from gaussian distribution $D_{\Lambda+u,s}$, if the coefficient vector $(a_0, ..., a_{n-1})$ is sampled by $D_{\Lambda+u,s}$. We further define the gaussian distribution $D_{\Lambda+u}^{\mathsf{Coeffs}}$ as the distribution of a polynomial $a = \sum_{i \in [n]} a_i x^i$ sampled from gaussian distribution $D_{\Lambda+u,s}$. We also extend this notion to the polynomial vector $a = (a_1, \cdots, a_n)$ component-wise.

Sub-Gaussian. It is convenient for our analyses to use sub-Gaussian random variables and their bounds. We defer the details to full version of this paper.

2.4   Rings and Ideal Lattices

Next, we briefly present the concepts and lemmas related to rings and ideal lattices required in this work. See the work of [27,28] for further details.

Rings. For an m-th cyclotomic polynomial $\Phi(x)$ (of degree $n = \varphi(m)$), define the polynomial quotient ring $R = \mathbb{Z}[x]/\Phi(x)$. For an integer q, denote R_q as the ring R/qR. For the polynomial ring R, we denote $[-\rho, \rho]_R \subset R$ as the set of elements in R with coefficients in $[-\rho, \rho] \cap \mathbb{Z}$. Any element in R can be considered as a vector of its coefficients. Namely, an element $a = \sum_{i \in [n]} a_i x^i \in R$ can be seen as the vector $a = (a_0, ..., a_{n-1})$. We call this map as coefficient embedding (denoted as $\mathsf{Coeffs}(\cdot)$). Furthermore, we can also represent a ring element $a \in R$ as a matrix in $\mathbb{Z}^{n \times n}$ by the following map $\mathsf{Rot} : R \to \mathbb{Z}^{n \times n}$:

$$\mathsf{Rot}(a) = \begin{bmatrix} \mathsf{Coeffs}(a)^\top \\ \mathsf{Coeffs}(xa \bmod \Phi(x))^\top \\ \vdots \\ \mathsf{Coeffs}(x^{n-1}a \bmod \Phi(x))^\top \end{bmatrix}.$$

Furthermore, we extend this map to ring vectors and matrices by applying it entry-wise, i.e., for a vector $a^\top = (a_1, \ldots, a_m) \in R^m$, we define $\mathsf{Rot}(a^\top) =$

$[\mathsf{Rot}(a_1)|\dots|\mathsf{Rot}(a_m)] \in \mathbb{Z}^{n \times nm}$, and the map for matrices can be defined similarly. In the case of power of 2 cyclotomic rings, i.e., $\Phi(x) = x^n + 1$ for n being some power of 2, the above rotation matrix $\mathsf{Rot}(a)$ is the anti-cyclic matrix.

Rings in This Work. Throughout this paper, we only work on power of 2 cyclotomic rings for their nice and simple mathematical structures. Thus, we will only present the related lemmas with respect to this type of rings.

Norms and Singular Value. The norms of ring vectors (or matrices) are defined by their corresponding coefficient embedding vectors (or matrices). The singular value of a ring matrix $\mathbf{R} \in R^{k \times k'}$ is defined by the singular value of its corresponding matrix obtained by Rot map, that is $s_1(\mathbf{R}) := \sup_{\|u\|=1} \|\mathsf{Rot}(\mathbf{R})u\|$.

The following lemma shows that R_q has exponentially many invertible elements, if the modulo q satisfies certain property.

Lemma 2.7 ([25]). *Let q be a prime such that $q \equiv 3 \bmod 8$ and n be a power of 2. Let $R_q = \mathbb{Z}_q[x]/\Phi_{2n}(x)$. Then, all $u \in R_q$ satisfying $\|\mathsf{Coeffs}(u)\|_2 < \sqrt{q}$ are invertible, i.e., $u \in R_q^*$.*

Ring Learning with Errors. The Learning With Errors (LWE) problem was introduced by Regev [32]. To improve efficiency of LWE-based schemes, the ring version of LWE, namely RLWE, was introduced [27,34]. For $s \in R_q$ and an error distribution ψ over R_q, the RLWE distribution $A_{s,\psi}$ over $R_q \times R_q$ is the distribution of the pair $(a, b = (a \cdot s) + e)$, where a is randomly sampled over R_q, and the error term e is independently sampled according ψ. Here we recall the RLWE problem as follows.

Definition 2.8 (Decision Ring-LWE Problem). *The decision Ring-LWE problem, denoted $R\text{-DLWE}_{n,\ell,q,\psi}$ is to distinguish between ℓ independent samples from $A_{s,\psi}$ for a random choice of a secret $s \leftarrow R_q$ of degree n, and the same number of uniformly random and independent samples from $R_q \times R_q$.*

The bit hardness can be defined following the framework [30] as a decision primitive, similar to the case of IBE in Definition 2.3. Particularly, the $R\text{-DLWE}_{n,\ell,q,\psi}$ problem can be formulated by a security game $\mathbf{Expt}_{\mathcal{B}}^{\mathsf{RLWE}}(1^n, \ell, q, \psi)$ where an adversary $\mathcal{B}$ is challenged with either ℓ samples from $A_{s,\psi}$ or the uniform distribution. Define $\mathsf{Adv}_{\mathcal{B}}^{\mathsf{RLWE}} = \alpha_{\mathcal{B}} \cdot (2\beta_{\mathcal{B}} - 1)^2$, where $\alpha_{\mathcal{B}}$ and $\beta_{\mathcal{B}}$ are the probability that $\mathcal{B}$ does not abort and the conditional probability that $\mathcal{B}$ outputs the correct bit conditioning on the non-abort event. Then the bit hardness of $R\text{-DLWE}$ is defined as follows.

Definition 2.9 (Bit Hardness of R-DLWE). *$R\text{-DLWE}_{n,\ell,q,\psi}$ is λ-bit hard, if for all (T, α, β)-adversary $\mathcal{B}$ in $\mathbf{Expt}_{\mathcal{B}}^{\mathsf{RLWE}}(1^n, \ell, q, \psi)$, we have $\frac{T}{\mathsf{Adv}_{\mathcal{B}}^{\mathsf{RLWE}}} \geq 2^\lambda$.*

Below we present a reduction from some lattice problem to R-DLWE, showing that the ring (D)LWE problem is as hard as the underlying lattice problem.

Lemma 2.10 (Theorem 1 of [25]). *Let α be the positive real, m be a power of 2, ℓ be an integer, $\Phi(x) = x^n + 1$ be the mth cyclotomic polynomial where $m = 2n$, and $R = \mathbb{Z}[x]/(\Phi(x))$. Let $q \equiv 3 \mod 8$ be a prime such that there is another prime $p \equiv 1 \mod m$ satisfying $p \leq q \leq 2p$. Let $\sigma_{\mathsf{RLWE}} := \alpha q \geq n^{3/2}\ell^{1/4}\omega(\log^{9/4}(n))$. Then, there is a PPT quantum reduction from $\tilde{O}(n/\alpha)$-approximate SIVP(or SVP) to $R\text{-DLWE}_{n,\ell,q,\chi}$ with $\chi = D_{\mathbb{Z}^n,\sigma_{\mathsf{RLWE}}}^{\mathsf{Coeffs}}$.*

Trapdoors for Rings. For positive integers b and $k > k' \geq \lceil \log(q) \rceil$, let $\boldsymbol{g}_b^\top = [1|b|b^2|...|b^{k'}|0] \in R^k$ be the gadget matrix. As stated in the work of [29], this gadget matrix has a public trapdoor $\mathbf{T}_g$ with small norm, i.e., $\|\mathbf{T}_g\| \leq \sqrt{b^2 + 1}$. Next we present several useful sampling algorithms from the work of [25, 29].

Lemma 2.11 ([25]). *Let n be a power of 2, q be prime larger than $4n$ such that $q \equiv 3 \mod 8$, b, ρ be positive integers satisfying $\rho < \frac{1}{2}\sqrt{q/n}$, and $\epsilon_s \in (0,1)$ be a small real regarding the smoothing parameter. Furthermore, define $\log_1(\cdot) := \log_2(\cdot)$. There are efficient algorithms such that:*

- $\mathsf{TrapGen}(n, k, \rho, q) \rightarrow (\boldsymbol{a}, \mathbf{T}_a)$ *([29], Lemma 5.3): A randomized algorithm that, when $k \geq 2\log_\rho(q)$, outputs a ring vector $\boldsymbol{a} \in R^k$ and a matrix $\mathbf{T}_a \in R^{k \times k}$, where $\mathsf{Rot}(\boldsymbol{a}^\top) \in \mathbb{Z}^{n \times nk}$ is full-rank matrix and $\mathsf{Rot}(\mathbf{T}_a) \in \mathbb{Z}^{nk \times nk}$ is a basis for $\Lambda^\perp((\mathsf{Rot}(\boldsymbol{a}^\top))$ such that $\boldsymbol{a}$ is $\frac{k}{2^{\frac{nk}{4}+2}}$-close to uniform and $\|\mathsf{Rot}(\mathbf{T}_a)\|_{\mathsf{GS}} < O\left(b\rho\sqrt{n\log_\rho(q)}\right)$.*

- $\mathsf{SampleLeft}(\boldsymbol{a}, \boldsymbol{b}, \mathbf{T}_a, u, \sigma) \rightarrow \boldsymbol{e}$ *([16]): A randomized algorithm that, on input the vectors $\boldsymbol{a}, \boldsymbol{b} \in R^k$, where $\mathsf{Rot}(\boldsymbol{a}^\top), \mathsf{Rot}(\boldsymbol{b}^\top) \in \mathbb{Z}^{n \times nk}$ are full-rank, an element $u \in R_q$, a matrix $\mathbf{T}_a$ such that $\mathsf{Rot}(\mathbf{T}_a) \in \mathbb{Z}^{nk \times nk}$ is a basis for $\Lambda^\perp((\mathsf{Rot}(\boldsymbol{a}^\top))$, and a Gaussian parameter $\sigma > \|\mathsf{Rot}(\mathbf{T}_a)\|_{\mathsf{GS}} \cdot \sqrt{\log(2n(1+1/\epsilon_s))/\pi}$, outputs a vector $\boldsymbol{e} \in R^{2k}$ sampled from a distribution which is $4(nk)^2\epsilon_s$-close to $D_{\Lambda_{\mathsf{Coeffs}(u)}^\perp\left(\mathsf{Rot}([\boldsymbol{a}^\top|\boldsymbol{b}^\top])\right),\sigma}$, i.e., $[\boldsymbol{a}^\top|\boldsymbol{b}^\top] \cdot \boldsymbol{e} = u$, and $\mathsf{Coeffs}(\boldsymbol{e})$ is distributed according to $D_{\Lambda_{\mathsf{Coeffs}(u)}^\perp\left(\mathsf{Rot}([\boldsymbol{a}^\top|\boldsymbol{b}^\top])\right),\sigma}$.*

- $\mathsf{SampleRight}(\boldsymbol{a}, \mathbf{R}, u, y, \boldsymbol{g}_b, \mathbf{T}_{g_b}, \sigma) \rightarrow \boldsymbol{e}$ *where $\boldsymbol{b} = \boldsymbol{a}\mathbf{R} + y \cdot \boldsymbol{g}_b$ ([1]): A randomized algorithm that, on input the ring vectors $\boldsymbol{a}, \boldsymbol{g}_b \in R^k$ such that $\mathsf{Rot}(\boldsymbol{a}^\top), \mathsf{Rot}(\boldsymbol{g}_b^\top) \in \mathbb{Z}^{n \times nk}$ are full-rank, elements $y \in R^*, u \in R$, a matrix $\mathbf{R} \in R^{k \times k}$, a matrix $\mathbf{T}_{g_b} \in R^{k \times k}$ such that $\mathsf{Rot}(\mathbf{T}_{g_b})$ is a basis for the lattice $\Lambda^\perp((\mathsf{Rot}(\boldsymbol{g}_b))$, and a Gaussian parameter $\sigma > s_1(\mathbf{R}) \cdot \|\mathsf{Rot}(\mathbf{T}_{g_b})\|_{\mathsf{GS}} \cdot \sqrt{\log(2n(1+1/\epsilon_s))/\pi}$, outputs a vector $\boldsymbol{e} \in R^{2k}$ sampled from a distribution which is $4(nk)^2\epsilon_s$-close to $D_{\Lambda_{\mathsf{Coeffs}(u)}^\perp\left(\mathsf{Rot}([\boldsymbol{a}^\top|\boldsymbol{b}^\top])\right),\sigma}$, i.e., $[\boldsymbol{a}^\top|\boldsymbol{b}^\top] \cdot \boldsymbol{e} = u$, and $\mathsf{Coeffs}(\boldsymbol{e})$ is distributed according to $D_{\Lambda_{\mathsf{Coeffs}(u)}^\perp\left(\mathsf{Rot}([\boldsymbol{a}^\top|\boldsymbol{b}^\top])\right),\sigma}$.*

- *([29]) Let $k \geq \lceil \log_b(q) \rceil$. There is a publicly known matrix $\mathbf{T}_{g_b}$ such that $\mathsf{Rot}(\mathbf{T}_{g_b})$ is a basis for the lattice $\Lambda^\perp(\mathsf{Rot}(\boldsymbol{g}_b^\top))$ and $\|\mathsf{Rot}(\mathbf{T}_{g_b})\|_{\mathsf{GS}} \leq \sqrt{b^2 + 1}$. Furthermore, there exists a deterministic polynomial time algorithm $\boldsymbol{g}_b^{-1}$ which takes input $\boldsymbol{u} \in R_q^k$, and outputs $\mathbf{R} = \boldsymbol{g}_b^{-1}(\boldsymbol{u}^\top)$ such that $\mathbf{R} \in [-b,b]_{R^{k \times k}}$, $\boldsymbol{g}_b^\top \cdot \mathbf{R} = \boldsymbol{u}^\top$, and $s_1(\mathbf{R}) \leq nkb$. Similarly, there exists a randomized polynomial time algorithm $\widehat{\boldsymbol{g}_b}^{-1}$ which takes input $\boldsymbol{u} \in R_q^k$, and* outputs $\mathbf{R} \leftarrow \widehat{g_b}^{-1}(\boldsymbol{u}^\top)$ such that $\boldsymbol{g}_b^\top \cdot \mathbf{R} = \boldsymbol{u}^\top$. Each coefficient in any entry of $\mathbf{R}$ follows a sub-Gaussian centered 0 with parameter $O(1)$, implying $s_1(\mathbf{R}) \leq \tilde{O}(b\sqrt{nk})$ with an overwhelming probability.

Remark 2.12. *Throughout this paper, we make an appointment that $\boldsymbol{g}_b^{-1}($ or $\widehat{g_b}^{-1})$ maps an integer vector $\boldsymbol{u} \in \mathbb{Z}_q^k$ to a integer matrix $\mathbf{R} \in [-b, b]_{\mathbb{Z}^{k\times k}} \subset \mathbb{Z}^{k\times k}$.*

The following lemma shows a simple upper bound of the norm of $\boldsymbol{g}^{-1}(\cdot)$'s output. Due to space limit, we defer the proof in full version of this paper.

Lemma 2.13. *For integers k, q, b satisfying the definition of $\boldsymbol{g}_b$, on input a vector $\boldsymbol{c} \in \mathbb{Z}_q^k$, the algorithm $\boldsymbol{g}_b^{-1}$ described in lemma 2.11 outputs the matrix $\boldsymbol{g}_b^{-1}(\boldsymbol{c}) \in [-b, b]_{R^{k\times k}} \subset R^{k\times k}$ such that $\|\boldsymbol{g}_b^{-1}(\boldsymbol{c}^\top)\| \leq bk$.*

Homomorphic Computation. In this work, we use the concept of GSW homomorphic encoding [3, 21]. We defer the concepts to full version of this paper.

3 New Homomorphic Equality Test and Tighter Analysis

In this section, we present our first main technique – a new homomorphic equality testing method. As discussed in the introduction, our goal can be described as follows: given $\mathsf{Encode}(x^\alpha)$ and $\beta \in \mathbb{Z}$, compute $\mathsf{Encode}(\tau)$ for $\tau = 1$ if $\alpha = \beta$ or otherwise $\tau = 0$. Below we present our method and then an optimization that achieves tighter parameters. Finally, we describe a connection with packing/unpacking GSW encodings using our new technique.

3.1 Homomorphic Equality Testing

As we mentioned in the preliminary, this work focuses on the cyclotomic rings of 2's power, which have simpler mathematical structures. Let $R = \mathbb{Z}[x]/\Phi_m(x)$ be the m-th cyclotomic ring where $m = 2^k$, modulus q be co-prime to m, and $R_q = R/qR$. For this setting, we have $\Phi_m(x) = x^n + 1$ where $n = \varphi(m) = m/2$.

As we discussed in the introduction, we can use the function $f(v) := \sum_{i=0}^{m-1} v^i$ to design an equality tester. Before we formally present the method, we first recall the following important notion that will be used in the design and analysis of our IBE scheme.

Particularly, the lattice IBE framework [1, 4, 25, 39] requires to design two *deterministic* ways to compute the homomorphic encodings. The required property can be formulated in the following notion of δ-expanding evaluation. The parameter δ measures the quality of the evaluation, playing a key factor in the noise analysis of the IBE scheme. Therefore, an important goal in this series of work is to minimize δ from the design and/or analysis.

Definition 3.1 (δ-expanding evaluation [4, 39]). *Two deterministic algorithm (PubEval, TrapEval) are δ-expanding with respect to function $f : \mathcal{X}^t \to \mathcal{Y}$, if they are efficient and have following properties:*

– PubEval($\{b_i \in R_q^k\}_{i\in[t]}, f$): *on input a function f and vectors of encodings* $\{b_i\}_{i\in[t]}$, *this algorithm outputs a ring vector* $b_f \in R_q^k$;
– TrapEval($a \in R_q^k, \{\mathbf{R}_i \in R^{k\times k}\}_{i\in[t]}, (z_i)_{i\in[t]}, f$): *the trapdoor evaluation algorithm outputs a matrix* $\mathbf{R}_f \in R^{k\times k}$ *such that for any* $\boldsymbol{z}^\top = (z_1, ..., z_t) \in \mathcal{X}^t$, $a \in R_q^k$, *and trapdoor information* $\{\mathbf{R}_i \in R^{k\times k}\}_{i\in[t]}$:

$$\mathsf{PubEval}\left(\{a^\top \cdot \mathbf{R}_i + z_i \cdot g_b^\top\}_{i\in[t]}, f\right) = a^\top \cdot \mathbf{R}_f + f(z) \cdot g_b^\top.$$

Furthermore, we have $\|\mathbf{R}_f\| \leq \delta \cdot \max_{i\in[t]} \|\mathbf{R}_i\|$.

This definition can be extended to a family of functions $\mathcal{F}$, where we require the algorithms to be δ-expanding with respect to all functions $f \in \mathcal{F}$.

In the following section, we present our design and analysis for the above equality test function in the term of δ-expanding homomorphic evaluation.

3.2 Our Construction

We first define the family of equality test functions as follow.

Definition 3.2 (Equality Test Function). *Define function* $\mathsf{Equal}_\beta(\cdot)$ *parameterized by* $\beta \in [m]$ *as follows: on input* $x^\alpha \in R$, *the function outputs 1 if* $\alpha \equiv \beta$ mod m *and 0 otherwise.*

We next present the algorithms and then analyze the expansion factor.

Construction 3.3. *We present algorithms* (PubEval, TrapEval) *for* Equal_β *for any* $\beta \in [m]$ *as follows.*

PubEval($\{b_\alpha\}, \mathsf{Equal}_\beta$) :
1. *Compute the encoding of* $x^{\alpha-\beta}$ *by* $b' := b_\alpha x^{-\beta}$.
2. *Compute* c_{m-1} *recursively as follows:*

$$c_j = \begin{cases} g_b & j = 0 \\ g_b^{-1}(c_{j-1}^\top)^\top \cdot b' + g_b & j \geq 1 \end{cases} \tag{1}$$

3. *Output* $g_b^{-1}(m^{-1}g_b^\top)^\top \cdot c_{m-1}$.

TrapEval($a, \{\mathbf{R}_\alpha\}, (x^\alpha), \mathsf{Equal}_\beta$) :
1. *Compute* $\mathbf{R}' := \mathbf{R}_\alpha \cdot x^{-\beta}$.
2. *Let* c_j*'s be vectors as defined as in the* PubEval *Eq. (1) with* $b_\alpha = a \cdot \mathbf{R}_\alpha + x^\alpha \cdot g_b$. *Then compute* $\mathbf{R}_{m-1}$ *recursively as follows:*

$$\mathbf{R}_j := \begin{cases} 0 & j = 0 \\ \mathbf{R}' \cdot g_b^{-1}(c_{j-1}^\top) + x^{\alpha-\beta} \cdot \mathbf{R}_{j-1} & j \geq 1 , \end{cases} \tag{2}$$

3. *Output* $\mathbf{R}_{m-1} \cdot g_b^{-1}(m^{-1}g_b^\top)$.

In the following theorem, we summarize the quality of the above algorithms. Due to space limit, we put the proof in full version of this paper.

Theorem 3.4. *The algorithms* (PubEval, TrapEval) *in Construction 3.3 are* $mn(kb)^2$*- expanding with respect to the function family* $\{\mathsf{Equal}_\beta(\cdot)\}_{\beta\in[m]}$.

3.3 An Optimization with Tighter Analysis

In this section, we present an optimization of the above homomorphic evaluation processes that achieves a tighter δ-expansion factor.

We notice that in the IBE settings, we need deterministic evaluation algorithms, so a randomized $\widehat{g_b}^{-1}(\cdot)$ cannot be applied to optimize parameters as the case of FHE evaluation, e.g., [3,29]. To tackle this challenge, we consider using a randomized $\widehat{g_b}^{-1}$ with a public seed, e.g., a PRF key K. In this way, we can make the $\widehat{g_b}^{-1}$ "deterministic," as everyone can derive the randomness to compute $\widehat{g_b}^{-1}$ from the public key K. Here we notice that we do not use PRF for security, but a way to generate randomness for $\widehat{g_b}^{-1}$. Thus it does not affect the overall security by publishing the seed of PRF in public.

To formalize the idea above, we define a slight variant of δ-homomorphic evaluation in the common random string (CRS) model,[5] where algorithms (PubEval, TrapEval) have access to a CRS selected randomly in the beginning.

Definition 3.5 (CRS δ-expanding Evaluation). *Algorithms* (PubEval, TrapEval) *are in the common random string (CRS) model if the algorithms have access to* crs *selected randomly in the beginning. Moreover, they are δ-expanding in the CRS model if with an overwhelming probability (i.e., $1-\mathsf{negl}(\lambda)$) over the choice of* crs, *the algorithms satisfies the requirement of δ-expanding in Definition 3.1.*

Then we can instantiate evaluation algorithms with a tighter δ expanding factor in the CRS model as below. Here we present a sketch.

Construction 3.3 in the CRS Model. Replacing the deterministic g_b^{-1} in Construction 3.3 by a randomized $\widehat{g_b}^{-1}$ under a public PRF key K, we can easily derive (PubEval, TrapEval) in the CRS model, achieving a better δ parameter. We summarize this optimization in the following theorem.

Theorem 3.6. *There exist* (PubEval, TrapEval) *that are $\tilde{O}(mb^2 k\sqrt{nk})$-expanding in the CRS model for the function family $\{\mathsf{Equal}_\beta(\cdot)\}_{\beta\in[m]}$.*

We defer the details about the construction and analysis to full version of this paper.

An Alternative Approach and Comparison. We notice that the homomorphic equality test can be done if the input is given in the bit representation. Particularly, consider $\mathsf{Equal}'_\beta(\alpha)$ where $\alpha \in [m]$ is given in the form $(\alpha_1, \ldots, \alpha_{\lceil \log m \rceil - 1}) \in \{0,1\}^{\lceil \log m \rceil - 1}$, then we can express $\mathsf{Equal}'_\beta(\alpha) := \prod_{i=0}^{\lceil \log m \rceil - 1} ((1 - \alpha_i)(1 - \beta_i) + \alpha_i \cdot \beta_i)$, where β_i is the i-th bit of $\beta \in [m]$. We can use the method of [3,12,15] for the homomorphic computation, and improve the expanding factor in the CRS model as the above. Particularly we have:

---

[5] We can define the common reference string model, where crs is selected according to some sampling algorithm. In this work, the common random string model suffices.

Theorem 3.7. *There   exist   algorithms   (PubEval, TrapEval)   that   are $O(nkb \log m)$- expanding in plain model, and are $\tilde{O}(b\sqrt{nk} \log m)$-expanding in the CRS model with respect to the function family $\{\mathsf{Equal}'_\beta(\cdot)\}_{\beta \in [m]}$.*

Compared with Construction 3.3, the bit-wise homomorphic evaluation method has a better expanding factor, but would require more input ciphertexts. This would affect our later IBE constructions – our IBE instantiation with Equal_β would require a smaller RLWE $1/\alpha$ (i.e., $1/n^{7.5+O(1)}$) yet smaller mpk, (i.e., $\omega(1)$ basic vectors), and the instantiation with Equal'_β would require a larger RLWE $1/\alpha$ (i.e., $1/n^{4.5+O(1)}$), yet larger mpk, (i.e., $\omega(\log \lambda)$ basic vectors). To our current knowledge, the asymptotic hardness of RLWE does not differ significantly for the two $1/\alpha$'s [2], so the instantiation of IBE with Equal_β as Construction 3.3 has better overall efficiency, asymptotically.

3.4   Application to Packing/Unpacking Homomorphic Encodings

Our equality test technique can be further used to pack/unpack GSW-type [3,21] homomorphic encodings. We defer the details in full version of this paper.

Particularly, we can compress $\log m$ bit-encodings into one encoding of a ring element without losing information. This technique can be generically used to improve FHE [3,21] for boolean computation, ABE [12] for circuits, and the theoretical state-of-the-arts IBE [39]. As a result , the mpk size in the IBE [39] can be shrunk by a factor of $\log m$ in the ring setting from our technique.

Our technique for the applications demonstrates another non-trivial advantage of RLWE over the plain LWE, which might be of independent interests.

4   New Partition Function and Homomorphic Evaluation

In this section, we describe our second main technique – an explicit design of the partition function required by our IBE scheme and homomorphic evaluation algorithms with a small expansion factor. Our design uses the algebraic structure of cyclotomic rings in a critical way, avoiding the route of Barrington's Theorem as the prior work [39]. As a result, our explicit partition function yields significantly better concrete parameters in the overall IBE scheme.

To describe the partition function, we first recall an insight from the work [4], stating that the IBE design with the trapdoor vanishing technique indeed only needs (weak) pairwise independent hash functions plus the random isolation technique of Valiant and Vazirani [35], which can generically replace the prior notions "admissible hash functions" or "abort-resistant hash functions." We state the following lemma from [4] to summarize this insight.

Lemma 4.1 ([4]). *Let $Q \subset \{0,1\}^n$ be an arbitrary subset, A,B be integers such that $B \leq A, |Q| \leq \delta B$ for some $\delta \in (0,1)$, and let $\mathcal{H} : \{0,1\}^n \to \mathcal{Y}$ be an almost pairwise independent hash function family which has the following properties:*

1 $\forall\ x \in \{0,1\}^n$, $\Pr_{h \in \mathcal{H}} [h(x) = 0] = \frac{1}{A}$.

2 For any distinct $x_1 \neq x_2 \in \{0,1\}^n$, $\Pr_{h \in \mathcal{H}}[h(x_1) = 0|h(x_2) = 0] < \frac{1}{B}$.

Then for any element $x \notin Q$, we have

$$\Pr_{h \in \mathcal{H}}\left[h(x) = 0 \wedge (h(x') \neq 0 \; \forall x' \in Q)\right] \in (\frac{1-\delta}{A}, \frac{1}{A}).$$

Thus, our goal in this section is to (1) design such a hash function family, and (2) design PubEval and TrapEval algorithms with a small average-case expanding factor for the hash family. These would suffice for our IBE scheme.

4.1 Our New Hash Function Family

In this section, we first describe a simplified version to illustrate the core idea, and then show how to transform this simplified version to our final design.

Design Idea. Our design uses an error correcting code ECC : $\mathcal{D} \to \mathbb{Z}_p^{\mathsf{L}}$ with relative distance $\varUpsilon$ as follows. We define a basic hash function $h : \mathcal{D} \to \mathbb{Z}_p$:

$$h_{\alpha,\beta}(z) = (\mathsf{ECC}(z)[\alpha] - \beta),$$

where $\alpha \in [\mathsf{L} + 1]$ selects the position of $\mathsf{ECC}(z)$ and $\beta \in \mathbb{Z}_p$ represents a shift. Here we use $\{1, \ldots, \mathsf{L}\}$ to index the position of the error correcting code, and assume $\mathsf{ECC}(z)[0] = 0$ for any $z \in \mathcal{D}$. This indexing will be convenient for describing our further constructions.

A hash family is naturally defined as $\mathcal{H} = \{h_{\alpha,\beta} : \alpha \in [\mathsf{L} + 1] \setminus \{0\}, \beta \in \mathbb{Z}_p\}$. It is easy to show that (1) $\Pr_{\alpha,\beta}[h_{\alpha,\beta}(z) = 0] = 1/p$ for any $z \in \mathcal{D}$ and (2) for any distinct $z_1 \neq z_2 \in \mathcal{D}$, we have $\Pr_{\alpha,\beta}\left[h_{\alpha,\beta}(z_1) = 0|h_{\alpha,\beta}(z_2) = 0\right] \leq 1 - \varUpsilon$. Intuitively, for $z_1 \neq z_2$, there is $\varUpsilon$ fraction of the positions in their error correcting codes that give different values, meaning with this probability over the choice of α, $\mathsf{ECC}(z_1)[\alpha] \neq \mathsf{ECC}(z_2)[\alpha]$. This would imply $h_{\alpha,\beta}(z_1) \neq h_{\alpha,\beta}(z_2)$, which can be used to derive the probability bound we want.

The basic hash family as is does not yet fulfill what we need for the IBE analysis, as usually the parameter Q (corresponding to the number of adversary's key queries) is larger than the parameter p we can set. To tackle this issue, we use the technique of parallel repetition in the following way. Let $t \in \mathbb{Z}$ be parameter, and $\boldsymbol{\alpha} \in ([\mathsf{L} + 1] \setminus \{0\})^t, \boldsymbol{\beta} \in \mathbb{Z}_p^t$ be parameters. We define $h_{\boldsymbol{\alpha},\boldsymbol{\beta}}^{\|,t} : \mathcal{D} \to \mathbb{Z}_p^t$ as

$$h_{\boldsymbol{\alpha},\boldsymbol{\beta}}^{\|,t}(z) = \left(h_{\alpha_1,\beta_1}(z), \ldots, h_{\alpha_t,\beta_t}(z)\right).$$

We can then show that (1) $\Pr_{\boldsymbol{\alpha},\boldsymbol{\beta}}\left[h_{\boldsymbol{\alpha},\boldsymbol{\beta}}^{\|,t}(z) = 0\right] = 1/p^t$ and (2) for any distinct $z_1 \neq z_2 \in \mathcal{D}$, we have $\Pr_{\boldsymbol{\alpha},\boldsymbol{\beta}}\left[h_{\boldsymbol{\alpha},\boldsymbol{\beta}}^{\|,t}(z_1) = 0|h_{\boldsymbol{\alpha},\boldsymbol{\beta}}^{\|,t}(z_2) = 0\right] \leq (1 - \varUpsilon)^t$.

Thus, by choosing an appropriate parameter t, the family $\mathcal{H}^t = \{h_{\boldsymbol{\alpha},\boldsymbol{\beta}}^{\|,t} : \boldsymbol{\alpha} \in ([\mathsf{L}+1] \setminus \{0\})^t, \boldsymbol{\beta} \in \mathbb{Z}_p^t\}$ and Lemma 4.1 can be used to analyze our IBE security.

Remark 4.2. *As we discussed in the introduction, using error correcting codes to design a partition function has been explored previously in the context of IBE and VRF. e.g., [8, 24, 39]. Our new insight is to integrate the ECC into the cyclotomic rings so that it can be easily computed homomorphically. More details follow.*

Our Final Construction – Hash in the Ring. However, to design a Ring-based IBE, using the above hash family (as is) still faces two major challenges: (1) the family $\mathcal{H}^t$ with output domain $\mathbb{Z}_p^t$ is not naturally compatible with the ring, and thus not convenient for our ring-based IBE design. (2) The second challenge is quite subtle – the IBE analysis [1,39] requires to compute (homomorphically) $\mathcal{H}^{t'}$ for a flexible $t' \in [t]$, yet in an oblivious way in t', i.e., the evaluation only depends on t but does not know t'. The purpose is to derive a more fine-grained security analysis for the IBE scheme. Therefore, the hash family must at least capture $\cup_{t' \in [t]} \mathcal{H}^{t'}$, and support this type of oblivious evaluation.

To tackle these issues, we propose a modified ring-based hash family $\mathcal{H}^{R,t}$ that captures all $\mathcal{H}^{t'}$ for $t' \leq t$ and matches the output domain with the ring R of the RLWE. At a high level, $\mathcal{H}^{R,t}$ embeds $\mathcal{H}^{t'}$ with output $\mathbb{Z}_p^{t'}$ for all $t' \in [t]$ into some subset of the ring R, which is naturally compatible with our Ring IBE design. Next we present our final design, starting with some important notations.

Important Notations. Let R be the m-th cyclotomic ring and $n = m/2$; p, t be integers such that $tp \leq n$; ECC $: \mathcal{D} \to \mathbb{Z}_p^{\mathsf{L}}$ with relative distance Υ be an error correcting code whose codeword is indexed by $\{1, \ldots, \mathsf{L}\}$ and $\mathsf{ECC}(z)[0] = 0$ for every $z \in \mathcal{D}$. Then, we present our design of the hash function as follow.

Definition 4.3. *For any $(\boldsymbol{\alpha}, \boldsymbol{\beta}) \in [\mathsf{L}+1]^t \times \mathbb{Z}_p^t$, we define hash function $H_{\boldsymbol{\alpha},\boldsymbol{\beta}}^{R,t} :$ $\mathcal{D} \to R$ as $H_{\boldsymbol{\alpha},\boldsymbol{\beta}}^{R,t}(z) := \sum_{i \in [t]} \left(x^{ip+\mathsf{ECC}(z)[\alpha_i]} - x^{ip+\beta_i} \right).$*

According to the property $\mathsf{ECC}(z)[0] = 0$, in the above hash we extend the range of $\boldsymbol{\alpha}$ to $[\mathsf{L}+1]^t$ without affecting the result. Under this design, we define the following classes of hash functions:

Definition 4.4. *For any $t' \in [t]$, define the class $\mathcal{H}^{R,t,t'}$ as follows.*

$$\mathcal{H}^{R,t,t'} = \left\{ H_{\boldsymbol{\alpha},\boldsymbol{\beta}}^{R,t} : \boldsymbol{\alpha}' \in ([\mathsf{L}+1] \setminus \{0\})^{t'}, \boldsymbol{\beta}' \in \mathbb{Z}_p^{t'}, \boldsymbol{\alpha}^\top = (\boldsymbol{\alpha}'^\top, \mathbf{0}^\top), \boldsymbol{\beta}^\top = (\boldsymbol{\beta}'^\top, \mathbf{0}^\top) \right\},$$

where $\mathbf{0}^\top = (0, 0, \ldots, 0) \in \mathbb{Z}_p^{t-t'}$, i.e., padding 0's to match the dimension t. Furthermore, define $\mathcal{H}^{R,t} = \cup_{t' \in [t]} \mathcal{H}^{R,t,t'}$.

Intuitively, for a fixed t', if the index $(\boldsymbol{\alpha}, \boldsymbol{\beta})$ is chosen randomly from the set $([\mathsf{L}+1] \setminus \{0\})^t \times \mathbb{Z}_p^t$, then the function $H^{R,t}$ behaves like $h^{\|,t'}$ as we elaborate next. Observe that we can view $H_{\boldsymbol{\alpha},\boldsymbol{\beta}}^{R,t}$ as a hash that embeds the vector $h_{\boldsymbol{\alpha},\boldsymbol{\beta}}^{\|,t'} \in \mathbb{Z}_p^{t'}$ into the ring R. From our setting that $\mathsf{ECC}(z)[0] = 0$, the padded $\mathbf{0}$'s will result in cancelled terms in $H^{R,t}$, i.e., $x^{ip+\mathsf{ECC}(z)[0]} - x^{ip} = 0$ for every $i \in [t'+1, t]$. Moreover, we notice that different coordinates in the output vector of $h^{\|,t'}$ will not interfere – the i-th coordinate of the vector, namely $h_{\alpha_i,\beta_i}(z)$, corresponds to the ring element $x^{ip+\mathsf{ECC}(z)[\alpha_i]} - x^{ip+\beta_i}$. As both $\mathsf{ECC}(z)[\alpha_i]$ and β_i take values between 0 and $p-1$, our design guarantees that $(x^{ip+\mathsf{ECC}(z)[\alpha_i]} - x^{ip+\beta_i})$ would not interfere with $(x^{jp+\mathsf{ECC}(z)[\alpha_i]} - x^{jp+\beta_i})$ for $i \neq j$. Formally we prove the following lemma.

Lemma 4.5. *For any code* $\mathsf{ECC} : \mathcal{D} \to \mathbb{Z}_p^{\mathsf{L}}$ *with relative distance* Υ, *ring* R *with dimension* n *such that* $tp \leq n$, *Then for any* $t' \leq t$, *the hash function family* $\mathcal{H}^{R,t,t'}$ *as in Definition 4.4 has following properties:*

1 *For any element* $z_1 \in \mathcal{D}$, $\Pr_{H \in \mathcal{H}^{R,t,t'}} \left[H(z_1) = 0 \right] = (1/p)^{t'}$.

2 *For any distinct elements* $z_1 \neq z_2 \in \mathcal{D}$, *we have*

$$\Pr_{H \in \mathcal{H}^{R,t,t'}} \left[H(z_1) = 0 | H(z_2) = 0 \right] < (1 - \Upsilon)^{t'}.$$

We defer the proof of this lemma in full version of this paper.

Two Further Important Properties. It is important to point out two further important properties that will be used in our IBE analysis.

- **(Obliviousness)** The computation of the hash $H_{\alpha,\beta}^{R,t}$ is oblivious to the choice of (α, β). That is to say, for any $t' \leq t$ and any choice of $(\alpha, \beta) \in ([L+1] \setminus \{0\})^t \times \mathbb{Z}_p^t$ the way to compute $H_{\alpha,\beta}^{R,t}$ remains the same. This is extremely important for our IBE design and proof of security.
- **(Invertibility)** We notice that if $H^{R,t}(z) \neq 0$, then it is also invertible in the ring R_q for any prime $q \equiv 3 \mod 8$ and $q \geq 2t$. This is because $\|H^{R,t}(z)\|_2 \leq \sqrt{2t} \leq \sqrt{q}$. By Lemma 2.7, any element with norm less than $\sqrt{q}$ is invertible in R_q for this type of prime q.

4.2 Homomorphic Evaluation of the Partitioning Function

To homomorphically evaluate the hash function, we first identify the high level goal: given input encodings $\{\mathsf{Encode}(x^{\alpha_i})\}_{i \in [t]}$, $\mathsf{Encode}\left(\sum_{i \in [t]} x^{ip+\beta_i}\right)$ and a hash input $z \in \mathcal{D}$ in the clear, our task is to output an encoding $\mathsf{Encode}\left(H_{\alpha,\beta}^{R,t}(z)\right)$.

To achieve this, we first observe that we can re-write the hash function as

$$H_{\alpha,\beta}^{R,t}(z) = -\sum_{i \in [t]} x^{ip+\beta_i} + \sum_{i \in [t]} \sum_{j \in [L+1]} \left(j \overset{?}{=} \alpha_i \right) x^{ip+\mathsf{ECC}(z)[j]},$$

where $\left(j \overset{?}{=} \alpha_i \right)$ outputs 1 if the equality holds and otherwise 0. Recall that we index the codeword by $[1, L]$ and we set $\mathsf{ECC}(z)[0] = 0$ for any $z \in \mathcal{D}$.

As the input z and iterators i, j are in the clear, the only non-trivial homomorphic computation is the equality test $\left(j \overset{?}{=} \alpha_i \right)$. The reader at this point might already observe that this is what we achieved in the prior Construction 3.3, if we further have $L + 1 \leq m$ (as our equality test function naturally only supports comparison of parameters in $[m]$). However, our application would require longer codewords, i.e., $L = m^\eta > m + 1$ for some $\eta > 1$, so this direct approach would not work. To solve this issue, we consider input encodings $\{\mathsf{Encode}(\alpha_{i,i'})\}_{i\in[t],i'\in[\eta]}$ where $(\alpha_{i,0},\ldots,\alpha_{i,(\eta-1)})$ is considered as the m-ary representation of $\alpha_i \in [L+1] \setminus \{0\}$. To test whether $j \overset{?}{=} \alpha_i$ for $j \in [L+1] \setminus \{0\}$, we can first compute the m-ary representation of j as $(j_0,\ldots,j_{\eta-1})$ and then check whether $j_{i'} = \alpha_{i,i'}$ for every $i' \in [\eta]$.

Using this insight, we present the procedure formally. To work under the syntax of $(\mathsf{PubEval}, \mathsf{TrapEval})$, we define the hash function in the following form where the computation is in the clear:

Definition 4.6 (Hash Function for Homomorphic Evaluation). *Let R be some cyclotomic ring with degree n being a power of 2, q be an integer, $R_q = R/qR$ and ECC be an error correcting code mapping $\mathcal{D} \to \mathbb{Z}_p^L$, satisfying the constraint $tp \leq n$ and further $L + 1 \leq m^n$. Suppose the function $\mathsf{Equal}_\beta(x^\alpha)$ parametered by β outputs $1 \in \mathbb{Z}_q$ if the input $x^{\tilde\alpha}$ satisfying $\alpha = \beta$ and $0 \in \mathbb{Z}_q$ otherwise. Define function $F_z(\{\alpha_{i,i'}\}_{i\in[t],i'\in[\eta]}, \tilde\beta)$ parameterized by $z \in \mathcal{D}$ as: on input $\{\alpha_{i,i'}\}_{i\in[t],i'\in[\eta]} \in [m]^{t\times n}$, $\tilde\beta \in R_q$, the function computes as follows.*

- *For each $j \in [L+1]$, denote j's m-ary representation as $(j[0],\ldots,j[\eta-1])$.*
- *For each $i \in [t], j \in [L+1]$, compute $b_{i,j} = \prod_{i'\in[\eta]} \mathsf{Equal}_{j[i']}(x^{\alpha_{i,i'}})$.*
- *Output $-\tilde\beta + \sum_{i\in[t],j\in[L+1]} b_{i,j} \cdot x^{ip+\mathsf{ECC}(z)[j]}$.*

Under the above notation, we present the homomorphic evaluation procedures.

Construction 4.7. *Given $(\mathsf{PubEval}, \mathsf{TrapEval})$ for $\{\mathsf{Equal}_\beta(\cdot)\}_{\beta\in[m]}$ (either in the plain or CRS model; ref. Sections 3.2 and 3.3) as subroutine, we construct $(\mathsf{PubEval}, \mathsf{TrapEval})$ for $\{F_z\}_{z\in\mathcal{D}}$ (in the plain or CRS model, respectively) as:*

$\mathsf{PubEval}\left(\left\{\{b_{\alpha_{i,i'}}\}_{i\in[t],i'\in[\eta]}, b_{\tilde\beta}\right\}, F_z\right)$:
1 *For $i \in [t], j \in [L+1], i' \in [\eta]$, (homomorphically) compute*

$$b_{i,j,i'} = \begin{cases} \mathsf{PubEval}(b_{\alpha_{i,0}}, \mathsf{Equal}_{j[0]}) & i' = 0, \\ \mathsf{PubEval}(b_{\alpha_{i,i'}}, \mathsf{Equal}_{j[i']}) \cdot g_b^{-1}\left(b_{i,j,(i'-1)}\right) & i' \geq 1. \end{cases}$$

Then, let $b_{i,j} := b_{i,j,(\eta-1)}$
2 *Output $b_H := -b_{\tilde\beta} + \sum_{i\in[t],j\in[L+1]} b_{i,j} \cdot x^{ip+\mathsf{ECC}(z)[j]}$*

$\mathsf{TrapEval}\left(a, \left\{\{\mathbf{R}_{\alpha_{ii'}}\}_{i\in[t],i'\in[\eta]} \subset R_q^{k\times k}, \mathbf{R}_{\tilde\beta} \in R_q^{k\times k}\right\}, (x^\alpha, \tilde\beta), F_z\right)$:
1 *For $i \in [t], j \in [L+1], i' \in [\eta]$, (homomorphically) compute*

$$\mathbf{R}'_{i,j,i'} := \mathsf{TrapEval}\left(a, \{\mathbf{R}_{\alpha_{i,i'}}\}, (x^{\alpha_{i,i'}}), \mathsf{Equal}_{j[i']}\right).$$

2 For $i' \in [\eta]$, let $\boldsymbol{b}_{i,j,i'}$ be the vector evaluated in PubEval algorithm with $\boldsymbol{b}_{\alpha_{i,i'}} = \boldsymbol{a} \cdot \mathbf{R}_{\alpha_{ii'}} + x^{\alpha_{i,i'}} \cdot \boldsymbol{g}_b$, and recursively compute

$$
\mathbf{R}_{i,j,i'} = \begin{cases} \mathbf{R}'_{i,j,0} & i' = 0, \\ \mathbf{R}'_{i,j,i'} \cdot \boldsymbol{g}_b^{-1}\left(\boldsymbol{b}_{i,j,i'-1}\right) + \mathsf{Equal}_{j[i']}(x^{\alpha_{i,i'}}) \cdot \mathbf{R}_{i,j,i'-1} & i' \geq 1. \end{cases}
$$

Then let $\mathbf{R}_{i,j} := \mathbf{R}_{i,j,(\eta-1)}$.
3 Output $\mathbf{R}_H := -\mathbf{R}_{\tilde{\beta}} + \sum_{i\in[t],j\in[\mathsf{L}+1]} \mathbf{R}_{i,j}$.

We can easily calculate the expansion factor for the above (PubEval, TrapEval) for the family $\{F_z\}_{z\in\mathcal{D}}$, assuming we have (PubEval, TrapEval) that is δ-expanding for the family $\{\mathsf{Equal}_j\}_{j\in[m]}$, either in the plain or CRS model. We present the detailed analysis in full version of this paper.

Moreover, we notice that for the case $\eta = 1$, i.e., $\mathsf{L} + 1 \leq m$, we do not need to do the m-ary decomposition, and thus can obtain a better expanding factor by avoiding several layers of homomorphic multiplications. By combining Theorems 3.4 and 3.6 with the above construction, we can obtain the following corollary, showing the existence of the algorithms (PubEval, TrapEval) respect to the function family $\{F_z\}_{z\in\mathcal{D}}$ in both plain and CRS models.

Corollary 4.8. *Consider parameters $tp \leq n$ and $\mathsf{L} + 1 \leq m^\eta$ and others as stated in Definition 4.6. Then there exist an algorithm pair (PubEval, TrapEval) with following two properties:*

1. *If $\eta = 1$, the algorithms are $(\mathsf{L} + 1)tmn(kb)^2$-expanding in the plain model, and $\tilde{O}(t\mathsf{L}mkb^2\sqrt{nk})$-expanding in the CRS model for the family $\{F_z\}_{z\in\mathcal{D}}$.*
2. *If $\eta > 1$, the algorithms are $(\mathsf{L} + 1)tmn^2(kb)^3\eta$-expanding in the plain model, and $\tilde{O}(t\mathsf{L}mnk^2b^3\eta)$-expanding in the CRS model for the family $\{F_z\}_{z\in\mathcal{D}}$.*

Alternatively, if we use the bit-wise equality test computation (i.e., $\mathsf{Equal}'_{\beta}()$) as the underlying building block, then by Theorems 3.7 with the above construction, we can obtain the following corollary.

Corollary 4.9. *Consider parameters $tp \leq n$ and others as stated in Definition 4.6. There exist an algorithm pair (PubEval, TrapEval) that are $(\mathsf{L} + 1)tnkb\log m$-expanding in the plain model, and $\tilde{O}(t\mathsf{L}b\sqrt{nk}\log m)$-expanding in the CRS model for the family $\{F_z\}_{z\in\mathcal{D}}$.*

5 IBE Design and Analysis

Now we present the design and improvement of analysis of IBE.

5.1 Construction

Our IBE construction uses the building block – algorithms (PubEval, TrapEval) for the function class $\{F_z\}_{z\in\mathcal{D}}$ as Construction 4.7. We note that the function class requires an error correcting code $\mathsf{ECC} : \{0,1\}^\ell \to \mathbb{Z}_p^\mathsf{L}$ where $\mathsf{L} + 1 \leq m^\eta$. Next we present the construction.

Construction 5.1. *For identity space* ID $= \{0,1\}^{\ell}$ *and message space* M $=$ $\{0,1\}^n$, *we define* IBE *scheme* $\Pi =$ (Setup, KeyGen, Enc, Dec) *as follows:*

Setup(1^{λ}) : *On input security parameter* 1^{λ}, *the* Setup *algorithm does:*
1. *Sample* $(\boldsymbol{a}, \mathbf{T}_{\boldsymbol{a}}) \leftarrow$ TrapGen(n, k, ρ, q), *where* $\boldsymbol{a} \in R_q^k$.
2. *Choose* $\eta t + 1$ *random ring vectors, i.e.,* $\boldsymbol{b}_{i,j} \xleftarrow{\$} R_q^k$ *for* $i \in [t], j \in [\eta]$, $\boldsymbol{b}_{\beta} \xleftarrow{\$} R_q^k$, *and a random ring element* $u \xleftarrow{\$} R_q$.
3. *Sample a PRF key* K *as the CRS for the homomorphic evaluation.*
4. *Output the master keys as:* mpk $= (\boldsymbol{a}, (\boldsymbol{b}_{i,j})_{i \in [t], j \in [\eta]}, \boldsymbol{b}_{\beta}, u, K)$, msk $= \mathbf{T}_{\boldsymbol{a}}$.

KeyGen(mpk, msk, id): *On input the master keys* mpk, msk *and an identity* id $\in$ ID, *the* KeyGen *algorithm does the following:*
1. *Define* F_{id} *as the function as in Definition 4.6 with index* id.
2. *Compute* $\boldsymbol{b}_{\mathsf{id}} =$ PubEval$(\{\boldsymbol{b}_{i,j}\}_{i \in [t], j \in [\eta]}, \boldsymbol{b}_{\beta}, F_{\mathsf{id}})$.
3. *Sample* $\boldsymbol{r} \in R_q^{2k}$ *by* SampleLeft$(\boldsymbol{a}, \boldsymbol{b}_{\mathsf{id}}, \mathbf{T}_{\boldsymbol{a}}, u, \sigma_1)$, *satisfying* $\boldsymbol{r}^{\top} \cdot \begin{bmatrix} \boldsymbol{a} \\ \boldsymbol{b}_{\mathsf{id}} \end{bmatrix} = u$.
4. *Output* $\mathsf{sk}_{\mathsf{id}} = \boldsymbol{r}$ *as a secret key of* id.

Enc(mpk, id, $\boldsymbol{m}$): *On input* mpk, id *and message* $\boldsymbol{m} \in$ M, *the algorithm does:*
1. *Set* $\mu = m_0 + m_1 x + \cdots + m_{n-1} x^{n-1} \in R_q$.
2. *Compute* $\boldsymbol{b}_{\mathsf{id}} =$ PubEval$(\{\boldsymbol{b}_{i,j}\}_{i \in [t], j \in [\eta]}, \boldsymbol{b}_{\beta}, F_{\mathsf{id}})$.
3. *Sample* $s \xleftarrow{\$} R_q$, *and sample* $e_1, e_2 \leftarrow (D_{\mathbb{Z}^n, \sigma_2}^{\mathsf{Coeffs}})^k$ *and* $e_3 \leftarrow D_{\mathbb{Z}^n, \sigma_{\mathsf{RLWE}}}^{\mathsf{Coeffs}}$.
4. *Compute* $c_0 = u \cdot s + e_3 + \lceil \frac{q}{2} \rceil \cdot \mu$, *and* $\boldsymbol{c}_1 = \begin{bmatrix} \boldsymbol{a} \\ \boldsymbol{b}_{\mathsf{id}} \end{bmatrix} \cdot s + \begin{bmatrix} \boldsymbol{e}_1 \\ \boldsymbol{e}_2 \end{bmatrix}$.
5. *Output the ciphertext* ct $= (c_0, \boldsymbol{c}_1) \in R_q \times R_q^{2k}$.

Dec(mpk, $\mathsf{sk}_{\mathsf{id}}$, ct) *On input the master public key* mpk, *the secret key* $\mathsf{sk}_{\mathsf{id}} = \boldsymbol{r}$ *and ciphertext* ct $= (c_0, \boldsymbol{c}_1)$, *the decryption algorithm does the following:*
1. *Output* $\boldsymbol{m}' = \lfloor \frac{2}{q} \cdot \mathsf{Coeffs}(c_0 - \boldsymbol{r}^{\top} \cdot \boldsymbol{c}_1) \rceil \bmod 2$, *where the rounding function* $\lfloor \cdot \rceil$ *is applied coefficient-wise.*

Correctness. Correctness of our IBE scheme is captured by the following Theorem. We defer the proof of it in full version of our paper.

Theorem 5.2. *For any positive number* ω, *and ring modulus* $q \geq 5(\sigma_{\mathsf{RLWE}} \cdot \omega + \sigma_1 \sigma_2 \sqrt{2nk} \cdot \omega)$, *the* IBE *scheme* Π *presented in construction 5.1 is correct except with probability* $2^{-2nk+2} + 4e^{-\pi \omega^2}$.

5.2   Security

In this section, we analyze security of our IBE construction. Below we first present a theorem for a reduction from RLWE to IBE with concrete parameters.

We first define and recall several notations. Let ECC $: \{0,1\}^{\ell} \rightarrow \mathbb{Z}_p^{\mathsf{L}}$ with relative distance Υ be the underlying error correcting code of the function family $\{F_{\mathsf{id}}\}_{\mathsf{id} \in \mathsf{ID}}$. We denote $c = 1/(1 - \Upsilon)$. For our instantiations, we have the relations $\mathsf{L} + 1 \leq m^{\eta}$ and $p > c > p/w$ for some small $w \in \mathbb{R}$, which can be set between $[2, \lambda]$ depending on the selection of the code. We denote ϵ_s as a small positive real regarding the smoothing parameter involved in SampleLeft and SampleRight algorithms. Asymptotically, we would set $\epsilon_s = \text{negl}(\lambda)$, and concretely $\epsilon_s = 2^{-3\lambda}$, ensuring that the parameter ε defined below satisfies $\varepsilon = \text{negl}(\lambda)$ or $\varepsilon \leq \frac{1}{2^{2\lambda}}$. Intuitively, this means the statistical distance incurred in the sampling algorithms (in the scheme and proof of security) would be negligible or bounded by $\varepsilon \leq \frac{1}{2^{2\lambda}}$. Then we have the following theorem.

Theorem 5.3. *Given any (T, α, β)-adversary $\mathcal{A}$ making Q' key queries against* $\mathbf{Expt}_{\mathcal{A}}^{\mathsf{IBE}}(1^\lambda)$, *there exists a (T', α', β')-adversary $\mathcal{B}$ against* $\mathbf{Expt}_{\mathcal{B}}^{\mathsf{RLWE}}(1^n, k + 1, q, \psi)$, *such that* $T' \leq T + \min\{O\left(\frac{Q'pw^{t'-1}}{(2\beta-1)^2}\right), (Lp)^{t'}\}$, $\alpha' \geq \frac{(5-2\beta)\alpha}{36Q'pw^{t'-1}} - \frac{1}{2}\varepsilon$, *and* $|\beta' - \frac{1}{2}| \geq \frac{1}{2}\left(\frac{11-6\beta}{8}\beta - (\frac{5-2\beta}{36Q'pw^{t'-1}\varepsilon} - 1)^{-1}\right) - \frac{1}{4}$, *where* $\varepsilon = \frac{k}{2^{\frac{nk}{4}}} + (Q'(nk)^2 + 1)8\epsilon_s$, $t' = \lceil \log_c(3Q') \rceil$.

As discussed in the introduction, our analysis improves the running time of the artificial abort technique of Waters [37]. We present the proof below.

Proof. Let $\mathcal{A}$ be a (T, α, β)-adversary who makes Q' key queries against the IBE game of $\mathbf{Expt}_{\mathcal{A}}^{\mathsf{IBE}}(1^\lambda)$, and our goal is to construct a RLWE adversary $\mathcal{B}$ that satisfies the parameters as the theorem statement. Before presenting the concrete construction of $\mathcal{B}$, we first define several hybrids, from which the design idea of $\mathcal{B}$ naturally reveals.

Hybrid 0: In this hybrid, $\mathcal{A}$ plays the original security experiment $\mathbf{Expt}_{\mathcal{A}}^{\mathsf{IBE}}(1^\lambda)$.
Hybrid 1: In this hybrid, $\mathcal{A}$ plays a slightly modified security experiment $\mathbf{Expt}_{\mathcal{A}}^{\mathsf{IBE}}(1^\lambda)'$ where the challenger has an additional ability to send a $\perp$ message to $\mathcal{A}$ at any step, and then $\mathcal{A}$ would immediately abort upon receiving this message. The particular modified experiment is defined as follows:
  – The setup phase is identical to $\mathbf{Expt}_{\mathcal{A}}^{\mathsf{IBE}}(1^\lambda)$ except that the challenger chooses a random partitioning function $H \xleftarrow{\$} \mathcal{H}^{R,t,t'}$ as Definition 4.4, where $t' = \lceil \log_c(3Q') \rceil$. Particularly, the challenger would sample random vectors $\alpha' \in [L+1]^{t'}, \beta' \in \mathbb{Z}_p^{t'}$, denotes $\alpha = (\alpha', 0) \in [L+1]^t, \beta = (\beta', 0) \in \mathbb{Z}_p^t$, and finally sets and keeps the hash function:

$$H(\mathsf{id}) = F_{\mathsf{id}}(\alpha, \beta) = H_{\alpha,\beta}^{R,t}(\mathsf{id}) = \sum_{i\in[t]} (x^{ip+\mathsf{ECC}(\mathsf{id})[\alpha_i]} - x^{ip+\beta_i}).$$

  – The challenger responds to identity queries and issues the challenge ciphertext exactly as in $\mathbf{Expt}_{\mathcal{A}}^{\mathsf{IBE}}(1^\lambda)$. Let $\mathsf{id}_1, \cdots, \mathsf{id}_{Q'}$ be the identities where the attacker queries and let id^* be the challenge identity, which is not in $\{\mathsf{id}_1, \cdots, \mathsf{id}_{Q'}\}$.
  – In the final phase, adversary $\mathcal{A}$ might output a bit b' as its guess or might have aborted at some prior step. If the adversary does not abort, then the challenger does the *abort check* and *artificial abort* as follow:
    1. **Abort check:** the challenger checks if:

$$H(\mathsf{id}) \neq 0 \text{ for all } \mathsf{id} \in Q', \text{ and } H(\mathsf{id}^*) = 0.$$

    If the condition does not hold, challenger sends $\perp$ to $\mathcal{A}$, and $\mathcal{A}$ will abort the game upon receiving $\perp$.

2. **Artificial abort:** the challenger samples a bit $\Gamma \in \{0,1\}$ such that $\Pr[\Gamma = 1] = 1 - \tilde{\gamma}(\mathsf{id}^*, \mathsf{id}_1, \cdots, \mathsf{id}_{Q'})$ where $\tilde{\gamma}(\cdot)$ is defined as follows:
   - Define γ to be the probability as follow:

$$\gamma = \Pr_{H \in \mathcal{H}^{R,t,t'}} \left[H(\mathsf{id}_i) \neq 0 \text{ for all } i \leq Q', \text{ and } H(\mathsf{id}^*) = 0 \right]. \qquad (3)$$

   - If $O\left(\frac{\log(2\beta-1)\cdot\log(\gamma^*)}{(2\beta-1)^2\gamma^*}\right) < (\mathsf{L}p)^{t'}$, then the challenger samples $O\left(\frac{\log(2\beta-1)\cdot\log(\gamma^*)}{(2\beta-1)^2\gamma^*}\right)$ pairs of (α', β') and computes the hash values of $H_{\alpha,\beta}^{R,t}(*)$ for the identities $(\mathsf{id}_1, \cdots, \mathsf{id}_{Q'}, \mathsf{id}^*)$ to compute an estimate γ' of γ, where $\gamma^* = \frac{2}{9Q'pw^{t'-1}}$. Otherwise, challenger computes the *exact value* of γ by enumerating all choices of α, β's of the hash function for $(\mathsf{id}_1, \cdots, \mathsf{id}_{Q'}, \mathsf{id}^*)$. Notice that there are $(\mathsf{L}p)^{t'}$ choices of (α, β). Set $\gamma' = \gamma$.
   - If $\gamma^* \leq \gamma'$, challenger sets $\tilde{\gamma}(\mathsf{id}^*, \mathsf{id}_1, \cdots, \mathsf{id}_{Q'}) = \gamma^*/\gamma'$, otherwise sets $\tilde{\gamma}(\mathsf{id}^*, \mathsf{id}_1, \cdots, \mathsf{id}_{Q'}) = 1$.
   If $\Gamma = 1$ the challenger sends $\perp$ to $\mathcal{A}$, and then $\mathcal{A}$ aborts the game. In this case we say that the challenger aborted the game due to an artificial abort.

Hybrid 2: In this hybrid, $\mathcal{A}$ plays $\mathbf{Expt}_{\mathcal{A}}^{\mathsf{IBE}}(1^\lambda)'$ the same as Hybrid 1 except for changing the way of generating the public vectors $\{b_{i,j}\}_{i\in[t],j\in[\eta]}, b_\beta$. Here, the challenger chooses $\alpha_i \in [\mathsf{L}+1]$ for $i \in [t]$ as Hybrid 1, and additionally $\mathbf{R}_{i,j}, \mathbf{R}_\beta \leftarrow [-\rho, \rho]_R^{k\times k}$ for $i \in [t], j \in [\eta]$. For each $i \in [t]$, the challenger further decomposes $\alpha_i \in [\mathsf{L}+1]$ into the m-ary representation $(\alpha_{i,0}, \dots, \alpha_{i,(\eta-1)})$. Then define the public matrices as follows:

$$b_{i,j}^\top = a^\top \cdot \mathbf{R}_{i,j} + x^{\alpha_{i,j}} \cdot g_b^\top \quad \text{and} \quad b_\beta^\top = a^\top \cdot \mathbf{R}_\beta + \sum_{i\in[t]} x^{ip+\beta_i} \cdot g_b^\top.$$

Hybrid 3: In this hybrid, $\mathcal{A}$ plays $\mathbf{Expt}_{\mathcal{A}}^{\mathsf{IBE}}(1^\lambda)'$ the same as Hybrid 2 except that we change the way to generate the public vector a and to respond the secret key queries. Formally, the challenger samples $a \xleftarrow{\$} R_q^k$ uniformly at random instead of running TrapGen algorithm. On the other hand, to respond a secret key query for id, the challenger first computes

$$\mathbf{R}_{\mathsf{id}} = \mathsf{TrapEval}(a, \{\mathbf{R}_{i,j}\}_{i\in[t],j\in[\eta]}, \mathbf{R}_\beta, (\alpha, \beta), F_{\mathsf{id}}).$$

By the homomorphic property, we know that $b_{\mathsf{id}}^\top = \mathsf{PubEval}(\{b_{i,j}\}_{i\in[t],j\in[\eta]}, b_\beta, F_{\mathsf{id}}) = a^\top \cdot \mathbf{R}_{\mathsf{id}} + F_{\mathsf{id}}(\alpha, \beta) \cdot g_b^\top$. Then the challenger runs

$$r \leftarrow \mathsf{SampleRight}(a, \mathbf{R}_{\mathsf{id}}, u, F_{\mathsf{id}}(\alpha, \beta), g_b, \mathbf{T}_{g_b}, \sigma)$$

satisfying $[a^\top | b_{\mathsf{id}}^\top] \cdot r = u \bmod q$. Finally, the challenger outputs the secret key $\mathsf{sk}_{\mathsf{id}} = r \in R_q^{2k}$.

Hybrid 4: In this hybrid, $\mathcal{A}$ plays $\mathbf{Expt}_{\mathcal{A}}^{\mathsf{IBE}}(1^{\lambda})'$ the same as Hybrid 3 except for the way that challenge ciphertext (c_0^*, c_1^*) is generated. The challenger first chooses $s \xleftarrow{\$} R_q$, $\boldsymbol{x} \leftarrow (D_{\mathbb{Z}^n, \sigma_{\mathsf{RLWE}}}^{\mathsf{Coeffs}})^k$ and sets $\boldsymbol{v} = \boldsymbol{a} \cdot s + \boldsymbol{x} \in R_q^k$. Then, the challenger samples $e_3 \leftarrow D_{\mathbb{Z}^n, \sigma_{\mathsf{RLWE}}}^{\mathsf{Coeffs}}$, and sets the challenge ciphertext as

$$c_0^* = u \cdot s + e_3 + \lceil \tfrac{q}{2} \rceil \mu \quad \text{and} \quad c_1^* = \mathsf{ReRand}\big([\mathbf{I}_k | \mathbf{R}_{\mathsf{id}^*}]^{\top}, \boldsymbol{v}, \sigma_{\mathsf{RLWE}}, \sigma_3\big),$$

where $\mathbf{I}_k$ is the identity matrix in $R^{k \times k}$ and $\sigma_3 = \frac{\sigma_2}{2\sigma_{\mathsf{RLWE}}}$. The syntax of the re-randomization algorithm is defined in full version of this paper.

Hybrid 5: In this hybrid, $\mathcal{A}$ plays $\mathbf{Expt}_{\mathcal{A}}^{\mathsf{IBE}}(1^{\lambda})'$ the same as Hybrid 4 except for the way that the challenge ciphertext is generated. Here, the challenger first chooses random c_0 from R_q and random $\boldsymbol{v}'$ from R_q^k, and samples $\boldsymbol{x} \leftarrow (D_{\mathbb{Z}^n, \sigma_{\mathsf{RLWE}}}^{\mathsf{Coeffs}})^k$. Then challenger sets the challenge ciphertext as

$$c_0^* = c_0 + \lceil \tfrac{q}{2} \rceil \mu \quad \text{and} \quad c_1^* = \mathsf{ReRand}\big([\mathbf{I}_k | \mathbf{R}_{\mathsf{id}^*}]^{\top}, \boldsymbol{v}, \sigma_{\mathsf{RLWE}}, \sigma_3\big),$$

where $\boldsymbol{v} = \boldsymbol{v}' + \boldsymbol{x}$, and σ_3 is defined as in Hybrid 4. As c_0 is uniformly random and independent of c_1^*, it serves as a one-time pad that perfectly hides μ. Thus the advantage of the adversary in this hybrid is exactly 0.

Next we are going to analyze the adversary's advantage in each hybrid. Similar as the previous analysis, we denote (T_i, α_i, β_i) as $\mathcal{A}$'s running time, non-abort probability, and successfully conditional guessing probability in Hybrid i for $0 \le i \le 5$. We note that $(T_0, \alpha_0, \beta_0) = (T, \alpha, \beta)$ by the condition of the theorem, and $\beta_5 = 1/2$ as the message is hidden by an one-time pad in Hybrid 5. Particularly, we derive the following lemmas. Due to space limit, we defer the proofs of Lemma 5.4, 5.5, 5.6 in full version of our paper.

Lemma 5.4. $T_1 = T_0 + \min\left\{O\left(\frac{\log(2\beta-1)\cdot\log(\gamma^*)}{(2\beta-1)^2\gamma^*}\right), (Lp)^{t'}\right\}$, $\alpha_1 \ge \alpha\gamma^* \cdot (1 - \frac{2\beta-1}{4})$, and $\beta_1 \ge \left(1 - \frac{3}{8}(2\beta-1)\right) \cdot \beta$, where $\gamma^* = \frac{2}{9Q'pw^{t'-1}}$.

Lemma 5.5. $T_1 = T_4$, $\alpha_4 \ge \alpha_1 - \varepsilon$ and $\beta_4 \ge \beta_1 - \varepsilon/(\alpha_1 - \varepsilon)$.

Lemma 5.6. There exists a (T', α', β')-adversary $\mathcal{B}$ against $\mathbf{Expt}_{\mathcal{B}}^{\mathsf{RLWE}}(1^n, k + 1, q, \psi)$ such that $T' \le T_4 + O\left(\frac{\log(2\beta-1)\cdot\log(\gamma^*)}{(2\beta-1)^2\gamma^*}\right)$, $\alpha' \ge \alpha_4/2$ and $\beta' \ge \beta_4/2 + 1/4$, where $\gamma^* = \frac{2}{9Q'pw^{t'-1}}$.

Combining Lemma 5.4, 5.5 and Lemma 5.6, it's easy to verify that $T' \le T + \min\{O(\frac{\log(2\beta-1)\cdot\log(\gamma^*)}{(2\beta-1)^2\gamma^*}), (Lp)^{t'}\}$, $\alpha' \ge \frac{1}{2}(\alpha\gamma^* \cdot (1 - \frac{2\beta-1}{4}) - \varepsilon) \ge \frac{(5-2\beta)\alpha}{36Q'pw^{t'-1}} - \frac{1}{2}\varepsilon$ and $\beta' \ge \frac{1}{2}((1 - \frac{6\beta-3}{8})\beta - (\gamma^*\alpha(1 - \frac{2\beta-1}{4})/\varepsilon - 1)^{-1}) + \frac{1}{4} \ge \frac{1}{2}\left(\frac{11-6\beta}{8}\beta - (\frac{5-2\beta}{36Q'pw^{t'-1}\varepsilon} - 1)^{-1}\right) + \frac{1}{4}$, and thus we have that $|\beta' - 1/2| \ge \frac{1}{2}\left(\frac{11-6\beta}{8}\beta - (\frac{5-2\beta}{36Q'pw^{t'-1}\varepsilon} - 1)^{-1}\right) - \frac{1}{4}$. This completes the proof. $\quad\square$

5.3 Asymptotic and Concrete Parameters

We also describe how to set both asymptotic and concrete parameters for our
IBE scheme in the full version of this paper. Due to space limit, we summarize
the results as follows:

Corollary 5.7 (Asymptotic Parameterization). *Assume* RLWE *is hard for
parameters* $n = \Theta(\lambda), 1/\alpha := \sigma_{\mathsf{RLWE}}/q = 1/\mathsf{poly}(\lambda)$. *Then Construction 5.1
is an adaptively secure* IBE. *The reductions cost* (T', ϵ') *satisfies* $T' = T +
\min\{O\left(p^t \log(p^t) \cdot \log(1/\epsilon)/\epsilon\right), (Lp)^t\}$, $\epsilon' \geq O\big(\epsilon/\lambda^{\frac{1}{\kappa}}Q\big)$, *where* T *and* ϵ *are the
running time and advantage of an* IBE *adversary, who makes* Q *key queries.*

Corollary 5.8 (Concrete   Parameterization). *Assume   the   RLWE   is*
$\max\{\lambda + \lceil\lceil\log_c(3Q)\rceil \cdot \frac{1}{\kappa}\log n\rceil + 10, \lceil\log_c(3Q)\rceil \cdot \frac{\kappa+4}{\kappa}\log n + \log(\frac{1}{\epsilon})\rceil + 10\}$-*bit
hard for parameters* $n, q, \sigma_{\mathsf{RLWE}}$, *where* $c = 1/(1-\Upsilon) = \sqrt[\kappa]{n}/(\kappa+3)$, *and* ϵ *is the
advantage of an* IBE *adversary. Then Construction 5.1 is an adaptively secure*
IBE, *and can achieve* λ-*bit security.*

Acknowledgement. We would like to thank the anonymous reviewers of TCC 2021
for their insightful advices. Feng-Hao Liu and Zhedong Wang are supported by an
NSF Award CNS-1657040 and an NSF Career Award CNS-1942400. Part of this work
was done while Zhedong Wang was a postdoc at Florida Atlantic University. Parhat
Abla and Han Wang are supported by the National Natural Science Foundation of
China under Grant Number NSFC61772516 and the National Key R&D Program of
China under Grant Number 2020YFA0712303, and Shandong Provincial Key Research
and Development Program under Grant Number 2019JZZY020127. Any opinions, findings, and conclusions or recommendations expressed in this material are those of the
author(s) and do not necessarily reflect the views of the sponsors.

References

1. Agrawal, S., Boneh, D., Boyen, X.: Efficient lattice (H)IBE in the standard model.
   In: Gilbert, H. (ed.) EUROCRYPT 2010. LNCS, vol. 6110, pp. 553–572. Springer,
   Heidelberg (2010). https://doi.org/10.1007/978-3-642-13190-5_28
2. Albrecht, M.R., Player, R., Scott, S.: On the concrete hardness of learning with
   errors. J. Math. Cryptology. **9**(3), 169–203 (2015). https://bitbucket.org/malb/
   lwe-estimator/src/master/
3. Alperin-Sheriff, J., Peikert, C.: Faster bootstrapping with polynomial error. In:
   Garay, J.A., Gennaro, R. (eds.) CRYPTO 2014. LNCS, vol. 8616, pp. 297–314.
   Springer, Heidelberg (2014). https://doi.org/10.1007/978-3-662-44371-2_17
4. Apon, D., Fan, X., Liu, F.-H.: Vector encoding over lattices and its applications.
   Cryptology ePrint Archive, Report 2017/455 (2017). http://eprint.iacr.org/2017/
   455
5. Barrington, D.A.: Bounded-width polynomial-size branching programs recognize
   exactly those languages in nc1. J. Comput. Syst. Sci. **38**(1), 150–164 (1989)
6. Beame, P.W., Cook, S.A., Hoover, H.J.: Log depth circuits for division and related
   problems. SIAM J. Comput. **15**(4), 994–1003 (1986)

7. Bellare, M., Ristenpart, T.: Simulation without the artificial abort: simplified proof and improved concrete security for waters IBE scheme. In: Joux, A. (ed.) EURO-CRYPT 2009. LNCS, vol. 5479, pp. 407–424. Springer, Heidelberg (2009). https://doi.org/10.1007/978-3-642-01001-9_24

8. Bitansky, N.: Verifiable random functions from non-interactive witness-indistinguishable proofs. In: Kalai, Y., Reyzin, L. (eds.) TCC 2017. LNCS, vol. 10678, pp. 567–594. Springer, Cham (2017). https://doi.org/10.1007/978-3-319-70503-3_19

9. Boneh, D., Boyen, X.: Efficient selective-id secure identity-based encryption without random oracles. In: Cachin, C., Camenisch, J.L. (eds.) EUROCRYPT 2004. LNCS, vol. 3027, pp. 223–238. Springer, Heidelberg (2004). https://doi.org/10.1007/978-3-540-24676-3_14

10. Boneh, D., Boyen, X.: Secure identity based encryption without random oracles. In: Franklin, M. (ed.) CRYPTO 2004. LNCS, vol. 3152, pp. 443–459. Springer, Heidelberg (2004). https://doi.org/10.1007/978-3-540-28628-8_27

11. Boneh, D., Franklin, M.: Identity-based encryption from the weil pairing. In: Kilian, J. (ed.) CRYPTO 2001. LNCS, vol. 2139, pp. 213–229. Springer, Heidelberg (2001). https://doi.org/10.1007/3-540-44647-8_13

12. Boneh, D., et al.: Fully key-homomorphic encryption, arithmetic circuit ABE and compact garbled circuits. In: Nguyen, P.Q., Oswald, E. (eds.) EUROCRYPT 2014. LNCS, vol. 8441, pp. 533–556. Springer, Heidelberg (2014). https://doi.org/10.1007/978-3-642-55220-5_30

13. Boyen, X., Li, Q.: Towards tightly secure lattice short signature and id-based encryption. In: Cheon, J.H., Takagi, T. (eds.) ASIACRYPT 2016. LNCS, vol. 10032, pp. 404–434. Springer, Heidelberg (2016). https://doi.org/10.1007/978-3-662-53890-6_14

14. Brakerski, Z., Lombardi, A., Segev, G., Vaikuntanathan, V.: Anonymous IBE, leakage resilience and circular security from new assumptions. In: Nielsen, J.B., Rijmen, V. (eds.) EUROCRYPT 2018. LNCS, vol. 10820, pp. 535–564. Springer, Cham (2018). https://doi.org/10.1007/978-3-319-78381-9_20

15. Brakerski, Z., Vaikuntanathan, V.: Lattice-based FHE as secure as PKE. In: Naor, M. (ed.) ITCS 2014, pp. 1–12. ACM (January 2014)

16. Cash, D., Hofheinz, D., Kiltz, E., Peikert, C.: Bonsai trees, or how to delegate a lattice basis. In: Gilbert, H. (ed.) EUROCRYPT 2010. LNCS, vol. 6110, pp. 523–552. Springer, Heidelberg (2010). https://doi.org/10.1007/978-3-642-13190-5_27

17. Cheon, J.H., Takagi, T. (eds.): ASIACRYPT 2016. LNCS, vol. 10032. Springer, Heidelberg (2016). https://doi.org/10.1007/978-3-662-53890-6

18. Döttling, N., Garg, S.: From selective IBE to Full IBE and selective HIBE. In: Kalai, Y., Reyzin, L. (eds.) TCC 2017. LNCS, vol. 10677, pp. 372–408. Springer, Cham (2017). https://doi.org/10.1007/978-3-319-70500-2_13

19. Gentry, C.: Practical identity-based encryption without random oracles. In: Vaudenay, S. (ed.) EUROCRYPT 2006. LNCS, vol. 4004, pp. 445–464. Springer, Heidelberg (2006). https://doi.org/10.1007/11761679_27

20. Gentry, C., Peikert, C., Vaikuntanathan, V.: Trapdoors for hard lattices and new cryptographic constructions. In: Ladner, R.E., Dwork, C. (eds.), 40th ACM STOC, pp. 197–206. ACM Press (May 2008)

21. Gentry, C., Sahai, A., Waters, B.: Homomorphic encryption from learning with errors: conceptually-simpler, asymptotically-faster, attribute-based. In: Canetti, R., Garay, J.A. (eds.) CRYPTO 2013. LNCS, vol. 8042, pp. 75–92. Springer, Heidelberg (2013). https://doi.org/10.1007/978-3-642-40041-4_5

22. Gilbert, H. (ed.): EUROCRYPT 2010. LNCS, vol. 6110. Springer, Heidelberg (2010). https://doi.org/10.1007/978-3-642-13190-5
23. Gorbunov, S., Vinayagamurthy, D.: Riding on asymmetry: efficient ABE for branching programs. In: Iwata, T., Cheon, J.H. (eds.) ASIACRYPT 2015. LNCS, vol. 9452, pp. 550–574. Springer, Heidelberg (2015). https://doi.org/10.1007/978-3-662-48797-6_23
24. Katsumata, S.: On the untapped potential of encoding predicates by arithmetic circuits and their applications. In: Takagi, T., Peyrin, T. (eds.) ASIACRYPT 2017. LNCS, vol. 10626, pp. 95–125. Springer, Cham (2017). https://doi.org/10.1007/978-3-319-70700-6_4
25. Katsumata, S., Yamada, S.: Partitioning via non-linear polynomial functions: more compact IBEs from ideal lattices and bilinear maps. In: Cheon, J.H., Takagi, T. (eds.) ASIACRYPT 2016. LNCS, vol. 10032, pp. 682–712. Springer, Heidelberg (2016). https://doi.org/10.1007/978-3-662-53890-6_23
26. Lai, Q., Liu, F.-H., Wang, Z.: Almost tight security in lattices with polynomial moduli – PRF, IBE, all-but-many LTF, and more. In: Kiayias, A., Kohlweiss, M., Wallden, P., Zikas, V. (eds.) PKC 2020. LNCS, vol. 12110, pp. 652–681. Springer, Cham (2020). https://doi.org/10.1007/978-3-030-45374-9_22
27. Lyubashevsky, V., Peikert, C., Regev, O.: On ideal lattices and learning with errors over rings. In: Gilbert, H. (ed.) EUROCRYPT 2010. LNCS, vol. 6110, pp. 1–23. Springer, Heidelberg (2010). https://doi.org/10.1007/978-3-642-13190-5_1
28. Lyubashevsky, V., Peikert, C., Regev, O.: A toolkit for ring-LWE cryptography. In: Johansson, T., Nguyen, P.Q. (eds.) EUROCRYPT 2013. LNCS, vol. 7881, pp. 35–54. Springer, Heidelberg (2013). https://doi.org/10.1007/978-3-642-38348-9_3
29. Micciancio, D., Peikert, C.: Trapdoors for lattices: simpler, tighter, faster, smaller. In: Pointcheval, D., Johansson, T. (eds.) EUROCRYPT 2012. LNCS, vol. 7237, pp. 700–718. Springer, Heidelberg (2012). https://doi.org/10.1007/978-3-642-29011-4_41
30. Micciancio, D., Walter, M.: On the bit security of cryptographic primitives. In: Nielsen, J.B., Rijmen, V. (eds.) EUROCRYPT 2018. LNCS, vol. 10820, pp. 3–28. Springer, Cham (2018). https://doi.org/10.1007/978-3-319-78381-9_1
31. Nielsen, J.B., Rijmen, V. (eds.): EUROCRYPT 2018. LNCS, vol. 10820. Springer, Cham (2018). https://doi.org/10.1007/978-3-319-78381-9
32. Regev, O.: On lattices, learning with errors, random linear codes, and cryptography. In: Gabow, H.N., Fagin, R. (eds.), 37th ACM STOC, pp. 84–93. ACM Press (May 2005)
33. Shamir, A.: Identity-based cryptosystems and signature schemes. In: Blakley, G.R., Chaum, D. (eds.) CRYPTO 1984. LNCS, vol. 196, pp. 47–53. Springer, Heidelberg (1985). https://doi.org/10.1007/3-540-39568-7_5
34. Stehlé, D., Steinfeld, R., Tanaka, K., Xagawa, K.: Efficient public key encryption based on ideal lattices. In: Matsui, M. (ed.) ASIACRYPT 2009. LNCS, vol. 5912, pp. 617–635. Springer, Heidelberg (2009). https://doi.org/10.1007/978-3-642-10366-7_36
35. Valiant, L.G., Vazirani, V.V.: NP is as easy as detecting unique solutions. In: 17th ACM STOC, pp. 458–463. ACM Press (May 1985)
36. Waters, B.: Dual system encryption: realizing fully secure IBE and HIBE under simple assumptions. In: Halevi, S. (ed.) CRYPTO 2009. LNCS, vol. 5677, pp. 619–636. Springer, Heidelberg (2009). https://doi.org/10.1007/978-3-642-03356-8_36
37. Waters, B.: Efficient identity-based encryption without random oracles. In: Cramer, R. (ed.) EUROCRYPT 2005. LNCS, vol. 3494, pp. 114–127. Springer, Heidelberg (2005). https://doi.org/10.1007/11426639_7

38. Yamada, S.: Adaptively secure identity-based encryption from lattices with asymptotically shorter public parameters. In: Fischlin, M., Coron, J.-S. (eds.) EUROCRYPT 2016. LNCS, vol. 9666, pp. 32–62. Springer, Heidelberg (2016). https://doi.org/10.1007/978-3-662-49896-5_2
39. Yamada, S.: Asymptotically compact adaptively secure lattice IBEs and verifiable random functions via generalized partitioning techniques. In: Katz, J., Shacham, H. (eds.) CRYPTO 2017. LNCS, vol. 10403, pp. 161–193. Springer, Cham (2017). https://doi.org/10.1007/978-3-319-63697-9_6
40. Zhang, J., Chen, Yu., Zhang, Z.: Programmable hash functions from lattices: short signatures and IBEs with small key sizes. In: Robshaw, M., Katz, J. (eds.) CRYPTO 2016. LNCS, vol. 9816, pp. 303–332. Springer, Heidelberg (2016). https://doi.org/10.1007/978-3-662-53015-3_11

Cryptographic Shallots: A Formal Treatment of Repliable Onion Encryption

Megumi Ando[1]([⊠]) and Anna Lysyanskaya[2]

[1] MITRE, Bedford, MA 01730, USA
megumi_ando@alumni.brown.edu
[2] Brown University, Providence, RI 02912, USA

Abstract. Onion routing is a popular, efficient, and scalable method for enabling anonymous communications. To send a message m to Bob via onion routing, Alice picks several intermediaries, wraps m in multiple layers of encryption—a layer per intermediary—and sends the resulting *onion* to the first intermediary. Each intermediary *peels off* a layer of encryption and learns the identity of the next entity on the path and what to send along; finally Bob learns that he is the recipient and recovers the message m.

Despite its wide use in the real world, the foundations of onion routing have not been thoroughly studied. In particular, although two-way communication is needed in most instances, such as anonymous Web browsing or anonymous access to a resource, until now no definitions or provably secure constructions have been given for two-way onion routing. Moreover, the security definitions that existed even for one-way onion routing were found to have significant flaws.

In this paper, we (1) propose an ideal functionality for a *repliable* onion encryption scheme; (2) give a game-based definition for repliable onion encryption and show that it is sufficient to realize our ideal functionality; and finally (3), our main result is a construction of repliable onion encryption that satisfies our definitions.

1 Introduction

Suppose Alice wants to send a message to Bob, anonymously, over a point-to-point network such as the Internet. What cryptographic techniques exist to make this possible? One popular approach is onion routing: Alice sends her message through intermediaries, who mix it with other traffic and forward it on to Bob. To make this approach secure from an adversary eavesdropping on the network, she needs to wrap her message in several layers of encryption, one for each intermediary, giving rise to the term *onion routing*.

As originally proposed by Chaum [10], onion routing meant that Alice just uses regular encryption to derive each subsequent layer of her onion before sending it on to the first intermediary. I.e., if the intermediaries are Carol (public key pk_C), David (public key pk_D), and Evelyn (public key pk_E), then to send message m to Bob (public key pk_B), Alice forms

K. Nissim and B. Waters (Eds.): TCC 2021, LNCS 13044, pp. 188–221, 2021.
https://doi.org/10.1007/978-3-030-90456-2_7

her onion by first encrypting m under pk_B, then encrypting the resulting destination-ciphertext pair (Bob, c_B) under pk_E, and so forth: $O = \mathsf{Enc}_{\mathsf{pk}_C}((\text{David}, \mathsf{Enc}_{\mathsf{pk}_D}((\text{Evelyn}, \mathsf{Enc}_{\mathsf{pk}_E}((\text{Bob}, \mathsf{Enc}_{\mathsf{pk}_B}(m))))))).$ If we use this approach using regular public-key encryption, then the "peeled" onion O' that Carol will forward to David is going to be a shorter (in bit length) ciphertext than O, because ciphertexts are longer than the messages they encrypt. So even if Carol serves as an intermediary for many onions, an eavesdropping adversary can link O and O' by their lengths, unless Carol happens to also be the first intermediary for another onion.

To ensure that all onions are the same length, no matter which layer an intermediary is responsible for, Camenisch and Lysyanskaya [5] introduced *onion encryption*, a tailor-made public-key encryption scheme where the adversary can't tell how far an intermediary, e.g. Carol, is from an onion's destination, even for adversarial Carol. They gave an ideal functionality [6] for uni-directional onion encryption and a cryptographic scheme that, they argued, UC-realized it. However, their work did not altogether solve the problem of anonymous communication via onion routing. As Kuhn et al. [21] point out, there were significant definitional issues. Also, as, for example, Ando et al. [2,3] show, onion routing by itself does not guarantee anonymity, as a sufficient number of onions need to be present before any mixing occurs.

Those issues aside, however, Camenisch and Lysyanskaya (CL) left open the problem of "repliable" onions. In other words, once Bob receives Alice's message and wants to respond, what does he do? This is not just an esoteric issue. If one wants to do basic online tasks anonymously—e.g., browse the Web incognito or anonymously fill out a feedback form—a two-way channel between the anonymous original sender (here, Alice) and their interlocutor (here, Bob) needs to be established. Although CL outlined an initial idea for how to reply to an onion, they don't provide any definitions or proofs. Babel [18], Mixminion [14], Minx [16], and Sphinx [15] all provide mechanisms for the recipient to reply to the sender but don't provide any formal definitions or proofs either. This left a gap between proposed ideas for a repliable onion encryption scheme and rigorous examinations of these ideas. For instance, Kuhn et al. [21] pointed out a fatal security flaw in the current state-of-the-art, Sphinx. They also pointed out some definitional issues in the CL paper and proposed fixes for some of these issues but left open the problem of formalizing repliable onion encryption.

The Challenge. Let us see why repliable onion encryption is not like other types of encryption. Traditionally, to be able to prove that an encryption scheme satisfies a definition of security along the lines of CCA2 security, we direct honest parties (for example, an intermediary Iris) to check whether a ciphertext (or, for our purposes, an onion) she has received is authentic or has been "mauled;" Iris can then refuse to decrypt a "mauled" ciphertext (correspondingly, process a "mauled" onion). Most constructions of CCA2-secure encryption schemes work along these lines; that way, in the proof of security, the decryption oracle does not need to worry about decrypting ciphertexts that do not pass such a validity check, making it possible to prove security. This approach was made more explicit by Cramer and Shoup [12,13] who defined encryption with tags, where tags defined the scope of a ciphertext, and a ciphertext would never be decrypted unless it was accompanied by the correct tag.

The CL construction of onion encryption also works this way; it uses CCA2-secure encryption with tags to make it possible for each intermediary to check the integrity of an onion it received. So when constructing an onion, the sender had to construct each layer so that it would pass the integrity check, and in doing so, the sender needed to know what each layer was going to look like. This was not a problem for onion security in the forward direction since the sender knew all the puzzle pieces—the message m and the path (e.g. Carol, David, Evelyn) to the recipient Bob—so the sender could compute each layer and derive the correct tag that would allow the integrity check to pass. But in the reverse direction, the recipient Bob needs to form a reply onion without knowing part of the puzzle pieces. He should not know what any subsequent onion layers will look like: if he did, then an adversarial Bob, together with an adversarial intermediary and the network adversary, will be able to trace the reply onion as it gets back to Alice. So he cannot derive the correct tag for every layer. The sender Alice cannot do so either since she does not know in advance what Bob's reply message is going to be. So it is not clear how a CCA2-style definition can be satisfied at all.

At the same time, it is important to make sure that reply onions are indistinguishable (even to intermediaries who process them) from forward onions. As pointed out in prior work [14], this is crucial because "replies may be very rare relative to forward messages, and thus much easier to trace." Thus, making sure that they are hidden among the more voluminous forward traffic is desirable.

Our First Contribution: A Definition of Secure Repliable Onion Encryption. We define security by describing an ideal functionality $\mathcal{F}_{\mathsf{ROES}}$ in the simplified UC model [7]; from now on we refer to it as the *SUC model*. We chose the SUC model so that our functionality and proof did not have to explicitly worry about network issues and other subtleties of the full-blown UC model [6].

As should be expected of secure onion routing, $\mathcal{F}_{\mathsf{ROES}}$ represents onions originating at honest senders or formed as replies to honest senders, using bit strings that are computed independently on the contents of messages, their destinations, whether the onion is traveling in the forward direction or is a reply, and identities and number of intermediaries that follow or precede an honest intermediary. To process an onion, an honest party P sends it to the functionality $\mathcal{F}_{\mathsf{ROES}}$, which then informs P what its role is—an intermediary, the recipient, or the original sender of this onion. If P is an intermediary, the functionality sends it a string that represents the next layer of the same onion (also formed independently of the input). If P is the recipient, P learns the contents of the message m and whether the onion can be replied to, and can direct the functionality to create a reply onion containing a reply message r. Finally, if P is the sender of the original onion, then he learns r, the reply; he also learns to which one of his previous outgoing onions this one is the response. We describe $\mathcal{F}_{\mathsf{ROES}}$ in Sect. 3.

It is important to note that our functionality $\mathcal{F}_{\mathsf{ROES}}$ is defined in such a way that it allows for a scheme in which checking that an onion has been "mauled" is not entirely the job of each intermediary. More precisely, we think of the onion as consisting of two pieces. The first piece is the *header* H that, in $\mathcal{F}_{\text{ROES}}$, is a pointer to a data structure that contains the onion's information. The second piece is the payload, the *content* C that can be thought of as a pointer to a data structure inside $\mathcal{F}_{\text{ROES}}$ that contains the message m. The content C does not undergo an integrity check until it gets to its destination. This is how we overcome the challenge (above) of having a definition that enables replies.

Our Second Contribution: A Game-Style Definition of Secure Repliable Onion Encryption. Although UC-style definitions of security are a good way to capture the security properties of a novel cryptographic object such as secure repliable onion encryption, they can be difficult to work with. The SUC model makes the job easier, but it is still cumbersome to prove that a construction SUC-realizes an ideal functionality, especially one as involved as $\mathcal{F}_{\text{ROES}}$. So to make it easier, we provide a game-style definition, called "repliable-onion security" in Sect. 4.

This definition boils down to a game between an adversary and a challenger. The challenger generates the key pairs for two participants under attack: a sender S and an honest intermediary I. Similar to CCA2-security for public-key encryption, the challenger also responds (before and after the creation of a challenge onion) to the adversary's queries to S and I; i.e. the adversary may send onions to the parties under attack and learn how these onions are peeled. The adversary then requests that a challenge repliable onion be formed by S; the adversary picks the recipient R for this onion, as well as the message m to be routed to R, and the identities and public keys of all the intermediaries on the path from S to R (other than S and I) and the return path from the recipient to the sender. The honest intermediary I must appear somewhere on this path: either (a) I is on the forward path from S to R, or (b) I is the recipient, or (c) I is on the return path from R to S. The challenger then tosses a coin, and depending on the outcome, forms the challenge onion in one of two ways; the adversary's job to win the game is to correctly guess the outcome of the coin toss. If the coin comes up heads, the challenger forms the onion correctly, using the routing path provided by the adversary. If it comes up tails, then the challenger makes a "switch:" he forms two unrelated onions, one from S to I, and the other from I back to S; the details depend on whether this is case (a), (b), or (c). He then patches up the oracles for S and I so as to be able to pretend that the challenge onion was formed correctly. For details, see Sect. 4.

In Sect. 5, we show that our game-based definition is sufficient to SUC-realize $\mathcal{F}_{\text{ROES}}$ and that its non-adaptive variant is necessary: any repliable onion encryption scheme SUC-realizing $\mathcal{F}_{\text{ROES}}$ will satisfy it.

Here is how we overcome the definitional challenge of having a CCA2-style definition while enabling replies. When forming a repliable onion, the sender S will generate not just the onion to send on to the first intermediary, but, as a byproduct of forming that onion, will generate all the onion layers—to be precise, the header H_i and the content C_i of the ith onion layer for every i—on the path from himself to the recipient R. However, in the return direction, S is unable to know in advance the content of the onion (otherwise the recipient cannot send a return message); but the sender can still form just the header parts $\{H_i\}$ of those onion layers. So it is the headers that must satisfy CCA2-style non-malleability, while the content accompanying the header can be "mauled" on its way to its destination, be it the recipient R, or, in the case of a reply onion, the original sender S. However, upon arrival to its destination, any "mauled" content should be peeled to $\perp$.

Our Main Contribution: Realizing Secure Repliable Onion Encryption. We resolve the problem that CL left open fifteen years ago of constructing provably secure repliable onion encryption. Namely, we give a scheme, which we call *shallot encryption*, for repliable onion encryption. Our scheme is based on a CCA2-secure cryptosystem with tags, a strong PRP (in other words, a block cipher), and a collision-resistant hash function.

In a nutshell, here is how our construction works. As we explained above, we split up the onion into two pieces, the header H and the content C. H contains (in layered encryption form) the routing information and symmetric keys that are needed to process C. C contains the message and, in case this is a forward onion, instructions for forming the reply onion; this part is wrapped in layers of symmetric encryption. This way, the original sender Alice can form the headers for all the layers of the reply onion even though she does not know the contents of the reply in advance; Bob's contribution to the reply onion is just the content C. Each intermediary is responsible for peeling a layer off of H, learning its key k, and applying a strong PRP keyed by k to the contents C. The adaptive security properties guarantee that H cannot be "mauled," but checking the integrity of C is postponed until the onion gets to its destination—recipient Bob or original sender Alice—who check it using a MAC key. This is also why our scheme is called *shallot* encryption: the layered structure of the resulting onion resembles a shallot! (Shallots are a sub-family of onions.) See Sect. 6 for details.

Related Work. Onion routing and mixes were introduced by David Chaum in 1981 [10]. Since then, tremendous interest from applied security researchers resulted in numerous implementations [11,14,22,23].

Tor [14,17] is the most widely used tool for anonymizing Internet communications; according to statistics shared by the Tor Project (https://www.torproject.org/), an estimated two million users use Tor daily. Tor's approach is not, strictly speaking, onion encryption as defined here because no public keys are used for encryption; also, its live connection design is vulnerable to traffic analysis [19,24,25].

Despite its practical relevance and widely used implementations, the theoretical foundations of onion routing are somewhat shaky. None of the implementation papers cited above provided definitions or proofs of security. In 2005, Camenisch and Lysyanskaya (CL) provided the first formal definition of secure onion encryption [5]; this was done in Canetti's UC framework [6]. They also gave a game-based definition (onion-security) that they claimed was equivalent to one in the UC model and the first provably secure onion encryption scheme. CL mentioned the possibility of having a reply option (as did Chaum), but their formal treatment did not extend to it.

In a recent paper, Kuhn et al. [21] found a mistake in CL's game-based definition. In a nutshell, CL's onion-security game proceeded as follows: An adversary attacking an honest participant P is given P's public key and specifies the input to the algorithm for forming an onion. This input includes the identities and public keys of all the intermediaries and the final recipient and the contents of the message m; P is somewhere on the routing path. The challenger either responds with a correctly formed onion or with an onion whose routing path is cut off at P, i.e., for the latter type, P is the recipient of a random unrelated message m'. Kuhn et al. pointed out that, although this property indeed hides where the onion is headed after P, it does not hide where the onion has been before it got to P. Thus, CL's proof that their onion-security definition was sufficient to UC-realize $\mathcal{F}_{\text{onion}}$ had a missing step, which Kuhn et al. found. Kuhn et al. also showed how to use this unfortunate theoretical mistake to attack Sphinx [15]. In addition to pointing out this flaw, Kuhn et al. proposed a new game-based definition that implied the realizability of CL's ideal functionality $\mathcal{F}_{\text{onion}}$. However, they do not tackle repliable onions.

2 Repliable Onion Encryption: Syntax and Correctness

Here, we give the formal input/output (I/O) specification for a repliable onion encryption scheme. In contrast to the CL I/O specification for uni-directional onion encryption scheme [5], a repliable onion encryption scheme contains an additional algorithm, FormReply, for forming return onions. This algorithm allows the recipient of a message contained in a repliable onion to respond to the anonymous sender of the message without needing to know who the sender is.

In this paper, an onion O is a pair, consisting of the (encrypted) content C and the header H, i.e., $O = (H, C)$. The maximum length of a path of an onion, be it the forward path or the return path, is N; we assume that N is one of the public parameters pp. The algorithm for forming onions, FormOnion, also takes as one of its parameters, the label ℓ. This is so that when the sender receives a reply message m' along with the label ℓ, the sender can identify to which message m' is responding.

Definition 1 (Repliable onion encryption scheme I/O). *The set $\Sigma = (G, \text{FormOnion}, \text{ProcOnion}, \text{FormReply})$ of algorithms satisfies the I/O specification of a* repliable onion encryption scheme *for the label space $\mathcal{L}(1^\lambda)$, the message space $\mathcal{M}(1^\lambda)$, and a set $\mathcal{P}$ of router names if:*

- *G is a probabilistic polynomial-time (p.p.t.) key generation algorithm. On input the security parameter 1^λ (written in unary), the public parameters pp, and the party name P, the algorithm G returns a key pair, i.e., $(\text{pk}(P), \text{sk}(P)) \leftarrow G(1^\lambda, \text{pp}, P)$.*
- *FormOnion is a p.p.t. algorithm for forming onions. On input*
  - *i. a label $\ell \in \mathcal{L}(1^\lambda)$ from the label space,*
  - *ii. a message $m \in \mathcal{M}(1^\lambda)$ from the message space,*

iii. a forward path $P^{\rightarrow} = (P_1, \ldots, P_d)$ *(d stands for destination),*

iv. the public keys $\mathsf{pk}(P^{\rightarrow})$ *associated with the parties in* $P^{\rightarrow}$,

v. a return path $P^{\leftarrow} = (P_{d+1}, \ldots, P_s)$ *(s stands for sender), and*

vi. the public keys $\mathsf{pk}(P^{\leftarrow})$ *associated with the parties in* $P^{\leftarrow}$,

the algorithm FormOnion *returns a sequence* $O^{\rightarrow} = (O_1, \ldots, O_d)$ *of onions for the forward path, a sequence* $H^{\leftarrow} = (H_{d+1}, \ldots, H_s)$ *of headers for the return path, and a key* κ, *i.e.,* $(O^{\rightarrow}, H^{\leftarrow}, \kappa) \leftarrow$ FormOnion$(\ell, m, P^{\rightarrow}, \mathsf{pk}(P^{\rightarrow}), P^{\leftarrow}, \mathsf{pk}(P^{\leftarrow}))$. *Note: the key* κ *contains some state information that the sender of the onion might need for future reference; a scheme can still satisfy our definition if* $\kappa = \perp$.

- ProcOnion *is a deterministic polynomial-time (d.p.t.) algorithm for processing onions. On input an onion* O, *a router name* P, *and the secret key* $\mathsf{sk}(P)$ *belonging to* P, *the algorithm* ProcOnion *returns* (role, output), *i.e.,* (role, output) $\leftarrow$ ProcOnion$(O, P, \mathsf{sk}(P))$. *When* role $= \mathsf{I}$ *(for "intermediary"), output is the pair* (O', P') *consisting of the peeled onion* O' *and the next destination* P' *of* O'. *When* role $= \mathsf{R}$ *(for "recipient"), output is the message* m *for recipient* P. *When* role $= \mathsf{S}$ *(for "sender"), output is the pair* (ℓ, m) *consisting of the label* ℓ *and the reply message* m *for sender* P.

- FormReply *is a d.p.t. algorithm for replying to an onion. On input a reply message* $m \in \mathcal{M}(1^{\lambda})$, *an onion* O, *a router name* P, *and the secret key* $\mathsf{sk}(P)$ *belonging to* P, *the algorithm* FormReply *returns the onion* O' *and the next destination* P' *of* O', *i.e.,* $(O', P') \leftarrow$ FormReply$(m, O, P, \mathsf{sk}(P))$. *Note:* FormReply *may output* $(\perp, \perp)$ *if* P *is not the correct recipient of* O.

2.1   Onion Evolutions, Forward Paths, Return Paths and Layerings

Here, we define what it means for a repliable onion encryption scheme to be correct. Before we do this, we first define what onion *evolutions*, *paths*, and *layerings* are; the analogous notions for the unrepliable onion encryption scheme were introduced by Camenisch and Lysyanskaya [5].

Let $\Sigma = (G, \mathsf{FormOnion}, \mathsf{ProcOnion}, \mathsf{FormReply})$ be a repliable onion encryption scheme for the label space $\mathcal{L}(1^{\lambda})$, the message space $\mathcal{M}(1^{\lambda})$, and the set $\mathcal{P}$ of router names. Let $\mathcal{H} \subseteq \mathcal{P}$ be parties with honestly formed keys. For any $P \notin \mathcal{H}$, let $\mathsf{sk}(P) = \perp$ (i.e., secret keys that were not formed honestly are not well-defined for the purposes of this experiment).

Let $O_1 = (H_1, C_1)$ be an onion received by party $P_1 \in \mathcal{H}$, not necessarily formed using FormOnion.

We define a sequence of onion-location pairs recursively as follows: Let d be the first onion layer of (H_1, C_1) that when peeled, produces either "R" or "S" (if it exists, otherwise $d = \infty$). For all $i \in [d-1]$, let $(\mathsf{role}_{i+1}, ((H_{i+1}, C_{i+1}), P_{i+1})) = $ ProcOnion$((H_i, C_i), P_i, \mathsf{sk}(P_i))$. Let $s = d$ if peeling (H_d, C_d) produces "S." Otherwise, let $m \in \mathcal{M}(1^{\lambda})$ be a reply message from the message space, and let $((H_{d+1}, C_{d+1}), P_{d+1}) = $ FormReply$(m, (H_d, C_d), P_d, \mathsf{sk}(P_d))$. Let s be the first onion layer of (H_{d+1}, C_{d+1}) that when peeled, produces either "R" or "S" (if it exists, otherwise $s = \infty$). For all $i \in \{d+1, \ldots, s-1\}$, let $(\mathsf{role}_{i+1}, ((H_{i+1}, C_{i+1}), P_{i+1})) = $ ProcOnion$((H_i, C_i), P_i, \mathsf{sk}(P_i))$.

We call the sequence $\mathcal{E}(H_1, C_1, P_1, m) = ((H_1, C_1, P_1), \dots, (H_s, C_s, P_s))$ of onion-location pairs the *"evolution of the onion (H_1, C_1) starting at party P_1 given m as the reply message."* The sequence $\mathcal{P}^{\rightarrow}(H_1, C_1, P_1, m) = (P_1, \dots, P_d)$ is its *forward path*; the sequence $\mathcal{P}^{\leftarrow}(H_1, C_1, P_1, m) = (P_{d+1}, \dots, P_s)$ is its *return path*; and the sequence $\mathcal{L}(H_1, C_1, P_1, m) = (H_1, C_1, \dots, H_d, C_d, H_{d+1}, \dots, H_s)$ is its *layering*.

Definition 2 (Correctness). *Let G, FormOnion, ProcOnion, and FormReply form a repliable onion encryption scheme for the label space $\mathcal{L}(1^\lambda)$, the message space $\mathcal{M}(1^\lambda)$, and the set $\mathcal{P}$ of router names.*

Let N be the upper bound on the path length (in public parameters pp). Let $P = (P_1, \dots, P_s)$, $|P| = s \le 2N$ be any list (not containing $\perp$) of router names in $\mathcal{P}$. Let $d \in [s]$ be any index in $[s]$ such that $d \le N$ and $s - d + 1 \le N$. Let $\ell \in \mathcal{L}(1^\lambda)$ be any label in $\mathcal{L}(1^\lambda)$. Let $m, m' \in \mathcal{M}(1^\lambda)$ be any two messages in $\mathcal{M}(1^\lambda)$.

For every party P_i in P, let $(\mathsf{pk}(P_i), \mathsf{sk}(P_i)) \leftarrow G(1^\lambda, \mathsf{pp}, P_i)$ be P_i's key pair. Let $P^{\rightarrow} = (P_1, \dots, P_d)$, and let $\mathsf{pk}(P^{\rightarrow})$ be a shorthand for the public keys associated with the parties in $P^{\rightarrow}$. Let $P^{\leftarrow} = (P_{d+1}, \dots, P_s)$, and let $\mathsf{pk}(P^{\leftarrow})$ be a shorthand for the public keys associated with the parties in $P^{\leftarrow}$.

Let $((H_1, C_1), \dots, (H_d, C_d), H_{d+1}, \dots, H_s, \kappa)$ be the output of FormOnion on input the label ℓ, the message m, the forward path $P^{\rightarrow} = (P_1, \dots, P_d)$, the public keys $\mathsf{pk}(P^{\rightarrow})$ associated with the parties in $P^{\rightarrow}$, the return path $P^{\leftarrow} = (P_{d+1}, \dots, P_s)$, and the public keys $\mathsf{pk}(P^{\leftarrow})$ associated with the parties in $P^{\leftarrow}$.

The scheme Σ is correct if with overwhelming probability in the security parameter λ,

  i. **Correct forward path.**
    – $\mathcal{P}^{\rightarrow}(H_1, C_1, P_1, m') = (P_1, \dots, P_d)$.
    – *For every $i \in [d]$ and content C such that $|C| = |C_i|$, $\mathcal{P}^{\rightarrow}(H_i, C, P_i, m') = (P_i, \dots, P_d)$.*

  ii. **Correct return path.**
    – $\mathcal{P}^{\leftarrow}(H_1, C_1, P_1, m') = (P_{d+1}, \dots, P_s)$.
    – *For every $i \in \{d+1, \dots, s\}$, reply message m'', and content C such that $|C| = |C_i|$, $\mathcal{P}^{\rightarrow}(H_i, C, P_i, m'') = (P_{d+1}, \dots, P_s)$.*

  iii. **Correct layering.** $\mathcal{L}(H_1, C_1, P_1, m') = (H_1, C_1, \dots, H_d, C_d, H_{d+1}, \dots, H_s)$,

  iv. **Correct message.** $\mathsf{ProcOnion}((H_d, C_d), P_d, \mathsf{sk}(P_d)) = (\mathsf{R}, m)$,

  v. **Correct reply message.** $\mathsf{ProcOnion}((H_s, C_s), P_s, \mathsf{sk}(P_s)) = (\mathsf{S}, (\ell, m'))$ *where (H_s, C_s) are the header and content of the last onion in the evolution $\mathcal{E}(H_1, C_1, P_1, m')$.*

Note that we define onion evolution, (forward and return) paths, and layering so that we can articulate what it means for an onion encryption scheme to be correct. We define correctness to mean that how an onion peels (the evolution, paths, and layerings) exactly reflects the reverse process of how the onion was built up. Thus, for our definition to make sense, both ProcOnion and FormReply must be deterministic algorithms.

3 $\mathcal{F}_{\text{ROES}}$: Onion Routing in the SUC Framework

Here, we provide a formal definition of security for a repliable onion encryption scheme. We chose to define security in the simplified universal composability (SUC) model [7] as opposed to the universal composability (UC) model [6] as this choice greatly simplifies how communication is modeled. Additionally, since SUC-realizability implies UC-realizability [7], we do not lose generality by simplifying the model in this manner. In the SUC model, the environment $\mathcal{Z}$ can communicate directly with each party P by writing inputs into P's input tape and by reading P's output tape. The parties communicate with each other and also with the ideal functionality through an additional party, the router $\mathcal{R}$.

3.1 Ideal Functionality $\mathcal{F}_{\text{ROES}}$

In this section, honest parties are capitalized, e.g., P, P_i; and corrupt parties are generally written in lowercase, e.g., p, p_i. An onion formed by an honest party is *honestly formed* and is capitalized, e.g., O, O_i; whereas, an onion formed by a corrupt party is generally written in lowercase, e.g., o, o_i. Recall that an onion O is a pair, consisting of the content C and the header H, i.e., $O = (H, C)$.

How should we define the ideal functionality of a repliable onion encryption scheme? Honestly formed onions in an onion routing protocol should mix at honest nodes. This property is what enables anonymity from the standard adversary who can observe the network traffic on all communication links. Ideally, onions should mix (i) even if the distances from their respective origins or the distances to their respective destinations differ, and (ii) regardless of whether they are forward or return onions. Here, we define the ideal functionality so that a scheme that realizes it necessarily satisfies properties (i) and (ii) above.

Intuitively, onions mix iff onion layers are (computationally) unrelated to each other. Let O' be the onion we get from peeling the onion O. If the values of O and O' are correlated with each other, then O cannot mix with other onions. Conversely, if the values O and O' are unrelated to each other, then O can mix with other onions. However, the adversary necessarily knows how some onions layers are linked together. If the corrupt party p peels onion o, getting peeled onion o', then p knows that o and o' are linked.

Thus, we settle on our idea for an ideal functionality $\mathcal{F}_{\text{ROES}}$ (ROES, for "repliable onion encryption scheme") as follows: Let a *segment* of a routing path be a subpath of the path consisting of a sequence of corrupt parties possibly ending with a single honest party. Note that if there are two consecutive honest parties, (Alice, Bob) on the routing path, then (Bob) is a segment of the path. Each routing path can be uniquely broken up into a sequence $(s_1, \ldots, s_u)$ of non-overlapping segments, such that each segment s_i contains exactly one honest participant, except for the last segment that may end in an adversarial recipient. For $i \neq j$, onion layers corresponding to segment s_i should be computationally unrelated to the layers corresponding to segment s_j.

Thus, the ideal functionality $\mathcal{F}_{\text{ROES}}$ forms the onion layers for each segment of a routing path separately and independently from each other. $\mathcal{F}_{\text{ROES}}$ internally keeps tracks of how these layers are linked using two data structures, OnionDict and PathDict. If $\mathcal{F}_{\text{ROES}}$ forms an onion layer O for Alice (the last party of a segment) that should peel to an onion layer O' for Bob (the first party of the next segment), then it keeps track of this link in OnionDict; the output (O', Bob) is stored under the label (Alice, O). $\mathcal{F}_{\text{ROES}}$ initially forms and stores the onion links only for the forward path and stores the return path in PathDict; onion links for the return path are generated later on when they are needed. To produce the onion layers for a segment, $\mathcal{F}_{\text{ROES}}$ runs the algorithm SampleOnion, which it gets from the ideal adversary $\mathcal{A}$.

Sometimes, the environment $\mathcal{Z}$ instructs an ideal party to process an onion O (or form a reply to an onion O), not stored in either OnionDict or PathDict. If the header of O is not honestly formed, then $\mathcal{F}_{\text{ROES}}$ processes it according to the algorithm ProcOnion (or FormReply) supplied by $\mathcal{A}$. Otherwise, if O is the result of "mauling" just the content of an honestly formed onion X that peels to X', then $\mathcal{F}_{\text{ROES}}$ returns the onion O' with the same header as X'. To do this, it runs the algorithm CompleteOnion, also provided by $\mathcal{A}$.

Suppose honest sender Sandy sent an onion to adversarial recipient Robert. Robert responds; eventually an honest intermediary Iris will receive an onion O which contains Robert's response to Sandy. When $\mathcal{F}_{\text{ROES}}$ is called by Iris with onion O, it will be tipped off to the fact that $O = (H, C)$ is a return onion from Robert to Sandy because the header H will be stored in PathDict. At this point, $\mathcal{F}_{\text{ROES}}$ knows what path the onion will have to follow from now on and will be able to create the correct onion layers using SampleOnion and store them in OnionDict. Once the return onion makes its way to Sandy, Sandy will ask $\mathcal{F}_{\text{ROES}}$ to process it; at this point, $\mathcal{F}_{\text{ROES}}$ will need to know the return message r that Robert sent to Sandy. The algorithm RecoverReply serves that purpose: from Robert's onion O (received by Iris) it recovers his response r.

So, at setup, the algorithms ProcOnion, FormReply, SampleOnion CompleteOnion, and RecoverReply are provided to $\mathcal{F}_{\text{ROES}}$ by $\mathcal{A}$.

Figure 1 gives a summary of the ideal functionality $\mathcal{F}_{\text{ROES}}$ for repliable onion encryption. Below, we provide a formal, detailed description of $\mathcal{F}_{\text{ROES}}$.

Setting Up. The ideal functionality $\mathcal{F}_{\text{ROES}}$ handles requests from the environment on behalf of the ideal honest parties. During setup, $\mathcal{F}_{\text{ROES}}$ gets the following from the ideal adversary $\mathcal{A}$. For each algorithm in items (iii)-(vi) below, we first describe the input of the algorithm in normal font and then, in italics, provide a brief preview of how the algorithm will be used. $\mathcal{F}_{\text{ROES}}$ only runs for a polynomial number of steps which is specified in the public parameters pp and can time out on running these algorithms from the ideal adversary.

i. The set $\mathcal{P}$ of participants.
ii. The set Bad of corrupt parties in $\mathcal{P}$ (see Remark 4).
iii. The repliable onion encryption scheme's G, ProcOnion, and FormReply algorithms. *G is used for generating the honest parties' keys. ProcOnion is used for processing onions formed by corrupt parties. FormReply is used for replying to onions formed by corrupt parties.*
iv. The p.p.t. algorithm SampleOnion$(1^\lambda, \text{pp}, p^\rightarrow, p^\leftarrow, m)$ that takes as input the security parameter 1^λ, the public parameters pp, the forward path $p^\rightarrow$, the

IdealSetup	IdealProcOnion($(H, C), P$)

1: Get from ideal adversary $\mathcal{A}$: $\mathcal{P}$, Bad, G, ProcOnion, FormReply, SampleOnion, CompleteOnion, RecoverReply.
2: Initialize dictionaries OnionDict and PathDict.
	1: If (P, H) is "familiar," i.e., stored in one of our dictionaries
	  - If (P, H, C) in OnionDict, return next stored onion layer.
	  - Else if exists $(P, H, (X \neq C))$ in OnionDict, return output of CompleteOnion and stored next party (if stored next party exists), or "$\perp$" (if next party doesn't exist).
	  - Else if $(P, H, \star)$ in PathDict, return output of IdealFormOnion on message recovered using RecoverReply and label and path stored in PathDict.

IdealFormOnion($\ell, m, P^{\rightarrow}, P^{\leftarrow}$)

1: Break forward path into segments.
2: Run SampleOnion on segments to generate onion layers.
3: Store onion layers in OnionDict.
4: Store label ℓ and (rest of) return path in PathDict.

> 2: Else if (P, H) is not familiar, return output of ProcOnion($(H, C), P, \mathsf{sk}(P)$).

IdealFormReply($m, (H, C), P$)

1: If (P, H, C) in PathDict, return output of IdealFormOnion on m and label and path stored in PathDict.
2: Else, return output of FormReply($m, (H, C), P, \mathsf{sk}(P)$).

Fig. 1. Summary of ideal functionality $\mathcal{F}_{\mathsf{ROES}}$.

(possibly empty) return path $p^{\leftarrow}$, and the (possibly empty) message m. The routing path $(p^{\rightarrow}, p^{\leftarrow}) = (p_1, \ldots, p_i, P_{i+1})$ is always a sequence $(p_1, \ldots, p_i)$ of adversarial parties, possibly ending in an honest party P_{i+1}. $\mathcal{F}_{\mathsf{ROES}}$ fails if SampleOnion ever samples a repeating header or key.

SampleOnion *is used to compute an onion to send to p_1 which will be "peelable" all the way to an onion for P_{i+1}. If the return path $p^{\leftarrow}$ is nonempty and ends in an honest party P_{i+1}, SampleOnion produces an onion o for the first party p_1 in $p^{\rightarrow}$ and a header H for the last party P_{i+1} in $p^{\leftarrow}$. Else if the return path $p^{\leftarrow}$ is empty, and the forward path $p^{\rightarrow}$ ends in an honest party P_{i+1}, SampleOnion produces an onion o for the first party p_1 in $p^{\rightarrow}$ and an onion O for the last party P_{i+1} in $p^{\rightarrow}$. Else if the return path $p^{\leftarrow}$ is empty, and the forward path $p^{\rightarrow}$ ends in a corrupt party p_i, SampleOnion produces an onion o for the first party p_1 in $p^{\rightarrow}$.*

v. The p.p.t. algorithm CompleteOnion($1^{\lambda}, \mathsf{pp}, H', C$) that takes as input 1^{λ}, pp, the the party P, the header H', and the content C, and outputs an onion $O = (H', C')$. $\mathcal{F}_{\mathsf{ROES}}$ fails if CompleteOnion ever produces a repeating onion. CompleteOnion *produces an onion (H', C') that resembles the result of peeling an onion with content C.*

vi. The d.p.t. algorithm RecoverReply($1^{\lambda}, \mathsf{pp}, O, P$) that takes as input 1^{λ}, pp, the onion O, and the party P, and outputs a label ℓ and a reply message m. *This algorithm is used for recovering the label ℓ and reply message m from the return onion O that carries the response from a corrupt recipient to an honest sender.*

Let sid denote the session id specific the parameters that the setup, above, creates. $\mathcal{F}_{\mathsf{ROES}}^{\mathsf{sid}}$ denotes the session of $\mathcal{F}_{\mathsf{ROES}}$ with this sid. $\mathcal{F}_{\mathsf{ROES}}^{\mathsf{sid}}$ generates a public key pair $(\mathsf{pk}(P), \mathsf{sk}(P))$ for each honest party $P \in \mathcal{P} \backslash \mathsf{Bad}$ using the key generation algorithm G and sends the public keys to their respective party. (If working within the global PKI framework, each party then relays his/her key to the global bulletin board functionality [9].) $\mathcal{F}_{\mathsf{ROES}}^{\mathsf{sid}}$ also creates the following (initially empty) dictionaries:

- The *onion dictionary* OnionDict supports:
  - A method $\mathsf{put}((P, H, C), (\mathsf{role}, \mathsf{output}))$ that stores under the label (P, H, C): the role "role" and the output "output." *Should participant P later direct $\mathcal{F}_{\mathsf{ROES}}^{\mathsf{sid}}$ to process onion $O = (H, C)$, it will receive the values* (role, output) *stored in* OnionDict *corresponding to* (P, H, C).
  - A method $\mathsf{lookup}(P, H, C)$ that looks up the entry (role, output) corresponding to the label (P, H, C). *This method will be used when P directs* $\mathcal{F}_{\mathsf{ROES}}^{\mathsf{sid}}$ *to process onion* $O = (H, C)$.
- The *return path dictionary* PathDict supports:
  - A method $\mathsf{put}((P, H, C), (P^{\leftarrow}, \ell))$ that stores under the label (P, H, C): the return path $P^{\leftarrow}$ and the label ℓ. *This method is used to store the return path $P^{\leftarrow}$ for the onion corresponding to label ℓ.*
  - A method $\mathsf{lookup}(P, H, C)$ that looks up entry $(P^{\leftarrow}, \ell)$ corresp. to the label (P, H, C). *Should P later direct* $\mathcal{F}_{\mathsf{ROES}}^{\mathsf{sid}}$ *to either reply to the onion* (H, C) *or to process an onion with header H, the stored return path $P^{\leftarrow}$ and label ℓ will be used to form the rest of the return onion layers.*

These data structures are stored internally at and accessible only by $\mathcal{F}_{\mathsf{ROES}}^{\mathsf{sid}}$.

Forming an Onion. After setup, the environment $\mathcal{Z}$ can instruct an honest party P to form an onion using the session id sid, the label ℓ, the message m, the forward path $P^{\rightarrow}$, and the return path $P^{\leftarrow}$. To form the onion, P forwards the instruction from $\mathcal{Z}$ to $\mathcal{F}_{\mathsf{ROES}}^{\mathsf{sid}}$ (via the router $\mathcal{R}$).

The goal of the ideal functionality $\mathcal{F}_{\mathsf{ROES}}^{\mathsf{sid}}$ is to create and maintain state information for handling an onion O (the response to the "form onion" request). O should be "peelable" by the parties in the forward path $P^{\rightarrow}$, internally associated with the return path $P^{\leftarrow}$, and for the purpose of realizing this functionality by an onion encryption scheme, each layer of the onion should look "believable" as onions produced from running FormOnion, ProcOnion, or FormReply. Importantly, O and its onion layers should reveal no information to $\mathcal{A}$:

- Each onion routed to an honest party P_i is formed initially with just (P_i) as the routing path and, therefore, reveals only that it is for P_i. When forming the onion, no message is part of the input; this ensures that the onion is information-theoretically independent of any message m.
- For every party p_i or P_i in the forward path, let $\mathsf{next}(i)$ denote the index of the next honest party $P_{\mathsf{next}(i)}$ following p_i. For example, if the forward path is $(P_1, p_2, p_3, P_4, P_5, p_6, p_7)$, then $\mathsf{next}(2) = 4$.

  Conceptually, each onion routed to an adversarial party p_i is formed by "wrapping" an onion layer for each corrupt party in $(p_i, \ldots, p_{\mathsf{next}(i)-1})$ (or

$(p_{i+1}, \ldots, p_{|P^\to|})$ if no honest party after p_i exists) around an onion formed for an honest party $P_{\text{next}(i)}$ (or a message if no honest party after p_i exists). This reveals at most the sequence $(p_i, \ldots, p_{\text{next}(i)-1}, P_{\text{next}(i)})$ (or the sequence $(p_i, \ldots, p_{|P^\to|})$ and the message m if no honest party after p_i exists). How this wrapping occurs depends on the internals of the SampleOnion algorithm provided by the ideal adversary.

To ensure these, $\mathcal{F}_{\text{ROES}}$ partitions the forward path $P^\to$ into segments:

Let P_f (f, for first) be the first honest party in the forward path. The first couple of segments are $(p_1, \ldots, p_{f-1}, P_f)$, $(p_{f+1}, \ldots, p_{\text{next}(f)-1}, P_{\text{next}(f)})$, etc.

For each segment $(p_i, \ldots, p_{j-1}, P_j)$, the ideal functionality $\mathcal{F}_{\text{ROES}}^{\text{sid}}$ samples onions (h_i, c_i) and (H_j, C_j) using the algorithm SampleOnion, i.e., $((h_i, c_i), (H_j, C_j)) \leftarrow$ SampleOnion$(1^\lambda, \text{pp}, (p_i, \ldots, p_{j-1}, P_j), (), \bot)$. As we explained when introducing the SampleOnion input/output structure, (h_i, c_i) is the onion that is intended for the participant $p_i \in$ Bad; once the adversarial participants take turns peeling it, the innermost layer (H_j, C_j) can be processed by the honest participant P_j.

If the recipient P_d is honest, this process will create all the onions in the forward direction. Suppose that the recipient p_d is corrupt. Let P_e (e, for end) be the last honest party in the forward path $P^\to$, and let $P_{\text{next}(d)}$ denote the first honest party in the return path $P^\leftarrow$. $\mathcal{F}_{\text{ROES}}^{\text{sid}}$ also runs SampleOnion$(1^\lambda, \text{pp}, (p_{e+1}, \ldots, p_d), (p_{d+1}, \ldots, p_{\text{next}(d)-1}, P_{\text{next}(d)}), m)$; as we explained when introducing the SampleOnion input/output structure, this produces an onion o_{e+1} and a header $H_{\text{next}(d)}$.

For every honest intermediary party P_i in the forward path, $\mathcal{F}_{\text{ROES}}^{\text{sid}}$ stores under the label (P_i, H_i, C_i) in the onion dictionary OnionDict the role "I," the $(i+1)^{st}$ onion layer (H_{i+1}, C_{i+1}), and destination P_{i+1}. The $(d+1)^{st}$ onion layer doesn't exist for the innermost layer (H_d, C_d) for an honest recipient P_d. In this case, $\mathcal{F}_{\text{ROES}}^{\text{sid}}$ stores just the role "R" and the message m.

If the recipient P_d is honest, $\mathcal{F}_{\text{ROES}}^{\text{sid}}$ stores the entry $((P_d, H_d, C_d), (P^\leftarrow, \ell))$ in the dictionary PathDict. Otherwise if the recipient p_d is corrupt, $\mathcal{F}_{\text{ROES}}^{\text{sid}}$ stores the entry $((P_{\text{next}(d)}, H_{\text{next}(d)}, *), (p^\leftarrow, \ell))$ in PathDict where $p^\leftarrow = (p_{\text{next}(d)+1}, \ldots, P_s)$. "$*$" is the unique symbol that means "any content."

Example. The recipient P_7 is honest. The forward path is $P^\to = (P_1, p_2, p_3, P_4, P_5, p_6, \boxed{P_7})$, and the return path is $P^\leftarrow = (p_8, p_9, P_{10}, p_{11}, P_{12})$. In this case, the first segment is (P_1), and the second segment is (p_2, p_3, P_4) and so on; and

$$(\bot, (H_1, C_1)) \leftarrow \text{SampleOnion}(1^\lambda, \text{pp}, (P_1), (), \bot)$$

$$((h_2, c_2), (H_4, C_4)) \leftarrow \text{SampleOnion}(1^\lambda, \text{pp}, (p_2, p_3, P_4), (), \bot)$$

$$(\bot, (H_5, C_5)) \leftarrow \text{SampleOnion}(1^\lambda, \text{pp}, (P_5), (), \bot)$$

$$((h_6, c_6), (H_7, C_7)) \leftarrow \text{SampleOnion}(1^\lambda, \text{pp}, (p_6, P_7), (), \bot).$$

$\mathcal{F}^{\mathsf{sid}}_{\mathsf{ROES}}$ stores in OnionDict and PathDict:

$$\mathsf{OnionDict.put}((P_1, H_1, C_1), (\mathsf{I}, ((h_2, c_2), p_2)))$$
$$\mathsf{OnionDict.put}((P_4, H_4, C_4), (\mathsf{I}, ((H_5, C_5), P_5)))$$
$$\mathsf{OnionDict.put}((P_5, H_5, C_5), (\mathsf{I}, ((h_6, c_6), p_6)))$$
$$\mathsf{OnionDict.put}((P_7, H_7, C_7), (\mathsf{R}, m)),$$
$$\mathsf{PathDict.put}((P_7, H_7, C_7), ((p_8, p_9, P_{10}, p_{11}, P_{12}), \ell)).$$

After updating OnionDict and PathDict, $\mathcal{F}^{\mathsf{sid}}_{\mathsf{ROES}}$ returns the first onion $O_1 = (H_1, C_1)$ to party P (via the router $\mathcal{R}$). Upon receiving O_1 from $\mathcal{F}$, P outputs the session id sid and O_1.

Processing an Onion. After setup, the environment $\mathcal{Z}$ can instruct an honest party P to process an onion $O = (H, C)$ for the session id sid. To process the onion, party P forwards the instruction to the ideal functionality $\mathcal{F}^{\mathsf{sid}}_{\mathsf{ROES}}$ (via the router $\mathcal{R}$).

Case 1: There is an entry (role, output) under the label (P, H, C) in OnionDict. In this case, $\mathcal{F}^{\mathsf{sid}}_{\mathsf{ROES}}$ responds to P (via the router $\mathcal{R}$) with (role, output).

Case 2: There is no entry under the label (P, H, C) in OnionDict, but there exists $X \neq C$ such that there is an entry $(\mathsf{I}, ((H', X'), P'))$ under the label (P, H, X) in OnionDict. This means that, P has received an onion with a properly formed header, but an improperly formed content. This is where we use the algorithm CompleteOnion to direct $\mathcal{F}_{\mathsf{ROES}}$ how to peel this "mauled" onion. Recall that CompleteOnion was provided by the adversary at setup. $\mathcal{F}^{\mathsf{sid}}_{\mathsf{ROES}}$ uses it to sample an onion $(H', C') \leftarrow \mathsf{CompleteOnion}(1^\lambda, \mathsf{pp}, H', C)$. $\mathcal{F}_{\mathsf{ROES}}$ then stores the new entry $(\mathsf{I}, ((H', C'), P'))$ under the label (P, H, C) in OnionDict, and responds to P with $(\mathsf{I}, ((H', C'), P'))$.

Case 3: There is no entry under the label (P, H, C) in OnionDict, but there exists $X \neq C$ such that there is an entry (R, m) under the label (P, H, X) in OnionDict. This means that P is the intended recipient of the onion (H, X) but instead just received the properly formed header H with "mauled" content C. In this case, $\mathcal{F}^{\mathsf{sid}}_{\mathsf{ROES}}$ responds to P with $(\mathsf{R}, \bot)$.

Case 4: There is no entry under the label (P, H, C) in OnionDict, but there exists $X \neq C$ such that there is an entry $(\mathsf{S}, (\ell, m))$ under the label (P, H, X) in OnionDict. This means that P was the original sender of an onion, and header H is the correct header for his reply onion; but the content C got "mauled" in transit: the correct reply onion was supposed to have content X (according to in OnionDict). $\mathcal{F}^{\mathsf{sid}}_{\mathsf{ROES}}$ responds to P with $(\mathsf{S}, \bot)$.

Case 5: There is no entry starting with (P, H) in OnionDict, but there is an entry $(P^\leftarrow, \ell)$ under the label $(P, H, *)$ in PathDict. This means that P is the first honest intermediary on the return path of an onion whose recipient was adversarial. $\mathcal{F}_{\mathsf{ROES}}$ needs to compute the reply message m' that the adversarial recipient meant to send back to the honest sender. This is the purpose of the RecoverReply algorithm that the adversary provides to $\mathcal{F}_{\mathsf{ROES}}$ at setup. Let m' be the message obtained by running $\mathsf{RecoverReply}(1^\lambda, \mathsf{pp}, O, P)$.

Next, $\mathcal{F}_{\mathsf{ROES}}$ computes the layers of the reply onion. If $P^{\leftarrow}$ is not empty, $\mathcal{F}_{\mathsf{ROES}}^{\mathsf{sid}}$ runs its "form onion" code (Sect. 3.1) with (ℓ, m') as the "message," $P^{\leftarrow}$ as the forward path, and the empty list "()" as the return path. (The code is run with auxiliary information for correctly labeling the last party in $P^{\leftarrow}$ as the sender.) $\mathcal{F}_{\mathsf{ROES}}^{\mathsf{sid}}$ responds to P with $(\mathsf{I}, ((H', C'), P'))$, where (H', C') is the returned onion, and P' is the first party in $P^{\leftarrow}$.

Otherwise if $P^{\leftarrow}$ is empty, then P is the recipient of the return onion, so $\mathcal{F}_{\mathsf{ROES}}^{\mathsf{sid}}$ responds to P with $(\mathsf{S}, (\ell, m'))$.

Case 6: $\mathcal{F}_{\mathsf{ROES}}^{\mathsf{sid}}$ doesn't know how to peel O (i.e., there is no entry starting with (P, H) in OnionDict and no entry under $(P, H, *)$ in PathDict). In this case, O does not have an honestly formed header; so, $\mathcal{F}_{\mathsf{ROES}}^{\mathsf{sid}}$ responds to P with $(\mathsf{role}, \mathsf{output}) = \mathsf{ProcOnion}(1^\lambda, \mathsf{pp}, O, P, \mathsf{sk}(P))$ (recall that ProcOnion is an algorithm supplied by the ideal adversary at setup).

The cases above cover all the possibilities. Upon receiving the response $(\mathsf{role}, \mathsf{output})$ from $\mathcal{F}_{\mathsf{ROES}}^{\mathsf{sid}}$, P outputs the session id sid and $(\mathsf{role}, \mathsf{output})$.

Forming a Reply. After setup, the environment $\mathcal{Z}$ can instruct an honest party P to form a reply using the session id sid, the reply message m, and an onion $O = (H, C)$. To form the return onion, P forwards the instruction to the ideal functionality $\mathcal{F}_{\mathsf{ROES}}^{\mathsf{sid}}$ (via the router $\mathcal{R}$).

Case 1: There is an entry $(P^{\leftarrow}, \ell)$ under the label (P, H, C) in PathDict. Then $\mathcal{F}_{\mathsf{ROES}}^{\mathsf{sid}}$ runs its "form onion" code (see Sect. 3.1) with (ℓ, m) as the "message," $P^{\leftarrow}$ as the forward path, and the empty list "()" as the return path. (The code is run with auxiliary information for correctly labeling the last party in $P^{\leftarrow}$ as the sender.) $\mathcal{F}_{\mathsf{ROES}}^{\mathsf{sid}}$ responds to P (via the router $\mathcal{R}$) with the returned onion O' and the first party P' in $P^{\leftarrow}$.

Case 2: No entry exists for (P, H, C) in PathDict. Then P is replying to an onion formed by an adversarial party, so $\mathcal{F}_{\mathsf{ROES}}^{\mathsf{sid}}$ replies to P with $(O', P') = \mathsf{FormReply}(1^\lambda, \mathsf{pp}, m, O, P, \mathsf{sk}(P))$. Upon receiving the response (O', P') from $\mathcal{F}_{\mathsf{ROES}}^{\mathsf{sid}}$, P outputs the session id sid and (O', P').

3.2 SUC-realizability of $\mathcal{F}_{\mathsf{ROES}}$

Recall what it means for a cryptographic scheme to SUC-realize $\mathcal{F}_{\mathsf{ROES}}$ [7].

Ideal Protocol. In the ideal onion routing protocol, the environment $\mathcal{Z}$ interacts with the participants by writing instructions into the participants' input tapes and reading their output tapes. Each input is an instruction to form an onion, process an onion, or form a return onion. When an honest party P receives an instruction from $\mathcal{Z}$, it forwards the instruction to $\mathcal{F}_{\mathsf{ROES}}$ via the router $\mathcal{R}$. Upon receiving a response from $\mathcal{F}_{\mathsf{ROES}}$ (via $\mathcal{R}$), P outputs the response. Corrupt parties are controlled by the adversary $\mathcal{A}$ and behave according to $\mathcal{A}$. $\mathcal{F}_{\mathsf{ROES}}^{\mathsf{sid}}$ does not interact with $\mathcal{A}$ after the setup phase. At the end of the protocol execution, $\mathcal{Z}$ outputs a bit b. Let $\mathsf{IDEAL}_{\mathcal{F}_{\mathsf{ROES}}, \mathcal{A}, \mathcal{Z}}(1^\lambda, \mathsf{pp})$ denote $\mathcal{Z}$'s output after executing the ideal protocol for security parameter 1^λ and public parameters pp.

Real Protocol. Let Σ be a repliable onion encryption scheme. The real onion routing protocol for Σ is the same as the ideal one (described above), except that the honest parties simply run Σ's algorithms to form and process onions. Let $\text{REAL}_{\Sigma,\mathcal{A},\mathcal{Z}}(1^\lambda, \text{pp})$ denote $\mathcal{Z}$'s output after executing the real protocol.

Definition 3 (SUC-realizability of $\mathcal{F}_{\text{ROES}}$). *The repliable onion encryption scheme Σ SUC-realizes the ideal functionality $\mathcal{F}_{\text{ROES}}$ if for every p.p.t. real-model adversary $\mathcal{A}$, there exists a p.p.t. ideal-model adversary $\mathcal{S}$ s.t. for every polynomial-time environment $\mathcal{Z}$, there exists a negligible function $\nu(\lambda)$ s.t.*
$$\left| \Pr\left[\text{IDEAL}_{\mathcal{F}_{\text{ROES}},\mathcal{S},\mathcal{Z}}(1^\lambda, \text{pp}) = 1 \right] - \Pr\left[\text{REAL}_{\Sigma,\mathcal{A},\mathcal{Z}}(1^\lambda, \text{pp}) = 1 \right] \right| \leq \nu(\lambda).$$

Remark 4. The set Bad of corrupted participants is selected non-adaptively, at setup time. Adaptive security is notoriously challenging to realize in the standard model for public-key encryption: As Canetti et al. [8] demonstrated, adaptively secure encryption requires non-committing encryption. A single-layer onion is already a public-key ciphertext, so any reasonable formulation of an onion routing ideal functionality would imply public-key encryption and, thus, would also require non-committing encryption. Non-committing encryption in the standard model requires that public keys can only be used once for a single ciphertext and, thus, is impossible in the standard PKI model. It is possible to realize it in the random-oracle (RO) model, and so in the RO model, adaptively secure onion routing may be possible. We leave this for future work, however.

Remark 5. In describing the ideal functionality, we made an implicit assumption that for every instruction to form an onion, the keys match the parties on the routing path. However, generally speaking, the environment $\mathcal{Z}$ can instruct an honest party to form an onion using the wrong keys for some of the parties on the routing path. Using the dictionary OnionDict, it is easy to extend our ideal functionality to cover this case: the ideal functionality would store in OnionDict, every onion layer for an honest party, starting from the outermost layer, until it reaches a layer with a mismatched key. To keep the exposition clean, we will continue to assume that router names are valid, and keys are as published.

Remark 6. As originally noted by Camenisch and Lysyanskaya [5], the environment is allowed to repeat the same input (e.g., a "process onion" request) in the UC framework (likewise, in the SUC framework). Thus, replay attacks are not only allowed in our model but inherent in the SUC framework. The reason that replay attacks are a concern is that they allow the adversary to observe what happens in the network as a result of repeatedly sending an onion over and over again—which intermediaries are involved, etc.—and that potentially allows the adversary to trace this onion. Our functionality does not protect from this attack (and neither did the CL functionality), but a higher-level protocol can address this by directing parties to ignore repeat "process onion" and "form reply" requests. Other avenues to address this (which can be added to our functionality, but we chose not to so as not to complicate it further) may include letting onions time out, so the time frame for repeating them could be limited.

Remark 7. The way that an ideal adversarial participant interacts with $\mathcal{F}_{\text{ROES}}$ to form an onion is by creating an onion in any way it wants and sending it over the network (which, in the SUC model, is controlled by the environment that writes to the participants' input tapes and reads their output tapes) to an ideal honest participant, who then calls $\mathcal{F}_{\text{ROES}}$ to process it. When an ideal honest party is a recipient of such an onion and replies to it with response r, this falls under case (2) of the IdealFormReply interface of $\mathcal{F}_{\text{ROES}}$. The resulting onion is returned to the ideal honest party who then puts it on its output tape, to be read by the environment, who, depending on the algorithm FormReply, immediately learns r without having to route the onion through the network. Thus, $\mathcal{F}_{\text{ROES}}$ itself does not need any additional interfaces to interact with an ideal adversarial participant.

4   Repliable-Onion Security: A Game-Based Definition

In the previous section, we gave a detailed description of an ideal functionality $\mathcal{F}_{\text{ROES}}$ of repliable onion encryption in the SUC model. However, given the complexity of the description, proving that an onion encryption scheme realizes $\mathcal{F}_{\text{ROES}}$ seems onerous. To address this, we provide an alternative, game-based definition of security that implies realizability of $\mathcal{F}_{\text{ROES}}$. We call this definition, *repliable-onion security.*

Informally, our repliable-onion security requires that the following three properties hold: (a) No adversary can tell (with a non-negligible advantage over random guessing) whether an honest transmitter of an honestly formed onion is the sender of the onion or an intermediary on the forward path. (b) Given an honestly formed onion O received by the recipient, no adversary can tell (with non-negligible advantage) whether the recipient is replying to O or sending an onion unrelated to O. (c) No adversary can tell (with non-negligible advantage) whether an honest transmitter of an honestly formed onion is the sender of the onion or an intermediary on the return path.

We formalize each of these three security properties by defining three corresponding security games. In each game, the adversary is given oracles for processing onions on behalf of the honest parties under attack. The adversary also selects additional inputs of each game, such as the identities of intermediaries, the message conveyed by the onion, etc.

In Fig. 2, we give the high-level description of the game ROSecurityGame and its three variants: (a), (b), and (c). The variants differ only in steps 4 and 5.

Formal Description of ROSecurityGame Variant (a). We now expand on what we described in Fig. 2 and provide a formal, detailed description of ROSecurityGame for the first variant, (a).

ROSecurityGame($1^\lambda, \Sigma$, CompleteOnion, $\mathcal{A}$)   is   parametrized   by   the security parameter 1^λ, the repliable onion encryption scheme Σ = $(G, \text{FormOnion}, \text{ProcOnion}, \text{FormReply})$, the p.p.t. algorithm CompleteOnion, and the adversary $\mathcal{A}$.

1: $\mathcal{A}$ picks honest parties' router names I and S. I is the honest intermediary router under attack, while S is the honest sender under attack.

2: $\mathcal{C}$ sets keys for honest parties I and S.

3: $\mathcal{A}$ gets access to oracles—$\mathcal{O}.\mathsf{PO}_I$, $\mathcal{O}.\mathsf{FR}_I$, $\mathcal{O}.\mathsf{PO}_S$, and $\mathcal{O}.\mathsf{FR}_S$— for processing onions and replying to them on behalf of I and S.

4: $\mathcal{A}$ provides input for the challenge onion: a label ℓ, a message m, a forward path $P^{\rightarrow} = (P_1, \ldots, P_d)$, a return path $P^{\leftarrow} = (P_{d+1}, \ldots, P_s)$, and keys associated with the routing path $(P^{\rightarrow}, P^{\leftarrow})$. If the return path is non-empty, it ends with S so that $P_s = S$. I appears somewhere on the routing path so that P_j is the first appearance of I on the path. The location of P_j determines which variant of the security game the adversary is playing:
   (a) P_j is an intermediary on the forward path (i.e., $j < d$),
   (b) P_j is the recipient (i.e., $j = d$) or
   (c) P_j is on the return path (i.e., $j > d$).

5: $\mathcal{C}$ flips a coin $b \leftarrow\$ \{0,1\}$. If $b = 0$, $\mathcal{C}$ forms the onion O as specified by $\mathcal{A}$. If $b = 1$, $\mathcal{C}$ forms the onion O with a "switch" at I and modifies ("rigs") the oracles accordingly.
   (a) To peel the challenge onion O on behalf of forward-path intermediary I, $\mathcal{O}.\mathsf{PO}_I$ will form (in answer to a query from $\mathcal{A}$) a new onion using the remainder of the routing path. To peel an onion $O' \neq O$ with the same header as the challenge onion, $\mathcal{O}.\mathsf{PO}_I$ uses the algorithm CompleteOnion.
   (b) To form a reply to the challenge onion O on behalf of I, $\mathcal{O}.\mathsf{FR}_I$ will form a new onion using the return path as the forward path (and the empty return path).
   (c) To peel the challenge onion O on behalf of the return-path intermediary I, $\mathcal{O}.\mathsf{PO}_I$ will form a new onion using the remainder of the return path as the forward path (and the empty return path).

6: $\mathcal{A}$ once again gets oracle access to $\mathcal{O}.\mathsf{PO}_I$, $\mathcal{O}.\mathsf{FR}_I$, $\mathcal{O}.\mathsf{PO}_S$, and $\mathcal{O}.\mathsf{FR}_S$.

7: $\mathcal{A}$ guesses b' and wins if $b' = b$.

Fig. 2. Summary of the repliable onion security game, ROSecurityGame. The parameters of the game are the security parameter λ, the repliable onion encryption scheme Σ, the p.p.t. algorithm CompleteOnion and the adversary $\mathcal{A}$.

1. The adversary $\mathcal{A}$ picks two router names $I, S \in \mathcal{P}$ ("I" for intermediary and "S" for sender) and sends them to the challenger $\mathcal{C}$.

2. The challenger $\mathcal{C}$ generates key pairs $(\mathsf{pk}(I), \mathsf{sk}(I))$ and $(\mathsf{pk}(S), \mathsf{sk}(S))$ for I and S using the key generation algorithm G and sends the public keys $(\mathsf{pk}(I), \mathsf{pk}(S))$ to $\mathcal{A}$.

3. $\mathcal{A}$ is given oracle access to (i) $\mathcal{O}.\mathsf{PO}_I(\cdot)$, (ii) $\mathcal{O}.\mathsf{FR}_I(\cdot, \cdot)$, (iii) $\mathcal{O}.\mathsf{PO}_S(\cdot)$, and (iv) $\mathcal{O}.\mathsf{FR}_S(\cdot, \cdot)$ where

   i–ii. $\mathcal{O}.\mathsf{PO}_I(\cdot)$ and $\mathcal{O}.\mathsf{FR}_I(\cdot, \cdot)$ are, respectively, the oracle for answering "process onion" requests made to honest party I and the oracle for answering "form reply" requests made to I.

   iii–iv. $\mathcal{O}.\mathsf{PO}_S(\cdot)$ and $\mathcal{O}.\mathsf{FR}_S(\cdot, \cdot)$ are, respectively, the oracle for answering "process onion" requests made to honest party S and the oracle for answering "form reply" requests made to S.

   Since ProcOnion and FormReply are deterministic algorithms, WLOG, the oracles don't respond to repeating queries.

4. $\mathcal{A}$ chooses a label $\ell \in \mathcal{L}(1^\lambda)$ and a message $m \in \mathcal{M}(1^\lambda)$. $\mathcal{A}$ also chooses names of participants on a forward path $P^{\rightarrow} = (P_1, \ldots, P_d)$, and a return path $P^{\leftarrow} = (P_{d+1}, \ldots, P_s)$ such that (i) if $P^{\leftarrow}$ is non-empty, then $P_s = S$, and

(ii) I appears somewhere on $P^\rightarrow$ before the recipient. For each $P_i \notin \{S, I\}$, $\mathcal{A}$ also chooses its public key $\mathsf{pk}(P_i)$. $\mathcal{A}$ sends to $\mathcal{C}$ the parameters for the challenge onion: ℓ, m, $P^\rightarrow$, the public keys $\mathsf{pk}(P^\rightarrow)$ of the parties in $P^\rightarrow$, $P^\leftarrow$ and the public keys $\mathsf{pk}(P^\leftarrow)$ of the parties in $P^\leftarrow$.

5. $\mathcal{C}$ samples a bit $b \leftarrow_\$ \{0, 1\}$.

   If $b = 0$, $\mathcal{C}$ runs FormOnion on the parameters specified by $\mathcal{A}$, i.e., $((O_1^0, \ldots, O_d^0), H^\leftarrow, \kappa) \leftarrow \mathsf{FormOnion}(\ell, m, P^\rightarrow, \mathsf{pk}(P^\rightarrow), P^\leftarrow, \mathsf{pk}(P^\leftarrow))$. In this case, the oracles—$\mathcal{O}.\mathsf{PO}_\mathsf{I}(\cdot)$, $\mathcal{O}.\mathsf{FR}_\mathsf{I}(\cdot, \cdot)$, $\mathcal{O}.\mathsf{PO}_\mathsf{S}(\cdot)$, and $\mathcal{O}.\mathsf{FR}_\mathsf{S}(\cdot, \cdot)$— remain unmodified.

   Otherwise, if $b = 1$, $\mathcal{C}$ performs the "switch" at honest party P_j on the forward path $P^\rightarrow$, where P_j is the first appearance of I on the forward path. $\mathcal{C}$ runs FormOnion twice. First, $\mathcal{C}$ runs it on input a random label $x \leftarrow_\$ \mathcal{L}(1^\lambda)$, a random message $y \leftarrow_\$ \mathcal{M}(1^\lambda)$, the "truncated" forward path $p^\rightarrow = (P_1, \ldots, P_j)$, and the empty return path "()," i.e., $((O_1^1, \ldots, O_j^1), (), \kappa) \leftarrow \mathsf{FormOnion}(x, y, p^\rightarrow, \mathsf{pk}(p^\rightarrow), (), ())$. $\mathcal{C}$ then runs FormOnion on a random label $x' \leftarrow_\$ \mathcal{L}(1^\lambda)$, the message m (that had been chosen by $\mathcal{A}$ in step 4), the remainder $q^\rightarrow = (P_{j+1}, \ldots, P_d)$ of the forward path, and the return path $P^\leftarrow$, i.e., $((O_{j+1}^1, \ldots, O_d^1), H^\leftarrow, \kappa') \leftarrow \mathsf{FormOnion}(x', m, q^\rightarrow, \mathsf{pk}(q^\rightarrow), P^\leftarrow, \mathsf{pk}(P^\leftarrow))$,

   We modify the oracles as follows. Let $O_j^1 = (H_j^1, C_j^1)$ and $O_{j+1}^1 = (H_{j+1}^1, C_{j+1}^1)$, and let H_s^1 be the last header in $H^\leftarrow$. $\mathcal{O}.\mathsf{PO}_\mathsf{I}$ does the following to "process" an onion $O = (H, C)$:

   i. If $O = O_j^1$ and $\mathsf{ProcOnion}(O, P_j, \mathsf{sk}(P_j)) = (\mathsf{R}, y)$, then return $(\mathsf{I}, (O_{j+1}^1, P_{j+1}))$.

   ii. If $O = O_j^1$ and $\mathsf{ProcOnion}(O, P_j, \mathsf{sk}(P_j)) \neq (\mathsf{R}, y)$, then fail.

   iii. If $O \neq O_j^1$ but $H = H_j^1$ and $\mathsf{ProcOnion}(O, P_j, \mathsf{sk}(P_j)) = (\mathsf{R}, \bot)$, then return $(\mathsf{I}, ((H_{j+1}^1, \mathsf{CompleteOnion}(H_{j+1}^1, C)), P_{j+1}))$.

   iv. If $O \neq O_j^1$ but $H = H_j^1$ and $\mathsf{ProcOnion}(O, P_j, \mathsf{sk}(P_j)) \neq (\mathsf{R}, \bot)$, then fail.

   $\mathcal{O}.\mathsf{PO}_\mathsf{S}$ does the following to "process" an onion O:

   v. If the header of O is H_s^1 and $\mathsf{ProcOnion}(O, P_s, \mathsf{sk}(P_s)) = (\mathsf{R}, m')$ for some message $m' \neq \bot$, then return $(\mathsf{S}, (\ell, m'))$.

   vi. If the header of O is H_s^1 and $\mathsf{ProcOnion}(O, P_s, \mathsf{sk}(P_s)) = (\mathsf{R}, \bot)$, then return $(\mathsf{S}, \bot)$.

   vii. If the header of O is H_s^1 and $\mathsf{ProcOnion}(O, P_s, \mathsf{sk}(P_s)) \neq (\mathsf{R}, m')$ for any message m', then fail.

   All other queries are processed as before.

   $\mathcal{C}$ sends to $\mathcal{A}$, the first onion O_1^b in the output of FormOnion.

6. $\mathcal{A}$ submits a polynomially-bounded number of (adaptively chosen) queries to oracles $\mathcal{O}.\mathsf{PO}_\mathsf{I}(\cdot)$, $\mathcal{O}.\mathsf{FR}_\mathsf{I}(\cdot, \cdot)$, $\mathcal{O}.\mathsf{PO}_\mathsf{S}(\cdot)$, and $\mathcal{O}.\mathsf{FR}_\mathsf{S}(\cdot, \cdot)$.

7. Finally, $\mathcal{A}$ guesses a bit b' and wins if $b' = b$.

Brief Formal Descriptions of ROSecurityGame Variants (b) and (c). Variant (b) differs from variant (a) in steps 4 and 5. In step 4, P_j is the recipient as opposed to an intermediary on the forward path. In step 5, the challenger still samples a random bit $b \leftarrow_\$ \{0, 1\}$ and, if $b = 0$, forms the challenge onion as specified by the adversary. If $b = 1$, the challenger runs FormOnion on input a random label, a random message, the forward path (provided by the adversary), and the empty path. The oracle for forming a reply on behalf of I is modified so that the oracle replies with the output of FormOnion on input a random label, a random message, the return path (provided by the adversary), and the empty path "()." For the full description, see Appendix A.

Variant (c) also differs from variant (a) in steps 4 and 5. In step 4, P_j is an intermediary on the return path $(P_{d+1}, \ldots, P_s)$, i.e., $j > d$, as opposed to an intermediary on the forward path $(P_1, \ldots, P_d)$. In step 5, the challenger still samples a random bit $b \leftarrow_\$ \{0,1\}$ and, if $b = 0$, forms the challenge onion as specified by the adversary. If $b = 1$, the challenger runs FormOnion on input a random label, a message (provided by the adversary), the forward path $(P_1, \ldots, P_d)$, and the subpath $(P_{d+1}, \ldots, P_j)$. The oracle for processing an onion on behalf of I is modified so that the oracle replies with the output of FormOnion on input a random label, a random message, the rest of the return path $(P_{j+1}, \ldots, P_s)$, and the empty path "()." For the full description, see Appendix A.

Definition 8 (Repliable-onion security). *A repliable onion encryption scheme Σ is* repliable-onion secure *if there exist a p.p.t. algorithm* CompleteOnion *and a negligible function $\nu : \mathbb{N} \mapsto \mathbb{R}$ such that every p.p.t. adversary $\mathcal{A}$ wins the security game* ROSecurityGame($1^\lambda, \Sigma,$ CompleteOnion, $\mathcal{A}$) *with negligible advantage, i.e.,* $\left|\Pr[\mathcal{A} \text{ wins } \text{ROSecurityGame}(1^\lambda, \Sigma, \text{CompleteOnion}, \mathcal{A})] - \frac{1}{2}\right| \leq \nu(\lambda)$.

Remark on Definition 8. An onion formed by running a secure onion encryption scheme and received (resp. transmitted) by an honest party P does not reveal how many layers are remaining (resp. came before) since the adversary cannot distinguish between the onion and another onion formed using the same parameters except with the path truncating at the recipient (resp. sender) P.

5   Repliable-Onion Security $\Rightarrow$ SUC-Realizability of $\mathcal{F}_{\mathsf{ROES}}$

Theorem 9. *If the onion encryption scheme Σ is correct (Definition 2) and repliable-onion secure (Definition 8), then it SUC-realizes the ideal functionality $\mathcal{F}_{\mathsf{ROES}}$ (Definition 3).*

To do this, we must show that for any static setting (fixed adversary $\mathcal{A}$, set Bad of corrupted parties, and public key infrastructure), there exists a simulator $\mathcal{S}$ such that for all $\mathcal{Z}$, there exists a negligible function $\nu : \mathbb{N} \mapsto \mathbb{R}$ such that $\left|\Pr\left[\text{IDEAL}_{\mathcal{F}_{\mathsf{ROES}}, \mathcal{S}, \mathcal{Z}}(1^\lambda, \mathsf{pp}) = 1\right] - \Pr\left[\text{REAL}_{\Sigma, \mathcal{A}, \mathcal{Z}}(1^\lambda, \mathsf{pp}) = 1\right]\right| \leq \nu(\lambda)$.

We first provide a description of the simulator $\mathcal{S}$:

Recall that during setup, the ideal adversary (i.e., $\mathcal{S}$) sends to the ideal functionality, (i) the set $\mathcal{P}$ of participants, (ii) the set Bad $\subseteq \mathcal{P}$ of corrupted parties, (iii) the onion encryption scheme's algorithms: G, ProcOnion, and FormReply, (iv) the algorithm SampleOnion, (v) the algorithm CompleteOnion, and (vi) the algorithm RecoverReply. (See Sect. 3.1 for the syntax of these algorithms.) In order for our construction to be secure, the simulator $\mathcal{S}$ must provide items (i)-(vi) to $\mathcal{F}_{\mathsf{ROES}}$ such that when the ideal honest parties respond to the environment, one input at a time, the running history of outputs looks like one produced from running the real protocol using the onion encryption scheme.

To complete the description of $\mathcal{S}$, we must provide internal descriptions of how the last three items above – SampleOnion, CompleteOnion, and RecoverReply – work. Since we are in the static setting, we will assume, WLOG, that these algorithms "know" who is honest, who is corrupt, and all relevant keys. See Fig. 3 for a summary of the simulator.

Send to $\mathcal{F}_{\mathsf{ROES}}$:	SampleOnion$(p^{\rightarrow}, p^{\leftarrow}, m)$
$\mathcal{P}$, Bad, G, ProcOnion, FormReply, SampleOnion, CompleteOnion, RecoverReply.	SampleOnion just runs FormOnion on the segments $p^{\rightarrow}$ and $p^{\leftarrow}$ using a random label and, depending on whether the first segment contains the corrupt recipient, either the correct message m (if it does) or a random one (if it doesn't).
CompleteOnion(H', C)	
Let CO be an algorithm such that no adversary can win ROSecurityGame with non-negligible probability. Such an algorithm must exist since Σ is repliable-onion secure. CompleteOnion = CO.	RecoverReply(O, P) Return the message from running ProcOnion$(O, P, \mathsf{sk}(P))$.

Fig. 3. Summary of simulator $\mathcal{S}$

Description of Simulator $\mathcal{S}$. We now expand on the summary in Fig. 3.

Sampling an Onion. Let $\mathcal{F}_{\mathsf{ROES}}^{\mathsf{sid}}$ denote the ideal functionality corresponding to the static setting. When the ideal functionality $\mathcal{F}_{\mathsf{ROES}}^{\mathsf{sid}}$ receives a request from the honest party P to form an onion using the label ℓ, the message m, the forward path $P^{\rightarrow}$, and the return path $P^{\leftarrow}$, $\mathcal{F}_{\mathsf{ROES}}^{\mathsf{sid}}$ partitions the routing path $(P^{\rightarrow}, P^{\leftarrow})$ into non-overlapping "segments" where each segment is a sequence of adversarial parties that must end in a single honest party, unless it ends in the adversarial recipient. (See Sect. 3.1 for a more formal description of these segments.) $\mathcal{F}_{\mathsf{ROES}}^{\mathsf{sid}}$ runs the algorithm SampleOnion independently on each segment of the routing path. Additionally, if the forward path ends in a corrupt party, $\mathcal{F}_{\mathsf{ROES}}^{\mathsf{sid}}$ runs SampleOnion on the last segment of the forward path and the first segment of the return path. Using SampleOnion in this way produces onions with the property that onions belonging to different segments are information-theoretically unrelated to each other.

The algorithm SampleOnion takes as input the security parameter 1^{λ}, the public parameters pp, the forward path $p^{\rightarrow}$, and the return path $p^{\leftarrow}$.

Case 0: The routing path $(p^{\rightarrow}, p^{\leftarrow})$ is not a sequence of adversarial parties, possibly ending in an honest party. In this case, the input is invalid, and SampleOnion returns an error.

Case 1: The return path $p^\leftarrow$ is non-empty and ends in an honest party P_j. In this case, SampleOnion first samples a random label $x \leftarrow_\$ \mathcal{L}(1^\lambda)$ and then runs FormOnion on the label x, the message m (from the "form onion" request), the forward path $p^\rightarrow = (p_1, \ldots, p_i)$, the public keys $\mathsf{pk}(p^\rightarrow)$ associated with the parties in $p^\rightarrow$, the return path $p^\leftarrow = (p_{i+1}, \ldots, P_j)$, and the public keys $\mathsf{pk}(p^\leftarrow)$ associated with the parties in $p^\leftarrow$. Finally, SampleOnion outputs the first onion o_1 and the last header H_j in the output $((o_1, \ldots, o_i), (h_{i+1}, \ldots, H_j), \kappa) \leftarrow$ FormOnion$(1^\lambda, \mathsf{pp}, x, m, p^\rightarrow, \mathsf{pk}(p^\rightarrow), p^\leftarrow, \mathsf{pk}(p^\leftarrow))$.

Case 2: The return path $p^\leftarrow$ is empty, and the forward path $p^\rightarrow$ ends in an honest party P_i. In this case, SampleOnion first samples a random label $x \leftarrow_\$ \mathcal{L}(1^\lambda)$ and a random message $y \leftarrow_\$ \mathcal{M}(1^\lambda)$ and then runs FormOnion on the label x, the message y, the forward path $p^\rightarrow = (p_1, \ldots, P_i)$, the public keys $\mathsf{pk}(p^\rightarrow)$ associated with the parties in $p^\rightarrow$, the empty return path "()," and the empty sequence "()" of public keys. Finally, SampleOnion outputs the first onion o_1 and the last onion O_i in the output $((o_1, \ldots, O_i), (), \kappa) \leftarrow$ FormOnion$(1^\lambda, \mathsf{pp}, x, y, p^\rightarrow, \mathsf{pk}(p^\rightarrow), (), ())$.

Case 3: The return path $p^\leftarrow$ is empty, and the forward path $p^\rightarrow$ ends in a corrupt party p_i. In this case, SampleOnion first samples a random label $x \leftarrow_\$ \mathcal{L}(1^\lambda)$ and then runs FormOnion on the label x, the message m (from the "form onion" request), the forward path $p^\rightarrow = (p_1, \ldots, p_i)$, the public keys $\mathsf{pk}(p^\rightarrow)$ associated with the parties in $p^\rightarrow$, the empty return path "()," and the empty sequence "()" of public keys. Finally, SampleOnion outputs the first onion o_1 in the output $((o_1, \ldots, o_i), h^\leftarrow, \kappa) \leftarrow$ FormOnion$(1^\lambda, \mathsf{pp}, x, m, p^\rightarrow, \mathsf{pk}(p^\rightarrow), (), ())$.

Completing an Onion. The environment $\mathcal{Z}$ can modify just the content of an honestly formed onion $O = (H, X)$, leaving the header H intact. When $\mathcal{Z}$ instructs an honest party P to process this kind of onion $O = (H, C)$, the ideal functionality $\mathcal{F}_{\mathsf{ROES}}^{\mathsf{sid}}$ runs the algorithm CompleteOnion to produce an onion (H', C') that (i) looks like the output of ProcOnion on (H, C) and (ii) has the same header H' that $\mathcal{F}_{\mathsf{ROES}}^{\mathsf{sid}}$ assigned to the peeled onion (H', X') of (H, X).

Since the onion encryption scheme Σ is repliable-onion secure (Definition 8), by definition, there exist an algorithm CO and a negligible function ν such that no adversary can win ROSecurityGame$(1^\lambda, \Sigma, \mathsf{CO}, \mathcal{A})$ with probability greater than $\nu(\lambda)$. We shall use this algorithm as the simulator's CompleteOnion algorithm, i.e., CompleteOnion = CO.

Recovering a Reply Message. The environment $\mathcal{Z}$ can instruct an honest party P to process a return onion O formed by a corrupt recipient p_d in response to an onion from an honest sender; P can be an intermediary party on the return path or the original sender. In such a situation, the ideal functionality $\mathcal{F}_{\mathsf{ROES}}^{\mathsf{sid}}$ runs the algorithm RecoverReply to recover the reply message from O.

The algorithm RecoverReply$(1^\lambda, \mathsf{pp}, O, P)$ simply runs ProcOnion$(O, P, \mathsf{sk}(P))$ and returns the message in the output (if it exists). If no message is returned, then RecoverReply outputs an error.

Proof Sketch of Theorem 9. We now show that the view that any environment $\mathcal{Z}$ obtains by running the real protocol is indistinguishable from its view when the honest participants run the ideal protocol $\mathcal{F}_{\mathsf{ROES}}$ with our simulator $\mathcal{S}$.

Proof Idea: An onion encryption scheme SUC-realizes $\mathcal{F}_{\mathsf{ROES}}$ if the environment cannot distinguish whether an honest onion's evolution (the sequence of onion layers) comes from a single call to FormOnion (the real setting), or if it is produced by $\mathcal{F}_{\mathsf{ROES}}$. Recall that, to form an honest onion's evolution, $\mathcal{F}_{\mathsf{ROES}}$ calls SampleOnion (which, for our simulator, is the same algorithm as FormOnion) multiple times, each call corresponding to a segment of the onion's routing path.

Our game-based definition of repliable-onion security has a very similar requirement: the adversary cannot distinguish whether the evolution of an honestly formed onion comes from a single FormOnion call or from two computationally unrelated FormOnion calls. More precisely, if the game picks $b = 0$, then no switch occurs, and the onion layers are formed "honestly," i.e., via a single call to FormOnion. If the game picks $b = 1$, then the onion layers are formed using a "switch:" the path is broken up into two segments, and for each segment of the path, the onion layers are formed using separate calls to FormOnion.

At the heart of our proof is a hybrid argument that shows that onion layers formed using i calls to FormOnion (so they have $i - 1$ such "switches") are indistinguishable from those formed by $i + 1$ such calls. Thus, we show that onion layers of the real protocol (produced by a single call to FormOnion) are indistinguishable from those in the ideal world (produced by $\mathcal{F}_{\mathsf{ROES}}$ that calls FormOnion separately for each segment of the routing path). Therefore, we conclude that if an onion encryption scheme is repliable-onion secure, then it SUC-realizes $\mathcal{F}_{\mathsf{ROES}}$. See the full version of this paper for the formal proof [1].

Is repliable-onion security necessary to SUC-realize $\mathcal{F}_{\mathsf{ROES}}$? Let us now address the converse of the theorem. Given an onion encryption scheme Σ that SUC-realizes $\mathcal{F}_{\mathsf{ROES}}$, does it follow that it is correct and repliable-onion secure?

In order to prove that it does, we would have to give a reduction $\mathcal{B}$ that acts as the environment towards honest participants I and S; $\mathcal{B}$'s goal is to determine whether I and S are running Σ or, instead, using $\mathcal{F}_{\mathsf{ROES}}$ with some simulator $\mathcal{S}$. $\mathcal{B}$ would obtain I's and S's public keys from the setup step of the system, and would pass them on to $\mathcal{A}$. Whenever $\mathcal{A}$ issues ProcOnion queries for I and S, $\mathcal{B}$ acts as the environment that sends these onions to I and S.

Next comes the challenge step, and this is where this proof would run into difficulty. In our repliable-onion security game, it is at this point that $\mathcal{A}$ specifies the names and public keys of the rest of the participants in the system. But our functionality assumed that this setup was done ahead of time; modeling it this way made the functionality more manageable and interacted well with the SUC model. However, we can show that a modified, non-adaptive version of repliable-onion security is, in fact, necessary to SUC-realize $\mathcal{F}_{\mathsf{ROES}}$. Let NAROSecurityGame($1^{\lambda}$, Σ, CompleteOnion, $\mathcal{A}$) be the ROSecurityGame security game modified as follows: instead of waiting until the challenge step to specify the names and public keys on the routing path of the challenge onion, $\mathcal{A}$ specifies them at the very beginning. Other than that, we define *non-adaptive repliable-onion security* completely analogously to repliable-onion security:

Definition 10 (Non-adaptive repliable-onion security). *A repliable onion encryption scheme* Σ *is* non-adaptive repliable-onion secure *if there exist a p.p.t. algorithm* CompleteOnion *and a negligible function* $\nu :$ $\mathbb{N} \mapsto \mathbb{R}$ *such that every p.p.t. adversary* $\mathcal{A}$ *wins the security game* NAROSecurityGame$(1^\lambda, \Sigma, \mathsf{CompleteOnion}, \mathcal{A})$ *with negligible advantage, i.e.,* $\left| \Pr \left[\mathcal{A} \text{ wins } \mathsf{NAROSecurityGame}(1^\lambda, \Sigma, \mathsf{CompleteOnion}, \mathcal{A}) \right] - \frac{1}{2} \right| \leq \nu(\lambda)$.

Theorem 11 is the closest we can show to the converse of Theorem 9:

Theorem 11. *If an onion encryption scheme* Σ *SUC-realizes the ideal functionality* $\mathcal{F}_{\mathsf{ROES}}$ *(Definition 3) then it is non-adaptive repliable-onion secure (Definition 10).*

Proof. The proof is by a hybrid argument. Let $\mathsf{Experiment}^0(1^\lambda, \mathcal{A})$ be the adversary's view in the non-adaptive repliable-onion security game when $b = 0$. Let I and S denote the names of the honest parties chosen by $\mathcal{A}$.

Let $\mathsf{Hybrid}^{real_0}(1^\lambda, \mathcal{A})$ be the same as $\mathsf{Experiment}^0$ except in organization. Here, we split up the NAROSecurityGame challenger into components: one component is responsible for executing Σ on behalf of participant S (i.e., generate S's keys, process and where possible, reply to onions routed to S, and form the challenge onion on behalf of S), another is responsible for executing Σ on behalf of I (i.e. i.e., generate I's keys and deal with onions routed to I), and the third component, $\mathcal{B}$ carries out everything else, including interacting with $\mathcal{A}$. When organized this way, it is easy to see that $\mathcal{B}$ and $\mathcal{A}$ jointly act as the environment (from the SUC model) for the real-world execution of Σ by the honest participants S and I. The environment here directs only one of the participants (S) to ever form an onion: just the one challenge onion. The output of $\mathsf{Hybrid}^{real_0}(1^\lambda, \mathcal{A})$ is the adversary's view.

Let $\mathsf{Hybrid}^{ideal_0}(1^\lambda, \mathcal{A})$ be the same as $\mathsf{Hybrid}^{real_0}(1^\lambda, \mathcal{A})$ except that the real execution of Σ is replaced with executing $\mathcal{F}_{\mathsf{ROES}}$. Hybrid^{real_0} and $\mathsf{Hybrid}^{ideal_0}$ are indistinguishable by the hypothesis. By construction of $\mathcal{F}_{\mathsf{ROES}}$, the layers of the sole onion that's ever created in $\mathsf{Hybrid}^{ideal_0}(1^\lambda, \mathcal{A})$ are computed by splitting the routing path into two segments: one ends in I and the other one in S.

Let us consider another game $\mathsf{Hybrid}^{ideal_1}(1^\lambda, \mathcal{A})$. This game is identical to $\mathsf{Hybrid}^{ideal_0}(1^\lambda, \mathcal{A})$ except in how it is internally organized. Here, acting as the environment responsible for supplying inputs to S, $\mathcal{B}$ will cause two onions to be formed. In case (a), both onions are formed by S: one with I as the recipient, and the second onion is formed using the rest of the routing path; in case (b), S sends a non-repliable onion to I who then replies to S by forming a fresh onion; in case (c), I forms an onion using the first segment of the path, and then a fresh onion with S as the recipient. The parts that are visible to $\mathcal{A}$ are just the onions themselves, and therefore $\mathsf{Hybrid}^{ideal_1}(1^\lambda, \mathcal{A})$ is identical to $\mathsf{Hybrid}^{ideal_0}(1^\lambda, \mathcal{A})$.

Next, define $\mathsf{Hybrid}^{real_1}(1^\lambda, \mathcal{A})$: here, the environment ($\mathcal{B}$ acting jointly with $\mathcal{A}$) interacts with S and I exactly as in $\mathsf{Hybrid}^{ideal_1}(1^\lambda, \mathcal{A})$, but S and I are running Σ instead of $\mathcal{F}_{\mathsf{ROES}}$ with $\mathcal{S}$. By the hypothesis, $\mathsf{Hybrid}^{real_1}(1^\lambda, \mathcal{A})$ is indistinguishable from $\mathsf{Hybrid}^{ideal_1}(1^\lambda, \mathcal{A})$. It is easy to see that $\mathsf{Hybrid}^{real_1}(1^\lambda, \mathcal{A})$ and $\mathsf{Hybrid}^{ideal_1}(1^\lambda, \mathcal{A})$ are identical when I appears only once in the routing path.

When I appears more than once in the routing path, the views are indistinguishable due to the realizability of $\mathcal{F}_{\mathsf{ROES}}$.

Finally, let $\mathsf{Experiment}^1(1^\lambda, \mathcal{A})$ be the adversary's view in the non-adaptive repliable-onion security game when $b = 1$. $\mathsf{Hybrid}^{real_1}(1^\lambda, \mathcal{A})$ and $\mathsf{Experiment}^1$ are identical by construction. Therefore, we have shown that $\mathsf{Experiment}^1(1^\lambda, \mathcal{A}) \approx \mathsf{Experiment}^1(1^\lambda, \mathcal{A})$, and therefore, Σ is non-adaptive repliable-onion secure.

6   Shallot Encryption

In this section, we provide our construction of a repliable onion encryption scheme dubbed "*Shallot Encryption Scheme*." Inspired by the Camenisch and Lysyanskaya (CL) approach [5], our construction forms each onion layer for a party P by encrypting the previous layer under a key k which, in turn, is encrypted under the public key of P and a tag t. Our construction differs from the CL construction in that the tag t is not a function of the layer's content. Instead, authentication of the message happens separately, using a message authentication code. The resulting object is more like a shallot than an onion; it consists of *two* separate layered encryption objects: the header and the content (which may contain a "bud," i.e., another layered encryption object, namely the header for the return onion). We still call these objects "onions" to be consistent with prior work, but the scheme overall merits the name "shallot encryption."

Let λ denote the security parameter. Let $F_{(.)}(\cdot, \cdot)$ be a pseudorandom function family such that, whenever $\mathsf{seed} \in \{0,1\}^k$, F_{seed} takes as input two k-bit strings and outputs a k-bit string. Such a function can be constructed from a regular one-input PRF in a straightforward fashion.

Let $\{f_k(\cdot)\}_{k\in\{0,1\}^*}$ and $\{g_k(\cdot)\}_{k\in\{0,1\}^*}$ be block ciphers, i.e., pseudorandom permutations (PRPs). We use the same key to key both block ciphers: one ($\{f_k(\cdot)\}_{k\in\{0,1\}^*}$) with a "short" blocklength $L_1(\lambda)$ is used for forming headers, and the other ($\{g_k(\cdot)\}_{k\in\{0,1\}^*}$) with a "long" blocklength $L_2(\lambda)$ is used for forming contents. This is standard and can be constructed from regular block ciphers. Following the notational convention introduced by Camenisch and Lysyanskaya [5], let $\{X\}_k$ denote $f_k(X)$ if $|X| = L_1(\lambda)$, or $g_k(X)$ if $|X| = L_2(\lambda)$, and let $\}X\{_k$ correspondingly denote $f_k^{-1}(X)$ or $g_k^{-1}(X)$.

Let $\mathcal{E} = (\mathsf{Gen}_\mathcal{E}, \mathsf{Enc}, \mathsf{Dec})$ be a CCA2-secure encryption scheme with tags [12], let $\mathsf{MAC} = (\mathsf{Gen}_{\mathsf{MAC}}, \mathsf{Tag}, \mathsf{Ver})$ be a message authentication code (MAC), and let h be a collision-resistant hash function.

Setting Up: Each party P_i forms a public key pair $(\mathsf{pk}(P_i), \mathsf{sk}(P_i))$ using the public key encryption scheme's key generation algorithm $\mathsf{Gen}_\mathcal{E}$, i.e., $(\mathsf{pk}(P_i), \mathsf{sk}(P_i)) \leftarrow \mathsf{Gen}_\mathcal{E}(1^\lambda, \mathsf{pp}, P_i)$.

Forming a Repliable Onion. Each onion consists of (1) the header (i.e., the encrypted routing path and associated keys) and (2) the content (i.e., the encrypted message).

Forming the Header: In our example, let Alice (denoted P_s) be the sender, and let Bob (denoted P_d, d for destination) be the recipient. To form a *repliable onion*, Alice receives as input a label ℓ, a message m, a *forward* path to

Bob: $P^{\rightarrow} = P_1, \ldots, P_{d-1}, P_d$, $|P^{\rightarrow}| = d \leq N$, and a *return* path to herself: $P^{\leftarrow} = P_{d+1}, \ldots, P_{s-1}, P_s$, $|P^{\leftarrow}| = s - d + 1 \leq N$. All other participants P_i are intermediaries.

Let "seed" be a seed stored in $\mathsf{sk}(P_s)$. Alice computes (i) an encryption key $k_i = F_{\mathsf{seed}}(\ell, i)$ for every party P_i on the routing path $(P^{\rightarrow}, P^{\leftarrow})$, (ii) an authentication key K_d for Bob using $\mathsf{Gen}_{\mathsf{MAC}}(1^\lambda)$ with $F_{\mathsf{seed}}(d, \ell)$ sourcing the randomness for running the key generation algorithm, and (iii) an authentication key K_s for herself using $\mathsf{Gen}_{\mathsf{MAC}}(1^\lambda)$ with $F_{\mathsf{seed}}(s, \ell)$ sourcing the randomness for running the key generation algorithm.

Remark: We can avoid using a PRF in exchange for requiring state; an alternative to using a PRF is to store keys computed from true randomness locally.

The goal of FormOnion is to produce an onion O_1 for the first party P_1 on the routing path such that P_1 processing O_1 produces the onion O_2 for the next destination P_2 on the routing path, and so on.

Suppose for the time being that both the forward path and the return path are of the maximum length N, i.e., $d = s - d + 1 = N$.

Let O be an onion that we want party P to "peel." The *header* of O is a sequence $H = (E, B^1, \ldots, B^{N-1})$. E is an encryption under P's public key and the tag $t = h(B^1, \ldots, B^{N-1})$ of the following pieces of information that P needs to correctly process the onion: (i) P's role, i.e., is P an intermediary, or the onion's recipient, or the original sender of the onion whose reply P just received; (ii) in case P is an intermediary or recipient, the encryption key k necessary for making sense of the rest of the onion; (iii) in case P is the original sender, the label ℓ necessary for making sense of the rest of the onion; and (iv) in case P is the recipient, the authentication key K.

If P is an intermediary, it will next process $(B^1, \ldots, B^{N-1})$ by inverting each of them, in turn, using the block cipher's key k, to obtain the values $\}B^1\{_k, \ldots, \}B^{N-1}\{_k$. The value $\}B^1\{_k$ reveals the destination P' and the ciphertext E' of the peeled onion. For each $1 < j < N$, the value $\}B^j\{_k$ is block $(B')^{j-1}$ of the peeled onion, so the header of the peeled onion will begin with $(E', (B')^1, \ldots, (B')^{N-2})$. The final block $(B')^{N-1}$ of the header is formed by computing the inverse of the PRP keyed by k of the all-zero string of length $L_1(\lambda)$, i.e., $(B')^{N-1} = \}0\ldots0\{_k$.

Therefore, sender Alice needs to form her onion so that each intermediary applying the procedure described above will peel it correctly. Using the keys $k_1, \ldots, k_d$ and K_d, Alice first forms the header $H_d = (E_d, B_d^1, \ldots, B_d^{N-1})$ for the last onion O_d on the forward path (the one to be processed by Bob): For every $i \in \{1, \ldots, N-1\}$, let $B_d^i = \}\ldots\}0\ldots0\{_{k_i}\ldots\{_{k_{d-1}}$. The tag t_d for integrity protection is the hash of these blocks concatenated together, i.e., $t_d = h(B_d^1, \ldots, B_d^{N-1})$. The ciphertext E_d is the encryption of (R, k_d, K_d) under the public key $\mathsf{pk}(P_d)$ and the tag t_d, i.e., $E_d \leftarrow \mathsf{Enc}(\mathsf{pk}(P_d), t_d, (\mathsf{R}, k_d, K_d))$. The headers of the remaining onions in the evolution are formed recursively. Let

$$B_{d-1}^1 = \{P_d, E_d\}_{k_{d-1}},$$
$$B_{d-1}^i = \{B_d^{i-1}\}_{k_{d-1}}, \qquad\qquad \forall i \in \{2, \ldots, N-1\},$$
$$t_{d-1} = h(B_{d-1}^1, \ldots, B_{d-1}^{N-1}),$$
$$E_{d-1} \leftarrow \mathsf{Enc}(\mathsf{pk}(P_{d-1}), t_{d-1}, (\mathsf{I}, k_{d-1}));$$

and so on. (WLOG, we assume that (P_d, E_d) "fits" into a block; i.e., $|P_d, E_d| \leq L_1(\lambda)$. A block cipher with the correct blocklength can be built from a standard one [4,20].)

Forming the Encrypted Content: Alice then forms the encrypted content for Bob. First, if the return path $P^\leftarrow$ is non-empty, Alice forms the header H_{d+1} for the return onion using the same procedure that she used to form the header H_1 for the forward onion, but using the return path $P^\leftarrow$ instead of the forward path $P^\rightarrow$ and encrypting (S, ℓ) instead of (R, k_s, K_s). That is, the ciphertext E_s of the "innermost" header H_s is the encryption $\mathsf{Enc}(\mathsf{pk}(P_s), t_s, (\mathsf{S}, \ell))$ rather than $\mathsf{Enc}(\mathsf{pk}(P_s), t_s, (\mathsf{R}, k_s, K_s))$. If the return path is empty, then H_{d+1}, k_s and K_s are the empty string.

When Bob processes the onion, Alice wants him to receive (i) the message m, (ii) the header H_{d+1} for the return onion, (iii) the keys k_s and K_s for forming a reply to the anonymous sender (Alice), and (iv) the first party P_{d+1} on the return path. So, Alice sets the "*meta-message*" M to be the concatenation of m, H_{d+1}, k_s, K_s, and P_{d+1}: $M = (m, H_{d+1}, k_s, K_s, P_{d+1})$.

Alice wants Bob to be able to verify that M is the meta-message, so she also computes the tag $\sigma_d = \mathsf{Tag}(K_d, M)$. (WLOG, (M, σ_d) "fits" exactly into a block; i.e., $|M| \leq L_2(\lambda)$.)

The encrypted content C_i for each onion O_i on the forward path is given by: $C_i = \{\ldots \{M, \sigma_d\}_{k_d} \cdots\}_{k_i}$. See Fig. 4 for a pictorial description of the how the repliable onion is formed.

We now explain what happens when $d \neq N$, or $s - d + 1 \neq N$: If either d or $s - d + 1$ exceed the upper bound N, then FormOnion returns an error. If d is strictly less than N, the header is still "padded" to $N - 1$ blocks by sampling N encryption keys as before. Likewise if $s - d + 1 < N$, the header is padded to $N - 1$ blocks in similar fashion. (Note that the size of each repliable onion is twice the size of a CL non-repliable onion [5] with maximum path length N.)

Processing a Repliable Onion. Let Carol be an intermediary node on the forward path from Alice to Bob. When Carol receives the onion $O_i = (H_i, C_i)$ consisting of the header $H_i = (E_i, B_i^1, \ldots B_i^{N-1})$ and the content C_i, she processes it as follows:

Carol first computes the tag $t_i = h(B_i^1, \ldots B_i^{N-1})$ for integrity protection and then attempts to decrypt the ciphertext E_i of the header using her secret key $\mathsf{sk}(P_i)$ and the tag t_i to obtain her role and key(s), i.e., $(\mathsf{I}, k_i) = \mathsf{Dec}(\mathsf{sk}(P_i), t_i, E_i)$. Carol succeeds in decrypting E_i only if the header has not been tampered with. In this case, she gets her role "I" and the key k_i and proceeds with processing the header and content:

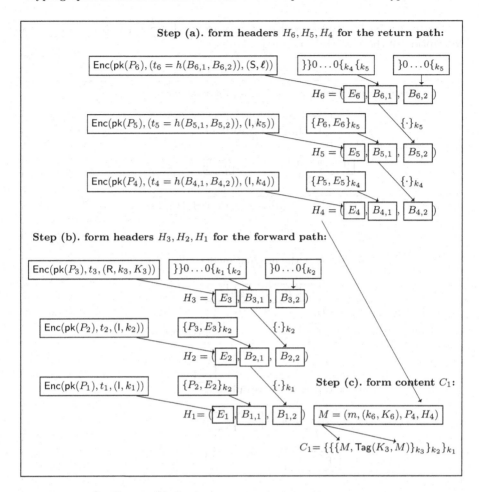

Fig. 4. Steps for forming the first shallot onion $O_1 = (H_1, C_1)$ when the forward path is $P^{\rightarrow} = (P_1, P_2, P_3)$, and the return path is $P^{\leftarrow} = (P_4, P_5, P_6)$: (a) steps for forming the headers H_6, H_5, H_4 for the return path, (b) steps for forming the headers H_3, H_2, H_1 for the forward path, and (c) steps for forming the content C_1.

Carol first decrypts the first block B_i^1 of the current header to retrieve the next destination P_{i+1} and ciphertext E_{i+1} of the processed header (header of the next onion), i.e., $(P_{i+1}, E_{i+1}) = \}B_i^1\{_{k_i}$. To obtain the first $N-2$ blocks of the processed header, Carol decrypts the last $N-2$ blocks of H: $B_{i+1}^j = \}B_i^{j+1}\{_{k_i}$ for all $j \in [N-2]$. To obtain the last block of the processed header, Carol "decrypts" the all-zero string "$0\ldots0$:" $B_{i+1}^{N-1} = \}0\ldots0\{_{k_i}$. To process the content, Carol simply decrypts the current content C_i: $C_{i+1} = \}C_i\{_{k_i}$.

Let David be an intermediary party on the return path. When David receives the onion O_j, he processes it exactly in the same way that Carol processed the onion O_i in the forward direction. (Critically, David does not know that he is on the return path as opposed to the forward path.) See Fig. 5 for a pictorial description of the how the onion is processed.

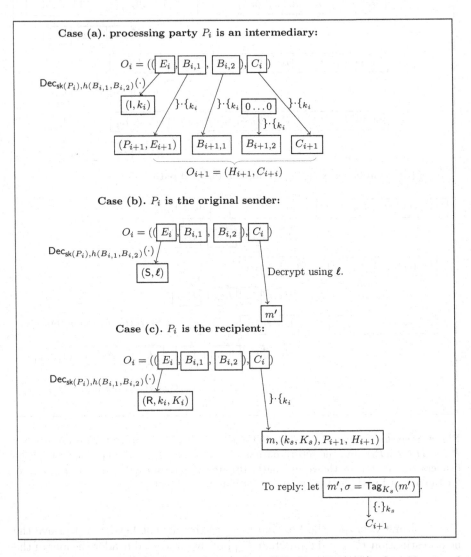

Fig. 5. Steps for processing a shallot onion $O_i = ((H_i, B_{i,1}, B_{i,2}), C_i)$ when $N = 3$ and when (a) the processing party P_i is an intermediary, (b) P_i is the original sender, and (c) P_i is the recipient. For (c), steps for forming the reply onion $O_{i+1} = (H_{i+1}, C_{i+1})$ for the next destination P_{i+1}.

Replying to the Anonymous Sender. When Bob receives the onion $O_d = (H_d, C_d)$, he processes it in the same way that the intermediary party Carol does, by running ProcOnion: Bob first decrypts the ciphertext E_d of the header to retrieve his role "R" and the keys k_d and K_d. If O_d hasn't been tampered with, Bob retrieves the meta-message $M = (m, H_{d+1}, k_s, K_s, P_{d+1})$ and the tag σ_d that Alice embedded into the onion by decrypting the content C_d using the key k_d: $((m, H_{d+1}, k_s, K_s, P_{d+1}), \sigma_d) = \}C_d\{k_d$. Bob can verify that the message is untampered by running the MAC's verification algorithm $\mathsf{Ver}(K_d, M, \sigma_d)$.

To respond to the anonymous sender (Alice) with the message m', Bob creates a new encrypted content using the keys k_s and K_s: $C_{d+1} = \{m', \mathsf{Tag}(K_s, m')\}_{k_s}$. Bob sends the reply onion $O_{d+1} = (H_{d+1}, C_{d+1})$ to the next destination P_{d+1}.

Reading the Reply. When Alice receives the onion O_s, she retrieves the reply from Bob by first processing the onion, by running $\mathsf{ProcOnion}$:

Alice first decrypts the ciphertext E_s of the header to retrieve her role "S" and the label ℓ. She reconstructs the each encryption key $k_i = F_{\mathsf{seed}}(\ell, i)$ and the authentication key K_s using the pseudo-randomness $F_{\mathsf{seed}}(s, \ell)$. (Alternatively, if she stored the keys locally, she looks up the keys associated with label ℓ in a local data structure). If O_s hasn't been tampered with, Alice retrieves the reply m' that Bob embedded into the onion by decrypting the content C_s using the keys $(k_{d+1}, \ldots, k_s)$: $(m', \sigma_s) = \}\{\ldots \{C_s\}_{k_{s-1}} \cdots \}_{k_{d+1}}\{k_s$. Alice can verify that the message is untampered by running $\mathsf{Ver}(K_s, m', \sigma_s)$.

7 Shallot Encryption Scheme Is Secure

Theorem 12. *Shallot Encryption Scheme (in Sect. 6) SUC-realizes the ideal functionality $\mathcal{F}_{\mathsf{ROES}}$ (Definition 3).*

By Theorem 9, it suffices to prove that Shallot Encryption Scheme is correct and repliable-onion secure under the assumption that (i) $\{f_k\}_{k \in \{0,1\}^*}$ is a PRP, (ii) $\mathcal{E}$ is a CCA2-secure encryption scheme with tags, (iii) MAC is a message authentication code, and (iv) h is a collision-resistant hash function.

<u>Proof Idea:</u> In cases (a) and (c) (in these cases, P_j is an intermediary, not the recipient), we can prove that $\mathcal{A}$'s view when $b = 0$ is indistinguishable from $\mathcal{A}$'s view when $b = 1$ using a hybrid argument. The gist of the argument is as follows: First, P_j's encryption key k_j is protected by CCA2-secure encryption, so it can be swapped out for the all-zero key "$0 \ldots 0$." Next, blocks $(N - j - 1)$ to $(N - 1)$ of the onion for P_{j+1} look random as they are all "decryptions" under k_j, so they can be swapped out for truly random blocks. Next, blocks 1 to $(N - j - 1)$ and the content of the onion for P_j look random as they are encryptions under k_j, so they can be swapped out for truly random blocks. At this point, the keys for forming O_{j+1} can be independent of the keys for forming O_j, and these onions may be formed via separate $\mathsf{FormOnion}$ calls; see Fig. 6.

Experiment^0—game with $b = 0$, same as Hybrid^1
Hybrid^1—make O_{j+1}, then O_1
Hybrid^2—same as Hybrid^1 except swap ℓ for random label
Hybrid^3—same as Hybrid^2 except swap k_j for fake key "0...0"
Hybrid^4—same as Hybrid^3 except swap $(B_{j+1}^{N-j-1}, \ldots, B_{j+1}^{N-1})$ for truly random blocks
Hybrid^5—same as Hybrid^4 except swap $(B_j^1, \ldots, B_j^{N-j-1})$ and C_j for truly random blocks
Hybrid^6—same as Hybrid^5 except swap onion for intermediary P_j for onion for recipient P_j
Hybrid^7—same as Hybrid^6 except swap truly random blocks and content in O_j for
   pseudo-random blocks $(B_j^1, \ldots, B_j^{N-j-1}, C_j)$
Hybrid^8—same as Hybrid^7 except swap truly random blocks in H_{j+1} for pseudo-random
   blocks $(B_{j+1}^{N-j-1}, \ldots, B_{j+1}^{N-1})$
Hybrid^9—same as Hybrid^8 except swap key "0...0" for real key k_j
Experiment^1—game with $b = 1$, same as Hybrid^9

Fig. 6. Road map of proof of Theorem 12

For case (b) (P_j is the recipient), we can use a simpler hybrid argument since only the content of a forward onion can be computationally related to the keys for the return path. Thus, we can swap out just the content for a truly random string. See the full paper for the full proof [1].

Acknowledgements. We thank the reviewers of this paper for their helpful comments. This work was funded in part by Facebook faculty research awards.

A   Security Game for Variants (b) and (c)

Variant (b). Below, we provide a description of steps 4 and 5 of the repliable-onion security game, ROSecurityGame, in Sect. 4 for case (b).

4. $\mathcal{A}$ chooses a label $\ell \in \mathcal{L}(1^\lambda)$ and a message $m \in \mathcal{M}(1^\lambda)$. $\mathcal{A}$ also chooses a forward path $P^\rightarrow = (P_1, \ldots, P_d)$ and a return path $P^\leftarrow = (P_{d+1}, \ldots, P_s)$ such that (i) if $P^\leftarrow$ is non-empty, then it ends with S, (ii) I appears in the routing path, and (iii) the first time it appears in the path is at the recipient P_d. $\mathcal{A}$ sends to $\mathcal{C}$ the parameters for the challenge onion: ℓ, m, $P^\rightarrow$, the public keys $\mathsf{pk}(P^\rightarrow)$ of the parties in $P^\rightarrow$, $P^\leftarrow$, and the public keys $\mathsf{pk}(P^\leftarrow)$ of the parties in $P^\leftarrow$.

5. $\mathcal{C}$ samples a bit $b \leftarrow_\$ \{0, 1\}$.
   If $b = 0$, $\mathcal{C}$ runs FormOnion on the parameters specified by $\mathcal{A}$, i.e., $((O_1^0, \ldots, O_d^0), H^\leftarrow, \kappa) \leftarrow \mathsf{FormOnion}(\ell, m, P^\rightarrow, \mathsf{pk}(P^\rightarrow), P^\leftarrow, \mathsf{pk}(P^\leftarrow))$. In this case, the oracles—$\mathcal{O}.\mathsf{PO_I}(\cdot)$, $\mathcal{O}.\mathsf{FR_I}(\cdot, \cdot)$, $\mathcal{O}.\mathsf{PO_S}(\cdot)$, and $\mathcal{O}.\mathsf{FR_S}(\cdot, \cdot)$—remain unmodified.
   Otherwise, if $b = 1$, $\mathcal{C}$ performs the "switch" at honest recipient P_d. $\mathcal{C}$ runs FormOnion on input a random label $x \leftarrow_\$ \mathcal{L}(1^\lambda)$, a random message $y \leftarrow_\$ \mathcal{M}(1^\lambda)$, the forward path $P^\rightarrow$, and the empty return path "()", i.e., $((O_1^1, \ldots, O_d^1), (), \kappa) \leftarrow \mathsf{FormOnion}(x, y, P^\rightarrow, \mathsf{pk}(P^\rightarrow), (), ())$.

We modify the oracles as follows. $\mathcal{O}.\mathsf{FR}_\mathsf{I}$ does the following to "form a reply" using message m' and onion $O = O_d^1$: $\mathcal{O}.\mathsf{FR}_\mathsf{I}$ runs FormOnion on a random label x', a random message y', the return path $P^\leftarrow$ as the forward path, and the empty return path "()", i.e., $((O_{j+1}^{m'}, \ldots, O_s^{m'}), (), \kappa^{m'}) \leftarrow$ FormOnion$(x', y', P^\leftarrow, \mathsf{pk}(P^\leftarrow), (), ())$, stores the pair $(O_s^{m'}, m')$ (such that the pair is accessible by $\mathcal{O}.\mathsf{POS}$), and returns $(O_{j+1}^{m'}, P_{j+1})$. $\mathcal{O}.\mathsf{POS}$ does the following to "process" an onion O:

   i. If $O = O'$ for some stored pair (O', m') and ProcOnion$(O, P_s, \mathsf{sk}(P_s)) = (\mathsf{R}, m')$, then return $(\mathsf{S}, (\ell, m'))$.

   ii. If $O = O'$ for some stored pair (O', m') and ProcOnion$(O, P_s, \mathsf{sk}(P_s)) \neq (\mathsf{R}, m')$, then fail.

   iii. If $O \neq O'$ for any stored pair (O', m') but $O = (H', C)$ for some stored pair $((H', C'), m')$ and ProcOnion$(O, P_s, \mathsf{sk}(P_s)) = (\mathsf{R}, \perp)$, then return $(\mathsf{S}, \perp)$.

   iv. If $O \neq O'$ for any stored pair (O', m') but $O = (H', C)$ for some stored pair $((H', C'), m')$ and ProcOnion$(O, P_s, \mathsf{sk}(P_s)) \neq (\mathsf{R}, \perp)$, then fail.

All other queries are processed as before.

Variant (c). Below, we provide a description of steps 4 and 5 of the repliable-onion security game, ROSecurityGame, in Sect. 4 for case (c).

4. $\mathcal{A}$ chooses a label $\ell \in \mathcal{L}(1^\lambda)$ and a message $m \in \mathcal{M}(1^\lambda)$. $\mathcal{A}$ also chooses a forward path $P^\rightarrow = (P_1, \ldots, P_d)$ and a return path $P^\leftarrow = (P_{d+1}, \ldots, P_s)$ such that (i) if $P^\leftarrow$ is non-empty, then it ends with S, (ii) I doesn't appear on the $P^\rightarrow$, and (iii) I appears somewhere on $P^\leftarrow$. $\mathcal{A}$ sends to $\mathcal{C}$ the parameters for the challenge onion: ℓ, m, $P^\rightarrow$, the public keys $\mathsf{pk}(P^\rightarrow)$ of the parties in $P^\rightarrow$, $P^\leftarrow$, and the public keys $\mathsf{pk}(P^\leftarrow)$ of the parties in $P^\leftarrow$.

5. $\mathcal{C}$ samples a bit $b \leftarrow_\$ \{0, 1\}$.

    If $b = 0$, $\mathcal{C}$ runs FormOnion on the parameters specified by $\mathcal{A}$, i.e., $((O_1^0, \ldots, O_d^0), H^\leftarrow, \kappa) \leftarrow$ FormOnion$(\ell, m, P^\rightarrow, \mathsf{pk}(P^\rightarrow), P^\leftarrow, \mathsf{pk}(P^\leftarrow))$. In this case, the oracles—$\mathcal{O}.\mathsf{PO}_\mathsf{I}(\cdot)$, $\mathcal{O}.\mathsf{FR}_\mathsf{I}(\cdot, \cdot)$, $\mathcal{O}.\mathsf{POS}(\cdot)$, and $\mathcal{O}.\mathsf{FRS}(\cdot, \cdot)$—remain unmodified.

    Otherwise, if $b = 1$, $\mathcal{C}$ performs the "switch" at honest party P_j on the return path $P^\leftarrow$, where P_j is the first appearance of I on the routing path. $\mathcal{C}$ runs FormOnion on input a random label $x \leftarrow_\$ \mathcal{L}(1^\lambda)$, the message m (that had been chosen by $\mathcal{A}$ in step 4), the forward path $P^\rightarrow$, and the "truncated" return path $p^\leftarrow = (P_{d+1}, \ldots, P_j)$, i.e., $(O^\rightarrow, (H_{d+1}^1, \ldots, H_j^1), \kappa) \leftarrow$ FormOnion$(x, m, P^\rightarrow, \mathsf{pk}(P^\rightarrow), p^\leftarrow, \mathsf{pk}(p^\leftarrow))$.

    We modify the oracles as follows. $\mathcal{O}.\mathsf{PO}_\mathsf{I}$ does the following to "process" an onion O:

   i. If $O = (H_j^1, C)$ for some content C and ProcOnion$(O, P_j, \mathsf{sk}(P_j)) = (\mathsf{R}, m')$ for some message m' (possibly equal to "$\perp$"), then runs FormOnion on a random label x', a random message y', the remainder the return path $q^\leftarrow = (P_{j+1}, \ldots, P_s)$ as the forward path, and the empty return path "()", i.e., $((O_{j+1}^{m'}, \ldots, O_s^{m'}), (), \kappa^{m'}) \leftarrow$ FormOnion$(x', y', q^\leftarrow, \mathsf{pk}(q^\leftarrow), (), ())$, stores the pair $(O_s^{m'}, m')$ (such that the pair is accessible by $\mathcal{O}.\mathsf{POS}$), and returns $(O_{j+1}^{m'}, P_{j+1})$.

ii. If $O = (H_j^1, C)$ for some content C and $\mathsf{ProcOnion}(O, P_j, \mathsf{sk}(P_j)) \neq$ (R, m') for some message m', then fails.

$\mathcal{O}.\mathsf{PO_S}$ does the following to "process" an onion O:

iii. If $O = O'$ for some stored pair (O', m') and $\mathsf{ProcOnion}(O, P_s, \mathsf{sk}(P_s)) =$ (R, m'), then return (S, (ℓ, m')).

iv. If $O = O'$ for some stored pair (O', m') and $\mathsf{ProcOnion}(O, P_s, \mathsf{sk}(P_s)) \neq$ (R, m'), then fail.

v. If $O \neq O'$ for any stored pair (O', m') but $O = (H', C)$ for some stored pair $((H', C'), m')$ and $\mathsf{ProcOnion}(O, P_s, \mathsf{sk}(P_s)) = (R, \perp)$, then return (S, $\perp$).

vi. If $O \neq O'$ for any stored pair (O', m') but $O = (H', C)$ for some stored pair $((H', C'), m')$ and $\mathsf{ProcOnion}(O, P_s, \mathsf{sk}(P_s)) \neq (R, \perp)$, then fail.

All other queries are processed as before.

References

1. Ando, M., Lysyanskaya, A.: Cryptographic shallots: a formal treatment of repliable onion encryption. Cryptology ePrint Archive, Report 2020/215 (2020). https://eprint.iacr.org/2020/215

2. Ando, M., Lysyanskaya, A., Upfal, E.: Practical and provably secure onion routing. In: Chatzigiannakis, I., Kaklamanis, C., Marx, D., Sannella, D. (eds.) ICALP 2018, volume 107 of LIPIcs, pp. 144:1–144:14. Schloss Dagstuhl (July 2018)

3. Ando, M., Lysyanskaya, A., Upfal, E.: On the complexity of anonymous communication through public networks. In: 2nd Conference on Information-Theoretic Cryptography, ITC 2021. Schloss Dagstuhl-Leibniz-Zentrum für Informatik (2021)

4. Boneh, D., Shoup, V.: A graduate course in applied cryptography. Draft 0.2 (2015)

5. Camenisch, J., Lysyanskaya, A.: A formal treatment of Onion routing. In: Shoup, V. (ed.) CRYPTO 2005. LNCS, vol. 3621, pp. 169–187. Springer, Heidelberg (2005). https://doi.org/10.1007/11535218_11

6. Canetti, R.: Universally composable security: a new paradigm for cryptographic protocols. In: 42nd FOCS, pp. 136–145. IEEE Computer Society Press (October 2001)

7. Canetti, R., Cohen, A., Lindell, Y.: A simpler variant of universally composable security for standard multiparty computation. In: Gennaro, R., Robshaw, M. (eds.) CRYPTO 2015. LNCS, vol. 9216, pp. 3–22. Springer, Heidelberg (2015). https://doi.org/10.1007/978-3-662-48000-7_1

8. Canetti, R., Feige, U., Goldreich, O., Naor, M.: Adaptively secure multi-party computation. In: 28th ACM STOC, pp. 639–648. ACM Press (May 1996)

9. Canetti, R., Shahaf, D., Vald, M.: Universally composable authentication and key-exchange with global PKI. In: Cheng, C.-M., Chung, K.-M., Persiano, G., Yang, B.-Y. (eds.) PKC 2016. LNCS, vol. 9615, pp. 265–296. Springer, Heidelberg (2016). https://doi.org/10.1007/978-3-662-49387-8_11

10. Chaum, D.L.: Untraceable electronic mail, return addresses, and digital pseudonyms. Commun. ACM 24(2), 84–90 (1981)

11. Cottrell, L.: Mixmaster and remailer attacks (1995)

12. Cramer, R., Shoup, V.: A practical public key cryptosystem provably secure against adaptive chosen ciphertext attack. In: Krawczyk, H. (ed.) CRYPTO 1998. LNCS, vol. 1462, pp. 13–25. Springer, Heidelberg (1998). https://doi.org/10.1007/BFb0055717

13. Cramer, R., Shoup, V.: Universal hash proofs and a paradigm for adaptive chosen ciphertext secure public-key encryption. In: Knudsen, L.R. (ed.) EUROCRYPT 2002. LNCS, vol. 2332, pp. 45–64. Springer, Heidelberg (2002). https://doi.org/10.1007/3-540-46035-7_4

14. Danezis, G., Dingledine, R., Mathewson, N.: Mixminion: design of a type III anonymous remailer protocol. In: 2003 IEEE Symposium on Security and Privacy, pp. 2–15. IEEE Computer Society Press (May 2003)

15. Danezis, G., Goldberg, I.: Sphinx: a compact and provably secure mix format. In: 2009 IEEE Symposium on Security and Privacy, pp. 269–282. IEEE Computer Society Press (May 2009)

16. Danezis, G., Laurie, B.: Minx: a simple and efficient anonymous packet format. In: Proceedings of the 2004 ACM Workshop on Privacy in the Electronic Society, pp. 59–65 (2004)

17. Dingledine, R., Mathewson, N., Syverson, P.F.: Tor: the second-generation onion router. In: Proceedings of the 13th USENIX Security Symposium, San Diego, CA, USA, 9–13 August 2004, pp. 303–320 (2004)

18. Gulcu, C., Tsudik, G.: Mixing e-mail with Babel. In: Proceedings of Internet Society Symposium on Network and Distributed Systems Security, pp. 2–16. IEEE (1996)

19. Johnson, A., Wacek, C., Jansen, R., Sherr, M., Syverson, P.F.: Users get routed: traffic correlation on tor by realistic adversaries. In: Sadeghi, A.-R., Gligor, V.D., Yung, M. (eds.) ACM CCS 2013, pp. 337–348. ACM Press (November 2013)

20. Katz, J., Lindell, Y.: Introduction to Modern Cryptography. Chapman and Hall/CRC (2014)

21. Kuhn, C., Beck, M., Strufe, T.: Breaking and (partially) fixing provably secure onion routing. In: 2020 IEEE Symposium on Security and Privacy, pp. 168–185. IEEE Computer Society Press (May 2020)

22. Möller, U., Cottrell, L.: Mixmaster protocol–v2. unfinished draft (January 2000)

23. Parekh, S.: Prospects for remailers. First Monday 1(2) (1996)

24. Sun, Y., Edmundson, A., Feamster, N., Chiang, M., Mittal, P.: Counter-RAPTOR: safeguarding tor against active routing attacks. In: 2017 IEEE Symposium on Security and Privacy, pp. 977–992. IEEE Computer Society Press (May 2017)

25. Wails, R., Sun, Y., Johnson, A., Chiang, M., Mittal, P.: Tempest: temporal dynamics in anonymity systems. PoPETs 2018(3), 22–42 (2018)

Grafting Key Trees: Efficient Key Management for Overlapping Groups

Joël Alwen[1], Benedikt Auerbach[2](✉)(iD), Mirza Ahad Baig[2](iD), Miguel Cueto Noval[2], Karen Klein[3], Guillermo Pascual-Perez[2](iD), Krzysztof Pietrzak[2], and Michael Walter[4](iD)

[1] AWS Wickr, New York, USA
alwenjo@amazon.com
[2] IST Austria, Klosterneuburg, Austria
{bauerbac,mbaig,mcuetono,gpascual,pietrzak}@ist.ac.at
[3] ETH Zurich, Zurich, Switzerland
karen.h.klein@protonmail.com
[4] Zama, Paris, France
michael.walter@zama.ai

Abstract. Key trees are often the best solution in terms of transmission cost and storage requirements for managing keys in a setting where a group needs to share a secret key, while being able to efficiently rotate the key material of users (in order to recover from a potential compromise, or to add or remove users). Applications include multicast encryption protocols like LKH (Logical Key Hierarchies) or group messaging like the current IETF proposal TreeKEM.

A key tree is a (typically balanced) binary tree, where each node is identified with a key: leaf nodes hold users' secret keys while the root is the shared group key. For a group of size N, each user just holds $\log(N)$ keys (the keys on the path from its leaf to the root) and its entire key material can be rotated by broadcasting $2\log(N)$ ciphertexts (encrypting each fresh key on the path under the keys of its parents).

In this work we consider the natural setting where we have many groups with partially overlapping sets of users, and ask if we can find solutions where the cost of rotating a key is better than in the trivial one where we have a separate key tree for each group.

We show that in an asymptotic setting (where the number m of groups is fixed while the number N of users grows) there exist more general key

B. Auerbach, M.A. Baig and K. Pietrzak—received funding from the European Research Council (ERC) under the European Union's Horizon 2020 research and innovation programme (682815 - TOCNeT); Karen Klein was supported in part by ERC CoG grant 724307 and conducted part of this work at IST Austria, funded by the ERC under the European Union's Horizon 2020 research and innovation programme (682815 - TOCNeT); Guillermo Pascual-Perez was funded by the European Union's Horizon 2020 research and innovation programme under the Marie Skłodowska-Curie Grant Agreement No. 665385; Michael Walter conducted part of this work at IST Austria, funded by the ERC under the European Union's Horizon 2020 research and innovation programme (682815 - TOCNeT).

K. Nissim and B. Waters (Eds.): TCC 2021, LNCS 13044, pp. 222–253, 2021.
https://doi.org/10.1007/978-3-030-90456-2_8

graphs whose cost converges to the cost of a single group, thus saving a factor linear in the number of groups over the trivial solution.

As our asymptotic "solution" converges very slowly and performs poorly on concrete examples, we propose an algorithm that uses a natural heuristic to compute a key graph for any given group structure. Our algorithm combines two greedy algorithms, and is thus very efficient: it first converts the group structure into a "lattice graph", which is then turned into a key graph by repeatedly applying the algorithm for constructing a Huffman code.

To better understand how far our proposal is from an optimal solution, we prove lower bounds on the update cost of continuous group-key agreement and multicast encryption in a symbolic model admitting (asymmetric) encryption, pseudorandom generators, and secret sharing as building blocks.

1   Introduction

Key Trees. In various group communication settings, including multicast encryption [7,15,16] or group messaging protocols [4,8], the most efficient constructions use a binary tree structure to manage keys. The general idea is to consider a balanced binary tree with edges directed from leaves to the root. One then identifies each node v with a key k_v (of a symmetric encryption scheme for multicast encryption and a public-key encryption scheme for group messaging). Each edge (u, v) corresponds to a ciphertext $\mathsf{Enc}_{k_u}(k_v)$ and each leaf node v with a user u_v. A user u_v will know the (secret) key k_v, and from the ciphertexts can then retrieve all the keys on the path from its leaf to the root ε. The root key k_ε is thus known to all users, and can be used for secure communication to or among the group members.

What makes this tree structure so appealing is the fact that in a group of size N, the key material of a user u can be completely rotated by replacing only the keys on the path from u to ε, which in a balanced tree has length at most $d = \lceil \log(N) \rceil$. Moreover, as the nodes in a tree all have indegree two, one only needs to compute two fresh ciphertexts for each new key (in practice just one as the new keys can be derived via a hash-chain).

These aspects are important as the number of keys a user requires basically defines the communication and computational efficiency of a key rotation, which is the main operation performed to add or remove users, or for a user to update their keys in order to recover from a potential compromise.

Groups. In this work we consider an extension of this setting to multiple groups. We are given a base set $[N] = \{1, \ldots, N\}$ of users with a set system $\mathcal{S} = \{S_1, \ldots, S_k\}$ (each $S_i \subseteq [N]$), and we ask for a key managing structure such that for any set $S_i \in \mathcal{S}$, the users in S_i share a group key. This is a natural and well motivated setting; consider for example a university, where one might want to have a shared key for all students attending particular lectures.

A trivial solution to this problem is to simply use a different key-tree for every group S_i, in this work we explore more efficient solutions.

Key-Graphs Beyond Trees. For a set system $\mathcal{S}$ as above, instead of using disjoint trees, any directed acyclic graph (DAG) $\mathcal{G} = (\mathcal{V}, \mathcal{E})$ with the following properties is sufficient to maintain group keys:

1. Every user $i \in [N]$ corresponds to a source v_i (a node of indegree 0).
2. Every group $S_i \in \mathcal{S}$ corresponds to a sink v_{S_i} (a node of outdegree 0).
3. For every $S_i \in \mathcal{S}$ and $j \in [N]$, there is a directed path from v_j to v_{S_i} if and only if $j \in S_i$.
4. The indegree of any node is at most 2.

The first three properties ensure that any user $j \in [N]$ can learn the keys associated with the nodes of groups they are in. The last property is not really necessary, but it is without loss of generality in the sense that any graph can be turned into a graph with at most as large update cost (as we show in Sect. 3), and where every node other than the leaves has indegree at most 2. We call this a key-derivation graph for $\mathcal{S}$.

Update Cost. If we rotate the keys of a user i we need to replace all keys that can be reached from v_i, which we denote by $\mathcal{D}(v_i)$, and encrypt each new key under the keys of its co-path. We thus define the update cost of a user $i \in [N]$ as $\sum_{v \in \mathcal{D}(v_i)}(\text{indeg}(v) - 1)$, which with item 4 above roughly simplifies to the number of v_i's descendants $|\mathcal{D}(v_i)|$. The update cost $\text{Upd}(\mathcal{G})$ of a DAG $\mathcal{G}$ is the sum over the update cost of all its leaves, which is proportional to the average update cost of users.

Towards constructing more efficient key-derivation schemes when we have multiple overlapping groups, we thus address the problem of determining how small the update cost of a key-derivation for a given set system $\mathcal{S} = \{S_1, \dots, S_k\}$ over $[N]$ can be, and how to find graphs which achieve, or at least come close to, this minimum.

Our Contributions. We look at this problem from two perspectives. To get an insight on how much can be saved compared to the trivial solution, we first adapt a qualitative, asymptotic perspective, where we assume a fixed set system, but the number of users N goes to infinity while the relative size of the sets and intersections remains the same. We prove a lower bound on the update cost in this setting and give an algorithm computing graphs matching this bound.

As this solution turns out to be far from optimal for certain concrete set systems, we then also look at a quantitative non-asymptotic setting, where we consider concrete bounds and care about things like additive constants. We propose an algorithm that seems better equipped to handle such systems and prove upper and lower bounds on the update costs of graphs generated by it. Finally, we prove lower bounds on the update cost of any continuous group-key agreement scheme and multicast encryption scheme in a symbolic model.

1.1   The Asymptotic Setting

Given a set system $\mathcal{S} = (S_1, \dots, S_k)$ over some base set $[n]$, we let $\mathcal{S}(N)$ denote the system with base set $[N]$ we get by considering each element in S with multiplicity N/n. E.g. if $\mathcal{S} = (\{1,2\}, \{2,3\})$ then $\mathcal{S}(6) = (\{1,2,4,5\}, \{2,3,5,6\})$.[1] Thus, as the number of users N grows the relative sizes of the groups and their intersections remain fixed.

Let $s_i := |S_i|/n$ denote the relative size of S_i and $s = \sum_{i=1}^{m} s_i$ be the average number of groups users are in. We assume wlog. That each user is in at least one group, implying $s \geq 1$. Let $\mathrm{Opt}(\mathcal{S})$ denote the update cost of the best key-graph for a set system $\mathcal{S}$ and $\mathrm{Triv}(\mathcal{S})$ the update cost of the Trivial algorithm (which makes a key-tree for every $S_i \in \mathcal{S}$). We will show that (the hidden constants in the big-Oh notation all depend on k, the number of groups).

$$\mathrm{Opt}(\mathcal{S}(N)) = N \log(N) + \Theta(N) \tag{1}$$

$$\mathrm{Triv}(\mathcal{S}(N)) = s \cdot N \log(N) - \Theta(N) \tag{2}$$

$$\text{thus} \quad \frac{\mathrm{Triv}(\mathcal{S}(N))}{\mathrm{Opt}(\mathcal{S}(N))} = s - o(1) \tag{3}$$

As s is the average number of groups users are in, this shows that

> *asymptotically* (for a fixed set system $\mathcal{S}$ but with increasing number N of users) the update cost of an optimal key-derivation graph depends only on N (but not on $\mathcal{S}$). In this regime, the gain we get by using more cleverly chosen key-derivation graphs (as opposed to using a key-tree for every group) can be up to linear in s, the number of groups an average user is in, but not, say, the number of groups $|\mathcal{S}|$.

While we do not know how to efficiently find the best key graph for a given set system $\mathcal{S}$, in Sect. 4 we define a family $\mathcal{G}_{ao}(\mathcal{S}(N))$ which is asymptotically optimal, i.e., matches Eq. 1. Intuitively, it first partitions the universe of users $[N]$ into the sets of users that are members of exactly the same groups. More precisely, for $I \subseteq [k]$ let P_I be the set of users that are members of the groups specified by I. Then, the asymptotically optimal algorithm builds a balanced binary tree for every P_I, and in a second step connects the roots of these trees to the appropriate group keys by another layer of binary trees. For an illustration of the trivial and asymptotically optimal algorithms see Fig. 1.

1.2   The Non-asymptotic Setting

Asymptotics can Kick in Slowly. The asymptotic setting gives a good idea about the efficiency we can expect once the number of users N is large compared to the number $k = |\mathcal{S}|$ of groups. Nevertheless, it should be noted that this asymptotic effect can kick in only slowly: assume the artificial example where for some small base set $[n]$ we have a set system $\mathcal{S} = \{S_1, \ldots, S_k\}$ with $k = 2^n - 1$ groups where for every non-empty subset of users we have a group. Then each user is in 2^{n-1} groups and thus needs at least that many keys, and so the $\Theta(1)$ term in the asymptotic update cost $\log(N) + \Theta(1)$ of a single user is also at least 2^{n-1}. For

---

[1] $\mathcal{S}(N)$ is only well defined if N/n is an integer, we ignore this technicality as we will be interested in the case $N \to \infty$.

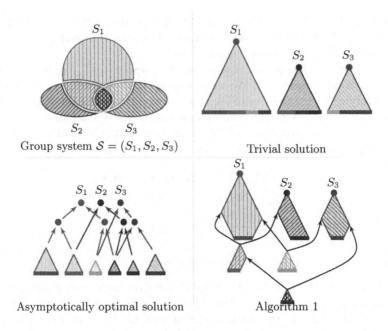

Fig. 1. Key graphs for group systems. Top left; Venn diagram of the considered group system. Top right; trivial key graph using one balanced binary tree per group. Bottom left; Asymptotically optimal key graph using one balanced binary tree per partition P_I. Bottom right; asymptotically optimal key graph obtained using Algorithm 1. In the depictions of key trees the horizontal thick lines indicates the users' personal keys.

the $\log(N)$ term to dominate we need $\log(N) \gg 2^{n-1}$, or $N \gg 2^{2^{n-1}}$, so the number of users needs to grow doubly exponential in the base set $[n]$.

Moving on to the non-asymptotic setting, consider a group system $\mathcal{S}$ for a fixed set of users $[N]$. The discussion above indicates that for $\mathcal{S}$ the asymptotic update cost per user of $\log(N)$ could be very far off the truth unless N becomes fairly large compared to the number of groups. This leaves the possibility that for concrete group systems where N is not huge relative to $\mathcal{S}$, already the trivial key-graph performs fairly well in practice. This, however, turns out to not be the case.

First, let us observe that the gap in update cost can never be larger than $\log(N)$, for any $\mathcal{S}$ over $[N]$

$$\mathrm{Triv}(\mathcal{S}) \leq \log(N) \cdot \mathrm{Opt}(\mathcal{S}) \tag{4}$$

To see this we observe that the update cost for every user $i \in [N]$ is at most a factor $\log(N)$ larger in the trivial solution: a user i that is in $s_i = |\{S \in \mathcal{S} : i \in S\}|$ groups has an update cost of at least s_i in any key graph, in particular in $\mathrm{Opt}(\mathcal{S})$, and at most $\sum_{S \in \mathcal{S}, i \in S} \log(|S|) \leq s_i \cdot \log(N)$ in the trivial key graph.

In Sect. 4.2 we will show that this is not merely a theoretical gap by giving an example of a natural system S for which the update costs of both the trivial and the asymptotically optimal algorithms match the gap of $\log(N)$.

A Greedy Algorithm Based on Huffman Codes. The discussion above indicates that for set systems mapping groups that we might encounter in practice, one should not simply use an asymptotically optimal solution, but aim for a solution that is optimal, or at least close to optimal, for all instances.

Algorithm 1 that we propose in Sect. 5 is an algorithm for computing a key-graph given a set system S. In a first step, the algorithm computes a "Boolean-lattice graph" for S, and in a second iteratively runs the algorithm to compute Huffman Codes to compute the key graph. As the algorithm is basically a composition of greedy algorithms, it is very efficient. We leave it as an open question whether it really is optimal, and if not, whether there's an efficient (polynomial time) algorithm to compute $\mathrm{Opt}(S)$ and find the corresponding key graph for a given S in general.[2]

We present Algorithm 1 in Sect. 5 and discuss its connection to Boolean lattices. Then, we derive concrete lower and upper bounds on its update cost, that can serve as a good estimate on how much it saves compared to the trivial algorithm and the asymptotically optimal algorithm of Sect. 1.1. We further show that Algorithm 1 and a class of algorithms generalizing the approach taken are optimal in the asymptotic setting. While the same is true for the algorithm discussed in Sect. 1.1, Algorithm 1 seems better suited for practical applications as key-derivation graphs constructed by it reflect the hierarchical structure inherent to such systems. An example of a key graph generated by it is in Fig. 1.

Our analysis concerns static group systems, but in the full version of this work [3] we show how known techniques that allow adding and removing users from groups in the settings of continuous group-key agreement and multicast encryption for a single group, can be adapted to key-derivation graphs generated by the greedy algorithm.

Lower Bounds. To get a feeling for how close to optimal our approach is, we prove a lower bound on the average update cost for arbitrary schemes for continuous group-key agreement (in Sect. 6) and multicast encryption (in the full version of this work [3]) that are based only on simple primitives such as encryption, pseudorandom generators, and secret sharing in a *symbolic security model*. This closely follows ideas from Micciancio and Panjwani [14], who considered such a symbolic model to analyze the worst-case update cost of multicast encryption schemes. We improve on their results by considering the setting of *multiple* potentially overlapping groups and proving a lower bound on the *average* communication complexity.

Our bound essentially shows that on average the cost of a user in any CGKA scheme or multicast encryption scheme for group system $S_1, \ldots, S_k$ constructed from the considered primitives satisfies

---

[2] The question whether a polynomial time algorithm for computing $\mathrm{Opt}(S)$ exists can be naturally asked in various ways. We discuss it in more detail in Sect. 7.

$$\text{Upd}(\mathcal{G}) \geq \frac{1}{N} \cdot \sum_{\emptyset \neq I \subseteq [k]} |P_I| \cdot \log(|P_I|) \ ,$$

where $P_I \subseteq [N]$ is the set of users *exactly* in the groups specified by index set $I \subseteq [k]$. We consider it an interesting open question to either improve on this bound or to construct an algorithm matching it.

1.3   Related Work

In the setting of a single group, key graphs have been used to construct secure multicast encryption, e.g. [7,15,16], and continuous group-key agreement (CGKA), e.g. [4,8]. In the setting of multiple groups, the approach to use binary trees for every set of users that are members of exactly the same groups similarly to the asymptotically optimal algorithm, has been suggested in [13,17]. However, the trees are then combined in a way that induces an overhead that is linear in the number of trees.

In [9], Cremers et al. consider the post-compromise security guarantees of CGKA protocols for multiple groups. They show that in certain update scenarios, protocols based on pairwise channels have better healing properties than protocols based on key trees, as updates in a single group also benefit all subgroups of it. We stress that these issues do not arise in our approach, as updates in our setting are global and thus affect all groups the updating user is a member of.

The symbolic security model was first introduced by Dolev and Yao [10] and used by Micciancio and Panjwani [14] to prove worst case bounds on the update cost of multicast encryption schemes for a single group. In the context of CGKA schemes it was recently used by Bienstock et al. [6], who analyze the communication cost of concurrent updates in CGKA schemes for a single group.

2   Preliminaries

2.1   Notation

Throughout the paper log denotes the logarithm with respect to base 2.

Graph Notation. Let $\mathcal{G} = (\mathcal{V}, \mathcal{E})$ be a directed acyclic graph (DAG). To node $v \in \mathcal{V}$ we associate the sets $\mathcal{A}(v) = \{v' \in \mathcal{V} \mid \exists \text{ path from } v' \text{ to } v\}$ of *ancestors* of v, and $\mathcal{D}(v) = \{v' \in \mathcal{V} \mid \exists \text{ path from } v \text{ to } v'\}$ of *descendants* of v. Here, we allow paths of length 0 and hence $v \in \mathcal{A}(v)$ and $v \in \mathcal{D}(v)$. Let $\mathcal{G}' = (\mathcal{V}', \mathcal{G}')$ be a subgraph of $\mathcal{G}$ and $v \in \mathcal{V}'$. We denote the set of parents of v by $\mathcal{P}(v)$. The set of *co-parents* $\mathcal{CP}(v, \mathcal{G}') \subseteq \mathcal{V}$ of v with respect to $\mathcal{G}'$ in $\mathcal{G}$ is the set of vertices that are parents of v in $\mathcal{G}$ but not in $\mathcal{G}'$.

Probability Distributions. Let X be a random variable with outcomes $x_1, \dots, x_\ell$ with probability $p_1, \dots, p_\ell$. Then we denote by $\mathbb{E}[X]$ its expectation and by $H(X) = -\sum_{i=1}^{\ell} p_i \log(p_i)$ its Shannon entropy.

2.2 Huffman Codes

Given a collection $v_1, \cdots, v_\ell$ of disconnected leaves of weight $w_1, \ldots, w_\ell \in \mathbb{N}$ a *Huffman Tree* is constructed as follows. From the set $\{v_1, \ldots, v_\ell\}$ two nodes v_{i_1}, v_{i_2} with the smallest weights are picked. Then a node v and edges $(v_{i_1}, v), (v_{i_2}, v)$ are added to the graph. v's weight is set to $w_{i_1} + w_{i_2}$ and the set of nodes to be considered updated to $\{v_1, \ldots, v_\ell\} \cup \{v\} \backslash \{v_{i_1}, v_{i_2}\}$. This step is repeated until all leaves are collected under a single root.

Since all nodes have indegree 2 the Huffman tree defines a prefix-free binary code for $(v_1, \ldots, v_\ell)$. We will make use of the following property of Huffman Codes.

Lemma 1 (Optimality of Huffman Codes [11]). *Consider a Huffman tree $\mathcal{T}$ over leaves $v_1, \ldots, v_\ell$ of weight $w_1, \ldots, w_\ell \in \mathbb{N}$. Let $w = \sum_{i=1}^{\ell} w_i$ and let $U_\mathcal{T}$ denote the probability distribution that picks leaf v_i with probability w_i/w proportional to its weight. Then, if $\mathrm{len}(U_\mathcal{T})$ denotes the random variable measuring the length of the path from a leaf picked according to $U_\mathcal{T}$ to the root, we have that the average length of such paths is bounded by*

$$H(U_\mathcal{T}) \leq \mathbb{E}[\mathrm{len}(U_\mathcal{T})] \leq H(U_\mathcal{T}) + 1 \ .$$

3 Key-Derivation Graphs for Multiple Groups

In this section we discuss key-derivation graphs for systems consisting of multiple groups. In Sect. 3.1 we briefly recall two applications of such graphs; continuous group-key agreement and multicast encryption. In Sect. 3.2 we formally define key-derivation graphs, discuss how key material in a graph is refreshed, and define its update cost.

3.1 Continuous Group-Key Agreement and Multicast Encryption

Continuous Group-Key Agreement. *Continuous group-key agreement* (CGKA) schemes [1] are an important building block in the construction of secure asynchronous group messaging schemes. As the name indicates, the goal of a CGKA scheme is to establish a common key that is to be used to secure the communication between members of a group. As groups can typically be long-lived, users need to also be able to frequently update the key material known to them, to on one hand, recover from a potential compromise and, on the other hand, ensure forward-secrecy of messages sent in the past.

In this work we are interested in the more general setting in which users $n \in [N]$ want to agree on keys for a system of groups $S_1, \ldots, S_k \subseteq 2^{[N]}$. After the groups have been established in a setup phase user n can use the procedure $\mathrm{Upd}(n)$ to produce an update message that rotates the key material known to them, thus eliminating any keys that may have leaked during a compromise. This update message is broadcast to the other users using the untrusted delivery server. Given their own secret keys, users are then able to retrieve the refreshed keys that should be known to them. A natural goal to aim for is to minimize the communication cost incurred by such update messages.

Naturally, one would like to additionally support dynamic operations, i.e., allow users to add and remove other users from groups in the system. While in this work we focus on the update costs of schemes for a system of static groups, in the full version of this work [3] we show that the known techniques of blanking and unmerged leaves used in the MLS protocol [4] can be adapted to schemes obtained from our approach.

Efficient CGKA protocols [4,8] (in the single group setting) establish a key-derivation graph in the setup phase that, in turn, allows user to update at a cost that is logarithmic in the number of group members.[3] In Sect. 3.2 we formally define key-derivation graphs and discuss how the updating process works.

Multicast Encryption. The goal of a *multicast encryption* scheme [7,15,16] is to establish a key for a group of users to enable them to decrypt ciphertexts broadcast to the group. Every user holds a personal long-term key, but opposed to CGKA there also exists a central authority that has access to all secret key material. After a setup phase, the central authority is able to add and remove users from the group by refreshing key material and broadcasting messages to the group. The central goal in the construction of multicast schemes is to minimize the communication complexity incurred by such operations. Typically, multicast encryption schemes also rely on key-derivation graphs.

As in the case of CGKA, we are interested in the more general setting of a system of potentially overlapping groups of users.

3.2   Key-Derivation Graphs

We now discuss key-derivation graphs. In our exposition we will focus on graphs for continuous group-key agreement. At the end of the section we discuss the differences to graphs for multicast encryption.

Consider a set of parties $[N]$ and a collection $\mathcal{S} \subseteq 2^{[N]}$ of subgroups of $[N]$. A key-derivation graph (kdg) for $[N]$ and $\mathcal{S}$ organizes key pairs in a way that allows the members of a particular subgroup to agree on a key, and further enables parties to refresh the key material known to them. Every node v in the graph is associated to a key pair $(\mathsf{pk}_v, \mathsf{sk}_v)$ of a public-key encryption scheme $(\mathsf{KGen}, \mathsf{Enc}, \mathsf{Dec})$, and edges (v, v') indicate that parties with access to sk_v also posses $\mathsf{sk}_{v'}$. The personal keys of users correspond to sources and every group is represented by a node that holds the corresponding secret group key. We formalize the structural requirements on the graph in the multi-group setting as follows.

---

[3] In order to ensure authenticity of update messages and to prevent the server from sending users inconsistent update messages these protocols employ additional techniques. We leave the question how to adapt these to key-derivation graphs for multiple groups to future work (See Sect. 7).

Definition 1. *Let $N \in \mathbb{N}$, $\mathcal{S} \subseteq 2^{[N]}$, and $\mathcal{G} = (\mathcal{V}, \mathcal{E})$ a DAG. We say that $\mathcal{G}$ is a* key-derivation graph *for universe of elements $[N]$ and groups $\mathcal{S}$ if*

1. *For every $n \in [N]$ there exists a source $v_n \in \mathcal{V}$ and for every $S \in \mathcal{S}$ there exists a node $v_S \in \mathcal{V}$. We further require that $v_n \neq v'_n$ for $n \neq n'$.*
2. *For $n \in [N]$ and $S \in \mathcal{S}$ we have $v_S \in \mathcal{D}(v_n)$ exactly if $n \in S$.*

In the definition above node v_n correspond to user n's personal key, and nodes v_S to group keys. The second property encodes correctness and security, intuitively saying that n is able to derive the group key of S exactly if $n \in S$.

Updates. Let $\mathcal{G}$ be a key-derivation graph for $[N]$ and $\mathcal{S}$. If party n wants to perform an update she has to refresh all key-material corresponding the subgraph $\mathcal{D}(v_n)$ known to her and communicate the change to the other parties. To this end she picks a spanning tree $\mathcal{T}_n = (\mathcal{V}', \mathcal{E}')$ of $\mathcal{D}(v_n)$, as well as a random seed Δ_{v_n}. Then starting from the source v_n, if v' is the ith child of node v she defines the seed of v' as $\Delta_{v'} = \mathsf{H}(\Delta_v, i)$, where H is a hash function. $\Delta_{v'}$ is then used to derive a new key-pair $(\mathsf{pk}_{v'}, \mathsf{sk}_{v'}) \leftarrow \mathsf{KGen}(\Delta_{v'})$ for v'. Finally, for every $v \in \mathcal{V}'$ and every co-parent $v' \in \mathcal{CP}(v, \mathcal{T}_n)$, n computes the ciphertext $c_{v,v'} = \mathsf{Enc}(\mathsf{pk}_{v'}, \Delta_v)$. The set of all ciphertexts together with the set of new public keys forms the update message. Finally, n deletes all seeds Δ_v.

We now show that the construction preserves correctness, i.e., users $n' \neq n$ are able to deduce all new secret keys in $\mathcal{D}(v_{n'})$ from the update message and thus in particular the group keys of all groups they are a member of. To this end, let $v \in \mathcal{D}(v_n) \cap \mathcal{D}(v_{n'})$. Then there exists a path $(v_{n'} = v_1, \ldots, v_\ell = v)$ in $\mathcal{D}(v_{n'})$. Let i be maximal with $v_i \notin \mathcal{D}(v_n)$ (Note that such i must exist as $v_{n'}$ is a source). By maximality of i the node v_i must be a coparent of v_{i+1} with respect to $\mathcal{D}(v_n)$. Thus, the update message contains an encryption of $\Delta_{v_{i+1}}$ to pk_{v_i}. As sk_{v_i} was not replaced by the update and is known to n' the user can recover $\Delta_{v_{i+1}}$ and in turn $\mathsf{sk}_{v_{i+1}}$. Now, n' can recover the remaining $\Delta_{v_{i+2}}, \ldots, \Delta_{v_\ell}$ and the corresponding secret keys as the seeds were either derived by hashing or, in the case that v_{j+1} is a coparent of v_j with respect to $\mathcal{D}(v_n)$, encrypted to the new key pk_{v_j}, the secret key of which was already recovered by n'.

Update Cost. Using the size of ciphertexts as a unit, the update cost of n is given by $\mathrm{Upd}(n) = \sum_{v \in \mathcal{T}_n} |\mathcal{CP}(v, \mathcal{T}_n)| = \sum_{v \in \mathcal{T}_n} (|\mathcal{P}(v)| - 1)$. Note that this quantity is independent of the particular choice of spanning tree $\mathcal{T}_n$. In this work we are interested in minimizing the *average* update cost, assuming that every user updates with the same probability. We define the *total update cost* $\mathrm{Upd}(\mathcal{G}) = \sum_{n \in [N]} \mathrm{Upd}(n)$ of $\mathcal{G}$. Note that $\mathrm{Upd}(\mathcal{G})/N$ is the average update cost of a user, and we can thus focus on trying to minimize $\mathrm{Upd}(\mathcal{G})$, which will allow for easier exposition. The following lemma shows that we can restrict our view to graphs in which every non-source has indegree 2. Note, that for graphs $\mathcal{G}$ with this property we have $|\mathcal{CP}(v, \mathcal{T}_n)| = 1$ for every n, $\mathcal{T}_n$, and $v \in \mathcal{T}_n$ that is not a source and thus in this case we can compute the update cost as

$$\mathrm{Upd}(\mathcal{G}) = \sum_{n \in [N]} (|\mathcal{T}_n| - 1) = \sum_{n \in [N]} (|\mathcal{D}(n)| - 1) = \sum_{n \in [N]} |\mathcal{D}(n)| - N . \quad (5)$$

Lemma 2. *Let* $n \in \mathbb{N}$, $\mathcal{S} \subseteq 2^{[N]}$, *and* $\mathcal{G}$ *a key-derivation graph for* $[N]$ *and* $\mathcal{S}$. *Then there exists a key-derivation graph* $\mathcal{G}'$ *for* $[N]$ *and* $\mathcal{S}$ *satisfying* $\mathrm{Upd}(\mathcal{G}') \leq \mathrm{Upd}(\mathcal{G})$ *such that for every non-source* $v \in \mathcal{V}'$ *we have* $\mathrm{indeg}(v) = 2$.

Due to space constraints we defer the proof to the full version of this work [3].

Key-Derivation Graphs for Multicast Encryption. Opposed to kdgs for CGKA key-derivation graphs for multicast encryption rely on symmetric encryption. Let (E, D) be a symmetric encryption scheme. Every node v in a kdg $\mathcal{G}$ for $[N]$ and $\mathcal{S}$ is associated to a key k_v, and an edge (v, v') indicates that a party with access to k_v knows $\mathsf{k}_{v'}$. We require structural requirements on $\mathcal{G}$ that are analogous to Definition 1. Updates with respect to leaf v_n, which for multicast encryption are computed by the central authority, and their update cost, are defined analogous to the setting of CGKA as well.

While the main goal of multicast encryption is not to recover from compromise of keys by updating, but instead to allow the central authority to dynamically change the structure of the groups $S_1, \dots, S_k$, the notion of an update with respect to a leaf v_n still turns out to be useful. Assume that the central authority performed an update for v_n starting with seed Δ. We can distinguish two cases. If Δ is not known to the owner n of leaf v_n then n lost access to all keys corresponding to $\mathcal{D}(v_n)$. Thus, by updating, the central authority can remove a party from *all* groups they are a member of. Assume on the other hand that the leaf was previously unpopulated and that Δ can be derived from n's long term key. Then n gained access to all group keys that can be reached from v_n. In the full version of this work [3] we discuss how updates can be used as the basic building block of implementing more fine grained operations, i.e., adding or removing a user from particular group S_i. The efficiency of these operations is significantly determined by the update cost as defined in this section.

3.3 Security

The main focus of this work is to investigate the communication complexity of key-derivation graphs for group systems. We do not give formal security proofs in this work. The structural requirements on kdgs and definition of update procedures are chosen with the goal of the resulting CGKA to achieve *post-compromise forward-secrecy* (PCFS) [2] roughly corresponding to *post-compromise security* (PCS) and *forward-secrecy* (FS) simultaneously. In the following paragraphs we provide an intuition on the security properties of kdgs. For ease of exposition we will discuss PCS and FS separately instead of PCFS.

Note that CGKA schemes constructed from kdgs employ further mechanisms to ensure authenticity and prevent a malicious sever to send users inconsistent update messages. We consider the construction of such mechanisms as well as a formal security analysis of kdgs to be important open questions for future work.

Preserving the Graph Invariant. We first discuss how updates preserve the invariant, that users n know exactly the secret keys corresponding to $\mathcal{D}(v_n)$, which by

Condition 2 of Definition 1 implies that n will never be able to derive a group key for some group they are not a member of. Note that if n is the updating user then they will only replace keys in $\mathcal{D}(v_n)$. If n receives an update message, on the other hand, then they will only be able to recover a key sk_v if either the corresponding seed Δ_v was encrypted to a key known to n or if Δ_v was derived by hashing from a seed $\Delta_{v'}$ recoverable by n. By iteratively applying this argument to $\Delta_{v'}$ we obtain that there must exist some $\Delta_{v''}$ that was encrypted to a key known to n such that v'' has a path to v. Thus, it must hold that $v \in \mathcal{D}(v_n)$. (Note that the one-wayness of the used hash function ensures that seeds derived by hashing can only be recovered from each other in the correct direction.)

Post-Compromise Security. The goal of PCS is to allow users whose secret state has been exposed to recover from this exposure by performing an update. Using the example of a single compromised user we now discuss how kdgs for group systems achieve this property. Assume that an adversary knows exactly the secret state of user n, i.e., all keys sk_v for $v \in \mathcal{D}(v_n)$, and that n then performs an update. Then the adversary is not able to deduce any of the replaced keys: Note that the initial random seed Δ_{v_n} is not encrypted to any key and thus cannot be leaked to the adversary. Thus, all other seeds Δ_v can only be derived by the adversary if Δ_v itself, or a seed from which Δ_v was derived by iterated hashing was encrypted to a key known to the adversary. However, the adversary only knows the keys corresponding to $\mathcal{D}(v_n)$ before the update, and those keys were replaced by freshly sampled ones before computing the ciphertexts. Thus, seeds are encrypted to either "old" keys not known to the adversary or new keys, and so after the update all keys are secure again.

Forward Secrecy. Forward secrecy requires that compromising a user's secret state does not allow the adversary to recover previous group keys. In key-derivation graphs old keys get deleted over time providing a limited form of forward-secrecy. Concretely, if a user n is corrupted all group keys before their last update remain secure. This holds, since seeds that were generated before this point in time and can be used to recover group keys were encrypted to keys no longer in n's memory. Note however, that group keys generated in between n's last update and the time of n's corruption might leak to the adversary. For example, a seed from which such keys can be derived might have been encrypted to the key sk_{v_n}, which remained unchanged until the corruption.

Improved Forward Secrecy Using Supergroups. CGKA constructions relying on kdgs like TreeKEM [5] rely on an additional mechanism to improve their forward-secrecy guarantees. Instead of directly using group keys sk_{v_S} to communicate within the group these keys are used to derive a so called *application secret* K that serves as the symmetric key for group communication. Whenever an update occurs, the new application secret of S is computed as $\mathsf{H}_2(\mathsf{sk}_{v_S}, K)$ the output of a hash function on input of the new group key and the previous application secret. Then, the old application secret is deleted from memory. The effect of this is that when a user's state leaks (including the current application secret K_t), no old application secret K_i can be recomputed from old update messages, unless K_{i-1} was already known to the adversary by former corruptions. In short, users gain the advantage of forward secrecy not only by issuing but also by processing updates of other users in S.

In the setting of a group system $\mathcal{S}$ we can further improve on this: Consider some group $S \in \mathcal{S}$ and let $S_1, \ldots, S_\ell$ be the maximal (with respect to inclusion) groups in $\mathcal{S}$ that contain S. We denote the application secrets for S and the S_i by K_S and K_{S_i} respectively. Now, whenever a member of any of the S_i issues an update the application secret of S is updated to $K_S \leftarrow \mathsf{H}_2(\mathsf{sk}_{v_S}, K_{S_1}, \ldots, K_{S_\ell})$.[4] Note that for every i since $S \subseteq S_i$ all members of S do indeed have access to K_{S_i} and thus are able to compute K_S, and that an update by users in S implies that all S_i are updated as well. The effect of this modification is that even updates by users *outside* of S—more precisely in any of the sets $S_i \backslash S$—imply forward secrecy of users in S. Note that this is in particular helpful in the case where $|S| \ll |S_i|$ and updates in the large group occur much more frequently than in the small group, for example in the case of two members of a large group having a private conversation.

3.4 The Trivial Algorithm

To construct a key-derivation graph for a single group S the parties $n \in S$ are typically arranged as the leaves of a balanced binary tree $\mathcal{T}$. The tree's root serves as the group key. In this case the length of paths from leaf to root is at most $\lceil \log(|S|) \rceil$ and in turn $\mathrm{Upd}(\mathcal{T}) \leq |S| \cdot \lceil \log(|S|) \rceil$. On the other hand, $\mathcal{T}$ defines a prefix-free binary code for the set S. Thus, by Shannon's source coding theorem the average length of paths from leaf to root is at least $\log(|S|)$ which implies $\mathrm{Upd}(\mathcal{T}) \geq |S| \cdot \log(|S|)$.

An Algorithm for Multiple Groups. A trivial approach to construct a key derivation graph for parties $[N]$ and group system $\mathcal{S} = \{S_1, \ldots, S_k\}$ is to simply apply the method described above to all S_i in parallel. That is, for $i \in [k]$ construct a balanced binary tree $\mathcal{T}_i$ with $|S_i|$ leaves such that for $n \in [N]$ the node v_n is a leaf of exactly the trees $\mathcal{T}_i$ with $n \in S_i$. Let $\mathcal{G}$ denote the resulting graph. The conditions of Definition 1 clearly hold and we can bound the total update cost of $\mathcal{G}$ by

$$\sum_{i \in [k]} |S_i| \cdot \log(|S_i|) \leq \mathrm{Upd}(\mathcal{G}) \leq \sum_{i \in [k]} |S_i| \cdot \lceil \log(|S_i|) \rceil \ .$$

Further, the update cost of a single user $n \in [N]$ is bounded by $\mathrm{Upd}(n) \leq \sum_{i:n \in S_i} \lceil \log(|S_i|) \rceil$.

4 Key-Derivation Graphs in the Asymptotic Setting

In this section we investigate the update cost of key-derivation graphs for multiple groups in an asymptotic setting. More precisely, for a system consisting of

---

[4] Regarding PCFS it might even be advantageous to include $K_{S'}$ for *all* $S' \supseteq S$.

a fixed number of groups, we consider the setting in which the number of users tends to infinity while the relative size of the groups stays constant. In Sect. 4.1 we first compute the asymptotically optimal update cost of key-derivation graphs and then show that the trivial algorithm does not achieve it. We then present an algorithm achieving the optimal update cost. In Sect. 4.2 we show that both approaches can perform badly for *concrete* group systems.

4.1 Key-Derivation Graphs in the Asymptotic Setting

We investigate the update cost of key derivation graphs in an asymptotic setting. That is, we consider N parties that form a subgroup system $\mathcal{S} = \{S_1, \ldots, S_k\}$ and fix values $p_I \in [0, 1]$ for $I \subseteq [k]$ that indicate the fraction of users that are members of exactly the groups specified by I.

More precisely, let $k \in \mathbb{N}_{\geq 2}$ be fixed and let $\{p_I\}_{I \subseteq [k]}$ be such that $\sum_{I \subseteq [k]} p_I = 1$. For $N \in \mathbb{N}$ let $\mathcal{S}(N) = \{S_1(N), \ldots, S_k(N)\} \subseteq 2^{[N]}$ be a subgroup system that satisfies $|P_I(N)| = N \cdot p_I$ for all I, where $P_I(N) = \bigcap_{i \in I} S_i(N) \setminus \bigcup_{j \in [k] \setminus I} S_j(N)$ is the set of users exactly in the groups specified by I.[5] Throughout this section we assume that $p_\emptyset = 0$, i.e., every user is in at least one group, and that at least two groups are non-empty. We are interested in the update cost of key-derivation graphs for $\mathcal{S}(N)$ when N tends to infinity.

Lower Bound in the Asymptotic Setting. We first compute a lower bound on the update cost of kdgs in the asymptotic setting. The bound follows from the following combinatorial result on *concrete* graphs, that will also turn out to be useful for our symbolic lower bound of Sect. 6. Recall that for graphs $\mathcal{G}' \subseteq \mathcal{G}$ and a vertex v the set $\mathcal{CP}(v, \mathcal{G}')$ is the set of co-parents of v with respect to $\mathcal{G}'$ in $\mathcal{G}$. Due to space constraints, we defer its proof to the full version of this work [3].

Lemma 3. *Let $M \in \mathbb{N}$ be fixed, $S_1, \ldots, S_k \subseteq [M]$, and let $\mathcal{G} = (\mathcal{V}, \mathcal{E})$ be a DAG such that there exist pairwise disjoint sets of sources V_n, $n \in [M]$, and nodes v_{S_i}, $i \in \{1, \ldots, k\}$ such that*

$$n \in S_i \quad \Rightarrow \quad \exists v_n \in V_n \text{ such that there is a path from } v_n \text{ to } v_{S_i} .$$

Further let $\mathcal{T}_n$ be a spanning forest of $\mathcal{D}(V_n) = \bigcup_{v_n \in V_n} \mathcal{D}(v_n)$. Then

$$M \cdot \mathbb{E}\Big[\sum_{v \in \mathcal{T}_n} |\mathcal{CP}(v, \mathcal{T}_n)| \Big] \geq \sum_{\emptyset \neq I \subseteq [k]} |P_I| \cdot \log(|P_I|) ,$$

where the expectation is to be understood with respect to the uniform distribution on $[N]$.

Note that Lemma 3 in the case $|V_n| = 1$ for all n can be seen as a lower bound on the total update cost of key-derivation graphs as defined in Sect. 3 since $M \cdot \mathbb{E}[\sum_{v \in \mathcal{T}_n} |\mathcal{CP}(v, \mathcal{T}_n)|] = \sum_{v \in \mathcal{T}_n} |\mathcal{CP}(v, \mathcal{T}_n)|$.

---

[5] $\mathcal{S}(N)$ is only well defined if $N \cdot p_I$ is an integer for all I, we ignore this technicality as we are interested in the case $N \to \infty$.

Turning to the asymptotic setting we have

$$\sum_{I\subseteq[k]} N \cdot p_I \cdot \log(N \cdot p_I) = N \cdot \sum_{I\subseteq[k]} p_I \log(N) + N \cdot \sum_{I\subseteq[k]} p_I \log(p_I)$$

$$= N\log(N) + N \cdot \sum_{I\subseteq[k]} \log(p_I) = N\log(N) + \Theta(N) \ ,$$

where we used that $\sum_I p_I = 1$. As we will show below, there exist key-derivation graphs matching this bound. We conclude that the optimal update cost in the asymptotic setting only depends on the overall number of users but not the particular set system:

$$\mathrm{Opt}(\mathcal{S}(N)) = N\log(N) + \Theta(N) \ .$$

Note, however, that the term $\Theta(N)$ hides a constant (with respect to N), that can be *exponential in k*.

Asymptotic Update Cost of the Trivial Algorithm. The trivial algorithm constructs a separate balanced binary tree for every group $S_i(N)$. For $i \in [k]$ let s_i be such that $N \cdot s_i = |S_i(N)|$ and further let $s = \sum_{i=1}^{k} s_i$ be the average number of groups a user are member of. Then, we can bound the update cost $\mathrm{Triv}(\mathcal{S}(N))$ of the trivial algorithm in the asymptotic setting as follows, showing that is does not match the optimal cost.

Claim. For $I \subseteq [k]$ let $p_I \in [0,1]$ be such that $\sum_{I\subseteq[k]} p_I = 1$ and $p_\emptyset = 0$. Let $\mathcal{S}(N)$ be the corresponding group system and s_i, s as defined above. Then

$$\mathrm{Triv}(\mathcal{S}(N)) = s \cdot N\log(N) + \Theta(N) \ .$$

Due to space constraints we defer the proof of this claim to the full version of this work [3].

An Asymptotically Optimal Graph. We will sketch how to construct an asymptotically optimal key graph $\mathcal{G}_{\mathrm{ao}}(N)$ for a given set system $\mathcal{S}$ over $[n]$. In a first step, for every I with $P_I(N) \neq \emptyset$, the algorithm constructs a balanced binary tree with root v_I using as leafs the elements of $P_I(N)$. Then, in a second step, for every group $S_i(N)$ it builds a balanced binary tree with root v_{S_i} using as leafs the nodes $\{v_I \mid I : i \in I\}$. An illustration of the algorithm's working principle is in Fig. 1. Correctness of the construction follows by inspection.

To bound the update cost $\mathrm{Upd}(\mathcal{G}_{\mathrm{oa}}(N))$ we split it in two parts; the first accounts for the contribution of the nodes generated during the first step, the second for the contribution of the second step. As $\sum_I p_I = 1$, the first part

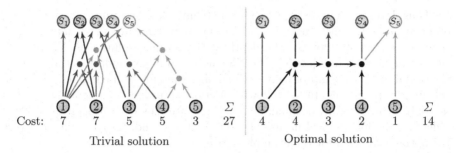

Fig. 2. Illustration of $\mathrm{Triv}(\mathcal{S}_N^\uparrow)$ (left) and $\mathrm{Opt}(\mathcal{S}_N^\uparrow)$ for $N = 5$. For each user, the update cost (i.e., the indegree 2 nodes reachable) is indicated.

contributes at most $\sum_{I\subseteq[k]} p_I \cdot N \cdot \log(N \cdot p_I) \leq N \cdot \log N$, while the contribution of the second part for every single user is constant as $\{v_I\}$ is independent of N, implying that with respect to the total update cost it is $\Theta(N)$. Thus, overall we get $\mathrm{Upd}(\mathcal{G}_{\mathrm{oa}}(N)) \leq N \cdot \log N + \Theta(N)$, matching the optimal update cost.

4.2 Update Cost for Concrete Group Systems

Now consider a concrete group system $\mathcal{S} = \{S_1, \ldots, S_k\}$ for a fixed set of users $[N]$. As already discussed in Sect. 1.2, it is possible that the number k of groups can be as large as $2^N - 1$. Thus, for concrete group systems the asymptotic update cost per user of $\log(N)$ (that contains hidden constants dependent on k) derived in Sect. 4.1 could be very far off the truth unless N becomes fairly large compared to the number of groups. This leaves the possibility that in the case where N is not huge relative to k, already the trivial key-graph performs fairly well in practice. In this section we show that this is not the case by giving an example where not only the trivial key-graph (which has a balanced tree for every set), but also our asymptotically optimal $\mathcal{G}_{\mathrm{oa}}$, perform poorly.

Recall that by Eq. 4 the update costs of the trivial and optimal solutions always satisfy $\mathrm{Triv}(\mathcal{S}) \leq \log(N) \cdot \mathrm{Opt}(\mathcal{S})$. The above argument seems very loose, but we show an example where we indeed have a gap of $\approx \log(N) - 1$ and thus almost match this seemingly loose $\log(N)$ bound. Define the "hierarchical" set system $\mathcal{S}_N^\uparrow$ over $[N]$ as

$$\mathcal{S}_N^\uparrow := \{S_1, \ldots, S_N\} \quad \text{where} \quad S_i = \{i, i+1, \ldots, N\} \ .$$

Note that while $\mathcal{S}_N^\uparrow$ is defined for all N, it is not asymptotic in the sense discussed in Sect. 4.1, as the number of groups grows with the number of users N. Further, for this group system the key derivation graphs output by the trivial and asymptotically optimal algorithms coincide, as for every P_I with $P_I \neq \emptyset$ we have $|P_I| = 1$. As the optimal solution for $\mathcal{S}$ is just a path, as illustrated in Fig. 2, we obtain update costs of $\mathrm{Triv}(\mathcal{S}_N^\uparrow) = \sum_{i=1}^N i \log(i) \approx \frac{N^2}{2} \log(N)$ and $\mathrm{Opt}(\mathcal{S}_N^\uparrow) = \sum_{i=1}^N i = \frac{N(N+1)}{2} \approx \frac{N^2}{2}$.

Thus $\text{Triv}(\mathcal{S}_N^\uparrow)/\text{Opt}(\mathcal{S}_N^\uparrow) \approx \log(N)$ matching the (4) bound. An interesting observation is the fact that an optimal solution can have much larger *depth* than the trivial one: for $\mathcal{S}_N^\uparrow$ the depth of the optimal solution is N, while in the trivial solution it is just $\log(N)$. The discussion above indicates that neither the trivial nor the asymptotically optimal algorithm are well-equipped to handle certain group systems. In the following section we propose an algorithm that is not only asymptotically optimal, but also generates key-derivation graphs better reflecting the hierarchical nature of group systems, and, in particular, recovers the optimal solution for the example above.

5 A Greedy Algorithm Based on Huffman Codes

In this section we propose an algorithm to compute key-derivation graphs for group systems. Its formal description is in Sect. 5.1. In Sect. 5.2 we compute bounds on its total update cost and compare it to the trivial algorithm and the asymptotically optimal algorithm of Sect. 4.1. Finally, in Sect. 5.3 we show that the algorithm, as well as a class generalizing it, are asymptotically optimal.

5.1 Algorithm Description

We now describe Algorithm 1 that, on input parties $[N]$ and a set of groups $\mathcal{S} \subseteq 2^{[N]}$, constructs a key-derivation graph. Its formal description is in Fig. 3.

Conceptually, the algorithm proceeds in two phases. The first phase (lines 1 to 11) determines the macro structure of the key-derivation graph. For reasons explained below we will refer to the graph generated in this phase as the *lattice graph*. In the second phase (lines 12 to 20), sources for the individual users are added at the correct position in the lattice graph, which afterwards is binarized to reduce the update size.

More precisely, at the beginning of the first phase the algorithm initializes a graph $\mathcal{G} = (\mathcal{V}, \mathcal{E})$ consisting of isolated nodes $v_{S'}$ with $S' \in \mathcal{S}$ that, looking ahead, will represent the group keys. Every node $v_{S'}$ is associated to a set $\mathsf{S}(v_{S'})$ that is initialized to group S'. The algorithm then determines nodes v_1, v_2 such that the intersection of their associated sets is maximal and adds a node v_3 as well as the edges $(v_3, v_1), (v_3, v_2)$ to the graph. The associated set of v_3 is set to $\mathsf{S}(v_1) \cap \mathsf{S}(v_2)$ and the associated sets of v_1 and v_2 are updated to $\mathsf{S}(v_1)\backslash\mathsf{S}(v_3)$ and $\mathsf{S}(v_2)\backslash\mathsf{S}(v_3)$ respectively. This step is repeated until the associated sets of all nodes are pairwise disjoint.

Let $\mathcal{G}_{\text{lat}} = (\mathcal{V}_{\text{lat}}, \mathcal{E}_{\text{lat}})$ denote the resulting lattice graph. In the second phase, for every node $v \in \mathcal{V}_{\text{lat}}$ for all $n \in \mathsf{S}(v)$, a source v_n representing user n together with edge (v_n, v') is added to the graph. Finally, for every node v with $\text{indeg}(v) \geq 3$, a Huffman tree from the parents to the node is built. Here, the weight of a source is 1, and the weight of non-sources is given as the number of sources below it.

Input: $(N, \mathcal{S})$

1: $\quad \mathcal{G} = (\mathcal{V}, \mathcal{E}) \leftarrow (\emptyset, \emptyset)$

2: $\quad$ **for** $S' \in \mathcal{S}$

3: $\quad\quad \mathcal{V} \leftarrow \mathcal{V} \cup \{v_{S'}\}$

4: $\quad\quad \mathsf{S}(v_{S'}) \leftarrow S'$

5: $\quad$ **while** the sets associated to $\mathcal{V}$ are not disjoint

6: $\quad\quad v_1, v_2 \leftarrow \underset{v_1, v_2 \in \mathcal{V}}{\arg\max}(|\mathsf{S}(v_1) \cap \mathsf{S}(v_2)|)$

7: $\quad\quad$ add the node v_3

8: $\quad\quad \mathsf{S}(v_3) \leftarrow \mathsf{S}(v_1) \cap \mathsf{S}(v_2)$

9: $\quad\quad \mathsf{S}(v_1) \leftarrow \mathsf{S}(v_1) \setminus \mathsf{S}(v_3)$

10: $\quad\quad \mathsf{S}(v_2) \leftarrow \mathsf{S}(v_2) \setminus \mathsf{S}(v_3)$

11: $\quad\quad$ add the edges $(v_3, v_1), (v_3, v_2)$

12: $\quad$ **for** $v \in \mathcal{V}$

13: $\quad\quad$ **for** $n \in \mathsf{S}(v)$

14: $\quad\quad\quad$ add the node v_n

15: $\quad\quad\quad$ add the edge (v_n, v)

16: $\quad\quad \mathsf{S}(v) \leftarrow \mathsf{S}(v) \setminus \{n\}$

17: $\quad$ compute the weight of each node as the number of sources below it

18: $\quad$ **for** every node with indegree > 1

19: $\quad\quad$ build a Huffman tree from the parents to the node

20: $\quad$ **return** $\mathcal{G}$

Fig. 3. Algorithm 1

Properties of the Lattice Graph. We now derive several properties of the lattice graph, which will be used to prove correctness and compute bounds on the total update cost of the generated key-derivation graph. Thus, let $\mathcal{G}_{\mathrm{lat}} = (\mathcal{V}_{\mathrm{lat}}, \mathcal{E}_{\mathrm{lat}})$ be the lattice graph generated on input of $[N]$ and set of k groups $\mathcal{S} = \{S_1, \ldots, S_k\} \subseteq 2^{[N]}$. For index set $I' \subseteq [k]$ we denoted by

$$P_{I'} := \bigcap_{i \in I'} S_i \setminus \bigcup_{j \in [k] \setminus I'} S_j \;,$$

the set of parties that are members of exactly the groups specified by I. Further, for $v \in \mathcal{V}_{\mathrm{lat}}$ we define

$$I(v) := \{i \in [k] \mid \text{exists path from } v \text{ to } v_{S_i}\} \;,$$

the index set of group nodes that can be reached from v. Finally, for a collection $\mathcal{V}' \subseteq \mathcal{V}$ of nodes we generalize the notation for associated sets to $\mathsf{S}(\mathcal{V}') := \cup_{v \in \mathcal{V}'} \mathsf{S}(v)$. We obtain the following.

Lemma 4. *Let $N, k \in \mathbb{N}$, $\mathcal{S} = \{S_1, \ldots, S_k\} \subseteq 2^{[N]}$, and let $\mathcal{G}_{\text{lat}} = (\mathcal{V}_{\text{lat}}, \mathcal{E}_{\text{lat}})$ be the lattice graph generated on input $([N], \mathcal{S})$. Then the following holds.*

1. *Let $v, v' \in \mathcal{V}_{\text{lat}}$ be such that $I(v) = I(v')$. Then $v = v'$.*
2. *$I(v) \neq \emptyset$ for all $v \in \mathcal{V}_{\text{lat}}$.*
3. *For every $v \in \mathcal{V}_{\text{lat}}$ and every $i \in I(v)$ there is exactly one path from v to v_{S_i}.*
4. *Consider the ancestor graph $\mathcal{A}(v)$ for $v \in \mathcal{V}_{\text{lat}}$. Then*

$$\bigcup_{v' \in \mathcal{A}(v)} \mathsf{S}(v') \subseteq \bigcap_{i \in I(v)} S_i .$$

   If $|I(v)| = 1$ then the equation holds with equality, i.e., $\bigcup_{v' \in \mathcal{A}(v_S)} \mathsf{S}(v') = S$ for all $S \in \mathcal{S}$.
5. *Consider some $v \in \mathcal{V}_{\text{lat}}$. Then we have $\mathsf{S}(v) = P_{I(v)}$.*

Due to space constraints, we defer the proof to the full version of this work [3]. We briefly discuss how Lemma 4 allows us to interpret the lattice graph as a subgraph of the Boolean lattice with respect to the power set of $[k]$, i.e., the graph $\mathcal{G}_B = (\mathcal{V}_B, \mathcal{E}_B)$ with $\mathcal{V}_B = \{v_I \mid I \subseteq [k]\}$ and edges $\mathcal{E}_B = \{(v_I, v_{I'}) \mid I, I' \subseteq [k] : I' \subseteq I)\}$. Indeed, Properties 1. and 2. allow us to map every $v \in \mathcal{V}_{\text{lat}}$ to a unique index set $I \subseteq [k]$. Since the existence of an edge $(v, v') \in \mathcal{E}_{\text{lat}}$ implies that $I(v) \supseteq I(v')$ all edges adhere to the structure of $\mathcal{G}_B$. Summing up, the map $\mathcal{G} \to \mathcal{G}_B; v \mapsto v_{I(v)}$ is an injective graph homomorphism. This allows us to identify nodes of the lattice graph with nodes of $\mathcal{G}_B$ and sometimes write $v_{I'}$ for a unique node $v \in \mathcal{V}_{\text{lat}}$ with $I(v) = I' \in \mathcal{P}([k])$. By Property 5. the associated set of v is P_I, the set of users exactly in the groups specified by I. Figure 4 depicts an example execution of Algorithm 1.

Correctness. We show that key-derivation graph $\mathcal{G}$ output by Algorithm 1 satisfies the correctness properties of Definition 1. Note that the first property holds by construction.

To see that the second property holds as well, consider the lattice graph. By Lemma 4, Property 4. for every group $S' \in \mathcal{S}$ the associated sets of the ancestors of $v_{S'}$ form a partition of S'. In the second phase of the algorithm a source v_n is added for every user and connected to corresponding node in the lattice graph. Thus, after this step the set of users with a path to $v_{S'}$ is exactly S'. As this property remains unaffected by the binarization step of line 19 the final key-derivation graph is indeed correct.

5.2 Total Update Cost

In this section we analyze the total update cost $\mathrm{Upd}(\mathcal{G}) = \sum_{n \in [N]} \mathrm{Upd}(n)$ of key-derivation graphs $\mathcal{G}$ generated by Algorithm 1. To this end, we will split $\mathrm{Upd}(\mathcal{G})$ into the contribution made by the constituting Huffman trees $\mathcal{T}$. Tree $\mathcal{T}$ has a single root and all non-sources in $\mathcal{T}$ have indegree 2. Let $\mathcal{L}(\mathcal{T})$ denote the set of leaves of $\mathcal{T}$. As argued in Lemma 2, the update cost of a leaf u with respect to $\mathcal{T}$ corresponds to the length $\mathrm{len}(u)$ of its path to the root. Note, however,

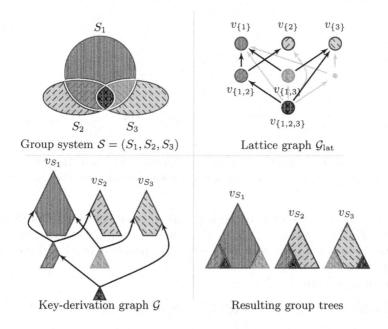

Group system $\mathcal{S} = (S_1, S_2, S_3)$ Lattice graph $\mathcal{G}_{\text{lat}}$

Key-derivation graph $\mathcal{G}$ Resulting group trees

Fig. 4. Working principle of the algorithm. Top left; Venn diagram of the considered group system. Top right; resulting lattice graph after the first phase. Node v_I has associated set $\mathsf{S}(v_I) = P_I$, the set of users in exactly the groups indicated by I. Nodes and edges of the Boolean lattice that are not part of $\mathcal{G}_{\text{lat}}$ are depicted in gray. Bottom left; final key derivation graph. Bottom right; resulting trees corresponding to groups S_1, S_2, S_3. Note that components of the same color are shared among different trees.

that leaves of $\mathcal{T}$ may represent more than one user in the key-derivation graph. Indeed, by construction of the algorithm, the weight w_u of u counts the number of leaves in $\mathcal{G}$ below u. Thus, the contribution of Huffman tree $\mathcal{T}$ towards the total update cost of $\mathcal{G}$ is given by $\mathrm{Upd}(\mathcal{T}) = \sum_{u \in \mathcal{L}(\mathcal{T})} w_u \mathrm{len}(u)$. If $U_{\mathcal{T}}$ is the probability distribution that picks $u \in \mathcal{L}(\mathcal{T})$ with probability proportional to its weight w_u, we can express the update cost of $\mathcal{T}$ in terms of the expected length from leaves to the root as

$$\mathrm{Upd}(\mathcal{T}) = \mathbb{E}[\mathrm{len}(U_{\mathcal{T}})] \cdot \sum_{u \in \mathcal{L}(\mathcal{T})} w_u \ . \tag{6}$$

We first consider Algorithm 1 for the simplest case of two subgroups and compare it to the trivial algorithm.

Example 1. Let $N \in \mathbb{N}$ and let $\mathcal{S}$ consist of two subgroups S_1, S_2 of sizes N_1 and N_2 respectively. Further assume that $|S_1 \cap S_2| = K$. Consider the key derivation graphs generated by the trivial algorithm and Algorithm 1, which in both cases decompose into several Huffman trees. The trivial algorithm essentially generates two trees T_1' and T_2', the first containing all members of S_1, the other all members

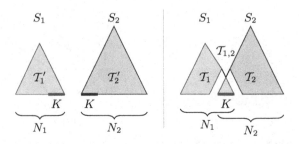

Fig. 5. Key-derivation graphs of the trivial algorithm (left) and Algorithm 1 (right) for two subgroups. Users that are members of both subgroups are marked in thick.

of S_2. Algorithm 1 first collects the K parties that are members of both groups in a tree $T_{1,2}$. The remaining $(N_1 - K)$ members of S_1 and the root of $T_{1,2}$ are collected in a tree T_1, the remaining $(N_2 - K)$ members of S_2 and the root of $T_{1,2}$ in a tree T_2 (See Fig. 5).

By Eq. 6 we have

$$\mathrm{Upd}(\mathcal{G}_{\mathrm{triv}}) = \mathrm{Upd}(T_1') + \mathrm{Upd}(T_2') = N_1\,\mathbb{E}[\mathrm{len}(U_{T_1'})] + N_2\,\mathbb{E}[\mathrm{len}(U_{T_2'})]$$

and

$$\begin{aligned}
\mathrm{Upd}(\mathcal{G}_{\mathrm{a1}}) &= \mathrm{Upd}(T_1) + \mathrm{Upd}(T_2) + \mathrm{Upd}(T_{1,2}) \\
&= N_1\,\mathbb{E}[\mathrm{len}(U_{T_1})] + N_2\,\mathbb{E}[\mathrm{len}(U_{T_2})] + K\,\mathbb{E}[\mathrm{len}(U_{T_{1,2}})]\ .
\end{aligned}$$

By optimality of Huffman codes (Lemma 1) we have that

$$H(U_T) \le \mathbb{E}[\mathrm{len}(U_T)] \le H(U_T) + 1$$

for $T \in \{T_1', T_2', T_1, T_2, T_{1,2}\}$, where $H(U_T)$ is the Shannon entropy of U_T. For T_1', T_2', and $T_{1,2}$ the leaves are distributed uniformly and we have $H(T_1') = \log(N_1)$, $H(T_2') = \log(N_2)$, $H(T_{1,2}) = \log(K)$. Let $i \in \{1,2\}$ and consider T_i. Then the first $N_i - K$ leaves have probability $1/N_i$ and the last leaf K/N_i. Thus $H(U_{T_i}) = (N_i - K)/N_i \log(N_i) + K/N_i \log(N_i/K) = \log(N_i) - K/N_i \log(K)$. Summing up we obtain

$$\begin{aligned}
&\mathrm{Upd}(\mathcal{G}_{\mathrm{triv}}) - \mathrm{Upd}(\mathcal{G}_{\mathrm{a1}}) \\
\ge\, & N_1 \log(N_1) + N_2 \log N_2 - N_1(\log(N_1) - K/N_1 \log(K) + 1) \\
& - N_2(\log(N_2) - K/N_2 \log(K) + 1) - K(\log(K) + 1) \\
=\, & K(\log(K) - 1) - (N_1 + N_2)\ .
\end{aligned}$$

Note that for $K \ge 2$ the first term is non-negative (For $K = 1$ it is easy to see that Algorithm 1 performs better than the trivial algorithm).

Before turning to arbitrary group systems, we derive a generalized statement on the update cost $\mathrm{Upd}(T)$ contributed by Huffman trees as defined above. Its proof is in the full version of this work [3].

Lemma 5. *Let* T *be a Huffman tree over leaves* $v_1, \ldots, v_\ell$ *of weight* $w_1, \ldots, w_\ell \in \mathbb{N}$. *Let* $w = \sum_{i=1}^{\ell} w_i$. *Then* T*'s update cost is bounded by*

$$w \log(w) - \sum_{i=1}^{\ell} w_i \log(w_i) \leq \mathrm{Upd}(T) \leq w(\log(w) + 1) - \sum_{i=1}^{\ell} w_i \log(w_i) \ .$$

Regarding general systems of subgroups we obtain the following result. Due to space constraints, we defer the proof to the full version of this work [3].

Theorem 1. *Let* $N \in \mathbb{N}$, $S_1, \ldots, S_k \subseteq [N]$, *and* $\mathcal{G}$ *the key-derivation graph output by Algorithm 1. Let* $\mathcal{G}_{\mathrm{lat}} = (\mathcal{V}_{\mathrm{lat}}, \mathcal{E}_{\mathrm{lat}})$ *be the corresponding lattice graph. Then*

$$\sum_{i=1}^{k} |S_i| \cdot \log(|S_i|) - \sum_{v \in \mathcal{V}_{\mathrm{lat}} : |I(v)| \geq 2} \left| \bigcup_{v' \in \mathcal{A}(v)} P_{I(v')} \right| \cdot \log \left(\left| \bigcup_{v' \in \mathcal{A}(v)} P_{I(v')} \right| \right)$$

$$\leq \mathrm{Upd}(\mathcal{G}) \leq \sum_{i=1}^{k} |S_i| \cdot (\log(|S_i|) + 1) \tag{7}$$

$$- \sum_{v \in \mathcal{V}_{\mathrm{lat}} : |I(v)| \geq 2} \left| \bigcup_{v' \in \mathcal{A}(v)} P_{I(v')} \right| \cdot \left(\log \left(\left| \bigcup_{v' \in \mathcal{A}(v)} P_{I(v')} \right| \right) - 1 \right), \tag{8}$$

where $\mathcal{A}(v)$ *denotes the set of ancestors of* v *in* $\mathcal{G}_{\mathrm{lat}}$, $I(v)$ *denotes the set* $\{i \in [k] \colon \exists \text{ path from } v \text{ to } v_{S_i}\}$, *and for* $I' \subseteq [N]$ *the set* $P_{I'} := \bigcap_{i \in I'} S_i \backslash \bigcup_{j \in [k] \backslash I'} S_j$ *indicates the users exactly in the subgroups corresponding to* I'.

The bounds of Theorem 1 depend on the structure of the lattice graph generated by the algorithm. Using Properties 4. and 5. of Lemma 4 to bound $|\mathsf{S}(\mathcal{A}(v'))|$ it is possible to obtain a weaker bound on $\mathrm{Upd}(\mathcal{G})$ that only depends on $[N]$ and $\mathcal{S}$.

We conclude the section by comparing the update cost of Algorithm 1 to that of the trivial algorithm and the asymptotically optimal algorithm of Sect. 4.1.

Comparison to the Trivial Algorithm. Note that the terms $\sum_{i=1}^{k} |S_i| \cdot \log(|S_i|)$ and $\sum_{i=1}^{k} |S_i| \cdot (\log(|S_i|) + 1)$ in Theorem 1 match the bounds on the update cost of the trivial algorithm derived in Sect. 3.4. Thus the second term of

$$\sum_{v \in \mathcal{V}_{\mathrm{lat}} : |I(v)| \geq 2} \left| \bigcup_{v' \in \mathcal{A}(v)} P_{I(v')} \right| \cdot \left(\log \left(\left| \bigcup_{v' \in \mathcal{A}(v)} P_{I(v')} \right| \right) - 1 \right)$$

provides a good estimate on how much Algorithm 1 saves compared to the trivial one. For the group system depicted in Fig. 4, for example, this would amount to $|S_1 \cap S_2| \cdot \log(|S_1 \cap S_2|) + |S_1 \cap S_3 \backslash S_2| \cdot \log(|S_1 \cap S_3 \backslash S_2|) + |S_1 \cap S_2 \backslash S_3| \cdot \log(|S_1 \cap S_2 \cap S_3|)$. Due to the "rounding error" of $+1$ in $\sum_{i=1}^{k} |S_i| \cdot (\log(|S_i|) + 1)$, Theorem 1 unfortunately does not allow us to conclude that the update cost of Algorithm 1 always improves on the one of the trivial algorithm. In the full version of this work [3], we provide an alternative analysis of $\mathrm{Upd}(\mathcal{G})$ that directly

244 J. Alwen et al.

compares the two algorithms and gives conditions that imply Algorithm 1 out-performing the trivial one.

Comparison to the Asymptotically Optimal Algorithm of Sect. 4.1. The algorithm of Sect. 4.1 in a first step constructs a binary tree for every non-empty partition $P_{I'}$ and then, in a second step, builds a binary tree for every group using the roots of the "partition trees" as leafs. We can interpret this as an algorithm that, similarly to Algorithm 1, in the first phase chooses a lattice graph $\mathcal{G}_{\text{lat}}$, concretely the graph that connects every node $v_{I'}$ directly with edges to all corresponding group nodes $\{v_{\{i\}} \mid i \in I'\}$, and in the second phase builds Huffman trees for every lattice node.[6]

Thus, by Lemma 5, we can lower bound the update cost of key graphs $\mathcal{G}_{\text{asopt}}$ generated by it by $\text{Upd}(\mathcal{G}_{\text{asopt}}) \geq \sum_{i=1}^{k} \Big(|S_i| \cdot \log(|S_i|) - \sum_{I' \subseteq [N]:i \in I' \land |I'| \geq 2} |P_{I'}| \cdot \log(|P_{I'}|) \Big) + \sum_{I' \subseteq [N]:|I'| \geq 2} |P_{I'}| \cdot \log(|P_{I'}|)$, which, taking into account that every I' with $|I'| = \ell$ corresponds to exactly ℓ groups, simplifies to

$$\text{Upd}(\mathcal{G}_{\text{asopt}}) \geq \sum_{i=1}^{k} |S_i| \cdot \log(|S_i|) - \sum_{I' \subseteq [N]:|I'| \geq 2} (|I'| - 1) |P_{I'}| \cdot \log(|P_{I'}|) . \quad (9)$$

For a comparison to Algorithm 1, consider a key derivation graph $\mathcal{G}_{\text{a1}}$ output by it. We now compute a lower bound on $\text{Upd}(\mathcal{G}_{\text{asopt}}) - \text{Upd}(\mathcal{G}_{\text{a1}})$. Let $\mathcal{G}'_{\text{lat}}$ be the lattice graph of $\mathcal{G}_{\text{a1}}$ and $v_{I'} \in \mathcal{G}'_{\text{lat}}$ such that $|I'| \geq 2$. Every non-sink in $\mathcal{G}'_{\text{lat}}$ has outdegree 2 and $v_{I'}$ is connected to all $v_{\{i\}}$ with $i \in I'$ by exactly one path. Thus, the subgraph of $\mathcal{G}'_{\text{lat}}$ induced by these paths is a binary tree with root $v_{I'}$ and $|I'|$ leafs, and thus consists of exactly $2|I'| - 1$ nodes, $|I'|$ of which have an index set of size 1. This implies that there exists $|I'| - 1$ many nodes $v_{I''}$ in $\mathcal{G}'_{\text{lat}}$ with $|I''| \geq 2$ such that $v_{I'} \in \mathcal{A}(v_{I''})$.

Using f as shorthand for the function $f : N \mapsto N \log(N)$ and $p_{I'} = |P_{I'}|$, we now can distribute the expressions $|P_{I'}| \cdot \log(|P_{I'}|)$ of Eq. 9 on the negative summands of Eq. 8 and obtain

$$\text{Upd}(\mathcal{G}_{\text{asopt}}) - \text{Upd}(\mathcal{G}_{\text{a1}}) \geq \sum_{v \in \mathcal{V}'_{\text{lat}}\, :\, |I(v)| \geq 2} \Big(f\Big(\sum_{v' \in \mathcal{A}(v)} p_{I(v')} \Big) - \sum_{v' \in \mathcal{A}(v)} f(p_{I(v')}) - 1 \Big) .$$

Since f grows super-linearly, the terms $f(\sum_{v' \in \mathcal{A}(v)} p_{I(v')}) - \sum_{v' \in \mathcal{A}(v)} f(p_{I(v')})$ are non-negative, and can even be of order N as for example $f(2N/2) - 2f(N/2) = N$. While, again due to the terms -1, we are unfortunately not able to conclude that Algorithm 1 is always more efficient, this shows that it still can save substantially in terms of update cost, in particular if the $p_{I'}$ are large.

---

[6] Formally, the algorithm as described in Sect. 4.1 collects all users that are *only* in group S_i in a tree before computing the tree for S_i, while in the lattice-graph variant these users are directly included in the tree for S_i. Note, however, that the latter approach can only improve the total update cost.

In this section we were considering the total update cost of key-derivation graphs generated by Algorithm 1, which relates to the average update cost of parties. As we have shown, this metric will typically improve compared to the trivial algorithm. However, it might still be possible, that the update cost of particular, fixed users increases. In the full version of this work [3] we show that while this may indeed happen, the increase is essentially bounded by a small constant.

5.3 Asymptotic Optimality of Boolean-Lattice Based Graphs

As discussed in Sect. 5.1, we can interpret our algorithm as follows. On input $([N], \mathcal{S} = \{S_1, \ldots, S_k\})$, in the first phase the algorithm picks a subgraph of the Boolean lattice $\mathcal{G}_B = (\mathcal{V}_B, \mathcal{E}_B)$ with respect to the power set of $[k]$, where

$$\mathcal{V}_B = \{v_I \mid I \subseteq [k]\} \quad \text{and} \quad \mathcal{E}_B = \{(v_I, v_{I'}) \mid I, I' \subseteq [k] : I' \subseteq I)\} .$$

We refer to this subgraph as the lattice graph. In the second phase, for $I \subseteq [k]$, a source for every party in P_I, i.e., the set of parties belonging exactly to the groups specified by I, is added and connected to node v_I. Each node in the graph is assigned a weight; sources have weight 1 and the weight of all other nodes is the sum of the weights of their parents. Finally, for every v_I a Huffman tree to its parents according to the weight distribution is built, resulting in the key-derivation graph.

In this section we consider key-derivation graphs for general choices of the lattice graph, i.e., key derivation graphs $\mathcal{G}$ obtained by executing the second phase of the algorithm as described above with respect to a lattice-graph $\mathcal{G}_{\text{lat}} = (\mathcal{V}_{\text{lat}}, \mathcal{E}_{\text{lat}}) \subseteq \mathcal{G}_B$.[7] We say $\mathcal{G}$ is the key-derivation graph associated to $\mathcal{G}_{\text{lat}}$, $[N]$ and $\mathcal{S}$. The following theorem shows that the update cost of every lattice-based key derivation graphs, and in particular graphs generated by Algorithm 1, is optimal in the asymptotic setting of Sect. 4. Due to space constraints, we defer its proof to the full version of this work [3].

Theorem 2. *Let* $k \in \mathbb{N}$ *be fixed, and for* $I \subseteq [k]$ *let* $p_I \in [0, 1]$ *be such that* $\sum_{I \subseteq [k]} p_I = 1$ *and* $p_\emptyset = 0$. *For* $N \in \mathbb{N}$ *let* $\mathcal{S}(N)$ *be the subgroup system associated to the* p_I.

Let $\mathcal{G}_{\text{lat}} = (\mathcal{V}_{\text{lat}}, \mathcal{E}_{\text{lat}})$ *be a subgraph of the Boolean-lattice graph with respect to* $[k]$ *satisfying that* $v_I \in \mathcal{V}_{\text{lat}}$ *for all* I *with* $p_I > 0$, *and let* $\mathcal{G}(N)$ *be the key-derivation graph associated to* $\mathcal{G}_{\text{lat}}$ *and* $\mathcal{S}(N)$. *Then*

$$\text{Upd}(\mathcal{G}(N)) \xrightarrow{N \to \infty} \sum_{I \subseteq [k]} |N \cdot p_I| \cdot \log(|N \cdot p_I|) + \Theta(N) = N \log(N) + \Theta(N) .$$

---

[7] Naturally, one would require that the resulting key-derivation graph satisfies correctness. However, this is not necessary for our analysis of its update cost.

6 Lower Bound on the Update Cost of CGKA

In this section we prove a lower bound on the average update cost of continuous group-key agreement schemes for multiple groups. As an intermediate step we will further prove a bound on the update cost of key-derivation graphs. To this aim, we follow the approach of Micciancio and Panjwani [14], who analyzed the worst-case communication complexity of multicast key distribution in a *symbolic* security model, where cryptographic primitives are considered as abstract data types. We will first recall their security model, adapt it to CGKA, and then prove how to extend their results to our setting. In the full version of this work [3], using a similar approach, we prove a lower bound for multicast encryption.

6.1 Symbolic Model

We first define a symbolic model in the style of Dolev and Yao [10] for CGKA schemes. It follows the approach of Micciancio and Panjwani [14], but as it admits the uses of public-key encryption also includes elements of the model of Bienstock et al. [6], who analyze the communication cost of concurrent updates in CGKA schemes.

Building Blocks. We restrict the analysis to schemes that are constructed from the following three primitives. Note that our construction is a special case of the constructions analyzed in this section.

- *Public-key Encryption:* Let $(\mathsf{KGen}, \mathsf{Enc}, \mathsf{Dec})$ denote a public-key encryption scheme, where
    - KGen on input of secret key sk returns the corresponding public key pk.
    - Enc takes as input a public key pk and a message m, and outputs a ciphertext $c \leftarrow \mathsf{Enc}(\mathsf{pk}, \mathsf{m})$.
    - Dec takes as input a secret key sk and a ciphertext c, and outputs a message $\mathsf{m} = \mathsf{Dec}(\mathsf{sk}, c)$. We assume perfect correctness: $\mathsf{Dec}(\mathsf{sk}, \mathsf{Enc}(\mathsf{pk}, \mathsf{m})) = \mathsf{m}$ for all sk, $\mathsf{pk} = \mathsf{KGen}(\mathsf{sk})$, and messages m.
- *Pseudorandom generator:* The algorithm G takes as input a secret key sk and expands it to a sequence of keys $\mathsf{G}_0(\mathsf{sk}), \ldots, \mathsf{G}_\ell(\mathsf{sk})$.
- *Secret sharing:* Let S, R denote the sharing and recovering procedures of a secret sharing scheme: For some access structure $\Gamma \subseteq 2^{[h]}$, the algorithm S takes as input a message m and outputs a set of shares $\mathsf{S}_1(\mathsf{m}), \ldots, \mathsf{S}_h(\mathsf{m})$ such that for any $I \in \Gamma$ it holds $\mathsf{R}(I, \{S_i(\mathsf{m})\}_{i \in I}) = \mathsf{m}$, but for any $I \not\subseteq \Gamma$ the message m cannot be recovered from $\{S_i(\mathsf{m})\}_{i \in I}$.

We consider the following data types that can be derived from other objects according to the following rules.

Data type		Grammar rules
Message m	$\leftarrow$	$\mathsf{sk}, \mathsf{pk}, \mathsf{Enc}(\mathsf{pk}, \mathsf{m}), S_1(\mathsf{m}), \ldots, S_h(\mathsf{m})$
Public key pk	$\leftarrow$	$\mathsf{KGen}(\mathsf{sk})$
Secret key sk	$\leftarrow$	$R, \mathsf{G}_0(\mathsf{sk}), \ldots, \mathsf{G}_\ell(\mathsf{sk})$

To describe the information that can be recovered from a set of messages M, the *entailment relation* is defined by the following rules:

$$\begin{aligned}
\mathsf{m} \in M &\Rightarrow& M \vdash \mathsf{m} \\
M \vdash \mathsf{sk} &\Rightarrow& M \vdash \mathsf{G}_0(\mathsf{sk}), \ldots, \mathsf{G}_l(\mathsf{sk}) \\
M \vdash \mathsf{Enc}(\mathsf{pk}, \mathsf{m}), \mathsf{sk} : \mathsf{pk} = \mathsf{KGen}(\mathsf{sk}) &\Rightarrow& M \vdash \mathsf{m} \\
\exists I \in \Gamma : \forall i \in I : M \vdash \mathsf{S}_i(\mathsf{m}) &\Rightarrow& M \vdash \mathsf{m}
\end{aligned}$$

By restricting to these relations we essentially assume *secure* encryption and secret sharing schemes. Examples and further comments (in the setting of multicast encryption) can be found in [14, Sect. 3.2]. The set of messages which can be recovered from M using relation $\vdash$ is denoted by $\mathsf{Rec}(M)$.

Continuous Group-Key Agreement. We now define continuous group-key agreement protocols in the symbolic model. We consider the case of CGKA for a static system of users $[N]$ and groups $S_1, \ldots, S_k \subseteq [N]$. Note that a lower bound for schemes in this setting in particular also excludes schemes which allow dynamic operations, i.e., adding and removing users from groups.

A CGKA scheme for $[N]$ and $S_1, \ldots, S_k$ specifies two procedures:

- Initially, Setup assigns each user $n \in [N]$ a personal set SK_n^0 of secret keys. Furthermore, Setup generates a set $\mathsf{msgs}(0)$ of so-called *rekey* messages to establish for every group S_j a group secret key $\mathsf{sk}_{S_j}^0$. We require that the initial sets of personal keys consist of uniformly random keys, and that for all $n' \neq n$ and $\mathsf{sk} \in \mathsf{SK}_n^0$ we have $\mathsf{sk} \notin \mathsf{Rec}(\mathsf{SK}_{n'}^0, \mathsf{msgs}(0))$.
- In round t, the algorithm Update takes as input a user identity $n \in [N]$, establishes new sets $\mathsf{SK}_{n'}^t$ for all users n', and outputs some rekey messages $\mathsf{msgs}(t)$ to establish for every group S_j an epoch t group key $\mathsf{sk}_{S_j}^t$. We do *not* require the new sets and group keys to be distinct from the ones of round $t - 1$. We denote the set of new uniformly random keys that were generated during the update procedure by the updating party by F_n^t.

Note that the only party generating new keys during update t is the updating party n. For ease of notation we define $\mathsf{F}_{n'}^t = \emptyset$ for all $n' \neq n$, and set $\mathsf{F}_{n'}^0 = \emptyset$ for all n'.

For *correctness*, we require that, (a) at all times members of a group are able to derive the current group key from their set of personal keys and the sent messages, and (b) if some user updated in round t, then all users are able to derive their new set of personal keys from their old one, the sent messages, and in the case of the updating party the new keys generated during the update. The latter condition accounts for the fact that changes to a user's set of personal keys need to be communicated to them.

More precisely, for (a) we require that for any subgroup structure and any sequence of updating users $(n_1, \ldots, n_t)$, for all $j \in [k]$ each member n of subgroup S_j can recover $\mathsf{sk}_{S_j}^t$:

$$\mathsf{sk}_{S_j}^t \in \mathsf{Rec}\left(\mathsf{SK}_n^t \cup \bigcup_{\iota \in [t]_0} \mathsf{msgs}(\iota)\right) .$$

For (b) we require that for any subgroup structure and any sequence of updating users $(n_1, \ldots, n_t)$, we have for all n that

$$\mathsf{SK}_n^t \subseteq \mathsf{Rec}\Big(\mathsf{SK}_n^{t-1} \cup \mathsf{F}_n^t \cup \bigcup_{\iota \in [t]_0} \mathrm{msgs}(\iota)\Big) .$$

For security, we assume the minimal requirement of *post-compromise security* (PCS), which essentially says that users can recover from compromise, which leaks their state and the keys generated during the time period of being compromised, by updating. Note that a lower bound in this setting in particular excludes protocols achieving stronger security notions desired in practice, like post compromise forward security [2].

More precisely, we formalize PCS as the condition that no group key can be recovered from members outside the group, and/or members' personal keys and the keys generated by them before their last update. To this end, for round t and user $n \in [N]$, let $t_{\mathrm{up}}(t, n)$ denote the round in which n performed their last update, where we set $t_{\mathrm{up}}(t, n) = 0$ if no such update occurred. I.e., we require that for any group system, any update pattern, in every round t we have that

$$\mathsf{sk}_{S_j}^t \notin \mathsf{Rec}\Big(\bigcup_{\substack{n \in [N] \setminus S_j, \\ t' \in [t]_0}} (\mathsf{SK}_n^{t'} \cup \mathsf{F}_n^{t'}) \cup \bigcup_{n \in S_j} \bigcup_{t' \in [t_{\mathrm{up}}(t,n)-1]_0} (\mathsf{SK}_n^{t'} \cup \mathsf{F}_n^{t'}) \cup \bigcup_{t' \in [t]_0} \mathrm{msgs}(t')\Big) .$$

Note that in the definition above, excluding all sets of personal secret keys since a user's last update is necessary even in the case that another user's update might have replaced them before round t, as otherwise SK_n^t and in turn $\mathsf{sk}_{S_j}^t$ could trivially be recovered by the two correctness conditions.

Our goal is to derive a lower bound on the communication complexity of CGKA schemes achieving PCS, i.e., the number of messages $|\cup_{t' \in [t]_0} \mathrm{msgs}(t')|$ sent by the protocol.

Key Graphs. The execution of any CGKA scheme can be reflected by a graph structure representing recoverability of the keys involved (cf. [14]). To define this graph, we first need to recall the definition of *useful* keys and messages.

A secret key sk is called *useless at time* t if it can be recovered from old key material, i.e., if

$$\mathsf{sk} \in \mathsf{Rec}\Big(\bigcup_{n \in [N]} \bigcup_{t' \in [t_{\mathrm{up}}(t,n)-1]_0} (\mathsf{SK}_n^{t'} \cup \mathsf{F}_n^{t'}) \cup \bigcup_{t' \in [t]_0} \mathrm{msgs}(t')\Big) ,$$

otherwise sk is called *useful.* As we will show below, if a CGKA scheme satisfies correctness and post-compromise security, then for all $t \in \mathbb{N}$, $n \in [N]$, $j \in [k]$ it must hold that at least one of the user's personal keys $\mathsf{sk}_n^t \in \mathsf{SK}_n^t$ as well as all group keys $\mathsf{sk}_{S_j}^t$ are useful at time t.

To decide whether a message is useful, one has to consider the information it contains, where messages can be arbitrarily nested applications of encryption Enc and secret sharing S. Thus, a message m is said to *encapsulate* a (pseudo)random key sk if $m = e_1(e_2(\ldots(e_j(sk))\ldots))$ where $e_i = \mathsf{Enc}_{\mathsf{pk}_i}$ or $e_i = \mathsf{S}_{h_i}$ (for some public key pk_i and $h_i \in [h]$). A message is then called *useful* if it encapsulates a useful key.

Definition 2 (Key graph [14]). *The* key graph $\mathcal{KG}_t = (\mathcal{V}_t, \mathcal{E}_t)$ *for a CGKA scheme at time t is defined as follows. $\mathcal{V}_t$ consists of all the keys that are useful at time t, and $\mathcal{E} \subseteq \mathcal{V} \times \mathcal{V}$ consists of all ordered pairs $(\mathsf{sk}_1, \mathsf{sk}_2)$ such that one of the following is true:*

1. *There exists $j \in [l]$ auch that $\mathsf{sk}_2 = \mathsf{G}_j(\mathsf{sk}_1)$.*
2. *There exists a message $m \in \bigcup_{j \in [t]_0} \mathrm{msgs}(j)$ with $m = e_1(\mathsf{Enc}(\mathsf{pk}_1, e_2(\mathsf{sk}_2)))$ with $\mathsf{pk}_1 = \mathsf{KGen}(\mathsf{sk}_1)$. Here e_1 and e_2 are some sequences of encryption and secret sharing, and we require that e_2 does not contain any encryption under a public key that has a matching secret key that is useful at time t.*

Edges of the second type are called communication edges.

One can show that for any node sk in $\mathcal{KG}$ there is at most one edge of the first type incident to sk (the proof is analogous to [14, Proposition 1]). Note that edges of the first type do not incur any communication cost, while edges of the second type require at least one message. Thus, in the following we will be interested in the number of communication edges. To this aim, we prove the following properties of key graphs. In particular, we show that even if a CGKA scheme does not rely on the use of a fixed key-derivation graph as discussed in Sect. 3, after every update the key graph must still have the properties of Definition 1.

We will rely on the following Lemma that can be proved analogously to [14, Lemma 1].

Lemma 6. *Consider a secure and correct CGKA scheme for $N \in \mathbb{N}$, $S_1, \ldots, S_k \subseteq [N]$. Then, for any $t \in \mathbb{N}$ and sequence of updates $(n_1, \ldots, n_t)$, the corresponding key graph $\mathcal{KG}_t$ satisfies the following. For every set of keys SK, and key sk_2 that is useful at time t, such that $\mathsf{sk}_2 \in \mathsf{Rec}\left(\mathsf{SK} \cup \bigcup_{t' \in [t]_0} \mathrm{msgs}(t')\right)$, there exists a useful $\mathsf{sk}_1 \in \mathsf{SK}$ such that there is a path from sk_1 to sk_2 in $\mathcal{KG}_t$ that only consists of keys sk with $\mathsf{sk} \in \mathsf{Rec}\left(\mathsf{SK} \cup \bigcup_{t' \in [t]_0} \mathrm{msgs}(t')\right)$.*

Note that the converse of Lemma 6 is not true, since, for example, a message $\mathsf{Enc}(\mathsf{pk}_1, \mathsf{S}_1(\mathsf{sk}_2))$ with useful keys $\mathsf{sk}_1, \mathsf{sk}_2$ and $\mathsf{pk}_1 = \mathsf{KGen}(\mathsf{sk}_1)$ incurs an edge $(\mathsf{sk}_1, \mathsf{sk}_2)$ while sk_2 can only be recovered from sk_1 if $\{1\} \in \Gamma$.

6.2 Lower Bound on the Average Update Cost

The communication complexity of a CGKA scheme after t updates is given by $\left|\bigcup_{t' \in [t]_0} \mathrm{msgs}(t')\right|$. To measure the efficiency of the scheme we will consider the *amortized communication complexity*

$$\mathrm{Com}_A := \left|\bigcup_{t' \in [t]_0} \mathrm{msgs}(t')\right|/t \ .$$

We now are ready to compute a bound on the expectation of $\mathrm{Com_A}$ in the scenario where, in every round, the updating party is chosen uniformly at random. In the full version of this work [3] we prove an analogous bound for multicast encryption that improves on [14, Theorem 1] in two aspects. It generalizes the bound to the setting of several, potentially overlapping groups, and further gives a bound on the *average* communication complexity of updates, as opposed to a worst case bound.

Theorem 3. *Consider a CGKA scheme* CGKA *for* $N \in \mathbb{N}$, $S_1, \ldots, S_k \subseteq [N]$ *that is secure in the symbolic model. Then the expected amortized average communication cost after* t *updates is bounded from below by*

$$\mathbb{E}[\mathrm{Com_A}] \geq (1 - 1/t) \cdot \frac{1}{N} \sum_{\emptyset \neq I \subseteq [k]} |P_I| \cdot \log(|P_I|) \ .$$

and the asymptotic (in the number of update operations) update cost of the protocol is at least $\frac{1}{N} \sum_{\emptyset \neq I \subseteq [k]} |P_I| \cdot \log(|P_I|)$.

Due to space constraints, we defer the proof to the full version of this work [3].

7   Open Problems

We conclude by discussing some open problems.

7.1   Optimal Key-Derivation Graphs

Unfortunately we are not able to tell how far from optimal the solutions generated by Algorithm 1 are for concrete group systems. We consider it an interesting open question to resolve this issue.

General kdgs. We first discuss this problem in its general form. I.e., given a system $\mathcal{S} = \{S_1, \ldots, S_k\}$ of subgroups of the set $[N]$ of users compute the key-derivation graph for $\mathcal{S}$ (as defined in Definition 1) that has minimal update cost. The question of whether a polynomial time algorithm for solving this problem exists can be naturally asked in various ways. E.g., when polynomial means polynomial in the number of users N (think of N being given in unary), or polynomial in a reasonable description of the set system $\mathcal{S}$, say, when we are given the sizes of all non-empty intersections of sets in $\mathcal{S}$. Here N can be exponential in the input length, so a potential solution would need to have a very succinct description. Algorithm 1 (which we do not know whether is optimal) can be turned into one of the latter kind by using an implicit representation during the Huffman coding step.

We are thankful to one reviewer of this work, who pointed out an interesting connection of key-derivation graphs for a group system $\mathcal{S} = \{S_1, \ldots, S_k\}$

to the *disjunctive complexity* of $\mathcal{S}$, which, given variables $x_1, \ldots, x_N \in \{0, 1\}$, corresponds to the size of the smallest circuit of fanin-2 OR-gates computing

$$\bigvee_{i \in S_1} x_i, \ldots, \bigvee_{i \in S_k} x_i . \tag{10}$$

Note that circuits computing (10) correspond exactly to key-derivation graphs for $\mathcal{S}$. So the two problems differ only by the used metric; while disjunctive complexity counts the number of non-sources in the graph, the update cost of a kdg weighs each of these nodes by the number of sources below it. As there exist upper and lower bound on the disjunctive complexity of group systems (see e.g. [12]), we consider it an interesting open questions whether these can be used to establish bounds on the update cost of kdgs. We want to point out, however, that this metric might be not fine-grained enough to capture certain properties of kdgs: E.g., for $N \in \mathbb{N}$ the systems $\mathcal{S}_1 = \{[N]\}$ and $\mathcal{S}_2 = \{[1], [2], \ldots, [N]\}$ both have disjunctive complexity $N - 1$, but their total update costs as kdgs are of order $N \cdot \log(N)$ and N^2 respectively.

Lattice Based kdgs. If we restrict our view to algorithms using Boolean-lattice based graphs as defined in Sect. 5.3, and are willing to make simplifying assumptions, the question of optimality translates to an optimization problem on graphs: we are going to (a) consider only lattice graphs $\mathcal{G}_{\text{lat}}$ where all nodes v are connected with their descendants $v' \in \mathcal{D}(v)$ by an *unique* path, and (b) assume in our analysis of the update cost that the algorithms second step (i.e., the generation of Huffman trees) is instead implemented with an idealized code, that has average codeword length matching the entropy of the leaf distribution. This essentially corresponds to ignoring the terms of $+1$ in Lemma 1.

Recall that for groups system $\{S_1, \ldots, S_k\}$ the nodes $v_I \in \mathcal{V}_{\text{lat}}$ of a lattice graph correspond to index sets $I \subseteq [k]$. It is easy to see that the correctness of $\mathcal{G}_{\text{lat}}$ together with condition (a), are equivalent to requiring that the only sinks in the graph are the singleton sets $\{i\}$, and that for every $v_I \in \mathcal{V}_{\text{lat}}$

$$I = I_1 \uplus \ldots \uplus I_\ell \tag{11}$$

holds, where $v_{I_1}, \ldots, v_{I_\ell}$ are the children of v_I and disjointness enforces unique paths.

The total update cost of a graph satisfying this property can be computed as follows. To every node v_I we associate the weight $w_I = \left| \bigcap_{i \in I} S_i \setminus \bigcup_{j \in [k] \setminus I} S_j \right|$ corresponding to the number of users exactly in the groups specified by I. Further, we inductively define the total weight t_I of v_I as

$$t_I = \begin{cases} w_I & \text{if } v_I \text{ is source} \\ w_I + \sum_{I' : v_{I'} \in \mathcal{P}(v_I)} t_{I'} & \text{else} \end{cases} ,$$

where $\mathcal{P}(v_I)$ denotes the set of parents of v_I. By assumptions (a) and (b), and Lemma 5, the update cost contributed by node v_I thus corresponds to

$$\text{Upd}(v_I) = t_I \log(t_I) - \sum_{I' : v_{I'} \in \mathcal{P}(v_I)} t_{I'} \log(t_{I'}) , \tag{12}$$

and we end up with the following optimization problem on lattice graphs.

Problem 1. Let $k \in \mathbb{N}$. Given weights $\{w_I\}_{I \subseteq [k]}$ with $w_I \in \mathbb{N}$ among the subgraphs of the Boolean lattice with respect to the power set of $[k]$ that satisfy Condition 11 find the subgraph $\mathcal{G}_{\text{lat}}$ of minimal total update cost

$$\text{Upd}(\mathcal{G}_{\text{lat}}) = \sum_{I \subseteq [k]} \text{Upd}(v_I) \ .$$

We consider it an interesting open question whether Algorithm 1 solves this problem and, if not, to find an efficient algorithm that does.

7.2   Security

In this work we focused on the communication complexity of key-derivation graphs and only gave an intuition on their security. Security proofs for secure group messaging are typically quite complex, and protocols rely on additional mechanisms (e.g. confirmation tag, transcript hash, and parent hash) ensuring that users of the system can not be tricked into inconsistent views of the graph. We consider it an important open question, to adapt these mechanisms to kdgs for several groups and give a formal security proof for the resulting CGKA protocols.

7.3   Efficiency of Dynamic Operations

In the full version of this work [3] we show that the techniques of blanking and unmerged leaves can be adapted to key-derivation graphs, in order to allow dynamic changes to the group membership. As is the case for singular groups, blanking and unmerged leaves decrease the efficiency of updates of a user n, since they destroy the binary structure of the graph, resulting in potentially more than a single ciphertext per node in $\mathcal{D}(v_n)$ having to be generated. However, the graph gradually recovers from this, assuming that parties with update trees overlapping $\mathcal{D}(v_n)$ update. It is an interesting open question how the decrease in efficiency compares to that of the trivial algorithm.

References

1. Alwen, J., Coretti, S., Dodis, Y., Tselekounis, Y.: Security analysis and improvements for the IETF MLS standard for group messaging. In: Micciancio, D., Ristenpart, T. (eds.) CRYPTO 2020. LNCS, vol. 12170, pp. 248–277. Springer, Cham (2020). https://doi.org/10.1007/978-3-030-56784-2_9
2. Alwen, J., Coretti, S., Jost, D., Mularczyk, M.: Continuous group key agreement with active security. In: Pass, R., Pietrzak, K. (eds.) TCC 2020. LNCS, vol. 12551, pp. 261–290. Springer, Cham (2020). https://doi.org/10.1007/978-3-030-64378-2_10

3. Alwen, J., et al.: Grafting key trees: efficient key management for overlapping groups. Cryptology ePrint Archive, Report 2021/1158 (2021). https://ia.cr/2021/1158

4. Barnes, R., Beurdouche, B., Millican, J., Omara, E., Cohn-Gordon, K., Robert, R.: The Messaging Layer Security (MLS) Protocol. Internet-Draft draft-ietf-mls-protocol-11, Internet Engineering Task Force (December 2020). Work in Progress. https://datatracker.ietf.org/doc/html/draft-ietf-mls-protocol-11

5. Bhargavan, K., Barnes, R., Rescorla, E.: TreeKEM: Asynchronous Decentralized Key Management for Large Dynamic Groups (May 2018)

6. Bienstock, A., Dodis, Y., Rösler, P.: On the price of concurrency in group ratcheting protocols. In: Pass, R., Pietrzak, K. (eds.) TCC 2020. LNCS, vol. 12551, pp. 198–228. Springer, Cham (2020). https://doi.org/10.1007/978-3-030-64378-2_8

7. Canetti, R., Garay, J.A., Itkis, G., Micciancio, D., Naor, M., Pinkas, B.: Multicast security: a taxonomy and some efficient constructions. In: IEEE INFOCOM 1999, New York, NY, USA, 21–25 March 1999, pp. 708–716 (1999)

8. Cohn-Gordon, K., Cremers, C., Garratt, L., Millican, J., Milner, K.: On ends-to-ends encryption: asynchronous group messaging with strong security guarantees. In: Lie, D., Mannan, M., Backes, M., Wang, X. (eds.) ACM CCS 2018, pp. 1802–1819. ACM Press (October 2018)

9. Cremers, C., Hale, B., Kohbrok, K.: Efficient post-compromise security beyond one group. Cryptology ePrint Archive, Report 2019/477 (2019). https://eprint.iacr.org/2019/477

10. Dolev, D., Yao, A.: On the security of public key protocols. IEEE Trans. Inf. Theor. **29**(2), 198–208 (1983)

11. Huffman, D.A.: A method for the construction of minimum-redundancy codes. Proc. IRE **40**(9), 1098–1101 (1952)

12. Jukna, S.: Boolean Function Complexity. Advances and Frontiers, vol. 27. Springer, Heidelberg (2012). https://doi.org/10.1007/978-3-642-24508-4

13. Mapoka, T.T., Shepherd, S., Abd-Alhameed, R., Anoh, K.O.: Novel rekeying approach for secure multiple multicast groups over wireless mobile networks. In: 2014 International Wireless Communications and Mobile Computing Conference (IWCMC), pp. 839–844. IEEE (2014)

14. Micciancio, D., Panjwani, S.: Optimal communication complexity of generic multicast key distribution. In: Cachin, C., Camenisch, J.L. (eds.) EUROCRYPT 2004. LNCS, vol. 3027, pp. 153–170. Springer, Heidelberg (2004). https://doi.org/10.1007/978-3-540-24676-3_10

15. Wallner, D.M., Harder, E.J., Agee, R.C.: Key management for multicast: issues and architectures. Internet Draft (September 1998). http://www.ietf.org/ID.html

16. Wong, C.K., Gouda, M., Lam, S.S.: Secure group communications using key graphs. IEEE/ACM Trans. Netw. **8**(1), 16–30 (2000)

17. Zhong, H., Luo, W., Cui, J.: Multiple multicast group key management for the internet of people. Concurrency Comput. Pract. Exp. **29**(3), e3817 (2017). e3817 CPE-15-0502.R1. https://doi.org/10.1002/cpe.3817

Updatable Public Key Encryption in the Standard Model

Yevgeniy Dodis[1], Harish Karthikeyan[1(✉)], and Daniel Wichs[2]

[1] New York University, New York City, USA
{dodis,karthik}@cs.nyu.edu
[2] Northeastern University and NTT Research, Boston, USA
wichs@ccs.neu.edu

Abstract. Forward security (FS) ensures that corrupting the current secret key in the system preserves the privacy or integrity of the prior usages of the system. Achieving forward security is especially hard in the setting of public-key encryption (PKE), where time is divided into periods, and in each period the receiver derives the next-period secret key from their current secret key, while the public key stays constant. Indeed, all current constructions of FS-PKE are built from hierarchical identity-based encryption (HIBE) and are rather complicated.

Motivated by applications to secure messaging, recent works of Jost et al. (Eurocrypt'19) and Alwen et al. (CRYPTO'20) consider a natural relaxation of FS-PKE, which they term *updatable PKE* (UPKE). In this setting, the transition to the next period can be initiated by any sender, who can compute a special *update ciphertext*. This ciphertext directly produces the next-period public key and can be processed by the receiver to compute the next-period secret key. If done honestly, future (regular) ciphertexts produced with the new public key can be decrypted with the new secret key, but past such ciphertexts cannot be decrypted with the new secret key. Moreover, this is true even if all other previous-period updates were initiated by untrusted senders.

Both papers also constructed a very simple UPKE scheme based on the CDH assumption in the random oracle model. However, they left open the question of building such schemes in the standard model, or based on other (e.g., post-quantum) assumptions, without using the heavy HIBE techniques. In this work, we construct two efficient UPKE schemes in the standard model, based on the DDH and LWE assumptions, respectively. Somewhat interestingly, our constructions gain their efficiency (compared to prior FS-PKE schemes from the same assumptions) by using tools from the area of circular-secure and leakage resilient public-key encryption schemes (rather than HIBE).

Y. Dodis—Partially supported by gifts from VMware Labs and Google, and NSF grants 1619158, 1319051, 1314568.

D. Wichs—Partially supported by NSF grants CNS-1413964, CNS-1750795 and the Alfred P. Sloan Research Fellowship.

K. Nissim and B. Waters (Eds.): TCC 2021, LNCS 13044, pp. 254–285, 2021.
https://doi.org/10.1007/978-3-030-90456-2_9

1   Introduction

For privacy applications, Forward Security (FS) refers to the ability to update sensitive information in a way that: (1) the system continues to be functional in the future; (2) compromise of the current secret state of the system does not affect the privacy of past secrets. For example, the famous authenticated Diffie-Hellman key agreement protocol,—where the party use long-term signing keys to authenticate the ephemeral public values g^a and g^b used to produce the shared key $k = g^{ab}$,—is forward-secure under the Decisional Diffie-Helman (DDH) assumption, even if the attacker later learns the long-term signing keys, as long as the no-longer-needed ephemeral secrets a and b were erased before this compromise.

In the symmetric-key world, forward security is also easy using a pseudorandom generator (PRG) G, provided the sender and the receiver can stay synchronized [12]. Given the current state s, the sender can produce $(r, s') \leftarrow G(s)$ to get the one-time symmetric key r, and the next state s', so that compromising s' does not affect the security of the one-time key r. One way to think about this is that PRGs allow one to produce an initial state s_0 that defines a "one-way chain" of pseudorandom states $s_0 \rightarrow s_1 \rightarrow s_2 \rightarrow \ldots$, which can only be traversed in the forward direction.

Forward-Secure PKE. Coming back to the public-key world, achieving FS for (non-interactive) Public-Key Encryption (PKE) turned out to be noticeably more complicated. The initial paper of Canetti et al. [24],—which up to this day is still essentially the state-of-the-art in the area,—defined FS-PKE as follows. The key generation outputs initial keys $(\mathsf{pk}_0, \mathsf{sk}_0)$, which implicitly defined two synchronized chains $\mathsf{pk}_0 \rightarrow \mathsf{pk}_1 \rightarrow \mathsf{pk}_2 \rightarrow \ldots$ and $\mathsf{sk}_0 \rightarrow \mathsf{sk}_1 \rightarrow \mathsf{sk}_2 \rightarrow \ldots$ which can be *independently* produced by multiple senders and a single receiver. The chains should be consistent in the sense that messages encrypted under pk_i should be decryptable by sk_i, and the secret-key chain should have the "one-wayness" property we want: exposing sk_i should not compromise the privacy of messages encrypted under prior public keys pk_j, for $j < i$.[1]

Canetti et al. [24] also showed how to build FS-PKE from any Hierarchical Identity-Based Encryption (HIBE) [34,35] scheme. As a result, as more HIBE schemes got built [14,15,22,25,30,31], we also get more FS-PKE schemes, even including purely theoretical schemes from very basic assumptions, like DDH/CDH, factoring, and super-low-noise LPN [22,30,31]. However, most of these schemes are quite complicated and inefficient (or rely on pairings/strong assumptions ??), at least compared to many simple PKE schemes that are available today. Unfortunately, closing the efficiency/complexity gap between FS-PKE and PKE remains open until this day.

Updatable PKE. As a step towards closing this gap, and motivated by independently interesting applications in the area of secure messaging schemes, two

---

[1] For efficiency reasons, [24] also insisted that $\mathsf{pk}_i = (\mathsf{pk}_0, i)$, meaning one can quickly go from pk_0 to pk_i, but this point will not be important for our discussion.

recent works of Jost *et al.* [38] and Alwen *et al.* [5] defined a relaxed notion of forward-secure PKE, called *updatable PKE* (UPKE). In this setting, any sender can initiate a "key update" by sending a special update ciphertext.[2] This ciphertext updates the receiver's public key and also, once processed by the receiver, will update their secret key. A malicious sender cannot harm security by sending a malicious key update generated with bad randomness. However, an honest sender is assured that, once the receiver processes an honestly generated key update, all ciphertexts produced in the past will remain secure even if the receiver's secret key is compromised in the future.

Note that in the setting of updatable PKE, we implicitly assume that there is an ordered sequence of update ciphertexts which will be decrypted by the receiver and that each sender can see this sequence and figure out the current public key at any time. For example, this holds if all the ciphertexts are sent by the same sender [38] (similar to the symmetric-key setting), or the ciphertexts could be sent by multiple senders, but there is some outside mechanism that will anyway serialize all these ciphertexts [5].

In the extreme cases, such as a secure group messaging application of [38], every sender S will initiate a key update after *each* ciphertext that it sends to the receiver R.[3] In particular, since S "trusts itself", S can be sure that the information in this ciphertext will be secure forever, the moment that R decrypts it (and moves its secret key forward), even if R gets corrupted later on. And this is true even if other senders S' that sent messages in the past were more careless, and might not have properly generated/erased the randomness of their updates, which were used to determine the public key under which S encrypted its message. In this sense, UPKE with key updates following every encryption provides a natural public-key analog of stream ciphers extensively used in symmetric-key cryptography, despite having multiple senders who do not necessarily trust each other's randomness. To put it differently, the security of each sender only depends on the quality/secrecy of its own randomness, while the correctness relies on the serialization of update ciphertexts sent by all the senders.

UPKE Syntax and Prior Constructions. A bit more precisely,[4] in addition to standard key generation, encryption, and decryption algorithms, the UPKE

---

[2] Of course, FS is trivial to achieve if the receiver can initiate the key update. Indeed, this type of key update is also happening in the secure messaging applications of [5, 38], trivially achieving FS when the receiver "speaks" and updates its key. However, we could also be in the scenario where the receiver is non-communicating for a long period of time, while many messages are being sent to *and processed by* the receiver. For example, the receiver could be part of a large secure messaging group [5] who only reads messages, but almost never posts messages. UPKE is precisely useful in this scenario.

[3] For the sake of generality, we will not necessarily insist on updating the public key after each ciphertext, but such extreme use is certainly an option for getting higher security.

[4] We use slightly different syntax than [5,38], but all our schemes are easily converted to meet the syntax of [5,38].

schemes have two special algorithms Upd-Pk and Upd-Sk. Any sender can run Upd-Pk on the current public-key pk_{i-1} to produce *update ciphertext* up_i and a new public key pk_i. In turn, the receiver will run Upd-Sk on the current secret key sk_{i-1} and update ciphertext up_i, to produce the new secret-key sk_i.

In terms of forward security, we require that exposure of any key sk_i should not compromise the privacy of messages encrypted under prior public keys pk_j, for $j < i$, *provided at least one "good" update happened from period j to i*. Hereby "good update" we mean that the randomness used by the sender to generate this update was not compromised by the attacker. Indeed, in the secure messaging applications of [5,38], all senders were assumed to be honest, although some of their local randomnesses could be compromised by the attacker. Following [5], our definition will actually be slightly stronger in that we will allow malicious randomness for the "bad updates". See Sect. 3.

To validate the usefulness of this relaxation, the works of [5,38] also gave an extremely fast and simple construction, which is orders of magnitude faster than HIBE-based FS-PKE schemes and is based on the CDH assumption in the random oracle model (ROM). The encryption scheme is just the standard hashed ElGamal encryption scheme: given public key $h = g^s$, encryption of m computes $(g^r, Hash(h^r) \oplus m)$, while decryption of (c, w) outputs $w \oplus Hash(c^s)$. To update the public/secret key, the sender chooses a random exponent δ, and simply *encrypts it using the standard encryption algorithm*. The new public key is $h' = hg^\delta$, and new secret key is $s' = s + \delta$. We notice, however, the random oracle model is critically used to break the circularity between encrypting the value δ, and later leaking the value $s' = s + \delta$ which depends on the secret key.

Our Main Contribution. In this work we build two efficient UPKE schemes in the *standard model.* Our first scheme is based on the DDH assumption and is approximately "security parameter less efficient" compared to the Hashed ElGamal UPKE scheme described above. Our second construction is also quite efficient and is based on the Learning-With-Errors (LWE) assumption. In particular, it gives the first efficient UPKE based on an assumption that is believed to be post-quantum secure. This was not known even in the random oracle model.

A rough summary of efficiency, security, usability, and assumptions trade-off for our schemes when compared to previous PKE, UPKE, and FS-PKE schemes is given in Table 1. It is clear from the table that our efficiency falls between that of PKE and FS-PKE (much closer to the former), we achieve the same (resp. much stronger) forward security as FS-PKE (resp. PKE), but we do require a stronger synchronization assumption than FS-PKE.

1.1 Our Technique: Using Circular Security and Leakage-Resilience

Looking at the random-oracle-based UPKE scheme of [5,38], we observe that the attacker learns the value $s' = s + \delta$, but also an encryption of δ. Namely, the attacker simultaneously gets: (a) encryption of (some function of the) secret-key, and (b) some leakage s' on the secret-key s. Of course, in that particular scheme, the leakage in (b) was trivial, since δ was completely random and therefore s'

Table 1. Comparison of different primitives. (κ is security parameter.)

Factors	PKE	UPKE [5,38] RO Model	UPKE (this work) Standard Model	FS-PKE
Efficiency	Very Efficient	$\approx$ PKE	$\approx$ PKE $\cdot \kappa$	Inefficient compared to PKE [a] (from HIBE)
Assumptions	DDH/CDH, Factoring, LWE	CDH	DDH, LWE	DDH/CDH, Factoring, LWE
Forward Security?	No	Yes	Yes	Yes
Synchronization	None	Strong (Updates)	Strong (Updates)	Weak (Time Periods)

[a] Here we compared to PKE based on the same assumption (DDH, LWE, etc.) to make this an "apple-to-apple" comparison. However, there are HIBEs [14,15] which are relatively efficient, but rely on pairings and use relatively strong assumptions.

is completely independent of s, while (so-called) key-dependent-message (KDM) security [13] in (a) was easily handled by the random oracle.

Nevertheless, we will find the abstractions in (a)+(b) useful when going to the standard model. In particular, we will follow the same template, but rely on circular-secure encryption schemes in the standard model under DDH/LWE (e.g., [8,17]) where the key s and/or the updates δ must consist of "small" values in some larger group $\mathbb{Z}_p$ and hence the leakage $s' = s + \delta$ in part (b) will no longer be trivial.[5] Luckily, these schemes are also leakage resilient and hence this non-trivial leakage does not hurt security.

Indeed, modulo several important technicalities,[6] both of our standard model constructions will effectively build UPKE from a regular PKE, which satisfies the following three properties simultaneously:

1. *Circular-secure and leakage-resilient (CS+LR):* Given encryption of the secret key s and any bounded-entropy leakage on s, the scheme is still semantically secure. See Sect. 4 for the precise definition.
2. *Key-Homomorphic:* Given a public key and a ciphertext pair that corresponds to some secret key s, together with some offset δ, we can convert them into a public key and a ciphertext pair that corresponds to the secret key $s' = s + \delta$ while preserving the encrypted message.
3. *Message-Homomorphic:* Given a ciphertext encrypting some value s, and offset s', we can convert it into a ciphertext encrypting $s' - s$.

Note that, for correctness, the scheme may restrict the secret key or the encrypted messages to be "small" values in a larger group over which the homomorphism holds.

We can now build UPKE as follows. We start with the circular-secure and leakage-resilient scheme and implement the updating mechanism by simply

---

[5] This is true for the DDH-based scheme of [17] since circular security requires encrypting in the exponent and decryption involves solving discrete log; therefore the encrypted values must be small. This is also true for the LWE-based scheme where the secret key must be small for correctness.

[6] Which is why we present the schemes separately, and the abstraction we give below is mainly for the intuition.

encrypting a random (small) offset δ and updating the public key appropriately using the key-homomorphic property. The receiver decrypts δ and updates their secret key s to $s' = s + \delta$. Note that the original key s should still have entropy when conditioned on the updated key s', so that we can use the leakage resilience of our scheme.

Reduction Idea. To get the intuition for our security proof, we first present the simplest special case where the challenge ciphertext for UPKE is requested in the very first time period, and there is a single honest update after the challenge, followed by the reveal of the resulting secret key s' to the attacker. As we will see, in this case, we will not even need to use the key-homomorphic property, but it is easy to see how key-homomorphic property will be needed for the general case. In our reduction, we will now need to utilize our UPKE attacker $\mathcal{A}$ for this simplest case, to build our CS+LR-attacker $\mathcal{A}'$.

$\mathcal{A}'$ will start with the challenge public key pk and will forward it to $\mathcal{A}$.

$\mathcal{A}$ will select two message m_0 and m_1 and give them to $\mathcal{A}'$.

$\mathcal{A}'$ will use these messages as its own challenge and will choose a probabilistic leakage function $s' = s + \delta$ for a random (unknown!) offset δ, where s is the original secret key of the CS+LR scheme.

Upon receiving this challenge ciphertext c^* and the value s' from its challenger, $\mathcal{A}'$ can simply forward c^* to $\mathcal{A}$, and also declare s' as the final value of the secret key after the update.

However, $\mathcal{A}'$ also needs to properly simulate the update ciphertext e which was supposed to encrypt the (unknown) value δ.

This is where $\mathcal{A}'$ will use the encryption e' of the secret key s, and the message-homomorphic property of the encryption scheme, to produce an encryption e of $\delta = s' - s$.

This completes the special case of the reduction. For the general case, where several (untrusted) updates could happen before the challenge is issued, we will also need to use the key-homomorphic property: both for

(a) converting the challenge ciphertext c^* in period 1 into the ciphertext encrypting the same message during the challenge period; as well as for

(b) converting the original encryption e' of s in period 1 into correctly distributed encryption e of δ during the exposure period.

While the high-level idea above will work for both of our DDH/LWE instantiations, in both cases we need to overcome certain challenges due to the need to correctly simulate various distributions in the above-sketched reduction.

Instantiating from DDH. We show that the BHHO cryptosystem [17] constructed from the DDH assumption satisfies the properties we need. In that cryptosystem the secret key is $s \in \mathbb{Z}_p^\ell$. Circular security holds when each component of the secret key is encrypted in the exponent, and decryption recovers the secret key by taking the discrete log. For this reason, the BHHO scheme needs to use a "short" $s \in \{0,1\}^\ell \subseteq \mathbb{Z}_p^\ell$. In our setting, we will set the initial key to a uniformly random $s_0 \in \{0,1\}^\ell$. Each update will choose some random offset $\delta_i \in \{0,1\}^\ell$ and will encrypt the value δ_i in the exponent; the updated key will be $s_{i+1} = s_i + \delta_i$ where the addition is performed over $\mathbb{Z}_p$. This scheme was shown to be circular secure [17] and leakage-resilient [46]; we show that the two security properties also hold simultaneously. It is also easy to see that the scheme is key and message homomorphic. When we use this scheme as a UPKE, we rely on the fact that when $\delta, s \in \{0,1\}^\ell$ are both chosen randomly then giving the sum $\delta + s$ (with addition over $\mathbb{Z}_p$) only reduces the entropy of s by $\ell \cdot \log(4/3) \leq \ell/2$ bits.

Instantiating from LWE. We show that the dual-Regev cryptosystem [33,48] constructed from the LWE assumption also satisfies the properties we need. The proof of circular security and leakage resilience are analogous to those of BHHO. One subtle issue that, while the dual-Regev scheme is key-homomorphic, when we update the key, we no longer get the correct ciphertext distribution – in particular, the "error term" distribution is perturbed. To fix this, we need to resort to the 'noise flooding/smudging" technique, where we add some super-polynomial noise to the ciphertext to hide small polynomial differences in the error term.

Follow Up Work. Following this work, the work of [28] defined an extension of UPKE called *fast-forwardable* UPKE (FF-UPKE). FF-UPKE addresses the problem that the UPKE receiver might be offline or otherwise miss many update ciphertexts, resulting in a situation where its current secret key sk_i is considerably behind the current public key pk_j: $i \ll j$. Of course, such "stale" receiver can still get to the current key sk_j, by downloading $\Delta = (j - i)$ key update messages, and performing Δ sequential secret key updates to "catch up". The goal of FF-UPKE is to achieve such "catching up" much faster: say, but only downloading a sub-linear (and, ideally, logarithmic) in Δ number of update ciphertexts (and, similarly, doing the sub-linear amount of work). [28] also built a generic FF-UPKE from any UPKE which they call *update-homomorphic*. Interestingly, minor modifications of our UPKE constructions turn out to be update-homomorphic. In contrast, the ROM-based UPKE [38] does not appear to be update-homomorphic and does not suffice for building FF-UPKE. Thus, as an unexpected application, the homomorphic properties of our construction,—which were needed to argue security of our scheme, but were not needed for the functionality,—turned out to be useful in a setting where random oracle does not appear to help.

1.2   Additional Theoretical Contributions

In the full version of our paper, we also consider two natural strengthenings of the basic chosen-plaintext attack (CPA) security of UPKE. First, we define the chosen-ciphertext attack (CCA) variant, where the attacker also has oracle access to the decryption oracle. Second, we consider extending the capability of untrusted senders in the CPA/CCA security game to produce *arbitrary* tuple of update ciphertext e and the corresponding new public key pk', rather than limiting their ability to selecting bad randomness r, and then *honestly* using r to produce the tuple (e, pk').

As initial feasibility results, for both variants, we show a generic way—using appropriate [27] notion of non-interactive zero-knowledge (NIZK) proofs—to extend the basic CPA notion of UPKE to meet the corresponding stronger requirement. Using the existing feasibility of such NIZK proofs from DDH/LWE, we get these stronger forms of UPKE can be met, under the corresponding assumption, in the standard model. Unlike our CPA constructions described above, here we do not give an *efficient* instantiation of the resulting schemes from DDH/LWE, leaving those to future work.

1.3   Related Work

Hierarchical Identity-Based Encryption (HIBE). As mentioned, Canetti et al. [24] also showed how to build FS-PKE (and therefore also UPKE) from any Hierarchical Identity-Based Encryption (HIBE) [14,15,22,25,30,31,34,35].

By plugging in prior constructions of HIBE from DDH/CDH [22,30,31], we would get an alternate construction of UPKE from DDH/CDH in the standard model. However, this construction is mainly of theoretical interest and is hugely impractical. In particular, it relies on complex garbled circuits that perform public-key operations. In more detail, if κ is the security parameter, the construction relies on a chain of $O(\kappa)$ garbled circuits, each of which outputs $O(\kappa)$ special ciphertexts (encrypted labels for next level garbled circuit), where each ciphertext consists of at least $O(\kappa)$ group elements; the fact that this is all computed inside a garbled circuit then adds at least another $O(\kappa)$ overhead on top. Lastly, going from HIBE to FS-PKE/UPKE adds another $O(\kappa)$ overhead, for a total complexity of at least $O(\kappa^5)$. So the complexity is at least $O(\kappa^3)$ worse than our scheme, even without getting into huge concrete overheads.

By plugging in prior constructions of HIBE from LWE [2,25], we would get an alternate construction of UPKE from LWE in the standard model. The resulting schemes could potentially be piratically efficient. However, our construction is still significantly simpler and more efficient for several reasons: (1) We do not rely on lattice trapdoors or GPV style pre-image sampling [33], which makes our scheme both conceptually simpler and practically more efficient. (2) Our secret key is a single lattice vector rather than an entire lattice basis. This makes our secret keys roughly an $O(\kappa)$ factor shorter. (3) We avoid the additional $O(\kappa)$ factor overhead in the transformation from HIBE to FS-PKE/UPKE.

Forward-Secure Signatures. Forward-Secure Signatures [6] are similar to FS-PKE, in that compromising the current signing key should not enable forgery of messages for previous periods. In particular, the tree-based FS-signature scheme of Bellare and Miner [11] was the inspiration for the HIBE-based FS-PKE of [24]. The above work was later extended by Malkin *et al.* [43]. Forward-secure signatures were also studied in the random oracle setting [1,36,41].

Other Key Evolving Encryption Schemes. The works of Jaeger and Stepanovs [37] and Poettering and Rössler [47] proposed two related notions of *key-updatable* PKE scheme, which provide an even stronger form of key-evolution than FS-PKE. In these schemes, key updates can be labeled by arbitrary, possibly adversarially chosen, strings. Unsurprisingly, the schemes in these works were also built from HIBE.

Circular and KDM Secure Encryption Schemes. Circular secure schemes allow the attacker to see encryptions of the secret key of the scheme. A natural extension of this notion studies a cycle of (sk_i, pk_i) pairs for $i = 1, \ldots, n$ where we encrypt sk_i under $pk_{i \mod n+1}$. This was defined as *key-dependent message security (KDM)* by Black *et al.* [13] and as *circular security* by Camenisch and Lysyanskaya [23]. The first cryptosystem in the standard model with a proof of KDM-security under a standard assumption was given by Boneh *et al.* [17]. Subsequently, constructions from the learning with errors (LWE) [8] and quadratic residuosity [20] assumptions were proposed. Construction for identity-based KDM-secure encryption [4] was also proposed. While the construction of Boneh *et al.* [17] was for affine functions, subsequent "KDM amplifications" transforms extended the class of functions significantly [7,10,21,44].

Leakage-Resilient Encryption Schemes. Most of the security models do not capture possible *side-channel attacks*. These attacks are designed to exploit unintended leakage that often stems from the physical environment. Akavia *et al.* [3] proposed a realistic framework that aimed to capture information about the leakage. Subsequent work by Naor and Segev [46] analyzed the resilience of public key cryptosystems to leakage. An important result was that they showed the (even slightly optimized version of the) BHHO scheme [17] was resilient to $|sk|(1 - o(1))$ bits of leakage. Subsequent work [26] showed the leakage resilience of both the BHHO scheme and the dual Regev encryption scheme [33,48] in the auxiliary input model. Brakerski *et al.* [22] studied both the leakage resilience and circular security of anonymous IBE. We point to the survey of leakage resilient cryptography by Kalai and Reyzin [39] for additional work in this domain.

Different "Updatable" Encryption. With an unfortunate naming collision, there has been a different kind of "updatable encryption schemes" considered in the literature [16,18,19,32,40,42]. These are *symmetric-key* encryption schemes that aim to accomplish key rotation in the cloud, specifically moving the ciphertexts under the old key to the new key. In particular, these schemes produce multiple encryptions of the same message under different keys and aim to produce update tokens that allow the update of old ciphertexts, without leaking the message content. In contrast, updatable schemes in this paper are *public-key*, encrypt different messages, and aim to achieve forward security. Thus, the notions are very different despite the partial naming collision.

2 Preliminaries

Notation. For a distribution X, we use $x \leftarrow_\$ X$ to denote that x is a random sample drawn from the distribution X. For a set S we use $x \leftarrow_\$ S$ to denote that x is chosen uniformly at random from the set S. We denote by U_d the uniform distribution over $\{0,1\}^d$.

Information-Theoretic Notions. The *prediction probability* is

$$\mathsf{Pred}(X) := \max_x \mathsf{P}[X = x].$$

We can also denote

$$\mathsf{Pred}(X|y) := \max_x \mathsf{P}[X = x | Y = y].$$

We define the conditional versions as

$$\mathsf{Pred}(X|Y) := \mathbf{E}_{y \leftarrow Y}\left[\mathsf{Pred}(X|y)\right].$$

The *(average-case) conditional min-entropy* is $\mathrm{H}_\infty(X|Y) = -\log(\mathsf{Pred}(X|Y))$. The *statistical distance* of X and Y is $\mathsf{SD}(X,Y) = \frac{1}{2}\sum_x |\mathsf{P}[X = x] - \mathsf{P}[Y = y]|$.

Theorem 1 (Leftover Hash Lemma). *Fix $\varepsilon > 0$. Let X be a random variable on $\{0,1\}^n$ with conditional min-entropy $\mathrm{H}_\infty(X|E) \geq k$. Let $\mathcal{H} = \{\mathcal{H}_n\}_{n \in \mathbb{N}}$ where $\mathcal{H}_n = \{h_s\}_{s \in \{0,1\}^d}$ for all n, be a universal hash family with output length $m \leq k - 2\log(1/\varepsilon)$. Then, $(h_{U_d}(X), U_d, E) \approx_\varepsilon (U_m, U_d, E)$*

Lemma 1 (Smudging Lemma [9]). *Let $B_1 = B_1(\kappa)$ and $B_2 = B_2(\kappa)$ be positive integers and let $e_1 \in [-B_1, B_1]$ be a fixed integer. Let $e_2 \leftarrow_\$ [-B_2, B_2]$ be chosen uniformly at random. Then the distribution of e_2 is statistically indistinguishable from $e_1 + e_2$ as long as $B_1/B_2 = negl(\kappa)$.*

Definition 1 (The Decisional Diffie Hellman Assumption (DDH)). *Let $\mathcal{G}$ be a probabilistic polynomial-time "group generator" that, given as a parameter 1^κ where κ is the security parameter, outputs the description of a group $\mathbb{G}$ that has prime order $p = p(\kappa)$. The decisional Diffie Hellman (DDH) assumption for $\mathcal{G}$ says that the following two ensembles are computationally indistinguishable:*

$$\{(g_1, g_2, g_1^r, g_2^r) : g_i \leftarrow \mathbb{G}, r \leftarrow \mathbb{Z}_p\} \approx_c \{(g_1, g_2, g_1^{r_1}, g_2^{r_2}) : g_i \leftarrow \mathbb{G}, r_i \leftarrow \mathbb{Z}_p\}$$

A lemma of Naor and Reingold [45] generalizes the above assumption for $m > 2$ generators.

Lemma 2 ([45]). *Under the DDH assumption on $\mathcal{G}$,*

$$\{(g_1, \ldots, g_m, g_1^r, \ldots, g_m^r) : g_i \leftarrow \mathbb{G}, r \leftarrow \mathbb{Z}_p\} \approx_c \{(g_1, \ldots, g_m, g_1^{r_1}, \ldots, g_m^{r_m}) : g_i \leftarrow \mathbb{G}, r_i \leftarrow \mathbb{Z}_p\}$$

Definition 2 (Learning with Errors Assumption (LWE)). *Consider integers n, m, q and a probability distribution χ on $\mathbb{Z}_q$, typically taken to be a normal distribution that has been discretized. Then, the LWE assumption states that the following two ensembles are computationally indistinguishable:*

$$\{A, A^T x + e : A \leftarrow_\$ \mathbb{Z}_q^{n \times m}, x \leftarrow_\$ \mathbb{Z}_q^n, e \leftarrow_\$ \chi^m\} \approx_c \{A, v : A \leftarrow_\$ \mathbb{Z}_q^{n \times m}, v \leftarrow_\$ \mathbb{Z}_q^m\}$$

3   Updatable Public Key Encryption (UPKE)

Jost *et al.* [38] introduced the notion of an Updatable Public Key Encryption (UPKE). This definition was later modified by the work of Alwen *et al.* [5]. Below, we present our variant of the UPKE.

Definition 3. *An updatable public key encryption (UPKE) scheme is a set of five polynomial-time algorithms* UPKE = (U-PKEG, U-Enc, U-Dec, Upd-Pk, Upd-Sk) *with the following syntax:*

- *Key generation:* U-PKEG *takes as parameter* 1^κ *where* κ *is the security parameter and outputs a fresh secret key* sk_0 *and a fresh initial public key* pk_0.
- *Encryption:* U-Enc *receives a public key* pk *and a message* m *to produce a ciphertext* c.
- *Decryption:* U-Dec *receives a secret key* sk *and a ciphertext* c *to produce message* m.
- *Update Public Key:* Upd-Pk *receives a public key* pk *to produce an update ciphertext* up *and a new public key* pk'.
- *Update Secret Key:* Upd-Sk *receives an update ciphertext* up *and secret key* sk *to produce a new secret key* sk'.

Correctness. Let (sk_0, pk_0) be the output of U-PKEG. For any sequence of randomness $\{r_i\}_{i=1}^{q}$, define the sequence of public keys and secret keys $\{(pk_i, sk_i)\}_{i=1}^{q}$ as follows: $(up_i, pk_i) \leftarrow$ Upd-Pk$(pk_{i-1}; r_i)$, $sk_i \leftarrow$ Upd-Sk(sk_{i-1}, up_i). Then, UPKE is correct if for any message m and for any $j \in [q]$,

$$P\left[\text{U-Dec}(sk_j, \text{U-Enc}(pk_j, m)) = m\right] = 1 .$$

3.1   IND-CR-CPA Security of UPKE

In this section, we define the security game. We will called this the IND-CR-CPA Security which is meant to capture INDistinguishibility under Chosen Randomness Chosen Plaintext Attack. Largely similar to the CPA security game, this also additionally allows the adversary to choose the randomness used to update the keys which is modeled by the following oracle access:

- $\mathcal{O}_{upd}(\cdot)$: $\mathcal{A}$ provides its choice of randomness r_i. The Challenger increments the time to $i + 1$. It then performs the following actions:

$$(up_{i+1}, pk_{i+1}) \leftarrow \text{Upd-Pk}(pk_i; r_i); \ sk_{i+1} \leftarrow \text{Upd-Sk}(sk_i, up_{i+1}) .$$

For any adversary $\mathcal{A}$ with running time t we consider the IND-CR-CPA security game:

- Sample $(sk_0, pk_0) \leftarrow$ U-PKEG(1^κ), $b \leftarrow_\$ \{0, 1\}$.
- $(m_0^*, m_1^*, state) \leftarrow_\$ \mathcal{A}^{\mathcal{O}_{upd}(\cdot)}(pk_0)$
- Compute $c^* \leftarrow_\$$ U-Enc$(pk_{q'}, m_b^*)$ where q' is the current time period.

- $state \leftarrow^\$ \mathcal{A}^{\mathcal{O}_{upd}(\cdot)}(c^*, state)$
- Choose uniformly random r^* and then compute

$$(\mathsf{up}^*, \mathsf{pk}^*) \leftarrow \mathsf{Upd\text{-}Pk}(\mathsf{pk}_q; r^*); \quad \mathsf{sk}^* \leftarrow \mathsf{Upd\text{-}Sk}(\mathsf{sk}_q, \mathsf{up}^*) .$$

where q is the current time period.
- $b' \leftarrow^\$ \mathcal{A}(\mathsf{pk}^*, \mathsf{sk}^*, \mathsf{up}^*, state)$.
- $\mathcal{A}$ wins the game if $b = b'$. The advantage of $\mathcal{A}$ in winning the above game is denoted by $\mathrm{Adv}^{\mathsf{UPKE}}_{\mathrm{crcpa}}(\mathcal{A}) = |\mathsf{P}\,[b = b'] - \frac{1}{2}|$.

Definition 4. *An updatable public-key encryption scheme* UPKE *is IND-CR-CPA-secure if for all PPT attackers* $\mathcal{A}$, *its advantage* $\mathrm{Adv}^{\mathsf{UPKE}}_{\mathrm{crcpa}}(\mathcal{A})$ *is negligible.*

Remark 1 (Comparison of the Security Models.). The work of Jost *et al.* [38] defined a notion which had an update procedure not specific to any public key. This was designed to support multiple instances, i.e. multiple key pairs, and where the offset generated by the public update could be applied to many public keys. While we consider the simpler setting of only one instance, which is also reflected in our syntax, we believe that our constructions trivially satisfy the stronger security model proposed by [38]. Our model also allows for $q \neq q'$, i.e., for the adversary to issue a challenge in one time period and corrupt in another time period. However, without loss of generality, we give the attacker the final secret key sk^* immediately following the honest post-challenge key update (at period q'), as this gives the most amount of information to the attacker.

Our definition is a generalization of the model proposed by Alwen *et al.* [5]: their notion forced an update of the keys after every encryption query, while ours separates the two processes for more flexibility.

4   Key-Dependent-Message-Secure Encryption Scheme

Let us recall the definition of a public-key encryption scheme.

Definition 5. *An encryption scheme is a set of three polynomial-time algorithms* $\mathcal{E} = (\mathsf{Gen}, \mathsf{Enc}, \mathsf{Dec})$ *with the following syntax:*

- *__Key generation:__* Gen *receives* 1^κ *where* κ *is the security parameter and outputs a fresh secret* sk *and outputs a fresh public key* pk.
- *__Encryption:__* Enc *receives a public key* pk *and a message* m *to produce a ciphertext* c.
- *__Decryption:__* Dec *receives a secret key* sk *and a ciphertext* c *to produce message* m.

Correctness. The correctness of an encryption scheme is such that $(\mathsf{pk}, \mathsf{sk}) \leftarrow \mathsf{Gen}(1^\kappa)$, $\forall m \in \mathcal{M}$,

$$\mathsf{P}\,[\mathsf{Dec}(\mathsf{sk}, \mathsf{Enc}(\mathsf{pk}, m)) = m] = 1$$

CS+LR Security. For any PPT adversary $\mathcal{A}$ we consider the following security game:

- Sample $(\mathsf{sk},\mathsf{pk}) \leftarrow^{\$} \mathsf{Gen}(1^\kappa)$, $b \leftarrow^{\$} \{0,1\}$.
- $L, f, m_0, m_1 \leftarrow^{\$} \mathcal{A}(\mathsf{pk})$ where L is the leakage function chosen by $\mathcal{A}$, m_0, m_1 are the challenge messages, and f is the function of the secret key that $\mathcal{A}$ wants to receive as encryption. L defines the leakage resilience and f defines the KDM security.
- Compute $C \leftarrow^{\$} \mathsf{Enc}(\mathsf{pk}, m_b)$, $C' \leftarrow^{\$} \mathsf{Enc}(\mathsf{pk}, f(\mathsf{sk}))^7$.
- $b' \leftarrow^{\$} \mathcal{A}(c_0, c_1, L(\mathsf{sk}))$.
- $\mathcal{A}$ wins the game if $b = b'$. The advantage of $\mathcal{A}$ in winning the above game is denoted by $\mathrm{Adv}^{\mathcal{E}}_{\mathrm{KDM}}(\mathcal{A}) = |\mathsf{P}\left[b = b'\right] - \frac{1}{2}|$.

Definition 6. *A public-key encryption scheme $\mathcal{E}$ is λ-CS+LR-secure if for all PPT attackers $\mathcal{A}$, and leakage functions L such that $\mathrm{H}_\infty(\mathsf{sk}|L(\mathsf{sk})) \geq |\mathsf{sk}| - \lambda$, its advantage $\mathrm{Adv}^{\mathcal{E}}_{\mathrm{cs+lr}}(\mathcal{A})$ is negligible.*

5   DDH Based Construction

This section presents construction from the DDH Assumption. We begin by presenting a slightly modified version of the PKE Scheme proposed by Boneh *et al.* [17] in Sect. 5.1. This scheme was shown to be independently circular secure and leakage resilient. We also show that the scheme is CS+LR secure in Sect. 5.2. We then present our construction of a UPKE scheme (Sect. 5.3), extended from the PKE scheme. We finally prove that the UPKE scheme is IND-CPA secure in Sect. 5.4.

5.1   The BHHO Cryptosystem

In this section, we present a modified version of the original BHHO Cryptosystem. This is presented as Construction 1.

Correctness. Let $m \in \mathbb{G}$. $\mathsf{Enc}(\mathsf{pk}, m) = (f_1 = g_1^r, \ldots, f_\ell = g_\ell^r, c = h^r \cdot m)$. Now, $\mathsf{Dec}(\mathsf{sk}, f_1, \ldots, f_\ell, c)$ outputs: $c \cdot (\prod_{i=1}^{\ell} f_i^{s_i})^{-1} = h^r \cdot m(\prod_{i=1}^{\ell} f_i^{s_i})^{-1} = (\prod_{i=1}^{\ell} g_i^{s_i})^r \cdot m \cdot (\prod_{i=1}^{\ell}(g_i^r)^{s_i})^{-1} = m$.

5.2   CS+LR Security of BHHO Cryptosystem

In this section, we provide proof of the combined circular security and leakage resilience of the BHHO Cryptosystem. Formally, we will prove the following theorem:

Theorem 2. *Under the DDH Assumption, Construction 1 is λ-CS+LR secure for leakage $\lambda = \ell - 2\log p - \omega(\log \kappa)$.*

---

[7] In our security proofs, the function f will be applied to each bit of the secret key.

Protocol BHHO Cryptosystem

$\mathsf{Gen}(1^\kappa)$

    Sample $s = (s_1, \ldots, s_\ell) \leftarrow_\$ \{0,1\}$ and
$g_1, \ldots, g_\ell \leftarrow_\$ \mathbb{G}$.
    Compute $h = \prod_{i=1}^\ell g_i^{s_i}$.
    return $\mathsf{sk} = s \in \mathbb{Z}_p^\ell$, $\mathsf{pk} = (g_1, \ldots, g_\ell, h) \in \mathbb{G}^{\ell+1}$.

$\mathsf{Enc}(\mathsf{pk}, m \in \mathbb{G})$

    Parse $\mathsf{pk} = (g_1, \ldots, g_\ell, h)$
    Sample $r \leftarrow_\$ \mathbb{Z}_p$
    for $i = 1, \ldots, \ell$ **do**
        Compute $f_i = g_i^r$
    return $C = (f_1, \ldots, f_\ell, c = h^r \cdot m) \in \mathbb{G}^{\ell+1}$

$\mathsf{Dec}(\mathsf{sk}, C)$

    Parse $C = (f_1, \ldots, f_\ell, c = h^r \cdot m)$ and $\mathsf{sk} = s = (s_1, \ldots, s_\ell) \in \mathbb{Z}_p^\ell$
    Compute $m' = c \cdot \left(\prod_{i=1}^\ell f_i^{s_i}\right)^{-1}$
    return m'

Construction 1. A modified version of the BHHO Cryptosystem where the bits of the secret key are not encoded as group elements. Let κ be the the security parameter. Let $\mathcal{G}$ be a probabilistic polynomial-time "group generator" that takes as input 1^κ and outputs the description of a group $\mathbb{G}$ with prime order $p = p(\kappa)$ and g is a fixed generator of $\mathbb{G}$.

However, before we can prove the theorem, we will prove that there exists an algorithm $\mathsf{Enc}'(\mathsf{pk}, i)$ such that $(\mathsf{pk}, \mathsf{Enc}(\mathsf{pk}, g^{s_i}), s) \approx_c (\mathsf{pk}, \mathsf{Enc}'(\mathsf{pk}, i), s)$. Consider the following definition of Enc':

$$\mathsf{Enc}'(\mathsf{pk}, i) = (f_1 = g_1^r, \ldots, f_{i-1} = g_{i-1}^r, f_i = g_i^r/g, f_{i+1} = g_{i+1}^r, \ldots, f_\ell = g_\ell^r, h^r)$$

We will first show that this ciphertext decrypts correctly to g^{s_i}.

$$\mathsf{Dec}(s, f_1, \ldots, f_\ell, c = h^r) = h^r \cdot \left(\prod_{i=1}^\ell f_i^{s_i}\right)^{-1} = h^r \left(\prod_{i=1}^\ell g_i^{s_i}\right)^{-r} g^{s_i} = h^r h^{-r} g^{s_i} = g^{s_i}$$

Lemma 3. *Under the DDH Assumption,* $(\mathsf{pk}, \mathsf{Enc}(\mathsf{pk}, g^{s_i}), s) \approx_c (\mathsf{pk}, \mathsf{Enc}'(\mathsf{pk}, i), s)$ *where* $(\mathsf{pk}, s) \leftarrow_\$ \mathsf{Gen}(1^\kappa)$

Proof. We will prove the lemma through a sequence of hybrids, outlined in Table 2.

Hybrid D_0. This is when Enc is used to encrypt g^{s_i}. It corresponds to the distribution:

$$(\mathsf{pk}, g_1^r, \ldots, g_\ell^r, h^r \cdot g^{s_i}, s : r \leftarrow_\$ \mathbb{Z}_p)$$

Hybrid D_1. This is same as Hybrid D_0 where we replace h^r by the steps of the decryption algorithm. It corresponds to the distribution

$$\left(\mathsf{pk}, f_1 = g_1^r, \ldots, f_\ell = g_\ell^r, \prod_{j=1}^\ell f_j^{s_j} \cdot g^{s_i}, s : r \leftarrow_\$ \mathbb{Z}_p\right)$$

Table 2. Proof outline for Lemma 3

Hybrid	Hybrid Definition	Security
D_0	Enc is used to encrypt g^{s_i}	Identical
D_1	D_0 except $h^r \cdot g^{s_i}$ replaced with $\prod_{j=1}^{\ell} f_j^{s_j} \cdot g^{s_i}$	
		DDH
D_2	D_1 except each $f_j \leftarrow_\$ \mathbb{G}$	
		Identical
D_3	D_2 except f_i is replaced by f_i/g where $f_i \leftarrow_\$ \mathbb{G}$	
		DDH
D_4	D_3 except $f_j = g_j^r$ where $r \leftarrow_\$ \mathbb{Z}_p$	
		Identical
D_5	Enc$'$ is used to encrypt g^{s_i}	

The distributions D_0 and D_1 are identical for the same value of $r \leftarrow_\$ \mathbb{Z}_p$. Therefore, there is no distinguishing advantage for any adversary $\mathcal{A}$.

Hybrid D_2. In this case, we sample each $f_i \leftarrow_\$ \mathbb{G}$. This corresponds to the distribution:

$$\left(\mathsf{pk}, f_1, \ldots, f_\ell, \prod_{j=1}^{\ell} f_j^{s_j} \cdot g^{s_i}, s : f_1, \ldots, f_\ell \leftarrow_\$ \mathbb{G} \right)$$

Claim. If DDH (as defined in Lemma 2) is hard for $\mathbb{G}$, then for every PPT $\mathcal{A}$, the advantage in distinguishing Hybrids D_1 and D_2 is negligible.

Proof. We will use an adversary $\mathcal{A}$ capable of distinguishing between the two distributions to create an adversary $\mathcal{B}$ that can win against the DDH Game. After receiving input from the challenger $(g_1, \ldots, g_\ell, f_1, \ldots, f_\ell)$, $\mathcal{B}$ generates $(\mathsf{pk}, \mathsf{sk} = s)$ and returns to $\mathcal{A}$: $(f_1, \ldots, f_\ell, \prod_{j=1}^{\ell} f_j^{s_j} \cdot g^{s_i}, s)$. It is easy to see that $\mathcal{B}$ perfectly simulates one of the hybrids based on the input it receives. This concludes the proof that $\mathcal{A}$ has negligible advantage in distinguishing the two hybrids.   □

Hybrid D_3. The same distribution as Hybrid 2, except that f_i is replaced by f_i/g.

$$\left(\mathsf{pk}, f_1, \ldots, f_{i-1}, f_i/g, f_{i+1}, \ldots, f_\ell, \prod_{j=1}^{\ell} f_j^{s_j} \cdot g^{s_i}, s : f_1, \ldots, f_\ell \leftarrow_\$ \mathbb{G} \right)$$

We know that for fixed g, f_i/g is indistinguishable from f_i where $f_i \leftarrow_\$ \mathbb{G}$. Therefore, the distributions are identical and $\mathcal{A}$ has no advantage in distinguishing the two distributions.

Hybrid D_4. This is corresponding to the distribution where $f_j = g_j^r$ where $r \leftarrow_\$ \mathbb{Z}_p$.

$$\left(\mathsf{pk}, g_1^r, \ldots, g_{i-1}^r, g_i^r/g, g_{i+1}^r, \ldots, g_\ell^r, \prod_{j=1}^{\ell} f_j^{s_j} \cdot g^{s_i}, s : r \leftarrow_\$ \mathbb{Z}_p \right)$$

Table 3. Proof outline for Theorem 2

Hybrid	Hybrid Definition	Security
D_0	The Original CS+LR Security Game, Enc is used	Corollary 1
D_1	D_0 except Enc' is used	
		Identical
D_2	D_1 except $h^r \cdot m_b$ replaced with $\prod_{j=1}^{\ell} f_j^{s_j} \cdot m_b$	
		DDH
D_3	D_2 except each f_i is replaced by $f_i \leftarrow_\$ \mathbb{G}$	
		Leftover Hash Lemma
D_4	D_3 except $\prod_{j=1}^{\ell} f_j^{s_j} \cdot m_b$ replaced by $U \leftarrow_\$ \mathbb{G}$	

Claim. If DDH (as defined in Lemma 2) is hard for $\mathbb{G}$, then for every PPT $\mathcal{A}$, the advantage in distinguishing Hybrids D_3 and D_4 is negligible.

The proof of this claim is similar to the proof of the earlier claim.

Hybrid 5. This is corresponding to the distribution $(\text{Enc}'(\text{pk}, i), s)$, $f_i = g_i^r/g$ where $r \leftarrow_\$ \mathbb{Z}_p$.

$$(\text{pk}, f_1 = g_1^r, \ldots, f_{i-1} = g_{i-1}^r, f_i = g_i^r/g, f_{i+1} = g_{i+1}^r, \ldots, f_\ell = g_\ell^r, h^r, s : r \leftarrow_\$ \mathbb{Z}_p)$$

It is clear that the input distribution in Hybrids D_4 and D_5 are identical for the same r and $\mathcal{A}$ has no advantage in distinguishing the two distributions. This is because: $\prod_{j=1}^{\ell} f_j^{s_j} \cdot g^{s_i} = \prod_{j \neq i} g_j^{r s_j} \cdot g_i^{r s_i}/g^{s_i} \cdot g^{s_i} = (\prod_{j=1}^{\ell} g_j^{s_j})^r = h^r$.   □

Therefore, we have shown that $(\text{Enc}(\text{pk}, g^{s_i}), s) \approx_c (\text{Enc}'(\text{pk}, i), s)$.

Further, note that each s_i is independently chosen. Additionally, each encryption/fake-encryption chooses its own independent randomness r. Therefore, we can independently replace each $\text{Enc}(\text{pk}, g^{s_i})$ with $\text{Enc}'(\text{pk}, i)$, and the resulting encryption of secret key is computationally indistinguishable from the one computed by Enc'. This proof can be shown by a sequence of hybrids, replacing one encryption at a time. Therefore, as a corollary we get that:

Corollary 1. *Under the DDH Assumption,*

$$(\text{pk}, \text{Enc}(\text{pk}, g^{s_1}), \ldots, \text{Enc}(\text{pk}, g^{s_\ell}), s) \approx_c (\text{pk}, \text{Enc}'(\text{pk}, 1), \ldots, \text{Enc}(\text{pk}, \ell), s)$$

With this corollary, we can prove the original theorem:

Theorem 2. *Under the DDH Assumption, Construction 1 is λ-CS+LR secure for leakage $\lambda = \ell - 2\log p - \omega(\log \kappa)$.*

Proof. We will prove the same through a sequence of hybrids, summarized in Table 3. Note that each of our hybrid distribution contains pk and $L(\text{sk} = s)$ in its definition. We drop these terms from the definition for simplicity and merely focus on the two ciphertexts which undergo the bulk of the changes.

Hybrid D_0. The original CS+LR Game. In this hybrid, $\mathcal{A}$ receives the following distribution:

$$\left(C = (f_1 = g_1^r, \ldots, f_\ell = g_\ell^r, h^r \cdot m_b), C' = (\mathsf{Enc}(\mathsf{pk}, g^{s_1}), \ldots, \mathsf{Enc}(\mathsf{pk}, g^{s_\ell})) : r \leftarrow_\$ \mathbb{Z}_p\right)$$

Hybrid D_1. The CS+LR Game but with C' consisting of the "fake encryption" algorithm. This corresponds to the distribution:

$$\left(C = (f_1 = g_1^r, \ldots, f_\ell = g_\ell^r, h^r \cdot m_b), C' = (\mathsf{Enc}'(\mathsf{pk}, 1), \ldots, \mathsf{Enc}'(\mathsf{pk}, \ell)) : r \leftarrow_\$ \mathbb{Z}_p\right)$$

In Corollary 1 we showed that the two distribution were indistinguishable even when conditioned on the secret key s. However, in the definition of D_0, D_1, we only provide partial leakage $L(s)$, and hence $\mathcal{A}$ has negligible advantage in distinguishing the two distributions.

Hybrid D_2. It is similar to hybrid D_1, but with $h^r \cdot m_b$ replaced by $\prod_{j=1}^{\ell} f_j^{s_j} \cdot m_b$. This is the following distribution:

$$\left(C = \left(f_1 = g_1^r, \ldots, f_\ell = g_\ell^r, \prod_{j=1}^{\ell} f_j^{s_j} \cdot m_b\right), C' : r \leftarrow_\$ \mathbb{Z}_p\right)$$

For the same r, the distributions from Hybrids D_2 and D_3 are identical. Therefore, $\mathcal{A}$ has no advantage in distinguishing the two hybrids.

Hybrid D_3. Similar to hybrid D_2, except each $f_i \leftarrow_\$ \mathbb{G}$. This is the following distribution:

$$\left(C = \left(f_1, \ldots, f_\ell, \prod_{j=1}^{\ell} f_j^{s_j} \cdot m_b\right), C' : f_1, \ldots, f_\ell \leftarrow_\$ \mathbb{G}\right)$$

Claim. If DDH is hard for $\mathbb{G}$, then for every PPT $\mathcal{A}$, the advantage in distinguishing hybrids D_2 and D_3 is negligible.

Proof. We will use an adversary $\mathcal{A}$ capable of distinguishing hybrids D_2 and D_3 to create $\mathcal{B}$ that can win against the DDH Game. $\mathcal{B}$ receives from the DDH Challenger: $(g_1, \ldots, g_\ell, f_1, \ldots, f_\ell)$. It chooses $s \leftarrow_\$ \{0,1\}^\ell$ and sets $\mathsf{pk} = (g_1, \ldots, g_\ell, h)$ where $h = \prod_{i=1}^{\ell} g_i^{s_i}$ and sets $\mathsf{sk} = s$. It then sends to $\mathcal{A}$: $(\mathsf{pk}, L(\mathsf{sk} = s), C = (f_1, \ldots, f_\ell, \prod_{j=1}^{\ell} f_j^{s_j} \cdot m_b), C' = (\mathsf{Enc}'(\mathsf{pk}, 1), \ldots, \mathsf{Enc}'(\mathsf{pk}, \ell)))$. It is easy to see that $\mathcal{B}$ perfectly simulates the distributions of hybrids D_2 and D_3 based on the input it receives. It merely forwards $\mathcal{A}$'s guess as its own. This concludes the proof that $\mathcal{A}$ has a negligible advantage in distinguishing hybrids D_2 and D_3. □

Hybrid D_4. Replace $\prod_{j=1}^{\ell} f_j^{s_j}$ with a random value $U \leftarrow_\$ \mathbb{G}$. This gives the distribution:

$$\left(C = (f_1, \ldots, f_\ell, U \cdot m_b), C' = (\mathsf{Enc}'(\mathsf{pk}, 1), \ldots, \mathsf{Enc}'(\mathsf{pk}, \ell)) : U, f_1, \ldots, f_\ell \leftarrow_\$ \mathbb{G}\right)$$

Claim. Hybrids D_3 and D_4 are statistically indistinguishable .

Proof. We can represent $f_i \leftarrow_\$ \mathbb{G}$ as g^{r_i} for random $r_i \leftarrow_\$ \mathbb{Z}_p$. Therefore, the term $\prod_{j=1}^{\ell} f_j^{s_j} = g^{\langle r, s \rangle}$ where $r = (r_1, \ldots, r_\ell)$. Now, note that distinguishing hybrids D_3 and D_4 is at least as hard as distinguishing the following two ensembles:

$$(r_1, \ldots, r_\ell, \langle r, s \rangle, C' : r_1, \ldots, r_\ell \leftarrow_\$ \mathbb{Z}_p); (r_1, \ldots, r_\ell, u, C' : u, r_1, \ldots, r_\ell \leftarrow_\$ \mathbb{Z}_p)$$

If one could distinguish the second pair of distributions, then they can efficiently calculate the value of g^{r_i} and $g^{\langle r, s \rangle}$, thereby distinguishing the original pair of distributions.

We will now complete the proof by showing that the second pair of distributions are statistically indistinguishable. To this end, we will use LHL, as defined in Theorem 1. We have that

$$\mathrm{H}_\infty(s|C', L(s), \mathsf{pk}) = \mathrm{H}_\infty(s|L(s), \mathsf{pk}) \geq \mathrm{H}_\infty(s|L(s)) - \log p \geq \ell - \lambda - \log p.$$

This is because C' is independent of the sk conditioned on pk, the value pk's component of h comes from a domain of size p, and L was a leakage function that satisfied $\mathrm{H}_\infty(s|L(s)) = \ell - \lambda$. Now, consider, the hash function family $\mathcal{H}$ consisting of $h_r(s) = \langle r, s \rangle \mod p$. The output length is $m = \log p$. This is a universal hash family. To apply LHL we need, $m = k - 2\log(1/\varepsilon)$. Here $k = \ell - \lambda - \log p$. Therefore, $\log p = \ell - \lambda - \log p - 2\log(1/\varepsilon)$. Or if $\lambda \leq \ell - 2\log p - 2\log(1/\varepsilon)$, for some negligible ε then the latter two distributions are statistically indistinguishable. □

It follows from the above claim that $\mathcal{A}$ has a negligible advantage in distinguishing hybrids D_3 and D_4. Further, in Hybrid 4, the message is masked by a random value and therefore $\mathcal{A}$ has no advantage in Hybrid D_4.

Combining the different hybrid arguments together, we get that any PPT algorithm $\mathcal{A}$ has a negligible advantage in the CS+LR security game. □

5.3 UPKE Construction

In this section, we present our construction of an updatable public key encryption based on the BHHO Cryptosystem. This is presented in Construction 2.

Correctness. Informally, correctness requires that any message m encrypted by an updated public key decrypts with the help of the corresponding updated secret key to the same message m, always.

- Let $(\mathsf{sk}, \mathsf{pk}) \leftarrow \mathsf{U\text{-}PKEG}(1^\kappa)$. Here, $\mathsf{sk} = s = (s_1, \ldots, s_\ell) \leftarrow_\$ \{0, 1\}^\ell$, and $\mathsf{sk} = (g_1, \ldots, g_\ell, \prod_{j=1}^{\ell} g_i^{s_i})$.
- Let r be the randomness used for the Upd-Sk procedure. Let $\delta = (\delta_1, \ldots, \delta_\ell)$ be the first ℓ bits of r. We have $(\mathsf{pk}', \mathsf{up}) \leftarrow \mathsf{Upd\text{-}Pk}(\mathsf{pk})$. Here, $\mathsf{pk}' = (g_1, \ldots, g_\ell, h \cdot \prod_{j=1}^{\ell} g_i^{\delta_i})$. $\mathsf{up} = (g_1^{r_1}, \ldots, g_\ell^{r_1}, h^{r_1} \cdot g^{\delta_1}), \ldots, (g_1^{r_\ell}, \ldots, g_\ell^{r_\ell}, h^{r_\ell} \cdot g^{\delta_\ell})$.

Protocol DDH-Based UPKE

U-PKEG(1^κ)

    Sample $s = (s_1, \ldots, s_\ell) \leftarrow\!\!\$ \{0,1\}$ and
    $g_1, \ldots, g_\ell \leftarrow\!\!\$ \mathbb{G}$.
    Compute $h = \prod_{i=1}^{\ell} g_i^{s_i}$.
    return sk $= s \in \mathbb{Z}_p^\ell$, pk $= (g_1, \ldots, g_\ell, h) \in \mathbb{G}^{\ell+1}$.

U-Enc(pk, $m \in \mathbb{G}$)

    Parse pk $= (g_1, \ldots, g_\ell, h)$
    Sample $r \leftarrow\!\!\$ \mathbb{Z}_p$
    for $i = 1, \ldots, \ell$ **do**
        Compute $f_i = g_i^r$
    return $C = (f_1, \ldots, f_\ell, c = h^r \cdot m) \in \mathbb{G}^{\ell+1}$

U-Dec(sk, C)

    Parse $C = (f_1, \ldots, f_\ell, c = h^r \cdot m)$ and sk $= s =$
    $(s_1, \ldots, s_\ell) \in \mathbb{Z}_p^\ell$
    Compute $m' = c \cdot \left(\prod_{i=1}^{\ell} f_i^{s_i}\right)^{-1}$
    return m'

Upd-Pk(pk)

    Parse pk $= (g_1, \ldots, g_\ell, h)$
    Sample $\delta = (\delta_1, \ldots, \delta_m) \leftarrow\!\!\$ \{0,1\}^\ell$
    Compute $h' = h \cdot \left(\prod_{i=1}^{\ell} g_i^{\delta_i}\right)$
    Encrypt δ bit-by-bit, i.e., up $=$
    (U-Enc(pk, g^{δ_1}), \ldots, U-Enc(pk, g^{δ_ℓ})).
    return (up, pk' $= (g_1, \ldots, g_\ell, h')$)

Upd-Sk(sk, up)

    Parse up $= (c_1, \ldots, c_\ell)$
    for $i = 1, \ldots, \ell$ **do**
        Compute $u_i = $ U-Dec(sk, c_i)
        if $u_i = 1$ **then**
            Set $\delta_i = 0$
        else
            Set $\delta_i = 1$
    Compute $s' = s + \delta$ where $\delta = (\delta_1, \ldots, \delta_\ell)$ and addition is element-by-element over $\mathbb{Z}_p$.
    return sk' $= (s')$

Construction 2. DDH Based Construction. Let κ be the the security parameter. Let $\mathcal{G}$ be a probabilistic polynomial-time "group generator" that takes as input 1^κ and outputs the description of a group $\mathbb{G}$ with prime order $p = p(\kappa)$ and g is a fixed generator of $\mathbb{G}$. Set $\ell = \lceil 5 \log p \rceil$.

- We will look at Upd-Sk now. It is easy to verify that Upd-Sk correctly decrypts each ciphertext in up to corresponding g^{δ_i}. This is either 1 when $\delta_i = 0$ or non-identity if $\delta = 1$. It then updates $s' = s + \delta$. Interestingly, while s was initialized to be a bit string, each element grows slowly over $\mathbb{Z}_p$.
- Consider U-Enc(pk', m). The resulting ciphertext is $(g_1^u, \ldots, g_\ell^u, h'^u \cdot m)$ for $u \leftarrow\!\!\$ \mathbb{Z}_p$.
- Consider U-Dec(sk', $g_1^u, \ldots, g_\ell^u, h'^u \cdot m)$). The decryption algorithm returns:

$$h'^u \cdot m \cdot \left(\prod_{j=1}^{\ell} (g_j^u)^{s_j'}\right)^{-1} = \left(h \cdot \prod_{j=1}^{\ell} g_j^{\delta_j}\right)^u \cdot m \cdot \left(\prod_{j=1}^{\ell} (g_j^u)^{s_j'}\right)^{-1}$$

$$= \left(\prod_{j=1}^{\ell} g_j^{s_j} \cdot \prod_{j=1}^{\ell} g_j^{\delta_j}\right)^u \cdot m \cdot \left(\prod_{j=1}^{\ell} (g_j^u)^{s_j + \delta_j}\right)^{-1} = m$$

- The same can be extended to additional updates. The key point to note is that the algorithms do not need s to be a bit string and therefore can, and indeed will grow.

5.4 Security of the UPKE Construction

Theorem 3. *Under the DDH Assumption, Construction 2 is IND-CR-CPA secure UPKE.*

Proof. We proved in Theorem 2 that Construction 1 is CS+LR secure with $\lambda = \ell - 2\log p - \omega(\log \kappa)$, under the DDH Assumption. We will use this as the starting point and use an adversary $\mathcal{A}$ against the IND-CPA game of the UPKE construction to construct an adversary $\mathcal{B}$ against the CS+LR Security game of the PKE Scheme.

- The reduction $\mathcal{B}$ receives from the challenger the public key pk_0 corresponding to some secret key s_0.
- It has a time period counter t initialized to 0
- $\mathcal{B}$ provides pk_0 to the adversary $\mathcal{A}$.
- $\mathcal{B}$ responds as follows to the oracle queries to $\mathcal{O}_{upd}(\cdot)$ as follows:
  For each input invocation, it increments the counter t to i and records the δ_i it receives as input.
- $\mathcal{B}$ then receives the challenge messages m_0^*, m_1^*.
- $\mathcal{B}$ then provides the *randomized* leakage function $L(\mathsf{sk}; \delta^*) = s_0 + \delta^*$ where the addition is element-by-element over $\mathbb{Z}_p$. Looking ahead, δ^* will correspond to the randomness for the fresh update before the secret key is provided to the $\mathcal{A}$. It also sets m_0^*, m_1^* as its challenge messages.
- $\mathcal{B}$ sends to its challenger the leakage function L, m_0^*, m_1^*. It also specifies the function f to be the encryption of each bit of the secret key in the exponent.
- In response, $\mathcal{B}$ receives C which is an encryption of m_b^* under pk_0, C' which is a encryption of s_0, bit-by-bit in the exponent, under pk_0, and a leakage z on s_0 defined by $z = s_0 + \delta^*$ for *unknown* $\delta^* \leftarrow_\$ \{0,1\}^\ell$. More formally,

$$C = \mathsf{U\text{-}Enc}(\mathsf{pk}_0, m_b^*); C' = (\mathsf{U\text{-}Enc}(\mathsf{pk}_0, g^{s_1}), \ldots, \mathsf{U\text{-}Enc}(\mathsf{pk}_0, g^{s_\ell}))$$

- At this point, let the time period be q'. Now, $\mathcal{A}$ expects $c^* = \mathsf{U\text{-}Enc}(\mathsf{pk}_{q'}, m_b^*)$. So $\mathcal{B}$ does the following to compute c^*:
  - $\mathcal{B}$ has $C = (\mathsf{U\text{-}Enc}(\mathsf{pk}_0, m_b^*))$ or $C = (f_1, \ldots, f_\ell, c = h^r \cdot m_b^*)$.
  - It computes $\Delta' = \sum_{i=1}^{q'} \delta_i$. $\Delta = (\Delta_1', \ldots, \Delta_\ell')$
  - To convert it into a public key corresponding to $s_{q'} = s_0 + \Delta'$, we do the following:

$$c^* = \left(f_1, \ldots, f_\ell, c \cdot \prod_{j=1}^{\ell} f_j^{\Delta_j'} \right)$$

  - This is where we employ the key homomorphism property.
- $\mathcal{B}$ sends to $\mathcal{A}$ the value of c^*.
- $\mathcal{B}$ continues to respond to $\mathcal{O}_{upd}(\cdot)$ queries as before. When $\mathcal{A}$ finally stops, let q be the time period. Now, $\mathcal{B}$ does the following:
  - To compute s^*:
    * It sets $\Delta = \sum_{i=1}^{q} \delta_i$. Again, the operation is element-by-element addition over $\mathbb{Z}_p$.
      Let $\Delta = (\Delta_1, \ldots, \Delta_\ell)$.
    * With the knowledge of z and Δ, $\mathcal{B}$ sets $s^* = s_{q+1} = z + \Delta$. Recall that $z = s_0 + \delta^*$ for random δ^*. In other words, $\mathcal{B}$ implicitly sets $\delta_{q+1} = \delta^*$, corresponding to the final secure update.

- To compute pk^*: With the knowledge of s^* it is also easy to generate the corresponding public key pk^* by merely computing the value of $h^* = \prod_{i=1}^{\ell} g_i^{s_i^*}$ where $s^* = (s_1^*, \ldots, s_\ell^*)$. Therefore, $\mathsf{pk}^* = (g_1, \ldots, g_\ell, h^*)$
- To compute up^*:
  * Recall that $\mathsf{up}^* = (\mathsf{U\text{-}Enc}(\mathsf{pk}_q, g^{\delta_1}), \ldots \mathsf{U\text{-}Enc}(\mathsf{pk}_q, g^{\delta_\ell}))$ where $\delta^* = (\delta_1, \ldots, \delta_\ell))$.
  * $\mathcal{B}$ has $C' = (\mathsf{U\text{-}Enc}(\mathsf{pk}_0, g^{s_1}), \ldots, \mathsf{U\text{-}Enc}(\mathsf{pk}_0, g^{s_\ell}))$ where $s_0 = (s_1, \ldots, s_\ell)$
  * Note that for all $i = 1, \ldots, \ell$, by definition, $\delta_i = z_i - s_i \in \mathbb{Z}_p$.
  * Let $\boldsymbol{ct}_i = \mathsf{Enc}(\mathsf{pk}_0, g^{s_i}) = (f_1, \ldots, f_\ell, c = h^r \cdot g^{s_i})$
  * For $i = 1, \ldots \ell$, then we transform each $\boldsymbol{ct}_i$ into $\boldsymbol{ct}'_i$ where

$$\boldsymbol{ct}'_i = \left(f'_1 = f_1^{-1}, \ldots, f'_\ell = f_\ell^{-1}, c' = \left(c \cdot g^{-z_i} \cdot \prod_{j=1}^{\ell} f_j^{-\Delta_j} \right)^{-1} \right)$$

  Now, $\mathsf{up}^* = (\boldsymbol{ct}'_1, \ldots, \boldsymbol{ct}'_\ell)$
- Send $(\mathsf{pk}^*, \mathsf{sk}^*, \mathsf{up}^*)$ to $\mathcal{A}$.
- $\mathcal{B}$ forwards $\mathcal{A}$'s guess as its own.

Analysis of Reduction. We first show that the leakage function defined here has sufficiently small entropy loss.

Claim. $H_\infty(s_0 | z) = \ell - \lambda$ where $\lambda = \ell(1 - \log_2(4/3))$

Proof. First note that the components of $z = (z_1, \ldots, z_\ell)$ and $s_0 = (s_1, \ldots, s_\ell)$ are independent of each other so $H_\infty(s_0 | z) = \sum_i H_\infty(s_i | z_i)$. Now, the distribution of z_i is given by

$$P[z_i = 0] = P[z_i = 2] = 1/4, P[z_i = 1] = 1/2$$

Further,

$$P[s_i = 0 | z_i = 0] = 1, P[s_i = 0 | z_i = 2] = 0, P[s_i = 0 | z_i = 1] = \frac{1}{2}$$

Therefore, $H_\infty(s_i | z_i) = -\log_2(1 \cdot P[z_i = 0] + 1 \cdot P[z_i = 2] + \frac{1}{2}P[z_i = 1]) = -\log(3/4)$ and $H_\infty(s_0 | z) = \ell \cdot \log_2(4/3)$. $\square$

We now show that the distribution of ciphertext is correct. We will show it is correct for any i. We have $c_i = (f_1, \ldots, f_\ell, c = h^r \cdot g^{s_i})$. First, we first transform it into a cipher text of $z - s_0$, under pk_0. This is message homomorphism. We then transform this ciphertext, under pk_0 to a ciphertext encrypting the same message under pk_q. This is the property of key homomorphism.

- Multiplying c with g^{-z_i} gives us a valid encryption of $g^{s_i - z_i}$. However, we have that $z_i - s_i = d_i$ where $\delta^* = (d_1, \ldots, d_\ell)$.

- To obtain the encryption of $g^{z_i - s_i}$ we merely take the inverse of all elements, and then multiply the last element by g^{z_i}. Therefore,

$$c_i' = (f_1' = g_1^{r'} = f_1^{-1}, \dots, f_\ell' = g_\ell^{r'} = f_\ell^{-1}, c' = c^{-1} \cdot g^{z_i} = h^{r'} \cdot g^{-s_i} \cdot g^{z_i})$$

with $r' = -r$.
- Now, note that $\mathsf{sk}_q = \mathsf{sk}_0 + \boldsymbol{\Delta} = (s_1 + \Delta_1, \dots, s_\ell + \Delta_\ell)$. The public key is therefore $\mathsf{pk}_q = (g_1, \dots, g_\ell, h_q)$ where $h_q = h \cdot \prod_{j=1}^{\ell} g_j^{\Delta_j}$. In order to transform a ciphertext $c_i' = (f_1', \dots, f_\ell', c')$ under pk_0 to a ciphertext under pk_q we modify the last component, c' as $c' \cdot \prod_{j=1}^{\ell} f_j'^{\Delta_j} = (c \cdot g^{-z_i} \cdot \prod_{j=1}^{\ell} f_j^{\Delta_j})^{-1}$.

Under this reduction, it is easy to see that $\mathcal{B}$ perfectly simulates the IND-CR-CPA game for $\mathcal{A}$. The advantage of $\mathcal{A}$ against the IND-CR-CPA is the same as the advantage of $\mathcal{B}$.   □

Choice of Parameters. We have from Theorem 2 that $\lambda \leq \ell - 2\log p - \omega(\log \kappa)$. We have also shown that our reduction needs $\ell - \lambda = \ell \cdot \log_2(4/3)$. Therefore, we have that $\ell \geq \frac{2}{\log_2(4/3)} \log p + \omega(\log \kappa)$. Or, $\ell = \lceil 5 \log p \rceil$.

6   Constructions Based on LWE

This section presents construction from the LWE Assumption. We begin by presenting a slightly modified version of the dual-Regev PKE Scheme [33,48] in Sect. 6.1. We show that the scheme is CS+LR secure in Sect. 6.2. We then present our construction of a UPKE scheme (Sect. 6.3), extended from the PKE scheme. We finally prove that the UPKE scheme is IND-CR-CPA secure in Sect. 6.4.

6.1   The Dual Regev or GPV Cryptosystem

The construction is presented as Construction 3.

Correctness. We show that the decryption algorithm is correct with overwhelming probability (over the choice of the randomness of $\mathsf{Gen}, \mathsf{Enc}$). The decryption algorithm computes:

$$\langle r, t \rangle = \langle r, A^T x + e \rangle = \langle r, A^T x \rangle + \langle r, e \rangle = \langle x, u \rangle + \langle r, e \rangle$$

$$pad - \langle r, t \rangle = \langle x, u \rangle + e' + b \left\lfloor \frac{p}{2} \right\rfloor - \langle r, t \rangle = b \left\lfloor \frac{p}{2} \right\rfloor + (e' - \langle e, r \rangle)$$

Now, note that $e' - \langle e, r \rangle$ is small in comparison to p. Therefore, the computed value is closer to $\lfloor p/2 \rfloor$ when $b = 0$ and the opposite when $b = 1$.

Protocol Dual Regev or GPV Cryptosystem

Gen(1^κ)

  Sample $A \leftarrow_\$ \mathbb{Z}_p^{n \times m}$
  Sample $r \leftarrow_\$ \{0,1\}^m$
  Compute $u = Ar$
  return (pk $= (A, u)$, sk $= (r)$)

Enc(pk, $b \in \{0,1\}$)

  Parse pk $= (A, u)$
  Sample $x \leftarrow_\$ \mathbb{Z}_p^n, e \leftarrow_\$ \chi^m, e' \leftarrow \chi'$
  Compute $t = A^T x + e$
  Compute $pad = \langle x, u \rangle + e' + b\lfloor p/2 \rfloor$
  return $c = (t, pad)$

Dec(sk, c)

  Parse $c = (t, pad)$ and sk $= r$
  Compute $b' = (pad - \langle r, t \rangle) \in \mathbb{Z}_p$
  return 0 if m' is closer to 0 than to $\lfloor p/2 \rfloor$ and 1
  otherwise.

Construction 3. The Dual Regev or GPV Cryptosystem. Let n, m, p be integer parameters of the scheme. We will assume that LWE holds where p is super-polynomial and χ is polynomially bounded. Then, we set χ' to be uniformly random over (say) $[-p/8, p/8]$.

6.2 CS+LR Security of the Dual-Regev Cryptosystem

In this section, we provide proof of the combined circular security and leakage resilience of the dual-Regev Cryptosystem. Formally, we will prove the following theorem:

Theorem 4. *Under the LWE Assumption, Construction 3 is λ-CS+LR secure with leakage $\lambda = m - (n + 1) \log p - \omega(\log \kappa)$.*

Before we can prove the above theorem, we show the existence of an encryption algorithm Enc' such that

$$(\mathsf{Enc}'(\mathsf{pk}, i), \mathsf{sk}) \approx_c (\mathsf{Enc}(\mathsf{pk}, r_i), \mathsf{sk}).$$

Consider: $\mathsf{Enc}'(\mathsf{pk}, i) := (t', pad')$ where:

- Let $x \leftarrow_\$ \mathbb{Z}_p^n, e \leftarrow_\$ \chi^m$ and $d = (d_1 = 0, \ldots, d_{i-1} = 0, d_i = -\lfloor p/2 \rfloor, d_{i+1} = 0, \ldots, d_m = 0)$. Then, $t' = A^T x + e + d$.
- $pad' = \langle x, u \rangle + e'$ where e' is chosen from a distribution χ' such that $e' + B$ is statistically indistinguishable from e' where $B \in \mathbb{Z}_p$.

Lemma 4. *Under the LWE Assumption, $(\mathsf{pk}, \mathsf{Enc}'(\mathsf{pk}, i), \mathsf{sk}) \approx_c (\mathsf{pk}, \mathsf{Enc}(\mathsf{pk}, r_i), \mathsf{sk})$. where $(\mathsf{pk}, \mathsf{sk}) \leftarrow_\$ \mathsf{Gen}(1^\kappa)$*

Proof Sketch. We will prove through a sequence of hybrids, summarized in Table 4. The complete proof of this Lemma can be found in the full version of the paper [29].

Further, note that r is independently chosen, bit by bit. In addition, each Enc, Enc' has independently chosen randomness. Therefore, as a corollary we get that:

Table 4. Proof outline for Lemma 4

Hybrid	Hybrid Definition	Security
D_0	Enc is used to encrypt r_i	Lemma 1
D_1	D_0 except $\langle x, u \rangle$ replaced with $\langle r, t \rangle$	
		LWE
D_2	D_1 except $t = A^T x + e$ replaced with $t \leftarrow^{\$} \mathbb{Z}_p^n$	
		Identical
D_3	D_2 except t replaced with $t + d$ where $d = (0, \ldots, 0, d_i = -\lfloor p/2 \rfloor, 0, \ldots, 0)$	
		LWE
D_4	D_3 except $t = A^T x + e$ where $x \leftarrow^{\$} \mathbb{Z}_p^n, e \leftarrow^{\$} \chi^m$	
		Lemma 1
D_5	Enc$'$ is used to encrypt r_i	

Corollary 2. *Under the LWE Assumption,*

$$(\mathsf{pk}, \mathsf{Enc}(\mathsf{pk}, r_1), \ldots, \mathsf{Enc}(\mathsf{pk}, r_m), \mathsf{sk}) \approx_c (\mathsf{pk}, \mathsf{Enc}'(\mathsf{pk}, 1), \ldots, \mathsf{Enc}'(\mathsf{pk}, m), \mathsf{sk})$$

We can now prove the original theorem:

Theorem 4. *Under the LWE Assumption, Construction 3 is λ-CS+LR secure with leakage $\lambda = m - (n+1)\log p - \omega(\log \kappa)$.*

Proof Sketch. We prove this similar to the proof of Theorem 2. This is done through a sequence of hybrids, summarized in Table 5. The complete proof of this Theorem can be found in the full version of the paper [29].

Table 5. Proof outline for Theorem 4

Hybrid	Hybrid Definition	Security
D_0	The Original CS+LR Security Game, Enc is used	Corollary 2
D_1	D_0 except Enc$'$ is used	
		Identical
D_2	D_1 except $\langle x, u \rangle$ replaced with $\langle r, t \rangle$	
		LWE
D_3	D_2 except $t = A^T x + e$ replaced with $t \leftarrow^{\$} \mathbb{Z}_p^n$.	
		Leftover Hash Lemma
D_4	D_3 except $\langle r, t \rangle$ replaced with $U \leftarrow \mathbb{Z}_p$	

6.3   UPKE Construction

In this section, we present our construction of an updatable public key encryption based on the dual-Regev cryptosystem. This is presented in Construction 4.

Protocol LWE-Based UPKE

U-PKEG(1^κ)

   Sample $\boldsymbol{A} \leftarrow_\$ \mathbb{Z}_p^{n \times m}$
   Sample $\boldsymbol{r} \leftarrow_\$ \{0,1\}^m$
   Compute $\boldsymbol{u} = \boldsymbol{A}\boldsymbol{r}$
   return $(\mathsf{pk} = (\boldsymbol{A}, \boldsymbol{u}), \mathsf{sk} = (\boldsymbol{r}))$

U-Enc($\mathsf{pk}, b \in \{0,1\}$)

   Parse $\mathsf{pk} = (\boldsymbol{A}, \boldsymbol{u})$
   Sample $\boldsymbol{x} \leftarrow_\$ \mathbb{Z}_p^n, \boldsymbol{e} \leftarrow_\$ \chi^m, e' \leftarrow \chi'$
   Compute $\boldsymbol{t} = \boldsymbol{A}^T \boldsymbol{x} + \boldsymbol{e}, pad = \langle \boldsymbol{x}, \boldsymbol{u} \rangle + e' + b\lfloor p/2 \rfloor$
   return $c = (\boldsymbol{t}, pad)$

U-Dec(sk, c)

   Parse $c = (\boldsymbol{t}, pad)$ and $\mathsf{sk} = \boldsymbol{r}$
   Compute $b' = (pad - \langle \boldsymbol{r}, \boldsymbol{t} \rangle) \in \mathbb{Z}_p$
   return 0 if m' is closer to 0 than to $\lfloor p/2 \rfloor$ and 1
   otherwise.

Upd-Pk(pk)

   Parse $\mathsf{pk} = (\boldsymbol{A}, \boldsymbol{u})$
   Sample $\boldsymbol{\delta} = (\delta_1, \ldots, \delta_m) \leftarrow_\$ \{0,1\}^m$
   Compute $\boldsymbol{u}' = \boldsymbol{u} + \boldsymbol{A}\boldsymbol{\delta}$
   Encrypt δ bit-by-bit, i.e., $\mathsf{up} = (\text{U-Enc}(\mathsf{pk}, \delta_1), \ldots, \text{U-Enc}(\mathsf{pk}, \delta_m))$.
   return $(\mathsf{up}, \mathsf{pk}' = (\boldsymbol{A}, \boldsymbol{u}'))$

Upd-Sk(sk, up)

   Parse $\mathsf{up} = (c_1, \ldots, c_m)$
   for $i = 1, \ldots, m$ **do**
      $\delta_i = \text{U-Dec}(\mathsf{sk}, c_i)$
   Compute $\boldsymbol{r}' = \boldsymbol{r} + \boldsymbol{\delta}$ where $\boldsymbol{\delta} = (\delta_1, \ldots, \delta_m)$
   return $\mathsf{sk}' = (\boldsymbol{r}')$

Construction 4. LWE Based Construction. Let n, m, p be integer parameters of the scheme. We will assume that LWE holds where p is super-polynomial and χ is polynomially bounded. Then, we set χ' to be uniformly random over (say) $[-p/8, p/8]$. Further, we have that $m \geq \frac{(n+1)}{\log_2(4/3)} \log p + \omega(\log \kappa)$.

Correctness. The property of correctness of UPKE requires that a bit b encrypted by an updated public key decrypts to the same bit b when the corresponding updated secret key is used.

- $(\mathsf{pk} = (\boldsymbol{A}, \boldsymbol{u} = \boldsymbol{A}\boldsymbol{r}), \mathsf{sk} = \boldsymbol{r}) \leftarrow$ U-PKEG(1^κ)
- We have the update bit $\boldsymbol{\delta} \leftarrow_\$ \{0,1\}^m$. We have the updated public key $\mathsf{pk}' = (\boldsymbol{A}, \boldsymbol{u}')$ where $\boldsymbol{u}' = \boldsymbol{u} + \boldsymbol{A}\boldsymbol{\delta}$. We also have $\mathsf{sk}' = \boldsymbol{r}' = \boldsymbol{r} + \boldsymbol{\delta}$
- Let us look at U-Enc(pk', b). It produces ciphertext $(\boldsymbol{t}, pad)$ where $\boldsymbol{t} = \boldsymbol{A}^T \boldsymbol{x} + \boldsymbol{e}$, $pad = \langle \boldsymbol{x}, \boldsymbol{u}' \rangle + e' + b\lfloor p/2 \rfloor$.
- Now, let us look at U-Dec($\boldsymbol{r}', (\boldsymbol{t}, pad)$). It computes

$$
\begin{aligned}
pad - \langle \boldsymbol{r}', \boldsymbol{t} \rangle &= \langle \boldsymbol{x}, \boldsymbol{u}' \rangle + e' + b\lfloor p/2 \rfloor - \langle \boldsymbol{r} + \boldsymbol{\delta}, \boldsymbol{A}^T \boldsymbol{x} + \boldsymbol{e} \rangle \\
&= \langle \boldsymbol{x}, \boldsymbol{A}\boldsymbol{r} + \boldsymbol{A}\boldsymbol{\delta} \rangle + e' + b\lfloor p/2 \rfloor - \langle \boldsymbol{r} + \boldsymbol{\delta}, \boldsymbol{A}^T \boldsymbol{x} + \boldsymbol{e} \rangle \\
&= \langle \boldsymbol{x}, \boldsymbol{A}(\boldsymbol{r} + \boldsymbol{\delta}) \rangle - \langle \boldsymbol{r} + \boldsymbol{\delta}, \boldsymbol{A}^T, \boldsymbol{x} \rangle + e' - \langle \boldsymbol{e}, \boldsymbol{r} \rangle + b\lfloor p/2 \rfloor \\
&= e' - \langle \boldsymbol{e}, \boldsymbol{r} \rangle + b\lfloor p/2 \rfloor
\end{aligned}
$$

- Now, note that $e' - \langle e, r \rangle$ is small in comparison to p. Therefore, the computed value is closer to $\lfloor p/2 \rfloor$ when $b = 0$ and the opposite when $b = 1$.

6.4 Security of the UPKE Construction

Theorem 5. *Under the LWE Assumption, Construction 4 is IND-CR-CPA secure UPKE.*

Proof. The proof is very similar to the proof of Theorem 3. We proved in Theorem 4 that the PKE scheme was CS+LR secure with $\lambda \leq m - (n+1) \log p - \omega(\log \kappa)$, under the LWE assumption. We will use this to construct $\mathcal{B}$ against the CS+LR game by using $\mathcal{A}$ against the IND-CPA Game.

- The reduction $\mathcal{B}$ receives from the challenger the public key pk_0 corresponding to some secret key s_0.
- It has a time period counter t initialized to 0
- $\mathcal{B}$ provides pk_0 to the adversary $\mathcal{A}$.
- $\mathcal{B}$ responds as follows to the oracle queries to $\mathcal{O}_{upd}(\cdot)$ as follows:
  For each input invocation, it increments the counter t to i and records the δ_i it receives as input.
- $\mathcal{B}$ then receives the challenge messages m_0^*, m_1^*.
- $\mathcal{B}$ then provides the *randomized* leakage function $L(\mathsf{sk}; \delta^*) = s_0 + \delta^*$ where the addition is element-by-element over $\mathbb{Z}_p$. Looking ahead, δ^* will correspond to the randomness for the fresh update before the secret key is provided to the $\mathcal{A}$. It also sets m_0^*, m_1^* as its challenge messages.
- $\mathcal{B}$ sends to its challenger the leakage function L, m_0^*, m_1^*. It also specifies the function f to be the encryption of each bit of the secret key.
- In response, $\mathcal{B}$ receives C which is an encryption of m_b^* under pk_0, C' which is a encryption of s_0, bit-by-bit, under pk_0, and a leakage z on r_0 defined by $z = r_0 + \delta^*$ for *unknown* $\delta^* \leftarrow_\$ \{0,1\}^m$. More formally,

$$C = \mathsf{U\text{-}Enc}(\mathsf{pk}_0, m_b^*); C' = (\mathsf{U\text{-}Enc}(\mathsf{pk}_0, r_1), \ldots, \mathsf{U\text{-}Enc}(\mathsf{pk}_0, r_m))$$

- At this point, let the time period be q'. Now, $\mathcal{A}$ expects $c^* = \mathsf{U\text{-}Enc}(\mathsf{pk}_{q'}, m_b^*)$. So $\mathcal{B}$ does the following to compute c^*:
  - $\mathcal{B}$ has $C = \mathsf{U\text{-}Enc}(\mathsf{pk}_0, m_b^*)$ or $C = (t = A^T x + e, pad = \langle x, u \rangle + e' + m_b^* \lfloor p/2 \rfloor)$.
  - It computes $\Delta' = \sum_{i=1}^{q'} \delta_i$.
  - It computes $pad^* = pad + \langle \Delta', t \rangle$ and sets $t^* = t$.
  - Now, $c^* = (t^*, pad^*)$
- $\mathcal{B}$ sends to $\mathcal{A}$ the value of c^*.
- $\mathcal{B}$ continues to respond to $\mathcal{O}_{upd}(\cdot)$ queries as before. When $\mathcal{A}$ finally stops, let q be the time period. Now, $\mathcal{B}$ does the following:
  - To compute $\mathsf{sk}^* = r^*$:
    * Set $\Delta = \sum_{i=1}^{q} \delta_i$.
    * With the knowledge of z, Δ, $\mathcal{B}$ sets $r^* = r_{q+1} = z + \Delta$.
  - To compute pk^*: With the knowledge of A, r^*, $\mathcal{B}$ computes $u^* = A r^*$. It sets $\mathsf{pk}^* = (A, u^*)$.
  - To compute up^*: $\mathcal{B}$ has bit-by-bit encryption of r_0. It needs to compute the bit-by-bit encryption of $\delta^* = z - r_0$. For simplicity, assume that z is a trit, i.e., taking value 0, 1, 2. Let $r_0 = (r_1, \ldots, r_m)$, $\delta^* = (d_1, \ldots, d_m)$ and $z = (z_1, \ldots, z_m)$. Recall that $r_i, d_i \in \{0, 1\}$ while $z_i \in \{0, 1, 2\}$. We will first look at how to transform $\mathsf{U\text{-}Enc}(\mathsf{pk}_0, r_i)$ to $\mathsf{U\text{-}Enc}(\mathsf{pk}_0, d_i)$.
    * If $z_i = 2$, then we have that $r_i = d_i = 1$. Therefore, $\mathsf{U\text{-}Enc}(\mathsf{pk}_0, r_i) = \mathsf{U\text{-}Enc}(\mathsf{pk}_0, d_i)$ and we do not need to do anything.

* Similarly if $z_i = 0$, then we have that $r_i = d_i = 0$. Once again, U-Enc(pk_0, r_i) = U-Enc(pk_0, d_i) and we do not need to do anything.
* If $z_i = 1$, then we merely need U-Enc(pk_0, r_i) to be modified to U-Enc($\mathsf{pk}_0, 1 - r_i$). To achieve this we merely add $\lfloor p/2 \rfloor$ to the second term in the ciphertext.

To convert U-Enc(pk_0, d_i) to U-Enc(pk_q, d_i) we do the following:
* Note that U-Enc(pk_0, d_i) = (t_0, pad_0) where $t_0 = A^T x + e$ and $pad_0 = \langle x, u_0 \rangle + e' + b\lfloor p/2 \rfloor$. Further, $u_q = u_0 + A\Delta$
* Let $t_q = t_0$, then $pad_q = pad_0 + \langle \Delta, t_0 \rangle$. with the choice
- Send ($\mathsf{pk}^*, \mathsf{sk}^*, \mathsf{up}^*$) to $\mathcal{A}$.
- $\mathcal{B}$ forwards $\mathcal{A}$'s guess as its own.

Analysis of the Reduction. We first show that the leakage function has sufficiently small entropy loss.

Claim. $H_\infty(r_0|z) = m - \lambda$, where $\lambda = m(1 - \log_2(4/3))$

The above is identical to Claim 5.4 in the proof of Theorem 3.

We then need to show that the distribution of ciphertext is correct. Specifically, the distribution of the update ciphertext. We have $t_0 = t_q$. We will show that pad_q is correctly distributed. By definition we have that: $pad_q = \langle x, u_q \rangle + e' + b\lfloor p/2 \rfloor$. Here, we compute pad_q as follows:

$$
\begin{aligned}
pad_q = pad_0 + \langle \Delta, t_0 \rangle &= \langle x, u_0 \rangle + e' + b\lfloor p/2 \rfloor + \langle \Delta, t_0 \rangle \\
&= \langle x, u_0 \rangle + e' + b\lfloor p/2 \rfloor + \langle \Delta, A^T x + e \rangle \\
&= \langle x, u_0 \rangle + \langle A\Delta, x \rangle + e' + \langle \Delta, e \rangle + b\lfloor p/2 \rfloor \\
&= \langle x, u_q \rangle + e' + \langle \Delta, e \rangle + b\lfloor p/2 \rfloor
\end{aligned}
$$

We can now use the definition of distribution e' and Lemma 1 to show that the computed distribution is statistically indistinguishable from the actual distribution.

Under this reduction, it is easy to see that $\mathcal{B}$ perfectly simulates the IND-CPA game for $\mathcal{A}$. The advantage of $\mathcal{A}$ against the IND-CPA is the same as the advantage of $\mathcal{B}$.   □

Choice of Parameters. From Theorem 4, we have that $m - \lambda \geq (n+1)\log p + \omega(\log \kappa)$. Further, we have from the above claim that $m - \lambda = m\log_2(4/3)$. Putting the two together, we get $m \geq \frac{n+1}{\log_2(4/3)}\log p + \omega(\log \kappa)$.

7 Towards Stronger Security

In this section, we begin by presenting the CCA extension of the CPA security game presented in Sect. 3. We later extend the CPA and CCA security to a stronger definition. Due to space constraints, we invite the readers to refer to the full version of this paper [29] for constructions that satisfy these definitions and proofs of security.

IND-CR-CCA Security of UPKE. In Sect. 3, we defined a CPA based security for an updatable public-key encryption. However, a natural extension is to consider CCA based security of the UPKE. We will call this IND-CR-CCA which is the abbreviation of INDistinguishability under Chosen Randomness Chosen Ciphertext Attack. In this setting, the adversary is given access to also the decryption oracle where the adversary can ask for decryption of a ciphertext under the current secret key on a ciphertext of its choice or creation. To model this access, we define two oracles:

- $\mathcal{O}_{upd}(\cdot)$: The challenger on receiving the randomness r_i from the adversary does the following:

$$(\mathsf{up}_i, \mathsf{pk}_i) \leftarrow \mathsf{Upd\text{-}Pk}(\mathsf{pk}_{i-1}; r_i); \quad \mathsf{sk}_i \leftarrow \mathsf{Upd\text{-}Sk}(\mathsf{sk}_{i-1}, \mathsf{up}_i) \ .$$

- $\mathcal{D}(\cdot)$: The challenger on receiving ciphertext c as input, returns $\mathsf{U\text{-}Dec}(sk_i, c)$ where i is the current epoch and sk_i is the secret key of the current epoch.

IND-CR-CCA Security. For any adversary $\mathcal{A}$ with running time t and we consider the
IND-CR-CCA security game:

- Sample $(\mathsf{sk}_0, \mathsf{pk}_0) \leftarrow \mathsf{U\text{-}PKEG}(1^\kappa)$, $b \leftarrow_{\$} \{0,1\}$.
- $(m_0^*, m_1^*, state) \leftarrow_{\$} \mathcal{A}^{\mathcal{O}_{upd}(\cdot), \mathcal{O}_{dec}(\cdot)}(\mathsf{pk}_0)$
- Compute $c^* \leftarrow_{\$} \mathsf{U\text{-}Enc}(\mathsf{pk}_{q'}, m_b^*)$ where q' is the current time period.
- Compute $state \leftarrow_{\$} \mathcal{A}^{\mathcal{O}_{upd}(\cdot), \mathcal{O}_{dec}(\cdot)}(c^*, state)$.
  - Here $\mathcal{A}$ is not allowed to query its $\mathcal{O}_{dec}(\cdot)$ oracle on the challenge ciphertext c^* until $\mathcal{A}$ makes at least one (arbitrary) query to its $\mathcal{O}_{upd}(\cdot)$ oracle.
- Choose uniformly random r^* and then compute

$$(\mathsf{up}^*, \mathsf{pk}^*) \leftarrow \mathsf{Upd\text{-}Pk}(\mathsf{pk}_q; r^*); \quad \mathsf{sk}^* \leftarrow \mathsf{Upd\text{-}Sk}(\mathsf{sk}_q, \mathsf{up}^*) \ .$$

  where q is the current time period.
- $b' \leftarrow_{\$} \mathcal{A}(\mathsf{pk}^*, \mathsf{sk}^*, \mathsf{up}^*, state)$. Note that the adversary is not given access to the decryption query as with knowledge of sk^*, it can perform the decryption on its own.
- $\mathcal{A}$ wins the game if $b = b'$. The advantage of $\mathcal{A}$ in winning the above game is denoted by $\mathrm{Adv}_{crcca}^{UPKE}(\mathcal{A}) = |P\,[b = b'] - \frac{1}{2}|$.

Definition 7. *An updatable public-key encryption scheme* UPKE *is IND-CR-CCA -secure if for all PPT attackers $\mathcal{A}$, its advantage $\mathrm{Adv}_{crcca}^{UPKE}(\mathcal{A})$ is negligible.*

Stronger CPA, CCA Security. In the definition of both the IND-CR-CPA and the IND-CR-CCA security, we allowed the adversary to provide bad randomness and the challenger honestly updated the public key based on this bad randomness. However, one can consider a stronger attack where the attacker could provide an arbitrary update ciphertext up and the new public key pk'. In other words, the adversary chooses the full *output* (up, pk′) of the public key update algorithm Upd-Pk, rather than its *input* r. The challenger will then check—using a special new algorithm (see below) Verify-Upd(pk, up, pk′)—that the supplied values are "consistent". If so, it will update the secret key using sk ← Upd-Sk(sk, up), as before. Otherwise, it will ignore this query of the attacker. With this intuition in mind, we formalize the changes in the syntax and security of UPKE.

Syntactic Changes. We introduce a new algorithm Verify-Upd(pk, up, pk′) where pk is the old public key, up is the update ciphertext and pk′ is the updated public key. This algorithm outputs 1 iff pk′ is consistently produced by up and pk.

Security Game Changes. We also change the definition of $\mathcal{O}_{upd}(\cdot)$. The new definition is as follows:

– $\mathcal{O}_{upd}(\cdot, \cdot)$: This takes as input two values up and pk′. It then runs $\tau \leftarrow$ Verify-Upd(pk, up, pk′). If $\tau = 1$, it runs sk′ ← Upd-Sk(sk, up), else it returns $\bot$.

References

1. Abdalla, M., Reyzin, L.: A new forward-secure digital signature scheme. In: Okamoto, T. (ed.) ASIACRYPT 2000. LNCS, vol. 1976, pp. 116–129. Springer, Heidelberg (2000). https://doi.org/10.1007/3-540-44448-3_10
2. Agrawal, S., Boneh, D., Boyen, X.: Efficient Lattice (H)IBE in the standard model. In: Gilbert, H. (ed.) EUROCRYPT 2010. LNCS, vol. 6110, pp. 553–572. Springer, Heidelberg (2010). https://doi.org/10.1007/978-3-642-13190-5_28
3. Akavia, A., Goldwasser, S., Vaikuntanathan, V.: Simultaneous hardcore bits and cryptography against memory attacks. In: Reingold, O. (ed.) TCC 2009. LNCS, vol. 5444, pp. 474–495. Springer, Heidelberg (2009). https://doi.org/10.1007/978-3-642-00457-5_28
4. Alperin-Sheriff, J., Peikert, C.: Circular and KDM security for identity-based encryption. In: Fischlin, M., Buchmann, J., Manulis, M. (eds.) PKC 2012. LNCS, vol. 7293, pp. 334–352. Springer, Heidelberg (2012). https://doi.org/10.1007/978-3-642-30057-8_20
5. Alwen, J., Coretti, S., Dodis, Y., Tselekounis, Y.: Security analysis and improvements for the IETF MLS standard for group messaging. In: Micciancio, D., Ristenpart, T. (eds.) CRYPTO 2020. LNCS, vol. 12170, pp. 248–277. Springer, Cham (2020). https://doi.org/10.1007/978-3-030-56784-2_9
6. Anderson, R.: Invited lecture. In: Fourth Annual Conference on Computer and Communications Security. ACM (1997)
7. Applebaum, B.: Key-dependent message security: generic amplification and completeness. J. Cryptol. **27**(3), 429–451 (2014)
8. Applebaum, B., Cash, D., Peikert, C., Sahai, A.: Fast cryptographic primitives and circular-secure encryption based on hard learning problems. In: Halevi, S. (ed.) CRYPTO 2009. LNCS, vol. 5677, pp. 595–618. Springer, Heidelberg (2009). https://doi.org/10.1007/978-3-642-03356-8_35

9. Asharov, G., Jain, A., López-Alt, A., Tromer, E., Vaikuntanathan, V., Wichs, D.: Multiparty computation with low communication, computation and interaction via threshold FHE. In: Pointcheval, D., Johansson, T. (eds.) EUROCRYPT 2012. LNCS, vol. 7237, pp. 483–501. Springer, Heidelberg (2012). https://doi.org/10.1007/978-3-642-29011-4_29

10. Barak, B., Haitner, I., Hofheinz, D., Ishai, Y.: Bounded key-dependent message security. In: Gilbert, H. (ed.) EUROCRYPT 2010. LNCS, vol. 6110, pp. 423–444. Springer, Heidelberg (2010). https://doi.org/10.1007/978-3-642-13190-5_22

11. Bellare, M., Miner, S.K.: A forward-secure digital signature scheme. In: Wiener, M. (ed.) CRYPTO 1999. LNCS, vol. 1666, pp. 431–448. Springer, Heidelberg (1999). https://doi.org/10.1007/3-540-48405-1_28

12. Bellare, M., Yee, B.: Forward-security in private-key cryptography. In: Joye, M. (ed.) CT-RSA 2003. LNCS, vol. 2612, pp. 1–18. Springer, Heidelberg (2003). https://doi.org/10.1007/3-540-36563-X_1

13. Black, J., Rogaway, P., Shrimpton, T.: Encryption-scheme security in the presence of key-dependent messages. In: Nyberg, K., Heys, H. (eds.) SAC 2002. LNCS, vol. 2595, pp. 62–75. Springer, Heidelberg (2003). https://doi.org/10.1007/3-540-36492-7_6

14. Boneh, D., Boyen, X.: Efficient selective-ID secure identity-based encryption without random Oracles. In: Cachin, C., Camenisch, J.L. (eds.) EUROCRYPT 2004. LNCS, vol. 3027, pp. 223–238. Springer, Heidelberg (2004). https://doi.org/10.1007/978-3-540-24676-3_14

15. Boneh, D., Boyen, X., Goh, E.-J.: Hierarchical identity based encryption with constant size ciphertext. In: Cramer, R. (ed.) EUROCRYPT 2005. LNCS, vol. 3494, pp. 440–456. Springer, Heidelberg (2005). https://doi.org/10.1007/11426639_26

16. Boneh, D., Eskandarian, S., Kim, S., Shih, M.: Improving speed and security in updatable encryption schemes, 2020. To appear in Asiacrypt 2020

17. Boneh, D., Halevi, S., Hamburg, M., Ostrovsky, R.: Circular-secure encryption from decision Diffie-Hellman. In: Wagner, D. (ed.) CRYPTO 2008. LNCS, vol. 5157, pp. 108–125. Springer, Heidelberg (2008). https://doi.org/10.1007/978-3-540-85174-5_7

18. Boneh, D., Lewi, K., Montgomery, H., Raghunathan, A.: Key Homomorphic PRFs and their applications. In: Canetti, R., Garay, J.A. (eds.) CRYPTO 2013. LNCS, vol. 8042, pp. 410–428. Springer, Heidelberg (2013). https://doi.org/10.1007/978-3-642-40041-4_23

19. Boyd, C., Davies, G.T., Gjøsteen, K., Jiang, Y.: Fast and secure updatable encryption. In: Micciancio, D., Ristenpart, T. (eds.) CRYPTO 2020. LNCS, vol. 12170, pp. 464–493. Springer, Cham (2020). https://doi.org/10.1007/978-3-030-56784-2_16

20. Brakerski, Z., Goldwasser, S.: Circular and leakage resilient public-key encryption under subgroup indistinguishability. In: Rabin, T. (ed.) CRYPTO 2010. LNCS, vol. 6223, pp. 1–20. Springer, Heidelberg (2010). https://doi.org/10.1007/978-3-642-14623-7_1

21. Brakerski, Z., Goldwasser, S., Kalai, Y.T.: Black-box circular-secure encryption beyond affine functions. In: Ishai, Y. (ed.) TCC 2011. LNCS, vol. 6597, pp. 201–218. Springer, Heidelberg (2011). https://doi.org/10.1007/978-3-642-19571-6_13

22. Brakerski, Z., Lombardi, A., Segev, G., Vaikuntanathan, V.: Anonymous IBE, leakage resilience and circular security from new assumptions. In: Nielsen, J.B., Rijmen, V. (eds.) EUROCRYPT 2018. LNCS, vol. 10820, pp. 535–564. Springer, Cham (2018). https://doi.org/10.1007/978-3-319-78381-9_20

23. Camenisch, J., Lysyanskaya, A.: An efficient system for non-transferable anonymous credentials with optional anonymity revocation. In: Pfitzmann, B. (ed.) EUROCRYPT 2001. LNCS, vol. 2045, pp. 93–118. Springer, Heidelberg (2001). https://doi.org/10.1007/3-540-44987-6_7

24. Canetti, R., Halevi, S., Katz, J.: A forward-secure public-key encryption scheme. In: Biham, E. (ed.) EUROCRYPT 2003. LNCS, vol. 2656, pp. 255–271. Springer, Heidelberg (2003). https://doi.org/10.1007/3-540-39200-9_16

25. Cash, D., Hofheinz, D., Kiltz, E., Peikert, C.: Bonsai trees, or how to delegate a lattice basis. J. Cryptol. **25**(4), 601–639 (2012)

26. Dodis, Y., Goldwasser, S., Tauman Kalai, Y., Peikert, C., Vaikuntanathan, V.: Public-key encryption schemes with auxiliary inputs. In: Micciancio, D. (ed.) TCC 2010. LNCS, vol. 5978, pp. 361–381. Springer, Heidelberg (2010). https://doi.org/10.1007/978-3-642-11799-2_22

27. Dodis, Y., Haralambiev, K., López-Alt, A., Wichs, D.: Efficient Public-Key Cryptography in the Presence of Key Leakage. In: Abe, M. (ed.) ASIACRYPT 2010. LNCS, vol. 6477, pp. 613–631. Springer, Heidelberg (2010). https://doi.org/10.1007/978-3-642-17373-8_35

28. Dodis, Y., Jost, D., Karthikeyan, H.: Forward-secure encryption with fast forwarding. Manuscript (2021)

29. Dodis, Y., Karthikeyan, H., Wichs, D.: Updatable public key encryption in the standard model (2021). https://cs.nyu.edu/~dodis/ps/upke.pdf

30. Döttling, N., Garg, S.: From selective IBE to full IBE and selective HIBE. In: Kalai, Y., Reyzin, L. (eds.) TCC 2017. LNCS, vol. 10677, pp. 372–408. Springer, Cham (2017). https://doi.org/10.1007/978-3-319-70500-2_13

31. Döttling, N., Garg, S.: Identity-based encryption from the Diffie-Hellman Assumption. In: Katz, J., Shacham, H. (eds.) CRYPTO 2017. LNCS, vol. 10401, pp. 537–569. Springer, Cham (2017). https://doi.org/10.1007/978-3-319-63688-7_18

32. Everspaugh, A., Paterson, K., Ristenpart, T., Scott, S.: Key rotation for authenticated encryption. In: Katz, J., Shacham, H. (eds.) CRYPTO 2017. LNCS, vol. 10403, pp. 98–129. Springer, Cham (2017). https://doi.org/10.1007/978-3-319-63697-9_4

33. Gentry, C., Peikert, C.., Vaikuntanathan, V.: Trapdoors for hard lattices and new cryptographic constructions. In: Ladner, R.E., Dwork, C. (eds.) 40th ACM STOC, pp. 197–206. ACM Press, May 2008

34. Gentry, C., Silverberg, A.: Hierarchical ID-based cryptography. In: Zheng, Y. (ed.) ASIACRYPT 2002. LNCS, vol. 2501, pp. 548–566. Springer, Heidelberg (2002). https://doi.org/10.1007/3-540-36178-2_34

35. Horwitz, J., Lynn, B.: Toward hierarchical identity-based encryption. In: Knudsen, L.R. (ed.) EUROCRYPT 2002. LNCS, vol. 2332, pp. 466–481. Springer, Heidelberg (2002). https://doi.org/10.1007/3-540-46035-7_31

36. Itkis, G., Reyzin, L.: Forward-secure signatures with optimal signing and verifying. In: Kilian, J. (ed.) CRYPTO 2001. LNCS, vol. 2139, pp. 332–354. Springer, Heidelberg (2001). https://doi.org/10.1007/3-540-44647-8_20

37. Jaeger, J., Stepanovs, I.: Optimal channel security against fine-grained state compromise: the safety of messaging. In: Shacham, H., Boldyreva, A. (eds.) CRYPTO 2018. LNCS, vol. 10991, pp. 33–62. Springer, Cham (2018). https://doi.org/10.1007/978-3-319-96884-1_2

38. Jost, D., Maurer, U., Mularczyk, M.: Efficient ratcheting: almost-optimal guarantees for secure messaging. In: Ishai, Y., Rijmen, V. (eds.) EUROCRYPT 2019. LNCS, vol. 11476, pp. 159–188. Springer, Cham (2019). https://doi.org/10.1007/978-3-030-17653-2_6

39. Kalai, Y.T., Reyzin, L.: A survey of leakage-resilient cryptography. Cryptology ePrint Archive, Report 2019/302 (2019). https://eprint.iacr.org/2019/302

40. Klooß, M., Lehmann, A., Rupp, A.: (R)CCA secure updatable encryption with integrity protection. In: Ishai, Y., Rijmen, V. (eds.) EUROCRYPT 2019. Part I, volume 11476 of LNCS, pp. 68–99. Springer, Heidelberg (2019)

41. Kozlov, A., Reyzin, L.: Forward-secure signatures with fast key update. In: Cimato, S., Persiano, G., Galdi, C. (eds.) SCN 2002. LNCS, vol. 2576, pp. 241–256. Springer, Heidelberg (2003). https://doi.org/10.1007/3-540-36413-7_18

42. Lehmann, A., Tackmann, B.: Updatable encryption with post-compromise security. In: Nielsen, J.B., Rijmen, V. (eds.) EUROCRYPT 2018. LNCS, vol. 10822, pp. 685–716. Springer, Cham (2018). https://doi.org/10.1007/978-3-319-78372-7_22

43. Malkin, T., Micciancio, D., Miner, S.: Efficient generic forward-secure signatures with an unbounded number of time periods. In: Knudsen, L.R. (ed.) EUROCRYPT 2002. LNCS, vol. 2332, pp. 400–417. Springer, Heidelberg (2002). https://doi.org/10.1007/3-540-46035-7_27

44. Malkin, T., Teranishi, I., Yung, M.: Efficient circuit-size independent public key encryption with KDM security. In: Paterson, K.G. (ed.) EUROCRYPT 2011. LNCS, vol. 6632, pp. 507–526. Springer, Heidelberg (2011). https://doi.org/10.1007/978-3-642-20465-4_28

45. Naor, M., Reingold, O.: Number-theoretic constructions of efficient pseudo-random functions. In: 38th FOCS, pp. 458–467. IEEE Computer Society Press, October 1997

46. Naor, M., Segev, G.: Public-key cryptosystems resilient to key leakage. In: Halevi, S. (ed.) CRYPTO 2009. LNCS, vol. 5677, pp. 18–35. Springer, Heidelberg (2009). https://doi.org/10.1007/978-3-642-03356-8_2

47. Poettering, B., Rösler, P.: Towards bidirectional ratcheted key exchange. In: Shacham, H., Boldyreva, A. (eds.) CRYPTO 2018. LNCS, vol. 10991, pp. 3–32. Springer, Cham (2018). https://doi.org/10.1007/978-3-319-96884-1_1

48. Regev, O.: On lattices, learning with errors, random linear codes, and cryptography. In: Gabow, H.N., Fagin, R., (eds.) 37th ACM STOC, pp. 84–93. ACM Press, May 2005

Towards Tight Adaptive Security of Non-interactive Key Exchange

Julia Hesse[1], Dennis Hofheinz[2], Lisa Kohl[3], and Roman Langrehr[2]([✉])

[1] IBM Research Europe - Zurich, Rüschlikon, Switzerland
jhs@zurich.ibm.com
[2] ETH Zurich, Zürich, Switzerland
{hofheinz,roman.langrehr}@inf.ethz.ch
[3] Cryptology Group, CWI Amsterdam, Amsterdam, The Netherlands
lisa.kohl@cwi.nl

Abstract. We investigate the quality of security reductions for non-interactive key exchange (NIKE) schemes. Unlike for many other cryptographic building blocks (like public-key encryption, signatures, or zero-knowledge proofs), all known NIKE security reductions to date are non-tight, i.e., lose a factor of at least the number of users in the system. In that sense, NIKE forms a particularly elusive target for tight security reductions.

The main technical obstacle in achieving tightly secure NIKE schemes are adaptive corruptions. Hence, in this work, we explore security notions and schemes that lie between selective security and fully adaptive security. Concretely:

WE EXHIBIT A TRADEOFF BETWEEN KEY SIZE AND REDUCTION LOSS. We show that a tighter reduction can be bought by larger public and secret NIKE keys. Concretely, we present a simple NIKE scheme with a reduction loss of $O(N^2 \log(\nu)/\nu^2)$, and public and secret keys of $O(\nu)$ group elements, where N denotes the overall number of users in the system, and ν is a freely adjustable scheme parameter.

Our scheme achieves full adaptive security even against multiple "test queries" (i.e., adversarial challenges), but requires keys of size $O(N)$ to achieve (almost) tight security under the matrix Diffie-Hellman assumption. Still, already this simple scheme circumvents existing lower bounds.

WE SHOW THAT THIS TRADEOFF IS INHERENT. We contrast the security of our simple scheme with a lower bound for all NIKE schemes in which shared keys can be expressed as an "inner product in the exponent". This result covers the original Diffie-Hellman NIKE scheme, as well as a large class of its variants, and in particular our simple scheme. Our lower bound gives a tradeoff between the "dimension" of any such scheme (which directly corresponds to key sizes in existing schemes), and the reduction quality. For $\nu = O(N)$, this shows our simple scheme and reduction optimal (up to a logarithmic factor).

WE EXHIBIT A TRADEOFF BETWEEN SECURITY AND KEY SIZE FOR TIGHT REDUCTIONS. We show that it is possible to circumvent the inherent tradeoff above by relaxing the desired security notion. Concretely, we

D. Hofheinz and R. Langrehr—Supported in part by ERC CoG grant 724307.

© International Association for Cryptologic Research 2021
K. Nissim and B. Waters (Eds.): TCC 2021, LNCS 13044, pp. 286–316, 2021.
https://doi.org/10.1007/978-3-030-90456-2_10

consider the natural notion of semi-adaptive security, where the adversary has to commit to a single test query after seeing all public keys. As a feasibility result, we bring forward the first scheme that enjoys compact public keys *and* tight semi-adaptive security under the conjunction of the matrix Diffie-Hellman and learning with errors assumptions.

We believe that our results shed a new light on the role of adaptivity in NIKE security, and also illustrate the special role of NIKE when it comes to tight security reductions.

Keywords: Tight reductions · Non-interactive key exchange · Pairings · Learning with errors

1   Introduction

NON-INTERACTIVE KEY EXCHANGE (NIKE). A non-interactive key exchange (NIKE) scheme assigns any two users P_i, P_j in a system a common shared key $K_{i,j}$. This assignment should happen without any communication, and be based only on a setup like a public-key infrastructure. A well-known example of a NIKE is the original Diffie-Hellman key exchange scheme [14], in which any party has a public key g^{x_i} with associated secret key x_i, and the shared key for parties with public keys g^{x_i}, g^{x_j} is computed as $K_{i,j} = g^{x_i x_j}$. For security, we would like that $K_{i,j}$ remains hidden to an outsider, i.e., without knowing any of the two involved secret keys.

NIKE schemes have been studied as an explicit cryptographic building block by Cash, Kiltz, and Shoup [9], followed by a more in-depth study of NIKE security notions and corresponding schemes by Freire, Hofheinz, Kiltz, and Paterson [19]. There are a variety of different NIKE schemes from various computational assumptions (e.g., [5,9,14,19,24,25,35]), and a number of NIKE applications including wireless networks [8], deniable authentication [15], and interactive key exchange [6].[1]

NIKE AND TIGHT SECURITY. One interesting particularity of NIKE schemes is the fact that it seems difficult to *tightly* reduce their security to a standard computational assumption. All known security reductions for NIKE schemes (against adaptive corruptions and to non-interactive assumptions in the standard model) lose a factor of at least N, the overall number of users in the system.[2] In fact, two works by Bader, Jager, Li, and Schäge [2] and Hesse, Hofheinz, and Kohl [25] give lower bounds (of $\mathcal{O}(N^2)$, resp. $\mathcal{O}(N)$) on the reduction loss of large classes of NIKE schemes and reductions.

---

[1] In this work, we focus on the public-key setting, i.e., we assume a public-key infrastructure. We note, however, that NIKE has also been considered in the identity-based setting [17,33,38].

[2] This means that we can currently only map NIKE adversaries with success probability ε and runtime t to adversaries on a suitable computational assumption with runtime $t' \approx t$ but success probability no more than $\varepsilon' \approx \varepsilon/N$.

This is quite remarkable, since for most other cryptographic building blocks (such as public-key encryption and digital signatures [26], zero-knowledge proofs [23], or interactive key exchange [1]), tight security proofs are known even in a multi-user setting. But apart from being a theoretical curiosity, this also means that currently, NIKE keysizes should be chosen rather conservatively, in order to account for a potential security loss in scenarios with a large number of users.

META-REDUCTIONS, AND WHAT MAKES TIGHT NIKE SECURITY PARTICU-LARLY HARD TO ACHIEVE. The mentioned works [2, 25] already give an indication of what the main technical obstacle to a tight NIKE reduction is. Namely, they employ a meta-reduction [4] that turns any reduction that is "too successful" (i.e., suffers only from a low reduction loss) into a stand-alone problem solver. We give more details on this technique in our technical overview below. This meta-reduction technique has been applied also to other settings (like digital signatures [10], key encapsulation [2], and hierarchical identity-based encryption [30]), but it always hinges on one crucial requirement on the investigated scheme and reduction.

To explain this crucial requirement, assume for concreteness a given NIKE security reduction Λ that is "too successful". A meta-reduction requires that Λ is of a special form, namely that Λ essentially simulates the whole NIKE security experiment (including corruptions) for any NIKE adversary that is given in a black-box way. Furthermore, in this simulation, Λ must be "committed" early on to the secret state of this simulation, and in particular to all NIKE shared keys, even if these shared keys are not revealed during the simulation. The reason for this "committed" requirement will become clearer below, but intuitively it enables a "rewinding attack" on the reduction Λ itself.[3]

Now NIKE and other cryptographic primitives differ in this technical requirement for the applicability of meta-reductions. Namely, for primitives like public-key encryption (PKE), it is relatively easy to construct a reduction that is not committed to its secret state in the above sense. To see why this is the case, observe that in a PKE setting, different user secret keys or ciphertexts are not correlated: corrupting one user (or decrypting one ciphertext) gives no information about other users' secret keys (or the decryption of other ciphertexts). Hence, a reduction that answers corruption or decryption queries does not commit itself to, e.g., decryption of a challenge ciphertext in any way.

On the other hand, corrupting one party P_i in a NIKE scheme immediately reveals all shared keys $K_{i,j}$ that P_i has with other (yet-uncorrupted) parties P_j. This also determines the secret keys of such P_j to the extent that the $K_{i,j}$ computed with these not-yet-revealed keys are fixed. Hence, corrupting parties will gradually determine the secret state of a simulation in a NIKE reduction (i.e., the functionality of secret keys of yet-uncorrupted parties). This problem does not appear in, say, PKE or signature schemes, and circumventing this

---

[3] In a nutshell, the meta-reduction extracts enough shared keys from Λ to take the role of a successful adversary in a rewound Λ-instance. If Λ is "too successful", this causes Λ to solve the underlying computational problem with these extracted keys. Hence, Λ solves the underlying problem essentially by interacting with itself.

"committing" property in NIKE schemes currently seems to be out of reach of known techniques.

THIS WORK: BEYOND LINEAR SECURITY LOSS. Motivated by this difficulty, in this work we examine this "committing" property closer for a general class of group-based NIKE schemes and slightly relaxed security notions. Specifically, for N again denoting the overall number of parties in the system we ask:

For which security notions can we obtain NIKE schemes with a security reduction to a standard assumption with a sublinear loss of $o(N)$?

We obtain positive and negative results:

– We start off with a simple and intuitive "inner-product-based" NIKE scheme NIKE_{ip} that enjoys full adaptive security and offers an interesting tradeoff between security loss and key sizes. Specifically, NIKE_{ip} is parameterized by $\nu > 0$, has public and secret keys that comprise $\mathcal{O}(\nu)$ group elements, and a reduction loss of $\mathcal{O}(N^2 \log(\nu)/\nu^2)$ to the matrix Diffie-Hellman assumption [18] (a relaxation of the decision linear assumption) in pairing-friendly groups. In particular, it is possible to set $\nu = N$ to obtain a scheme with an (almost) tight reduction to a standard computational assumption, but which also suffers from large keys.

While the scheme itself is not very efficient for large ν, it shows a conceptually simple way to conduct a "non-committing" reduction. Essentially, our reduction does not have the problematic "committing" property discussed above because each secret key contains enough entropy to be not quite determined by up to ν corruptions of arbitrary other users. This means that previous lower bounds [2,25] do not apply to this scheme.

We also note that our NIKE_{ip} is the first to obtain tight security against multiple (i.e., up to ν) "test queries", i.e., adversarial challenges. This essentially means that the scheme guarantees the security of not only a single, but many shared keys even after a number of adaptive corruptions. While this property is implied with polynomial loss by security with respect to a single test query, previous reductions (including the previously "most tightly" secure scheme from [25]) did not consider multiple test queries.

One can view our result also as a feasibility result about the possibility of tight *bounded* security (much like the notion of bounded chosen-ciphertext security for PKE schemes [12]) for NIKE schemes.

– Next, we demonstrate that this tradeoff between reduction loss and key sizes is to some extent inherent when trying to achieve adaptive NIKE security. Concretely, we show that a large class of group-based NIKE schemes (that includes the original Diffie-Hellman scheme, as well as variations such as the scheme from [25] and our NIKE_{ip}) must become "committed enough" after ν corruptions whenever keys are of size $o(\nu)$ group elements.

Our result manifests the tradeoff between key sizes and reduction loss of NIKE_{ip}, and in fact for a large and natural class of NIKE schemes. We stress that the previous lower NIKE bounds [2,25] do not offer similar tradeoffs, since they did not consider key sizes at all.

- Finally, motivated by the previous tradeoff, we investigate ways to achieve tight security with (asymptotically) compact keys by relaxing the desired security notion. We find a different tradeoff, and now trade security for tightness. Namely, we construct a NIKE NIKE$_{sa}$ with keys whose size do not depend on N, and with an (almost) tight security reduction that however only achieves semi-adaptive security. By "semi-adaptive security", we mean that an adversary is restricted not in the type or number of corruptions, but in the timing and number of test queries (i.e., challenges). Concretely, an adversary may not ask any test query after a certain, a-priori bounded number of ν corruptions (or queries for shared keys between honest parties) have been made. Semi-adaptive security interpolates between a mild form of selective security (in which an adversary has to commit in advance to the parties whose shared keys it wants to be challenged on) and full adaptive security.

Our semi-adaptively secure NIKE$_{sa}$ uses NIKE$_{ip}$ above as a conceptually simple building block, and additionally relies on FHE techniques. Its security can be reduced (with logarithmic loss) to the conjunction of the matrix Diffie-Hellman problem and the learning with errors (LWE) problem [36].

We believe that this result shows that even if we cannot achieve full adaptive security with compact keys and tightly, we are not limited to merely selective security. Due to lack of space, we present this contribution in full detail only in the full version of this work.

1.1   Technical Overview

SETTING. Formally, a NIKE is a tuple of algorithms (Setup, KeyGen, SharedKey), where Setup generates public parameters, KeyGen on input of the public parameters returns a key pair (pk, sk), and SharedKey on input of the public parameters, a public key pk$_i$ and a secret key sk$_j$ returns a shared key $K_{i,j}$. Correctness requires that for all honestly generated key pairs we have $K_{i,j} = K_{j,i}$.

SECURITY MODEL. The simplest NIKE security notion to achieve is *selective security*, where the adversary commits to the key pair of users to be challenged (i.e. for which the adversary either receives the real shared key or a random key) *before* seeing any public key. To model realistic attack scenarios, what we would like to capture in the security notion is *fully adaptive security* (also called *CKS-heavy security* [19] after the inventors Cash, Kiltz and Shoup of the notion [9]). Here, the adversary can arbitrarily query oracles $\mathcal{O}_{extr}$, $\mathcal{O}_{revH}$ and $\mathcal{O}_{test}$. $\mathcal{O}_{extr}$ models the adversary's ability to corrupt a user and reveals the corresponding secret key and $\mathcal{O}_{revH}$ models the ability of the adversary to observe shared keys in the system and reveals the shared keys between two users. Finally, the purpose of $\mathcal{O}_{test}$ is to model that an adversary should still not be able to distinguish the (non-revealed) shared keys between any pair of uncorrupted users from random. More precisely, $\mathcal{O}_{test}$ given a tuple of users either returns the real shared key between the users or a random key (depending on an initially flipped bit). Giving the adversary the power to ask corruption queries adaptively poses a challenge for the security reduction. Consider for example the Diffie-Hellman key exchange.

There, public key/ secret key tuples are of the form (g^x, x) and a shared key is computed as $(g^{x_i})^{x_j} = (g^{x_j})^{x_i}$. Thus, the reduction either *knows* x – and therefore cannot make use of an adversary distinguishing shared keys involving x from random – or *does not know* x, and can therefore not answer with the secret key if the adversary decides to corrupt the user.

From Selective to Adaptive Security with Loss $\Omega(N^2)$. This can be solved by partitioning proofs, reducing the adaptive security to selective security. More precisely, the reduction guesses the "test query" of the adversary (i.e., the parties involved in the query that the adversary tries to distinguish from random) ahead of time and embeds the underlying challenge only in the two corresponding public keys. The problem of this approach is the security loss: With N overall users in the system, this strategy will only be successful with probability $1/N^2$. This means that the security guarantee decreases when the number of users in the system grows, which one has to account for by choosing larger concrete parameters (e.g. group sizes). Further, an upper bound on the number of users might not be known at the time of setup. In this paper we therefore aim for directly proving adaptive security.

Relaxing the Security Notion: Semi-Adaptive Security. We introduce the notion of ν-*semi-adaptive*, which lies in between selective and adaptive security: Here, the adversary has to ask *all* test queries within the first ν-corruptions (but can ask arbitrary extract and reveal queries later), where any user involved in a extract, reveal or test-query counts as one corruption. In the special case of 2-semi-adaptive security the adversary has to commit to a single test query after seeing all public keys.

Security with Dishonest Key Registration (DKR). The security experiments described so far do not give the adversary the opportunity to register keys dishonestly, i.e., publish arbitrary public keys that are not necessarily in the image of KeyGen. This can of course occur in realistic scenarios and is ultimately the security notion to aim for. In this paper we restrict ourselves to security with honest key registration as described above, since the difficulty of constructing NIKEs with tight security occurs when going from selective to adaptive security, rather than going from HKR to DKR security. In fact, using standard methods one can *tightly* transform an HKR-secure NIKE into a DKR-secure one, basically by adding a simulation-sound proof of knowledge of the secret key to the public key (see e.g. [9,25]).

RELATED WORK. We give a comparison of our result with previous work in Tables 1 and 2. In order to explain the challenges when constructing tightly secure NIKE, in the following we give a brief explanation of previous techniques used to give upper and lower bounds on tightly secure NIKE.

We first recall the *commitment problem* that occurs when proving security of the Diffie-Hellman NIKE. Namely, the reduction either *knows* a secret key or *does not know* a secret key, since each group element has a unique discrete logarithm. Building on the ideas put forward by Coron [11], Bader, Jager, Li, and Schäge [2] presented a lower bound on the tightness of NIKE schemes for

Table 1. Comparison of existing NIKE schemes. $|pk|$ denotes the size of the public keys, measured in numbers of group elements and exponents. HKR and DKR denote fully adaptive security [19] with honest and dishonest key registrations (where 1-HKR/1-DKR refers to the corresponding notion in the single-test-query setting). N denotes the number of parties the adversary interacts with, $2 \leq \nu \leq N$ is arbitrary and poly is a polynomial independent of ν and N. Further, note that losses of the constructions from [9] and [19] stem from applying a generic transformation to level the security guarantees of compared schemes. DDH and CDH correspond to the decisional and computational Diffie-Hellman assumption, ROM stands for random oracle model and "Fact." for Factoring. DBDH stands for decisional bilinear Diffie-Hellman, DLIN for Decision Linear and LWE for Learning With Errors. Finally, note that in all cases DLIN can be replaced by the 2-Matrix Decision Diffie-Hellman assumption (MDDH). More generally, we can build on the k-MDDH assumption at the cost of increasing the public key size and security loss by a factor of k.

	$|pk|$	Sec. model	$\mathcal{O}$(Sec. loss)	Assumption	Pairing
Diffie–Hellman [14]	$1 \times \mathbb{G}$	HKR	N^2	DDH	-
HPS-based [25]	$3 \times \mathbb{G}$	1-HKR	N	DDH	-
CKS08 [9]	$2 \times \mathbb{G}$	DKR	N^2	CDH (ROM)	-
FHKP13 [19]	$1 \times \mathbb{Z}_n$	DKR	N^2	Fact. (ROM)	-
FHKP13 [19]	$2 \times \mathbb{G} + 1 \times \mathbb{Z}_p$	DKR	N^2	DBDH	asymm.
HPS-based [25]	$12 \times \mathbb{G}$	1-DKR	N	DLIN	symm.
ν-dim NIKE$_\text{ip}$ (Sect. 3)	$(\nu + 2) \times \mathbb{G}$	HKR	$(N/\nu)^2 \log \nu$	DLIN	symm.
N-dim NIKE$_\text{ip}$ (Sect. 3)	$(N + 2) \times \mathbb{G}$	HKR	$\log N$	DLIN	symm.
ν-dim NIKE$_\text{sa}$ (fullv.)	$\nu \cdot$ poly	ν-semi-ad.	$\log N$	DLIN, LWE	symm.
2-dim NIKE$_\text{sa}$ (fullv.)	poly	semi-ad.	$\log N$	DLIN, LWE	symm.

which public keys are *fully* committing to their secret keys and therefore their shared keys. Generally, the idea of a meta-reduction is to turn a "too successful" reduction into a stand-alone problem solver for the underlying (non-interactive) cryptographic assumption. The meta-reduction of Bader, Jager, Li, and Schäge [2] systematically rewinds the reduction Λ to run with all N^2 possible pairs of challenge users, arguing that in any run the reduction *either has to abort* or *indeed return the unique secret key*. Now, if the reduction does not abort with

Table 2. Lower bounds on the security loss of NIKE. Here, the public keys of NIKE$_\text{ip}$ are of size $O(\nu)$. Our lower bound only applies to the HPS-based NIKE [25] when instantiated with the decisional Diffie-Hellman-based hash proof system [13]. We note that (in settings where it applies) the lower bound of [25] gives better constants than ours. We highlight the best known lower bound for each construction in green.

	Diffie-Hellman KE	HPS-based KE [25]	NIKE$_\text{ip}$ (Sect. 3)
BJLS [2]	$\Omega(N^2)$	-	-
HHK [25]	$\Omega(N)$	$\Omega(N)$	-
This work (Sect. 4)	$\Omega(N)$	$\Omega(N)$	$\Omega(N/\nu)$

probability larger than $1/N^2$ (i.e., the reduction does not abort on at least 2 out of the $\binom{N}{2}$ possible runs), it follows that one can extract *all* secret keys from the reduction, and thereby perfectly simulate an external "perfect" adversary. (Note that for this to be true it is crucial that the reduction is limited to giving out *unique* secret keys, and therefore the shared keys are also unique.) Altogether, this shows that whenever the reduction is successful with probability larger than $1/N^2$, it could have solved the underlying problem itself. Since this is a contradiction to the hardness of the underlying assumption, it shows that the security loss of $\Omega(N^2)$ for Diffie-Hellman (and, more generally, NIKEs with "committing" public keys) is inherent.

Bypassing the Commitment Problem with Semi-Functional Public Keys. Hesse et al. [25] showed how to bypass the lower bound by allowing to switch to non-committing public keys. Essentially, their scheme allows to introduce "semi-functional" public keys which are computationally indistinguishable from public keys produced by KeyGen. This allows a reduction to escape the fully committed setting by introducing semi-functional public keys that do not necessarily fix the shared key with other (semi-functional or normal) public keys in the system. Their construction still suffers from a security loss of $\Omega(N)$, since their semi-functional public keys do not have secret keys and can thus be recognized upon corruption. Since a reduction needs to plant at least one such public key in order to escape full shared key commitment, a security loss of N is inherent. This lower bound on the security loss was formally shown in [25] for all schemes where normal public keys are committing *and* can be efficiently recognized given a corresponding secret key.

Considering Weaker NIKE Security Notions. By allowing an arbitrary number of adaptive test queries but no corruptions, as was done e.g. in [9], tight security turns out easy to achieve. In fact, even the standard Diffie-Hellman key exchange can be shown (almost) tightly secure with respect to this notion, by simply embedding the underlying challenge into all public keys. Tight security (with a loss of factor $O(\log N)$) then follows by the re-randomizability of the decisional Diffie-Hellman assumption. However, going from test-query-only to adaptive security with corruption introduces a security loss of $\Omega(N^2)$. Since we are not aware of a tighter reduction for the scheme of [9] in the setting of adaptive security with corruptions, we do not consider their scheme tight in the sense of our paper.

Hesse et al. [25] consider a restriction of the above described security notion where the adversary is only allowed a single test query (but at any point of time). Since the generic reduction from the single-test-query setting to the multi-test-query introduces an overhead of $\Omega(N^2)$, in this paper we focus on the multi-test-query setting.

Technical Idea 1: Overcoming Binding Public Keys

OUR CONSTRUCTION. In this work we overcome the limitation of [25] with a NIKE scheme $\mathrm{NIKE_{ip}}$ where both normal and semi-functional public keys have corresponding secret keys. Our construction is based on symmetric pairing groups. Let g be a group generator of the source group. We write $[x]$ for g^x and for a matrix $\mathbf{M} = (m)_{i,j}$ we write $[\mathbf{M}]$ for $([m])_{i,j}$. The public parameters of our NIKE are

$$\mathsf{pp} := ([\mathbf{D}], [\mathbf{MD}]),$$

where $\mathbf{D}$ is a uniformly random $(\nu+2) \times 2$ matrix and $\mathbf{M}$ is a uniformly random symmetric $(\nu+2) \times (\nu+2)$ matrix. The parameter $\nu \in \mathbb{N}_{\geq 2}$ will become important in the security proof. An normal key pair is now generated as follows: We sample a uniformly random 2-dimensional vector $\mathbf{w}$ and set

$$\mathsf{pk} := [\mathbf{Dw}] \qquad \text{and} \qquad \mathsf{sk} := [\mathbf{MDw}].$$

The shared key between two users is the inner product of one user's public key and the other user's secret key, computed with the pairing. To see that correctness holds, let $(\mathsf{pk}_1 = [\mathbf{Dw}_1], \mathsf{sk}_1 = [\mathbf{MDw}_1])$ and $(\mathsf{pk}_2 = [\mathbf{Dw}_2], \mathsf{sk}_1 = [\mathbf{MDw}_2])$ be two honestly generated key pairs. Then

$$\mathtt{SharedKey}(\mathsf{pp}, \mathsf{pk}_1, \mathsf{sk}_2) = e([\mathbf{w}_1^\top \mathbf{D}^\top], [\mathbf{MDw}_2]) = [\mathbf{w}_1^\top \mathbf{D}^\top \mathbf{MDw}_2]_T$$

$$= [\mathbf{w}_2^\top \mathbf{D}^\top \mathbf{M}^\top \mathbf{Dw}_1]_T \overset{(*)}{=} [\mathbf{w}_2^\top \mathbf{D}^\top \mathbf{MDw}_1]_T$$

$$= e([\mathbf{w}_2^\top \mathbf{D}^\top], [\mathbf{MDw}_1]) = \mathtt{SharedKey}(\mathsf{pp}, \mathsf{pk}_2, \mathsf{sk}_1).$$

The equality $(*)$ uses the symmetry of $\mathbf{M}$.

One can interpret the public parameters by setting $(\mathbf{d}_1 | \mathbf{d}_2) := \mathbf{D}$ as two exemplary key pairs

$$\mathsf{pp} := ((\mathsf{pk}_1 = [\mathbf{d}_1], \mathsf{sk}_1 = [\mathbf{Md}_1]), (\mathsf{pk}_2 = [\mathbf{d}_2], \mathsf{sk}_2 = [\mathbf{Md}_2])).$$

The user-generated keys are then random linear combinations of these exemplary key pairs. It is necessary to have at least two exemplary keys, because if the honest user keys would be linear combinations of just one exemplary key, one could use the pairing to check efficiently if a public key is in the subspace spanned by the exemplary public key. This would make it impossible for our reduction to use public keys that are not in the linear span of the exemplary public keys.

SEMI-FUNCTIONAL PUBLIC KEYS WITH SECRET KEYS. To argue security, we have to introduce semi-functional public and secret keys. A semi-functional public key is $[\mathbf{u}]$ where $\mathbf{u}$ is chosen uniformly at random from the full space (instead of only the linear span of $\mathbf{D}$'s column vectors). Accordingly, the corresponding semi-functional secret key is $[\mathbf{Mu}]$.

The semi-functional key pairs are indistinguishable from the normal key pairs by the matrix decisional Diffie-Hellman (MDDH) assumption. It states that vectors (represented in a group) from a 2-dimensional subspace (i.e. our normal keys) are indistinguishable from uniformly random vectors (i.e. our semi-functional keys). The MDDH assumption is implied by the well-known 2-linear assumption [18]. Due to the random self-reducibility of the MDDH assumptions, this implication holds even for arbitrary many vectors with security loss only $\mathcal{O}(\log \nu)$.

The semi-functional keys have the desired "less committing" property. Indeed, note that with publishing the public parameters the reduction is not completely committed to the matrix $\mathbf{M}$, since $\mathbf{MD}$ contains only little information about $\mathbf{M}$. Now for each semi-functional public key $\mathbf{u}$ the corresponding semi-functional secret key $\mathbf{Mu}$ leaks some new information about $\mathbf{M}$ and after ν secret keys have been used, the reduction is completely committed to $\mathbf{M}$. If we would apply a suitable basis change transformation to $\mathbf{M}$ (such that the column vectors of $\mathbf{D}$, and the used semi-functional secret keys become unit vectors), each semi-functional secret key corresponds to a row (due to the symmetry also a column) of $\mathbf{M}$ and each shared key corresponds to one entry of the matrix, as depicted by Fig. 1.

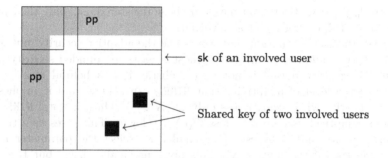

Fig. 1. The symmetric matrix $\mathbf{M}$ in the basis where the column vectors of $\mathbf{D}$ and the semi-functional public keys of the involved users are the standard basis vectors. The normal secret keys (and shared keys where at least one user has a normal public key) live in the gray area. The pp can be seen as two key pairs and normal public and secret keys are linear combinations of these public and secret keys.

Since in our scheme there are secret keys for the semi-functional public keys, it circumvents the main bottleneck of the approach of [25]: Our reduction turns all public keys into semi-functional ones, and does not have to rely on any guessing argument. In contrast to [25], our semi-functional keys are committing with respect to normal keys. But, since we turn all keys to semi-functional, it is completely sufficient that semi-functional keys are not committing with respect to other semi-functional public keys. This approach is summarized in Table 3.

LIMITING THE NUMBER OF INVOLVED USERS. When ν semi-functional secret keys have been leaked, (i.e., they have been leaked through an $\mathcal{O}_{\mathsf{extr}}$ query or used to answer an $\mathcal{O}_{\mathsf{revH}}$ or $\mathcal{O}_{\mathsf{extr}}$ query,) the reduction is completely committed to $\mathbf{M}$. In this situation we can still argue, that each test query leaked one entry of the matrix $\mathbf{M}$ that was not revealed in any other query and therefore looks uniformly random to the adversary. However, any further leakage of another semi-functional secret key could potentially leak one of the test-query entries. Thus we have to limit the adversary to involve at most ν users in the security game, where a user counts as involved, when he appeared in at least one $\mathcal{O}_{\mathsf{extr}}$,

Table 3. Effect of all combinations of normal and semi-functional public keys on the shared key $K_{i,j}$ in the HPS-based NIKE [25] and our $\mathsf{NIKE_{ip}}$.

	pk_j normal	pk_j semi-functional
pk_i normal	committed	not committed
	committed	committed
pk_i semi-functional	not committed	does not exist
	committed	Up to ν users involved: not committed Beyond: committed

$\mathcal{O}_{\mathsf{revH}}$, or $\mathcal{O}_{\mathsf{test}}$ query. (Users that have only been registered, i.e., only their public key was revealed, do not count as involved.)

We call the security notion that works like the adaptive security, but where the adversary is allowed to involve at most ν users, ν-bounded security. Even though this security notion is not very realistic, it is a helpful tool because it captures the level of adaptivity that $\mathsf{NIKE_{ip}}$ can achieve and it implies full adaptive security with security loss only $\mathcal{O}((N/\nu)^2)$. Thus, in total $\mathsf{NIKE_{ip}}$ can be proven adaptively secure with loss $\mathcal{O}((N/\nu)^2 \log \nu)$. This gives us a tradeoff between key size and tightness. The smaller we select the parameter ν, the smaller the size of the matrix $\mathbf{M}$. This gives us smaller keys, but the semi-functional keys will become committing earlier in the security game, leading to a larger security loss.

A curiosity of $\mathsf{NIKE_{ip}}$ is that the roles of the public key and secret key are completely symmetric. That is, when all users swap their public and secret key, $\mathsf{NIKE_{ip}}$ is still secure (and in the security proof we simply have to replace $\mathbf{M}$ by $\mathbf{M}^{-1}$).

Our scheme bypasses the lower bound of [25], because their lower bound requires, informally speaking, that whenever two key pairs look like valid to the adversary, the shared key between them is already determined by the public keys. This is not the case here: Two secret keys could differ by an entry of $\mathbf{M}$ that is unknown to adversary (thus both look like corresponding secret keys for the same public key), but, with a suitable public key of another valid key pair, this entry of $\mathbf{M}$ does not cancel out in the secret key computation and thus the two secret keys yield different shared keys.

Technical Idea 2: Lower Bound for Large Class of NIKEs
INNER-PRODUCT NIKE AND A NEW ARGUMENT FOR COMMITTING REDUCTIONS. To extend the existing results on lower bounds, we need to further broaden the class of NIKE schemes that the meta-reduction technique works for. The goal is to allow potential reductions to introduce keys that are less "committing" than in the previous bounds described above. Towards this goal, we observe that all DH-like NIKE schemes in the literature, including our $\mathsf{NIKE_{ip}}$ described above, have the following joint property: public and secret keys

Towards Tight Adaptive Security of NIKE   297

can be represented as $\mathbb{Z}_q^d$-vectors $\mathbf{x}, \mathbf{y}$, and shared keys are computed as (an invertible function of) the inner product $\langle \mathbf{x}, \mathbf{y}' \rangle$. We call such NIKE schemes *d-dimensional ip-NIKE*. The Diffie-Hellman key exchange, for example, allows for key pair (g^x, x) to be written as tuple (x, x) of the same one-dimensional vector $x \in \mathbb{Z}_q$. Shared keys between vector tuples $(x_i, x_i), (x_j, x_j)$ are computed as $(g^{x_i})^{x_j} = g^{\langle x_i, x_j \rangle} = g^{\langle x_j, x_i \rangle} = (g^{x_j})^{x_i}$. Intuitively, using only one-dimensional vectors as in DH-KE means that public keys commit already to all shared keys. Vectors of higher dimensions, though, allow a reduction to encode more information, and eventually escape a setting where all shared keys are fixed. We can now formalize this intuition by exploiting linearity of the inner product. Namely, for a d-dimensional inner-product NIKE, a meta-reduction can create a fully committed setting in case vector dimensions are smaller than the number of users. For this, assume unique[4] public key vectors $\mathbf{x}_1, \ldots, \mathbf{x}_m$ of $m \approx N$ corrupted users and public key vectors $\mathbf{x}, \mathbf{x}'$ for yet uncorrupted $\mathsf{pk}, \mathsf{pk}'$. Let further $\mathbf{y}_1, \ldots, \mathbf{y}_m, \mathbf{y}, \mathbf{y}'$ denote corresponding secret key vectors. We stress that the meta-reduction is not able to compute any of these values, and we only use them to argue that the reduction is committed. If d is smaller than m, $\mathbf{x}$ lies in the span of the m other vectors with noticeable probability, yielding $\sum_{i=1}^m \beta_i \mathbf{x}_i = \mathbf{x}$ for a $\mathbb{Z}_q^m$-vector β. This already determines the (exponent of the) shared key $\langle \mathbf{x}, \mathbf{y}' \rangle$ between $\mathbf{x}$ and $\mathbf{x}'$ as a linear combination of the (exponents of) shared keys between each $\mathbf{x}_1, \ldots, \mathbf{x}_n$ and $\mathbf{x}'$. To see this, we write

$$\langle \mathbf{x}, \mathbf{y}' \rangle = \langle \sum_{i=1}^m \beta_i \mathbf{x}_i, \mathbf{y}' \rangle = \sum_{i=1}^m \beta_i \langle \mathbf{x}_i, \mathbf{y}' \rangle = \sum_{i=1}^m \beta_i \langle \mathbf{y}_i, \mathbf{x}' \rangle,$$

where the latter equality follows from the correctness of the NIKE. Since the reduction already committed to the m shared key exponents $\langle \mathbf{y}_i, \mathbf{x}' \rangle_{i \in [m]}$ through corruptions of $\mathsf{pk}_1, \ldots, \mathsf{pk}_m$, we can conclude that the secret key between pk and pk' is fixed through its exponent $\langle \mathbf{x}, \mathbf{y}' \rangle$. We refer the reader to the "uniqueness lemma" (Lemma 5) for full details.

A meta-reduction can exploit this committed setting by rewinding the reduction, a technique that was already used to prove the previous lower bounds [2, 25]. And indeed, we can show that any tight reduction must have key dimensions close to N, in order to avoid the linear dependencies described above that would result in commitment of all shared keys in the span. We now describe our meta-reduction and resulting lower bound in detail.

OUR NEW LOWER BOUND. We are now ready to explain our lower bound. The general strategy of a meta-reduction is to first describe an inefficient "hypothetical" adversary $\mathcal{A}$ with success probability $\varepsilon_{\mathcal{A}}$, and then show that the hypothetical adversary can be efficiently simulated by rewinding the reduction except when some event "bad" occurs. Since the reduction has to work with the hypothetical adversary, this means that – except with probability $\Pr[\mathsf{bad}]$ – the reduction

---

[4] For our results we require uniqueness of a corresponding *public* key vector given the public key, which holds for all DH-based schemes from the literature including our first NIKE.

298 J. Hesse et al.

must also work with the simulated adversary, i.e., without external help. Since by assumption the reduction on its own cannot have more than negligible advantage in solving the underlying problem, this essentially shows that the success probability of the reduction can be upper bounded by $\Pr[\mathsf{bad}] \cdot \varepsilon_\mathcal{A} + \mathsf{negl}$ for a negligible function negl, i.e. lose a factor of $1/\Pr[\mathsf{bad}]$. For arguing that the simulated adversary perfectly simulates the hypothetical adversary we crucially rely on the uniqueness lemma, which ensures that all shared keys are fixed after the reduction gave out sufficiently many secret keys.

2-step-Adaptive Security. For proving our lower bound we introduce the *2-step-adaptive* security notion, where an adversary after receiving the public keys can first ask the secret keys for an arbitrary large set D, and then has to commit to a challenge tuple of public keys (outside D). The adversary wins if after receiving the remaining secret keys (except the ones involved in the challenge tuple), it returns the shared key between the challenge parties. It is straightforward to see that adaptive security implies this weaker security notion, and therefore any lower bound on 2-step-adaptive security readily carries over to adaptive security.

The Hypothetical Adversary. The idea of the hypothetical adversary is to enforce uniqueness of the challenge shared key by choosing the set D in a suitable way. By the uniqueness lemma this can be achieved by choosing D such that the corresponding public key vectors span all public keys. (Note that if a NIKE is a d-dimensional inner-product NIKE, there always exist such a set of size at most d.) Once the shared key between the challenge key pairs is fixed, the adversary can simply brute-force any tuple of secret keys corresponding to the challenge public keys that are consistent with all secret keys in D, and use these to compute the shared key. Since the shared key is unique, the hypothetical adversary will always be successful.[5]

Simulating the Hypothetical Adversary. The problem in simulating the hypothetical adversary is that the following cannot be done efficiently:

(1) *Extract* the public key vectors to find a spanning subset D, and
(2) Obtain the secret keys by *brute-force* to compute the challenge shared key.

The strategy of the meta-reduction to is therefore to:

(1) *Guess* a set D (and hope it is spanning), and
(2) Obtain secret keys by *rewinding the reduction* to compute the challenge shared key.

It turns out productive to choose $|D| \approx N/2$. The reason for this is as follows: On the one hand, for maximizing the probability that D is spanning, D should be chosen as large as possible. On the other hand, for extracting the secret keys from the reduction it is crucial that the reduction can be rewound while already

---

[5] To capture adversaries with arbitrary success probability $\varepsilon_\mathcal{A}$, the hypothetical adversary can simply flip a biased coin and only output the shared key with probability $\varepsilon_\mathcal{A}$.

being committed to the secret keys in D (since otherwise, the reduction could give out secret keys that are not consistent with the secret keys in D). In order to argue that the reduction either has to return valid secret keys for each $i \in [N] \backslash D$ or abort with high probability, we have to choose $[N] \backslash D$ large (essentially, the success probability will scale with $1 - 1/(N - |D|)$).

Success Probability of the Simulated Adversary. Finally, the meta-reduction can compute the shared key with the help of this extracted secret keys. By the uniqueness lemma we obtain that this shared key is unique if both strategies of the meta-reduction are successful, i.e. if (1) D is indeed *spanning*, and (2) the reduction returns *valid and consistent secret keys* for both public keys involved in the challenge.[6] We can show that the event bad that either of these is not satisfied only occurs with probability in the order of d/N. This results in the following informal theorem:

Theorem (Lower Bound): Any simple reduction from a non-interactive complexity assumption to the adaptive-security of a d-dimensional inner-product NIKE has to lose a factor in the order of $\Omega(N/d)$.

Our lower bound thus yields that $\mathsf{NIKE_{ip}}$, which is a ν-dimensional ip-NIKE (see Definition 5 for the formal definition), with secret keys of size $O(\nu)$ has an inherent security loss of at least $\Omega(N/\nu)$. We contrast that with the security loss of our security proof for the core NIKE, which is $O((N/\nu)^2 \log \nu)$. Thus, for $\nu = N$ the security reduction that we give in Sect. 3 is essentially optimal. We give a comparison of our lower bound with others in Table 2.

Technical Idea 3: Extension to "Semi-adaptive" Security
MOTIVATION: CONTROLLING ENTROPY LEAKAGE. The lower bound just presented appears to limit what we can prove about our first NIKE scheme $\mathsf{NIKE_{ip}}$. Specifically, it appears that we require a large setting of ν (i.e., large keys) for (almost) a tight security reduction. Taking a step back, the intuitive reason why we cannot obtain a better reduction is the following: every secret key revealed through a corruption query leaks entropy about the hidden matrix $\mathbf{M}$. This is intended, since in fact this fresh entropy is used to statistically blind shared keys. However, since the entropy contained in $\mathbf{M}$ is limited, this argument guarantees fresh entropy only for a bounded number of corruptions. After $\mathcal{O}(\nu)$ corruptions, $\mathbf{M}$ is fully determined, and any *additional* corruptions (or shared key or test queries) will result in (jointly) non-uniform shared keys. In particular, the security argument breaks down completely if more than $\mathcal{O}(\nu)$ corruptions are made, even if those are made after all shared key or test queries.

OUR GOAL: ν-SEMI-ADAPTIVE SECURITY. We now set out to mitigate this limitation, and better *control* the entropy released through secret keys. We will

---

[6] Even though only one secret key is necessary to compute the shared key, we can only be sure that the reduction is committed to the shared key when given both secret keys, since the reduction could switch to a semi-functional public key (without valid secret key).

unfortunately not be able to achieve full adaptive security with small keys. Instead, our goal will be a NIKE scheme with small keys, but in which more than $\mathcal{O}(\nu)$ corruptions are possible only *after* all test queries have been made. To more concrete: we will achieve what we call ν-semi-adaptive security, which denotes security against the following type of attacks. An adversary may request up to ν corruptions, shared key, or test queries (in any combination). After that, any number of corruption or shared key queries, *but no test queries* are allowed. This notion is hence weaker than adaptive security, but also does allow for some degree of ("early") adaptivity. Like our basic scheme NIKE$_\mathsf{ip}$, our ν-semi-adaptively secure scheme NIKE$_\mathsf{sa}$ will have keys of size $\mathcal{O}(\nu)$ group elements, and its security reduction will be (almost) tight, i.e., only lose a factor of $\mathcal{O}(\log \nu)$.

As discussed above, our result can also be seen as a tradeoff between security and key size: the larger its keys are, the closer to (full) adaptive security the achieved security notion is. We reach full adaptive security only with large keys (of size $\mathcal{O}(N)$ group elements), but smaller keys still yield a less adaptively but (almost) tightly secure scheme.

BUILDING BLOCK: NON-INTERACTIVE TAG EXCHANGE. We now explain the main technical ideas of our semi-adaptively secure NIKE$_\mathsf{sa}$. In a nutshell, we use NIKE$_\mathsf{ip}$ as a *tag generator*, or as what we call a "non-interactive tag exchange" (NITE) scheme. A NITE is defined like a NIKE, except that (a) we call shared keys "tags" now, and (b) we require "ν-programmability" instead of indistinguishability for security. ν-programmability requires that there is a dedicated "programming algorithm" that allows to semi-adaptively program tags in the following way: given up to ν pairs of parties $(P_{i,1}, P_{i,2})$ and corresponding "target tags" T_i, output corresponding secret keys that yield T_i as tag between $P_{i,1}$ and $P_{i,2}$. This programming succeeds even *after* all public keys are fixed, and in an adaptive way (such that the T_i can be fixed one at a time, depending on all public keys and earlier T_i). For security, we require that this programming is not detectable, even given *all* secret keys (programmed or not). We can interpret NIKE$_\mathsf{ip}$ as a NITE: shared keys are interpreted as tags, and programming works by adjusting $\mathbf{A}$ adaptively so that the desired tag values are computed.[7] Note that this process works only for programming up to $\mathcal{O}(\nu)$ tag values, since the entropy in $\mathbf{A}$ is limited. On the other hand, the notion of programmability also captures the security that NIKE$_\mathsf{ip}$ achieves when eventually all secret keys are revealed.

LEVERAGING NITE PROGRAMMABILITY. The security of a NITE scheme requires programmable tags, but does not require "unopened" tags to remain hidden in any way (e.g., in the sense of NIKE indistinguishability). Hence, we cannot immediately use a NITE scheme as NIKE. Instead, our NIKE$_\mathsf{sa}$ uses a NITE scheme to generate common (but not necessarily secret) shared tags for

---

[7] This is a slight oversimplification. In fact, programming requires to also make public keys semi-functional, as in the security proof of NIKE$_\mathsf{ip}$ sketched above. Our formal programmability definition will allow for such adjustments during programming.

any two parties, who will then employ a "tag-based NIKE" (TNIKE) as a second stage to compute the actual NIKE shared keys. Analogously to tag-based encryption [28], a TNIKE is simply a NIKE in which shared key computation takes a tag as additional input. For correctness of $\mathsf{NIKE_{sa}}$ in the usual sense, this tag should of course be the same for both parties.

Before describing a concrete TNIKE scheme, we describe its crucial abstract property: our TNIKE scheme has "punctured" secret keys, i.e., secret keys that allow to compute shared keys for all but one tag value. This puncturing point (i.e., the tag upon which shared key computation fails) is uniformly random, but not obvious from the corresponding public key. Similar puncturing techniques have been used as a technical tool to achieve adaptive security in various contexts before (e.g., [7,16,27,32,34,37,39]). In our security proof, we will program the tags output by the NITE scheme such that *all tags that refer to NIKE test queries will be programmed to be exactly the puncturing points of the corresponding secret keys*.[8] This programming is not detectable thanks to the NITE's security, and leads to a situation in which all test queries are randomized.

OUR CONCRETE CONSTRUCTION. Armed with this intuition, we now give more details on our actual TNIKE construction. To illustrate the main ideas, we only describe a slightly simplified version of our construction for minimal ν, i.e., such that it achieves only a small degree of semi-adaptivity. The construction is based on the learning with errors (LWE) problem, and assumes public parameters $\mathsf{pp} := \mathbf{A} \xleftarrow{\$} \mathbb{Z}_p^{n \times m}$. A public key contains

$$\mathsf{pk} := (\mathbf{SA} + \mathbf{E}, \mathbf{V} = \mathbf{AU} + \tau\mathbf{G}),$$

where $\mathbf{S}$ is a random matrix, $\mathbf{E}$ and $\mathbf{U}$ are a "noise" matrices with small entries, $\mathbf{G}$ is the fixed "gadget matrix" of [31], and τ is the (uniformly random) tag at which the corresponding secret key will be punctured. Note that $\mathbf{V}$ is actually an encryption of τ under the fully homomorphic encryption (FHE) scheme of Gentry, Sahai, and Waters [21].[9] The corresponding secret key is of the form

$$\mathsf{sk} := (\mathbf{S}, \mathbf{U}, \tau).$$

To compute the shared key between two users, assume a public key pk as above, a secret key $\mathsf{sk}' = (\mathbf{S}', \mathbf{U}', \tau')$ from another user, and a tag T. We first homomorphically and deterministically compute an FHE encryption $\mathbf{V}^\star = \mathbf{AU}^\star + b\mathbf{G}$ from $\mathbf{V}$, where $b \in \{0,1\}$ with $b = 1$ iff $\tau = T$. (Note that this really denotes the punctured point τ encrypted in $\mathbf{V}$, not the one from sk'. Hence, b is hidden at this point.) The corresponding shared key K is a rounded version of $\mathbf{S}'\mathbf{V}^\star$, i.e.,

$$K = \mathsf{round}(\mathbf{S}'\mathbf{V}^\star).$$

---

[8] This is again an oversimplification: for a particular choice of tag, one involved party P_i will not be able to compute the TNIKE shared key, while the other party P_j will be able to compute a shared key that depends on entropy in P_j's secret key.

[9] In this overview, we neglect the fact that τ should be a small scalar. Our full scheme will actually encrypt τ bitwise.

The other involved party, using $\mathsf{pk}' = (\mathbf{S}'\mathbf{A} + \mathbf{E}', \mathbf{V}')$ and $\mathsf{sk} = (\mathbf{S}, \mathbf{U}, \tau)$, computes the same shared key differently: it uses $\mathbf{U}$ to obtain the encryption random coins $\mathbf{U}^\star$ with $\mathbf{V}^\star = \mathbf{A}\mathbf{U}^\star + b\mathbf{G}$ (for b as above) and computes

$$K' = \mathsf{round}((\mathbf{S}'\mathbf{A} + \mathbf{E}')\mathbf{U}^\star) = \mathsf{round}(\mathbf{S}'\mathbf{A}\mathbf{U}^\star + \mathbf{E}'\mathbf{U}^\star) \overset{(*)}{=} \mathsf{round}(\mathbf{S}'\mathbf{A}\mathbf{U}^\star),$$

where $(*)$ holds with high probability for a suitable rounding function, since $\mathbf{E}'$ and $\mathbf{U}$ have small entries. Indeed, $K = K'$ whenever $T \neq \tau$ (so that $b = 0$ and $\mathbf{V}^\star = \mathbf{A}\mathbf{U}^\star$). But for $T = \tau$, the rounded value

$$\mathbf{S}'\mathbf{V}^\star = \mathbf{S}'\mathbf{U}^\star + \mathbf{S}'\mathbf{G}$$

in K contains the term $\mathbf{S}'\mathbf{G}$, which extracts randomness from $\mathbf{S}'$ (that, using a proper setup of $\mathbf{A}$, does not appear in pk'). Hence, the tag $T = \tau$ is special, in that K is randomized by entropy from $\mathbf{S}'$ only for this T. Note that the value K' does not contain this extra term, and so in fact does not satisfy $K' = K$ for $T = \tau$. Of course, since in "normal operation", tags are independently and uniformly random values, $T = \tau$ happens only with negligible probability, and this affects correctness of the scheme only negligibly.

Before going further, we note that this overview over our TNIKE scheme neglects a few things: we did not discuss suitable dimensions, the rounding function, or a suitable encoding of large tags τ. Besides, we did not discuss a generalization to larger values of ν (which require programming more values τ_i into each key). Finally, we did not discuss how both parties coordinate on their role in the computation of K (i.e., on whose $\mathbf{V}$ is used as a basis of computation). All of those questions have simple, albeit sometimes tedious technical answers, and we will discuss all of these issues inside.

THE SECURITY OF OUR CONSTRUCTION. We now briefly sketch the proof of 1-semi-adaptive security of $\mathsf{NIKE}_{\mathsf{sa}}$, which is composed of our NITE and TNIKE schemes. So assume a 1-semi-adaptive adversary $\mathcal{A}$ that obtains all public keys, and then may ask a single test query. After this, and without loss of generality, $\mathcal{A}$ obtains all secret keys of parties not involved in that test query. We need to show that $\mathcal{A}$'s success in distinguishing between real and random answers is negligible, and, for a tight reduction, does not scale in the number of users. To do so, consider the following short sequence of game hops:

Game 0 is the original 1-semi-adaptive NIKE security game with a test query that is answered with the real shared key.

Game 1 changes how the tags for the test query are computed: here, the tag for the test query is adaptively programmed to be the puncturing point τ of the corresponding user. Note that the corresponding shared key can still be computed for $\mathcal{A}$ in the same way that K is computed above. By programmability of the NITE scheme, and using the security of the used FHE scheme, this change goes unnoticed by $\mathcal{A}$.[10]

---

[10] We note that to obtain *tight* security at this point, we will temporarily switch the used FHE scheme into a lossy mode of encryption [3,22].

Game 2 replaces the result of the test query with an independently chosen random shared key. This change is statistical, and can be justified with the observations above about hidden entropy in $\mathbf{S}'$.

We give full details of the proof (and additional discussion) in the full version of this paper.

2 Preliminaries

We use $x \overset{\$}{\leftarrow} S$ to denote the process of sampling an element x from a set S uniformly at random. For a probability distribution $\mathcal{D}$, we write $x \leftarrow \mathcal{D}$ to denote that the random variable x is distributed according to $\mathcal{D}$. If $\mathcal{A}$ is a (probability) algorithm then we write $x \overset{\$}{\leftarrow} \mathcal{A}(b)$ to denote the random variable x outputted by $\mathcal{A}$ on input b. We use $\mathsf{Sym}_n(\mathbb{Z}_q)$ (for $n \in \mathbb{N}$, q prime) to denote the set of symmetric $n \times n$ over $\mathbb{Z}_q$. Initially, all partial maps (denoted by $f : A \dashrightarrow B$) are totally undefined in our games. We write $x[i]$ for the i-th bit of the binary representation of x. We write $(a, \_) := (x, y)$ and $(\_, b) := (x, y)$ to define $a := x$ and $b := y$, respectively. $T(\mathcal{A})$ denotes the running time of $\mathcal{A}$.

2.1 Pairing Group Assumptions

Throughout this paper, SymGGen denotes a probabilistic polynomial-time (PPT) algorithm that on input 1^λ returns a description $\mathcal{PG} := (\mathbb{G}, \mathbb{G}_T, q, g, e)$ of a symmetric pairing group, where $\mathbb{G}$ and $\mathbb{G}_T$ are cyclic groups of order q for a λ-bit prime q. The group element g is a generator of $\mathbb{G}$. The function $e : \mathbb{G} \times \mathbb{G} \to \mathbb{G}_T$ is an efficient computable (non-degenerated) bilinear map (i.e., a pairing). Define $g_T := e(g, g)$, which is a generator in $\mathbb{G}_T$.

We use the implicit representation of group elements as in [18]. For $s \in \{\epsilon, T\}$ and $a \in \mathbb{Z}_q$ define $[a]_s = ag_s \in \mathbb{G}_s$ as the implicit representation of a in $\mathbb{G}_s$. Similarly, for a matrix $\mathbf{A} = (a_{ij}) \in \mathbb{Z}_q^{n \times m}$ we define $[\mathbf{A}]_s$ as the implicit representation of $\mathbf{A}$ in $\mathbb{G}_s$. Note that it is efficient to compute $[\mathbf{AB}]_s$ given $([\mathbf{A}]_s, \mathbf{B})$ or $(\mathbf{A}, [\mathbf{B}]_s)$ with matching dimensions. Furthermore, $e([\mathbf{A}], [\mathbf{B}]) := [\mathbf{AB}]_T$ can be efficiently computed given $[\mathbf{A}]$ and $[\mathbf{B}]$ with the pairing e.

Many assumptions in paring groups can be expressed as matrix decisional Diffie-Hellman (MDDH) assumption [18]. For a definition of the (Q-fold) MDDH assumption, see [18] or the full version of this paper.

We use the Q-fold uniform matrix distribution, because the uniform distribution allows us to give a tight reduction to the standard 1-fold version, as shown by the following Lemma. Gay et al. already provided a tight reduction [20], but their proof is flawed[11] as pointed out by [29]. The proof can be found in the full version.

---

[11] They correctly prove that $\mathcal{U}_{\ell,k}$-MDDH is tightly equivalent to $\mathcal{U}_k$-MDDH, but the proof can not show that Q-fold $\mathcal{U}_{\ell,k}$-MDDH is tightly equivalent to Q-fold $\mathcal{U}_k$-MDDH.

Lemma 1 (Random self-reducibility of $\mathcal{U}_{\ell,k}$-MDDH). *For every $\ell > k$ and every PPT adversary $\mathcal{A}$ there exists an adversary $\mathcal{B}$ with*

$$\mathsf{Adv}^{\mathsf{mddh},Q}_{\mathcal{A},\mathcal{U}_{\ell,k},\mathsf{SymGGen},s}(\lambda) \leq \left\lceil \log\left(\frac{\ell}{k}\right) \right\rceil k \left(\mathsf{Adv}^{\mathsf{mddh}}_{\mathcal{B},\mathcal{U}_k,\mathsf{SymGGen},s}(\lambda) + \frac{3}{q-1} \right),$$

where $\mathcal{PG} \leftarrow \mathsf{SymGGen}(1^\lambda)$ and $T(\mathcal{B}) \approx T(\mathcal{A}) + Q \cdot \mathrm{poly}(\lambda)$, where poly *is a polynomial independent of $\mathcal{A}$.*

2.2 Non-Interactive Key Exchange

Definition 1 (NIKE). *A* NIKE *scheme with identity space $\mathcal{IDS}$ and key space $\mathcal{K}$ consists of three polynomial-time algorithms* (Setup, KeyGen, SharedKey), *where*

- Setup *is a randomized algorithm that takes the unary encoded security parameter 1^λ and samples public parameters* pp
- KeyGen *is a randomized algorithm that takes the parameters* pp *and an identity* id $\in \mathcal{IDS}$ *and samples a key pair* (pk, sk)
- SharedKey *is a deterministic algorithm that takes the parameters* pp, *an identity* id_1 *with its corresponding public key* pk_1 *and another identity* id_2 *with its corresponding secret key* sk_2 *and outputs a shared key K*

Definition 2 (Correctness). *We say that a* NIKE (Setup, KeyGen, SharedKey) *for identity space $\mathcal{IDS}$ is statistically correct, if the correctness error*

$$\sup_{\mathsf{id}_1,\mathsf{id}_2 \in \mathcal{IDS}} \Pr[\mathsf{SharedKey}(\mathsf{pp},\mathsf{id}_1,\mathsf{pk}_1,\mathsf{id}_2,\mathsf{sk}_2) \neq \mathsf{SharedKey}(\mathsf{pp},\mathsf{id}_2,\mathsf{pk}_2,\mathsf{id}_1,\mathsf{sk}_1) \mid$$

$$\mathsf{pp} \leftarrow \mathsf{Setup}(1^\lambda), (\mathsf{pk}_1,\mathsf{sk}_1) \leftarrow \mathsf{KeyGen}(\mathsf{pp},\mathsf{id}_1), (\mathsf{pk}_2,\mathsf{sk}_2) \leftarrow \mathsf{KeyGen}(\mathsf{pp},\mathsf{id}_2)]$$

is negligible in λ. A NIKE *is perfectly correct if its correctness error is zero.*

The standard security notion for a NIKE is adaptive security. It is a real-or-random notion that allows the adversary to register users, corrupt users, reveal shared keys and get challenged adaptively and arbitrary often. One could strengthen this security notion by giving the adversary an additional oracle that allows him to learn the shared keys of a user and a self-generated public key (dishonest key registration). This security notion can be achieved tightly with little overhead using the generic transformation of [25].

Our first construction in Sect. 3 achieves a weaker security notion, that we call ν-bounded security, for any $\nu \in \mathbb{N}_{\geq 2}$ with keys that grow linearly in ν. ν-bounded security is defined as adaptive security, but the adversary may only use up to ν users for corruption, revealing shared keys, and challenges. It can still register arbitrary many users and choose adaptively the subset of ν users for the other queries. While this security notion is arguably too weak for most realistic scenarios, it is useful because it implies adaptive security with security loss only $\mathcal{O}((N/\nu)^2)$.

In the full version we show how to strengthen our result to achieve ν-semi-adaptive security. This notion is defined like ν-bounded security, except that the adversary can still make $\mathcal{O}_{\text{extr}}$, $\mathcal{O}_{\text{revH}}$ (and $\mathcal{O}_{\text{regH}}$) queries after exceeding the limit of ν involved users. Clearly, ν-semi-adaptive security tightly implies ν-bounded security, but is a more realistic security notion.

Definition 3 (Adaptive, ν-bounded, and ν-semi-adaptive security). *We say that a NIKE* NIKE $=$ (Setup, KeyGen, SharedKey) *is ν-bounded, ν-semi-adaptively, or adaptively secure (for $\nu \geq 2$), if for all PPT adversaries $\mathcal{A}$*

$$\mathsf{Adv}_{\texttt{NIKE}}^{\mathcal{A}\text{xxx}}(\lambda) := 2\Pr[\mathsf{Exp}_{\mathcal{A},\texttt{NIKE}}^{\text{xxx}}(\lambda) \Rightarrow 1] - 1$$

is negligible for xxx $=$ ν-bounded, xxx $=$ ν-semi-adaptive *or* xxx $=$ adaptive, *respectively. The games* $\mathsf{Exp}_{\mathcal{A},\texttt{NIKE}}^{\text{xxx}}(\lambda)$ *are defined in Fig. 2.*

The following argument shows that ν-bounded security implies adaptive security via a non-tight reduction. The reduction forwards the registration queries of up to ν users to the ν-bounded experiment and generates all other keys itself. Then the reduction can randomize the shared keys in the test queries between two users when both of their registrations have been forwarded. Via a hybrid argument, the reduction can randomize all test queries step by step. We defer the formal proof to the full version.

Lemma 2. *For every NIKE* NIKE *and every PPT adversary $\mathcal{A}$ against the adaptive security of* NIKE, *there exists a PPT adversary $\mathcal{B}$ against the ν-bounded security for any $\nu \in \{2, \ldots, N\}$ with*

$$\mathsf{Adv}_{\mathcal{A},\texttt{NIKE}}^{\text{adaptive}}(\lambda) \leq \frac{1}{2}\left\lceil \frac{N}{\lfloor \nu/2 \rfloor} + 1 \right\rceil^2 \left(\mathsf{Adv}_{\mathcal{B},\texttt{NIKE}}^{\nu\text{-bounded}}(\lambda) + (N_{\text{rev}} + N_{\text{test}})\varepsilon_{\texttt{NIKE}}(\lambda) \right)$$

and $T(\mathcal{B}) \approx T(\mathcal{A}) + N \operatorname{poly}(\lambda)$ for a polynomial poly independent of $\mathcal{A}$, where N is the maximum number of users that $\mathcal{A}$ registers, N_{rev} and N_{test} are the maximum number of $\mathcal{A}$'s $\mathcal{O}_{\text{revH}}$ and $\mathcal{O}_{\text{test}}$ queries, respectively, and $\varepsilon_{\texttt{NIKE}}(\lambda)$ is the correctness error of NIKE.

For our lower bound on tightness of adaptive NIKE security reductions, we define a relatively weak notion called *2-step-adaptive security*. The experiment is depicted in Fig. 3. It allows the adversary to see $n - 2$ secret keys in two loads, and commit to one challenge pair of public keys after seeing the first load. Finally, 2-step-adaptive is the only notion in this paper which is computational, meaning that the adversary has to provide the shared key of the challenge pair in order to win the experiment. To ease presentation of our lower bound proof, the adversary is split into three stateful algorithms $\mathcal{A}_1, \mathcal{A}_2, \mathcal{A}_3$.

$\mathsf{Exp}_{\mathcal{A},\mathrm{NIKE}}^{\mathrm{adaptive}}(\lambda)$:

  $\mathrm{pp} \leftarrow \mathsf{Setup}(1^{\lambda})$
  $Q_{\mathrm{extr}} := \emptyset;\ Q_{\mathrm{rev}} := \emptyset;\ Q_{\mathrm{test}} := \emptyset;$
  $\boxed{Q_{\mathrm{inv}} := \emptyset}$
  $\mathrm{pks} : \mathcal{IDS} \dashrightarrow \mathcal{PK}$
  $\mathrm{sks} : \mathcal{IDS} \dashrightarrow \mathcal{SK}$
  $b \xleftarrow{\$} \{0,1\}$
  $b^{\star} \leftarrow \mathcal{A}^{\mathcal{O}_{\mathrm{regH}}(\cdot), \mathcal{O}_{\mathrm{extr}}(\cdot), \mathcal{O}_{\mathrm{revH}}(\cdot,\cdot), \mathcal{O}_{\mathrm{test}}(\cdot,\cdot)}(\mathrm{pp})$
  $\mathbf{if}\ Q_{\mathrm{rev}} \cap Q_{\mathrm{test}} = \emptyset \wedge \nexists A \in Q_{\mathrm{test}} :$
    $A \cap Q_{\mathrm{extr}} = \emptyset\ \boxed{\wedge\ |Q_{\mathrm{inv}}| \le \nu}\ \mathbf{then}$
    $\mathbf{return}\ b \stackrel{?}{=} b^{\star}$
  $\mathbf{else}$
    $\mathbf{return}\ 0$

$\mathcal{O}_{\mathrm{regH}}(\mathrm{id} \in \mathcal{IDS})$:

  $\mathbf{if}\ \mathrm{pks}(\mathrm{id}) \ne \perp \mathbf{then\ return} \perp$
  $(\mathrm{pk}, \mathrm{sk}) \leftarrow \mathsf{KeyGen}(\mathrm{pp}, \mathrm{id})$
  $\mathrm{pks}(\mathrm{id}) := \mathrm{pk};\ \mathrm{sks}(\mathrm{id}) := \mathrm{sk}$
  $\mathbf{return}\ \mathrm{pk}$

$\mathcal{O}_{\mathrm{extr}}(\mathrm{id} \in \mathcal{IDS})$:

  $\mathbf{if}\ \mathrm{sks}(\mathrm{id}) \ne \perp \mathbf{then}$
    $Q_{\mathrm{extr}} := Q_{\mathrm{extr}} \cup \{\mathrm{id}\};$
    $\boxed{Q_{\mathrm{inv}} := Q_{\mathrm{inv}} \cup \{\mathrm{id}\}}$
    $\mathbf{return}\ \mathrm{sks}(\mathrm{id})$
  $\mathbf{return} \perp$

$\mathcal{O}_{\mathrm{revH}}(\mathrm{id}_1 \in \mathcal{IDS}, \mathrm{id}_2 \in \mathcal{IDS})$:

  $\mathbf{if}\ \mathrm{pks}(\mathrm{id}_1) \ne \perp \wedge \mathrm{sks}(\mathrm{id}_2) \ne \perp \mathbf{then}$
    $Q_{\mathrm{rev}} := Q_{\mathrm{rev}} \cup \{\{\mathrm{id}_1, \mathrm{id}_2\}\}$
    $\boxed{Q_{\mathrm{inv}} := Q_{\mathrm{inv}} \cup \{\mathrm{id}_1, \mathrm{id}_2\}}$
    $\mathrm{pk}_1 := \mathrm{pks}(\mathrm{id}_1);\ \mathrm{sk}_2 := \mathrm{sks}(\mathrm{id}_2)$
    $\mathbf{return}\ \mathsf{SharedKey}(\mathrm{pp}, \mathrm{id}_1, \mathrm{pk}_1, \mathrm{id}_2, \mathrm{sk}_2)$
  $\mathbf{return} \perp$

$\mathcal{O}_{\mathrm{test}}(\mathrm{id}_1^{\star} \in \mathcal{IDS}, \mathrm{id}_2^{\star} \in \mathcal{IDS})$:

  $\mathbf{if}\ \mathrm{pks}(\mathrm{id}_1^{\star}) \ne \perp \wedge \mathrm{sks}(\mathrm{id}_2^{\star}) \ne \perp \wedge \{\mathrm{id}_1^{\star},$
  $\mathrm{id}_2^{\star}\} \notin Q_{\mathrm{test}} \mathbf{then}$
    $Q_{\mathrm{test}} := Q_{\mathrm{test}} \cup \{\{\mathrm{id}_1^{\star}, \mathrm{id}_2^{\star}\}\}$
    $\boxed{Q_{\mathrm{inv}} := Q_{\mathrm{inv}} \cup \{\mathrm{id}_1^{\star}, \mathrm{id}_2^{\star}\}}$
    $\boxed{\mathbf{if}\ |Q_{\mathrm{inv}}| > \nu \mathbf{then\ return} \perp}$
    $\mathrm{pk}_1 := \mathrm{pks}(\mathrm{id}_1^{\star});\ \mathrm{sk}_2 := \mathrm{sks}(\mathrm{id}_2^{\star})$
    $K_0^{\star} \leftarrow \mathsf{SharedKey}(\mathrm{pp}, \mathrm{id}_1^{\star}, \mathrm{pk}_1, \mathrm{id}_2^{\star}, \mathrm{sk}_2)$
    $K_1^{\star} \xleftarrow{\$} \mathcal{K}$
    $\mathbf{return}\ K_b^{\star}$
  $\mathbf{return} \perp$

Fig. 2. Experiment for adaptive security, $\boxed{\nu\text{-semi-adaptive security}}$, and $\overline{\nu\text{-bounded security}}$ of a NIKE scheme NIKE with identity space $\mathcal{IDS}$ and shared key space $\mathcal{K}$. $\mathcal{PK}$ denotes the public key space and $\mathcal{SK}$ denotes the secret key space. The partial maps pks and sks are initially totally undefined. The set Q_{inv} keeps track of all users involved in the game, that is, users that have been used in at least one $\mathcal{O}_{\mathrm{extr}}$, $\mathcal{O}_{\mathrm{revH}}$ or $\mathcal{O}_{\mathrm{test}}$ query (users that have been only registered but not used since then are not counted as involved users). In the ν-bounded experiment the adversary may involve at most ν users. In the ν-semi-adaptive experiment the adversary may not ask $\mathcal{O}_{\mathrm{test}}$ queries any more after more than ν users have been involved.

Definition 4 (2-step-adaptive security). *A NIKE* NIKE = (Setup, KeyGen, SharedKey) *is 2-step-adaptively secure, if for all PPT adversaries* $(\mathcal{A}_1, \mathcal{A}_2, \mathcal{A}_3)$

$$\mathsf{Adv}_{\mathrm{NIKE}}^{\text{2-step-adaptive}}(\mathcal{A}_1, \mathcal{A}_2, \mathcal{A}_3) := \Pr[\mathsf{Exp}_{\mathcal{A}=(\mathcal{A}_1, \mathcal{A}_2, \mathcal{A}_3), N, \mathrm{NIKE}}^{\text{2-step-adaptive}}(\lambda) \to 1]$$

is negligible. The experiment is defined in Fig. 3.

$$\mathsf{Exp}^{\text{2-step-adaptive}}_{\mathcal{A}=(\mathcal{A}_1,\mathcal{A}_2,\mathcal{A}_3),N,\texttt{NIKE}}(\lambda):$$

   $\mathsf{pp} \xleftarrow{\$} \texttt{NIKE.Setup}(1^\lambda)$
   $\textbf{for } i \in \{1, \dots, N\} \textbf{ do}$
      $(\mathsf{pk}_i, \mathsf{sk}_i) \leftarrow \texttt{NIKE.KeyGen}(\mathsf{pp})$
   $(st_1, D) \leftarrow \mathcal{A}_1(\mathsf{pp}, \mathsf{pk}_1, \dots, \mathsf{pk}_N)$
   $(st_2, \{i^\star, j^\star\}) \leftarrow \mathcal{A}_2(st_1, (\mathsf{sk}_i)_{i \in D})$
   $K^\star \leftarrow \mathcal{A}_3(st_2, (\mathsf{sk}_i)_{i \in [N] \setminus (D \cup \{i^\star, j^\star\})})$
   $\textbf{if } K^\star = \texttt{NIKE.SharedKey}(\mathsf{pk}_{i^\star}, \mathsf{sk}_{j^\star}) \textbf{ then}$
      $\textbf{return } 1$
   $\textbf{else}$
      $\textbf{return } 0$

Fig. 3. Experiment for 2-step-adaptive security of a NIKE scheme NIKE with shared key space $\mathcal{K}$, for any $N \in \mathbb{N}$. If $i^\star \in D$ or $j^\star \in D$, the experiment aborts.

It is straightforward to verify that 2-step-adaptive security is implied by adaptive security. The relations between the security notions considered in this paper are shown in Fig. 4.

3   An Inner-Product-Based NIKE Scheme

We present our NIKE $\texttt{NIKE}_{\textsf{ip}}$ in Fig. 5 that tightly achieves ν-bounded security for arbitrary $\nu \geq 2$. However, this comes at the price of public and secret key size $\mathcal{O}(\nu)$. Together with Lemma 2, this gives an adaptively secure NIKE with a trade-off between key size and security loss. The security can be based on any MDDH assumption in symmetric pairing groups. Correctness follows from

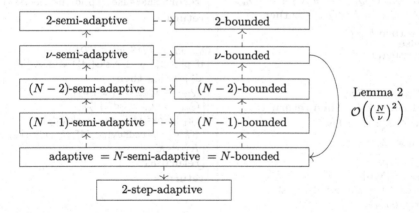

Fig. 4. Relations between NIKE security notions for $\nu \in \{2, \dots, N-2\}$ used in this paper. Dashed arrows mean "tightly implies" and solid arrows mean "implies with specified loss".

$$\text{SharedKey}(\text{pp}, \text{id}_i, \text{pk}_i, \text{id}_j, \text{sk}_j) = e([(\mathbf{Dw}_i)^\top], [\mathbf{MDw}_j]) = [\mathbf{w}_i^\top \mathbf{D}^\top \mathbf{MDw}_j]_T =$$
$$[\mathbf{w}_j^\top \mathbf{D}^\top \mathbf{MDw}_i]_T = e([(\mathbf{Dw}_j)^\top], [\mathbf{MDw}_i]) = \text{SharedKey}(\text{pp}, \text{id}_j, \text{pk}_j, \text{id}_i, \text{sk}_i).$$

Setup(1^λ):
$\lfloor \mathcal{G} := (\mathbb{G}, \mathbb{G}_T, q, g, e) \leftarrow \text{SymGGen}(1^\lambda)$
$\mathbf{D} \leftarrow \mathcal{U}_{k+\nu,k}$
$\mathbf{M} \overset{\$}{\leftarrow} \text{Sym}_{k+\nu}(\mathbb{Z}_q)$
$\text{return pp} := (\mathcal{G}, [\mathbf{D}], [\mathbf{MD}])$

SharedKey$(\text{pp}, \text{id}_1, \text{pk}_1, \text{id}_2, \text{sk}_2)$:
$\lfloor \text{return } e(\text{pk}_1^\top, \text{sk}_2)$

KeyGen(pp, id):
$\lfloor \text{parse pp} =: (\mathcal{G}, [\mathbf{D}], [\mathbf{MD}])$
$\mathbf{w} \overset{\$}{\leftarrow} \mathbb{Z}_q^k$
$\text{pk} := [\mathbf{Dw}]$
$\text{sk} := [\mathbf{MDw}]$
$\text{return } (\text{pk}, \text{sk})$

Fig. 5. Our inner-product-based NIKE_{ip} using symmetric pairing groups.

$G_0 \quad \boxed{G_1}$

Exp$_{\mathcal{A},\text{NIKE}}^{\nu\text{-bounded}}(\lambda)$:
$\lfloor \mathcal{G} := (\mathbb{G}, \mathbb{G}_T, q, g, e) \leftarrow \text{SymGGen}(1^\lambda)$
$\mathbf{D} \leftarrow \mathcal{U}_{k+\nu,k}$
$\mathbf{M} \overset{\$}{\leftarrow} \text{Sym}_{k+\nu}(\mathbb{Z}_q)$
$\text{pp} := (\mathcal{G}, [\mathbf{D}], [\mathbf{MD}])$
$Q_{\text{extr}} := \emptyset; \ Q_{\text{rev}} := \emptyset; \ Q_{\text{test}} := \emptyset$
$Q_{\text{inv}} := \emptyset$
$\text{pks} : \mathcal{IDS} \dashrightarrow \mathcal{PK}$
$\text{sks} : \mathcal{IDS} \dashrightarrow \mathcal{SK}$
$b \overset{\$}{\leftarrow} \{0,1\}$
$b^\star \leftarrow \mathcal{A}^{\mathcal{O}_{\text{regH}}(\cdot), \mathcal{O}_{\text{extr}}(\cdot), \mathcal{O}_{\text{revH}}(\cdot,\cdot), \mathcal{O}_{\text{test}}(\cdot,\cdot)}(\text{pp})$
$\text{if } Q_{\text{rev}} \cap Q_{\text{test}} = \emptyset \wedge \nexists A \in Q_{\text{test}} :$
$A \cap Q_{\text{extr}} = \emptyset \wedge |Q_{\text{inv}}| \leq \nu \text{ then}$
$\mid \text{return } b \overset{?}{=} b^\star$
else
$\lfloor \text{return } 0$

$\mathcal{O}_{\text{regH}}(\text{id} \in \mathcal{IDS})$:
$\text{if } \text{pks}(\text{id}_i) \neq \perp \text{ then return } \perp$
$\mathbf{w} \overset{\$}{\leftarrow} \mathbb{Z}_q^k; \ \mathbf{u} := \mathbf{Dw}$
$\boxed{\mathbf{u} \overset{\$}{\leftarrow} \mathbb{Z}_q^{k+\nu}}$
$\text{pk} := [\mathbf{u}]$
$\text{sk} := [\mathbf{Mu}]$
$\text{pks}(\text{id}_i) := \text{pk}; \ \text{sks}(\text{id}_i) := \text{sk}$
$\lfloor \text{return pk}$

$\mathcal{O}_{\text{extr}}(\text{id} \in \mathcal{IDS})$:
$\text{if } \text{sks}(\text{id}) \neq \perp \text{ then}$
$\mid Q_{\text{extr}} := Q_{\text{extr}} \cup \{\text{id}\}; \ Q_{\text{inv}} := Q_{\text{inv}} \cup \{\text{id}\}$
$\lfloor \text{return } \text{sks}(\text{id})$
$\lfloor \text{return } \perp$

$\mathcal{O}_{\text{revH}}(\text{id}_1 \in \mathcal{IDS}, \text{id}_2 \in \mathcal{IDS})$:
$\text{if } \text{pks}(\text{id}_1) \neq \perp \wedge \text{sks}(\text{id}_2) \neq \perp \text{ then}$
$\mid Q_{\text{rev}} := Q_{\text{rev}} \cup \{\{\text{id}_1, \text{id}_2\}\}$
$\mid Q_{\text{inv}} := Q_{\text{inv}} \cup \{\text{id}_1, \text{id}_2\}$
$\mid \text{pk}_1 := \text{pks}(\text{id}_1); \ \text{sk}_2 := \text{sks}(\text{id}_2)$
$\lfloor \text{return SharedKey}(\text{pp}, \text{id}_1, \text{pk}_1, \text{id}_2, \text{sk}_2)$
$\lfloor \text{return } \perp$

$\mathcal{O}_{\text{test}}(\text{id}_1^\star \in \mathcal{IDS}, \text{id}_2^\star \in \mathcal{IDS})$:
$\text{if } \text{pks}(\text{id}_1^\star) \neq \perp \wedge \text{sks}(\text{id}_2^\star) \neq \perp \wedge \{\text{id}_1^\star,$
$\text{id}_2^\star\} \notin Q_{\text{test}} \text{ then}$
$\mid Q_{\text{test}} := Q_{\text{test}} \cup \{\{\text{id}_1^\star, \text{id}_2^\star\}\}$
$\mid Q_{\text{inv}} := Q_{\text{inv}} \cup \{\text{id}_1^\star, \text{id}_2^\star\}$
$\mid \text{pk}_1 := \text{pks}(\text{id}_1^\star); \ \text{sk}_2 := \text{sks}(\text{id}_2^\star)$
$\mid K_0^\star \leftarrow \text{SharedKey}(\text{pp}, \text{id}_1^\star, \text{pk}_1, \text{id}_2^\star, \text{sk}_2)$
$\mid K_1^\star \overset{\$}{\leftarrow} \mathcal{K}$
$\lfloor \text{return } K_b^\star$
$\lfloor \text{return } \perp$

Fig. 6. Hybrids for the security proof of the NIKE from Fig. 5. The partial maps pks and sks are initially totally undefined.

Theorem 1 (Security). *For every PPT adversary $\mathcal{A}$ against ν-bounded security of* $\mathsf{NIKE_{ip}}$, *there exists a PPT adversary $\mathcal{B}$ solving $\mathcal{U}_k$-MDDH*

$$\mathsf{Adv}^{\nu\text{-bounded}}_{\mathcal{A},\mathsf{NIKE_{ip}}}(\lambda) \leq \left\lceil \log\left(1 + \frac{\nu}{k}\right) \right\rceil k \left(\mathsf{Adv}^{\mathsf{mddh}}_{\mathcal{B},\mathcal{U}_k,\mathsf{SymGGen},s}(\lambda) + \frac{1}{q-1} \right) + \frac{1}{q-1}$$

and $T(\mathcal{B}) \approx T(\mathcal{A}) + N\,\mathrm{poly}(\lambda)$ for a polynomial poly independent of $\mathcal{A}$.

The proof uses a hybrid argument with hybrids G_0 and G_1 given in Fig. 6.

Lemma 3 ($\mathsf{G}_0 \rightsquigarrow \mathsf{G}_1$). *For every PPT adversary $\mathcal{A}$ there exists an PPT adversary $\mathcal{B}$ such that*

$$\left|\Pr[\mathsf{G}_0^{\mathcal{A}}(\lambda) \Rightarrow 1] - \Pr[\mathsf{G}_1^{\mathcal{A}}(\lambda) \Rightarrow 1]\right| \leq \left\lceil \log\left(1 + \frac{\nu}{k}\right) \right\rceil k \left(\mathsf{Adv}^{\mathsf{mddh}}_{\mathcal{B},\mathcal{U}_k,\mathsf{SymGGen},s}(\lambda) \right.$$
$$\left. + \frac{1}{q-1} \right)$$

and $T(\mathcal{B}) \approx T(\mathcal{A}) + N\,\mathrm{poly}(\lambda)$ for a polynomial poly independent of $\mathcal{A}$.

Proof. The real game G_0 uses normal keys (i.e. the public key is a chosen from the linear span of $\mathbf{D}$'s column vectors). In the game G_1 all keys are semi-functional (i.e. the public key is a chosen uniformly at random). Given an N-fold $\mathcal{U}_k$-MDDH challenge $[\mathbf{D}], ([\mathbf{u}_i])_{1 \leq i \leq N}$ one can simulate the games G_0 and G_1 efficiently when $\mathbf{A}$ in known over $\mathbb{Z}_q$. If the vectors $\mathbf{u}_i$ are sampled from the linear span of $\mathbf{D}$ this yields the game G_0 and if the vectors $\mathbf{u}_i$ are sampled uniformly random, this yields the game G_1. By reducing the N-fold $\mathcal{U}_k$-MDDH assumption to the $\mathcal{U}_k - \mathsf{MDDH}$ assumption with Lemma 1, the statement follows.   □

Lemma 4 (G_1). *For every PPT adversary $\mathcal{A}$ there exists an PPT adversary $\mathcal{B}$ such that*
$$\left|\Pr[\mathsf{G}_1^{\mathcal{A}}(\lambda) \Rightarrow 1]\right| \leq \frac{1}{2} + \frac{1}{q-1}$$

and $T(\mathcal{B}) \approx T(\mathcal{A}) + N\,\mathrm{poly}(\lambda)$ for a polynomial poly independent of $\mathcal{A}$.

Proof. Without loss of generality, assume the adversary involves exactly ν users. Let us assume, that the column vectors of $\mathbf{D}$ and the public keys of all involved users (users with id $\in Q_{\mathsf{inv}}$ at the end of the game) are linearly independent. Since all the public keys are uniformly random vectors in G_1, this happens with probability at least $1 - 1/(q-1)$. Initially, the symmetric bilinear form $B(\mathbf{v}, \mathbf{w}) := \mathbf{v}^\top \mathbf{M} \mathbf{w}$ is uniformly random to the adversary. Now suppose the adversary makes a $\mathcal{O}_{\mathsf{test}}$ query with two users $\mathsf{id}_1^\star$ and $\mathsf{id}_2^\star$. Let $[\mathbf{u}_1^\star]$ and $[\mathbf{u}_2^\star]$ be the public keys of $\mathsf{id}_1^\star$ and $\mathsf{id}_2^\star$, respectively and let $[\mathbf{u}_1], \ldots, [\mathbf{u}_{\nu-2}]$ be the public keys of all other users. We show the shared key between the tested users, $[B(\mathbf{u}_1^\star, \mathbf{u}_2^\star)]_T$, is statistically independent of all the other information the adversary learns about B during the game.

Assume all $\mathcal{O}_{\text{revH}}$ queries and other $\mathcal{O}_{\text{test}}$ queries involve at least one involved user different to $\{\text{id}_1^*, \text{id}_2^*\}$, because if the adversary makes a $\mathcal{O}_{\text{revH}}$ query with id_1^* and id_2^* the adversary has lost trivially and a duplicated $\mathcal{O}_{\text{test}}$ query would only return $\bot$. Thus these queries can not reveal any information about B that is not revealed by $\mathbf{M}(\mathbf{D}|\mathbf{u}_1|\cdots|\mathbf{u}_{\nu-2})$. The public parameters only reveal $\mathbf{MD}$ and any $\mathcal{O}_{\text{extr}}$ query only reveals $\mathbf{Mu}_i$ for an $i \in \{1,\ldots,\nu-2\}$. In total the adversary learns from all queries except the analyzed $\mathcal{O}_{\text{test}}$ query only $\mathbf{M}(\mathbf{D}|\mathbf{u}_1|\cdots|\mathbf{u}_{\nu-2})$. Since the column vectors of $\mathbf{D}$ together with $\{\mathbf{u}_1,\ldots,\mathbf{u}_{\nu-2},\mathbf{u}_1^*,\mathbf{u}_2^*\}$ are assumed to be a linear independent set, $B(\mathbf{u}_1^*,\mathbf{u}_2^*) = (\mathbf{u}_1^*)^\top \mathbf{Mu}_2^*$ is uniformly random given $\mathbf{M}(\mathbf{D}|\mathbf{u}_1|\cdots|\mathbf{u}_{\nu-2})$. We can apply the above argument to each of the adversaries $\mathcal{O}_{\text{test}}$ queries. Consequently, the adversaries advantage in G_1 is 0 under the stated assumptions. □

Proof (of Therorem 1.) Combining Lemmata 3 and 4 proves Theorem 1.   □

Corollary 1. *The NIKE* $\mathsf{NIKE}_{\text{ip}}$ *is adaptively secure with a security loss of* $\mathcal{O}((N/\nu)^2 \log \nu)$ *under the decision linear (DLIN) assumption.*

Proof. The DLIN assumption implies the $\mathcal{U}_k$-MDDH for $k \geq 2$ [18], so we can set $k = 2$. The NIKE then achieves ν-bounded security with loss $\mathcal{O}(\log \nu)$ by Theorem 1. With Lemma 2 we can achieve adaptive security by increasing the security loss by a factor of $\mathcal{O}((N/\nu)^2)$.   □

4   Lower Bound

In this section, we show that for all NIKEs that follow a special structure, there is an in some sense inherent trade-off between key sizes and quality of the reduction. Compared to previous lower bounds on NIKE reductions [2,25], we do not make the generic assumption that pairs of public keys already determine the corresponding shared key. Instead, we leave room for a reduction to adaptively determine secret keys upon corruptions, as long as they follow the inner product structure we require. We use the notions of Non-Interactive Complexity Assumption (NICA, [2], Def. 4 and 5) and Simple Reductions [2], Def. 6 and 7, where the latter is adapted to the reduction breaking our 2-step-adaptive security in a straightforward way.

We now formalize the notion of *inner-product NIKE*. The intuition behind this definition is as follows. Basically, we require an (inefficient) algorithms **Extract** that can be used to extract the key vectors $(\mathbf{x},\mathbf{y})$ from a valid pair of public and secret keys, such that $(\mathbf{x},\mathbf{y})$ can be used to compute the shared key as an inner product. As we will see in the next section, this inner-product structure will enforce uniqueness of the shared keys, as soon as sufficiently many secret keys are fixed. The verification algorithm is necessary to ensure that the reduction can only give out public and secret keys that satisfy some structural requirements (e.g. be of the right form and dimension). The public extraction algorithm **PExtract** together with the *binding* requirement is necessary to ensure that the public keys are committing to the vector $\mathbf{x}$, even before the secret keys are given out. Finally, we therefore require the function f to be invertible, since it will be crucial that there is a one-to-one correspondence between the inner product and the shared key algorithm (note though that the inverse does not have to be efficiently computable).

Definition 5 (Inner-product NIKE). *Let $p \in \mathbb{N}$ a prime. We say a NIKE NIKE = (Setup, KeyGen, SharedKey) is a d-dimensional inner-product NIKE (ip-NIKE) over $\mathbb{Z}_p$, if there exists:*

- *a PPT algorithm* Ver *taking as input public parameters* pp, *and a key pair* (pk, sk) *and returning a bit* $b \in \{0, 1\}$,
- *an (inefficient) deterministic extractor* Extract *that takes as input public parameters* pp, *and a key pair* (pk, sk) *and returns a tuple* $(\mathbf{x}, \mathbf{y}) \in \mathbb{Z}_p^d \times \mathbb{Z}_p^d$,
- *an (inefficient) deterministic extractor* PExtract *taking as input* pp *and* pk *and returning a vector* $\mathbf{x} \in \mathbb{Z}_p^d$,
- *and a function* f *taking as input public parameters* pp *and an element* $z \in \mathbb{Z}_p$ *and returning a element in the image of* NIKE.SharedKey.

such that the following properties hold.

(i) *Verifiable keys. For all* (pk, sk) *in the image of* NIKE.KeyGen(pp) *it holds* Ver(pp, pk, sk) = 1.

(ii) *Ip-computable shared keys. For all public parameters* pp, *and all key pairs* (pk, sk), (pk', sk') *with* Ver(pp, pk, sk) = Ver(pp, pk', sk') = 1, *for* $(\mathbf{x}, \mathbf{y}) \leftarrow$ Extract(pp, pk, sk) *and* $(\mathbf{x}', \mathbf{y}') \leftarrow$ Extract(pp, pk', sk') *it holds*

$$\text{SharedKey}(\text{pp}, \text{pk}, \text{sk}') = f(\text{pp}, \langle \mathbf{x}, \mathbf{y}' \rangle).$$

(iii) *Binding public keys. For all* (pk, sk) *with* Ver(pk, sk) = 1 *for* $\mathbf{x} \leftarrow$ PEx-tract(pp, pk) *and* $(\tilde{\mathbf{x}}, \tilde{\mathbf{y}}) \leftarrow$ Extract(pp, pk, sk) *it holds* $\mathbf{x} = \tilde{\mathbf{x}}$.

(iv) *Invertibility of* f. *The induced function* $f_{\text{pp}} = f(\text{pp}, \cdot)$ *is injective with inverse* f_{pp}^{-1}.

We call a key pair (pk, sk) *with* Ver(pp, pk, sk) = 1 *valid. By the ip-dimension of an inner-product NIKE* NIKE, *we denote the minimal dimension d, such that* NIKE *satisfies the definition of d-dimensional inner-product NIKE.*

4.1 Lower Bound for Inner-product NIKEs

In order to show our lower bound, we first prove that after giving out sufficiently many public key/secret key pairs for a NIKE that satisfies the inner-product form, the reduction is committed to all shared keys. More precisely, let $\{\text{pk}_i\}_{i \in I}$ such that the corresponding vectors $\mathbf{x}_i \leftarrow$ PExtract(pp, pk_i) span the whole space $\mathbb{Z}_p^d$.[12] We further fix secret keys for pk_i for all $i \in I$ such that $(\text{pk}_i, \text{sk}_i)$ are all valid and *consistent* with each other, meaning that for all i, j, we have

---

[12] For simplicity of this explanation we assume for now that such a set of keys exists, but stress that our results do not rely on it.

$\mathsf{SharedKey}(\mathsf{pp}, \mathsf{pk}_i, \mathsf{sk}_j) = \mathsf{SharedKey}(\mathsf{pp}, \mathsf{pk}_j, \mathsf{sk}_i)$. We will show that such a set of keys fix not only the shared keys between the public keys within $\{\mathsf{pk}_i\}_{i \in I}$, but the shared keys between *all* possible valid public keys in the system. Therefore, if d is significantly smaller than N, then with high probability, any large enough random subset of key pairs will span the whole space of public keys and thereby already fix all shared keys (computed as inner products) in the system. This will be crucial in our meta reduction, where we use uniqueness of shared keys in order to efficiently simulate a hypothetical perfect adversary, thereby essentially showing that the reduction either has to abort with large probability or would be able to solve the underlying problem itself.

Lemma 5 (Unique shared keys for ip-NIKEs). *Let $d, p, \lambda \in \mathbb{N}$ and $\mathsf{NIKE} = (\mathsf{Setup}, \mathsf{KeyGen}, \mathsf{SharedKey}, \mathsf{Ver}, \mathsf{Extract}, \mathsf{PExtract})$ a d-dimensional ip-NIKE over $\mathbb{Z}_p$. Let $I \subset [N]$. Let $\mathsf{pp} \in \{0,1\}^\star$ and let $\{(\mathsf{pk}_i, \mathsf{sk}_i)\}_{i \in I}, (\mathsf{pk}, \mathsf{sk}), (\mathsf{pk}', \mathsf{sk}')$ be such that:*

(a) All key pairs are valid: $\mathsf{Ver}(\mathsf{pp}, \mathsf{pk}_i, \mathsf{sk}_i) = 1$ for all $i \in I$ and $\mathsf{Ver}(\mathsf{pp}, (\mathsf{pk}, \mathsf{sk})) = \mathsf{Ver}(\mathsf{pp}, \mathsf{pk}', \mathsf{sk}') = 1$.

(b) The key pairs in I are pairwise consistent: $\mathsf{SharedKey}(\mathsf{pp}, \mathsf{pk}_i, \mathsf{sk}_j) = \mathsf{SharedKey}(\mathsf{pp}, \mathsf{pk}_j, \mathsf{sk}_i)$ for all $i, j \in I$ with $i \neq j$.

(c) The key pairs $(\mathsf{pk}, \mathsf{sk})$ and $(\mathsf{pk}', \mathsf{sk}')$ are consistent with the key pairs in I: $\mathsf{SharedKey}(\mathsf{pp}, \mathsf{pk}, \mathsf{sk}_i) = \mathsf{SharedKey}(\mathsf{pp}, \mathsf{pk}_i, \mathsf{sk})$ and $\mathsf{SharedKey}(\mathsf{pp}, \mathsf{pk}', \mathsf{sk}_i) = \mathsf{SharedKey}(\mathsf{pp}, \mathsf{pk}_i, \mathsf{sk}')$ for all $i \in I$.

(d) The public keys $\mathsf{pk}, \mathsf{pk}'$ are "in the span" of $\{\mathsf{pk}_i\}_{i \in I}$: for $\mathbf{x}_i \leftarrow \mathsf{PExtract}(\mathsf{pp}, \mathsf{pk}_i)$ and $\mathbf{x} \leftarrow \mathsf{PExtract}(\mathsf{pp}, \mathsf{pk})$, $\mathbf{x}' \leftarrow \mathsf{PExtract}(\mathsf{pp}, \mathsf{pk}')$ it holds that $\mathbf{x}, \mathbf{x}'$ are in the span of $\{\mathbf{x}_i\}_{i \in I}$.

Then it holds that $\mathsf{SharedKey}(\mathsf{pp}, \mathsf{pk}, \mathsf{sk}') = \mathsf{SharedKey}(\mathsf{pp}, \mathsf{pk}', \mathsf{sk})$. *In other words, the shared key between the users holding* pk' *and* pk *is consistent.*

Proof. Let $(\mathbf{x}_i, \mathbf{y}_i) \leftarrow \mathsf{Extract}(\mathsf{pp}, \mathsf{pk}_i, \mathsf{sk}_i)$, $(\mathbf{x}, \mathbf{y}) \leftarrow \mathsf{Extract}(\mathsf{pp}, \mathsf{pk}, \mathsf{sk})$, and $\mathbf{x}' \leftarrow \mathsf{PExtract}(\mathsf{pp}, \mathsf{pk}')$. Note that $\mathbf{x}$ can be extracted from pk independently of the corresponding secret key due to the "binding public keys" property Definition 5 (iii). We can rely on the latter property since key pairs are valid because of condition (a). Again because of (a), shared keys are ip-computable, and we have

$$\mathsf{SharedKey}(\mathsf{pp}, \mathsf{pk}, \mathsf{sk}') = \mathsf{SharedKey}(\mathsf{pp}, \mathsf{pk}', \mathsf{sk})$$

$$\overset{\text{Def. 5 (ii)}}{\Longleftrightarrow} f_{\mathsf{pp}}(\langle \mathbf{x}, \mathbf{y}' \rangle) = f_{\mathsf{pp}}(\langle \mathbf{x}', \mathbf{y} \rangle)$$

$$\overset{f_{\mathsf{pp}} \text{ invertible}}{\Longleftrightarrow} \langle \mathbf{x}, \mathbf{y}' \rangle = \langle \mathbf{x}', \mathbf{y} \rangle,$$

and thus it suffices to show equality of these inner products. Due to validity of all involved key pairs and condition (b), for all $i, j \in I$ with $i \neq j$, it holds:

$$\langle \mathbf{x}_i, \mathbf{y}_j \rangle \overset{\text{Def. 5 (ii)}}{=} f_{\mathsf{pp}}^{-1}(\mathsf{SharedKey}(\mathsf{pp}, \mathsf{pk}_i, \mathsf{sk}_j))$$
$$\overset{\text{Cond. (b)}}{=} f_{\mathsf{pp}}^{-1}(\mathsf{SharedKey}(\mathsf{pp}, \mathsf{pk}_j, \mathsf{sk}_i)) \overset{\text{Def. 5 (ii)}}{=} \langle \mathbf{x}_j, \mathbf{y}_i \rangle. \tag{1}$$

Analogously, by to validity of all involved key pairs and condition (c) for all $i \in I$, we have:

$$\langle \mathbf{x}_i, \mathbf{y} \rangle = \langle \mathbf{x}, \mathbf{y}_i \rangle \quad \text{and} \quad \langle \mathbf{x}_i, \mathbf{y}' \rangle = \langle \mathbf{x}', \mathbf{y}_i \rangle. \tag{2}$$

By condition (d) from the lemma statement, we can find $\beta, \gamma \in \mathbb{Z}_p^{|I|}$ with $\sum_{j=1}^{|I|} \beta_j \mathbf{x}_j = \mathbf{x}$ and $\sum_{i=1}^{|I|} \gamma_i \mathbf{x}_i = \mathbf{x}'$. First, note that for all $i \in I$ we have

$$\langle \mathbf{x}_i, \sum_{j=1}^{|I|} \beta_j \mathbf{y}_j \rangle = \sum_{j=1}^{|I|} \beta_j \langle \mathbf{x}_i, \mathbf{y}_j \rangle \overset{\text{Eq. 1}}{=} \sum_{j=1}^{|I|} \beta_j \langle \mathbf{x}_j, \mathbf{y}_i \rangle = \langle \mathbf{x}, \mathbf{y}_i \rangle \overset{\text{Eq. 2}}{=} \langle \mathbf{x}_i, \mathbf{y} \rangle. \tag{3}$$

With this, it follows that

$$\langle \mathbf{x}, \mathbf{y}' \rangle \overset{\text{Cond. (d)}}{=} \langle \sum_{j=1}^{|I|} \beta_j \mathbf{x}_j, \mathbf{y}' \rangle = \sum_{j=1}^{|I|} \beta_j \langle \mathbf{x}_j, \mathbf{y}' \rangle \overset{\text{Eq. 2}}{=} \sum_{j=1}^{|I|} \beta_j \langle \mathbf{x}', \mathbf{y}_j \rangle = \langle \mathbf{x}', \sum_{j=1}^{|I|} \beta_j \mathbf{y}_j \rangle.$$

Finally, we have

$$\langle \mathbf{x}', \sum_{j=1}^{|I|} \beta_j \mathbf{y}_j \rangle = \sum_{i=1}^{|I|} \gamma_i \langle \mathbf{x}_i, \sum_{j=1}^{|I|} \beta_j \mathbf{y}_j \rangle \overset{\text{Eq. 3}}{=} \sum_{i=1}^{|I|} \gamma_i \langle \mathbf{x}_i, \mathbf{y} \rangle = \langle \mathbf{x}', \mathbf{y} \rangle,$$

which concludes the proof. $\square$

Note that this in particular implies that the shared key is *independent of the choice of secret keys* sk, sk' *satisfying conditions (a) and (c)*.

Relying on the fact that after giving out sufficiently many secret keys, all shared keys are uniquely determined, we are able to prove a trade-off between the tightness of the reduction and the dimension of an inner-product NIKE. We formalize this in the following theorem, which we prove in the full version, and give an interpretation of our result below.

Theorem 2. *Let $\mathcal{N} = (G, U, V)$ be a non-interactive complexity assumption, let $N, d \in \mathbb{N}$ with $4d + 6 < N$, and let $p \in \mathbb{N}$ a prime. Let* NIKE *be a perfectly correct 2-step-adaptively-secure d-dimensional ip-NIKE over $\mathbb{Z}_p$ with shared key space $\mathcal{K}$, public key space $\mathcal{PK}$ and secret key space $\mathcal{SK}$. Then, for any simple $(\varepsilon_\Lambda, \varepsilon_A)$-reduction from breaking the NICA $\mathcal{N}$ to breaking the N-user 2-step-adaptive security of* NIKE*, there exists a PPT adversary $\mathcal{B}$ on the NICA $\mathcal{N}$, such that*

$$\varepsilon_\Lambda \leq \frac{4d + 6}{N} \cdot \varepsilon_A + \text{Adv}_{\mathcal{N}, \mathcal{B}}^{\text{nica}}.$$

INTERPRETATION. Theorem 2 says that if any reduction is successfully breaking the underlying NICA $\mathcal{N}$ with probability noticeably larger than $(4d + 6)/N$, the reduction can be turned into a standalone $\mathcal{N}$ solver, without help of an external adversary. More precisely, assuming $\mathcal{N}$ is hard we obtain

$$\varepsilon_\Lambda \leq \frac{4d+6}{N} \cdot \varepsilon_\mathcal{A} + \text{negl}$$

for a negligible function negl. This implies a security loss of at least $N/(4d+6)$.

We can thus conclude that any inner-product NIKE that satisfies 2-step-adaptive security has to either have a significant loss, or ip-dimension proportional to the number of users N. In particular, this gives strong evidence that a fully-adaptive NIKEs with tight security only exist for an a priori fixed number of users, but not for a dynamic setting where users continuously join or leave. Altogether, using the relations between security notions depicted in Fig. 4, we obtain the following informal corollary:

Corollary 2. *Any simple reduction from a non-interactive complexity assumption $\mathcal{N}$ to the X-security of a d-dimensional ip-NIKE has to lose a factor in the order of Y, where N is the number of public keys, $\mathcal{N}$ is assumed to be hard and $(X, Y) \in \{(\text{2-step-adaptive}, \Omega(N/d)), (\text{adaptive}, \Omega(N/d)), (\nu\text{-semi-adaptive}, \Omega(\nu^2/(N \cdot d)))\}$.*

References

1. Bader, C., Hofheinz, D., Jager, T., Kiltz, E., Li, Y.: Tightly-secure authenticated key exchange. In: Dodis, Y., Nielsen, J.B. (eds.) TCC 2015. LNCS, vol. 9014, pp. 629–658. Springer, Heidelberg (2015). https://doi.org/10.1007/978-3-662-46494-6_26

2. Bader, C., Jager, T., Li, Y., Schäge, S.: On the impossibility of tight cryptographic reductions. In: Fischlin, M., Coron, J.-S. (eds.) EUROCRYPT 2016. LNCS, vol. 9666, pp. 273–304. Springer, Heidelberg (2016). https://doi.org/10.1007/978-3-662-49896-5_10

3. Bellare, M., Hofheinz, D., Yilek, S.: Possibility and impossibility results for encryption and commitment secure under selective opening. In: Joux, A. (ed.) EUROCRYPT 2009. LNCS, vol. 5479, pp. 1–35. Springer, Heidelberg (2009). https://doi.org/10.1007/978-3-642-01001-9_1

4. Boneh, D., Venkatesan, R.: Breaking RSA may not be equivalent to factoring. In: Nyberg, K. (ed.) EUROCRYPT 1998. LNCS, vol. 1403, pp. 59–71. Springer, Heidelberg (1998). https://doi.org/10.1007/BFb0054117

5. Boneh, D., Zhandry, M.: Multiparty key exchange, efficient traitor tracing, and more from indistinguishability obfuscation. In: Garay, J.A., Gennaro, R. (eds.) CRYPTO 2014. LNCS, vol. 8616, pp. 480–499. Springer, Heidelberg (2014). https://doi.org/10.1007/978-3-662-44371-2_27

6. Boyd, C., Mao, W., Paterson, K.G.: Key agreement using statically keyed authenticators. In: Jakobsson, M., Yung, M., Zhou, J. (eds.) ACNS 2004. LNCS, vol. 3089, pp. 248–262. Springer, Heidelberg (2004). https://doi.org/10.1007/978-3-540-24852-1_18

7. Boyen, X., Mei, Q.: BrentWaters. Direct chosen ciphertext security from identity-based techniques. In: Atluri, V., Meadows, C., Juels, J. (eds.) ACM CCS 2005. ACM Press, November 2005. pp. 320–329. https://doi.org/10.1145/1102120.1102162

8. Capar, C., Goeckel, D., Paterson, K.G., Quaglia, E.A., Towsley, D., Zafer, M.: Signal-flow-based analysis of wireless security protocols. Inf. Comput. **226**, 37–56 (2013). https://doi.org/10.1016/j.ic.2013.03.004

9. Cash, D., Kiltz, E., Shoup, V.: The Twin Diffie-Hellman problem and applications. In: Smart, N. (ed.) EUROCRYPT 2008. LNCS, vol. 4965, pp. 127–145. Springer, Heidelberg (2008). https://doi.org/10.1007/978-3-540-78967-3_8

10. Coron, J.-S.: On the exact security of full domain hash. In: Bellare, M. (ed.) CRYPTO 2000. LNCS, vol. 1880, pp. 229–235. Springer, Heidelberg (2000). https://doi.org/10.1007/3-540-44598-6_14

11. Coron, J.-S.: Optimal security proofs for PSS and other signature schemes. In: Knudsen, L.R. (ed.) EUROCRYPT 2002. LNCS, vol. 2332, pp. 272–287. Springer, Heidelberg (2002). https://doi.org/10.1007/3-540-46035-7_18

12. Cramer, R., et al.: Bounded CCA2-secure encryption. In: Kurosawa, K. (ed.) ASIACRYPT 2007. LNCS, vol. 4833, pp. 502–518. Springer, Heidelberg (2007). https://doi.org/10.1007/978-3-540-76900-2_31

13. Cramer, R., Shoup, V.: Universal hash proofs and a paradigm for adaptive chosen ciphertext secure public-key encryption. In: Knudsen, L.R. (ed.) EUROCRYPT 2002. LNCS, vol. 2332, pp. 45–64. Springer, Heidelberg (2002). https://doi.org/10.1007/3-540-46035-7_4

14. Diffie, W., Hellman, M.E.: New directions in cryptography. IEEE Trans. Inf. Theory **22**(6), 644–654 (1976)

15. Dodis, Y., Katz, J., Smith, A., Walfish, S.: Composability and on-line deniability of authentication. In: Reingold, O. (ed.) TCC 2009. LNCS, vol. 5444, pp. 146–162. Springer, Heidelberg (2009). https://doi.org/10.1007/978-3-642-00457-5_10

16. Dolev, D., Dwork, C., Naor, M.: Nonmalleable cryptography. SIAM J. Comput. **30**(2), 391–437 (2000)

17. Dupont, R., Enge, A.: Provably secure non-interactive key distribution based on pairings. Discrete Appl. Math. **154**(2), 270–276 (2006)

18. Escala, A., Herold, G., Kiltz, E., Ràfols, C., Villar, J.: An algebraic framework for diffie-hellman assumptions. In: Canetti, R., Garay, J.A. (eds.) CRYPTO 2013. LNCS, vol. 8043, pp. 129–147. Springer, Heidelberg (2013). https://doi.org/10.1007/978-3-642-40084-1_8

19. Freire, E.S.V., Hofheinz, D., Kiltz, E., Paterson, K.G.: Non-interactive key exchange. In: Kurosawa, K., Hanaoka, G. (eds.) PKC 2013. LNCS, vol. 7778, pp. 254–271. Springer, Heidelberg (2013). https://doi.org/10.1007/978-3-642-36362-7_17

20. Gay, R., Hofheinz, D., Kiltz, E., Wee, H.: Tightly CCA-secure encryption without pairings. In: Fischlin, M., Coron, J.-S. (eds.) EUROCRYPT 2016. LNCS, vol. 9665, pp. 1–27. Springer, Heidelberg (2016). https://doi.org/10.1007/978-3-662-49890-3_1

21. Gentry, C., Sahai, A., Waters, B.: Homomorphic encryption from learning with errors: conceptually-simpler, asymptotically-faster, attribute-based. In: Canetti, R., Garay, J.A. (eds.) CRYPTO 2013. LNCS, vol. 8042, pp. 75–92. Springer, Heidelberg (2013). https://doi.org/10.1007/978-3-642-40041-4_5

22. Gorbunov, S., Vaikuntanathan, V., Wichs, D.: Leveled fully homomorphic signatures from standard lattices. In: Servedio, R.A., Rubinfeld, R. (eds.) 47th ACM STOC, pp. 469–477. ACM Press, June 2015. https://doi.org/10.1145/2746539.2746576

23. Groth, J., Sahai, A.: Efficient non-interactive proof systems for bilinear groups. In: Smart, N. (ed.) EUROCRYPT 2008. LNCS, vol. 4965, pp. 415–432. Springer, Heidelberg (2008). https://doi.org/10.1007/978-3-540-78967-3_24

24. Guo, S., Kamath, P., Rosen, A., Sotiraki, K.: Limits on the efficiency of (ring) LWE based non-interactive key exchange. In: Kiayias, A., Kohlweiss, M., Wallden, P., Zikas, V. (eds.) PKC 2020. LNCS, vol. 12110, pp. 374–395. Springer, Cham (2020). https://doi.org/10.1007/978-3-030-45374-9_13

25. Hesse, J., Hofheinz, D., Kohl, L.: On tightly secure non-interactive key exchange. In: Shacham, H., Boldyreva, A. (eds.) CRYPTO 2018. LNCS, vol. 10992, pp. 65–94. Springer, Cham (2018). https://doi.org/10.1007/978-3-319-96881-0_3

26. Hofheinz, D., Jager, T.: Tightly secure signatures and public-key encryption. In: Safavi-Naini, R., Canetti, R. (eds.) CRYPTO 2012. LNCS, vol. 7417, pp. 590–607. Springer, Heidelberg (2012). https://doi.org/10.1007/978-3-642-32009-5_35

27. Hofheinz, D., Kiltz, E., Shoup, V.: Practical Chosen Ciphertext Secure Encryption from Factoring. J. Cryptol. **26**(1), 102–118 (2011). https://doi.org/10.1007/s00145-011-9115-0

28. Kiltz, E.: Chosen-ciphertext security from tag-based encryption. In: Halevi, S., Rabin, T. (eds.) TCC 2006. LNCS, vol. 3876, pp. 581–600. Springer, Heidelberg (2006). https://doi.org/10.1007/11681878_30

29. Langrehr, R., Pan, J.: Tightly secure hierarchical identity-based encryption. J. Cryptol. **33**(4), 1787–1821 (2020). https://doi.org/10.1007/s00145-020-09356-x

30. Lewko, A., Waters, B.: Why Proving HIBE systems secure is difficult. In: Nguyen, P.Q., Oswald, E. (eds.) EUROCRYPT 2014. LNCS, vol. 8441, pp. 58–76. Springer, Heidelberg (2014). https://doi.org/10.1007/978-3-642-55220-5_4

31. Micciancio, D., Peikert, C.: Trapdoors for lattices: simpler, tighter, faster, smaller. In: Pointcheval, D., Johansson, T. (eds.) EUROCRYPT 2012. LNCS, vol. 7237, pp. 700–718. Springer, Heidelberg (2012). https://doi.org/10.1007/978-3-642-29011-4_41

32. Naor, M., Reingold, M., Rosen, A.: Pseudo-random functions and factoring (extended abstract). In: 32nd ACM STOC. ACM Press, pp. 11–20, May 2000. https://doi.org/10.1145/335305.335307

33. Paterson, K.G., Srinivasan, S.: Building Key-private public-key encryption schemes. In: Boyd, C., González Nieto, J. (eds.) ACISP 2009. LNCS, vol. 5594, pp. 276–292. Springer, Heidelberg (2009). https://doi.org/10.1007/978-3-642-02620-1_20

34. Peikert, C., Waters, B.: Lossy trapdoor functions and their applications. In: 40th ACM STOC. Ladner, R.E., Dwork, C. (eds.) ACM Press, May 2008, pp. 187–196. https://doi.org/10.1145/1374376.1374406

35. Pointcheval, D., Sanders, O.: Forward secure non-interactive key exchange. In: Abdalla, M., De Prisco, R. (eds.) SCN 2014. LNCS, vol. 8642, pp. 21–39. Springer, Cham (2014). https://doi.org/10.1007/978-3-319-10879-7_2

36. Regev, O.: Quantum computation and lattice problems. In: 43rd FOCS. IEEE Computer Society Press, Nov. 2002, pp. 520–529. https://doi.org/10.1109/SFCS.2002.1181976

37. Sahai, A., Waters, B.: How to use indistinguishability obfuscation: deniable encryption, and more. In: Shmoys, D.B., (eds.) 46th ACM STOC, pp. 475–484. ACM Press (2014). https://doi.org/10.1145/2591796.2591825

38. Sakai, R., Ohgishi, K., Kasahara, M.: Cryptosystems based on pairing. In: SCIS 2000. Okinawa, Japan, January 2000

39. Waters, B.: Dual system encryption: realizing fully secure IBE and HIBE under simple assumptions. In: Halevi, S. (ed.) CRYPTO 2009. LNCS, vol. 5677, pp. 619–636. Springer, Heidelberg (2009). https://doi.org/10.1007/978-3-642-03356-8_36

On the Impossibility of Purely Algebraic Signatures

Nico Döttling[1] , Dominik Hartmann[2](✉) , Dennis Hofheinz[3], Eike Kiltz[2] ,
Sven Schäge[4] , and Bogdan Ursu[3]

[1] CISPA Saarbrücken, Saarbrücken, Germany
[2] Ruhr-University Bochum, Bochum, Germany
{dominik.hartmann,eike.kiltz}@rub.de
[3] Department of Computer Science, ETH Zurich, Zurich, Switzerland
{hofheinz,bogdan.ursu}@inf.ethz.ch
[4] Eindhoven University of Technology, Eindhoven, The Netherlands

Abstract. The existence of one-way functions implies secure digital signatures, but not public-key encryption (at least in a black-box setting). Somewhat surprisingly, though, *efficient* public-key encryption schemes appear to be much easier to construct from concrete algebraic assumptions (such as the factoring of Diffie-Hellman-like assumptions) than efficient digital signature schemes. In this work, we provide one reason for this apparent difficulty to construct efficient signature schemes.

Specifically, we prove that a wide range of *algebraic* signature schemes (in which verification essentially checks a number of linear equations over a group) fall to conceptually surprisingly simple linear algebra attacks. In fact, we prove that in an algebraic signature scheme, sufficiently many signatures can be linearly combined to a signature of a fresh message. We present attacks both in known-order and hidden-order groups (although in hidden-order settings, we have to restrict our definition of algebraic signatures a little). More explicitly, we show:
- the insecurity of all algebraic signature schemes in Maurer's generic group model (in pairing-free groups), as long as these schemes do not rely on other cryptographic assumptions, such as hash functions.
- the insecurity of a natural class of signatures in hidden-order groups, where verification consists of linear equations over group elements.

We believe that this highlights the crucial role of *public* verifiability in digital signature schemes. Namely, while public-key encryption schemes do not require any publicly verifiable structure on ciphertexts, it is exactly this structure on signatures that invites attacks like ours and makes it hard to construct efficient signatures.

1 Introduction

Digital Signatures and Public-Key Encryption. Digital signatures and public-key encryption (PKE) schemes are two of the most fundamental cryptographic primitives. Both of them are crucial to securing communication, and are used

© International Association for Cryptologic Research 2021
K. Nissim and B. Waters (Eds.): TCC 2021, LNCS 13044, pp. 317–349, 2021.
https://doi.org/10.1007/978-3-030-90456-2_11

in countless applications. From a theoretical perspective, these primitives are comparable, but somewhat different in strength: it is known that existentially, digital signatures are equivalent to one-way functions [41, 45]. (That is, secure digital signatures can be constructed from one-way functions and vice versa.) However, PKE schemes appear to be strictly stronger (in a black-box sense) than one-way functions [31]. In this sense, it is easier to construct digital signatures than PKE schemes.

On the other hand, current *efficient* constructions of signatures and PKE schemes from stronger (in particular group-based) assumptions paint a different picture. For instance, efficient PKE schemes are known from the factoring [29] and DDH [16, 34] assumptions. But *efficient* signature schemes from the factoring or DDH assumptions appear to require random oracles [5, 33, 47], stronger assumptions [17], or tradeoffs in efficiency [30]. Hence, it seems that efficient signatures are somewhat harder to construct than PKE schemes. This leads to the obvious question that motivates this work:

What makes efficient (standard-model) digital signature schemes harder to construct than PKE schemes?

We note that while lower bounds for digital signature schemes exist, they are either limited to very special types of signature schemes (like structure-preserving signatures [1, 2, 25, 26] in the pairing setting), or to bounds on the efficiency of constructions from symmetric primitives [4, 23]. To the best of our knowledge, e.g., the (space or time) complexity of group-based signature schemes (without pairings) is not well-understood.

The Role of Public Verifiability. Of course, signature and PKE schemes have a very different syntax (and different goals). However, one unique property of digital signatures is that of *public verifiability*. Specifically, even an adversary can verify the validity of a signature, while it can in general not verify the consistency of a PKE ciphertext (i.e., that it was generated with the encryption procedure). In a security reduction, this difference allows a wider range of techniques to modify ciphertexts in a security reduction than signatures. In fact, a popular technique for PKE security reductions starts by making the ciphertext inconsistent [16, 18, 34]. Similar techniques for signatures exist [24], but currently require a very specific algebraic setup in order to be compatible with public verifiability.

In a nutshell, public verifiability enforces a certain publicly verifiable structure on signatures that does not need to be present in PKE ciphertexts. For many known signature schemes (e.g., [8, 17, 21, 30, 47, 52]), verifying this structure amounts to checking whether different group elements or exponents stored in the signature fulfill one or more polynomial equations (whose coefficients are derived from public key, message, and signature). The simpler these equations, the more efficient the signature scheme becomes.

Our Results. In this paper, we use the above observations as a motivation to look at a very simple class of signature schemes we call "algebraic". An algebraic signature scheme is one in which public keys and signatures consist of group elements (and possibly some additional auxiliary information), and verification consists in checking whether these group elements satisfy some linear relations (whose coefficients are influenced by the auxiliary information). This class of signatures is simple and natural, and would seem a promising starting point for constructing efficient signature schemes. We provide impossibility results in two settings:

- In pairing-free groups of known order, we show that all algebraic signature schemes in Maurer's generic group model are insecure, as long as these signature schemes do not rely on other cryptographic assumptions, such as random oracles.
- In hidden-order groups, we establish the insecurity of a natural subclass of algebraic signatures (essentially those without auxiliary information). As a further extension, we show that BLS signatures are insecure when the BLS hash function is instantiated with a specific type of programmable hash function, such as Waters' programmable hash function used in his signature scheme [52].

In both settings, we show that in algebraic signature schemes, it is always possible to linearly combine sufficiently many existing signatures (for distinct messages) to another signature for a fresh message. (The specific methods to do that depend on the setting, however.)

As a simple special case, assume a signature scheme for which valid signatures $(\sigma_1, \ldots, \sigma_k)$ satisfy a single equation of the form

$$\sigma_1 P_1 + \ldots + \sigma_k P_k = P_0$$

over an additive group $(\mathbb{G}, +)$, where the $P_i = P_i(\mathsf{vk}, m) \in \mathbb{G}$ are publicly computable from verification key and message, and the σ_i are exponents from the signature.

Now if the P_i are also (publicly) computed in a linear fashion from a few base elements $X_1, \ldots, X_n \in \mathbb{G}$ in the verification key, each signature gives a linear equation

$$\sigma'_1 X_1 + \ldots + \sigma'_n X_n = 0$$

(with known σ'_i) for the X_i. After seeing sufficiently many valid signatures, the σ'_i (and hence the σ_i) for a fresh random message m^* can be derived by linear algebra. Hence, such a signature scheme is insecure.

Extensions. We extend this idea also to more equations, groups of unknown order (in which linear algebra has to be replaced with computations over the integers), and to randomized signatures. Our results cover typical settings of groups with known order (as used, e.g., with Diffie-Hellman-like assumptions), and with unknown order (as used, e.g., for factoring- and RSA-based constructions).

On the Efficiency of Our Attacks. The basic attack outlined above is efficient in the sense that only linear algebra operations over matrices of exponents are made. When generalizing to unknown-order settings, these operations become linear algebra operations over the integers (which are more expensive, but remain polynomially efficient).

However, we will also generalize these ideas to schemes in which signatures contain arbitrary "tags" t (i.e., non-algebraic bitstrings that may influence the selection of the $P_i = P_i(\mathsf{vk}, m, t)$). Such tags can model, e.g., random coins chosen during signing. In general, it is not immediately clear how to adapt the above attack idea to such "tagged" signatures, since the attack only yields forgery coefficients σ_i, but no suitable t.

In this general setting, we give an attack that is "pseudo-efficient" in the generic group model. More specifically, our attack uses only a polynomial number of group operations, but brute-forces a suitable t (and thus becomes computationally infeasible for larger t). This attack shows that even for "tagged" signatures with such a t, security cannot come from hardness assumptions in the group alone. We stress that this generalized attack brute-forces only t, and becomes efficient also in terms of running time for logarithmically-short t. In fact, for empty t, it coincides with the basic attack described above.

What Do Our Results Say About Existing Paradigms for Signature Schemes? Our characterization also helps to understand what differentiates somewhat less efficient schemes like (implicitly [30] or explicitly [39]) tree-based schemes: in tree-based schemes, the polynomial equations checked have very diverse coefficients (in the sense that every message uses a unique set of coefficients). Our results do not apply in such settings, since we may end up with more variables than linear equations for these variables.

A Note on Generic Group Models. Since our first result employs generic groups, it is worthwhile to comment on our choice of Maurer's generic group model. Generic group models (GGMs) formalize the idea that algorithms, both schemes and adversaries, can only make algebraic use of a group, in other words only use the group *as a black box*. This is typically formalized by giving such algorithms access to the group via a *group oracle*, which takes as input $\mathbb{Z}_p$ elements and returns *handles* to group elements. The group oracle also performs group operations by taking handles of group elements and returning the handle of the resulting group element.

This idea can be implemented in different nuances. In Shoup's generic group model [51], the handles are chosen by a random injective function from $\mathbb{Z}_p$ into a set of sufficiently long bit-strings, i.e. each group element is represented by a unique but otherwise uniformly random handle. In this model, the group oracle can be immediately used to implement a random oracle [55] . As a consequence, in Shoup's generic group model, Schnorr's signature scheme [47] (using random-oracle-like features of the generic group as in [14]) is provably secure. But this means that in this model there do in fact exist fully succinct signature schemes, yet via a non-standard use of the group.

In Maurer's generic group model [37], the group oracle is stateful and handles are computed lazily via a counter. Consequently, the handles do not carry additional entropy and the group oracle cannot be used to implement a random oracle. Furthermore, it seems to be difficult to even define a consistent hash function on group elements, as the labels depend on the order in which the group elements were queried.

More Applications. But while conceptually proving what *cannot* work to construct efficient signature schemes, we also showcase our techniques for a known signature scheme. Namely, we show that the pairing-based Boneh-Lynn-Shacham signature scheme [11], whose security is proved in the random oracle model, *cannot* be implemented with a suitable algebraic hash function (such as Waters' programmable hash function used in his signature scheme [52]).

1.1 Related Work

Impossibility results in idealized and restricted models have a rich history, dating back to the seminal work of Impagliazzo and Rudich [32] who established impossibility of constructing key-agreement from one-way functions in a black-box way. In this vein, Boneh et al. [12] showed that Identity-Based Encryption (IBE) [10,15,50] cannot be constructed from trapdoor permutations in a black-box way. Papakonstantinou et al. [42] generalized this result to show that IBE cannot be constructed by making only black-box use of a *cryptographic group without pairings*[1]. The techniques of [42] set the blueprint for a line of follow-up works, including this work, in arguing that public information (such as the master public key for an IBE scheme) imposes a system of linear constraints, and every time an adversary is provided a user secret key, one of two events must occur. (1) Either the dimension of this system decreases in the adversary's view or (2) the adversary could have generated this user key by himself from information which was already available to him. In this way, it can be argued that the size of public parameters dictate a (polynomial) upper bound for how many key-queries such an IBE can be secure. Roughly, by exhausting this bound an adversary can force event (2) to happen after a polynomial number of key queries, thereby breaking security of the IBE scheme. The impossibility result of [42] is provided in Shoup's generic group model. Pass and Shelat [43] showed that achieving VBB obfuscation is impossible to achieve by only making black-box use of constant degree graded encoding. In their work, the ideal graded encoding scheme is modeled akin to Shoup's generic group model, in that handles to group elements are (unique) uniformly random bit strings. On a technical level, [43] shows that ideal multilinear maps in any such construction are *useless*, in that they can be compiled out while still obtaining an approximately correct VBB obfuscator (which were shown to be impossible [6]). The core idea is, in the same vein as in [42],

---

[1] Identity-based Encryption was later shown to be possible from the Computational Diffie-Hellman (CDH) assumption in cryptographic groups by making non-black-box use of the underlying group [19].

to learn as system of linearly independent polynomials via black-box access to the ideal multilinear maps. This in turn allows emulation of zero-test queries in the obfuscated program without access to the ideal multilinear maps. This result was generalized by Mahmoody, Mohammed and Nematihaji [36] to the setting of ideal non-commutative rings. Zhandry and Zhang [54] adapted the compilation technique of [43] to order revealing encryption, showing that this primitive cannot be constructed in Shoup's generic group model. While Shoup's model is in some sense closer to the plain model than Maurer's model by providing explicit representations of group elements, this aspect leads to many numerous technical obstacles. A recent line of work has focused on studying limitations of construction techniques for pivotal cryptographic primitives in Maurer's model. Rotem, Segev and Shahaf [46] showed that any generic construction (in Maurer's model) of a delay function in a *group of known order* is insecure, giving evidence that the use of hidden order groups in known constructions [7,44,53] might indeed be necessary. Schul-Ganz and Segev [49] provided a tight version of the impossibility result of [42] in Maurer's model, in showing that any IBE scheme whose public parameters contain n group elements will support at most n identity secret keys. We remark using a simple technique known as Naor's trick, any IBE scheme can be transformed into a signature scheme. Consequently, on the surface our results also imply the results of [49]. However, [49] consider IBE schemes allowing arbitrary (yet generic) decryption algorithms, whereas in this work we consider signature schemes with algebraic verification, i.e. signature schemes where verification can be expressed as a (generic) equation system. In this sense, our results do not immediately imply the results of [49], and further study in this direction is necessary.

1.2   Technical Outline

We will now provide a high level overview of our generic attacks. As purely combinatorial techniques suffice to achieve signatures of size logarithmic in the size of the message space [35,39,41], we will first suitably restrict the class of signature schemes under consideration.

Algebraic Signature Schemes. We will consider signature schemes which only make *algebraic* use of a cryptographic group. By algebraic, we mean that the group is only accessed via the standard group operations, but not by making use of representations of group elements. Essentially our notion of algebraic signature schemes is characterized by the property that verification checks a set of linear equations in the group. Specifically, assume in the following that we are working over a cyclic group $\mathbb{G}$ with generator P isomorphic to $\mathbb{Z}_p$. To simplify notation, we will write group operations additively. We say a signature scheme over an additive group $\mathbb{G}$ is algebraic, if it meets the following structural requirements.

- Signing keys sk are arbitrary bit-strings, whereas verification keys consist of a vector of n group elements $\mathbf{X} = (X_1, \ldots, X_n)^\mathsf{T}$ and a bit-string s.
- The signing algorithm produces signatures σ which consist of a vector of k group elements $\mathbf{Y} = (Y_1, \ldots, Y_k)^\mathsf{T}$ and a bit string t.

– The verification algorithm $\mathsf{Verify}(\mathsf{vk}, m, \sigma)$ is described by two efficiently computable functions A and B, where $A(s, m, t)$ returns a $\mathbb{Z}_p^{\ell \times n}$ matrix and $B(s, m, t)$ returns a $\mathbb{Z}_p^{\ell \times k}$ matrix, respectively. The signature σ is accepted if the group-equations

$$A(s, m, t) \cdot \mathbf{X} = B(s, m, t) \cdot \mathbf{Y}$$

hold over the additive group $(\mathbb{G}, +)$.

We call this type of signature scheme *algebraic*, as the verification algorithm only makes algebraic use of the group, i.e. no bit-representations of group elements are used. Note further that this definition does not impose any restrictions on the signing algorithm, i.e. the signing algorithm may compute arbitrary functions of the signing key and the message. While at first glance this notion might seem overly restrictive, we will argue below that any signature scheme which only makes algebraic use of a group must be of this form. This notion does not include pairing-based constructions in the generic group model, since only linear verification equations are considered. Therefore constructions like [8,9] are not covered by our results.

Learning Linear Functions. We will now turn to showing that any algebraic signature scheme can be efficiently attacked in the generic group model, where we measure the adversary's efficiency only in terms of its group oracle queries. Our starting point is a basic fact about the learnability of linear functions. Consider an experiment where a challenger chooses some function F, and then plays the following game with an adversary $\mathcal{A}$. The challenger chooses an input $\mathbf{x}_i$ from some distribution $\mathcal{X}$ and for each $\mathbf{x}_i$, $\mathcal{A}$ can either decide to see $F(\mathbf{x}_i)$ or provide a guess for $F(\mathbf{x}_i)$, where in the latter case if the adversary guesses correctly it wins. Clearly, for general functions F this experiment is hopeless for the adversary, as F could, e.g., be a pseudorandom function with large output domain.

On the other hand, things are different if F is a linear function. Say $F : \mathsf{V} \to \mathsf{U}$ is a linear function between two vector spaces V and U over some field $\mathbb{F}$, where V is (say) of dimension n. Now, every time $\mathcal{A}$ is given a new input $\mathbf{x}_i \in \mathsf{V}$, then one out of two things must happen.

1. It holds that $\mathbf{x}_i$ is in the span of $\mathbf{x}_1, \ldots, \mathbf{x}_{i-1}$. In this case, it follows from the linearity of F that $F(\mathbf{x}_i)$ is uniquely specified by the input-output pairs $(\mathbf{x}_1, F(\mathbf{x}_1)), \ldots, (\mathbf{x}_{i-1}, F(\mathbf{x}_{i-1}))$. Thus, in this case $\mathcal{A}$ can win the experiment with probability 1, simply by solving a linear equation system for $F(\mathbf{x}_i)$.
2. It holds that $\mathbf{x}_i$ is not in the span of $\mathbf{x}_1, \ldots, \mathbf{x}_{i-1}$. In this case, $\mathcal{A}$ will learn new information about F.

Noting that the dimension of V is n, it follows that case 2 can happen at most n times. Consequently, after at most n rounds the adversary will win the experiment with probability 1.

Learning Affine Relations. The discussion in the previous paragraph does not immediately translate into an attack against algebraic signatures, as the signing algorithm is not necessarily a linear function. However, we will now modify the above argument such that it yields an efficient attack against algebraic signatures over prime order groups.

First note that for an algebraic signature scheme, knowing the discrete logarithms $\mathbf{x} = (x_1, \ldots, x_n)^\mathsf{T}$ of the group elements $\mathbf{X} = (X_1, \ldots, X_n)^\mathsf{T}$ is sufficient to forge signatures: Due to correctness of the signature scheme, we know that for any message m there exists a valid signature $\sigma = (\mathbf{Y}, t)$, i.e., it holds that

$$A(s, m, t) \cdot \mathbf{X} = B(s, m, t) \cdot \mathbf{Y}.$$

Consequently, it also holds

$$A(s, m, t) \cdot \mathbf{x} = B(s, m, t) \cdot \mathbf{y}.$$

in $\mathbb{Z}_p$. But this means that, given the discrete logarithms $\mathbf{x}$ of $\mathbf{X}$, we can find a signature for any message m by exhaustively searching over all possible values of t and testing for each t whether the equation system $B(s, m, t) \cdot \mathbf{y} = A(s, m, t) \cdot \mathbf{x}$ has a solution $\mathbf{y}$. If for a given t such a $\mathbf{y}$ exists, $(t, \mathbf{Y} = \mathbf{y}P)$ is a valid signature of the message m.

Towards developing the actual attack, we will now discuss a twist of the above idea. Assume the adversary already knows $(m_1, \sigma_1), \ldots, (m_{i-1}, \sigma_{i-1})$, where $\sigma_j = (\mathbf{Y}_j, t_j)$.

Then we can define a set $\mathsf{T}_{i-1} \subseteq \mathbb{Z}_p^n$ of *candidate vectors* $\mathbf{x}$ which could be the discrete logarithms of $\mathbf{X}$. A vector $\mathbf{x}$ is in T_{i-1}, if for all indices $j \in \{1, \ldots, i-1\}$ it holds that $A(s, m_j, t_j) \cdot \mathbf{x} = B(s, m_j, t_j) \cdot \mathbf{Y}_j$. In other words, T_{i-1} consists of all vectors $\mathbf{x}$ such that for $j \in \{1, \ldots, i-1\}$ the (m_j, σ_j) are valid message-signature pairs under the verification key $\mathbf{x}$.

Note that while membership in the set T_{i-1} can be decided using a polynomial number of group queries, we cannot efficiently compute the set T_{i-1} given the message-signature pairs $(m_1, \sigma_1), \ldots, (m_{i-1}, \sigma_{i-1})$. However observe that T_{i-1} is an affine subspace of $\mathbb{Z}_p^n$, as it is the solution-space of a non-homogenous linear equation system.

Ignoring the issue that we cannot efficiently compute T_{i-1} for the moment, we can now mount a similar learning argument as above. For an additional message-signature pair (m_i, σ_i), define T_i analogous to T_{i-1} taking the additional message-signature pair into account. So for every new message m_i, one out of two cases may happen:

1. By learning the signature σ_i of m_i the space T_i does not shrink, i.e., it holds that $\mathsf{T}_i = \mathsf{T}_{i-1}$.
2. By learning the signature σ_i the space T *does shrink*, i.e., $\mathsf{T}_i \subsetneq \mathsf{T}_{i-1}$.

Note that if the first case happens, an adversary $\mathcal{A}$ which knows T_{i-1} might have just as well computed σ_i *on its own*. Again ignoring the issue that this can't be implemented with a polynomial number of group operations, the adversary could exhaustively search over all $\sigma = (\mathbf{Y}, t)$ and pick one for which $\mathsf{T}_i = \mathsf{T}_{i-1}$. In the second case however, since both T_i and T_{i-1} are affine spaces, the dimension of T_i must be strictly smaller than the dimension of T_{i-1}. Since the space $\mathsf{T}_0 = \mathbb{Z}_p^n$ has dimension n, case 2 can happen at most n times.

Impossibility of Algebraic Signatures Against Generic Adversaries. We will now address the issue that in the above sketch computing the affine spaces T_i cannot be achieved with a polynomial number of group operations. Upon closer inspection, the above argument only hinges on the fact that the dimension of T_{i-1} is decreasing. Since T_i is an affine space, it can be expressed as the sum of any point in T_i and a linear space W_i. By standard linear algebra, it holds that W_i is the intersection of the kernels of the $A(s, m_j, t_j)$. Clearly, W_i has the same dimension as T_i, i.e., whenever the dimension of T_i decreases, the dimension if W_i decreases as well.

However, instead of looking at T_i or W_i we will look at the *dual space* of T_i, that is the set of all homogeneous linear equations satisfied by all elements in T_i.

Specifically, for a verification key $\mathsf{vk} = (\mathbf{X}, s)$, a message m and a signature $\sigma = (\mathbf{Y}, t)$ we define the space

$$\mathsf{K}(m, t) = \mathrm{LKer}(B(s, m, t)) \cdot A(s, m, t),$$

where $\mathrm{LKer}(B(s, m, t))$ is the left-kernel of $B(s, m, t)$.

Notice that for every $\mathbf{v} \in \mathsf{K}(m, t)$ we can write $\mathbf{v}^\mathsf{T} = \mathbf{w}^\mathsf{T} A(s, m, t)$ for a $\mathbf{w}^\mathsf{T} \in \mathrm{LKer}(B(s, m, t))$ and it holds that

$$\mathbf{v}^\mathsf{T} \cdot \mathbf{X} = \mathbf{w}^\mathsf{T} \cdot A(s, m, t)\mathbf{X} = \mathbf{w}^\mathsf{T} \cdot B(s, m, t)\mathbf{Y} = 0,$$

as $\mathbf{w}^\mathsf{T} \in \mathrm{LKer}(B(s, m, t))$. In the main body we show that $\mathsf{K}(m, t)$ precisely characterizes the linear constraints imposed on the unknown vector $\mathbf{x}$ by s, m and t, that is if it holds for all $\mathbf{v}^\mathsf{T} \in \mathsf{K}(m, t)$ that $\mathbf{v}^\mathsf{T} \cdot \mathbf{X} = 0$ then there exists a $\mathbf{Y}$ such that $A(s, m, t)\mathbf{X} = B(s, m, t)\mathbf{Y}$. We further define L_i to be the set of linear constraints imposed by all $(m_1, \sigma_1), \ldots, (m_i, \sigma_i)$, that is

$$\mathsf{L}_i = \bigoplus_{j=1}^{i} \mathsf{K}(m_j, t_j),$$

where $\oplus$ denotes the sum of vector spaces[2]. Note that $\mathsf{K}(m_i, t_i)$ and hence the L_i can be efficiently computed from the bit-strings s and $(m_1, t_1), \ldots, (m_i, t_i)$. While the space T_i of candidates for $\mathbf{x}$ potentially shrinks when we add a new message-signature pair, the space L_i of linear relations that must be satisfied by all the $\mathbf{x}$ grows. As before, we will distinguish two cases concerning a new message-signature pair (m_i, σ_i).

---

[2] The sum of vector spaces is the set of all vectors in the ambient space which can be linearly combined from vectors in these spaces.

1. In the first case it holds that $L_i = L_{i-1}$, in other words it holds that $K(m_i, t_i) \subseteq L_{i-1}$
2. In the second case it holds that $L_{i-1} \not\subseteq L_i$, i.e. $K(m_i, t_i)$ contains new linear relations about $\mathbf{X}$.

We can routinely argue as before via a simple dimension argument that case 2 can happen at most n times. On the other hand, if case 1 happens for some (m_i, t_i), we can now efficiently forge a signature as follows. If $K(m_i, t_i) \subseteq L_{i-1}$, then by the above discussion there exists a $\mathbf{Y}$ such that $A(s, m_i, t_i)\mathbf{X} = B(s, m_i, t_i)\mathbf{Y}$. But the critical observation now is that this is a linear equation system for which we can find a solution $\mathbf{Y} \in \mathbb{G}^k$ (which is guaranteed to exist by the above discussion) by e.g. computing a *weak left-inverse*[3] H of $B(s, m, t)$ and setting

$$\mathbf{Y} = H \cdot A(s, m_i, t_i)\mathbf{X}.$$

Since H can be efficiently computed from $B(s, m, t)$, we can obtain $\mathbf{Y}$ from $\mathbf{X}$ by applying a polynomial number of computable $\mathbb{Z}_p$ operations to $\mathbf{X}$.

Consequently, the final attack can be described as follows, defining the spaces L_i as above. Initialize $L_0 = \{0\}$ and repeat for pairwise distinct messages $m_1, \ldots, m_{n+1}$. For message m_i, check if there exists t_i such that $K(m_i, t_i) \subseteq L_{i-1}$. If so, compute $\mathbf{Y}_i$ as above, set $\sigma_i = (\mathbf{Y}_i, t_i)$ and output the forge (m_i, σ_i). Otherwise, query a signature $\sigma_i = (\mathbf{Y}_i, t_i)$ from the signing oracle, set $L_i \leftarrow L_{i-1} \oplus K(m_i, t_i)$ and continue.

Notice that while this attack needs to brute-force over all choices of the t_i, it only makes a polynomial number of queries to the group oracle. In fact we will show the slightly stronger statement that even if the adversary only receives a fixed number of random message/signature pairs, the above attack will work with overwhelming probability.

Algebraic Signatures in Groups of Unknown Order. For the above attack, we've constructed an adversary which makes a polynomial number of queries to the group oracle, but is otherwise unbounded. We will now consider a more restricted class of algebraic signatures over groups of *unknown order* and provide a fully efficient attack against this class of signatures by using a tweak on the above ideas. In this setting, we will not model the group as a generic group but rather provide efficient attacks against a simplified variant of algebraic signatures in any group of unknown order. Inspecting the above attack, the only inefficient part of the attack is the exhaustive search over the signature component t. In our notion of simplified algebraic signatures we will therefore require that the signature consists only of the group elements $\mathbf{Y}$.

Furthermore, in the unknown group order setting, we will model the publicly computable matrices $A(\mathsf{vk}, m)$ and $B(\mathsf{vk}, m)$ used by the verification algorithm as integer matrices. For a technical reason, in our notion of simplified signatures we will also require that the matrix B only depends on vk, but not on m.

---

[3] A weak left-inverse of a matrix B is a matrix H for which it holds that $BHB = B$. For any matrix B the weak left-inverse H can be efficiently computed e.g. via gaussian elimination.

Clearly, if the group order is not known, we cannot immediately extend the above argument, as we have used linear algebra over fields to compute the spaces of linear relations L_i. Now assume that for a verification key vk the adversary is given message-signature pairs $(m_1, \mathbf{Y}_1), \ldots, (m_{Q_s}, \mathbf{Y}_{Q_s})$, i.e. from the view of the adversary the following linear relations hold over the group:

$$A(\mathsf{vk}, m_1) \cdot \mathbf{X} = B(\mathsf{vk}) \cdot \mathbf{Y}_1$$

$$\vdots$$

$$A(\mathsf{vk}, m_{Q_s}) \cdot \mathbf{X} = B(\mathsf{vk}) \cdot \mathbf{Y}_{Q_s}.$$

Noting that the $A(\mathsf{vk}, m_i)$ are integer matrices in $\mathbb{Z}^{\ell \times n}$, then if the number of signatures Q_s issued to the adversary is greater than $\ell \cdot n$, we will observe integer linear relations between the $A(\mathsf{vk}, m_i)$, i.e. there exist $\alpha_1, \ldots, \alpha_{Q_s} \in \mathbb{Z}$ such that

$$\sum_{i=1}^{Q_s} \alpha_i A(\mathsf{vk}, m_i) = 0.$$

Assuming that $\alpha_{Q_s} \neq 0$, we can express $\alpha_{Q_s} A(\mathsf{vk}, m_{Q_s})$ as

$$\alpha_{Q_s} A(\mathsf{vk}, m_{Q_s}) = - \sum_{i=1}^{Q_s-1} \alpha_i A(\mathsf{vk}, m_i).$$

Note that if $\alpha_{Q_s} = 1$, we can in fact forge a signature of the message m_{Q_s} given the message-signatures pairs $(m_1, \mathbf{Y}_1), \ldots, (m_{Q_s-1}, \mathbf{Y}_{Q_s-1})$ as follows. Computing

$$\mathbf{Y}_{Q_s}^* = - \sum_{i=1}^{Q_s-1} \alpha_i \mathbf{Y}_i,$$

it holds that

$$B(\mathsf{vk})\mathbf{Y}_{Q_s}^* = - \sum_{i=1}^{Q_s-1} \alpha_i B(\mathsf{vk})\mathbf{Y}_i = - \sum_{i=1}^{Q_s-1} \alpha_i A(\mathsf{vk}, m_i)\mathbf{X}$$

$$= \alpha_{Q_s} A(\mathsf{vk}, m_{Q_s})\mathbf{X} = A(\mathsf{vk}, m_{Q_s})\mathbf{X}.$$

Our main effort in Sect. 4 is devoted to showing for a sufficiently large but poly-bounded Q_s there indeed do exist $\alpha_1, \ldots, \alpha_{Q_s} \in \mathbb{Z}$ with $\alpha_{Q_s} = 1$ such that

$$\sum_{i=1}^{Q_s} \alpha_i A(\mathsf{vk}, m_i) = 0.$$

A particular challenge of establishing this is that the existence of a signature for m_{Q_s} only guarantees such a linear relation modulo N (where N is the unknown group order). But to implement our attacks we need such a linear relation over $\mathbb{Z}$. We will further show that such a linear relation can be efficiently found using integer linear algebra techniques.

2   Preliminaries

2.1   Notation

We denote the security parameter by λ and assume that all algorithms implicitly take 1^λ as an additional input. For $n \in \mathbb{N}$, we define the set $[n] := \{1, \ldots, n\}$. For a finite set S, $s \xleftarrow{\$} S$ denotes sampling s uniformly at random from S. Similarly, we write $s \xleftarrow{\$} A(x)$ for the output of a probabilistic algorithm A on input x and fresh random coins, and $s \leftarrow A(x)$ for deterministic algorithms. A probabilistic algorithm is PPT or efficient, if its runtime is polynomial in the security parameter and its inputs. For a cyclic group $\mathbb{G}$ of order N with generator P, we write $\mathcal{G} = (\mathbb{G}, N, P)$. We write all groups in additive notation and assume that the bit length of N is in $\mathcal{O}(\lambda)$. Specifically, the multiplication of a matrix of exponents and a group element vector is defined in the natural way, i.e. for $M = (m_{i,j}) \in \mathbb{Z}_N^{n \times k}$ and $\mathbf{x} = (X_1, \ldots, X_k)^\mathsf{T} \in \mathbb{G}^k$, we define $M \cdot \mathbf{x} := (X_1', \ldots, X_n')^\mathsf{T}$ with $X_i' = \sum_{j=1}^k m_{i,j} X_j$ for $i \in [n]$.

We will also use symmetric pairing groups, which we denote as $\mathcal{G} = (\mathbb{G}, \mathbb{G}_T, N, P, e)$, where $e : \mathbb{G} \times \mathbb{G} \to \mathbb{G}_T$ and both $\mathbb{G}, \mathbb{G}_T$ are of order N, with $\mathbb{G}$ being generated by P.

We denote column vectors as lowercase bold $\mathbf{x} \in \mathbb{Z}^n$. For a matrix $M \in \mathbb{Z}^{n \times k}$, we denote by $\mathbf{m}_{*i}$ the ith column of M and $\mathbf{m}_{j*}^\mathsf{T}$ the jth row of M. The free module generated by the columns of a matrix $M \in \mathbb{Z}^{n \times k}$ is defined as $\mathsf{ColumnSpace}(M) := \{\mathbf{a} \in \mathbb{Z}^n : \text{there exists } \mathbf{c} \in \mathbb{Z}^k \text{ with } \mathbf{a} = \sum_{j=1}^k c_j \mathbf{m}_{*j}\}$. Alternatively, we can also see $\mathsf{ColumnSpace}$ as an integer lattice in $\mathbb{Z}^n$.

Let K be a field and V be a K-vector space. For a vector subspace U of V, we write $\mathsf{U} \subseteq \mathsf{V}$. For a (finite) set of vector subspaces $\mathsf{U}_i \subseteq \mathsf{V}$ for $i \in I$, we denote the *direct sum* as $\mathsf{U} = \bigoplus_{i \in I} \mathsf{U}_i$, i.e. the smallest vector subspace $\mathsf{U} \subseteq \mathsf{V}$ s.t. $\mathsf{U}_i \subseteq \mathsf{U}$ for $i \in I$. Vectors of group elements are bold, upper case letters and vectors of group exponents are bold, lower case letters. All vectors are column vectors unless stated otherwise.

For a matrix A, we write its left-kernel as $\mathrm{LKer}(A) := \{\mathbf{x} \mid \mathbf{x}^\mathsf{T} \cdot A = \mathbf{0}\}$, which is a vector subspace of A's domain. The product of a vector space V with a matrix A is defined in the natural way as $\mathsf{V} \cdot A := \{\mathbf{x}^\mathsf{T} \cdot A \mid \mathbf{x} \in \mathsf{V}\}$.

We will need the following lemma about the extended gcd (greatest common divisor) algorithm in Sect. 4.

Lemma 1. *Consider any two integers $a, b \in \mathbb{Z}$. If a divides b, then the extended gcd algorithm outputs a as the greatest common divisor, along with the Bezout coefficients $(1, 0)$. Similarly, If b divides a, then the algorithm outputs b as the greatest common divisor, along with the Bezout coefficients $(0, 1)$. Recall that the Bezout coefficients are any integers α, β that satisfy the identity $\alpha a + \beta b = \gcd(a, b)$.*

2.2   Generic Group Model

In the generic group model, the group structure is hidden from an adversary. We use the definition of Maurer [38], since, in contrast to the model of Shoup [51], it doesn't allow for hash functions on group elements, since this would already result in short signatures, e.g. [47].

Specifically, the group is encapsulated in a black box, which has registers for group elements and only exposes them through labels to the outside. These labels are simply running register numbers and (unlike in Shoup's model) are not unique to a group element. (That is, several labels can reference the same group element.) A generic adversary can only interact with the group via a group operation oracle $\mathcal{O}_{\mathrm{grp}}$ and an equality test oracle $\mathcal{O}_{\mathrm{eq}}$. The group operation oracle takes two labels as input, internally computes the group operation on the group elements corresponding to the labels, writes the new group element to a new register and outputs the label of the new register. The equality test oracle takes two labels and outputs 1 iff the group elements corresponding to the labels are equal. For simplicity, we also add a multiplication oracle $\mathcal{O}_{\mathrm{mul}}$, which takes a label and an integer and returns a label to the group element multiplied by the integer, and assume that the GGM always outputs the same label for the same group element since this specific label can always be found by a generic adversary with polynomially many queries to the equality check oracle.

An adversary is called *generic*, if it works with only access to the generic group model. As the GGM is an information theoretic model, the running time of a generic adversary is typically measured by the number of its queries to the group oracles. It is called *pseudo-efficient*, if it makes polynomially many queries in the security parameter to its group oracles, yet its overall running time is (potentially) unbounded. If furthermore the overall running time is also polynomially bounded, then we call it *efficient*.

We will present a pseudo-efficient generic adversary in Sect. 3 and an efficient, standard model adversary in Sect. 4. Note that although a pseudo-efficient adversary in the generic group model doesn't immediately present an adversary on the schemes covered by our impossibility result, it is sufficient to rule out black-box constructions from generic groups alone. In other words, the result tells us that in order to make a signature scheme secure, we need another source of complexity, which we "factor out" through letting our adversary be unbounded outside of the generic group.

2.3   Signatures

We recall the standard definitions of syntax and security for digital signatures.

Definition 2 (Digital Signatures).   *A digital signature scheme* SIG = {KeyGen, Sign, Verify} *consists of the following algorithms.*

- *The key generation algorithm* KeyGen *is probabilistic and on input of the security parameter* 1^λ *outputs a verification key and secret key* (vk, sk). *We assume that* vk *implicitly defines the (finite) message space* $\mathcal{M}$, *which is superpolynomial in* λ.
- *The signing algorithm* Sign *takes a message* $m \in \mathcal{M}$ *and a secret key* sk *as input and returns a signature* σ.

- *The deterministic verification algorithm* Verify *takes a verification key, a message* $m \in \mathcal{M}$ *and a signature* σ *as input and returns 1 for accept and 0 for reject.*

We require that for all $(vk, sk) \xleftarrow{\$} \mathsf{KeyGen}(1^\lambda)$ *and every message* $m \in \mathcal{M}$ *we have*

$$Pr[\mathsf{Verify}(vk, m, \mathsf{Sign}(sk, m)) = 1] = 1.$$

Definition 3 (UF-CMA Security). *We define the advantage of an adversary* $\mathcal{A}$ *against* UF-CMA *security (unforgeability against chosen message attack) of a signature scheme* SIG *as*

$$Adv_{\mathcal{A},\mathsf{SIG}}^{\mathsf{UF\text{-}CMA}}(\lambda) = Pr \left[\begin{array}{c|c} \mathsf{Verify}(vk, m^*, \sigma^*) = 1 & (vk, sk) \xleftarrow{\$} \mathsf{KeyGen}(1^\lambda) \\ \wedge\, m^* \notin \{m_1, \ldots, m_q\} & (m^*, \sigma^*) \xleftarrow{\$} \mathcal{A}^{\mathsf{Sign}(sk,\cdot)}(vk) \end{array} \right],$$

where $m_1, \ldots m_q$ *is the set of all messages queried to the signing oracle* $\mathsf{Sign}(sk, \cdot)$.

We can similarly define the notion UF-q-CMA, which is parametrized by the number q of signature queries the adversary is allowed to make, for some $q < |\mathcal{M}|$.

A weaker form of security is captured by unforgeability against random message attacks (UF-q-RMA security), where the adversary receives a set of q random messages and signatures.

Definition 4 (UF-q-RMA Security). *Let* $q < |\mathcal{M}|$. *We define the advantage of an adversary* $\mathcal{A}$ *against* UF-q-RMA *security (unforgeability against random message attack) of a signature scheme* SIG *as*

$$Adv_{\mathcal{A},\mathsf{SIG}}^{\mathsf{UF\text{-}}q\text{-}\mathsf{RMA}}(\lambda) = Pr \left[\begin{array}{c|c} & (vk, sk) \xleftarrow{\$} \mathsf{KeyGen}(1^\lambda) \\ \mathsf{Verify}(vk, m^*, \sigma^*) = 1 & \forall i \in [q] : m_i \xleftarrow{\$} \mathcal{M} \setminus \{m_1, \ldots, m_{i-1}\} \\ \wedge\, m^* \notin \{m_1, \ldots, m_q\} & \forall i \in [q] : \sigma_i \xleftarrow{\$} \mathsf{Sign}(sk, m_i) \\ & (m^*, \sigma^*) \xleftarrow{\$} \mathcal{A}(vk, (m_i, \sigma_i)_{i \in [q]}) \end{array} \right].$$

Note that in UF-q-RMA security the messages are uniformly random without repetition, i.e., all messages are distinct. Moreover, we decided to make the parameter q explicit since it simplifies the exposition of our impossibility results. (In an alternative definition more closely related to UF-CMA security, the adversary would first specify the number of signatures q it would like to see. All our negative results also hold in this notion.)

3 Signature Schemes over Groups of Prime Order

In this section, we will show our impossibility result for signatures in the generic group model for prime order groups.

3.1 Algebraic Signatures

We now introduce our abstraction of algebraic signatures over a generic group $\mathbb{G}$. Intuitively, these signatures are limited by the fact that one doesn't have access to the representation of group elements. Specifically, in Mauer's GGM, one can't even define a consistent (hash) function on group elements not provided by the GGM itself, as the label of each group element depends on the order in which they are received and are therefore not consistent. This makes it hard to map group elements to group exponents consistently. Hence, in algebraic signatures all exponents in the verification have to be independent of the group elements of the signature and the verification key.

Definition 5. *An* algebraic signature scheme SIG *over* $\mathcal{G} = (\mathbb{G}, p, P)$ *of prime order* p *with parameters* $n, k, \ell, \kappa \in \mathbb{N}$ *polynomial in the security parameter* λ *is a digital signature scheme with the following structural properties.*

- *There exists efficiently computable functions* $A : \{0,1\}^* \times \mathcal{M} \times \{0,1\}^\kappa \to \mathbb{Z}_p^{\ell \times n}$ *and* $B : \{0,1\}^* \times \mathcal{M} \times \{0,1\}^\kappa \to \mathbb{Z}_p^{\ell \times k}$. *If* s, m *and* t *are clear, we write* $A = A(s, m, t)$ *and* $B = B(s, m, t)$.
- $\mathsf{KeyGen}(1^\lambda)$ *outputs a keypair* (vk, sk) *with* $sk \in \{0,1\}^*$ *and*

$$vk = (\mathbf{X} = (X_1, \ldots, X_n)^\mathsf{T}, s) \in \mathbb{G}^n \times \{0,1\}^*.$$

- $\mathsf{Sign}(sk, m)$ *outputs a signature*

$$\sigma = (\mathbf{Y} = (Y_1, \ldots, Y_k)^\mathsf{T}, t) \in \mathbb{G}^k \times \{0,1\}^\kappa.$$

- $\mathsf{Verify}(vk, m, \sigma)$ *returns 1 iff*

$$A(s, m, t) \cdot \mathbf{X} = B(s, m, t) \cdot \mathbf{Y}.$$

Recall that group $(\mathbb{G}, +)$ is written in additive form. Hence Verify checks whether ℓ group equations are fulfilled simultaneously.

3.2 Preparation

If B as in Definition 5 would be invertible for some m^*, t^*, then finding such a pair suffices to break the signature scheme. So we only consider signature schemes where this is not the case and use a different approach. As outlined in the introduction, our adversary will try to learn linear relations on the verification key elements and find a message for which a signature exists that verifies for all possible verification keys satisfying the linear relations already known. These relations form an affine space, but computing it requires group oracle queries. Since the number of group oracle queries an adversary is allowed to make is limited, we will not look at the relations directly but at the *dual space*, as it can be computed without group oracle access. Specifically, we will look for vectors $\mathbf{z} \in \mathbb{Z}_p^n$ s.t. $\mathbf{z}^\mathsf{T} \cdot \mathbf{x} = \mathbf{0}$. These can be found with the help of the following Lemma 6.

Lemma 6. *Let* $A \in \mathbb{Z}_p^{\ell \times n}, B \in \mathbb{Z}_p^{\ell \times k}$ *and* $\mathbf{x} \in \mathbb{Z}_p^n$ *for some prime* p. *Then the following statements are equivalent:*

$$\exists \mathbf{y} \in \mathbb{Z}_p^k : \quad A \cdot \mathbf{x} = B \cdot \mathbf{y} \tag{1}$$

$$\forall \mathbf{z} \in \mathrm{LKer}(B) : \quad \mathbf{z}^\mathsf{T} \cdot A \cdot \mathbf{x} = 0 \tag{2}$$

$$\forall \mathbf{v} \in \mathrm{LKer}(B) \cdot A : \quad \mathbf{v}^\mathsf{T} \cdot \mathbf{x} = 0. \tag{3}$$

Notice that each signature will satisfy Eq. (1) and since A and B are $\mathbb{Z}_p$ matrices, the $\mathbf{v}$ in Eq. (3) can be computed without the group oracle. The specific usage of Lemma 6 will be described in Sect. 3.3.

Proof. We show the statement by proving circular implications in the order $(1) \Rightarrow (2) \Rightarrow (3) \Rightarrow (1)$.
$(1) \Rightarrow (2)$: clear.
$(2) \Rightarrow (3)$: Let $\mathbf{v} \in \mathrm{LKer}(B) \cdot A$. Then there is a $\mathbf{z} \in \mathrm{LKer}(B)$, s.t. $\mathbf{v}^\mathsf{T} = \mathbf{z}^\mathsf{T} \cdot A$. Then we have $\mathbf{v}^\mathsf{T} \cdot \mathbf{x} = \mathbf{z}^\mathsf{T} \cdot A \cdot \mathbf{x} \overset{(2)}{=} 0$. Since $\mathbf{v}$ was chosen arbitrarily, this holds for all $\mathbf{v} \in \mathrm{LKer}(B) \cdot A$ and (3) follows.
$(3) \Rightarrow (1)$: We prove $\neg(1) \Rightarrow \neg(3)$. If B spans $\mathbb{Z}_p^\ell$, the step is trivial. So assume that B doesn't span $\mathbb{Z}_p^\ell$. Define an $\ell \times \ell$-matrix H s.t. H maps the columns of B to 0 and all vectors linearly independent of B to themselves. Such a matrix exists due to the basis extension theorem and is a non-zero matrix as long as B doesn't have full rank ℓ. Since we assume $\neg(1)$, $A \cdot \mathbf{x}$ is not in the span of B and $H \cdot A \cdot \mathbf{x} \neq 0$ unless $A \cdot \mathbf{x} = 0$ (which would contradict $\neg(1)$). However all rows of H are in the left kernel of B. H is non-zero, so there is at least one such non-zero row vector $\mathbf{w}$ and $\mathbf{w} \cdot A \cdot \mathbf{x} \neq 0$ but $\mathbf{w} \in \mathrm{LKer}B$, which shows $\neg(3)$.

3.3 Impossibility of Secure Algebraic Signatures

Theorem 7 (Impossibility of Algebraic Signatures with UF-q-RMA Security). *Let* SIG *be an algebraic signature scheme with parameters* $n, k, \ell, \kappa \in \mathbb{N}$ *over group* $\mathbb{G}$ *of prime order* p. *Then there exists a generic group adversary* $\mathcal{A}$ *with*

$$Adv_{\mathcal{A},\mathsf{SIG}}^{\mathit{UF\text{-}n\text{-}RMA}}(\lambda) \geq \frac{1}{n+1}$$

Specifically, $\mathcal{A}$ *makes* $Q_{\mathrm{mul}} = \ell(n+k)$ *group multiplication queries to* $\mathcal{O}_{\mathrm{mul}}$, $Q_{\mathrm{grp}} = \ell(n+k-2)$ *group operation queries to* $\mathcal{O}_{\mathrm{grp}}$, *and additional* $2^\kappa \cdot poly(n, k, \ell, \log(p))$ *computation steps.*

Note that adversary $\mathcal{A}$ is potentially pseudo-efficient as it makes polynomially many queries to its group oracles but its overall running time is exponential in κ.

We now provide an intuition for the proof. The central ingredient is Lemma 6, which is used in two ways during the proof. First, each signature is a valid solution to the verification equation system, so Eq. (3) holds and $\mathrm{LKer}(B(s, m, t)) \cdot A$ is exactly the space of linear relations on the verification key imposed by the signature. A and B output matrices over $\mathbb{Z}_p$, hence this space can be computed without GGM queries. On the other hand, if the adversary finds a message/bitstring pair (m^*, t^*) for which A and B satisfy Eq. (3), it knows that a solution to the verification equation exists for (m^*, t^*). Since $\mathbb{Z}_p$ is a field, the solution can be found with standard linear algebra techniques.

We will show that for a random message m^*, the probability that there exists a t^* s.t. (m^*, t^*) satisfies Eq. (3) is non-negligible. Intuitively, if we sample $n + 1$ random messages and get signatures for n of them, we either learn the complete space of linear relations on the verification key or at least one of the messages doesn't introduce a new linear relation. In either case, at least one of the $n + 1$ messages satisfies Eq. (3) and the adversary can forge a signature for that message.

Proof. We describe a generic attacker $\mathcal{A}$ with the properties stated above. First, $\mathcal{A}$ receives a verification key $vk = (\mathbf{X}, s)$ and $q := n$ message/signature pairs $(m_i, \sigma_i)_{i \in [n]}$, where $m_i \xleftarrow{\$} \mathcal{M} \setminus \{m_1, \ldots, m_{i-1}\}$ and $\sigma_i := (\mathbf{Y}_i, t_i) \xleftarrow{\$} \mathsf{Sign}(vk, m_i)$. Next, $\mathcal{A}$ computes

$$\mathsf{L} := \bigoplus_{j=1}^{n} \mathsf{LKer}(B(s, m_j, t_j)) \cdot A(s, m_j, t_j)$$

where $\bigoplus$ is the sum of the vector subspaces and $B(s, m_j, t_j)$ and $A(s, m_j, t_j)$ are the defining matrices from Defintion 5. Note that L is a vector subspace of $\mathbb{Z}_p^n$. Then $\mathcal{A}$ chooses a random message $m^* \xleftarrow{\$} \mathcal{M} \setminus \{m_1, \ldots, m_n\}$ and for every $t \in \{0, 1\}^\kappa$, $\mathcal{A}$ computes

$$\mathsf{K}(m^*, t) := \mathsf{LKer}(B(s, m^*, t)) \cdot A(s, m^*, t),$$

where s is the bit string from vk. $\mathcal{A}$ checks whether $\mathsf{K}(m^*, t) \subseteq \mathsf{L}$, i.e. if $\mathsf{K}(m^*, t)$ is a vector subspace of L. If $\mathcal{A}$ finds a pair (m^*, t^*) for which this condition holds, it continues. Otherwise, $\mathcal{A}$ aborts.

For the pair (m^*, t^*), $\mathcal{A}$ sets up the linear equation system

$$A(s, m^*, t^*) \cdot \mathbf{X} = B(s, m^*, t^*) \cdot \mathbf{Y}^*$$

and tries to solve it for $\mathbf{Y}^*$. If it finds a solution, it outputs its forgery $\sigma^* := (\mathbf{Y}^*, t^*)$ on message m^* and aborts otherwise.

We proceed to the analysis of $\mathcal{A}$.

RUNNING TIME. First, note that $\mathcal{A}$ can check whether the condition $\mathsf{K}(m, t) \subseteq \mathsf{L}$ on the vector spaces holds without making any GGM queries and $\mathcal{A}$ can compute L without verifying the received signatures. Therefore $\mathcal{A}$ does not require any GGM queries before trying to solve the linear equation system, which takes at most $\ell(n + k)$ group multiplication queries and $\ell(n + k - 2)$ group operation queries, which yields the stated number of queries. Since $\mathcal{A}$ chooses a random message m^* and searches over all strings $t \in \{0, 1\}^\kappa$ to find a fitting t^* and computes the vector space $\mathsf{K}(m^*, t^*)$ for each potential t^*, its additional computation is bounded by $2^\kappa \cdot poly((n, k, \ell, \log(p)))$, where the polynomial term consists mostly of subspace computations and membership tests. Therefore $\mathcal{A}$ is pseudo-efficient, unless $\kappa \in \mathcal{O}(\log(\lambda))$.

CORRECTNESS. To show correctness, we fix a verification key $vk = (\mathbf{X}, s)$ in the execution of $\mathcal{A}$.

For the moment, assume that $\mathcal{A}$ samples the distinct random messages $m_1, \ldots, m_{n+1}$ and chooses the i-th message as its forgery and queries the remaining n to the signing oracle. Define

$$\mathsf{L}_i := \bigoplus_{j \in [n+1] \setminus \{i\}} \mathsf{K}(m_j, t_j)$$

where t_j is some bitstring used in the signatures returned by the challenger for message m_j.

Then there exists at least one $i \in [n+1]$ s.t. $\mathsf{K}(m_i, t_i) \subset \mathsf{L}_i$ for some t_i.

Assume for contradiction, that no such i exists, i.e. $\mathsf{K}(m_i, t_i) \not\subset \mathsf{L}_i$ for all $i \in [n+1]$ and $t_i \in \{0,1\}^\kappa$. But then the dimension of $L'_i = \bigoplus_{k \in [n+1] \setminus \{i,j\}} K(m_k, t_k)$ is smaller than the dimension of L_i for all $i \in [n+1], j \in [n+1] \setminus \{i\}$, since $K(m_j, t_j)$ increases the dimension of L_j and therefore is not included in any of the other $\mathsf{K}(m_i, t_i)$ and especially not in $\mathsf{K}(m_i, t_i)$. With the same argument, removing each $K(m_j, t_j)$ reduces the dimension of L_i by at least one. However since the dimension of L_i is at most $n-1$ (as otherwise $\mathsf{L}_i = \mathbb{Z}_p^n$ and then $\mathsf{K}(m_i, t_i) \subseteq \mathsf{L}_i$), removing n messages would reduce its dimension to -1, which is a contradiction.

So by choosing a random message from a set of $n+1$ messages, the adversary chooses a message m^* which satisfies Eq. (3) together with some t^* with probability at least $\frac{1}{n+1}$. But since all messages are random, this is the same as saying that the probability of the last message, i.e. m_{n+1} being this message is at least $\frac{1}{n+1}$ and this also holds if the first n messages are randomly chosen by the challenger and only the last message is chosen by the attacker.

Therefore $\mathcal{A}$ finds a pair (m^*, t^*) such that $A(s, m^*, t^*)$ and $B(s, m^*, t^*)$ satisfy Eq. 3 from Lemma 6 for the verification key vector $\mathbf{X}$ with probability at least $\frac{1}{n+1}$. This implies that the verification equation system has a solution and it can be found using standard linear algebra techniques since $\mathbb{Z}_p$ is a field. Since a signature is valid, iff it satisfies the verification equation this solution is exactly a valid signature and $\mathcal{A}$ wins the UF-n-RMA game.

4   Signature Schemes over Groups of Unknown Order

In this section, we describe a linear attack concerning a specific form of signatures over groups of unknown order. This attack has implications in particular on factoring- and RSA-based signatures. We start first by defining a particular type of signatures that we can attack. We call this type of signatures simplified algebraic signatures.

4.1   Simplified Algebraic Signatures

Unlike in the previous case where the group order was known, here the signatures rely on the algebraic structure of a group of (potentially) unknown order, such as in RSA signatures.

Compared to our formalization of algebraic signatures from Definition 5, the verification key of *simplified* algebraic signatures does not contain the s element anymore. This change is without loss of generality: namely, since the results in this section can be formulated in the standard model (without generic groups), linear coefficients can depend on the full representation of group elements in the verification key. Any additional information (that was previously contained in s) can now be encoded with group elements in vk.

Furthermore, signatures in simplified algebraic signature schemes do not contain the string t anymore. This is in fact a restriction, and it is caused by the fact that our attacks from this section need to be efficient. Hence, we cannot afford to run a brute-force search over a suitable t during an attack here (unlike in the attack from Sect. 3). Moreover, observe that the matrix B is not allowed to depend on the message m, which is another difference when compared to Definition 5, a restriction which stems from the limitations of our attack.

Definition 8. *Let λ denote the security parameter and $\mathcal{G} = (\mathrm{G}, N, P)$ be a group of order $N \in \mathbb{N}$ (that may or may not be known, with N having $O(\lambda)$ bits). A simplified algebraic signature scheme* SIG *over $\mathcal{G}$ with parameters $n, k, \ell \in \mathbb{N}$ (polynomial in λ) is a digital signature scheme with the following structural properties.*

- *There exist efficiently computable functions $A : \{0,1\}^* \times \mathcal{M} \to \mathbb{Z}_N^{\ell \times n}$ and $B : \{0,1\}^* \to \mathbb{Z}_N^{\ell \times k}$. If m is clear, we write $A := A(vk, m)$ and $B := B(vk)$ respectively.*
- KeyGen(1^λ) *outputs a keypair (vk, sk) with $sk \in \{0,1\}^*$ and*

$$vk = (\mathbf{X} = (X_1, \ldots, X_n)^\top) \in \mathrm{G}^n.$$

- Sign(sk, m) *outputs a signature*

$$\sigma = (\mathbf{Y} = (Y_1, \ldots, Y_k)^\top) \in \mathrm{G}^k.$$

- Verify(vk, m, σ) *returns 1 iff*

$$A(vk, m) \cdot \mathbf{X} = B(vk) \cdot \mathbf{Y}.$$

4.2   Hermite Normal Form

We present one of the main technical tools we are going to use in this section and which allows us to utilize linear algebra over the ring of integers.

Definition 9 (Hermite Normal Form [3,40]). *An $n \times m$ matrix H over $\mathbb{Z}$ is in* Hermite Normal Form (HNF) *if $H = \mathbf{0}$ or $H \neq \mathbf{0}$ and there exists an integer r with $1 \leq r \leq \min(n, m)$, such that:*

- *the first r columns are non-zero, i.e., $\mathbf{h}_{*j} \neq \mathbf{0}$ for all $j \in [r]$.*
- *there is a sequence of integers $1 \leq n_1 < n_2 < \ldots < n_r \leq n$, such that:*

- $h_{i,j} = 0$ for $j \in [m], i < n_j$. Also, $h_{i,j} = 0$ for $j > r$ and any $i \in [n]$.
- $h_{n_j,j} > 0$, for all $1 \leq j \leq r$. Moreover, all entries of H on rows n_j for $j \in [r]$ are non-negative and $h_{n_j,j}$ is strictly greater than all other elements on the n_j^{th} row, namely: $0 \leq h_{n_j,k} < h_{n_j,j}$ for all $j \in [r], k \in [j-1]$.

Note that r from Definition 9 coincides with the column-rank of H. Matrix H will therefore be in HNF if it has the following shape, where $\mathbf{0}$ denotes the all-zero matrix in $\mathbb{Z}^{n,m-r}$ and $*$ stands for any element of $\mathbb{Z}$:

$$
\begin{pmatrix}
0 & 0 & & 0 & & \\
\vdots & \vdots & & & & \\
0 & 0 & & & & \\
h_{n_1,1} & 0 & & \vdots & & \\
* & \vdots & & & & \\
* & 0 & & 0 & & \\
* & h_{n_2,2} & & \vdots & & \mathbf{0} \\
* & * & \ddots & 0 & & \\
* & * & \ddots & h_{n_r,r} & & \\
* & * & \ddots & \vdots & & \\
* & * & \ddots & * & & \\
\end{pmatrix}
$$

The top-most non-zero element $h_{n_j,j}$, $j \in [r]$ on each column is called a *pivot*. The second condition in Definition 9 tells us that all elements on a row with a pivot are non-negative and must be strictly smaller than the pivot. No condition is enforced on elements that are on a row without a pivot, meaning they might be negative.

Note that we use this (more-general) definition (see for example [3]) because we need to accommodate matrices which are not-necessarily square, and for which the column-rank is not necessarily maximal.

Lemma 10 (Existence and uniqueness of HNF [48]). *For any matrix $M \in \mathbb{Z}^{n \times m}$, there exists a unique matrix $\mathsf{HNF}(M) \in \mathbb{Z}^{n \times m}$ in Hermite Normal Form such that:*

$$\mathsf{ColumnSpace}(\mathsf{HNF}(M)) = \mathsf{ColumnSpace}(M).$$

Lemma 11 (A polynomial-time algorithm for HNF [22]). *For any $n \times m$ matrix M, computing its Hermite Normal Form can be realized in polynomial time.*

The following lemma is well-known:

Lemma 12. *Let $A \in \mathbb{Z}^{n \times m}, H = \mathsf{HNF}(A)$ and $\mathbf{c} \in \mathbb{Z}^n$. If $\mathbf{c} \in \mathsf{ColumnSpace}(H)$ then we can find in polynomial time (in the bitlength of its input) integer vectors $\boldsymbol{\beta}$ and $\boldsymbol{\alpha}$ such that $\mathbf{c} = H \cdot \boldsymbol{\beta}$ and $\mathbf{c} = A \cdot \boldsymbol{\alpha}$.*

4.3   An Inefficient AddColumn Procedure for Matrices in HNF

In this section we describe a straightforward inefficient algorithm which on input matrix H in Hermite Normal Form and column vector $\mathbf{d}$, will compute the HNF of $[H \mid \mathbf{d}]$. While inefficient, this algorithm will simplify our proof by allowing us to analyze the impact of successively adding columns to a matrix H on its HNF. Since the HNF is unique, the reasoning we come to using the inefficient algorithm will extend to the efficient one, since we are only concerned with what happens to the HNF, and not its intermediate results.

The AddColumn Algorithm

Input: $n \times m$ matrix $H = [B \mid \mathbf{0}]$ in Hermite Normal Form and column vector $\mathbf{d}$. Assume without loss of generality that $H = B$.
Output: $\mathsf{HNF}([H \mid \mathbf{d}])$.

The algorithm iterates over the non-zero columns of H as follows.

1. **Initialization**: The algorithm initializes $E(0) = B$ and $\mathbf{c}(0) = \mathbf{d}$. At step i, matrix $E(i)$ is initialized as $E(i) \leftarrow E(i-1)$ and vector $\mathbf{c}(i) \leftarrow \mathbf{c}(i-1)$. Additionally, at step i, vector $\mathbf{c}(i)$ has its first $i-1$ elements set to 0. Values $r(i), n_1(i), \ldots, n_r(i)$ correspond to the $r, n_1 \ldots n_r$ values of $E(i)$ from Definition 9. Since these indices may change, they depend on the iteration number i. If $\mathbf{c}(i)_i$ is 0, then we skip iteration i and move on to step $i+1$. Otherwise, if $\mathbf{c}(i)_i \neq 0$, we let s be the smallest index such that $n_s(i-1) \geq i$. We write:

$$E(i) = \begin{pmatrix} 0 & & & & 0 \\ \vdots & & & & 0 \\ 0 & & & & 0 \\ e_{n_1(i),1}(i) & & & & 0 \\ e_{n_1(i)+1,1}(i) & \ddots & & & \\ \vdots & & e_{n_s(i),s}(i) & & \\ & & \vdots & F(i) & \\ e_{n,1}(i) & & e_{n,s}(i) & & \end{pmatrix}$$

In the right lower corner of $E(i)$ is matrix $F(i) \in \mathbb{Z}^{(n-n_s(i)) \times (m-s)}$, which does not change during iteration i. All entries $e(i)_{k,j}$ with $k < n_j(i)$ are 0, for all $j \in [r]$ and $k \in [n_j(i) - 1]$. We also have $e(i)_{k,j} = 0$, for all $k \in [n]$ and $j > r(i)$.

2. **Column Index Selection**: Recall that s is the smallest index such that $n_s(i-1) \geq i$. What this means is that the sth column is the first column of $E(i)$ that can be modified using element $\mathbf{c}(i)_i$. Now, we distinguish the following cases:

   (a) **Column Insertion Step**: If $n_s(i-1) > i$, we insert vector $\mathbf{c}(i)$ before the sth column of $E(i)$. Namely, $\mathbf{c}(i)$ becomes the sth column of $E(i)$ and matrix $E(i)$ increases its column dimension by 1. We then set $\mathbf{c}(i)$ to the all-zero vector and after the modular reduction phase (which we will soon describe as well), we will output $E(i)$ as the HNF of $[H|\mathbf{d}]$.

(b) **GCD step**: Otherwise, we have $n_s(i-1) = i$. We then know that $e(i)_{i,s} \neq 0$, since $e(i)_{i,s}$ is the top-most non-zero element on the sth column (the pivot). We compute $g \leftarrow \gcd(e(i)_{i,s}, c(i)_i) = \alpha e(i)_{i,s} + \beta c(i)_i$, where $\alpha, \beta \in \mathbb{Z}$ are the Bezout coefficients computed by the extended greatest common divisor algorithm. We aim to replace $e_{i,s}(i)$ with $g = \gcd(e(i)_{i,s}, c(i)_i)$, while preserving the column space of $E(i)$:

  – The sth column of $E(i)$ is modified as $\mathbf{e}(i)_{*s} \leftarrow \alpha \mathbf{e}(i)_{*s} + \beta \mathbf{c}(i)$. Note that the first $(i-1)$ entries of $c(i)$ are 0, which means that $e(i)_{i,s}$ remains the top-most non-zero element on the sth column (the pivot), as required by the HNF condition (Definition 9).
  – Vector $\mathbf{c}(i) \leftarrow \mathbf{c}(i) - (c(i)_i/g) \cdot \mathbf{e}(i)_{*s}$. This replaces the ith component of $\mathbf{c}(i)$ with 0.

3. **Modular Reduction Phase**: Finally, the algorithm has to ensure that $0 \leq e(i)_{n_j,k} < e(i)_{n_j,j}$ for all $k \in [m], j \in [r]$. This is done by reducing the large entries modulo the pivots (the top-most non-zero elements on each column). To preserve the column space, the algorithm uses the following procedure:

> **for** $j = 1$ **to** m **do**
>   **for** $k = j+1$ **to** r **do**
>   **if** $e(i)_{n_k(i),j} \geq e(i)_{n_k(i),k}$ **then**
> $\mathbf{e}(i)_{*j} \leftarrow \mathbf{e}(i)_{*j} - \left\lfloor \frac{e(i)_{n_k(i),j}}{e(i)_{n_k(i),k}} \right\rfloor \mathbf{e}(i)_{*k}$
>   **else if** $e(i)_{n_k(i),j} < 0$ **then**
> $\mathbf{e}(i)_{*j} \leftarrow \mathbf{e}(i)_{*j} + \left\lceil \frac{e(i)_{n_k(i),j}}{e(i)_{n_k(i),k}} \right\rceil \mathbf{e}(i)_{*k}$
>   **end if**
>   **end for**
> **end for**

At this stage $E(i)$ is in HNF and $\mathbf{c}(i)$ has its first i entries equal to 0. The algorithm is now ready to move on to the next i, making the same computations for $E(i+1)$. Note that all operations of AddColumn are expressed as operations on the columns of the matrix $E(i)$. This means that $E(i)$ has the same column space as $E(i-1)$.

4. **Output**: If the algorithm made no column insertions, then the output is $[E(n)\|\mathbf{0}]$, where here $\mathbf{0} \in \mathbb{Z}^{n\times 1}$. If at some point the algorithm made a column insertion, the output will be $E(n)$.

REMARK ON THE RUNNING TIME OF AddColumn. The algorithm described above is (potentially) inefficient because the intermediate values computed by the algorithm are not shown to be bounded. A polynomial time algorithm for computing $\text{HNF}([H \mid \mathbf{b}])$ can be found in [22, 40].

Lemma 13 (Decreasing pivots). *Consider $n, m \in \mathbb{N}^*$. Let $H \in \mathbb{Z}^{n\times m}$ be a matrix in HNF and of column-rank r. Consider a column vector $\mathbf{b}$ and let $H' := \text{AddColumn}(H, \mathbf{b}) = \text{HNF}([H \mid \mathbf{b}])$. Let $r, n_1, \ldots, n_r$ be the column-rank* and pivot indices of H, and $r', n'_1, \ldots, n'_r$ the values corresponding to H' (as in Definition 9).

Then we must have one of the following cases:

1. $r' > r$, i.e. the column rank of H' is strictly greater than the one of H.
2. $r' = r$ and then the positions of the pivots remain the same ($n_j = n'_j$, for all $j \in [r]$). Moreover, all pivot entries of H' are smaller than or equal to the corresponding pivot elements of H, i.e. $h'_{n_j,j} \leq h_{n_j,j}$, for all $j \in [n]$. Furthermore, at least a pivot entry of H' is smaller by at least a factor of 2 than the corresponding pivot of H, i.e. $h'_{n_j,j} \leq h_{n_j,j}/2$, for some $j \in [r]$.
3. $\mathbf{b} \in \mathsf{ColumnSpace}(H)$.

Proof. We consider the following statements:

- $r' < r$ **cannot hold.** Let $E(i)$ and $\mathbf{c}(i)$ be the intermediary values computed by AddColumn. We show first that $r' < r$ cannot hold. Observe that the algorithm may insert one column (and only one) during its execution, which introduces a new pivot element. Apart from that, each pivot element in H' is computed as the greatest common divisor of a non-zero pivot element in $E(i)$ and a non-zero element of $\mathbf{c}(i)$. Moreover, the modular reduction phase does not modify the value of the pivots. Therefore, pivots in H cannot be set to 0 and thus $r \leq r'$.
- **Case 1 does not hold implies pivot positions are the same.** If $r = r'$, this implies that the algorithm never inserts the vector $\mathbf{c}(i)$ as a column of $E(i)$. As explained in the previous paragraph, pivots in H' are computed as the greatest common divisor of a non-zero pivot and $E(i)$ and a non-zero element of $\mathbf{c}(i)$. Additionally, since pivots in $E(i)$ cannot become 0 and no column insertion is made, the pivot positions also remain unchanged.
- **Case 1 does not hold implies smaller pivots.** By contradiction, assume for now that the pivot entries $h'_{n_j,j}$ are not smaller or equal than $h_{n_j,j}$, for all $j \in [r]$. Since we are in the case of no column insertions, observe that $e(j)_{n_i,i}$ can only change its value in iteration n_i of AddColumn. This means that $h'_{n_i,i}$ is equal to the value $e(i)_{n_i,i}$ has at the end of iteration n_i. Then, since $h_{n_i,i} \neq 0$, $e(i)_{n_i,i} = \gcd(h_{n_i,i}, c(i)_{n_i})$, therefore $e(i)_{n_i,i}$ divides $h_{n_i,i}$. Thus, we have $e(i)_{n_i,i} \leq h_{n_i,i}$, which implies $h'_{n_i,i} \leq h_{n_i,i}$.
- **Case 1 does not hold and equal pivots imply Case 3.** Now assume by contradiction that $h'_{n_j,j} = h_{n_j,j}$, for all $j \in [r]$. This means that $e(i)_{n_j,j}$ remain the same throughout the execution of the AddColumn algorithm. From the description of AddColumn, we have that $e(i)_{n_j,j} = \gcd(e(i-1)_{n_j,j}, c(i)_{n_j})$. We use Lemma 1 and notice that, if the pivot elements $e(i)_{n_j,j}$ never change, then neither can the non-zero elements which are not pivots. That is because they already satisfy $0 \leq e_{n_k,j} < e_{n_k,k}$, for all $k \in [r], j \in [k-1]$ at the start of the algorithm, so the modular reduction phase cannot further reduce these elements.

  Recall that we defined $s(i)$ as the smallest index such that $n_s(i-1) \geq i$. Since by hypothesis, case 1 does not hold, this implies that $n_s(i-1) = i$. But then, it must hold that, at the beginning of iteration i, $e(i)_{n_{s(i)},s(i)}$ was already equal to $\gcd(e(i)_{n_{s(i)},s(i)}, c(i)_{n_{s(i)}})$. Therefore, $c(i)_{n_{s(i)}}$ is already divisible by $e(i)_{n_{s(i)},s(i)}$ at the beginning of iteration i. Since this holds for all iterations $i \in [n]$, this implies that $\mathbf{b}$ can be expressed as a linear combination of the columns of H, therefore $\mathbf{b} \in \mathsf{ColumnSpace}(H)$.

- **Case 1 and Case 3 do not hold imply Case 2.** Let's now assume that $\mathbf{b} \notin \mathsf{ColumnSpace}(H)$. From the argument above, we know that for some iteration $i \in [n]$ and index $s(i) \in [r]$, at least one pivot element $e(i)_{n_{s(i)},s(i)} < e(i - 1)_{n_{s}(i),s(i)}$. But $e(i)_{n_{s}(i),s(i)} = \gcd(e(i-1)_{n_s(i),s(i)}, c(i)_i)$, so $e(i)_{n_{s(i)},s(i)}$ must be smaller by at least a factor of 2 than $e(i-1)_{n_{s(i)},s(i)}$. Since $e(i)_{n_{s(i)},s(i)}$ is not changed in iterations $(i+1)\ldots n$, this implies that $h'_{n_{s(i)},s(i)} \le h_{n_{s(i)},s(i)}/2$.

This concludes the proof of Lemma 13.

4.4 Impossibility of Simplified Algebraic Signatures

Theorem 14 (Impossibility of Simplified Algebraic Signatures with UF-Q_S-CMA Security). *Let* SIG *be a simplified algebraic signature scheme with parameters* $\lambda, n, k, \ell \in \mathbb{N}$ *over group* $\mathbb{G}$ *of (possibly) unknown order* N *and message space superpolynomial in* λ. *Then there exists a PPT adversary* $\mathcal{A}$ *with*

$$Adv_{\mathcal{A},\mathsf{SIG}}^{UF\text{-}Q_S\text{-}CMA}(\lambda) = 1$$

The adversary makes at most $Q_S = (n\ell)^2 \cdot |\tau_{max}|$ *signature queries, where* $|\tau_{max}|$ *is the bitlength of the largest entry in the matrices* $A(vk, m)$ *for the messages that will be queried (we will argue that* $|\tau_{max}| = \mathrm{poly}(n \log(N) + |m|)$). *In addition,* $|\mathcal{M}|$ *does not have to be superpolynomial, it suffices to require* $|\mathcal{M}| \ge Q_S + 1$.

Letting T_{linear} *denote an upper bound on the run-time of all invocations of the polynomial-time HNF algorithm and* $T_{\max}$ *be an upper-bound on the polynomial running time of functions* A, *our attack runs in* $O(Q_S \cdot (T_{\max} + T_{\mathrm{linear}})) = O\big((n\ell)^2 \cdot |\tau_{\max}| \cdot (T_{\max} + T_{\mathrm{linear}})\big)$.

Proof. We describe our PPT adversary $\mathcal{A}$. Recall that $A(vk, m)$ is efficiently computable, this means that there exists a value τ_{max} whose bitlength is greater or equal than all the entries of the matrices $A(vk, m)$ that will be queried. Since the input length of the functions computing $A(vk, m)$ is $n \log(N) + |m|$, we have that the bitlength $|\tau_{\max}|$ is polynomially small with $|\tau_{max}| = \mathrm{poly}(n \log(N) + |m|)$.

1. **Setup Phase.** The challenger runs KeyGen, generating sk and $vk = \mathbf{X}$ and sends vk to $\mathcal{A}$.
2. **Discovery Phase.** Let $\mathbf{a}_{i*}(vk, m)^\top$ denote the ith row of $A(vk, m)$ and $\mathbf{b}_{j*}(vk)^\top$ be the jth row of $B(vk)$. The adversary initializes matrix $H(0)$ to be the empty matrix. At iteration i, the adversary picks a uniformly random message $m_i \xleftarrow{\$} \mathcal{M} \setminus \{m_1, \ldots, m_{i-1}\}$. It then computes the column vector $\mathbf{c}(i) = [\mathbf{a}_{1*}(vk, m_i)^\top | \ldots | \mathbf{a}_{\ell*}(vk, m_i)^\top]^\top \in \mathbb{Z}^{n\ell}$ and builds

matrix $D(i) = [H(i-1)|\mathbf{c}(i)] \in \mathbb{Z}^{n\ell \times i}$. Let $H(i) = \mathsf{HNF}(D(i))$, where $\mathsf{HNF}(D(i))$ denotes the (column-style) HNF of matrix $D(i)$. The adversary checks whether $H(i) = [H(i-1)|\mathbf{0}]$, if that is the case, it means that $\mathbf{c}(i) \in \mathsf{ColumnSpace}(H(i-1))$ (i.e. $\mathbf{c}(i)$ is in the linear span of the columns of $H(i-1)$). Let $\mathbf{h}(i-1)_{*j}$ denote the jth column of $H(i-1)$. Using linear algebra over $\mathbb{Z}$ (see for example [48]), the adversary can efficiently compute a linear combination of the columns of $H(i-1)$. More specifically, it can find a vector $\boldsymbol{\beta} \in \mathbb{Z}^i$ such that $\mathbf{c}(i) = \sum_j \beta_j \mathbf{h}(i-1)_{*j}$ through a matrix-vector multiplication (whose complexity can be bounded by T_{linear}). From Lemma 12, this allows us to also recover a vector $\boldsymbol{\alpha} \in \mathbb{Z}^i$ such that $\mathbf{c}(i) = \sum_j \alpha_j \mathbf{c}(j)$, where $\mathbf{c}(i)$ was defined as $\mathbf{c}(i) = [\mathbf{a}_{1*}(vk, m_i)^\top | \dots | \mathbf{a}_{\ell*}(vk, m_i)^\top]^\top \in \mathbb{Z}^{n\ell}$.
3. **Signing Queries:** Consider $j \in [i-1]$, then for all $\alpha_j \neq 0$, the adversary makes a signing query on m_j and receives signature $\mathbf{Y}_{m_j} = (Y_{m_j,1} \dots Y_{m_j,k})$.
4. **Forgery Phase:** Consider the following matrix of group elements:

$$\mathbf{W} = \begin{pmatrix} \mathbf{Y}_{m_1}^\top \\ \vdots \\ \mathbf{Y}_{m_{i-1}}^\top \end{pmatrix} \in \mathbb{G}^{(i-1) \times k}$$

At this stage, the adversary can compute a forged signature for message $m^* = m_i$ as $(\mathbf{Y}^*)^\top = \boldsymbol{\alpha}^\top \mathbf{W}$ and it outputs the forgery $\mathbf{Y}^*$.

CORRECTNESS OF THE ATTACK. Let's assume for now that the adversary has output a forgery. Since $\mathbf{c}(i) = \sum_j \alpha_j \mathbf{c}(j)$, where $\mathbf{c}(j)$ was defined as $\mathbf{c}(i) = [\mathbf{a}_{1*}(vk, m_i)^\top | \dots | \mathbf{a}_{\ell*}(vk, m_i)^\top]^\top$, we have the following intermediary result:

$$\sum_{j=1}^{i-1} \left(\alpha_j \cdot A(vk, m_j) \right) = A(vk, m^*). \tag{4}$$

The forgery is an accepting signature, because:

$$
\begin{aligned}
B(vk)\mathbf{Y}^* &= B(vk)\mathbf{W}^\top \boldsymbol{\alpha} \\
&= \left(B(vk)\mathbf{Y}_{m_1} | \dots | B(vk)\mathbf{Y}_{m_{i-1}} \right) \cdot \boldsymbol{\alpha} \\
&\overset{(*)}{=} \left(A(vk, m_1)\mathbf{X} | \dots | A(vk, m_{i-1})\mathbf{X} \right) \cdot \boldsymbol{\alpha} \\
&= \sum_{j=1}^{i-1} \left(\alpha_j \cdot A(vk, m_j)\mathbf{X} \right) = \left(\sum_{j=1}^{i-1} \alpha_j \cdot A(vk, m_j) \right)\mathbf{X} \\
&= A(vk, m^*)\mathbf{X}.
\end{aligned}
$$

Equality $(*)$ holds because signatures $\mathbf{Y}_{m_j}$ are correct for all $j \in [i-1]$. We have shown that $A(vk, m)\mathbf{X} = B(vk)\mathbf{Y}^*$, which implies that the forgery is a valid signature. The last equation uses Eq. 4.

RUNNING TIME. The adversary can only compute a forgery if for some iteration i, it holds that $\mathbf{c}(i) \in \mathsf{ColumnSpace}(H(i-1))$. We show that this must occur after a polynomial number of iterations. From Lemma 13, we have that at least one of the following cases must hold:

1. The column rank of $H(i)$ is strictly larger than the rank of $H(i-1)$.
2. The rank is unchanged, so are the positions of the pivots, but at least one pivot of $H(i)$ decreases by at least a factor of 2. Furthermore, all other pivots are smaller than or equal to the previous ones, i.e. $h(i)_{n_j,j} \le h(i-1)_{n_j,j}$, for all $j \in [n]$.
3. Or $\mathbf{c}(i) \in \mathsf{ColumnSpace}(H(i-1))$.

Note that even though Lemma 13 is proven by reasoning about the inefficient algorithm AddColumn, since the HNF is unique, the proof also applies to poly-time HNF algorithms (Lemma 11). Therefore, at each iteration, we have the following possibilities:

1. The rank of $H(i)$ increases. This can only happen at most $n\ell$ times.
2. Column-rank and pivot positions are unchanged, but at least one pivot decreases by a factor of 2, while no other pivot increases. Since the HNF is applied on matrices $A(vk, m)$ with each entry bounded by $\tau_{\max}$, this can happen at most $|\tau_{\max}| \cdot n\ell$ times (we can have at most $n\ell$ pivots). The pivots become smaller by one bit, until they become 1, and do not decrease further.
3. It holds that $\mathbf{c}(i) \in \mathsf{ColumnSpace}(H(i-1))$, and we can forge a signature.

Therefore, this means that after at most $(n\ell)^2 \cdot |\tau_{\max}|$ iterations, we will end up in the third case, when $H(i) = [H(i-1)|\mathbf{0}]$ and we can compute a forgery. Since computing the HNF is a polynomial-time algorithm and the number of iterations is polynomial, this means that the adversary also runs in polynomial time.

Theorem 15 (Impossibility of Simplified Algebraic Signatures with UF-q-RMA Security). *Let* SIG *be a simplified algebraic signature scheme with parameters $n, k, \ell \in \mathbb{N}$ over group $\mathbb{G}$ of (possibly) unknown order N, and let Q_S be defined as in Theorem 14. There exists a PPT adversary $\mathcal{A}$ with*

$$Adv_{\mathcal{A},\mathsf{SIG}}^{\mathsf{UF}\text{-}Q_S\text{-}\mathsf{RMA}}(\lambda) = \frac{1}{Q_S+1}$$

The proof of Theorem 15 can be found in the full version of this paper [20].

Remark 16. We can also consider a slight generalization of Definition 8 to account for the additional element t from Definition 5. Specifically, we could allow verification to check equations of the form:

$$A(vk, m, t) \cdot \mathbf{X} = B(vk) \cdot \mathbf{Y}.$$

The value $t \in \{0,1\}^\kappa$ is then part of the signature. Note that unlike in Definition 5, matrices B are not allowed to depend on t here. Our attack can be generalized to this setting and remains in polynomial-time, as long as $\kappa = O(\log(\lambda))$.

5 Extension: BLS Signatures Instantiated with Algebraic Hash Functions Are Insecure

It is well-known that Waters' hash function [13,52] (which is prominently used in his signature scheme from [52] to imitate useful features of a random oracle) cannot be used to securely implement the random oracle in the Boneh-Lynn-Shacham signature scheme [11]. Intuitively, the reason for this is that Waters' hash function has certain algebraic properties that, e.g., make it easy to find distinct preimages A, B, C, D with $\mathsf{H}(A) + \mathsf{H}(B) - \mathsf{H}(C) = \mathsf{H}(D)$ (where addition and subtraction take place in the target domain of H, a cyclic group). These algebraic relations directly translate to simple algebraic relations among BLS signatures, which can be exploited as in Sect. 3.3.

In this section, we generalize this observation and show that BLS signatures [11] cannot be securely implemented with *any* "algebraic" standard-model hash function (such as a programmable hash function [28]).

Definition 17 (Algebraic hash function). *An algebraic hash function over a group $\mathbb{G}$ and with message space $\mathcal{M}$ consists of two PPT algorithms:*

- *A key generation algorithm* HGen *that outputs an evaluation key hk. We assume that hk specifies a vector* $\mathbf{X} = (X_1, \ldots, X_n)^\mathsf{T} \in \mathbb{G}^n$ *of group elements.*
- *An evaluation algorithm* Eval *that, on input hk and* $m \in \mathcal{M}$, *outputs a hash value*

$$\mathsf{H}_{hk}(m) = A(hk, m)^\mathsf{T} \cdot \mathbf{X} \in \mathbb{G}$$

for a public and efficiently computable function A with output in $\mathbb{Z}^n$.

In a nutshell, algebraic hash functions construct their output through generic group operations from a sequence $\mathbf{X}$ of public group elements (defined in the hashing key hk). Popular constructions of programmable hash functions (e.g., [27,28,52] are algebraic hash functions.

In this section, we want to show that the attack in Theorem 14 can be adjusted to also work against another type of signatures, which we refer to as plain algebraic signatures in pairing groups. This class of signatures generalizes the BLS signature when the BLS hash function is modelled as an algebraic hash function. What is different from Definition 8, is that Definition 18 supports verification equations which apply a pairing operation on certain elements of the verification key along with other parts of the verification key. In particular, this means that the signature can consist of group elements whose implicit exponents correspond to quadratic relations in the implicit exponents of the group elements in the verification key.

Definition 18 (Plain Algebraic Signatures in Pairing Groups). *Let λ denote the security parameter and $\mathcal{G} = (\mathbb{G}, \mathbb{G}_T, N, P, e)$ be a symmetric pairing group of order $N \in \mathbb{N}$ (that may or may not be known, with N having $O(\lambda)$ bits). Consider also* (HGen, Eval) *to be an algebraic hash function. A plain algebraic signature scheme* SIG *over $\mathcal{G}$ with parameters $k, \gamma \in \mathbb{N}$ (polynomial in λ) is a digital signature scheme with the following structural properties.*

- *There exist efficiently computable functions* $A : \{0,1\}^* \times \mathcal{M} \rightarrow \mathbb{Z}_N^{\gamma \times 1}$ *and* $B : \{0,1\}^* \rightarrow \mathbb{Z}_N^{1 \times k}$. *If m is clear, we write* $A := A(hk, m)$ *and* $B := B(vk)$ *respectively.*
- KeyGen(1^λ) *outputs a keypair (vk, sk) with* $sk \in \{0,1\}^*$ *and*

$$vk = (X, \mathbf{X}^{hk}) = (X, (X_1^{hk}, \ldots, X_\gamma^{hk})^\top) \in \mathbb{G} \times \mathbb{G}^\gamma,$$

where $hk := \mathbf{X}^{hk}$ *is the hash key of the algebraic hash function, generated using the* HGen *algorithm.*
- Sign(sk, m) *outputs a signature σ, with:*

$$\sigma = (\mathbf{Y} = (Y_1, \ldots, Y_k)^\top) \in \mathbb{G}^k.$$

- Verify(vk, m, σ) *returns 1 iff*

$$e(\mathsf{H}_{hk}(m), X) = e(A(hk, m)^\intercal \cdot \mathbf{X}^{hk}, X) = e(P, B(vk) \cdot \mathbf{Y}).$$

The result in Theorem 14 extends to the signatures in Definition 18:

Theorem 19 (Impossibility of Plain Algebraic Signatures in Pairing Groups, with UF-CMA Security). *Let* SIG *be a plain algebraic signature scheme in pairing groups with parameters* $\lambda, k, \gamma \in \mathbb{N}$ *over a symmetric pairing group* $(\mathbb{G}, \mathbb{G}_T, e)$ *of (possibly) unknown order N and message space superpolynomial in λ. Then there exists a PPT adversary $\mathcal{A}$ with*

$$Adv_{\mathcal{A},\mathsf{SIG}}^{UF\text{-}CMA}(\lambda) = 1$$

The adversary makes at most $Q_S = \gamma^2 \cdot |\tau_{max}|$ *signature queries, where* $|\tau_{max}|$ *is the bitlength of the largest entry in the matrices $A(hk, m)$ for the messages that will be queried (we have* $|\tau_{max}| = \mathrm{poly}(\gamma \log(N) + |m|)$*). In addition, $|\mathcal{M}|$ does not have to be superpolynomial, it suffices to require* $|\mathcal{M}| \geq Q_S + 1$.

Letting T_{linear} *denote an upper bound on the run-time of all invocations of the polynomial-time HNF algorithm and* T_{max} *be an upper-bound on the polynomial running time of functions A, our attack runs in* $O(Q_S \cdot (T_{\text{max}} + T_{\text{linear}})) = O\left(\gamma^2 \cdot |\tau_{\text{max}}| \cdot (T_{\text{max}} + T_{\text{linear}})\right)$.

Proof Sketch. As in the proof of Theorem 14, the adversary iteratively obtains signatures for many messages $m_1 \ldots m_i$ and constructs an HNF matrix describing the column space generated by column vectors $A(hk, m_1)^\top \ldots A(hk, m_i)^\top$. Since $A(hk, m)$ is a row vector, the goal is to find a message m^* with $A(hk, m^*)^\top \in$ ColumnSpace$(A(hk, m_1)^\top | \ldots | A(hk, m_i)^\top)$ and to retrieve an integer vector $\alpha \in \mathbb{Z}^i$, such that $A(hk, m^*) = \sum_{j=1}^i \alpha_j A(hk, m_i)$. The forgery signature $\mathbf{Y}^*$ is then computed as $\mathbf{Y}^* = \sum_{j=1}^i \alpha_j \mathbf{Y}_j$. Let us check that this indeed satisfies correctness:

$$e\left(A(hk, m^*)^\top \cdot \mathbf{X}^{hk}, X\right) = e\left(\sum_{j=1}^i \alpha_j A(hk, m_i)^\top \cdot \mathbf{X}^{hk}, X\right) =$$

$$\overset{\text{Correctness of } \mathbf{Y}_j}{=} \sum_{j=1}^i \alpha_j e(P, B(vk) \cdot \mathbf{Y}_j) = e(P, B(vk) \cdot \mathbf{Y}^*)$$

Arguing that the algorithm succeeds in forging after Q_S iterations is identical to the reasoning in Theorem 14.

BLS SIGNATURES. In the following, we will prove a result about the BLS signature scheme [11]. We will not formally define BLS signatures, since it will only be important which signatures are considered valid by BLS. In the BLS scheme, public keys are of the form $vk := X = x \cdot P \in \mathbb{G}$ for a group $\mathbb{G}$ of order p generated by P, and uniformly random $x \in \mathbb{Z}_p$. We also assume a hash function H, whose parameters may be added to vk if the function is parameterized. Valid signatures for a message m are of the form

$$\sigma = x \cdot \mathsf{H}(m).$$

BLS signatures consist of only one group element Y, and verification is performed by a pairing operation:
$$e(\mathsf{H}(m), X) = e(P, Y).$$

Boneh, Lynn, and Shacham [11] prove that if the used hash function H is modeled as a random oracle, then their scheme is UF-CMA secure under the computational Diffie-Hellman assumption in $\mathbb{G}$. In contrast, we prove that if H is algebraic (in the sense of Definition 17), then the scheme is insecure:

Theorem 20. *When implemented with an algebraic hash function H, the BLS scheme described above is UF-q-RMA-insecure for a polynomial $q = q(\gamma)$ in the number of public group elements of H.*

To show Theorem 20, observe that BLS (when implemented with an algebraic hash function), is a plain signature in the sense of Definition 18. Hence, Theorem 20 follows Theorem 19. Furthermore, if the order p of the used group G is prime, then tracing the steps of our attack actually shows that $q(\gamma) \leq \gamma + 1$.

Remark 21 (Waters Signatures). Note that Waters signatures [52] make use of programmable hash functions and symmetric pairing groups, and are known to be secure in the standard model. The attack in Theorem 19 does not extend to Waters signatures, because their verification equation pairs $\mathsf{H}(m)$ with parts of the signature, which is not allowed in Definition 18.

Remark 22 (Further generalization of plain and simplified algebraic signatures). We could also consider a definition of signature that captures the verification equations in both Definition 8 and Definition 18. By adjusting our attacks to concatenate the $A(hk, m)$ vectors from Definition 18 to the $\mathbf{c}(i)$ vectors of the attack in Theorem 14, one can obtain an attack against this slightly generalized signature class.

Acknowledgements. We thank Mark Zhandry and the anonymous reviewers for their helpful comments. Nico Döttling was supported by the Helmholtz Association within the project "Trustworthy Federated Data Analytics" (TFDA) (funding number ZT-I-OO1 4). Dennis Hofheinz and Bogdan Ursu were supported in part by ERC grant 724307. Dominik Hartmann was supported by the Deutsche Forschungsgemeinschaft

(DFG, German Research Foundation) under German's Excellence Strategy - EXC 2092 CASA - 390781972, and the German Federal Ministry of Education and Research (BMBF) iBlockchain project. Eike Kiltz was supported by the BMBF iBlockchain project, the EU H2020 PROMETHEUS project 780701, DFG SPP 1736 Big Data, and by the Deutsche Forschungsgemeinschaft (DFG, German research Foundation) as part of the Excellence Strategy of the German Federal and State Governments – EXC 2092 CASA - 390781972. Sven Schäge was supported by the German Federal Ministry of Education and Research (BMBF), Project DigiSeal (16KIS0695) and Huawei Technologies Düsseldorf, Project vHSM. Part of this work was done while Sven Schäge was at Ruhr-University Bochum.

References

1. Abe, M., Ambrona, M., Ohkubo, M., Tibouchi, M.: Lower bounds on structure-preserving signatures for bilateral messages. In: Catalano, D., De Prisco, R. (eds.) SCN 2018. LNCS, vol. 11035, pp. 3–22. Springer, Cham (2018). https://doi.org/10.1007/978-3-319-98113-0_1

2. Abe, M., Groth, J., Haralambiev, K., Ohkubo, M.: Optimal structure-preserving signatures in asymmetric bilinear groups. In: Rogaway, P. (ed.) CRYPTO 2011. LNCS, vol. 6841, pp. 649–666. Springer, Heidelberg (2011). https://doi.org/10.1007/978-3-642-22792-9_37

3. W.A. Adkins, S.H. Weintraub, J.H. Ewing, F.W. Gehring, and P.R. Halmos. Algebra: An Approach Via Module Theory. Graduate Texts in Mathematics. Springer, New York (1992). https://doi.org/10.1007/978-1-4612-0923-2

4. Barak, B., Mahmoody-Ghidary, M.: Lower bounds on signatures from symmetric primitives. In: 48th Annual Symposium on Foundations of Computer Science, pp. 680–688, Providence, RI, USA, 20–23 October, IEEE Computer Society Press (2007)

5. Bellare, M., Rogaway, P.: Random oracles are practical: a paradigm for designing efficient protocols. In: Denning, D.E., Pyle, R., Ganesan, R., Sandhu, R.S., Ashby, V. (eds.), ACM CCS 93: 1st Conference on Computer and Communications Security, pp. 62–73, Fairfax, Virginia, USA, 3–5 November 1993, ACM Press (1993)

6. Bitansky, N., Paneth, O.: On the impossibility of approximate obfuscation and applications to resettable cryptography. In: Boneh, D., Roughgarden, T., Feigenbaum, J. (eds.), 45th Annual ACM Symposium on Theory of Computing, pp. 241–250, Palo Alto, CA, USA, 1–4 June 2013, ACM Press (2013)

7. Boneh, D., Bonneau, J., Bünz, B., Fisch, B.: Verifiable delay functions. In: Shacham, H., Boldyreva, A. (eds.) CRYPTO 2018. LNCS, vol. 10991, pp. 757–788. Springer, Cham (2018). https://doi.org/10.1007/978-3-319-96884-1_25

8. Boneh, D., Boyen, X.: Short signatures without random oracles. In: Cachin, C., Camenisch, J.L. (eds.) EUROCRYPT 2004. LNCS, vol. 3027, pp. 56–73. Springer, Heidelberg (2004). https://doi.org/10.1007/978-3-540-24676-3_4

9. Boneh, D., Boyen, X., Shacham, H.: Short group signatures. In: Franklin, M. (ed.) CRYPTO 2004. LNCS, vol. 3152, pp. 41–55. Springer, Heidelberg (2004). https://doi.org/10.1007/978-3-540-28628-8_3

10. Boneh, D., Franklin, M.: Identity-based encryption from the Weil pairing. In: Kilian, J. (ed.) CRYPTO 2001. LNCS, vol. 2139, pp. 213–229. Springer, Heidelberg (2001). https://doi.org/10.1007/3-540-44647-8_13

11. Boneh, D., Lynn, B., Shacham, H.: Short signatures from the Weil pairing. In: Boyd, C. (ed.) ASIACRYPT 2001. LNCS, vol. 2248, pp. 514–532. Springer, Heidelberg (2001). https://doi.org/10.1007/3-540-45682-1_30
12. Boneh, D., Papakonstantinou, P.A., Rackoff, C., Vahlis, Y., Waters, B.: On the impossibility of basing identity based encryption on trapdoor permutations. In: 49th Annual Symposium on Foundations of Computer Science, pp. 283–292, Philadelphia, PA, USA, 25–28 October 2008, IEEE Computer Society Press (2008)
13. Chaum, D., Evertse, J.-H., van de Graaf, J.: An improved protocol for demonstrating possession of discrete logarithms and some generalizations. In: Chaum, D., Price, W.L. (eds.) EUROCRYPT 1987. LNCS, vol. 304, pp. 127–141. Springer, Heidelberg (1988). https://doi.org/10.1007/3-540-39118-5_13
14. Chen, Y., Lombardi, A., Ma, F., Quach, W.: Does fiat-shamir require a cryptographic hash function? Cryptology ePrint Archive, Report 2020/915 (2020). https://eprint.iacr.org/2020/915
15. Cocks, C.: An identity based encryption scheme based on quadratic residues. In: Honary, B. (ed.) Cryptography and Coding 2001. LNCS, vol. 2260, pp. 360–363. Springer, Heidelberg (2001). https://doi.org/10.1007/3-540-45325-3_32
16. Cramer, R., Shoup, V.: A practical public key cryptosystem provably secure against adaptive chosen ciphertext attack. In: Krawczyk, H. (ed.) CRYPTO 1998. LNCS, vol. 1462, pp. 13–25. Springer, Heidelberg (1998). https://doi.org/10.1007/BFb0055717
17. Cramer, R., Shoup, V.: Signature schemes based on the strong RSA assumption. In: Motiwalla, J., Tsudik, G. (eds.), ACM CCS 99: 6th Conference on Computer and Communications Security, pp. 46–51. Singapore, 1–4 November 1999. ACM Press (1999)
18. Cramer, R., Shoup, V.: Universal hash proofs and a paradigm for adaptive chosen ciphertext secure public-key encryption. In: Knudsen, L.R. (ed.) EUROCRYPT 2002. LNCS, vol. 2332, pp. 45–64. Springer, Heidelberg (2002). https://doi.org/10.1007/3-540-46035-7_4
19. Döttling, N., Garg, S.: Identity-based encryption from the Diffie-Hellman assumption. In: Katz, J., Shacham, H. (eds.) CRYPTO 2017. LNCS, vol. 10401, pp. 537–569. Springer, Cham (2017). https://doi.org/10.1007/978-3-319-63688-7_18
20. Döttling, N., Hartmann, D., Hofheinz, D., Kiltz, E., Schäge, S., Ursu, B.: On the Impossibility of Purely Algebraic Signatures. Cryptology ePrint Archive, Report 2021/738 (2021). https://ia.cr/2021/738
21. ElGamal, T.: A public key cryptosystem and a signature scheme based on discrete logarithms. In: Blakley, G.R., Chaum, D. (eds.) CRYPTO 1984. LNCS, vol. 196, pp. 10–18. Springer, Heidelberg (1985). https://doi.org/10.1007/3-540-39568-7_2
22. Frumkin, M.A.: Polynomial time algorithms in the theory of linear Diophantine equations. In: Karpiński, M. (ed.) FCT 1977. LNCS, vol. 56, pp. 386–392. Springer, Heidelberg (1977). https://doi.org/10.1007/3-540-08442-8_106
23. Gennaro, R., Gertner, Y., Katz, J., Trevisan, L.: Bounds on the efficiency of generic cryptographic constructions. SIAM J. Comput. **35**(1), 217–246 (2005)
24. Gerbush, M., Lewko, A., O'Neill, A., Waters, B.: Dual form signatures: an approach for proving security from static assumptions. In: Wang, X., Sako, K. (eds.) ASIACRYPT 2012. LNCS, vol. 7658, pp. 25–42. Springer, Heidelberg (2012). https://doi.org/10.1007/978-3-642-34961-4_4
25. Ghadafi, E.: further lower bounds for structure-preserving signatures in asymmetric bilinear groups. In: Buchmann, J., Nitaj, A., Rachidi, T. (eds.) AFRICACRYPT 2019. LNCS, vol. 11627, pp. 409–428. Springer, Cham (2019). https://doi.org/10.1007/978-3-030-23696-0_21

26. Ghadafi, E.: Partially structure-preserving signatures: Lower bounds, constructions and more. IACR ePrint Archive, report 2020/477 (2020). http://eprint.iacr.org/2020/477

27. Hofheinz, D., Jager, T., Kiltz, E.: Short signatures from weaker assumptions. In: Lee, D.H., Wang, X. (eds.) ASIACRYPT 2011. LNCS, vol. 7073, pp. 647–666. Springer, Heidelberg (2011). https://doi.org/10.1007/978-3-642-25385-0_35

28. Hofheinz, D., Kiltz, E.: Programmable hash functions and their applications. In: Wagner, D. (ed.) CRYPTO 2008. LNCS, vol. 5157, pp. 21–38. Springer, Heidelberg (2008). https://doi.org/10.1007/978-3-540-85174-5_2

29. Hofheinz, D., Kiltz, E., Shoup, V.: Practical chosen ciphertext secure encryption from factoring. J. Cryptology **26**(1), 102–118 (2013)

30. Hohenberger, S., Waters, B.: Short and stateless signatures from the RSA assumption. In: Halevi, S. (ed.) CRYPTO 2009. LNCS, vol. 5677, pp. 654–670. Springer, Heidelberg (2009). https://doi.org/10.1007/978-3-642-03356-8_38

31. Impagliazzo, R., Rudich, S.: Limits on the provable consequences of one-way permutations. In: 21st Annual ACM Symposium on Theory of Computing, pp. 44–61, Seattle, WA, USA, 15–17 May 1989, ACM Press (1989)

32. Impagliazzo, R., Rudich, S.: Limits on the provable consequences of one-way permutations. In: Goldwasser, S. (ed.) CRYPTO 1988. LNCS, vol. 403, pp. 8–26. Springer, New York (1990). https://doi.org/10.1007/0-387-34799-2_2

33. Katz, J., Wang, N.: Efficiency improvements for signature schemes with tight security reductions. In: Jajodia, S., Atluri, V., Jaeger, T. (eds.), ACM CCS 2003: 10th Conference on Computer and Communications Security, pp. 155–164, Washington, DC, USA, 27–30 October 2003, ACM Press (2003)

34. Kurosawa, K., Desmedt, Y.: A new paradigm of hybrid encryption scheme. In: Franklin, M. (ed.) CRYPTO 2004. LNCS, vol. 3152, pp. 426–442. Springer, Heidelberg (2004). https://doi.org/10.1007/978-3-540-28628-8_26

35. Lamport, L.: Constructing digital signatures from a one way function. Technical report, October 1979

36. Mahmoody, M., Mohammed, A., Nematihaji, S.: On the impossibility of virtual black-box obfuscation in idealized models. In: Kushilevitz, E., Malkin, T. (eds.) TCC 2016. LNCS, vol. 9562, pp. 18–48. Springer, Heidelberg (2016). https://doi.org/10.1007/978-3-662-49096-9_2

37. Maurer, U.M.: Towards the equivalence of breaking the Diffie-Hellman protocol and computing discrete logarithms. In: Desmedt, Y.G. (ed.) CRYPTO 1994. LNCS, vol. 839, pp. 271–281. Springer, Heidelberg (1994). https://doi.org/10.1007/3-540-48658-5_26

38. Maurer, U.: Abstract models of computation in cryptography. In: Smart, N.P. (ed.) Cryptography and Coding 2005. LNCS, vol. 3796, pp. 1–12. Springer, Heidelberg (2005). https://doi.org/10.1007/11586821_1

39. Merkle, R.C.: A digital signature based on a conventional encryption function. In: Pomerance, C. (ed.) CRYPTO 1987. LNCS, vol. 293, pp. 369–378. Springer, Heidelberg (1988). https://doi.org/10.1007/3-540-48184-2_32

40. Micciancio, D., Warinschi, B.: A linear space algorithm for computing the hermite normal form. In: Proceedings of the 2001 International Symposium on Symbolic and Algebraic Computation, ISSAC 2001, pp. 231–236, New York, Association for Computing Machinery (2001)

41. Naor, M., Yung, M.: Universal one-way hash functions and their cryptographic applications. In: 21st Annual ACM Symposium on Theory of Computing, pp. 33–43, Seattle, WA, USA, 15–17 May 1989, ACM Press (1989)

42. Papakonstantinou, P.A., Rackoff, C., Vahlis, Y.: How powerful are the DDH hard groups? Electron. Colloquium Comput. Complex. **19**, 167 (2012)
43. Pass, R., Shelat, A.: Impossibility of VBB obfuscation with ideal constant-degree graded encodings. In: Kushilevitz, E., Malkin, T. (eds.) TCC 2016. LNCS, vol. 9562, pp. 3–17. Springer, Heidelberg (2016). https://doi.org/10.1007/978-3-662-49096-9_1
44. Pietrzak, K.: Simple verifiable delay functions. In: Blum, A. (ed), ITCS 2019: 10th Innovations in Theoretical Computer Science Conference, vol. 124, pp. 60:1–60:15, San Diego, CA, USA, 10–12 January 2019, LIPIcs (2019)
45. Rompel, J.: One-way functions are necessary and sufficient for secure signatures. In: 22nd Annual ACM Symposium on Theory of Computing, pp. 387–394, Baltimore, MD, USA, 14–16 May 1990, ACM Press (1990)
46. Rotem, L., Segev, G., Shahaf, I.: Generic-group delay functions require hidden-order groups. In: Canteaut, A., Ishai, Y. (eds.) EUROCRYPT 2020. LNCS, vol. 12107, pp. 155–180. Springer, Cham (2020). https://doi.org/10.1007/978-3-030-45727-3_6
47. Schnorr, C.P.: Efficient identification and signatures for smart cards. In: Brassard, G. (ed.) CRYPTO 1989. LNCS, vol. 435, pp. 239–252. Springer, New York (1990). https://doi.org/10.1007/0-387-34805-0_22
48. Schrijver, A.: Theory of Linear and Integer Programming. Wiley Series in Discrete Mathematics & Optimization. Wiley, Hoboken (1998)
49. Schul-Ganz, G., Segev, G.: Generic-group identity-based encryption: A tight impossibility result. Information-Theoretic Cryptography (2021)
50. Shamir, A.: Identity-based cryptosystems and signature schemes. In: Blakley, G.R., Chaum, D. (eds.) CRYPTO 1984. LNCS, vol. 196, pp. 47–53. Springer, Heidelberg (1985). https://doi.org/10.1007/3-540-39568-7_5
51. Shoup, V.: Lower Bounds for Discrete Logarithms and Related Problems. In: Fumy, W. (ed.) EUROCRYPT 1997. LNCS, vol. 1233, pp. 256–266. Springer, Heidelberg (1997). https://doi.org/10.1007/3-540-69053-0_18
52. Waters, B.: Efficient identity-based encryption without random oracles. In: Cramer, R. (ed.) EUROCRYPT 2005. LNCS, vol. 3494, pp. 114–127. Springer, Heidelberg (2005). https://doi.org/10.1007/11426639_7
53. Wesolowski, B.: Efficient verifiable delay functions. In: Ishai, Y., Rijmen, V. (eds.) EUROCRYPT 2019. LNCS, vol. 11478, pp. 379–407. Springer, Cham (2019). https://doi.org/10.1007/978-3-030-17659-4_13
54. Zhandry, M., Zhang, C.: Impossibility of order-revealing encryption in idealized models. In: Beimel, A., Dziembowski, S. (eds.) TCC 2018. LNCS, vol. 11240, pp. 129–158. Springer, Cham (2018). https://doi.org/10.1007/978-3-030-03810-6_5
55. Zhandry, M., Zhang, C.: The relationship between idealized models under computationally bounded adversaries. Cryptology ePrint Archive, Report 2021/240 (2021). https://eprint.iacr.org/2021/240

Policy-Compliant Signatures

Christian Badertscher[1] , Christian Matt[2] , and Hendrik Waldner[3(✉)]

[1] IOHK, Zurich, Switzerland
christian.badertscher@iohk.io
[2] Concordium, Zurich, Switzerland
cm@concordium.com
[3] University of Edinburgh, Edinburgh, Scotland
hendrik.waldner@ed.ac.uk

Abstract. We introduce *policy-compliant signatures (PCS)*. A PCS scheme can be used in a setting where a central authority determines a global policy and distributes public and secret keys associated with sets of attributes to the users in the system. If two users, Alice and Bob, have attribute sets that jointly satisfy the global policy, Alice can use her secret key and Bob's public key to sign a message. *Unforgeability* ensures that a valid signature can only be produced if Alice's secret key is known and if the policy is satisfied. *Privacy* guarantees that the public keys and produced signatures reveal nothing about the users' attributes beyond whether they satisfy the policy or not. PCS extends the functionality provided by existing primitives such as attribute-based signatures and policy-based signatures, which do not consider a designated receiver and thus cannot include the receiver's attributes in the policies. We describe practical applications of PCS which include controlling transactions in financial systems with strong privacy guarantees (avoiding additional trusted entities that check compliance), as well as being a tool for trust negotiations.

We introduce an indistinguishability-based privacy notion for PCS and present a generic and modular scheme based on standard building blocks such as signatures, non-interactive zero-knowledge proofs, and a (predicate-only) predicate encryption scheme. We show that it can be instantiated to obtain an efficient scheme that is provably secure under standard pairing-assumptions for a wide range of policies.

We further model PCS in UC by describing the goal of PCS as an enhanced ideal signature functionality which gives rise to a simulation-based privacy notion for PCS. We show that our generic scheme achieves this composable security notion under the additional assumption that the underlying predicate encryption scheme satisfies a stronger, fully adaptive, simulation-based attribute-hiding notion.

1 Introduction

Digital signatures provide authenticity to messages in the sense that everyone can verify that a signed message was indeed signed by a specific sender, and

© International Association for Cryptologic Research 2021
K. Nissim and B. Waters (Eds.): TCC 2021, LNCS 13044, pp. 350–381, 2021.
https://doi.org/10.1007/978-3-030-90456-2_12

not modified afterwards. Attribute-based signatures [26] and policy-based signatures [4] extend this concept by introducing policies that the sender needs to satisfy to generate a valid signature. We take this one step further and introduce *policy-compliant signatures (PCS)* with policies that take into account attributes of both, the sender and the receiver. This is useful in settings where messages have a designated receiver. A prevalent example of such a setting are blockchain applications, in which a sender signs a transaction sending funds to a given receiver. If such a system is used within a corporation and PCS are used for generating these signatures, the company can set a policy, restricting who can send funds to whom.

In more detail, a PCS scheme allows a central authority to generate a master public key and a master secret key for a given policy. The authority can then use the master secret key to generate public/private key pairs associated with a set of attributes. The signer Alice then uses her private signing key and the receiver Bob's public key to create a signature for a message. The signature can be publicly verified using all public keys. It is only valid if Alice's and Bob's attributes together satisfy the global policy.

Security Requirements. Unforgeability of ordinary signature schemes ensures that valid signatures cannot be produced without knowledge of the secret key, and that signed messages cannot be modified without invalidating the signature. The unforgeability notion of PCS additionally requires that even with access to the secret key, it should not be possible for a malicious sender to craft a valid signature if the policy is not satisfied by the sender and the receiver.

In addition to unforgeability, PCS provide privacy for the sender's and receiver's attributes. Our privacy notion captures three different attack scenarios: First, outsiders only seeing the public keys and signatures between two parties should not learn anything about the attributes of these parties beyond the fact whether they satisfy the policy. Secondly, a (possibly malicious) sender should not learn anything about the receiver's attributes except whether their attributes satisfy the policy. And finally, a (possibly malicious) receiver should not learn anything about the sender's attributes except whether their attributes satisfy the policy.

The Core Challenge to Obtain PCS. Consider the following attempt to obtain the functionality of a PCS scheme: A central authority is in charge of checking compliance of every single transaction by ensuring that whenever a sender S with attributes x sends a message to a receiver R with attributes x^*, the policy specified by $F(x, x^*)$ is satisfied. While conceptually simple, it does not satisfy our needs: One goal of PCS is to avoid a central authority assisting in the signature generation and verification because this results in a central point of failure in the execution of the system. Stated differently, the authority shall only be used to issue the credentials but the (non-interactive) signature generation and verification must be possible only with the public values associated to the receiver and the secret values of the sender.

In a second attempt, we let the authority issue ordinary signature key pairs (pk, sk) and a certificate of the respective attributes C_x to each participant in the system. To send a message m, a sender S signs the message m and proves, using a non-interactive zero-knowledge proof, that the attributes associated with the certificates of the sender and the receiver satisfy the policy $F(x, x^*)$. This second attempt looks more appealing, but it has the drawback that the sender must be aware of the recipient's attributes since otherwise no proof can be generated about the compliance with attributes not owned by the sender—especially if the certificate C_{x^*} is supposed to (computationally) hide the attributes of the receiver.[1]

We see that the main challenge to obtain PCS is to ensure that only valid signatures can be generated by a sender without a trusted authority assisting in the signature generation while the attributes of any entity in the system are hidden at any time, even from the sender. At first sight, this appears contradictory as it excludes any solution where the sender "proves" a joint statement including a receiver, using only public information about the receiver, which hides the receiver's attributes. The key idea to overcome this issue is to employ a specific form of predicate encryption that allows every participant to only learn a single bit of information upon generating a signature. This single leaked bit is $F(x, x^*)$ and the process does not leak anything beyond this evaluation. We additionally show that this specific form of predicate encryption is in fact *necessary* to obtain PCS.

1.1   Applications of PCS

Applications to Financial Payment Systems. PCS can be used in all settings in which messages are sent to designated receivers and a global policy about the senders and receivers needs to be publicly verifiable. This naturally occurs in financial transactions, such as paying online services when purchasing, for example, digital content (such as movies) or services (such as online games or lotteries) that are region-dependent or age restricted. Typically, such services require additional authentication upon payment such as identity card information through scanning or manual input. PCS signatures can merge the act of authentication with the basic task of signing a transaction. A policy can be expressed as a list of requirements for say n categories of services S_i. For age and/or country restrictions, a policy might be given by $(\text{Age} \geq 18 \wedge S_1) \vee (\text{Age} \geq 16 \wedge \text{Country} = \text{CH} \wedge S_2) \vee \dots$. Assume Alice obtained a key-pair from a credential management entity that is tied to her country of residence (akin to obtaining an ID card), and each service of Bob is assigned the correct category (identified also by a PCS public key for credential S_i). Then the payment system needs no additional check of the policy if the transactions are signed using a PCS scheme.

---

[1] For the same reason, attempts to derive PCS in a black-box way from existing policy-based primitives fail (cf. Section 1.3) because they would require to implement a policy only based on the public key of the receiver, which does not allow to efficiently obtain their attributes.

If a transaction is successful, (an honest) Bob can be sure that the client had access to appropriate private credentials. Thanks to the public verifiability, the transaction can be validated by an external auditor and by the attribute hiding property of PCS the exact combination of client attributes and service is not leaked (to the auditor) by the signature system.

Furthermore, in blockchain systems such as Bitcoin [28], a transaction transferring funds from a sender Alice to a receiver Bob contains a signature from Alice on the transaction details. Before adding such a transaction to a new block, the miners verify the validity of the transaction including the signature. When the used signature scheme is replaced by a PCS scheme, such transactions are only valid if the global policy allows Alice to send funds to Bob. This can be useful if the blockchain is used in a corporate environment where the money flow needs to be restricted in certain ways, e.g., defined by a legal system. Imagining a toy example, one could define a new company-wide digital token T with address format $addr = (pk_{\mathrm{pcs}}, \ldots)$. A transaction transferring tokens T from $addr_A$ to $addr_B$ can only be valid if a (publicly verifiable) PCS signature confirms this transaction. By issuing credentials to employees and to facilities (such as canteens) within the company, and defining the policy to steer token flow (e.g., employees are allowed to exchange tokens or consume the tokens at company facilities), such tokens can be bound to a specific purpose at the sole cost of having to verify PCS signatures and address formats. The security of PCS makes it impossible for any sender to violate the company policy, both by accident or malice. This renders other compliance checks for this policy obsolete, such as techniques that are only triggered after suspicious transactions are observed and that often result in a complete revocation of a user's privacy [9,15]. The attribute-hiding property of PCS further ensures that no information about the attributes of the transacting entities beyond that they satisfy the policy is revealed by the signatures and addresses (in the above toy example, we would not reveal whether it is a transaction between employees or between an employee and a facility). Thanks to this, the pseudonymity of the used blockchain system is preserved.

Applications to Trust Negotiations. Another application of PCS are trust-negotiation systems [19,25]. Assume Alice and Bob work for an intelligence agency and need to exchange secret information. Further assume these agencies have a policy on who is allowed to exchange information with whom, e.g., based on the divisions and ranks of the involved parties as in role-based access control systems. In [25], the example assumes Alice has top-level clearance and before sending a message M, she must make sure that Bob also has top-level clearance. In the language of [25], what PCS brings to this setting is a simple implementation of the following two-party protocol: The common input are the access-control policy F (defined on the space of party credentials), and the agency's public parameters pp_{agency} (equivalent to a company-wide public-key infrastructure). Alice's private inputs are her message M and her credentials $cred_A$, and Bob's private input is his credentials $cred_B$. The output out_A of Alice and out_B of Bob are defined to be

$$out_A = \begin{cases} 1, & \text{if } F(cred_A, cred_B) \\ 0, & \text{otherwise} \end{cases} \qquad out_B = \begin{cases} M, & \text{if } F(cred_A, cred_B) \\ \bot, & \text{otherwise} \end{cases}.$$

Assuming the agency has set up the public-key infrastructure, the above functionality is realized as follows: Alice encrypts the message M with Bob's (encryption) public key and signs the corresponding ciphertext with a PCS scheme (using her secret signing key, and Bob's signature public key). If the resulting signature is valid, then Alice sends the packet to Bob and otherwise does not send the message. If the policy is satisfied, then Bob learns the message. Otherwise, Bob learns nothing. The PCS scheme itself does not leak anything beyond the fulfillment of the policy.

1.2   Our Contributions and Organization of this Paper

PCS Notion. As a conceptual contribution, we introduce the notion of PCS (see Section 3). In addition to the syntactical requirements, we define unforgeability (in Section 3.2). This includes policy enforcement, i.e., unforgeability ensures that a signature that verifies with respect to the public verification key of the sender A and the receiver B can only be produced when possessing the secret signing key of A and if the attributes of A and B satisfy the policy.

Furthermore, we define an indistinguishability-based attribute hiding notion (in Section 3.3). This notion intuitively guarantees that an adversary cannot distinguish public keys and signatures generated for different sets of attributes, as long as the policy does not separate them.

Generic Construction and Concrete Instantiation. We first provide an efficient generic construction of PCS from standard tools using digital signatures, (predicate-only) predicate encryption, and NIZK in Sect. 4. We show that relying on predicate-only PE is a tight fit for our goal in the sense that any PCS scheme gives rise to a related PE scheme. This settles an important feasibility question regarding constructions and efficiency for PCS in general.

Our generic construction is not only theoretically interesting, it also admits efficient instantiations (w.r.t. the indistinguishability-based attribute-hiding notion) based on standard pairing assumptions coupled with Groth-Sahai proofs for the rich class of predicates expressible by inner-products [22]. The policies that are realizable on top of the inner-product functionality range from CNF formulas and exact threshold clauses (with conjunctive or disjunctive clauses) to hidden-vector-encryption which in turn opens up the field for PCS to efficiently implement subset predicates, comparison predicates and their conjunctions as defined in [8].

Composable PCS and SIM-Based Notion. Finally, we cast PCS as an ideal, enhanced signature functionality in the spirit of [2,11] to model the ideal composable guarantees of PCS. We then derive a simpler simulation-based attribute hiding notion (in Section 5.1) and prove that an unforgeable and sim-based secure PCS scheme realizes the ideal signature functionality. By definition of the ideal system, the sim-based notion guarantees that everything an attacker can learn from the public keys and signatures can be efficiently produced by a simulator given only the public information and the information for which signatures the policy is satisfied. This allows to capture precisely which information is leaked by a PCS scheme. We show that our generic construction achieves this notion if the underlying PE scheme satisfies a related (fully adaptive) simulation-based notion, which is stronger than what has been considered in the literature so far, notably in [17].

1.3 Related Work

We provide an overview of cryptographic primitives which have been introduced in the context of attribute-based and policy-dependent constructions to shed light on the role and necessity of PCS in this space.

Attribute-Based Signatures and Policy-Based Signatures. Attribute-based signatures (ABS) [26] have similar goals to PCS: In an ABS scheme, an authority can generate secret signing keys associated to a set of attributes. The signer can then sign messages for some policy and the resulting signature is only valid if the signer's attributes satisfy the policy. Policy-based signatures [4] generalize this concept by allowing the policies to depend not only the sender's attributes but also on the signed messages. A clear distinction from PCS is that they do not allow the policies to depend on the receiver's attributes. Thus, the notions and security guarantees are very different.

Another difference between PCS and ABS is that an ABS scheme allows the sender to choose the policy for each message at the time of signing, whereas the policy in PCS schemes is fixed by the authority during the setup. This gives ABS more flexibility. Note, however, that allowing the sender to choose the policy in PCS schemes would be detrimental to our privacy guarantees: We want to protect the receiver's attributes even from malicious senders. Allowing the sender to choose many different policies and then verify the resulting signatures would allow a malicious sender to find the precise attributes of all receivers.

Finally, ABS provide an additional security guarantee that PCS do not offer, namely unlinkability of signatures. That is, given two signatures, one cannot determine whether they have been produced by the same signer; one only learns that somebody satisfying the policies signed. In a PCS scheme, this is not required since it is not needed for the applications we have in mind. For example, when used in a blockchain system providing pseudonymity, the signatures are anyway linked to the pseudonyms of the senders and receivers of transactions. Trying to hide the signer would thus not be useful in this context.

Designated Verifier Signatures. Designated verifier signatures have been introduced by Jakobsson et al. [21]. As in our setting, they consider signatures produced for a designated receiver. They require that only this receiver can verify the signatures. Furthermore, the receiver should not be able to convince others of the validity of such signatures. This is in contrast to PCS, which can be verified publicly. The setting and security requirements are thus very different.

Matchmaking Encryption. The high-level goals of PCS and matchmaking encryption (ME) introduced by Ateniese et al. [1] seem similar, but turn out to be quite distinctive due to the respective applications in mind. ME captures a non-interactive variant of a secret-handshake (with payload), that is, in addition to the functionality that PCS supports. In ME, the sender has the freedom to define the receiver's policy and the receiver can in addition to its private key (for the attributes), receive an additional policy decryption key that captures a policy on the sender's attributes under which the receiver is able to decrypt the ciphertext. These two receiver private keys can conceptually be merged into one single attribute-policy decryption key, which results in a seemingly simpler notion that is realizable from standard FE (capturing the policy as a specific function). This notion is dubbed arranged ME (A-ME).

In a nutshell, our unforgeability requirements are stronger and require that even if sender and receiver collude, they should not be able to produce a valid (publicly verifiable) signature (authenticity of ME is a guarantee for an honest receiver not to be fooled by a ciphertext of a sender that does not possess the required attributes). Second, the ME authenticity game does not provide an oracle to the adversary for computations on the private key, therefore disallowing all attacks that are based on malleable ciphertexts, which is problematic for our needs. This aspect also influences the obtained privacy guarantees. In the ME security game, the adversary only obtains a single value (the ciphertext) that is a function of the sender's secret key. For ME, this makes a lot of sense as it is used to replace a handshake with a single payload message. We, however, need a signing oracle and hence obtain strictly stronger privacy. For the sake of self-containment, we sketch an (A-)ME scheme which does not provide the attribute hiding property of PCS in the full version.

Finally, constructions of PCS for simple policies like CNF, conjunctions of equalities or comparisons, are in the standard model and have practical instantiations. In contrast, even for simple equality policies where the FE and randomized FE are not needed as building blocks, the constructions of [1] are in the random oracle model.

Access Control Encryption. The notion of access control encryption (ACE) [3,16] is a cryptographic primitive that allows to control the information flow within a system. ACE is not suitable to achieve the task we need. First, the system relies crucially on a third-party called the sanitizer which is a role that does not fit into our setting. Secondly, ACE only protects the information flow within the system (when running through a sanitizer), whereas in our system, corrupted parties might meet offline trying to generate a valid joint signature, which must be part of the attack model.

Predicate Encryption and Attribute-Based Encryption. Predicate encryption and attribute-based encryption allow decryption of ciphertexts only for users with secret keys matching a certain policy. While PCS are signatures and not encryption schemes, they are still related because of the required privacy notion. In particular, our indistinguishability-based and simulation-based attribute hiding properties are closely related to the respective notions for these encryption schemes.

The notion of predicate encryption has first been considered in [8,22]. In the work of Boneh and Waters [8], the authors construct a scheme that allows for comparison, subset and arbitrary conjunctive queries. In the succeeding work of Katz et al. [22], the authors present a scheme for the inner product functionality and the authors also observe that the inner product functionality is sufficient for polynomial predicate evaluations as well as DNF and CNF formulas. We mention more regarding the common policies of these schemes below. Since the results of Boneh and Waters [8] and Katz et al. [22], more works for the same functionality class have been proposed [29,30], as well as for the stronger notion of partially-hiding predicate encryption [17,31]. Partially-hiding predicate encryption is a generalization of predicate encryption in which the ciphertext is extended with public attributes. The function associated with the functional key is then first applied on the public information and the result is then used together with hidden attribute of the ciphertext.

2   Preliminaries

We denote the security parameter with $\lambda \in \mathbb{N}$ and use 1^λ as its unary representation. We call a randomized algorithm $\mathcal{A}$ *probabilistic polynomial time* (PPT) if there exists a polynomial $p(\cdot)$ such that for every input x the running time of $\mathcal{A}(x)$ is bounded by $p(|x|)$. A function $\mathrm{negl} : \mathbb{N} \to \mathbb{R}^+$ is called *negligible* if for every positive polynomial $p(\lambda)$, there exists $\lambda_0 \in \mathbb{N}$ such that for all $\lambda > \lambda_0 \colon \mathrm{negl}(\lambda) < 1/p(\lambda)$. If clear from the context, we sometimes omit λ for improved readability. The set $\{1, \ldots, n\}$ is denoted as $[n]$ for $n \in \mathbb{N}$. For the equality check of two elements, we use "=". The assign operator is denoted with ":=", whereas randomized assignment is denoted with $a \leftarrow A$, with a randomized algorithm A and where the randomness is not explicit. If the randomness is explicit, we write $a := A(x; r)$ where x is the input and r is the randomness. For algorithms $\mathcal{A}$ and $\mathcal{B}$, we write $\mathcal{A}^{\mathcal{B}(\cdot)}(x)$ to denote that $\mathcal{A}$ gets x as an input and has oracle access to $\mathcal{B}$, that is, the response for an oracle query q is $\mathcal{B}(q)$.

Further preliminaries on digital signature schemes, non-interactive zero-knowledge proofs and predicate encryption can be found in the full version.

3   Policy-Compliant Signatures

In this section, we introduce the notion of policy-compliant signature (PCS) schemes together with the notion of unforgeability and indistinguishability-based attribute hiding. We start by describing the syntax of PCS schemes, which consists of four algorithms, responsible for the setup of the parameters, the key generation and the signature generation and verification.

Definition 3.1 (Policy-Compliant Signatures). *Let* $\{X_\lambda\}_{\lambda \in \mathbb{N}}$ *be a family of attribute sets and denote by* $\mathcal{X}_\lambda$ *the powerset of* X_λ. *Further let* $\mathcal{F} = \{\mathcal{F}_\lambda\}_{\lambda \in \mathbb{N}}$ *be a family of sets* $\mathcal{F}_\lambda$ *of predicates* $F \colon \mathcal{X}_\lambda \times \mathcal{X}_\lambda \rightarrow \{0, 1\}$. *Then a policy-compliant signature (PCS) scheme for the functionality class* $\mathcal{F}_\lambda$ *is a tuple of four PPT algorithms* PCS = (Setup, KeyGen, Sign, Verify):

Setup$(1^\lambda, F)$: *On input a unary representation of the security parameter* λ *and a policy* $F \in \mathcal{F}_\lambda$, *output a master public and secret key pair* (mpk, msk).

KeyGen(msk, x): *On input the master secret key* msk *and a set of attributes* $x \in \mathcal{X}_\lambda$, *output a public and secret key pair* (pk, sk).

Sign(mpk, sk$_S$, pk$_R$, m): *On input the master public key* mpk, *a sender secret key* sk$_S$, *a receiver public key* pk$_R$ *and a message* m, *output either a signature* σ *or* $\perp$.

Verify(mpk, pk$_S$, pk$_R$, m, σ): *On input the master public key* mpk, *a sender public key* pk$_S$, *a receiver public key* pk$_R$, *a message* m *and a signature* σ, *output either* 0 *or* 1.

A Policy-Compliant Signature scheme is called correct, *if for all messages* m, *policies* $F \in \mathcal{F}_\lambda$, *and sets of attributes* $x_1, x_2 \in \mathcal{X}_\lambda$, *for all pairs* (mpk, msk) *in the support of* Setup$(1^\lambda, F)$, *all key pairs* (pk$_S$, sk$_S$) *and* (pk$_R$, sk$_R$) *in the corresponding support of* KeyGen(msk, x_1) *and* KeyGen(msk, x_2), *respectively,*

$$\Pr\left[\text{Verify}(\text{mpk}, \text{pk}_S, \text{pk}_R, m, \text{Sign}(\text{mpk}, \text{sk}_S, \text{pk}_R, m)) = F(x_1, x_2)\right]$$
$$\geq 1 - \text{negl}(\lambda),$$

where the probability is over the random coins of Sign *and* Verify.

3.1   Adversarial Capabilities in the Security Games

Before diving into the security properties, we briefly explain the adversarial capabilities. The adversary can (using the oracle QKeyGen or QKeyGenLR) obtain public keys for chosen attributes, which models honest parties in the system of which the public key is known; (using the oracle QCor) obtain the secret key corresponding to a given public key, which models the adversary corrupting a party; and (using the oracle QSign) obtain signatures relative to chosen public keys, which models the adversary seeing signatures from honest parties.

More formally, in a context where a master secret key msk is defined (as will be the case in our security experiments), we capture the above by defining the following stateful oracles that maintain the initially empty sets $\mathcal{QK}$, $\mathcal{QC}$, and $\mathcal{QS}$.

Key-Generation Oracle QKeyGen$(\cdot)$: On the ith input of an attribute set x_i, generate (pk$_i$, sk$_i$) $\leftarrow$ KeyGen(msk, x_i), add $(i, \text{pk}_i, \text{sk}_i, x_i)$ to $\mathcal{QK}$, and return pk$_i$.

Left-or-Right Key-Generation Oracle QKeyGenLR$(\cdot, \cdot)$: On the ith input of a pair of attribute sets $x_{i,0}$ and $x_{i,1}$, generate (pk$_i$, sk$_i$) $\leftarrow$ KeyGen(msk, $x_{i,\beta}$), add $(i, \text{pk}_i, \text{sk}_i, x_{i,0}, x_{i,1})$ to $\mathcal{QK}$, and return pk$_i$. In this case, the bit β is defined by the security game.

Corruption Oracle QCor($\cdot$): On input an index i, if $\mathcal{QK}$ contains an entry $(i, \cdot, \mathsf{sk}_i, \cdot) \in \mathcal{QK}$ or $(i, \cdot, \mathsf{sk}_i, \cdot, \cdot) \in \mathcal{QK}$ for some sk_i, then add that entry from $\mathcal{QK}$ to $\mathcal{QC}$ and return sk_i. Otherwise, return $\bot$.

Signing Oracle QSign($\cdot, \cdot, \cdot$): On input a (sender) index i, a (receiver) public key pk', and a message m, if $\mathcal{QK}$ contains an entry $(i, \mathsf{pk}_i, \mathsf{sk}_i, \cdot) \in \mathcal{QK}$ or $(i, \mathsf{pk}_i, \mathsf{sk}_i, \cdot, \cdot) \in \mathcal{QK}$ for some pk_i and sk_i, then return $\sigma \leftarrow$ PCS.Sign($\mathsf{mpk}, \mathsf{sk}_i, \mathsf{pk}', m$) and add $(i, \mathsf{pk}_i, \mathsf{pk}', m, \sigma)$ to $\mathcal{QS}$. Otherwise, return $\bot$.

3.2 Existential Unforgeability

The unforgeability notion captures that an adversary $\mathcal{A}$ is not able to create a valid signature for a public key that belongs to an uncorrupted party. Additionally, the adversary should also not be able to create a valid signature for a pair of public keys that do not fulfill the policy. More precisely, any signature for a new message m^* that successfully verifies, with respect to arbitrary sender and receiver public keys, constitutes a forgery unless the adversary has obtained the private key corresponding to the public key associated to the sender's attribute set x, and the receiver public key is associated to attribute set x^* obtained via the key generation oracle, and $F(x, x^*) = 1$. An interesting special case is regarding collisions of public keys. Here a forgery is valid unless the adversary has corrupted all indexes i corresponding to that public key.[2] Note that as a further special case that the adversary cannot create a valid signature w.r.t. public keys that have not been output by the key generation authority (formally, the condition on the last line in Fig. 1 is trivially true). Looking ahead, this game-based notion in fact captures all unforgeability properties we motivated for PCS: we show in Sect. 5 that Definition 3.2 implies ideal unforgeability properties when modeling PCS as an enhanced signature functionality.

We capture these requirements using an existential unforgeability game:

Definition 3.2 (Existential Unforgeability of a PCS Scheme). *Let* PCS = (Setup, KeyGen, Sign, Verify) *be a PCS scheme as defined in Definition 3.1. We define the experiment* EUF-CMA^{PCS} *in Fig. 1 and define the advantage of an adversary* $\mathcal{A} = (\mathcal{A}_1, \mathcal{A}_2)$ *by*

$$\mathsf{Adv}_{\mathsf{PCS}, \mathcal{A}}^{\mathrm{EUF\text{-}CMA}}(\lambda) = \Pr[\mathrm{EUF\text{-}CMA}^{\mathsf{PCS}}(1^\lambda, \mathcal{A}) = 1].$$

A PCS scheme PCS *is called* existential unforgeable under adaptive chosen message attacks *or* existential unforgeable *for short if for any polynomial-time adversary* $\mathcal{A} = (\mathcal{A}_1, \mathcal{A}_2)$, *there exists a negligible function* negl *such that:* $\mathsf{Adv}_{\mathsf{PCS}, \mathcal{A}}^{\mathrm{EUF\text{-}CMA}}(\lambda) \leq \mathrm{negl}(\lambda)$.

---

[2] This is vital to our use case of PCS: as long as a given user is not corrupted, no one is able to produce valid signatures that could be considered valid signatures of that party.

$$\begin{array}{l}
\hline
\textbf{EUF-CMA}^{\mathsf{PCS}}(1^\lambda, \mathcal{A}) \\
\hline
(F, \mathsf{st}) \leftarrow \mathcal{A}_1(1^\lambda) \\
(\mathsf{mpk}, \mathsf{msk}) \leftarrow \mathsf{Setup}(1^\lambda, F) \\
(\mathsf{pk}, \mathsf{pk}^*, m^*, \sigma^*) \leftarrow \mathcal{A}_2^{\mathsf{QKeyGen}(\cdot), \mathsf{QCor}(\cdot), \mathsf{QSign}(\cdot,\cdot,\cdot)}(\mathsf{st}, \mathsf{mpk}) \\
\textbf{Output:}\ \mathsf{Verify}(\mathsf{mpk}, \mathsf{pk}, \mathsf{pk}^*, m^*, \sigma^*) = 1 \wedge \\
\quad\quad\Big[\big[\exists (\cdot, \mathsf{pk}, \cdot, \cdot) \in \mathcal{QK} \setminus \mathcal{QC} \wedge (\cdot, \mathsf{pk}, \mathsf{pk}^*, m^*, \cdot) \notin \mathcal{QS} \big] \vee \\
\quad\quad\quad \forall (i, \mathsf{pk}, \cdot, x_i), (\cdot, \mathsf{pk}^*, \cdot, x^*) \in \mathcal{QK} : F(x_i, x^*) = 0 \Big] \\
\hline
\end{array}$$

Fig. 1. Unforgeability game of PCS.

3.3 Indistinguishability-Based Attribute Hiding

We formalize the notion of attribute hiding as a security game. In this security game, the adversary has access to a left-or-right key-generation oracle that it can query multiple times using pairs of attribute sets (x_0, x_1) to obtain the key for x_β, where β is a random bit sampled in the beginning of the game. The goal of the adversary is to guess the bit β. To achieve this, it additionally has access to a corruption oracle with with it can obtain the secret keys corresponding to previously obtained public keys. This is only allowed for public keys that previously have been generated for the same attribute set, i.e. $x_0 = x_1$. Furthermore, the adversary is also allowed to query a signing oracle to obtain signatures generated for sender and receiver key pairs of its choice.

To prevent the adversary from trivially distinguishing between the generated public keys, we need to exclude two kinds of trivial attacks: first, if x_β is seen as the receiver attributes, then distinguishing is trivial if the adversary possesses a secret key for the attribute set x such that $F(x, x_\beta) \neq F(x, x_{1-\beta})$. Second, if a signing query is asked for a pair of challenge keys such that $F(x_\beta, x'_\beta) \neq F(x_{1-\beta}, x'_{1-\beta})$, where x_β and $x_{1-\beta}$ are the attribute sets potentially associated with the sender key and x'_β and $x'_{1-\beta}$ are the attribute sets potentially associated with the receiver key, then distinguishing is trivial. Any other interaction is deemed valid.

Definition 3.3 (IND-Based Attribute Hiding). *Let* PCS $=$ (Setup, KeyGen, Sign, Verify) *be a PCS scheme as defined in Definition 3.1. For* $\beta \in \{0,1\}$, *we define the experiment* $\mathsf{AH}_\beta^{\mathsf{PCS}}$ *in Fig. 2, where all oracles are defined as in Section 3.1. The advantage of an adversary* $\mathcal{A} = (\mathcal{A}_1, \mathcal{A}_2)$ *is defined by*

$$\mathsf{Adv}_{\mathsf{PCS}, \mathcal{A}}^{\mathsf{AH}}(\lambda) = |\Pr[\mathsf{AH}_0^{\mathsf{PCS}}(1^\lambda, \mathcal{A}) = 1] - \Pr[\mathsf{AH}_1^{\mathsf{PCS}}(1^\lambda, \mathcal{A}) = 1]|.$$

We call an adversary valid if all of the following hold with probability 1 over the randomness of the adversary and all involved algorithms:

- *for every* $(i, \cdot, \cdot, x_{i,0}, x_{i,1}) \in \mathcal{QC}$ *and for all* $(\cdot, \cdot, \cdot, x_{j,0}, x_{j,1}) \in \mathcal{QK}$, *we have* $x_{i,0} = x_{i,1} =: x_i$ *and* $F(x_i, x_{j,0}) = F(x_i, x_{j,1})$,

– *and for all* $(i, \cdot, \mathsf{pk}_j, \cdot, \cdot) \in \mathcal{QS}$, *and* $(i, \cdot, \cdot, x_{i,0}, x_{i,1}), (\cdot, \mathsf{pk}_j, \cdot, x_{j,0}, x_{j,1}) \in \mathcal{QK}$, *we have* $F(x_{i,0}, x_{j,0}) = F(x_{i,1}, x_{j,1})$.

A PCS scheme PCS *is called* attribute hiding *if for any valid polynomial-time adversary* $\mathcal{A} = (\mathcal{A}_1, \mathcal{A}_2)$, *there exists a negligible function* negl *such that:* $\mathsf{Adv}^{\mathrm{AH}}_{\mathrm{PCS}, \mathcal{A}}(\lambda) \leq \mathsf{negl}(\lambda)$.

$\mathbf{AH}^{\mathrm{PCS}}_{\beta}(1^{\lambda}, \mathcal{A})$

$(F, \mathsf{st}) \leftarrow \mathcal{A}_1(1^{\lambda})$

$(\mathsf{mpk}, \mathsf{msk}) \leftarrow \mathsf{PCS.Setup}(1^{\lambda}, F)$

$\alpha \leftarrow \mathcal{A}_2^{\mathsf{QKeyGenLR}(\cdot, \cdot), \mathsf{QCor}(\cdot), \mathsf{QSign}(\cdot, \cdot, \cdot)}(\mathsf{st}, \mathsf{mpk})$

Output: α

Fig. 2. The Attribute-Hiding game for PCS.

4 Construction of a Policy-Compliant Signature Scheme

We present in Sect. 4.1 our policy-compliant signature scheme, show that it is correct in Sect. 4.2, proof its security in Sects. 4.3 and 4.4, and show in Sect. 4.5 how the scheme, which is quite generic, can be instantiated from standard assumptions.

4.1 The Scheme

The high-level idea of the scheme is to let PCS signatures generated by the signer contain proofs that part of the target's public key can be decrypted. Recall that the challenge of our notion is to publish a *single* public-key that hides all attributes, but where *all* a priori legitimate parties can figure out the bit of information whether they jointly satisfy the policy. For this step, we use a predicate-only predicate encryption scheme for the specific functionality class induced by the policy. To allow for the evaluation of the global policy on the inputs of the sender and the receiver using a predicate encryption scheme, we define a deterministic encoding function $\mathsf{SubPol}(F, x) = (\mathsf{SubPol}_1(F, x), \mathsf{SubPol}_2(F, x))$ that takes as input the global policy F and a set of attributes x and outputs a sub-policy encoding f_x (output of SubPol_1) and the attribute encoding x (output of SubPol_2) for the associated PE scheme. Functionally, we have

$$\mathsf{SubPol}(F, x) = (\mathsf{SubPol}_1(F, x), \mathsf{SubPol}_2(F, x)),$$
$$\text{s.t. } \forall x, x' \in \mathcal{X} : F(x, x') = \underbrace{\mathsf{SubPol}_1(F, x)(\mathsf{SubPol}_2(F, x'))}_{=f_x(x')}. \tag{1}$$

We note that the usage of PE is not a coincidence here as there is an interesting theoretical connection between PCS and PE which we give in the full version. To turn the scheme into a secure PCS scheme, we still need to protect the integrity which entails the binding of public-keys and the proof-of-decryption, as well as binding public keys to the authority. Here, we make use of two types of signatures, namely existentially unforgeable signatures as well as strongly unforgeable signatures. Finally, a NIZK proof is used to establish the core relation of Fig. 4 to prove the above binding and correct decryption.

The full scheme is given in Fig. 3. Later in Sects. 4.3 and 4.4 we prove the concrete security of the scheme. The implied succinct asymptotic security statement can be stated as follows:

Theorem 4.1 (Security of our PCS Construction (Asymptotic version)). *The PCS scheme* PCS *in Fig. 3 (w.r.t. policies $F \in \mathcal{F}$) is unforgeable and attribute hiding, if the signature schemes* $\mathsf{DS}_{\mathsf{priv}}$ *and* DS_{P} *are unforgeable, the signature scheme* $\mathsf{DS}_{\mathsf{pub}}$ *is strongly unforgeable,* PE *is an attribute-hiding (predicate-only) predicate encryption scheme (for the induced predicates from Eq. (1)), and* NIZK *is a secure non-interactive zero-knowledge proof of knowledge system for the relation R_{ZK} of Fig. 4.*

4.2 Correctness

The correctness of the construction described in Fig. 3 follows from the correctness of the predicate encryption scheme, the signature schemes, and the non-interactive zero-knowledge proof. Note that for the sake of exposition, we assume perfect correctness. However, even if any of the underlying building blocks has negligible correctness failure, this propagates through our scheme and would make it violate correctness only with negligible probability. Consider any two attribute sets x, y with $F(x, y) = 1$ (the other case for $F(x, y) = 0$ is straightforward) and let $(\mathsf{mpk}, \mathsf{msk}) \leftarrow \mathsf{Setup}(1^\lambda)$, $(\mathsf{pk}_x, \mathsf{sk}_x) \leftarrow \mathsf{KeyGen}(\mathsf{msk}, x)$, $(\mathsf{pk}_y, \mathsf{sk}_y) \leftarrow \mathsf{KeyGen}(\mathsf{msk}, y)$ and $\sigma \leftarrow \mathsf{Sign}(\mathsf{mpk}, \mathsf{pk}_y := (\mathsf{vk}_y, \mathsf{ct}_y, \sigma^y_{\mathsf{pub}}), \mathsf{sk}_x :=$ $(\mathsf{vk}_x, \mathsf{sk}^{\mathsf{DS}}_x, \mathsf{sk}_{f_x}, \sigma^x_{\mathsf{priv}}), m)$ for an arbitrary message m. We have $\sigma \neq \bot$ because the check during the signature generation whether $\mathsf{PE.Dec}(\mathsf{sk}_{f_x}, \mathsf{ct}_y) = 1$ will be satisfied for $F(x, y) = 1$ due to the correctness of the scheme PE and the requirement in Eq. (1). Furthermore, the signature on the sender's public key verifies by the correctness of the signature scheme $\mathsf{DS}_{\mathsf{pub}}$ during the signing process. In the signature verification step, the calls to Verify for the signatures schemes $\mathsf{DS}_{\mathsf{pub}}, \mathsf{DS}_{\mathsf{priv}}$ and DS_{P} always return 1 by the correctness of the signature schemes $\mathsf{DS}_{\mathsf{pub}}, \mathsf{DS}_{\mathsf{priv}}$ and DS_{P}. Furthermore, NIZK.Verify always returns 1 by the correctness of NIZK. This proves the correctness of the PCS scheme.

4.3 Existential Unforgeability

After showing the correctness of our construction, we prove its unforgeability.

Setup($1^\lambda, F$):	Sign($\mathsf{mpk}, \mathsf{sk}, \mathsf{pk}_R, m$):
$\mathsf{CRS} \leftarrow \mathsf{NIZK.Setup}(1^\lambda)$	Parse $\mathsf{mpk} = (F, \mathsf{CRS}, \mathsf{vk}_{\mathsf{pub}}, \mathsf{vk}_{\mathsf{priv}})$
$\mathsf{msk}_{\mathsf{PE}} \leftarrow \mathsf{PE.Setup}(1^\lambda)$	$\quad \mathsf{sk} = (\mathsf{vk}_S, \mathsf{sk}_S, \mathsf{sk}_{f_x}, \sigma_{\mathsf{priv}})$
$(\mathsf{vk}_{\mathsf{pub}}, \mathsf{sk}_{\mathsf{pub}}) \leftarrow \mathsf{DS}_{\mathsf{pub}}.\mathsf{Setup}(1^\lambda)$	$\quad \mathsf{pk}_R = (\mathsf{vk}_R, \mathsf{ct}_R, \sigma_{\mathsf{pub}})$
$(\mathsf{vk}_{\mathsf{priv}}, \mathsf{sk}_{\mathsf{priv}}) \leftarrow \mathsf{DS}_{\mathsf{priv}}.\mathsf{Setup}(1^\lambda)$	If $\mathsf{DS}_{\mathsf{pub}}.\mathsf{Verify}(\mathsf{vk}_{\mathsf{pub}},$
$\mathsf{mpk} := (F, \mathsf{CRS}, \mathsf{vk}_{\mathsf{pub}}, \mathsf{vk}_{\mathsf{priv}})$	$\qquad\qquad (\mathsf{vk}_R, \mathsf{ct}_R), \sigma_{\mathsf{pub}}) = 0$
$\mathsf{msk} := (\mathsf{msk}_{\mathsf{PE}}, \mathsf{sk}_{\mathsf{pub}}, \mathsf{sk}_{\mathsf{priv}})$	$\quad$ Return $\bot$
Return $(\mathsf{mpk}, \mathsf{msk})$	If $\mathsf{PE.Dec}(\mathsf{sk}_{f_x}, \mathsf{ct}_R) = 0$
	$\quad$ Return $\bot$
	$\pi \leftarrow \mathsf{Prove}(\mathsf{CRS},$
KeyGen(msk, x):	$\qquad\qquad (\mathsf{vk}_{\mathsf{priv}}, \mathsf{vk}_S, \mathsf{vk}_R, \mathsf{ct}_R),$
Parse $\mathsf{msk} := (\mathsf{msk}_{\mathsf{PE}}, \mathsf{sk}_{\mathsf{pub}}, \mathsf{sk}_{\mathsf{priv}})$	$\qquad\qquad (\mathsf{sk}_{f_x}, \sigma_{\mathsf{priv}}))$
$(\mathsf{vk}_{\mathsf{P}}, \mathsf{sk}_{\mathsf{P}}) \leftarrow \mathsf{DS}_{\mathsf{P}}.\mathsf{Setup}(1^\lambda)$	with L defined corresponding to Fig. 4.
$(f_x, x) = \mathsf{SubPol}(F, x)$	$\sigma' \leftarrow \mathsf{DS}_{\mathsf{P}}.\mathsf{Sign}(\mathsf{sk}_S, (m, \pi))$
$\mathsf{ct} \leftarrow \mathsf{PE.Enc}(\mathsf{msk}_{\mathsf{PE}}, x)$	Return $\sigma := (\pi, \sigma')$
$\mathsf{sk}_{f_x} \leftarrow \mathsf{PE.KeyGen}(\mathsf{msk}_{\mathsf{PE}}, f_x)$	
$\sigma_{\mathsf{pub}} \leftarrow \mathsf{DS}_{\mathsf{pub}}.\mathsf{Sign}(\mathsf{sk}_{\mathsf{pub}}, (\mathsf{vk}_{\mathsf{P}}, \mathsf{ct}))$	Verify($\mathsf{mpk}, \mathsf{pk}_S, \mathsf{pk}_R, m, \sigma$):
$\sigma_{\mathsf{priv}} \leftarrow \mathsf{DS}_{\mathsf{priv}}.\mathsf{Sign}(\mathsf{sk}_{\mathsf{priv}}, (\mathsf{vk}_{\mathsf{P}}, \mathsf{sk}_{f_x}))$	Parse $\mathsf{mpk} = (F, \mathsf{CRS}, \mathsf{vk}_{\mathsf{pub}}, \mathsf{vk}_{\mathsf{priv}})$
$\mathsf{pk} := (\mathsf{vk}_{\mathsf{P}}, \mathsf{ct}, \sigma_{\mathsf{pub}})$	$\quad \mathsf{pk}_S = (\mathsf{vk}_S, \mathsf{ct}_S, \sigma_{\mathsf{pub}}^S)$
$\mathsf{sk} := (\mathsf{vk}_{\mathsf{P}}, \mathsf{sk}_{\mathsf{P}}, \mathsf{sk}_{f_x}, \sigma_{\mathsf{priv}})$	$\quad \mathsf{pk}_R = (\mathsf{vk}_R, \mathsf{ct}_R, \sigma_{\mathsf{pub}}^R)$
Return $(\mathsf{pk}, \mathsf{sk})$	$\quad \sigma = (\pi, \sigma')$
	(Return 0 if parsing fails or $\sigma = \bot$)
	Return
	$\mathsf{DS}_{\mathsf{pub}}.\mathsf{Verify}(\mathsf{vk}_{\mathsf{pub}}, (\mathsf{vk}_R, \mathsf{ct}_R), \sigma_{\mathsf{pub}}^R)$
	$\wedge \mathsf{DS}_{\mathsf{pub}}.\mathsf{Verify}(\mathsf{vk}_{\mathsf{pub}}, (\mathsf{vk}_S, \mathsf{ct}_S), \sigma_{\mathsf{pub}}^S)$
	$\wedge \mathsf{NIZK.Verify}(\mathsf{CRS}, (\mathsf{vk}_{\mathsf{priv}}, \mathsf{vk}_R,$
	$\qquad\qquad\qquad\qquad \mathsf{vk}_S, \mathsf{ct}_R), \pi)$
	$\wedge \mathsf{DS}_{\mathsf{P}}.\mathsf{Verify}(\mathsf{vk}_S, (\pi, m), \sigma')$

Fig. 3. The Policy-Compliant Signature Scheme. It uses a NIZK proof system NIZK, a predicate encryption scheme PE, and three digital signature schemes $\mathsf{DS}_{\mathsf{pub}}, \mathsf{DS}_{\mathsf{priv}}$ and DS_{P}.

Relation R_{ZK}:

Instance: $x = (\mathsf{vk}_{\mathsf{priv}}, \mathsf{vk}_S, \mathsf{vk}_R, \mathsf{ct}_R)$

Witness: $w = (\mathsf{sk}_{f_\infty}, \sigma_{\mathsf{priv}})$

$R_{ZK}(x, w) = 1$ if and only if:

   $\mathsf{DS}_{\mathsf{priv}}.\mathsf{Verify}(\mathsf{vk}_{\mathsf{priv}}, (\mathsf{vk}_S, \mathsf{sk}_{f_\infty}), \sigma_{\mathsf{priv}}) = 1$ and $\mathsf{PE}.\mathsf{Dec}(\mathsf{sk}_{f_\infty}, \mathsf{ct}_R) = 1$

Fig. 4. Relation used for the PCS scheme in Fig. 3.

Theorem 4.2. *Let* $\mathsf{DS}_{\mathsf{pub}} = (\mathsf{DS}_{\mathsf{pub}}.\mathsf{Setup}, \mathsf{DS}_{\mathsf{pub}}.\mathsf{Sign}, \mathsf{DS}_{\mathsf{pub}}.\mathsf{Verify})$ *be a SUF-CMA secure signature scheme and let* $\mathsf{DS}_{\mathsf{priv}} = (\mathsf{DS}_{\mathsf{priv}}.\mathsf{Setup}, \mathsf{DS}_{\mathsf{priv}}.\mathsf{Sign}, \mathsf{DS}_{\mathsf{priv}}.\mathsf{Verify})$ *and* $\mathsf{DS}_{\mathsf{P}} = (\mathsf{DS}_{\mathsf{P}}.\mathsf{Setup}, \mathsf{DS}_{\mathsf{P}}.\mathsf{Sign}, \mathsf{DS}_{\mathsf{P}}.\mathsf{Verify})$ *be a EUF-CMA secure signature scheme and let* $\mathsf{NIZK} = (\mathsf{NIZK}.\mathsf{Setup}, \mathsf{NIZK}.\mathsf{Prove}, \mathsf{NIZK}.\mathsf{Verify})$ *be an extractable proof system, then the construction* $\mathsf{PCS} = (\mathsf{Setup}, \mathsf{KeyGen}, \mathsf{Enc}, \mathsf{Dec})$, *defined in Fig. 3, is existentially unforgeable. Namely, for any PPT adversary* $\mathcal{A}$, *there exist PPT adversaries* $\mathcal{B}, \mathcal{B}', \mathcal{B}''$ *and* $\mathcal{B}'''$, *such that*

$$\mathsf{Adv}_{\mathsf{PCS},\mathcal{A}}^{\mathsf{EUF\text{-}CMA}}(\lambda) \leq \mathsf{Adv}_{\mathsf{DS}_{\mathsf{pub}},\mathcal{B}}^{\mathsf{SUF\text{-}CMA}}(\lambda) + 2q \cdot \mathsf{Adv}_{\mathsf{DS}_{\mathsf{P}},\mathcal{B}'}^{\mathsf{EUF\text{-}CMA}}(\lambda)$$
$$+ \mathsf{Adv}_{\mathsf{DS}_{\mathsf{priv}},\mathcal{B}''}^{\mathsf{EUF\text{-}CMA}}(\lambda) + \mathsf{Adv}_{\mathsf{NIZK},\mathcal{B}'''}^{\mathsf{Ext}}(\lambda),$$

where q *denotes the number of queries to* $\mathsf{QKeyGen}$.

Proof (Sketch). To prove the unforgeability of our PCS scheme, we introduce several bad events and bound their respective probabilitises by the unforgeability of the different signature schemes as well as the extractability of the NIZK proof system.

The first event that we need to bound is the event that an adversary generates a valid key toegether with a valid signature, without querying the key generation oracle. This event cannot occur due to the strong unforgeability of the signature scheme $\mathsf{DS}_{\mathsf{pub}}$. We need strong unforgeability here to prevent an adversary from turning an existing key into a new key by generating a different, valid, signature for this key. The second event that we need to bound is the event that the adversary is able to generate a valid signature using an existing key for which it does not know the corresponding secret key. This event can directly be bounded by the existential unforgeability of the signature scheme DS_{P}. The third, and last, event that we need to bound is the event in which the adversary creates a valid signature for two keys that do not fulfill the policy. The occurrence of this event can be bound by the extractability of the NIZK proof system and the unforgeability of the signature scheme $\mathsf{DS}_{\mathsf{priv}}$ and DS_{P}. In more detail, if an adversay is able to create a valid signature for a key pair, where the corresponding attributes do not fulfill the policy, then it has either (1) generated a NIZK proof for an incorrect statement, which is a contradiction to the extractability of the NIZK proof system; (2) has generated a valid witness for the NIZK proof by forging a signature of the $\mathsf{DS}_{\mathsf{priv}}$ signature scheme. This event is a contradiction to the existential unforgeability of the $\mathsf{DS}_{\mathsf{priv}}$ signature scheme. The third, and

Game	CRS, π		pk	justification
G_0	$\mathsf{CRS} \leftarrow \mathsf{NIZK.Setup}(1^\lambda)$ $\pi \leftarrow \mathsf{NIZK.Prove}(\mathsf{CRS}, x, w)$		$\mathsf{KeyGen}(\mathsf{msk}, x_0)$	
G_1	$\mathsf{CRS} \leftarrow \mathcal{S}_1(1^\lambda)$ $\pi \leftarrow \mathcal{S}_2(\mathsf{CRS}, \tau, x)$		$\mathsf{KeyGen}(\mathsf{msk}, x_0)$	Zero-knowledge of NIZK
G_2	$\mathsf{CRS} \leftarrow \mathcal{S}_1(1^\lambda)$ $\pi \leftarrow \mathcal{S}_2(\mathsf{CRS}, \tau, x)$		$\mathsf{KeyGen}(\mathsf{msk}, \boxed{x_1})$	AH of PE
G_3	$\mathsf{CRS} \leftarrow \mathsf{NIZK.Setup}(1^\lambda)$ $\pi \leftarrow \mathsf{NIZK.Prove}(\mathsf{CRS}, x, w)$		$\mathsf{KeyGen}(\mathsf{msk}, x_1)$	Zero-knowledge of NIZK

Fig. 5. Overview of the games to prove the indistinguishability of attribute-hiding of the policy-compliant signature scheme described in Fig. 3.

last, possiblity of the adversary to produce a forgery would be to if it obtained two public keys which allowed for a "mix and match" attack, which however is exlcuded by bounding the collision probability of the keys. The proof then follows by showing that if none of these bad events occur, then no PCS forgery exists.

The formal proof of this theorem can be found in the full version.   □

4.4 Indistinguishability-Based Attribute Hiding

We next prove that our PCS scheme is attribute hiding.

Theorem 4.3. *Let* $\mathsf{PE} = (\mathsf{PE.Setup}, \mathsf{PE.KeyGen}, \mathsf{PE.Enc}, \mathsf{PE.Dec})$ *be a predicate encryption scheme, let* $\mathsf{NIZK} = (\mathsf{NIZK.Setup}, \mathsf{NIZK.Prove}, \mathsf{NIZK.Verify})$ *be a NIZK proof system and let* $\mathsf{DS_{pub}} = (\mathsf{DS_{pub}.Setup}, \mathsf{DS_{pub}.Sign}, \mathsf{DS_{pub}.Verify})$ *be a strongly unforgeable signature scheme, then the construction* $\mathsf{PCS} = (\mathsf{Setup}, \mathsf{KeyGen}, \mathsf{Enc}, \mathsf{Dec})$, *defined in Fig. 3, is attribute hiding. Namely, for any valid PPT adversary* $\mathcal{A}$, *there exist PPT adversaries* $\mathcal{B}, \mathcal{B}'$ *and* $\mathcal{B}''$, *such that:*

$$\mathsf{Adv}^{\mathsf{AH}}_{\mathsf{PCS}, \mathcal{A}}(\lambda) \leq 2 \cdot \mathsf{Adv}^{\mathsf{ZK}}_{\mathsf{NIZK}, \mathcal{B}}(\lambda) + \mathsf{Adv}^{\mathsf{AH}}_{\mathsf{PE}, \mathcal{B}'}(\lambda) + \mathsf{Adv}^{\mathsf{SUF\text{-}CMA}}_{\mathsf{DS_{pub}}, \mathcal{B}''}(\lambda).$$

Proof. To prove this statement, we use a hybrid argument with the games defined in Fig. 5. Note that G_0 corresponds to the game $\mathsf{AH}^{\mathsf{PCS}}_0(1^\lambda, \mathcal{A})$ and G_3 to the game $\mathsf{AH}^{\mathsf{PCS}}_1(1^\lambda, \mathcal{A})$. This results in:

$$\mathsf{Adv}^{\mathsf{AH}}_{\mathsf{PCS}, \mathcal{A}}(1^\lambda) = |\Pr[\mathsf{AH}^{\mathsf{PCS}}_0(1^\lambda, \mathcal{A}) = 1] - \Pr[\mathsf{AH}^{\mathsf{PCS}}_1(1^\lambda, \mathcal{A}) = 1]|$$
$$= |\Pr[\mathsf{G}_0(\lambda, \mathcal{A}) = 1] - \Pr[\mathsf{G}_3(\lambda, \mathcal{A}) = 1]|.$$

We describe the different games in more detail:

Game G_1: In this game, we change from an honestly generated CRS and honestly generated proofs to a simulated CRS and simulated proofs. The transition from G_0 to G_1 is justified by the zero-knowledge property of NIZK. Namely, we can exhibit a PPT adversary $\mathcal{B}_0$ such that:

$$|\Pr[G_0(\lambda, \mathcal{A}) = 1] - \Pr[G_1(\lambda, \mathcal{A}) = 1]| \leq \mathsf{Adv}_{\mathsf{NIZK}, \mathcal{B}_0}^{\mathsf{ZK}}(\lambda).$$

Game G_2: In this game, we change the attributes used for the generation of the challenge public keys pk_i from $x_{i,0}$ to $x_{i,1}$ for all i. The transition from G_1 to G_2 is justified by the attribute-hiding property of PE and the strong unforgeability of $\mathsf{DS}_{\mathsf{pub}}$. Intuitively, we rely on the strong unforgeability of the signature scheme $\mathsf{DS}_{\mathsf{pub}}$ to prevent an adversary from learning any information about the challenge keys by obtaining a signature for a maliciously generated key. Namely, we can exhibit PPT adversaries $\mathcal{B}_1$ and $\mathcal{B}_2$ such that:

$$|\Pr[G_1(\lambda, \mathcal{A}) = 1] - \Pr[G_2(\lambda, \mathcal{A}) = 1]| \leq \mathsf{Adv}_{\mathsf{PE}, \mathcal{B}_1}^{\mathsf{AH}}(\lambda) + \mathsf{Adv}_{\mathsf{DS}_{\mathsf{pub}}, \mathcal{B}_2}^{\mathsf{SUF\text{-}CMA}}(\lambda).$$

Game G_3: This game is the $\mathsf{AH}_1^{\mathsf{PCS}}(1^\lambda, \mathcal{A})$ game. In this game, we change back from a simulated CRS and simulated proofs π to an honestly generated CRS and honestly generated proofs π. As the transition from G_0 to G_1, this transition is justified by the zero-knowledge property of NIZK. Namely, we can exhibit a PPT adversary $\mathcal{B}_3$ such that:

$$|\Pr[G_2(\lambda, \mathcal{A}) = 1] - \Pr[G_3(\lambda, \mathcal{A}) = 1]| \leq \mathsf{Adv}_{\mathsf{NIZK}, \mathcal{B}_3}^{\mathsf{ZK}}(\lambda).$$

Putting everything together, we obtain the theorem.   □

We present the proofs for the different transitions in the full version.

4.5   Efficient Instantiations Based on Inner-Product PE

In this section, we show that our generic PCS scheme can be instantiated efficiently for certain policies such as the ones mentioned in the introduction. Since the most efficient predicate-only PE schemes are known for the inner-product functionality class in the standard model, we focus on this instantiation and briefly recall the associated realizable policies established in [8,22]. The two functionality classes we recall are:

Inner-Product Functionality. The functionality class is defined as $\mathcal{F}_{N,k}^{\mathsf{IP}} = \{F_{N,k}^{\mathsf{IP}} : \mathbb{Z}_N^k \times \mathbb{Z}_N^k \to \{0,1\}\}$ by the equation

$$F_{N,k}^{\mathsf{IP}}(\boldsymbol{x}, \boldsymbol{y}) = \begin{cases} 1 & \text{if } \langle \boldsymbol{x}, \boldsymbol{y} \rangle = 0 \bmod N, \\ 0 & \text{if } \langle \boldsymbol{x}, \boldsymbol{y} \rangle \neq 0 \bmod N. \end{cases}$$

Hidden-Vector Functionality. Define $\Sigma_* = \Sigma \cup \{*\}$ with $\Sigma = \{0,1\}$. The functionality class is defined as $\mathcal{F}_k^{\mathsf{HV}} = \{F_k^{\mathsf{HV}} : \Sigma_*^k \times \Sigma^k \to \{0,1\}\}$ by the equation

$$F_k^{\mathsf{HV}}(\boldsymbol{x}, \boldsymbol{y}) = \begin{cases} 1 & \text{if } \forall i \in [k] \ (x_i = y_i \text{ or } x_i = *), \\ 0 & \text{otherwise.} \end{cases}$$

In the following, we call a predicate encryption scheme that implements the IP functionality inner-product encryption (IPE) and refer to a predicate encryption scheme that implements the HV functionality as hidden-vector encryption (HVE). Note that the predicates in the associated PE schemes correspond to the functions $F_{N,k}^{\mathsf{IP}}(\boldsymbol{x}, \cdot)$ and $F_k^{\mathsf{HV}}(\boldsymbol{x}, \cdot)$ parameterized by the vector $\boldsymbol{x}$ corresponding to the first argument of the above functions, respectively. As shown in [22], HVE with dimension ℓ can be realized generically based on IPE of dimension 2ℓ.

Instantiating the Generic Scheme. The elements of our generic construction are digital signatures, predicate encryption, and NIZK. For inner-product predicates there exist efficient PE schemes for the assumed indistinguishability-based security [29,30] (and also for a certain type of simulation-based security [17]). For the signature scheme used by the authority to generate σ_{pub} and the signature scheme used by the client, we can use BLS signatures [6] (or BB signatures [5] to avoid switching to an idealized model). For the signature scheme used by the authority to generate σ_{priv}, we however have to pay attention, as it is used as part of the witness in a NIZK computation. The only source of practical inefficiency comes from the additional usage of the NIZK proof for the relation $R_{\mathsf{ZK}}(x,w) \leftrightarrow \mathsf{DS}_{\mathsf{priv}}.\mathsf{Verify}(\mathsf{vk}_{\mathsf{priv}}, (\mathsf{vk}_S, \mathsf{sk}_{f_x}), \sigma_{\mathsf{priv}}) \wedge \mathsf{Dec}(\mathsf{sk}_{f_x}, \mathsf{ct}_R) = 1$, as it combines a generic signature verification with a proof of decryption of the PE scheme. Note that there are two signature schemes involved: the signature scheme with which the authority produces σ_{priv} is the crucial one in this section. For the "inner signature" (the one used by a party to sign the final message) it will only be convenient to assume that vk_S is encoded as a group element of some cyclic group (which is the case for the variants discussed above). Note that the NIZK relation does not involve signatures of the inner scheme, just the representation of the public key as part of the statement.

To avoid the potential source of inefficiency from the NIZK we can use predicate encryption and signature schemes that align well with the use of the Groth-Sahai framework [18,20] to verify the relation R_{ZK}. We achieve such a combination by using the (pairing-based) structure-preserving signature (SPS) scheme from Kiltz et al. [23] in combination with the (pairing-based) inner-product PE scheme from Okamoto et al. [29] that yields pairing product equations to verify relation R_{ZK}.

In a nutshell, pairing groups are represented as a tuple $(\mathbb{G}_1, \mathbb{G}_2, \mathbb{G}_T, q, g_1, g_2, e)$ where $\mathbb{G}_1, \mathbb{G}_2, \mathbb{G}_T$ are cyclic groups of prime order q, g_1 and g_2 are generators of $\mathbb{G}_1$ and $\mathbb{G}_2$, respectively. Finally, $e : \mathbb{G}_1 \times \mathbb{G}_2 \mapsto \mathbb{G}_T$ is an efficiently computable non-degenerate bilinear map and $g_T := e(g_1, g_2)$ is a generator of the target group. Groth-Sahai proofs implement a NIZK for a collection of product pairing equations of the form

$$\prod_{i=1}^{s} e(x_i, A_i) \cdot \prod_{i=1}^{s'} e(B_i, y_i) \cdot \prod_{i=1}^{s'} \prod_{j=1}^{s} e(x_i, y_i)^{\gamma_{i,j}} = t_T$$

where $A_i \in \mathbb{G}_1$, $B_i \in \mathbb{G}_2$, $t_T \in \mathbb{G}_T$ and $\gamma_{i,j} \in \mathbb{Z}_q$ are constants (and part of the statement to be proven), and $x_i \in \mathbb{G}_1$ as well as $y_i \in \mathbb{G}_2$ are the private witness variables (and s, s' are integers). A priori, GS proofs for product pairing equations are only witness-indistinguishable unless certain additional constraints are met [20]. But even if those conditions are not met, efficient transformations can turn GS NIWI into full NIZK proofs (with extractability for group elements) with low overhead as shown in [13] by creating an OR-Proof system (allowing a simulator to always find a witness) and using the controlled malleability of the GS proof systems. We refer to [14, Theorem 3.2 and Appendix B] for the full details. As mentioned above, we instantiate the paring-based primitives from [29] (encryption) and [23] (signature):

- In the PE scheme of [29], ciphertexts are represented as pairs $\mathsf{ct} = (c_1, c_2)$, where $c_2 \in \mathbb{G}_T$ is the blinded plaintext m and has the form $c_2 = m \cdot g^\zeta$ (for a random ζ chosen during encryption) and c_1 is an N-vector $c_1 = (A_1, \dots A_N)$ with $A_i \in \mathbb{G}_1$ (for an integer parameter N of the scheme). The decryption key for functionality f_x is represented by an N-vector $\mathsf{sk}_{f_x} = (k_1, \dots, k_N)$ with $k_i \in \mathbb{G}_2$. The decryption operation is $m' \leftarrow c_2 / \prod_{i=1}^{N} e(A_i, k_i)$. Note that to turn the scheme into a predicate-only PE scheme, we can fix $m = \mathbb{I}_{G_T}$ and do not need the extra blinding of the ciphertext (fixing $\zeta := 1$) and hence the decryption operation satisfies the equation $c_2 = g_T = e(g_1, g_2) = \prod_{i=1}^{N} e(A_i, k_i)$.
- In the SPS scheme of [23], a signature string is a tuple $\sigma = (s_1, s_2, s_3, s_4)$ with $s_4 \in \mathbb{G}_2$, and $s_i \in \mathbb{G}_1^{1 \times (k+1)}$, $i \in \{1, 2, 3\}$ for an integer parameter k. The public key of this system consists of four matrices $\mathbf{M}_i$, where $\mathbf{M}_1, \mathbf{M}_2 \in \mathbb{G}_2^{k+1 \times k}$, $\mathbf{M}_3 \in \mathbb{G}_2^{n+1 \times k}$, and $\mathbf{M}_4 \in \mathbb{G}_2^{k+1 \times k}$ (where n is the parameter specifying the message length). Verifying a signature σ with respect to this public key amounts to the following collection of $2k+1$ pairing product equations, where a message $x \in \mathbb{G}_1^n$ is encoded as $m := (g_1, x_1, \dots, x_n)$: For each $j \in [k]$ we check that

$$\prod_{i=1}^{k+1} e((s_1)_i, (\mathbf{M}_4)_{j,i})$$
$$= \prod_{i=1}^{k+1} e((m)_i, (\mathbf{M}_3)_{j,i}) \cdot \prod_{i=1}^{k+1} e((s_2)_i, (\mathbf{M}_1)_{j,i}) \cdot \prod_{i=1}^{k+1} e((s_3)_i, (\mathbf{M}_2)_{j,i})$$

holds, as well as $e((s_2)_j, s_4) = e((s_3)_j, g_2)$ is satisfied for each $j \in [k+1]$.

Therefore, the relation in Fig. 4 can be expressed as proving a satisfying assignment of the above pairing product equations, where the (private) decryption key and the private signature are the private witness variables of the above equations, whereas the ciphertext and public keys can be treated as the constants (and hence part of the statement).

Instantiating Logical Formulas. By applying the techniques of [22] in our setting, we can implement various policies expressed as logical formulas. While all previous techniques are applicable to our setting, we only dive into simple reductions for completeness, as the core principle is the same for any technique mapping a logical formula to inner-products or hidden-vector functionalities.

IPE and Threshold Clauses. Assume a finite list of variables P_i, $i = 1 \ldots q$, where each variable can take on values p_i from a finite set $\mathcal{P}$. Assume a policy F is expressed as a combination of sender and receiver properties. We assume that the policy is expressed as a list of requirements, each requirement being a clause, and where one requires that exactly d out of k of the requirements (clauses) must be satisfied (e.g., $d = 1$ as in our introductory example).

That is, we have a set of clauses $\{K_i\}_{i \in [k]}$, each with n_i sender properties and m_i receiver properties of the form

$$K_i = (P^{(s)}_{idx(i,1)} = p_{i,1} \wedge \cdots \wedge P^{(s)}_{idx(i,n_i)} = p_{i,n_i} \wedge P^{(r)}_{idx(i,n_i+1)}$$

$$= p_{i,n_i+1} \wedge \cdots \wedge P^{(r)}_{idx(i,n_i+m_i)} = p_{i,n_i+m_i}),$$

which we call a conjunctive clause. Here, $P^{(s)}_{idx(i,j)}$ resp. $P^{(r)}_{idx(i,j)}$ denote variables P_h indexed via an indexing function $h = idx(i,j)$ (which is induced by such a finite policy). Note that the variables constrain the sender (superscript (s)) and the receiver (superscript (r)).

Our goal is to map the policy F to the functionality class $\mathcal{F}^{\mathsf{IP}}_{k+1}$. In particular, we must show how the authority performs the mapping $(f_{\boldsymbol{x}}, \boldsymbol{x}) \leftarrow \mathsf{SubPol}(F, (\overline{x}_1, \ldots, \overline{x}_n))$ in the scheme of Fig. 3, where $\overline{x}_1, \ldots, \overline{x}_n$ is the assignment of attributes to each P_i of a user Alice (note that we omit treating null values for simplicity). The authority performs the following computation:

1. The authority precomputes which clauses Alice cannot satisfy anymore, and which ones she potentially can satisfy with a matching receiver. The authority defines for all $i \in [k]$:

$$X_i := \begin{cases} 1 & \text{if } \bigwedge_{j=1}^{n_i} (\overline{x}_{idx(i,j)} = p_{i,j}) = 1, \\ 0 & \text{otherwise.} \end{cases}$$

The first part of the output of the subpolicy algorithm SubPol is $f_{\boldsymbol{x}}(\cdot) := F^{\mathsf{IP}}_{N,k+1}((X_1, \ldots, X_k, 1), \cdot)$, where we assume $N > k$.

2. The authority precomputes which clauses Alice cannot satisfy if she is the receiver, and which ones she potentially can satisfy with a matching sender.

The authority defines:

$$
Y_i := \begin{cases} 1 & \text{if } \bigwedge_{j=1}^{m_i} (\overline{x}_{idx(i,n_i+j)} = p_{i,n_i+j}) = 1, \\ 0 & \text{otherwise}, \end{cases}
$$

for all $i \in [k]$. The second part of the output of the subpolicy algorithm SubPol is $x := (Y_1, \ldots, Y_k, -d)$.

We observe that if a sender obtains a secret key generated based on the vector $(X_1, \ldots, X_k, 1)$ and signs (as shown in Fig. 3) a message for a receiver public key that contains the ciphertext generated based on vector $(Y_1, \ldots, Y_k, -d)$ as shown above, we have

$$
\langle (X_1, \ldots, X_k, 1), (Y_1, \ldots, Y_k, -d) \rangle = 0
$$
$$
\Longleftrightarrow \langle (X_1, \ldots, X_k), (Y_1, \ldots Y_k) \rangle = d
$$

because $N > k$ (which is assumed to avoid wraparound complications). Since each of the products $X_i \cdot Y_i$ signals the joint fulfillment of the original clause K_i (thanks to the precomputation step), this means that exactly d clauses are jointly satisfied, which corresponds to the policy F.

We note that if the policy F has disjunctive clauses instead, that is for each $i \in [k]$

$$
K_i = (P^{(s)}_{idx(i,1)} = p_{i,1} \vee \cdots \vee P^{(s)}_{idx(i,n_i)} = p_{i,n_i} \vee P^{(r)}_{idx(i,n_i+1)}
$$
$$
= p_{i,n_i+1} \vee \cdots \vee P^{(r)}_{idx(i,n_i+m_i)} = p_{i,n_i+m_i}),
$$

(where for $d = k$ we obtain CNF formulas) an analogous reasoning yields that the reduction to inner products for dimension $2k + 1$ can be achieved by having the authority follow the above steps but define for all $i \in [k]$, $X_{2i-1} := 1$ and

$$
X_{2i} := \begin{cases} 1 & \text{if } \bigvee_{j=1}^{n_i} (\overline{x}_{idx(i,j)} = p_{i,j}) = 1, \\ 0 & \text{otherwise}, \end{cases}
$$

as well as for all $i \in [k]$

$$
Y_{2i-1} := \begin{cases} 1 & \text{if } \bigvee_{j=1}^{m_i} (\overline{x}_{idx(i,n_i+j)} = p_{i,n_i+j}) = 1, \\ 0 & \text{otherwise}, \end{cases}
$$

$$
Y_{2i} := \begin{cases} 0 & \text{if } \bigvee_{j=1}^{m_i} (\overline{x}_{idx(i,n_i+j)} = p_{i,n_i+j}), \\ 1 & \text{otherwise}. \end{cases}
$$

The authority finally computes $f_x(\cdot) := F^{\mathrm{IP}}_{N,2k+1}((X_1,\ldots,X_{2k},1),\cdot)$ and $x :=$ $(Y_1,\ldots,Y_{2k},-d)$ (and generates the associated keys and ciphertext as prescribed in Fig. 3). The above is seen to represent the policy F by observing that each clause i is represented by two variables such that the sum $X_{2i-1}\cdot Y_{2i-1}+X_{2i}\cdot Y_{2i}$ equals 0 if no party satisfies the clause, and 1 in any other case.

HVE and CNF Formulas. HVE opens up the space for many policies and is itself realizable from the inner product functionality [8,22]. For example, for CNF formulas, i.e., as above with $d = k$, where k is the number of disjunctive clauses, the reduction to HVE for dimension k is straightforward: The authority defines

$$X_i = \begin{cases} * & \text{if } \bigvee_{j=1}^{n_i} (\overline{x}_{idx(i,j)} = p_{i,j}) = 1, \\ 1 & \text{otherwise.} \end{cases}$$

and

$$Y_i = \begin{cases} 1 & \text{if } \bigvee_{j=1}^{m_i} (\overline{x}_{idx(i,n_i+j)} = p_{i,n_i+j}) = 1, \\ 0 & \text{otherwise.} \end{cases}$$

The the authority computes $f_x(\cdot) := F^{\mathrm{HV}}_k((X_1,\ldots,X_k),\cdot)$ and $x := (Y_1,\ldots,Y_k)$ and generates the associated keys and ciphertext as prescribed in Fig. 3.

This accurately represents the CNF policy F: A sender can only decrypt the ciphertext in the public key of a receiver if for each clause i, either the sender already satisfies that clause and thus the resulting vector has the wildcard symbol $*$ at this position, or the receiver has a satisfying assignment and hence its vector must be equal to 1 at this position to match the sender's value.

5   Universal Composability and SIM-Based PCS

Simulation-based security has the advantage that, instead of arguing and excluding trivial attacks, we follow the real/ideal world paradigm, where in the ideal-world, the leakage to the simulator and the unforgeability properties are captured in an explicit fashion.

The ideal PCS Functionality. In this section, we cast policy compliant signature as an enhanced signature functionality following [2,11] that incorporates all of our declared goals for this primitive. We give the description in Section 5. The difference to a standard signature functionality are at a high-level the following:

- There is a distinct trusted party, denoted M that is responsible for the setup. M is responsible to generate the signing keys for parties with respect to the attributes they possess. Note that at this level of abstraction, we do not discuss *how* the authority decides to assign an attribute to a party. This will be managed by the higher-level protocols. The attributes of honest parties do not leak to the adversary, which captures that the obtained public key does not leak any attributes. However, the adversary learns by definition of the signature algorithm, whether the corrupted parties are allowed to send messages to the new honest parties.

- On signing operations, only valid signatures are recorded. That is, if party P_i with attributes x_{P_i} signs a message m for party P_j with attributes x_{P_j}, then the record $(m, \sigma, v_M, v_{P_i}, v_{P_j}, 1)$ is only stored if $F(x_{P_i}, x_{P_j}) = 1$, where v_M denotes the public parameters and v_{P_i}, v_{P_j} are the unique public keys associated with parties P_i and P_j, respectively.
- On verification queries of the form (VERIFY, sid, $m, \sigma, v'_M, v'_A, v'_B$), the functionality ensures aside of completeness and unforgeability w.r.t. honest signers also that no valid signature can be generated for any combination of v'_A, v'_B unless the public keys are associated to attributes x'_A and x'_B such that $F(x'_A, x'_B) = 0$.
- On top of unforgeability, privacy guarantees that the adversary learns at most the policy evaluation $F(x_i, x_j)$ (associated with the respective keys) for every signing query. For corrupted parties, the adversary learns their attributes $\tilde{x}$ (since it learns all inputs and outputs by that party upon corruption by default) as well as all evaluations $F(\tilde{x}, x_j)$.

Functionality $\mathsf{Func}_{\mathsf{PolSig}}^{M, \mathcal{F}}$

The functionality interacts with an arbitrary party set $\mathcal{P} := \{P_1, \ldots, P_n\}$ and adversary $\mathcal{S}$. The functionality is parameterized by a distinct identity $M \notin \mathcal{P}$ of the credential manager and the class of supported policies $\mathcal{F}$.

Initialize $F \leftarrow \perp, x_{P_i}, v_{P_i} \leftarrow \perp$ for all $P_i \in \mathcal{P} \setminus \{M\}$ and $v_M \leftarrow \perp$. The functionality maintains the initialized party set $\mathcal{I} := \{P_i \in \mathcal{P} \mid v_{P_i} \neq \perp\}$ (and we omit the explicit inclusion of parties for simplicity).

Policy Initialization. Upon input (POLICY-GEN, sid, F) from party M do the following: if $v_M \neq \perp$ or $F \notin \mathcal{F}$, ignore the request; otherwise, provide (POLICY-GEN, sid, F) to $\mathcal{S}$. Upon receiving (POLICY-GEN, sid, v) from $\mathcal{S}$, output (POLICY-GEN, sid, v) to M and set $v_M \leftarrow v$.

Key Generation. Upon input (KEY-GEN, sid, P, x) from party M, where $P \in \mathcal{P} \setminus \mathcal{I}$, do the following: ignore the request if $v_M = \perp$; otherwise define $x_{P_i} \leftarrow x$ and compute:

1. Provide the leakage information $\{(\hat{P}, P_i) \mapsto F(x_{\hat{P}}, x_{P_i}) \mid \text{for all corrupted } \hat{P} \in \mathcal{I}\}\}$ to $\mathcal{S}$.
2. Provide (KEY-GEN, sid, P_i) to $\mathcal{S}$. Upon receiving (VERIFICATION-KEY, sid, P_i, v) from $\mathcal{S}$, verify that for all $P \in \mathcal{I}$ $v_P \neq v$, and if this is the case, set $v_{P_i} \leftarrow v$ and output (VERIFICATION-KEY, sid, x, v) to P_i. If v is not unique, ignore the input from $\mathcal{S}$.

Signing. On input (SIGN, sid, m, v) from party $P \in \mathcal{I}$:

- If $v = v_{P_j}$ for some $P_j \in \mathcal{I}$ and $F(x_P, x_{P_j}) = 1$ then provide (SIGN, sid, $m, P, v, 1$) to $\mathcal{S}$. Upon receiving (SIGNATURE, sid, m, P, v, σ) from

$\mathcal{S}$, verify that no entry $(m, \sigma, v_M, v_P, v_{P_j}, 0)$ is stored. If it is, then output an error message to P and halt. Else, output (SIGNATURE, sid, m, v, σ) to P, and store the entry $(m, \sigma, v_M, v_P, v_{P_j}, 1)$.

- In any other case, provide (SIGN, sid, $m, P, v, 0$) to $\mathcal{S}$ and when receiving (SIGNATURE, sid, m, s) from $\mathcal{S}$, output (SIGNATURE, sid, m, v, s) to P. *(This case guarantees that such messages are not considered as signed.)*

Verification. Upon input (VERIFY, sid, $m, \sigma, v'_M, v'_A, v'_B$) from any party P, hand (VERIFY, sid, $m, \sigma, v'_M, v'_A, v'_B$) to $\mathcal{S}$. Upon receiving (VERIFIED, sid, $m, v'_M, v'_A, v'_B, \phi$) from $\mathcal{S}$ do:

1. If $v'_M = v_M$, $v'_A = v_{P_i}$, $v'_B = v_{P_j}$ for some $P_i, P_j \in \mathcal{I}$ and the entry $(m, \sigma, v_M, v_{P_i}, v_{P_j}, 1)$ is recorded, then set $f = 1$. *(Condition 1 guarantees completeness: If the verification keys are the registered ones and σ is a legitimately generated signature for m, then the verification succeeds.)*
2. Else, if $v'_M = v_M$, $v'_A = v_{P_i}$, $v'_B = v_{P_j}$ for some $P_i, P_j \in \mathcal{I}$ and P_i is not corrupted and no entry $(m, \sigma, v_M, v_{P_i}, v_{P_j}, 1)$ for any σ' is recorded, then set $f = 0$ and record the entry $(m, \sigma, v_M, v_{P_i}, v_{P_j}, 0)$. *(Condition 2 guarantees unforgeability: For any combination of generated public keys, the signer is not corrupted, and never signed m, then the verification fails.)*
3. Else, if $v'_M = v_M$, $v'_A = v_{P_i}$, $v'_B = v_{P_j}$ for some $P_i, P_j \in \mathcal{I}$ and no entry $(m, \sigma, v_M, v_{P_i}, v_{P_j}, 1)$ for any σ' is recorded, then set $f = 0$ if $F(x_{P_i}, x_{P_j}) = 0$, and otherwise set $f \leftarrow \phi$. Record the entry $(m, \sigma, v_M, v_{P_i}, v_{P_j}, f)$. *(Condition 3 guarantees policy compliance of dishonest signers: For any combination of generated public keys, even if everyone is corrupted the verification must fail if the policy is not satisfied.)*
4. Else, if $v'_M = v_M$ but we have that $\forall P_i \in \mathcal{I} : v'_A \neq v_{P_i}$ or $\forall P_i \in \mathcal{I} : v'_B \neq v_{P_i}$, then set $f \leftarrow 0$ and record the entry $(m, \sigma, v_M, v'_A, v_{B'}, 0)$. *(Condition 4 ensures that no valid signatures can exist w.r.t. public keys not issued by the credential manager.)*
5. Else, if there is an entry (m, σ, v', f') stored, then let $f = f'$. *(Condition 5 guarantees consistency: All verification requests with identical parameters will result in the same answer.)*
6. Else, let $f = \phi$ and record the entry $(m, \sigma, v'_M, v'_A, v'_B, \phi)$. *(If no condition applies, then let the adversary decide.)*
7. Finally, output (VERIFIED, sid, m, f) to P.

Corruption Mode. The party M is not corruptible. For all other parties P_i, the functionality supports the standard corruption mode [12], that is, upon input (CORRUPT, P_i) on the backdoor tape, send all previous inputs to $\mathcal{S}$ and hand over the control of P_i's input and output tapes to $\mathcal{S}$ and providing the adversary all capabilities that an honest party has. Additionally, whenever a party P_i gets corrupted, provide the leakage information $\{(P_i, P_j) \mapsto F(x_{P_i}, x_{P_j}) \mid P_j \in \mathcal{I}\}$.

Blueprint Usage of the Scheme in UC. As with signatures [2,11], a PCS scheme PCS = (Setup, KeyGen, Sign, Verify) can be mapped in a straightforward way to a UC protocol tailored to realize the low-level functionality $\mathsf{Func}_{\mathsf{PolSig}}^{M,\mathcal{F}}$ (low level in the sense that it exports the interface without much abstraction). The main difference to an ordinary signature scheme is the presence of a trusted party assisting in the key generation step. That is, we have a trusted (credential) manager M incorruptible by definition[3], where we assume secure point-to-point channels between M and each P_i. The protocol π_M^{PCS} can be specified as follows:

- **Party M:**
  - On input (POLICY-GEN, sid, F), run $\mathsf{Setup}(1^\lambda, F)$ and generate the output (POLICY-GEN, sid, mpk). Store msk internally.
  - On input (KEY-GEN, sid, P, x), run $\mathsf{KeyGen}(\mathsf{msk}, x)$ and send the message $(x, (\mathsf{pk}, \mathsf{sk}))$ to party P over a secure channel.
- **Party P_i:**
  - Upon receiving (for the first time) the message $(x, (\mathsf{pk}, \mathsf{sk}))$ from M on the secure channel, store it internally and output (VERIFICATION-KEY, sid, x, pk). If the party has initialized its public key already, messages from M are ignored.
  - On input (SIGN, sid, m, v), if this party has already a secret key sk, then execute $\sigma \leftarrow \mathsf{Sign}(v, \mathsf{sk}, m)$ and return (SIGNATURE, sid, m, v, σ).
  - On input (VERIFY, sid, $m, \sigma, v_M', v_A', v_B'$), return the output (VERIFIED, sid, m, $\mathsf{Verify}(v_M', v_A', v_B', m, \sigma)$).

With this composable understanding in mind, we now set out to establish a concise and simpler SIM-based PCS notion in the spirit of [7,24,27] that implies the UC realization of the ideal PCS functionality, which we show formally in Theorem 5.2. Looking ahead, the proof of Theorem 5.2 reveals that all the ideal unforgeability properties (Conditions 2, 3, and 4) of $\mathsf{Func}_{\mathsf{PolSig}}^{M,\mathcal{F}}$ follow from the game-based unforgeability notion defined in Definition 3.2, which is thereby validated to capture what we intended to model.

5.1   Simulation-Based Attribute Hiding

Our starting point is the already established game-based notion, where the adversary gets access to a variety of oracles, as defined in Sect. 3.1. Following [7,24,27], we consider a simulator $\mathcal{S} = (\mathcal{S}_{\mathsf{Setup}}, \mathcal{S}_{\mathsf{KG}}, \mathcal{S}_{\mathsf{Cor}}, \mathcal{S}_{\mathsf{Sgn}})$, where $\mathcal{S}_{\mathsf{Setup}}$ simulates Setup and $\mathcal{S}_{\mathsf{KG}}$, $\mathcal{S}_{\mathsf{Cor}}$, and $\mathcal{S}_{\mathsf{Sgn}}$ simulate the oracles QKeyGen, QCor, and QSign, respectively. These simulator algorithms have a shared state and in addition to the inputs to the oracles, get a *leakage set* $\mathcal{L}$. The set $\mathcal{L}$ is initially empty and gets augmented during the experiment analogous to how the simulator in the UC functionality obtains information.

Definition 5.1 (SIM-Based AH). *Let* $\mathsf{PCS} = (\mathsf{Setup}, \mathsf{KeyGen}, \mathsf{Sign}, \mathsf{Verify})$ *be a PCS scheme as defined in Definition 3.1. We define the experiments* $\mathsf{Real}^{\mathsf{PCS}}(1^\lambda, \mathcal{A})$ *and* $\mathsf{Ideal}^{\mathsf{PCS}}(1^\lambda, \mathcal{A}, \mathcal{S})$ *for a PPT adversary* $\mathcal{A}$ *and a PPT simulator* $\mathcal{S} = (\mathcal{S}_{\mathsf{Setup}}, \mathcal{S}_{\mathsf{KG}}, \mathcal{S}_{\mathsf{Cor}}, \mathcal{S}_{\mathsf{Sgn}})$ *in Fig. 6. In the real world, the adversary*

---

[3] Formally, the property of such trusted third parties to be incorruptible is modeled by instructing its protocol machine to ignore the corruption request on the backdoor tape.

has access to oracles as defined in Sect. 3.1. The simulator algorithms have a shared state s, which is modelled as giving them s as input, and allowing all of them to update the state s. In the ideal experiment, the initially empty sets $\mathcal{IQK}$ and $\mathcal{IQC}$ are maintained. Furthermore, all but $\mathcal{S}_{\mathsf{Setup}}$ get as an additional input the leakage set $\mathcal{L}$, which is initially empty. The sets are updated according to the following rules:

- *When $\mathcal{A}$ queries the key generation oracle using x_j, the following gets added to $\mathcal{L}$ (before $\mathcal{S}_{\mathrm{KG}}$ is invoked):*

$$\{(i,j) \mapsto F(x_i, x_j) \mid (i, \mathsf{pk}_i, x_i) \in \mathcal{IQC}\}.$$

  After the simulator $\mathcal{S}_{\mathrm{KG}}$ has been invoked, (j, pk_j, x_j) is added to $\mathcal{QK}$, where pk_j is the output of $\mathcal{S}_{\mathrm{KG}}$.
- *When $\mathcal{A}$ makes a corruption query i with $(i, \mathsf{pk}_i, x_i) \in \mathcal{QK}$, then the following gets added to $\mathcal{L}$ (before $\mathcal{S}_{\mathrm{Cor}}$ is invoked):*

$$\big(x_i, \{(i,j) \mapsto F(x_i, x_j) \mid (j, \mathsf{pk}_j, x_j) \in \mathcal{IQK}\}\big).$$

  Additionally, $(i, \mathsf{pk}_i, x_i) \in \mathcal{IQK}$ is also added to $\mathcal{IQC}$.
- *When $\mathcal{A}$ makes a signing query (i, pk_R, m), the following gets added to $\mathcal{L}$:*

$$\{(i,j) \mapsto F(x_i, x_j) \mid (i, \mathsf{pk}_i, x_i), (j, \mathsf{pk}_R, x_j) \in \mathcal{IQK}\}.$$

This models that adversaries learn whether a pair of keys satisfy the policy by observing a signature for these keys.

The advantage of a PPT adversary $\mathcal{A}$ in the experiment is defined as:

$$\mathsf{Adv}^{\mathsf{Sim}}_{\mathsf{PCS},\mathcal{A},\mathcal{S}}(\lambda) = |\Pr[\mathrm{Real}^{\mathsf{PCS}}(1^\lambda, \mathcal{A}) = 1] - \Pr[\mathrm{Ideal}^{\mathsf{PCS}}(1^\lambda, \mathcal{A}, \mathcal{S}) = 1]|.$$

A PCS scheme PCS is simulation attribute hiding, if for any PPT adversary $\mathcal{A}$ there exists a PPT simulator $\mathcal{S}$, such that $\mathsf{Adv}^{\mathsf{Sim}}_{\mathsf{PCS},\mathcal{A},\mathcal{S}}(\lambda) \leq \mathrm{negl}(\lambda)$, where $\mathrm{negl}(\cdot)$ is a negligible function.

We conclude with the following theorem:

Theorem 5.2. *Protocol π^{PCS}_M securely realizes $\mathsf{Func}^{M,\mathcal{F}}_{\mathsf{PolSig}}$ if PCS is existentially unforgeable (Definition 3.2) and simulation-based attribute hiding (Definition 5.1).*

Proof. We prove the theorem in two main steps. First we assume a hybrid world with a functionality like $\mathsf{Func}^{M,\mathcal{F}}_{\mathsf{PolSig}}$ but which does not protect the privacy of any party's attributes, but only enforces the ideal unforgeability guarantees. We show that there is a UC simulator $\mathcal{S}_{uc}$ that can simulate the real-world perfectly unless the environment (together with the dummy adversary) provoke an event that implies a forgery of the PCS scheme as captured by game **EUF-CMA**^{PCS} in Fig. 1. The second step of the proof is to switch to the true ideal world with $\mathsf{Func}^{M,\mathcal{F}}_{\mathsf{PolSig}}$. We re-design the previous simulator to obtain $\mathcal{S}'_{uc}$ that uses

$$\begin{array}{|l|}
\hline
\mathbf{Real}^{\mathsf{PCS}}(1^\lambda, \mathcal{A}) \\
\hline
(F, \tau) \leftarrow \mathcal{A}_1(1^\lambda) \\
(\mathsf{mpk}, \mathsf{msk}) \leftarrow \mathsf{Setup}(1^\lambda, F) \\
\alpha \leftarrow \mathcal{A}^{\mathsf{QKeyGen}(\cdot), \mathsf{QCor}(\cdot), \mathsf{QSign}(\cdot,\cdot,\cdot)}(\tau, \mathsf{mpk}) \\
\hline
\mathbf{Output:}\ \alpha \\
\hline
\end{array}$$

$$\begin{array}{|l|}
\hline
\mathbf{Ideal}^{\mathsf{PCS}}(1^\lambda, \mathcal{A}, \mathcal{S}) \\
\hline
(F, \tau) \leftarrow \mathcal{A}_1(1^\lambda) \\
(\mathsf{mpk}, s) \leftarrow \mathcal{S}_{\mathsf{Setup}}(1^\lambda, F) \\
\alpha \leftarrow \mathcal{A}^{\mathcal{S}_{\mathsf{KG}}(s,\mathcal{L}), \mathcal{S}_{\mathsf{Cor}}(s,\mathcal{L},\cdot), \mathcal{S}_{\mathsf{Sgn}}(s,\mathcal{L},\cdot,\cdot,\cdot)}(\tau, \mathsf{mpk}) \\
\hline
\mathbf{Output:}\ \alpha \\
\hline
\end{array}$$

Fig. 6. Real and ideal experiments for the simulation-based attribute hiding definition for the scheme PCS. Both experiments interact with an adversary $\mathcal{A}$. The ideal experiment additionally interacts with a simulator $\mathcal{S} = (\mathcal{S}_{\mathsf{Setup}}, \mathcal{S}_{\mathsf{KG}}, \mathcal{S}_{\mathsf{Cor}}, \mathcal{S}_{\mathsf{Sgn}})$. The simulator gets the initially empty leakage set $\mathcal{L}$, which grows during the experiment as described in Definition 5.1.

the assumed simulator $\mathcal{S}_{pcs} = (\mathcal{S}_{\mathsf{Setup}}, \mathcal{S}_{\mathsf{KG}}, \mathcal{S}_{\mathsf{Cor}}, \mathcal{S}_{\mathsf{Sgn}})$ required by Definition 5.1. Any environment that notices this switch to $\mathcal{S}'_{uc}$ can be used to distinguish $\mathbf{Real}^{\mathsf{PCS}}$ and $\mathbf{Ideal}^{\mathsf{PCS}}$.

In more detail, we have the following hybrid worlds:

Hybrid H_0: This is the real-world process with protocol π_M^{PCS}.

Hybrid H_1: Here we assume an "ideal functionality" Func_{hyb} that acts like $\mathsf{Func}_{\mathsf{PolSig}}^{M,\mathcal{F}}$ but with the following difference:

· On input (KEY-GEN, sid, P, x), behave as $\mathsf{Func}_{\mathsf{PolSig}}^{M,\mathcal{F}}$ does but additionally output x to the adversary.

Designing a simulator for this world follows the pattern of the signature simulator of [11] with additional setup, that is. We define the simulator $\mathcal{S}_{uc}$:

- On input (POLICY-GEN, sid, F) from Func_{hyb}, execute $\mathsf{Setup}(1^\lambda, F)$ and then return to the functionality (POLICY-GEN, sid, mpk). Store msk for future use.

- On input (KEY-GEN, sid, P_i) alongside the leakage set $\{(\hat{P}, P_i) \mapsto F(x_{\hat{P}}, x_{P_i}) \mid$ for all corrupted $\hat{P} \in \mathcal{I}\}\}$, *and the additional leakage information* x specific to Func_{hyb}, the simulator executes $\mathsf{KeyGen}(\mathsf{msk}, x)$, stores the obtained key-pair (pk, sk) as $(P_i, \mathsf{pk}, \mathsf{sk})$ for future use. Provide (VERIFICATION-KEY, sid, P_i, pk) to the functionality.

- On input (SIGN, sid, m, P, v, b) from Func_{hyb}, obtain the record $(P, \mathsf{pk}, \mathsf{sk})$ and execute $\sigma \leftarrow \mathsf{Sign}(v, \mathsf{sk}, m)$ (give up activation if this party has not yet obtained its key). Return to the functionality (SIGNATURE, sid, m, P, v, σ).

- On input (VERIFY, sid, $m, \sigma, v'_M, v'_A, v'_B$) from Func_{hyb}, let $\phi \leftarrow \mathsf{Verify}(v'_M, v'_A, v'_B, m, \sigma)$ and return (VERIFIED, sid, $m, v'_M, v'_A, v'_B, \phi$) to the functionality.

- On a corruption request for party P_i, $\mathcal{S}_{uc}$ corrupts P_i in the ideal functionality (and formally also obtains leakage set $\{(P_i, P_j) \mapsto F(x_{P_i}, x_{P_j}) \,|\, P_j \in \mathcal{I}\}$ that is not needed here since the simulator has full knowledge of attributes), checks for a previously stored record $(P_i, \mathsf{pk}, \mathsf{sk})$ and if such a record exists returns sk. (And from now onward, the simulator acts as relay between environment and functionality.)

Hybrid H_2: This hybrid is the ideal functionality (i.e., the ideal protocol for) $\mathsf{Func}_{\mathsf{PolSig}}^{M,\mathcal{F}}$ together with simulator $\mathcal{S}'_{uc}$. We define $\mathcal{S}'_{uc}$ by stating what the difference is compared to $\mathcal{S}_{uc}$. This will be handy when arguing about the indistinguishability of this and the previous hybrid.

- On input (POLICY-GEN, sid, F) from $\mathsf{Func}_{\mathsf{PolSig}}^{M,\mathcal{F}}$, simulator $\mathcal{S}'_{uc}$ executes $(\mathsf{mpk}, s) \leftarrow \mathcal{S}_{\mathsf{Setup}}(1^\lambda, F)$ (instead of Setup) and stores s for future use (instead of msk). Initialize the leakage set $\mathcal{L} \leftarrow \emptyset$. The interaction with the functionality is just like $\mathcal{S}_{uc}$.
- On input (KEY-GEN, sid, P_i) alongside the leakage set $L = \{(\hat{P}, P_i) \mapsto F(x_{\hat{P}}, x_{P_i}) \,|\, \text{for all corrupted } \hat{P} \in \mathcal{I}\}$—but *without the additional leakage x from above*–from $\mathsf{Func}_{\mathsf{PolSig}}^{M,\mathcal{F}}$, $\mathcal{S}'_{uc}$ computes $\mathcal{L} \leftarrow \mathcal{L} \cup L$ and executes $\mathcal{S}_{\mathsf{KG}}(s, \mathcal{L})$ to obtain pk and an updated state s. The simulator stores the tuple $(P_i, \mathsf{pk}, \bot)$ (no secret key is stored). The remaining interaction with the functionality is identical to $\mathcal{S}_{uc}$.
- On input (SIGN, sid, m, P, v, b) from $\mathsf{Func}_{\mathsf{PolSig}}^{M,\mathcal{F}}$, the simulator updates the leakage set $\mathcal{L}$ only if there is an entry $(P', v, \cdot)$ by adding the tuple (P, P', b). Next, retrieve a previously stored record $(P, \mathsf{pk}, \bot)$ and generate the signature $\sigma \leftarrow \mathcal{S}_{\mathsf{Sgn}}(s, \mathcal{L}, P, v, m)$ (which also updates the state s). The interaction between the simulator and the functionality is the same as in $\mathcal{S}_{uc}$.
- On input (VERIFY, sid, $m, \sigma, v'_M, v'_A, v'_B$) from $\mathsf{Func}_{\mathsf{PolSig}}^{M,\mathcal{F}}$, the simulator behaves identically to $\mathcal{S}_{uc}$.
- On a corruption request for party P_i, $\mathcal{S}'_{uc}$ corrupts P_i in $\mathsf{Func}_{\mathsf{PolSig}}^{M,\mathcal{F}}$, and includes the additional leakage information $L = \{x_{P_i}\} \cup \{(P_i, P_j) \mapsto F(x_{P_i}, x_{P_j}) \,|\, P_j \in \mathcal{I}\}$ by computing $\mathcal{L} \leftarrow \mathcal{L} \cup L$. Next, it retrieves the record $(P_i, \mathsf{pk}, \cdot)$ and if such a record exists returns $\mathsf{sk} \leftarrow \mathcal{S}_{\mathsf{Cor}}(s, \mathcal{L}, P_i)$ (which also updates s) and returns sk. (And from now on, the simulator acts as relay between environment and functionality.)

In the full version, we state and prove two claims that show the indistinguishability of hybrid H_0 and H_1 and the indistinguishability of H_1 and H_2. Combining both claims yields that for any UC environment (and without loss of generality in the dummy adversary model, see [10]) the (real) protocol execution of π_M^{PCS} is indistinguishable from the ideal protocol execution with functionality $\mathsf{Func}_{\mathsf{PolSig}}^{M,\mathcal{F}}$ and ideal adversary (i.e., simulator) $\mathcal{S}'_{uc}$. The theorem follows. $\quad\square$

5.2 On the SIM-Based Security of our Generic Scheme

If we assume that the underlying predicate-only predicate encryption scheme of our construction in Fig. 3 satisfies the strong simulation-based PE security notion

378 C. Badertscher et al.

as defined in the full version, then the generic scheme achieves the simulation-based and therefore the composable notion of PCS. We note that the requirement in the simulation-based PE security is the adaptive (and thus stronger) version of what is proven so far in the literature, such as in [17,29]. We leave it as an interesting open problem to realize PE schemes that fulfill the stronger (adaptive) simulation-based security notion based on reasonable assumptions. We note that such schemes require idealized models such as proofs in the bilinear generic group model [24] or the random oracle model.

Theorem 5.3. *Let* PE $=$ (PE.Setup, PE.KeyGen, PE.Enc, PE.Dec) *be a simulation secure predicate encryption scheme, let further* NIZK $=$ (NIZK.Setup, NIZK.Prove, NIZK.Verify) *be a NIZK proof system and let* $\mathsf{DS_{pub}}$ $=$ (DS$_{pub}$.Setup, DS$_{pub}$.Sign, DS$_{pub}$.Verify) *be a strong unforgeable signature scheme, then there exists a simulator* S *such that the construction* PCS $=$ (Setup, KeyGen, Enc, Dec), *defined in Fig. 3, is simulation private. Namely, for any PPT adversary* A *there exist PPT adversaries* B, B' *and* B'', *such that:*

$$\mathsf{Adv}_{\mathsf{PCS},A,S}^{\mathrm{Sim}}(\lambda) \leq \mathsf{Adv}_{\mathsf{NIZK},B}^{\mathrm{ZK}}(\lambda) + \mathsf{Adv}_{\mathsf{PE},B',S'}^{\mathrm{Sim}}(\lambda) + \mathsf{Adv}_{\mathsf{DS_{pub}},B''}^{\mathrm{SUF\text{-}CMA}}(\lambda).$$

Proof. The simulator S for the proof of this theorem is described in the full version. Informally, the simulator S uses the simulators of the predicate encryption scheme to generate the keys. For answering signature queries, the simulator S additionally receives the policy evaluation of the associated attributes of the keys that are used for the signature query. Since S knows if the statement is part of the language of the NIZK system, it can use the NIZK simulator to generate a valid proof for the statement relying on the zero-knowledge property of the NIZK system.

As in the proof of Theorem 4.3, we assume that the adversary A only queries the signing oracle using public keys that previously have been output by one of the key oracles or has been a reply to the challenge query. The argument here is the same as in the proof of Theorem 4.3, which results in the summand $\mathsf{Adv}_{\mathsf{DS_{pub}},B''}^{\mathrm{SUF\text{-}CMA}}(\lambda)$ of the bound in the theorem.

To show that the ideal world with the simulator S is indistinguishable from the real world, we use a hybrid argument where the hybrids are formally defined in the full version. Note that $\mathsf{H_0}$ corresponds to the real world $\mathrm{Real}^{\mathsf{PCS}}(1^\lambda, A)$ and $\mathsf{H_2}$ to the ideal world $\mathrm{Ideal}^{\mathsf{PCS}}(1^\lambda, A, S)$. This results in:

$$\mathsf{Adv}_{\mathsf{PCS},A,S}^{\mathrm{Sim}}(\lambda) = |\Pr[\mathsf{H_0}(\lambda, A) = 1] - \Pr[\mathsf{H_2}(\lambda, A) = 1]|.$$

We describe the different games in more detail:

Hybrid $\mathsf{H_1}$: In this hybrid, we change from an honestly generated CRS and honestly generated proofs to a simulated CRS and simulated proofs. The transition from $\mathsf{H_0}$ to $\mathsf{H_1}$ is justified by the zero-knowledge property of NIZK. Namely, we can exhibit a PPT adversary B_0 such that:

$$|\Pr[\mathsf{H_0}(\lambda, A) = 1] - \Pr[\mathsf{H_1}(\lambda, A) = 1]| \leq \mathsf{Adv}_{\mathsf{NIZK},B_0}^{\mathrm{ZK}}(\lambda).$$

Hybrid H_2**:** This hybrid is the $\mathsf{Ideal}^{\mathsf{PCS}}(1^\lambda, \mathcal{A})$ world. In this hybrid, we change from honestly generated keys to simulated keys. The transition from H_1 to H_2 is justified by the simulation policy hiding property of PE. Namely, we can exhibit a PPT adversary $\mathcal{B}_1$ such that:

$$| \Pr[H_1(\lambda, \mathcal{A}) = 1] - \Pr[H_2(\lambda, \mathcal{A}) = 1]| \leq \mathsf{Adv}^{\mathsf{Sim}}_{\mathsf{PE}, \mathcal{B}_1, \mathcal{S}'}(\lambda).$$

Putting everything together, we obtain the theorem.   □

We present the proofs for the different transitions in the full version.

References

1. Ateniese, G., Francati, D., Nuñez, D., Venturi, D.: Match me if you can: matchmaking encryption and its applications. In: Boldyreva, A., Micciancio, D. (eds.) CRYPTO 2019. LNCS, vol. 11693, pp. 701–731. Springer, Cham (2019). https://doi.org/10.1007/978-3-030-26951-7_24

2. Backes, M., Hofheinz, D.: How to break and repair a universally composable signature functionality. In: Zhang, K., Zheng, Y. (eds.) ISC 2004. LNCS, vol. 3225, pp. 61–72. Springer, Heidelberg (2004). https://doi.org/10.1007/978-3-540-30144-8_6

3. Badertscher, C., Matt, C., Maurer, U.: Strengthening access control encryption. In: Takagi, T., Peyrin, T. (eds.) ASIACRYPT 2017. LNCS, vol. 10624, pp. 502–532. Springer, Cham (2017). https://doi.org/10.1007/978-3-319-70694-8_18

4. Bellare, M., Fuchsbauer, G.: Policy-based signatures. In: Krawczyk, H. (ed.) PKC 2014. LNCS, vol. 8383, pp. 520–537. Springer, Heidelberg (2014). https://doi.org/10.1007/978-3-642-54631-0_30

5. Boneh, D., Boyen, X.: Short signatures without random oracles. In: Cachin, C., Camenisch, J.L. (eds.) EUROCRYPT 2004. LNCS, vol. 3027, pp. 56–73. Springer, Heidelberg (2004). https://doi.org/10.1007/978-3-540-24676-3_4

6. Boneh, D., Lynn, B., Shacham, H.: Short signatures from the Weil pairing. In: Boyd, C. (ed.) ASIACRYPT 2001. LNCS, vol. 2248, pp. 514–532. Springer, Heidelberg (2001). https://doi.org/10.1007/3-540-45682-1_30

7. Boneh, D., Sahai, A., Waters, B.: Functional encryption: definitions and challenges. In: Ishai, Y. (ed.) TCC 2011. LNCS, vol. 6597, pp. 253–273. Springer, Heidelberg (2011). https://doi.org/10.1007/978-3-642-19571-6_16

8. Boneh, D., Waters, B.: Conjunctive, subset, and range queries on encrypted data. In: Vadhan, S.P. (ed.) TCC 2007. LNCS, vol. 4392, pp. 535–554. Springer, Heidelberg (2007). https://doi.org/10.1007/978-3-540-70936-7_29

9. Camenisch, J., Lysyanskaya, A.: An efficient system for non-transferable anonymous credentials with optional anonymity revocation. In: Pfitzmann, B. (ed.) EUROCRYPT 2001. LNCS, vol. 2045, pp. 93–118. Springer, Heidelberg (2001). https://doi.org/10.1007/3-540-44987-6_7

10. Canetti, R.: Universally composable security: a new paradigm for cryptographic protocols. In: 42nd FOCS, pp. 136–145. IEEE Computer Society Press (October 2001). https://doi.org/10.1109/SFCS.2001.959888

11. Canetti, R.: Universally composable signatures, certification and authentication. Cryptology ePrint Archive, Report 2003/239 (2003). https://eprint.iacr.org/2003/239

12. Canetti, R.: Universally composable security. J. ACM **67**(5) (September 2020). https://doi.org/10.1145/3402457
13. Chase, M., Kohlweiss, M., Lysyanskaya, A., Meiklejohn, S.: Malleable proof systems and applications. In: Pointcheval, D., Johansson, T. (eds.) EUROCRYPT 2012. LNCS, vol. 7237, pp. 281–300. Springer, Heidelberg (2012). https://doi.org/10.1007/978-3-642-29011-4_18
14. Chase, M., Kohlweiss, M., Lysyanskaya, A., Meiklejohn, S.: Malleable proof systems and applications. Cryptology ePrint Archive, Report 2012/012 (2012). https://eprint.iacr.org/2012/012
15. Damgård, I., Ganesh, C., Khoshakhlagh, H., Orlandi, C., Siniscalchi, L.: Balancing privacy and accountability in blockchain identity management. In: Paterson, K.G. (ed.) CT-RSA 2021. LNCS, vol. 12704, pp. 552–576. Springer, Cham (2021). https://doi.org/10.1007/978-3-030-75539-3_23
16. Damgård, I., Haagh, H., Orlandi, C.: Access control encryption: enforcing information flow with cryptography. In: Hirt, M., Smith, A. (eds.) TCC 2016. LNCS, vol. 9986, pp. 547–576. Springer, Heidelberg (2016). https://doi.org/10.1007/978-3-662-53644-5_21
17. Datta, P., Okamoto, T., Takashima, K.: Adaptively simulation-secure attribute-hiding predicate encryption. In: Peyrin, T., Galbraith, S. (eds.) ASIACRYPT 2018. LNCS, vol. 11273, pp. 640–672. Springer, Cham (2018). https://doi.org/10.1007/978-3-030-03329-3_22
18. Escala, A., Groth, J.: Fine-tuning groth-sahai proofs. In: Krawczyk, H. (ed.) PKC 2014. LNCS, vol. 8383, pp. 630–649. Springer, Heidelberg (2014). https://doi.org/10.1007/978-3-642-54631-0_36
19. Frikken, K.B., Li, J., Atallah, M.J.: Trust negotiation with hidden credentials, hidden policies, and policy cycles. In: NDSS 2006. The Internet Society (February 2006)
20. Groth, J., Sahai, A.: Efficient non-interactive proof systems for bilinear groups. In: Smart, N. (ed.) EUROCRYPT 2008. LNCS, vol. 4965, pp. 415–432. Springer, Heidelberg (2008). https://doi.org/10.1007/978-3-540-78967-3_24
21. Jakobsson, M., Sako, K., Impagliazzo, R.: Designated verifier proofs and their applications. In: Maurer, U. (ed.) EUROCRYPT 1996. LNCS, vol. 1070, pp. 143–154. Springer, Heidelberg (1996). https://doi.org/10.1007/3-540-68339-9_13
22. Katz, J., Sahai, A., Waters, B.: Predicate encryption supporting disjunctions, polynomial equations, and inner products. In: Smart, N. (ed.) EUROCRYPT 2008. LNCS, vol. 4965, pp. 146–162. Springer, Heidelberg (2008). https://doi.org/10.1007/978-3-540-78967-3_9
23. Kiltz, E., Pan, J., Wee, H.: Structure-preserving signatures from standard assumptions, revisited. In: Gennaro, R., Robshaw, M. (eds.) CRYPTO 2015. LNCS, vol. 9216, pp. 275–295. Springer, Heidelberg (2015). https://doi.org/10.1007/978-3-662-48000-7_14
24. Kim, S., Lewi, K., Mandal, A., Montgomery, H., Roy, A., Wu, D.J.: Function-hiding inner product encryption is practical. In: Catalano, D., De Prisco, R. (eds.) SCN 2018. LNCS, vol. 11035, pp. 544–562. Springer, Cham (2018). https://doi.org/10.1007/978-3-319-98113-0_29
25. Li, N., Du, W., Boneh, D.: Oblivious signature-based envelope. In: Borowsky, E., Rajsbaum, S. (eds.) 22nd ACM PODC. pp. 182–189. ACM (July 2003). https://doi.org/10.1145/872035.872061
26. Maji, H.K., Prabhakaran, M., Rosulek, M.: Attribute-based signatures. In: Kiayias, A. (ed.) CT-RSA 2011. LNCS, vol. 6558, pp. 376–392. Springer, Heidelberg (2011). https://doi.org/10.1007/978-3-642-19074-2_24

27. Matt, C., Maurer, U.: A definitional framework for functional encryption. In: Fournet, C., Hicks, M. (eds.) CSF 2015 Computer Security Foundations Symposium, pp. 217–231. IEEE Computer Society Press (2015). https://doi.org/10.1109/CSF.2015.22

28. Nakamoto, S.: Bitcoin: A peer-to-peer electronic cash system. manuscript (2009). http://www.bitcoin.org/bitcoin.pdf

29. Okamoto, T., Takashima, K.: Adaptively attribute-hiding (hierarchical) inner product encryption. In: Pointcheval, D., Johansson, T. (eds.) EUROCRYPT 2012. LNCS, vol. 7237, pp. 591–608. Springer, Heidelberg (2012). https://doi.org/10.1007/978-3-642-29011-4_35

30. Okamoto, T., Takashima, K.: Fully secure unbounded inner-product and attribute-based encryption. In: Wang, X., Sako, K. (eds.) ASIACRYPT 2012. LNCS, vol. 7658, pp. 349–366. Springer, Heidelberg (2012). https://doi.org/10.1007/978-3-642-34961-4_22

31. Wee, H.: Attribute-hiding predicate encryption in bilinear groups, revisited. In: Kalai, Y., Reyzin, L. (eds.) TCC 2017. LNCS, vol. 10677, pp. 206–233. Springer, Cham (2017). https://doi.org/10.1007/978-3-319-70500-2_8

Simple and Efficient Batch Verification Techniques for Verifiable Delay Functions

Lior Rotem[✉]

School of Computer Science and Engineering, Hebrew University of Jerusalem,
91904 Jerusalem, Israel
lior.rotem@cs.huji.ac.il

Abstract. We study the problem of *batch verification* for verifiable delay functions (VDFs), focusing on proofs of correct exponentiation (PoCE), which underlie recent VDF constructions. We show how to compile any PoCE into a batch PoCE, offering significant savings in both communication and verification time. Concretely, given any PoCE with communication complexity c, verification time t and soundness error δ, and any pseudorandom function with key length $\mathsf{k_{prf}}$ and evaluation time t_{prf}, we construct:

- A batch PoCE for verifying n instances with communication complexity $m \cdot c + \mathsf{k_{prf}}$, verification time $m \cdot t + n \cdot m \cdot O(t_{\mathsf{op}} + t_{\mathsf{prf}})$ and soundness error $\delta + 2^{-m}$, where λ is the security parameter, m is an adjustable parameter that can take any integer value, and t_{op} is the time required to evaluate the group operation in the underlying group. This should be contrasted with the naïve approach, in which the communication complexity and verification time are $n \cdot c$ and $n \cdot t$, respectively. The soundness of this compiler relies only on the soundness of the underlying PoCE and the existence of one-way functions.
- An improved batch PoCE based on the low order assumption. For verifying n instances, the batch PoCE requires communication complexity $c + \mathsf{k_{prf}}$ and verification time $t + n \cdot (t_{\mathsf{prf}} + \log(s) \cdot O(t_{\mathsf{op}}))$, and has soundness error $\delta + 1/s$. The parameter s can take any integer value, as long as it is hard to find group elements of order less than s in the underlying group. We discuss instantiations in which s can be exponentially large in the security parameter λ.

If the underlying PoCE is constant round and public coin (as is the case for existing protocols), then so are all of our batch PoCEs, implying that they can be made non-interactive using the Fiat-Shamir transform.

Additionally, for RSA groups with moduli which are the products of two safe primes, we show how to efficiently verify that certain elements are not of order 2. This protocol, together with the second compiler above and any (single-instance) PoCE in these groups, yields an efficient batch PoCE in safe RSA groups. To complete the picture, we also show how to

L. Rotem—supported by the Adams Fellowship Program of the Israel Academy of Sciences and Humanities and by the European Union's Horizon 2020 Framework Program (H2020) via an ERC Grant (Grant No. 714253).

K. Nissim and B. Waters (Eds.): TCC 2021, LNCS 13044, pp. 382–414, 2021.
https://doi.org/10.1007/978-3-030-90456-2_13

extend Pietrzak's protocol (which is statistically sound in the group QR_N^+ when N is the product of two safe primes) to obtain a statistically-sound PoCE in safe RSA groups.

1   Introduction

Verifiable delay functions (VDFs), recently formalized by Boneh et al. [BBB+18], have proven to be extremely useful in a wide array of exciting applications. These include, among others, verifiable randomness beacons (e.g., [LW15] and also [GS98, BCG15, BGZ16, PW18, HYL20, GLO+21]), resource-efficient blockchains [CP19], computational time-stamping (e.g., [CE12, LSS20] and the references therein) and time-based proofs of replication (e.g., [Ler14, ABB+16, Pro17, BDG17, Fis19]). Roughly speaking, a VDF is a function $f : \mathcal{X} \to \mathcal{Y}$ which is defined with respect to a delay parameter T and offers the following sequentiality guarantee: It should not be possible to compute f on a randomly-chosen input in time less than T, even with preprocessing and polynomially-many parallel processors. However, the function should be computable in time polynomial in T. Moreover, the function should be efficiently verifiable: For an input $x \in \mathcal{X}$, it should be possible to produce alongside the output $y \in \mathcal{Y}$, a short proof π asserting that indeed $y = f(x)$. Verifying the proof should be much quicker than computing the function anew.

Proofs of Correct Exponentiation. The main VDF candidates currently known are based on the "repeated squaring" function in groups of unknown order, such as RSA groups or class groups of imaginary quadratic fields. This function – first introduced for delay purposes by Rivest, Shamir and Wagner [RSW96] – is defined by $x \mapsto x^{2^T}$, where T is the delay parameter and the exponentiation is with respect to the group operation. The recent and elegant works of Wesolowski [Wes19], of Pietrzak [Pie19] have augmented the repeated squaring function with non-interactive proofs, yielding full-fledged candidate VDF constructions (see also the survey of Boneh et al. [BBF18] covering these constructions). Both of these proofs are based on applying the Fiat-Shamir heuristic [FS86] to *succinct proofs of correct exponentiation*. These are protocols in which a (possibly malicious) prover tries to convince a verifier that $y = x^e$, for a joint input consisting of two group elements x and y and an arbitrary (and potentially very large) exponent e.[1] The succinctness of these protocols manifests itself both in their communication complexity, and in the verifier's running time, which is much lesser than the time it would take the verifier to compute x^e on her own. Very recently, in an independent and concurrent work, Block et al. [BHR+21] showed how to generalize Pietrzak's protocol to obtain a proof of correct exponentiation that is information-theoretically secure in any group of unknown order.

---

[1] Often, these protocols offer only computational soundness guarantee. Nevertheless, we use the name *proofs* (rather than *arguments*) throughout, for more concise presentation and for consistency with previous works (e.g., [BBF19]).

Verifying Multiple VDF Outputs. In many of the applications of VDFs, one might be (and in some cases even likely to be) interested in verifying not only one but many VDF outputs at once. Examples for such scenarios include (but are not restricted to) verifying that a storage service maintains multiple replicas of the same file via a VDF-based proof of replication; verifying the shared randomness produced by a VDF-based randomness beacon during the last several epochs; and verifying the time-stamps of multiple files stamped using a VDF-based time-stamping scheme. Unfortunately, verifying multiple VDF outputs naïvely, by verifying the proof for each of them separately and independently, comes at a premium: If one wishes to verify n individual VDF proofs, each of which is ℓ bits long and takes time t to verify, then verifying all of them using the aforesaid naïve approach results in a total proof size (and hence communication overhead) of $n \cdot \ell$ and verification time of $n \cdot t$.

Existing Approaches. The related and fundamental problem of verifying many exponentiations in cryptographic groups, traces back to the seminal work of Bellare, Garay and Rabin [BGR98], which presented elegant batch verification algorithms. However, their work, motivated by the task of batch verification of signatures, did not consider the setting of an external prover and the efficiency considerations attached to it (i.e., succinctness). Moreover, their more efficient approach and its analysis rely on cyclic groups of prime order, which seem somewhat unlikely to accommodate VDF constructions [RSS20] (see Sect. 1.2). In the context of VDF verification, Wesolowski[2] recently presented a "batch version" of his proof of correct exponentiation. Alas, the soundness of this batch proof is proven under the adaptive root assumption, which is a new and rather strong assumption in groups of unknown order. In particular this assumption is stronger than the low order assumption which underlies Pietrzak's protocol [BBF18,Pie19],[3] and making this assumption is of course undesirable when starting from the information-theoretically sound protocol of Block et al. [BHR+21]. This state of affairs urges the search for succinct and efficient batch proofs of correct exponentiation which rely on weaker assumptions than the adaptive root assumption.

1.1   Our Contributions

We present simple and efficient batch verification techniques for proofs of correct exponentiation, extending the basic techniques of Bellare, Garay and Rabin

---

[2] In the updated longer version of his work [Wes20].

[3] For example, in cyclic groups of prime (and publicly known) order, the low order assumption holds information-theoretically, whereas the adaptive root assumption does not hold. Moreover, even in groups which are believed to be of unknown order, the adaptive root assumption seems to be a stronger one: For instance, for a modulus N which is the product of two safe primes, the low order assumption holds information-theoretically in the group of quadratic residues modulo N. This is in contrast to the adaptive root assumption which is at least as strong as assuming the hardness of factoring N. See Sect. 2 for details.

to the external-prover setting and to composite-order groups. In conjunction with current VDF candidates based on proofs of correct exponentiation for the repeated squaring function [RSW96, Wes19, Pie19, BHR+21], our techniques immediately give rise to VDFs with batch verification. Our compilers rely on weaker assumptions than currently-known batching techniques for verifiable delay functions, paving the way to a variety of new instantiations.

Batch Proofs of Correct Exponentiation. We define the notion of a *batch proof of correct exponentiation*. This is a protocol in which a prover and a verifier share as input n pairs $(x_1, y_1), \ldots, (x_n, y_n)$ of group elements and an exponent $e \in \mathbb{N}$, and the prover attempts to convince the verifier that $x_i^e = y_i$ for each $i \in [n]$.[4] Loosely speaking, we say that a batch proof of correct exponentiation has soundness error δ if in case $x_i^e \neq y_i$ for some $i \in [n]$, no efficient (malicious) prover can convince a verifier to accept with probability greater than $\delta + \mathsf{negl}(\lambda)$, where $\lambda \in \mathbb{N}$ is the security parameter (see Sect. 3 for the formal definition).

A General Compiler. As our first main contribution, we show how to compile any proof of correct exponentiation into a batch proof of correct exponentiation, offering significant savings in both communication and verification time, relative to the naïve transformation. The soundness of this compiler essentially relies on an information-theoretic argument, which is then derandomized using a pseudorandom function. This makes it a generic compiler which can be applied in any group, as long as the underlying proof of correct exponentiation is sound in this group, hence also making it compatible with the new proof of correct exponentiation of Block et al. [BHR+21].

Theorem 1.1 (informal). *Let $\mathbb{G}$ be a group and assume the existence of a one-way function and of a proof of correct exponentiation in $\mathbb{G}$ with communication complexity $c = c(\lambda, e)$, verification time $t = t(\lambda, e)$ and soundness error $\delta = \delta(\lambda)$, where $\lambda \in \mathbb{N}$ is the security parameter and $e \in \mathbb{N}$ is the exponent. Then, for any $n, m \in \mathbb{N}$, there exists a batch proof of correct exponentiation for n pairs of elements in the group $\mathbb{G}$, with communication complexity $c_{\mathsf{batch}} = c \cdot m + \lambda$, verification time $t_{\mathsf{batch}} = m \cdot t + n \cdot m \cdot \mathsf{poly}(\lambda)$ and soundness error $\delta_{\mathsf{batch}} = \delta + 2^{-m}$.*

An Improved Compiler Based on the Low Order Assumption. Our second main contribution is an improved compiler, whose soundness is based on the low order assumption in groups of unknown order, recently introduced by Boneh et al. [BBF18]. Roughly speaking, for an integer ℓ, the ℓ-low order assumption asserts that one cannot efficiently come up with a group element $z \neq 1$ and an exponent $\omega < \ell$ such that $z^\omega = 1$. This compiler enjoys significant improvements over our general compiler: The communication complexity is now completely independent of the desired soundness guarantee (i.e., one can reduce the soundness error without increasing communication), and the running time of the verifier is also improved. Concretely, we prove the following theorem.

---

[4] Note that our definition of batch proofs of correct exponentiation deals with scenarios in which all instances should be verified with respect to the same exponent. We discuss this point further in Sect. 3, and leave it as an interesting open question to construct batch proofs for different exponents.

Theorem 1.2 (informal). *Let $\mathbb{G}$ be a group and assume the existence of a one-way function and of a proof of correct exponentiation in $\mathbb{G}$ with communication complexity $c = c(\lambda, e)$, verification time $t = t(\lambda, e)$ and soundness error $\delta = \delta(\lambda)$, where $\lambda \in \mathbb{N}$ is the security parameter and $e \in \mathbb{N}$ is the exponent. Assume that the ℓ-low order assumption holds in $\mathbb{G}$ for an integer $\ell = \ell(\lambda)$. Then, for any $n \in \mathbb{N}$ and $s \leq \ell$, there exists a batch proof of correct exponentiation for n pairs of elements in the group $\mathbb{G}$, with communication complexity $c_{\mathsf{batch}} = c + \lambda$, verification time $t_{\mathsf{batch}} = t + O(n \cdot \log(s) \cdot \mathsf{poly}(\lambda))$, and soundness error $\delta_{\mathsf{batch}} = \delta + 1/s$.*

In Sect. 6, we also discuss why the low order assumption is necessary for our compiler to yield the soundness guarantees of Theorem 1.2.

Instantiating the Compiler. The compiler from Theorem 1.2 relies on the same techniques as those underlying Wesolowski's [Wes20] batch proof (which, as mentioned above, can be traced back to Bellare, Garay and Rabin [BGR98]). However, our compiler is modular and our analysis of its soundness is based solely on the low order assumption (compared to Wesolowski's reliance on the adaptive root assumption). This means that our compiler can be applied to both the protocols of Wesolowski and of Pietrzak, without making any further assumptions beyond those required by their single-instance protocols (and one-way functions for derandomization purposes). Concretely, there are currently three main candidates for families of groups in which the low order assumption is plausible:[5]

- **The groups QR_N and QR_N^+.** The low order assumption holds information-theoretically in the group QR_N of quadratic residues modulo N when N is the product of two safe primes (as well as in the isomorphic group QR_N^+ of *signed* quadratic residues modulo N, in which group membership is efficiently recognizable). It may also rely on the assumption that the low order problem is computationally hard in these groups for other choices of N. The reader is referred to Sect. 2 for further details regarding these groups.
- **RSA groups.** The low order assumption cannot hold in the RSA group $\mathbb{Z}_N^*$ since $-1 \in \mathbb{Z}_N$ is always of order two in this group. Boneh et al. [BBF18] suggested to work over the quotient group $\mathbb{Z}_N^*/\{\pm 1\}$ instead. We consider two additional possibilities. One is to settle on a slightly weaker soundness guarantee: If the verifier accepts, it must be the case that $x_i^e \in \{y_i, -y_i\}$ for every $i \in [n]$. Observe, that this requirement indeed seems compatible with many of the applications of VDFs mentioned above.[6] When N is the product of two safe primes, we show (following Seres and Burcsi [SB20]) that this weaker notion of soundness for our compiler is actually implied by the

---

[5] For a more in-depth discussion see Sect. 6 and the work of Boneh et al. [BBF18].

[6] For example, when it comes to proofs of replication, if a file is retrievable given an encoding y which is the output of a VDF, then it is also retrievable given $-y$. As an additional example, in the context of verifiable randomness beacons, this weakened soundness guarantee gives a malicious prover the ability to convince the verifier that the shared randomness is $-y$, when in fact it should be y, but no more than that.

hardness of factoring N. The second option is to compose our compiler with an additional protocol, specifically tailored in order to prove that $y_i \neq -x_i^e$ for each i. We discuss this approach below.

– **Class groups of imaginary quadratic fields.** The security of the low order assumption in these groups is still unclear [BBF18,BKS+20], but at least for now, there are possible parameters for which the low order assumption remains unbroken in these groups.

Strong Soundness in RSA Groups via Proofs of Order. As discussed above, when our compiler from Theorem 1.2 is used within RSA groups, we can obtain only a weaker form of soundness. The issue is that a malicious prover can still convince the verifier that $x_i^e = y_i$ for every i, even though there exists an index j for which $y_j/x_j^e = -1$. To remedy this situation we present a protocol that allows the prover to convince the verifier that $\mathsf{order}(y_i/x_i^e) \neq 2$ for every i, and hence in particular $y_i/x_i^e \neq -1$ for every i. The protocol builds on the work of Di Crescenzo et al. [CKK+17], but extends it in a non-trivial manner to save in communication (or proof size, when Fiat-Shamir is applied). It enjoys efficient verification and information-theoretic soundness when the modulus N of the RSA group is the product of two safe primes, and it can be made succinct (i.e., with communication complexity is independent of the number n of pairs of group elements) using a pseudorandom function. Hence, in such groups, executing this protocol in parallel to our compiler from Theorem 1.2 yields a full-fledged sound compiler in RSA groups, without compromising on weaker soundness notions or making strong assumptions. In Theorem 1.3 below, by "safe RSA groups" we mean RSA groups whose modulus is the product of two λ-bit safe primes.

Theorem 1.3 (informal). *Assume the existence of a one-way function and of a proof of correct exponentiation in safe RSA groups with communication complexity $c = c(\lambda, e)$, verification time $t = t(\lambda, e)$ and soundness error $\delta = \delta(\lambda)$, where $\lambda \in \mathbb{N}$ is the security parameter and $e \in \mathbb{N}$ is the exponent. Then, for any $n, m \in \mathbb{N}$ and $s < 2^{\lambda-1}$, there exists a batch proof of correct exponentiation for n pairs of elements in safe RSA groups, with communication complexity $c_{\mathsf{batch}} = c + O(\lambda)$, verification time $t_{\mathsf{batch}} = t + O(n \cdot m \cdot \log(s) \cdot \mathsf{poly}(\lambda))$, and soundness error $\delta_{\mathsf{batch}} = \delta + 1/s + 2^{-m}$.*

A Statistically-Sound Proof of Correct Exponentiation in RSA Groups. To complete the picture, we present a proof of correct exponentiation in standard (safe) RSA groups.[7] The protocol is obtained by extending Pietrzak's protocol [Pie19] with techniques similar to those used to prove Theorem 1.3. The protocol actually achieves statistical soundness in safe RSA groups, with very little overhead in terms of communication and verification time when compared to Pietrzak's protocol.

Theorem 1.4 (informal). *There exists a statistically-sound proof of correct exponentiation in safe RSA groups, whose communication complexity and verification time essentially match those of Pietrzak's protocol.*

---

[7] This is in contrast to the quotient group $\mathbb{Z}_N^* \setminus \{\pm 1\}$ or the subgroups QR_N and QR_N^+ of $\mathbb{Z}_N^*$.

Though the statistically-sound proof of correct exponentiation of Block et al. [BHR+21] can also be instantiated in safe RSA groups, their protocol incurs a factor λ overhead in communication complexity when compared to Pietrzak's protocol. In contrast, our protocol only incurs an overhead of factor 2 in communication complexity.

Interpreting Our Results. We make two clarifications in order to help the reader interpret the above results. Firstly, we emphasize that the parameters m (from Theorems 1.1 and 1.3) and s (from Theorems 1.2 and 1.3) do not scale with the number n of pairs (x_i, y_i) to be verified, and can be fine-tuned at will to achieve the desired tradeoff between the soundness error of the batch protocol on the one hand, and the communication complexity and verifier's running time on the other hand. Secondly, we stress that in all of the above theorems, the polynomials referred to by poly are fixed polynomials that depend only on λ, and do not scale with neither n nor the exponent e. These two points have several important implications:

- The communication overhead incurred by our compilers is completely independent of n.
- The verification time depends linearly on n, but in all of our compilers, we manage to "decouple" the terms which depend on n from the terms which depend on the original verification time t in the underlying proof of correct exponentiation protocol (and hence we also decouple n from the exponent e). This should be contrasted with the naïve solution discussed above, in which the verification time is $t \cdot n$. Moreover, observe that some linear dependency on n seems unavoidable, since merely reading the verifier's input takes time at least n.
- One can set m to be super-logarithmic in the security parameter λ (e.g., by setting $m(\lambda) = \log(\lambda) \cdot \log^*(\lambda)$) in Theorems 1.1 and 1.3, and s to be super-polynomial in Theorems 1.2 and 1.3, to obtain protocols with negligible soundness error, with only slightly greater communication complexities and verification times than those of the underlying proof of correct exponentiation.

Applying the Fiat-Shamir Heuristic. All of our compilers add only a single *public coin* message from the verifier to the prover. Consequently, if the Fiat-Shamir heuristic [FS86] can be applied in the random oracle model to the underlying proof of correct exponentiation, then it can be applied to resulted batch proof as well (as long as m and s are set such that the soundness error is negligible). In particular, the Fiat-Shamir heuristic may be applied to the compiled versions (via our compilers) of the protocols of Wesolowski [Wes19], of Pietrzak [Pie19], and of Block et al. [BHR+21] to obtain non-interactive batch proofs of correct exponentiation. See Sect. 5 and the related work of Lombardi and Vaikuntanathan [LV20] for a more exhaustive discussion on the matter.

Communication in the Interactive Setting. As illustrated below, we use pseudorandom functions in order to shrink the length of the public coin message from the verifier to the prover. This is necessary only in the interactive setting, since when the Fiat-Shamir heuristic is applied this message is computed locally by the prover (and hence does not affect the proof's length). Indeed, verification of VDFs is typically considered to be non-interactive, but we nevertheless believe that exploring interactive verification of VDFs is interesting and well-justified by applications in which verification is done by a single verifier in an online manner, such as VDF-based proofs of storage. Using an interactive protocol in such settings eliminates the need to rely on the Fiat-Shamir transform.

1.2   Additional Related Work and Open Problems

Batch Verification for Group Exponentiation. The line of works that seems most related to ours was initiated by the seminal work of Bellare, Garay and Rabin [BGR98] (following up on the works of Fiat [Fia89], Naccache et al. [NMV+94] and of Yen and Laih [YL95][8]) and considers the following problem: Let $\mathbb{G}$ be a cyclic group and let g be a generator of the group. The task, given n exponents $x_1, \ldots, x_n$ and n group elements $h_1, \ldots, h_n$, is to verify that $g^{x_i} = h_i$ for each $i \in [n]$. Bellare et al. presented several approaches for solving this problem, exhibiting different savings in terms of computational costs vis-à-vis the naïve solution of raising g to the power of each x_i.

Our compilers are inspired by two elegant techniques of Bellare et al. – the "random subsets" technique and the "random exponents" technique – but there are some key differences between their work and ours. Firstly, we embed these techniques within the framework of succinct proofs of correct exponentiation (which we extend to the batch setting). This setting presents its own set of unique technical challenges, the main one being reducing the communication overhead (or proof size, in the non-interactive setting). This challenge does not arise in the setting considered in their work (and in follow-up works), which is motivated by batch verification of signatures. Secondly, the random exponents technique as proposed by Bellare et al. and its analysis explicitly and inherently assumes that the group at hand is of prime order. Such groups do not seem to enable VDF constructions, as Rotem, Segev and Shahaf [RSS20] recently showed how break the sequentiality of any such construction in the generic-group model. We extend the approach underlying the random exponents technique to composite-order groups.

In a concurrent and independent work, Block et al. [BHR+21] also extended the random subsets technique of Bellare et al. that we use to derive Theorem 1.1, in the context of hidden-order groups (though they did not explicitly observe the connection between the work of Bellare et al. and theirs). Their motivation was to extend Pietrzak's protocol [Pie19] to obtain an information-theoretically sound protocol, while ours is proof batching, but the application of the random subsets technique is quite similar in both cases.

Di Crescenzo et al. [CKK+17] considered the related problem of batch delegation of exponentiation in RSA groups, while extending the random exponents technique of Bellare, Garay and Rabin. Our treatment of RSA groups is also

---

[8] See also [CHP07] and the many references therein.

inspired by the techniques of Di Crescenzo et al. but their protocol includes a communication overhead which is linear in the number n of exponentiations to be delegated (and verified) – which in our setting, is exactly what we are trying to avoid. We manage to get rid of this dependency altogether.

A long line of follow-up works succeeded the work of Bellare et al. suggesting various improvements to their techniques in various settings (see for example [BP00, CL06, CY07, CHP07, CL15] and the references therein). An interesting open question is whether some of these techniques can be used in order to improve our results.

Other VDF Candidates. This work focuses on VDF candidates which are based on the repeated squaring function in groups of unknown order. Other candidates have also been proposed over the last couple of years. Some of which are based on different assumptions, such as candidates based on super-singular isogenies [FMP+19, Sha19], and the VeeDo VDF candidate in prime fields [Sta20]; while other constructions (e.g., [EFK+20, DGM+20]) achieve various desired properties. An interesting possible direction for future research is to enable batch verification to these candidate VDFs as well, either relying on our techniques or presenting new ones tailored specifically for these candidates.

Necessity of One-Way Functions in the Interactive Setting. Informally put, our protocols use some function f to derandomize a long public coin message from the verifier to the prover. In our proposed instantiations, f is implemented using a cryptographic pseudorandom generator or pseudorandom function (both are known to exist assuming one-way functions [GGM86, Nao91, HIL+99]), and we show that the soundness of this approach is "as good" as the soundness before the derandomization. However, in all of our protocols, we only need the output of f on a uniformly-random input to satisfy some specific statistical property. Hence, an interesting open question is whether our reliance on one-way functions is necessary, or can f be instantiated without them while still offering comparable security guarantees. One possibility is to use a Nissan-Wigderson type pseudorandom generator [NW94, IW97], relying on worst-case assumptions. Another is to use ϵ-biaset sets (see for example [NN93, AGH+92, Ta-17] and the references therein), though this approach seems to inherently yield a slightly worse communication to soundness tradeoff.

1.3   Technical Overview

In this section we provide a high-level overview of the techniques used throughout the paper. In this overview, we ignore various technical subtleties that arise in the full proofs.

The Basic Random Subset Compiler. We start by describing the basic idea which underlines the generic compiler guaranteed by Theorem 1.1. Let Π be any (single-instance) proof of correct exponentiation, and let $(x_1, y_1), \ldots, (x_n, y_n)$ and $e \in \mathbb{N}$ be the n pairs of group elements and the exponent that are shared by the prover and the verifier as input. Recall that the prover wishes to convince the verifier that $y_i = x_i^e$ for each $i \in [n]$. The basic technical observation underlying the compiler is that if for some index $i \in [n]$ it holds that $y_i \neq x_i^e$, then with probability at least $1/2$ over the choice of a uniformly random subset $\mathcal{S}$ of $[n]$, it holds that $\prod_{j \in \mathcal{S}} y_j \neq \left(\prod_{j \in \mathcal{S}} x_j \right)^e$. This observation then naturally lends itself to obtain a batch proof of correct exponentiation: First, the verifier simply chooses such a subset $\mathcal{S}$ uniformly at random and sends it to the prover. Then, the verifier and the prover execute Π on shared input $(x' = \prod_{j \in \mathcal{S}} x_j, y' = \prod_{j \in \mathcal{S}} y_j, e)$; that is, the prover uses Π to convince the verifier that indeed $y' = (x')^e$. By the above observation, if Π has soundness error δ, then the compiled batch protocol has soundness error at most $\delta + 1/2$. The reader is referred to Sect. 4 for a formal description of the compiler and its analysis.

Amplifying Soundness and Reducing Communication. The above compiler suffers from two main drawbacks: The soundness error of the resulted batch protocol is at least $1/2$, and its communication complexity is necessarily linear in the number n of pairs of group elements, since a uniformly chosen subset of $[n]$ has n bits of entropy. Fortunately, this situation is easy to remedy by introducing two simple modifications to the protocol. First, instead of choosing just one subset $\mathcal{S}$ of $[n]$, the verifier chooses m such subsets $\mathcal{S}_1, \ldots, \mathcal{S}_m$ for some integer m which parameterizes the compiler. Then, the verifier and the prover run m parallel executions of the underlying protocol Π, where in the ith execution, they run on shared input $(x_i' = \prod_{j \in \mathcal{S}_i} x_j, y_i' = \prod_{j \in \mathcal{S}_i} y_j, e)$. Suppose that $y_j \neq x_j^e$ for some $j \in [n]$. Using the observation from the previous paragraph, it is straightforward that if $\mathcal{S}_1, \ldots, \mathcal{S}_m$ are chosen independently and uniformly at random from all subsets of $[n]$, then the probability that $y_i' = (x_i')^e$ for each $i \in [m]$ is at most 2^{-m}. Hence, if Π has soundness error δ, then the compiled batch protocol has soundness error at most $\delta + 2^{-m}$ (regardless of whether the soundness of the underlying protocol Π is amplified via parallel repetition).

In order to attend to the large communication complexity of the compiled protocol (now the verifier has to send $k \cdot n$ bits to the prover), we derandomize the choice of the sets $\mathcal{S}_1, \ldots, \mathcal{S}_m$. Instead of sampling these sets explicitly and sending their description to the prover, the verifier now samples and sends a short key k to a pseudorandom function PRF. This key can now succinctly represent $\mathcal{S}_1, \ldots, \mathcal{S}_m$; for example by letting $j \in \mathcal{S}_i$ if and only if $\mathsf{PRF}_k(i, j) = 1$, for every $i \in [m]$ and $j \in [n]$. Roughly speaking, the security of the pseudorandom function guarantees that if $y_j \neq x_j^e$ for some $j \in [n]$, then the probability that $y_i' = (x_i')^e$ for each $i \in [m]$ is at most $2^{-m} + \mathsf{negl}(\lambda)$, where λ is the security parameter. See Sect. 5 for a formal description and analysis of the strengthened protocol.

The Random Exponents Compiler. We now describe the idea behind our improved compiler based on the low order assumption (Theorem 1.2). The observation is that the basic Random Subset Compiler as described above can be viewed in a more general manner: The verifier chooses $\alpha_1, \ldots, \alpha_n \leftarrow \{0, 1\}$, and then the two parties invoke the underlying protocol Π on joint input $x' = \prod_{i \in [n]} x_i^{\alpha_i}$, $y' = \prod_{i \in [n]} y_i^{\alpha_i}$ and e. The idea is to now let the verifier choose

$\alpha_1, \ldots, \alpha_n$ from a large domain; concretely, from the set $[s]$ for some appropriately chosen parameter $s \in \mathbb{N}$. As before, after the verifier chooses $\alpha_1, \ldots, \alpha_n$ and sends them over to the prover, the two parties invoke the underlying protocol Π on shared input (x', y', e) for asserting that $y' = (x')^e$. It should be noted that as in the Random Subset Compiler, the choice of $\alpha_1, \ldots, \alpha_n$ can be derandomized using a pseudorandom function in order to save in communication, without significantly affecting the soundness of the compiler.

The proof of soundness of the compiled protocol now has to rely on the s-low order assumption, which roughly speaking, says that it should be hard to find a group element x and a positive integer $\omega < s$ such that $x^\omega = 1$. We wish to argue that if the s-low order assumption holds in the group at hand and $y_j \neq x_j^e$ for some $j \in [n]$, then enlarging the domain from which $\alpha_1, \ldots, \alpha_n$ are drawn (up to and including $[s]$) proportionally reduces the probability that $y' = (x')^e$. This is done by a reduction, which we now informally describe, to the s-low order assumption. For the formal statement and reduction, we refer the reader to Sect. 6.

Let $(x_1, y_1), \ldots, (x_n, y_n)$ be n pairs of elements in a group $\mathbb{G}$ such that at least one index i satisfies $y_i \neq x_i^e$, and let i^* be the first such index. Consider the following algorithm A for finding a low order element in $\mathbb{G}$. A first samples $n + 1$ integers $\alpha_1, \ldots, \alpha_{i^*-1}, \alpha_{i^*+1}, \ldots, \alpha_n, \beta, \beta'$ uniformly at random from $[s]$. Then, it checks that $\left(x_{i^*}^\beta \cdot \prod_{i \in [n] \setminus \{i^*\}} x_i^{\alpha_i} \right)^e = y_{i^*}^\beta \cdot \prod_{i \in [n] \setminus \{i^*\}} y_i^{\alpha_i}$, that $\left(x_{i^*}^{\beta'} \cdot \prod_{i \in [n] \setminus \{i^*\}} x_i^{\alpha_i} \right)^e = y_{i^*}^{\beta'} \cdot \prod_{i \in [n] \setminus \{i^*\}} y_i^{\alpha_i}$, and that $\beta \neq \beta'$. If any of these conditions does not hold, it aborts. Otherwise, if all of these conditions check out, A outputs the group element $z = y_{i^*}/x_{i^*}^e$ together with the exponent $\omega = |\beta - \beta'|$. It is easy to verify that if both of the equalities checked by A hold, then this implies that $z^\omega = 1$, while the inequality checked by A implies that indeed $\omega \neq 0$. Now assume towards contradiction that the probability that $y' = (x')^e$ is at least $1/s + \epsilon$ for some $\epsilon > 0$. Then, a careful analysis shows that the probability that A does not abort is at least ϵ^2. Informally, this implies that if the s-low order assumption holds in $\mathbb{G}$ and the underlying protocol Π has soundness error δ, then the compiled batch protocol has soundness error at most $\delta + 1/s + \mathsf{negl}(\lambda)$.

Strong Soundness in Safe RSA Groups. Recall that, as mentioned in Sect. 1.1, the s-low order assumption cannot hold in the group $\mathbb{Z}_N^*$ for any $s \geq 2$, since $N - 1$ is always an element of order 2 in the group. Therefore, the Random Exponents Compiler obtains a weaker form of soundness when applied in $\mathbb{Z}_N^*$, guaranteeing only that $y_i = \pm x_i^e$. To counter this problem, we present a protocol for proving that $\mathsf{order}(y_i/x_i^e) \neq 2$ for every i. Our basic approach follows a technique by Di Crescenzo et al. [CKK+17] for proving that $\mathsf{order}(y/x^e) \neq 2$ for $x, y \in \mathbb{Z}_N^*$ and an odd exponent e. In their protocol, the prover computes $w = x^{(e+1)/2}$ and sends it to the verifier, who then accepts if and only if $w^2 = x \cdot y$. The idea is that if N is the product of two safe primes and $\mathsf{order}(y/x^e) = 2$, then $x \cdot y$ must be a quadratic non-residue modulo N. This is true since, as we prove, all group elements of order 2 in $\mathbb{Z}_N^*$, including y/x^e, are quadratic non-residues modulo N. Now observe that $x \cdot y = (y/x^e) \cdot x^{e+1}$. Since e is odd, x^{e+1} is a quadratic residue modulo N, and we conclude that $x \cdot y$ is a quadratic non-residue modulo N. This means that w^2, which is of course a quadratic residue modulo N, cannot be equal to $x \cdot y$ and the verifier will inevitably reject.

Generalizing this approach to arbitrary exponents is fairly straightforward, by having the prover compute w as $x^{\lceil(e+1)/2\rceil}$ and then having the verifier check that $w^2 = x^{1+(e+1 \mod 2)} \cdot y$. The more acute issue is that when moving to the batch setting, the naïve way for verifying that $\mathsf{order}(y_i/x_i^e) \neq 2$ for every $i \in [n]$ is by running the above protocol n times in parallel, which results in communication complexity which is linear in n. To avoid this overhead, we combine the ideas of Di Crescenzo et al. with techniques from our Random Subset Compiler. Concretely, in our final protocol, the verifier chooses a key k to a pseudorandom function, to succinctly represent m random subsets $\mathcal{S}_1, \ldots, \mathcal{S}_m$ of $[n]$, and sends k to the prover. The prover then computes $w_j := \prod_{i \in \mathcal{S}_j} x_i^{\lceil(e+1)/2\rceil}$ for every $j \in [m]$ and sends $w_1, \ldots, w_m$ to the verifier. Finally, the verifier computes $t_j := \prod_{i \in \mathcal{S}_j} x_i^{1+(e+1 \mod 2)} \cdot y_i$ for every $j \in [m]$ and accepts if and only if $t_j = w_j^2$ for all j-s. A careful analysis shows that if $\mathsf{order}(y_i/x_i^e) = 2$ for some $i \in [n]$ and the subsets $\mathcal{S}_1, \ldots, \mathcal{S}_m$ uniformly and independently at random, then each t_j is a quadratic non-residue with probability at least $1/2$. This implies that the verifier will accept with probability at most $2^{-m} + \mathsf{negl}(\lambda)$. We refer the reader to the full version for a detailed description of our protocol and a formal analysis of its soundness.

A Statistically-Sound Protocol in Safe RSA Groups. Our statistically-sound proof of correct exponentiation in RSA groups is obtained by extending the protocol of Pietrzak [Pie19] using techniques similar to those detailed above. We start by recalling Pietrzak's protocol. Suppose that the prover wishes to convince the verifier that $y = x^{2^T}$ for a group $\mathbb{G}$, elements $x, y \in \mathbb{G}$ and an integer T, and assume for ease of presentation that $T = 2^t$ for some $t \in \mathbb{N}$. In the beginning of the protocol, the prover computes $z = x^{2^{T/2}}$ and sends z to the verifier. Now the prover wishes to prove to the verifier that indeed $z = x^{2^{T/2}}$ and $y = z^{2^{T/2}}$, since if $y \neq x^{2^T}$ then it must be that $z \neq x^{2^{T/2}}$ or $y \neq z^{2^{T/2}}$. One possibility is to recurse on both claims, until the exponent is small enough for the verifier to verify the claims herself. However, in this manner the number of sub-claims will blowup very quickly, resulting in a lengthy proof and in a long verification time. So instead, Pietrzak's idea is to merge both claims using (implicitly) the random exponents technique of Bellare, Garay and Rabin [BGR98]. The verifier samples a random integer $r \leftarrow [2^\lambda]$ and sends it to the prover, and then the two parties recurse on the (single) instance $(x' = x^r \cdot z, y' = z^r \cdot y, T' = T/2)$. That is, the prover now needs to convince the verifier of the claim $y' = (x')^{T'}$, where T' is half the size of T. Suppose now that all elements in the group are of order at least 2^λ.[9] In this case, if $y \neq x^{2^T}$ then there is at most one value of $r \in [2^\lambda]$ for which $y' = (x')^{T'}$ and hence $\Pr\left[y' = (x')^{T'}\right] \leq 2^{-\lambda}$ over the choice of r. This recursion continues for $\log T = t$ rounds until $T = 1$, in which case the verifier can simply check the relation $y = x^2$ herself using a single squaring in the group.

In order to extend this protocol to the group $\mathbb{Z}_N^*$ for a modulus N that is the product of two safe primes, we use similar techniques to those used above for extending the Random Exponents Compiler. Concretely, consider a round in Piertzak's protocol in which the prover wants to prove that $y = x^{2^T}$. In addition to $z = x^{2^{T/2}}$, the prover now also computes $w = x^{2^{T/2-1}+1}$ and sends it to the verifier. The verifier then checks that $x^2 \cdot z = w^2$, and if that is not the case then the verifier rejects immediately. This additional verification is made in each of the $\log T$ rounds of the protocol, and if the verifier does not reject in any of the rounds and the check for $T = 1$ goes through, then the verifier accepts.

To analyze the soundness of our protocol, suppose that all group elements (other than the identity) are either of order 2 or have order at least 2^λ; this is the case for $\mathbb{Z}_N^*$ where N is the product of two large enough safe primes. Let x and y be group elements such that $y \neq x^{2^T}$, and assume that z and w are the group elements which the prover sends to the verifier. If $x^2 \cdot z \neq w^2$, then the verifier will surely reject and we are done, so for the rest of the analysis we assume that $x^2 \cdot z = w^2$. Consider two cases:

- If $z = x^{2^{T/2}}$, then for any $r \in [2^\lambda]$ it holds that $(x^r \cdot z)^{2^{T/2}} = z^r \cdot x^{2^T} \neq z^r \cdot y$. In other words, $\Pr\left[y' = (x')^{T'}\right] = 0$, where $x' = x^r \cdot z$, $y' = z^r \cdot y$, $T' = T/2$ and the probability is taken over $r \leftarrow [2^\lambda]$.

- If $z \neq x^{2^{T/2}}$, then we prove that there is at most one value $r \in [2^\lambda]$ for which $(x^r \cdot z)^{2^{T/2}} = z^r \cdot y$. Assume towards contradiction otherwise; that is, that there are two *distinct* integers $r, r' \in [2^\lambda]$ for which this equality holds. Rearranging, this means that $(x^{2^{T/2}}/z)^d = 1$ for $d = r - r'$. Since $x^{2^{T/2}} \neq z$ and $d < 2^\lambda$, we obtain that the order of $x^{2^{T/2}}/z$ is greater than 1 and lesser than 2^λ, and hence this order must be 2. On the one hand, this means that $x^{2^{T/2}}/z$ is a quadratic non-residue modulo N (recall that all elements of order 2 in a safe RSA group are quadratic non-residues), and hence z is a quadratic non-residue modulo N. But on the other hand, our assumption that $x^2 \cdot z = w^2$ implies that z is a quadratic residue modulo N, arriving at a contradiction.

Over all, we obtain that in each round whose input (x, y, T) satisfies $y \neq x^{2^T}$, the probability that the input (x', y', T') to the next round will satisfy $y' = (x')^{T'}$ is at most $2^{-\lambda}$ over the choice of $r \leftarrow [2^\lambda]$. The soundness of our protocol then follows by taking a union bound over all rounds. We refer the reader to the full version for a detailed description of our protocol and a formal analysis of its soundness.

---

[9] Recall that Boneh et al. [BBF18] proved computational soundness by extending this analysis to the case where there are elements of order less than 2^λ, but these are hard to find. We focus here on statistical soundness, as this is what we will obtain in safe RSA groups.

1.4   Paper Organization

The remainder of this paper is organized as follows. First, in Sect. 2 we present the basic notation, mathematical background and standard cryptographic primitives that are used throughout the paper. In Sect. 3 we formally define proofs of correct exponentiation and their batch variant. In Sect. 4 we present a simplified version of our Random Subsets Compiler for general groups; and then in Sect. 5 we present the necessary amendments required in order to obtain the full-fledged compiler. In Sect. 6 we present our improved compiler and analyze its security based on the low order assumption.

Due to space limitations some of our contributions appear in the full version of this paper. In particular, in the full version we give tighter security analyses for our more efficient compiler in the specific cases of QR_N^+ and RSA groups. In addition, we show how to obtain strong soundness for this compiler in safe RSA groups, and present our new proof of correct exponentiation in such groups.

2   Preliminaries

In this section we present the basic notions and standard cryptographic tools that are used in this work. For an integer $n \in \mathbb{N}$ we denote by $[n]$ the set $\{1, \dots, n\}$. For a set $\mathcal{X}$, we denote by $2^{\mathcal{X}}$ the power set of $\mathcal{X}$; i.e., the set which contains all subsets of $\mathcal{X}$ (including the empty set and $\mathcal{X}$ itself). For a distribution X we denote by $x \leftarrow X$ the process of sampling a value x from the distribution X. Similarly, for a set $\mathcal{X}$ we denote by $x \leftarrow \mathcal{X}$ the process of sampling a value x from the uniform distribution over $\mathcal{X}$. A function $\nu : \mathbb{N} \to \mathbb{R}^+$ is *negligible* if for any polynomial $p(\cdot)$ there exists an integer N such that for all $n > N$ it holds that $\nu(n) \leq 1/p(n)$.

Pseudorandom Functions. We use the following standard notion of a pseudorandom function. Let $\mathsf{PRF} = (\mathsf{PRF.Gen}, \mathsf{PRF.Eval})$ be a function family over domain $\{\mathcal{X}_\lambda\}_{\lambda \in \mathbb{N}}$ with range $\{\mathcal{Y}_\lambda\}_{\lambda \in \mathbb{N}}$ and key space $\{\mathcal{K}_\lambda\}_{\lambda \in \mathbb{N}}$, such that:

- $\mathsf{PRF.Gen}$ is a probabilistic polynomial-time algorithm, which takes as input the security parameter $\lambda \in \mathbb{N}$ and outputs a key $K \in \mathcal{K}_\lambda$.
- $\mathsf{PRF.Eval}$ is a deterministic polynomial-time algorithm, which takes as input a key $K \in \mathcal{K}_\lambda$ and a domain element $x \in \mathcal{X}_\lambda$ and outputs a value $y \in \mathcal{Y}_\lambda$.

For ease of notation, for a key $K \in \mathcal{K}_\lambda$, we denote by $\mathsf{PRF}_K(\cdot)$ the function $\mathsf{PRF.Eval}(K, \cdot)$. We also assume without loss of generality that for every $\lambda \in \mathbb{N}$, it holds that $\mathcal{K}_\lambda = \{0,1\}^\lambda$ and that $\mathsf{PRF.Gen}(1^\lambda)$ simply samples K from $\{0,1\}^\lambda$ uniformly at random. Using these conventions, the following definition captures the standard notion of a pseudorandom function family.

Definition 2.1. *A function family* $\mathsf{PRF} = (\mathsf{PRF.Gen}, \mathsf{PRF.Eval})$ *is* pseudorandom *if for every probabilistic polynomial-time algorithm* D, *there exists a negligible function* $\nu(\cdot)$ *such that*

$$\mathsf{Adv}_{\mathsf{PRF}, \mathsf{D}}(\lambda) \stackrel{\mathsf{def}}{=} \left| \Pr_{K \leftarrow \{0,1\}^\lambda} \left[\mathsf{D}(1^\lambda)^{\mathsf{PRF}_K(\cdot)} = 1 \right] - \Pr_{f \leftarrow \mathcal{F}_\lambda} \left[\mathsf{D}(1^\lambda)^{f(\cdot)} = 1 \right] \right| \leq \nu(\lambda),$$

for all sufficiently large $\lambda \in \mathbb{N}$, where $\mathcal{F}_\lambda$ is the set of all functions mapping $\mathcal{X}_\lambda$ into $\mathcal{Y}_\lambda$.

RSA Groups and the Factoring Assumption. We will use to following formalization in order to reason about ensembles of RSA moduli and the hardness of finding their factorizations. Let ModGen be a probabilistic polynomial-time algorithm, which takes as input the security parameter $\lambda \in \mathbb{N}$, and outputs a bi-prime modulus $N = p \cdot q$ and possibly additional parameters pp.

Definition 2.2. *The factoring assumption holds with respect to modulus generation algorithm* ModGen *if for every probabilistic polynomial time algorithm* A, *there exists a negligible function $\nu(\cdot)$ such that*

$$\Pr\left[\begin{matrix} p' \cdot q' = N \\ p', q' \in \{2, \ldots, N-1\} \end{matrix} \middle| \begin{matrix} (N, \mathsf{pp}) \leftarrow \mathsf{ModGen}(1^\lambda) \\ (p', q') \leftarrow \mathsf{A}(N, \mathsf{pp}) \end{matrix}\right] \leq \nu(\lambda),$$

for all sufficiently large $\lambda \in \mathbb{N}$.

The following simple lemma (see for example [Bon99]) states that it is easy to find a factorization of an RSA modulus N given a non-trivial square root of unity in the RSA group $\mathbb{Z}_N^*$.

Lemma 2.3. *There exist a deterministic algorithm* A, *such that for every pair (p, q) of primes and every group element $x \in \mathbb{Z}_N^*$ for which $x^2 = 1$ and $x \notin \{1, -1\}$, where $N = p \cdot q$, it holds that* A(N, x) *outputs p and q. Moreover,* A *runs in time polynomial in $\log(N)$.*

Using Safe Primes. We will sometimes focus on the case in which the RSA modulus N is the product of two *safe* primes. That is, $N = p' \cdot q'$, such that p' and q' are primes and there exist primes p and q for which $p' = 2p + 1$ and $q' = 2q + 1$. In this case, the order of the RSA group $\mathbb{Z}_N^*$ is $\varphi(N) = 4 \cdot p \cdot q$, where $\varphi(\cdot)$ is Euler's totient function.

The Group QR_N^+. Another group of interest in this work is the group QR_N of quadratic residues modulo N, where N is an RSA modulus generated by the modulus generation algorithm ModGen. This is the group defined by

$$QR_N \overset{\text{def}}{=} \left\{x^2 \mod N : x \in \mathbb{Z}_N^*\right\}.$$

The order of the group QR_N is $\varphi(N)/4$. If N is the product of two safe primes $p' = 2p + 1$ and $q' = 2q + 1$, this means the order of QR_N is $p \cdot q$.

We will also consider the group QR_N^+ of *signed* quadratic residues modulo N, defined by

$$QR_N^+ \overset{\text{def}}{=} \{|x| : x \in QR_N\},$$

where the absolute value operator $|\cdot|$ is with respect to the representation of $\mathbb{Z}_N^*$ elements as elements in $\{-(N-1)/2, \ldots, (N-1)/2\}$. This is because membership in QR_N^+ can be decided in polynomial time[10] and we will implicitly use this fact when reasoning about these groups. The map $|\cdot|$ acts as an isomorphism from QR_N to QR_N^+, and hence QR_N^+ is also of order $\varphi(N)/4$. For a more in-depth discussion on the use of QR_N^+ instead of QR_N see [FS00, HK09, Pie19].

Working Over General Groups. Some of the results in this paper are more general, and do not assume working over a specific group. In these cases, the algorithm ModGen will be replaced by a group generation algorithm GGen. This is a probabilistic polynomial-time algorithm which takes in as input the security parameter and outputs a description of a group $\mathbb{G}$, and possibly additional public parameters pp. All groups in this paper are assumed to be abelian and we will not note this explicitly hereinafter. We will also implicitly assume that for all groups considered in this paper, their group operation is implementable in time polynomial in the security parameter λ.

The Low Order Assumption. We will rely on the following formalization of the low order assumption, put forth by Boneh et al. [BBF18] as a prerequesite for instantiating Pietrzak's protocol [Pie19] in general groups. For a group $\mathbb{G}$, let $1_\mathbb{G}$ denote the identity element of the group.

Definition 2.4. *Let* GGen *be a group generation algorithm, and let* $d = d(\lambda)$ *be an integer function of the security parameter* $\lambda \in \mathbb{N}$. *We say that the d-low order assumption holds with respect to* GGen *if for every probabilistic polynomial-time algorithm* A, *there exists a negligible function* $\nu(\cdot)$ *such that*

$$\mathsf{Adv}_{\mathsf{GGen},d,\mathsf{A}}^{\mathsf{LowOrd}}(\lambda) \overset{\text{def}}{=} \Pr\left[\mathsf{LowOrd}_{d,\mathsf{A}}^{\mathsf{GGen}}(\lambda) = 1\right] \leq \nu(\lambda)$$

for all sufficiently large $\lambda \in \mathbb{N}$, *where the experiment* $\mathsf{LowOrd}_{d,\mathsf{A}}^{\mathsf{GGen}}(\lambda)$ *is defined as follows:*

1. $\mathbb{G} \leftarrow \mathsf{GGen}(1^\lambda)$.
2. $(x, \omega) \leftarrow \mathsf{A}(\mathbb{G})$.
3. *Output 1 if* $x \neq 1_\mathbb{G}$; $\omega < d$; *and* $x^\omega = 1_\mathbb{G}$. *Otherwise, output 0.*

Pietrzak observed (although not in this terminology) that the d-low order assumption holds information-theoretically in the group QR_N^+, whenever N is the product of two safe primes $p' = 2p + 1$ and $q' = 2q + 1$, and $d \leq \min\{p, q\}$.

In cases where $\mathbb{G}$ is naturally embedded in some ring R and $-1_\mathbb{G} \in \mathbb{G}$ (that is, the additive inverse of the multiplicative identity is an element of the group),[11] we can consider a weakening of Definition 2.4, requiring that the adversary is unable to come up with a low order element other than $\pm 1_\mathbb{G}$.

---

[10] This is the case since, as observed by Fischlin and Schnorr [FS00], $QR_N^+ = \mathbb{J}_N^+$, where $\mathbb{J}_N$ is the group of elements with Jacobi symbol $+1$ and $\mathbb{J}_N^+ \overset{\text{def}}{=} \mathbb{J}_N / \pm 1$. Hence, deciding whether an integer x is in QR_N^+ amounts to checking that $x \geq 0$ and that its Jacobi symbol is $+1$.

[11] This is indeed the case for RSA groups, which are embedded in the ring $\mathbb{Z}_N$.

Definition 2.5. *Let* GGen *be a group generation algorithm, and let* $d = d(\lambda)$ *be an integer function of the security parameter* $\lambda \in \mathbb{N}$. *We say that the* weak d-low order assumption *holds with respect to* GGen *if for every probabilistic polynomial-time algorithm* A, *there exists a negligible function* $\nu(\cdot)$ *such that*

$$\mathsf{Adv}^{\mathsf{WeakLO}}_{\mathsf{GGen},d,\mathsf{A}}(\lambda) \overset{\text{def}}{=} \Pr\left[\mathsf{WeakLO}^{\mathsf{GGen}}_{d,\mathsf{A}}(\lambda) = 1\right] \leq \nu(\lambda)$$

for all sufficiently large $\lambda \in \mathbb{N}$, *where the experiment* $\mathsf{WeakLO}^{\mathsf{GGen}}_{d,\mathsf{A}}(\lambda)$ *is defined as follows:*

1. $\mathbb{G} \leftarrow \mathsf{GGen}(1^\lambda)$.
2. $(x,\omega) \leftarrow \mathsf{A}(\mathbb{G})$.
3. *Output 1 if* $x \notin \{1_\mathbb{G}, -1_\mathbb{G}\}$; $\omega < d$; *and* $x^\omega = 1_\mathbb{G}$. *Otherwise, output 0.*

Seres and Burcsi [SB20] recently proved (as a special case) that in RSA groups with a modulus N which is the product of two safe primes $p' = 2p + 1$ and $q' = 2q + 1$, the weak d-low order assumption for $d \leq \min\{p,q\}$ is equivalent to factoring N.

3 Succinct Proofs of Correct Exponentiation

In this section we review the notion of succinct proofs of correct exponentiation. First, in Sect. 3.1, we define proofs of correct exponentiation for a single instance and then, in Sect. 3.2, we extend the definition to account for the task of batch verification.

3.1 The Basic Definition

Loosely speaking, a proof of correct exponentiation is a protocol executed by two parties, a prover and a verifier, with a common input (x, y, e), where x and y are elements in some group $\mathbb{G}$ and e is an integer. The goal of the prover is to convince the verifier that $y = x^e$. Of course, the verifier can just compute x^e and compare the result to y on her own, but we will be interested in protocols in which the verifier works much less than that. Concretely, we are typically interested in protocols in which the verifier runs in time $\ll \mathsf{poly}(\log(e), \lambda)$, which is the time it will take the verifier to compute x^e on her own, assuming that the group operation is implementable in time polynomial in the security parameter $\lambda \in \mathbb{N}$.

More formally, a proof of correct exponentiation (PoCE) is a triplet $\pi = (\mathsf{GGen}, \mathsf{P}, \mathsf{V})$ of probabilistic polynomial-time algorithms, where GGen is a group generation algorithm (recall Sect. 2), P is the prover and V is the verifier. We denote by $\langle \mathsf{P}(\mathsf{aux}), \mathsf{V}\rangle(\mathsf{input})$ the random variable corresponding to the output of V when the joint input to P and to V is input and P additionally receives the private auxiliary information aux. In case P receives no auxiliary information, we write $\langle \mathsf{P}, \mathsf{V}\rangle(\mathsf{input})$. The properties which should be satisfied by a PoCE are defined in the following definition.

Definition 3.1. *Let* $\delta = \delta(\lambda)$ *be a function of the security parameter* $\lambda \in \mathbb{N}$, *and let* $t = t(\lambda, e)$ *and* $c = c(\lambda, e)$ *be functions of* $\lambda \in \mathbb{N}$ *and of the exponent* $e \in \mathbb{N}$. *A triplet* $\pi = (\mathsf{GGen}, \mathsf{P}, \mathsf{V})$ *of probabilistic polynomial-time algorithms is said to be a* (δ, c, t)-*proof of correct exponentiation (PoCE) if the following conditions hold:*

1. **Completeness:** *For every* $\lambda \in \mathbb{N}$, *for every* $(\mathbb{G}, \mathsf{pp})$ *in the support of* $\mathsf{GGen}(1^\lambda)$ *and for every input* $(x, y, e) \in \mathbb{G}^2 \times \mathbb{N}$ *such that* $x^e = y$, *it holds that*
$$\Pr\left[\langle \mathsf{P}, \mathsf{V} \rangle (\mathbb{G}, \mathsf{pp}, x, y, e) = 1\right] = 1,$$
   where the probability is over the randomness of P *and of* V.
2. δ-**Soundness:** *For every pair* $\mathsf{P}^* = (\mathsf{P}_1^*, \mathsf{P}_2^*)$ *of probabilistic polynomial-time algorithms, there exists a negligible function* $\nu(\cdot)$ *that*
$$\mathsf{Adv}_{\pi, \mathsf{P}^*}^{\mathsf{PoCE}} \stackrel{\text{def}}{=} \Pr\left[\begin{matrix} \langle \mathsf{P}_2^*(\mathsf{st}), \mathsf{V} \rangle (\mathbb{G}, \mathsf{pp}, x, y, e) = 1 \\ x^e \neq y \end{matrix} \middle| \begin{matrix} (\mathbb{G}, \mathsf{pp}) \leftarrow \mathsf{GGen}(1^\lambda) \\ (x, y, e, \mathsf{st}) \leftarrow \mathsf{P}_1^*(\mathbb{G}, \mathsf{pp}) \end{matrix}\right]$$
$$\leq \delta(\lambda) + \nu(\lambda),$$
   for all sufficiently large $\lambda \in \mathbb{N}$.
3. **Succinctness:** *For every* $\lambda \in \mathbb{N}$, *for every* $(\mathbb{G}, \mathsf{pp})$ *in the support of* $\mathsf{GGen}(1^\lambda)$ *and for every input* $(x, y, e) \in \mathbb{G}^2 \times \mathbb{N}$, *it holds that: The total length of all messages exchanged between* P *and* V *in a random execution of the protocol on joint input* $(\mathbb{G}, \mathsf{pp}, x, y, e)$ *is at most* $c(\lambda, e)$ *with probability 1, where the probability is over the randomness of* P *and of* V.
4. **Efficient verification:** *For every* $\lambda \in \mathbb{N}$, *for every* $(\mathbb{G}, \mathsf{pp})$ *in the support of* $\mathsf{GGen}(1^\lambda)$ *and for every input* $(x, y, e) \in \mathbb{G}^2 \times \mathbb{N}$, *it holds that: The running time of* V *in a random execution of the protocol on joint input* $(\mathbb{G}, \mathsf{pp}, x, y, e)$ *is at most* $t(\lambda, e)$ *with probability 1, where the probability is over the randomness of* P *and of* V.

3.2   Batch Proofs of Correct Exponentiation

We now turn to define *batch* proofs of correct exponentiation. In such proofs, the joint input is composed of $2n$ group elements $x_1, \ldots, x_n, y_1, \ldots, y_n$ and an exponent e, for some $n \in \mathbb{N}$. The prover now wishes to convince the verifier that $x_i^e = y_i$ for each of the $i \in [n]$. The definition is a natural extension of Definition 3.1, except that now the communication complexity and the running time of the verifier may both scale with the integer n. It might also make sense to consider the case where the soundness error δ is also a function of n, but this will not be the case in our protocols, and hence we do not account for this case in our definition. The formal definition below uses the same notation as did Definition 3.1.

Definition 3.2. *Let* $\delta = \delta(\lambda)$ *be a function of the security parameter* $\lambda \in \mathbb{N}$, *and let* $t = t(\lambda, e, n)$ *and* $c = c(\lambda, e, n)$ *be function of* λ, *of the exponent* $e \in \mathbb{N}$ *and of* $n \in \mathbb{N}$. *A triplet* $\pi = (\mathsf{GGen}, \mathsf{P}, \mathsf{V})$ *of probabilistic polynomial-time algorithms is said to be a* (δ, c, t)-*batch proof of correct exponentiation (BPoCE) if the following conditions hold:*

1. **Completeness:** *For every integers $\lambda, n \in \mathbb{N}$, every $(\mathbb{G}, \mathsf{pp})$ in the support of $\mathsf{GGen}(1^\lambda)$ and every input $(\vec{x} = (x_1, \ldots, x_n), \vec{y} = (y_1, \ldots, y_n), e) \in \mathbb{G}^n \times \mathbb{G}^n \times \mathbb{N}$ such that $x_i^e = y_i$ for every $i \in [n]$, it holds that*

$$\Pr\left[\langle \mathsf{P}, \mathsf{V} \rangle (\mathbb{G}, \mathsf{pp}, \vec{x}, \vec{y}, e) = 1\right] = 1,$$

   where the probability is over the randomness of P and of V.

2. **δ-Soundness:** *For every pair $\mathsf{P}^* = (\mathsf{P}_1^*, \mathsf{P}_2^*)$ of probabilistic polynomial-time algorithms, there exists a negligible function $\nu(\cdot)$ such that*

$$\mathsf{Adv}_{\pi, \mathsf{P}^*}^{\mathsf{BPoCE}} \stackrel{\text{def}}{=} \Pr\left[\begin{array}{c} \langle \mathsf{P}_2^*(\mathsf{st}), \mathsf{V} \rangle (\mathbb{G}, \mathsf{pp}, \vec{x}, \vec{y}, e) = 1 \\ \exists i \in [n], x_i^e \neq y_i \end{array} \middle| \begin{array}{c} (\mathbb{G}, \mathsf{pp}) \leftarrow \mathsf{GGen}(1^\lambda) \\ (n, \vec{x}, \vec{y}, e, \mathsf{st}) \leftarrow \mathsf{P}_1^*(\mathbb{G}, \mathsf{pp}) \end{array}\right]$$
$$\leq \delta(\lambda) + \nu(\lambda),$$

   for all sufficiently large $\lambda \in \mathbb{N}$, where $\vec{x} = (x_1, \ldots, x_n)$ and $\vec{y} = (y_1, \ldots, y_n)$.

3. **Succinctness:** *For every $\lambda, n \in \mathbb{N}$, for every $(\mathbb{G}, \mathsf{pp})$ in the support of $\mathsf{GGen}(1^\lambda)$ and for every input $(\vec{x}, \vec{y}, e) \in \mathbb{G}^n \times \mathbb{G}^n \times \mathbb{N}$, it holds that: The total length of all messages exchanged between P and V in a random execution of the protocol on joint input $(\mathbb{G}, \mathsf{pp}, \vec{x}, \vec{y}, e)$ is at most $c(\lambda, e, n)$ with probability 1, where the probability is over the randomness of P and of V.*

4. **Efficient verification:** *For every $\lambda, n \in \mathbb{N}$, for every $(\mathbb{G}, \mathsf{pp})$ in the support of $\mathsf{GGen}(1^\lambda)$ and for every input $(\vec{x}, \vec{y}, e) \in \mathbb{G}^n \times \mathbb{G}^n \times \mathbb{N}$, it holds that: The running time of V in a random execution of the protocol on joint input $(\mathbb{G}, \mathsf{pp}, \vec{x}, \vec{y}, e)$ is at most $t(\lambda, e, n)$ with probability 1, where the probability is over the randomness of P and of V.*

On Using a Single Exponent. The above definition considers the setting of a single exponent for all n pairs of group elements; that is, the joint input includes a single exponent $e \in \mathbb{N}$ for which the prover contends that $x_i^e = y_i$ for all $i \in [n]$. Note that this setting is indeed in line with the motivation described in Sect. 1 of batch verification of many VDF outputs based on the repeated squaring function. This is the case, since in this scenario the exponent e is determined by the delay parameter T. In the examples mentioned in Sect. 1, a scenario in which all outputs were computed with respect to the same delay parameter is reasonable. It might still be of interest, both theoretically and for specific applications (see for example [BBF19]), to construct batch proofs of correct exponentiation with different exponents, and we leave it is as an interesting open question.

4   Warm-Up: The Random Subset Compiler

In this section we present a simplified version of our general compiler, which we call "The Random Subset Compiler" following Bellare, Garay and Rabin [BGR98]. This simplified version is based on a technique introduced by Bellare et al. for related, yet distinct, purposes (recall Sect. 1.2). In our context of proofs of correct exponentiation, this technique introduces quite a large communication overhead and a considerable amount of additional soundness error. Nevertheless, we start off with this simplified version as it already captures the main ideas behind the full-fledged compiler. Then, in Sect. 5 we show how to simultaneously amplify the soundness guarantees of our compiler and considerably reducing the communication overhead.

Let $\delta = \delta(\lambda)$ be a function of the security parameter $\lambda \in \mathbb{N}$, and let $c = c(\lambda, e)$ and $t = t(\lambda, e)$ be functions of λ and of the exponent $e \in \mathbb{N}$. Our compiler uses as a building block any (δ, c, t)-PoCE (recall Definition 3.1) $\pi = (\mathsf{GGen}, \mathsf{P}, \mathsf{V})$ and produces a protocol $\mathsf{Batch}_1(\pi) = (\mathsf{GGen}, \mathsf{P}_{\mathsf{Batch}}, \mathsf{V}_{\mathsf{Batch}})$, which is a (δ', c', t')-BPoCE for $\delta' = \delta + 1/2$ and for related functions $c' = c'(\lambda, e, n)$ and $t' = t'(\lambda, e, n)$.

The Protocol $\mathsf{Batch}_1(\pi)$

Joint input: Public parameters $(\mathbb{G}, \mathsf{pp})$ generated by $\mathsf{GGen}(1^\lambda)$, vectors $\vec{x} = (x_1, \dots, x_n)$ and $\vec{y} = (y_1, \dots, y_n)$ of group elements, and an exponent $e \in \mathbb{N}$.

1. $\mathsf{V}_{\mathsf{Batch}}$ samples $\mathcal{I} \leftarrow 2^{[n]}$ and sends $\mathcal{I}$ to $\mathsf{P}_{\mathsf{Batch}}$.
2. Both $\mathsf{V}_{\mathsf{Batch}}$ and $\mathsf{P}_{\mathsf{Batch}}$ compute $x_{\mathsf{prod}} = \prod_{i \in \mathcal{I}} x_i$ and $y_{\mathsf{prod}} = \prod_{i \in \mathcal{I}} y_i$.
3. $\mathsf{V}_{\mathsf{Batch}}$ and $\mathsf{P}_{\mathsf{Batch}}$ execute the protocol π on joint input $(\mathbb{G}, \mathsf{pp}, x_{\mathsf{prod}}, y_{\mathsf{prod}}, e)$, where $\mathsf{V}_{\mathsf{Batch}}$ plays the role of V and $\mathsf{P}_{\mathsf{Batch}}$ plays the role of P. Let $b \in \{0, 1\}$ be the output of V in this execution.
4. $\mathsf{V}_{\mathsf{Batch}}$ outputs b.

Theorem 4.1 below establishes the completeness, soundness, succinctness and verifier efficiency of $\mathsf{Batch}_1(\pi)$. It uses the following notation: We let $t_{\mathsf{op}}(\lambda)$ denote a bound on the time required to apply the binary group operation on two group elements, in a group $\mathbb{G}$ generated by $\mathsf{GGen}(1^\lambda)$.

Theorem 4.1. *Assume that π is a (δ, c, t)-PoCE. Then, $\mathsf{Batch}_1(\pi)$ is a (δ', c', t')-BPoCE, where for every $\lambda, e, n \in \mathbb{N}$:*

- $\delta'(\lambda) = \delta(\lambda) + 1/2$.
- $c'(\lambda, n, e) = c(\lambda, e) + n$.
- $t'(\lambda, n, e) = t(\lambda, e) + O(n \cdot t_{\mathsf{op}}(\lambda))$.

We start by presenting our main technical lemma, which we will use in the proof of Theorem 4.1 as well as in subsequent sections.

Lemma 4.2. *Let $\mathbb{G}$ be a group. For every integers $n, e \in \mathbb{N}$ and vectors $\vec{x}, \vec{y} \in \mathbb{G}^n$ the following holds: If there exists an index $i \in [n]$ such that $x_i^e \neq y_i$, then*

$$\Pr_{\mathcal{I} \leftarrow 2^{[n]}} \left[\left(\prod_{i \in \mathcal{I}} x_i \right)^e \neq \prod_{i \in \mathcal{I}} y_i \right] \geq \frac{1}{2}.$$

Proof of Lemma 4.2. For a subset $\mathcal{I} \subseteq [n]$, we say that $\mathcal{I}$ is *biased* if $\left(\prod_{i \in \mathcal{I}} x_i \right)^e \neq \prod_{i \in \mathcal{I}} y_i$, and otherwise we say that $\mathcal{I}$ is *balanced*. Denote by $\mathcal{S}_{\mathsf{Balanced}}$ and by $\mathcal{S}_{\mathsf{Biased}}$ the set of all balanced subsets of $[n]$ and the set of all biased subsets of $[n]$, respectively.

Suppose that there exists an index $i \in [n]$ such that $x_i^e \neq y_i$, and let i^* be an arbitrary such index (e.g., the minimal index for which the inequality holds). We wish to show that $|S_{\text{Balanced}}| \leq |S_{\text{Biased}}|$, as this will conclude the proof of the lemma. To this end, consider a partition $\mathcal{P}$ of $2^{[n]}$ to 2^{n-1} pairs as follows:

$$\mathcal{P} = \{(\mathcal{I}, \mathcal{I} \cup \{i^*\}) \ : \ i^* \notin \mathcal{I}\}.$$

In each pair $(\mathcal{I}, \mathcal{I} \cup \{i^*\})$ in $\mathcal{P}$, at most one subset of $\mathcal{I}$ and $\mathcal{I} \cup \{i^*\}$ can be balanced. This is the case since if $\mathcal{I} \in S_{\text{Balanced}}$, then it must be that $\mathcal{I} \cup \{i^*\} \in S_{\text{Biased}}$ since

$$\prod_{i \in \mathcal{I} \cup \{i^*\}} x_i^e = (x_i^*)^e \cdot \prod_{i \in \mathcal{I}} x_i^e$$

$$= (x_i^*)^e \cdot \prod_{i \in \mathcal{I}} y_i \tag{1}$$

$$\neq y_{i^*} \cdot \prod_{i \in \mathcal{I}} y_i$$

$$= \prod_{i \in f(\mathcal{I})} y_i, \tag{2}$$

where Eq. (1) holds because $\mathcal{I}$ is balanced, and (2) holds due to the assumption that $x_{i^*}^e \neq y_{i^*}$. Since at most one subset in each pair of the 2^{n-1} pairs in $\mathcal{P}$ is balanced, it holds that $|S_{\text{Balanced}}| \leq |S_{\text{Biased}}|$ concluding the proof. ∎

We are now ready to prove Theorem 4.1, establishing the completeness, soundness, verifier efficiency and succinctness of our protocol π_{Batch}.

Proof of Theorem 4.1. Completeness follows immediately from the completeness of π and the fact that if $x_i^e = y_i$ for every $i \in [n]$, then it also holds that $\left(\prod_{i \in \mathcal{I}} x_i\right)^e = \prod_{i \in \mathcal{I}} y_i$ for any choice of $\mathcal{I} \in 2^{[n]}$.

We now turn to prove that $\text{Batch}_1(\pi)$ satisfies δ'-soundness for $\delta' = \delta + 1/2$. Let $P_{\text{Batch}}^* = (P_{\text{Batch},1}^*, P_{\text{Batch},2}^*)$ be a malicious prover attempting to break the soundness of $\text{Batch}_1(\pi)$. Consider the following pair $P^* = (P_1^*, P_2^*)$ attempting to break the soundness of π. On input $(\mathbb{G}, \text{pp})$ generated by $\text{GGen}(1^\lambda)$, the algorithm P_1^* is defined as follows:

1. Invoke $(n, \vec{x}, \vec{y}, e, \text{st}) \leftarrow P_{\text{Batch},1}^*(\mathbb{G}, \text{pp})$, where $\vec{x} = (x_1, \ldots, x_n)$ and $\vec{y} = (y_1, \ldots, y_n)$.
2. Sample $\mathcal{I} \leftarrow 2^{[n]}$.
3. Compute $x_{\text{prod}} = \prod_{i \in \mathcal{I}} x_i$ and $y_{\text{prod}} = \prod_{i \in \mathcal{I}} y_i$.
4. Set $\text{st}' = (\text{st}, \vec{x}, \vec{y}, \mathcal{I})$.
5. Output $(x_{\text{prod}}, y_{\text{prod}}, e, \text{st}')$.

Then, the algorithm P_2^*, running on private input st' and interacting with the verifier V on joint input $(\mathbb{G}, \text{pp}, x_{\text{prod}}, y_{\text{prod}}, e)$, is defined as follows:

1. Parse st' as $(\text{st}, \vec{x}, \vec{y}, \mathcal{I})$.

2. Invoke $\mathsf{P}^*_{\mathsf{Batch},2}$ on input st and simulate to $\mathsf{P}^*_{\mathsf{Batch},2}$ an execution of $\mathsf{Batch}_1(\pi)$ on joint input $(\mathbb{G}, \mathsf{pp}, \vec{x}, \vec{y}, e)$:

   (a) Send $\mathcal{I}$ to $\mathsf{P}^*_{\mathsf{Batch},2}$ as the first message of the verifier in $\mathsf{Batch}_1(\pi)$.

   (b) Let V play the role of $\mathsf{V}_{\mathsf{Batch}}$ in all subsequent rounds, by relaying all messages from $\mathsf{P}^*_{\mathsf{Batch},2}$ to V and vice versa.

We now turn to bound $\mathsf{Adv}^{\mathsf{PoCE}}_{\pi,\mathsf{P}^*}$. To that end, we define the following events:

- Let $\mathsf{NotEqual}$ denote the event in which for some $i \in [n]$, it holds that $x_i^e \neq y_i$, where $n, \vec{x}, \vec{y}$ and e are outputted by $\mathsf{P}^*_{\mathsf{Batch},1}$ in Step 1 of P^*_1, $\vec{x} = (x_1, \ldots, x_n)$ and $\vec{y} = (y_1, \ldots, y_n)$.
- Let $\mathsf{BiasedSet}$ be the event in which

$$\left(\prod_{i \in \mathcal{I}} x_i\right)^e \neq \prod_{i \in \mathcal{I}} y_i,$$

where $n, \vec{x}, \vec{y}$ and e are as before and $\mathcal{I}$ is the random subset sampled by P^*_1 in Step 2.
- Let PWin be the event in which P^* wins; that is, V outputs 1 and $\mathsf{BiasedSet}$ holds.
- Let $\mathsf{PBatchWin}$ be the event in which $\mathsf{P}^*_{\mathsf{Batch}}$ wins in the simulation of $\mathsf{Batch}_1(\pi)$ by P^*: The simulated $\mathsf{V}_{\mathsf{Batch}}$ outputs 1 and $\mathsf{NotEqual}$ holds.

Equipped with this notation, it holds that

$$\begin{aligned}
\mathsf{Adv}^{\mathsf{PoCE}}_{\pi,\mathsf{P}^*} &= \Pr\left[\mathsf{PWin}\right] \\
&\geq \Pr\left[\mathsf{PWin}|\mathsf{PBatchWin} \wedge \mathsf{BiasedSet}\right] \cdot \Pr\left[\mathsf{PBatchWin} \wedge \mathsf{BiasedSet}\right] \\
&= \Pr\left[\mathsf{PBatchWin} \wedge \mathsf{BiasedSet}\right], \quad\quad\quad\quad\quad\quad\quad\quad\quad\quad (3)
\end{aligned}$$

where Eq. (3) holds since conditioned on $\mathsf{PBatchWin}$, it holds that $\mathsf{V}_{\mathsf{Batch}}$ (in the simulation of $\mathsf{Batch}_1(\pi)$) outputs 1. This implies that V outputs 1, and hence that $\Pr\left[\mathsf{PWin}|\mathsf{PBatchWin} \wedge \mathsf{BiasedSet}\right] = 1$. By total probability,

$$\begin{aligned}
\Pr\left[\mathsf{PBatchWin} \wedge \mathsf{BiasedSet}\right] & \\
&= \Pr\left[\mathsf{PBatchWin}\right] - \Pr\left[\mathsf{PBatchWin} \wedge \overline{\mathsf{BiasedSet}}\right] \\
&= \mathsf{Adv}^{\mathsf{BPoCE}}_{\mathsf{Batch}_1(\pi),\mathsf{P}^*_{\mathsf{Batch}}} - \Pr\left[\mathsf{PBatchWin} \wedge \overline{\mathsf{BiasedSet}}\right] \quad\quad (4) \\
&\geq \mathsf{Adv}^{\mathsf{BPoCE}}_{\mathsf{Batch}_1(\pi),\mathsf{P}^*_{\mathsf{Batch}}} - \Pr\left[\mathsf{NotEqual} \wedge \overline{\mathsf{BiasedSet}}\right] \quad\quad (5) \\
&\geq \mathsf{Adv}^{\mathsf{BPoCE}}_{\mathsf{Batch}_1(\pi),\mathsf{P}^*_{\mathsf{Batch}}} - \Pr\left[\overline{\mathsf{BiasedSet}}|\mathsf{NotEqual}\right], \quad\quad (6)
\end{aligned}$$

where Eq. (4) holds since P^* perfectly simulates $\mathsf{Batch}_1(\pi)$ to $\mathsf{P}^*_{\mathsf{Batch}}$; and Eq. (5) is true since $\mathsf{PBatchWin}$ is contained in $\mathsf{NotEqual}$, and hence $\mathsf{PBatchWin} \wedge \overline{\mathsf{BiasedSet}}$ is contained in $\mathsf{NotEqual} \wedge \overline{\mathsf{BiasedSet}}$.
We are left with bounding $\Pr\left[\overline{\mathsf{BiasedSet}}|\mathsf{NotEqual}\right]$. Indeed, Lemma 4.2 immediately implies that

$$\Pr\left[\mathsf{BiasedSet}\,\middle|\,\mathsf{NotEqual}\right] \leq \frac{1}{2}. \tag{7}$$

Taking Eq. (3), (6) and (7) together and rearranging, we get that

$$\mathsf{Adv}^{\mathsf{BPoCE}}_{\mathsf{Batch}_1(\pi),\mathsf{P}^*_{\mathsf{Batch}}} \leq \mathsf{Adv}^{\mathsf{PoCE}}_{\pi,\mathsf{P}^*} + \frac{1}{2},$$

which implies – since π satisfies δ-soundness – that there exists a negligible function $\nu(\cdot)$ such that

$$\mathsf{Adv}^{\mathsf{BPoCE}}_{\mathsf{Batch}_1(\pi),\mathsf{P}^*_{\mathsf{Batch}}} \leq \delta(\lambda,e) + \frac{1}{2} + \nu(\lambda),$$

for all sufficiently large $\lambda \in \mathbb{N}$.

We have proved that $\mathsf{Batch}_1(\pi)$ satisfies δ'-soundness for $\delta' = \delta + 1/2$. To conclude the proof, we are left with bounding the verifier's running time t' and the communication complexity c' of $\mathsf{Batch}_1(\pi)$. As for the running time of $\mathsf{V}_{\mathsf{Batch}}$: The verifier samples a random subset $\mathcal{I}$, computes $\prod_{i\in\mathcal{I}} x_i$ and $\prod_{i\in\mathcal{I}} y_i$ and participates in a single execution of π. Since the products computed by $\mathsf{V}_{\mathsf{Batch}}$ include at most n group elements each, it follows that her running time is $t' = O(n \cdot t_{\mathsf{op}}(\lambda)) + t$. The communication in $\mathsf{Batch}_1(\pi)$ includes the subset $\mathcal{I}$, which can be encoded using n bits, and all messages exchanged in a single execution of π. Therefore, the total communication is $c' = c + n$. This concludes the proof of Theorem 4.1. ∎

5 Amplifying Soundness and Reducing Communication

In this section, we address the two main drawbacks of the compiler from Sect. 4; namely, its large soundness error, and the fact that the communication complexity is linearly dependent on the number n of pairs (x_i, y_i). In order to do so, we introduce an improved compiler, which differs from the one found in Sect. 4 in two respects. First, the verifier now chooses m random subsets $\mathcal{I}_1, \ldots, \mathcal{I}_m \subseteq [n]$ for some integer m which is a parameter of the protocol, and the parties invoke m parallel executions of the underlying protocol π on the m inputs which are induced by these subsets. Note that sending the representation of m random subsets of $[n]$ requires that the verifier sends additional $m \cdot n$ bits to the prover. To avoid this communication overhead, we let the verifier succinctly represent these m subsets via a single key to pseudorandom function, thus reducing the additive communication overhead to just λ bits, where $\lambda \in \mathbb{N}$ is the security parameter. As we will show, this essentially does not harm the soundness guaranteed by the protocol.

We now turn to formally present our compiler. Let $\delta = \delta(\lambda)$ a be a function of the security parameter $\lambda \in \mathbb{N}$, and let $c = c(\lambda, e)$ and $t = t(\lambda, e)$ be functions of λ and of the exponent $e \in \mathbb{N}$. Our compiler is parameterized by an integer $m \in \mathbb{N}$, and uses the following building blocks:

- A (δ, c, t)-PoCE $\pi = (\mathsf{GGen}, \mathsf{P}, \mathsf{V})$ (recall Definition 3.1).
- A pseudorandom function family PRF, such that for every $\lambda \in \mathbb{N}$ and for every key $K \in \{0,1\}^\lambda$, the function PRF_K maps inputs in $\{0,1\}^{\lceil \log(m \cdot n) \rceil}$ to outputs in $\{0,1\}$. For ease of notation, for integers $j \in [m]$ and $i \in [n]$, we will write $\mathsf{PRF}_K(j\|i)$, with the intention (but without noting it explicitly) that the input to the function is a bit string representing the integers j and i.

The compiler produces a protocol $\mathsf{Batch}_2^m(\pi) = (\mathsf{GGen}, \mathsf{P}_{\mathsf{Batch}}, \mathsf{V}_{\mathsf{Batch}})$, which is a (δ', c', t')-BPoCE for $\delta' = \delta + 2^{-m}$ and for related functions $c' = c'(\lambda, e, n)$ and $t' = t'(\lambda, e, n)$.

The Protocol $\mathsf{Batch}_2^m(\pi)$

Joint input: Public parameters $(\mathbb{G}, \mathsf{pp})$ generated by $\mathsf{GGen}(1^\lambda)$, vectors $\vec{x} = (x_1, \ldots, x_n)$ and $\vec{y} = (y_1, \ldots, y_n)$ of $\mathbb{G}$ elements, and an exponent $e \in \mathbb{N}$.

1. $\mathsf{V}_{\mathsf{Batch}}$ samples $K \leftarrow \{0,1\}^\lambda$ and sends K to $\mathsf{P}_{\mathsf{Batch}}$.
2. For $j = 1, \ldots, m$:
   (a) Both $\mathsf{V}_{\mathsf{Batch}}$ and $\mathsf{P}_{\mathsf{Batch}}$ compute $\mathcal{I}_j = \{i \in [n] : \mathsf{PRF}_K(j\|i) = 1\}$.
   (b) Both $\mathsf{V}_{\mathsf{Batch}}$ and $\mathsf{P}_{\mathsf{Batch}}$ compute $u_j = \prod_{i \in \mathcal{I}_j} x_i$ and $w_j = \prod_{i \in \mathcal{I}_j} y_i$.
3. $\mathsf{V}_{\mathsf{Batch}}$ and $\mathsf{P}_{\mathsf{Batch}}$ execute in parallel m executions of the protocol π, where in the j-th execution, the joint input is $(\mathsf{pp}, u_j, w_j, e)$. In each execution, $\mathsf{V}_{\mathsf{Batch}}$ plays the role of V and $\mathsf{P}_{\mathsf{Batch}}$ plays the role of P. For each $j \in [m]$, let $b_j \in \{0,1\}$ be the output of V in the j-th execution.
4. $\mathsf{V}_{\mathsf{Batch}}$ outputs $b := \bigwedge_{j=1}^m b_j$.

Theorem 5.1 establishes the completeness, soundness, succinctness and verifier efficiency of $\mathsf{Batch}_2^m(\pi)$. Recall that we denote by $t_{\mathsf{op}} = t_{\mathsf{op}}(\lambda)$ the time required to apply the binary group operation on two group elements, in a group $\mathbb{G}$ generated by $\mathsf{GGen}(1^\lambda)$. We also denote by $t_{\mathsf{prf}} = t_{\mathsf{prf}}(\lambda, m, n)$ the time required to compute $\mathsf{PRF}_K(z)$ for $K \in \{0,1\}^\lambda$ and $z \in \{0,1\}^{\lceil \log(m \cdot n) \rceil}$.

Theorem 5.1. *Assume that* PRF *is a pseudorandom function and that π is a (δ, c, t)-PoCE. Then, $\mathsf{Batch}_2^m(\pi)$ is a (δ', c', t')-BPoCE, where:*

- $\delta'(\lambda) = \delta(\lambda) + 2^{-m}$.
- $c'(\lambda, n, e) = m \cdot c(\lambda, e) + \lambda$.
- $t'(\lambda, n, e) = m \cdot t(\lambda, e) + \lambda + O(m \cdot n \cdot (t_{\mathsf{op}} + t_{\mathsf{prf}}))$.

Before proving Theorem 5.1, a couple of remarks are in order.

Applying the Fiat-Shamir Heuristic. If the Fiat-Shamir heuristic [FS86] can be applied to π in the random oracle model, then it can also be applied to $\mathsf{Batch}_2^m(\pi)$ as well, as long as $m = \omega(\log(\lambda))$ (and hence 2^{-m} is a negligible function of the security parameter $\lambda \in \mathbb{N}$). This is the case since our compiler only adds a single *public coin* message from the verifier to the prover. In particular, the Fiat-Shamir heuristic may be applied whenever π is a constant-round public-coin protocol with negligible soundness error, which is indeed the case for the protocol of Wesolowski [Wes19]. It should be noted that even though the protocol of Pietrzak [Pie19] is not constant-round, the Fiat-Shamir heuristic may still be applied to it in the random oracle model, and so it can also be applied to the compiled version thereof using our compiler.

Replacing PRF with a Pseudorandom Generator. Our use of PRF enables us to handle cases in which n is not a-priori bounded and can be chosen by the malicious prover (this is in line with Definition 3.2). However, in many cases it makes sense to consider values of n which *are* a-priori bounded. In such cases, we can replace our use of the pseudorandom function with a pseudorandom generator PRG mapping seeds of length λ to outputs of length $m \cdot n$.[12] Instead of sampling a key K, the verifier will now sample a seed $s \leftarrow \{0,1\}^\lambda$ to PRG and send it over to the prover. Then, both the prover and the verifier can compute $y = \mathsf{PRG}(s)$ and parse y as the natural encoding of m subsets $\mathcal{I}_1, \ldots, \mathcal{I}_m$ of $[n]$ (i.e., for each $j \in [m]$, the vector $(y_{(j-1)\cdot n+1}, \ldots, y_{j\cdot n})$ is the characteristic vector of $\mathcal{I}_j$). In practice, PRG can be efficiently implemented via a cryptographic hash function (e.g., SHA).

Proof of Theorem 5.1. We start by analyzing the communication complexity and the verifier's running time. Per the running time of the verifier: It samples a random key $K \leftarrow \{0,1\}^\lambda$, taking time λ; makes $m \cdot n$ invocation of PRF, taking time $m \cdot n \cdot t_{\mathsf{prf}}$; computes $2m$ products of at most n group elements each, taking time $O(m \cdot n \cdot t_{\mathsf{op}})$; and participates in m executions of π, which takes time $m \cdot t$. It follows that her running time is $t' = t + \lambda + O(m \cdot n \cdot (t_{\mathsf{op}} + t_{\mathsf{prf}}))$. The communication in $\mathsf{Batch}_2^m(\pi)$ includes the key K and all messages exchanged in m executions of π, resulting in a total communication complexity of $c' = m \cdot c + \lambda$. The δ'-soundness of $\mathsf{Batch}_2^m(\pi)$ follows immediately from the following lemma and the pseudorandomness of PRF.

Lemma 5.2. *For every pair* $\mathsf{P}^*_{\mathsf{Batch}} = (\mathsf{P}^*_{\mathsf{Batch},1}, \mathsf{P}^*_{\mathsf{Batch},2})$ *of probabilistic polynomial time algorithms, there exist a probabilistic polynomial-time algorithm* D *and a negligible function* $\nu(\cdot)$ *such that*

$$\mathsf{Adv}^{\mathsf{BPoCE}}_{\mathsf{Batch}_2^m(\pi), \mathsf{P}^*_{\mathsf{Batch}}} \leq \delta + 2^{-m} + \mathsf{Adv}_{\mathsf{PRF}, \mathsf{D}}(\lambda) + \nu(\lambda)$$

for all sufficiently large $\lambda \in \mathbb{N}$.

Due to space limitations, the proof of Lemma 5.2 can be found in the full version of the paper.

6 An Improved Compiler from the Low Order Assumption

In this section we present an improved compiler, which enjoys significant communication improvements over our general compiler from Sect. 5. Concretely, the communication complexity of the resulted protocol is completely independent

---

[12] We implicitly assume here that m and n are both polynomially-bounded functions of the security parameter.

of the additional soundness error (the verification time, though also improved, still depends on it).[13] The cost is that this compiler, unlike the previous one, relies on an algebraically-structured computational assumption – the low order assumption (recall Definition 2.4). However, this caveat does not seem overly restrictive when to compiler is applied to either the protocol of Pietrzak or to that of Wesolowski [Pie19, Wes19], both of which rely either on this assumption or stronger ones. Our compiler is inspired by an approach presented by Bellare, Garay and Rabin [BGR98] (which also implicitly underlies the batch proof of Wesolowski [Wes20]), while introducing some new ideas for the setting of succinct BPoCE (see Sects. 1.2 and 1.3 for details).

6.1   The Compiler

We now present the compiler. Let GGen be a group generation algorithm (recall Sect. 2). Let $\delta = \delta(\lambda)$ a be a function of the security parameter $\lambda \in \mathbb{N}$, and let $c = c(\lambda, e)$ and $t = t(\lambda, e)$ be functions of λ and of the exponent $e \in \mathbb{N}$. Our compiler is parameterized by an integer s, and uses the following building blocks:

- A (δ, c, t)-PoCE $\pi = (\mathsf{GGen}, \mathsf{P}, \mathsf{V})$.
- A pseudorandom function family PRF, such that for every $\lambda \in \mathbb{N}$ and for every key $K \in \{0, 1\}^\lambda$, the function PRF_K maps inputs in $\{0, 1\}^{\lceil \log(n) \rceil}$ to outputs in $[s]$.[14] For ease of notation, for an integer $i \in [n]$, we will write $\mathsf{PRF}_K(i)$, with the intention (but without noting it explicitly) that the input to the function is a bit string representing the integer i.

The compiler produces a protocol $\mathsf{Batch}_3^s(\pi) = (\mathsf{GGen}, \mathsf{P}', \mathsf{V}')$, which is a (δ', c', t')-BPoCE for related functions $\delta' = \delta'(\lambda)$, $c' = c'(\lambda, e, n)$ and $t' = t'(\lambda, e, n)$.

The Protocol $\mathsf{Batch}_3^s(\pi)$

Joint input: Public parameters $(\mathbb{G}, \mathsf{pp})$ generated by $\mathsf{GGen}(1^\lambda)$, vectors $\vec{x} = (x_1, \ldots, x_n)$ and $\vec{y} = (y_1, \ldots, y_n)$ of group elements, and an exponent $e \in \mathbb{N}$.

1. V' samples $K \leftarrow \{0, 1\}^\lambda$ and sends K to P'.
2. For $i = 1, \ldots, n$: Both V' and P' compute $\alpha_i := \mathsf{PRF}_K(i)$.
3. Both V' and P' compute $x = \prod_{i \in [n]} x_i^{\alpha_i}$ and $y = \prod_{i \in [n]} y_i^{\alpha_i}$.
4. V' and P' execute the protocol π on joint input $(\mathbb{G}, \mathsf{pp}, x, y, e)$, where V' plays the role of V and P' plays the role of P. Let $b \in \{0, 1\}$ be the output of V in this execution.
5. V' outputs b.

---

[13] Recall that in the compiler from Sect. 5, in order to obtain an additive soundness loss of 2^{-m}, the communication had to grow linearly with m.

[14] Given any efficient algorithm Samp for sampling from the uniform distribution over $[s]$ using $r = r(s)$ random coins, PRF can be implemented by invoking a PRF mapping $\{0, 1\}^{\lceil \log(n) \rceil}$ into $\{0, 1\}^r$ and then applying Samp using the output of the PRF as random coins.

Similarly to our discussion in Sect. 5, if the Fiat-Shamir heuristic [FS86] can be applied to π in the random oracle, then it can also be applied to $\mathsf{Batch}_3^s(\pi)$. Moreover, if the number n of pairs (x_i, y_i) is a-priori bounded, then the use of PRF can be replaced by a pseudorandom generator in a similar manner to what was done in Sect. 5.

Theorem 6.1 establishes the completeness, soundness, succinctness and verifier efficiency of $\mathsf{Batch}_3^s(\pi)$, in cases where the low order assumption holds with respect to GGen. Recall that we denote by $t_{\mathsf{op}} = t_{\mathsf{op}}(\lambda)$ the time required to apply the binary group operation on two group elements in $\mathbb{G}$ that is generated by $\mathsf{GGen}(1^\lambda)$. We also denote by $t_{\mathsf{prf}} = t_{\mathsf{prf}}(\lambda, s, n)$ the time required to compute $\mathsf{PRF}_K(z)$ for $K \in \{0,1\}^\lambda$ and $z \in \{0,1\}^{\lceil \log(n) \rceil}$.

Theorem 6.1. *Assume that* PRF *is a pseudorandom function, that* π *is a* (δ, c, t)-*PoCE, and that the s-low order assumption holds with respect to* GGen. *Then,* $\mathsf{Batch}_3^s(\pi)$ *is a* (δ', c', t')-*BPoCE, where:*

- $\delta'(\lambda) = \delta(\lambda) + 1/s$.
- $c'(\lambda, n, e) = c(\lambda, e) + \lambda$.
- $t'(\lambda, n, e) = t(\lambda, e) + \lambda + n \cdot t_{\mathsf{prf}} + O(n \cdot \log(s) \cdot t_{\mathsf{op}})$.

Instantiating the Compiler. Basing the compiler on the general low order assumption gives rise to several possible instantiations. In particular:

- **The groups QR_N and QR_N^+.** The low order assumption holds unconditionally in the group QR_N of quadratic residues modulo N when N is the product of two safe primes, as well as in the (isomorphic) group QR_N^+ of *signed* quadratic residues modulo N (recall Sect. 2). Concretely, if $N = (2p + 1) \cdot (2q + 1)$ for prime p and q, then QR_N and QR_N^+ contain no elements of order less than $\min\{p, q\}$. In the context of VDFs, this was observed by Pietrzak [Pie19] and by Boneh et al. [BBF18]. However, it is also plausible that the assumption holds computationally in the groups QR_N and QR_N^+ when the factors of N are not safe primes.
- **RSA groups.** It is tempting to instantiate our compiler within the RSA group $\mathbb{Z}_N^*$ as perhaps the best-understood group of unknown order. Alas, the low order assumption cannot hold in $\mathbb{Z}_N^*$ since $-1 \in \mathbb{Z}_N$ is always of order two in this group. One possible ramification, suggested by Boneh et al. is to work over the quotient group $\mathbb{Z}_N^*/\{\pm 1\}$. Another possibility is to settle on a slightly weaker soundness guarantee for BPoCEs, which allows a malicious prover to convince the verifier that $y_i = x_i^e$ for every i, even though for some indices $y_i = -x_i^e$. This weakened soundness guarantee is defined in the full version and can be shown to follow from the weak low order assumption (Definition 2.5), using essentially the same proof as the proof of Theorem 6.1. Moreover, Seres and Burcsi [SB20] have shown that when N is the product of two safe primes, breaking the weak low order assumption in $\mathbb{Z}_N^*$ is equivalent to factoring the modulus N.[15] A third option is to compose our compiler

---

[15] Their proof can also be used, essentially unchanged, to show that (the strong variant of) the low order assumption in $\mathbb{Z}_N^* \{\pm 1\}$ is equivalent to factoring N.

with an additional protocol, specifically dedicated to proving that $y_i \neq -x_i^e$ for each i. We present and analyze such a protocol in the paper's full version.

– **Class groups of imaginary quadratic fields.** These groups were suggested in the context of VDFs by Wesolowski [Wes19] as candidate groups of unknown order. The security of the low order assumption in these groups is still unclear [BBF18,BKS+20]; but at least until proven otherwise, it is possible that our compiler can be instantiated in a sub-family of these groups as well. See the recent work of Belabas et al. [BKS+20] for further details on the possible choice of parameters for such groups.

On the Tightness of the Reduction. In Sect. 6.2 we prove the soundness of our compiler based on the low order assumption. This general reduction, however, suffers from a cubic security loss: Given a prover which breaks the soundness of the resulting BPoCE with advantage $\delta + 1/s + \epsilon$, we construct an adversary breaking the low order assumption with advantage $O(\epsilon^3)$. Coming up with a tight reduction to the general low order assumption seems to be beyond current techniques. Hence, instead, in the full version of the paper, we give specific proofs for the soundness of our compiler in the groups QR_N^+ and $\mathbb{Z}_N^*$. In the former, our proof is information-theoretic, while in the latter, it relies on a tight reduction to the factoring assumption.

Necessity of the Low Order Assumption. We note that our reliance on the s-low-order assumption in Theorem 6.1 is necessary. To see why that is, suppose that we work in a group $\mathbb{G}$ in which the assumption does not hold; that is, given the group description it is easy to find a group element z and an integer $\omega < s$ such that $z^\omega = 1_\mathbb{G}$. In this case, the attacker can output an instance $((x_i, y_i)_{i \in [n]}, e)$ such that n and e are arbitrary integers, $x_1, \ldots, x_n$ are arbitrary group elements, $y_i = x_i^e$ for every $i \in \{2, \ldots, n\}$ and $y_1 = z \cdot x_1^e$. The verifier V' will incorrectly accept whenever the group elements x and y computed by P' and V' in Step refStep:CombinedInstance of the protocol satisfy $y = x^e$. This occurs when the exponents $\alpha_1, \ldots, \alpha_n$ satisfy $\left(\prod_{i=1}^n x_i^{\alpha_i}\right)^e = \prod_{i=1}^n y_i^{\alpha_i}$. By the choices made by the attacker, this equality holds whenever $z^{\alpha_1} = 1_\mathbb{G}$, which happens with probability at least $1/s$.

Proof of Theorem 6.1. We first analyze the communication complexity and the running time of the verifier, and then in Sect. 6.2, we base the soundness of $\mathsf{Batch}_3^s(\pi)$ on the low order assumption. As for the running time of verifier: It samples a random key $K \leftarrow \{0,1\}^\lambda$, taking time λ; makes n invocation of PRF, taking time $n \cdot t_{\mathsf{prf}}$; raises n elements to exponents which are bounded by s, which takes time $O(n \cdot \log(s) \cdot t_{\mathsf{op}})$; computes the product of n group elements, taking time $(n-1) \cdot t_{\mathsf{op}}$; and participates in a single execution of π, which takes time t. It follows that her running time is $t' = t + \lambda + n \cdot t_{\mathsf{prf}} + O(n \cdot (\log(s) + 1) \cdot t_{\mathsf{op}})$. The communication in $\mathsf{Batch}_3^s(\pi)$ includes the key K and all messages exchanged in a single execution of π, resulting in a total communication of $c' = c + \lambda$.

6.2   Soundness Analysis Based on the Low Order Assumption

The proof of soundness for $\mathsf{Batch}_3^s(\pi)$ follows the same outline as did the corresponding proof in Sect. 5, and is by reduction to the δ-soundness of π, to the pseudorandomness of PRF and to the low order assumption with respect to GGen. Since the reduction and its analysis are extremely similar to those presented in Sect. 5, we forgo presenting them explicitly here, and instead concentrate on the main differences.

Concretely, the only major difference between the soundness analysis of $\mathsf{Batch}_3^s(\pi)$ and the analysis of $\mathsf{Batch}_2^m(\pi)$ in Sect. 5, is that instead of relying on Lemma 4.2 in order to lower bound the probability that $x^e \neq y$ (where x and y are computed from $\vec{x}, \vec{y}$ as defined in Step refStep:CombinedInstance of $\mathsf{Batch}_3^s(\pi)$), we rely on Lemma 6.2 and Corollary 6.3 found below. Loosely, relying on the low order assumption with respect to GGen, Lemma 6.2 and its corollary assert that if there is some $i \in [n]$ for which $x_i^e \neq y_i$, then with probability at most $1/s + \mathsf{negl}(\lambda)$ over the choice of $\alpha_1, \dots, \alpha_n \leftarrow [s]$, it holds that $x^e = y$.[16]

Lemma 6.2. *Let $\mathbb{G}$ be a group. For every integers $n, e \in \mathbb{N}$, any integer s, any number $\epsilon \in (0,1)$ and any vectors $\vec{x}, \vec{y} \in \mathbb{G}^n$ the following holds: If there exists an index $i \in [n]$ such that $x_i^e \neq y_i$ and*

$$
\Pr_{\alpha_1,\dots,\alpha_n \leftarrow [s]} \left[\left(\prod_{i \in [n]} x_i^{\alpha_i} \right)^e = \prod_{i \in [n]} y_i^{\alpha_i} \right] > \frac{1}{s} + \epsilon,
$$

then there exists an algorithm A which receives as input $\vec{x}, \vec{y}$ and e, runs in time $\mathsf{poly}(\lambda, n, \log(e))$, and with probability at least ϵ^2 outputs $(u, \omega) \in \mathbb{G} \times \mathbb{N}$ such that $u \neq 1_{\mathbb{G}}$, $1 < \omega < s$ and $u^\omega = 1_{\mathbb{G}}$.

Corollary 6.3 below follows from Lemma 6.2 and from the definition of the low order assumption (Definition 2.4).

Corollary 6.3. *Let GGen be a group generation algorithm and let $s = s(\lambda)$ be a function of the security parameter λ. If the s-low order assumption holds with respect to GGen, then for any probabilistic polynomial-time algorithm P_0^*, there exists a negligible function $\nu(\cdot)$ such that*

$$
\Pr \left[\begin{array}{l} \exists i \in [n], x_i^e \neq y_i \\ \left(\prod_{i \in [n]} x_i^{\alpha_i} \right)^e = \prod_{i \in [n]} y_i^{\alpha_i} \end{array} \middle| \begin{array}{l} (\mathbb{G}, \mathsf{pp}) \leftarrow \mathsf{GGen}(1^\lambda) \\ (n, \vec{x}, \vec{y}, e) \leftarrow \mathsf{P}_0^*(\mathbb{G}, \mathsf{pp}) \\ \alpha_1, \dots, \alpha_n \leftarrow [s] \end{array} \right] \leq \frac{1}{s} + \nu(\lambda),
$$

for all sufficiently large $\lambda \in \mathbb{N}$.

---

[16] Observe that in $\mathsf{Batch}_3^s(\pi)$, the exponents $\alpha_1, \dots, \alpha_n$ are not chosen uniformly at random from $[s]$, but using the pseudorandom function PRF. This is handled in exactly the same manner in which it was handled in the previous section. The reader is referred to the full version for further details.

Due to space limitations, the proofs of Lemma 6.2 and Corollary 6.3 can be found in the paper's full version.

References

[ABB+16] Armknecht, F., Barman, L., Bohli, J.-M., Karame, G.O.: Mirror: enabling proofs of data replication and retrievability in the cloud. In: Proceedings of the 25th USENIX Conference on Security Symposium, SEC 2016, pp. 1051–1068 (2016)

[AGH+92] Alon, N., Goldreich, O., Håstad, J., Peralta, R.: Simple constructions of almost k-wise independent random variables. Random Struct. Algorithms **3**(3), 289–304 (1992)

[BBB+18] Boneh, D., Bonneau, J., Bünz, B., Fisch, B.: Verifiable delay functions. In: Shacham, H., Boldyreva, A. (eds.) CRYPTO 2018. LNCS, vol. 10991, pp. 757–788. Springer, Cham (2018). https://doi.org/10.1007/978-3-319-96884-1_25

[BBF18] Boneh, D., Bünz, B., Fisch, B.: A survey of two verifiable delay functions. Cryptology ePrint Archive, Report 2018/712 (2018)

[BBF19] Boneh, D., Bünz, B., Fisch, B.: Batching techniques for accumulators with applications to IOPs and stateless blockchains. In: Boldyreva, A., Micciancio, D. (eds.) CRYPTO 2019. LNCS, vol. 11692, pp. 561–586. Springer, Cham (2019). https://doi.org/10.1007/978-3-030-26948-7_20

[BCG15] Bonneau, J., Clark, J., Goldfeder, S.: On bitcoin as a public randomness source. Cryptology ePrint Archive, Report 2015/1015 (2015)

[BDG17] Benet, J., Dalrymple, D., Greco, N.: Proof of replication (2017). https://filecoin.io/proof-of-replication.pdf. Accessed 16 Sep 2021

[BGR98] Bellare, M., Garay, J.A., Rabin, T.: Fast batch verification for modular exponentiation and digital signatures. In: Nyberg, K. (ed.) EUROCRYPT 1998. LNCS, vol. 1403, pp. 236–250. Springer, Heidelberg (1998). https://doi.org/10.1007/BFb0054130

[BGZ16] Bentov, I., Gabizon, A., Zuckerman, D.: Bitcoin beacon. arXiv:605.04559 (2016)

[BHR+21] Block, A.R., Holmgren, J., Rosen, A., Rothblum, R.D., Soni, P.: Time- and space-efficient arguments from groups of unknown order. In: Malkin, T., Peikert, C. (eds.) CRYPTO 2021. LNCS, vol. 12828, pp. 123–152. Springer, Cham (2021). https://doi.org/10.1007/978-3-030-84259-8_5

[BKS+20] Belabas, K., Kleinjung, T., Sanso, A., Wesolowski, B.: A note on the low order assumption in class group of an imaginary quadratic number fields. Cryptology ePrint Archive, Report 2020/1310 (2020)

[Bon99] Boneh, D.: Twenty years of attacks on the RSA cryptosystem. Not. AMS **46**(2), 203–213 (1999)

[BP00] Boyd, C., Pavlovski, C.: Attacking and repairing batch verification schemes. In: Okamoto, T. (ed.) ASIACRYPT 2000. LNCS, vol. 1976, pp. 58–71. Springer, Heidelberg (2000). https://doi.org/10.1007/3-540-44448-3_5

[CE12] Clark, J., Essex, A.: CommitCoin: carbon dating commitments with Bitcoin. In: Financial Cryptography and Data Security, FC 2012, pp. 390–398 (2012)

[CHP07] Camenisch, J., Hohenberger, S., Pedersen, M.Ø.: Batch verification of short signatures. In: Naor, M. (ed.) EUROCRYPT 2007. LNCS, vol. 4515, pp. 246–263. Springer, Heidelberg (2007). https://doi.org/10.1007/978-3-540-72540-4_14

[CKK+17] Crescenzo, G.D., Khodjaeva, M., Kahrobaei, D., Shpilrain, V.: Computing multiple exponentiations in discrete log and RSA groups: from batch verification to batch delegation. In: IEEE Conference on Communications and Network Security (CNS), pp. 531–539 (2017)

[CL06] Cheon, J.H., Lee, D.H.: Use of sparse and/or complex exponents in batch verification of exponentiations. IEEE Trans. Comput. **55**(12), 1536–1542 (2006)

[CL15] Cheon, J.H., Lee, M.-K.: Improved batch verification of signatures using generalized sparse exponents. Comput. Stand. Interfaces **40**, 42–52 (2015)

[CP19] Cohen, B., Pietrzak, K.: The Chia network blockchain (2019). https://www.chia.net/assets/ChiaGreenPaper.pdf. Accessed 16 Sep 2021

[CY07] Cheon, J.H., Yi, J.H.: Fast batch verification of multiple signatures. In: Okamoto, T., Wang, X. (eds.) PKC 2007. LNCS, vol. 4450, pp. 442–457. Springer, Heidelberg (2007). https://doi.org/10.1007/978-3-540-71677-8_29

[DGM+20] Döttling, N., Garg, S., Malavolta, G., Vasudevan, P.N.: Tight verifiable delay functions. In: Galdi, C., Kolesnikov, V. (eds.) SCN 2020. LNCS, vol. 12238, pp. 65–84. Springer, Cham (2020). https://doi.org/10.1007/978-3-030-57990-6_4

[EFK+20] Ephraim, N., Freitag, C., Komargodski, I., Pass, R.: Continuous verifiable delay functions. In: Canteaut, A., Ishai, Y. (eds.) EUROCRYPT 2020. LNCS, vol. 12107, pp. 125–154. Springer, Cham (2020). https://doi.org/10.1007/978-3-030-45727-3_5

[Fia89] Fiat, A.: Batch RSA. In: Brassard, G. (ed.) CRYPTO 1989. LNCS, vol. 435, pp. 175–185. Springer, New York (1990). https://doi.org/10.1007/0-387-34805-0_17

[Fis19] Fisch, B.: Tight proofs of space and replication. In: Ishai, Y., Rijmen, V. (eds.) EUROCRYPT 2019. LNCS, vol. 11477, pp. 324–348. Springer, Cham (2019). https://doi.org/10.1007/978-3-030-17656-3_12

[FMP+19] De Feo, L., Masson, S., Petit, C., Sanso, A.: Verifiable delay functions from supersingular isogenies and pairings. In: Galbraith, S.D., Moriai, S. (eds.) ASIACRYPT 2019. LNCS, vol. 11921, pp. 248–277. Springer, Cham (2019). https://doi.org/10.1007/978-3-030-34578-5_10

[FS86] Fiat, A., Shamir, A.: How to prove yourself: practical solutions to identification and signature problems. In: Odlyzko, A.M. (ed.) CRYPTO 1986. LNCS, vol. 263, pp. 186–194. Springer, Heidelberg (1987). https://doi.org/10.1007/3-540-47721-7_12

[FS00] Fischlin, R., Schnorr, C.: Stronger security proofs for RSA and Rabin bits. J. Cryptol. **13**(2), 221–244 (2000)

[GGM86] Goldreich, O., Goldwasser, S., Micali, S.: How to construct random functions. J. ACM **33**(4), 792–807 (1986)

[GLO+21] Galindo, D., Liu, J., Ordean, M., Wong, J.-M.: Fully distributed verifiable random functions and their application to decentralised random beacons. In: IEEE European Symposium on Security and Privacy (2021, to appear)

[GS98] Goldschlag, D.M., Stubblebine, S.G.: Publicly verifiable lotteries: applications of delaying functions. In: Financial Cryptography, FC 1998, pp. 214–226 (1998)

[HIL+99] Håstad, J., Impagliazzo, R., Levin, L.A., Luby, M.: A pseudorandom generator from any one-way function. SIAM J. Comput. **28**(4), 1364–1396 (1999)

[HK09] Hofheinz, D., Kiltz, E.: The group of signed quadratic residues and applications. In: Halevi, S. (ed.) CRYPTO 2009. LNCS, vol. 5677, pp. 637–653. Springer, Heidelberg (2009). https://doi.org/10.1007/978-3-642-03356-8_37

[HYL20] Han, R., Yu, R., Lin, H.: RANDCHAIN: decentralised randomness beacon from sequential proof-of-work. In: IEEE International Conference on Blockchain, pp. 442–449 (2020)

[IW97] Impagliazzo, R., Wigderson, A.: P = BPP if E requires exponential circuits: Derandomizing the XOR lemma. In: Proceedings of the 29th Annual ACM Symposium on Theory of Computing, pp. 220–229 (1997)

[Ler14] Lerner, S.D.: Proof of unique blockchain storage (2014). https://bitslog.com/2014/11/03/proof-of-local-blockchain-storage/. Accessed 16 Sep 2021

[LSS20] Landerreche, E., Stevens, M., Schaffnerevan, C.: Non-interactive cryptographic timestamping based on verifiable delay functions. In: Financial Cryptography and Data Security, FC 2020, pp. 541–558 (2020)

[LV20] Lombardi, A., Vaikuntanathan, V.: Fiat-Shamir for repeated squaring with applications to PPAD-hardness and VDFs. In: Micciancio, D., Ristenpart, T. (eds.) CRYPTO 2020. LNCS, vol. 12172, pp. 632–651. Springer, Cham (2020). https://doi.org/10.1007/978-3-030-56877-1_22

[LW15] Lenstra, A.K., Wesolowski, B.: A random zoo: sloth, unicorn, and trx. Cryptology ePrint Archive, Report 2015/366 (2015)

[Nao91] Naor, M.: Bit commitment using pseudorandomness. J. Cryptol. **4**(2), 151–158 (1991)

[NMV+94] Naccache, D., et al.: Can D.S.A. be improved?—Complexity trade-offs with the digital signature standard. In: De Santis, A. (ed.) EUROCRYPT 1994. LNCS, vol. 950, pp. 77–85. Springer, Heidelberg (1995). https://doi.org/10.1007/BFb0053426

[NN93] Naor, M., Naor, J.: Small-bias probability spaces: efficient constructions and applications. SIAM J. Comput. **22**(4), 838–856 (1993)

[NW94] Nisan, N., Wigderson, A.: Hardness vs randomness. J. Comput. Syst. Sci. **49**(2), 149–167 (1994)

[Pie19] Pietrzak, K.: Simple verifiable delay functions. In: Proceedings of the 10th Conference on Innovations in Theoretical Computer Science, pp. 60:1–60:15 (2019)

[Pro17] Protocol Labs: Filecoin: a decentralized storage network (2017). https://filecoin.io/filecoin.pdf. Accessed 16 Sep 2021

[PW18] Pierrot, C., Wesolowski, B.: Malleability of the blockchain's entropy. Cryptogr. Commun. **10**(1), 211–233 (2018)

[RSS20] Rotem, L., Segev, G., Shahaf, I.: Generic-group delay functions require hidden-order groups. In: Canteaut, A., Ishai, Y. (eds.) EUROCRYPT 2020. LNCS, vol. 12107, pp. 155–180. Springer, Cham (2020). https://doi.org/10.1007/978-3-030-45727-3_6

[RSW96] Rivest, R.L., Shamir, A., Wagner, D.A.: Time-lock puzzles and timed-release crypto (1996)

[SB20] Seres, I.A., Burcsi, P.: A note on low order assumptions in RSA groups. Cryptology ePrint Archive, Report 2020/402 (2020)

[Sha19] Shani, B.: A note on isogeny-based hybrid verifiable delay functions. Cryptology ePrint Archive, Report 2019/205 (2019)

[Sta20] StarkWare: Presenting: VeeDo (2020). https://medium.com/starkware/presenting-veedo-e4bbff77c7ae. Accessed 16 Sep 2021

[Ta-17] Ta-Shma, A.: Explicit, almost optimal, epsilon-balanced codes. In: Proceedings of the 49rd Annual ACM Symposium on Theory of Computing, pp. 238–251 (2017)

[Wes19] Wesolowski, B.: Efficient verifiable delay functions. In: Ishai, Y., Rijmen, V. (eds.) EUROCRYPT 2019. LNCS, vol. 11478, pp. 379–407. Springer, Cham (2019). https://doi.org/10.1007/978-3-030-17659-4_13

[Wes20] Wesolowski, B.: Efficient verifiable delay functions. J. Cryptol. **33**, 2113–2147 (2020)

[YL95] Yen, S.-M., Laih, C.-S.: Improved digital signature suitable for batch verification. IEEE Trans. Comput. **44**(7), 957–959 (1995)

Non-malleable Vector Commitments via Local Equivocability

Lior Rotem[✉] and Gil Segev

School of Computer Science and Engineering, Hebrew University of Jerusalem,
91904 Jerusalem, Israel
{lior.rotem,segev}@cs.huji.ac.il

Abstract. Vector commitments (VCs), enabling to commit to a vector and locally reveal any of its entries, play a key role in a variety of both classic and recently-evolving applications. However, security notions for VCs have so far focused on passive attacks, and non-malleability notions considering active attacks have not been explored. Moreover, existing frameworks that may enable to capture the non-malleability of VCs seem either too weak (non-malleable non-interactive commitments that do not account for the security implications of local openings) or too strong (non-malleable zero-knowledge sets that support both membership and non-membership proofs).

We put forward a rigorous framework capturing the non-malleability of VCs, striking a careful balance between the existing weaker and stronger frameworks: We strengthen the framework of non-malleable non-interactive commitments by considering attackers that may be exposed to local openings, and we relax the framework of non-malleable zero-knowledge sets by focusing on membership proofs. In addition, we strengthen both frameworks by supporting (inherently-private) updates to entries of committed vectors, and discuss the benefits of non-malleable VCs in the context of both UTXO-based and account-based stateless blockchains, and in the context of simultaneous multi-round auctions (that have been adopted by the US Federal Communications Commission as the standard auction format for selling spectrum ranges).

Within our framework we present a direct approach for constructing non-malleable VCs whose efficiency essentially matches that of the existing standard VCs. Specifically, we show that any VC can be transformed into a non-malleable one, relying on a new primitive that we put forth. Our new primitive, *locally-equivocable commitments with all-but-one binding*, is evidently both conceptually and technically simpler compared to multi-trapdoor mercurial trapdoor commitments (the main building block underlying existing non-malleable zero-knowledge sets), and admits more efficient instantiations based on the same number-theoretic assumptions.

L. Rotem and G. Segev—Supported by the European Union's Horizon 2020 Framework Program (H2020) via an ERC Grant (Grant No. 714253).
L. Rotem—Supported by the Adams Fellowship Program of the Israel Academy of Sciences and Humanities.

K. Nissim and B. Waters (Eds.): TCC 2021, LNCS 13044, pp. 415–446, 2021.
https://doi.org/10.1007/978-3-030-90456-2_14

1   Introduction

Vector commitments (VCs) [LY10, CF13] enable to non-interactively commit to a vector $(x_1, \ldots, x_q)$ while offering the useful property of *local opening*: The committer can reveal any individual entry x_i without the overhead of revealing the entire vector. At the same time, VCs are also required to be *position binding*: The committer should not be able to reveal any entry of an even maliciously-committed vector to more than a single value.

The main measure of efficiency for VCs, which makes them extremely useful for a variety of applications but highly non-trivial to construct, is their succinctness: Both the size of the commitment and the size of the local openings should be sublinear in the number q of elements in the committed vector. Whereas the classic notion of a Merkle tree [Mer87] can be seen as a VC in which the size of the commitment is independent of q and the size of local openings scales logarithmically with q, Libert and Yung [LY10] and Catalano and Fiore [CF13] presented constructions in which both sizes are independent of q.

Starting already with Merkle's early work, VCs consistently play a key role in a wide range of applications as a communication-efficient method for authenticating rather large amounts of data by allowing users to retrieve small parts of the data alongside short proofs of authenticity. Such applications include, for example, verifiable databases and authenticated data structures (e.g., [NN98, MND+04, BGV11, SvDJ+12, KSS+16, CFG+20]), zero-knowledge sets (e.g., [MRK03, LY10, CRF+11, CHL+13]), cryptographic accumulators [BdM93] (which have many applications on their own right – see for example [BP97, GR97, CL02, DKN+04, Ngu05, ABC+12, MGG+13, FVY14] and the references therein), stateless blockchains (e.g., [STS99, Tod16, But17, BBF19, TAB+20]), and succinct arguments (e.g., [Kil92, Mic94, BBF19, LM19, OWW+20]).

Non-malleable Commitments. Another long line of research regarding commitment schemes, initiated by the seminal work of Dolev, Dwork and Naor [DDN00], deals with the construction of *non-malleable* commitments. Roughly speaking, a commitment scheme is non-malleable if an adversary which receives a commitment to some value x, cannot produce a commitment to some "non-trivially related" value x'. Non-malleable commitments have established themselves as instrumental in a host of cryptographic tasks, especially those requiring to protect against man-in-the-middle attacks. Numerous constructions of non-malleable commitments have been suggested over the years, satisfying various flavors of security notions and achieving different efficiency tradeoffs, based on wide range of cryptographic assumptions (e.g., [CIO98, DDN00, FF00, CKO+01, Bar01, CF01, PR05, PR08, PPV08, LPV08, LP09, PW10, Wee10, LP11, GLO+12, GPR16, COS+17, Khu17] and the many references therein).

This Work: Non-malleable Vector Commitments. The fundamental importance of VCs and of non-malleable commitments motivates the study of non-malleable VCs with the premise of significantly strengthening the security and improving the efficiency of the wide range of applications in which they play a key role. For example, non-malleable VCs would directly give rise to verifiable databases, authenticated data structures and cryptographic accumulators offering non-malleability guarantees. As additional, less direct examples, in Sect. 1.2 we discuss the benefits of using non-malleable VCs as building blocks in the contexts of stateless blockchains and simultaneous multi-round auctions.

However, the notion of non-malleable VCs has not yet been explored, and the existing framework and constructions of standard non-malleable commitments do not take into account the significant security implications of local openings. A closely-related notion, which has been thoroughly explored, is that of non-malleable zero-knowledge sets (ZKS), introduced in the beautiful work of Gennaro and Micali [GM06] (extending the notion of standard ZKS [MRK03]). Non-malleable ZKS can be seen as a substantial strengthening of non-malleable VCs, supporting *non-membership* proofs in addition to membership proofs. The work of Gennaro and Micali initiated an exciting line of research leading to constructions of non-malleable ZKS based on gradually weaker assumptions and with increasingly better parameters (see [LY10, CF13] and the references therein). However, these constructions rely on the useful yet intricate notion of multi-trapdoor mercurial trapdoor commitments [GM06], specifically tailored to support non-membership proofs (see also [CHL+13, CDV06] for basic background on mercurial commitments). As prominent applications of VCs generally do not require non-membership proofs (as we exemplify in Sect. 1.2), this raises the following question:

> *Can non-malleable VCs be constructed within a simplified framework*
> *both* **conceptually** *(e.g., simpler and more intuitive notions)*
> *and* **technically** *(e.g., direct and more efficient constructions)?*

1.1 Our Contributions

Notion of Non-malleability for VCs. We put forward a strong notion of non-malleability for vector commitment schemes. Our framework strikes a careful balance between the weaker notion of non-malleable non-interactive commitments [CIO98, CKO+01] and the considerably stronger notion of non-malleable zero-knowledge sets [GM06]. Concretely, we generalize the notion of non-malleable non-interactive commitments by incorporating the adversarial adaptivity and additional information resulting from local openings. That is, the key difference from the notion of non-malleable non-interactive commitments is that we aim at achieving non-malleability against adversaries which may have already been exposed to several local openings. Looking ahead, this key difference is the reason that simple attempts of combining VCs and non-malleable commitments do not seem to suffice for realizing our notion (as we demonstrate in Sect. 3.2).

Warm-Up: Merkle Trees are Non-malleable in the Random-Oracle Model. As a first step within our framework, we examine the non-malleability of existing vector commitments schemes and observe that they are easily malleable (some of them by design in order to support public updates). Then, as a warm-up towards our main result, we show that a Merkle tree does satisfy our requirements when its underlying hash function is modeled as a random oracle [BR93] (and we show that this does not generally hold in the standard model):

Theorem 1.1 (informal). *Let* H *be a hash function and let* treeVC *be the Merkle tree vector commitment scheme that obtained via* H. *Then,* treeVC *is a non-malleable vector commitment scheme when* H *is modeled as a random oracle.*

Theorem 1.1 demonstrates the feasibility of realizing our notion of non-malleable vector commitments via a direct construction whose proof is not explicitly based on multi-trapdoor mercurial trapdoor commitments. However, the non-malleability of this construction heavily relies on the random-oracle model and, more importantly, the construction has local openings whose size scales logarithmically with the number q of elements in the committed vector.

Main Result: Efficient Non-malleable VCs Via Locally Equivocability. We present a direct approach for constructing non-malleable VCs whose efficiency essentially matches that of the existing standard VCs. Inspired by constructions of non-malleable zero-knowledge sets [GM06, LY10, CF13] (and, more generally, of non-malleable cryptographic primitives [DDN00]), we show that any vector commitment scheme can be transformed into a non-malleable one, relying on a new primitive that we put forth. Our new primitive, *locally-equivocable commitments with all-but-one binding*, is evidently both conceptually and technically simpler when compared to multi-trapdoor mercurial trapdoor commitments, as we discuss below. We prove the following theorem:

Theorem 1.2 (informal). *Any vector commitment scheme can be transformed into a non-malleable one using: (1) a locally-equivocable commitment scheme with all-but-one binding, (2) a one-time strongly-unforgeable signature scheme, and (3) a universal one-way hash family.*

We note that our notions of non-malleability and our construction extend to accumulators [BdM93], which can be viewed as VCs for vectors whose length is not necessarily bounded ahead of time. Specifically, in our construction, the underlying VC can be replaced with an accumulator, and the underlying locally-equivocable commitment scheme can be replaced with one that supports an a-priori unbounded number of commitments (this is already the case with our number-theoretic constructions).

Intuitive, Simple & Efficient: Locally-Equivocable Commitments with All-But-One Binding. Our new notion of commitments is obtained by augmenting the standard notion of tag-based commitments with the following two requirements:

- **Local equivocability:** A committer can generate several equivocal commitments with respect to a single common-reference string.

- **All-but-one binding:** Equivocal commitments generated with respect to a predetermined tag τ should be binding with respect to any other tag even when given the trapdoor associated with τ.

This new notion is evidently both conceptually and technically simpler than the notion of multi-trapdoor mercurial trapdoor commitments. From the conceptual perspective, it has a short and intuitive description. This is evident not only from the above informal description, but also from the fact that in addition to the standard setup, commitment and decommitment procedures, our notion consists of only 3 additional procedures, whereas the notion of a multi-trapdoor mercurial trapdoor commitment consists of 7 additional procedures (already in its non-vector variant) together with a non-trivial number of correctness and security requirements.

From the technical perspective, on the one hand we observe that our new notion strengthens Fischlin's notion of identity-based trapdoor commitments [Fis01, Ch. 2.6]; whereas on the other hand we nevertheless show that Fischlin's highly-efficient number-theoretic constructions satisfy our strengthened notion [Fis01, Ch. 3.3]. Specifically, this yields constructions based on the discrete logarithm assumption and on the RSA assumption, in which commitments consist of a *single* group element. This should be contrasted with the known constructions of multi-trapdoor mercurial trapdoor commitments based on the same assumptions in which commitments consist of *two* group elements. The difference between producing one or two group elements might not be significant on its own, but both in our construction and in those based on multi-trapdoor mercurial trapdoor commitments the underlying commitment scheme is used for producing q commitments (where q is the number of elements in the committed vector), and this translates into a more significant difference between producing q and $2q$ group elements.

In addition to these highly-efficient number-theoretic constructions, we also present a construction based on the existence of any standard commitment scheme (and thus based on the existence of any one-way function [Nao91, HIL+99]). However, this construction is mainly of theoretical significance as it supports only an a-priori bounded of number q of equivocal commitments, and the length of its common-reference string is linear in this bound. Such guarantees still suffice for our non-malleable vector commitment, but lead to somewhat impractical efficiency guarantees.

Extension: Non-malleable Dynamic VCs. Catalano and Fiore [CF13] constructed VCs in which individual entries of the committed vector can be updated *publicly* (i.e., without knowledge of the committer's private state). Such public updates, however, are inherently incompatible with the motivation underlying the notion of non-malleability, and indeed with our definition of non-malleable VCs. In light of this inherent limitation, we show that our framework and construction can nevertheless support updates in a *private* manner, requiring knowledge of the private state generated by the committer in order to update entries of the underlying vector.

We extend our definition of non-malleable VCs to support dynamic VCs as well, essentially requiring that non-malleability is maintained even when the adversary receives a vector commitment which has undergone adversarially-chosen updates. We then revisit our construction from Theorem 1.2 and show that if the underlying VC supports private updates,[1] then so does our resulting non-malleable VC (which is indeed non-malleable with respect to our extended definition).

Theorem 1.3 (informal). *Any privately-updatable vector commitment scheme can be transformed into a non-malleable privately-updatable one using: (1) a locally-equivocable commitment scheme with all-but-one binding, (2) a strongly-unforgeable signature scheme, and (3) a universal one-way hash family.*

1.2   Applications

The notion of non-malleable commitments is over three decades old [DDN00], and has found a variety of applications. Since our notion of non-malleable VCs strengthens this notion in the non-interactive setting, it can be applied in any case in which non-interactive non-malleable commitments can be used, while offering significant efficiency improvement via local openings. Specifically, VCs play a key role in a wide range of applications both as an intermediate building block and as a direct communication-efficient method for authenticating large amounts of data (allowing users to retrieve small parts of the data alongside short proofs of their authenticity). Here, we focus our attention on discussing the benefits of non-malleable VCs in the contexts of stateless blockchains and simultaneous multi-round auctions.

Stateless Blockchains. VCs are used as a direct communication-efficient method for authenticating large amounts of data in stateless blockchains both in the UTXO model (e.g., Bitcoin [Nak08]) and in the account model (e.g., Ethereum [But14]).[2] In both models, transactions and smart-contracts consist of local opening of VCs, where the VCs represent a compressed version of a current state, and are stored by validating parties. Their local openings are verified either as unspent transactions in the UTXO model, or as account balances and various other user-specific properties in the account model (see for example, [BBF19, GRW+20, BBB+18, TAB+20], for extensive discussions and additional related work – which is far beyond the context of our work).

In such scenarios, the basic security properties of VCs are generally insufficient in order to guarantee cross-transaction independence (also known as transaction non-malleability [BCG+14]). Specifically, in such highly interactive scenarios, attackers may indeed observe both VCs and local openings, then manipulate the VCs to represent a malleated state (e.g., either in an implicitly-malicious

---

[1] Note that a VC which supports public updates trivially supports private updates.

[2] In fact, in some cases, accumulators are used instead of vector commitments. As noted about, our notions of non-malleability and our construction apply also to accumulators.

manner by issuing honest yet tailored transactions that lead to specific state updates, or in an explicitly-malicious manner by potentially controlling to some extent some of the verifying parties), and then produce local openings with respect to the malleated VCs – as captured by our notion for non-malleable VCs. Thus, relying on non-malleable VCs in the context of stateless blockchains can significantly reduce both storage and communication while guaranteeing cross-transaction independence.

Simultaneous Multi-round Auctions. One of the most classic and direct applications of (non-malleable) commitments is that of sealed-bid auctions [DDN00], and in this context our notion of non-malleable VCs seems particularly suitable for Simultaneous Multi-Round Auctions (SMRA) [Bic17, Ch. 6]. Such auctions provide a widespread multi-round format for selling multiple items. SMRAs were designed for the US Federal Communications Commission in the early 1990s, and since then they have become the standard auction format for selling spectrum worldwide.

SMRAs proceed in rounds, where in each round some or all bidders bid for multiple items, and each item may either be sold or not sold in each round depending of the specific rules of the auction and the submitted bids. After each round is closed the auctioneer discloses which items were won, who wins each of these items, and at what price. Depending on the specific rules of the auction, there are differences in the level of information revealed about other bidders' bids. In some cases all bids are publicly revealed after each round, whereas in other cases only prices of the currently winning bids are publicly revealed.

From the perspective of using vector commitments, submitting each bidder's bids for all available items in each round using a VC, and then publicly revealing local openings for the required (e.g., winning) bids according to the rules of the auction, can lead to significant communication savings (at least in the case of spectrum ranges, the number of ranges may be rather large – although not as large as in the context of using VCs for stateless blockchains). However, this enables a malicious bidder to malleate vector commitments (i.e., bids) provided in earlier rounds or even in the same round after having seen some of their local openings, and to generate a vector commitment (i.e., a bid) to related values together with corresponding local openings at a later stage – as captured by our notion of non-malleable VCs. Thus, relying on non-malleable VCs in the context of SMRAs can significantly reduce communication while guaranteeing cross-round and cross-bid independence.

1.3   Overview of Our Approach

In this section we provide a high-level overview of our notion of non-malleability and of our main construction of a non-malleable vector commitment scheme (Theorem 1.2). For brevity, the main ideas underlying our additional results are described within the corresponding sections.

The starting point of our work is the notion of a vector commitment scheme $\mathcal{VC} = (\mathsf{VC.Setup}, \mathsf{VC.Commit}, \mathsf{VC.Open}, \mathsf{VC.Verify})$ [CF13] with the following syntax: The algorithms VC.Setup and VC.Commit are invoked in order to produce a common-reference string crs, and in order to produce a commitment vcom for a vector $(x_1, \ldots, x_q)$, respectively. In turn, the algorithms VC.Open and VC.Verify are then invoked in order to produce a local opening π_i for each entry $i \in [q]$ of the committed vector, and in order to verify it, respectively. In terms of security, a vector commitment scheme should provide *position binding*, essentially asking that no efficient algorithm can generate a commitment vcom together with two valid openings for the same entry $i \in [q]$ corresponding to different values x_i and x_i'. The main measure of efficiency for vector commitments, which makes them non-trivial to construct, is their succinctness. This is captured by asking for upper bounds on the sizes of the resulting commitments and local openings (e.g., asking that both sizes are nearly independent of the length q of the committed vector). We refer the reader to Sect. 2.2 for the formal description of the position binding and succinctness requirements.

Our Notion of Non-malleability. Based on the standard notion of non-malleability for non-interactive commitment schemes [CIO98, CKO+01], any non-malleable vector commitment scheme should at least satisfy the following informal property: An efficient adversary which receives a commitment vcom to a vector $\vec{x} = (x_1, \ldots, x_q)$, should not be able to produce (and then open) a vector commitment $\widehat{\text{vcom}}$ to some vector $\hat{\vec{x}} = (\widehat{x_1}, \ldots, \widehat{x_q})$ which is "non-trivially related" to $\vec{x}$. However, this property does not capture the adversarial adaptivity and additional information resulting from local openings. Therefore, our notion of non-malleability for vector commitments asks that the above property holds even when the adversary can request local openings for some of the entries of $\vec{x}$ before deciding on $\widehat{\text{vcom}}$, and then open only some of the entries $\hat{\vec{x}}$ after obtaining local opening for all other entries of $\vec{x}$.

This is formalized by considering a "real" security experiment involving an adversary and an "ideal" security experiment involving a simulator. At a high level, in the real experiment, the adversary is provided with a commitment vcom to a vector $\vec{x} = (x_1, \ldots, x_q)$, and is allowed to request local openings $(\pi_i)_{i \in \mathcal{I}}$ for any subset $\mathcal{I} \subseteq [q]$ of the entries of $\vec{x}$ for producing a commitment $\widehat{\text{vcom}}$. Then, the adversary is provided with local openings for all other entries of $\vec{x}$, and outputs local openings $(\widehat{\pi}_j)_{j \in \mathcal{J}}$ for a subset $\mathcal{J} \subseteq [q]$ of the entries of a malleated vector $(\widehat{x_1}, \ldots, \widehat{x_q})$ (although, note that $\widehat{\text{vcom}}$ is not required to actually correspond to any such malleated vector). In the ideal experiment, the simulator is provided only with a description of the distribution $\mathcal{D}$ from which $\vec{x}$ is sampled (i.e., without the commitment vcom) and the values $(x_i)_{i \in \mathcal{I}}$ (i.e., without the local openings $(\pi_i)_{i \in \mathcal{I}}$), and outputs malleated values $(\widehat{x}_j)_{j \in \mathcal{J}}$.

The outputs of both experiments consist of the values $(x_i)_{i \in [q]}$ and $(\widehat{x}_j)_{j \in [q]}$, where in the real experiment we replace with $\bot$ each value $\widehat{x}_j$ for which either $j \notin \mathcal{J}$ or $\widehat{\pi}_j$ does not properly verify, and in the ideal experiment we replace with $\bot$ each value $\widehat{x}_j$ for which $j \notin \mathcal{J}$. Our notion of non-malleability then asks that for any efficient adversary there exists an efficient simulator such that the outputs of the two experiments are computationally indistinguishable. We refer the reader to Sect. 3 for our formal definition, and for an in-depth discussion of its various technical aspects (including, the underlying distribution $\mathcal{D}$, the relation between the sets $\mathcal{I}$ and $\mathcal{J}$, and more).

Our Main Construction. Given any vector commitment scheme $\mathcal{VC}$ we transform it into a non-malleable one as follows. In order to commit to a vector $(x_1, \ldots, x_q)$ we first sample a signing key sk and a corresponding verification key vk for a one-time strongly-unforgeable signature scheme. Then, for each $i \in [q]$ we generate a commitment c_i to the value x_i using a locally-equivocable commitment scheme $\mathcal{LE}$ with all-but-one binding (our newly-introduced primitive augmenting the standard notion of tag-based commitments with two additional requirements). Each of these q commitments is generated with respect to the tag $\tau = h(vk)$ for a universal one-way hash function h. Then, we commit to the vector $(c_1, \ldots, c_q)$ using the underlying vector commitment scheme $\mathcal{VC}$, and output the resulting vector commitment vcom, the verification key vk and a signature σ on vcom using the signing key sk.

In turn, for every $i \in [q]$, a local opening of the value x_i consists of the commitment c_i and its corresponding decommitment d_i, and of a local opening π_i of the commitment c_i with respect to the vector commitment vcom. The verification algorithm first verifies the one-time signature σ, and then verifies the decommitment d_i and the local opening π_i. We refer the reader to Sect. 5 for a formal description of our construction.

Note that from a foundational perspective, the required building blocks can all be based on the existence of any vector commitment scheme. Specifically, any vector commitment scheme implies the existence of a one-way function, which in turns implies the existence of a locally-equivocable commitment scheme with all-but-one binding, a one-time strongly unforgeable signature scheme and a universal one-way hash family. In addition, from a more practical perspective, the above building blocks can all be realized based on a variety of number-theoretic assumptions leading to practical implementations (see the full version of the paper for practical number-theoretic constructions of locally-equivocable commitments with all-but-one binding, and for a construction based on one-way functions).

Focusing on the main measures of efficiency for vector commitments, namely the lengths of resulting commitments and local openings, and the verification time of the local openings, we observe the following:

- A commitment produced by our scheme consists of a commitment produced by the underlying vector commitment scheme, and of a verification key and a signature which can be instantiated with any practical strongly-unforgeable signature scheme[3]. Thus, the length of commitments produced by our scheme is essentially dominated by that of the underlying vector commitment scheme, which can be as short as a single group element.
- A local opening produced by our scheme consists of a local opening produced by the underlying vector commitment scheme together with a commitment

---

[3] See, for example, [BSW06, BS07] and the many references therein for a variety of practical strongly-unforgeable signature schemes both in the random-oracle model and in the standard model.

and a decommitment produced by the underlying locally-equivocable commitment scheme with all-but-one binding. Relying on existing constructions of vector commitment schemes and on our number-theoretic constructions of locally-equivocable commitment schemes with all-but-one binding (which can be found in the full version), leads to local openings that are essentially as short as three group elements.

- The verification of a local opening produced by our scheme consists of a verification of a local opening produced by the underlying vector commitment scheme, a decommitment of the underlying locally-equivocable commitment scheme with all-but-one binding, and a signature verification. Once again, relying on our number-theoretic constructions of locally-equivocable commitment schemes with all-but-one binding and on practical signature schemes, this is dominated by the verification time of the underlying vector commitment scheme.

Proving the Security of Our Main Construction. Recall that for proving the security of our construction, we have to show that for any efficient adversary there exists an efficient simulator for which the outputs of the above-mentioned real and ideal experiments are computationally indistinguishable. Given the informal flavor of the current exposition, we refer the reader to the full version of the paper for an overview of the simulator's description and of the indistinguishably of the two experiments (in addition, of course, to the formal proof of security). For avoiding additional notation and various additional technical details, here we focus only on the adversary's behavior in the real experiment.

Consider an adversary $\mathcal{A}$ that is provided in the real experiment with a commitment vcom to a vector $\vec{x} = (x_1, \ldots, x_q)$. Recall that, in our construction, the commitment vcom is of the form $\mathsf{vcom} = \mathsf{vcom}_0 \| vk \| \sigma$, where vcom_0 is a commitment produced using the underlying vector commitment scheme $\mathcal{VC}$ to the vector of commitments $(c_1, \ldots, c_q)$ produced using the locally-equivocable scheme $\mathcal{LE}$ to $(x_1, \ldots, x_q)$ with respect to the tag $h(vk)$ (for a universal one-way hash function h included in the common-reference string), vk is a verification key for a one-time strongly-unforgeable signature scheme, and σ is a signature on vcom_0 produced using the corresponding signing key. The adversary $\mathcal{A}$ requests local openings $(\pi_i)_{i \in \mathcal{I}}$ for some subset $\mathcal{I} \subseteq [q]$ of the entries of $\vec{x}$, and produces a commitment $\widehat{\mathsf{vcom}} = \widehat{\mathsf{vcom}_0} \| \widehat{vk} \| \widehat{\sigma}$. Then, the adversary is provided with local openings for all other entries of $\vec{x}$, and outputs local openings $(\widehat{\pi}_j)_{j \in \mathcal{J}}$ for a subset $\mathcal{J} \subseteq [q]$. Our proof considers the following three cases (the first and second cases are straightforward, and the third case is the main technical argument):

- **Case 1: $\widehat{vk} = vk$.** This case reduces to the one-time strong unforgeability of the signature scheme, unless $\widehat{\mathsf{vcom}_0} = \mathsf{vcom}_0$ or the signature σ does not verify properly (and in these cases our simulator guarantees that the outputs of the real and ideal experiments are identical).
- **Case 2: $\widehat{vk} \neq vk$ but $h(\widehat{vk}) = h(vk)$.** This case reduces to the universal one-wayness of h.

– **Case 3: $h(\widehat{vk}) \neq h(vk)$.** In this case we rely on the position binding of the underlying vector commitment scheme $\mathcal{VC}$, and on the equivocability[4] and all-but-one binding of the locally-equivocable scheme $\mathcal{LE}$. Our main observation is that essentially any advantage that may be obtained in the real experiment must follow from the adversary's ability to choose the values $(\widehat{x}_j)_{j \in \mathcal{J}}$ to which it opens the commitment $\widehat{vcom}$ *after* issuing $\widehat{vcom}$. That is, any such advantage must follow from the adversary's ability to produce a commitment $\widehat{vcom}$ and then to provide local openings to more than a single tuple of values $(\widehat{x}_j)_{j \in \mathcal{J}}$. These local openings are obtained by relying on the fact that generating $c_1, \ldots, c_q$ using the equivocation algorithms of $\mathcal{LE}$ is indistinguishable from the real experiment and does not bind them to a single tuple of values with respect to the tag $\tau = h(vk)$. Thus, we can rewind the adversary to obtain corresponding local openings with respect to the tag $\widehat{\tau} = h(\widehat{vk})$. But, if $\mathcal{A}$ can open, say, the j-th location of $\widehat{vcom}$ in two different ways, we show that this contradicts either the position binding of $\mathcal{VC}$ or the all-but-one binding of $\mathcal{LE}$.

1.4   Open Problems

Our framework and constructions lead to various open problems, and here we discuss two such problems focusing on further extending our approach both in the context of vector commitments and in the more general context of non-interactive non-malleable commitments.

Non-malleable Subvector Commitments. The recent works of Lai and Malavolta [LM19] and of Boneh, Bünz and Fisch [BBF19] introduced the notion of VCs with *subvector openings*. These are VCs which allow the committer to open k entries of the committed vector simultaneously, with a proof whose length is sublinear in k. Our construction, being quite modular, does not seem to support such concise openings, and an interesting open problem is to construct non-malleable VCs that do support subvector openings. A possible starting point may be the recent work Gorbunov et al. [GRW+20], presenting the notion of commitments with aggregatable proofs. Constructing commitments which satisfy both this notion and our notion of local equivocability with all-but-one binding would seem to enable the construction of non-malleable subvector commitments, using our underlying approach for constructing non-malleable VCs.

Implications to Non-malleable Commitments. Finally, note that any non-malleable vector commitment scheme is also a non-interactive non-malleable commitment scheme (when the vector is of length 1). In that respect, our work presents a general and unified framework for constructing non-interactive non-malleable commitments, capturing both the generic construction of Di Crescenzo, Ishai and Ostrovsky from any one-way function [CIO98] and the efficient number-theoretic constructions of Di Cresccenzo, Katz, Ostrovsky and Smith

---

[4] In our formal proof, we actually rely on the equivocability guarantee earlier in order to enable the simulator to invoke the adversary in the ideal experiment.

[CKO+01]. As such, it may enable to construct efficient non-interactive non-malleable commitments based on new assumptions (e.g., isogenies or lattice-based assumptions) by constructing equivocable tag-based commitments with all-but-one binding based on such assumptions.

1.5 Paper Organization

The remainder of this paper is organized as follows. First, in Sect. 2 we present the basic notation and standard cryptographic primitives that are used throughout the paper. In Sect. 3 we present our framework for non-malleable VCs, show that existing VCs do not satisfy our requirements, and demonstrate that simple attempts of combining VCs and non-malleable commitments do not suffice for realizing our notion. In Sect. 4 we introduce our notion of a locally-equivocable commitment scheme with all-but-one binding, and in Sect. 5 we present our construction of a non-malleable VC.

Due to space limitations some of our contributions appear in the full version of this paper. In particular, in the full version we give a formal proof of security for our construction of a non-malleable VC. We also show that a Merkle tree is a non-malleable VC in the random-oracle model, and present our constructions of locally-equivocable commitment schemes with all-but-one binding. Finally, we show that our framework and construction extend to the dynamic setting.

2 Preliminaries

In this section we present the basic notions and standard cryptographic tools that are used in this work. For an integer $n \in \mathbb{N}$ we denote by $[n]$ the set $\{1, \ldots, n\}$. For a distribution X we denote by $x \leftarrow X$ the process of sampling a value x from the distribution X. Similarly, for a set $\mathcal{X}$ we denote by $x \leftarrow \mathcal{X}$ the process of sampling a value x from the uniform distribution over $\mathcal{X}$. A function $\nu : \mathbb{N} \to \mathbb{R}^+$ is *negligible* if for any polynomial $p(\cdot)$ there exists an integer N such that for all $n > N$ it holds that $\nu(n) \leq 1/p(n)$.

2.1 Equivocable Commitment Schemes

We rely on the standard notion of a (non-interactive) equivocable commitment scheme which can be realized based on the existence of any one-way function [Nao91, CIO98]. An equivocable commitment scheme over a domain $\mathcal{X} = \{\mathcal{X}_\lambda\}_{\lambda \in \mathbb{N}}$ is a 5-tuple $\mathcal{EQ} = (\mathsf{EQ.Setup}, \mathsf{EQ.Commit}, \mathsf{EQ.Decommit}, \mathsf{EQ.Equiv_1}, \mathsf{EQ.Equiv_2})$ of polynomial-time algorithms defined as follows:

- The algorithm $\mathsf{EQ.Setup}$ is a probabilistic algorithm that receives as input the security parameter $\lambda \in \mathbb{N}$ and outputs a common-reference string crs.
- The algorithm $\mathsf{EQ.Commit}$ is a probabilistic algorithm that receives as input the security parameter $\lambda \in \mathbb{N}$, a common-reference string crs, an element $x \in \mathcal{X}_\lambda$, and outputs a commitment c and a decommitment d.

- The algorithm EQ.Decommit is a deterministic algorithm that receives as input the security parameter $\lambda \in \mathbb{N}$, a common-reference string crs, a commitment c and a decommitment d, and outputs an element $x \in \mathcal{X}_\lambda$ or the rejection symbol $\perp$.
- The algorithm EQ.Equiv$_1$ is a probabilistic algorithm that receives as input the security parameter $\lambda \in \mathbb{N}$, and outputs a common-reference string $\widehat{\text{crs}}$, a commitment $\widehat{c}$ and a state st.
- The algorithm EQ.Equiv$_2$ is a deterministic algorithm that receives as input the security parameter $\lambda \in \mathbb{N}$, a state st and an element $x \in \mathcal{X}_\lambda$, and outputs a decommitment $\widehat{d}$.

Correctness. We rely on the standard notion of correctness for commitment schemes. That is, for any security parameter $\lambda \in \mathbb{N}$ and for any $x \in \mathcal{X}_\lambda$ it should hold that

$$\Pr\left[\text{EQ.Decommit}(1^\lambda, \text{crs}, c, d) = x\right] = 1,$$

where crs $\leftarrow$ EQ.Setup(1^λ) and $(c, d) \leftarrow$ EQ.Commit(1^λ, crs, x), and the probability is taken over the internal randomness of all algorithms.

Equivocability. We rely on the following notion of equivocability [CIO98, CKO+01]:

Definition 2.1. *A commitment scheme* $\mathcal{EQ}$ = (EQ.Setup, EQ.Commit, EQ.De-commit, EQ.Equiv$_1$, EQ.Equiv$_2$) *over a domain* $\mathcal{X} = \{\mathcal{X}_\lambda\}_{\lambda \in \mathbb{N}}$ *is equivocable if the following requirements hold:*

- **Equivocation correctness:** *For any* $\lambda \in \mathbb{N}$ *and* $x \in \mathcal{X}_\lambda$ *it holds that*

$$\Pr\left[\text{EQ.Decommit}(1^\lambda, \widehat{\text{crs}}, \widehat{c}, \widehat{d}) = x\right] = 1,$$

  where $(\widehat{\text{crs}}, \widehat{c}, \text{st}) \leftarrow$ EQ.Equiv$_1$(1^λ) *and* $\widehat{d} :=$ EQ.Equiv$_2$(1^λ, st, x), *and the probability is taken over the internal randomness of all algorithms.*
- **Equivocation indistinguishability:** *For any probabilistic polynomial-time algorithm* $\mathcal{A}$ *there exists a negligible function* $\nu(\cdot)$ *such that*

$$\mathbf{Adv}_{\mathcal{EQ},\mathcal{A}}^{\text{Equiv}}(\lambda) \stackrel{\text{def}}{=} \left|\Pr\left[\text{Equiv}_{\mathcal{EQ},\mathcal{A}}^{(0)}(\lambda)\right] - \Pr\left[\text{Equiv}_{\mathcal{EQ},\mathcal{A}}^{(1)}(\lambda)\right]\right| \leq \nu(\lambda)$$

  for all sufficiently large $\lambda \in \mathbb{N}$, *where for each* $b \in \{0, 1\}$ *the experiment* Equiv$_{\mathcal{EQ},\mathcal{A}}^{(b)}(\lambda)$ *is defined as follows:*
  1. $(x, \text{st}_\mathcal{A}) \leftarrow \mathcal{A}(1^\lambda)$.
  2. $\text{crs}_0 \leftarrow$ EQ.Setup(1^λ).
  3. $(c_0, d_0) \leftarrow$ EQ.Commit(1^λ, crs, x).
  4. $(\text{crs}_1, c_1, \text{st}_1) \leftarrow$ EQ.Equiv$_1$(1^λ).
  5. $d_1 =$ EQ.Equiv$_2$(1^λ, st$_1$, x).
  6. $b' \leftarrow \mathcal{A}(\text{st}_\mathcal{A}, \text{crs}_b, c_b, d_b)$.
  7. *Output* b'.

Binding. We rely on the standard notion of computational binding for commitment schemes.

Definition 2.2. *A commitment scheme* $\mathcal{EQ}$ = (EQ.Setup, EQ.Commit, EQ.De-commit, EQ.Equiv$_1$, EQ.Equiv$_2$) *over a domain* $\mathcal{X} = \{\mathcal{X}_\lambda\}_{\lambda \in \mathbb{N}}$ *is binding if for any probabilistic polynomial-time algorithm* $\mathcal{A}$ *there exists a negligible function* $\nu(\cdot)$ *such that*

$$\mathbf{Adv}^{\mathsf{Bind}}_{\mathcal{EQ},\mathcal{A}} \overset{\mathsf{def}}{=} \Pr\left[\mathsf{Bind}_{\mathcal{EQ},\mathcal{A}}(\lambda) = 1\right] \leq \nu(\lambda)$$

for all sufficiently large $\lambda \in \mathbb{N}$, *where the experiment* $\mathsf{PosBind}_{\mathcal{EQ},\mathcal{A}}(\lambda)$ *is defined as follows:*

1. crs $\leftarrow$ EQ.Setup(1^λ)
2. $(c, (d, x), (d', x')) \leftarrow \mathcal{A}(1^\lambda, \mathsf{crs})$.
3. *Output 1 if the following conditions hold:*
   - $x \neq x'$ *and* $x, x' \in \mathcal{X}_\lambda$.
   - EQ.Decommit(1^λ, crs, c, d) = x.
   - EQ.Decommit(1^λ, crs, c, d') = x'.
   Otherwise, output 0.

2.2 Vector Commitment Schemes

We follow the notion of a vector commitment scheme as formalized by Libert and Yung [LY10] and Catalano and Fiore [CF13]. As discussed in Sect. 1.1, here we consider the static setting (i.e., vector commitment schemes without updates). In the full version of the paper, we extend our approach to the dynamic setting.

Definition 2.3. *A vector commitment scheme over a domain* $\mathcal{X} = \{\mathcal{X}_\lambda\}_{\lambda \in \mathbb{N}}$ *is a quadruple* $\mathcal{VC}$ = (VC.Setup, VC.Commit, VC.Open, VC.Verify) *of algorithms defined as follows:*

- *The algorithm* VC.Setup *is a probabilistic algorithm that receives as input the security parameter* $\lambda \in \mathbb{N}$ *and a polynomial* $q = q(\lambda)$ *and outputs common-reference string* crs.
- *The algorithm* VC.Commit *is a probabilistic algorithm that receives as input the security parameter* $\lambda \in \mathbb{N}$, *a common-reference string* crs *and a vector* $(x_1, \ldots, x_q) \in (\mathcal{X}_\lambda)^q$, *and outputs a commitment* vcom *and a state* st.
- *The algorithm* VC.Open *is a probabilistic algorithm that receives as input the security parameter* $\lambda \in \mathbb{N}$, *a common-reference string* crs, *a commitment* vcom, *a state* st *and an index* $i \in [q]$, *and outputs a proof* π.
- *The algorithm* VC.Verify *is a deterministic algorithm that receives as input the security parameter* $\lambda \in \mathbb{N}$, *a common-reference string* crs, *a commitment* vcom, *an index* $i \in [q]$, *an element* $x \in \mathcal{X}_\lambda$ *and a proof* π, *and outputs a bit* $b \in \{0, 1\}$.

Correctness. A vector commitment scheme $\mathcal{VC}$ = (VC.Setup, VC.Commit, VC.Open, VC.Verify) over a domain $\mathcal{X} = \{\mathcal{X}_\lambda\}_{\lambda \in \mathbb{N}}$ is correct if for any $\lambda \in \mathbb{N}$, for any polynomial $q = q(\lambda)$, for any vector $(x_1, \ldots, x_q) \in (\mathcal{X}_\lambda)^q$, and for any index $i \in [q]$, it holds that

$$\Pr\left[\text{VC.Verify}\left(1^\lambda, \text{crs}, \text{vcom}, i, x_i, \pi\right) = 1\right] = 1,$$

where crs $\leftarrow$ VC.Setup(1^λ), (vcom, st) $\leftarrow$ VC.Commit$(1^\lambda, \text{crs}, (x_1, \ldots, x_q))$ and $\pi \leftarrow$ VC.Open$(1^\lambda, \text{crs}, \text{vcom}, \text{st}, i)$; and the probability is taken over the randomness of all algorithms.

Security. Catalano and Fiore introduced the following notion of position binding for capturing the security of vector commitment schemes.

Definition 2.4. *A vector commitment scheme* $\mathcal{VC}$ = (VC.Setup, VC.Commit, VC.Open, VC.Verify) *over a domain* $\mathcal{X} = \{\mathcal{X}_\lambda\}_{\lambda \in \mathbb{N}}$ *is* position binding *if for any polynomial* $q = q(\lambda)$ *and for any probabilistic polynomial-time algorithm* $\mathcal{A}$ *there exists a negligible function* $\nu(\cdot)$ *such that*

$$\mathbf{Adv}_{\mathcal{VC},q,\mathcal{A}}^{\text{PosBind}} \stackrel{\text{def}}{=} \Pr\left[\text{PosBind}_{\mathcal{VC},q,\mathcal{A}}(\lambda) = 1\right] \le \nu(\lambda)$$

for all sufficiently large $\lambda \in \mathbb{N}$, *where the experiment* $\text{PosBind}_{\mathcal{VC},q,\mathcal{A}}(\lambda)$ *is defined as follows:*

1. crs $\leftarrow$ VC.Setup$(1^\lambda, q)$
2. (vcom, i, x_i, x_i', π, π') $\leftarrow \mathcal{A}(1^\lambda, q, \text{crs})$.
3. *Output 1 if the following conditions hold:*
   - $x_i \neq x_i'$.
   - VC.Verify $\left(1^\lambda, \text{crs}, \text{vcom}, i, x_i, \pi\right) = 1$.
   - VC.Verify $\left(1^\lambda, \text{crs}, \text{vcom}, i, x_i', \pi'\right) = 1$.
   Otherwise, output 0.

Succinctness. The main measure of efficiency for vector commitments, which makes them non-trivial to construct, is their succinctness. This may be captured by asking for upper bounds $\ell_{\text{Commit}}(\lambda, q)$ and $\ell_{\text{Open}}(\lambda, q)$ on the size of the commitment and the size of the local openings, respectively, as follows.

Definition 2.5. *A vector commitment scheme* $\mathcal{VC}$ = (VC.Setup, VC.Commit, VC.Open, VC.Verify) *over a domain* $\mathcal{X} = \{\mathcal{X}_\lambda\}_{\lambda \in \mathbb{N}}$ *is* $(\ell_{\text{Commit}}, \ell_{\text{Open}})$-succinct *if for any* $\lambda \in \mathbb{N}$, *for any polynomial* $q = q(\lambda)$, *for any common-reference string* crs *produced by* VC.Setup$(1^\lambda, q)$, *for any vector* $(x_1, \ldots, x_q) \in (\mathcal{X}_\lambda)^q$, *and for any commitment and state* (vcom, st) *produced by* VC.Commit$(1^\lambda, \text{crs}, (x_1, \ldots, x_q))$ *the following two requirements are satisfied:*

- *The bit-length of* vcom *is at most* $\ell_{\text{Commit}}(\lambda, q)$.
- *For any index* $i \in [q]$ *and for any proof* π *produced by* VC.Open$(1^\lambda, \text{crs}, \text{vcom}, \text{st}, i)$, *the bit-length of* π *is at most* $\ell_{\text{Open}}(\lambda, q)$.

2.3   One-Time Strongly-Unforgeable Signature Schemes

We rely on the standard notion of a one-time strongly-unforgeable signature scheme, which is known to exist based on the existence of any one-way function [Lam79,NY89,Rom90] (and thus, in particular, based on any of the number-theoretic assumptions that we consider in this paper). A signature scheme is a tuple $\mathcal{SIG} = (\mathsf{Sig.Gen}, \mathsf{Sig.Sign}, \mathsf{Sig.Verify})$ of algorithms defined as follows:

- The algorithm $\mathsf{Sig.Gen}$ is a probabilistic algorithm that receives as input the security parameter $\lambda \in \mathbb{N}$ and outputs a pair (sk, vk) of a signing key and a verification key.
- The algorithm $\mathsf{Sig.Sign}$ is a (possibly) probabilistic algorithm that receives as input a signing key sk and a message m and outputs a signature σ.
- The algorithm $\mathsf{Sig.Verify}$ is a deterministic algorithm that receives as input a verification key vk, a message m and a signature σ, and outputs a bit $b \in \{0,1\}$.

In terms of correctness, the standard requirement for signature schemes asks that

$$\Pr\left[\mathsf{Sig.Verify}_{vk}(m, \mathsf{Sig.Sign}_{sk}(m)) = 1\right] = 1$$

for every $\lambda \in \mathbb{N}$ and for every message m, where $(sk, vk) \leftarrow \mathsf{Sig.Gen}(1^\lambda)$, where the probability is taken over the internal randomness of all algorithms. In terms of security, we rely on the following standard notion of one-time strong unforgeability.

Definition 2.6. *A signature scheme* $\mathcal{SIG} = (\mathsf{Sig.Gen}, \mathsf{Sig.Sign}, \mathsf{Sig.Verify})$ *is one-time strongly unforgeable if for every probabilistic polynomial-time algorithm* $\mathcal{A}$ *there exists a negligible function* $\nu(\cdot)$ *such that*

$$\mathbf{Adv}^{\mathsf{Forge}}_{\mathcal{SIG},\mathcal{A}}(\lambda) \overset{\text{def}}{=} \Pr\left[\mathsf{Forge}_{\mathcal{SIG},\mathcal{A}}(\lambda) = 1\right] \leq \nu(\lambda)$$

for all sufficiently large $\lambda \in \mathbb{N}$, *where the experiment* $\mathsf{Forge}_{\mathcal{SIG},\mathcal{A}}(\lambda)$ *is defined as follows:*

1. $(sk, vk) \leftarrow \mathsf{Sig.Gen}(1^\lambda)$.
2. $(m, \mathsf{st}_{\mathcal{A}}) \leftarrow \mathcal{A}(1^\lambda, vk)$.
3. $(m^*, \sigma^*) \leftarrow \mathcal{A}(\mathsf{st}_{\mathcal{A}}, \sigma)$, *where* $\sigma \leftarrow \mathsf{Sig.Sign}_{sk}(m)$.
4. *If* $\mathsf{Sig.Verify}_{vk}(m^*, \sigma^*)$ *and* $(m^*, \sigma^*) \neq (m, \sigma)$ *then output 1 and otherwise output 0.*

2.4   Universal One-Way Hash Functions

We rely on the standard notion of universal one-way hash functions, which is known to exist based on the existence of any one-way function [NY89,Rom90] (and thus, in particular, based on any of the number-theoretic assumptions that we consider in this paper). A hash family from domain $\mathcal{X} = \{\mathcal{X}_\lambda\}_{\lambda \in \mathbb{N}}$ to range $\mathcal{Y} = \{\mathcal{Y}_\lambda\}_{\lambda \in \mathbb{N}}$ is a collection $\mathcal{H} = \{\mathcal{H}_\lambda\}_{\lambda \in \mathbb{N}}$ where each $\mathcal{H}_\lambda$ consists of functions

$h : \mathcal{X}_\lambda \rightarrow \mathcal{Y}_\lambda$. For simplifying our notation we let $h \leftarrow \mathcal{H}_\lambda$ denote the process of sampling a function h from $\mathcal{H}_\lambda$ without explicitly describing a sampling algorithm, where h denotes both the description of the sampled function and its evaluation algorithm.

Definition 2.7. *A hash family $\mathcal{H}$ from domain $\mathcal{X} = \{\mathcal{X}_\lambda\}_{\lambda \in \mathbb{N}}$ to range $\mathcal{Y} = \{\mathcal{Y}_\lambda\}_{\lambda \in \mathbb{N}}$ is a* universal one-way hash family *if for every probabilistic polynomial-time algorithm $\mathcal{A}$ there exists a negligible function $\nu(\cdot)$ such that*

$$\mathbf{Adv}_{\mathcal{H},\mathcal{A}}^{\mathsf{UOWHF}}(\lambda) \overset{\text{def}}{=} \Pr\left[\mathsf{UOWHF}_{\mathcal{H},\mathcal{A}}(\lambda) = 1\right] \leq \nu(\lambda)$$

for all sufficiently large $\lambda \in \mathbb{N}$, where the experiment $\mathsf{UOWHF}_{\mathcal{H},\mathcal{A}}(\lambda)$ is defined as follows:

1. *$(x, \mathsf{st}) \leftarrow \mathcal{A}(1^\lambda)$.*
2. *$h \leftarrow \mathcal{H}_\lambda$.*
3. *$x' \leftarrow \mathcal{A}(\mathsf{st}, h)$.*
4. *If $x \neq x'$ and $h(x) = h(x')$ then output 1, and otherwise output 0.*

3 Non-malleable Vector Commitments

In this section we begin by presenting our notion of non-malleability for vector commitment schemes. Then, in Sect. 3.1 we show that existing vector commitment schemes do not satisfy it (some of them by design in order to support public updates). As mentioned in Sect. 1.1, the key difference from the standard notion of non-malleable non-interactive commitments is that we aim at achieving non-malleability even with respect to adversaries which have already been exposed to several local openings. This key difference is the reason that simple attempts of combining VCs and non-malleable commitments, that we discuss in Sect. 3.2, do not suffice for realizing our new notion.

Loosely speaking, a vector commitment scheme is non-malleable if an efficient adversary which receives a vector commitment vcom to a vector $\vec{x} = (x_1, \ldots, x_q)$, cannot produce (and open) a vector commitment $\widehat{\mathsf{vcom}}$ to some vector $\vec{\widehat{x}} = (\widehat{x_1}, \ldots, \widehat{x_q})$ which is "non-trivially related" to $\vec{x}$. This property should hold even when the adversary can request local openings for some of the entries of $\vec{x}$ before deciding on $\widehat{\mathsf{vcom}}$; and open only some of the entries $\vec{\widehat{x}}$. Definition 3.1 below uses the term "valid distribution" which is formally clarified following the definition. As discussed in Sect. 1.1, we start by considering the static setting of vector commitments without updates. In the full version, we extend our approach to the dynamic setting.

Definition 3.1. *A vector commitment $\mathcal{VC} = (\mathsf{VC.Setup}, \mathsf{VC.Commit}, \mathsf{VC.Open}, \mathsf{VC.Verify})$ over a domain $\mathcal{X} = \{\mathcal{X}_\lambda\}_{\lambda \in \mathbb{N}}$ is* non-malleable *if for any polynomially-bounded integer $q = q(\lambda)$ and for any probabilistic polynomial-time algorithm $\mathcal{A}$ there exist a probabilistic polynomial-time algorithm $\mathcal{S}$ such that the following holds:*

For any probabilistic polynomial-time algorithm $\mathcal{R}$ and for any valid distribution $\mathcal{D} = \{\mathcal{D}_\lambda\}_{\lambda \in \mathbb{N}}$ over $\{(\mathcal{X}_\lambda)^q\}_{\lambda \in \mathbb{N}}$, there exists a negligible function $\nu(\cdot)$ such that

$$\mathbf{Adv}_{\mathcal{VC},q,\mathcal{A},\mathcal{S},R,\mathcal{D}}^{\mathsf{NM}}(\lambda)$$

$$\stackrel{\text{def}}{=} \left| \Pr\left[\mathcal{R}\left(\mathsf{Real}_{\mathcal{VC},q,\mathcal{A},\mathcal{D}}(\lambda)\right) = 1\right] - \Pr\left[\mathcal{R}\left(\mathsf{Ideal}_{\mathcal{VC},q,\mathcal{S},\mathcal{D}}(\lambda)\right) = 1\right]\right| \leq \nu(\lambda)$$

for all sufficiently large $\lambda \in \mathbb{N}$, where the experiments $\mathsf{Real}_{\mathcal{VC},q,\mathcal{A},\mathcal{D}}(\lambda)$ and $\mathsf{Ideal}_{\mathcal{VC},q,\mathcal{S},\mathcal{D}}(\lambda)$ are defined as follows:

The Experiment $\mathsf{Real}_{\mathcal{VC},q,\mathcal{A},\mathcal{D}}(\lambda)$:

1. $\mathsf{crs} \leftarrow \mathsf{VC.Setup}(1^\lambda, q)$.
2. $(x_1, \ldots, x_q) \leftarrow \mathcal{D}_\lambda$.
3. $(\mathsf{vcom}, \mathsf{st}) \leftarrow \mathsf{VC.Commit}(1^\lambda, \mathsf{crs}, (x_1, \ldots, x_q))$.
4. $(\mathcal{I}, \mathsf{st}_\mathcal{A}) \leftarrow \mathcal{A}(1^\lambda, \mathsf{crs}, \mathsf{vcom})$ *where* $\mathcal{I} \subseteq [q]$.
5. $\pi_i \leftarrow \mathsf{VC.Open}(1^\lambda, \mathsf{crs}, \mathsf{vcom}, \mathsf{st}, i)$ *for each* $i \in [q]$.
6. $(\widehat{\mathsf{vcom}}, \mathcal{J}, \mathsf{st}_\mathcal{A}) \leftarrow \mathcal{A}\left(\mathsf{st}_\mathcal{A}, (x_i)_{i \in \mathcal{I}}, (\pi_i)_{i \in \mathcal{I}}\right)$, *where* $\mathcal{J} \subseteq [q]$.
7. $((\widehat{x}_j)_{j \in \mathcal{J}}, (\widehat{\pi}_j)_{j \in \mathcal{J}}) \leftarrow \mathcal{A}\left(\mathsf{st}_\mathcal{A}, (x_i)_{i \in \overline{\mathcal{I}}}, (\pi_i)_{i \in \overline{\mathcal{I}}}\right)$, *where* $\overline{\mathcal{I}} = [q] \setminus \mathcal{I}$.
8. *If* $\widehat{\mathsf{vcom}} = \mathsf{vcom}$ *or if* $\mathsf{VC.Verify}\left(1^\lambda, \mathsf{crs}, \widehat{\mathsf{vcom}}, j, \widehat{x}_j, \widehat{\pi}_j\right) = 0$ *for some* $j \in \mathcal{J}$, *then output* $((x_1, \ldots, x_q), (\bot)^q, \mathcal{I})$.
   Otherwise, output $((x_1, \ldots, x_q), (\widehat{x_1}, \ldots, \widehat{x_q}), \mathcal{I})$, *where* $\widehat{x}_j = \bot$ *for each* $j \in [q] \setminus \mathcal{J}$.

The Experiment $\mathsf{Ideal}_{\mathcal{VC},q,\mathcal{S},\mathcal{D}}(\lambda)$:

1. $(x_1, \ldots, x_q) \leftarrow \mathcal{D}_\lambda$.
2. $(\mathcal{I}, \mathsf{st}_\mathcal{S}) \leftarrow \mathcal{S}(1^\lambda, \mathcal{D})$.
3. $(\mathcal{J}, (\widehat{x}_j)_{j \in \mathcal{J}}) \leftarrow \mathcal{S}(\mathsf{st}_\mathcal{S}, (x_i)_{i \in \mathcal{I}})$.
4. *Output* $((x_1, \ldots, x_q), (\widehat{x_1}, \ldots, \widehat{x_q}), \mathcal{I})$ *where* $\widehat{x}_i = \bot$ *for every* $i \in [q] \setminus \mathcal{J}$.

Succinctness. Recall that the main measure of efficiency for vector commitments, which makes them non-trivial to construct, is their succinctness: Both the size of the commitment and the size of the local openings should be sublinear in the number q of elements in the committed vector. That is, the standard notion of vector commitments does not require any hiding guarantees [CF13], and thus can be trivially satisfied if succinctness is not required (in this case a vector commitment scheme can simply output the vector itself). When additionally requiring a vector commitment scheme to hide all entries of the committed vector for which local openings were not provided, the task becomes non-trivial even when succinctness is not required (since this introduces a selective decommitment problem whenever an attacker can request local openings after having seen the commitment).

Our notion of non-malleability implies, in particular, such a hiding guarantee, and is therefore non-trivial to realize even when succinctness is not required. Nevertheless, as discussed in Sect. 1.1, the non-malleable vector commitments resulting from our transformation are essentially as succinct as the existing standard vector commitments that do not require any hiding guarantees.

Valid Distributions. Definition 3.1 considers *valid* distributions, and here we formally define this notion. On the face of it, one can hope to consider all distributions that are samplable in polynomial time. However, exactly as in case of non-malleable zero-knowledge sets [GM06], our notion of non-malleable vector commitments faces a "selective decommitment" problem (since it considers attackers which may be exposed to several adaptively-chosen local openings). One approach to overcome this difficulty, which is the approach that we follow in this work, is to restrict our attention to considering the natural subclass of all efficiently samplable distributions that was considered by Gennaro and Micali [GM06]). This subclass consists of all distributions that are not only efficiently samplable, but also all of their marginal distributions are efficiently samplable.

That is, we say that a distribution $\mathcal{D} = \{\mathcal{D}_\lambda\}_{\lambda \in \mathbb{N}}$ over $\{(\mathcal{X}_\lambda)^q\}_{\lambda \in \mathbb{N}}$ is valid if the following holds: For every $\lambda \in \mathbb{N}$, for every $\vec{x} = (x_1, \ldots, x_{q(\lambda)})$ in the support of $\mathcal{D}_\lambda$, and for every subset $\mathcal{I} = (i_1, \ldots, i_{|\mathcal{I}|}) \subseteq [q(\lambda)]$, it is possible to efficiently sample a vector $\vec{y}$ from the conditional distribution $\mathcal{D}_\lambda | (\forall i \in \mathcal{I} : y_i = x_i)$. We denote the process of sampling the entries of $\vec{y}$ in $\overline{\mathcal{I}} = [q] \setminus \mathcal{I}$ by $(y_j)_{j \in \overline{\mathcal{I}}} \leftarrow \mathcal{D} | (\mathcal{I}, (x_i)_{i \in \mathcal{I}})$. Note that this requirement is fairly reasonable, and in particular, it is satisfied by any product distribution $\mathcal{D}$ over $(\mathcal{X}_\lambda)^q$.

An alternative approach, as pointed out by Gennaro and Micali, is to rely on an underlying commitment scheme that provides a certain form of security against selective decommitment attacks. In their context, it seems that the underlying commitment scheme would have to be at least both mercurial and provide security against selective decommitment attacks (realizing this alternative approach for non-malleable zero-knowledge sets still remains an interesting open problem). Similarly, in our context it would have to be at least locally equivocable with all-but-one binding (as we define in Sect. 4) and provide security against selective decommitment attacks. We leave the exploration of this alternative approach as an avenue for further research.

$\mathcal{J}$ Cannot be Chosen Later. Note that we allow the adversary $\mathcal{A}$ in the experiment $\mathrm{Real}_{\mathcal{VC},q,\mathcal{A},R,\mathcal{D}}(\lambda)$ to choose the subset $\mathcal{J}$ at the latest stage possible. This is true because had we let A choose $\mathcal{J}$ in Step 7 of the experiment, then $\mathcal{A}$ could have encoded information about $(x_j)_{j \in \overline{\mathcal{I}}}$ within their choice of $\mathcal{J}$. For example, assume that we let the adversary choose $\mathcal{J}$ in Step 7 of $\mathrm{Real}_{\mathcal{VC},q,\mathcal{A},R,\mathcal{D}}(\lambda)$ (after observing $(x_j)_{j \in \overline{\mathcal{I}}}$), and consider an adversary which chooses $\mathcal{J}$ to be of size 1 if the parity of the bit-description of $x_{j_1} \| \cdots \| x_{j_{|\overline{\mathcal{I}}|}}$ is 1, and chooses $\mathcal{J}$ to be of size 0 if this parity is 0, where $\overline{\mathcal{I}} = \{j_1, \ldots, j_{|\overline{\mathcal{I}}|}\}$. Of course, this cannot be simulated, since the simulator never gets access to $x_{j_1}, \ldots, x_{j_{|\overline{\mathcal{I}}|}}$.

Invalid Openings. Whenever the adversary $\mathcal{A}$ provides an invalid opening for *any* index in $\mathcal{J}$, then the output of the real experiment is set to be of the form $((x_1, \ldots, x_q), (\perp)^q, \mathcal{I})$. We argue that this choice is indeed a necessary one. To see why that is the case, consider the following alternative (and faulty) approach: For all $j \in \mathcal{J}$ for which $\mathcal{A}$ provides invalid openings set $\widehat{x}_j = \perp$, but for all indices for which $\mathcal{A}$ provides valid openings, keep the $\widehat{x}_j$'s in the output of the experiment as is (that is, as outputted by $\mathcal{A}$ in Step 7). The problem with this approach is that it effectively gives $\mathcal{A}$ the power to choose $\mathcal{J}$ in Step 7 of the experiment, for example by outputting $\mathcal{J} = [q]$ in Step 6 and then providing valid openings for a different set $\mathcal{J}' \subsetneq [q]$ in Step 7. As explained above, such a definition cannot be satisfied, as it allows $\mathcal{A}$ to encode information about $(x_j)_{j \in \bar{\mathcal{I}}}$ via the set of validly-opened positions.

Letting $\mathcal{J}$ Intersect $\mathcal{I}$. At first glance, it might seem uncanny that we let the adversary choose the set $\mathcal{J}$ such that it includes locations for which the adversary has seen openings before producing $\widehat{\mathsf{vcom}}$ (i.e., it intersects $\mathcal{I}$). On the face of it, this allows for trivial attacks, since the adversary can trivially commit, via $\widehat{\mathsf{vcom}}$, to values that are related to $(x_i)_{i \in \mathcal{I}}$. However, Definition 3.1 "discounts" such trivial attacks from the adversary's advantage, by allowing the simulator to access values $(x_i)_{i \in \mathcal{I}}$ as well.

Choosing $\mathcal{I}$ Adaptively. We note that Definition 3.1 can be strengthened, by allowing the adversary in $\mathsf{Real}_{\mathcal{VC}, q, \mathcal{A}, R, \mathcal{D}}(\lambda)$ to choose the set $\mathcal{I}$ in an adaptive manner. That is, to choose the indices included in $\mathcal{I}$ one by one, each index being chosen after $\mathcal{A}$ has observed the values x_i (and the associated proof π_i) for each previous chosen index i. Our construction in Sect. 5 remains secure under this strengthened definition, and its proof of security readily extends to it.

Reusability. One might consider a strengthening of Definition 3.1, by providing the adversary with many vector commitments $\mathsf{vcom}_1, \ldots, \mathsf{vcom}_k$ (and to local openings of their choice) to vectors $\vec{v_1}, \ldots, \vec{v_k}$, and requiring that they cannot produce (and later open) a vector commitment $\widehat{\mathsf{vcom}}$ to a vector $\vec{v}$ which is non-trivially related to $\vec{v_1}, \ldots, \vec{v_k}$. Such a strengthening is in line with the notion of a *reusable* non-malleable non-interactive commitment scheme [DG03] and more generally, with the notion of concurrent non-malleable commitments [DDN00]. We believe that our framework and constructions can be generalized to support such a definition, and we leave this task to future work.

3.1   Existing Schemes Do Not Satisfy Our Notion

Merkle Trees in the Standard Model. Consider the Merkle tree construction of vector commitments with respect to a hash function $h : \{0,1\}^{2\lambda} \to \{0,1\}^{\lambda}$. That is, a commitment vcom to a vector $\vec{x} \in \{0,1\}^{\lambda \times q}$ is the root of the binary hash tree whose left leaves (i.e., leaves which are left children) are the values of $\vec{x}$; the right leaves are assigned some predetermined arbitrary values; and the value of each node is obtained by applying h to the concatenation of its children.[5] In the full version we present a formal description of this construction, and show that if h is modeled as a random oracle, then this construction is indeed non-malleable per Definition 3.1. Alas, if h is instantiated via a standard-model collision resistant hash function, this is not necessarily the case. Loosely speaking, this is because the function h itself may be malleable.

As a concrete and simple example, consider the case in which $h(z) = z_1 \| h'(z_2 \| \cdots \| z_{2\lambda})$, where $z = z_1 \| \cdots \| z_{2\lambda} \in \{0,1\}^{2\lambda}$ and $h' : \{0,1\}^{2\lambda - 1} \to \{0,1\}^{\lambda-1}$ is a collision-resistant hash function. It is not hard to verify that h is also collision resistant; but still, the vector commitment it induces is malleable.

---

[5] We embed the entries of $\vec{x}$ only as left leaves as to avoid trivial attacks. Doing so, the opening of say, the i-th entry does not trivially reveal any other entries.

In fact, this vector commitment is not even completely hiding: Consider the following attacker which first request to see an opening of the first entry x_1 of $\vec{x}$ (by outputting $\mathcal{I} = \{1\}$ in Step 4 of the real experiment of Definition 3.1). This opening includes the value assigned to the sibling of the parent of x_1 (which is the parent of x_2); denote this value by $y = y_1 \| \cdots \| y_\lambda \in \{0,1\}^\lambda$. Then y_1 is equal to the first bit of x_2. This means that the adversary can commit from scratch to some vector $(\widehat{x_1}, \ldots, \widehat{x_q})$ such that the first bit of $\widehat{x_2}$ is also y_1 (and the other entries are chosen arbitrarily), satisfying a non-trivial relation with $\vec{x}$. This is just one simple example, and many more examples exist for the malleability of standard-model instantiation of Merkle trees.

Algebraic Constructions. More recent algebraic constructions of vector commitments turn out to be malleable as well. To start, consider the constructions of Catalano and Fiore [CF13], based on either the discrete logarithm assumption or the RSA assumption. In both of these construction, a user commits to a vector $\vec{x}$ of integers, by computing $\mathsf{vcom} = \prod_{i \in [q]} g_i^{x_i}$, where $g_1, \ldots, g_q$ are publicly-known group elements. It is not hard to see, that an attacker receiving vcom can produce a commitment $\widehat{\mathsf{vcom}}$ to any affinely-related vector $a \cdot \vec{x} + \vec{z}$, by computing $\mathsf{vcom}^a \cdot \prod_{i \in [q]} g_i^{z_i}$.

Lai and Malavolta [LM19] recently generalized the constructions of Catalano and Fiore to Euclidean rings (they also presented an additional construction in bilinear groups, which falls into the same template as the constructions of Catalano and Fiore, and hence the same attack applies to it). Concretely, they consider a module over a ring R, consisting of an Abelian group $(\mathbb{G}, \times)$ and a binary operation $\circ : R \times \mathbb{G} \to \mathbb{G}$. A vector commitment to a vector $\vec{x} \in \mathcal{X}^q$ is then computed by the inner product $\langle \vec{x}, \vec{S} \rangle = (x_1 \circ S_1) \times \cdots \times (x_q \circ S_q)$, where $\mathcal{X} \subseteq R$ is a subset satisfying some natural property and $\vec{S}$ is a vector of publicly-known group elements. Unsurprisingly, the afore-described attack easily generalizes to this construction as well. For any $a \in R$ and $z \in R^q$, an attacker which receies a commitment vcom to a vector $\vec{x} \in \mathcal{X}^q$ can compute a commitment to any affinely-related vector $a \cdot \vec{x} + \vec{z}$, where $(+, \cdot)$ are the two ring operations, by computing $(a \circ \mathsf{vcom}) \times \langle \vec{z}, \vec{S} \rangle$. Note that this attack works as long as $a \cdot \vec{x} + \vec{z}$ lies in $\mathcal{X}$.

3.2   Simple Attempts that Fail

For obtaining an initial understanding of the challenges in constructing non-malleable vector commitments, consider the following two constructions which are based on rather simple and direct combinations of vector commitments and non-malleable commitments, and fail to satisfy Definition 3.1. In what follows, $\mathsf{nm}\mathcal{COM}$ is a standard non-malleable commitments scheme and $\mathcal{VC}$ is a (potentially malleable) vector commitment scheme.

Applying $\mathsf{nm}\mathcal{COM}$ and then $\mathcal{VC}$. As a first attempt, consider what happens when in order to commit to some vector $\vec{x}$, one first applies $\mathsf{nm}\mathcal{COM}$ locally to each entry of $\vec{x}$ to obtain q commitments $c_1, \ldots, c_q$; and then uses $\mathcal{VC}$ to commit to these commitments. The problem with this approach is that $\mathcal{VC}$ might be malleable. For example, if $\mathcal{VC}$ appends a random bit to the end of each commitment, then an adversary which receives a commitment vcom to a vector $\vec{x}$ produced using the approach described above, can easily produce a different commitment $\widehat{\text{vcom}}$ to the same $\vec{x}$ by flipping the last bit of vcom. It might be also the case that $\mathcal{VC}$ is malleable in the following sense: Given a commitment vcom to a vector $\vec{x}$ produced using $\mathcal{VC}$, it is easy to "replace" some of the entries of the vector underlying vcom, resulting in a commitment to a related vector $\vec{x}'$ which identifies with $\vec{x}$ on some of its locations. If this is the case, then such an attack is also possible for the combined vector commitment scheme which first applies nm$\mathcal{COM}$ locally.[6]

Applying $\mathcal{VC}$ and then nm$\mathcal{COM}$. Consider a construction which, in order to commit to a vector $\vec{x}$, first applies $\mathcal{VC}$ to produce a commitment vcom_0 and commits to vcom_0 using nm$\mathcal{COM}$ to produce a commitment vcom. Alas, this approach also does not meet Definition 3.1. The main issue is unique to the setting of non-malleable vector commitments: Per Definition 3.1, an adversary can request to see openings of individual entries of $\vec{x}$ before outputting their own commitment $\widehat{\text{vcom}}$. These openings must include in particular the intermediate commitment vcom_0. Hence, if $\mathcal{VC}$ is malleable, then the adversary, having observed vcom_0 can come up with a different commitment $\widehat{\text{vcom}_0}$ with respect to $\mathcal{VC}$ for some related vector $\vec{x}'$. Then, the adversary can simply commit to $\widehat{\text{vcom}_0}$ using nm$\mathcal{COM}$ to produce the desired commitment $\widehat{\text{vcom}}$.

4 Locally-Equivocable Commitments with All-But-One Binding

In this section we introduce the notion of a locally-equivocable commitment scheme with all-but-one binding, which serves as one of the main building-blocks underlying our construction of a non-malleable vector commitment scheme. Our notion is obtained by augmenting the standard notion of a non-interactive tag-based commitment scheme with two additional requirements, namely local equivocability and all-but-one binding.

In addition, we present both a somewhat theoretical realization of the our new notion based on the existence of any one-way function, and two efficient number-theoretic realizations: A construction based on the discrete logarithm assumption, and a construction based on the RSA assumption. In both cases, the common-reference string consists of 2–3 group elements (in addition to

---

[6] Another issue which may arise, is that nm$\mathcal{COM}$ might not be *concurrent* non-malleable (see, for example, [DDN00,PR05,PR08,LPV08] and the references therein). In this case, an adversary which observes some of the local commitments and openings produced via nm$\mathcal{COM}$ may be able to come up with nm$\mathcal{COM}$ commitments to related values. This issue, however, can be relatively easily resolved by using a commitment scheme which offers non-malleability even against adversaries which observe at most q commitments and openings.

the description of the group), and a commitment consists of a single group element. As discussed in Sect. 1.1, these number-theoretic constructions were described by Fischlin in his Ph.D. thesis [Fis01] (and also used by Crescenzo, Katz, Ostrovsky and Smith [CKO+01] in their number-theoretic constructions of non-malleable non-interactive commitment schemes[7]). Although our notion of a locally-equivocable commitment scheme with all-but-one binding strengthens Fischlin's notion of identity-based trapdoor commitments (as we discuss below), we nevertheless show that these constructions satisfy our notion. Our constructions are provided in the full version.

Formally, a locally-equivocable commitment scheme with all-but-one binding over a domain $\mathcal{X} = \{\mathcal{X}_\lambda\}_{\lambda \in \mathbb{N}}$ and a tag space $\mathcal{T} = \{\mathcal{T}_\lambda\}_{\lambda \in \mathbb{N}}$ is a 6-tuple $\mathcal{LE} = (\mathsf{LE.Setup}, \mathsf{LE.Commit}, \mathsf{LE.Decommit}, \mathsf{LE.AltSetup}, \mathsf{LE.Equiv}_1, \mathsf{LE.Equiv}_2)$ of polynomial-time algorithms defined as follows:

- The algorithm $\mathsf{LE.Setup}$ is a probabilistic algorithm that receives as input the security parameter $\lambda \in \mathbb{N}$ and a polynomially-bounded integer $q = q(\lambda)$, and outputs a common-reference string crs.
- The algorithm $\mathsf{LE.Commit}$ is a probabilistic algorithm that receives as input the security parameter $\lambda \in \mathbb{N}$, a common-reference string crs, an element $x \in \mathcal{X}_\lambda$, an index $i \in [q]$ and a tag $\tau \in \mathcal{T}_\lambda$, and outputs a commitment c and a decommitment d.[8]
- The algorithm $\mathsf{LE.Decommit}$ is a deterministic algorithm that receives as input the security parameter $\lambda \in \mathbb{N}$, a common-reference string crs, a commitment c, a decommitment d, an index $i \in [q]$ and a tag $\tau \in \mathcal{T}_\lambda$, and outputs an element $x \in \mathcal{X}_\lambda$ or the rejection symbol $\bot$.
- The algorithm $\mathsf{LE.AltSetup}$ is a probabilistic algorithm that receives as input the security parameter $\lambda \in \mathbb{N}$ and a polynomially-bounded integer $q = q(\lambda)$, and outputs a state st_0.
- The algorithm $\mathsf{LE.Equiv}_1$ is a probabilistic algorithm that receives as input the security parameter $\lambda \in \mathbb{N}$ a state st_0, a polynomially-bounded integer $q = q(\lambda)$ and a tag $\tau \in \mathcal{T}_\lambda$, and outputs a common-reference string $\widehat{\mathsf{crs}}$, commitments $\widehat{c}_1, \ldots, \widehat{c}_q$ and a state st_1.
- The algorithm $\mathsf{LE.Equiv}_2$ is a deterministic algorithm that receives as input the security parameter $\lambda \in \mathbb{N}$, an element $x \in \mathcal{X}_\lambda$, an index $i \in [q]$, a state st_1 and a tag $\tau \in \mathcal{T}_\lambda$, and outputs a decommitment $\widehat{d}$.

A commitment scheme as described above should satisfy the standard correctness requirement of commitment schemes. That is, for any security parameter $\lambda \in \mathbb{N}$, for any tag $\tau \in \mathcal{T}_\lambda$, for any polynomially-bounded $q = q(\lambda)$, for any $i \in [q]$ and for any $x \in \mathcal{X}_\lambda$ it holds that

$$\Pr\left[\mathsf{LE.Decommit}(1^\lambda, \mathsf{crs}, c, d, i, \tau) = x\right] = 1,$$

---

[7] Although Crescenzo et al. did not explicitly frame their construction as relying on an underlying equivocable commitment scheme, we follow a somewhat more fine-grained abstraction via our local equivocability and all-but-one binding properties.

[8] We note that the commitment and decommitment algorithms $\mathsf{LE.Commit}$ and $\mathsf{LE.Decommit}$ receive the index $i \in [q]$ as input for technical reasons that come up in our generic construction based on one-way functions.

where crs $\leftarrow$ LE.Setup($1^\lambda, q$) and $(c, d) \leftarrow$ LE.Commit(1^λ, crs, x, i, τ), and the probability is taken over the internal randomness of all algorithms.

The following two definitions formally capture our local equivocability and all-but-one binding requirements.

Definition 4.1 (Local equivocability). *A commitment scheme* $\mathcal{LE} =$ (LE.Setup, LE.Commit, LE.Decommit, LE.AltSetup, LE.Equiv$_1$, LE.Equiv$_2$) *over a domain* $\mathcal{X} = \{\mathcal{X}_\lambda\}_{\lambda \in \mathbb{N}}$ *and a tag space* $\mathcal{T} = \{\mathcal{T}_\lambda\}_{\lambda \in \mathbb{N}}$ *is* locally equivocable *if the following requirements hold:*

- **Equivocation correctness:** *For any* $\lambda \in \mathbb{N}$, *for any* $\tau \in \mathcal{T}_\lambda$, *for any polynomially-bounded* $q = q(\lambda)$, *for any* $i \in [q]$ *and for any* $x \in \mathcal{X}_\lambda$ *it holds that*

$$\Pr\left[\text{LE.Decommit}(1^\lambda, \widehat{\text{crs}}, \widehat{c}_i, \widehat{d}, i, \tau) = x\right] = 1,$$

  where $(\widehat{\text{crs}}, \widehat{c}_1, \ldots, \widehat{c}_q, \text{st}_1) \leftarrow$ LE.Equiv$_1$(1^λ, LE.AltSetup(1^λ), q, τ) *and* $\widehat{d} =$ LE.Equiv$_2$($1^\lambda, x, i, \text{st}_1$), *and the probability is taken over the internal randomness of all algorithms.*

- **Equivocation indistinguishability:** *For any probabilistic polynomial-time algorithm* $\mathcal{A}$, *there exists a negligible function* $\nu(\cdot)$ *such that for any polynomially bounded* $q = q(\lambda)$ *it holds that*

$$\mathbf{Adv}_{\mathcal{LE}, q, \mathcal{A}}^{\text{LocalEquiv}}(\lambda)$$

$$\stackrel{\text{def}}{=} \left|\Pr\left[\text{IndParam}_{\mathcal{LE}, q, \mathcal{A}, 0}(\lambda)\right] - \Pr\left[\text{IndParam}_{\mathcal{LE}, q, \mathcal{A}, 1}(\lambda)\right]\right| \leq \nu(\lambda)$$

  for all sufficiently large $\lambda \in \mathbb{N}$, *where for any bit* $b \in \{0, 1\}$ *the experiment* IndParam$_{\mathcal{LE}, q, \mathcal{A}, b}(\lambda)$ *is defined as follows:*
  1. $(\tau, x_1, \ldots, x_q, \text{st}_\mathcal{A}) \leftarrow \mathcal{A}(1^\lambda)$.
  2. crs$_0 \leftarrow$ LE.Setup($1^\lambda, q$).
  3. $(c_{0,i}, d_{0,i}) \leftarrow$ LE.Commit(1^λ, crs, x_i, i, τ) *for each* $i \in [q]$.
  4. st$_0 \leftarrow$ LE.AltSetup($1^\lambda, q$).
  5. $(\text{crs}_1, c_{1,1}, \ldots, c_{1,q}, \text{st}_1) \leftarrow$ LE.Equiv$_1$(1^λ, st$_0, q, \tau$).
  6. $d_{1,i} =$ LE.Equiv$_2$($1^\lambda, x_i, i, \text{st}_1$) *for each* $i \in [q]$.
  7. $b' \leftarrow \mathcal{A}(\text{st}_\mathcal{A}, \text{crs}_b, (c_{b,i})_{i \in [q]}, (d_{b,i})_{i \in [q]})$.
  8. *Output* b'.

Intuitively, the all-but-one binding property requires that an adversary which generates equivocable public parameters (via the LE.Equiv$_1$ algorithm) using a tag τ of their choice, cannot break the binding property with respect to these parameters and a different tag $\tau' \neq \tau$.

Definition 4.2 (All-but-one binding). *A commitment scheme* $\mathcal{LE} =$ (LE.Setup, LE.Commit, LE.Decommit, LE.AltSetup, LE.Equiv$_1$, LE.Equiv$_2$) *over a domain* $\mathcal{X} = \{\mathcal{X}_\lambda\}_{\lambda \in \mathbb{N}}$ *and a tag space* $\mathcal{T} = \{\mathcal{T}_\lambda\}_{\lambda \in \mathbb{N}}$ *is* all-but-one binding *if for any probabilistic polynomial-time algorithm* $\mathcal{A}$ *there exists a negligible function* $\nu(\cdot)$ *such that for polynomially-bounded* $q = q(\lambda)$ *it holds that*

$$\mathbf{Adv}_{\mathcal{LE}, q, \mathcal{A}}^{\text{ABOBind}}(\lambda) \stackrel{\text{def}}{=} \Pr\left[\text{ABOBind}_{q, \mathcal{A}}^{\mathcal{LE}}(\lambda) = 1\right] \leq \nu(\lambda)$$

for all sufficiently large $\lambda \in \mathbb{N}$, where the experiment $\mathsf{ABOBind}_{q,\mathcal{A}}^{\mathcal{LE}}(\lambda)$ *is defined as follows:*

1. $(\tau, \mathsf{st}_{\mathcal{A}}) \leftarrow \mathcal{A}(1^{\lambda})$, *where* $\tau \in \mathcal{T}_{\lambda}$.
2. $\mathsf{st}_0 \leftarrow \mathsf{LE.AltSetup}(1^{\lambda}, q)$.
3. $\rho \leftarrow \{0,1\}^r$, *where* $r = r(\lambda)$ *is the number of random coins used by* $\mathsf{LE.Equiv}_1$ *on security parameter* $\lambda \in \mathbb{N}$.
4. $(\widehat{\mathsf{crs}}, \widehat{c}_1, \ldots, \widehat{c}_q, \mathsf{st}_1) = \mathsf{LE.Equiv}_1(1^{\lambda}, \mathsf{st}_0, q, \tau; \rho)$.
5. $(c, d, d', i, \tau') \leftarrow \mathcal{A}(\mathsf{st}_{\mathcal{A}}, \mathsf{st}_0, \rho)$.
6. $x = \mathsf{LE.Decommit}(1^{\lambda}, \widehat{\mathsf{crs}}, c, d, i, \tau')$ *and* $x' = \mathsf{LE.Decommit}(1^{\lambda}, \widehat{\mathsf{crs}}, c, d', i, \tau')$.
7. *Output* 1 *if* $\tau' \neq \tau$, $x \neq \bot$, $x' \neq \bot$ *and* $x \neq x'$. *Otherwise, output* 0.

Comparing Our Notion to Identity-Based and Simulation-Sound Trapdoor Commitments. Having formally defined our notion of a locally-equivocable commitment scheme with all-but-one binding, we can now compare it to Fischlin's notion of an identity-based trapdoor commitment scheme [Fis01, Ch. 2.6]. Both notions are obtained by augmenting the standard notion of a non-interactive tag-based commitment scheme with equivocability and all-but-one binding requirements. Our requirements, however, are more strict compared to those of Fischlin, both in terms of equivocability and in terms of all-but-one binding.

First, in terms of equivocability, Fischlin asks for an equivocation algorithm that produces an equivocable common-reference string and a *single* equivocable commitment which should be indistinguishable from an honestly-generated common-reference string and an honestly-generated commitment. However, for our construction of a non-malleable vector commitment scheme, producing a single equivocable commitment seems insufficient. Thus, we ask for an equivocation algorithm that produces an equivocable common-reference string and q equivocable commitments (where $q = q(\lambda)$ is any predetermined polynomial) which should be indistinguishable from an honestly-generated common-reference string and an honestly-generated vector of q independent commitments. We note that such a requirement does not necessarily follow from the case $q = 1$ due to potential dependencies between the equivocable common-reference string and the single equivocable commitment that may be efficiently identifiable when producing more than a single equivocable commitment (this is evident in our generic construction based any non-interactive equivocable commitment scheme, where the common-reference string grows with q).

Second, in terms of all-but-one binding, Fischlin asks that when generating an equivocable common-reference string with respect to a predetermined tag τ, commitments with respect to all other tags should still be binding even when given the trapdoor associated with τ. For our construction we strengthen this requirements, and ask that commitments with respect to all other tags should still be binding even when given the trapdoor associated with τ and the internal randomness of the equivocation algorithm.

An additional related notion is that of a simulation-sound trapdoor commitment scheme, put forth by Garay, MacKenzie, and Yang [GMY03], which can be seen as augmenting standard trapdoor commitments [Rey01, Ch. A.5] with tags. Garay et al. also considered an enhanced binding property, requiring that binding with respect to a tag τ should be preserved, even if the attacker can obtain a single "fake" opening (using the trapdoor) for any commitment with respect to τ, as well as an unbounded number of openings for any commitment with respect to any other tag $\tau' \neq \tau$. This notion seems to be incomparable to our notion of locally-equivocable commitments with all-but-one binding. First, the trapdoor in simulation-sound trapdoor commitments is a global trapdoor generated by the honest parameters generation algorithm. There are no alternative procedures to generate equivocable parameters and commitments, and the trapdoor is not tied to any particular tag. This means that knowledge of the trapdoor allows one to open any (honestly generated) commitment to any value they desires. Second, whereas in our enhanced binding property the attacker receives the trapdoor associated with a tag τ of their choice, the attacker in the notion of Garay et al. does not receive the trapdoor, but only openings computed using it (this is unavoidable, since knowledge of the trapdoor in their notion allows the attacker to break binding with respect to all tags).

5   Our Construction of a Non-malleable Vector Commitment Scheme

Our construction relies on the following building blocks:

- A vector commitment scheme $\mathcal{VC}$ = (VC.Setup, VC.Commit, VC.Open, VC. Verify) over a domain $\mathcal{X} = \{\mathcal{X}_\lambda\}_{\lambda \in \mathbb{N}}$ (see Sect. 2.2).[9]
- A locally-equivocable commitment scheme with all-but-one binding $\mathcal{LE}$ = (LE.Setup, LE.Commit, LE.Decommit, LE.AltSetup, LE.Equiv$_1$, LE.Equiv$_2$) over the domain $\mathcal{X} = \{\mathcal{X}_\lambda\}_{\lambda \in \mathbb{N}}$ and a tag space $\mathcal{T} = \{\mathcal{T}_\lambda\}_{\lambda \in \mathbb{N}}$ (see Sect. 4) with tags of length $t = t(\lambda)$ bits.
- A one-time strongly-unforgeable signature scheme $\mathcal{SIG}$ = (Sig.Gen, Sig.Sign, Sig.Verify) (see Sect. 2.3). Let $v = v(\lambda)$ denote the bit-length of the verification keys that are produced by Sig.Gen(1^λ).
- A universal one-way hash family $\mathcal{H} = \{\mathcal{H}_\lambda\}_{\lambda \in \mathbb{N}}$ (see Sect. 2.4), where each $\mathcal{H}_\lambda$ consists of functions mapping $v(\lambda)$-bit strings to $t(\lambda)$-bit strings for every security parameter $\lambda \in \mathbb{N}$.

As discussed in Sect. 1.3, from a foundational perspective, the above building blocks can all be based on the existence of any vector commitment scheme. Additional, from a more practical perspective, the above building blocks can all be realized based on a variety of number-theoretic assumptions leading to practical implementations.

Given the above building blocks, our construction of a non-malleable vector commitment scheme, denoted nm$\mathcal{VC}$ = (nmVC.Setup, nmVC.Commit, nmVC.Open, nmVC.Verify), is defined as follows:

---

[9] We emphasize that the security of our construction does not rely on $\mathcal{VC}$ providing any flavor of hiding or succinctness, and this is discussed below in the overview of our proof.

A non-malleable vector commitment scheme nm$\mathcal{VC}$

nmVC.Setup($1^\lambda, q$):

1. Sample $\mathsf{crs_{LE}} \leftarrow \mathsf{LE.Setup}(1^\lambda, q)$, $\mathsf{crs_{VC}} \leftarrow \mathsf{VC.Setup}(1^\lambda, q)$ and $h \leftarrow \mathcal{H}_\lambda$.
2. Output $\mathsf{crs} = \mathsf{crs_{LE}} \| \mathsf{crs_{VC}} \| h$.

nmVC.Commit($1^\lambda, \mathsf{crs}, (x_1, \ldots, x_q)$):

1. Parse crs as $\mathsf{crs_{LE}} \| \mathsf{crs_{VC}} \| h$.
2. Sample $(sk, vk) \leftarrow \mathsf{Sig.Gen}(1^\lambda)$ and compute $\tau = h(vk)$.
3. For each $i \in [q]$ compute $(c_i, d_i) \leftarrow \mathsf{LE.Commit}(1^\lambda, \mathsf{crs_{LE}}, x_i, i, \tau)$.
4. Compute $(\mathsf{vcom_0}, \mathsf{sto}) \leftarrow \mathsf{VC.Commit}(1^\lambda, \mathsf{crs_{VC}}, (c_1, \ldots, c_q))$ and $\sigma \leftarrow \mathsf{Sig.Sign}_{sk}(\mathsf{vcom_0})$.
5. Output $(\mathsf{vcom}, \mathsf{st})$, where $\mathsf{vcom} = \mathsf{vcom_0} \| vk \| \sigma$ and $\mathsf{st} = \mathsf{sto} \| c_1 \| \cdots \| c_q \| d_1 \| \cdots \| d_q$.

nmVC.Open($1^\lambda, \mathsf{crs}, \mathsf{vcom}, \mathsf{st}, i$):

1. Parse crs as $\mathsf{crs_{LE}} \| \mathsf{crs_{VC}} \| h$, vcom as $\mathsf{vcom_0} \| vk \| \sigma$ and st as $\mathsf{sto} \| c_1 \| \cdots \| c_q \| d_1 \| \cdots \| d_q$.
2. Compute $\pi_0 \leftarrow \mathsf{VC.Open}(1^\lambda, \mathsf{crs_{VC}}, \mathsf{vcom_0}, \mathsf{sto}, i)$.
3. Output $\pi = c_i \| d_i \| \pi_0$.

nmVC.Verify($1^\lambda, \mathsf{crs}, \mathsf{vcom}, i, x, \pi$):

1. Parse crs as $\mathsf{crs_{LE}} \| \mathsf{crs_{VC}} \| h$, vcom as $\mathsf{vcom_0} \| vk \| \sigma$ and st as π as $c_i \| d_i \| \pi_0$.
2. Compute $\tau := h(vk)$.
3. Output 1 if all of the following conditions hold:
   - $\mathsf{Sig.Verify}_{vk}(\mathsf{vcom_0}, \sigma) = 1$.
   - $\mathsf{VC.Verify}(1^\lambda, \mathsf{crs_{VC}}, \mathsf{vcom_0}, i, c_i, \pi_0) = 1$.
   - $\mathsf{LE.Decommit}(1^\lambda, \mathsf{crs_{LE}}, c_i, d_i, i, \tau) = x$.

   Otherwise, output 0.

Finally, we note that for simplifying our construction and its proof, the length of the secret state $\mathsf{st} = \mathsf{sto} \| c_1 \| \cdots \| c_q \| d_1 \| \cdots \| d_q$ produced by the commitment algorithm nmVC.Commit in the above description depends linearly on q but this can be easily avoided whenever the committed vector $(x_1, \ldots, x_q)$ is additionally provided. Specifically, given $x_1, \ldots, x_q$, the entire sequence of values $c_1, \ldots, c_q, d_1, \ldots, d_q$ can be replaced with a single key K for a pseudorandom function PRF that will allow the algorithm nmVC.Open to recompute any of these values when needed. Specifically, instead of computing $(c_i, d_i) \leftarrow \mathsf{LE.Commit}(1^\lambda, \mathsf{crs_{LE}}, x_i, i, \tau)$ by feeding the algorithm LE.Commit with a fresh random string $r_i \leftarrow \{0, 1\}^*$, we can instead feed it with a pseudorandom string $r_i = \mathsf{PRF}_K(\mathsf{crs_{LE}}, x_i, i, \tau)$ which is reproducible via knowledge of K and x_i.

Security. The following theorem captures the security of our construction, showing that it satisfies our notion of non-malleability for vector commitment schemes (recall Definition 3.1) based on the security of its underlying building blocks:

(1) a vector commitment scheme $\mathcal{VC}$, (2) a locally-equivocable commitment scheme with all-but-one binding $\mathcal{LE}$, (3) a one-time strongly-unforgeable signature scheme $\mathcal{SIG}$, and (4) a universal one-way hash family $\mathcal{H}$.

Theorem 5.1. *For every probabilistic polynomial-time algorithm $\mathcal{A}$ and polynomial $q = q(\lambda)$, there exists a probabilistic polynomial-time algorithm $\mathcal{S}_{\mathcal{A}}$ such that the following holds: For any probabilistic polynomial-time algorithm $\mathcal{R}$, there are probabilistic polynomial-time algorithms $\mathcal{B}_1, \mathcal{B}_2, \mathcal{B}_3, \mathcal{B}_4$ and $\mathcal{B}_5$ such that*

$$\mathbf{Adv}^{\mathsf{NM}}_{\mathsf{nm}\mathcal{VC},q,\mathcal{A},\mathcal{S}_{\mathcal{A}},\mathcal{R},\mathcal{D}}(\lambda) \leq \mathbf{Adv}^{\mathsf{LocalEq}}_{\mathcal{LE},q,\mathcal{B}_1}(\lambda) + \mathbf{Adv}^{\mathsf{Forge}}_{\mathcal{SIG},\mathcal{B}_2}(\lambda) + \mathbf{Adv}^{\mathsf{UOWHF}}_{\mathcal{H},\mathcal{B}_3}(\lambda)$$

$$+2 \cdot \left(\mathbf{Adv}^{\mathsf{ABOBind}}_{\mathcal{LE},q,\mathcal{B}_4}(\lambda) + \mathbf{Adv}^{\mathsf{PosBind}}_{\mathcal{VC},q,\mathcal{B}_5}(\lambda) \right)$$

for every $\lambda \in \mathbb{N}$.

Due to space limitations, the formal proof of Theorem 5.1 is provided in the full version.

References

[ABC+12] Ahn, J.H., Boneh, D., Camenisch, J., Hohenberger, S., Shelat, A., Waters, B.: Computing on authenticated data. In: Proceedings of the 9th Theory of Cryptography Conference, pp. 169–191 (2012)

[Bar01] Barak, B.: How to go beyond the black-box simulation barrier. In: Proceedings of the 42nd Annual IEEE Symposium on Foundations of Computer Science, pp. 106–115 (2001)

[BBB+18] Bünz, B., Bootle, J., Boneh, D., Poelstra, A., Wuille, P., Maxwell, G.: Bulletproofs: short proofs for confidential transactions and more. In: Proceedings of the IEEE Symposium on Security and Privacy, pp. 315–334 (2018)

[BBF19] Boneh, D., Bünz, B., Fisch, B.: Batching techniques for accumulators with applications to IOPs and stateless blockchains. In: Advances in Cryptology - CRYPTO 2019, pp. 561–586 (2019)

[BCG+14] Ben-Sasson, E., et al.: Zerocash: decentralized anonymous payments from bitcoin. In: Proceedings of the IEEE Symposium on Security and Privacy, pp. 459–474 (2014)

[BdM93] Benaloh, J., de Mare, M.: One-way accumulators: a decentralized alternative to digital signatures. In: Advances in Cryptology - EUROCRYPT 1993, pp. 274–285 (1993)

[BGV11] Benabbas, S., Gennaro, R., Vahlis, Y.: Verifiable delegation of computation over large datasets. In: Advances in Cryptology - CRYPTO 2011, pp. 111–131 (2011)

[Bic17] Bichler, M.: Market Design: A Linear Programming Approach to Auctions and Matching. Cambridge University Press, Cambridge (2017)

[BP97] Barić, N., Pfitzmann, B.: Collision-free accumulators and fail-stop signature schemes without trees. In: Advances in Cryptology - EUROCRYPT 1997, pp. 480–494 (1997)

[BR93] Bellare, M., Rogaway, P.: Random oracles are practical: a paradigm for designing efficient protocols. In: Proceedings of the 1st ACM Conference on Computer and Communications Security, pp. 62–73 (1993)

[BS07]   Bellare, M., Shoup, S.: Two-tier signatures, strongly unforgeable signatures, and fiat-Shamir without random oracles. In: Proceedings of the 10th International Conference on Theory and Practice of Public-Key Cryptography, pp. 201–216 (2007)

[BSW06] Boneh, D., Shen, E., Waters, B.: Strongly unforgeable signatures based on computational Diffie-Hellman. In: Proceedings of the 9th International Conference on Theory and Practice of Public-Key Cryptography, pp. 229–240 (2006)

[But14] Buterin, V.: Ethereum: a next-generation smart contract and decentralized application platform. Available at https://ethereum.org/en/whitepaper/ (2014)

[But17] Buterin, V.: The stateless client concept (2017). Available at https://ethresear.ch/t/the-stateless-client-concept/172

[CDV06] Catalano, D., Dodis, Y., Visconti, I.: Mercurial commitments: minimal assumptions and efficient constructions. In: Proceedings of the 3rd Theory of Cryptography Conference, pp. 120–144 (2006)

[CF01]   Canetti, R., Fischlin, M.: Universally composable commitments. In: Advances in Cryptology - CRPYTO 2001, pp. 19–40 (2001)

[CF13]   Catalano, D., Fiore, D.: Vector commitments and their applications. In: Proceedings of the 16th International Conference on Practice and Theory in Public-Key Cryptography, pp. 55–72 (2013)

[CFG+20] Campanelli, M., Fiore, D., Greco, N., Kolonelos, D., Nizzardo, L.: Incrementally aggregatable vector commitments and applications to verifiable decentralized storage. In: Advances in Cryptology - ASIACRYPT 2020, pp. 3–35 (2020)

[CHL+13] Chase, M., Healy, A., Lysyanskaya, A., Malkin, T., Reyzin, L.: Mercurial commitments with applications to zero-knowledge sets. J. Cryptol. 26(2), 251–279 (2013)

[CIO98] Crescenzo, G.D., Ishai, Y., Ostrovsky, R.: Non-interactive and non-malleable commitment. In: Proceedings of the 30th Annual ACM Symposium on the Theory of Computing, pp. 141–150 (1998)

[CKO+01] Crescenzo, G.D., Katz, J., Ostrovsky, R., Smith, A.D.: Efficient and non-interactive non-malleable commitment. In Advances in Cryptology - EUROCRYPT 2001, pp. 40–59 (2001)

[CL02]   Camenisch, J., Lysyanskaya, A.: Dynamic accumulators and application to efficient revocation of anonymous credentials. In: Advances in Cryptology - CRYPTO 2002, pp. 61–76 (2002)

[COS+17] Ciampi, M., Ostrovsky, R., Siniscalchi, L., Visconti, I.: Four-round concurrent non-malleable commitments from one-way functions. In: Advances in Cryptology - CRYPTO 2017, pp. 127–157 (2017)

[CRF+11] Catalano, D., Raimondo, M.D., Fiore, D., Messina, M.: Zero-knowledge sets with short proofs. IEEE Trans. Inf. Theory 57(4), 2488–2502 (2011)

[DDN00] Dolev, D., Dwork, C., Naor, M.: Nonmalleable cryptography. SIAM J. Comput. 30(2), 391–437 (2000)

[DG03]   Damgard, I., Groth, J.: Non-interactive and reusable non-malleable commitment schemes. In: Proceedings of the 35th Annual ACM Symposium on the Theory of Computing, pp. 426–437 (2003)

[DKN+04] Dodis, Y., Kiayias, A., Nicolosi, A., Shoup, V.: Anonymous identification in ad hoc groups. In: Advances in Cryptology - EUROCRYPT 2004, pp. 609–626 (2004)

[FF00] Fischlin, M., Fischlin, R.: Efficient non-malleable commitment schemes. In: Advances in Cryptology - CRYPTO 2000, pp. 413–431 (2000)

[Fis01] Fischlin, M.: Trapdoor commitment schemes and their applications. PhD Thesis, University of Frankfurt (available at https://www.math.uni-frankfurt.de/~dmst/research/phdtheses/mfischlin.dissertation.2001.html) (2001)

[FVY14] Fromknecht, C., Velicanu, D., Yakoubov, S.: A decentralized public key infrastructure with identity retention. Cryptology ePrint Archive, Report 2014/803 (2014)

[GLO+12] Goyal, V., Lee, C.-K., Ostrovsky, R., Visconti, I.: Constructing non-malleable commitments: a black-box approach. In: Proceedings of the 53rd Annual IEEE Symposium on Foundations of Computer Science, pp. 51–60 (2012)

[GM06] Gennaro, R., Micali, S.: Independent zero-knowledge sets. In: Proceedings of the 33th International Colloquium on Automata, Languages and Programming, pp. 34–45 (2006)

[GMY03] Garay, J.A., MacKenzie, P., Yang, K.: Strengthening zero-knowledge protocols using signatures. In: Advances in Cryptology - EUROCRYPT 2003, pp. 177–194 (2003)

[GPR16] Goyal, V., Pandey, O., Richelson, S.: Textbook non-malleable commitments. In: Proceedings of the 48th annual ACM Symposium on Theory of Computing, pp. 1128–1141 (2016)

[GR97] Gennaro, R., Rohatgi, P.: How to sign digital streams. In: Advances in Cryptology - CRYPTO 1997, pp. 180–197 (1997)

[GRW+20] Gorbunov, S., Reyzin, L., Wee, H., Zhang, Z.: Pointproofs: aggregating proofs for multiple vector commitments. In: Proceedings of the 27th ACM Conference on Computer and Communications Security, pp. 2007–2023 (2020)

[HIL+99] Håstad, J., Impagliazzo, R., Levin, L.A., Luby, M.: A pseudorandom generator from any one-way function. SIAM J. Comput. 28(4), 1364–1396 (1999)

[Khu17] Khurana, D.: Round optimal concurrent non-malleability from polynomial hardness. In: Proceedings of the 15th Theory of Cryptography Conference, pp. 139–171 (2017)

[Kil92] Kilian, J.: A note on efficient zero-knowledge proofs and arguments. In: Proceedings of the 24th Annual ACM Symposium on Theory of Computing, pp. 723–732 (1992)

[KSS+16] Krupp, J., Schröder, D., Simkin, M., Fiore, D., Ateniese, G., Nürnberger, S.: Nearly optimal verifiable data streaming. In: Proceedings of the 19th International Conference on Practice and Theory in Public-Key Cryptography, pp. 417–445 (2016)

[Lam79] Lamport, L.: Constructing digital signatures from a one way function. Technical Report SRI-CSL-98, SRI International Computer Science Laboratory (1979)

[LM19] Lai, R.W.F., Malavolta, G.: Subvector commitments with application to succinct arguments. In: Advances in Cryptology - CRYPTO 2019, pp. 530–560 (2019)

[LP09] Lin, H., Pass, R.: Non-malleability amplification. In: Proceedings of the 41st annual ACM Symposium on Theory of Computing, pp. 189–198 (2009)

[LP11]   Lin, H., Pass, R.: Constant-round non-malleable commitments from any one-way function. In: Proceedings of the 43rd Annual ACM Symposium on Theory of Computing, pp. 705–714 (2011)

[LPV08] Lin, H., Pass, R., Venkitasubramaniam, M.: Concurrent non-malleable commitments from any one-way function. In: Proceedings of the 5th Theory of Cryptography Conference, pp. 571–588 (2008)

[LY10]   Libert, B., Yung, M.: Concise mercurial vector commitments and independent zero-knowledge sets with short proofs. In: Proceedings of the 7th Theory of Cryptography Conference, pp. 499–517 (2010)

[Mer87] Merkle, R.C.: A digital signature based on a conventional encryption function. In: Advances in Cryptology - CRYPTO 1987, pp. 369–378 (1987)

[MGG+13] Miers, I., Garman, C., Green, M., Rubin, A.D.: Zerocoin: anonymous distributed e-cash from bitcoin. In: IEEE Symposium on Security and Privacy, pp. 397–411 (2013)

[Mic94] Micali, S.: CS proofs. In: Proceedings of the 35th Annual IEEE Symposium on the Foundations of Computer Science, pp. 436–453 (1994)

[MND+04] Martel, C., Nuckolls, G., Devanbu, P., Gertz, M., Kwong, A., Stubblebine, S.G.: A general model for authenticated data structures. Algorithmica **39**(1), 21–24 (2004)

[MRK03] Micali, S., Rabin, M.O., Kilian, J.: Zero-knowledge sets. In: Proceedings of the 44th Annual IEEE Symposium on Foundations of Computer Science, pp. 80–91 (2003)

[Nak08] Nakamoto, S.: Bitcoin: a peer-to-peer electronic cash system. Available at https://bitcoin.org/bitcoin.pdf (2008)

[Nao91] Naor, M.: Bit commitment using pseudorandomness. J. Cryptol. **4**(2), 151–158 (1991)

[Ngu05] Nguyen, L.: Accumulators from bilinear pairings and applications. In: Topics in Cryptology - CT-RSA 2005, pp. 275–292 (2005)

[NN98]   Naor, M., Nissim, K.: Certificate revocation and certificate update. In: Proceedings of the 7th USENIX Security Symposium, pp. 217–228 (1998)

[NY89]   Naor, M., Yung, M.: Universal one-way hash functions and their cryptographic applications. In: Proceedings of the 21st Annual ACM Symposium on Theory of Computing, pp. 33–43 (1989)

[OWW+20] Ozdemir, A., Wahby, R., Whitehat, B., Boneh, D.: Scaling verifiable computation using efficient set accumulators. In: Proceedings of the 29th USENIX Security Symposium, pp. 2075–2092 (2020)

[PPV08] Pandey, O., Pass, R., Vaikuntanathan, V.: Adaptive one-way functions and applications. In: Advances in Cryptology - CRYPTO 2008, pp. 57–74 (2008)

[PR05]   Pass, R., Rosen, A.: Concurrent non-malleable commitments. In: Proceedings of the 46th Annual IEEE Symposium on Foundations of Computer Science, pp. 563–572 (2005)

[PR08]   Pass, R., Rosen, A.: New and improved constructions of nonmalleable cryptographic protocols. SIAM J. Comput. **38**(2), 702–752 (2008)

[PW10]   Pass, R., Wee, H.: Constant-round non-malleable commitments from subexponential one-way functions. In: Advances in Cryptology - EUROCRYPT 2010, pp. 638–655 (2010)

[Rey01] Reyzin, L.: Zero-knowledge with public keys. PhD Thesis, Massachusetts Institute of Technology (available at https://www.cs.bu.edu/~reyzin/phd-thesis.html) (2001)

[Rom90] Rompel, J.: One-way functions are necessary and sufficient for secure signatures. In: Proceedings of the 22nd Annual ACM Symposium on Theory of Computing, pp. 387–394 (1990)

[STS99] Sander, T., Ta-Shma, A.: Auditable, anonymous electronic cash. In: Advances in Cryptology - CRYPTO 1999, pp. 555–572 (1999)

[SvDJ+12] Stefanov, E., van Dijk, M., Jules, A., Opera, A.: Iris: a scalable cloud file system with efficient integrity checks. In: Proceedings of the 28th Annual Computer Security Applications Conference, pp. 229–238 (2012)

[TAB+20] Tomescu, A., Abraham, I., Buterin, V., Drake, J., Feist, D., Khovratovich, D.: Aggregatable subvector commitments for stateless cryptocurrencies. In: Proceedings of the 12th International Conference on Security and Cryptography for Networks, pp. 45–64 (2020)

[Tod16] Todd, P.: Making UTXO set growth irrelevant with low-latency delayed TXO commitments (2016). Available at https://petertodd.org/2016/delayed-txo-commitments

[Wee10] Wee, H.: Black-box, round-efficient secure computation via non-malleability amplification. In: Proceedings of the 51st Annual IEEE Symposium on Foundations of Computer Science, pp. 531–540 (2010)

Non-malleable Time-Lock Puzzles and Applications

Cody Freitag[1], Ilan Komargodski[2,3], Rafael Pass[1], and Naomi Sirkin[1(✉)]

[1] Cornell Tech, New York City, USA
{cfreitag,rafael,nephraim}@cs.cornell.edu
[2] Hebrew University, Jerusalem, Israel
ilank@cs.huji.ac.il
[3] NTT Research, Palo Alto, USA

Abstract. Time-lock puzzles are a mechanism for sending messages "to the future", by allowing a sender to quickly generate a puzzle with an underlying message that remains hidden until a receiver spends a moderately large amount of time solving it. We introduce and construct a variant of a time-lock puzzle which is *non-malleable*, which roughly guarantees that it is impossible to "maul" a puzzle into one for a related message without solving it.

Using non-malleable time-lock puzzles, we achieve the following applications:
- The first fair non-interactive multi-party protocols for coin flipping and auctions in the plain model without setup.
- Practically efficient fair multi-party protocols for coin flipping and auctions proven secure in the (auxiliary-input) random oracle model.

As a key step towards proving the security of our protocols, we introduce the notion of functional non-malleability, which protects against tampering attacks that affect a specific function of the related messages. To support an unbounded number of participants in our protocols, our time-lock puzzles satisfy functional non-malleability in the fully concurrent setting. We additionally show that standard (non-functional) non-malleability is impossible to achieve in the concurrent setting (even in the random oracle model).

1 Introduction

Time-lock puzzles (TLPs), introduced by Rivest, Shamir, and Wagner [45], are a cryptographic mechanism for committing to a message, where a sender can (quickly) generate a puzzle with a solution that remains hidden until the receiver spends a moderately large amount of time solving it (even in the presence of parallel processors). Rivest et al. [45] gave a very efficient construction of TLPs where security relies on the repeated squaring assumption. This assumption postulates, roughly, that it is impossible to significantly speed up repeated modular exponentiations in a group of unknown order, even when using many parallel processors. This construction and assumption have proven extremely useful in various (and sometimes unexpected) applications [9,15,19,33,36,44,50], some of which have already been implemented and deployed in existing systems.

ⓒ International Association for Cryptologic Research 2021
K. Nissim and B. Waters (Eds.): TCC 2021, LNCS 13044, pp. 447–479, 2021.
https://doi.org/10.1007/978-3-030-90456-2_15

Non-malleability. In a Man-In-the-Middle (MIM) attack, an eavesdropper tries to actively maul intermediate messages to compromise the integrity of the underlying values. To address such attacks, Dolev, Dwork and Naor [18] introduced the general concept of non-malleability in the context of cryptographic commitments. Roughly speaking, non-malleable commitments are an extension of plain cryptographic commitments (that guarantee binding and hiding) with the additional property that no adversary can maul a commitment for a given value into a commitment to a "related" value. As this is a fundamental concept with many applications, there has been a tremendous amount of research on this topic [1, 11, 12, 22–24, 27, 29–33, 35, 39–41, 43, 49].

Non-malleable TLPs and Applications. To date, non-malleability has not been considered in the context of TLPs (or other timed primitives).[1] Indeed, the construction of TLPs of [45] *is malleable*.[2] This fact actually has negative consequences in various settings where TLPs could be useful. For instance, consider a scenario where n parties perform an auction by posting bids on a public bulletin board. To implement this fairly, a natural approach is to use a commit-and-reveal style protocol, where each party commits to its bid on the board, and once all bids are posted each party publishes its opening. Clearly, one has to use non-malleable commitments to guarantee that bids are independent (otherwise, a malicious party can potentially bid for the maximal other bid plus 1). However, non-malleability is not enough since there is a fairness issue: a malicious party may refuse to open after seeing all other bids and so other parties will never know what the unopened bid was.

Using non-malleable TLPs to "commit" to the bids solves this problem. Indeed, the puzzle of a party who refuses to reveal its bid can be recovered after some moderately large amount of time by all honest parties. This style of protocol can also be used for fair multi-party collective coin flipping where n parties wish to agree on a common unbiased coin. There, each party encodes a random bit via a TLP and all parties will eventually agree on the parity of those bits.[3] This gives a highly desirable collective coin flipping protocol with an important property that we refer to as *optimistic efficiency*: when all parties are honest and publish their "openings" immediately after seeing all puzzles, the protocol terminates and all parties agree on an unbiased bit. As we will see, no other known protocol for this (highly important) task has this property. Even

---

[1] The concurrent works of [3, 4, 28] consider similar notions of non-malleability for time-lock puzzles. See Sect. 1.3 for a detailed comparison.

[2] The puzzle of [45] for a message s and difficulty T is a tuple $(g, N, T, s \oplus g^{2^T} \bmod N)$, where N is an RSA group modulus and g is a random element from $\mathbb{Z}_N$. The puzzle is trivially malleable since the message is one-time padded.

[3] In the context of coin flipping, if a malicious party aborts prematurely, this can bias the output [13] causing the fairness issue mentioned above. Boneh and Naor [9] used timed primitives and interaction to circumvent the issue in the two-party case, but we care about the multi-party case and prefer to avoid interaction as much as possible.

ignoring optimistic efficiency, such a protocol yields a fully non-interactive coin flipping protocol where each participant solves all published puzzles.

1.1 Our Results

To present our results, we start with a high level definition of a non-malleable TLP. Recall that for some secret s and difficulty t, a time-lock puzzle enables sampling a puzzle z which can be solved in time t to recover s, but guarantees that s remains hidden to any adversary running in time less than t.

For non-malleability, we require that any man-in-the-middle (MIM) attacker $\mathcal{A}$ that receives a puzzle z "on the left" cannot output a different puzzle $\tilde{z}$ "on the right" to a related value. Formally, we consider the (inefficient) distribution $\mathsf{mim}_{\mathcal{A}}(t, s)$ that samples a puzzle z to s, gets $\tilde{z} \leftarrow \mathcal{A}(z)$, and outputs the value $\tilde{s}$ computed by solving $\tilde{z}$. However, if $z = \tilde{z}$, then $\tilde{s} = \bot$ (since simply forwarding the commitment does not count as a valid mauling attack). Then, non-malleability requires that for any solution s and MIM attacker with depth much less than t (so it cannot break hiding), the distribution for a value s given by $\mathsf{mim}_{\mathcal{A}}(t, s)$ is indistinguishable from the distribution $\mathsf{mim}_{\mathcal{A}}(t, 0)$ for an unrelated value, 0. We emphasize that indistinguishability should hold even against arbitrary polynomial time or even *unbounded* distinguishers that, in particular, can solve the TLP. We also consider the natural extension to the bounded *concurrent* setting [42], where the MIM attacker $\mathcal{A}$ receives n_{left} concurrent puzzles on the left and attempts to generate n_{right} puzzles on the right to related values. In this setting, the distinguisher receives the solutions to all n_{right} puzzles. We refer to this as $(n_{\mathsf{left}}, n_{\mathsf{right}})$-concurrency.

We next give our main results. First, we present our results on non-malleable time-lock puzzles, and we discuss the various notions of non-malleability that we consider in this setting. Next, we show how to additionally satisfy a strong public verifiability property using a specific time-lock puzzle based on repeated squaring. Finally, we discuss the applications of our constructions for fair multi-party protocols.

Non-malleable Time-Lock Puzzles. We give two different constructions of non-malleable TLPs. We emphasize that, as explained above, this primitive is not only natural on its own right, but also has important applications to the design of secure protocols for various basic tasks. Our first construction is practically efficient, relies on the existence of any given TLP [6,45], and is proven secure in the (auxiliary-input) random oracle model [47].

Theorem 1.1 (Informal; See Theorem 4.2 and Corollary 4.3). *For every $n_{\mathsf{left}}, n_{\mathsf{right}}, L \in \mathrm{poly}(\lambda)$, assuming that there is a TLP (supporting 1-bit messages) that is secure for attackers of size $2^{3n_{\mathsf{right}} \cdot L} \cdot \mathrm{poly}(\lambda)$, there exists an $(n_{\mathsf{left}}, n_{\mathsf{right}})$-concurrent non-malleable TLP supporting messages of length L. The scheme is proven secure in the auxiliary-input random oracle model.*

In terms of security, our reduction is *depth preserving*: if the given TLP is secure against attackers of depth $T(\lambda)/\alpha(\lambda)$, where $\alpha(\cdot)$ is a fixed polynomial independent of T denoting the advantage of an attacker, then the resulting non-malleable TLP is secure against attackers of depth $T(\lambda)/\alpha'(\lambda)$ for a related fixed polynomial $\alpha'(\cdot)$. In particular, the dependence on T in hardness is preserved. Additionally, note that if $n_{\text{right}} \cdot L \in O(\log \lambda)$, then the underlying TLP only needs to be polynomially secure.

Instantiating the TLP with the construction of [45], our scheme is extremely efficient: encoding a message requires a single invocation of a random oracle and few (modular) exponentiations. Additionally, our construction is very simple to describe: to generate a puzzle for a solution s with randomness r, we sample a puzzle for (s, r) using randomness which itself depends (via the random oracle) on s and r.[4] Nevertheless, the proof of security turns out to be somewhat tricky and non-trivial; see Sect. 2 for details.

We prove that our scheme is non-malleable against all polynomial-size attackers that cannot solve the puzzles (and this is inherent as the latter ones can easily maul any puzzle). We even allow the attacker's description to depend arbitrarily on the random oracle. We formalize this notion by showing that our TLP is non-malleable in the *auxiliary-input* random oracle model, a model that was introduced by Unruh [47] (see also [14]) in order to capture preprocessing attacks, where a non-uniform attacker obtains an advice string that depends arbitrarily on the random oracle. Thus, in a sense, our construction does *not* require any form of attacker-independent setup.

Our second construction is proven secure in the plain model (without any form of setup) and is based on the non-malleable code for bounded polynomial depth tampering functions due to [15]. This construction relies on a variety of assumptions (including keyless hash functions and non-interactive witness indistinguishable proofs) and is less practically efficient. While the main technical ideas for the construction and proof are given in [15], the threat model they consider is weaker than what we require for non-malleable TLPs; for example, they only consider plain (non-concurrent) non-malleability and do not require security against re-randomization attacks (mauling a code word for m into a different code word for m). We show how to extend their construction to our setting, and prove the following theorem.

Theorem 1.2 (Informal). *Assume a time-lock puzzle, a keyless multi-collision resistant hash function, a non-interactive witness indistinguishable proof for* NP, *and injective one-way functions, all sub-exponentially secure. Then, there exists a bounded concurrent non-malleable time-lock puzzle secure against polynomial size adversaries.*

---

[4] We note that our construction is conceptually similar to the Fujisaki-Okamoto (FO) transformation [21] used to generically transform any CPA-secure public-key encryption scheme into a CCA-secure one using a random oracle. However, since our setting and required guarantees are different, the actual proof turns out to be much more delicate and challenging.

We emphasize that both of our constructions only achieve *bounded* concurrency, where the number of instances the attacker participates in is a priori bounded (and the scheme may depend on this bound). We show that the stronger notion of *full* concurrency, which does not place such limitations and is achievable in all other standard settings of non-malleability, is actually impossible to achieve for TLPs. Therefore, our result is best possible in this sense.

Theorem 1.3 (Informal). *There is no fully concurrent non-malleable TLP (even in the random oracle model).*

In a nutshell, the impossibility from Theorem 1.3 is proven by the following generic MIM attack. Given a puzzle z, if the number of "sessions" the attacker can participate in is at least as large as $|z|$, they can essentially generate $|z|$ puzzles encoding *the bits of* z. Since the distinguisher of the MIM game (which is now given those bits) can run in arbitrary polynomial time, it can simply solve the original puzzle and recover the original solution in full. We emphasize that this attack only requires a polynomial-time distinguisher. This attack is circumvented in the bounded concurrency setting (Theorem 1.1) by setting the length of the puzzle to be longer than the concurrency bound. Specifically, to support n concurrent puzzles on the right, we can set the message length to $L \cdot n$, which is what results in exponential security loss $2^{L \cdot n}$ as discussed above.

Functional Non-malleability. We note that the attack on fully concurrent non-malleable time-lock puzzles crucially relies on the fact that the *distinguisher* in the MIM game can solve the underlying puzzles. However, it is easy to see that if the distinguisher is restricted to bounded depth, this attack fails. One could define a *weaker* notion of non-malleability where the MIM distinguisher is depth-bounded, but this results in a weaker security guarantee. In particular, we show in the full version of the paper that there exists a natural TLP construction that satisfies this (weaker) definition yet has a valid mauling attack.[5]

In light of this observation, we introduce a new definition of non-malleability that *generalizes* the standard definition considered in Theorem 1.1. We call the notion *functional* non-malleability and, as the name suggests, the security notion is parameterized by a class of functions $\mathcal{F}$. Denote by L the bit-length of the messages we want to support and by n the number of sessions that the MIM attacker participates in on the right. We think of $f \in \mathcal{F}$ as some *bounded depth* function of the form $f: (\{0,1\}^L)^n \to \{0,1\}^m$, which is the target function of the input messages that the MIM adversary is trying to bias. Specifically, the distinguisher of the MIM game now receives the output of the function f when applied to the values underlying the puzzles given by the MIM adversary. When $\mathcal{F}$ includes all identity functions (which are bounded depth and have output length $m = n \cdot L$), functional non-malleability implies the standard definition of concurrent non-malleability (as the distinguisher just gets all the messages from the n mauled puzzles).

---

[5] As we discuss in the Sect. 1.3, concurrent works allow the distinguisher to be bounded depth.

Naturally, it makes sense to ask what guarantees can we get if we a priori restrict f, say in its output length, without limiting the number of sessions n. This turns out to particularly useful when the application at hand only requires non-malleability against a specific form of tampering functions (this indeed will be the case for us below). Concretely, let $\mathcal{F}_m$ be the class of all functions whose output length is at most m bits and which can be computed in depth polynomial in the security parameter λ and in $\log(n \cdot L)$ (using the notation given above). Then, we have the following result.

Theorem 1.4 (Informal; See Theorem 4.2). *Assuming that there exists a TLP, then for every $m \in \text{poly}(\lambda)$ there exists a fully concurrent functional non-malleable TLP for the class of functions $\mathcal{F}_m$. The scheme is proven secure in the auxiliary-input random oracle model assuming the given TLP is secure for all attackers of size at most $2^{3m} \cdot \text{poly}(\lambda)$.*

The above construction is *depth preserving* in the same way as the construction from Theorem 1.1. Further, note that as long as $m \in O(\log \lambda)$, we only require standard polynomial hardness from the given TLP. We remark that Theorem 1.4 will turn out to be instrumental for our applications we discuss below. We also believe that the abstraction of functional non-malleability is important on its own right and view it as an independent contribution. We also show how to achieve fully concurrent functional non-malleability for our plain model construction.

Publicly Verifiable Time-Lock Puzzles. In addition to non-malleability, we construct TLPs that also have a public verifiability property: after a party solves the puzzle, they can publish the underlying solution together with a proof which can be later used by anyone to *quickly* verify the correctness of the solution. We emphasize that this must hold even if the solver determines that the puzzle has no valid solution. We believe this primitive is of independent interest.

We build our non-malleable, publicly verifiable TLP assuming a very weak form of (partially) trusted setup. The setup of our TLP consists of a set of many public parameters where we only assume that at least one of them was generated honestly. We call this model the All-But-One-string (ABO-string) model.[6] We design this to fit into our multi-party protocol application (see Theorem 1.7 below) in such a way where the parties themselves will generate this setup in the puzzle generation phase. Indeed, as we discuss below, publicly verifiable TLPs in the ABO-string model will imply coin flipping *without setup*.

Theorem 1.5 (Informal). *Assuming the repeated squaring assumption, there exists a publicly verifiable non-malleable TLP in the ABO-string model. The construction is proven secure in the auxiliary-input random oracle model.*

---

[6] Our ABO-string model is a variant of the multi-string model of Groth and Ostrovsky [25], where it is assumed that a majority of the public parameters are honestly generated.

Our construction is depth preserving and has security which depends on the message length. In particular, the security of the resulting TLP is the same as in the constructions in Theorem 1.1 and Theorem 1.4, depending on the type of non-malleability desired for the resulting TLP.

To construct our publicly verifiable TLP, we use a *strong trapdoor VDF* which is why our construction is not generic from any time-lock puzzle. Somewhat surprisingly, we need to leverage specific properties of the trapdoor VDF of Pietrzak's [44] using the group of signed quadratic residues QR_N^+ where N is a product of safe primes.[7] For an overview of our construction, see Sect. 2.2.

Fair Multi-Party Auctions and Coin Flipping. As we mentioned above, an appealing application of non-malleable TLPs is for tasks such as fair multi-party auctions or coin flipping. Our protocols (for both tasks) are extremely efficient and consist of just two phases: first each party "commits" to their bid/randomness using some puzzle, and then after all puzzles are made public, each party publishes its solution. If some party refuses to open their puzzle, a force-opening phase is performed. Alternatively, we can instantiate our protocols in the fully non-interactive setting where all parties solve every other puzzle.

In what follows, we focus on the task of fair multi-party coin flipping, which is a core building block in recent proof-of-stake blockchain designs; see below. The application to auctions follows in a similar manner. It is convenient to consider our protocol in a setting where there is a public bulletin board. Any party can publish a puzzle to the bulletin board during the commit phase and then publish its solution after some pre-specified amount of time has elapsed.

Relying only our concurrent, functional non-malleable (not necessarily publicly verifiable) TLP constructions, all of our protocols (both non-interactive and two-phase) satisfy fairness, informally defined as follows:

- **Fairness:** No malicious adversary (controlling all but one party) can bias the output of the protocol, even by aborting early. Namely, as long as there is at least one honest participating party, the output will be a (nearly) uniformly random value.

Our two-phase "commit-and-reveal" style protocols have the additional efficiency guarantee:

- **Optimistic Efficiency:** If all participating parties are honest, then the protocol terminates within two message rounds (without the need to wait the pre-specified amount of time for the second phase), and all parties can efficiently verify the output of the protocol.

Using our construction of a publicly verifiable non-malleable TLP, we satisfy the following public verifiability property:

---

[7] For this, we assume that sampling uniformly random safe primes can be done efficiently; this is a pretty common assumption, see [48] for more details.

- **Public Verifiability:** In the case that any participating party is dishonest and does not publish their solution, any party can break the puzzle in a moderate amount of time and provide a publicly verifiable proof of the solution. We even require that an honest party can prove that a published puzzle has *no* valid solution.

We focus on two main results from the above discussion, although we get a variety of different protocols depending on what TLP we start with and how we instantiate the protocol. First, we construct fully non-interactive protocols in the plain model without any setup.

Theorem 1.6 (Informal; see Theorem 5.3**).** *Assume a time-lock puzzle, a keyless multi-collision resistant hash function, a non-interactive witness indistinguishable proof for* NP, *and injective one-way functions, all sub-exponentially secure. Then, there exist fully non-interactive, fair multi-party coin flipping and auction protocols. The protocols support an unbounded number of participants and require no setup.*

Next, we achieve efficient, publicly verifiable two-phase protocols in the auxiliary input random oracle model.

Theorem 1.7 (Informal; See Theorem 5.1**).** *Assuming the repeated squaring assumption, there exist two-phase fair multi-party coin flipping and auction protocols that satisfy optimistic efficiency and public verifiability. The protocols support an unbounded number of participants and require no trusted setup. Security is proven in the auxiliary-input random oracle.*

The differences between the protocols achieved in these two theorems is that the first is non-interactive and has no setup, while the second is two rounds and is in the random oracle model, yet leverages this to achieve public verifiability and better concrete efficiency. We emphasize that both of the protocols support polynomial-length outputs, relying on sub-exponential security of the underlying time-lock puzzle.

We also emphasize that our protocols support an a priori unbounded number of participants. This may seems strange in light of our impossibility from Theorem 1.3. We bypass this lower bound (as mentioned above) by observing that for most natural applications (including coin flipping and auctions), the notion of functional non-malleability from Theorem 1.4 suffices. The key insight is that we only need indistinguishability with respect to specific depth-bounded functions with a priori bounded output lengths (e.g., parity for coin flipping, or taking the maximum for auctions). Since the output length in both cases is known, we can actually support *full* concurrency which translates into having an unbounded number of participants.

For auctions, we note that our protocols are the first multi-party protocols *under any assumption* that satisfy fairness against malicious adversaries and requires no adversary-independent setup—using the timed commitments of [9] works only in the two-party setting and additionally relies on trusted setup, and using the homomorphic time-lock puzzles of [36] does not satisfy fairness in the presence of malicious adversaries. For coin flipping, our two-round protocol is the first multi-party protocol that is fair against malicious adversaries while satisfying optimistic efficiency. Next, we provide a more in depth comparison of our non-interactive coin flipping protocol with existing solutions.

Simulation-Based Fairness. As mentioned above, we show that our protocols are fair in the sense that no malicious adversary can bias the output of the protocol. This suffices for applications which only use the *output* of the protocol. To capture applications that additionally depend on the protocol transcript, we show that our protocol satisfies simulation security with full fairness in the programmable random oracle model. This guarantees that the protocol execution in the presence of a malicious adversary (even one aborting early) can be simulated to a uniformly random output in an ideal model where every honest party receives the output (regardless of whether any malicious party aborts early).

Non-interactive Coin Flipping. We emphasize that our non-interactive coin flipping protocol of Theorem 1.6 is the first such protocol without any form of setup in the plain model. Specifically, we mean that there is no common random string or any assumed common function. Still, our practically efficient protocol of Theorem 1.7 as a non-interactive protocol still enjoys some benefits over existing schemes.

In the non-interactive setting, Boneh et al. [7] proposed a VDF-based protocol. Specifically, each party publishes a random string r_i and then the agreed upon coin is defined by running a VDF on the seed $H(r_1 \| \ldots \| r_n)$, where H is a random oracle. As the VDF must be evaluated to obtain the output, this type of protocol does not satisfy optimistic efficiency. Nevertheless, the VDF-based protocol has the advantage that only a single slow computation needs to be computed, whereas our non-interactive protocol requires n such computations for n participants (which can be done in parallel). Malavolta and Thyagarajan [36] address this inefficiency in the context of time-lock puzzles (which do allow for the option of optimistic efficiency) by constructing *homomorphic* time-lock puzzles, where many separate puzzles can be combined into a single puzzle to be solved. However, their TLP scheme is malleable and so cannot be directly used to obtain a fair protocol against malicious adversaries.[8] In the two-phase setting, however, our publicly verifiable protocol has the property that only a single honest party needs to solve each puzzle, and this computation can easily be delegated to an external server.

The VDF-based scheme of [7] can be based on repeated squaring in a group of unknown order based on the publicly verifiable proofs of [44,50]. In this setting, the protocols can either be instantiated using RSA groups that require attacker-independent trusted setup, or based on class groups that rely only on

---

[8] It is possible to make this protocol maliciously secure using concurrent non-malleable zero-knowledge proofs [2,32,34,38], proving that each party acted honestly, but this (1) makes the construction significantly less efficient, and (2) requires either trusted setup and additional hardness assumptions, or additional rounds of interaction.

a common random string. As we do in this work, the common random string can be implemented in the ABO-string model using a random oracle (which the attacker may depend on arbitrarily). Therefore, when restricting our attention to protocols without attacker-independent setup, the previous VDF-based protocols are based on less standard assumptions on class groups, whereas we give a protocol that can be instantiated from more standard assumptions on RSA groups with better concrete efficiency.

Privacy. Let us remark that the protocols that we described guarantee fairness but not privacy. The latter, however, can be obtained in specific applications by composing our protocols with existing privacy-preserving tools such as Anonize [26].

1.2 Related Work

Timed Commitments. Boneh and Naor [9] introduced timed commitments, which can be viewed as a publicly verifiable and interactive TLP. They additionally require that the puzzle (which is an interactive commitment) convinces the receiver that if they brute-force the solution, they will succeed. Because of this additional property, their commitment scheme is interactive and relies on a less standard assumption called the generalized Blum-Blum-Shub assumption. Their scheme is additionally malleable.

Fair Coin Flipping in Blockchains. Generating unbiased bits is one of the largest bottlenecks in modern proof-of-stake crypto-currency designs [5,16,17]. Recall that in a proof-of-stake blockchains, the idea is, very roughly speaking, to enforce "one vote per unit of stake". This is usually implemented by choosing random small committees at every epoch and letting that committee decide on the next block. The main question is how to obtain "pure" randomness so that the chosen committee is really "random".

One option is to use the hash of an old-enough block as the randomness. Unfortunately, it is known that the hash of a block is not completely unbiased: an attacker can essentially fully control about logarithmically many of its bits. In existing systems, this is mitigated by "blowing up" parameters to compensate for the (small yet meaningful) advantage the attacker has, making those systems much less efficient. Using a mechanism that generates unbiased bits, we could make proof-of-stake crypto-currencies much more efficient.

1.3 Concurrent Work

Several related papers [3,4,28] have been developed concurrently and independently to this work.[9] The works of Baum et al. [3,4] formalize and construct

---

[9] We emphasize that only Sect. 1.3, Appendix A, and the separation regarding the different notions of non-malleability (given in the full version) were added based on these works. All other definitions and results that appear are completely independent of these works.

various (publicly verifiable) time-based primitives, including TLPs, under the Universal Composability (UC) framework [10]. Katz et al. [28] (among other results, less related to ours) introduce and construct non-malleable non-interactive timed commitments. While the notions that are introduced and studied are related, the results are all incomparable as each paper has a somewhat different motivation which leads to different definitions and results.

Comparison with [28]. Let us start by comparing definitions. Katz et al. consider a CCA-style definition adapted to the depth-bounded setting. In the classical setting of unbounded polynomial-time attackers, CCA security definitions are usually stronger than "only" non-malleability, but this is not generally true in the depth-bounded setting.

In more detail, they consider a depth-bounded version of CCA security, where the attacker (who is also the distinguisher) is bounded to run in time less than the hardness of the timed primitive. We, on the other hand, allow the distinguisher of the MIM game to be unbounded (while only the attacker is bounded). We believe this is an important distinction and we provide more insights into the differences between the bounded and unbounded distinguisher settings in the full version. Specifically, we show that non-malleability with a depth-bounded distinguisher is (essentially) equivalent to our definition of functional non-malleability with output length 1. We also give a construction separating the definitions of non-malleability with an unbounded vs. depth-bounded distinguisher, showing that non-malleability in the bounded distinguisher setting gives a strictly weaker security guarantee.

Regarding the primitives constructed, recall that timed commitments [9] (ignoring non-malleability for now) allow one to commit to a message m in such a way that the commitment hides m up to some time T, yet the verifier can be sure that it can be force opened to *some* value after roughly T time. In contrast, plain TLPs are not necessarily guaranteed to contain valid messages. In this context, our notion of publicly-verifiable TLPs is in between these two notions: we treat puzzles without a solution as invalid (say encoding $\perp$) but we additionally provide a way to publicly verify that this is the case after it has been solved. Nevertheless, we note that the construction of Katz et al. does not imply a TLP since their commitment procedure takes T time (while TLP generation should take time essentially independent of T).

Additionally, their constructions achieve non-malleability through the use of NIZKs following the Naor-Yung [37] paradigm for CCA-secure encryption. Known (even interactive) zero-knowledge proofs for correctness of time-lock puzzles are quite expensive (see, e.g., Boneh-Naor [9] which requires parallel repetition). Using generic NIZKs (even in the random oracle model) would be even worse.

Regarding assumptions, their construction is proven secure in the algebraic group model [20] and relies on trusted setup, while ours is proven secure in the (auxiliary-input) random oracle model and hence requires no trusted setup independent of the adversary. Both constructions rely on repeated squaring as the source of depth-hardness, and theirs additionally makes use of NIZKs (which require setup).

Comparison with [3,4]. Baum et al. consider a UC-style definition, which is generally stronger than non-malleability. In this setting, the environment takes the place of the distinguisher in the MIM game. Their definition is closer to ours as the environment may run for an arbitrary polynomial number of rounds and thus does not restrict the depth of the distinguisher. In terms of modeling, the construction of a UC-secure TLP in [4] relies on a programmable random oracle, whereas our construction relies on a non-programmable (auxiliary-input) random oracle. In fact, they prove that their notion of UC security cannot be achieved in the non-programmable random oracle model.

In a follow-up work [3], they show that their time-lock puzzle construction satisfies a notion of public verifiability. However, they achieve public verifiability only for honestly generated puzzles, that is, one can prove that a puzzle has a solution s, but cannot prove that a puzzle has no solution. In our terminology, we refer to this as one-sided public verifiability In contrast, our construction achieves full verifiability. This property is crucial for our efficient coin flipping protocol since it allows only one honest party to (attempt to) solve any invalid puzzle. With only one-sided public verifiability, every participant would need to solve all invalid puzzles, and the output of the coin-flip can only be efficiently verified (in time less than T) in the case that all puzzles are honestly generated.

1.4 Paper Organization

In Sect. 2, we give an overview of our techniques. Next, we give preliminaries in Sect. 3. In Sect. 4, we give our construction of functional non-malleable time-lock puzzles in the random oracle model. In Sect. 5, we give our construction of fair multi-party coin flipping. In Appendix A we discuss the various notions of non-malleability for TLPs introduced in this and related works. Additional results are provided in the full version, including our non-malleable TLP construction in the plain model, an impossibility result for unbounded concurrency, our publicly verifiable TLP construction, our simulation-secure coin flipping protocol, and a separation between unbounded and depth-bounded non-malleability.

2 Technical Overview

In Sect. 2.1, we give an overview of our non-malleable time-lock puzzle construction (in the random oracle model) and its proof of security. Then in Sect. 2.2, we overview our construction of publicly verifiable (and non-malleable) time-lock puzzles from repeated squaring. Finally in Sect. 2.3, we discuss how our non-malleable time-lock puzzle constructions can be used for fair multi-party coin flipping with various desirable properties.

We start by recalling the definition of TLPs, as necessary to give an overview of our techniques. A TLP consists of two algorithms (Gen, Sol). Gen is a probabilistic procedure that takes as input an embedded solution s and a time parameter t, and outputs a puzzle z. Sol is a deterministic procedure that on input a puzzle z for time bound t, outputs a solution in depth (or parallel time) roughly t. We note that TLPs can be thought of as a fine-grained analogue to commitments where "hardness" of the puzzle means that the puzzles are hiding against distinguishers of depth less than t. On the other hand, hiding *can be broken* in depth t (using Sol). Additionally, we require that Sol always finds the correct underlying solution s for a puzzle z. This corresponds to perfect binding in the language of commitments.

2.1 Non-malleability for Time-Lock Puzzles

In this section, we overview our non-malleable time-lock puzzle construction in the random oracle model (for the plain model construction, we refer the reader to the overview in [15], as the main ideas are the same). Our construction relies on any time-lock puzzle TLP and a common random oracle $\mathcal{O}$. We now describe our non-malleable TLP, which we denote nmTLP. In order to generate a puzzle for a solution s that can be broken in time t, nmTLP.Gen uses randomness r and feeds $s\|r$ into the random oracle to get a string r_{tlp}. It then uses TLP.Gen to create a puzzle with difficulty t for $s\|r$ using randomness r_{tlp}. That is,

$$\text{nmTLP.Gen}(t, s; r) := \text{TLP.Gen}(t, s\|r; \mathcal{O}(s\|r)).$$

Note that in order to solve the puzzle output by nmTLP.Gen, it suffices to just solve the puzzle generated using TLP.Gen, which takes time t. In other words, nmTLP.Sol(t, z) simply computes $s\|r = \text{TLP.Sol}(t, z)$ and outputs s. In fact, the solver can even check to make sure that the solutions s is valid by checking that $s = \text{TLP.Gen}(t, s; r)$.

We note that our construction is conceptually similar to the Fujisaki-Okamoto (FO) transformation [21] for transforming CPA-secure encryption to CCA-secure encryption using a random oracle. However, as we will see below, our proof is substantially different. In particular, the FO transformation achieves unbounded CCA security, which we show is impossible in our setting!

Hardness. To show the hardness of nmTLP relative to a random oracle, we rely on the hardness of TLP in the plain model, against attackers of depth much less than t. At a high level, we show that breaking the hardness of nmTLP requires either guessing the randomness r used to generate the randomness $r_{\text{tlp}} = \mathcal{O}(s\|r)$ for the underlying puzzle, or directly breaking the hardness of TLP, both of which are infeasible for bounded attackers. To formalize this, we consider any depth-bounded distinguisher $\mathcal{D}^{\mathcal{O}}$, who receives as input a nmTLP puzzle z corresponding to solution s_0 or s_1 and distinguishes the two cases with non-negligible probability. By construction, z actually corresponds to a TLP puzzle for $s_0\|r_0$ or $s_1\|r_1$, so we would like to use $\mathcal{D}$ to construct a distinguisher against the hardness of TLP.

We first note that if $\mathcal{D}$ never makes a query to $\mathcal{O}$ containing the randomness r_b underlying z, then we can simulate $\mathcal{O}$ by lazily sampling it in the plain model, and hence use $\mathcal{D}$ as a distinguisher for the hardness of TLP. If $\mathcal{D}$ does make a query containing r_b, then with overwhelming probability it must have received a puzzle corresponding to $s_b\|r_b$ (since in this case, r_{1-b} is independent of $\mathcal{D}$ and its input z). Moreover, all of its queries up until that point have uniformly random answers independent of z, so we can simulate them as well, up until receiving this query. Therefore, in both cases, we can carry out this attack in the plain model and rely on the hardness of TLP.

Non-malleability. To show non-malleability of nmTLP, we want to argue that any depth-bounded man-in-the-middle (MIM) attacker $\mathcal{A}$ cannot maul a puzzle z for s (received on the left) to a puzzle $\tilde{z}$ (output on the right) for a related value $\tilde{s} \neq s$. At a high level, whenever $\mathcal{A}$ changes the underlying value s to $\tilde{s}$, then the output of the random oracle on $\tilde{s}$ is now uniformly random and independent of z. Indeed, we show that for any fixed puzzle $\tilde{z}$ and a value $\tilde{s}$, a randomly generated puzzle for $\tilde{s}$ will not be equal to $\tilde{z}$ with high probability (otherwise we show how to break the hardness of TLP). So, intuitively, the only way to generate a *valid* puzzle $\tilde{z}$ for $\tilde{s}$ is to "know" the underlying value $\tilde{s}$, but hardness intuitively implies that no depth-bounded adversary can "know" s.

We formalize this intuition by a hybrid argument to show that the MIM distribution $\tilde{s} \leftarrow \mathsf{mim}_\mathcal{A}(t, s)$ is indistinguishable from $\mathsf{mim}_\mathcal{A}(t, 0)$. At a high level, we first replace the inefficient distribution $\mathsf{mim}_\mathcal{A}(t, s)$ by a low-depth circuit $\mathcal{B}$. At this point, we want to use the hiding property to indistinguishably swap the puzzle to 0, so the hybrid is now unrelated to s. We describe the key ideas for these hybrids below.

For the first hybrid, the key insight is that we can compute $\mathsf{mim}_\mathcal{A}(t, s)$ *in low depth* using an algorithm $\mathcal{B}$ by simply looking at the oracle queries made by $\mathcal{A}$. In this sense, we are relying on the extractability property of random oracles to say that $\mathcal{A}$ must know any valid value $\tilde{s}$ it generates a puzzle for. Specifically, let $\tilde{z}$ be the output of $\mathcal{A}$. For every query $(s_i\|r_i)$ that $\mathcal{A}$ makes to $\mathcal{O}$, $\mathcal{B}$ outputs s_i if $\tilde{z} = \mathsf{nmTLP}(t, s_i\|r_i; \mathcal{O}(s_i\|r_i))$. If there are no such queries, $\mathcal{B}$ outputs $\bot$. $\mathcal{B}$ requires depth comparable to the depth of $\mathcal{A}$ since all of these checks can be done in parallel. Furthermore, the output of $\mathcal{B}$ is indistinguishable from the true output given the above observation that $\mathcal{A}$ cannot output a valid puzzle for a value it doesn't query.

For the next hybrid, we would like to indistinguishably replace the underlying puzzle for s with a puzzle for 0, which would suffice to show non-malleability. Because $\mathcal{B}$ is low-depth, it seems that we should be able to use the hiding property of nmTLP to say that the output of $\mathcal{B}$ does not depend on the underlying value s. Specifically, we want to conclude that if the output of $\mathcal{B}$ (who outputs many bits) is statistically far when the underlying value is s versus 0, then there exists a distinguisher (who outputs a single bit) that can distinguish puzzles for s

and 0. Towards this claim, we show how to "flatten" any (possibly unbounded) distinguisher $\mathcal{D}$ who distinguishes between the output of $\mathcal{B}$ in the case where the underlying value is s versus 0. Specifically, we encode the truth table of $\mathcal{D}$ as a low-depth distinguishing circuit of size roughly $2^{|s|}$ to make this reduction go through. As a result, we need to rely on a sub-exponentially security of the underlying TLP when $|s| = \lambda$. Namely, the underlying TLP cannot be broken by sub-exponential sized circuits with depth much less than t. However, when $|s| \in O(\log \lambda)$, we only need to rely on *polynomial* security of the underlying TLP.

Impossibility of Fully Concurrent Non-malleability. Ideally, we would like to achieve fully concurrent non-malleability, meaning that any MIM attacker that receives any polynomial n number of puzzles on the left cannot maul them to n puzzles for related values. However, we show that this is impossible to achieve.

Consider an arbitrary TLP for a polynomial time bound t. We construct a MIM attacker $\mathcal{A}$ that receives only a single puzzle z on the left with solution s where the length of z is L. Then, $\mathcal{A}$ can split z into L bits and output a puzzle on the right for each bit *of the puzzle* z. Then, the values underlying the puzzles output by $\mathcal{A}$ when viewed together yield z, which is related to the value s! More formally, there exists a polynomial time distinguisher that solves the puzzle z in polynomial time t and can distinguish $\mathcal{A}$'s output in the case when it receives a puzzle for s or an unrelated value, say 0.

This implies that for any n which is greater than the size of a puzzle, the TLP cannot be non-malleable against MIM attackers who output at most n puzzles on the right. At a high level, the impossibility follows from the fact that hardness does not hold against arbitrary polynomial-time distinguishers (which usually *is* the case for hiding of standard commitments).

Despite this impossibility, we show that we actually *can* achieve concurrent non-malleability against a *specific class of distinguishers* in the non-malleability game. We refer to this notion as concurrent *functional* non-malleability.

Achieving Concurrent Functional Non-malleability. In many applications, we only need a form of non-malleability to hold with respect to certain classes of functions. For example, in our application to coin flipping, we only need that a puzzle z with solution s cannot be mauled to a set of puzzles $\widetilde{z}_1, \ldots, \widetilde{z}_n$ with underlying values $\widetilde{s}_1, \ldots, \widetilde{s}_n$ such that $\bigoplus_{i \in [n]} \widetilde{s}_i$ "depends on" s. With this in mind, we define a concurrent functional non-malleability with respect to a class of functions $\mathcal{F}$. We say that a TLP satisfies *functional* non-malleability for a class $\mathcal{F}$ if the output of $f(\mathrm{mim}_{\mathcal{A}}(t, s))$ is indistinguishable from $f(\mathrm{mim}_{\mathcal{A}}(t, 0))$ for any $f \in \mathcal{F}$, which also naturally generalizes to the concurrent setting. We note that functional non-malleability for a class $\mathcal{F}$ actually implies standard non-malleability whenever the class $\mathcal{F}$ contains the identity function, so functional non-malleability generalizes the standard notion of non-malleability.

Going back to the proof of standard (non-concurrent) non-malleability for our construction nmTLP, we observe that the security we need for the underlying time-lock puzzle we use depends on $2^{|s|}$ where $|s|$ is the size of the puzzle solutions. Specifically, given any distinguisher in the non-malleability that had input of size $|s|$, we were able to construct a distinguisher for hardness of size $2^{|s|}$. In fact, this exact same proof works in the context of concurrent functional non-malleability for functions f that have *low depth* and bounded output length m. We require f to be low depth so the reduction constitutes a valid attack against hardness, and then we only require security proportional to 2^m!

We briefly discuss how our nmTLP construction works for concurrent functional non-malleability for the class $\mathcal{F}_m$ of function with low depth and output length m. Specifically, for every m, we define a scheme nmTLP$_m$ assuming that TLP is secure against attackers of size roughly 2^m. Because TLP requires security against 2^m size attackers, our construction nmTLP$_m$ also only achieves security against 2^m size attackers. As such, our nmTLP.Gen algorithm needs to use at least $\Omega(m + \lambda)$ bits of randomness (otherwise an attacker could cycle through all choices of randomness to break security). Recall that nmTLP$_m$.Gen with randomness r outputs a puzzle using TLP.Gen with solution $s\|r$. As a result, if we want to support solutions of size $|s|$ in nmTLP$_m$, we need our underlying TLP to support solutions of size $O(|s| + m + \lambda)$. By correctness, this implies that our schemes outputs puzzles of size roughly $O(|s| + m + \lambda)$.

Bounded Concurrent Non-malleability. Our construction of time-lock puzzles for concurrent functional non-malleability can also be seen as a construction for bounded concurrent (plain) non-malleability. Specifically, consider the case where the MIM attacker outputs at most n puzzles on the right. We can think of this as functional non-malleability where the low depth function is simply identity on $n \cdot |s|$ bits. From the above discussion, this implies a protocol assuming a TLP with security against size $2^{n \cdot |s|}$ attackers, with puzzles of size roughly $O(n \cdot |s| + \lambda)$.

Security in the Auxiliary-Input Random Oracle Model. Finally, we note that the most of our constructions and formal proofs are in the auxiliary-input random oracle model (AI-ROM) introduced by Unruh [47]. In this model, the non-uniform attacker is allowed to depend arbitrarily on the random oracle, so there is no attacker-independent non-uniform advice. At a high level, we use the result from [47] to conclude that the view of any bounded-size MIM attacker $\mathcal{A}$ with oracle access to $\mathcal{O}$ (where $\mathcal{A}$ may depend arbitrarily on $\mathcal{O}$) is indistinguishable the view of $\mathcal{A}$ with access to a "lazily sampled" oracle $\mathcal{P}$ that is fixed at a set of points F (which depend on $\mathcal{A}$). Formally, in the non-malleability analysis, we switch to an intermediate hybrid where the MIM attacker has access to a partially fixed, lazily sampled oracle $\mathcal{P}$. Then, because the MIM attacker $\mathcal{A}$ must maul honestly generated puzzles that have high entropy, we show that it is necessary for $\mathcal{A}$ to query the oracle $\mathcal{P}$ outside the fixed set of points F. From this, we carefully show that a similar analysis follows as discussed above for the ROM.

2.2   Publicly Verifiable Time-Lock Puzzles

We observe that the non-malleable time-lock puzzle construction nmTLP we described above has a very natural—yet incomplete—public verifiability property. Solving a puzzle yields both the solution s and the randomness r use to generate that puzzle. As such, anyone who solves a valid puzzle can send the opening r to another party, and convince them that s is the unique valid solution to the puzzle. However, we emphasize that this only works for *valid* puzzles and solutions.

Consider the following problematic scenario for our nmTLP construction. Suppose a party "commits" to a value via a puzzle z and refuses to open the commitment. As we said before, if z is a valid puzzle, any party can solve the puzzle, get the solution s and an opening r that proves that s is the unique solution. What if the puzzle corresponds to *no solution*? We refer to this scenario by saying that the puzzle corresponds to the solution $\perp$. In this case (by definition), there is no solution s and opening r for any such that $z = \mathsf{Gen}(t, s; r)$. Anyone who solve the invalid puzzle—which requires a lot of computational power—*will* be able to conclude that the puzzle is malformed, but they will not be able to convince anyone else that this is the case. Ideally, we would have a time-lock puzzle where Sol additionally outputs a publicly verifiable proof π that the solution it computes is correct, even if the solution may be $\perp$! We refer to such a time-lock puzzle as a *publicly verifiable* time-lock puzzle. We next discuss the definition and our construction of publicly verifiable time-lock puzzles.

Defining Public Verifiability. More formally, a publicly verifiable time-lock puzzle consists of algorithms (Gen, Sol, Verify). As with normal time-lock puzzles, $\mathsf{Gen}(t, s)$ outputs a puzzle z. The algorithm $\mathsf{Sol}(t, z)$ outputs the solution s as well as a proof π that it computed s correctly. Finally $\mathsf{Verify}(t, z, (s, \pi))$ checks that s is indeed the correct solution for the puzzle z (corresponding to $\mathsf{Sol}(t, z)$), using the proof π. In addition to (Gen, Sol) being a valid time-lock puzzle, we require that Sol and Verify constitute a sound non-interactive argument. In fact, we require a very strong notion of soundness. We need it to be the case that even for maliciously chosen puzzles that have no solution, the time-lock puzzle is still sound—even against the adversary that generated the malformed puzzle. In other words, we require that no attacker can compute a puzzle z, a value s', and a proof π' such that $\mathsf{Verify}(t, z, (s', \pi'))$ accepts yet s' is not the value s computed by $\mathsf{Sol}(t, z)$, which may be $\perp$.

Ideally, we would want a publicly verifiable time-lock puzzle that requires *no setup*. We instead consider a weak form of setup which we refer to as the All-But-One-string (ABO-string) model. In this model, Sol and Verify additionally take as input a string $\mathsf{mcrs} = (\mathsf{crs}_1, \ldots, \mathsf{crs}_n) \in (\{0, 1\}^\lambda)^n$, and we require that soundness holds as long as one of the values of crs_i is sampled uniformly (without necessarily knowing which one); this is why we refer to it as the all-but-one string model. We note that in multi-party protocols, the ABO-string model is realistic as each participant $i \in [n]$ can post a value for crs_i. Then, we require soundness to hold as long as one participant is honest, which is a reasonable assumption in this multi-party setting.

Constructing Publicly Verifiable Time-Lock Puzzles. Our construction of a publicly verifiable time-lock puzzle follows the blueprint of Rivest, Shamir, and Wagner [45] for constructing time-lock puzzles from repeated squaring. Namely, we use the output of a sequential function (repeated squaring in a suitable group) essentially as one-time pad to mask the value underlying the time-lock puzzle. As in [45], we require that the sequential function has a trapdoor so that puzzles can be generated efficiently. Unlike [45], we additionally require that the sequential function is publicly verifiable to enable publicly verifiability for the time-lock puzzle. Finally, we apply the non-malleability transformation described above to achieve full public verifiability. In what follows, we describe each of these steps in more detail.

For the underlying sequential function, we use what we call a *strong trapdoor verifiable delay function* (VDF). A VDF (introduced by Boneh et al. [7]) is a publicly verifiable sequential function that can be computed in time t but not much faster, even with lots of parallelism. A trapdoor VDF (formalized by Wesolowski [50]) additionally has a trapdoor for quick evaluation. We require a trapdoor VDF in the ABO-string model that satisfies additional properties required by our application. While the properties we define—and achieve—are heavily tailored towards our application, we believe some of the techniques may be of independent interest. More specifically, a strong trapdoor VDF comes with a Sample algorithm to generate inputs for an evaluation algorithm Eval. We emphasize that, even in the ABO-string model, Sample is independent of any form of setup. Previous definitions of VDFs require the proof to be sound with probability over an *honestly sampled* input. In contrast, we require that the proof is sound for any maliciously chosen input that is in the support of the Sample algorithm. We note that this property is satisfied by a variant of Pietrzak's VDF [44] based on repeated squaring. At a high level, this is because Pietrzak's VDF is sound (at least in the random oracle model) for any group of unknown order where no adversary can find a group of low order (see e.g.[8] for further discussion), so by using any RSA group with no low order elements (as in [44]), the proof is sound even if the group is maliciously chosen (yet still a valid RSA group), which gives the strong property we need. We note that the proof of soundness for our strong trapdoor VDF in the ABO-string and auxiliary-input random oracle model follows by a similar argument to that of [44] in the (plain) random oracle model after applying Unruh's result [47].

Next, we construct what we refer to as a *one-sided* publicly verifiable time-lock puzzle in the ABO-string model by using the strong trapdoor VDF in the RSW-style construction described above. By one-sided, we mean that completeness and soundness hold only for puzzles in the support of Gen (again, we emphasize that this is in contrast to a randomly sampled puzzle). Then, our full construction applies our non-malleability transformation to a one-sided publicly verifiable time-lock puzzle. We already argued that the non-malleability transformation provides a form of public verifiability for puzzles z in the support of Gen. Namely, anyone can prove to another party that a valid puzzle z has a solution s, but the proof may not be sound when trying to prove that a puzzle has no solution. However, we next show that if the underlying puzzle satisfies one-sided public verifiability, then the resulting (non-malleable) publicly verifiable TLP is sound for any $z \in \{0,1\}^*$ (possibly not in the support of Gen).

Proof of Full Public Verifiability. Let (Gen, Sol, Verify) be the TLP resulting from applying our non-malleability transformation to a one-sided PV TLP (Gen$_{\mathsf{tlp}}$, Sol$_{\mathsf{tlp}}$, Verify$_{\mathsf{tlp}}$). Consider any puzzle $z \in \{0,1\}^*$. If z is in the support of Gen, we want to ensure that no one can prove that $s' = \bot$ is a valid solution. At the same time, if z is not in the support of Gen, we want to ensure that no one can prove that $s' \neq \bot$ is a valid solution.

When we run Sol(t, z), we first run Sol$_{\mathsf{tlp}}(t, z)$ and get a solution $s_{\mathsf{tlp}} = \hat{s}\|\hat{r}$ with a proof π_{tlp}. If $\hat{r}$ is a valid opening for the proposed solution $\hat{s}$, then Sol can simply output the solution $s = \hat{s}$ and the proof $\pi = \hat{r}$. If $\hat{r}$ is not a valid opening for $\hat{s}$, Sol must output $\bot$ and a proof π that this is the case. We set $\pi = (s_{\mathsf{tlp}}, \pi_{\mathsf{tlp}})$, which intuitively gives anyone else a way to "shortcut" the computation of Sol$_{\mathsf{tlp}}$.

Now suppose that an adversary tries to falsely convince you that a puzzle z with no solution has a solution $s' \neq \bot$ using a proof $\pi' = r'$. To do so, it must be the case that r' is a valid opening for s' with respect to Gen. But if that were the case, then z *would have a solution*, in contradiction.

On the other hand, suppose that an adversary tries to falsely convince you that a puzzle z with solution s has no solution, i.e. $s' = \bot$, using a proof $\pi' = (s'_{\mathsf{tlp}}, \pi'_{\mathsf{tlp}})$. Since z has a solution, it means that z is in the support of Gen$_{\mathsf{tlp}}$. By one-sided public verifiability, this means that π'_{tlp} is a valid proof that $s'_{\mathsf{tlp}} = \hat{s}\|\hat{r}$ is the correct solution to z with respect to Gen$_{\mathsf{tlp}}$. So if $\hat{r}$ is not a valid opening for $\hat{s}$ with respect to Gen, we know the adversary must be lying. In other words, the only way the adversary can cheat is by cheating in the underlying one-sided PV TLP on a puzzle z in the support of Gen$_{\mathsf{tlp}}$.

Discussion of Our Non-malleable PV TLP. We note that the publicly verifiable time-lock puzzle we described above can be made to satisfy the same non-malleability guarantees as we discuss in Sect. 2.1 (as we construct it using the same transformation but with a specific underlying time-lock puzzle). Thus, assuming the repeated squaring assumption, we get a publicly verifiable time-lock puzzle that satisfies concurrent function non-malleability for any class of low depth functions $\mathcal{F}_m$ with output length m. Our construction is in the ABO-string model, and we prove security in the auxiliary-input random oracle model (which is needed for soundness of the strong trapdoor VDF in the ABO-string model in addition to the non-malleability transformation). This model is reasonable for our practical applications to multi-party protocols, as we will see below. Due to the fact that this is a non-black box construction, we note that it does not apply to our non-malleable TLP construction in the plain model.

We also note that our explicit repeated squaring assumption states that repeated squaring in RSA groups for n-bit integers cannot be sped up even by adversaries of size roughly 2^m. The repeated squaring assumption is closely related to the assumption on factoring (which has recently been formalized in different generic models by the works of [28,46]). The current best known algorithms for factoring run in time at least $2^{n^{1/3}}$. In the case where $m \in O(\log \lambda)$, for example, we only require that polynomial-size attackers cannot speed up repeated squaring, which is a relatively mild assumption. In the case where m is larger, say $m = \lambda$, then we need to choose n to be at least λ^3 (based on known algorithms for factoring). This gives an example of the various trade-offs we get for the security and efficiency of our construction depending on the class of low depth functions $\mathcal{F}_m$ that we want non-malleability for.

2.3 Fair Multi-party Protocols

We will focus on coin flipping for concreteness, and note that for auctions the ideas are similar. We give a protocol in auxiliary-input random oracle model, and one in the plain model, depending on which non-malleable TLP construction we use to instantiate it (which result in different guarantees). Here, we describe our random oracle protocol, which captures the main ideas and various properties we can achieve.

At a high level, the coin flipping protocol is very simple. Each party chooses a random bit and publishes a time-lock puzzle that encodes the chosen bit. After all puzzles are published, each party opens their puzzle by revealing the bit that they used as well as the randomness used to generate the puzzle. Any puzzle that is not opened can be "solved" after a moderately large amount of time t. Once all puzzles have been opened, the agreed upon bit (i.e., the output of the protocol) is the XOR of all revealed bits. The above protocol template is appealing because it naturally satisfies optimistic efficiency: if all parties are honest and open their puzzles, the protocol terminates immediately. When using time-lock puzzles which are both non-malleable (as discussed in Sect. 2.1) and publicly verifiable (as discussed in Sect. 2.2), we achieve the following highly desirable properties:

- **Fairness:** No malicious party can bias the output of the protocol.
  This crucially relies on non-malleability for the underlying time-lock puzzle. For a protocol with n participants, we need the time-lock puzzle to satisfy n-concurrent non-malleability. This guarantees that as long as one party is honest, the output of the protocol will be (at least statistically close to) a uniformly random bit.
- **Unbounded participants:** Anyone can participate in the protocol.
  This property might come as a surprise since we show fully concurrent non-malleability is impossible to achieve. However, we emphasize that our time-lock puzzle achieves fully concurrent *functional* non-malleability for the XOR

function. This allows us to deal with any a priori unbounded number of participants, which is important in many decentralized and distributed settings.

- **Public verifiability:** Only one party needs to solve each unopened puzzle, and can provide a publicly verifiable proof that it solved it correctly.

This follows immediately by the public verifiability property we achieve for the underlying time-lock puzzle. Without this property, any unopened puzzles may need to be solved by every party that want to know the output of the protocol, which is prohibitively expensive. However, public verifiability instead opens up the application to *any* party, not even involved in the protocol. Furthermore, this work can even be delegated to an external server since trust is guaranteed by the attached proof.

We note that our non-malleable and publicly verifiable time-lock puzzle is defined in the All-But-One-string (ABO-string) model, which is required for public verifiability. To implement this model, we have each participant i publish a fresh random string $\mathsf{crs}_i \leftarrow \{0,1\}^\lambda$ in addition to its puzzle z_i. Then, whenever some party tries to solve (or verify) a puzzle, it puts all of the random strings together as a multi-common random string $\mathsf{mcrs} = (\mathsf{crs}_1, \ldots, \mathsf{crs}_n)$ from all n participants, and uses this for the publicly verifiable proof. As long as a single party is honest and publishes a random string crs_i independent of all other participants, then the publicly verifiable proof system will be sound.

Simulation-Based Fairness. Finally, we discuss how fairness in the above protocol can be strengthened to a simulation-style definition. Consider running our protocol to get a value s, where s is the XOR of bits underlying the adversary's and honest players' time-lock puzzles. In our simulation-secure protocol, we will set the output to $\mathcal{O}(s)$ where $\mathcal{O}$ is a programmable random oracle. This enables a simulator running in polynomial time to solve the adversary's puzzles and program $\mathcal{O}(s)$ to the desired output value. It then suffices to show that the adversary $\mathcal{A}$ does not detect this change in the oracle, meaning that $\mathcal{A}$ does not query s before publishing its time-lock puzzles. We observe that if $\mathcal{A}$ does indeed query s, it implies an adversary against the game-based fairness of our protocol, that runs $\mathcal{A}$ to get s and outputs a TLP to s along with $\mathcal{A}$'s puzzles, thus biasing the output to $s \oplus s = 0$. We note that this shows that game-based fairness for a standard commit-and-reveal style protocol (with TLPs instead of commitments) can be generically transformed into a simulation-secure protocol by feeding the output into a programmable random oracle.

3 Preliminaries

We first define time-lock puzzles without any additional properties.

Definition 3.1. *Let* $B \colon \mathbb{N} \to \mathbb{N}$. *A* B-*hard time-lock puzzle (TLP) is a tuple* $(\mathsf{Gen}, \mathsf{Sol})$ *with the following syntax:*

- $z \leftarrow \mathsf{Gen}(1^\lambda, t, s)$: *A PPT algorithm that on input a security parameter $\lambda \in \mathbb{N}$, a difficulty parameter $t \in \mathbb{N}$, and a solution $s \in \{0,1\}^\lambda$, outputs a puzzle $z \in \{0,1\}^*$.*
- $s = \mathsf{Sol}(1^\lambda, t, z)$: *A deterministic algorithm that on input a security parameter $\lambda \in \mathbb{N}$, a difficulty parameter $t \in \mathbb{N}$, and a puzzle $z \in \{0,1\}^*$, outputs a solution $s \in (\{0,1\}^\lambda \cup \{\bot\})$.*

We require $(\mathsf{Gen}, \mathsf{Sol})$ to satisfy the following properties.

- **Correctness:** *For every $\lambda, t \in \mathbb{N}$, solution $s \in \{0,1\}^\lambda$, and $z \in \mathrm{Supp}\big(\mathsf{Gen}(1^\lambda, t, s)\big)$, it holds that $\mathsf{Sol}(1^\lambda, t, z) = s$.*
- **Efficiency:** *There exist a polynomial p such that for all $\lambda, t \in \mathbb{N}$, $\mathsf{Sol}(1^\lambda, t, \cdot)$ is computable in time $t \cdot p(\lambda, \log t)$.*
- **B-Hardness:** *There exists a positive polynomial function α such that for all functions T and non-uniform distinguishers $\mathcal{A} = \{\mathcal{A}_\lambda\}_{\lambda \in \mathbb{N}}$ satisfying $\alpha(\lambda) \le T(\lambda) \in B(\lambda) \cdot \mathrm{poly}(\lambda)$, $\mathsf{size}(\mathcal{A}_\lambda) \in \mathcal{B}(\lambda) \cdot \mathrm{poly}(\lambda)$, and $\mathsf{depth}(\mathcal{A}_\lambda) \le T(\lambda)/\alpha(\lambda)$ for all $\lambda \in \mathbb{N}$, there exists a negligible function negl such that for all $\lambda \in \mathbb{N}$, and $s, s' \in \{0,1\}^\lambda$,*

$$\Big| \Pr\Big[\mathcal{A}_\lambda(\mathsf{Gen}(1^\lambda, T(\lambda), s)) = 1\Big] - \Pr\Big[\mathcal{A}_\lambda(\mathsf{Gen}(1^\lambda, T(\lambda), s')) = 1\Big]\Big| \le \mathsf{negl}(\lambda),$$

where the probabilities are over the randomness of Gen and $\mathcal{A}_\lambda$.

When $B(\lambda) \in \mathrm{poly}(\lambda)$, we say that the TLP is polynomially-hard.

In the above definition, we assume for simplicity that the solutions s are λ-bits long. We can naturally generalize this to consider the case where solutions have some specified length $L(\lambda)$. We emphasize that the notion of B-hardness above suffices to capture both polynomial security and sub-exponential security, as it captures hardness against adversaries of size $B(\lambda)$, up to polynomial factors.

Non-malleable Time-Lock Puzzles. To formalize non-malleability in the context of time-lock puzzles, we introduce a Man-In-the-Middle (MIM) adversary. Because time-lock puzzles are designed to be broken in some depth t, we restrict our MIM adversary to have at most depth $t/\alpha(\lambda)$ for a function α denoting the advantage of the adversary. Furthermore, we allow for concurrent MIM adversaries that possibly interact with many senders and receivers at the same time.

Definition 3.2 (MIM Adversaries). *Let $n_L, n_R, B_{\mathsf{nm}}, \alpha, T \colon \mathbb{N} \to \mathbb{N}$. An $(n_L, n_R, B_{\mathsf{nm}}, \alpha, T)$-Man-In-the-Middle (MIM) adversary is a non-uniform algorithm $\mathcal{A} = \{\mathcal{A}_\lambda\}_{\lambda \in \mathbb{N}}$ satisfying $\mathsf{depth}(\mathcal{A}_\lambda) \le T(\lambda)/\alpha(\lambda)$ and $\mathsf{size}(\mathcal{A}_\lambda) \in \mathcal{B}_{\mathsf{nm}}(\lambda) \cdot \mathrm{poly}(\lambda)$ for all $\lambda \in \mathbb{N}$ that receives $n_L(\lambda)$ puzzles on the left and outputs $n_R(\lambda)$ puzzles on the right.*

We next define the MIM distribution, which corresponds to the values underlying the puzzles output by the MIM adversary. To capture adversaries that simply forward one of the puzzles on the left to a receiver on the right, we set the value for any forwarded puzzle to be $\bot$.

Definition 3.3 (MIM Distribution]). *Let $n_L, n_R, B_{nm}, \alpha, T \colon \mathbb{N} \to \mathbb{N}$. Let $\mathcal{A} = \{\mathcal{A}_\lambda\}_{\lambda \in \mathbb{N}}$ be an $(n_L, n_R, B_{nm}, \alpha, T)$-MIM adversary. For any $\lambda \in \mathbb{N}$ and $\vec{s} = (s_1, \ldots, s_{n_L(\lambda)}) \in (\{0,1\}^\lambda)^{n_L(\lambda)}$, we define the distribution*

$$(\widetilde{s}_1, \ldots, \widetilde{s}_{n_R(\lambda)}) \leftarrow \mathsf{mim}_{\mathcal{A}}(1^\lambda, T(\lambda), \vec{s})$$

as follows. $\mathcal{A}_\lambda$ receives puzzles $z_i \leftarrow \mathsf{Gen}(1^\lambda, T(\lambda), s_i)$ for all $i \in [n_L(\lambda)]$ and outputs puzzles $(\widetilde{z}_1, \ldots, \widetilde{z}_{n_R(\lambda)})$. Then for each $i \in [n_R(\lambda)]$, we define

$$\widetilde{s}_i = \begin{cases} \bot & \text{if there exists a } j \in [n_L(\lambda)) \text{ such that } \widetilde{z}_i = z_j, \\ \mathsf{Sol}(1^\lambda, T(\lambda), \widetilde{z}_i) & \text{otherwise.} \end{cases}$$

Intuitively, a time-lock puzzle is non-malleable if the MIM distribution of a bounded depth attacker does not depend on the solutions underlying the puzzles it receives on the left. We formalize this definition below.

Definition 3.4 (Concurrent Non-malleable). *Let $n_L, n_R, B_{nm} \colon \mathbb{N} \to \mathbb{N}$. A time-lock puzzle is (n_L, n_R)-concurrent non-malleable against adversaries of size B_{nm} if there exists a positive polynomial α such that for every function T with $\alpha(\lambda) \leq T(\lambda) \in B_{nm}(\lambda) \cdot \mathrm{poly}(\lambda)$ for all $\lambda \in \mathbb{N}$, and every $(n_L, n_R, B_{nm}, \alpha, T)$-MIM adversary $\mathcal{A} = \{\mathcal{A}_\lambda\}_{\lambda \in \mathbb{N}}$, the following holds.*

For any distinguisher $\mathcal{D}$, there exists a negligible function negl such that for all $\lambda \in \mathbb{N}$ and $\vec{s} = (s_1, \ldots, s_{n_L(\lambda)}) \in (\{0,1\}^\lambda)^{n_L(\lambda)}$,

$$\left| \Pr\left[\mathcal{D}(\mathsf{mim}_{\mathcal{A}}(1^\lambda, T(\lambda), \vec{s})) = 1 \right] - \Pr\left[\mathcal{D}(\mathsf{mim}_{\mathcal{A}}(1^\lambda, T(\lambda), (0^\lambda)^{n_L(\lambda)})) = 1 \right] \right|$$
$$\leq \mathsf{negl}(\lambda).$$

When $B_{nm}(\lambda) = 1$, we say the TLP is (n_L, n_R)-concurrent non-malleable. When this only holds against non-uniform PPT distinguishers $\mathcal{D}$, we say that the time-lock puzzle is computationally (n_L, n_R)-concurrent non-malleable.

Relation to Non-malleable Commitments.

When defining non-malleability for TLPs, a natural attempt is to view TLPs as commitments, and give a definition analogous to non-malleable commitments. This is usually formalized as either non-malleability with respect to commitment, or non-malleability with respect to extraction. The former notion requires that no man-in-the-middle adversary can maul a commitment z to s into a commitment $\widetilde{z}$ whose unique underlying value is related to s, whereas the latter notion requires that $\mathcal{E}(\widetilde{z})$ is unrelated to s, where $\mathcal{E}$ is a given extractor. When $\mathcal{E}$ has the guarantee that it outputs the committed value on valid commitments and $\bot$ on invalid ones, these notions are equivalent. However, when considering extractors that may output arbitrary values when given invalid commitments, these notions are incomparable in general. In the context of time-lock puzzles, we observe that Sol is the natural extractor for Gen, and moreover that non-malleability should capture adversaries that maul a puzzle into one that solves to a related value. Therefore, our definition above is analogous to non-malleability with respect to extraction, where Sol is the extractor.

Next, we consider standard variants for the definition of non-malleable above.

Definition 3.5. *We say the a TLP satisfies the following non-malleability properties when Definition 3.4 holds against* $(n_L, n_R, B_{nm}, \alpha, T)$-*MIM adversaries for the following settings of* n_L *and* n_R:

- *fully concurrent non-malleable if the definition holds against any* $n_L, n_R \in \text{poly}(\lambda)$,
- *one-many non-malleable if the definition holds for any* $n_R(\lambda) \in \text{poly}(\lambda)$ *and* $n_L = 1$,
- n-*concurrent non-malleable if the definition holds for* $n_L = n_R = n$,
- *one-*n *non-malleable for* $n_L(\lambda) = 1$ *and* $n_R = n$,
- *and simply non-malleable (not concurrent) for* $n_L(\lambda) = n_R(\lambda) = 1$.

4   Non-malleable Time-Lock Puzzles

We start by defining the notion of functional non-malleability for time-lock puzzles. Then, we give the transformation from any time-lock puzzle to one that satisfies concurrent functional non-malleability for depth bounded functions, in the auxiliary input random oracle model, and discuss how this result implies a time-lock puzzle satisfying bounded concurrent (standard) non-malleability.

Functional Non-malleability. In the following definition, we focus on the case of unbounded concurrency, but note that can be defined for restricted cases as in Definition 3.5.

Definition 4.1 (Concurrent Functional Non-malleable). *Let* B_{nm}, L: $\mathbb{N} \to \mathbb{N}$, *and* (Gen, Sol) *be a time-lock puzzle for messages of length* $L(\lambda)$. *Let* $\mathcal{F}$ *be a class of functions of the form* $f: (\{0,1\}^{L(\lambda)})^* \to \{0,1\}^*$. *We say that* (Gen, Sol) *is concurrent functional non-malleable for* $\mathcal{F}$ *against* B_{nm}-*size adversaries if for any function* $f \in \mathcal{F}$ *and polynomial* n, *there exists a polynomial* α *such that for every function* T *with* $\alpha(\lambda) \leq T(\lambda) \in B_{nm}(\lambda) \cdot \text{poly}(\lambda)$ *for all* $\lambda \in \mathbb{N}$, *every* $(n, n, B_{nm}, \alpha, T)$-*MIM adversary* $\mathcal{A} = \{\mathcal{A}_\lambda\}_{\lambda \in \mathbb{N}}$, *the following holds.*

For any distinguisher $\mathcal{D}$, *there exists a negligible function* negl *such that for all* $\lambda \in \mathbb{N}$ *and* $\vec{s} = (s_1, \ldots, s_{n(\lambda)}) \in (\{0,1\}^{L(\lambda)})^{n(\lambda)}$,

$$\left| \Pr\left[\vec{\tilde{s}} \leftarrow \text{mim}_{\mathcal{A}}(1^\lambda, T(\lambda), \vec{s}) : \mathcal{D}(f(\vec{\tilde{s}})) = 1 \right] \right.$$

$$\left. - \Pr\left[\vec{\tilde{s}} \leftarrow \text{mim}_{\mathcal{A}}(1^\lambda, T(\lambda), (0^{L(\lambda)})^{n(\lambda)}) : \mathcal{D}(f(\vec{\tilde{s}})) = 1 \right] \right| \leq \text{negl}(\lambda).$$

When $B_{nm}(\lambda) = 1$, *we say the TLP is concurrent functional non-malleable for* $\mathcal{F}$. *When the above only holds against non-uniform PPT distinguishers* $\mathcal{D}$, *we say the TLP is computationally functional non-malleable for* $\mathcal{F}$.

We note that functional non-malleability for a class $\mathcal{F}$ that contains the identity function id implies standard non-malleability as $\mathcal{D}(\text{id}(\vec{\tilde{s}})) = \mathcal{D}(\vec{\tilde{s}})$.

4.1   Non-malleable Time-Lock Puzzle Construction

In this section, we give our construction of a fully concurrent functional non-malleable time-lock puzzle for functions with bounded depth and output length. We rely on the following building blocks and parameters.

- A function m denoting the output length for our function non-malleability. We require $m(\lambda) \in \text{poly}(\lambda)$. Throughout this section, where λ is clear from context, we let $m = m(\lambda)$.
- A B_{tlp}-hard time-lock puzzle $\text{TLP} = (\text{Gen}_{\text{tlp}}, \text{Sol}_{\text{tlp}})$ for $B_{\text{tlp}}(\lambda) = 2^{3m}$. We let $\lambda_{\text{tlp}} = \lambda_{\text{tlp}}(\lambda) \in \text{poly}(\lambda, m)$ be the bits of randomness needed for TLP on security parameter λ, for solutions of length $2m + 2\lambda$.
- A class of functions $\mathcal{F}_m$ of the form $f \colon (\{0,1\}^\lambda)^* \to \{0,1\}^{m(\lambda)}$. We assume that there exists a polynomial d such that for every polynomial n, every function $f \in \mathcal{F}_m$ can be computed in depth $d(\lambda, \log n(\lambda))$ and polynomial size on inputs of length at most $\lambda \cdot n(\lambda)$.
- A random oracle $\mathcal{O} \in \text{RF}_{2\lambda+2m}^{\lambda_{\text{tlp}}}$, where $\mathcal{O}$ on input $(s, r) \in \{0,1\}^{\lambda+(2m+\lambda)}$ outputs a random value $r' \in \{0,1\}^{\lambda_{\text{tlp}}}$.

Our construction $\text{nmTLP}_m = (\text{Gen}, \text{Sol})$ in the random oracle model:

- $z = \text{Gen}^{\mathcal{O}}(1^\lambda, t, s; r)$:
  1. Get $r' = \mathcal{O}(s, r)$.
  2. Output $z = \text{Gen}_{\text{tlp}}(1^\lambda, t, (s\|r); r')$.
- $s = \text{Sol}^{\mathcal{O}}(1^\lambda, t, z)$:
  1. Compute $s' = \text{Sol}_{\text{tlp}}(1^\lambda, t, z)$ and parse $s' = s\|r$.
  2. If $z = \text{Gen}^{\mathcal{O}}(1^\lambda, t, s; r)$, output s.
  3. If not, output $\bot$.

Theorem 4.2 (Fully Concurrent Functional Non-Malleable TLPs). *Let $m(\lambda) \in \text{poly}(\lambda)$, $B_{\text{hard}}(\lambda) = 2^{m(\lambda)}$, and $B_{\text{tlp}}(\lambda) = 2^{3m(\lambda)}$. Assuming TLP is a B_{tlp}-hard time-lock puzzle, then nmTLP_m is a B_{hard}-hard fully concurrent functional non-malleable time-lock puzzle in the AI-ROM for the class of functions $\mathcal{F}_m$.*

We observe the following corollaries to the above theorem:

- If $m(\lambda) \in O(\log(\lambda))$ then we can simply assume a polynomially-hard TLP.
- For any $m(\lambda) \in \text{poly}(\lambda)$, our theorem follows by assuming a sub-exponentially secure TLP. Specifically, it suffices that there exists a constant $\gamma \in (0, 1)$ such that $B_{\text{tlp}}(\lambda) = 2^{\lambda^\gamma}$, and we can instantiate this with $\lambda_{\text{tlp}} = (\lambda + 3m(\lambda))^{1/\gamma}$ bits of randomness.

We also observe that the above theorem can be used to get n-bounded concurrency for any polynomial n, simply by setting the output length m of the functions in $\mathcal{F}_m$ to $\lambda \cdot n(\lambda)$. Specifically, let f_{id} be the identity function with input and output length $\lambda \cdot n(\lambda)$. Since $f_{\text{id}} \in \mathcal{F}_{\lambda \cdot n(\lambda)}$, a fully concurrent functional non-malleable TLP for $\mathcal{F}_{\lambda \cdot n(\lambda)}$ implies an n-concurrent non-malleable TLP, which gives the following corollary.

Corollary 4.3 (n-Concurrent Non-Malleable TLPs). *Let* $n(\lambda) \in$ poly(λ), $B_{\text{hard}}(\lambda) = 2^{\lambda \cdot n(\lambda)}$, *and* $B_{\text{tlp}}(\lambda) = 2^{3\lambda \cdot n(\lambda)}$. *Assuming* TLP *is a* B_{tlp}-*hard time-lock puzzle, then* nmTLP$_{\lambda \cdot n(\lambda)}$ *is a* B_{hard}-*hard n-concurrent non-malleable time-lock puzzle in the AI-ROM.*

The proof of Theorem 4.2 is deferred to the full version.

5   Applications to Multi-party Coin Flipping and Auctions

In this section, we discuss our fair multi-party protocols. We focus on the case of multi-party coin flipping and address auctions in Remark 1 below. We note that this section focuses on game-based fairness, and the extension to simulation security is given in the full version.

Our multi-party coin flipping protocol is based generically on any time-lock puzzle. Fairness follows when the time-lock puzzle satisfies concurrent functional non-malleability for the XOR function $f_\oplus$. Specifically, in order to produce L bits of randomness, we need concurrent functional non-malleability for the function $f_\oplus: (\{0,1\}^L)^* \to \{0,1\}^L$ that on input $(r_1, \ldots, r_n)$ outputs $\bigoplus_{r_i \neq \perp} r_i$. Our protocol satisfies various additional properties, depending on the time-lock puzzle:

- Given a publicly verifiable time-lock puzzle, the resulting protocol is publicly verifiable. In this setting, our protocol can either be made interactive, or non-interactive.
- If the time-lock puzzle is not publicly verifiable, the resulting protocol is non-interactive, and does not achieve public verifiability.

In what follows, we present our results in the public verifiability setting, and discuss differences with the non-publicly verifiable setting when relevant.

We describe our protocol in a public bulletin board model, where any party may "publish" a message that all other parties will see within some fixed time. Our protocol consists four phases: a commit phase, open phase, force open phase, and output phase. The commit and open phases consist of a single synchronous round of communication where all participating parties publish a message on the bulletin board. The force open phase can be computed by any party, and only needs to be computed by a single (honest) party if the underlying time-lock puzzle is publicly verifiable. Once all puzzles have been opened (or force opened), any party can run the output phase to get the output of the protocol. In the non-interactive version of the protocol, the open phase is omitted and every party runs the force open phase themselves, and uses the resulting values to compute the output of the protocol locally. When we refer to an *honest* participant, we mean a party that runs the protocol as specified, independent of all other participants.

For any $L: \mathbb{N} \to \mathbb{N}$, let (Gen, Sol, Verify) be a publicly verifiable time-lock puzzle (in the ABO string model) with message length $L(\lambda)$ that satisfies concurrent functional non-malleability for the function $f_\oplus$ (which has output length

$L(\lambda)$). We additionally let $\alpha(\lambda)$ be the advantage of any attacker guaranteed by the functional non-malleability of the time-lock puzzle. The protocol takes as common input a security parameter λ and a polynomial time bound $t = T(\lambda)$ that satisfies the following requirements. First, we require that the commit phase takes time less than $T(\lambda)/\alpha(\lambda)$ such that functional non-malleability (and hence hardness) are preserved during the protocol. At the same time, the commit phase needs to be long enough so that all participants can generate and publish their puzzles.

- **Commit phase:** Each participant i samples $s_i \leftarrow \{0,1\}^{L(\lambda)}$ and $r_i, \mathsf{crs}_i \leftarrow \{0,1\}^\lambda$, computes $z_i = \mathsf{Gen}(1^\lambda, t, s_i; r_i)$, and publishes z_i and crs_i. Let $\mathsf{mcrs} = (\mathsf{crs}_1, \ldots, \mathsf{crs}_n)$. Any puzzle that is a copy of a previously posted puzzle is ignored.
- **Open phase:** Each participant i that published in the commit phase publishes the solution s_i and with an opening r_i.
- **Force open phase:** For each puzzle z_j, if either (a) there is no published solution s_j and opening r_j or (b) if $z_j \neq \mathsf{Gen}(1^\lambda, t, s_j; r_j)$, compute and publish $(s_j, \pi_j) \leftarrow \mathsf{Sol}(1^\lambda, \mathsf{mcrs}, t, z_j)$ (where s_j might be $\perp$).
- **Output phase:** If for every puzzle z_j and solution s_j, either (a) there is a published opening r_j such that $z_j = \mathsf{Gen}(1^\lambda, t, s_j; r_j)$ or (b) a published proof π_j such that $\mathsf{Verify}(1^\lambda, \mathsf{mcrs}, t, z_j, (s_j, \pi_j)) = 1$, then output $s = \bigoplus_{s_j \neq \perp} s_j$.

We note that the protocol above does not assume an a priori bound on the number of participants. Furthermore, there is no external setup needed by the protocol. All participants, however, do publish a random string $\mathsf{crs}_i \leftarrow \{0,1\}^\lambda$ that can be used to implement the ABO-string model for $(\mathsf{Gen}, \mathsf{Sol}, \mathsf{Verify})$.

Theorem 5.1. *Let $L(\lambda) \in \mathrm{poly}(\lambda)$. Assume the existence of a publicly verifiable time-lock puzzle for $L(\lambda)$ bit messages in the ABO-string model that satisfies concurrent function non-malleability for $f_\oplus$ with $L(\lambda)$ bit output. Then, there exists a multi-party coin flipping protocol that outputs $L(\lambda)$ bits and satisfies optimistic efficiency, fairness, and public verifiability. The protocol supports an unbounded number of participants and requires no adversary-independent trusted setup.*

We obtain the following result by using our publicly verifiable non-malleable TLP construction (given in the full version) with the above theorem.

Corollary 5.2. *Let $B, L \colon \mathbb{N} \to \mathbb{N}$ where $B(\lambda) = 2^{3L(\lambda)}$. Assuming the B-repeated squaring assumption for RSWGen, there exists a multi-party coin flipping protocol that outputs $L(\lambda)$ bits and satisfies optimistic efficiency, fairness, and public verifiability. The protocol supports an unbounded number of participants and requires no adversary-independent trusted setup. Security is proven in the auxiliary-input random oracle model.*

Finally, we note that if we instead start with our non-malleable time-lock puzzle in the plain model (which is not publicly verifiable) the non-interactive

474   C. Freitag et al.

variant of our protocol gives non-interactive coin flipping in the plain model. In particular, we obtain the following theorem based on our plain model construction (given in the full version).

Theorem 5.3. *Let* $L\colon \mathbb{N} \to \mathbb{N}$ *and* $S(\lambda) = 2^{\lambda + L(\lambda)}$. *Assume a time-lock puzzle, a keyless multi-collision resistant hash function, a non-interactive witness indistinguishable proof for* NP, *and injective one-way functions, all sub-exponentially secure, where in particular the time-lock puzzle is secure against polynomial-depth adversaries of size* S. *Then, there exist fully non-interactive fair multi-party coin flipping protocol that outputs* $L(\lambda)$ *bits, where fairness holds against non-uniform polynomial time distinguishers. The protocol supports an unbounded number of participants and requires no setup.*

We note that if we only consider protocols that output $L(\lambda) \in O(\log \lambda)$ bits, then fairness against polynomial time distinguishers implies statistical fairness. This is because if there is an unbounded distinguisher for $O(\log \lambda)$ bits, we can construct a polynomial time distinguisher that simply hard codes the truth table of the unbounded distinguisher.

We remark how we can adapt our protocol to deal with auctions.

Remark 1 (Multi-Party Auctions). For our application to auctions, we consider a standard second-price, sealed-bid auction, in which the auctioned item is assigned to the highest bidder who pays the second highest bid for the item. We assume some form of authenticated channels so we can know the bidders' identities in order to distribute the auctioned items. We leave these as external implementation details for the protocol. The main protocol proceeds as follows.

In the commit phase, each participant computes a time-lock puzzle to their bid. The open and force open phases are identical to the case of coin flipping. Then in the output phase, we need to determine the identity of the highest bidder and the value of the second highest bid.

The function that computes the output consists of finding the top two values in a set. This can be computed in low depth (doing a tree of comparisons in parallel) and has output length $\log n + \log M$ where n is the number of participants and M is a bound on the largest valid bid. Thus, using our publicly verifiable time-lock puzzle that satisfies concurrent functional non-malleability for this function, the resulting protocol is secure assuming $n \cdot M \cdot \text{poly}(\lambda)$ security for the repeated squaring assumption. Assuming n and M are polynomially bounded, we only need polynomial security assumptions.

The proof of Theorem 5.1 is deferred to the full version.

Acknowledgements. This work was supported in part by NSF Award SATC-1704788, NSF Award RI-1703846, NSF Award DGE-1650441, AFOSR Award FA9550-18-1-0267, DARPA Award HR00110C0086, and a JP Morgan Faculty Award. Ilan Komargodski is supported in part by an Alon Young Faculty Fellowship and by an ISF grant (No. 1774/20). This research is based upon work supported in part by the Office of the Director of National Intelligence (ODNI), Intelligence Advanced Research

Projects Activity (IARPA), via 2019-19-020700006. The views and conclusions contained herein are those of the authors and should not be interpreted as necessarily representing the official policies, either expressed or implied, of ODNI, IARPA, or the U.S. Government. The U.S. Government is authorized to reproduce and distribute reprints for governmental purposes notwithstanding any copyright annotation therein.

A   Discussion of Non-malleable Definitions

We briefly discuss the different notions of non-malleability studied in this work. Specifically, we compare standard non-malleability (Definition 3.4), non- malleability against depth-bounded distinguishers, and functional non-malleability (Definition 4.1). In Sect. 1.3, we also discuss the definitions considered in the concurrent works of [3,4,28].

Common to all of our definitions, there is a depth-bounded man-in-the-middle (MIM) attacker, which we call $\mathcal{A}$, that on input a puzzle z with solution s tries to output a different puzzle $\tilde{z}$ to a related value $\tilde{s}$. Here, $\mathcal{A}$ is depth-bounded relative to the difficulty of the puzzle, so it should not be able to solve the puzzle. The definitions vary in what it means for $\tilde{s}$ to be "related" to s. For our standard notion of non-malleability, we require that no unbounded distinguisher $\mathcal{D}$ on input $\tilde{s}$ can tell if it came from the experiment starting with s or the all-zero string. In the definition of non-malleability against depth-bounded distinguishers, $\mathcal{D}$ is restricted to be depth-bounded in the same way as $\mathcal{A}$. In the case of functional non-malleability, the (unbounded) distinguisher $\mathcal{D}$ receives instead as input $f(\tilde{s})$ where f is a low-depth function. We parameterize functional non-malleability by an output length m. When $m = |s|$, this captures plain non-malleability by considering f to be the identity function. When $m = 1$, this captures depth-bounded distinguisher non-malleability as f essentially plays the role of the depth-bounded distinguisher $\mathcal{D}$. In Theorem 4.2, we show how to construct a time-lock puzzle satisfying functional non-malleability for any output length m assuming a time-lock puzzle that is $2^m \cdot \mathrm{poly}(\lambda)$ secure.

When considering concurrent non-malleability, the MIM attacker $\mathcal{A}$ receives possibly multiple puzzles $z_1, \ldots, z_{n_L}$ that have solutions $s_1, \ldots, s_{n_L}$ as input and tries to output multiple puzzles $\tilde{z}_1, \ldots, \tilde{z}_{n_R}$ (different from its inputs) corresponding to $\tilde{s}_1, \ldots, \tilde{s}_{n_R}$. In the most general form, we can consider some distinguisher $\mathcal{D}$ that receives as input $f(\tilde{s}_1, \ldots, \tilde{s}_{n_R})$ and tries to tell if it came from the experiment starting with $s_1, \ldots, s_{n_L}$ or with n_L all-zero strings. We show in the full version that if the MIM attacker can encode a time-lock puzzle into the value $f(\tilde{s}_1, \ldots, \tilde{s}_{n_R})$ (where f may be the identity), then the construction cannot be secure against an unbounded distinguisher. In particular, if the function's output length m is greater than the output length of the time-lock puzzle, the scheme may not be secure. On the other hand, our construction of Theorem 4.2 works for functional non-malleability even in the fully concurrent setting, as the output length of f is bounded. So, as long as the output length of the function f is sufficiently small, we can support unbounded concurrency.

Finally, our separation in the full version gives a construction that satisfies plain (non-concurrent) non-malleability against depth-bounded distinguishers yet does not satisfy non-malleability against unbounded distinguishers. We remark that in the setting where the message length for the puzzle is 1 bit, these notions are equivalent by simply considering the depth-bounded distinguisher that outputs the bit it gets as input. Moreover, it can be shown that they are equivalent as long as the message length is in $O(\log \lambda)$. Therefore, this separation necessarily relies on the fact that the message length for the puzzle is in $\omega(\log \lambda)$.

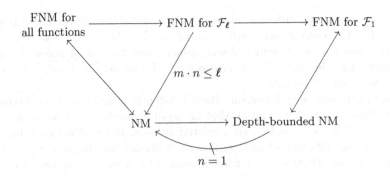

Fig. 1. Relationship between notions of non-malleability. An arrow from A to B indicates that any construction satisfying A also satisfies B. Here, m is the message length, n is the concurrency, and $\mathcal{F}_\ell$ is class of depth-bounded functions with ℓ-bit output.

We summarize the various relationships between the definitions in Fig. 1.

References

1. Barak, B.: Constant-round coin-tossing with a man in the middle or realizing the shared random string model. In: 43rd Symposium on Foundations of Computer Science FOCS, pp. 345–355 (2002)
2. Barak, B., Prabhakaran, M., Sahai, A.: Concurrent non-malleable zero knowledge. In: 47th Annual IEEE Symposium on Foundations of Computer Science (FOCS), pp. 345–354 (2006)
3. Baum, C., David, B., Dowsley, R., Nielsen, J.B., Oechsner, S.: Craft: composable randomness and almost fairness from time. Cryptology ePrint Archive, Report 2020/784 (2020). https://eprint.iacr.org/2020/784
4. Baum, C., David, B., Dowsley, R., Nielsen, J.B., Oechsner, S.: TARDIS: a foundation of time-lock puzzles in UC. In: Canteaut, A., Standaert, F.-X. (eds.) EUROCRYPT 2021. LNCS, vol. 12698, pp. 429–459. Springer, Cham (2021). https://doi.org/10.1007/978-3-030-77883-5_15
5. Bentov, I., Pass, R., Shi, E.: Snow white: provably secure proofs of stake. IACR Cryptol. ePrint Arch. **2016**, 919 (2016)
6. Bitansky, N., Goldwasser, S., Jain, A., Paneth, O., Vaikuntanathan, V., Waters, B.: Time-lock puzzles from randomized encodings. In: ITCS (2016)
7. Boneh, D., Bonneau, J., Bünz, B., Fisch, B.: Verifiable delay functions. In: Shacham, H., Boldyreva, A. (eds.) CRYPTO 2018. LNCS, vol. 10991, pp. 757–788. Springer, Cham (2018). https://doi.org/10.1007/978-3-319-96884-1_25

8. Boneh, D., Bünz, B., Fisch, B.: A survey of two verifiable delay functions. IACR Cryptol. ePrint Arch. **2018**, 712 (2018)
9. Boneh, D., Naor, M.: Timed commitments. In: Bellare, M. (ed.) CRYPTO 2000. LNCS, vol. 1880, pp. 236–254. Springer, Heidelberg (2000). https://doi.org/10.1007/3-540-44598-6_15
10. Canetti, R.: Universally composable security: a new paradigm for cryptographic protocols. In: FOCS, pp. 136–145. IEEE Computer Society (2001)
11. Ciampi, M., Ostrovsky, R., Siniscalchi, L., Visconti, I.: Concurrent non-malleable commitments (and more) in 3 rounds. In: Robshaw, M., Katz, J. (eds.) CRYPTO 2016. LNCS, vol. 9816, pp. 270–299. Springer, Heidelberg (2016). https://doi.org/10.1007/978-3-662-53015-3_10
12. Ciampi, M., Ostrovsky, R., Siniscalchi, L., Visconti, I.: Four-round concurrent non-malleable commitments from one-way functions. In: Katz, J., Shacham, H. (eds.) CRYPTO 2017. LNCS, vol. 10402, pp. 127–157. Springer, Cham (2017). https://doi.org/10.1007/978-3-319-63715-0_5
13. Cleve, R.: Limits on the security of coin flips when half the processors are faulty (extended abstract). In: Proceedings of the 18th Annual ACM Symposium on Theory of Computing, STOC, pp. 364–369 (1986)
14. Coretti, S., Dodis, Y., Guo, S., Steinberger, J.: Random oracles and non-uniformity. In: Nielsen, J.B., Rijmen, V. (eds.) EUROCRYPT 2018. LNCS, vol. 10820, pp. 227–258. Springer, Cham (2018). https://doi.org/10.1007/978-3-319-78381-9_9
15. Dachman-Soled, D., Komargodski, I., Pass, R.: Non-malleable codes for bounded parallel-time tampering. In: Malkin, T., Peikert, C. (eds.) CRYPTO 2021. LNCS, vol. 12827, pp. 535–565. Springer, Cham (2021). https://doi.org/10.1007/978-3-030-84252-9_18
16. Daian, P., Pass, R., Shi, E.: Snow White: robustly reconfigurable consensus and applications to provably secure proof of stake. In: Goldberg, I., Moore, T. (eds.) FC 2019. LNCS, vol. 11598, pp. 23–41. Springer, Cham (2019). https://doi.org/10.1007/978-3-030-32101-7_2
17. David, B., Gaži, P., Kiayias, A., Russell, A.: Ouroboros praos: an adaptively-secure, semi-synchronous proof-of-stake blockchain. In: Nielsen, J.B., Rijmen, V. (eds.) EUROCRYPT 2018. LNCS, vol. 10821, pp. 66–98. Springer, Cham (2018). https://doi.org/10.1007/978-3-319-78375-8_3
18. Dolev, D., Dwork, C., Naor, M.: Non-malleable cryptography (extended abstract). In: Proceedings of the 23rd Annual ACM Symposium on Theory of Computing, STOC, pp. 542–552 (1991)
19. Ephraim, N., Freitag, C., Komargodski, I., Pass, R.: Continuous verifiable delay functions. IACR Cryptol. ePrint Arch. **2019**, 619 (2019)
20. Fuchsbauer, G., Kiltz, E., Loss, J.: The algebraic group model and its applications. In: Shacham, H., Boldyreva, A. (eds.) CRYPTO 2018. LNCS, vol. 10992, pp. 33–62. Springer, Cham (2018). https://doi.org/10.1007/978-3-319-96881-0_2
21. Fujisaki, E., Okamoto, T.: Secure integration of asymmetric and symmetric encryption schemes. J. Cryptol. **26**(1), 80–101 (2013)
22. Goyal, V.: Constant round non-malleable protocols using one way functions. In: Fortnow, L., Vadhan, S.P. (eds.) Proceedings of the 43rd ACM Symposium on Theory of Computing, STOC, pp. 695–704 (2011)
23. Goyal, V., Lee, C., Ostrovsky, R., Visconti, I.: Constructing non-malleable commitments: a black-box approach. In: 53rd Annual IEEE Symposium on Foundations of Computer Science, FOCS, pp. 51–60 (2012)

24. Goyal, V., Pandey, O., Richelson, S.: Textbook non-malleable commitments. In: Proceedings of the 48th Annual ACM SIGACT Symposium on Theory of Computing, STOC, pp. 1128–1141 (2016)
25. Groth, J., Ostrovsky, R.: Cryptography in the multi-string model. J. Cryptol. **27**(3), 506–543 (2014)
26. Hohenberger, S., Myers, S., Pass, R., Shelat, A.: An overview of ANONIZE: a large-scale anonymous survey system. IEEE Secur. Priv. **13**(2), 22–29 (2015)
27. Kalai, Y.T., Khurana, D.: Non-interactive non-malleability from quantum supremacy. In: Boldyreva, A., Micciancio, D. (eds.) CRYPTO 2019. LNCS, vol. 11694, pp. 552–582. Springer, Cham (2019). https://doi.org/10.1007/978-3-030-26954-8_18
28. Katz, J., Loss, J., Xu, J.: On the security of time-lock puzzles and timed commitments. In: Pass, R., Pietrzak, K. (eds.) TCC 2020. LNCS, vol. 12552, pp. 390–413. Springer, Cham (2020). https://doi.org/10.1007/978-3-030-64381-2_14
29. Khurana, D.: Round optimal concurrent non-malleability from polynomial hardness. In: Kalai, Y., Reyzin, L. (eds.) TCC 2017. LNCS, vol. 10678, pp. 139–171. Springer, Cham (2017). https://doi.org/10.1007/978-3-319-70503-3_5
30. Khurana, D., Sahai, A.: How to achieve non-malleability in one or two rounds. In: 58th IEEE Annual Symposium on Foundations of Computer Science, FOCS, pp. 564–575 (2017)
31. Lin, H., Pass, R.: Non-malleability amplification. In: Proceedings of the 41st Annual ACM Symposium on Theory of Computing, STOC, pp. 189–198 (2009)
32. Lin, H., Pass, R.: Constant-round non-malleable commitments from any one-way function. In: Proceedings of the 43rd ACM Symposium on Theory of Computing, STOC, pp. 705–714 (2011)
33. Lin, H., Pass, R., Soni, P.: Two-round and non-interactive concurrent non-malleable commitments from time-lock puzzles. In: 58th IEEE Annual Symposium on Foundations of Computer Science, FOCS, pp. 576–587. IEEE Computer Society (2017)
34. Lin, H., Pass, R., Tseng, W.-L.D., Venkitasubramaniam, M.: Concurrent non-malleable zero knowledge proofs. In: Rabin, T. (ed.) CRYPTO 2010. LNCS, vol. 6223, pp. 429–446. Springer, Heidelberg (2010). https://doi.org/10.1007/978-3-642-14623-7_23
35. Lin, H., Pass, R., Venkitasubramaniam, M.: Concurrent non-malleable commitments from any one-way function. In: Canetti, R. (ed.) TCC 2008. LNCS, vol. 4948, pp. 571–588. Springer, Heidelberg (2008). https://doi.org/10.1007/978-3-540-78524-8_31
36. Malavolta, G., Thyagarajan, S.A.K.: Homomorphic time-lock puzzles and applications. In: Boldyreva, A., Micciancio, D. (eds.) CRYPTO 2019. LNCS, vol. 11692, pp. 620–649. Springer, Cham (2019). https://doi.org/10.1007/978-3-030-26948-7_22
37. Naor, M., Yung, M.: Public-key cryptosystems provably secure against chosen ciphertext attacks. In: STOC, pp. 427–437. ACM (1990)
38. Ostrovsky, R., Pandey, O., Visconti, I.: Efficiency preserving transformations for concurrent non-malleable zero knowledge. In: Micciancio, D. (ed.) TCC 2010. LNCS, vol. 5978, pp. 535–552. Springer, Heidelberg (2010). https://doi.org/10.1007/978-3-642-11799-2_32
39. Pandey, O., Pass, R., Vaikuntanathan, V.: Adaptive one-way functions and applications. In: Wagner, D. (ed.) CRYPTO 2008. LNCS, vol. 5157, pp. 57–74. Springer, Heidelberg (2008). https://doi.org/10.1007/978-3-540-85174-5_4

40. Pass, R., Rosen, A.: Concurrent non-malleable commitments. In: 46th Annual IEEE Symposium on Foundations of Computer Science (FOCS), pp. 563–572 (2005)

41. Pass, R., Rosen, A.: New and improved constructions of non-malleable cryptographic protocols. In: Proceedings of the 37th Annual ACM Symposium on Theory of Computing, STOC, pp. 533–542 (2005)

42. Pass, R., Rosen, A.: Concurrent nonmalleable commitments. SIAM J. Comput. **37**(6), 1891–1925 (2008)

43. Pass, R., Wee, H.: Constant-round non-malleable commitments from sub-exponential one-way functions. In: Gilbert, H. (ed.) EUROCRYPT 2010. LNCS, vol. 6110, pp. 638–655. Springer, Heidelberg (2010). https://doi.org/10.1007/978-3-642-13190-5_32

44. Pietrzak, K.: Simple verifiable delay functions. In: 10th Innovations in Theoretical Computer Science Conference, ITCS, pp. 60:1–60:15 (2019)

45. Rivest, R.L., Shamir, A., Wagner, D.A.: Time-lock puzzles and timed-release crypto,: technical report. Massachusetts Institute of Technology, Cambridge, MA, USA (1996)

46. Rotem, L., Segev, G.: Generically speeding-up repeated squaring is equivalent to factoring: sharp thresholds for all generic-ring delay functions. In: Micciancio, D., Ristenpart, T. (eds.) CRYPTO 2020. LNCS, vol. 12172, pp. 481–509. Springer, Cham (2020). https://doi.org/10.1007/978-3-030-56877-1_17

47. Unruh, D.: Random oracles and auxiliary input. In: Menezes, A. (ed.) CRYPTO 2007. LNCS, vol. 4622, pp. 205–223. Springer, Heidelberg (2007). https://doi.org/10.1007/978-3-540-74143-5_12

48. Von Zur Gathen, J., Shparlinski, I.E.: Generating safe primes. J. Math. Cryptol. **7**(4), 333–365 (2013)

49. Wee, H.: Black-box, round-efficient secure computation via non-malleability amplification. In: FOCS (2010)

50. Wesolowski, B.: Efficient verifiable delay functions. In: Ishai, Y., Rijmen, V. (eds.) EUROCRYPT 2019. LNCS, vol. 11478, pp. 379–407. Springer, Cham (2019). https://doi.org/10.1007/978-3-030-17659-4_13

Vector and Functional Commitments
from Lattices

Chris Peikert[1,2(✉)], Zachary Pepin[1], and Chad Sharp[1]

[1] University of Michigan, Ann Arbor, USA
cpeikert@umich.edu
[2] Algorand, Inc., Boston, USA

Abstract. Vector commitment (VC) schemes allow one to commit concisely to an ordered sequence of values, so that the values at desired positions can later be proved concisely. In addition, a VC can be statelessly updatable, meaning that commitments and proofs can be updated to reflect changes to individual entries, using knowledge of just those changes (and not the entire vector). VCs have found important applications in verifiable outsourced databases, cryptographic accumulators, and cryptocurrencies. However, to date there have been relatively few post-quantum constructions, i.e., ones that are plausibly secure against quantum attacks.

More generally, functional commitment (FC) schemes allow one to concisely and verifiably reveal various functions of committed data, such as linear functions (i.e., inner products, including evaluations of a committed polynomial). Under falsifiable assumptions, all known functional commitments schemes have been limited to "linearizable" functions, and there are no known post-quantum FC schemes beyond ordinary VCs.

In this work we give post-quantum constructions of vector and functional commitments based on the standard Short Integer Solution lattice problem (appropriately parameterized):

- First, we present new statelessly updatable VCs with significantly shorter proofs than (and efficiency otherwise similar to) the only prior post-quantum, statelessly updatable construction (Papamanthou *et al.*, EUROCRYPT 13). Our constructions use private-key setup, in which an authority generates public parameters and then goes offline.
- Second, we construct functional commitments for *arbitrary (bounded) Boolean circuits* and branching programs. Under falsifiable assumptions, this is the first post-quantum FC scheme beyond ordinary VCs, and the first FC scheme of any kind that goes beyond linearizable functions. Our construction works in a new model involving an authority that generates the public parameters and remains online to provide public, reusable "opening keys" for desired functions of committed messages.

© International Association for Cryptologic Research 2021
K. Nissim and B. Waters (Eds.): TCC 2021, LNCS 13044, pp. 480–511, 2021.
https://doi.org/10.1007/978-3-030-90456-2_16

1   Introduction

Commitment schemes are an essential cryptographic primitive. They provide the cryptographic equivalent of a "locked box," allowing one to publicly lock some desired value away and to later reveal it. By analogy, two central desiderata of such schemes are as follows. First, it should be *binding*: once a (possibly adversarially generated) commitment is published, there should be no way to open it to two different values. Second, it may also be *hiding*: no one should be able to see inside the box. That is, the commitment reveals essentially nothing about the underlying value.

First constructed and formalized in work by Libert and Yung [LY10] and by Catalano and Fiore [CF13], *vector commitment* (VC) schemes generalize commitments to ordered sequences of values. More specifically, one can commit to a d-dimensional vector $\mathbf{m}$ and later open the commitment at any desired indices, i.e., prove that the ith entry of $\mathbf{m}$ is m_i. Here the notion of binding is replaced with *position binding*: it should be infeasible to open a commitment at a position i as two different message entries $m_i \neq m_i'$. For hiding, we may require that the commitment and openings reveal nothing about the *unopened* message entries. (However, many applications of VCs turn out not to need hiding.) In order to rule out trivial implementations, commitments and proofs are required to be *concise*, meaning that they should be smaller than the entire message vector, i.e., sublinear in d (and the smaller the better).

Additionally, VCs often need to be *updatable*, meaning it is possible to update commitments and proofs to reflect changes in the underlying vector entries, faster than the trivial solution of just computing new commitments and proofs from scratch. Updatability can even be *stateless* (also known as *distributed*) [CPSZ18], meaning that updates require only the position at which the message vector changed, and the old and new entries (or even just their difference).

Libert, Ramanna, and Yung [LRY16] generalized the concept of VCs to the notion of *functional commitments* (FCs), with a focus on *linear* functions. For some particular class of functions $\mathcal{F}$, FCs allow one to commit to a vector $\mathbf{m}$ and then, for any desired functions $f \in \mathcal{F}$, open the function-value pairs $(f, y = f(\mathbf{m}))$. (Traditional VCs can be seen as FCs for the class $\mathcal{F} = \{f_i(\mathbf{m}) = m_i\}_{i \in [d]}$ of "coordinate projection" functions.) A special case of linear FCs, defined earlier by Kate, Zaverucha, and Goldberg [KZG10] considers committing to a *polynomial* and then opening its evaluations at desired points.

Applications. Vector commitments have found numerous cryptographic applications. Catalano and Fiore [CF13] demonstrated their usefulness for publicly verifiable databases with efficient updates and, more broadly, verifiable outsourcing of storage [BGV11], updatable zero-knowledge sets and databases [MRK03,Lis05], cryptographic accumulators [BdM93], and pseudonymous credentials [KZG10]. More recently, Chepurnoy *et al.* [CPSZ18] used statelessly updatable VCs to construct an architecture for cryptocurrencies with stateless transaction validation.

Beyond VCs, functional commitments for polynomials [KZG10] and, more generally, linear functions [LRY16] have additionally found applications in verifiable secret sharing [CGMA85], content extraction signatures [SBZ01], proof-carrying data systems, and zero-knowledge SNARKs [BFS20,BDFG20].

Constructions. Merkle trees [Mer87] provide the first instantiation of VCs, with $O(1)$ commitment size and $O(\log d)$ proof size (both as functions solely of the dimension d), but they are not statelessly updatable. Libert and Yung [LY10] gave a construction that can serve as a statelessly updatable VC (and more), based on a "q-type" pairing assumption where q is the vector dimension, with $O(1)$-sized commitments and openings. Catalano and Fiore [CF13] gave two constructions of statelessly updatable VCs, based respectively on the Computational Diffie-Hellman (CDH) assumption over pairing-friendly groups and the RSA assumption, where each commitment and opening is a single group element. Chepurnoy *et al.* [CPSZ18] gave a construction based on the q-Strong Bilinear Diffie-Hellman assumption, which has smaller public parameters than the aforementioned CDH-based scheme (linear in d rather than quadratic) but slightly slower proof updates, and improved time complexity for proof updates versus the aforementioned RSA-based scheme ($O(\log d \log \log d)$ versus $O(d)$).

The work of [KZG10] gave a polynomial commitment scheme where commitments and proofs are each a single group element, and which is secure under the q-Strong Diffie-Hellman assumption. More generally, the work of [LRY16] gave an FC scheme for *linear* functions $f_{\mathbf{w}}(\mathbf{m}) = \langle \mathbf{w}, \mathbf{m} \rangle$, based on a subgroup decision assumption on pairing-friendly composite-order groups, in which commitments and proofs are each a single group element. Recently, the work of [LP20] gave a functional commitment scheme for what the authors called the class of "semi-sparse" polynomials. This class is an example of a *linearizable* function class, i.e., every function f in the class can be (efficiently) decomposed as $f(\mathbf{m}) = L_f(P(\mathbf{m}))$ for some polynomial-time "preprocessing" function P (which depends only on the class, and not the specific function f) and a linear function L_f (which may depend on f). For any linearizable class, an FC can be generically implemented via a linear FC (though perhaps not as efficiently as with a specialized construction), simply by having the committer commit to $P(\mathbf{m})$.

For *non-linearizable* function classes, we are not aware of *any* FC construction, apart from a straightforward generic construction mentioned in [LRY16]: it combines any succinct commitment scheme with any succinct noninteractive argument of knowledge for NP (such as PCP-based ones [Kil92,Mic94] or more specialized ones like Bulletproofs [BBB+18]), for proving functions of the committed data. However, the latter component cannot be based on a *falsifiable* assumption via a black-box security reduction [GW11]; indeed, existing constructions like the ones cited above tend to rely on strong heuristics like the random oracle model. In summary, we do not have any FC for a non-linearizable function class based on a falsifiable assumption.

There has also been quite limited work on *post-quantum* vector commitment schemes, i.e., ones which are plausibly secure against quantum attacks. Merkle trees instantiated with a post-quantum hash function may be used, though they suffer from relatively inefficient and necessarily stateful updates. Papamanthou *et al.* [PSTY13] gave a Merkle-tree-like construction based on the Short Integer Solution (SIS) lattice problem, which straightforwardly yields a statelessly updatable VC scheme. At present, we are unaware of any post-quantum FC schemes beyond the aforementioned VC schemes and generic FC construction (requiring non-falsifiable assumptions); in particular, even constructing a post-quantum *linear* FC from a falsifiable assumption is an open problem.

1.1   Our Contributions

We present two main sets of results. First, in Sect. 3 we give new constructions of vector commitments based on the (post-quantum) SIS lattice problem. The first of these is a "base" VC construction that is statelessly updatable; it is most appropriate for only moderately large d, due to the public parameters' quadratic dependence on d. Then, for larger dimensions d^h, we give a specialized tree transformation of our SIS-based VC that preserves stateless updates (unlike generic Merkle trees). This transformation uses a main idea from [PSTY13], but our construction's proofs are significantly more concise, by a d factor, because the transformation is based on a VC rather than a hash function. For a detailed comparison with the prior work on VCs see Figs. 1 and 2 and the associated discussion in Sect. 1.2, and for an overview of the constructions see Sect. 1.3.

Our second main contribution, given in Sect. 4, is a functional commitment scheme for *arbitrary (bounded) Boolean circuits* and branching programs, also based on SIS (appropriately parameterized). Under falsifiable assumptions, this is the first functional commitment scheme that goes beyond linearizable functions, and is also the first post-quantum construction of functional commitments beyond vector commitments, e.g., for linear functions. Indeed, we specialize our general construction to linear functions over large finite fields, resulting in a relatively simple and potentially practical scheme.

Our functional commitment construction works in a model, which we introduce in this work, involving a trusted authority that sets up the public parameters and *remains online* to provide "opening keys" ok_f for any desired functions f of committed messages. We stress that, unlike superficially similar models (e.g., for identity- or attribute-based encryption), these opening keys are not tied to any particular party and do not need to be transmitted via a secret channel; they can be announced publicly and used by all committers any number of times. See Sect. 1.3 for an overview of the construction.

As an additional contribution, in the full version we give a formal definition and analysis of a generic tree transformation on VCs, which converts a VC for d-dimensional vectors into one for d^h-dimensional vectors for any desired positive integer h. The transformation is like a Merkle tree of height h and arity d, using the underlying VC rather than a hash function to commit to each node's children. The key advantage is that to open an entry, one only needs to open each step of the entry's root-to-leaf path, but *no "sibling" information is required*. This immediately saves about a factor of d in the proof size, thus allowing for the use of a larger arity d and hence smaller height h, which reduces proof size even further. This main idea has previously been used in other contexts like signatures [DN94] and zero-knowledge databases [CRFM08], and even VCs [Kus18] (where it is called a "Verkle tree"), though without a formal analysis or treatment of updates.

1.2   Comparisons to Related Work

For the purposes of comparison, we divide existing VC schemes into "primitive" and "tree-based" schemes. Primitive schemes operate directly on the input vector and are typically based on some concrete cryptographic assumption (RSA, CDH, SIS, etc.). A tree-based scheme transforms another (usually primitive) VC scheme, and treats its input vector as a tuple of subvectors, somehow recursively committing to each subvector and then committing to the tuple of results using the underlying scheme. Tree-based VCs are most suitable for vectors of large dimension, and generally sacrifice proof and/or commitment size for smaller public parameters.

Primitive Schemes. Here and in Fig. 1 we briefly compare our base SIS vector commitment scheme to other primitive VCs from the literature [CF13, CPSZ18]. The primary advantage of our scheme is that it is plausibly secure against quantum attacks, whereas the others are broken by them. However, this comes at the cost of commitment and proof sizes that are *logarithmic*, rather than *constant*, in the vector dimension d. Our scheme, along with the others in question, has stateless updates but requires private-coin setup, in contrast to the only other known post-quantum VC schemes (discussed below).

Scheme	$|vp|$	$|cp|$	$|c|$	$|\pi|$	Setup	Stateless	PQ
[CF13] (RSA)	d	d	1	1	Private	✓	✗
[CF13] (CDH)	d	d^2	1	1	Private	✓	✗
[CPSZ18]	d	d	1	1	Private	✓	✗
Construction 1	d	d^2	$\log d$	$\log d$	Private	✓	✓

Fig. 1. A comparison of "primitive" VC schemes. Object sizes are expressed asymptotically as functions of the vector dimension d, with logarithmic factors elided from the sizes of verifier parameters vp and committer parameters cp (but not commitments c or proofs π). PQ indicates that the scheme is plausibly secure against quantum attacks.

Tree-Based Schemes. Here and in Fig. 2 we compare tree-based schemes that commit to vectors of (typically large) dimension D, using a tree of some chosen arity d and height $h = \log_d D$. It is important to bear in mind that asymptotically different values of d and h are optimal for different schemes, so the object sizes as functions of these parameters cannot be compared directly across schemes.

   Selecting optimal parameters for Merkle trees is straightforward: simply minimize the asymptotic proof size $dh = d \log_d D$, yielding optimal values $d = O(1)$ and $h = O(\log d)$. For the remaining schemes, choosing larger d (and thereby smaller $h = \log_d D$) reduces the commitment and proof sizes, at the cost of larger public parameters. Therefore, one should maximize d subject to some reasonable constraint on the sizes of the public parameters. For large dimensions D, a plausible choice is $d = D^\epsilon$ for some small constant $\epsilon > 0$, yielding $h = 1/\epsilon = O(1)$; we use this setting for the following comparisons.

Like the scheme described in [PSTY13], our specialized tree transformation (Construction 2) has stateless updates. However, ours has smaller proofs at the cost of larger public parameters, both by a factor of d. This seems like an advantageous tradeoff in most applications, since many proofs (about many commitments) are given for a single set of public parameters.

In comparison with Merkle trees, the primary benefit of our specialized tree transform is that it has stateless updates. However, its proof sizes are slightly larger than those of Merkle trees ($O(\log^2 D)$ rather than $O(\log D)$), and its commitment sizes are logarithmic rather than constant.

The generic tree transformation for VCs (in the full version) instantiated with our SIS-based scheme (Construction 1) has constant-factor improvements, by h or h^2, in commitment size and proof size compared to our specialized scheme and that of [PSTY13], with an additional factor-of-d improvement in proof size over [PSTY13]. Unlike those other works, however, it requires stateful updates.

Though not post-quantum, instantiating the generic tree transformation with the CDH-based scheme of [CF13] (which has constant-sized commitments and proofs) demonstrates more clearly the structural advantage it has over Merkle trees. Since sibling information is not necessary, the proof size depends only on $h = O(1)$. However, this comes at the cost of private setup and larger public parameters.

Scheme	$\lvert vp \rvert$	$\lvert cp \rvert$	$\lvert c \rvert$	$\lvert \pi \rvert$	Setup	Stateless	PQ
Merkle tree	1	1	1	hd	Public	✗	✓
[PSTY13]	$h^2 d$	$h^2 d$	$h \log d$	$h^3 d \log^2 d$	Public	✓	✓
Construction 2	$h^2 d$	$h^2 d^2$	$h \log d$	$h^3 \log^2 d$	Private	✓	✓
Generic tree with 1 (SIS)	d	d^2	$\log d$	$h \log d$	Private	✗	✓
Generic tree with [CF13] (CDH)	d	d^2	1	h	Private	✗	✗

Fig. 2. A comparison of "tree-based" VC schemes. Object sizes are expressed as functions of the tree arity d and height h (handling a vector dimension $D = d^h$), with logarithmic factors elided from the sizes of the verifier parameters vp and committer parameters cp (but not the commitments c or proofs π). PQ indicates that the scheme is plausibly secure against quantum attacks (for Merkle trees, when using a PQ hash function).

Other Related Work. The work of [BGJS16] considered a variant of functional commitment (potentially with a bounded number of function queries), which does not require succinctness but also does not need any trusted setup, and showed that it is implied by verifiable functional encryption (and thereby from assumptions on pairing-friendly groups).

The work of [HW15] considers a primitive called "somewhat statistically binding" (SSB) hash, which is a strengthening of vector commitments: the commitment and openings of individual entries are concise, and additionally, the commitment is *statistically* binding at one (hidden) location. However, the construction relies on Merkle trees plus (comparatively heavy) fully homomorphic encryption, so it has no better efficiency than ordinary Merkle trees, nor is it statelessly updatable.

1.3   Technical Overview

In this section we give a brief overview of the key ideas underlying our constructions; we assume some basic familiarity with the abstract functionality of "trapdoors" for lattices [GPV08] and "third-generation" fully homomorphic encryption/commitments [GSW13, GVW15].

SIS-Based Vector Commitments. Our base VC scheme is conceptually inspired by the ones proposed in [CF13]. To convey the key ideas, we describe a technically simpler, unoptimized version of our scheme for vectors whose entries belong to $\mathcal{M} = \{0,1\}^\ell$ for some desired ℓ. To generate the public parameters, we first choose a uniformly random matrix $\mathbf{U} = [\mathbf{U}_0 \mid \cdots \mid \mathbf{U}_{d-1}] \in \mathbb{Z}_q^{n \times \ell d}$, where each $\mathbf{U}_i \in \mathbb{Z}_q^{n \times \ell}$. Then we generate d (statistically close to) uniformly random matrices $\mathbf{A}_i \in \mathbb{Z}_q^{n \times m}$ along with respective trapdoors $\mathbf{T}_i$. We use each trapdoor $\mathbf{T}_i$ to sample a "short" (discrete Gaussian-distributed) $\mathbf{R}_i \in \mathbb{Z}^{m \times \ell(d-1)}$ such that $\mathbf{A}_i \mathbf{R}_i = \mathbf{U}_{-i}$, where $\mathbf{U}_{-i} \in \mathbb{Z}_q^{n \times \ell(d-1)}$ is $\mathbf{U}$ with its ith block $\mathbf{U}_i$ removed. The public parameters are $\mathbf{U}$ and all the $\mathbf{A}_i$ and $\mathbf{R}_i$ matrices.

The commitment to a vector $\mathbf{m} \in \{0,1\}^{\ell d}$ is simply $\mathbf{c} = \mathbf{U}\mathbf{m} \in \mathbb{Z}_q^n$.[1] To open the commitment at position i as $\mathbf{m}_i \in \{0,1\}^\ell$, output the proof $\mathbf{p}_i = \mathbf{R}_i \mathbf{m}_{-i} \in \mathbb{Z}^m$ (which is short), where $\mathbf{m}_{-i} \in \{0,1\}^{\ell(d-1)}$ is $\mathbf{m}$ with its ith ℓ-bit block removed. The verifier simply checks that $\mathbf{p}_i$ is sufficiently short and that $\mathbf{c} = \mathbf{A}_i \mathbf{p}_i + \mathbf{U}_i \mathbf{m}_i$, which holds since

$$\mathbf{A}_i \mathbf{p}_i + \mathbf{U}_i \mathbf{m}_i = \mathbf{A}_i \mathbf{R}_i \mathbf{m}_{-i} + \mathbf{U}_i \mathbf{m}_i = \mathbf{U}_{-i} \mathbf{m}_{-i} + \mathbf{U}_i \mathbf{m}_i = \mathbf{U}\mathbf{m} = \mathbf{c}.$$

Breaking position binding of this scheme means producing a tuple $(\mathbf{c}^*, i, \mathbf{m}_i, \mathbf{m}'_i, \mathbf{p}, \mathbf{p}')$ such that for commitment $\mathbf{c}^*$ and position i, proofs $\mathbf{p}, \mathbf{p}'$ respectively verify for distinct $\mathbf{m}_i \neq \mathbf{m}'_i$, i.e., $\mathbf{p}, \mathbf{p}'$ are sufficiently short and

$$\mathbf{c}^* = \mathbf{A}_i \mathbf{p} + \mathbf{U}_i \mathbf{m}_i = \mathbf{A}_i \mathbf{p}' + \mathbf{U}_i \mathbf{m}'_i.$$

From this, we have that $\mathbf{x} := \begin{bmatrix} \mathbf{p}_i - \mathbf{p}'_i \\ \mathbf{m}_i - \mathbf{m}'_i \end{bmatrix} \neq \mathbf{0}$ is an SIS solution to the (statistically close to) uniformly random matrix $[\mathbf{A}_i \mid \mathbf{U}_i]$. Our security reduction shows how to embed an external SIS instance as this matrix, and generate all the rest of the public parameters to have the proper joint distribution (even though the reduction does not have a trapdoor for $\mathbf{A}_i$).

---

[1] In this overview we aim only for position binding, and dispense with hiding.

In our actual construction, we use the "trapdoor puncturing" technique of [PW08, ABB10, MP12] to reduce the size of the public parameters, allowing us to generate each $\mathbf{A}_i$ from a single uniformly random matrix $\mathbf{A} \in \mathbb{Z}_q^{n \times m}$. The (stateless) updatability of this scheme follows from the linearity of commitments and openings.

Specialized Tree Transformation. In the full version, we construct a generic tree transformation for VC schemes for vectors of high dimension d^h, which uses any VC for dimension d as a black box. (Its practical efficiency was analyzed in [Kus18], but without a formal security analysis or treatment of updates.) The main idea is very similar to that of Merkle trees [Mer87], but with the public hash function replaced by a vector commitment scheme. In particular, it can be instantiated with our SIS-based VC scheme, where commitments in $\mathbb{Z}_q^n$ are treated as messages by representing them as bit vectors. More formally, we can use the nonlinear "bit decomposition" transformation $\mathbf{G}^{-1} \colon \mathbb{Z}_q^n \to \mathbb{Z}^w$, where $w \approx n \log q$ and we take $\ell = w$ in the above construction, to bring commitments back into the message space (and this can be inverted by multiplying by the "gadget" matrix $\mathbf{G} \in \mathbb{Z}_q^{n \times w}$). However, this nonlinearity makes the commitment function of the transformed scheme non-linear, and thus breaks stateless updatability.

To preserve linearity and thereby stateless updatability, we give a specialized tree transformation of our SIS-based VC scheme, which takes inspiration from the Merkle-tree-like construction of [PSTY13]. For simplicity, we briefly outline this transformation for small parameters $d = h = 2$ (though a significantly larger d yields better efficiency).

The public parameters are identical to those of the base scheme (for $d = 2$), and using them we additionally define a matrix

$$\mathbf{U}^{(2)} := \mathbf{U}(\mathbf{I}_2 \otimes \mathbf{G}^{-1}(\mathbf{U})) = [\mathbf{U}_0 \mathbf{G}^{-1}(\mathbf{U}) \mid \mathbf{U}_1 \mathbf{G}^{-1}(\mathbf{U})] \in \mathbb{Z}_q^{n \times \ell d^2}.$$

To commit to a vector $\overline{\mathbf{m}} = (\overline{\mathbf{m}}_{00}, \overline{\mathbf{m}}_{01}, \overline{\mathbf{m}}_{10}, \overline{\mathbf{m}}_{11}) \in \{0,1\}^{\ell d^h} = \{0,1\}^{4\ell}$, we compute $\overline{\mathbf{c}} = \mathbf{G}^{-1}(\mathbf{U}^{(2)})\overline{\mathbf{m}}$; observe that this is a linear function of $\overline{\mathbf{m}}$, which ultimately allows for stateless updates. Also notice that

$$\mathbf{G}\overline{\mathbf{c}} = \mathbf{U}^{(2)}\overline{\mathbf{m}} = \mathbf{U}(\mathbf{I}_2 \otimes \mathbf{G}^{-1}(\mathbf{U}))\overline{\mathbf{m}}$$

is a commitment (under the base scheme) to $\overline{\mathbf{m}}' := (\mathbf{I}_2 \otimes \mathbf{G}^{-1}(\mathbf{U}))\overline{\mathbf{m}} \in \mathbb{Z}^{\ell d}$, which is relatively short. Additionally, $\overline{\mathbf{m}}'$ itself can be seen essentially as a pair of commitments, as

$$
\begin{aligned}
\overline{\mathbf{m}}' &= (\mathbf{I}_2 \otimes \mathbf{G}^{-1}(\mathbf{U}))\overline{\mathbf{m}} \\
&= \begin{bmatrix} \mathbf{G}^{-1}(\mathbf{U}) \begin{bmatrix} \overline{\mathbf{m}}_{00} \\ \overline{\mathbf{m}}_{01} \end{bmatrix} \\ \mathbf{G}^{-1}(\mathbf{U}) \begin{bmatrix} \overline{\mathbf{m}}_{10} \\ \overline{\mathbf{m}}_{11} \end{bmatrix} \end{bmatrix} =: \begin{bmatrix} \mathbf{c}_0 \\ \mathbf{c}_1 \end{bmatrix},
\end{aligned}
$$

because $\mathbf{Gc}_i \in \mathbb{Z}_q^n$ is a commitment (under the base scheme) to $(\overline{\mathbf{m}}_{i0}, \overline{\mathbf{m}}_{i1})$. So, to prove a particular entry of the message $\overline{\mathbf{m}}$, say $\overline{\mathbf{m}}_{01}$, we simply provide $\mathbf{c}_0$ and a proof that it is the 0th entry of $\overline{\mathbf{m}}'$ (viewing $\mathbf{G}\overline{\mathbf{c}}$ as a commitment to $\overline{\mathbf{m}}'$), along with a proof that $\overline{\mathbf{m}}_{01}$ is the 1st entry committed to by $\mathbf{Gc}_0$. Breaking position binding of this scheme requires breaking position binding of the base scheme somewhere along this path.

We stress that the above proof structure is more concise than for Merkle trees and [PSTY13], because the proofs need not contain any "sibling" information. Essentially, our construction opens a vector commitment at each level, just as in the generic VC transformation, but in a manner that preserves linearity and hence stateless updates. This also allows for the use of a larger tree arity d, which reduces the tree height and thereby the number of elements in proofs. However, preserving statelessness in this way does come at a cost: in the general version of the transformation, the norm of $\overline{\mathbf{m}}'$ can grow linearly with its dimension ℓd^h, so the SIS parameters of the underlying VC scheme must be increased to accommodate these larger messages. This introduces a poly-logarithmic dependence on d^h in the sizes of commitments and proofs. The SIS-based Merkle-like construction of [PSTY13] (when used as a VC) has exactly the same dependence, so our commitment sizes match, and our proof sizes are strictly better by a d factor. (See Fig. 2.)

Functional Commitments for Arbitrary Functions. In Sect. 4 we give an SIS-based construction of functional commitments for arbitrary Boolean functions of bounded size S, via an online authority that provides opening keys for desired functions. The construction relies heavily upon the fully homomorphic commitment scheme that was implicit in the homomorphic encryption scheme of Gentry, Sahai, and Waters [GSW13], and was made explicit by Gorbunov, Vaikuntanathan, and Wichs [GVW15]. We remark that while the latter work gives a commitment scheme in which one can commit to data and then later open any bounded function of it, this falls short of a true functional commitment scheme because the commitment is not *succinct*—its size is a substantial factor larger than the data itself. In our construction, the sizes of both the commitments and proofs depend only on the complexity of the supported functions, and not directly on the message size. More specifically, they grow poly-logarithmically in the size and polynomially in the depth of the functions; see Sect. 4.3 for details.

In our construction, the commitment function is essentially identical to the first stage (homomorphic evaluation) of the correlation-intractable hash functions of [CCH+19, PS19]. However, in those works' main application (noninteractive zero knowledge proofs), the resulting output is never "opened." In functional commitments, the result needs to be opened in several different ways, once for each function that is proved about the committed message.

We also mention that using just tagged-trapdoor techniques, which predate the above-referenced fully homomorphic schemes but provide only linear homomorphism, we specialize our functional commitment scheme to arbitrary linear functions over large finite fields. The resulting scheme is asymptotically quite efficient, especially when adapted to use rings, and potentially practical. In this overview we just focus on the general scheme for arbitrary functions, and refer to Sect. 4.3 for the linear specialization.

Public Parameters and Commitment. The public parameters in our scheme are a uniformly random matrix $\mathbf{C} \in \mathbb{Z}_q^{n \times Sw}$ (where again, $w \approx n \log q$ is the width of the gadget matrix $\mathbf{G} \in \mathbb{Z}_q^{n \times w}$) and a (statistically close to) uniform matrix $\mathbf{A} \in \mathbb{Z}_q^{n \times m}$, which is generated with a trapdoor $\mathbf{T}$ that serves as the authority's secret key. Using standard tagged-trapdoor techniques, for each size-S function f we implicitly define a public matrix $\mathbf{A}_f \in \mathbb{Z}_q^{n \times m}$ that is efficiently computable from $\mathbf{A}$ and f; the authority's trapdoor $\mathbf{T}$ allows it to sample short preimages with respect to any of these $\mathbf{A}_f$.

It is helpful to interpret the public parameter $\mathbf{C}$ as a homomorphic commitment to some as-yet-unspecified function(s) f, with respect to some corresponding public key. To commit to a message m, one simply computes $\mathbf{C}_m = \mathsf{Eval}(U_m, \mathbf{C})$, i.e., the homomorphic evaluation of the universal function $U_m(f) := U(f, m) = f(m)$ on the committed function f. Therefore, we can think of $\mathbf{C}_m$ as a homomorphic commitment to $f(m)$—but we again stress that f is still unspecified.[2] We stress that it is vital that the homomorphic evaluation can indeed be done using just $\mathbf{C}$ and m, and not the unspecified public key relative to which $\mathbf{C}$ is viewed as a commitment.

Opening. In order to prove for a commitment $\mathbf{C}_m$ that $f(m) = y$ for some desired f, one first needs an appropriate opening key from the authority. Such a key is simply some randomness that opens $\mathbf{C}$ as a homomorphic commitment to the desired function f, *with respect to public key* $\mathbf{A}_f$. That is, the authority uses its trapdoor $\mathbf{T}$ to sample a "short" integer matrix such that $\mathbf{C} = \mathsf{FHCom}_{\mathbf{A}_f}(f; \mathbf{R}_f)$. We point out that each opening key essentially equivocates $\mathbf{C}$ as committing to a different value—but this does not violate security in any way, because these openings are with respect to *different* $\mathbf{A}_f$. (Indeed, it is important that the authority publishes at most one opening key for each function, which can be ensured by standard techniques.)

With an opening key $\mathbf{R}_f$ in hand, one proves that $f(m) = y$ by "tracing" the evolution of the randomness through the homomorphic computation of $\mathbf{C}_m$ from $\mathbf{C}$. More specifically, a key feature of the homomorphic commitment scheme is that, given the function U_m and the "short" randomness $\mathbf{R}_f$ underlying the commitment $\mathbf{C} = \mathsf{FHCom}_{\mathbf{A}_f}(f; \mathbf{R}_f)$, one can efficiently compute "relatively short" randomness $\mathbf{R}_{f,m}$ underlying $\mathbf{C}_m$, i.e., for which

$$\mathbf{C}_m := \mathsf{Eval}(U_m, \mathbf{C}) = \mathsf{FHCom}_{\mathbf{A}_f}(y = f(m); \mathbf{R}_{f,m}).$$

To prove that $f(m) = y$, one just computes and reveals this $\mathbf{R}_{f,m}$. The verifier checks that it is sufficiently short and that $\mathbf{C}_m = \mathsf{FHCom}_{\mathbf{A}_f}(y; \mathbf{R}_{f,m})$.

---

[2] As an optimization, for Boolean functions f the matrix $\mathbf{C}_m$ can be further compressed to just a single vector $\mathbf{c}_m \in \mathbb{Z}_q^n$; we omit the details in this overview.

For security, we prove that under the SIS assumption (appropriately param-eterized), it is infeasible for an adversary to break *function binding*, i.e., to out-put a tuple $(\mathbf{C}^*, f^*, y, y', \mathbf{R}, \mathbf{R}')$ such that $y \neq y'$ and yet the verifier accepts on both $(\mathbf{C}^*, f^*, y, \mathbf{R})$ and $(\mathbf{C}^*, f^*, y', \mathbf{R}')$. We prove this for a *selective function attack*, where the adversary must announce the targeted function f^* before seeing the public parameters, but may produce the rest of its output $(\mathbf{C}^*, y, y', \mathbf{R}, \mathbf{R}')$ after getting arbitrary opening keys for functions f of its choice, *even including* $f = f^*$. It is well known that security against such selective attacks can be boosted to security against fully adaptive attacks using complexity leveraging, i.e., the reduction is loose by a factor of the size of the function class. In addition, there are lattice-trapdoor techniques for obtaining adaptive security in related settings (e.g., [CHKP10, Yam16]), which seem compatible with our construction techniques.

1.4   Open Problems and Future Work

Our work raises several interesting questions for further research. First, recall that all of our constructions require private-coin setup (i.e., a trusted authority that uses private randomness to generate the public parameters). An important question is whether there are lattice-based or other post-quantum vector com-mitments with public setup and having similar or better properties, including for updates. (Recall that post-quantum Merkle trees can have public setup, but require stateful updates.)

Recall that our functional commitment scheme requires an *online* authority to generate opening keys for the desired functions, using some secret trapdoor.[3] A very interesting question is whether functional commitments for some large non-linear function class can be obtained using an *offline* authority, which only generates and publishes some setup parameters, based on a falsifiable assump-tion.[4] Even more ambitiously, can such a scheme be constructed with just *pub-lic*-coin setup?

Finally, the literature contains several variants of vector commitments. For example, *subvector* commitments [LM19, CFG+20] allow one to open a commit-ted vector at any subset of positions, via a proof that is smaller than proofs for all the positions individually. Subvector commitments can even be *aggregat-able* [TAB+20], meaning that openings for two different subsets can be aggre-gated, producing an opening for their union. So far, subvector commitments have been constructed only from assumptions on pairing-friendly groups. It is a very interesting question whether any kind of subvector commitments (with or without aggregation) can be constructed from lattices or other post-quantum assumptions.

---

[3] However, if the class has only polynomially many functions, then the authority can publish all the opening keys and then go offline (disappear).

[4] Recall that the naive construction proposed in [LRY16], which combines a succinct commitment scheme with a succinct noninteractive argument for NP, cannot have a black-box security proof from a falsifiable assumption [GW11].

2   Preliminaries

For any non-negative integer i, denote $[i] = \{0, \ldots, i - 1\}$ (where $[0] = \emptyset$). For a real vector $\mathbf{v}$, let $\|\mathbf{v}\| := (\sum_i v_i^2)^{1/2}$ denote its Euclidean norm and $\|\mathbf{v}\|_1 = \sum_i |v_i|$ denote its ℓ_1 norm. For a real matrix $\mathbf{V}$, let $\|\mathbf{V}\| := \max_j \|\mathbf{v}_j\|$ denote the maximum Euclidean norm of its column vectors $\mathbf{v}_j$, and let $s_1(\mathbf{V}) := \max_{\mathbf{u} \neq \mathbf{0}} \|\mathbf{V}\mathbf{u}\| / \|\mathbf{u}\|$ denote its maximum singular value (also known as its spectral norm). Observe that for any matrix $\mathbf{V}$ and vector $\mathbf{u}$, we have $\|\mathbf{V}\mathbf{u}\| \leq \|\mathbf{V}\| \cdot \|\mathbf{u}\|_1$ by the triangle inequality.

2.1   Vector Commitments

Definition 1 (Vector commitment). *A* vector commitment scheme *with message space $\mathcal{M}$, commitment space $\mathcal{C}$, and proof space $\mathcal{P}$ (which may be functions of the setup parameters) is a set of algorithms with the following interfaces:*

– Setup$(1^\lambda, 1^d)$ *outputs (public) committer parameters cp and verifier parameters vp.*
– Commit$(cp, \mathbf{m} \in \mathcal{M}^d)$ *outputs a commitment $c \in \mathcal{C}$ and some committer state st.*
– Open$(cp, st, i \in [d])$ *outputs a proof p_i for the ith entry of the committed message associated to st.*
– Verify$(vp, c \in \mathcal{C}, i \in [d], m \in \mathcal{M}, p \in \mathcal{P})$ *either accepts or rejects.*

These algorithms should satisfy the following correctness condition: for any $d = \mathrm{poly}(\lambda)$, $\mathbf{m} \in \mathcal{M}^d$, and $i \in [d]$, and for $(cp, vp) \leftarrow$ Setup$(1^\lambda, 1^d)$, $(c, st) \leftarrow$ Commit$(cp, \mathbf{m})$, and $p_i \leftarrow$ Open(cp, st, i), Verify(vp, c, i, m_i, p_i) accepts with probability $1 - \mathrm{negl}(\lambda)$ (over all the randomness of the experiment).

Additionally, the scheme is updatable *if it has a set of algorithms with the following interfaces:*

– PrepareUpdates$(cp, st, j \in [d], m'_j \in \mathcal{M})$ *outputs a commitment update δ_c, a proof update δ_p, and a state update δ_s for changing the jth entry of the committed message vector to m'_j.*
– UpdateC$(vp, c \in \mathcal{C}, \delta_c)$ *deterministically outputs an updated commitment c'.[5]*
– UpdateP$(vp, i \in [d], p_i \in \mathcal{P}, \delta_p)$ *deterministically outputs an updated proof p'_i.*
– UpdateS(cp, st, δ_s) *deterministically outputs an updated committer state st'.*

Additionally, the scheme is statelessly updatable *if* PrepareUpdates *can be implemented via:*

– PrepareUpdates$^{no\text{-}st}(cp, j \in [d], m_j \in \mathcal{M}, m'_j \in \mathcal{M})$, *which has the same outputs as* PrepareUpdates, *and differs only in its inputs: it does not get the committer state st, and instead receives only the old and new jth entries m_j, m'_j of the message vector $\mathbf{m}$. Then* PrepareUpdates *can be written generically in terms of* PrepareUpdates$^{no\text{-}st}$ *(assuming that $\mathbf{m}$ is part of st, which is without loss of generality).*

---

[5] The determinism is without loss of generality, because PrepareUpdates can include any needed random coins in δ_c; the same also applies for UpdateP, δ_p and UpdateS, δ_s.

Moreover, the scheme is differentially updatable *if* PrepareUpdates$^{no\text{-}st}$ *(and hence* PrepareUpdates*) can be implemented via:*

- PrepareUpdates$^{diff}(cp, j \in [d], \delta)$, *which has the same outputs as* PrepareUpdates$^{no\text{-}st}$, *and differs only in its inputs: rather than receiving* m_j *and* m'_j *separately, it receives only the "difference"* $\delta = m'_j - m_j$, *where* $-$ *denotes some abstract operation on* $\mathcal{M}$ *(whose output may be more compact than its two inputs). Then* PrepareUpdates$^{no\text{-}st}$ *can be written generically in terms of* PrepareUpdates^{diff}.

These algorithms should satisfy the following correctness condition: for any $d = \text{poly}(\lambda)$, *any* $(cp, vp) \leftarrow \text{Setup}(1^\lambda, 1^d)$, *any* $\mathbf{m}, \mathbf{m}' \in \mathcal{M}^d$ *that differ in at most the* j*th coordinate, and any* $i \in [d]$, *the outputs of the following two experiments are statistically indistinguishable; if they are identically distributed, we say that the updatability is* perfect*:*

1. *Let* $(c, st) \leftarrow \text{Commit}(cp, \mathbf{m})$, $p_i \leftarrow \text{Open}(cp, st, i)$, $(\delta_c, \delta_p, \delta_s) \leftarrow$ PrepareUpdates(cp, st, j, m'_j),[6] $c' \leftarrow \text{UpdateC}(vp, c, \delta_c)$, $p'_i \leftarrow \text{UpdateP}(vp, i, p_i, \delta_p)$, $st' \leftarrow \text{UpdateS}(cp, st, \delta_s)$. *Output* (st', c', p'_i).
2. *Let* $(c', st') \leftarrow \text{Commit}(cp, \mathbf{m}')$, $p'_i \leftarrow \text{Open}(cp, st', i)$. *Output* (st', c', p'_i).

In words, the results of updating a commitment and proof to a new entry of the message vector should be essentially the same as generating a "fresh" commitment and proof on the updated message vector. (The state information is included in the results for compositionality, so that the same goes for polynomially many updates.)

Remark 1. We note that our vector commitment interface differs slightly from the one introduced in [CF13]. First, we split our public parameters into separate committer and verifier parameters, to highlight the different values needed by each role. Second, we break out PrepareUpdates from the algorithms that do the actual updating, to delineate what work can be performed by the committer rather than the verifier. However, any VC implementing our interface can trivially be converted to the interface from [CF13], simply by merging the public parameters, and merging the code in PrepareUpdates that generates δ_c and δ_p into UpdateC and UpdateP, respectively.

Position Binding. We now recall the main security property of vector commitments, known as position binding. Essentially, it should be infeasible to output a (possibly malformed) commitment along with two valid openings for different message entries at a particular position.

---

[6] For statelessly updatable schemes, this step can be replaced by PrepareUpdates$^{no\text{-}st}(cp, j, m_j, m'_j)$, and for differentially updatable ones, it can be replaced by PrepareUpdates$^{diff}(cp, j, \delta = m'_j - m_j)$.

Definition 2. *A vector commitment scheme VCS is position binding if, for every $d = d(\lambda) = \text{poly}(\lambda)$ and every probabilistic polynomial-time adversary $\mathcal{A}$,*

$$\mathbf{Adv}_{VCS}^{pba}(\mathcal{A}) := \Pr[m \neq m' \text{ and } \textsf{Verify}(vp, c^*, i, m, p) = \textsf{Verify}(vp, c^*, i, m', p') = accept] = \text{negl}(\lambda),$$

where the probability is over the choice of $(cp, vp) \leftarrow \textsf{Setup}(1^\lambda, 1^d)$, $(c^*, i, m, p, m', p') \leftarrow \mathcal{A}(1^\lambda, 1^d, cp, vp)$.

Position binding alone is a sufficient security property for many applications of vector commitments, and can be obtained entirely with deterministic algorithms, excepting Setup; indeed, our own constructions achieve this. Of course, a deterministic Commit algorithm cannot hide the message vector, at least not in the sense of indistinguishability.

2.2 Short Integer Solution and (Tagged) Trapdoors

We recall the Short Integer Solution (SIS), and its hardness based on worst-case lattice problems.

Definition 3. *The (homogeneous) $SIS_{n,q,m,\beta}$ problem is: given a uniformly random matrix $\mathbf{A} \in \mathbb{Z}_q^{n \times m}$, find a non-zero integral vector $\mathbf{z} \in \mathbb{Z}^m$ such that $\mathbf{Az} = \mathbf{0}$ (mod $*$)q and $\|\mathbf{z}\| \leq \beta$. The normal form of the problem is to find a non-zero integral vector $\mathbf{z} = (\mathbf{x} \in \mathbb{Z}^m, \mathbf{e} \in \mathbb{Z}^n)$ such that $\mathbf{Ax} = \mathbf{e}$ (mod $*$)q and $\|\mathbf{z}\| \leq \beta$.*

When $q \geq \beta \cdot \tilde{O}(\sqrt{n})$ and m is polynomial in n and $\log q$, solving $SIS_{n,q,m,\beta}$ (in either its homogeneous or normal form) is at least as hard as approximating certain worst-case lattice problems on n-dimensional lattices to within a $\beta \cdot \tilde{O}(\sqrt{n})$ factor [MR04,GPV08].

Gadget and Trapdoors. Our constructions use standard techniques for SIS-based trapdoors and preimage sampling as developed in [GPV08,MP12]. These rely on a publicly known "gadget" matrix $\mathbf{G} \in \mathbb{Z}_q^{n \times w}$ for some w. The prototypical example is $\mathbf{G} = \mathbf{I}_n \otimes (1, 2, \ldots, 2^{\lceil \log_2 q \rceil - 1})$ where $w = n\lceil \log_2 q \rceil$, but any other suitable $\mathbf{G}$ supporting an efficient preimage-sampling algorithm can work just as well in our applications (possibly after adjusting parameters); see [MP12] for the precise requirements.

The basic gadget-based inversion operation is a deterministic function denoted $\mathbf{G}^{-1} \colon \mathbb{Z}_q^n \to \mathbb{Z}^w$, which for some small $g = g_{\mathbf{G}}$ satisfies $\mathbf{G} \cdot \mathbf{G}^{-1}(\mathbf{u}) = \mathbf{u}$ and $\|\mathbf{G}^{-1}(\mathbf{u})\| \leq g$ for all $\mathbf{u} \in \mathbb{Z}_q^n$.[7] (For example, $g_{\mathbf{G}} = 1$ for the prototypical gadget $\mathbf{G}$ defined above.) We extend the definition of $\mathbf{G}^{-1}$ to matrices simply by applying it column-wise.

The more advanced inversion operation is the (randomized) preimage-sampling algorithm, whose properties are described below in Theorem 1. For this purpose the gadget matrix $\mathbf{G}$ comes with a small factor $\omega = \omega_{\mathbf{G}}$ that appears in

---

[7] We stress that $\mathbf{G}^{-1}$ is a *function*, not a matrix, and it does not necessarily satisfy $\mathbf{G}^{-1}(\mathbf{G} \cdot \mathbf{z}) = \mathbf{z}$ for $\mathbf{z} \in \mathbb{Z}^w$.

the bounds associated with the sampling algorithm. (E.g., for the prototypical $\mathbf{G}$ given above, we can take ω to be any $\omega(\sqrt{\log n})$ function.)

Preimage sampling works for "tagged" trapdoors, which rely on an efficiently computable *invertible-differences* encoding from elements of some particular set F to $\mathbb{Z}_q^{n \times n}$. In such an encoding, for any distinct $f, f' \in F$, the difference $\mathbf{H}_{f'} - \mathbf{H}_f$ between their respective encodings $\mathbf{H}_{f'}, \mathbf{H}_f$ is invertible. A standard construction (see, e.g., [PW08, ABB10, MP12]) for prime q uses any (efficiently computable) injective map from F into the finite field $\mathbb{F}_{q^n}$, which is viewed as an n-dimensional vector space over $\mathbb{F}_q$ with some arbitrary basis. Then relative to that basis, multiplication by any fixed (nonzero and hence invertible) field element $f \in \mathbb{F}_{q^n}$ basis corresponds, via an additive homomorphism, to multiplication by an (invertible) matrix $\mathbf{H}_f \in \mathbb{Z}_q^{n \times n}$; this correspondence therefore yields an invertible-differences encoding. (This can be extended to arbitrary nonprime q in a natural way; see, e.g., [MP12].)

The following theorem summarizes the trapdoor functionality that our constructions will use; our presentation abstracts away the precise distributions sampled by the various algorithms. Typically SampleD samples from a discrete Gaussian distribution (as in [GPV08]), but the theorem holds equally well (but with somewhat looser bounds) for other distributions over the integers, like uniform over a sufficiently wide interval; see [LW15].

Theorem 1 ([GPV08, MP12]). *There are probabilistic polynomial-time algorithms* TrapGen, SampleD, SamplePre *and a "gadget" matrix* $\mathbf{G} \in \mathbb{Z}_q^{n \times w}$ *having the following properties, where* $m = \bar{m} + w$:

1. TrapGen($\bar{\mathbf{A}} \in \mathbb{Z}_q^{n \times \bar{m}}, \mathbf{H}^* \in \mathbb{Z}_q^{n \times n}$) *outputs some* $(\mathbf{A} \in \mathbb{Z}_q^{n \times m}, \mathbf{T} \in \mathbb{Z}^{\bar{m} \times m})$ *such that* $s_1(\mathbf{T}) \le s_T = O(\sqrt{m})$ *and*

$$\mathbf{A} = \bar{\mathbf{A}}\mathbf{T} + [\mathbf{0} \mid \mathbf{H}^*\mathbf{G}] \in \mathbb{Z}_q^{n \times m}.$$

2. *For any* $\bar{m} \ge 2n \log q$ *and any* $\mathbf{H}^* \in \mathbb{Z}_q^{n \times n}$, *and for uniformly random* $\bar{\mathbf{A}} \leftarrow \mathbb{Z}_q^{n \times \bar{m}}$ *and* $(\mathbf{A}, \mathbf{T}) \leftarrow$ TrapGen($\bar{\mathbf{A}}, \mathbf{H}^*$), *the distribution of* $\mathbf{A} \in \mathbb{Z}_q^{n \times m}$ *is within* negl(n) *statistical distance of uniform.*

3. *For any* $\mathbf{H}^*, \mathbf{H} \in \mathbb{Z}_q^{n \times n}$ *such that* $\mathbf{H}^* - \mathbf{H}$ *is invertible, any* $(\mathbf{A}, \mathbf{T}) \leftarrow$ TrapGen($\bar{\mathbf{A}}, \mathbf{H}^*$) *for any* $\bar{\mathbf{A}} \in \mathbb{Z}_q^{n \times \bar{m}}$, *any* $s \ge s_T \cdot \omega$, *any positive integer* k, *and letting* $\mathbf{A}' = \mathbf{A} - [\mathbf{0} \mid \mathbf{H}\mathbf{G}]$:

   (a) *For* $\mathbf{R} \leftarrow$ SampleD($1^{m \times k}, s$) *the distribution of* $\mathbf{U} = \mathbf{A}'\mathbf{R} \in \mathbb{Z}_q^{n \times k}$ *is within* $k \cdot$ negl(n) *statistical distance of uniform.*

   (b) *For any* $\mathbf{U} \in \mathbb{Z}_q^{n \times k}$, SamplePre($\mathbf{T}, \mathbf{A}', \mathbf{U}, s$) *outputs some* $\mathbf{R} \in \mathbb{Z}^{m \times k}$ *such that* $\|\mathbf{R}\| \le s\sqrt{m}$, $s_1(\mathbf{R}) = O(s\sqrt{m+k})$, *and the distribution of* $\mathbf{R}$ *is within* $k \cdot$ negl(n) *statistical distance of* $D_{\mathbf{A}', \mathbf{U}, s}$, *the conditional distribution of* $\mathbf{R} \leftarrow$ SampleD($1^{m \times k}, s$) *conditioned on the event* $\mathbf{A}'\mathbf{R} = \mathbf{U}$.

   In particular, the output distributions of the following two experiments are within $k \cdot$ negl(n) *statistical distance:*

   – *choose* $\mathbf{R} \leftarrow$ SampleD($1^{m \times k}, s$) *and output* $(\mathbf{R}, \mathbf{U} = \mathbf{A}'\mathbf{R} \in \mathbb{Z}_q^{n \times k})$.

   – *choose uniformly random* $\mathbf{U} \leftarrow \mathbb{Z}_q^{n \times k}$ *and* $\mathbf{R} \leftarrow$ SamplePre($\mathbf{T}, \mathbf{A}', \mathbf{U}, s$), *and output* $(\mathbf{R}, \mathbf{U})$.

We stress that the distribution $D_{\mathbf{A}',\mathbf{U},s}$ from Item 3b does not involve $\mathbf{T}$, so SamplePre's output essentially reveals nothing about its $\mathbf{T}$ argument. More precisely, in probability experiments we can replace calls to $\mathsf{SamplePre}(\mathbf{T}, \mathbf{A}', \mathbf{U}, s)$, which use $\mathbf{T}$, with (not necessarily efficient) samplings from $D_{\mathbf{A}',\mathbf{U},s}$, which do not use $\mathbf{T}$.

3   Vector Commitments

In this section we construct a vector commitment scheme based on the SIS problem (for suitable parameters). By convention, in this section we let n be the security parameter.

3.1   Construction

We let messages be vectors over $\mathcal{M} = I^\ell$ for some desired ℓ and interval $I \subset \mathbb{Z}$ of contiguous integers of maximum magnitude $M_I = \max_{i \in I}|i|$, e.g., $I = \{0, 1\}$ and $M_I = 1$.

The construction uses a suitable gadget matrix $\mathbf{G} \in \mathbb{Z}_q^{n \times w}$ and an injective, efficiently computable invertible-differences encoding that maps any $i \in [d+1]$ to a matrix $\mathbf{H}_i \in \mathbb{Z}_q^{n \times n}$, so that $\mathbf{H}_{i'} - \mathbf{H}_i$ is invertible for any distinct $i, i' \in [d+1]$; see Sect. 2.2 for instantiations. (In fact, because we will later need to take $q \gg d$, if q is prime then we can simply take $\mathbf{H}_i = i\mathbf{I}$ to be a scaled identity matrix.)

Construction 1 (SIS-based vector commitment). For suitable parameters $\bar{m}, s, \gamma$ (which are functions of the security parameter n), define the following differentially updatable vector commitment scheme.

- Setup($1^n, 1^d$): choose uniformly random $\bar{\mathbf{A}} \leftarrow \mathbb{Z}_q^{n \times \bar{m}}$ and let $(\mathbf{A}, \mathbf{T}) \leftarrow \mathsf{TrapGen}(\bar{\mathbf{A}}, \mathbf{H}_d)$. In all that follows, let $m = \bar{m} + w$ and for any $i \in [d]$ let

$$\mathbf{A}_i = \mathbf{A} - [\mathbf{0} \mid \mathbf{H}_i\mathbf{G}] \in \mathbb{Z}_q^{n \times m}. \qquad (1)$$

  Choose uniformly random $\mathbf{U} = [\mathbf{U}_0 \mid \cdots \mid \mathbf{U}_{d-1}] \leftarrow \mathbb{Z}_q^{n \times \ell d}$, where each $\mathbf{U}_j \in \mathbb{Z}_q^{n \times \ell}$.

  For each $i \in [d]$ let $\mathbf{R}_{i,i} = \mathbf{0} \in \mathbb{Z}^{m \times \ell}$, and for each $j \in [d] \setminus \{i\}$, let $\mathbf{R}_{i,j} \leftarrow \mathsf{SamplePre}(\mathbf{T}, \mathbf{A}_i, \mathbf{U}_j, s)$. Observe that $i \neq d$ and hence $\mathbf{H}_d - \mathbf{H}_i \in \mathbb{Z}_q^{n \times n}$ is invertible, as needed by SamplePre (see Item 3 of Theorem 1). In particular,

$$\mathbf{R}_{i,j} \in \mathbb{Z}^{m \times \ell} \text{ is "short" and } \mathbf{A}_i\mathbf{R}_{i,j} = \mathbf{U}_j. \qquad (2)$$

  Output the committer parameters $cp = (\mathbf{U}, \mathbf{R} = (\mathbf{R}_{i,j})_{i,j \in [d]} \in \mathbb{Z}^{md \times \ell d})$ and the verifier parameters $vp = (\mathbf{A}, \mathbf{U})$.
- Commit($cp, \mathbf{m} \in \mathcal{M}^d = I^{\ell d}$): output commitment $\mathbf{c} = \mathbf{U}\mathbf{m} = \sum_{j \in [d]} \mathbf{U}_j\mathbf{m}_j \in \mathbb{Z}_q^n$ and state $st = \mathbf{m}$.
- Open($cp, st = \mathbf{m}, i \in [d]$): output $\mathbf{p}_i = \mathbf{R}_{i,\star}\mathbf{m} = \sum_{j \in [d]} \mathbf{R}_{i,j}\mathbf{m}_j \in \mathbb{Z}^m$.
- Verify($vp, \mathbf{c} \in \mathbb{Z}_q^n, i \in [d], \mathbf{m}_i \in \mathcal{M}, \mathbf{p}_i \in \mathbb{Z}^m$): accept if $\|\mathbf{p}_i\| \leq \gamma$ and $\mathbf{c} = \mathbf{A}_i\mathbf{p}_i + \mathbf{U}_i\mathbf{m}_i$; otherwise, reject.

In addition, define the following update algorithms.

- PrepareUpdates^{diff}($cp, j \in [d], \boldsymbol{\delta} \in \mathbb{Z}^\ell$): output commitment update[8] $\delta_c = \tilde{\mathbf{c}} = \mathbf{U}_j \boldsymbol{\delta} \in \mathbb{Z}_q^n$, proof update[9] $\delta_p = (\mathbf{r}_i)_{i\in[d]}$ where $\mathbf{r}_i = \mathbf{R}_{i,j}\boldsymbol{\delta} \in \mathbb{Z}^m$, and state update $\delta_s = (j, \boldsymbol{\delta})$.
- UpdateC($vp, \mathbf{c} \in \mathbb{Z}_q^n, \delta_c = \tilde{\mathbf{c}} \in \mathbb{Z}_q^n$): output $\mathbf{c}' = \mathbf{c} + \tilde{\mathbf{c}} \in \mathbb{Z}_q^n$.
- UpdateP($vp, i, \mathbf{p}_i \in \mathbb{Z}^m, \delta_p = (\mathbf{r}_i)_{i\in[d]}$): output $\mathbf{p}'_i = \mathbf{p}_i + \mathbf{r}_i \in \mathbb{Z}^m$.
- UpdateS($cp, st = \mathbf{m}, \delta_s = (j, \boldsymbol{\delta})$): output $st' = \mathbf{m}'$, which is $\mathbf{m}$ with its jth $\mathcal{M}$-entry $\mathbf{m}_j$ replaced by $\mathbf{m}'_j = \mathbf{m}_j + \boldsymbol{\delta}$.

Parameters and Sizes. An appropriate choice of the parameters $\bar{m}, s, \gamma$ is as follows:

- let $\bar{m} = \lceil 2n \log q \rceil$ so that Item 2 of Theorem 1 applies;
- let $s = s_T \cdot \omega$ where ω and $s_T = O(\sqrt{m})$ are as in Sect. 2.2, so that $s_1(\mathbf{T}) \leq s_T$ and SamplePre can sample with parameter s, by Items 1 and 3 (respectively) of Theorem 1;
- let $\gamma = O(s M_I \sqrt{(m + \ell d)\ell d}) = O(s M_I(m + \ell d))$ be sufficiently large so that the norm of a proof $\mathbf{p}_i = \mathbf{R}_{i,\star}\mathbf{m}$ is bounded by γ. (This is because $s_1(\mathbf{R}_{i,\star}) = O(s\sqrt{m + \ell d})$ by Item 3b of Theorem 1, and $\|\mathbf{m}\| \leq M_I\sqrt{\ell d}$ because $\mathbf{m} \in I^{\ell d}$.)[10]

Letting the modulus q be sufficiently large relative to β (Equation (3)), as needed for the hardness of the relevant SIS problem, we obtain the following asymptotic object sizes.

- Commitments are in $\mathbb{Z}_q^n$ and hence have size $O(n \log q)$ bits.
- Proofs are vectors in $\mathbb{Z}^m$ of Euclidean norm bounded by $\gamma < q$, and hence can have size $O(n \log q)$ bits.
- Committer parameters are dominated by the $d^2 - d$ short matrices $\mathbf{R}_{i,j} \in \mathbb{Z}^{m \times \ell}$, and hence have size $\tilde{O}(n\ell d^2)$ bits. This can be reduced by a factor of n using a ring-based construction and Ring-SIS.
- Verifier parameters are dominated by the d matrices $\mathbf{U}_j \in \mathbb{Z}_q^{n \times m}$, and hence have size $O(n^2 d \log q)$ bits. This also can be reduced by a factor of n using rings. Separately, the verifier parameters can be reduced to just the size of $\mathbf{A} \in \mathbb{Z}_q^{n \times m}$, which is $O(n^2 \log^2 q)$ bits (or $O(n \log^2 q)$ bits using rings), by including the appropriate authenticated $\mathbf{U}_i$ in each proof.

---

[8] Alternatively, depending on how much space it requires to represent $\boldsymbol{\delta}$ compared to an element of $\mathbb{Z}_q^n$, it may be preferable to output $\delta_c = (j, \boldsymbol{\delta})$ as the commitment update, and have UpdateC compute $\mathbf{U}_j \boldsymbol{\delta}$.

[9] Alternatively, if UpdateP has access to all the $\mathbf{R}_{i,j}$ (via the committer parameters), then we can output a smaller proof update $\delta_p = \boldsymbol{\delta}$, and UpdateP can compute $\mathbf{r}_i = \mathbf{R}_{i,j}\boldsymbol{\delta}$ itself.

[10] A smaller γ can be used if we have a tighter bound on $\|\mathbf{m}\|$, e.g., if we know from the surrounding application that $\mathbf{m}$ is sparse.

Combinable Commitments and Proofs. The scheme also has the following combinability properties.[11] Suppose we have several commitments $\mathbf{c}_j = \mathbf{U}\mathbf{m}_j$ to respective message vectors $\mathbf{m}_j \in \mathbb{Z}^{\ell d}$ for $j = 1,\dots,t$. Gathering these into the columns of matrices $\mathbf{C} \in \mathbb{Z}_q^{n \times t}$ and $\mathbf{M} \in \mathbb{Z}^{\ell d \times t}$ (respectively), we have $\mathbf{C} = \mathbf{U}\mathbf{M}$. Then for any integer vector $\mathbf{e} \in \mathbb{Z}^t$ representing a linear combination of the message vectors, $\mathbf{c} := \mathbf{C}\mathbf{e} = \mathbf{U}(\mathbf{M}\mathbf{e}) \in \mathbb{Z}_q^n$ is the commitment to the combined message $\mathbf{m} := \mathbf{M}\mathbf{e} \in \mathbb{Z}^{\ell d}$.

Proofs are similarly combinable, for any fixed position. Let $\mathbf{p}_i^j \in \mathbb{Z}^m$ denote the opening of $\mathbf{c}_j$ at position i, and collect these into the columns of a matrix $\mathbf{P}_i \in \mathbb{Z}^{m \times t}$. Then $\mathbf{P}_i = \mathbf{R}_{i,\star}\mathbf{M}$, and hence $\mathbf{p}_i := \mathbf{P}_i\mathbf{e} = \mathbf{R}_{i,\star}\mathbf{m}$ is the proof for position i of the combined message $\mathbf{m} = \mathbf{M}\mathbf{e}$. Note that the entries of $\mathbf{m}$ may be larger than those of the $\mathbf{m}_j$—their magnitudes depend on the norm of $\mathbf{e}$—so the norm bound γ used in Verify and related parameters need to be adjusted accordingly.

In the full version we discuss variants of this scheme, including a more efficient one based on Ring-SIS.

3.2   Correctness

Lemma 1. *For the parameters given above, Construction 1 is a correct, perfectly updatable vector commitment scheme (according to Definition 1).*

Proof. We first show that openings are accepted by the verifier. Let $(cp, vp) \leftarrow$ Setup$(1^n, 1^d)$ and let $\mathbf{m} \in \mathcal{M}^d$, $\mathbf{c} = $ Commit$(cp, \mathbf{m}) = \mathbf{U}\mathbf{m}$ and $\mathbf{p}_i = $ Open$(cp, \mathbf{m}, i) = \mathbf{R}_{i,\star}\mathbf{m}$ for some $i \in [d]$. Then

$$\mathbf{A}_i\mathbf{p}_i = \mathbf{A}_i\sum_{j\in[d]}\mathbf{R}_{i,j}\mathbf{m}_j = \sum_{j\in[d]}(\mathbf{A}_i\mathbf{R}_{i,j})\mathbf{m}_j = \sum_{j\in[d]\setminus\{i\}}\mathbf{U}_j\mathbf{m}_j,$$

since by definition of Setup we have that $\mathbf{A}_i\mathbf{R}_{i,j} = \mathbf{U}_j$ for $i \neq j$ (Equation (2)) and $\mathbf{R}_{i,i} = \mathbf{0}$. Finally, we have

$$\sum_{j\in[d]\setminus\{i\}}\mathbf{U}_j\mathbf{m}_j = \mathbf{U}\mathbf{m} - \mathbf{U}_i\mathbf{m}_i = \mathbf{c} - \mathbf{U}_i\mathbf{m}_i,$$

as required. Moreover, by our choice of γ above we have that $\|\mathbf{p}_i\| = \|\mathbf{R}_{i,\star}\mathbf{m}\| \leq \gamma$. Therefore, Verify$(vp, \mathbf{c}, i, \mathbf{m}_i, \mathbf{p}_i)$ accepts.

Due to space limitations, we defer the proof of perfect differential updatability to the full version. $\square$

3.3   Security

Theorem 2. *Construction 1 is position binding if $SIS_{n,q,\bar{m}+\ell,\beta}$ is hard for*

$$\beta := 2\sqrt{\gamma^2 s_T^2 + M_I^2 \cdot \ell} = O(\gamma \cdot s_T) = O(M_I \cdot m(m + \ell d)) \cdot \omega. \qquad (3)$$

---

[11] We use the term *combinability* rather than *aggregatability* because the latter is often used for the ability to combine proofs for several different locations, which we do not see how to do for our construction.

More specifically, for any adversary $\mathcal{A}$ against the position binding of the scheme, there is an $SIS_{n,q,\bar{m}+\ell,\beta}$ adversary $\mathcal{B}$ for which

$$\mathbf{Adv}^{SIS}(\mathcal{B}) \geq \frac{1}{d}\mathbf{Adv}^{pba}(\mathcal{A}) - \mathrm{negl}(n),$$

and whose running time is essentially that of $\mathcal{A}$, plus a small polynomial in n.

Proof. Let $\mathcal{A}$ be any adversary that attacks the position binding (Definition 2) of Construction 1. That is, for some $d = \mathrm{poly}(n)$, and letting $(cp, vp) \leftarrow \mathsf{Setup}(1^n, 1^d)$, $\mathcal{A}(1^n, 1^d, cp, vp)$ attempts to output some $(\mathbf{c}, i, \mathbf{m}, \mathbf{m}', \mathbf{p}, \mathbf{p}')$ with distinct $\mathbf{m}, \mathbf{m}' \in I^{\ell d}$ and where $\mathsf{Verify}(vp, \mathbf{c}, i, \mathbf{m}, \mathbf{p})$, $\mathsf{Verify}(vp, \mathbf{c}, i, \mathbf{m}', \mathbf{p}')$ both accept.

We use $\mathcal{A}$ to construct an SIS adversary $\mathcal{B}$ which, on input $[\bar{\mathbf{A}} \mid \bar{\mathbf{U}}] \in \mathbb{Z}_q^{n \times (\bar{m}+\ell)}$, seeks to output a nonzero vector $\mathbf{x} \in \mathbb{Z}^{\bar{m}+\ell}$ such that $[\bar{\mathbf{A}} \mid \bar{\mathbf{U}}]\mathbf{x} = \mathbf{0}$ and $\|\mathbf{x}\| \leq \beta$. It operates as follows:

1. Choose uniformly random $i^* \in [d]$ as a guess of the position where $\mathcal{A}$ will attempt to break binding.
2. Let $(\mathbf{A}, \mathbf{T}) \leftarrow \mathsf{TrapGen}(\bar{\mathbf{A}}, \mathbf{H}_{i^*})$ and note that $s_1(\mathbf{T}) \leq s_T$ and $\mathbf{A}_{i^*} = \mathbf{A} - [\mathbf{0} \mid \mathbf{H}_{i^*}\mathbf{G}] = \bar{\mathbf{A}}\mathbf{T} \in \mathbb{Z}_q^{n \times m}$, by Item 1 of Theorem 1.
3. Define $\mathbf{U}_{i^*} = \bar{\mathbf{U}}$.
4. For each $j \neq i^*$ let $\mathbf{R}_{i^*,j} \leftarrow \mathsf{SampleD}(1^{m \times \ell}, s)$ and set $\mathbf{U}_j = \mathbf{A}_{i^*}\mathbf{R}_{i^*,j} \in \mathbb{Z}_q^{n \times \ell}$.
5. For each $i \neq i^*$ and $j \neq i$, let $\mathbf{R}_{i,j} \leftarrow \mathsf{SamplePre}(\mathbf{T}, \mathbf{A}_i, \mathbf{U}_j, s)$.
6. For each $i \in [d]$ let $\mathbf{R}_{i,i} = \mathbf{0}$.
7. Let $cp = (\mathbf{U} = (\mathbf{U}_j)_{j \in [d]} \in \mathbb{Z}_q^{n \times \ell d}, \mathbf{R} = (\mathbf{R}_{i,j})_{i,j \in [d]} \in \mathbb{Z}^{md \times \ell d})$ and $vp = (\mathbf{A}, \mathbf{U})$.
8. Let $(\mathbf{c}, i, \mathbf{m}, \mathbf{m}', \mathbf{p}, \mathbf{p}') \leftarrow \mathcal{A}(1^n, 1^d, cp, vp)$.
9. If $i \neq i^*$, abort. Otherwise, output $\mathbf{x} = \begin{bmatrix} \mathbf{T}(\mathbf{p} - \mathbf{p}') \\ \mathbf{m} - \mathbf{m}' \end{bmatrix} \in \mathbb{Z}^{\bar{m}+\ell}$.

By inspection, it is clear that $\mathcal{B}$ runs in the same time as $\mathcal{A}$, plus a small polynomial.

First, we show that if $\mathcal{A}$ successfully breaks binding at position $i = i^*$, then $\mathcal{B}$ outputs an SIS solution for $[\bar{\mathbf{A}} \mid \bar{\mathbf{U}}]$. In this case, we have $\mathbf{m} \neq \mathbf{m}'$ and both $\mathsf{Verify}(vp, \mathbf{c}, i^*, \mathbf{m}, \mathbf{p})$ and $\mathsf{Verify}(vp, \mathbf{c}, i^*, \mathbf{m}', \mathbf{p}')$ accept, so $\mathbf{c} = \mathbf{A}_{i^*}\mathbf{p} + \mathbf{U}_{i^*}\mathbf{m} = \mathbf{A}_{i^*}\mathbf{p}' + \mathbf{U}_{i^*}\mathbf{m}'$ and $\|\mathbf{p}\|, \|\mathbf{p}'\| \leq \gamma$. Recalling from above that $\mathbf{A}_{i^*} = \bar{\mathbf{A}}\mathbf{T}$, we therefore have

$$[\bar{\mathbf{A}} \mid \bar{\mathbf{U}}]\mathbf{x} = [\bar{\mathbf{A}} \mid \bar{\mathbf{U}}]\begin{bmatrix} \mathbf{T}(\mathbf{p} - \mathbf{p}') \\ \mathbf{m} - \mathbf{m}' \end{bmatrix}$$

$$= \bar{\mathbf{A}}\mathbf{T}(\mathbf{p} - \mathbf{p}') + \bar{\mathbf{U}}(\mathbf{m} - \mathbf{m}')$$

$$= \mathbf{A}_{i^*}(\mathbf{p} - \mathbf{p}') + \mathbf{U}_{i^*}(\mathbf{m} - \mathbf{m}')$$

$$= (\mathbf{A}_{i^*}\mathbf{p} + \mathbf{U}_{i^*}\mathbf{m}) - (\mathbf{A}_{i^*}\mathbf{p}' + \mathbf{U}_{i^*}\mathbf{m}')$$

$$= \mathbf{c} - \mathbf{c} = \mathbf{0}.$$

Moreover, $\mathbf{x} \neq \mathbf{0}$ because $\mathbf{m} \neq \mathbf{m}'$, and by the triangle inequality and the above bound $s_1(\mathbf{T}) \leq s_T$ we have

$$\|\mathbf{x}\| = \sqrt{\|\mathbf{T}(\mathbf{p} - \mathbf{p}')\|^2 + \|\mathbf{m} - \mathbf{m}'\|^2} \leq \sqrt{(2\gamma \cdot s_T)^2 + (2M_I \cdot \ell)^2} = \beta.$$

Therefore, $\mathbf{x}$ is an SIS solution for $[\bar{\mathbf{A}} \mid \bar{\mathbf{U}}]$.

It remains to analyze the probability that $\mathcal{A}$ breaks position binding at position $i = i^*$ in the above experiment run by $\mathcal{B}$. To do this we consider the following hybrid experiments.

- H_0 corresponds exactly to the "real" attack experiment with Setup, with some convenient presentational changes to aid comparison with the other experiments.
  1. Sample $i^* \leftarrow [d]$ uniformly at random.
  2. Sample $\bar{\mathbf{A}} \in \mathbb{Z}_q^{n \times \bar{m}}$ uniformly at random and $(\mathbf{A}, \mathbf{T}) \leftarrow \mathsf{TrapGen}(\bar{\mathbf{A}}, \mathbf{H}_d)$.
  3. Sample $\mathbf{U}_{i^*} \in \mathbb{Z}_q^{n \times \ell}$ uniformly at random.
  4. For each $j \neq i^*$, choose uniform $\mathbf{U}_j \leftarrow \mathbb{Z}_q^{n \times \ell}$ and let $\mathbf{R}_{i^*,j} \leftarrow \mathsf{SamplePre}(\mathbf{T}, \mathbf{A}_{i^*}, \mathbf{U}_j, s)$.
  5. For each $i \neq i^*$ and $j \neq i$, let $\mathbf{R}_{i,j} \leftarrow \mathsf{SamplePre}(\mathbf{T}, \mathbf{A}_i, \mathbf{U}_j, s)$.
  6. Set $\mathbf{R}_{i,i} = \mathbf{0}$ for all $i \in [d]$.
  7. Set $cp = (\mathbf{U}, \mathbf{R} = (\mathbf{R}_{i,j})_{i,j\in[d]})$ and $vp = (\mathbf{A}, \mathbf{U} = (\mathbf{U}_j)_{j\in[d]})$.
  8. Let $(\mathbf{c}, i, \mathbf{m}, \mathbf{m}', \mathbf{p}, \mathbf{p}') \leftarrow \mathcal{A}(1^n, 1^d, cp, vp)$.
  Note that H_0 is identical to the position-binding attack experiment against the scheme, as the choice of i^* only affects the order in which the $\mathbf{R}_{i,j}$ and $\mathbf{U}_j$ are selected. This does not affect the distribution of (cp, vp), and indeed, i^* is independent of the input to $\mathcal{A}$. Hence, the probability of the event GOOD that $\mathcal{A}$ breaks position binding at index $i = i^*$ is $d^{-1} \cdot \mathbf{Adv}^{\mathrm{pba}}(\mathcal{A})$.
- H_1 is identical to H_0 except that we replace Step 4 with the following:
  4. For each $j \neq i^*$, sample $\mathbf{R}_{i^*,j} \leftarrow \mathsf{SampleD}(1^{m \times \ell}, s)$ and let $\mathbf{U}_j = \mathbf{A}_{i^*}\mathbf{R}_{i^*,j} \in \mathbb{Z}_q^{n \times \ell}$.
  By Item 3 of Theorem 1, each independent $(\mathbf{R}_{i^*,j}, \mathbf{U}_j)$ pair generated in H_0 is within $\ell \cdot \mathrm{negl}(n)$ statistical distance of the corresponding pair generated in H_1. Because $\ell = \mathrm{poly}(n)$, the probability of the event GOOD in H_1 is within $\mathrm{negl}(n)$ of its probability in H_0.
- H_2 is identical to H_1 except we replace Step 5 with the following:
  5. For $i \neq i^*$ and $j \neq i$, (inefficiently) sample $\mathbf{R}_{i,j} \leftarrow D_{\mathbf{A}_i, \mathbf{U}_j, s}$.
  Note that $\mathbf{T}$ is unused in H_2, because the experiment instead samples inefficiently (e.g., using brute force); this is acceptable because we will only make *statistical* comparisons between H_2 and its adjacent experiments. For each i, we have $i \neq d$ and hence $\mathbf{H}_d - \mathbf{H}_i \in \mathbb{Z}_q^{n \times n}$ is invertible. So by Item 3b of Theorem 1, each of the independent $\mathbf{R}_{i,j}$ (for $i \neq i^*$ and $j \neq i$) sampled from $\mathsf{SamplePre}(\mathbf{T}, \mathbf{A}_i, \mathbf{U}_j, s)$ in H_1 is within $\ell \cdot \mathrm{negl}(n)$ statistical distance of the corresponding $\mathbf{R}_{i,j}$ sampled from $D_{\mathbf{A}_i, \mathbf{U}_j, s}$ in H_2. Hence, the probability of the event GOOD in H_2 is within $\mathrm{negl}(n)$ of its probability in H_1.
- H_3 is identical to H_2 except that we replace Step 2 with the following:
  2. Sample $\bar{\mathbf{A}} \in \mathbb{Z}_q^{n \times \bar{m}}$ uniformly at random and let $(\mathbf{A}, \mathbf{T}) \leftarrow \mathsf{TrapGen}(\bar{\mathbf{A}}, \mathbf{H}_{i^*})$.

By Item 2 of Theorem 1, for uniformly random $\bar{\mathbf{A}}$ we have that the $\mathbf{A}$ obtained from $\mathsf{TrapGen}(\bar{\mathbf{A}}, \mathbf{H})$ is within $\mathrm{negl}(n)$ statistical distance from uniform, for *any* tag $\mathbf{H}$. Hence, the $\mathbf{A}$ generated in H_2 is within $\mathrm{negl}(n)$ statistical distance from the $\mathbf{A}$ generated in H_3. Note that this is *not* necessarily true for the $\mathbf{T}$s generated in each experiment, however $\mathbf{T}$ is entirely unused (following its creation) in both experiments. Hence, the probability of the event GOOD in H_3 is within $\mathrm{negl}(n)$ of its probability in H_2.

- H_4 is identical to H_3 except that we replace Step 5 with the following:

    5. For each $i \neq i^*$ and $j \neq i$, sample $\mathbf{R}_{i,j} \leftarrow \mathsf{SamplePre}(\mathbf{T}, \mathbf{A}_i, \mathbf{U}_j, s)$.

    For all $i \neq i^*$ we have that $\mathbf{H}_{i^*} - \mathbf{H}_i \in \mathbb{Z}_q^{n \times n}$ is invertible. So by Item 3b of Theorem 1, each (independently chosen) $\mathbf{R}_i$ that is generated in this way is within $\mathrm{negl}(n)$ statistical distance of the corresponding one in H_3. By the same reasoning given above for H_2 versus H_1, the probability of the event GOOD in H_4 is within $\mathrm{negl}(n)$ of its probability in H_3.

    Finally, notice that H_4 is identical to the experiment that $\mathcal{B}$ simulates to $\mathcal{A}$, because the $\bar{\mathbf{A}}$ and $\mathbf{U}_{i^*} = \bar{\mathbf{U}}$ from the SIS instance are uniformly random and independent.

Combining all of the above completes the proof of the theorem.   □

3.4   Specialized Tree Transformation

In the vector commitment scheme from Construction 1, the sizes of the committer and verifier parameters are respectively quadratic and linear in the message dimension d, which makes the construction unsuitable as-is for large dimensions. In the full version, we give a formal treatment of a generic d-ary tree construction that transforms a VC scheme for dimension d into one for dimension d^h for any desired positive integer h, with no increase in the sizes of the parameters or commitments. Only the proof and proof-update sizes increase, growing linearly in h but independently of d. However, this transformation fails to preserve the combinability of commitments and proofs, as well as the stateless updatability property of the base scheme, which is important for distributed VCs [CPSZ18].

Here we give a specialized tree-like transformation of our SIS-based VC scheme. In contrast with the generic transform, ours preserves combinability and (differential) stateless updates, essentially because commitments are linear in the committed messages, but at the price of somewhat larger objects and a stronger SIS assumption. The transformation is based on the main idea from [PSTY13], which was used in the context of an SIS-based Merkle-tree-like construction (which can be used as a VC). In that context, a proof must include all of the "sibling" information for each step in a root-to-leaf path, so the proof size ends up being proportional to $hd \log^2(d^h)$. (The $\log^2(d^h)$ factor comes from the length of the proofs along the path as well as the sizes of the integers within them.) Here we show that the main idea from [PSTY13] also applies to our SIS-based VC scheme, but with the advantage that *proofs need not contain any sibling information*, so the proof size grows only as $h \log^2(d^h) = h^3 \log^2 d$.

In summary, our construction is quantitatively a strict improvement over the VC obtained from [PSTY13], for any choice of arity d and tree height h (but at the price of private setup). Its efficiency profile also recommends using a moderately large d and correspondingly smaller h, which can ultimately yield the same asymptotic proof size as for the *generic* tree transformation for VCs, while preserving combinability and (differential) stateless updates (but at the price of private setup and a stronger SIS assumption).

Construction 2 (SIS-based tree vector commitment). Let $\mathbf{G} \in \mathbb{Z}_q^{n \times w}$ be a suitable gadget matrix with associated magnitude bound $g_{\mathbf{G}}$ for the $\mathbf{G}^{-1}$ operation; see Sect. 2.2 for details. (This gadget need not be the same as the one used in Construction 1.)

Let message vectors be over $\overline{\mathcal{M}} = \overline{I}^w$ for some desired range $\overline{I} = \{-M_{\overline{I}}, \ldots, M_{\overline{I}}\} \subset \mathbb{Z}$. Let h be any positive integer, and adopt the algorithms defined in Construction 1 for dimension-d vectors over $\mathcal{M} = I^w$, where $I = \{-M_I, \ldots, M_I\}$ for $M_I = M_{\overline{I}} \cdot g_{\mathbf{G}} \cdot w \cdot d^h$.[12] Define the following algorithms:

- $\overline{\mathsf{Setup}}_h(1^n, 1^{d^h})$: output $(cp = (\mathbf{U} = [\mathbf{U}_0 \mid \cdots \mid \mathbf{U}_{d-1}], \_), vp) \leftarrow \mathsf{Setup}(1^n, 1^d)$. In all that follows, let $\mathbf{S}^{(1)} = \mathbf{I}_{wd} \in \mathbb{Z}^{wd \times wd}$ and $\mathbf{U}^{(1)} = \mathbf{U} \in \mathbb{Z}_q^{n \times wd}$, and for $1 < k \le h$ let

$$\mathbf{S}^{(k)} = \mathbf{I}_d \otimes \mathbf{G}^{-1}(\mathbf{U}^{(k-1)}) \in \mathbb{Z}^{wd \times wd^k}$$
$$\mathbf{U}^{(k)} = \mathbf{U}\mathbf{S}^{(k)} \in \mathbb{Z}_q^{n \times wd^k}.$$

  Note that $\mathbf{U}^{(k)} = [\mathbf{U}_0^{(k)} \mid \cdots \mid \mathbf{U}_{d^k-1}^{(k)}]$ can be viewed as a block matrix where each $\mathbf{U}_{\overline{\jmath}}^{(k)} \in \mathbb{Z}_q^{n \times w}$ and $\overline{\jmath} \in [d^k]$. Moreover, each such block can be computed independently given just $\mathbf{U}$ and $\overline{\jmath}$, without needing to compute the entire matrix.[13]

- For $1 \le k \le h$, $\overline{\mathsf{Commit}}_k(cp, \overline{\mathbf{m}} \in \overline{\mathcal{M}}^{d^k} = \overline{I}^{wd^k})$ does:
  - let $\overline{\mathbf{c}} = \mathbf{G}^{-1}(\mathbf{U}^{(k)})\overline{\mathbf{m}} \in I^w = \mathcal{M}$,[14]
  - output $(\overline{\mathbf{c}}, \overline{st} = \overline{\mathbf{m}})$.

- $\overline{\mathsf{Open}}_1 = \mathsf{Open}$. For $1 < k \le h$, $\overline{\mathsf{Open}}_k(cp, \overline{st} = \overline{\mathbf{m}} \in \overline{\mathcal{M}}^{d^k}, \overline{\imath} \in [d^k])$ does:
  - write $\overline{\imath} = id^{k-1} + \overline{\imath}'$ where $i \in [d]$ and $\overline{\imath}' \in [d^{k-1}]$,
  - parse $\overline{\mathbf{m}} = (\overline{\mathbf{m}}_0, \ldots, \overline{\mathbf{m}}_{d-1})$ where each $\overline{\mathbf{m}}_i \in \overline{\mathcal{M}}^{d^{k-1}}$,
  - let $\mathbf{p}_i \leftarrow \mathsf{Open}(cp, \mathbf{S}^{(k)}\overline{\mathbf{m}} \in I^{wd} = \mathcal{M}^d, i)$,

---

[12] The factor $M_{\overline{I}} \cdot w \cdot d^h$ in M_I may be replaced by an upper bound on $\|\mathbf{m}\|_1$ for only those message vectors $\mathbf{m}$ that may be used in an application, e.g., sparse vectors.

[13] Specifically, $\mathbf{U}_{\overline{\jmath}}^{(k)} = \mathbf{U}_j \mathbf{G}^{-1}(\mathbf{U}_{\overline{\jmath}'}^{(k-1)})$ where $\overline{\jmath} = jd^{k-1} + \overline{\jmath}'$ for $\overline{\jmath} \in [d^k]$, $j \in [d]$, and $\overline{\jmath}' \in [d^{k-1}]$. Unrolling this fully, $\mathbf{U}_{\overline{\jmath}}^{(k)} = \mathbf{U}_{j_{k-1}}\mathbf{G}^{-1}(\mathbf{U}_{j_{k-2}}\mathbf{G}^{-1}(\cdots \mathbf{G}^{-1}(\mathbf{U}_{j_1}\mathbf{G}^{-1}(\mathbf{U}_{j_0}))\cdots))$ where $j_{k-1}\cdots j_1 j_0$ is the base-d representation of $\overline{\jmath}$.

[14] Note that $\mathbf{G}\overline{\mathbf{c}} = \mathbf{U}\mathbf{S}^{(k)}\overline{\mathbf{m}} \in \mathbb{Z}_q^n$ is the commitment output of $\mathsf{Commit}(cp, \mathbf{S}^{(k)}\overline{\mathbf{m}})$, but we cannot necessarily compute $\overline{\mathbf{c}}$ from that output.

- let $(\overline{\mathbf{c}}_i, \_) \leftarrow \overline{\mathsf{Commit}}_{k-1}(cp, \overline{\mathbf{m}}_i),$[15]
  - let $\overline{p}'_{\bar{\imath}'} \leftarrow \overline{\mathsf{Open}}_{k-1}(cp, \overline{\mathbf{m}}_i, \bar{\imath}'),$
    - output $\overline{p}_{\bar{\imath}} = (\mathbf{p}_i, \overline{\mathbf{c}}_i, \overline{p}'_{\bar{\imath}'}).$
- $\overline{\mathsf{Verify}}_1(vp, \overline{\mathbf{c}} \in I^w = \mathcal{M}, \bar{\imath} \in [d], \overline{\mathbf{m}}_{\bar{\imath}} \in \mathcal{M}, \overline{p}_{\bar{\imath}}) = \mathsf{Verify}(vp, \mathbf{G}\overline{\mathbf{c}}, \bar{\imath}, \overline{\mathbf{m}}_{\bar{\imath}}, \overline{p}_{\bar{\imath}}).$
  For $1 < k \leq h$, $\overline{\mathsf{Verify}}_k(vp, \overline{\mathbf{c}} \in I^w = \mathcal{M}, \bar{\imath} \in [d^k], \overline{\mathbf{m}}_{\bar{\imath}} \in \mathcal{M}, \overline{p}_{\bar{\imath}})$ does:
  - define $i, \bar{\imath}'$ in terms of $\bar{\imath}$ as in $\overline{\mathsf{Open}}_k$ and parse $\overline{p}_{\bar{\imath}} = (\mathbf{p}_i, \overline{\mathbf{c}}_i, \overline{p}'_{\bar{\imath}'}),$
  - if $\mathsf{Verify}(vp, \mathbf{G}\overline{\mathbf{c}}, i, \overline{\mathbf{c}}_i, \mathbf{p}_i)$ rejects, then reject,
  - if $\overline{\mathsf{Verify}}_{k-1}(vp, \overline{\mathbf{c}}_i, \bar{\imath}', \overline{\mathbf{m}}_{\bar{\imath}}, \overline{p}'_{\bar{\imath}'})$ rejects, then reject; else, accept.

Update algorithms follow rather straightforwardly from the linearity of the commitment, and are given in the full version.

Object Sizes. Instantiating the underlying scheme with parameters discussed above and choosing sufficiently large q relative to β (where β is as in Eq. (3)), so that $\log q = O(h \log d + \log n) = O(h \log d)$ under the (very mild) assumption that the vector dimension $d^h = n^{\Omega(1)}$ is at least polynomial in n, we obtain the following asymptotic object sizes.

- A commitment is a vector in $\mathcal{M} = I^w$, with each entry bounded by $M_I = M_{\bar{I}} \cdot g_{\mathbf{G}} \cdot w \cdot d^h$. Since $w = O(n \log q) = O(nh \log d)$, a commitment requires $O(wh \log d) = O(nh^2 \log^2 d)$ bits to represent.
- A proof consists of $h - 1$ vectors in $\mathcal{M}$ and h proofs from the underlying scheme; the latter are vectors in $\mathbb{Z}^m$ of Euclidean norm bounded by γ. Since $m = O(n \log q) = O(nh \log d)$ and $\log \gamma = O(h \log d)$, a full proof requires $O(nh^3 \log^2 d)$ bits to represent.
- The committer parameters cp are dominated by the $d^2 - d$ short matrices $\mathbf{R}_{i,j} \in \mathbb{Z}^{m \times w}$ from the underlying scheme, and hence have size $\tilde{O}(n^2 h^2 d^2)$. This can be reduced by a factor of n using a ring-based construction
- The verifier parameters vp are dominated by the d matrices $\mathbf{U}_j \in \mathbb{Z}_q^{n \times w}$, and hence have size $O(n^2 h^2 d \log^2 d)$ bits. This also can be reduced by a factor of n using a ring-based construction.

In the full version, we prove that for any positive integer h, Construction 2 is correct, perfectly updatable, and position binding.

4   Functional Commitments (with Authority)

In this section we define *functional commitments with authority*, which enable concise commitments and proofs of *arbitrary functions* (from a particular family) of committed messages. We introduce a new model in which a trusted authority both performs the system setup, and remains online to give out *opening keys* ok_f that enable committers to open desired functions f of committed messages. We stress that, unlike with identity/attribute-based encryption, where each key extracted by the authority must be transmitted confidentially to its

---

[15] Alternatively, the computation of all the d^{h-1} intermediate commitments $\overline{\mathbf{c}}_i$ could be done at commitment time, and stored in st.

intended recipient and kept secret, with functional commitments all opening keys can be made public and used by any party. For example, any party can query the authority for any supported function f, and the authority can post the opening key ok_f on a public bulletin board for all to see and use.

Of course, if the supported function family has only polynomially many functions, then the authority can immediately post all the associated opening keys and then go offline forever. However, many families of interest have super-polynomially (or even exponentially) many functions, so in these cases the authority needs to remain online to answer new queries. It is a very interesting question whether our construction can be modified to remove the need for an online authority.

4.1 Definitions

Here we formally define functional commitments with authority, and the security notions we consider for them.

Definition 4. *A* functional commitment scheme with authority *for a function class $\mathcal{F}$, and having message space $\mathcal{M}$, commitment space $\mathcal{C}$, and proof space $\mathcal{P}$ (all of which may depend on the security parameter), is a tuple of algorithms with the following interfaces:*

- Setup(1^λ) *outputs* committer parameters cp, verifier parameters vp, *and an* extraction key ek.
- Extract($ek, f \in \mathcal{F}$) *outputs an* opening key ok_f *for the function f.*
- Commit($cp, m \in \mathcal{M}$) *outputs a* commitment $c \in \mathcal{C}$ *and some* auxiliary data aux.
- Open(cp, aux, ok_f) *outputs a* proof $p_{f,m} \in \mathcal{P}$ *for the value of $f(m)$, where m is the committed message associated to aux.*
- Verify($vp, c \in \mathcal{C}, f \in \mathcal{F}, y, p_{f,m}$) *either accepts or rejects.*

The scheme should satisfy the following correctness property: for any $m \in \mathcal{M}$ and $f \in \mathcal{F}$, and for $(cp, vp, ek) \leftarrow$ Setup(1^λ), $ok_f \leftarrow$ Extract(ek, f), $(c, aux) \leftarrow$ Commit(cp, m), and $p_{f,m} \leftarrow$ Open(cp, aux, ok_f), Verify($vp, c, f, y = f(m), p_{f,m}$) should accept with $1 - \text{negl}(\lambda)$ probability (over all the randomness of the experiment).

Definition 5. *For a functional commitment scheme with authority FCS, the* selective-function attack *game with an adversary is defined as follows:*

1. *The adversary is given the security parameter 1^λ and outputs a function $f^* \in \mathcal{F}$ to the challenger.*
2. *The challenger lets $(cp, vp, ek) \leftarrow$ Setup(1^λ) and gives cp, vp to the adversary.*
3. *The adversary is given adaptive oracle (query) access to* Extract($ek, \cdot$).[16]

---

[16] Note that we allow the adversary to query the oracle on any $f \in \mathcal{F}$, even $f = f^*$. This is because having an opening key for f^* does not inherently allow for breaking function binding for f^*—as opposed to, say, identity-based encryption, where a decryption key for the target identity trivially allows decryption of the challenge ciphertext.

4. *Finally, the adversary outputs a commitment c^* and two value-proof pairs (y,p) and (y',p'). It wins the game if $y \neq y'$ and both $\mathsf{Verify}(vp,c^*,f^*,y,p)$ and $\mathsf{Verify}(vp,c^*,f^*,y',p')$ accept.*

The advantage *of an adversary $\mathcal{A}$ in the above game, denoted $\mathbf{Adv}_{FCS}^{sfa}(\mathcal{A})$, is the probability that it wins the game (as a function of the security parameter).*

We say that FCS has the selective function binding *property if $\mathbf{Adv}_{FCS}^{sfa}(\mathcal{A}) = \mathrm{negl}(\lambda)$ for every probabilistic polynomial-time adversary $\mathcal{A}$.*

Remark 2. One can strengthen Definition 5 by changing the attack game so that the adversary does not specify the target function f^* until Item 4 (rather than in Item 1, before seeing the public parameters and the queried opening keys); we call the resulting security notion *adaptive*, or *full*, functional binding. Generically, any scheme with selective security also has adaptive security, up to a loose reduction whose advantage is smaller by a factor of the size of the function family. (This follows by the standard technique of complexity leveraging—i.e., initially "guessing" the function f^* that the adversary will eventually choose, and succeeding when this guess turns out to be correct.)

4.2   Homomorphic Commitments

A main tool used in our functional commitment scheme is a homomorphic commitment implicit in the FHE scheme of Gentry, Sahai, and Waters (GSW) [GSW13], and made explicit in the works of Gorbunov, Vaikuntanathan, and Wichs (GVW) [GVW15] and Peikert and Shiehian [PS19], which we recall in this section. For better parameters and efficiency when working with certain function families (e.g., linear functions), we generalize the scheme somewhat using standard "tagged trapdoor" and homomorphic techniques developed in works such as [PW08, AFV11, MP12, Xag13]. The following theorem abstracts what we need from these works and others like [BV14, AP14]; see the cited works and the full version for further details on the implementations of the claimed algorithms.

Theorem 3 (Homomorphic commitment). *Let $\mathcal{U}$ denote one of the following families $\mathcal{U}_{linear}$, $\mathcal{U}_{circuit}$, $\mathcal{U}_{BP}$ of "size-T" functions from X^S to X^L, for a certain domain X, input size S, and output length L:*

- *for $X = \mathbb{Z}_q^{n \times n}$, $T = S$, and $L = 1$, the family $\mathcal{U}_{linear}$ of functions $U_{\mathbf{M}}$ with $\mathbf{M} = (\mathbf{M}_1, \ldots, \mathbf{M}_S) \in X^S$, defined as $U_{\mathbf{M}}(\mathbf{F}) := \sum_{i=1}^S \mathbf{F}_i \mathbf{M}_i$ for $\mathbf{F} = (\mathbf{F}_1, \ldots, \mathbf{F}_S) \in X^S$;*
- *for $X = \{0,1\}$, the set $\mathcal{U}_{circuit}$ of size-T, depth-D Boolean circuits $U \colon \{0,1\}^S \to \{0,1\}^L$;*
- *for $X = \{0,1\}$, the set $\mathcal{U}_{BP}$ of size-T (for a given width) branching programs $U \colon \{0,1\}^S \to \{0,1\}^L$.*

There exist deterministic polynomial-time algorithms Encode, Eval having the following properties. Each input in square brackets is optional, and when provided, the additional output (also in square brackets) is also produced. The algorithm's main output is the same whether or not the optional input is provided.

1. $\mathsf{Eval}(U \in \mathcal{U}, \mathbf{C} \in \mathbb{Z}_q^{n \times Sw}[, \mathbf{R}_x \in \mathbb{Z}^{m \times Sw}])$ *outputs a commitment matrix* $\mathbf{C}_U \in \mathbb{Z}_q^{n \times Lw}$ *[and an integral matrix* $\mathbf{R}_{U,x} \in \mathbb{Z}^{m \times Lw}$*].*
   If $\mathbf{C} = \mathbf{AR}_x + \mathsf{Encode}(x)$ *for some* $\mathbf{A} \in \mathbb{Z}_q^{n \times m}$ *and* $x \in X^S$, *then* $\mathbf{C}_U = \mathbf{AR}_{U,x} + \mathsf{Encode}(U(x))$, *and:*
   (a) for $\mathcal{U} = \mathcal{U}_{linear}$, $\|\mathbf{R}_{U,x}\| \leq \|\mathbf{R}_x\| \cdot Sw$;
   (b) for $\mathcal{U} = \mathcal{U}_{circuit}$, $\|\mathbf{R}_{U,x}\| \leq \|\mathbf{R}_x\| \cdot (w+1)^D$;
   (c) for $\mathcal{U} = \mathcal{U}_{BP}$, $\|\mathbf{R}_{U,x}\| \leq \|\mathbf{R}_x\| \cdot w^{O(1)} \cdot T$.
2. *There is an efficient deterministic polynomial-time algorithm that, given any invertible* $\mathbf{Y} \in \mathbb{Z}_q^{n \times n}$ *and any* $\mathbf{u} \in \mathbb{Z}_q^n$, *outputs a binary* $\mathbf{e} = \mathbf{G}^{-1}(\mathbf{Y}^{-1}\mathbf{u}) \in \{0,1\}^w$ *such that* $\mathsf{Encode}(\mathbf{Y}) \cdot \mathbf{e} = \mathbf{Y}(\mathbf{Ge}) = \mathbf{u}$.
3. *There is an efficient deterministic polynomial-time algorithm that, given any* $\mathbf{M} \in \mathbb{Z}_q^{n \times L}$, *outputs a binary* $\mathbf{e} \in \{0,1\}^{Lw}$ *such that* $\mathsf{Encode}(\mathbf{y}) \cdot \mathbf{e} = \mathbf{My} \in \mathbb{Z}_q^n$ *for every* $\mathbf{y} \in \{0,1\}^L$.

4.3   Functional Commitment Construction

Here we give a functional commitment (with authority) for various families $\mathcal{F}$ of functions from a given message space $\mathcal{M}$ to X^L, for some domain X and output length L (typically, $X = \mathbb{Z}_q^{n \times n}$ or $X = \{0,1\}$).

Let $\mathcal{F}' = \mathcal{F} \cup \{d\}$ where $d \notin \mathcal{F}$ is some distinguished "dummy" function, and define the family of functions

$$\mathcal{U} := \{U_m \colon \mathcal{F}' \to X^L\}_{m \in \mathcal{M}}$$
$$U_m(f) := f(m);$$

we emphasize that this switches the roles of the message m and function f, letting the message define a function U_m that takes f as input data.

The construction requires homomorphic evaluation of any $U_m \in \mathcal{U}$ (for known $m \in \mathcal{M}$) on a commitment to a function f under the GSW/GVW scheme; let S denote the size of f under a suitable representation for this purpose. Naturally, the choice of function family $\mathcal{F}$ influences the scheme's efficiency and parameters (norm bound γ, modulus q, etc.); we describe some example instantiations of interest following the construction.

The construction also uses an injective, efficiently computable invertible-differences encoding that maps any $f \in \mathcal{F}'$ to a matrix $\mathbf{H}_f \in \mathbb{Z}_q^{n \times n}$, so that $\mathbf{H}_f - \mathbf{H}_{f'}$ is invertible for any distinct $f, f' \in \mathcal{F}'$. (See Sect. 2.2 for instantiations.) For simplicity we assume that the family $\mathcal{F}'$ is small enough to support such an encoding. Alternatively, we can map each f to a *tuple* $(\mathbf{H}_{f,1}, \ldots, \mathbf{H}_{f,t})$ for sufficiently large t so that $\mathbf{H}_{f,i} - \mathbf{H}_{f',i}$ is invertible for some i (and modify the construction below in the natural way), or we can first apply a collision-resistant (or even just universal one-way) hash function to f and use an invertible-differences encoding on the hash values.[17]

---

[17] No homomorphic properties (only invertible differences) are needed for this encoding of the functions, so hashing is acceptable.

Construction 3 (SIS-based functional commitment). Let function families $\mathcal{F}, \mathcal{F}' = \mathcal{F} \cup \{d\}$ (which may depend on the security parameter n) and $\mathcal{U} = \{U_m(\cdot)\}$ be as described above. For suitable parameters $\bar{m}, s, \gamma$, we define the following functional commitment scheme (with authority) for the family $\mathcal{F}$.

- Setup(1^n): choose uniform $\bar{\mathbf{A}} \leftarrow \mathbb{Z}_q^{n \times \bar{m}}$ and let $(\mathbf{A} \in \mathbb{Z}_q^{n \times m}, \mathbf{T} \in \mathbb{Z}^{\bar{m} \times m}) \leftarrow$ TrapGen($\bar{\mathbf{A}}, \mathbf{H}_d$), where $d \in \mathcal{F}'$ is the special "dummy" function. In all that follows, for any $f \in \mathcal{F}$ let

$$\mathbf{A}_f = \mathbf{A} - [\mathbf{0} \mid \mathbf{H}_f \mathbf{G}] \in \mathbb{Z}_q^{n \times m}. \tag{4}$$

  Choose uniformly random $\mathbf{C} \leftarrow \mathbb{Z}_q^{n \times Sw}$. Output the committer parameters $cp = \mathbf{C}$, the verifier parameters $vp = \mathbf{A}$, and the extraction key $ek = (\mathbf{C}, \mathbf{A}, \mathbf{T})$.
- Extract($ek = (\mathbf{C}, \mathbf{A}, \mathbf{T}), f \in \mathcal{F}$): output $\mathbf{R}_f \leftarrow$ SamplePre($\mathbf{T}, \mathbf{A}_f, \mathbf{C} -$ Encode(f), s) as the opening key. Observe that $f \neq d$ and hence $\mathbf{H}_d - \mathbf{H}_f \in \mathbb{Z}_q^{n \times n}$ is invertible, as needed by SamplePre (see Item 3 of Theorem 1). In particular, $\mathbf{R}_f \in \mathbb{Z}^{m \times Sw}$ is "short" and

$$\mathbf{C} = \mathbf{A}_f \mathbf{R}_f + \text{Encode}(f), \tag{5}$$

  i.e., $\mathbf{R}_f$ is randomness that opens $\mathbf{C}$ as a commitment to f with respect to $\mathbf{A}_f$. *Note:* for security, it is *essential* that repeated calls to Extract on the same input (ek, f) produce the *same* output $\mathbf{R}_f$. This can be ensured by the standard techniques of memoization (e.g., using a public bulletin board of all prior queries and answers), or by applying a pseudorandom function to (ek, f) to generate randomness for the call to SamplePre, so that $\mathbf{R}_f$ is a deterministic function of the input.
- Commit($cp = \mathbf{C}, m \in \mathcal{M}$): output $\mathbf{C}_m = \text{Eval}(U_m, \mathbf{C}) \in \mathbb{Z}_q^{n \times Lw}$ and $aux = m$. [For Boolean functions the commitment can be compressed significantly; see Sect. 4.3 below.]
- Open($cp = \mathbf{C}, aux = m \in \mathcal{M}, ok_f = \mathbf{R}_f$): compute $(\mathbf{C}_m, \mathbf{R}_{m,f}) = \text{Eval}(U_m, \mathbf{C}, \mathbf{R}_f)$ and output $\mathbf{R}_{m,f} \in \mathbb{Z}^{m \times Lw}$.
  [For Boolean functions the proof can be compressed significantly; see Sect. 4.3 below.]
- Verify($vp = \mathbf{A}, \mathbf{C}^*, f \in \mathcal{F}, \mathbf{y} \in X^L, \mathbf{R}^*$): accept if $\|\mathbf{R}^*\| \leq \gamma$ and $\mathbf{C}^* = \mathbf{A}_f \mathbf{R}^* + \text{Encode}(\mathbf{y})$, i.e., if $\mathbf{R}^*$ is sufficiently short randomness that opens $\mathbf{C}^*$ as a commitment to $\mathbf{y}$ with respect to $\mathbf{A}_f$. Otherwise, reject.

Combinability. Similarly to our SIS-based vector commitments from Sect. 3, the functional commitment scheme has the following combinability property: given commitments $\mathbf{C}_m, \mathbf{C}_{m'}$ and respective proofs $\mathbf{R}_{m,f}, \mathbf{R}_{m',f}$ that $f(m) = \mathbf{y}, f(m') = \mathbf{y}'$ for some function f, we can take the same arbitrary small linear combination of each pair to get a combined commitment and a proof (under a suitably relaxed norm bound) that $f(m) + f(m') = \mathbf{y} + \mathbf{y}'$. For linear functions f this is equivalent to $f(m + m') = \mathbf{y} + \mathbf{y}'$, but we caution that in general it may not correspond to the application of f on any legal message.

Parameters. Here we give a convenient choice of parameters that works for all of our instantiations:

- let $\bar{m} = \lceil 2n \log q \rceil$ so that the output $\mathbf{A}$ of TrapGen is statistically close to uniform;
- let $s = s_T \cdot \omega$ where ω and $s_T = O(\sqrt{m})$ are as in Sect. 2.2, so that $s_1(\mathbf{T}) \leq s_T$ and SamplePre can sample with parameter s, by Items 1 and 3 (respectively) of Theorem 1;
- let γ be defined based on the particular function family $\mathcal{F}$, as in the following instantiations.

Instantiation: Linear Functions over Finite Fields. Let $\mathbb{F} = \mathbb{F}_{p^n}$ for some prime p that divides q, let $\mathcal{M} = \mathbb{F}^S$ for some $S = S(\lambda)$, and let $\mathcal{F}'$ be the family of all $\mathbb{F}$-linear functions from $\mathbb{F}^S$ to $\mathbb{F}$. We can represent any such function as a vector $\boldsymbol{f} = (f_1, \ldots, f_S) \in \mathbb{F}^S$ of field elements, and can define $U_{\boldsymbol{m}}(\boldsymbol{f}) := \sum_{i=1}^S f_i m_i \in \mathbb{F}$ for each $\boldsymbol{m} \in \mathbb{F}^S$. By simulating $\mathbb{F}$ using the matrix ring $\mathcal{R} = \mathbb{Z}_q^{n \times n}$ (simply by reducing modulo p), Theorem 3 with family $\mathcal{U}_{\text{linear}}$ yields a suitable homomorphic commitment. For this instantiation, following Item 1a of Theorem 3 we set

$$\gamma = \gamma_{\text{linear}} := s\sqrt{m} \cdot Sw.$$

Let the "dummy" function $d \in \mathcal{F}'$ be the trivial function that always outputs zero, leaving the family $\mathcal{F} = \mathcal{F}' \setminus \{d\}$ of all *nontrivial* linear functions as the one supported by the scheme (note that the trivial function is not needed, since its output is fixed).

Remark 3. The restriction to linear functions over *finite fields*, rather than more general matrix rings $\mathbb{Z}_p^{n \times n}$ where p divides q, is mostly for convenience of presentation in the SIS-based security proof (see the full version). Using more sophisticated techniques and exploiting the fact that every column of the trapdoor $\mathbf{T}$ is well hidden information theoretically (conditioned on the adversary's view), it is plausible that the proof could be adapted to work for the full matrix ring $\mathbb{Z}_p^{n \times n}$ (though we do not do so here, to keep the proof simpler).

Instantiation: Boolean Functions of Bounded Complexity. Let $\mathcal{F}'$ be the family of all functions from some set $\mathcal{M}$ to $\{0,1\}^L$ that are computable by Boolean circuits of some depth $D' = D'(\lambda)$ and size $S = S(\lambda) = \text{poly}(\lambda)$, under a suitable representation as binary strings. There is a (uniformly generated) universal Boolean circuit U of size $T = T(S) = \text{poly}(S)$ and depth $D = O(D')$ for which $U(f, m) = f(m)$ for all $f \in \mathcal{F}', m \in \mathcal{M}$. Defining the size-$T$, depth-$D$ circuits $U_{\boldsymbol{m}}(\cdot) = U(\cdot, m)$, Theorem 3 with the family $\mathcal{U}_{\text{circuit}} = \{U_{\boldsymbol{m}}(\cdot)\}$ yields a suitable homomorphic commitment. For this instantiation, following Item 1b of Theorem 3 we set

$$\gamma = \gamma_{\text{circuit}} := s\sqrt{m} \cdot (w+1)^D.$$

We proceed analogously for the family $\mathcal{F}'$ of functions from $\mathcal{M}$ to $\{0,1\}^L$ computable by size-S branching programs of some fixed width, using a (uniformly generated) universal branching program $U(f, m)$ of some size $T = T(S) = $

poly(S), and invoking Theorem 3 with the family $\mathcal{U}_{\mathrm{BP}} = \{U_m(\cdot) = U(\cdot, m)\}$ yields a suitable homomorphic commitment. For this instantiation, following Item 1c of Theorem 3 we set

$$\gamma = \gamma_{\mathrm{BP}} := s\sqrt{m} \cdot w^{O(1)} \cdot T.$$

In both instantiations we let the "dummy" function $d \in \mathcal{F}'$ be the trivial function that always outputs zero, leaving the family $\mathcal{F} = \mathcal{F}'\backslash\{d\}$ of all *nontrivial* size-S circuits (or branching programs) as the one supported by the scheme. (There is no need to suport the trivial function, since its output is fixed.)

Compressing Commitments and Proofs. Finally, for functions with outputs in $\{0,1\}^L$ for some $L \leq n$, we can reduce the sizes of the commitments and proofs by a factor of Lw.[18] Define $\mathbf{M} \in \mathbb{Z}_q^{n \times L}$ to be the identity matrix $\mathbf{I} \in \mathbb{Z}_q^{L \times L}$ padded with $n - L$ all-zero rows, and let $\mathbf{e} \in \{0,1\}^{Lw}$ be as in Item 3 of Theorem 3. Then any commitment $\mathbf{C}_m \in \mathbb{Z}_q^{n \times Lw}$ can be replaced by the single column vector $\mathbf{c}_m = \mathbf{C}_m \cdot \mathbf{e} \in \mathbb{Z}_q^n$, and any proof $\mathbf{R}_{m,f} \in \mathbb{Z}^{m \times Lw}$ can be replaced by $\mathbf{r}_{m,f} = \mathbf{R}_{m,f} \cdot \mathbf{e} \in \mathbb{Z}^m$. We then redefine $\mathsf{Verify}(\mathbf{A}, \mathbf{c}^*, f, \mathbf{y} \in \{0,1\}^L, \mathbf{r}^*)$ to accept if $\|\mathbf{r}^*\| \leq \gamma' := \gamma\|\mathbf{e}\|_1 \leq \gamma Lw$ and $\mathbf{c}^* = \mathbf{A}_f \mathbf{r}^* + \binom{\mathbf{y}}{\mathbf{0}}$. This works because $\|\mathbf{r}_{m,f}\| \leq \|\mathbf{R}_{m,f}\| \cdot \|\mathbf{e}\|_1$, and $\mathsf{Encode}(\mathbf{y}) \cdot \mathbf{e} = \mathbf{My} = \binom{\mathbf{y}}{\mathbf{0}}$. We note that the above-described combinability property is also preserved.

Lemma 2. *For the instantiations and parameters given above, Construction 3 is a correct functional commitment scheme with authority.*

Proof. Let $m \in \mathcal{M}$ and $f \in \mathcal{F}$ be arbitrary, and let:

- $(cp = \mathbf{C}, vp = \mathbf{A}, ek = (\mathbf{C}, \mathbf{A}, \mathbf{T})) \leftarrow \mathsf{Setup}(1^n)$,
- $ok_f = \mathbf{R}_f \leftarrow \mathsf{Extract}(ek, f) = \mathsf{SamplePre}(\mathbf{T}, \mathbf{A}_f, \mathbf{C} - \mathsf{Encode}(f), s)$
  (note that $f \neq d$ and s is large enough, so $\mathsf{SamplePre}$ works on these arguments), and
- $(\mathbf{C}_m, \mathbf{R}_{m,f}) = \mathsf{Open}(\mathbf{C}, m, \mathbf{R}_f) = \mathsf{Eval}(U_m, \mathbf{C}, \mathbf{R}_f)$
  (note that $\mathbf{C}_m = \mathsf{Commit}(\mathbf{C}, m) = \mathsf{Eval}(U_m, \mathbf{C})$ by definition of Eval).

We show that $\mathsf{Verify}(\mathbf{A}, \mathbf{C}_m, f, y = f(m), \mathbf{R}_{m,f})$ accepts. By definition of Extract and Item 3 of Theorem 1, we have $\|\mathbf{R}_f\| \leq s\sqrt{m}$ and

$$\mathbf{C} = \mathbf{A}_f \mathbf{R}_f + \mathsf{Encode}(f),$$

so by the correctness of $U_m(\cdot) = U(\cdot, m)$ and of $\mathsf{Eval}(U_m, \mathbf{C}, \mathbf{R}_f)$ (Theorem 3) we have

$$\mathbf{C}_m = \mathbf{A}_f \mathbf{R}_{m,f} + \mathsf{Encode}(U_m(f)) = \mathbf{A}_f \mathbf{R}_{m,f} + \mathsf{Encode}(y),$$

as required. In addition, $\|\mathbf{R}_{m,f}\| \leq \gamma$ because $\|\mathbf{R}_{m,f}\|/\|\mathbf{R}_f\|$ is bounded as given in Item 1 of Theorem 3, so Verify accepts.

---

[18] For $L > n$, we can simply treat the function as the concatenation of multiples functions, and extract keys and generate proofs for each of them individually.

Finally, for the compressed variant with commitment $\mathbf{c}_m := \mathbf{C}_m \mathbf{e}$ and proof $\mathbf{r}_{m,f} := \mathbf{R}_{m,f} \cdot \mathbf{e}$, we have

$$\mathbf{c}_m = \mathbf{A}_f \mathbf{r}_{m,f} + \mathsf{Encode}(y) \cdot \mathbf{e} = \mathbf{A}_f \mathbf{r}_{m,f} + \begin{pmatrix} \mathbf{y} \\ \mathbf{0} \end{pmatrix}$$

and has norm $\|\mathbf{r}\| \leq \|\mathbf{R}_{m,f}\| \cdot \|\mathbf{e}\|_1 \leq \gamma \|\mathbf{e}\|_1 = \gamma'$, so Verify accepts.   □

Theorem 4. *For the instantiations and parameters given above, Construction 3 satisfies selective function binding (Definition 5) if normal-form $SIS_{n,q,\bar{m},\beta}$ is hard for sufficiently large $\beta = O(\gamma w \sqrt{m})$ [or for the compressed variant, $\beta = O(\gamma' \sqrt{m})$ where $\gamma' = \gamma \|\mathbf{e}\|_1$ for the special short vector $\mathbf{e}$ used for compression].*

More specifically, for any adversary $\mathcal{A}$ against the selective function binding of the scheme that makes at most $Q = Q(n)$ queries to its $\mathsf{Extract}$ oracle, there is a normal-form $SIS_{n,q,\bar{m},\beta}$ adversary $\mathcal{B}$ for which

$$\mathbf{Adv}^{SIS}(\mathcal{B}) \geq \mathbf{Adv}^{sfa}(\mathcal{A}) - (Q + 1) \cdot \mathrm{negl}(n),$$

and whose running time is that of $\mathcal{A}$ plus a small polynomial in n.

Due to space constraints, the proof of Theorem 4 is deferred to the full version. (It has many similarities with the proof of Theorem 2.)

Acknowledgments. We thank the anonymous TCC reviewers for many helpful comments and suggestions. This material is based upon work supported by DARPA under Agreement No. HR00112020025. Any opinions, findings and conclusions or recommendations expressed in this material are those of the author(s) and do not necessarily reflect the views of the United States Government or DARPA.

References

[ABB10] Agrawal, S., Boneh, D., Boyen, X.: Efficient lattice (H)IBE in the standard model. In: EUROCRYPT, pp. 553–572 (2010)

[AFV11] Agrawal, S., Freeman, D.M., Vaikuntanathan, V.: Functional encryption for inner product predicates from learning with errors. In: ASIACRYPT (2011)

[AP14] Alperin-Sheriff, J., Peikert, C.: Faster bootstrapping with polynomial error. In: CRYPTO, pp. 297–314 (2014)

[BBB+18] Bünz, B., Bootle, J., Boneh, D., Poelstra, A., Wuille, P., Maxwell, G.: Bulletproofs: short proofs for confidential transactions and more. In: IEEE Symposium on Security and Privacy, pp. 315–334 (2018)

[BDFG20] Boneh, D., Drake, J., Fisch, B., Gabizon, A.: Halo infinite: Recursive zk-SNARKs from any additive polynomial commitment scheme. Cryptology ePrint Archive, Report 2020/1536 (2020). https://eprint.iacr.org/2020/1536

[BdM93] Benaloh, J.C., de Mare, M.: One-way accumulators: a decentralized alternative to digital sinatures (extended abstract). In: EUROCRYPT, vol. 765, pp. 274–285 (1993)

510   C. Peikert et al.

[BFS20] Bünz, B., Fisch, B., Szepieniec, A.: Transparent SNARKs from DARK compilers. In: EUROCRYPT, pp. 677–706 (2020)
[BGJS16] Badrinarayanan, S., Goyal, V., Jain, A., Sahai, A.: Verifiable functional encryption. In: ASIACRYPT, pp. 557–587 (2016)
[BGV11] Benabbas, S., Gennaro, R., Vahlis, Y.: Verifiable delegation of computation over large datasets. In: CRYPTO, pp. 111–131 (2011)
[BV14] Brakerski, Z., Vaikuntanathan, V.: Lattice-based FHE as secure as PKE. In: ITCS, pp. 1–12 (2014)
[CCH+19] Canetti, R., et al.: Fiat-Shamir: from practice to theory. In: STOC, pp. 1082–1090 (2019)
[CF13] Catalano, D., Fiore, D.: Vector commitments and their applications. In: PKC, pp. 55–72 (2013)
[CFG+20] Campanelli, M., Fiore, D., Greco, N., Kolonelos, D., Nizzardo, L.: Incrementally aggregatable vector commitments and applications to verifiable decentralized storage. In: ASIACRYPT, pp. 3–35 (2020)
[CGMA85] Chor, B., Goldwasser, S., Micali, S., Awerbuch, B.: Verifiable secret sharing and achieving simultaneity in the presence of faults (extended abstract). In: FOCS, pp. 383–395 (1985)
[CHKP10] Cash, D., Hofheinz, D., Kiltz, E., Peikert, C.: Bonsai trees, or how to delegate a lattice basis. J. Cryptol. 25(4), 601–639 (2012). Preliminary version in Eurocrypt 2010
[CPSZ18] Chepurnoy, A., Papamanthou, C., Srinivasan, S., Zhang, Y.: EDRAX: a cryptocurrency with stateless transaction validation. Cryptology ePrint Archive, Report 2018/968 (2018). https://eprint.iacr.org/2018/968
[CRFM08] Catalano, D., Raimondo, M.D., Fiore, D., Messina, M.: Zero-knowledge sets with short proofs. IEEE Trans. Inf. Theory 57(4), 2488–2502 (2011). Preliminary version in EUROCRYPT 2008
[DN94] Dwork, C., Naor, M.: An Efficient Existentially Unforgeable Signature Scheme and its Applications. In: Desmedt, Y.G. (ed.) CRYPTO 1994. LNCS, vol. 839, pp. 234–246. Springer, Heidelberg (1994). https://doi.org/10.1007/3-540-48658-5_23
[GPV08] Gentry, C., Peikert, C., Vaikuntanathan, V.: Trapdoors for hard lattices and new cryptographic constructions. In: STOC, pp. 197–206 (2008)
[GSW13] Gentry, C., Sahai, A., Waters, B.: Homomorphic encryption from learning with errors: conceptually-simpler, asymptotically-faster, attribute-based. In: CRYPTO, pp. 75–92 (2013)
[GVW15] Gorbunov, S., Vaikuntanathan, V., Wichs, D.: Leveled fully homomorphic signatures from standard lattices. In: STOC, pp. 469–477 (2015)
[GW11] Gentry, C., Wichs, D.: Separating succinct non-interactive arguments from all falsifiable assumptions. In: STOC, pp. 99–108 (2011)
[HW15] Hubácek, P., Wichs, D.: On the communication complexity of secure function evaluation with long output. In: ITCS, pp. 163–172 (2015)
[Kil92] Kilian, J.: A note on efficient zero-knowledge proofs and arguments. In: STOC, pp. 723–732 (1992)
[Kus18] Kuszmaul, J.: Verkle trees (2018). Unpublished manuscript, available at https://math.mit.edu/research/highschool/primes/materials/2018/Kuszmaul.pdf
[KZG10] Kate, A., Zaverucha, G.M., Goldberg, I.: Constant-size commitments to polynomials and their applications. In: ASIACRYPT, pp. 177–194 (2010)
[Lis05] Liskov, M.D.: Updatable zero-knowledge databases. In: ASIACRYPT, pp. 174–198 (2005)

[LM19]   Lai, R.W.F., Malavolta, G.: Subvector commitments with application to succinct arguments. In: CRYPTO, pp. 530–560 (2019)

[LP20]   Lipmaa, H., Pavlyk, K.: Succinct functional commitment for a large class of arithmetic circuits. In: ASIACRYPT, pp. 686–716 (2020)

[LRY16] Libert, B., Ramanna, S.C., Yung, M.: Functional commitment schemes: from polynomial commitments to pairing-based accumulators from simple assumptions. In: ICALP, pp. 30:1–30:14 (2016)

[LW15]   Lyubashevsky, V., Wichs, D.: Simple lattice trapdoor sampling from a broad class of distributions. In: PKC, pp. 716–730 (2015)

[LY10]   Libert, B., Yung, M.: Concise mercurial vector commitments and independent zero-knowledge sets with short proofs. In: TCC, pp. 499–517 (2010)

[Mer87] Merkle, R.C.: A digital signature based on a conventional encryption function. In: CRYPTO, pp. 369–378 (1987)

[Mic94] Micali, S.: CS proofs. In: FOCS, pp. 436–453 (1994)

[MP12]   Micciancio, D., Peikert, C.: Trapdoors for lattices: simpler, tighter, faster, smaller. In: EUROCRYPT, pp. 700–718 (2012)

[MR04]   Micciancio, D., Regev, O.: Worst-case to average-case reductions based on Gaussian measures. SIAM J. Comput. 37(1), 267–302 (2007). Preliminary version in FOCS 2004

[MRK03] Micali, S., Rabin, M.O., Kilian, J.: Zero-knowledge sets. In: FOCS, pp. 80–91 (2003)

[PS19]   Peikert, C., Shiehian, S.: Noninteractive zero knowledge for NP from (plain) learning with errors. In: CRYPTO, pp. 89–114 (2019)

[PSTY13] Papamanthou, C., Shi, E., Tamassia, R., Yi, K.: Streaming authenticated data structures. In: EUROCRYPT, pp. 353–370 (2013)

[PW08]   Peikert, C., Waters, B.: Lossy trapdoor functions and their applications. SIAM J. Comput. 40(6), 1803–1844 (2011). Preliminary version in STOC 2008

[SBZ01] Steinfeld, R., Bull, L., Zheng, Y.: Content extraction signatures. In: ICISC, pp. 285–304 (2001)

[TAB+20] Tomescu, A., Abraham, I., Buterin, V., Drake, J., Feist, D., Khovratovich, D.: Aggregatable subvector commitments for stateless cryptocurrencies. In: SCN, Lecture Notes in Computer Science, pp. 45–64 (2020)

[Xag13] Xagawa, K.: Improved (hierarchical) inner-product encryption from lattices. In: PKC, pp. 235–252 (2013)

[Yam16] Yamada, S.: Adaptively secure identity-based encryption from lattices with asymptotically shorter public parameters. In: EUROCRYPT, pp. 32–62 (2016)

Author Index

Printed in the United States
by Baker & Taylor Publisher Services